Strategic Management
Concepts and Cases

Strategic Management
Concepts and Cases

Arthur A. Thompson, Jr.
A. J. Strickland III
both of
The University of Alabama

Fifth Edition

Homewood, IL 60430

Cover photo: Brian Leng/All Stock

Associate publisher: Martin F. Hanifin
Developmental editor: Elizabeth J. Rubenstein
Project editor: Paula M. Buschman
Production manager: Bette K. Ittersagen
Artist: Benoit and Associates
Compositor: Better Graphics, Inc.
Typeface: 10/12 Times Roman
Printer: R. R. Donnelley & Sons Company

Library of Congress Cataloging-in-Publication Data

Thompson, Arthur A., 1940–
    Strategic management: concepts and cases / Arthur A. Thompson and
A. J. Strickland III. —5th ed.
      p.   cm.
   ISBN 0-256-07837-8—ISBN 0-256-09863-8 (International ed.)
   ISBN 0-256-08493-9
  1. Strategic planning. 2. Strategic planning—Case studies.
  I. Strickland, A. J. (Alonzo J.) II. Title.
  HD30.28.T53   1990
  658.4′012—dc20   89–29577
                                           CIP

Printed in the United States of America

3 4 5 6 7 8 9 0 DO 7 6 5 4 3 2 1

. . . .

To Hasseline and Kitty

Preface

The hallmarks for this fifth edition are "new, much enhanced, and in step with the strategic management challenges of the 1990s." Seventy percent of the cases are new, including nine international cases and four ethics cases. The concepts chapters provide quantum improvements in readability and coverage, with much more space devoted to global competition, multinational strategies, ethics, and values. Plus, we've created a total teaching package—text, cases, an all-new global simulation game, case analysis software, a readings book, videos, color transparencies, lecture notes and transparency masters, a computerized test bank, and an expanded *Instructor's Manual*. It adds up to the biggest revision we've ever done and to an array of new features and new options.

What's New in the Text Chapters

Rapid-fire development of the strategic management literature dictates making important edition-to-edition changes to freshen the coverage, update treatments, and keep the presentation close to the cutting edge. In this edition, the two most noteworthy enhancements involve: (1) internationalizing the entire treatments of strategic analysis and strategy formation to create a solid global perspective, and (2) adding four lengthy sections linking ethics and values to the tasks of crafting and implementing strategy. Also, we have given extra attention to the use of incentive compensation and reward systems as a major strategy-implementing tool, included a section on the role of employee training in the implementation process, created a new chapter on company situation analysis, streamlined and reorganized the presentation of industry and competitive analysis, provided chapter-end Key Points summaries to spotlight important concepts and tools, included 20 new Illustration Capsules, used an array of international examples, and livened up the writing style significantly. Every chapter has been overhauled and every page has undergone significant rewriting and rethinking to elevate the caliber of the presentation.

Even though the overall structure of this edition parallels the last, we've made numerous adjustments in content, emphasis, and organizational arrangement:

- Chapter 1 has been recast to lay out more sharply and concisely just what strategy-making, strategy-implementing, and strategic managing are all about. The separate roles of line managers, strategic planners, and boards of directors are spelled out.

- Chapter 2 stresses the direction-setting entrepreneurial tasks—defining the business, establishing strategic objectives, and crafting a strategy. Two new sections describe how ethics, values, and social responsibility considerations shape the choice of strategy.

- The chapter on industry and competitive analysis has been streamlined and simplified. The conceptual framework is applicable to any market situation, whether local, national, or global. This framework weaves together all the basic tools for appraising a company's external strategic situation—the determinants of industry structure, the concept of driving forces, Porter's model of competition, the technique of strategic group mapping, competitor analysis, the identification of key success factors, and the assessment of long-term industry attractiveness.

- The new chapter on company situation analysis is built around diagnosing how well the present strategy is working, SWOT analysis, competitive strength assessments, strategic cost or value chain analysis, and identification of strategic issues confronting the company.

- A much-revised chapter on competitive strategy and competitive advantage goes through the whole range of business strategy approaches—striving to be the low-cost producer, differentiation, focusing, offensive strategies, defensive strategies, and vertical integration strategies. More attention is paid to how a sustainable competitive advantage can be won.

- Chapter 6, Matching Strategy to the Situation, examines the major strategy alternatives in generic types of industry environments and company situations. Coverage of strategic issues and alternatives in globally competitive markets stands out as a centerpiece in this chapter. In addition to a new table contrasting multicountry and global strategies, students are introduced to the concepts of critical markets, global market dominance, and global scale economies.

- Chapter 7, Corporate Diversification Strategies, has new sections on how diversification builds shareholder value, the roles of cost sharing and skills transfer in creating competitive advantage via diversification, and the competitive advantages that accrue to diversified multinational corporations in a globally competitive business world.

- Chapter 8 stresses the tools for sizing up the different businesses a diversified company is in and managing strategic fit relationships to capture competitive advantage opportunities.

- Strategy implementation is framed around six principal tasks: building a capable organization, linking the budgeting process to the strategic plan, putting strategy-supportive policies and administrative practices into place, tying the reward structure to the achievement of strategic objectives, shaping the corporate culture, and exercising strategic leadership. Chapter 9 deals with the first three tasks and Chapter 10 with the last three.

- Chapter 10 includes a new section on establishing ethical standards and values, a second new section on enforcing ethical behavior, and a third new section on the CEO's role in setting an ethical example.
- There is enhanced coverage of corporate social responsibility and corporate citizenship in establishing a mission (Chapter 2) and setting forth a culture-shaping statement of corporate values and beliefs (Chapter 10).
- Greater emphasis has been placed on using incentive compensation approaches to strengthen employee commitment to strategy implementation (Chapter 10). This discussion complements the material in the Nucor, Lincoln Electric, Mary Kay Cosmetics, and Wal-Mart cases.
- Key Points sections at the ends of the chapters draw attention to strategic principles and crucial analytical steps, thus serving as handy references for case analysis and for thinking about the big picture in strategic terms.
- Four of the twenty new Illustration Capsules involve international companies and three involve values and ethics.

All in all, we are confident you will find the text portion of this edition better organized, more tightly written, comfortably mainstream, and as close to the cutting edge of both theory and practice as basic textbook discussions can be. We think previous adopters will be very pleased and nonadopters have ample reason to take a fresh look.

The Collection of Cases

Of the 38 cases selected for this edition, 26 are new and 2 of the holdovers have been revised and updated. The cases have been grouped into five sections. The first group of five cases concentrates on the role and tasks of the manager as chief strategy-maker and chief strategy-implementer. A second group of 14 cases deals with analyzing and crafting business-level strategy. There are five cases involving corporate diversification situations. In the fourth section, there are 10 cases covering the ins and outs of implementing strategy. An all-new section of four cases highlights the links between strategy and ethics management. Scattered throughout the lineup are nine cases concerning international companies, globally competitive industries, and cross-cultural situations. Quite possibly, it is the best lineup of cases from beginning to end we've ever been able to assemble.

Special attention has been given to including a rich diversity of interesting companies, products, and situations. The nine international cases, in conjunction with the new material in the text chapters, give a solid global perspective to this edition. Two of the cases, Grand Theatre and Public Service of New Mexico, have videotape segments that can be shown during the class discussion. Then there are four cases involving firms listed in *The 100 Best Companies to Work For in America,* three cases about young start-up companies, eight cases dealing with the strategic problems of family-owned or relatively small entrepreneurial businesses, two cases about companies whose founder-CEO now rank among the world's billionaires, and a nonprofit organization case. Nineteen cases involve public companies that students can further research in the library.

We have continued our traditional practice of choosing cases that senior-level students can suitably handle and that provoke lively classroom discussions. At least 18 of the cases involve companies or products with which students are likely to be familiar. The researchers who contributed cases to this edition had done a first-rate job of preparing cases that contain valuable teaching points, illustrate what's happening out in the field, and allow students to apply the tools of strategic analysis. We believe you will find the case collection in this edition chock full of interest, effective in the classroom, tightly linked to the text treatments in Chapters 1 through 10, and representative of contemporary strategic problems and analytical applications.

The Business Strategy Game Option

The biggest and most significant addition to the fifth edition's package is an optional supplement called *The Business Strategy Game*. Three considerations caused us to create this globalized industry simulation as an integrated companion for use with the text and cases:

1. Simulations are uncommonly effective teaching-learning tool that also add valuable excitement and stimulation to the course.
2. We saw a growing need for a 1990s-style simulation that captures the international dimensions of strategic management and that gives students an up-close understanding of the global competitive challenges facing managers in one industry after another.
3. We believed students could profit greatly from a simulation where developing and executing five-year strategic plans are an integral part of the exercise.

Moreover, the speed of today's personal computers, along with the number-crunching power of spreadsheet software, made it possible to design a next-generation game that not only entails minimal gear-up time on the instructor's part but also is easy to administer.

About the Simulation.   The product for *The Business Strategy Game* is athletic footwear—chosen because it is a product students personally know about, buy, and wear regularly. The industry setting is global—companies can manufacture and sell their brands in the United States, Europe, or Asia. Competition is head-to-head—each team of students must match its strategic wits against the other company teams. Companies can focus their efforts on one geographic market, two, or all three; they can establish a one-country production base or they can manufacture in all three geographic markets. Demand conditions, tariffs, and wage rates vary from area to area.

The company that students manage has plants to operate; a work force to compensate; inventories to control; accounting and cost data to examine; capital expenditure decisions to make; marketing and sales campaigns to wage; shareholders to worry about; sales forecasts to consider; and gyrations in exchange rates, interest rates, and the stock market to take into account. Students must evaluate whether to pursue a low-cost producer strategy, a differentiation strategy, or a focus strategy. They have to decide whether to produce off-shore in Asia where wage rates are very low or to avoid import tariffs and transocean shipping costs by producing in every primary geographic market. And they must endeavor to maximize shareholder wealth via increased dividend payments and stock price appreciation. Each team of students is challenged to use their entrepreneurial and strategic skills to become the next Nike or Reebok and ride the wave of growth to the top of the worldwide athletic footwear industry.

A built-in five-year decision-making feature allows students to (1) craft a five-year strategic plan and (2) extrapolate out the ramifications of the upcomings year's decision on the next four years. All the number-crunching is done by the computer in seconds. With this feature, students can project the long-range consequences of current decisions, make intelligent short-run versus long-run tradeoffs, and create a five-year set of decisions (in effect, a five-year strategic plan) which is revised and updated as the game unfolds. A special "Calc" feature allows students to ask "what if" and to compare alternative strategic actions in a matter of seconds. *The Business Strategy Game* can be used with any IBM or compatible PC capable of running Lotus 1–2–3. This simulation is suitable for both senior and MBA courses.

Special Features. Instructors who adopt *The Business Strategy Game* will find several features that make things run smoothly and easily:

- Everything is done on disks: students enter their decisions on disks; during processing, complete industry and company results are written back on the disks. It takes only a few minutes to collect the disks or return them. A printout of the industry scoreboard and a printout of the instructor's report are automatically generated during processing.
- Decisions can be processed in 40 minutes (less than 25 minutes on a fast PC); simple procedures allow most or all of the processing to be delegated to a student assistant.
- Students will find it convenient and uncomplicated to use the PC to play *The Business Strategy Game* even if they have had no prior exposure to PCs; no programming of any kind is involved. Full instructions are presented in the *Player's Manual* and on the screens themselves.
- A scoreboard of company performance is automatically calculated for each decision period. Instructors determine the weights to be given to each of five performance measures—revenues, after-tax profits, return on stockholders' investment, stock price, and bond rating; the overall performance score can be used to grade team performance.

An *Instructor's Manual* describes how to integrate the game into the course, provides tips on how to administer the game (based on our 15 years of experience in using a simulation every semester), and contains step-by-step processing instructions.

The Value a Simulation Adds.   First and foremost, the exercise of running a simulated company over a number of decision periods helps develop students' business judgment. They learn about risk-taking. They weigh the merits of profits now against profits later. They get valuable practice in assessing the long-term consequences of short-term decisions. And by having to live with the decisions they make, they experience what it means to be accountable and responsible for achieving satisfactory results. Second, students learn an enormous amount from working with the numbers; exploring options; and trying to unite production, marketing, finance, and human resource decisions into a coherent strategy. The effect is to help students integrate a lot of material and gain a total enterprise perspective. Third, students' entrepreneurial instincts blossom as they get caught up in the competitive spirit of the game. The resulting entertainment value helps instructors maintain a high level of involvement in the course throughout the term.

Instructors will find *The Business Strategy Game* a welcome addition to the package of options and supplements. A simulation game has been a standard part of the strategic management course at our school for over 20 years; it is *the single most effective exercise* we've found for pulling the pieces of the business puzzle together for students and giving them an integrative, capstone experience. We've class tested *The Business Strategy Game* with eight sections over two semesters. It has gotten very high marks from the students.

The STRAT–ANALYST™ Software Option

We introduced this optional supplement with the fourth edition as a way of incorporating the calculating power of PCs into the case analysis part of the strategic management course. Because it proved both popular and effective, a number of enhancements have been added for this edition. As before, STRAT–ANALYST works on all IBM or compatible personal computers with 512K memories and the capability to run Lotus 1–2–3™, version 2.01 or higher, or the Student Version. Having Lotus 1–2–3 drive the STRAT–ANALYST disks is a strong plus because it gives students access to a host of calculating and data-manipulating powers and because most university PC labs have the Lotus 1–2–3 package available for students' use.

This version of STRAT–ANALYST has three main sections. The first section contains preprogrammed, customized templates for each of 16 cases calling for substantial number-crunching. With these templates, students can:

- Obtain calculations showing financial ratios, profit margins and rates of return, common-size income statements and balance sheets, and annual compound rates of change.
- Calculate Altman's bankruptcy index (a method for predicting when a company may be headed into deep financial trouble).

- Do what-if scenarios and compare the projected outcomes for one strategic option versus another.
- Make five-year best-case, expected-case, and worst-case projections of performance using the what-if approach.
- Construct line graphs, bar graphs, pie charts, and scatter diagrams using any of the case data or calculations on file.
- Get report-ready printouts for all these calculations and graphs.

Not only is this section of STRAT–ANALYST a big timesaver for students but it also gets them into the habit of always looking at the story the numbers tell about a company's performance and situation. Because students can do a more systematic number-crunching analysis with STRAT–ANALYST than without it, instructors can insist on and expect thorough financial assessments. STRAT–ANALYST's graphing capabilities are particularly valuable to students in preparing written assignments and visual aids for oral presentations. The what-if features make it easier to quantify the effects of particular strategic actions and to examine the outcomes of alternative scenarios. Five-year projections of performance can be generated in less than 10 minutes.

The second section of STRAT–ANALYST features an easy-to-use, step-by-step generic procedure for conducting a comprehensive, strategic situation analysis. The two-part menu includes:

- Industry and competitive situation analysis (keyed to Table 3–5 in the text).
- Company situation analysis (keyed to Table 4–4 in the text).

Students can choose to go through either or both situation analysis options as appropriate; when finished, they get neatly organized, final-copy printouts of their analyses in report formats which are convenient for instructors to grade. Hints for using each situational analysis tool are provided directly on STRAT–ANALYST to guide students in the right direction. The benefit of these two menu options is that students are prompted into considering the full array of concepts and tools and doing a *systematic* situation analysis rather than trying to get by with spotty analysis and weakly justified opinions.

The third section of STRAT–ANALYST offers two menu selections for developing recommmendations:

1. Action recommendations pertaining to strategy formulation—development of a basic strategic direction (mission and objectives), proposing an overall business strategy, recommending specific moves to gain competitive advantage, and specifying functional area support strategies.
2. Action recommendations for implementing/executing the chosen strategy and correcting whatever assortment of internal administrative and operating problems may exist.

Both selections walk students step-by-step through areas where actions may need to be taken. A Hints screen appears at each step.

The whole intent of STRAT–ANALYST is to give students a major assist in doing higher-caliber strategic analysis and to cut the time it takes them to do thorough case preparation. This software should also build student comfort levels and skills in the use of PCs for managerial analysis purposes. The instructor profits too—from improved student performance and from increased flexibility in varying the nature of case analysis assignments. Start-up instructions for STRAT-ANALYST are on pages 991–998 in this book; once the disks are booted up, all other directions needed by users appear right on the screens.

The Readings Book Option

For instructors who want to incorporate samples of the strategic management literature into the course, a companion volume, *Readings in Strategic Management,* containing 40 selections is available. Thirty-two of the readings are new to the third edition; almost two-thirds have been published since 1985. All are quite readable, and all are suitable for seniors and MBA students. Most of the selections are articles reprinted from leading journals; they add in-depth treatment to important topic areas covered in the text and put readers at the cutting edge of academic thinking and research on the subject. Some of the articles are drawn from practitioner sources and stress how particular tools and concepts relate directly to actual companies and managerial practices. Seven articles examine the role of the general manager and strategy; eleven articles concern strategic analysis and strategy formation at the business unit level; six articles deal with strategy in diversified companies; nine articles relate to various aspects of strategy implementation; and seven articles are about strategy and ethics management. Five of these articles deal with the international dimensions of strategic management. In tandem, the readings package provides an effective, efficient vehicle for reinforcing and expanding the text-case approach.

The Expanded Instructor's Package

A series of instructional aids has been developed to assist adopters in successfully using the fifth edition. The *Instructor's Manual* contains suggestions for using the text materials, various approaches to course design and course organization, a sample syllabus, alternative course outlines, over 600 multiple choice questions, discussion questions, a comprehensive teaching note for each case, plus eight classic cases from previous editions. There is a computerized test bank for generating examinations, a set of color transparencies depicting the figures and tables in the 10 text chapters, and a manual of transparency masters that thoroughly cover text concepts and support the instructor's lectures on the material. A videotape containing interviews with key individuals is available for use with the Grand Theatre and Public Service Company of New Mexico cases.

In concert, the textbook, the three companion supplements, and the expanded instructor's package form the most complete, best integrated lineup of teaching materials of any of our previous editions. The package offers wide latitude in course design, full access to the range of computer-assisted instructional techniques, an assortment of visual aids, and plenty of opportunity to keep the nature of student assignments varied and interesting. Our intent has been to give you everything you need to offer a course that is not only very much in keeping with the strategic management challenges and issues of the 1990s but also capable of winning enthusiastic student approval.

Acknowledgments

We have benefited from the help of many people during the evolution of this book. Students, adopters, and reviewers have generously supplied an untold number of insightful comments and helpful suggestions. Our intellectual debt to those academics, writers, and practicing managers who have blazed new trails in the strategy field will be obvious to any reader familiar with the literature of strategic management.

We are particularly indebted to the case researchers whose casewriting efforts appear herein and to the companies whose cooperation made the cases possible. To each one goes a very special thank-you. The importance of good, timely cases cannot be overestimated in contributing to a substantive study of strategic management issues and practices. From a research standpoint, cases in strategic management are invaluable in exposing the generic strategic issues companies face, in forming hypotheses about strategic behavior, and in drawing experience-based generalizations about the practice of strategic management. Pedagogically, cases about strategic management give students essential practice in diagnosing and evaluating strategic situations, in learning to use the tools and concepts of strategy analysis, in sorting through various strategic options, in crafting strategic action plans, and in figuring out successful ways to implement and execute the chosen strategy. Without a continuing stream of fresh, well-researched, and well-conceived cases, the discipline of strategic management would quickly fall into disrepair, losing much of its energy and excitement. There's no question, therefore, that first-class case research constitutes a valuable scholarly contribution.

The following reviewers made valuable contributions to the fifth edition: S. A. Billon, University of Delaware; Charles H. Byles, Oklahoma State University; Gerald L. Geisler, Sangamon State University; Rose Knotts, North Texas State University; Joseph Rosenstein, University of Texas at Arlington; James B. Thurman, George Washington University; and Ivan Able, Baruch College.

We are also indebted to W. Harvey Hegarty, Roger Evered, Charles B. Saunders, Rhae M. Swisher, Claude I. Shell, R. Thomas Lenz, Michael C. White, Dennis Callahan, R. Duane Ireland, William E. Burr II, C. W. Millard, Richard Mann, Kurt Christensen, Neil W. Jacobs, Louis W. Fry, D. Robley Wood, George J. Gore, and William R. Soukup. These reviewers were of considerable help in directing our efforts at various stages in the evolution of the manuscript through the first four editions.

Naturally, as custom properly dictates, we are responsible for whatever errors of fact, deficiencies in coverage or exposition, and oversights that remain. As always we value your recommendations and thoughts about the book. Your comments regarding coverage and content will be most welcome, as will your calling our attention to specific errors. Please write us at P.O. Box 870225, Department of Management and Marketing, Tuscaloosa, Alabama 35487-0225.

Arthur A. Thompson, Jr.
A. J. Strickland III

A Special Note to Students

The ground that strategic management covers is challenging, wide-ranging, and exciting. The center of attention is *the total enterprise*—the environment in which it operates, the direction management intends to head, management's strategic plan for getting the enterprise moving in this direction, and the managerial tasks of implementing and executing the chosen strategy successfully. We'll be examining the foremost issue in running a business enterprise: What must managers do, and do well, to make the company a winner rather than a loser in the game of business?

The answer that emerges again and again, and which becomes the theme of the course is that good strategy making and good strategy implementing are always the most reliable signs of good management. The task of this course is to expose you to the reasons why good strategic management nearly always produces good company performance and to instruct you in the methods of crafting a well-conceived strategy and then successfully executing it.

During the course, you can expect to learn what the role and tasks of the strategy-maker are. You will grapple with what strategy means and with all the ramifications of figuring out which strategy is best in light of a company's overall situation. You will get a workout in sizing up a variety of industry and competitive situations, in using the tools of strategic analysis, in considering the pros and cons of strategic alternatives, and in crafting an attractive strategic plan. You will learn about the principal managerial tasks associated with implementing the chosen strategy successfully. You will become more skilled as a strategic thinker and you will develop your powers of business judgment. The excitement comes, believe it or not, from the extra savvy you will pick up about playing the game of business and from the blossoming of your entrepreneurial and competitive instincts.

In the midst of all this, another purpose is accomplished: to help you integrate and apply what you've learned in prior courses. Strategic management is a big picture course. It deals with the grand sweep of how to manage. Unlike your other business courses where the subject matter was narrowly aimed at a particular function or piece of the business—accounting, finance, marketing, production, human resources, or information systems—this course deals with the company's entire makeup and situation from both inside and outside. Nothing is ignored or assumed away. The task is to arrive at solid judgments about how all the relevant factors add up. This makes strategic management an integrative, capstone course in which you reach back to use concepts and techniques covered in previous courses. For perhaps the first time you'll see how the various pieces of the business puzzle fit together and why the different parts of a business need to be managed in strategic harmony for the organization to operate in winning fashion.

No matter what your major is, the content of this course has all the ingredients to be the best course you've taken—best in the sense of learning a lot about business and holding your interest from beginning to end. Dig in, get involved, and make the most of what the course has to offer. As you tackle the subject matter, ponder Ralph Waldo Emerson's observation, "Commerce is a game of skill which many people play, but which few play well." What we've put between these covers is aimed squarely at helping you become a wiser, shrewder player. Good luck!

A. A. T.
A. J. S.

Contents

I

The Concepts and Techniques
of Strategic Management

1 The Strategic Management Process

"Cheshire Puss," she [Alice] began . . . "would you please tell me which way I ought to go from here?"
"That depends on where you want to get to," said the cat.
Lewis Carroll

My job is to make sure the company has a strategy and that everybody follows it.
Kenneth H. Olsen
CEO, Digital Equipment Corp.

This book is about the managerial tasks of crafting and implementing strategy. *An organization's strategy is delineated in the pattern of moves and approaches devised by management to produce successful organization performance.* Strategy, in effect, is a managerial game plan for running the organization. Managers develop strategies to give order to how an organization goes about its business and to achieve target objectives. Without a strategy, there is no established course to follow, no roadmap to manage by, no coherent action plan for producing the intended results.

Strategy formulation and implementation are core management functions. Among all the things that managers do, few affect organizational performance more lastingly than how well the management team handles the tasks of charting the organization's long-term direction, developing strategic moves and approaches, and executing the strategy in ways that produce the intended results. Indeed, *good strategy and good strategy implementation are the most trustworthy signs of good management.*

There is strong reason to associate "good management" with how well managers craft and execute strategy. It is hard to justify a top grade for managers who design shrewd strategies but fail to execute them well; weak implementation opens the door for organizational performance to fall short of full potential. Competent execution of a mediocre strategy scarcely qualifies managers for a gold-star award either. The standards for judging whether an organization is well managed, therefore, include good strategy-making *combined* with good strategy execution. The better conceived an organization's strategy and the more flawless its execution, the greater the chance that the organization will perform up to potential.

This is not to say that doing a good job of strategy-making and strategy-implementing will *guarantee* excellent organizational performance every year. Organizations can always go downhill for short periods because of adverse conditions beyond management's ability to foresee or react to. But the bad luck of adverse events never excuses weak performance year after year. It is always management's responsibility to adjust to adverse conditions by undertaking strategic defenses and managerial approaches that produce par performance despite a normal run of adversity.

THE FIVE TASKS OF STRATEGIC MANAGEMENT

The strategic management function has five interrelated components:

1. *Developing a concept of the business and forming a vision of where the organization needs to be headed*—in effect, infusing the organization with a sense of purpose, providing long-term direction, and establishing a *mission*.
2. *Translating the mission into specific long-range and short-range performance objectives*.
3. *Crafting a strategy* to achieve the targeted performance.
4. *Implementing and executing the chosen strategy* efficiently and effectively.
5. *Evaluating performance, reviewing the situation, and initiating corrective adjustments* in mission, objectives, strategy, or implementation in light of actual experience, changing conditions, new ideas, and new opportunities.

A model of the process is shown in Figure 1–1. Let's take a brief look at each one of these components to provide perspective for the chapters that follow.

Developing a Vision and a Mission

The foremost direction-setting question facing the senior managers of any enterprise is "What is our business and what will it be?" Developing a thoughtful answer to this question pushes managers to consider what the organization's business makeup should be and to develop a clearer vision of where the organization needs to be headed over the next 5 to 10 years. Management's answer to "What is our business and what will it be?" begins the process of carving out a meaningful direction for the organization to take and of establishing a strong organizational identity. Management's vision of what the organization seeks to do and to become is commonly termed the organization's *mission*. A mission state-

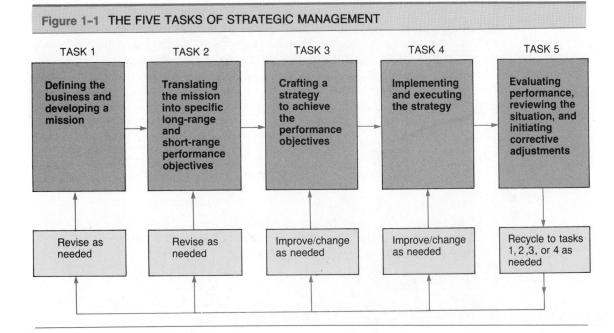

Figure 1–1 THE FIVE TASKS OF STRATEGIC MANAGEMENT

ment broadly outlines the organization's future course and serves to communicate "who we are, what we do, and where we're headed." Some examples of *company mission statements* are presented in Illustration Capsule 1.

ILLUSTRATION CAPSULE 1

EXAMPLES OF COMPANY MISSION STATEMENTS

Presented below are six actual company mission statements:

MCI Communications

MCI's mission is leadership in the global telecommunications services industry.

Public Service Company of New Mexico

Our mission is to work for the success of the people we serve by providing our CUSTOMERS reliable electric service, energy information, and energy options that best satisfy their needs.

(continued)

American Red Cross

The mission of the American Red Cross is to improve the quality of human life; to enhance self-reliance and concern for others; and to help people avoid, prepare for, and cope with emergencies.

Hewlett-Packard Company

Hewlett-Packard is a major designer and manufacturer of electronic products and systems for measurement and computation. HP's basic business purpose is to provide the capabilities and services needed to help customers worldwide improve their personal and business effectiveness.

Otis Elevator

Our mission is to provide any customer a means of moving people and things up, down, and sideways over short distances with higher reliability than any similar enterprise in the world.

Deluxe Checks

The mission of Deluxe Checks is to provide all banks, S&L's, and investment firms with error-free financial instruments delivered in a timely fashion.

Source: Company annual reports.

Setting Objectives

The act of setting objectives serves the purpose of converting the mission and direction into something specific to shoot for, something specific to achieve. Setting challenging but achievable objectives helps guard against complacency, internal confusion over what to accomplish, and mediocre organizational performance. Both short-range and long-range objectives are needed. *Short-range objectives* spell out what management needs to work toward over the next year or two; *long-range objectives* direct managers to consider what they can do *now* to boost the organization's performance over the longer term.

Objective-setting ideally is something *all managers* do. Every organization unit needs concrete, measurable performance targets that specify what it will do to assist in meeting the overall or organizationwide objectives. When the set of overall organizationwide objectives is broken down into specific targets for each organization unit and when lower-echelon managers are held accountable for achieving the objectives in their area of responsibility, a results-oriented climate emerges, and the whole organization ends up pointed in the intended direction.

Examples of the kinds of objectives that companies set in pursuing their missions are shown in Illustration Capsule 2.

ILLUSTRATION CAPSULE 2

EXAMPLES OF CORPORATE OBJECTIVES: NIKE, LOTUS DEVELOPMENT, AND CITICORP

Nike's Objectives (as stated in 1987)

- Protect and improve NIKE's position as the number one athletic brand in America, with particular attention to the company's existing core businesses in running, basketball, tennis, football, baseball, and kid's shoes and newer businesses with good potential like golf and soccer.
- Build a strong momentum in the growing fitness market, beginning with walking, workout, and cycling.
- Intensify the company's effort to develop products that women need and want.
- Explore the market for products specifically designed for the requirements of maturing Americans.
- Direct and manage the company's international business as it continues to develop.
- Continue the drive for increased margins through proper inventory management and fewer, better products.

Lotus Development Corporation's Objectives (as stated in 1986)

- To provide customer-driven solutions to practical business and professional problems.
- To advance the standards which our anchor products have set.
- To introduce complementary and companion products which make our software more valuable to existing users and accessible to new users.
- To create and acquire new products which offer data pathways into our existing software and which create entirely new categories of software.
- To invest in new strategic initiatives which will improve long-term competitiveness.
- To continue to improve our financial performance by continuing to strengthen our organization and deepen both our management and development teams.

(continued)

Citicorp's Objectives (as stated in 1988)

- To build shareholder value through:
    Sustained growth (12–18%) in earnings per share.
    A continued commitment to building customer-oriented
        businesses worldwide.
    Superior rates of return on equity (18%).
    A strong balance sheet.
    A business balanced by customer, product, and geography.

Source: Company annual reports.

Crafting a Strategy

Strategy-making brings into play the critical managerial issue of *how* to achieve the targeted results in light of the organization's situation and prospects. Objectives are the "ends," and *strategy* is the "means" of achieving them. The task of forming a strategy starts with hard analysis of the organization's internal and external situation. Armed with an understanding of the "big picture," managers can better devise a strategy of how to generate the targeted results.

Definitionally, *strategy is the pattern of organizational moves and managerial approaches used to achieve organizational objectives and to pursue the organization's mission.* The pattern of moves and approaches already taken indicates what the prevailing strategy is; the planned moves and approaches signal how the prevailing strategy is to be embellished or changed. Thus, while strategy represents the managerial game plan for running an organization, this plan does not consist of just good intentions and actions yet to be taken. An organization's strategy is nearly always a blend of prior moves, approaches already in place, and new actions being mapped out. Indeed, the biggest part of an organization's strategy usually consists of prior approaches and practices that are working well enough to continue. An organization's strategy that is mostly new most of the time signals erratic decision-making and weak "strategizing" on the part of managers. Major changes in strategy can be expected on occasion, especially in crisis situations, but they cannot be made often without creating internal chaos and confusion among customers.

Crafting a strategy has a *strongly entrepreneurial character* in the sense that managers have to choose among alternative business directions and pursue moves that entail at least some venturesomeness and risk-taking. How boldly/cautiously managers push out in new directions and whether they press for improved organizational performance are often good indicators of their enterprising spirit. The entrepreneurial risks inherent in managerial strategy-making are becoming complacent when the present strategy is working well and being overly analytical and hesitant when a strategy starts to grow stale. The entrepreneurial challenge is to keep the organization's strategy fresh, to maintain the organization's capacity for dealing with changing conditions, and to steer the organization into doing the right things at the right time.

The enterprising quality of strategy formation extends to all managers, not just senior executives. Entrepreneurship is involved when a sales manager crafts a *narrow* strategy to boost sales by equipping sales reps' cars with mobile telephones. And entrepreneurship is involved when senior executives devise a *broad* companywide strategy to become the low-cost producer in the industry and then use the cost advantage to undercut rivals' prices, grab some of their customers, and gain market share. Hence, entrepreneurial strategy-making falls on the shoulders of managers up and down the organizational hierarchy, in functional departments and in remote operating units (plants and district offices) as well as at the top of the organizational pyramid. Strategy-making is not something just top managers do; it is something all managers do—every manager needs an entrepreneurial game plan for the area he/she is in charge of.

From the perspective of the whole organization, the task of "strategizing" is an ongoing exercise.[1] While "the whats" of an organization's mission and long-term objectives, once chosen, may remain unaltered for several years, "the hows" of strategy are always evolving, partly to respond to an ever-changing external environment, partly from the proactive efforts of managers to create new windows of opportunity, and partly from fresh ideas about how to make the strategy work better. On occasion, major changes emerge when a new strategic move is put to the test in the real world or when a crisis strikes and managers see that the organization's strategy needs radical reorientation. As a consequence, refinements and additions to the strategic plan, interspersed with periodic quantum leaps, are a normal part of managerial "strategizing."

The ongoing stream of strategic moves and approaches means that an organization's strategy forms over a period of time and then reforms, always consisting of some mix of holdover approaches and freshly planned moves. Aside from crisis situations (where many strategic moves may have to be made very quickly, producing a substantially new strategy almost overnight) and new company start-ups (where strategy exists more in the form of plans and intended actions), a company's strategy is formed in bits and pieces, as events unfold and as managerial experience with the situation accumulates. Everything cannot be planned out in advance, and even the best-laid plans must be responsive to changing conditions. Strategy-making thus proceeds on two fronts—one proactively thought through in advance, the other conceived in response to new developments, special opportunities, and experience with the successes and failures of prior strategic moves, approaches, and actions. Figure 1–2 indicates the different moves and approaches that delineate a company's strategy.

The three tasks of defining the business, setting objectives, and forming a strategy all involve direction-setting. Together, they specify where the organiza-

---

[1] Henry Mintzberg, "Crafting Strategy," *Harvard Business Review* 65, no. 4 (July-August 1987), pp. 66–75; and James B. Quinn, *Strategies for Change: Logical Incrementalism* (Homewood, Ill.: Richard D. Irwin, 1980), Chap. 2, especially pp. 58–59.

Figure 1–2 THE COMPONENTS OF COMPANY STRATEGY

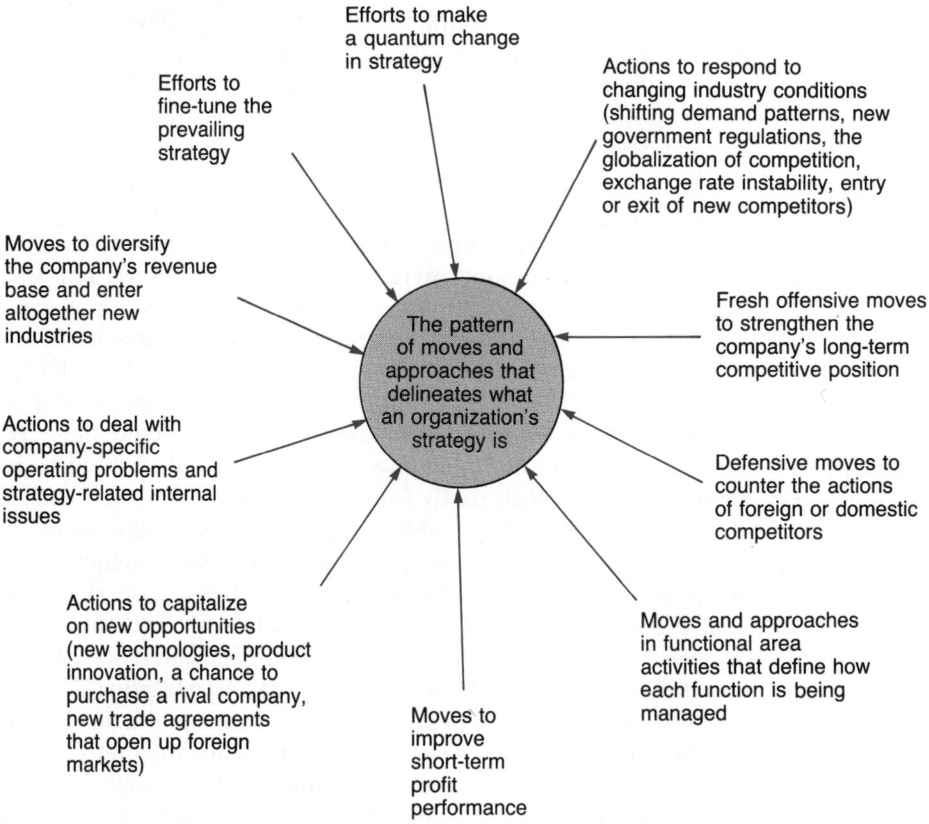

tion is headed and how management intends to achieve the targeted results. Together, they constitute a *strategic plan*. In some companies, especially large corporations that are committed to regular strategy reviews and formal strategic planning, the strategic plan is explicit and written (although some parts of the plan may be omitted if they are too sensitive to reveal before they are actually undertaken). In other companies, the strategic plan is not put on paper but rather exists in the form of understandings among managers about what is to be carried over from the past and what new actions are to be taken. Organizational objectives are the part of the strategic plan most often put in writing and circulated widely among managers and employees.

Illustration Capsule 3 presents an outline of Sara Lee Corporation's mission, objectives, and strategies as an example of how the three direction-setting steps join together.

ILLUSTRATION CAPSULE 3

SARA LEE CORPORATION: MISSION, OBJECTIVES, AND STRATEGY

In a recent annual report, the management of Sara Lee Corporation set forth the company's mission, objectives, and strategy:

Mission

Sara Lee Corporation's mission is to be the leading brand-name food and consumer packaged goods company with major market share positions in key consumer markets worldwide.

We manufacture and market high-quality, marketing-sensitive products with growth potential. These products, which are sold through common distribution channels, include

- Packaged food products,
- Food products and services for the foodservice industry,
- Consumer personal products, and
- Household and personal care products.

Objectives

Size alone—that is, being the largest by some quantitative measure—does not define leadership. We aspire to be a larger company only to the extent that size and scale contribute to achieving more important measures of pre-eminence.

First, and above all, the leading company must be an outstanding financial performer for its stockholders. We must produce dependable and consistent financial returns which rank high in absolute terms as well as relative to our peer competitors.

Second, our product positions must be very high quality, compete in significant market segments, and command exceptionally strong market shares.

Third, our management people and processes must be of the highest caliber and appropriate to the times.

And fourth, we must be recognized as a corporation with an especially high sense of responsibility to our employees and public constituencies.

(continued)

Corporate Strategies

1. *Invest to accelerate internal growth.* Direct and focus investment spending on strategic opportunities to build share and to accelerate unit volume growth in key product positions.

2. *Develop the lowest cost position in all product categories.* Emphasize and measure operating efficiencies and cost structures in all areas of the corporation to reduce costs consistently and to increase return on sales without sacrificing quality.

3. *Make acquisitions.* Acquire businesses which fit Sara Lee Corporation's strategic focus and which provide increased opportunity for growth consistent with our mission.

4. *Leverage brand names and strategically link businesses for synergy.* Generate growth by building and extending brand positions, and improve returns by strategically combining divisions and developing synergies among businesses.

5. *Pursue cross-channel distribution for established products, brands and positions.* Increase unit volume and return on sales with cross-channel distribution.

Source: 1987 Annual Report.

Strategy Implementation and Execution

The strategy-implementing function consists of seeing what it will take to make the strategy work and then getting it done on schedule—*the skill comes in knowing how to achieve results*. The job of implementing strategy is primarily an action-driven *administrative task* that cuts across many internal matters. The specific administrative elements necessary to put the strategy into place include:

- Building an organization capable of carrying out the strategy successfully.
- Developing budgets that steer resources into those internal activities critical to strategic success.
- Motivating people in ways that induce them to pursue the target objectives energetically and, if need be, modifying their duties and job behavior to better fit the requirements of successful strategy execution.
- Tying the reward structure to the achievement of the targeted results.
- Creating a work environment that is conducive to successful strategy implementation.
- Installing strategy-supportive policies and procedures.
- Exerting the internal leadership needed to drive implementation forward and to keep improving on how the strategy is being executed.

The administrative aim is to create "fits" between the way things are done and what it takes for effective strategy execution. The stronger the fits, the better the execution of strategy. The most important fits are between strategy and organizational capabilities, between strategy and the reward structure, between strategy and internal policies and procedures, and between strategy and the organization's culture (the latter emerges from the values and beliefs shared by organizational members and from management's human relations practices). Fitting the ways the organization does things internally to what it takes for effective strategy execution is what unites the organization firmly behind the accomplishment of strategy.

The strategy-implementing task is easily the most complicated and time-consuming part of strategic management. It cuts across virtually all facets of managing, and actions must be initiated from many points within the organization. The strategy-implementer's agenda emerges from careful assessment of what the organization must do differently and better to carry out the strategic plan proficiently. Each manager has to think through the answer to "What has to be done in my area of responsibility to carry out my piece of the strategic plan, and how can I best get it done?" The amount of internal change needed to put the strategy into place depends on how much strategic change is called for, how far out of alignment internal practices are with the requirements of strategy, and how well strategy and organizational culture are already matched. Once the needed changes and actions are identified, management must supervise all the details of implementation and apply enough pressure on the organization to convert objectives into results. Depending on the amount of internal change involved, full implementation can take several months to several years.

Evaluating Performance, Reviewing the Situation, and Initiating Corrective Adjustments

None of the previous four tasks are one-time exercises. Circumstances always crop up and make corrective adjustments desirable. Long-term direction may need to be altered, the business redefined, and management's vision of the organization's future course narrowed or broadened. Performance targets may need raising or lowering in light of past experience and future prospects. Strategy may need to be modified because of shifts in long-term direction, because new objectives have been set, or because changing conditions make fine-tuning or major overhaul necessary.

The search for even better strategy execution is also continuous. Sometimes an aspect of implementation does not go as well as intended and changes have to be made. Progress in putting strategy in place typically occurs unevenly—faster in some areas and slower in others. Some things get done easily; others prove nettlesome. Implementation comes through the pooling effect of many administrative decisions about how to do things and how to create stronger fits between strategy and internal operating practices. Budget revisions, policy changes, reorganization, personnel changes, culture-changing actions, and revised compensation practices are typical ways of trying to make strategy work better.

WHY STRATEGIC MANAGEMENT IS AN ONGOING PROCESS

Because each one of the five tasks of strategic management requires constant evaluation and a decision whether to continue with things as they are or to make changes, *the process of managing strategy is ongoing*—nothing is final and all prior actions are subject to modification. Strategic management is a process filled with constant motion. Changes in the organization's situation, either from the inside or outside or both, constantly drive strategic adjustments. This is why Figure 1–1 is explicit about recycling to any of the tasks as needed.

The task of evaluating performance and initiating corrective adjustments is both the end and the beginning of the strategic management cycle. The march of external and internal events guarantees that revisions in the four previous components will be needed sooner or later. It is always incumbent on management to push for better performance—to find ways to improve the existing strategy and how it is being executed. Changing external conditions add further impetus to the need for periodic revisions in a company's mission, performance objectives, strategy, and approaches to strategy execution. Most of the time, the adjustments involve fine-tuning, but occasions for a quantum strategic reorientation do arise—sometimes prompted by significant external developments and sometimes by sharply sliding financial performance. Strategy managers must stay close enough to the situation to detect when changing conditions require a strategic response and when they don't. It is their job to read the winds of change, recognize significant changes early, and capitalize on events as they unfold.[2]

Characteristics of the Process

While developing a mission, setting objectives, forming a strategy, implementing and executing the strategic plan, and evaluating performance form the elements of managing strategy, actually performing the tasks is not so cleanly divided and neatly sequenced. There is much interplay among the five tasks. For example, considering what strategic actions to take raises issues about whether and how the strategy can be satisfactorily implemented. Deciding on a company mission involves setting objectives for the organization to achieve (both involve directional priorities). Establishing challenging but achievable objectives must take into account both current performance and the strategy options available for improving performance. Deciding on a strategy is entangled with decisions about long-term direction and whether objectives have been set too high or too low.

Second, the five strategic management tasks are not done in isolation. They are carried out in the midst of all other managerial responsibilities—supervision of day-to-day operations, dealing with unexpected crises, going to meetings, preparing reports, handling people problems, and taking on special assignments and civic duties. Thus, while the job of managing strategy is the most important

---

[2] Mintzberg, "Crafting Strategy," p. 74.

function management performs insofar as organizational success or failure is concerned, it isn't all managers must do or be concerned about.

Third, strategy management makes erratic demands on a manager's time. An organization's situation does not change in an orderly or predictable way. Hence strategic issues and decisions take up big chunks of management time in some weeks and months and little or none in others.

Last, the big day in, day out time-consuming aspect of strategic management is trying to get the best strategy-supportive performance out of every individual and trying to perfect the current strategy by refining its content and execution. Managing strategy is mostly managing the strategy in place, not developing and instituting strategic change. The really valuable strategic management skill lies less in actually formulating strategic change than in knowing *when* to do so.[3] Perpetual changes in strategy are not only dysfunctional but also are unnecessary—most of the time, there's more to be gained from improving execution of the present strategy.

WHO ARE THE STRATEGY MANAGERS?

An organization's chief executive officer (CEO) is the most visible and most important *strategy manager*. The CEO, as captain of the ship, bears full responsibility for leading the tasks of formulating and implementing the strategic plan for the organization as a whole, irrespective of the fact that others have a hand in the process. The CEO functions as chief direction-setter, chief objective-setter, chief strategy-maker and chief strategy-implementer for the total enterprise. What the CEO views as important usually moves to the top of the strategic priority list, and the CEO has the final word on key strategic decisions.

Vice presidents for production, marketing, finance, human resources, and other functional departments have important strategy-making and strategy-implementing responsibilities as well. Normally, the production v-p oversees production strategy; the marketing v-p heads up the marketing strategy effort; the financial v-p is in charge of financial strategy; and so on. Usually functional vice presidents are also involved in proposing and developing key elements of the overall strategy, working closely with the CEO to hammer out a consensus and make certain parts of the strategy more effective. Only rarely are all the key pieces of organization strategy personally fashioned by the CEO.

But managerial positions with strategy-making and strategy-implementing responsibility are by no means restricted to these few senior executives; in very real ways, *every manager is a strategy-maker and strategy-implementer for the area he/she has authority over and supervises*. This is because every part of a company—be it a business unit, division, operating department, plant, or district office—has a strategic role to carry out. And the manager in charge of that unit, with guidance from superiors, usually ends up doing some or most of the strategy-

---

[3] Mintzberg, "Crafting Strategy," p. 73.

making for the unit and carrying the burden of implementing whatever strategic choices are made. Obviously, though, managers who are farther down in the managerial hierarchy have a narrower, more specific strategy-making/strategy-implementing role than managers closer to the top of the pyramid.

Another reason why lower-echelon managers are strategy-makers and strategy-implementers is that the more geographically scattered and diversified an organization's operations are, the more impossible it becomes for a few senior executives to handle all the strategic planning that needs to be done. It is just too hard for managers in the corporate office to gain enough command of all the situational details out in the various geographical areas and operating units to be able to prescribe appropriate strategies. What usually happens is that some of the strategy-making responsibility is delegated to those lower-level managers who head the organizational subunits where specific strategic results must be achieved. Delegating a lead strategy-making role to those managers who will be deeply involved in carrying out the strategy in their areas fixes accountability for strategic success or failure. When the managers who implement the strategy are also its architects, it is hard for them to shift the blame or make excuses if they don't achieve the target results.

A company that has diversified into several different businesses has four distinct levels of strategy managers:

- *The chief executive officer and other senior corporate-level executives* who have primary responsibility and personal authority for big strategic decisions affecting the total enterprise and the collection of individual businesses the enterprise has diversified into.
- *Managers who have profit-and-loss responsibility for subsidiary business units* and who are expected to exercise a major leadership role in formulating and implementing strategy for the individual business they head.
- *Functional area managers within a given business unit* who have direct authority over a major piece of the business (manufacturing, marketing and sales, finance, R&D, personnel) and therefore must support the business unit's overall strategy with strategic actions in their own areas.
- *Managers of major operating departments and geographic field units* who have frontline responsibility for putting together the details of strategic efforts in their areas and for carrying out their pieces of the overall strategic plan at the grass roots level.

A single-business enterprise has no more than three of these levels—business-level strategy managers, functional area strategy managers, and operating-level strategy managers. Together, they form a management team responsible for directing the strategic efforts of the total enterprise in that one business. Proprietorships, partnerships, and small owner-managed enterprises, however, typically have only one or two strategy managers since the whole strategy-making/strategy-implementing function can be handled by just a few key people.

Managerial jobs involving strategy formulation and implementation abound in not-for-profit organizations as well. For example, a multicampus state university has four strategy-managing levels: (1) the president of the whole university system is a strategy manager with broad direction-setting responsibility and strategic decision-making authority over all the campuses; (2) the chancellor for each campus customarily has strategy-making/strategy-implementing authority over all academic, student, athletic, and alumni matters plus budgetary, programmatic and coordinative responsibilities for the whole campus; (3) the academic deans of various colleges or schools have lead responsibility for charting future direction at the college-level, steering resources into some programs and out of others, and otherwise devising a collegewide plan to fulfill the college's teaching-research-service mission; and (4) the heads of various academic departments within a college or school are strategy managers with first-line strategy-making/strategy-implementing responsibility for the department's undergraduate and graduate program offerings, faculty research efforts, and all other activities relating to the department's mission, objectives, and future direction. In federal and state government, heads of local, district, and regional offices function as strategy managers in their efforts to be responsive to the specific needs and situations of the geographical area their office serves (a district manager in Portland may need a slightly different strategy than does the district manager in Orlando). In municipal governments, heads of various departments (police, fire, water and sewer, parks and recreation, health and so on) are strategy managers because they have line authority for the operations of their department and thus can influence departmental objectives, the formation of a strategy to achieve these objectives, and how the strategy is implemented.

Managerial jobs with strategy-making/strategy-implementing roles are thus commonplace. The ins and outs of strategy formulation and implementation are a *basic* aspect of managing, *not* just something for top-level managers to deal with.[4]

The Role and Tasks of Strategic Planners

If senior and middle managers have lead roles in strategy-making and strategy-implementing in their areas of responsibility, what do strategic planners do? Is there a legitimate place in big companies for a strategic planning department staffed with specialists in planning and strategic analysis? The answer is yes. But the department's role and tasks should consist chiefly of helping to gather and organize information that strategy managers need, establishing and administering an annual strategy review cycle whereby all strategy managers reconsider and refine their strategic plans, and then coordinating the process of reviewing and

---

[4] Since the scope of a manager's strategy-making/strategy-implementing role varies according to the manager's position in the organizational hierarchy, our use of the word *organization* includes whatever kind of organizational unit the strategy manager is in charge of—an entire company or not-for-profit organization, a business unit within a diversified company, a major geographic division, an important functional unit within a business, or an operating department or field unit reporting to a specific functional area head. This way we can avoid using the awkward phrase "the organization or organizational subunit" to indicate the scope of a manager's strategy-making/strategy-implementing responsibilities. It should be clear from the context of the discussion whether the subject applies only to the total enterprise or to most or all management levels.

approving the strategic plans developed in various parts of the company. The value added by strategic planners comes in their facilitating and coordinating the strategic planning efforts of line managers, helping managers at all levels crystalize the strategic issues that ought to be addressed, providing information, helping with the analysis of industry and competitive conditions if asked, and generating information on the company's strategic performance. But strategic planners should not be charged with making strategic decisions, preparing detailed strategic plans (for someone else to implement), or making strategic action recommendations that usurp the strategy-making responsibilities of managers in charge of major operating units.

When strategic planners are asked to go beyond the function of providing specialized staff assistance and to prepare a comprehensive strategic plan for top management's consideration, either of two adverse consequences may occur. One is that some managers will gladly toss the tough strategic problems in their areas onto the desks of strategic planners to let the planners do their strategic thinking for them. The planners, not knowing as much about the situation as the managers, are in a weaker position to design a workable action plan, and in any event, they cannot be held responsible for implementing what they recommend. Putting responsibility for strategy-making into the hands of planners and responsibility for implementation into the hands of line managers makes it hard to fix accountability for unacceptably poor strategic results. It also deludes senior managers into thinking they don't have to be personally involved in leading the organization down a clear-cut path and crafting a strategy capable of generating above-average results. The hard truth is that strategy-making is simply not a staff function, nor is it something that can be handed off to an advisory committee of lower-ranking managers.

The second adverse consequence of having strategic planners take a lead strategy-making role is that line managers have no ownership stake in the plan. When senior and middle managers have no personal stake in, or real emotional commitment to, the strategic agenda proposed by the planners, they are prone to give lip service to the plan, make a few token implementation efforts, then quickly get back to "business as usual" knowing that the formal written plan concocted by the planners does not represent their own "real" managerial agenda. The written strategic plan, because it lacks credibility and true top-management commitment, soon becomes a paper document collecting dust on managers' shelves. The end result is that few managers take the work product of the strategic planning staff seriously enough to pursue wholehearted implementation—planning is viewed as just another bureaucratic exercise.

Either consequence renders formal strategic planning efforts ineffective and opens the door for a strategy-making vacuum conducive to organizational drift or to fragmented, uncoordinated strategic decisions. The odds are then heightened that the organization will have no strong strategic rudder and insufficient top-down direction. The flaws in having staffers or advisory committees formulate strategies for areas they do not manage are: (1) they cannot be held strictly accountable if their recommendations don't produce the desired results (since they don't have authority for directing implementation) and (2) what they recommend won't be well accepted or enthusiastically implemented by those who "have to sing the song the planners have written." But when managers are expected to be the chief strategy-makers and strategy-implementers for the areas they head, it is their own strategy and their own implementation approach that are being put to the test of workability. The "buy in" to their own strategy and implementation efforts is certainly stronger than it is for someone else's efforts. Hence they are likely to be more committed to making the plan work (their future careers with the organization are at more risk!), and they can be held strictly accountable for achieving the target results in their area.

The Strategic Role of the Board of Directors

With senior and middle managers having lead responsibility for crafting and implementing strategy, the chief strategic role of an organization's board of directors is to see that the overall task of managing strategy is adequately done.[5] Boards of directors normally review important strategic moves and approve strategic plans—a procedure that makes the board ultimately responsible for the strategic actions taken. But directors rarely can or should play a direct role in formulating the strategy they must approve. The immediate task of directors in ratifying strategy and new direction-setting moves is to ensure that the proposals presented to them have been adequately analyzed and thought through and that the proposed strategy is superior to available alternatives; flawed proposals are customarily withdrawn for revision by management.[6] The longer-range task of directors is to evaluate the caliber of senior managers' strategy-making and strategy-implementing skills. Here it is necessary to determine whether the current CEO is doing a good job of strategic management (as a basis for awarding salary increases and bonuses and deciding on retention or removal) and, also, to evaluate the strategic skills of other senior executives in line to succeed the current CEO.

THE BENEFITS OF A "STRATEGIC APPROACH" TO MANAGING

The message of this book is that doing a good job of managing inherently requires doing a good job of strategic management. Today's managers have to think strategically about their company's position and about the impact of changing conditions. They have to monitor the external situation closely enough to know *when* to institute strategy change. They have to know the business well enough to know *what kind* of strategic changes to initiate. Simply said, the fundamentals of strategic management need to drive the whole approach to managing organiza-

---

[5] Kenneth R. Andrews, *The Concept of Corporate Strategy*, 3rd ed. (Homewood, Ill.: Richard D. Irwin, 1987), p. 123.

[6] Ibid.

tions.[7] The chief executive officer of one successful company put it well when he said:

> In the main, our competitors are acquainted with the same fundamental concepts and techniques and approaches that we follow, and they are as free to pursue them as we are. More often than not, the difference between their level of success and ours lies in the relative thoroughness and self-discipline with which we and they develop and execute our strategies for the future.

The advantages of first-rate strategic thinking and conscious strategy management (as opposed to freewheeling improvisation, gut feel, and drifting along) include (1) providing better guidance to the entire organization on the crucial point of "what it is we are trying to do and to achieve," (2) making management more alert to change, new opportunities, and threatening developments, (3) providing managers with a much-needed rationale to evaluate competing budget requests for investment capital and new staff—a rationale that argues strongly for steering resources into strategy-supportive, results-producing areas, (4) helping to unify the numerous strategy-related decisions by managers across the organization, and (5) creating a more *proactive* management posture and counteracting tendencies for decisions to be reactive and defensive.[8]

The fifth advantage of being proactive rather than merely reactive frequently enhances long-term performance. Business history shows that high-performing enterprises often *initiate* and *lead,* not just *react* and *defend.* They see strategy as a tool for securing a sustainable competitive advantage and for pushing performance to superior levels. Ideally, devising and executing a powerful, opportunistic strategy will propel a firm to a leadership position above and apart from industry rivals, so its earnings will prosper and its products/services will become *the* standard for industry comparison.

A Recap of Important Terms

Let's conclude this introductory overview of the managerial tasks of formulating and implementing strategy by reiterating the meaning of key terms that will be used again in the chapters to come:

> *Organization mission*—management's customized answer to the question "What is our business and what will it be?" A mission statement broadly outlines the organization's future direction and serves as a guiding concept for what the organization is to do and to become.

---

[7] For a lucid discussion of the importance of the strategic management function, see V. Ramanujam and N. Venkatraman, "Planning and Performance: A New Look at an Old Question," *Business Horizons* 30, no. 3 (May-June 1987), pp. 19–25; and Henry Mintzberg, "The Strategy Concept: Another Look at Why Organizations Need Strategies," *California Management Review* 30, no. 1 (Fall 1987), pp. 25–32.

[8] Kenneth R. Andrews, *The Concept of Corporate Strategy,* rev. ed. (Homewood, Ill.: Richard D. Irwin, 1980), pp. 15–16, 46, 123–29; and Seymour Tilles, "How to Evaluate Corporate Strategy," *Harvard Business Review* 41, no. 4 (July-August 1963), p. 116.

Performance objectives—the organization's targets for achievement.

Long-range objectives—the achievement levels to be reached either within the next three to five years or else on an ongoing basis year after year.

Short-range objectives—the near-term performance targets; they establish the pace for achieving the long-range objectives.

Strategy—the managerial action plan for achieving organizational objectives; strategy is mirrored in the *pattern* of moves and approaches devised by management to produce the desired performance. Strategy is the *how* of pursuing the organization's mission and reaching target objectives.

Strategic plan—a statement outlining an organization's mission and future direction, near-term and long-term performance targets, and strategy in light of the organization's external and internal situation.

Strategy formulation—refers to the entire direction-setting management function of an organization's mission, setting specific performance objectives, and forming a strategy. The end product of strategy formulation is a strategic plan.

Strategy implementation—the full range of managerial activities associated with putting the chosen strategy into place, supervising its pursuit, and achieving the targeted results.

In the chapters to come, we will probe the strategy-related tasks of managers and the methods of strategic analysis more intensively. When you get to the end of the book we think you will see why the two things that usually separate the best-managed organization from the rest are (1) superior strategy-making and entrepreneurship and (2) competent implementation and execution of the chosen strategy. An organization's management team—whether it devises and implements new strategies, is preoccupied with implementing prior strategies better, or does nothing to change either strategy or the organization's basic method of operating—is still the organization's chief strategy-maker and chief strategy-implementer. The quality of managerial strategy-making and strategy-implementing has a significant impact on organization performance. A company that has no clear-cut direction, vague or undemanding objectives, or a muddled or flawed strategy is much more likely to drift, to tolerate subpar performance, and to lose its competitiveness.

SUGGESTED READINGS

Andrews, Kenneth R. *The Concept of Corporate Strategy,* 3rd Ed. Homewood, Ill.: Richard D. Irwin, 1987, chap. 1.

Gluck, Frederick W. "A Fresh Look at Strategic Management." *Journal of Business Strategy* 6, no. 2 (Fall 1985), pp. 4–21.

Kelley, C. Aaron. "The Three Planning Questions: A Fable." *Business Horizons* 26, no. 2 (March–April 1983), pp. 46–48.

Kotter, John P. *The General Managers.* New York: Free Press, 1982.

Levinson, Harry, and Stuart Rosenthal. *CEO: Corporate Leadership in Action.* New York: Basic Books, 1987.

Mintzberg, Henry. "Crafting Strategy." *Harvard Business Review* 65, no. 4 (July–August 1987), pp. 66–75.

————. "The Strategy Concept: Five Ps for Strategy." *California Management Review* 30, no. 1 (Fall 1987), pp. 11–24.

————. "The Strategy Concept: Another Look at Why Organizations Need Strategies." *California Management Review* 30, no. 1 (Fall 1987), pp. 25–32.

Quinn, James Brian. *Strategies for Change: Logical Incrementalism.* Homewood, Ill.: Richard D. Irwin, 1980, chaps. 2 and 3.

Ramanujam, V., and N. Venkatraman. "Planning and Performance: A New Look at an Old Question." *Business Horizons* 30, no. 3 (May–June 1987), pp. 19–25.

Yip, George S. "Who Needs Strategic Planning?" *Journal of Business Strategy* 6, no. 2 (Fall 1985), pp. 22–29.

2

The Three Strategy-Making Tasks: Developing a Mission, Setting Objectives, and Forming a Strategy

· · · · · · · · · · · · · · · ·

Management's job is not to see the company as it is . . . but as it can become.
John W. Teeter
CEO, Greyhound Corp.

· · · · · · · · · · · · · · · ·

Without a strategy the organization is like a ship without a rudder, going around in circles. It's like a tramp; it has no place to go.
Joel Ross and Michael Kami

· · · · · · · · · · · · · · · ·

You've got to come up with a plan. You can't wish things will get better.
John F. Welch
CEO, General Electric

This chapter provides a more in-depth look at each of the three strategy-making tasks: defining the business and developing a mission, setting performance objectives, and forming a strategy to produce the desired results. We will also examine the nature of strategy-making at each managerial level in the organizational hierarchy and present four generic approaches managers can take in performing the strategy-making task.

DEVELOPING A MISSION: THE FIRST DIRECTION-SETTING TASK

Management's vision of what the organization is trying to do and to become over the long-term is commonly referred to as the organization's *mission*. A *mission statement* specifies what activities the organization intends to pursue and what course management has charted for the future. It outlines "who *we* are, what *we* do, and where *we* are headed." Mission statements are thus personalized in the sense that they set an organization apart from others in its industry and give it its own special identity, character, and path for development. For example, the mission of a major New York bank like Chase Manhattan has little in common with a locally owned small town bank even though both organizations are technically in the banking industry. Without a concept of what the organization should and should not do and a vision of where the organization needs to be going, a manager is ill-equipped to function effectively as either leader or strategy-maker. There are three distinct aspects to the task of formulating a mission:

* Understanding what business an organization is really in.
* Deciding when to change the mission and alter the organization's strategic course.
* Communicating the mission in ways that are clear, exciting, and inspiring.

Understanding and Defining the Business

Defining what business an organization is in is not always obvious or easy. Is IBM in the computer business (a product-oriented definition), in the information and data processing business (a computer-needs type of definition), or in the electronics business (a technology-oriented definition)? Is Coca-Cola in the soft-drink business (in which case its strategic vision can be trained narrowly on the actions of Pepsi, 7 Up, Dr Pepper, Canada Dry, and Schweppes), or is it in the beverage industry (in which case management must think strategically about positioning Coca-Cola products in a market that includes fruit juices, alcoholic drinks, milk, bottled water, coffee, and tea)? This is not a trivial question for Coca-Cola. Many young adults get their morning caffeine fix by drinking cola instead of coffee; with a beverage industry perspective as opposed to a soft-drink industry perspective, Coca-Cola management is more likely to perceive a long-term growth opportunity in winning youthful coffee drinkers over to its colas.

Defining what business an organization is really in is a composite of three factors:[1]

1. Customer needs—*what* is being satisfied.
2. Customer groups—*who* is being satisfied.
3. The technologies used and functions performed—*how* customers needs are satisfied.

Defining a business in terms of what to satisfy, who to satisfy, and how the organization will go about producing the satisfaction adds completeness to the definition. It also directs management to look outward toward customers and markets as well as inward in forming its concept of "who we are and what we

---

[1] Derek F. Abell, *Defining the Business: The Starting Point of Strategic Planning* (Englewood Cliffs, N.J.: Prentice Hall, 1980), p. 169.

do.''[2] A good example of a business definition that incorporates all three aspects is a paraphrase of Polaroid's business definition during the early 1970s: ''perfecting and marketing instant photography to satisfy the needs of more affluent U.S. and West European families for affection, friendship, fond memories, and humor.'' For years, McDonald's business definition has centered on ''serving hot, tasty food quickly in a clean restaurant for a good value'' to a broad base of customers worldwide. McDonald's serves over 20 million customers daily at over 10,000 restaurants in over 40 countries. Illustration Capsule 4 describes how Circle K, the second largest convenience store retailer in the United States, views its mission and business.

The Polaroid, McDonald's, and Circle K examples all adhere closely to the three necessary components of a mission statement: the specific needs served by the company's basic product(s) or service(s), the targeted customer groups, and the technology and functions the company employs in providing its product/service. It takes all three to define what business a company is really in. Just knowing what products or services a firm provides is never enough. Products or services per se are not important to customers; what turns a product or service into a business is the need or want being satisfied. Without the need or want there is no business. Customer groups are relevant to the definition because they indicate the market to be served: the geographic domain to be covered and the types of buyers the firm is going after. Technology used and functions performed are important because they indicate how the company will satisfy the customer's need and how much of the industry's production chain its activities will span. In this latter regard, a firm can be *specialized,* participating in one aspect of the whole industry's production chain, or *fully integrated,* operating in all parts of the industry chain. Circle K, for instance, is a specialized firm operating only in the retail end of the chain; it doesn't manufacture the items it retails. The major international oil companies like Exxon, Mobil, and Chevron, however, are fully integrated; they lease drilling sites, drill wells, pump crude oil out of the wells, transport crude oil in their own ships and pipelines to their own refineries, and sell gasoline and other refined products through their own networks of branded distributors and service station outlets. Because of the disparity in functions performed and technology employed, the business of a retailer like Circle K is thus much narrower and quite different from a fully integrated enterprise like Exxon. Between these two extremes firms can stake out *partially integrated* positions, participating only in selected stages of the industry. So one way of distinguishing how one firm's business differs from another's, especially among firms in the same industry, is by looking at which functions they perform in the chain.

---

[2] There is a tendency sometimes for companies to view their mission in terms of making a profit. However, profit is more correctly an *objective* and a *result* of what the company does. Missions based on making a profit are incapable of distinguishing one type of profit-seeking enterprise from another—the mission and business of Sears are plainly different from the mission and business of Delta Airlines, even though both try to earn a profit.

ILLUSTRATION CAPSULE   4

CIRCLE K's MISSION STATEMENT

We believe our primary business is not so much retail as it is service oriented.

Certainly, our customers buy merchandise in our stores. But they can buy similar items elsewhere, and perhaps pay lower prices.

But they're willing to buy from Circle K because we give them added value for their money.

That added value is service and convenience.

Our Mission
As a service company, our mission is to:

Satisfy our customers' immediate needs and wants by providing them with a wide variety of goods and services at multiple locations.

Our Customers
We will not place a limit on the conveniences we offer customers.

They buy at Circle K much differently than at a supermarket. They come to our stores for specific purchases, which they make as quickly as possible. They want immediate service and are willing to pay a premium for it.

Our Stores
We will build our stores at locations most accessible to our customers.

We will organize our merchandise to (1) facilitate quick purchases and (2) encourage other purchases.

We will maintain our stores so they will always be brightly lit, colorful, clean, and comfortable places for our customers and our employees.

Our Goods and Services
We will not be one store—but a dozen stores in one.

We are a gas station, a fast-food restaurant, a grocery store, drugstore, liquor store, newsstand, video rental shop, small bank—and more.

Source: 1987 Annual Report.

A Broad or Narrow Business Definition?   For a small Hong Kong printing company to define its business broadly as ''Asian-language communications'' has no practical direction-setting value. With such a definition the company could pursue limitless courses, most well beyond the scope and capability of a small Hong Kong printer. Mission statements and business definitions have to be narrow enough to pin down the real arena of business interest. Otherwise they cannot serve as boundaries for what to do and not do and as beacons of where managers intend to take the company. Consider the following definitions based on broad-narrow scope:

Broad definition	Narrow definition
Beverages	Soft drinks
Footwear	Athletic footwear
Furniture	Wrought iron lawn furniture
Global mail delivery	Overnight package delivery
Travel and tourism	Ship cruises in the Caribbean

Broad-narrow definitions are always relative. Being in "the furniture business" is probably too broad a concept for a company set on being the largest manufacturer of wrought iron lawn furniture in North America. On the other hand, soft drinks has proved too narrow a scope for a growth-oriented company like Coca-Cola, which, with its beverage industry perspective, acquired Minute-Maid and Hi-C (to capitalize on growing consumer interest in fruit juice products) and Taylor Wine Company (using the California Cellars brand to establish a foothold in wines).[3] The U.S. Postal Service operates with a broad definition; it provides all kinds of global mail delivery services to all types of senders. Federal Express, however, operates with a narrow business definition based on handling overnight package delivery for customers who have unplanned emergencies and tight deadlines.

Diversified firms frequently take a more expansive view of their business scope. The language they use in their mission statements is narrow enough to define their customer-market-technology arenas but open-ended and adaptable enough to incorporate expansion into desirable new businesses. Alcan, Canada's leading aluminum company, used this type of language in its mission statement:

> Alcan is determined to be the most innovative diversified aluminum company in the world. To achieve this position, Alcan will be one, global, customer-oriented enterprise committed to excellence and lowest cost in its chosen aluminum businesses, with significant resources devoted to building an array of new businesses with superior growth and profit potential.

Morton-Thiokol, a substantially more diversified enterprise, used simultaneous broad-narrow terms to define its business:

> We are an international, high-technology company serving the diverse needs of government and industry with products and services ranging from massive solid rocket motors to small ordnance devices, from polymers to disc brake pads, from

---

[3] Coca-Cola's foray into wines was not deemed successful enough to warrant continuation; the division was divested about five years after initial acquisition.

heavy denier yarns to woven carpet backing, from snow-grooming vehicles to trigger sprayers.

John Hancock's mission statement communicates a shift from its long-standing base in insurance to a broader mission in insurance, banking, and diversified financial services:

> At John Hancock, we are determined not just to compete but to advance, building our market share by offering individuals and institutions the broadest possible range of products and services. Apart from insurance, John Hancock encompasses banking products, full brokerage services and institutional investment, to cite only a few of our diversified activities. We believe these new directions constitute the right moves . . . the steps that will drive our growth throughout the remainder of this century.

Where Entrepreneurship Comes In

A member of Maytag's board of directors summed it up well when Maytag unexpectedly made a major acquisition that began to transform it from a domestic company into an international one: "Times change, conditions change." Changing conditions make it incumbent on managers to keep looking toward the future, always checking for *when* it's time to steer a new course and adjust the mission. The key question is "What new directions should we be moving in *now* to get ready for the changes we see coming in our business?" Redirecting the enterprise in light of new developments and changes on the horizon reduces the chances of getting caught in a poor market position or being in the wrong business at the wrong time. For example, Philip Morris, the leading U.S. manufacturer of cigarettes, in anticipation of long-term deterioration in cigarette demand, has positioned itself as a major contender in the food products industry by acquiring two of the largest manufacturers, General Foods and Kraft. Many U.S. companies are broadening their missions geographically and forming joint ventures with European companies to position themselves for the dismantling of trade barriers in the European Community in 1992.

Good entrepreneurship entails alertness to changing customer wants and needs, to why some customers are dissatisfied with the current products and services they are using, to the kinds of problems customers are having with the industry's product, to new technological potential out in the wings, to changing international trade conditions, and to other important signs of growing or shrinking business opportunity. Appraising new customer-market-technology developments ultimately leads to entrepreneurial judgments about which of several forks in the road to take. It is a strategy leader's job to peer far down each of the forks, evaluate the risks and prospects of each path, and make direction-setting decisions to position the enterprise to be a successful performer in the years ahead. *A well-chosen mission prepares a company for the future*. Many companies in consumer electronics and telecommunications, believing that their future products will incorporate microprocessors and other elements of computer technology, are expanding their missions and establishing positions in the various phases of the computer business to have access to the needed technology. Numerous companies in manufacturing, seeing the swing to internationalization and global competition, are broadening their missions from serving domestic markets to serving global markets. Coca-Cola, Kentucky Fried Chicken, and McDonald's are pursuing market opportunities in China, Europe, Japan, and the Soviet Union; the Japanese automobile companies are working to establish a much bigger presence in the European car market; CNN, Turner Broadcasting's successful all-news cable channel, is pushing hard to win its way into European homes and become the first all-news channel for Europe. Thus a company's mission always has a time dimension; it is subject to change whenever senior management concludes that the present mission is no longer adequate.

Communicating the Mission

Communicating the mission to subordinate managers and employees is almost as important a task as developing the mission. Effective mission statements are inspiring—they call for the best in one way or another.[4] If senior management couches the organization's mission in platitudes, the words are likely to have a hollow ring that leaves lower-level managers and employees uninspired—they gain neither challenge nor a sense of direction from motherhood-and-apple-pie-style verbiage. Similarly, if senior executives fail to communicate the mission in ways that induce buy-in and a sense of purpose, or if they don't provide a convincing rationale for why the organization has to move in new directions, the mission statement will do little to change employees' attitudes, thinking, and behavior. Such an outcome makes it that much harder to move the organization down the chosen path. The skill in wording a mission statement comes in choosing simple, concise terminology that speaks loudly and clearly to all concerned and leaves no doubt about the future course management has charted. Then it needs to be repeated over and over in a challenging, convincing fashion. A simple, clear, often-repeated, inspiring mission statement will turn heads in the intended direction and begin a new organizational march. As this occurs, the first step in organizational direction-setting has been taken. Illustration Capsule 5 provides an example of an inspiration-oriented mission statement.

ILLUSTRATION CAPSULE   5

THE BEATRICE MISSION

We have a bold mission. It will challenge us. It will test us. Nothing else is worthy of Beatrice. Nothing else will reward us more.

   Over the next five years, Beatrice will emerge as the world's premier marketer of food and consumer products . . . *the* power in the consumer

(continued)

---

[4] Tom Peters, *Thriving on Chaos* (New York: Harper & Row, 1988), pp. 486–8.

marketplace, wherever we choose to compete. Each of our brands will be a leader in its category.

Our first priority will be total dedication to anticipating and satisfying consumer needs. We intend to improve the consumer's life by providing products of superior quality, value and convenience. We will place the consumer first in every decision we make and in everything we do. Only this course of action will enable us to satisfy the needs of our employees for personal growth and meaningful careers. Only this course will enable our suppliers, distributors, trade partners and shareholders to prosper along with us.

The common theme that runs through all the uncommon efforts of the Beatrice family is our unfailing commitment to quality and value. In meeting this challenge we will constantly break new ground, foster new ideas, develop new technologies and establish new rules in the world marketplace. Our presence will be felt in a strong and positive way everywhere that our products are sold. This dedication extends to a true concern for the well-being of all the communities in which we operate.

Quality . . . value . . . dedication to the consumer . . . a commitment to excellence and originality . . . maintaining our obligations to our employees, our shareholders, our suppliers, distributors, trading partners and to our communities.

These are the solid cornerstones on which the future of Beatrice will be built. These are the standards by which all of us will be judged.

Source: 1987 Annual Report.

In drawing together what has been said about the task of developing a mission, it should be apparent that a well-conceived, well-said mission statement has real managerial value: (1) it crystalizes top management's own view about the firm's long-term direction and makeup, (2) it helps keep the direction-related actions of lower-level managers on the right path, (3) it communicates an organizational purpose and identity that can inspire employees and provide enduring challenge in their work, (4) it helps managers avoid either visionless or rudderless management, and (5) it helps an organization prepare for the future.

ESTABLISHING LONG-RANGE AND SHORT-RANGE OBJECTIVES: THE SECOND DIRECTION-SETTING TASK

The act of establishing objectives converts the mission and directional course into specific performance targets to be achieved. At the same time, it begins the necessary process of training the energies of *each part* of the organization on what needs to be accomplished. Objectives are needed for each *key result* that managers deem important to success.[5] Specific key result areas where objectives are

---

[5] The literature of management is filled with references to *goals* and *objectives*. These terms are used in a variety of ways, many of them conflicting. Some writers use the term *goals* to refer

usually needed include overall size and rank in the industry, annual growth in revenues and earnings, return on investment, annual dividend increases, market share, reputation for product quality and/or technological leadership, recognition as a "blue chip" company, ability to ride out ups and downs in the economy, degree of diversification, financial strength, customer service, and cost competitiveness. Illustration Capsule 6 provides a sampling of strategic objectives of some well-known corporations.

ILLUSTRATION CAPSULE   6

STRATEGIC OBJECTIVES OF WELL-KNOWN CORPORATIONS

Federal Express: To become the largest and best transportation company in the world.

Alcan Aluminum: To be the lowest-cost producer of aluminum.

To outperform the average return on equity of the Standard & Poor's Industrial Stock Index.

General Electric: To become the most competitive enterprise in the world by being number one or number two in market share in every business the company is in.

Black & Decker: To continue new product introductions and globalization.

Atlas Corp.:   To become a low-cost, medium-size gold producer, producing in excess of 125,000 ounces of gold a year and building gold reserves of 1,500,000 ounces.

Quaker Oats Co.:   To achieve return on equity at 20 percent or above, "real" earnings growth averaging 5 percent or better over time, be a leading marketer of strong consumer brands, and improve the profitability of low-return businesses or divest them.

---

to the long-run results an organization seeks to achieve and the term *objectives* to refer to immediate, short-run performance targets. Some writers reverse the usage, referring to objectives as the desired long-run results and goals as the desired short-run results. Others use the terms interchangeably. And still others use the term *goals* to refer to general organizationwide performance targets and the term *objectives* to mean the specific targets set by subordinate managers in response to the broader, more inclusive goals of the whole organization. In our view, there's little point in getting bogged down in semantic distinctions between the terms *goals* and *objectives;* the important thing is to recognize that the results an enterprise seeks to attain vary both in scope and in time perspective. In nearly every instance, organizations need long-range and short-range performance targets. It is managerially irrelevant which targets are called "goals" and which are called "objectives." To avoid creating any more of a semantic jungle, we use the single term *objectives* to refer to the performance targets and results an organization seeks to attain. We use the adjectives *long-range* (or long-run) and *short-range* (or short-run) to identify the relevant time frame, and we try to describe objectives to indicate their intended scope and level in the organization.

Both long-range and short-range objectives are needed. Long-range objectives serve two purposes. First, they raise the issue of what actions to take *now* in order to reach the targeted long-range performance *later* (a manager can seldom wait until the end of year 4 to begin working on what needs to be achieved in year 5!). Second, having long-range objectives pushes managers to weigh the impact of today's decisions on longer-range performance. Without the pressure to meet long-range performance targets, managers invariably base decisions on what is most expedient in the near-term.

Short-range objectives spell out the immediate and near-term results to be achieved. They indicate the *speed* at which the organization needs to move along its charted path as well as the *level of performance* being aimed for. They represent a commitment by managers to produce specified results in a specified time frame. This means objectives must spell out *how much by when*. Short-range objectives can be the same as long-range objectives when an organization is already performing at the target long-range level. For instance, if a company has an ongoing objective of 15 percent profit growth every year and is currently achieving this objective, then the company's long-range and short-range profit objectives coincide. The most important situation where short-range objectives differ from long-range objectives occurs when managers are trying to elevate organizational performance and cannot reach the long-range/ongoing target in just one year; short-range objectives then serve as steps for reaching the ultimate target.

The Value of Performance Objectives

Unless an organization's mission and direction are translated into *measurable* performance targets, and until real pressure is put on managers to show progress in reaching these targets, the organization's mission statement will likely end up as nice words, good intentions, and unrealized dreams of accomplishment. The hard knocks of experience tell a powerful story about why objective-setting is a critical task in the strategic management process: *companies whose managers set objectives for each key result area and then aggressively pursue actions calculated to achieve their performance targets are strong candidates to outperform the companies whose managers operate with hopes, prayers, and good intentions.*

It is essential that performance objectives be stated in *quantifiable* or measurable terms and that they contain a *deadline for achievement*. This means avoiding statements like "maximize profits," "reduce costs," "become more efficient," or "increase sales," which specify neither how much nor when. Spelling out strategic targets in measurable terms and then holding managers accountable for reaching their assigned targets within a specified time frame (1) substitutes purposeful, strategic decision-making for aimless actions and confusion over what to accomplish and (2) provides a set of benchmarks for judging the organization's actual strategic performance.

The "Challenging but Achievable" Test

Objectives should not represent whatever levels of achievement management decides would be "nice." Wishful thinking has no place in objective-setting. For objectives to serve as a tool for *stretching* an organization to reach its full potential, they must meet the criterion of being *challenging but achievable*. Satisfying this criterion means setting objectives in the light of several important "inside-outside" considerations:

- What performance levels will industry and competitive conditions realistically allow?
- What results will it take for the organization to be a successful performer?
- What performance is the organization capable of *when pushed*?

In effect, therefore, setting challenging but achievable objectives requires managers to judge what performance is possible in light of external conditions against what performance the organization is really capable of achieving. The tasks of objective-setting and strategy-making often become intertwined at this point. Whereas strategy is management's tool for achieving strategic targets, the choice of a strategy hinges on the organization setting financial performance objectives high enough to execute management's strategy, to make other needed moves, and to please investors and the financial community.

The Need for Objectives at All Management Levels

For strategic thinking and strategy-driven decision-making to penetrate deeply into the organizational hierarchy, performance targets must be established not only for the organization as a whole but also for each of the organization's separate businesses and product lines and down to each functional area and department within the business-unit/product-line structure.[6] Only when every manager, from the chief executive officer down to the lowest strategy manager, is held accountable for achieving specific results in the units they head is the objective-setting process complete enough to ensure that the whole organization is pointed down the chosen trail and that each part of the organization knows what it needs to accomplish.

The objective-setting process is more top-down than it is bottom-up. An example will clarify how strategic objectives at one managerial level drive objectives and strategies of the next level down. Suppose the senior executives of a diversified corporation establish a corporate profit objective of $5 million for next year. Suppose further, after discussion between corporate management and the general managers of the firm's five different businesses, each business is given the challenging but achievable profit objective of $1 million (i.e., if the five business divisions contribute $1 million each in profit, the corporation can reach its $5 million profit objective). Observe so far, with respect to profit only, that corporate executives have set a priority of $5 million in total profit for the year and that the general managers of each business division have been assigned responsibility for $1 million in profit by year-end. A concrete result has thus been agreed on and

───────

[6] Peter F. Drucker, *Management: Tasks, Responsibilities, Practices* (New York: Harper & Row, 1974), p. 100. See also Charles H. Granger, "The Hierarchy of Objectives," *Harvard Business Review* 42, no. 3 (May-June 1963), pp. 63–74.

translated into measurable action commitments to achieve something at two levels in the managerial hierarchy. Next, suppose the general manager of business unit X, after some analytical calculations and discussions with functional area managers, concludes that reaching the $1 million profit objective will require selling 100,000 units at an average price of $50 and producing them at an average cost of $40 (the $10 profit margin multiplied by 100,000 units yields a $1 million profit). Consequently, the general manager and the manufacturing manager may settle on a manufacturing objective of 100,000 units at a unit cost of $40; the general manager and the marketing manager may agree on a sales objective of 100,000 units and an average selling price of $50. In turn, the marketing manager may break the sales objective of 100,000 units into unit sales targets for each salesperson, for each sales territory, and/or for each item in the product line. In similar fashion, objectives are agreed on for every other key area.

The top-down process of establishing performance targets for each manager and organizational subunit not only leads to a clearer definition of what results are expected and who is responsible for achieving them but also provides a valuable degree of unity and cohesion to the decisions and actions taken in different parts of the organization. Generally speaking, organizationwide objectives and strategy need to be established first so they can drive the objective-setting and strategy-making of lower-level organizational units. Top-down objective-setting/ strategizing provides guidance from above and helps lower-level organization units formulate objectives and strategies that are in step with and contribute to those of the total enterprise. With bottom-up objective-setting, organizationwide objectives that emerge from aggregating lower-level objectives may be neither strategically coherent nor bear any resemblance to top management's priorities.

CRAFTING A STRATEGY: THE THIRD DIRECTION-SETTING TASK

Organizations need strategies in order to have guidelines for *how* to achieve objectives and *how* to pursue the organization's mission. Strategy-making is all about *how*—about choosing from the array of options. Without a strategy or overall game plan, there's no overarching consistency to strategic actions and decisions, and the organization will struggle inefficiently and ineffectively to generate a coherent response to the situation and problems it confronts. In addition, organizations need strategies in order to outcompete rivals, to maneuver through threatening environments, and to focus their efforts.[7] In forming a strategy out of the many options that exist, the strategist acts as a forger of responses to market change, a seeker of new opportunities, and a synthesizer of the different moves and approaches taken at various times in various parts of the organization.

As we emphasized in the opening chapter, strategy-making is not just a task for senior executives. In large, diversified enterprises, decisions about what approaches to take and what new moves to initiate involve senior executives in the corporate office, heads of business units and product divisions, functional

---

[7] See Henry Mintzberg, "The Strategy Concept II: Another Look at Why Organizations Need Strategies," *California Management Review* 30, no. 1 (Fall 1987), pp. 25–32.

Table 2-1 THE STRATEGY-MAKING HIERARCHY: WHO HAS PRIMARY RESPONSIBILITY FOR WHAT KINDS OF STRATEGY ACTIONS

Strategy level	Primary strategy development responsibility	Strategy-making functions and areas of focus
Corporate strategy	CEO, other key executives (decisions are typically reviewed/approved by boards of directors)	• Building and managing a high-performing portfolio of business units (making acquisitions, strengthening existing business positions, divesting businesses that no longer fit into management's plans) • Capturing the synergy among related business units and turning it into competitive advantage • Establishing investment priorities and steering corporate resources into businesses with the most attractive opportunities • Reviewing/revising/unifying the major strategic approaches and moves proposed by business unit managers
Line-of-business strategies	General manager/head of business unit (decisions are typically reviewed/approved by senior corporate executive, usually CEO)	• Devising moves and approaches to compete successfully and to secure a competitive advantage • Forming responses to changing external conditions • Uniting the strategic initiatives of key functional departments • Taking action to address company-specific issues and operating problems

Functional strategies	Functional managers (decisions are typically reviewed/approved by business unit head)	• Crafting functional area/departmental moves and approaches to support business strategy and to achieve functional/departmental performance objectives; functional strategies are needed in such areas as:
		  R&D/technology
		  Production/manufacturing
		  Marketing and sales/distribution
		  Finance
		  Human resources
		• Reviewing/revising/unifying strategy-related moves and approaches proposed by lower-level managers

Operating strategies	Field unit heads/lower-level managers within functional areas (decisions are reviewed/approved by functional area head/department head)	• Crafting still narrower and more specific approaches/moves aimed at supporting functional and business strategies and at achieving field unit/departmental objectives

department heads (manufacturing, marketing and sales, finance, human resources, and the like) within business-units and divisions, and managers of geographic units, plants, and areas within major functional departments. Four levels of strategy-making stand out: corporate strategy, business strategy, functional strategy, and operating strategy. Table 2–1 summarizes who has the primary responsibility for each strategy level and what the areas of focus are at each level.

Corporate Strategy

Corporate strategy is the overall managerial game plan for a diversified company. Corporate strategy is companywide—an umbrella over all businesses that the company is in. Business strategy, by contrast, pertains to the managerial plan for just a single business or business unit. Corporate strategy is what makes the

Figure 2–1 IDENTIFYING THE CORPORATE STRATEGY OF A DIVERSIFIED COMPANY

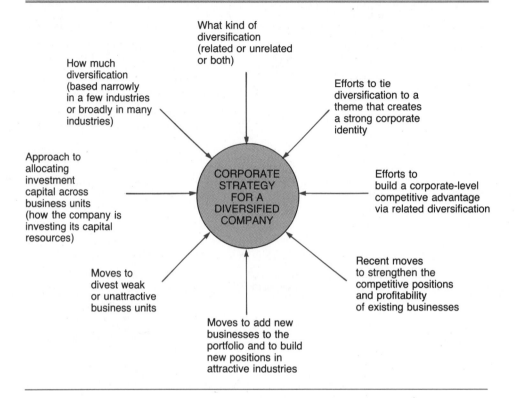

diversified corporate whole add up to more than the sum of its business unit parts.[8] It consists of the moves made to establish business positions in different industries and of the approaches made to managing the company's business units, both individually and as a group (see Figure 2–1). There are four areas of focus in crafting corporate strategy for a diversified company:

1. *Making the moves to accomplish diversification.* The first concern in diversification is what the portfolio of businesses should consist of—specifically, what industries to diversify into, whether to enter the chosen industries by starting a new business from scratch, or whether to acquire a company already in business (an established leader, an up-and-coming company, or a troubled company with turnaround potential). This piece of corporate strategy establishes whether diversification is based narrowly in a few industries or broadly in many industries, and it shapes how the company will be positioned in each of the target industries.

---

[8] Michael E. Porter, "From Competitive Advantage to Corporate Strategy," *Harvard Business Review* 65, no. 3 (May–June 1987), pp. 43–59.

2. *Managing the diversified portfolio and initiating moves to boost the combined performance of existing businesses.* As positions are created in the chosen industries, corporate strategy-making concentrates on ways to get better performance out of the business-unit portfolio. Decisions must be reached about how to strengthen the long-term competitive positions, and thus the profitability, of the businesses the corporation has invested in. Corporate parents can help their business units be more successful by supplying much-needed funds for new capacity and efficiency improvements, by supplying missing skills and managerial know-how, by acquiring another company in the same industry and merging the two operations into a stronger business, and/or by acquiring new businesses that strongly complement existing businesses. The overall plan for managing the portfolio usually involves pursuing rapid-growth strategies in the most promising businesses, keeping the other core businesses healthy, initiating turnaround efforts in weak-performing businesses with potential, and divesting businesses that are no longer attractive or that don't fit into management's long-range plans.

3. *Finding ways to capture the synergy among related business units and turn it into competitive advantage.* When a company pursues related diversification, some business units in the corporate porfolio end up having related technologies, similar operating characteristics, the same distribution channels, common customers, or some other synergistic relationship. These relationships often create opportunities to transfer skills, share expertise, or share facilities in ways that reduce cost, strengthen the competitiveness of some of the corporation's products, or enhance the capabilities of particular business units—any of which can represent a significant source of competitive advantage. The more that different businesses in the portfolio are related, the greater the opportunities for skills transfer and/or sharing and the bigger the window for creating competitive advantage via related diversification. Indeed, one of the factors that makes diversification attractive is achieving synergistic *strategic fit* among some business units so their combined performance is *greater* than each unit could achieve independently. The essence of strategic fit is a $2 + 2 = 5$ effect, an outcome that boosts overall corporate performance and shareholder value.

4. *Establishing investment priorities and steering corporate resources into the most attractive business units.* A corporation's different businesses are usually not equally attractive from the standpoint of future capital investment. The task here is to rank the attractiveness of investing more capital in each of the businesses and to channel resources into areas where earnings potentials are higher and away from areas where they are lower. The strategy may include divesting business units that are chronically poor performers or that are in industries that have been judged unattractive to the company. Divestiture frees up unproductive investments for redeployment to promising business units or for financing attractive new acquisitions.

Business Strategy

The term *business strategy* (or business-level strategy) refers to the managerial game plan for a single business. It is mirrored in the pattern of approaches and moves crafted by management to produce successful performance in *one specific*

Figure 2–2   IDENTIFYING STRATEGY FOR A SINGLE-BUSINESS COMPANY

Moves made
to deal with
changing industry
conditions and
other emerging
developments in the
external environment

Approach to vertical
integration (full, partial,
none) and other moves
to establish the
company's competitive
scope within the
industry

Basic competitive approach:
  Low-cost/low price?
  Differentiation
  (what kind?)
  Focus on a specific
  market niche?

BUSINESS
STRATEGY
(the managerial
plan for a single
line of
business)

Moves to secure
a competitive
advantage

Approach to
manufacturing
and operations

Key functional
strategies

Approach to
marketing,
promotion
and distribution

Recent moves
to strengthen
competitive
position and
improve performance

R&D/technology
approaches

Approach to
human resources/
labor relations

Financial
approaches

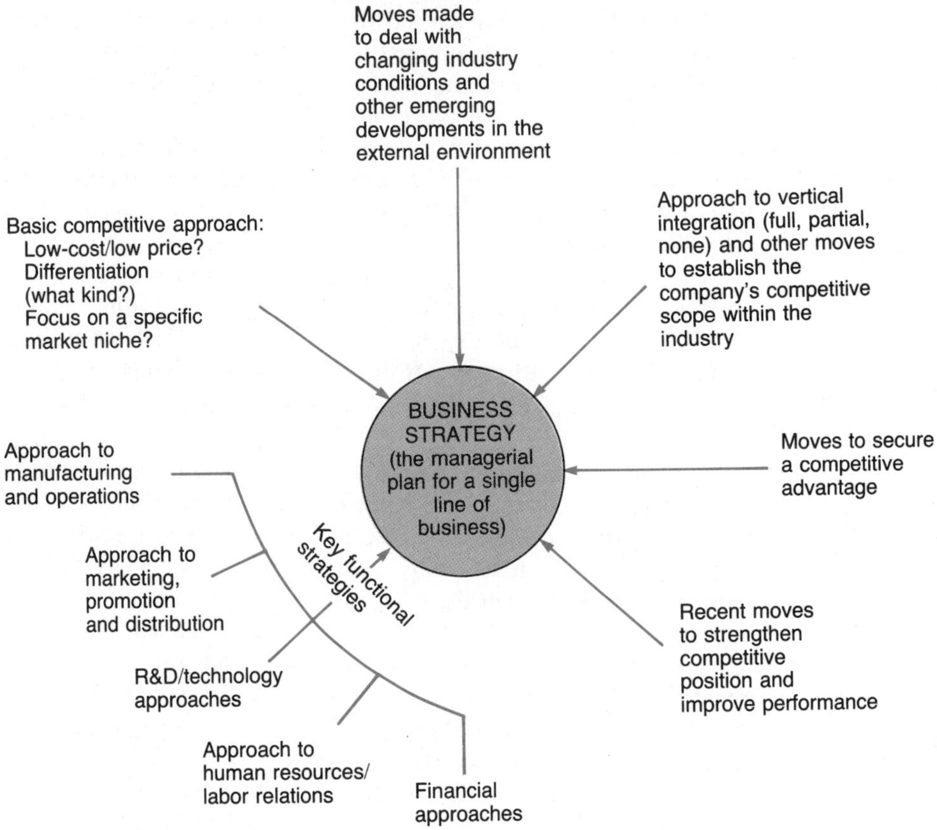

line of business. The various elements of business strategy are shown in Figure
2–2. For a stand-alone, single-business company, corporate strategy and business
strategy are one and the same since there is only one business to form a strategy
for; the distinction between corporate strategy and business strategy is relevant
only when diversification enters the strategic picture.

   *The central thrust of business strategy is how to build and strengthen the
company's long-term competitive position in the marketplace.* Toward this end,
business strategy deals with (1) forming responses to changes underway in the
industry, the economy at large, the regulatory and political arena, and other
relevant areas, (2) crafting competitive moves and market approaches that can
lead to sustainable competitive advantage, (3) uniting the strategic initiatives of
functional departments, and (4) addressing company-specific strategic issues and
operating problems facing the business.

   Clearly, business strategy must include whatever moves and new approaches
managers deem prudent in light of market forces, economic trends and develop-

ments, buyer demographics, new legislation and regulatory requirements, and other such broad external factors. A good strategy must be well-matched to the external situation; as the external environment changes in significant ways, adjustments in strategy eventually become desirable. Whether a company's response to external change is prompt or slow tends to be a function of how long events must unfold before managers can assess any implications for the business and how much longer it will take them to form a strategic response. Some external changes, of course, require little or no response, while others call for significant strategy alterations. And some external changes are more difficult to respond to than others—for example, cigarette manufacturers face a tough challenge responding to the mounting campaign against smoking.

What separates a powerful business strategy from a mediocre one is the strategist's ability *to forge a series of moves and approaches capable of producing sustainable competitive advantage*. With a competitive advantage, a company has good prospects for above-average profitability and success in the industry. Without competitive advantage, a company risks being outcompeted by stronger rivals and locked into mediocre performance. Crafting a business strategy that yields sustainable competitive advantage has several facets: deciding where a firm has the best chance to win a competitive edge, developing product/service attributes that appeal to buyers and set the company apart from rivals, and countering the competitive moves of rival companies. The pattern of moves and approaches that form a company's strategy for competing successfully is typically both offensive and defensive in makeup—some actions are aggressive and amount to direct attacks on the market positions of competitors; others are intended to counteract fresh moves made by rivals. The three basic competitive approaches are (1) striving to be the industry's low-cost producer (thereby aiming for a cost-based competitive advantage over rivals), (2) pursuing differentiation based on such advantages as quality, performance, service, styling, or technological superiority, and (3) focusing on a narrow market niche and winning a competitive edge by catering to buyers' needs and tastes better than rivals.

Internally, business strategy involves taking actions to develop the skills and capabilities needed to secure competitive advantage. Successful business strategies usually aim at creating a distinctive competence in one or more functional activities performed by the company and then using this competence as a basis for opening up a competitive advantage over rivals. A *distinctive competence* is something a firm does especially well in comparison to rival companies. It can relate to R&D, technical expertise, manufacturing capability, sales and distribution, customer service, or anything else that is a competitively important aspect of creating, producing, or marketing the company's product or service. On a broader internal front, business strategy must also be concerned with how to manage the various functional activities within the business (purchasing, production, R&D, finance, human resources, sales and marketing, and distribution). Strategic actions are needed in each functional activity to *support* the company's competitive approach and overall business strategy. Coordinating the strategy-related actions of the various functional areas adds power to the business strategy.

Business strategy must also include action plans to address any special strategy-related issues unique to the company (such as whether to add new capacity, replace an obsolete plant, increase R&D funding for a promising technology, or reduce interest expenses). Such custom-tailoring of strategy to fit a company's specific situation is one of the reasons why every company in an industry has a somewhat different business strategy.

Lead responsibility for business strategy falls in the lap of the manager in charge of the business. Even if the business head does not personally wield a heavy hand in the business strategy-making process, preferring to delegate much of the task to others, he or she is still accountable for the strategy and the results it produces. The business head, as chief strategist, has at least two other responsibilities. One is seeing that supporting strategies in each of the major functional areas of the business are well-conceived and consistent with each other. The other is getting major strategic moves approved by higher authority (the board of directors and/or corporate level officers) if needed, and keeping them informed of important new developments, deviations from plan, and potential strategy revisions. In diversified companies, business-unit heads also must ensure that the business strategy adequately supports the achievement of corporate objectives and is consistent with corporate strategy themes.

Functional Area Strategy

The term *functional area strategy* refers to the functional-specific approaches and moves crafted by management. Functional strategies represent the managerial game plan for running particular parts of a business. A functional area strategy is needed for every major activity within a business—R&D, production, marketing and sales, distribution, finance, human resources, information systems, and the like. Functional strategies add detail to business strategy and indicate how functional activities will be managed. The primary role of functional strategy is to *support* the overall business strategy. Another role is to specify how functional managers plan to achieve functional area performance objectives. Thus, functional strategy in the production/manufacturing area consists of the managerial game plan for *how* manufacturing activities will be conducted to achieve manufacturing objectives and to support business strategy. Functional strategy in the finance area consists of the array of financial moves and approaches that are planned to achieve specific financial objectives and to support business strategy. And so on.

Lead responsibility for functional area strategy-making is normally delegated to the managers in charge of each functional unit unless, for some reason, the business-unit head decides to exert a strong influence. Functional managers usually work in concert with key subordinates, other functional area heads, and the business head in devising functional approaches and moves to recommend for final review and approval. Reviewing each functional area head's strategy proposals gives the business-unit head an opportunity to unify all functional strategies behind the business strategy and the achievement of business objectives. When all of the principal functional activities within a business are consistent and strongly support the business strategy, the entire business strategy obtains added power. Plainly, a business's marketing strategy, production strategy, finance strategy, and human resources strategy should be working in concert rather than at cross-purposes.

Operating Strategy

Operating strategy refers to the even narrower and more detailed approaches and moves devised by lower-level functional managers and geographic-unit managers to achieve the strategy-supporting performance objectives established in their areas of responsibility. Operating strategy, while of lesser scope than the higher levels of strategy-making, is still important from the standpoint of strategic completeness. Even the smallest organizational units, if they are important enough to exist, are important enough to have performance targets to achieve. Managers of these units need to devise approaches and make moves to achieve these objectives, thereby putting them in a strategy-making role too. For instance, the manager of a company's eastern region needs a strategy customized to that region's particular situation; the manager of plant X needs a strategy for accomplishing plant X's objectives, carrying out plant X's role in the overall manufacturing game plan, and dealing with whatever strategic problems exist for plant X. So it goes for all the managers of key operating units.

To further indicate the nature of operating strategy, consider the following instances of how the managers of various operations craft narrow pieces of strategy that end up supporting higher-level strategies in important ways:

- A company with a low-price, high-volume business strategy and a need to achieve low manufacturing costs launches a companywide effort to boost worker productivity by 10 percent. To contribute to the productivity-boosting objective: (1) the hiring director develops a new employee recruiting program to screen out all but the most highly motivated, best-qualified job applicants; (2) the director of information systems devises a way to use office technology to boost the productivity of office workers; (3) the employee benefits director devises an improved incentive-compensation plan to reward increased output by manufacturing employees; and (4) the purchasing director launches a search for time-saving tools and equipment.

- A distributor of plumbing equipment emphasizes quick delivery and accurate order-filling as keystones of its customer service approach. To support this strategy, the warehouse manager (1) develops an inventory stocking strategy that allows 99 percent of all orders to be completely filled without back ordering any item and (2) has a warehouse staffing strategy of maintaining a large enough work force to ship any order within 24 hours.

Coordinating the Strategy-Making Effort

While each managerial level needs a strategic game plan to achieve the objectives set at that level, management direction-setting and strategy-making tasks are not complete until the separate pieces and layers of strategy-making are unified into a coherent, coordinated pattern. Harmonizing the objective-setting, strategy-mak-

Figure 2–3 THE NETWORKING OF MISSIONS, OBJECTIVES, AND STRATEGIES DOWN
THROUGH THE MANAGERIAL HIERARCHY

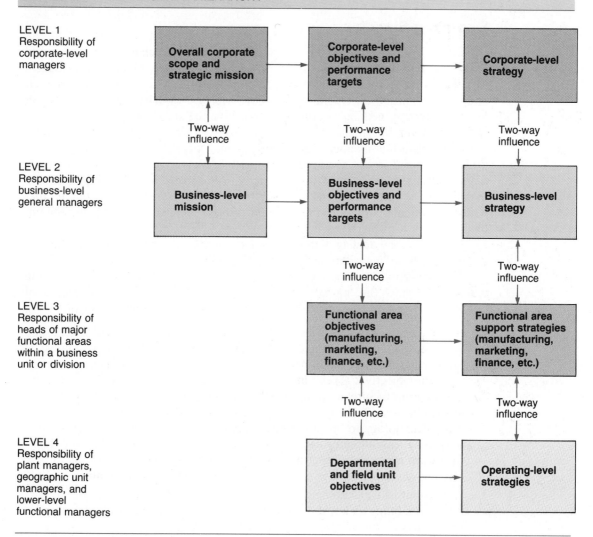

ing effort piece-by-piece and level-by-level usually occurs via the review and
approval process. Figure 2–3 shows the networking of objectives and strategies
down through the managerial hierarchy. The key point is that, while each level of
management needs a strategic game plan to achieve the objectives set at that level,
vertical linkages in both objectives and strategy unify the objective-setting and
strategy-making activities of many managers into a coherent, coordinated pattern.
Tight linkages in the objectives and strategies of each organizational unit prevent
each unit from marching off in its own direction. Generally, corporate and busi-

ness missions, objectives, and strategy need to be established first, so they can drive the objective-setting and strategy-making of lower-level organizational units; without a top-down objective-setting/strategizing approach, one cannot expect lower-level organization units to formulate objectives and strategies that are in step with and contribute to those of the total enterprise. To get an idea what happens to an organization when senior managers fail to exercise strong top-down direction-setting and strategic leadership, imagine what would happen to a football team's offensive performance if neither the coach nor the quarterback decided to exercise leadership in calling a play for the team, but instead instructed each player to choose whatever play he thought would work best and then run it when the center decided to snap the ball.

An organization's strategy is not well formulated until the separate pieces and layers of strategy-making mesh together well—much like the pieces of a puzzle. The power of business strategy is enhanced when functional area and operating-level strategies form a unified, reinforcing pattern of approaches. When all the pieces of business strategy pull together, individual organizational departments can't blunt the priorities of what is best for the total enterprise.[9] Likewise, in a multibusiness enterprise, welding diverse business-level strategies together in some coherent fashion improves the power of corporate strategy. Figure 2–3 underscores that an organization's strategic plan is the sum total of the directional actions and decisions it must make in trying to accomplish its objectives. In effect, *a strategic plan is a collection of strategies.*

THE FACTORS THAT SHAPE STRATEGY

Many, many factors enter into the forming of a strategy. Figure 2–4 is a simple model of the primary factors that come into play and how strategy finally emerges. The interplay of these factors is always complex and always industry- and company-specific. Each situation, in other words, is different enough to have its own elements of uniqueness. This is why careful analysis of a firm's external and internal situation is an essential prelude to strategy-making. As a rule, strategy-making is not truly successful unless it

- Produces "goodness of fit" between an organization's external and internal situation.
- Helps build a sustainable competitive advantage.
- Elevates company performance.

These, indeed, are the tests of a winning strategy. Let's take a brief look at the broad considerations that enter into the strategy-making process.

---

[9] Functional area managers sometimes are more interested in doing what is best for their own areas, in building their own empire, and in consolidating their personal power and organizational influence than they are in cooperating with other functional managers to unify behind the overall business strategy. Consequently, functional area support strategies may work at cross-purposes, forcing the business-level general manager to expend time and energy refereeing functional strategy conflicts and building support for a more unified approach.

Figure 2–4   FACTORS SHAPING THE CHOICE OF COMPANY STRATEGY

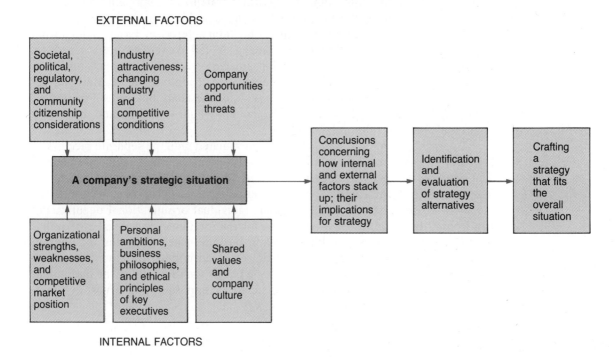

Societal, Political, Regulatory, and Citizenship Considerations

In a broad sense, the choice of strategy is always bounded by what is legal, by what is in compliance with government policies and regulatory requirements, by what is socially acceptable, and by what constitutes community citizenship. Special interest groups, the glare of investigative reporting, a fear of unwanted political action, and public expectations of corporate citizenship and integrity are all capable of forcing incremental changes in company strategies. Rising societal concerns over health and nutrition, alcohol and drug abuse, hazardous waste disposal, sexual harassment, equal pay for equal work, trade and budget deficits, and the impact of plant closings on local communities have impacted the strategies of many companies. Public concerns over the rising tide of foreign imports and political debate over how to correct the chronic U.S. trade deficit have been driving forces in the strategic decisions of Japanese and European companies to locate plants in the United States. Heightened awareness of the dangers of cholesterol have caused several food products companies to stop using low-cost palm oil and coconut oil in their products. The specter of acid rain legislation has prompted electric utilities and coal-mining companies to explore new technologies and strategies for burning coal more cleanly.

Factoring in societal priorities, community concerns, and the potential for onerous legislation and regulatory requirements has become a standard part of external situation analysis at more and more companies. Intense public pressure and adverse media coverage have made such a practice essential. The task of making an organization's strategy "socially responsible" means: (1) keeping organizational activities in tune with what is generally perceived as the public interest; (2) responding positively to emerging societal priorities and expectations; (3) demonstrating a willingness to take action ahead of regulatory confrontation; (4) balancing stockholder interests against the larger interests of society as a whole; and (5) being a "good citizen" in the community.

The swing to increased corporate social responsibility is showing up in company mission statements. John Hancock, for example, concludes its mission statement with the following sentence:

> In pursuit of this mission, we will strive to exemplify the highest standards of business ethics and personal integrity; and shall recognize our corporate obligation to the social and economic well-being of our community.

Union Electric, a St. Louis-based utility company, includes the following statement in its official corporate policy:

> As a private enterprise entrusted with an essential public service, we recognize our civic responsibility in the communities we serve. We shall strive to advance the growth and welfare of these communities and shall participate in civic activities which fulfill that goal . . . for we believe this is both good citizenship and good business.

Industry Attractiveness and Competitive Conditions

An industry's long-term attractiveness is a big strategy-determining factor. Unless a firm believes the industry environment presents an attractive situation, it is better off investing company resources elsewhere. Assuming the industry is attractive, then a firm's strategic options depend on a variety of industry-specific considerations: the drivers of change in the industry, competitive forces, the strategies and likely moves of rival companies, the industry's price-cost-profit economics, and the basic requirements for competitive success. A company's assessment of the industry and competitive environment has a direct bearing on how it should try to position itself in the industry and on its basic competitive approach.

Specific Company Opportunities and Threats

The particular opportunities a company has and the threats it faces are key influences on strategy. Strategy needs to be deliberately crafted to capture some or all of a company's best opportunities, especially the ones that can enhance its long-term competitive position and profitability. Likewise, strategy should be geared to providing as good a defense as possible against external threats to the company's well-being and future performance. Identifying the company's opportunities and threats is a first-order consideration.

Organizational Strengths, Weaknesses, and Competitive Capabilities

Experience shows that in matching strategy to a firm's internal situation, management should build strategy around what the company does well and avoid strategies whose success depends heavily on something the company does poorly or has never done at all—in short, *strategy must be well-matched to company strengths, weaknesses, and competitive capabilities.* Pursuing an opportunity without the organizational competence and resources to capture it is foolish. An organization's strengths make some opportunities and strategies attractive; likewise its internal weaknesses and its present competitive market position make certain strategies risky or even out of the question.

In this regard, one of the most pivotal strategy-shaping internal considerations is whether a company has or can build a distinctive competence. The importance of a distinctive competence to strategy formation rests with (1) the unique capability it gives an organization in capitalizing on a particular opportunity, (2) the competitive edge it may give a firm in the marketplace, and (3) the potential for using it as the cornerstone of strategy. The best path to competitive advantage is when a firm has a distinctive competence in one of the key requirements for market success, rivals do not have offsetting competences, and rivals are not able to attain a similar competence except at high cost and/or over an extended period of time.[10]

Even if an organization has no distinctive competence (and many do not), it still must shape its strategy to suit its particular skills and available resources. It never makes sense to develop a strategic plan that cannot be executed with the skills and resources a firm is able to muster.

The Personal Ambitions, Business Philosophies, and Ethical Beliefs of Managers

Crafting a strategy is rarely so dominated by objective analysis as to eliminate any room for the subjective imprint of managers. Managers do not dispassionately assess what strategic course to steer. Their decisions are often influenced by their own vision of how to compete and position the enterprise and by what image and standing they want the company to have. Both casual observation and formal studies indicate that the ambitions, values, business philosophies, attitudes toward risk, and ethical beliefs of managers usually have important influences on strategy.[11] Sometimes the influence of the manager's personal values and experiences is conscious and deliberate; at other times it may be unconscious. As

---

[10] David T. Kollat, Roger D. Blackwell, and James F. Robeson, *Strategic Marketing* (New York: Holt, Rinehart & Winston, 1972), p. 24.

[11] See, for instance, William D. Guth and Renato Tagiuri, "Personal Values and Corporate Strategy," *Harvard Business Review* 43, no. 5 (September-October 1965), pp. 123–32; Kenneth R. Andrews, *The Concept of Corporate Strategy,* rev. ed. (Homewood, Ill.: Richard D. Irwin, 1980), chap. 4; and Richard F. Vancil, "Strategy Formulation in Complex Organizations," *Sloan Management Review* 17, no. 2 (Winter 1976), pp. 4–5.

Professor Andrews has noted in explaining the relevance of personal factors to strategy, "Somebody has to have his heart in it."[12]

Several examples of how business philosophies and personal values enter into strategy-making are particularly noteworthy. Japanese managers are strong proponents of strategies that take a long-term view and that aim at building market share and competitive position. In contrast, some corporate executives and Wall Street financiers have drawn criticism for overemphasizing short-term profits at the expense of long-term competitive positioning and for being more attracted to strategies involving a financial play on assets (leveraged buyouts and stock buybacks) rather than using corporate resources to make long-term strategic investments. Japanese companies also display a quite different philosophy regarding the role of suppliers. Their favorite strategic approach is to enter into long-term partnership arrangements with key suppliers to improve the quality and reliability of component parts and to reduce inventory requirements. In other countries the prevailing philosophy of managers has been to use adversarial strategies with suppliers, the aim being to do business short-term with whoever offers the best price and delivery.

Attitudes toward risk also have a big influence on strategy. Risk-averters are inclined toward "conservative" strategies that minimize downside risk, have a quick payback, and produce sure short-term profits. On the other hand, risk-takers lean more toward opportunistic strategies where bold moves can produce a big payoff over the long term. Risk-takers prefer innovation to imitation and bold offensives to defensive conservatism.

Managerial values also influence whether a firm's strategy is ethical. Managers with high ethical standards take pains to see that their companies observe a strict code of ethics in all aspects of the business. Accepting kickbacks from suppliers, giving kickbacks to key customers, badmouthing rivals' products, and contributing to political campaigns in return for political influence are examples of forbidden practices. Strategy-related instances where company ethics are called into question include charging excessive interest rates on credit card balances, employing bait-and-switch sales tactics, and continuing to market products suspected of having safety problems or whose ingredients are known health hazards.

The Influence of Shared Values and Company Culture on Strategy

Every organization's policies, values, traditions, behaviors, and ways of doing things become so ingrained that the organization takes on a distinctive culture. Some companies are noted for being pioneers and exhibiting innovative leadership; others are noted for their concern for employees and a strong people-orientation. Still others are dominated by such traits as a long-standing dedication to superior craftsmanship, a proclivity for financial wheeling and dealing, a desire to grow rapidly by acquiring other companies, a strong social consciousness, or

---

[12] Andrews, *The Concept of Corporate Strategy,* p. 85.

unusual emphasis on customer service and total customer satisfaction. In recent years, companies have increasingly attempted to set forth their shared values and to make them more explicitly known. One company set forth its statement of shared values thusly:

> We are market-driven. We believe that functional excellence, combined with teamwork across functions and profit centers, is essential to achieving superb execution. We believe that people are central to everything we will accomplish. We believe that honesty, integrity, and fairness should be the cornerstone of our relationships with consumers, customers, suppliers, stockholders, and employees.

IBM's founder, Thomas Watson once stated, "We must be prepared to change all the things we are in order to remain competitive in the environment, but we must never change our three basic beliefs: (1) respect for the dignity of the individual, (2) offering the best customer service in the world, and (3) excellence." AT&T's nearly century-old value system emphasizes (1) universal service, (2) fairness in handling personnel matters, (3) a belief that work should be held in balance with commitments to one's family and community, and (4) relationships (from one part of the organization to another). AT&T's management views these values as essential in a technologically dynamic, highly structured company. At both IBM and AT&T, the value system is deeply ingrained and widely shared by managers and employees, so much so that a definite corporate culture has emerged—the shared values are not empty slogans; they are a way of life within the company.[13]

In companies with strong cultures, certain key values and cultural traits are typically reflected in strategy; in some cases these traits even dominate the choice of strategy. This is because culture-related values and policies become embedded in the thoughts and actions of executives, in the way the enterprise shapes its responses to external events, and in the skills and expertise it builds into the company structure, thereby creating a culture-driven bias about what strategy to select and what strategy the firm may be most capable of executing.

LINKING STRATEGY WITH ETHICS

Strategy ought to be ethical. It should involve rightful actions, not wrongful ones; otherwise it won't pass the test of moral scrutiny. This means more than conforming to what is legal. Ethical and moral standards go beyond the prohibitions of law and the language of "thou shalt not" to the issue of *duty* and the language of "should and should not." Ethics concerns human duty and the principles on which these duties rest.[14]

---

[13] For more details, see Richard T. Pascale, "Perspectives on Strategy: The Real Story behind Honda's Success," in Glenn Carroll and David Vogel, *Strategy and Organization: A West Coast Perspective* (Marshfield, Mass.: Pitman Publishing, 1984), p. 60.

[14] Harry Downs, "Business Ethics: The Stewardship of Power," *Strategic Management Planning,* forthcoming.

Every business has duties to five constituencies: owners/shareholders, employees, customers, suppliers, and the community at large. Each of these constituencies is a stakeholder in the enterprise with certain expectations as to what the enterprise should do and how it should do it; each affects the organization and is affected by it.[15] Owners/shareholders, for instance, expect return on their investment. Even though individual investors differ in their preferences for profits now versus profits later, their desire to take risks, and their willingness to exercise social responsibility, business executives have a moral duty to pursue profitable management of the owners' investment.

The duty to employees arises out of respect for the worth and dignity of individuals who devote their energies to the business and who depend on the business for their economic well-being. Principled strategy-making demands that employee-related decisions be made equitably and compassionately, with concern for due process and the impact that strategic change has on employees' lives. At best, the chosen strategy should be advantageous to employees in the areas of wage and salary levels, career opportunities, job security, and overall working conditions; at worst, the chosen strategy should not disadvantage employees. Even in crisis situations where adverse employee impact cannot be avoided, businesses have an ethical duty to minimize whatever hardships have to be imposed in the form of work force reductions, plant closings, job transfers, relocations, retraining, and loss of income.

The duty to the customer arises out of expectations that attend the purchase of a good or service. Inadequate appreciation of this duty has led to product liability laws and a host of rules and regulations to protect consumers. All kinds of strategy-related ethical issues still arise here however. Should a seller inform consumers *fully* about the contents of its product, especially if it contains ingredients that, though officially approved for use, are suspected of having potentially harmful effects? Is it ethical for the makers of alcoholic beverages to sponsor college events, given that many college students are under 21? Is it ethical for cigarette manufacturers to advertise at all (even though it is legal)? Is it ethical for airlines to withhold information about terrorist bomb threats from the public? Is it ethical for manufacturers to produce and sell products they know have faulty parts or defective designs that may not become apparent until after the warranty expires? In submitting bids on a contract to do work for a customer, is it unethical to try to gain inside information not available to other bidders? Is it ethical to give some customers special treatment?

A company's ethical duty to its suppliers arises out of the market relationship that exists between them. They are both partners and adversaries. They are partners in the sense that the quality of suppliers' parts affects the quality of a firm's own product. They are adversaries in the sense that the supplier wants the highest price and profit it can get while the buyer wants a cheaper price, better quality, and speedier service. A business confronts several ethical issues in its supplier relationships: Is it ethical to threaten to cease doing business with a

---

[15] Ibid.

supplier unless the supplier agrees not to do business with key competitors? Is it ethical to accept gifts from suppliers? Is it ethical to pay a supplier in cash?

The ethical duty to the community-at-large stems from the business's status as a citizen of the community and as an institution of society. Communities and society are reasonable in expecting businesses to be good citizens—to pay their fair share of taxes for fire and police protection, waste removal, streets and highways, and so on and to exercise care in the impact their activities have on the environment and on the communities in which they operate. The community and public interest should be accorded the same recognition and attention as the other four constituencies. Whether a company is a good community citizen is ultimately demonstrated by the way it supports community activities, in the ways employees are encouraged to participate in community activities, in the care with which it handles the health and safety aspects of its operations, in the responsibility it accepts for overcoming environmental pollution, in the relationships it has with regulatory bodies and with employee unions, and in its efforts to exhibit high ethical standards.

NCR Corporation, a $6 billion computer and office equipment company, recently cast its entire mission statement in terms of its duty to shareholders, customers, employees, suppliers, and the community at large. See Illustration Capsule 7.

ILLUSTRATION CAPSULE   7

ETHICS AND VALUES AT NCR CORPORATION

In 1988, NCR management set forth a corporate mission statement that formally recognized the company's duty to serve the interests of all stakeholders, not just those of stockholders. The mission of "creating value for our stakeholders" represented a blend of ethical principles and values:

- NCR is a successful, growing company dedicated to achieving superior results by assuring that its actions are aligned with stakeholder expectations. Stakeholders are all constituencies with a stake in the fortunes of the company. NCR's primary mission is to create value for our stakeholders.
- We believe in conducting our business activities with integrity and respect while building mutually beneficial and enduring relationships with all of our stakeholders.
- We take customer satisfaction personally: we are committed to providing superior value in our products and services on a continuing basis.

(continued)

- We respect the individuality of each employee and foster an environment in which employees' creativity and productivity are encouraged, recognized, valued and rewarded.
- We think of our suppliers as partners who share our goal of achieving the highest quality standards and the most consistent level of service.
- We are committed to being caring and supportive corporate citizens within the world-wide communities in which we operate.
- We are dedicated to creating value for our shareholders and financial communities by performing in a manner that will enhance returns on investments.

Source: 1987 Annual Report.

Carrying Out Ethical Responsibilities. It is management, not constituent groups, who is responsible for managing the enterprise. Thus, it is management's perceptions of its ethical duties and of constituents' claims that drive whether and how strategy is linked to ethical behavior. Managers can broaden their outlook by considering decisions from each constituent's point of view. Conflicts among the claims and views of the five constituencies usually prevent management from deferring to any single interest in strategic decisions. In forming a strategy for the enterprise, it is the strategy-maker's job to evaluate the strategic options in light of each constituent's claims and then to strike a rational, objective, and equitable balance. If any of the five constituencies conclude that management is not doing its duty, they have their own avenues for recourse. Concerned investors can act through the annual shareholders' meeting, by appealing to the board of directors, or by selling their stock. Concerned employees can unionize and bargain collectively, or they can seek employment elsewhere. Customers can switch their purchases to competitors. Suppliers can find other buyers or pursue other market alternatives. The community and society can do anything from staging protest marches to stimulating political and governmental action.[16]

A management that truly cares about business ethics and corporate social responsibility is proactive rather than reactive in linking strategic action and ethics. It steers away from ethically or morally questionable business opportunities. As a matter of policy, management does not do business with suppliers that engage in activities the company does not condone. As a matter of policy, it recruits and hires employees whose values and behavior are in keeping with the company's principles and ethical standards. It cares about *how* it does business, and its actions reflect a strong corporate conscience. It recognizes that an unethical company has difficulty attracting and keeping high-caliber employees.

[16] Ibid.

APPROACHES TO PERFORMING THE STRATEGY-MAKING TASK

Companies and managers perform the strategy-making task differently. In small, owner-managed companies, strategy-making is developed informally. Often the strategy is never written but exists mainly in the entrepreneur's own mind and in oral understandings with key subordinates. The largest firms, however, tend to develop their plans via an annual strategic planning cycle (complete with prescribed procedures, forms, and timetables) that includes broad management participation, lots of studies, and multiple meetings to probe and question. The larger and more diverse an enterprise, the more managers feel it is better to have a structured process that is done annually, involves written plans, and requires management scrutiny and official approval at each level.

Along with variations in the organizational process of formulating strategy come variations in the way the manager, as chief entrepreneur and organizational leader, personally participates in the actual work of strategic analysis and strategic choice. The four basic strategy-making styles used by managers are:[17]

The Master Strategist Approach—Here the manager personally functions as chief strategist and chief entrepreneur, exercising *strong* influence over the kinds and amount of analysis conducted, over the strategy alternatives to be explored, and over the details of strategy. This does not mean that the manager personally does all the work; what it does mean is that the manager personally becomes the chief architect of strategy and wields a proactive hand in shaping some or all of the major pieces of strategy. The manager acts as strategy commander and has a big ownership stake in the chosen strategy.

The Delegate It to Others Approach—Here the manager in charge delegates the exercise of strategy-making to others, perhaps a strategic planning staff or a task force of trusted subordinates. The manager then personally stays off to the side, keeps in touch with how things are progressing via reports and oral conversations, offers guidance if need be, smiles or frowns as "trial balloon" recommendations are informally run by him/her for reaction, then puts a stamp of approval on the "strategic plan" after it has been formally presented and discussed and a consensus emerges. But the manager rarely has much ownership in the recommendations and, privately, may not see much urgency in pushing *truly hard* to implement some or much of what has been stated in writing in the company's "official strategic plan." Also, it is generally understood that "of course, we may have to proceed a bit differently if conditions change"—which gives the manager flexibility to go slow or ignore those approaches/moves that "on further reflection may not be the thing to do at this time." This strategy-making style has the advantage of letting the manager pick and choose from the smorgasbord of strategic ideas that bubble up from below, and it allows room for broad participation and input from many managers and areas. The weakness is that a manager can end up so detached from the process of formal strategy-making that no real strategic leadership is exercised—indeed, the impression that subordinates get is

---

[17] This discussion is based on David R. Brodwin and L. J. Bourgeois, "Five Steps to Strategic Action," in Glenn Carroll and David Vogel, *Strategy and Organization: A West Coast Perspective* (Marshfield, Mass.: Pitman Publishing, 1984), pp. 168–78.

that, all the lip service to the contrary, strategic planning is not an activity worth a big claim on the boss's personal time and attention. The stage is then set for rudderless direction-setting; often the strategy-making that does occur is short-run oriented and reactive.

The Collaborative Approach—This is a middle approach whereby the manager enlists the help of key subordinates in hammering out a consensus strategy that all "the key players" will back and do their best to implement successfully. The biggest strength of this style of managing the formulation process is that those who are charged with strategy formulation are also those who are charged with implementing the chosen strategy. Giving subordinate managers a clear-cut ownership stake in the strategy they subsequently must implement enhances commitment to successful execution. And, when subordinates have had a hand in proposing their part of the overall strategy, they can be held accountable for making it work—the "I told you it was a bad idea" alibi won't fly.

The Champion Approach—In this style of presiding over strategy formulation, the manager is interested neither in a big personal stake in the details of strategy nor in the time-consuming tedium of leading others through participative brainstorming or a collaborative "group wisdom" exercise. Rather, the idea is to encourage subordinate managers to develop, champion, and implement sound strategies. Here strategy moves upward from the "doers" and the "fast-trackers." Executives serve as judges, evaluating the strategy proposals reaching their desks. This approach is especially well-suited for large diversified corporations where it is impossible for the CEO to be on top of all the strategic and operating problems facing each of many business divisions. Therefore, if the CEO is to exploit the fact that many people in the enterprise can see strategic opportunities that he cannot, then he must give up some control over strategic direction in order to foster strategic opportunities and new strategic initiatives. The CEO may articulate general strategic themes as organizationwide guidelines for strategic thinking, but the real skill is stimulating and rewarding new strategy proposals put forth by a champion who believes in the opportunity and badly wants the blessing to go after it. With this approach, the total "strategy" is strongly influenced by the sum of the championed initiatives that get approved.

These four basic managerial approaches to forming a strategy illuminate several aspects about how strategy emerges. In situations where the manager-in-charge personally functions as the chief architect of strategy, the choice of what strategic course to steer is often influenced by his/her own vision of how to position the enterprise and by the manager's ambitions, values, business philosophies, and sense of what moves to make next. The primary weakness of the master strategist approach is that the caliber of the strategy depends so heavily on the strategy-making skills of the individual functioning as strategy commander. Highly centralized strategy-making can work fine when the manager-in-charge has a powerful, insightful vision of what needs to be done and how to do it. But it can break down in a large, complex organization where many strategic initiatives are needed and the CEO's grasp of the situation is stretched thinly over many issues and problems.

On the other hand, when the manager-in-charge delegates much of the strategy-making task to others, the resulting strategy seldom bears his/her personal stamp. Often, the strategy that emerges is shaped by influential subordinates, by powerful functional departments, or by political coalitions that have a strong interest in promoting their particular version of what the strategy ought to be. "Politics" and the exercise of power are most likely to come into play in situations where there is no strong consensus on what strategy to adopt; this opens the door for a political solution to emerge. The collaborative approach is conducive to political strategy formation as well, since powerful departments and individuals have ample opportunity to build a consensus for their favored strategic approach. However, the big danger of a delegate-it-to-others approach is a serious lack of top-down direction and strategic leadership.

The strength of the champion approach is also its weakness. The value of championing is that it encourages innovative ideas to bubble up from below. Individuals with attractive strategic proposals are given room and resources to try them out. Such an approach helps keep strategy fresh and renews an organization's capacity for innovation. On the other hand, the championed actions, because they come from many places in the organization, may lack coordination and form no coherent pattern. A manager must work conscientiously to ensure that what is championed adds power to the overall organization strategy; otherwise, strategic initiatives may be launched in directions that have no integrating links or overarching rationale. The value of top-down strategy-making is to add cohesion and unity to the strategy-making necessarily done in the lower echelons of the organization.

KEY POINTS

Management's direction-setting task involves developing a mission, setting objectives, and forming a strategy. Early on in the direction-setting process, managers need to form a vision of where to lead the organization and to answer "What is our business and what will it be?" A well-conceived mission statement helps channel organizational efforts along the course management has charted and contributes to a strong sense of organizational identity. Effective visions are clear, challenging, and inspiring; they prepare a firm for the future and they make sense in the marketplace. Their role is to produce employee "buy-in" and to serve as a beacon of long-term direction.

The second direction-setting step is to establish short-range and long-range objectives for the organization to achieve. Objectives translate the mission statement into specific performance targets. The agreed-on objectives need to be challenging but achievable, and they need to spell out precisely how much by when. In other words, objectives should be measurable and should involve deadlines for achievement. Objectives are needed at all organizational levels.

The third direction-setting step entails forming strategies to achieve the objectives set in each area of the organization. A corporate strategy is needed to achieve corporate-level objectives; business strategies are needed to achieve business-unit performance objectives; functional strategies are needed to achieve the performance targets set in each major functional department; and operating-level strategies are needed to achieve the objectives set in each operating and geographic unit. In effect, an organization's strategic plan is a collection of strategies. As shown in Table 2–1, different strategic issues are addressed at each level of managerial strategy-making. Typically, the strategy-making task needs to be more top-down than bottom-up, since the role of lower-level strategy is to support and complement higher-level strategic thrusts and to contribute to the achievement of higher-level, companywide objectives.

Strategy is shaped by both outside and inside considerations. The major external considerations are societal, political, regulatory, and community factors; industry attractiveness; and the company's market opportunities and threats. The primary internal considerations are company strengths, weaknesses, and competitive capabilities; managers' personal ambitions, philosophies, and ethics; and the company's culture and shared values. A good strategy must be well matched to all these situational considerations.

There are essentially four basic ways to manage the strategy formation process in an organization: the master strategist approach where the manager-in-charge personally functions as the chief architect of strategy, the delegate-it-to-others approach, the collaborative approach, and the champion approach. All four have strengths and weaknesses. All four can succeed or fail depending on how well the approach is managed and depending on the strategy-making skills and judgments of the individuals involved.

SUGGESTED READINGS

Andrews, Kenneth R. *The Concept of Corporate Strategy,* 3rd ed. Homewood, Ill.: Richard D. Irwin, 1987, chaps. 2, 3, 4, and 5.

Foster, Lawrence W. "From Darwin to Now: The Evolution of Organizational Strategies." *Journal of Business Strategy* 5, no. 4 (Spring 1985), pp. 94–98.

Granger, Charles H. "The Hierarchy of Objectives." *Harvard Business Review* 42, no. 3 (May-June 1964), pp. 63–74.

McLellan, R., and G. Kelly. "Business Policy Formulation: Understanding the Process." *Journal of General Management* 6, no. 1 (Autumn 1980), pp. 38–47.

Morris, Elinor. "Vision and Strategy: A Focus for the Future." *Journal of Business Strategy* 8, no. 2 (Fall 1987), pp. 51–58.

Mintzberg, Henry. "Crafting Strategy." *Harvard Business Review* 65, no. 4 (July-August 1987), pp. 66–77.

Quinn, James Brian. *Strategies for Change: Logical Incrementalism.* Homewood, Ill.: Richard D. Irwin, 1980, chaps. 2 and 4.

3 Industry and Competitive Analysis

....

Analysis is the critical starting point of strategic thinking.
Kenichi Ohmae

....

Awareness of the environment is not a special project to be undertaken only when warning of change becomes deafening.
Kenneth R. Andrews

Crafting a strategy is an analysis-driven exercise, not an activity where managers can succeed by sheer effort and creativity. Judgments about what strategy to pursue ideally need to be grounded in a probing assessment of a company's external environment and internal situation. Unless a company's strategy ends up being well matched to the full range of external and internal situational considerations, it's suitability is suspect.

THE ROLE OF SITUATION ANALYSIS IN STRATEGY-MAKING

While the phrase *situation analysis* tends to conjure up images of collecting reams of information and sorting through descriptive facts and figures, such a concept doesn't fit here at all. From a strategy-making standpoint, *the purpose of situation analysis is to draw out the features in a company's internal/external environment that most directly frame its window of strategic options and opportunities.* The effort concentrates on generating solid answers to a well-defined set of strategic questions, then using these answers first to form a more understandable picture of the company's strategic situation and second to identify strategic action alternatives.

In studying the methods of strategic situation analysis, it is customary to begin with single-business companies instead of diversified enterprises. This is because strategic analysis of diversified companies draws on many of the concepts and techniques used in evaluating the strategic situations of single-business companies. In business-level strategic analysis, the two biggest situational considerations are (1) industry and competitive conditions (these are the heart of a single-business company's "external environment") and (2) a company's own internal situation and competitive position. This chapter examines the techniques of *industry and competitive analysis,* the term commonly used to refer to external situation analysis of a single-business company. Chapter 4 covers the tools of *company situation analysis*. Industry and competitive analysis looks broadly at a company's *macroenvironment;* company situation analysis examines the narrower territory of a firm's immediate *microenvironment*.

Figure 3–1 presents the external-internal framework of strategic situation analysis for a single-business company. It indicates both the analytical steps involved and the connection to developing business strategy. Note the logical flow from analysis of the company's external and internal situation to evaluation of alternatives to choice of strategy. This flow makes situation analysis the starting point in the process of forming a strategic plan for a single-business enterprise. Indeed, as we shall see in the rest of this chapter and in Chapter 4, really understanding the strategic aspects of a company's macro- and microenvironments is an essential precondition to doing a good job of establishing a mission, setting objectives, and crafting business strategy. Note also that the three criteria for deciding whether a strategy is "good" are whether it fits the situation, whether it helps build competitive advantage, and whether it is likely to boost company performance.

THE METHODS OF INDUSTRY AND COMPETITIVE ANALYSIS

Industries differ widely in their economic characteristics, competitive situations, and future outlooks. The pace of technological change can range from fast to slow. Capital requirements can be big or small. The market can be worldwide or local. Sellers' products can be standardized or highly differentiated. Competitive forces can be strong or weak and can center on price or on any of several nonprice variables. Buyer demand can be rising briskly or declining. Industry conditions differ so much that leading companies in unattractive industries are hard-pressed to earn respectable profits, while even weak companies in attractive industries can turn in good performances.

Industry and competitive analysis utilizes a toolkit of concepts and techniques to get a clear fix on changing industry conditions and on the nature and strength of competitive forces. It is a way of thinking strategically about an industry's overall situation and drawing conclusions about whether the industry is an attractive

Figure 3–1   FROM SITUATION ANALYSIS TO STRATEGIC CHOICES

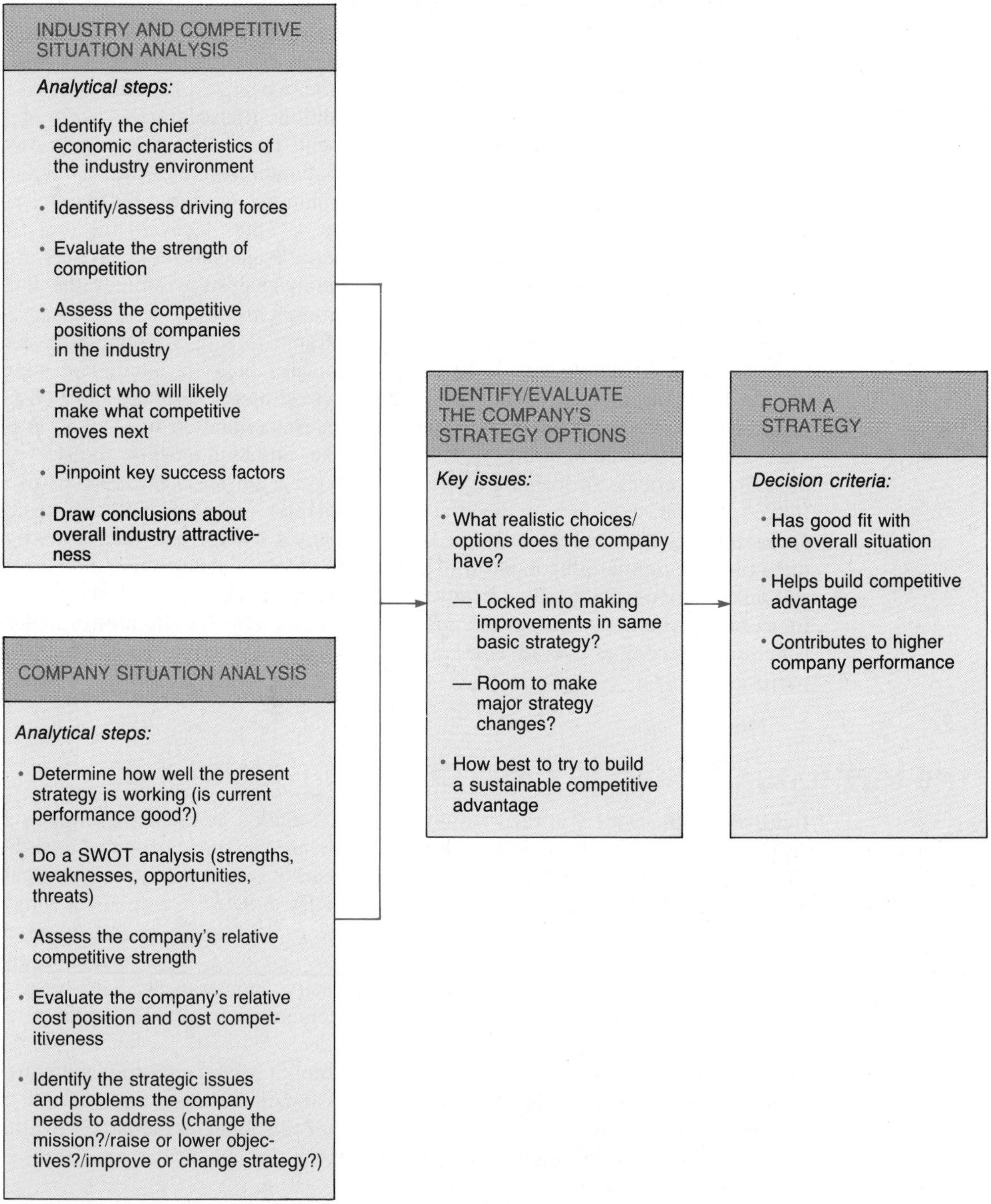

INDUSTRY AND COMPETITIVE SITUATION ANALYSIS

Analytical steps:

- Identify the chief economic characteristics of the industry environment

- Identify/assess driving forces

- Evaluate the strength of competition

- Assess the competitive positions of companies in the industry

- Predict who will likely make what competitive moves next

- Pinpoint key success factors

- Draw conclusions about overall industry attractiveness

COMPANY SITUATION ANALYSIS

Analytical steps:

- Determine how well the present strategy is working (is current performance good?)

- Do a SWOT analysis (strengths, weaknesses, opportunities, threats)

- Assess the company's relative competitive strength

- Evaluate the company's relative cost position and cost competitiveness

- Identify the strategic issues and problems the company needs to address (change the mission?/raise or lower objectives?/improve or change strategy?)

IDENTIFY/EVALUATE THE COMPANY'S STRATEGY OPTIONS

Key issues:

- What realistic choices/ options does the company have?
    - Locked into making improvements in same basic strategy?
    - Room to make major strategy changes?

- How best to try to build a sustainable competitive advantage

FORM A STRATEGY

Decision criteria:

- Has good fit with the overall situation

- Helps build competitive advantage

- Contributes to higher company performance

investment for company funds. The framework of industry and competitive analysis hangs on seven key questions:

1. What are the chief economic characteristics of the industry?
2. What are the drivers of change in the industry and what impact will they have?
3. What competitive forces are at work in the industry and how strong are they?
4. Which companies are in the strongest/weakest competitive positions?
5. Who will likely make what competitive moves next?
6. What key factors will determine competitive success or failure?
7. How attractive is the industry in terms of its prospects for above-average profitability?

With solid answers to these questions, a business strategist can deduce what the company's most realistic strategic options are and form a strategy well matched to changing industry conditions and to competitive forces.

Let's turn now to the steps of industry and competitive analysis to examine exactly what is involved and the analytical tools that come into play.

Profiling the Industry's Dominant Economic Characteristics

Because industries differ so significantly in their basic character and structure, industry and competitive analysis begins with an overview of the industry's dominant economic traits. As a working definition, we use the word *industry* to mean a group of firms whose products have so many of the same attributes that they compete for the same buyers. The factors to consider in pinpointing the industry's primary economic features are fairly standard:

- Market size.
- Scope of competitive rivalry (local, regional, national, or global).
- Market growth rate and where the industry is in the growth cycle (early development, rapid growth and takeoff, early maturity, late maturity and saturation, stagnant and aging, decline and decay).
- Number of rivals and their relative sizes—is the industry fragmented with many small companies or concentrated and dominated by a few large companies?
- The number of buyers and their relative sizes.
- The prevalence of backward and forward integration.
- Ease of entry and exit.
- The pace of technological change in both production process innovation and new product introductions.
- Whether the product(s)/service(s) of rival firms are highly differentiated, weakly differentiated, or essentially identical.
- The extent to which economies of scale are present in manufacturing, transportation, or mass marketing.

- Whether high rates of capacity utilization are crucial to achieving low-cost production efficiency.
- Whether the industry has a strong learning and experience curve such that average unit cost declines as *cumulative* output (and thus the experience of "learning by doing") builds up.
- Capital requirements.
- Whether industry profitability is above/below par.

Table 3-1 illustrates a profile of an industry's chief economic characteristics.

An industry's economic characteristics are important because of the implications they have for strategy. For example, when an industry entails heavy capital investment in plant and equipment, a firm can ease the resulting burden of high fixed costs by pursuing a strategy that promotes high utilization of fixed assets and generates more revenue per dollar of fixed-asset investment. Thus commercial airlines employ strategies to boost the revenue productivity of their expensive jet aircraft fleets by cutting ground time at airport gates (to get in more flights per day with the same plane) and by discounting fares to fill up otherwise empty seats on each flight. In consumer goods industries like beer, fast food, tires, and home appliances, where sizable scale economies accrue from building extensive dealer networks and using national advertising to pull products through the in-place dealer channels, company strategies aim at gaining good distribution access and

---

Table 3-1 A SAMPLE PROFILE OF AN INDUSTRY'S DOMINANT ECONOMIC CHARACTERISTICS

Market Size: $400–$500 million annual revenues; 4 million tons, total volume.

Scope of Competitive Rivalry: Primarily regional; producers rarely sell outside a 250-mile radius of plant due to high cost of shipping long distances.

Market Growth Rate: 2–3 percent annually.

Stage in Life Cycle: Mature.

Number of Companies in Industry: About 30 companies with 110 plant locations and capacity of 4.5 million tons. Market shares range from a low of 3 percent to a high of 21 percent.

Customers: About 2,000 buyers; most are industrial chemical firms.

Degree of Vertical Integration: Mixed; 5 of the 10 largest companies are integrated backward into mining operations and also forward in that sister industrial chemicals divisions buy over 50 percent of the output of their plants; all other companies are engaged solely in manufacturing.

Ease of Entry/Exit: Moderate entry barriers exist in the form of capital requirements to construct a new plant of minimum efficient size (cost equals $10 million) and ability to build a customer base inside a 250-mile radius of plant.

Technology/Innovation: Production technology is standard and changes have been slow; biggest changes are occurring in products—about 1–2 newly formulated specialty chemicals products are being introduced annually accounting for nearly all of industry growth.

Product Characteristics: Highly standardized; the brands of different producers are essentially identical (buyers perceive little real difference from seller to seller).

Scale Economies: Moderate; all companies have virtually equal manufacturing costs but scale economies exist in shipping in multiple carloads to same customer and in purchasing large quantities of raw materials.

Experience Curve Effects: Not a factor in this industry.

Capacity Utilization: Manufacturing efficiency is highest between 90–100 percent of rated capacity; below 90 percent utilization, unit costs run significantly higher.

Industry Profitability: Subpar to average; the commodity nature of the industry's product results in intense price-cutting when demand slackens, but prices firm up during periods of strong demand. Profits track the strength of demand for the industry's products.

Figure 3–2 COMPARISON OF EXPERIENCE CURVE EFFECTS FOR 10 PERCENT, 20 PERCENT, AND 30 PERCENT COST REDUCTIONS FOR EACH DOUBLING OF CUMULATIVE PRODUCTION VOLUME

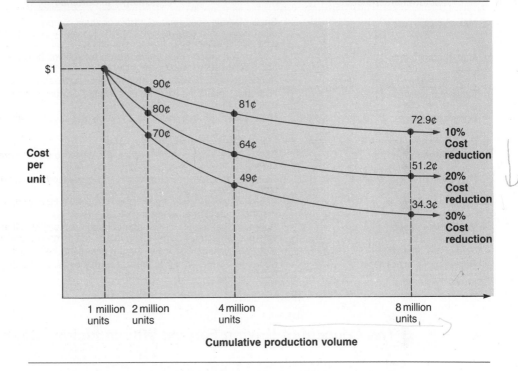

trying to capture a market share big enough to support spending tens of millions of dollars annually on advertising.

In industries characterized by one product advance after another, companies are driven to invest enough time and money in R&D to keep their technical skills and innovative capability abreast of competitors—a product innovation strategy becomes a condition of survival. Finally, in industries like semiconductor manufacturing, the *learning/experience* curve effect causes unit costs to decline about 20 percent each time *cumulative* production volume doubles. With a 20 percent experience curve effect, if the first 1 million chips cost $1 each, by a production volume of 2 million the unit cost is down to $.80 (80 percent of $1), by a production volume of 4 million the unit cost drops to $.64 (80 percent of $.80), and so on. When an industry is characterized by a strong experience curve effect, a company that moves first to initiate production of a new-style product and develops a strategy to capture the largest market share can win the competitive advantage of being the low-cost producer. The bigger the experience curve effect, the bigger the cost advantage of the company with the largest *cumulative* production volume, as shown in Figure 3–2.

Table 3–2 highlights some important ways in which an industry's economic characteristics can affect industry and competitive conditions.

Table 3-2   EXAMPLES OF THE STRATEGIC IMPORTANCE OF AN INDUSTRY'S KEY ECONOMIC CHARACTERISTICS

Factor/characteristic	Strategic importance
• Market size	• Small markets don't tend to attract big/new competitors; large markets often draw the interest of corporations looking to acquire companies with established competitive positions in attractive industries.
• Market growth rate	• Fast growth breeds new entry; growth slowdowns spawn increased rivalry and a shakeout of weak competitors.
• Capacity surpluses or shortages	• Surpluses push prices and profit margins down; shortages pull them up.
• Industry profitability	• High-profit industries attract new entrants; depressed conditions encourage exit.
• Entry/exit barriers	• High barriers protect positions and profits of existing firms; low barriers make existing firms vulnerable to entry.
• Product is a big-ticket item for buyers	• More buyers will shop for lowest price.
• Standardized products	• Buyers have more power because it is easier to switch from seller to seller.
• Rapid technological change	• Raises risk factor; investments in technology facilities/equipment may become obsolete before they wear out.
• Capital requirements	• Big requirements make investment decisions critical; timing becomes important; creates a barrier to entry and exit.
• Vertical integration	• Raises capital requirements; often creates competitive differences and cost differences among fully versus partially versus nonintegrated firms.
• Economies of scale	• Increases volume and market share needed to be cost competitive.
• Rapid product innovation	• Shortens product life cycle; increases risk because of opportunities for leapfrogging.

The Concept of Driving Forces: Why Industries Change

An industry's economic features say a lot about the basic nature of the industry environment but very little about the ways in which the environment may be changing. All industries are characterized by trends and new developments that, either gradually or speedily, produce changes important enough to require a strategic response from participating firms. The popular hypothesis about industries going through evolutionary phases or life-cycle stages helps explain industry change but is, at best, incomplete.[1] The life-cycle stages are strongly keyed to the overall industry growth rate (which is why such terms as rapid growth, early maturity, saturation, and decline are used to describe the stages). Yet there are more causes of industry change than the industry's position on the growth curve.

While it is important to judge an industry's stage of growth, there is more analytical value in identifying the specific forces giving rise to industry change. Industry conditions change *because forces are in motion that create incentives or pressures for change.*[2] The most dominant of these forces are called *driving forces* because they have the biggest influences on what kind of changes will take place in the industry's structure and environment. Driving forces analysis has two

---

[1] For a more extended discussion of the problems with the life-cycle hypothesis, see Michael E. Porter, *Competitive Strategy: Techniques for Analyzing Industries and Competitors* (New York: Free Press, 1980), pp. 157–62.

[2] Ibid., p. 162.

steps: identifying what the driving forces are and evaluating their impact on the industry.

The Most Common Driving Forces.   Many events can affect an industry powerfully enough to qualify as driving forces. Some of these are one-of-a-kind, but most fall into one of several basic categories. The most common driving forces are:[3]

- *Changes in the long-term industry growth rate*—Increases or decreases in industry growth are a powerful influence in the investment decisions of existing firms to expand capacity. A strong upsurge in long-term demand frequently attracts new firms to the market, and a shrinking market often causes some firms to exit the industry. Shifts in industry growth up or down are thus a force for industry change because they affect the balance between industry supply and buyer demand, entry and exit, and how hard it will be for a firm to capture additional sales.

- *Changes in who buys the product and how they use it*—Shifts in buyer composition and the emergence of new ways to use the product have potential for forcing adjustments in customer service offerings (credit, technical assistance, maintenance and repair), creating a need to market the industry's product through a different mix of dealers and retail outlets, prompting producers to broaden/narrow their product lines, increasing/decreasing capital requirements, and changing sales and promotion approaches. The computer industry has been transformed by the surge of buyers for personal and mid-size computers. Consumer interest in cordless telephones and mobile telephones has opened a major new buyer segment for telephone equipment manufacturers.

- *Product innovation*—Product innovation can broaden an industry's customer base, rejuvenate industry growth, and widen the degree of product differentiation among rival sellers. Successful new product introductions strengthen the market position of the innovating companies, usually at the market share expense of companies who either stick with their old products or are slow to follow with their own versions of the new product. Industries where product innovation has been a key driving force include copying equipment, cameras and photographic equipment, computers, electronic video games, toys, prescription drugs, frozen foods, and personal computer software.

- *Technological change*—Advances in technology can dramatically alter an industry's landscape, making it possible to produce new and/or better products at lower cost and opening up whole new industry frontiers. Technological change can also generate changes in capital requirements, minimum efficient plant sizes, the desirability of vertical integration, and learning or experience curve effects.

- *Marketing innovation*—When firms introduce successful new ways to mar-

---

[3] What follows draws on the discussion in Porter, *Competitive Strategy*, pp. 164–83.

ket their products, they can spark a burst of buyer interest, widen industry demand, increase product differentiation, and/or lower unit costs—any or all of which can precipitate changes in the competitive positions of rival firms and force strategy revisions.

- *Entry or exit of major firms*—The entry of one or more foreign companies into a market once dominated by domestic firms nearly always produces a big shakeup in industry conditions. Likewise, when an established domestic firm from another industry attempts entry either by acquisition or by launching its own start-up venture, it usually intends to apply its skills and resources in some innovative fashion. The outcome of major entry can be a ''new ballgame'' not only with new key players but also with new rules for competing. Similarly, exit of a major firm changes industry structure by reducing the number of market leaders (perhaps increasing the dominance of the leaders who remain) and causing a rush to capture the exiting firm's customers.

- *Diffusion of technical know-how*—As knowledge about how to perform a particular activity or to execute a particular manufacturing technology spreads, any technically-based competitive advantage held by firms originally possessing this know-how erodes. The diffusion of such know-how can occur through scientific journals, trade publications, on-site plant tours, word-of-mouth among suppliers and customers, and the hiring away of knowledgeable employees. It can also occur when the possessors of technological know-how license others to use it for a royalty fee or team up with a company interested in turning the technology into a new business venture. Quite often, technological know-how can be acquired by simply buying a company that has the wanted skills, patents, or manufacturing capabilities. In recent years technology transfer across national boundaries has emerged as one of the most important driving forces in the internationalization of markets and global competition. As companies in more countries gain access to technical know-how, they upgrade their manufacturing capabilities in a long-term effort to compete head-on against established companies. Examples of where technology transfer has turned a largely domestic industry into an increasingly global one include automobiles, tires, consumer electronics, telecommunications, and computers.

- *Increasing globalization of the industry*—Global competition is usually associated with shifting patterns of competitive advantage among key players. Industries move toward globalization for any of several reasons. Certain firms launch long-term strategies to win a globally dominant market position; demand for the industry's product emerges in more and more countries; trade barriers drop; technology transfer opens the door for more companies in more countries to enter the industry arena on a major scale; significant labor cost differences among countries create a strong reason to locate plants for labor-intensive products in low-wage countries (wages in South Korea, Taiwan, and Singapore, for example, are about one-fourth those in the United States); significant cost economies accrue to firms with world-scale volumes as opposed to national-scale volumes; and the growing ability of multinational companies to transfer their production, marketing, and management know-how from country to country at significantly lower cost than companies with a one-country customer base gives multinational competitors a significant competitive advantage over domestic-only competitors. Globalization is most likely to be a driving force in industries (*a*) based on natural resources (supplies of crude oil, copper, and cotton, for example, are geographically scattered), (*b*) where low-cost production is a critical consideration (making it imperative to locate plant facilities in countries where the lowest costs can be achieved), and (*c*) where one or more growth-oriented, market-seeking companies are pushing hard to gain a significant competitive position in as many attractive country markets as they can.

* *Changes in cost and efficiency*—In industries where economies of scale are emerging or where strong learning curve effects are allowing firms with the most production experience to undercut rivals' prices, large market share becomes such a distinct advantage that all firms are driven to adopt volume-building strategies—a "race for growth" dominates the industry. Likewise, sharply rising costs for a key input (either raw materials or labor) can cause a scramble to either (*a*) line up reliable supplies of the input at affordable prices or (*b*) search out lower-cost substitute inputs. Any time important changes in cost or efficiency take place in an industry, the door is open for rivals' positions to change radically concerning who has how big a cost advantage.

* *Emerging buyer preferences for a differentiated instead of a commodity product (or for a more standardized product instead of strongly differentiated products)*—Sometimes growing numbers of buyers begin to decide that a standard "one-size-fits-all" product with a bargain price meets their needs as effectively as premium priced brands offering a broad choice of features and options. Such a swing in buyer demand can drive industry change, shifting patronage away from sellers of more expensive differentiated products to sellers of cheaper commodity products and creating a very price-competitive market environment—a development that can so dominate the marketplace it limits the strategic freedom of industry producers to do much more than compete hard on price. On the other hand, a shift away from standardized products occurs when sellers are able to win a bigger and more loyal buyer following by bringing out new features, making style changes, offering options and accessories, and creating image differences via advertising and packaging. Then the driver of change is the struggle among rivals to out-differentiate one another. Industries evolve differently depending on whether the forces in motion are acting to increase or decrease the emphasis on product differentiation.

* *Regulatory influences and government policy changes*—Regulatory and governmental actions can often force significant changes in industry practices and strategic approaches. Deregulation has been a big driving force in the airline, banking, natural gas, and telecommunications industries. Drunk driving laws and drinking age legislation recently became driving forces in

the alcoholic beverage industry. In international markets, newly enacted policies of host governments to open up their domestic markets to foreign participation or to close off foreign participation to protect domestic companies are a major factor in shaping whether the competitive struggle between foreign and domestic companies occurs on a level playing field or whether it is one-sided (owing to government favoritism).

- *Changing societal concerns, attitudes, and lifestyles*—Emerging social issues and changing attitudes and lifestyles can be powerful instigators of industry change. Consumer concerns about salt, sugar, chemical additives, cholesterol, and nutrition have forced the food industry to reexamine food processing techniques, redirect R&D efforts into whole new areas, and introduce scores of healthier products. Safety concerns have been major drivers of change in the automobile, toy, and outdoor power equipment industries, to mention a few. Increased interest in physical fitness has produced whole new industries to supply exercise equipment, jogging clothes and shoes, and medically supervised diet programs. Social concerns about air and water pollution have been major forces in industries that discharge waste products into the air and water. Growing antismoking sentiment has posed a major long-term threat to the cigarette industry.

- *Reductions in uncertainty and business risk*—A young, emerging industry is typically characterized by much uncertainty over potential market size, how much time and money will be needed to surmount technological problems, an unproven cost structure, and how to distribute the products and access potential buyers. Such high-risk ventures attract only the most entrepreneurial companies. Over time, however, as uncertainty about the industry's viability dissipates and pioneering firms prove successful, more conservative firms are usually enticed to enter the industry. Often, the entrants are larger, financially strong firms hunting for attractive growth industries in which to invest. In international markets, conservatism is prevalent in the early stages of globalization. There is a strong propensity for firms to guard against risk by relying initially on exporting, licensing, and joint ventures to enter foreign markets. Then, as experience accumulates in making a success out of foreign operations and as perceived risk levels decline, companies move quicker and more aggressively to form wholly owned subsidiaries and to pursue a full-scale, multicountry competitive strategy.

The foregoing list of *potential* driving forces in an industry indicates why it is too simplistic to view industry change only in terms of the life-cycle model and why it is essential to probe for the *causes* underlying the emergence of new industry conditions.

However, while *many* forces of change may be at work in a given industry, no more than three or four are likely to qualify as *driving* forces in the sense that they will act as *the major determinants* of how the industry evolves and operates. Thus, strategic analysts must resist the temptation to label everything they see changing as driving forces; the analytical task is to evaluate the forces of industry change carefully enough to separate the major factors from the minor ones.

Driving forces analysis has practical strategy-making value. In the first place, the driving forces in an industry indicate to managers what external factors will have the greatest effect on the company's business over the next several years. Second, to position the company to deal with these forces, managers must assess the implications and consequences of each driving force—that is, they must project what impact the driving forces will have on the industry. Third, strategy-makers obviously need to craft a strategy that is directly responsive to the driving forces and their effects on the industry.

Environmental Scanning Techniques.   One way to get a jump on what driving forces are likely to emerge is to utilize environmental scanning techniques as an early detector of "new straws in the wind." *Environmental scanning* is a term used to describe a broad-ranging, mind-stretching effort to monitor and interpret social, political, economic, ecological, and technological events in an attempt to spot budding trends and conditions that could eventually impact the industry. Environmental scanning involves time frames well beyond the next one to three years—for example, it could involve judgments about the demand for energy in the year 2000, what kinds of household appliances will be needed in the "house of the future," what people will be doing with computers 20 years from now, or what will happen to our forests if the demand for paper continues to grow at its present rate. Environmental scanning thus attempts to look broadly at "first-of-its-kind" happenings, what kinds of new ideas and approaches are catching on, and extrapolate their possible implications 5 to 20 years into the future. The purpose and value of environmental scanning is to raise the consciousness of managers about potential developments that could have an important impact on industry conditions and pose new opportunities and threats.

Environmental scanning can be accomplished using such techniques as systematic monitoring and study of current events, futures research, scenarios, and the Delphi method (a technique for finding consensus among a group of "knowledgeable experts"). Environmental scanning methods are highly qualitative and subjective and can involve much speculation. The appeal of environmental scanning, notwithstanding its speculative nature, is that it helps managers to lengthen their planning horizon, to translate an inkling of a future opportunity or threat into a clearer strategic issue (for which they can begin to develop a strategic answer), and to think strategically about macroenvironmental factors.[4] Companies that undertake formal environmental scanning on a fairly continuous and comprehensive level include General Electric, AT&T, Coca-Cola, Ford, General Motors, Du Pont, and Shell Oil.

---

[4] For further discussion of the nature and use of environmental scanning, see Roy Amara and Andrew J. Lipinski, *Business Planning for an Uncertain Future: Scenarios and Strategies* (New York: Pergamon Press, 1983); Harold E. Klein and Robert E. Linneman, "Environmental Assessment: An International Study of Corporate Practice," *Journal of Business Strategy* 5, no. 1 (Summer 1984), pp. 55–75; and Ian H. Wilson, "Environmental Scanning and Strategic Planning," *Business Environment/Public Policy: 1979 Conference Papers* (St. Louis: American Assembly of Collegiate Schools of Business, 1980), pp. 159–63.

Analyzing the Strength of Competitive Forces

A cornerstone of industry and competitive analysis is to dig deeply into the industry's competitive process—the main sources of competitive pressures and how strong these pressures are. This analytical step is particularly essential because managers cannot devise a competitively successful strategy without insight into the industry's unique set of competitive characteristics and "rules of the game."

Even though competitive pressures in one industry are never precisely the same as in another, how competition works from industry to industry is similar enough to use a common analytical framework in gauging its nature and intensity. Indeed, as a general rule, *competition in an industry is a composite of five competitive forces:*

1. The rivalry among competing sellers in the industry.
2. The potential entry of new competitors.
3. The market attempts of companies in other industries to win customers over to their own *substitute* products.
4. The bargaining power and leverage exercisable by suppliers of inputs.
5. The bargaining power and leverage exercisable by buyers of the product.

The *five-forces model* of competition analysis, as diagrammed in Figure 3–3, is extremely helpful in systematically diagnosing the principal competitive pressures in a market and assessing how strong and important each one is.[5] Not only is it the most widely used technique of competition analysis, but it is also uncommonly straightforward to use.

The Rivalry among Competing Sellers.   The most powerful of the five competitive forces is *usually* the competitive battle among rival firms.[6] The vigor with which sellers use the competitive weapons at their disposal to jockey for a stronger market position and win a competitive edge over rivals signals the strength of this competitive force. *Competitive strategy* is the narrower portion of business strategy dealing with management's *competitive approaches for achieving market success, its offensive moves to secure a competitive edge over rival firms, and its defensive moves to protect its competitive position.*[7]

---

[5] For a thoroughgoing treatment of the five-forces model by its originator, see Porter, *Competitive Strategy,* chap. 1.

[6] Parts of this section are based on the discussion in Arthur A. Thompson, "Competition as a Strategic Process," *Antitrust Bulletin* 25, no. 4 (Winter 1980), pp. 777–803.

[7] The distinction between *competitive strategy* and *business strategy* is useful here. As we defined it in Chapter 2, business strategy not only addresses squarely the issue of how to compete, but it also embraces all of the functional area support strategies, how management plans to respond to changing industry conditions of all kinds (not just those that are competition-related), and how management intends to address the full range of strategic issues confronting the business. Competitive strategy, however, is narrower in scope and zeros in on the firm's competitive approach, the competitive edge strived for, and specific moves to outmaneuver rival companies.

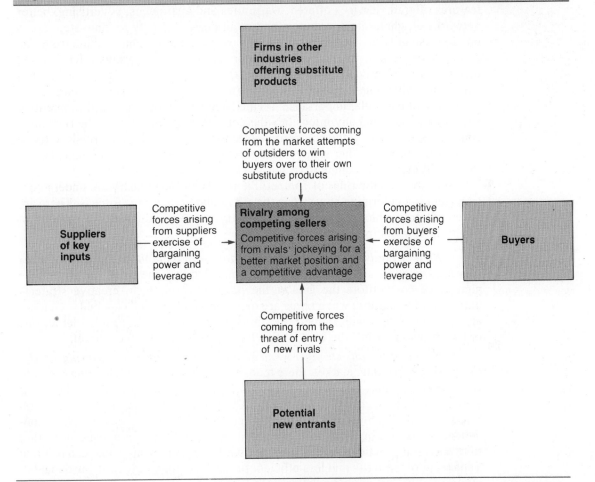

Figure 3–3 THE "FIVE-FORCES" MODEL OF COMPETITION: A KEY ANALYTICAL TOOL

Source: Adapted from Michael E. Porter, "How Competitive Forces Shape Strategy," *Harvard Business Review* 57, no. 2 (March–April 1979). pp. 137–45.

The challenge in crafting a winning competitive strategy, of course, is *how to gain an edge over rivals*. The big complication is that the success of any one firm's strategy hinges on what strategies its rivals employ and the resources rivals are willing and able to put behind their strategies. The "best" strategy for one firm in its maneuvering for competitive advantage depends, in other words, on the competitive strength and competitive strategies of rival companies. And whenever a firm makes a strategic move, rivals may retaliate with offensive or defensive countermoves. Thus competitive rivalry turns out to be a game of strategy, of move and countermove, played under "warlike" conditions according to the rules of business competition—in effect, *competitive markets are economic battlefields*.

Competitive battles among rival sellers can assume many forms and shades of intensity. The weapons used for competing include price, quality, performance features offered, services offered, warranties and guarantees, advertising, better networks of wholesale distributors and retail dealers, ability to innovate, and so on. The use of these weapons can change over time as emphasis shifts from one competitive weapon to another and as competitors make various offensive and defensive moves. Rivalry is thus dynamic; the current scene is always modified as companies initiate new moves and countermoves. Two principles of competitive rivalry are of particular importance: (1) the employment of a powerful competitive strategy by one company intensifies the competitive pressures on the remaining companies and (2) how the competitive weapons are being used by rivals to try to outmaneuver one another shapes "the rules of competition" in the industry and the requirements for competitive success.

Once the specific rules of competitive rivalry in the industry are understood, managers can determine how strong this particular competitive force is. There are several factors which, industry after industry, seem to influence the *strength* of rivalry among competing sellers:[8]

1. *Rivalry tends to intensify as the number of competitors increases and as they become more equal in size and capability.* Up to some point, the greater the number of competitors the greater the probability of fresh, creative strategic initiatives. In addition, when rivals are more equal in size and capability, chances are greater that they will compete on a fairly even footing, making it harder for one or two firms to "win" the competitive battle and dominate the market.

2. *Rivalry is usually stronger when demand for the product is growing slowly.* In a rapidly expanding market, there tends to be enough business for everybody to grow. Indeed, it may take all of a firm's financial and managerial resources just to keep abreast of the growth in buyer demand, much less to steal rivals' customers. But when growth slows or when market demand drops unexpectedly, expansion-minded firms and/or firms with excess capacity often cut prices and use other sales-increasing tactics, thereby igniting a battle for market share that can result in a shakeout of the weak and less-efficient firms. The industry then "consolidates" into a smaller, but individually stronger, group of sellers.

3. *Rivalry is more intense when industry conditions tempt competitors to use price cuts or other competitive weapons to boost unit volume.* Whenever fixed costs are high and marginal costs are low, firms are under strong economic pressure to produce at or near full capacity. Hence, if market demand weakens and capacity utilization begins to fall off, rival firms frequently resort to secret price concessions, special discounts, rebates, and other sales-increasing tactics. A similar situation arises when a product is perishable, seasonal, or costly to hold in inventory.

4. *Rivalry is stronger when the costs incurred by customers in switching from one brand to another are low.* The lower the costs of switching, the easier it is for

---

[8] These indicators of what to look for in evaluating the intensity of interfirm rivalry are based on Porter, *Competitive Strategy,* pp. 17–21.

rival sellers to attempt raids on one another's customers. On the other hand, high switching costs give a seller some protection from such raids.

5. *Rivalry is stronger when one or more competitors are dissatisfied with their market position and initiate moves to bolster their standing at the expense of rivals.* Firms that are losing ground or find themselves in financial trouble are often driven into taking aggressive action. Such moves as acquisition of smaller rivals, the introduction of new products, a boost in advertising, special price promotions, and the like can all trigger a new round of competitive maneuvering and a heightened battle for market share.

6. *Rivalry increases in proportion to the size of the payoff from a successful strategic move.* The greater the potential reward, the more likely some firm will aggressively pursue a strategy to capture the perceived opportunity. The size of the strategic payoff varies partly with the speed of retaliation. When competitors can be expected to respond slowly (or not at all), the initiator of a fresh competitive strategy can reap the benefits in the intervening period and perhaps gain a first-mover advantage that is not easily surmounted. The greater the benefits of moving first, the more likely some firm will accept the risk of pioneering.

7. *Rivalry tends to be more vigorous when it costs more to get out of a business than to stay in and compete.* The higher the exit barriers (and thus the more costly it is to abandon a market), the stronger the incentive for firms to remain and compete as best they can, even though they may be earning low profits or even incurring a loss.

8. *Rivalry becomes more volatile and unpredictable the more diverse competitors are in terms of their strategies, personalities, corporate priorities, resources, and countries of origin.* A diverse group of sellers is more likely to spawn one or more mavericks willing to rock the boat with unconventional moves and approaches, thus generating a more lively and uncertain competitive environment. The added presence of new, lower-cost foreign-based competitors intent on gaining market share is a surefire factor in boosting the intensity of rivalry.

9. *Rivalry increases when strong companies outside the industry acquire weak firms in the industry and launch aggressive, well-funded moves to transform their newly acquired competitors into major market contenders.* Philip Morris is a classic example. This leading cigarette firm with excellent marketing know-how shook up the whole beer industry's approach to marketing by acquiring stodgy Miller Brewing Company in the late 1960s. In short order, Philip Morris revamped the marketing of Miller High Life and pushed it to the number two best-selling brand. PM also pioneered low-calorie beers with the introduction of Miller Lite— a move that made light beer the fastest-growing segment in the beer industry.

The jockeying for position among competitors unfolds in round after round of moves and countermoves. Thus, the strategist's job is to identify the current weapons of competitive rivalry, to stay on top of how the game is being played, and to judge how much pressure competitive rivalry is going to put on profitability. Competitive rivalry is "intense" when the actions of competitors are driving down industry profits; rivalry is "moderate" when most companies can earn acceptable profits; and rivalry is "weak" when most companies in the industry can earn above-average returns on investment. Chronic use of cutthroat competitive tactics among rival sellers tends to make an industry inherently unattractive.

The Competitive Force of Potential Entry.   New entrants to a market bring new production capacity, the desire to establish a secure place in the market, and sometimes substantial resources with which to compete.[9] Just how serious the competitive threat of entry is in a particular market depends on two classes of factors: *barriers to entry* and the *expected reaction of incumbent firms to new entry*. A barrier to entry exists whenever it is hard for a newcomer to break into the market and/or the economics of the business put a potential entrant at a price/cost disadvantage relative to its competitors. There are several major sources of entry barriers:[10]

- *Economies of scale*—Important scale economies deter entry because they force potential entrants to enter on a large-scale basis (a costly and perhaps risky move) or accept a cost disadvantage (and consequently lower profitability). Large-scale entry could result in chronic overcapacity in the industry and/or it could so threaten the market shares of existing firms that they are pushed into aggressive retaliation (in the form of price cuts, increased advertising and sales promotion, and similar steps) to maintain their position. Either way, the entrant's outlook is for lower profits. Entrants may encounter scale-related barriers not just in production, but in advertising, marketing and distribution, financing, after-sale customer service, raw materials purchasing, and R&D as well.

- *Inability to gain access to technology and specialized know-how*—Many industries require technological capability and skills not readily available to a new entrant. Key patents can effectively bar entry as can lack of skilled personnel and a lack of familiarity with certain technologies and complicated manufacturing techniques. Existing firms often carefully guard the know-how that gives them a technological edge. Unless new entrants can gain access to such proprietary knowledge, they will lack the technical capability to compete on an equal footing.

- *The existence of learning and experience curve effects*—When achieving lower unit costs is partly or mostly a function of experience in producing the product and other learning curve benefits, a new entrant is put at a disadvantage in competing with existing firms having more accumulated know-how.

- *Brand preferences and customer loyalty*—Buyers usually have some attachment to existing brands. European consumers, for example, are fiercely loyal to European brands of major household appliances. High brand loyalty means that a potential entrant must be prepared to spend

---

[9] Michael E. Porter, "How Competitive Forces Shape Strategy," *Harvard Business Review* 57, no. 2 (March–April 1979), p. 138.

[10] Porter, *Competitive Strategy*, pp. 7–17.

enough money on advertising and sales promotion to overcome customer loyalties and build its own clientele. Substantial time and money can be involved. In addition, in some circumstances it is difficult or costly for a customer to switch to a new brand, in which case a new entrant must persuade buyers that its brand is worth the switching costs. To overcome the switching cost barrier, new entrants may have to offer buyers a bigger price cut or an extra margin of quality or service. All this can mean lower expected profit margins for new entrants—something that increases the risk to start-up companies dependent on sizable, early profits to support their new investment.

- *Capital requirements*—The larger the total dollar investment needed to enter the market successfully, the more limited the pool of potential entrants. The most obvious capital requirements are associated with manufacturing plant and equipment, working capital to finance inventories and customer credit, introductory advertising and sales promotion to establish a clientele, and covering start-up losses.

- *Cost disadvantages independent of size*—Existing firms may have cost advantages not available to potential entrants regardless of the entrant's size. These advantages can include access to the best or cheapest raw materials, possession of patents and proprietary technological know-how, the benefits of any learning and experience curve effects, having plants built and equipped at preinflation prices, favorable locations, and lower borrowing costs.

- *Access to distribution channels*—In the case of consumer goods, a potential entrant may face the barrier of gaining adequate distribution access. Wholesale distributors may be reluctant to take on a product that lacks buyer recognition. A network of retail dealers may have to be set up from scratch. Retailers have to be convinced to give a new brand ample display space and an adequate trial period. The more existing producers have the present distribution channels tied up, the tougher entry will be. Potential entrants, to overcome this barrier, may have to "buy" distribution access by offering better margins to dealers and distributors or by giving advertising allowances and other promotional incentives. The result is that the potential entrant's profits may be squeezed unless and until its product gains such market acceptance that distributors and retailers want to carry it because of its popularity.

- *Regulatory policies*—Government agencies can limit or even bar entry by controlling licenses and permits. Regulated industries like banking, insurance, radio and television stations, liquor retailing, and railroads all feature government-controlled entry. In international markets, host governments commonly limit foreign entry and must approve all foreign investment applications. Stringent government-mandated safety regulations and environmental pollution control standards also make entry more expensive.

- *Tariffs and international trade restrictions*—National governments commonly use tariffs and trade restrictions (antidumping rules, local content requirements, and quotas) to raise entry barriers for foreign firms. In 1988, due to tariffs imposed by the South Korean government, a Ford Taurus cost South Korean car buyers over $40,000. European governments require that certain Asian products, from electronic typewriters to copying machines, contain 40 percent European-made parts. And to protect European chipmakers from low-cost Asian competition, such governments have a rigid formula for calculating floor prices for computer memory chips.

Even if a potential entrant is willing to tackle the problems of entry barriers, it may be dissuaded by its expectations about how existing firms will react to new entry.[11] Will incumbent firms "move over" grudgingly and let the new entrant take a viable share of the market, or will they launch a vigorous, "survival of the fittest" defense of their market positions—including price cuts, increased advertising, new product improvements, and whatever else is calculated to give a new entrant (as well as other rivals) a hard time? A potential entrant is likely to have second thoughts when incumbent firms send strong signals that they will be aggressive in defending their market positions against entry and when they have substantial financial resources with which to wage a defense. An entrant may also turn away when incumbent firms are in a position to use leverage with distributors and customers to keep their business.

The best test of whether potential entry is a strong or weak competitive force is to ask if existing firms should be concerned about potential entry. When the answer is no, potential entry is not a source of competitive pressure. When the answer is yes, as it is in industries where lower-cost foreign competitors are seeking new markets, then potential entry is a strong force that requires defensive or maybe offensive strategic action.

One additional point needs to be made about the threat of entry as a competitive force: the threat of entry changes as industry prospects grow brighter or dimmer and as entry barriers rise or fall. For example, the expiration of a key patent can greatly increase the threat of entry. A technological discovery can create an economy of scale advantage where none existed before. New actions by incumbent firms to increase advertising, strengthen distributor-dealer relations, step up R&D, or improve product quality can erect higher roadblocks to entry. In international markets, entry barriers for foreign-based firms fall as tariffs are lowered, as domestic wholesalers and dealers seek out lower-cost foreign-made goods, and as domestic buyers become more willing to purchase foreign brands.

The Competitive Force of Substitute Products.   Firms in one industry are, quite often, in close competition with firms in another industry because their respective products are good substitutes. The producers of eyeglasses compete with the makers of contact lenses. The producers of wood stoves compete with such substitutes as kerosene heaters and portable electric heaters. The sugar industry has felt major competition from companies that produce artificial sweeteners. The producers of plastic containers confront strong competition from the makers of glass bottles and jars, manufacturers of paperboard cartons, and producers of tin

---

[11] Porter, "How Competitive Forces Shape Strategy," p. 140, and Porter, *Competitive Strategy,* p. 14–15.

cans and aluminum cans. Aspirin manufacturers must take into account how their product compares with other pain relievers and headache remedies.

The competitive force of closely related substitute products enters into play in several ways. First, the presence of readily available and competitively priced substitutes places a ceiling on the prices an industry can afford to charge for its own product without giving customers an incentive to switch to substitutes and then suffering market erosion.[12] This price ceiling, at the same time, puts a lid on the profits that industry members can earn unless they find ways to cut costs. When substitutes are cheaper than the industry's product, industry members come under heavy competitive pressure to reduce their prices and to find ways to absorb the price cuts with cost reductions. Second, the availability of substitutes inevitably invites customers to make quality and performance comparisons as well as price comparisons. For example, firms that buy glass bottles and jars from glassware manufacturers constantly monitor whether they can just as effectively package their products in paper cartons or tin cans. The competitive pressure from substitute products thus pushes industry rivals to hunt for ways to convince customers their product is more advantageous than substitutes. Usually this means devising a competitive strategy that differentiates the industry's product from substitute products via some combination of cheaper price, better quality, better service, and more desirable performance features.

Another determinant of whether substitutes are a strong or weak competitive force is whether it is difficult or costly for the industry's customers to switch to substitute products.[13] Typical switching costs include employees retraining costs, the cost to purchase additional equipment, payments for technical help in making the changeover, the time and cost in testing the quality and reliability of the substitute, and the psychic costs of severing old supplier relationships and establishing new ones. If switching costs are high, sellers of substitutes must offer a major cost or performance benefit in order to steal the industry's customers away. When switching costs are low, it is easier for sellers of substitutes to convince buyers to change over to their product.

As a rule, then, the lower the price of substitutes, the higher their quality and performance, and the lower the user's switching costs, the more intense are the competitive pressures posed by substitute products. The best indicators of the competitive strength of substitute products are the rate at which their sales are growing and the market inroads they are making. Other indicators are their plans for expansion of capacity and their profits.

The Power of Suppliers. Whether the suppliers to an industry are a weak or strong competitive force depends on market conditions in the supplier industry and the significance of the item they supply.[14] The competitive force of suppliers is greatly diminished whenever the item they provide is a standard commodity

---

[12] Porter, "How Competitive Forces Shape Strategy," p. 142, and Porter, *Competitive Strategy*, pp. 23–24.

[13] Porter, *Competitive Strategy*, p. 10.

[14] Ibid., pp. 27–28.

available on the open market from a large number of suppliers with ample capability to fill orders. Then it is relatively simple to multiple-source whatever is needed, choosing to buy from whichever suppliers offer the best deal. In such cases, suppliers can win concessions only when supplies become tight and users are so anxious to secure what they need that they agree to terms more favorable to suppliers. Suppliers are likewise in a weak bargaining position whenever there are good substitute inputs and switching is neither costly nor difficult. For example, the power of the suppliers of aluminum cans to soft drink bottlers is checked by the latter's ability to use plastic containers and glass bottles. Suppliers also have less leverage when the industry they are supplying is a *major* customer. Here the well-being of suppliers becomes closely tied to the well-being of their major customer. This usually means suppliers have a big incentive to protect the customer industry via reasonable prices, improved quality, and the development of new products and services that might enhance their customers' competitive positions, sales, and profits. Indeed, when industry members form a close working relationship with major suppliers, they may be able to realize substantial benefits in the form of better quality components, just-in-time deliveries, and reduced inventory costs.

On the other hand, powerful suppliers can put an industry in a profit squeeze via price increases that cannot fully be passed on to the industry's consumers. Suppliers become a potentially strong competitive force in this regard when the item they provide makes up a sizable fraction of the costs of an industry's product, is crucial to the industry's production process, and/or significantly affects the quality of the industry's product. Likewise, a supplier (or group of suppliers) gains bargaining leverage the more difficult or costly it is for users to switch from one supplier to another. Big suppliers with good reputations and growing demand for their output are harder to wring concessions from than small suppliers striving to broaden their customer base and fill their production capacity.

Suppliers are also more powerful when they can supply a component cheaper than industry members can make it themselves. For instance, the producers of outdoor power equipment (lawnmowers, rotary tillers, snowblowers, and so on) find it cheaper to source the small engines they need from outside specialists in small engine manufacture rather than to manufacture their own in-house because the volume they need is too small to justify the investment and master the process. Small engine specialists, by supplying many kinds of engines to the whole power equipment industry, obtain a big enough sales volume to capture scale economies, become proficient in all the techniques, and achieve costs well below what power equipment firms could realize by making their own engines in-house. Small engine suppliers then are in a position to price the item below what it would cost the user to self-manufacture but far enough above their own costs to generate an attractive profit margin. In such situations, the bargaining position of suppliers is strong *until* the volume of parts needed internally becomes large enough to justify backward integration. Then the balance of power shifts away from the supplier. The more credible the threat of backward integration into the suppliers' business becomes, the more that companies gain an upper hand over suppliers in negotiating favorable supply terms.

A final instance in which an industry's suppliers play an important competitive role is when suppliers, for one reason or another, do not have the capability or the incentive to provide items of adequate quality. For example, if auto parts suppliers in the United States provide lower-quality components to the U.S. automobile manufacturers, they can so increase the warranty and defective goods costs of the auto firms that the latter's profits, reputation, and competitive position in the world automobile market are seriously impaired.

The Power of Buyers. Just as with suppliers, the competitive strength of buyers can range from strong to weak. Buyers have substantial bargaining leverage in a number of situations.[15] The most obvious is when buyers are large and purchase a sizable percentage of the industry's output. The bigger buyers are and the larger the quantities they purchase, the more clout they have in negotiating with sellers. Often, large buyers are successful in using the leverage of their size and their volume purchases to obtain price concessions and other favorable terms. Buyers also gain power when their costs of switching to competing brands or to competing substitutes are relatively low. Any time buyers have the flexibility to fill their needs by sourcing from several sellers rather than having to use just one brand, they have added room to negotiate with sellers. When the industry's product is pretty much standard from seller to seller, it is generally easy for buyers not only to find alternative sellers but also to switch from seller to seller at little or no cost. The more strongly differentiated sellers' products are, however, the less able buyers are to switch without incurring sizable switching costs.

One last point: all buyers are not likely to possess equal degrees of bargaining power with sellers, and some may be less sensitive than others to price, quality, or service. For example, in the apparel industry major manufacturers, on the one hand, confront significant customer power in selling direct to retail chains like Sears or K mart, and on the other, they find themselves in a position to get much better prices selling to apparel boutiques.

The Strategic Implications of the Five Competitive Forces. The unique analytical contribution of Figure 3–3 is the systematic way it exposes the makeup of competitive forces. *Analysis of the competitive environment requires that the strength of each one of the five competitive forces be assessed.* The collective impact of these forces determines what competition is like in a given market. As a rule, the stronger competitive forces are, the lower is the collective profitability of participant firms. The most brutally competitive situation occurs when the five forces combine to create pressures so oppressive that the industry outlook is for prolonged subpar profitability or even losses for most or all firms. The competitive structure of an industry is clearly "unattractive" from a profit-making standpoint if rivalry among sellers is strong, entry barriers are low, competition from substitutes is strong, and both suppliers and customers are able to exercise considerable bargaining leverage. On the other hand, when an industry offers superior long-term profit prospects, it can be said that competitive forces are not

---

[15] Ibid., pp. 24–27.

unduly strong and the competitive structure of the industry is "favorable" and "attractive." The "ideal" competitive environment from a profit-making perspective is where both suppliers and customers are in a weak bargaining position, there are no good substitutes, entry barriers are relatively high, and rivalry among present sellers is only moderate. However, even where some of the five competitive forces are strong, an industry is competitively attractive if a firm's strategy provides a good enough defense against the five forces that the enterprise ends up with a competitive advantage and with the ability to earn above-average profits.

In coping with competitive forces, successful strategists search for competitive approaches that will (1) insulate the firm as much as possible from the five competitive forces, (2) influence the industry's competitive rules in the company's favor, and (3) provide a strong position from which to "play the game" of competition as it unfolds in the industry. Strategists cannot do this task well without first perceptively analyzing the whole competitive picture of the industry via the five forces model.

Assessing the Competitive Positions of Rival Companies

The next step in examining the industry's competitive structure is to study the respective positions of rival companies in the industry. One technique for revealing the competitive positions of industry participants is *strategic group mapping*.[16] This analytical tool serves as a convenient bridge between looking at the industry as a whole and considering the standing of each firm separately. It is useful when an industry is populated with so many competitors that it is not practical to examine each one in depth.

A strategic group consists of those rival firms with similar competitive approaches and positions in the market.[17] Companies in the same strategic group can resemble one another in several ways: they may have comparable product line breadth, use the same kinds of distribution channels, be vertically integrated to much the same degree, offer buyers similar services and technical assistance, use essentially the same product attributes to appeal to similar types of buyers, emphasize the same distribution channels, depend on identical technological approaches, and/or sell in the same price/quality range. An industry contains only one strategic group when all sellers approach the market with essentially identical strategies. At the other extreme, there are as many strategic groups as there are competitors when each rival pursues a distinctively different competitive approach and occupies a substantially different competitive position in the marketplace.

The procedure for constructing a strategic group map and deciding which firms belong in which strategic group is straightforward:

• Identify the competitive characteristics that differentiate firms in the industry—typical variables are price/quality range (high, medium, low),

---

[16] Ibid., chap. 7.

[17] Ibid., pp. 129–30.

geographic coverage (local, regional, national, global), degree of vertical integration (none, partial, full), product line breadth (wide, narrow), use of distribution channels (one, some, all), and degree of service offered (no frills, limited, full service).

- Plot the firms on a two-variable map using pairs of these differentiating characteristics.
- Assign firms that fall in about the same strategy space to the same strategic group.
- Draw circles around each strategic group, making the circles proportional to the size of the group's respective share of total industry sales revenues.

This produces a two-dimensional *strategic group map* such as the one for the beer industry portrayed in Illustration Capsule 8.

To map the positions of strategic groups accurately in the industry's overall "strategy space," several guidelines need to be observed.[18] First, the two variables selected as axes for the map should *not* be highly correlated; if they are, the circles on the map will fall along a diagonal and the map will tell nothing more about the relative positions of competitors than would considering one of the variables by itself. For instance, if companies with broad product lines use multiple distribution channels while companies with narrow lines use a single distribution channel, then one of the variables is redundant. We can learn just as much about who is positioned how by looking at broad versus narrow product lines as by adding in single versus multiple distribution channels. Second, the variables chosen as axes for the map should expose big differences in how rivals have positioned themselves to compete in the marketplace. This, of course, requires identifying the characteristics that differentiate rival firms and then using these differences as variables for the axes and as the basis for deciding which firm belongs in which strategic group. Third, the variables used as axes don't have to be either quantitative or continuous; rather, they can be discrete variables or defined in terms of distinct classes and combinations. Fourth, drawing the sizes of the circles on the map proportional to the combined sales of the firms in each strategic group allows the map to reflect the relative sizes of each strategic group. Fifth, if more than two good competitive variables can be used as axes for the map, then several maps can be drawn to give different exposures to the competitive positioning relationships present in the industry's structure. Because there need not be one best map for portraying how competing firms are positioned in the market, it is advisable to experiment with different pairs of competitive variables.

Strategic group analysis is helpful in deepening understanding of competitive rivalry.[19] To begin with, changing industry conditions often favor some strategic groups and hurt others. Sometimes driving forces so disadvantage certain strategic groups that firms in the adversely affected groups try to shift to a more favorably situated group. How hard such a move proves to be is a function of

---

[18] Ibid., pp. 152–54.

[19] Ibid., pp. 130, 132–38, and 154–55.

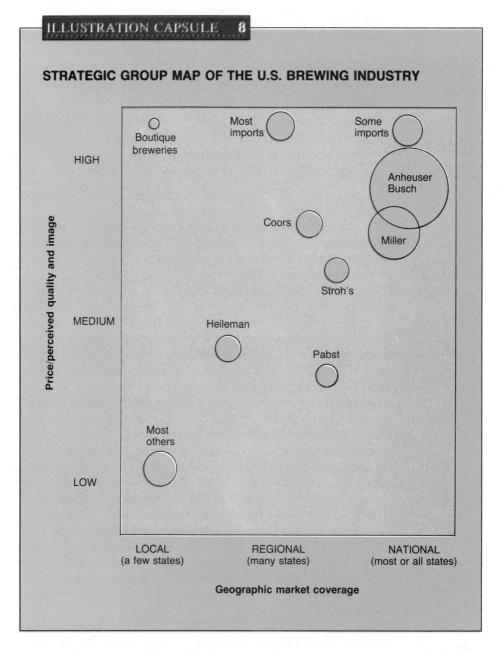

ILLUSTRATION CAPSULE   8

STRATEGIC GROUP MAP OF THE U.S. BREWING INDUSTRY

whether the entry barriers into the target strategic group are high or low. Rival firms' attempts to enter a new strategic group nearly always increase competitive pressures. If certain firms are known to be trying to change their competitive positions on the map, then attaching arrows to the circles showing the targeted direction helps clarify the picture of competitive jockeying among rivals.

A second thing to watch for is whether the profit potential of different strategic groups varies due to the strengths and weaknesses in each group's market position. Differences in profitability can occur because of differing degrees of bargaining leverage with suppliers or customers and differing degrees of exposure to competition from substitute products outside the industry.

Generally speaking, the closer the various strategic groups are to each other on the map, the stronger competitive rivalry tends to be. Although firms in the same strategic group are the closest rivals, the next closest rivals are in the immediately adjacent groups. Often, firms in strategic groups that are *far apart* on the map compete hardly at all. For instance, Heineken Brewing Co. in Amsterdam and Dixie Brewing Co. in New Orleans both sell beer, but the prices and perceived qualities of their products are much too different to generate any competition between them. For the same reason, Timex is not a meaningful competitive rival of Rolex, and Subaru is not a close competitor of Lincoln or Mercedes-Benz.

Competitor Analysis: Predicting What Moves Which Rivals Are Likely to Make Next

Studying the actions and behavior of one's closest competitors is essential. Unless a company pays watchful attention to what competitors are doing, it ends up "flying blind" into competitive battle. It is foolish to expect to outmaneuver rival companies without knowing what strategies they are using and what moves they are likely to make next. What actions rivals are taking and are likely to take next have direct bearing on what a company's own best strategic moves are—whether it will need to defend against specific actions taken by rivals or whether rivals' moves provide an opening for a new offensive thrust.

Identifying Competitors' Strategies. A quick profile of key competitors can be gotten by looking at where they are in the industry, their strategic objectives as revealed by actions recently taken, and their basic competitive approaches. Table 3–3 provides an easy-to-use scheme for summing up the objectives and strategies of rival companies. Such a summary, along with the information provided from the strategic group map, usually suffices to evaluate the seriousness of the competitive threat that specific rivals pose.

Evaluating Who the Industry's Major Players Are Going to Be. It is usually obvious who the *current* major contenders are, but these same firms are not necessarily positioned strongly for the future. Some may be losing ground or be ill-equipped to compete on the industry's future battleground. Smaller companies may be moving into real contention and poised to go on the offensive against larger but weaker rivals. In fast-moving, high-technology industries and in globally competitive industries, companies can and do fall from the leadership ranks; others, for one reason or another, end up being acquired. Today's industry leaders don't automatically become tomorrow's.

In deciding whether a competitor is favorably or unfavorably positioned to gain market ground, attention needs to center on why there is potential for it to do better or worse than other rivals. Usually, how securely a company holds its present market share is a function of its vulnerability to driving forces and competitive pressures, whether it has a competitive advantage or disadvantage,

Table 3-3 CATEGORIZING THE OBJECTIVES AND STRATEGIES OF COMPETITORS

Competitive scope	Strategic intent	Market share objective	Competitive position/situation	Strategic posture	Competitive strategy

• Local
• Regional
• National
• Multicountry
• Global
	• Be the dominant leader
	• Overtake the present industry leader
	• Be among the industry leaders (top 5)
	• Move into the top 10
	• Move up a notch or two in the industry rankings
	• Overtake a particular rival (not necessarily the leader)
	• Maintain position
	• Just survive
		• Aggressive expansion via both acquisition and internal growth
		• Expansion via internal growth (boost market share at the expense of rival firms)
		• Expansion via acquisition
		• Hold onto present share (by growing at a rate *equal* to the industry average)
		• Give up share if necessary to achieve short-term profit objectives (stress profitability, not volume)
			• Getting stronger; on the move
			• Well-entrenched; able to maintain its present position
			• Stuck in the middle of the pack
			• Going after a different market position (trying to move from a weaker to a stronger position)
			• Struggling; losing ground
			• Retrenching to a position that can be defended
				• Mostly offensive
				• Mostly defensive
				• A combination of offense and defense
				• Aggressive risk-taker
				• Conservative follower
					• Striving for low cost leadership
					• Mostly focusing on a market niche
					  High end
					  Low end
					  Geographic
					  Buyers with special needs
					  Other
					• Pursuing differentiation based on
					  Quality
					  Service
					  Technological superiority
					  Breadth of product line
					  Image and reputation
					  Other attributes

Note: Since a focus strategy can be aimed at any of several market niches and a differentiation strategy can be keyed to any of several attributes, it is best to be explicit about what kind of focus strategy or differentiation strategy a given firm is pursuing. All focusers do not pursue the same market niche, and all differentiators do not pursue the same differentiating attributes.

and whether it is the likely target of offensive attack from other industry participants. Trying to identify which rivals are poised to gain market position and which rivals seem destined to lose market share helps a strategist figure out what kinds of moves key rivals are likely to make next.

Predicting Competitors' Next Moves.   This is the hardest yet most useful part of competitor analysis. Good clues about what moves a specific competitor may make next come from finding out how much pressure the rival is under to improve its financial performance. Aggressive rivals on the move are strong candidates for some type of new strategic initiative. Content rivals are likely to continue their present strategy with only minor fine-tuning. Ailing and troubled rivals can be performing so poorly that fresh strategic moves, either offensive or defensive, are virtually certain.

Since managers generally operate on assumptions about the industry's future and on beliefs about their firm's situation, insights into their strategic thinking also come from examining their public pronouncements about what it will take to be successful in the industry, listening to what they are saying about their own firm's situation, gathering information from the grapevine about what they are doing, and studying their past actions and leadership styles. Another thing to consider is whether the rival has the flexibility to make any major strategic changes or whether it is locked into pursuing its same basic strategy with minor adjustments.

To succeed in predicting a competitor's next moves, an analyst must get a good "feel" for the rival's situation, how its managers think, and what their options are. Doing the necessary detective work can be tedious and time-consuming since the information comes in bits and pieces from many sources. But it is a task worth doing well because the payoff is more time to ready whatever countermoves may be necessary and a potential to beat them to the punch by moving first.

Pinpointing the Key Factors for Competitive Success

Key success factors (KSFs) are the major determinants of financial and competitive success in a particular industry. Key success factors highlight the things all firms in the industry must pay close attention to—the specific outcomes crucial to success in the marketplace and the functional skills with the most direct bearing on company profitability. In beer, the KSFs are utilization of brewing capacity (to keep manufacturing costs low), a strong network of wholesale distributors (to gain access to as many retail outlets as possible), and clever advertising (to induce beer drinkers to buy a particular brand and thereby pull beer sales through the established wholesale/retail channels). In apparel manufacturing, the KSFs are fashion design (to create buyer appeal) and manufacturing efficiency (to keep selling prices competitive). In tin and aluminum cans, where the cost of shipping empty cans is substantial, the keys are having plants located close to end-use customers and having the ability to market plant output within economical shipping distances (regional market share proves far more crucial than national share).

Identification of key success factors is a top-priority strategic consideration. At the very least, management needs to know the industry well enough to conclude what is more important to competitive success and what is less important. At most, KSFs can serve as *the cornerstones* on which business strategy is built—frequently, a company can win a competitive advantage by concentrating on being distinctively better than rivals in one or more of the industry's key success factors.

Key success factors vary from industry to industry and even from time to time within the same industry as driving forces and competitive conditions change.

Table 3–4 provides a shopping list of the most common types of key success factors. However, rarely does any one industry have more than three or four key success factors at any one time. And even among these three or four, one or two usually outrank the others in importance. Strategic analysts, therefore, have to resist the temptation to include factors that have only minor importance on their list of key success factors—the purpose of identifying key success factors is to make judgments about what things are more important to competitive success and what things are less important. To compile a list of everything that matters even a little bit defeats the purpose of training management's eyes on the factors truly crucial to long-term competitive success.

Drawing Conclusions About Overall Industry Attractiveness

While each of the preceding analytical steps has added something new to the picture of the industry and competitive environment, the role of this final step is to review the overall situation and develop reasoned conclusions about the relative attractiveness or unattractiveness of the industry, both near-term and long-term. An assessment that the industry is attractive typically calls for some kind of an aggressive, expansion-oriented strategic approach. If the industry and competitive situation are judged relatively unattractive, companies will consider strategies to protect their profitability, and the weakest companies may seriously consider leaving the industry.

The factors to be especially alert for in drawing conclusions about industry attractiveness are:

- The industry's growth potential.
- Whether the industry will be favorably or unfavorably impacted by the prevailing driving forces.
- Potential for the entry/exit of major firms (probable entry reduces attractiveness to existing firms; the exit of a major firm or several weak firms opens up market share growth opportunities for the remaining firms).
- The stability/dependability of demand (as affected by seasonality, the business cycle, the volatility of consumer preferences, inroads from substitutes, and the like).
- Whether competitive forces will become stronger or weaker.
- The severity of problems/issues confronting the industry as a whole.
- The degrees of risk and uncertainty in the industry's future.
- Whether the industry's overall profit prospects are above average or below average.

Table 3–4 TYPES OF KEY SUCCESS FACTORS

Technology-Related KSFs
* Scientific research expertise (important in such fields as pharmaceuticals, medicine, space exploration, other "high-tech" industries)
* Production process innovation capability
* Product innovation capability
* Expertise in a given technology

Manufacturing-Related KSFs
* Low-cost production efficiency (achieve scale economies, capture experience curve effects)
* Quality of manufacture (fewer defects, less need for repairs)
* High utilization of fixed assets (important in capital intensive/high fixed-cost industries)
* Low-cost plant locations
* Access to adequate supplies of skilled labor
* High labor productivity (important for items with high labor content)
* Low-cost product design and engineering (reduces manufacturing costs)
* Flexibility to manufacture a range of models and sizes; take care of custom orders

Distribution-Related KSFs
* A strong network of wholesale distributors/dealers
* Gaining ample space on retailer shelves
* Having company-owned retail outlets
* Low distribution costs
* Fast delivery

Marketing-Related KSFs
* A well-trained, effective sales force
* Available, dependable service and technical assistance
* Accurate filling of buyer orders (few back orders or mistakes)
* Breadth of product line and product selection
* Merchandising skills
* Attractive styling/packaging
* Customer guarantees and warranties (important in mail-order retailing, big-ticket purchases, new product introductions)

Skills-Related KSFs
* Superior talent (important in professional services)
* Quality control know-how
* Design expertise (important in fashion and apparel industries)
* Expertise in a particular technology
* Ability to come up with clever, catchy ads
* Ability to get newly developed products out of the R&D phase and onto the market very quickly

Organizational Capability
* Superior information systems (important in airline travel, car rental, credit card, and lodging industries)
* Ability to respond quickly to shifting market conditions (streamlined decision-making, short lead times to bring new products to market)
* More experience and managerial know-how

Other Types of KSFs
* Favorable image/reputation with buyers
* Recognition as a leader
* Convenient locations (important in many retailing businesses)
* Pleasant, courteous employees
* Access to financial capital (important in newly emerging industries with high degrees of business risk and in capital intensive industries)
* Patent protection
* Overall low cost (not just in manufacturing)

Aside from these industrywide considerations, it is important to realize that an industry that is relatively unattractive overall can still be attractive to a company already favorably situated in the industry or to an outsider with the resources to acquire an existing company and the skills to turn it into a major industry contender. Appraising industry attractiveness from the standpoint of a particular company in the industry means looking at the following *additional aspects:*

- The company's competitive position in the industry and whether its position is likely to grow stronger or weaker (being a well-entrenched leader in an otherwise lackluster industry can still produce good profitability).
- The company's potential to capitalize on the vulnerabilities of weaker rivals (thereby converting an unattractive *industry* situation into a potentially interesting *company* opportunity).
- Whether the company is somewhat insulated from, or able to defend against, the factors that make the industry as a whole unattractive.
- Whether continued participation in this industry adds importantly to the firm's ability to be successful in other industries in which it has business interests.

The conclusions drawn about the attractiveness of the industry and competitive situation should have a major bearing on a company's strategic options and ultimate choice of strategy.

KEY POINTS

In this chapter we introduced several concepts and analytical approaches—driving forces, the five forces model of competition, strategic groups and strategic group mapping, competitor analysis, key success factors, and industry attractiveness considerations. They form the cornerstones of external situation analysis.

Table 3–5 provides a *format* for conducting industry and competitive analysis. It pulls together the concepts and thought processes we covered into a simple analytical framework and, if completed conscientiously, yields a readily digested bottom-line analysis of the industry and competitive environment.

Two final points are worth keeping in mind. First, the task of analyzing a company's external situation cannot be reduced to a mechanical, formula-like exercise in which facts and data are plugged in and definitive conclusions come pouring out. There can be several appealing scenarios about how an industry will evolve and what future competitive conditions will be like. For this reason, strategic analysis always leaves room for differences of opinion about how all the factors add up and how industry and competitive conditions will change. However, while no strategy analysis methodology can guarantee a single conclusive diagnosis, it doesn't make sense to shortcut strategic analysis and rely on opinion and casual observation. Managers become better strategists when they know what analytical questions to pose, can use situation analysis techniques to find answers, and have the skills to read clues about which way the winds of industry and competitive change are blowing. This is why we concentrated on suggesting the right questions to ask, explaining concepts and analytical approaches, and indicating the kinds of things to look for.

Second, in practice the process of industry and competitive analysis is incremental and ongoing, the result of gradually accumulated understanding and continuous rethinking and retesting of how all the relevant factors add up. Sweeping

Table 3-5 INDUSTRY AND COMPETITIVE ANALYSIS SUMMARY PROFILE

1. DOMINANT ECONOMIC CHARACTERISTICS OF THE INDUSTRY ENVIRONMENT (market growth, geographic scope, industry structure, scale economies, experience curve effects, capital requirements, and so on)

2. DRIVING FORCES

3. COMPETITION ANALYSIS
- Rivalry among competing sellers (a strong, moderate, or weak force/weapons of competition)

- Threat of potential entry (a strong, moderate, or weak force/assessment of entry barriers)

- Competition from substitutes (a strong, moderate, or weak force/why)

- Power of suppliers (a strong, moderate, or weak force/why)

- Power of customers (a strong, moderate, or weak force/why)

4. COMPETITIVE POSITION OF MAJOR COMPANIES/STRATEGIC GROUPS
- Favorably positioned/why

- Unfavorably positioned/why

5. COMPETITOR ANALYSIS
- Strategic approaches/predicted moves of key competitors

- Who to watch and why

6. KEY SUCCESS FACTORS

7. INDUSTRY PROSPECTS AND OVERALL ATTRACTIVENESS
- Factors making the industry attractive

- Factors making the industry unattractive

- Special industry issues/problems

- Profit outlook (favorable/unfavorable)

industry and competitive analyses need to be done periodically, but in the interim managers have to update and reexamine the picture as events unfold. The path leading to important strategic actions is usually the product of a *gradual* buildup of clues and documentation that important changes in the external environment are occurring, a *gradual* understanding of the implications of these changes, and gradually reaching conclusions about what future conditions in the industry will be like.

SUGGESTED READINGS

Ghemawat, Pankaj. "Building Strategy on the Experience Curve." *Harvard Business Review* 64, no. 2 (March–April 1985), pp. 143–49.

Linneman, Robert E., and Harold E. Klein. "Using Scenarios in Strategic Decision Making." *Business Horizons* 28, no. 1 (January–February 1985), pp. 64–74.

Ohmae, Kenichi. *The Mind of the Strategist*. New York: Penguin Books, 1983, chaps. 3, 6, 7, and 13.

Porter, Michael E. "How Competitive Forces Shape Strategy." *Harvard Business Review* 57, no. 2 (March–April 1979), pp. 137–45.

————. *Competitive Strategy: Techniques for Analyzing Industries and Competitors.* New York: Free Press, 1980, chap. 1.

————. *Competitive Advantage*. New York: Free Press, 1985, chap. 2.

4 Company Situation Analysis

Understand what really makes a company "tick."
Charles R. Scott
CEO, Intermark Corp.

If you think what exists today is permanent and forever true, you inevitably get your head handed to you.
John Reed
Chairman, Citicorp

The secret of success is to be ready for opportunity when it comes.
Disraeli

In the last chapter we saw how to use industry and competitive analysis to assess the relative attractiveness of a company's external environment. This chapter concerns how to evaluate a particular company's strategic situation in that environment. Company situation analysis revolves around five questions:

1. How well is the present strategy working?
2. What are the company's strengths, weaknesses, opportunities, and threats?
3. Is the company competitive on cost?
4. How strong is the company's competitive position?
5. What strategic issues does the company face?

In exploring these questions, we will introduce three new analytical techniques: SWOT analysis, strategic cost analysis, and competitive strength assessment. These tools are widely used in strategic analysis because they indicate how strongly a company holds its industry position and whether the present strategy is capable of boosting long-term performance.

HOW WELL IS THE PRESENT STRATEGY WORKING?

In evaluating how well a company's present strategy is working, one needs to start with what the strategy is (see Figure 2–2 in Chapter 2 to refresh your recollection of the key components of business strategy). The first thing to understand is the company's competitive approach—whether it is striving for low-cost leadership, trying to differentiate itself from rivals, or focusing narrowly on certain specific customer groups and market niches. Another important consideration is the firm's competitive scope within the industry—its degree of vertical integration and its geographic market coverage. The company's functional area support strategies in production, marketing, finance, human resources, and so on need to be identified and understood as well. In addition, the company may have initiated some recent strategic moves (for instance, a price cut, stepped-up advertising, entry into a new geographic area, or merger with a competitor) that are integral to its strategy and that aim at securing a particular competitive advantage and/or improved competitive position. Examining the rationale for each piece of the strategy—for each competitive move and each functional approach—should clarify what the present strategy is.

While it makes sense to evaluate the logical consistency of a strategy, judge how well-formulated a strategy is, and determine if any part of the strategy is flawed, the best evidence of how well a company's strategy is working comes from looking at the company's recent strategic performance. The most obvious indicators of strategic performance include (1) whether the firm's market share is rising or falling, (2) whether the firm's profit margins are increasing or decreasing and how large they are relative to rival firms, (3) trends in the firm's net profits and return on investment, and (4) whether the firm's sales are growing faster or slower than the market as a whole. The better a company's current strategic performance, the less likely the need for radical changes in strategy. The weaker a company's strategic performance, the more its current strategy must be questioned.

SWOT ANALYSIS

SWOT is an acronym for a company's strengths, weaknesses, opportunities, and threats. A SWOT analysis consists of sizing up a firm's internal strengths and weaknesses and its external opportunities and threats. It is an easy-to-use tool to get a quick *overview* of a firm's strategic situation. SWOT analysis is grounded on the principle that strategy must produce a strong fit between a company's internal capability (its strengths and weaknesses) and its external situation (reflected in part by its opportunities and threats).

Identifying Strengths and Weaknesses

Table 4–1 provides a list of things to look for to identify a company's internal strengths and weaknesses. A *strength* is something a company is good at doing or a characteristic that gives it an important capability. A strength can be a skill, a competence, a particular organizational resource or competitive asset, or something the company has done that puts it in a position of market advantage (like having a better product, stronger name recognition, superior technology, or better customer service). A *weakness* is something a company lacks or does poorly (in comparison to others) or a condition that puts it at a disadvantage. A weakness can be strategically important or not, depending on how much it matters in the competitive battle the company is in.

Table 4–1 SWOT ANALYSIS—WHAT TO LOOK FOR IN SIZING UP A COMPANY'S STRENGTHS, WEAKNESSES, OPPORTUNITIES, AND THREATS

Potential internal strengths

- A distinctive competence
- Adequate financial resources
- Good competitive skill
- Well thought of by buyers
- An acknowledged market leader
- Well-conceived functional area strategies
- Access to economies of scale
- Insulated (at least somewhat) from strong competitive pressures
- Proprietary technology
- Cost advantages
- Better advertising campaigns
- Product innovation skills
- Proven management
- Ahead on experience curve
- Better manufacturing capability
- Superior technological skills
- Other?

Potential internal weaknesses

- No clear strategic direction
- Obsolete facilities
- Subpar profitability because . . .
- Lack of managerial depth and talent
- Missing some key skills or competence
- Poor track record in implementing strategy
- Plagued with internal operating problems
- Falling behind in R&D
- Too narrow a product line
- Weak market image
- Weaker distribution network
- Below-average marketing skills
- Unable to finance needed changes in strategy
- Higher overall unit costs relative to key competitors
- Other?

Potential external opportunities

- Serve additional customer groups
- Enter new markets or segments
- Expand product line to meet broader range of customer needs
- Diversify into related products
- Vertical integration
- Falling trade barriers in attractive foreign markets
- Complacency among rival firms
- Faster market growth
- Other?

Potential external threats

- Entry of lower-cost foreign competitors
- Rising sales of substitute products
- Slower market growth
- Adverse shifts in foreign exchange rates and trade policies of foreign governments
- Costly regulatory requirements
- Vulnerability to recession and business cycle
- Growing bargaining power of customers or suppliers
- Changing buyer needs and tastes
- Adverse demographic changes
- Other?

Once a company's internal strengths and weaknesses are identified, the two lists have to be carefully evaluated. Some strengths are more important than others because they count for more in determining performance, in competing successfully, and in forming a powerful strategy. Likewise, some weaknesses can prove fatal, while others don't much matter or can be easily remedied.

From a strategy-making perspective, a company's strengths are significant because they can be the cornerstones of strategy and the basis on which to build competitive advantage. Strategy should be grounded on a company's best skills and market strengths. If a company doesn't have the competence and resources it needs to craft an attractive strategy, management must move quickly to build the required capabilities. At the same time, a good strategy necessarily needs to aim at correcting weaknesses that make the company vulnerable or that disqualify it from pursuing an attractive opportunity. The point here is simple: *an organization's strategy must be well suited to what it is capable of doing.* Achieving this condition means evaluating a company's strengths and weaknesses and deciding how to match them up with strategy effectively.

One of the "trade secrets" of first-rate strategic management is launching initiatives internally to turn a company strength into a distinctive competence. *A distinctive competence is something a company does especially well in comparison to its competitors.* In practice, there are many types of distinctive competence: manufacturing excellence, unusually good quality control, better service, more know-how in low-cost manufacturing, superior design capability, an ability to choose good retail locations, innovativeness in new product development, better merchandising and product display, better mastery of an important technology, a better feel for customer needs and tastes, a more effective sales force, and being better at working with customers on new applications and uses of the product. *The importance of distinctive competence to strategy formation rests with (1) the unique capability it gives an organization in going after a particular market opportunity, (2) the competitive edge it may give a firm in the marketplace, and (3) the potential for using the distinctive competence as the cornerstone of strategy.* It is always easier to develop competitive advantage in a market when a firm has a distinctive competence in one of the key requirements for market success, when rival companies have no offsetting competences, and when rivals can't match the competence without spending much time and money.

Identifying Opportunities and Threats

Table 4–1 also displays some of the things to be alert for in identifying a company's external opportunities and threats. Market opportunity is a big factor in shaping a company's strategy. However, there is an important distinction between *industry opportunities* and *company opportunities.* Not every company in an industry is well positioned to pursue each opportunity that exists in the industry—some are always better situated than others and some companies may be hopelessly out of contention. *The prevailing and emerging industry opportunities most relevant to a particular company are those in which the company has a competitive advantage or those that offer important avenues for growth.*

Often, certain factors in a company's external environment pose *threats* to its well-being. Threats can stem from the emergence of cheaper technologies, the introduction of new or better products by rivals, the entry of low-cost foreign competitors into a company's market stronghold, new regulations that are more burdensome to a company than to its competitors, vulnerability to a rise in interest rates, the potential of a hostile takeover, unfavorable demographic shifts, unfavorable shifts in foreign exchange rates, political upheaval in a foreign country where the company has facilities, and the like.

Identifying opportunities and threats is important, not only because they affect the attractiveness of a company's situation but also because they drive the formation of business-level strategy. To be adequately matched to a company's situation, strategy must (1) be aimed at pursuing opportunities best suited to the company's capabilities and (2) provide a defense against external threats. SWOT analysis is therefore more than an exercise in making four lists. It is essential to evaluate the strength, weakness, opportunity, and threat listings in terms of what conclusions can be drawn about the company's situation and what their implications are. Some of the pertinent strategy-making questions to consider, once the SWOT listings have been compiled, are:

- Does the company have any internal strengths or a distinctive competence to build an attractive strategy around? If the company has no distinctive competence, is there potential for turning one of its strengths into a distinctive competence?

- Do the company's weaknesses make it competitively vulnerable and/or do they disqualify the company from pursuing certain opportunities? Which weaknesses does strategy need to correct?

- Which opportunities does the company have the skills and resources to pursue with a real chance of success? *Remember:* Opportunity without the means to capture it is an illusion. An organization's strengths and weaknesses make it better suited to pursuing some opportunities than others. An objective appraisal of what a firm can do and what it shouldn't try to do always needs to guide the choice of strategy.

- What threats should management be worried most about, and what strategic moves does management need to consider in formulating a good defense?

STRATEGIC COST ANALYSIS AND ACTIVITY-COST CHAINS

One of the most telling signs of a company's situation is its cost position relative to competitors. Cost comparisons are especially critical in a commodity-product industry where price competition typically dominates and lower-cost companies have the upper hand. But even in industries where products are differentiated and competition is based on factors other than price, competing companies have to keep costs *in line with* rivals or risk jeopardizing their competitive position.

Competitors do not necessarily, or even usually, incur the same costs in supplying their products to end-users. Disparities in costs among rival producers can stem from:

- Differences in the prices paid for raw materials, components parts, energy, and other items purchased from suppliers.
- Differences in basic technology and the age of plants and equipment. (Because rival companies usually invest in plants and key pieces of equipment at different times, their facilities have somewhat different technological efficiencies and different fixed costs. Older facilities are typically less efficient, but if they were less expensive to construct or if they were acquired used at bargain prices, they *may* still be reasonably cost competitive with modern facilities.)
- Differences in internal operating costs owing to the economies of scale associated with different size plants, learning and experience curve effects, different wage rates, different productivity levels, different administrative overhead expenses, different tax rates, and the like.
- Differences in rival firms' exposure to inflation rates and changes in foreign exchange rates (as can occur in global industries where competitors have plants located in different nations).
- Differences in marketing costs, sales and promotion expenditures, and advertising expenses.
- Differences in inbound transportation costs and outbound shipping costs.
- Differences in forward channel distribution costs (the costs and markups added by distributors, wholesalers, and retailers in performing their functions of getting the product from the point of manufacture to the end-users).

For a company to be competitively successful, its costs must be in line with those of rival producers. However, product differentiation creates justification for some cost disparity. The need to be cost competitive is not so stringent as to *require* the costs of every firm in the industry to be *equal*, but, as a rule, the higher a firm's costs above those of the low-cost producers, the more vulnerable its market position becomes. Given the numerous opportunities for cost disparities among competing companies, a company must be alert to how its costs compare with rivals' costs. This is where *strategic cost analysis* comes in.

Strategic cost analysis focuses on a firm's relative cost position vis-á-vis its rivals. The primary analytical tool of strategic cost analysis is the construction of an *activity-cost chain* showing the makeup of costs from raw materials purchased to the price paid by ultimate customers.[1] The activity-cost chain thus goes beyond a company's own internal cost structure. It includes the buildup of cost (and thus the "value-added") at each stage in the whole industry chain of producing the product and distributing it to final users, as shown in Figure 4–1. Constructing an activity-cost chain for all of an industry's principal stages is especially revealing to a manufacturing firm. Its overall ability to furnish its product to end-users at a competitive price can easily depend on cost factors originating either *backward* in

---

[1] The ins and outs of strategic cost analysis are discussed at greater length in Michael E. Porter, *Competitive Advantage* (New York: The Free Press, 1985), chap. 2. What follows is a distilled adaptation of the approach pioneered by Porter.

Figure 4–1 GENERIC ACTIVITY-COST CHAIN FOR A REPRESENTATIVE INDUSTRY SITUATION

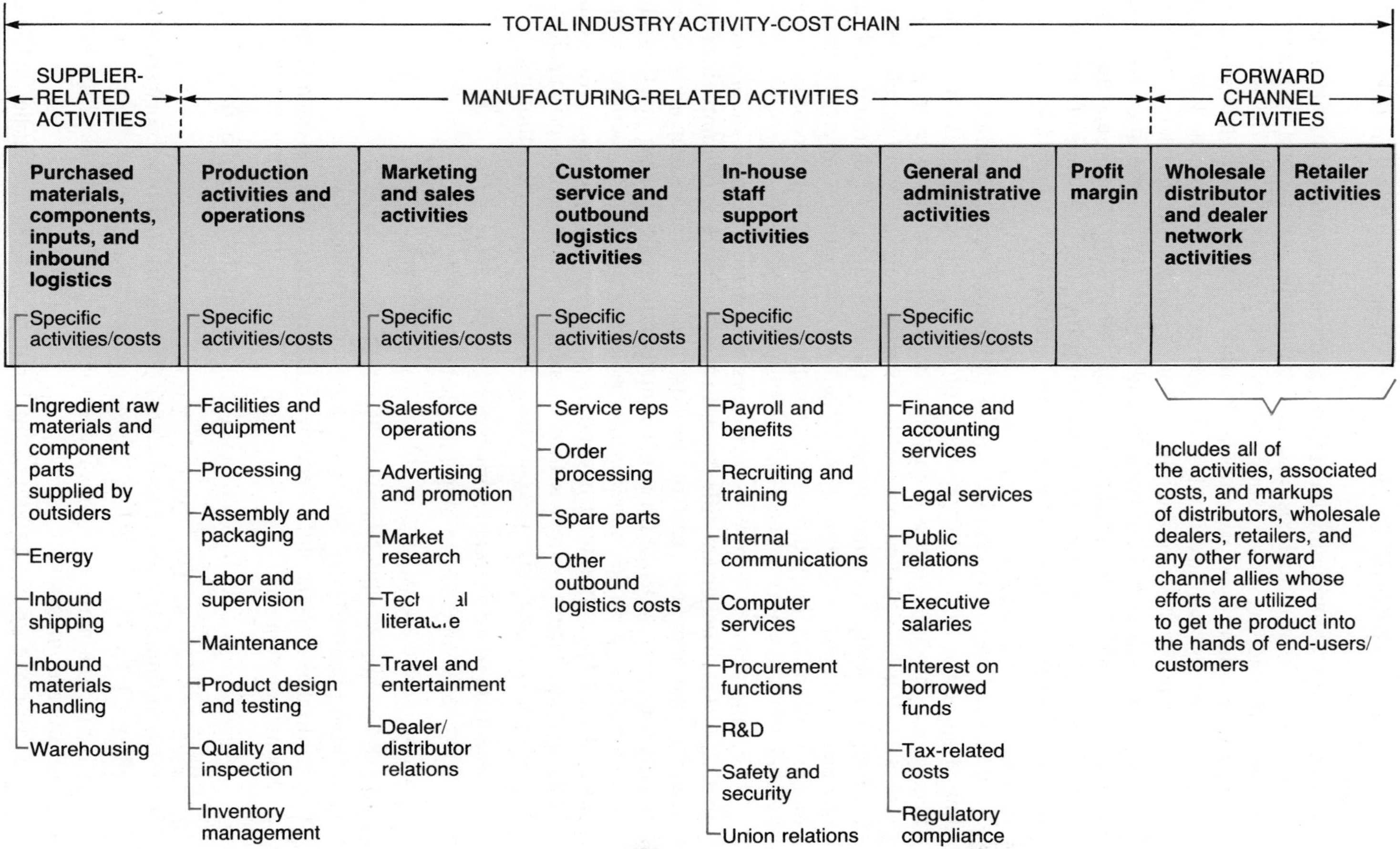

←—————— TOTAL INDUSTRY ACTIVITY-COST CHAIN ——————→

SUPPLIER-RELATED ACTIVITIES	MANUFACTURING-RELATED ACTIVITIES						FORWARD CHANNEL ACTIVITIES	
Purchased materials, components, inputs, and inbound logistics	Production activities and operations	Marketing and sales activities	Customer service and outbound logistics activities	In-house staff support activities	General and administrative activities	Profit margin	Wholesale distributor and dealer network activities	Retailer activities
Specific activities/costs	Specific activities/costs	Specific activities/costs	Specific activities/costs	Specific activities/costs	Specific activities/costs			
Ingredient raw materials and component parts supplied by outsiders	Facilities and equipment	Salesforce operations	Service reps	Payroll and benefits	Finance and accounting services			
Energy	Processing	Advertising and promotion	Order processing	Recruiting and training	Legal services			
Inbound shipping	Assembly and packaging	Market research	Spare parts	Internal communications	Public relations			
Inbound materials handling	Labor and supervision	Technical literature	Other outbound logistics costs	Computer services	Executive salaries			
Warehousing	Maintenance	Travel and entertainment		Procurement functions	Interest on borrowed funds			
	Product design and testing	Dealer/distributor relations		R&D	Tax-related costs			
	Quality and inspection			Safety and security	Regulatory compliance			
	Inventory management			Union relations				

Includes all of the activities, associated costs, and markups of distributors, wholesale dealers, retailers, and any other forward channel allies whose efforts are utilized to get the product into the hands of end-users/customers the suppliers' portion of the activity-cost chain or *forward* in the distribution channel portion.

The task of constructing an activity-cost chain is not easy. It requires breaking a firm's own historical cost accounting data into several principal cost categories and developing cost estimates for the backward and forward channel portions. In addition, it requires estimating the same cost elements and cost chains for rivals—an advanced art in competitive intelligence. But despite the tediousness of the task and the imprecision of some of the estimates, the payoff in exposing the cost competitiveness of one's position and the attendant strategic alternatives makes it a valuable analytical tool. Illustration Capsule 9 shows a simplified activity-cost chain comparison for the various brands of beer produced by Anheuser-Busch (the industry leader) and Adolph Coors (the third-ranking brewer).

The most important application of the activity-cost technique is to expose how a particular firm's cost position compares with those of its rivals. What is needed is competitor versus competitor cost estimates for a given product. The size of a company's cost advantage/disadvantage can vary from item to item in the product line, from customer group to customer group (if different distribution channels are used), and from plant to plant (if plants employ different technologies or are located in widely different geographic locations—different countries, for example).

Looking again at Figure 4–1, observe that there are three main areas in the cost chain where important differences in the *relative* costs of competing firms can occur: in the suppliers' part of the cost chain, in each company's respective activity segments, or in the forward channel portion of the chain. If a firm's lack of cost competitiveness lies either in the backward or forward sections of the cost chain, it may have to extend beyond its own in-house operations to reestablish cost competitiveness. When a firm's cost disadvantage lies principally in the backward end of the activity-cost chain, it has six strategic options:

- Negotiate more favorable prices with suppliers.
- Work with suppliers to help them achieve lower costs.
- Integrate backward to gain control over material costs.
- Try to use lower-priced substitute inputs.
- Search out sources of savings in inbound shipping costs.
- Try to make up the difference by initiating cost savings elsewhere in the overall cost chain.

When a firm's cost disadvantage occurs in the forward end of the cost chain, it has three corrective options:

- Push for more favorable terms with distributors and other forward channel allies.
- Change to a more economical distribution strategy, including the possibility of forward integration.
- Try to make up the difference by initiating cost savings earlier in the cost chain.

ILLUSTRATION CAPSULE   9

ACTIVITY-COST CHAINS FOR ANHEUSER-BUSCH AND COORS BEERS

In the table below are average cost estimates for the combined brands of beer produced by Anheuser-Busch and Coors. The example shows raw material costs, other manufacturing costs, and forward channel distribution costs. The data are for 1982.

Activity-cost elements	Estimated average cost breakdown for combined Anheuser-Busch brands		Estimated average cost breakdown for combined Adolph Coors brands	
	Per 6-pack of 12-oz. cans	Per barrel equivalent	Per 6-pack of 12-oz. cans	Per barrel equivalent
1. Manufacturing costs:				
Direct production costs:				
Raw material ingredients	$0.1384	$ 7.63	$0.1082	$ 5.96
Direct labor	0.1557	8.58	0.1257	6.93
Salaries for nonunionized personnel	0.0800	4.41	0.0568	3.13
Packaging	0.5055	27.86	0.4663	25.70
Depreciation on plant and equipment	0.0410	2.26	0.0826	4.55
Subtotal	0.9206	50.74	0.8396	46.27
Other expenses:				
Advertising	0.0477	2.63	0.0338	1.86
Other marketing costs and general administrative expenses	0.1096	6.04	0.1989	10.96
Interest	0.0147	0.81	0.0033	0.18
Research and development	0.0277	1.53	0.0195	1.07
Total manufacturing costs	$1.1203	$ 61.75	$1.0951	$ 60.34
2. Manufacturer's operating profit	0.1424	7.85	0.0709	3.91
3. Net selling price	1.2627	69.60	1.1660	64.25
4. Plus federal and state excise taxes paid by brewer	0.1873	10.32	0.1782	9.82
5. Gross manufacturer's selling price to distributor/wholesaler	1.4500	79.92	1.3442	74.07
6. Average margin over manufacturer's cost	0.5500	30.31	0.5158	28.43
7. Average wholesale price charged to retailer (inclusive of taxes in item 4 above but exclusive of other taxes)	$2.00	$110.23	$1.86	$102.50
8. Plus other assorted state and local taxes levied on wholesale and retail sales (this varies from locality to locality)	0.60		0.60	
9. Average 20% retail markup over wholesale cost	0.40		0.38	
10. Average price to consumer at retail	$3.00		$2.84	

Note: The difference in the average cost structures for Anheuser-Busch and Adolph Coors is, to some substantial extent, due to A-B's higher proportion of super-premium beer sales. A-B's super-premium brand, Michelob, was far and away the bestseller in its category and somewhat more costly to brew than premium and popular-priced beers.

Source: Compiled by Tom McLean, Elsa Wischkaemper, and Arthur A. Thompson, Jr. from a wide variety of documents and field interviews.

When the source of a firm's cost disadvantage is internal, several options are available:

- Initiate internal budget-tightening measures.
- Try to boost the productivity of workers and high-cost equipment.
- See if certain activities can be farmed out to contractors cheaper than they can be done internally.
- Invest in cost-saving technological improvements.
- Innovate around the troublesome cost components as new investments are made in plant and equipment.
- Redesign the product to achieve cost reduction.
- Try to make up the internal cost disadvantage by achieving cost savings in the backward and forward portions of the cost chain.

The construction of activity-cost chains is a valuable tool in company situation analysis because of what it reveals about a firm's cost competitiveness. Examining the makeup of a company's own activity-cost chain and comparing it to the chains of important rivals indicates who has how much of a cost advantage/disadvantage and which cost components are responsible. Such information is essential in forming a strategy to eliminate a cost disadvantage or create a cost advantage.

COMPETITIVE STRENGTH ASSESSMENT

In addition to the cost competitiveness diagnosis that activity-cost chain analysis provides, a more broad-based assessment needs to be made of a company's overall competitive position and competitive strength. Particular elements to single out for evaluation are (1) how strongly the firm holds its present competitive position, (2) whether the firm's position can be expected to improve or deteriorate if the present strategy is continued (allowing for fine-tuning), (3) how the firm ranks *relative to key rivals* on each important measure of competitive strength and industry key success factor, (4) the firm's net competitive advantage, and (5) the firm's ability to defend its position in light of industry driving forces, competitive pressures, and the anticipated moves of rivals.

Table 4–2 runs down the factors that often come into play in determining whether a firm's competitive position is improving or slipping. Again, more is needed than just a listing of the signs of improvement or slippage. The important thing is to assess how strong the company's position is and what is causing it to change, and to begin thinking through what strategic actions are needed to improve the company's position.

The really telling part of this aspect of company situation analysis, however, comes in formally appraising the firm's competitive strength versus key rivals on each key success factor and important competitive variable. Much of the information for this piece of company analysis comes from what has been done before. Industry analysis reveals the key success factors. Competitor analysis provides a basis for judging the strengths and capabilities of key rivals. Step one is to make a list of key success factors and any other relevant measure of competitive strength.

Table 4–2 THE SIGNS OF STRENGTH AND WEAKNESS IN A COMPANY'S COMPETITIVE POSITION

Signs of competitive strength	Signs of competitive weakness
• Important distinctive competences • Strong market share (or a leading market share) • A pacesetting or distinctive strategy • Growing customer base and customer loyalty • Above-average market visibility • In a favorably situated strategic group • Concentrating on fastest-growing market segments • Strongly differentiated products • Cost advantages • Above-average profit margins • Above-average marketing skills • Above-average technological and innovational capability • A creative, entrepreneurially alert management • In position to capitalize on opportunities	• No really good competitive advantage • Losing ground to rival firms • Below average growth in revenues • Short on financial resources • A slipping reputation with customers • Trailing in product development • In a strategic group destined to lose ground • Weak in areas where there is the most market potential • A higher-cost producer • Too small to be a major factor in the marketplace • No real distinctive competences • Not in good position to deal with emerging threats • Weak product quality

Step two is to rate the firm and its key rivals on each factor. Rating scales from 1 to 5 or 1 to 10 can be used (or ratings of stronger ($+$), weaker ($-$), and about equal ($=$) may suffice, especially if the information base is thin). Step 3 is to judge the company's overall competitive strength, noting specifically where the company is strongest and weakest and determining how much of a competitive edge, if any, the company has.

Table 4–3 provides two examples of how to do competitive strength assessments. The first one employs an *unweighted rating scale;* with unweighted ratings each key success factor/competitive strength measure is assumed to be equally important. The sum of the ratings gives an overall strength rating. However, it is conceptually stronger to use a weighted rating system because different measures are unlikely to be *equally* important determinants of competitive strength. In a commodity-product industry, for instance, being the low-cost supplier is the biggest determinant of competitive strength. In an industry with strong product differentiation, the most significant measures of competitive strength may be brand awareness, amount of advertising, reputation for quality, and distribution capability.

In a *weighted rating system* each relevant measure of competitive strength is assigned a weight based on its perceived importance. The largest weight could be as high as .75 (maybe even higher) in situations where one particular competitive variable is overwhelmingly decisive. Lesser competitive strength indicators can carry weights of .05 or .10. However, *the sum of the weights must add up to 1.0.* Weighted strength ratings are calculated by multiplying the assigned rating of each strength measure (using the 1 to 5 or 1 to 10 rating scale) by the assigned weight (a rating score of 4 times a weight of .20 gives a weighted rating of .80). The sum of the weighted ratings on each strength measure gives the company's overall strength rating. Comparisons of the weighted strength scores indicate how well the company stacks up against its competitors.

Table 4–3   ILLUSTRATIONS OF UNWEIGHTED AND WEIGHTED COMPETITIVE STRENGTH ASSESSMENTS

A. Sample of an Unweighted Competitive Strength Assessment (Rating scale: 1 = weakest; 10 = strongest)

Key success factor/Strength measure	ABC Co.	Rival 1	Rival 2	Rival 3	Rival 4
Quality/product performance	8	5	9	5	6
Reputation/image	8	7	10	5	6
Raw material access/cost	5	5	6	3	4
Technological skills	8	5	5	3	4
Advertising effectiveness	9	7	10	5	6
Marketing/distribution	9	7	9	5	6
Financial resources	5	4	7	3	4
Relative-cost position	5	9	6	3	4
Ability to compete on price	5	9	7	3	4
Unweighted overall strength rating	62	58	69	35	44

B. Sample of a Weighted Competitive Strength Assessment (Rating scale: 1 = weakest; 10 = strongest)

Key success factor/Strength measure	Weight	ABC Co.	Rival 1	Rival 2	Rival 3	Rival 4
Quality/product performance	0.10	8/0.80	5/0.50	9/0.90	5/0.50	6/0.60
Reputation/image	0.10	8/0.80	7/0.70	10/1.00	5/0.50	6/0.60
Raw material access/cost	0.05	5/0.25	5/0.25	6/0.30	3/0.15	4/0.20
Technological skills	0.05	8/0.40	5/0.25	5/0.25	3/0.15	4/0.20
Manufacturing capability	0.05	9/0.45	7/0.35	10/0.50	5/0.25	6/0.30
Marketing/distribution	0.05	9/0.45	7/0.35	9/0.45	5/0.25	6/0.30
Financial strength	0.10	5/0.50	4/0.40	7/0.70	3/0.30	4/0.40
Relative-cost position	0.25	5/1.25	9/2.25	6/1.50	3/0.75	4/1.00
Ability to compete on price	0.25	5/1.25	9/2.25	7/1.75	3/0.75	4/1.00
Sum of weights	1.00					
Weighted overall strength rating		6.15	7.30	7.35	3.60	4.60

The bottom half of Table 4–3 shows a sample competitive strength assessment for ABC Company using a weighted rating system. Note that the two methods shown result in a different ordering of the companies. In both examples, all companies are assigned the same scores on the rating scale. Yet ABC Company drops from second to third in strength and Rival 1 jumps from third into a virtual tie for first because Rival 1 is strong on the two factors that count the most. The use of weights can thus make a significant difference in the outcome of the assessment and in the conclusions drawn about a company's competitive strength.

The competitive strength assessment provides valuable insight into a company's competitive situation. The ratings show how a company stacks up against its rivals, factor by factor or measure by measure, thus revealing where the company is strongest and weakest and against whom. Moreover, comparisons of the overall competitive strength scores indicate whether the company is at a net competitive advantage or disadvantage against each rival. The company with the largest overall competitive strength rating is said to have a net competitive advantage over each rival. The size of the advantage is reflected in the amount by which its competitive strength score exceeds those of other companies. The net competitive advantage/disadvantage of the other companies is indicated by how much their overall competitive strength scores come out above/below the scores of each other rival.

Where a company is competitively strong and where it is weak have direct implications in crafting a strategy to improve the company's competitive position. As a general rule, a company should endeavor to capitalize on its competitive strengths and shore up or protect against its competitive weaknesses. In other words, it should build its strategy on its competitive strengths and make strategic moves to alleviate its competitive weaknesses. At the same time, the competitive strength ratings done for rival companies provide clear indications of which rivals may be vulnerable to competitive attack and the areas where they are weakest. When a company has important competitive strengths in areas where certain rivals are comparatively weak, it may make sense to design offensive moves to exploit the advantage.

DETERMINING THE STRATEGIC ISSUES THAT NEED TO BE ADDRESSED

The final step of company situation analysis is to identify all the important strategic issues management needs to address in forming an overall game plan for the company. The issues that emerge are necessarily peculiar to the company's situation and the particulars of its strategy. However, most of the issues should be apparent from the four preceding steps of company situation analysis and from the industry and competitive situation confronting the firm.

The primary considerations in coming up with the issues that need to be placed on the company's strategic action agenda are:

- Whether the present strategy is adequate in light of the driving forces at work in the industry.
- How closely the present strategy is geared to the industry's *future* key success factors.
- How good a defense the present strategy offers against the five competitive forces—future ones, not so much past or present ones.
- Whether the present strategy adequately protects the company against external threats and internal weaknesses.
- Whether the company is vulnerable to competitive attack by one or more rivals.
- Whether additional moves are needed to improve the company's cost position, to capitalize on emerging opportunities, or to boost the company's competitive position.

These considerations should indicate whether the company can continue the same basic strategy with minor adjustments or whether major overhaul is called for.

Table 4–4 COMPANY SITUATION ANALYSIS

1. STRATEGIC PERFORMANCE INDICATORS

Performance indicator	19__	19__	19__	19__	19__
Market share	____	____	____	____	____
Sales growth	____	____	____	____	____
Net profit margin	____	____	____	____	____
Return on equity investment	____	____	____	____	____
Other?	____	____	____	____	____

2. INTERNAL STRENGTHS

INTERNAL WEAKNESSES

EXTERNAL OPPORTUNITIES

EXTERNAL THREATS

3. COMPETITIVE STRENGTH ASSESSMENT

Rating Scale: 1 = Weakest; 10 = Strongest

Key success factor/ competitive variable	Weight	Firm A	Firm B	Firm C	Firm D	Firm E
Quality/product performance	____	___	___	___	___	___
Reputation/image	____	___	___	___	___	___
Raw material access/cost	____	___	___	___	___	___
Technological skills	____	___	___	___	___	___
Manufacturing capability	____	___	___	___	___	___
Marketing/distribution	____	___	___	___	___	___
Financial strength	____	___	___	___	___	___
Relative cost position	____	___	___	___	___	___
Other?	====	===	===	===	===	===
Overall strength rating	____	___	___	___	___	___

4. CONCLUSIONS CONCERNING COMPETITIVE POSITION
(Improving/slipping? Competitive advantages/disadvantages?)

5. MAJOR STRATEGIC ISSUES/PROBLEMS THE COMPANY MUST ADDRESS

The better matched a company's strategy is to its external environment and internal situation, the less need there is to contemplate shifts in strategy. On the other hand, when the present strategy is not well suited for the road ahead, the task of crafting a new strategy assumes high priority.

KEY POINTS

There are five steps to conducting a company situation analysis:

1. *Evaluating how well the current strategy is working.* This involves looking at the company's recent strategic performance and determining whether the various pieces of strategy are logically consistent.

2. *Doing a SWOT analysis.* A company's strengths are important because they can serve as major building blocks for strategy; company weaknesses are important because they may represent vulnerabilities that need correction. External opportunities and threats come into play because a good strategy necessarily aims at capturing attractive opportunities and defending against threats to the company's well-being.

3. *Evaluating the company's cost position relative to competitors* (using the concepts of strategic cost analysis and activity-cost chains if appropriate). Strategy must always aim at keeping costs sufficiently in line with rivals to preserve the company's ability to compete.

4. *Assessing the company's competitive position and competitive strength.* This step looks at how a company matches up against rivals on the chief determinants of competitive success. The competitive strength rankings indicate where a company is strong and weak; as a rule, a company's competitive strategy should be built on its competitive strengths and aim at shoring up areas where it is competitively vulnerable. Also, the areas where company strengths match up against competitor weaknesses suggest the potential for offensive attack.

5. *Determining the strategic issues and problems the company needs to address.* The purpose of this analytical step is to develop a complete strategy-making agenda using the results of both company situation analysis and industry and competitive analysis. The emphasis here is on understanding how well the present strategy fits the company's external and internal situation.

Table 4–4 contains a generalized framework for doing a company situation analysis. It incorporates the concepts and analytical techniques discussed in this chapter and, if used conscientiously, leads to insightful conclusions about the suitability of a company's present strategy and what strategic issues confront the company. Such is the purpose of company situation analysis.

SUGGESTED READINGS

Andrews, Kenneth R. *The Concept of Corporate Strategy,* 3rd ed. Homewood, Ill.: Richard D. Irwin, 1987, chap. 3.

Fahey, Liam, and H. Kurt Christensen. "Building Distinctive Competences into Competitive Advantages." In Liam Fahey, *The Strategic Planning Management Reader*. Englewood Cliffs, N.J.: Prentice-Hall, 1989, pp. 113–18.

Hax, Arnoldo C., and Nicolas S. Majluf. *Strategic Management: An Integrative Perspective*. Englewood Cliffs, N.J.: Prentice-Hall, 1984, chap. 15.

Henry, Harold W. "Appraising a Company's Strengths and Weaknesses." *Managerial Planning,* July–August 1980, pp. 31–36.

Paine, Frank T., and Leonard J. Tischler. "Evaluating Your Costs Strategically." In Liam Fahey, *The Strategic Planning Management Reader*. Englewood Cliffs, N.J.: Prentice-Hall, 1989, pp. 118–23.

Stevenson, Howard H. "Defining Corporate Strengths and Weaknesses." *Sloan Management Review* 17, no. 2 (Winter 1976), pp. 1–18.

5 Strategy and Competitive Advantage

Competing in the marketplace is like war. You have injuries and casualties, and the best strategy wins.
John Collins

Competitive advantage is at the heart of a firm's performance in competitive markets.
Michael E. Porter

Any business strategy, to be capable of sustained success, must be grounded in competitive advantage. A company gains competitive advantage when its position gives it an edge in coping with competitive forces and in attracting buyers. Many different positioning advantages exist: making the highest-quality product on the market, providing customer service superior to rivals, being recognized as a low-price seller, being in the best geographic location, having a product that does the best job performing a particular function, making a more reliable and longer-lasting product, and offering the most value for the money (a combination of good quality, good service, and acceptable price). Whichever positioning strategy a company pursues, in order to achieve competitive advantage a viable number of customers must end up buying the firm's product because of the "superior value" they perceive it has. Superior value is usually created in one of two ways: either by offering buyers a good product at a lower price or by using some differentiating technique to provide a "better" product that buyers think is worth a premium price.

This chapter spotlights how a company can achieve or defend a competitive advantage.[1] We begin with a discussion of the basic types of competitive strategies and then focus on how various competitive strategies, complemented with assorted offensive and defensive maneuvers, produce a position of advantage in the marketplace. In the chapter's final two sections we see how vertical integration strategies and first-mover advantages and disadvantages come into play.

THE THREE GENERIC TYPES OF COMPETITIVE STRATEGY

Competitive strategy is composed of all the specific moves and approaches a firm has taken and is taking to compete successfully in a given industry. In plainer terms, a firm's competitive strategy concerns how management is trying to knock the socks off rival companies and otherwise cope with the five competitive forces. It can be mostly offensive or mostly defensive, shifting from one to the other as seems appropriate.

Companies the world over have imaginatively explored virtually every conceivable approach to competing successfully and winning an edge in the marketplace. And because company managements custom tailor strategy to fit the specifics of their own company's situation and market environment, there are countless competitive strategy variations. In this sense, there are as many competitive strategies as there are companies trying to compete. However, beneath all the nuances, three *generic* competitive strategy approaches stand out:

1. Striving to be the overall low-cost producer in the industry (a *low-cost leadership strategy*).
2. Seeking to differentiate one's product offering in one way or another from rivals' products (a *differentiation strategy*).
3. Focusing on a narrow portion of the market rather than going after the whole market (a *focus* or *niche strategy*).[2]

Table 5–1 profiles the distinctive features of the three generic strategies.

Striving to Be the Low-Cost Producer

The impetus for striving to be the industry's low-cost producer is a market comprised of many price-sensitive buyers. The idea is to open up a sustainable cost advantage over competitors and then use the lower-cost edge as a basis for either underpricing competitors and gaining market share or earning a higher profit margin selling at the going market price. A cost advantage generates superior profitability only when it is not eaten away by the need to underprice competitors to win adequate sales volumes. Achieving low-cost leadership typ-

---

[1] The definitive work on this subject is Michael E. Porter, *Competitive Advantage* (New York: Free Press, 1985). The treatment in this chapter draws heavily on Porter's pioneering effort.

[2] The classification scheme follows that presented in Michael E. Porter, *Competitive Strategy: Techniques for Analyzing Industries and Competitors* (New York: Free Press, 1980), chap. 2, especially pp. 35–39 and 44–46.

Table 5-1 DISTINCTIVE FEATURES OF THE GENERIC COMPETITIVE STRATEGIES

Type of feature	Low-cost leadership	Differentiation	Focus
Strategic target	• A broad cross-section of the market.	• A broad cross-section of the market.	• A narrow market niche where buyer needs and preferences are distinctively different from the rest of the market.
Basis of competitive advantage	• Lower costs than competitors.	• An ability to offer buyers *something different* from competitors.	• Lower cost in serving the niche or an ability to offer niche buyers something customized to their requirements and tastes.
Product line	• A good basic product with few frills (acceptable quality and limited selection).	• Many product variations, wide selection, strong emphasis on the chosen differentiating features.	• Customized to fit the specialized needs of the target segment.
Production emphasis	• A continuous search for cost reduction without sacrificing acceptable quality and essential features.	• Invent ways to create value for buyers.	• Tailor-made for the niche.
Marketing emphasis	• Try to make a virtue out of product features that lead to low cost.	• Build in whatever features buyers are willing to pay for. • Charge a premium price to cover the extra costs of differentiating features.	• Communicate the focuser's unique ability to satisfy the buyer's specialized requirements.
Sustaining the strategy	• Economical prices/good value. • All elements of strategy aim at contributing to a sustainable cost advantage—the key is to manage costs down, year after year, in every area of the business.	• Communicate the points of difference in credible ways. • Stress constant improvement and use innovation to stay ahead of imitative competitors. • Concentrate on a few key differentiating features; use them to create a reputation and brand image.	• Remain totally dedicated to serving the niche better than other competitors; don't blunt the firm's image and efforts by entering other segments and adding other product categories to widen market appeal.

ically means making low cost *relative to competitors* the theme of the firm's entire business strategy—though low cost is not so zealously pursued that a firm's product ends up being too stripped down to generate buyer appeal.

Opening up a Cost Advantage. To achieve a cost advantage, a firm's cumulative costs across its activity-cost chain must be lower than competitors' cumulative costs. There are two ways to open up a cost advantage over rivals:

- Do a better job of increasing efficiency and containing costs.
- Revamp the activity-cost chain to bypass some cost-producing activities altogether.

Both approaches can be used simultaneously. Successful low-cost producers usually achieve their cost advantages from every cost-saving approach they can think of. Normally, low-cost producers have a very cost-conscious organizational culture symbolically reinforced with Spartan facilities, limited perks and frills for executives, intolerance of waste, intensive screening of budget requests, and broad employee participation in cost control efforts. Even though such firms are champions of frugality, they tend to commit funds aggressively to cost-saving improvements.

A firm intent on being a low-cost producer has to scrutinize each cost-creating activity and identify what drives the cost of the activity. Then it needs to use its knowledge about the cost drivers and innovatively seek ways to manage the costs of each activity down further and further. Where possible, whole activities need to be cut out of the activity-cost chain entirely. Companies can achieve dramatic cost advantages from restructuring the cost chain and eliminating unnecessary cost-producing activities. Illustration Capsule 10 describes how two companies won strong competitive positions by revamping the makeup of their industry's traditional activity-cost chain.

Examples of firms that are well known for their low-cost leadership strategies are Lincoln Electric in arc welding equipment, Briggs and Stratton in small horsepower gasoline engines, BIC in ballpoint pens, Black and Decker in tools, Design and Manufacturing in dishwashers (marketed under Sears' Kenmore brand), Beaird-Poulan in chain saws, Ford in heavy-duty trucks, General Electric in major home appliances, Wal-Mart in discount retailing, and Southwest Airlines in commercial airline travel.

The Appeal of Being a Low-Cost Producer. Being the low-cost producer in an industry provides some attractive defenses against the five competitive forces:

- As concerns *rival competitors,* the low-cost company is in the best position to compete offensively on the basis of price, to defend against price war conditions, to use the appeal of a lower price as a weapon for grabbing sales (and market share) from rivals, and to earn above-average profits (based on bigger profit margins or greater sales volume) in markets where price competition thrives. *A low-cost producer wields heavy influence in setting the industry's price floor.*

ILLUSTRATION CAPSULE **10**

WINNING A COST ADVANTAGE: IOWA BEEF PACKERS AND FEDERAL EXPRESS

Iowa Beef Packers and Federal Express have been able to win strong competitive positions by restructuring the traditional activity-cost chains in their industries. In beef packing, the traditional cost chain involved raising cattle on scattered farms and ranches, shipping them live to labor-intensive, unionized slaughtering plants, and then transporting whole sides of beef to grocery retailers whose butcher departments cut them into smaller pieces and packaged them for sale to grocery shoppers.

Iowa Beef Packers revamped the traditional chain with a radically different strategy—large automated plants employing nonunion labor were built near economically transportable supplies of cattle, and the meat was partially butchered at the processing plant into smaller high-yield cuts (sometimes sealed in plastic casing ready for purchase), boxed, and shipped to retailers. IBP's inbound cattle transportation expenses, traditionally a major cost item, were cut significantly by avoiding the weight losses that occurred when live animals were shipped long distances; major outbound shipping cost savings were achieved by not having to ship whole sides of beef with their high waste factor. Iowa Beef's strategy was so successful that it was, in 1985, the largest U.S. meatpacker, surpassing the former industry leaders, Swift, Wilson, and Armour.

Federal Express innovatively redefined the activity-cost chain for rapid delivery of small parcels. Traditional firms like Emery and Airborne Express operated by collecting freight packages of varying sizes, shipping them to their destination points via air freight and commercial airlines, and then delivering them to the addressee. Federal Express opted to focus only on the market for overnight delivery of small packages and documents. These were collected at local drop points during the late afternoon hours, flown on company-owned planes during early evening hours to a central hub in Memphis where from 11 P.M. to 3 A.M. each night, all parcels were sorted, then reloaded on company planes, and flown during the early morning hours to their destination points, where they were delivered the next morning by company personnel using company trucks. The cost structure so achieved by Federal Express was low enough to permit it to guarantee overnight delivery of a small parcel anywhere in the United States for a price as low as $11. In 1986, Federal Express had a 58 percent market share of the air-express package-delivery market versus a 15 percent share for UPS, 11 percent for Airborne Express, and 10 percent for Emery/Purolator.

Source: Based on information in Michael E. Porter, *Competitive Advantage* (New York: Free Press, 1985), p. 109.

- As concerns *buyers,* the low-cost company has partial profit margin protection from powerful customers, since the latter will rarely be able to bargain price down past the survival level of the next most cost-efficient seller.
- As concerns *suppliers,* the low-cost producer is more insulated than competitors from powerful suppliers *if* greater internal efficiency is the primary source of its cost advantage.
- As concerns *potential entrants,* the low-cost producer can use price-cutting to make it harder for a new rival to win customers; the pricing power of the low-cost producer acts as a barrier for a new entrant to hurdle.
- As concerns *substitutes,* a low-cost producer is in a more favorable position than higher-cost rivals to use low price as a defense against the attempts of substitutes to gain a market inroad.

Consequently, a low-cost producer's ability to set the industry's price floor and still earn a profit erects barriers around its market position. Any time price competition becomes a major market force, less efficient rivals get squeezed the most. Firms in a low-cost position relative to rivals have a significant edge in appealing to buyers who base their purchase decision on low price.

A competitive strategy based on low-cost leadership is particularly powerful when:

1. Price competition among rival sellers is a dominant competitive force.
2. The industry's product is an essentially standardized, commodity-type item readily available from a variety of sellers (a condition that enables buyers to shop for the best price).
3. There are few ways to achieve product differentiation that have value to buyers; or, to put it another way, buyers don't much care about the differences from brand to brand.
4. Most buyers use the product in the same ways and thus have common user requirements.
5. Buyers incur low switching costs in changing from one seller to another, thus giving them the flexibility to shop for the best price.
6. Buyers are large and have significant bargaining power.

The Risks a Low-Cost Producer Takes.   However, a low-cost competitive approach has its risks and drawbacks. Technological breakthroughs can open up cost reductions for rivals that nullify a low-cost producer's past investments and hard-won gains in efficiency. Rival firms may find it easy and/or inexpensive to imitate the leader's low-cost methods, thus making any advantage short-lived. A company driving hard to push its costs down can become so fixated on cost reduction that it fails to see some significant market changes beginning to occur—like buyers' growing preference for added quality or service, subtle shifts in buyers' uses of the product, and declining buyer sensitivity to price—thus getting left behind as buyer interest swings to other differentiating features. In sum, heavy investments in cost reduction can lock a firm into both its present technology and present strategy, leaving it vulnerable to new state-of-the-art technologies and to growing customer interest in something other than a cheaper price.

Differentiation Strategies

Differentiation strategies come into play whenever buyers' needs and preferences are too diverse to be fully satisfied by a standardized product. A successful differentiator studies buyers' needs and behavior carefully to learn what they consider important and valuable. Then the company incorporates one, or maybe several, of those differentiating features into its product offering to create buyer preferences for its brand over the brands of rivals. Competitive advantage results when a differentiator has unique ability, compared to rivals, to satisfy buyers who are looking for the featured attributes. Successful differentiation allows a firm to

- command a premium price for its product, and/or
- sell more units (because additional buyers are won over by the differentiating features), and/or
- gain greater buyer loyalty to its brand (because some buyers become strongly attached to the differentiating features).

Differentiation enhances profitability whenever the price premium commanded outweighs any added costs associated with achieving differentiation. Differentiation is unsuccessful when the forms of uniqueness a firm pursues are not valued highly enough by buyers to justify incurring the costs.

The approaches to differentiating one's product from rival firms take many forms: a different taste (Dr Pepper and Listerine), special features (Jenn-Air's indoor cooking tops with a vented built-in grill for barbecuing), superior service (Federal Express in overnight package delivery), spare parts availability (Caterpillar guarantees 48-hour spare parts delivery to any customer anywhere in the world or else the part is furnished free), overall value to the customer (McDonald's), engineering design and performance (Mercedes in automobiles), prestige and distinctiveness (Rolex in watches), product reliability (Johnson & Johnson in baby products), quality manufacture (Karastan in carpets and Honda in automobiles), technological leadership (3M Corporation in bonding and coating products), a full range of services (Merrill Lynch), a complete line of products (Campbell in soups), and top-of-the-line image and reputation (Brooks Brothers and Ralph Lauren in menswear, Kitchen Aid in dishwashers, and Cross in writing instruments).

Achieving Differentiation.   *Anything a firm can do to create buyer value represents a potential basis for differentiation.* Once good sources of value are identified, the value-creating attributes have to be built into a firm's product at an acceptable cost. A firm can incorporate attributes that raise the product's performance or make it more economical to use. A third option is to incorporate features that enhance buyer satisfaction in tangible or intangible ways during use. Differentiation possibilities can grow out of activities performed anywhere in the activity-cost chain. McDonald's gets high ratings on its french fries partly because it has strict specifications on the potatoes it purchases from its supplier. The quality of Japanese cars stems primarily from Japanese skills in manufacturing and quality control. IBM boosts buyer value by providing its customers with an extensive array of services and technical support. L.L. Bean makes its mail-order customers feel secure in their purchases by providing an unconditional guarantee with no time limit: "All of our products are guaranteed to give 100 percent satisfaction in every way. Return anything purchased from us at anytime if it proves otherwise. We will replace it, refund your purchase price, or credit your credit card, as you wish." The commercial airlines use their otherwise empty seats during off-peak travel periods (i.e., their excess capacity) as the basis for awarding free travel to frequent fliers.

What Makes Differentiation Attractive.   Differentiation provides some buffer against the strategies of rivals because buyers become loyal to the brand or model they like best and often are willing to pay a little (perhaps a lot!) more for it. In addition, successful differentiation (1) erects entry barriers in the form of customer loyalty and uniqueness that newcomers find hard to hurdle, (2) mitigates the bargaining power of large buyers since the products of alternative sellers are less attractive to them, and (3) puts a firm in a better position to fend off threats from substitutes because customers become attached to its brand. To the extent that differentiation allows a seller to charge a higher price and bolster profit margins, then a seller is in a stronger economic position to withstand the efforts of powerful suppliers to jack up their prices. Thus, as with cost leadership, successful differentiation creates lines of defense for dealing with the five competitive forces.

The most appealing types of differentiation strategies are those least subject to quick or inexpensive imitation. Here is where having a distinctive competence comes into play. When a firm has skills and competence that competitors cannot match easily, it can use this distinctive ability as a basis for successful differentiation. Areas where efforts to differentiate are likely to produce an attractive, longer-lasting competitive edge are:

- Differentiation based on *technical superiority*.
- Differentiation based on *quality*.
- Differentiation based on *giving customers more support services*.
- Differentiation based on the appeal of *more value for the money*.

As a rule, differentiation strategies work best in situations where (1) there are many ways to differentiate the product or service and some buyers perceive these differences as valuable, (2) buyer needs and uses of the item are diverse, and (3) few rival firms are following a similar differentiation approach.

Real Value, Perceived Value, and Signals of Value.   Buyers seldom pay for value they do not perceive, no matter how real the unique extras may be.[3] Thus the price premium that a differentiation strategy commands is a reflection of *the value actually delivered* to the buyer and *the value perceived* by the buyer (even if not actually delivered). The difference between actual value and perceived value emerges whenever buyers have a difficult time assessing in advance what their

---

[3] This discussion draws from Porter, *Competitive Advantage*, pp. 138–42. Porter's insights here are particularly important to formulating differentiating strategies because they highlight the relevance of "intangibles" and "signals."

experience with the product will be. Incomplete knowledge on the part of buyers often causes them to judge value on the basis of such *signals* as seller's word-of-mouth reputation, how attractively the product is packaged, how extensively the brand is advertised and thus how "well-known" it is, the content of the ads and the image they project, the manner in which information is presented in brochures and sales presentations, the attractiveness and aura of quality associated with the seller's facilities, the list of customers a seller has, the market share the firm has, the time the firm has been in business, the price being charged (where price denotes "quality"), and the professionalism, appearance, and personality of the seller's employees. These signals of value may be as important as actual value (1) when the nature of differentiation is subjective or hard to quantify, (2) when buyers are making their first-time purchases, (3) when repurchase is infrequent, and (4) when buyers are unsophisticated. A seller whose differentiation strategy delivers only modest extra value but who signals that extra value effectively may be able to command a higher price than a firm that actually delivers higher value but signals it poorly.

Keeping the Cost of Differentiation in Line.   Attempts to achieve differentiation usually raise costs. The trick to profitable differentiation is either to keep the costs of differentiating below the price premium the differentiation can command (this widens the profit margin per unit sold) or to offset thinner profit margins with enough added volume to increase total profits (larger volume can make up for smaller margins provided differentiation adds enough extra sales). In pursuing differentiation, a firm must be careful not to get its overall unit costs so far out of line with competitors that the resulting price premium it has to charge puts the brand out of the range buyers are willing to pay. From a cost perspective, the most attractive differentiating activities are those in which a firm can enjoy either a cost advantage over competitors or a price premium that more than offsets the added costs. There may also be good reason to add extra differentiating features that are not costly but add to buyer satisfaction—for example, fine restaurants typically provide such extras as a slice of lemon in the water glass, valet parking, and complimentary after-dinner mints.

The Risks of Pursuing Differentiation.   There are, of course, no guarantees that differentiation will produce a meaningful competitive advantage. If buyers see little value in uniqueness (i.e., a "standard" item meets their needs), then a low-cost strategy can easily defeat a differentiation strategy. In addition, differentiation is defeated when competitors can quickly copy the differentiating attempt. Rapid imitation means that real differentiation is never actually achieved since competing brands keep changing in like ways despite sellers' continued efforts to create uniqueness. Thus, to be successful at differentiation, a firm must search out durable sources of uniqueness that cannot be quickly or cheaply imitated. Aside from these considerations, other common pitfalls to pursuing differentiation include:[4]

---

[4] Ibid., pp. 160–62.

- Trying to differentiate on the basis of something that does not lower the cost or enhance the buyer's well-being, as perceived by the buyer.
- Overdifferentiating such that price is too high relative to competitors or that product quality or service levels go well past buyers' needs.
- Trying to charge too high a price premium (the bigger the premium, the more buyers can be lured away by lower-priced competitors).
- Ignoring the need to signal value and depending only on the "real" bases of differentiation.
- Not understanding or identifying what buyers consider as value.

Focus and Specialization Strategies

Focusing starts by choosing a market niche where buyers have distinctive preferences or requirements. The niche can be defined by geographic uniqueness, by specialized requirements in using the product, or by special product attributes that appeal only to niche members. *A focuser's basis for competitive advantage is either lower costs than competitors in serving the market niche or an ability to offer niche members something different from other competitors.* A focus strategy based on low cost depends on there being a target segment with requirements less costly to satisfy compared to the rest of the market. A focus strategy based on differentiation depends on there being a target segment that demands unique product attributes.

Examples of firms employing a focus strategy include Tandem Computers (a specialist in "nonstop" computers for customers who need a "fail-safe" system), Rolls Royce (in super luxury automobiles), Apple Computer in desktop publishing (its computers can create reports and graphics with typeset quality); Fort Howard Paper (specializing in paper products for industrial and commercial enterprises only); commuter airlines like Skywest and Atlantic Southeast (specializing in low-traffic, short-haul flights linking major airports with smaller cities 50 to 250 miles away); and Bandag (which specializes in truck tire recapping and promotes its recaps aggressively at over 1,000 truck stops).

Using a focus strategy to achieve a cost breakthrough is a fairly common technique. Budget-priced motel chains like Days Inn, Motel 6, and LaQuinta have lowered their investment and operating cost per room by using a no-frills approach and catering to price-conscious travelers. Discount stock brokerage houses have lowered costs by focusing on customers mainly interested in buy-sell transactions who are willing to forgo all the investment research, investment advice, and financial services offered by full-service firms like Merrill Lynch. Pursuing a cost advantage via focusing works well when a firm can find ways to lower costs significantly by limiting its customer base to a well-defined buyer segment.

When Focusing Is Attractive.   The most attractive segments for focusing have one or more of the following characteristics:

- The segment is big enough to be profitable.
- The segment has good growth potential.

- The segment is not crucial to the success of major competitors.
- The focusing firm has the skills and resources to serve the segment effectively.
- The focuser can defend itself against challengers by the customer goodwill it has built up and its superior ability to serve buyers in the segment.

A focuser's specialized skills in serving the target market niche provide a basis for defending against the five competitive forces. Rivals do not have the same ability to serve the focused firm's target clientele. The focused firm's distinctive competence gives it a competitive edge that serves as a barrier to entry in its market niche. Its distinctive competence also acts as a hurdle that substitutes must overcome. The bargaining leverage of powerful customers is blunted somewhat by their own unwillingness to shift their business to firms less capable of serving their needs.

Focusing works best (1) when it is costly or difficult for broad-line rivals to serve the target market niche well, (2) when no other rival is attempting to *specialize* in the same target segment, (3) when a firm's resources do not permit it to go after a wide segment of the total market, and (4) when industry segments differ widely in size, growth rate, profitability, and intensity of the five competitive forces making some segments more attractive than others.

The Risks of a Focus Strategy. Focusing carries several risks. One is the possibility that broad-range competitors will find effective ways to match the focused firm in serving the narrow target market. The second is the potential for the niche buyers' preferences and needs to drift toward the product attributes desired by the market as a whole; such an erosion of the differences across buyer segments opens the door for broad-based rivals to enter the target markets of the focused firms. A third is that the segment's attractiveness becomes so appealing it is soon inundated with competitors, causing profits to be split among many firms.

USING OFFENSIVE STRATEGIES TO SECURE COMPETITIVE ADVANTAGE

An offensive strategy, if successful, can open up a competitive advantage over rivals.[5] How long it takes to create an edge is a function of the industry's competitive characteristics. The buildup period, shown in Figure 5-1, can be short, as in service businesses, which need little in the way of equipment and distribution system support to implement a new offensive move. Or the buildup can take much longer, as in capital intensive and technologically sophisticated industries where it can take several years to debug a new technology, bring new capacity on line, and win consumer acceptance of a new product. Ideally, the buildup period is short; the longer it takes the more likely rivals will spot the move, see its potential, and begin a response. The size of the advantage (indicated

---

[5] Ian C. MacMillan, "How Long Can You Sustain a Competitive Advantage?" reprinted in Liam Fahey, *The Strategic Planning Management Reader* (Englewood Cliffs, N.J.: Prentice-Hall, 1989), pp. 23–24.

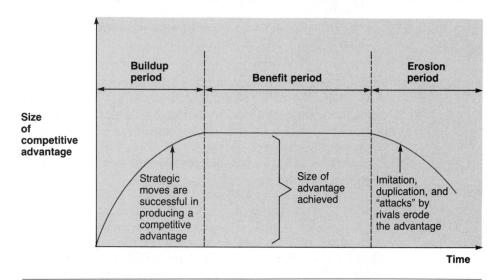

Figure 5–1 THE BUILDING AND ERODING OF COMPETITIVE ADVANTAGE

on the vertical scale in Figure 5–1) can be large (as in pharmaceuticals where patents on an important new drug produce a substantial advantage) or small (as in apparel where popular new designs can be imitated quickly). After buildup comes the benefit period. The length of the benefit period is governed by how long it takes rivals to respond effectively enough to begin closing the gap. The length of the response lag is crucial for three reasons: it limits the period in which the leader can expect to earn above-average profits; it determines how long the firm will have to recoup the investment made in creating the advantage; and it indicates how long the firm has to develop new offensive moves to sustain its edge. As competitors respond with serious counteroffensives, the competitive advantage begins to erode. *Any competitive advantage currently held will eventually be eroded by the actions of competent, resourceful competitors.*[6] Thus, to sustain its initial advantage, a firm must devise a second offensive. To be ready for the competitors' challenge when it comes, the groundwork for this "second act" needs to be laid while the firm is benefiting from its current competitive advantage.

There are six basic ways to mount strategic offensives:[7]

- Attack competitor strengths

---

[6] Ian C. MacMillan, "Controlling Competitive Dynamics by Taking Strategic Initiative," *The Academy of Management Executive* 2, no. 2 (May 1988), p. 111.

[7] Philip Kotler and Ravi Singh, "Marketing Warfare in the 1980s," *The Journal of Business Strategy* 1, no. 3 (Winter 1981), pp. 30–41; Philip Kotler, *Marketing Management* 5th ed. (Englewood Cliffs, N.J.: Prentice Hall, 1984), pp. 401–6; and Ian C. MacMillan, "Preemptive Strategies," *Journal of Business Strategy* 4, no. 2 (Fall 1983), pp. 16–26.

- Attack competitor weaknesses
- Grand offensives
- End-run offensives
- Guerrilla offensives
- Preemptive strikes

Attacking Competitor Strengths

There are two good reasons to go head-to-head against rival companies, pitting one's own strengths against theirs, price for price, model for model, and promotion tactic for promotion tactic. The first is to try to gain market share by outmatching the strengths of weaker rivals; attacking weaker rivals where they are strongest is attractive whenever it can bring a decisive market victory and a commanding edge over struggling competitors. The other reason is to whittle away at the competitive advantage of one or more rivals; here success is measured by how much the competitive gap closes up. The merits of a strength-against-strength offensive attack, of course, depend on how the costs of the offensive compare to the competitive benefits. For this type of offensive to succeed, the initiator needs enough competitive strength and resources to take at least some market share from the targeted rivals. Failing this, such an offensive makes no sense and is generally doomed from the start.

All-out attacks on competitor strengths can involve initiatives on any of several fronts—price-cutting, running comparison ads, adding new features that appeal to a rival's customers, constructing major new plant capacity in a rival's backyard, and bringing out new models to match their's model for model. A common ploy is for the aggressor to attack with an equally good product offering and a lower price.[8] This can produce market share gains if the targeted rival has strong reasons for not resorting to price cuts of its own and if the challenger convinces buyers that its product is just as good. However, whether such a strategy increases profits depends on whether the gains in volume offset the bottom-line impact of thinner margins per unit sold.

Another type of price-aggressive attack is based on first achieving overall low-cost leadership and then attacking competitors with a lower price.[9] Cost-related price-cutting is perhaps the strongest basis for launching and sustaining a price-aggressive offensive. Without a cost advantage, price-cutting works only if the aggressor has more financial resources and can outlast its rivals in a war of attrition.

Attacking Competitor Weaknesses

This offensive approach involves concentrating one's competitive strengths and resources directly against the weaknesses of rivals. Common weaknesses for attack are:

---

[8] Kotler, *Marketing Management*, p. 402.

[9] Ibid., p. 403.

- Geographic regions where the rival has low market share and/or is exerting less competitive effort.
- Buyer segments that the rival is neglecting and/or is less equipped to serve.
- Situations where rivals lag on quality and product performance and potential exists to switch their most performance-conscious customers to the challenger's better quality offering.
- Situations where rivals have done a poor job of providing adequate customer service, making it relatively easy for a service-oriented challenger to win the disenchanted customers.
- Instances where the defenders have under-advertised and otherwise not established a strong marketing presence, thereby allowing a challenger with strong marketing skills to move in.
- Gaps in the product line of market leaders, giving a challenger the opportunity to develop the gaps into strong, new market segments.
- Situations where the market leaders have failed to spot certain buyer needs, giving an aggressor the chance to jump in and serve them.

As a general rule, attacks on competitor weaknesses have a better chance of succeeding than attacks on strengths, provided the weaknesses represent important vulnerabilities and the rival is caught by surprise with no ready defense.[10]

Grand Offensives

There are times when aggressors launch a grand competitive offensive involving several major initiatives in an effort to throw a rival off-balance, divert its attention in many directions, and force it into channeling resources to protect its front, sides, and rear simultaneously. Hunt's tried such an offensive several years ago in an attempt to wrest market share from Heinz in the ketchup market. Simultaneously, Hunt's introduced two new ketchup flavors (pizza and hickory) to disrupt consumers' taste preferences, to try to create new product segments, and to capture more retail shelf space in stores. It lowered its price to 70 percent of Heinz's price, it offered sizable trade allowances to retailers, and it raised its advertising budget to over twice the level of Heinz's.[11] The offensive failed because not enough Heinz users tried the Hunt's brands, and many of those who switched to Hunt's soon switched back to Heinz. Grand offensives have their best chance of success when a challenger, because of superior resources, can overpower its rivals by outspending them across-the-board long enough to buy its way into a position of market leadership and competitive advantage.

End-Run Offensives

End-run offensives avoid direct assault on entrenched positions and aim instead at being first to occupy new ground. End-runs involve such moves as being first to

---

[10] For a discussion of the use of surprise, see William E. Rothschild, "Surprise and the Competitive Advantage," *Journal of Business Strategy* 4, no. 3 (Winter 1984), pp. 10–18.

[11] As cited in Kotler, *Marketing Management*, p. 404.

expand into new geographic markets, trying to create new segments by introducing products with different attributes and performance features to better meet buyer needs, and leapfrogging into next-generation technologies to supplant existing products and/or production processes. The whole idea of an end-run is to gain a significant first-mover advantage in a new arena and force competitors into playing catch-up. The most successful end-runs change the rules of the competitive game in the aggressor's favor.

Guerrilla Offensives

Guerrilla offensives are particularly well-suited to small challengers who have neither the resources nor the market visibility to mount a broad-based attack on the industry leaders. A guerrilla offensive uses the hit-and-run principle, attacking in those locations and at those times in which the underdog can compete under conditions that suit it rather than its bigger competitors. There are several options for designing a guerrilla offensive:[12]

1. Focus the offensive on a narrow, well-defined segment weakly defended by competitors.

2. Attack fronts where rivals are overextended and have spread their resources most thinly (possibilities include going after their customers located in less-populated geographic areas, enhancing delivery schedules at times when competitors' deliveries are running behind, adding to quality when rivals have quality control problems, and boosting technical services when buyers are confused by competitors' proliferation of models and optional features).

3. Make small, scattered, at-random raids on the leaders with such harassing tactics as selective lowballing on price, intense bursts of promotional activity, and legal actions charging antitrust violations, patent infringement, and unfair advertising.

Preemptive Strikes

Preemptive strikes involve moving first to secure an advantageous position that rivals cannot or are discouraged from duplicating. There are several ways to win a prime strategic position with preemptive moves:[13]

- *Expanding production capacity well ahead of market demand in hopes of discouraging rivals from following with expansions of their own.* When rivals are "bluffed" out of adding capacity by a fear of creating long-term excess supply conditions and having to struggle with the bad profit eco-

---

12 For more details, see MacMillan, "How Business Strategists Can Use Guerrilla Warfare Tactics," pp. 63–65; Kathryn R. Harrigan, *Strategic Flexibility* (Lexington, Mass.: Lexington Books, 1985), pp. 30–45; and Liam Fahey, "Guerrilla Strategy: The Hit-and-Run Attack," in Fahey, *The Strategic Planning Management Reader,* pp. 194–97.

13 The use of preemptive moves is treated comprehensively in Ian C. MacMillan, "Preemptive Strategies," *Journal of Business Strategy,* pp. 16–26. What follows in this section is based on MacMillan's article.

nomics of underutilized plants, the preemptor stands to win a bigger market share as market demand grows and its own plant capacity becomes filled.

* *Tying up the best (or the most) raw material sources and/or the most reliable, high-quality suppliers via long-term contracts or backward vertical integration.* This move can effectively relegate rivals to struggling for second-best supply positions.

* *Securing the best geographic locations.* Big first-mover advantages are often locked in by quickly moving to obtain the most favorable sites along a heavily traveled thoroughfare, at a new interchange or intersection, in a new shopping mall, in a natural beauty spot, or close to cheap transportation, raw material supplies, or market outlets, and so on.

* *Obtaining the business of prestigious customers.*

* *Establishing a "psychological" image and position in the minds of consumers that is unique and hard to copy and that establishes a compelling appeal and rallying cry.* Examples include Avis's well-known "We try harder" theme; Frito-Lay's guarantee to retailers of "99.5 percent service;" Holiday Inn's assurance of "no surprises," and Prudential's "piece-of-the-rock" image of safety and permanence.

* *Securing exclusive or dominant access to the best distributors in an area.*

Preemption has been used successfully on a number of occasions. General Mills' Red Lobster restaurant chain was notably successful in securing access to excellent seafood suppliers and in getting prime locations for its restaurant sites. DeBeers became the dominant world distributor of diamonds by tying up most of the important diamond mines. DuPont's aggressive capacity expansions in titanium dioxide, while not blocking all competitors from expanding, did discourage enough to give it a leadership position in the titanium dioxide industry. Coca-Cola has won a strong position in the fountain segment of the soft-drink industry by winning the business of McDonald's. Price Waterhouse's image as the most prestigious public accounting firm has always been linked to its list of blue-chip corporate clients.

To be successful, a preemptive move doesn't have to totally block rivals from following or copying; it merely needs to give a firm a "prime" position. A prime position is one that is easier to defend and that makes a material difference in how the game of competition unfolds in the industry.

Choosing Who to Attack

Aggressor firms need to analyze which of their rivals to attack as well as how to attack them. There are basically three types of firms to attack:[14]

---

[14] Kotler, *Marketing Management*, p. 400.

1. *Attack the market leader(s).* This entails high risk but can carry a potentially big payoff. It makes the best sense when the leader in terms of size and market share is not a "true leader" in terms of serving the market well. The signs of leader vulnerability include unhappy buyers, low profitability, strong emotional commitment to a technology it has pioneered, a history of regulatory problems, and being "stuck in the middle" lacking real strength based on low-cost leadership or differentiation. Attacks on leaders can also succeed when the challenger is able to revamp its activity-cost chain or otherwise innovate to gain a lock on a fresh cost-based or differentiation-based competitive advantage.[15] Attacks on leaders need not have the objective of making the aggressor the new leader; however, a challenger may "win" by simply wresting enough sales from the leader to make the aggressor a far stronger runner-up.

2. *Attack runner-up firms.* Launching offensives against weaker runner-up firms whose positions are vulnerable often has strong appeal and carries relatively low risk. In such cases, frontal attacks may well work, even if the challenger has smaller resources to work with because the targeted rival's vulnerabilities are so readily exploitable.

3. *Attack small local and regional firms that are not doing the job and whose customers are primed to switch to a better brand.*

As we have said, successful strategies are grounded in competitive advantage. This goes for offensive strategies, too. The competitive advantage areas that usually form the strongest basis for launching a strategic offensive include:[16]

- Coming up with a lower-cost product design.
- Making changes in production operations that lower costs or enhance differentiation.
- Developing product features that deliver superior performance to buyers or that lower buyers' user costs.
- Giving buyers more responsive after-sale support.
- Escalating the marketing effort in an undermarketed industry.
- Pioneering a new distribution channel.
- Bypassing wholesale distributors and selling direct to the end-user.

It is virtually imperative that a strategic offensive be tied to what a firm does best—its internal strengths and capabilities. As a rule, these strengths represent either a *key skill* (cost reduction, customer service skills, technical expertise) or a uniquely *strong functional capability* (engineering and product design, manufacturing expertise, advertising and promotion, distribution access).[17]

---

[15] Porter, *Competitive Advantage,* p. 518.

[16] Ibid., pp. 520–22.

[17] For more details, see MacMillan, "Controlling Competitive Dynamics," pp. 112–16.

USING DEFENSIVE STRATEGIES TO PROTECT COMPETITIVE ADVANTAGE

In a competitive market, all firms are subject to attacks from rivals. Offensive attacks can come both from new entrants in the industry and from established firms seeking to improve their market positions. The purpose of defensive strategy is to lower the risk of being attacked, to lessen the intensity of any attack that occurs, and to influence challengers to opt for less threatening offensive strategies. While defensive strategy usually doesn't enhance a firm's competitive advantage, it should definitely be capable of strengthening a firm's competitive position and thus sustaining whatever competitive advantage the firm has.

There are several basic ways for a firm to protect its competitive position. One approach involves trying to block the avenues challengers can take in mounting an offensive; the options here include:[18]

* Broadening the product line to close off vacant niches and gaps to would-be challengers.
* Introducing models or brands that match the characteristics challengers' models already have or might have.
* Keeping prices low on models that most closely match competitors' offerings.
* Signing exclusive agreements with dealers and distributors to keep competitors from using the same ones.
* Granting dealers and distributors sizable volume discounts in order to discourage them from experimenting with other suppliers.
* Offering free or low-cost training to buyers' personnel in the use of the firm's product.
* Making it harder for competitors to get buyers to try their brands by (1) giving special price discounts to buyers who are considering trial use of rival brands, (2) resorting to high levels of couponing and sample giveaways to buyers most prone to experiment, and (3) leaking information about impending new products or price changes that cause buyers to postpone switching.
* Raising the amount of financing provided to dealers and/or to buyers.
* Reducing delivery times for spare parts.
* Increasing warranty coverages.
* Patenting feasible alternative technologies.
* Maintaining a participation in alternative technologies.
* Protecting proprietary know-how in products, production technologies, and other parts of the activity-cost chain.
* Signing exclusive contracts with the best suppliers to block access of aggressive rivals.

---

[18] Porter, *Competitive Advantage*, pp. 489–94.

- Purchasing natural resource reserves in excess of present needs to preempt them from competitors.
- Avoiding suppliers that also serve competitors.
- Challenging rivals' products or practices in regulatory proceedings.

Moves such as these serve to fortify the firm's present position, but they also present competitors with a moving target. A successful defense has to do more than just strengthen a firm's present position. Specifically, a defender must adjust to changing industry conditions rather promptly to avoid "out-of-date" vulnerability. A mobile defense is thus preferable to a stationary one. On occasion, being a first-mover blocks a rival quite effectively; defensive strategy is not exclusively reactive and responsive to the moves of challengers.

A second approach to defensive strategy entails signaling challengers that there is a real threat of strong retaliation if the challenger attacks. The goal is to dissuade challengers from attacking at all (by raising their expectations that the resulting battle will be more costly to the challenger than it is worth) or, at the least, to divert them to arenas that are less threatening to the defender. Would-be challengers can be signaled by:[19]

- Publicly announcing management's commitment to maintain the firm's present market share.
- Publicly announcing plans to construct adequate production capacity to meet forecast demand growth and sometimes building ahead of demand.
- Leaking advance information about a new product generation, a breakthrough in production technology, or the planned introduction of important new brands or models, thereby raising the risk perceived by challengers that such a move will actually be forthcoming and, hopefully, inducing them to delay moves of their own until they see if the signals are credible.
- Publicly committing the firm to a policy of matching the prices or other terms offered by competitors (that is, touting and then following through on a "we will not be undersold" theme).
- Maintaining a war chest of cash reserves or other quickly tappable sources of liquidity.
- Making an occasional strong counter response to the moves of weak competitors to enhance the firm's image as a tough defender.

Another way to dissuade rivals involves trying to lower the profit inducement for challengers to launch an offensive. When a firm's or an industry's profitability is enticingly high, challengers are more willing to hurdle high defensive barriers and combat strong retaliation. A defender can deflect attacks, especially from new entrants, by deliberately forgoing some short-run profits and by using accounting techniques that obscure true profitability.

---

[19] Ibid., pp. 495–97. This listing here is selective; Porter offers a greater number of options.

VERTICAL INTEGRATION STRATEGIES

Vertical integration strategies extend a firm's competitive scope within the same industry. They involve expanding the firm's range of activities backward into sources of supply and/or forward toward end-users of the final product. Thus, if a manufacturer elects to build a new plant to make certain component parts rather than purchase them from outside suppliers, it remains in essentially the same industry as before. The only change is that it has business units in two stages of production in the industry's total activity-chain. Similarly, if a personal computer manufacturer elects to integrate forward by opening 100 retail stores to market its brands directly to users, it remains in the personal computer business even though its competitive scope extends further forward in the industry chain.

Moves to vertically integrate can aim at full integration—participating in all stages of the process of getting products in the hands of final users—or partial integration—building positions in just some stages of the industry's total production-distribution chain. A firm can accomplish vertical integration with its own start-up entry into other stages in the industry's activity-chain, or it can acquire an enterprise already positioned in the stage where it wishes to integrate.

The Appeal of Vertical Integration

The only good reason for investing company resources in vertical integration is to strengthen the firm's competitive position.[20] Unless vertical integration produces sufficient cost-savings to justify the extra investment or unless it yields competitive advantage, it has no real profit or strategic payoff.

Integrating backward to supply raw materials or component parts can generate cost-savings only if the volume needed is big enough to capture the same scale economies suppliers have. The cost-savings potential of backward integration is usually biggest when suppliers have sizable profit margins or when the item being supplied is a major cost component. The competitive advantage of backward vertical integration arises when a company, by supplying its own parts, ends up with a better-quality part and thereby significantly enhances the performance of its final product.

Backward integration can also spare a firm the uncertainty of being dependent on suppliers of crucial raw materials or support services and lessen the firm's vulnerability to powerful suppliers intent on jacking up the prices of important component materials at every opportunity. Stockpiling, fixed-price contracts, or the use of substitute inputs may not be attractive ways for dealing with uncertain supply conditions or with economically powerful suppliers. When this is the case, backward integration can be an organization's most profitable and competitively secure option for accessing reliable supplies of essential materials and support services at favorable prices.

---

[20] See Kathryn R. Harrigan, "Matching Vertical Integration Strategies to Competitive Conditions," *Strategic Management Journal* 7, no. 6 (November–December 1986), pp. 535–56; for specific advantages and disadvantages of vertical integration, see Kathryn R. Harrigan, *Strategic Flexibility* (Lexington, Mass.: Lexington Books, 1985), p. 162.

The strategic impetus for forward integration has much the same roots. Undependable sales and distribution channels can give rise to costly inventory pileups and frequent underutilization of capacity, thereby undermining the economies of a steady, near-capacity production operation. In such cases, it is often advantageous for a firm to set up its own wholesale-retail distribution network in order to gain dependable channels through which to push its products to end-users. Sometimes even a few percentage point increases in the average rate of capacity utilization can boost manufacturing margins enough to make forward integration economical. On other occasions, forward vertical integration into distribution and retailing is cheaper than going through independent distributors and dealers, thus providing a source of relative cost advantage.

For a raw materials producer, integrating forward into manufacturing may help achieve greater product differentiation and allow escape from the price-oriented competition of a commodity business. Often, in the early phases of the vertical product flow, intermediate goods are "commodities" in the sense that they have essentially identical technical specifications irrespective of producer (as is the case with crude oil, poultry, sheet steel, cement, and textile fibers). Competition in the markets for commodity or commodity-like products is usually fiercely price-competitive, with the shifting balance between supply and demand giving rise to volatile profits. However, the closer the production stage to the ultimate consumer, the greater the opportunities for a firm to break out of a commodity-like competitive environment and differentiate its end-product via design, service, quality features, packaging, promotion, and so on. Often, product differentiation causes the importance of price to shrink in comparison to other competitive variables and allows for improved profit margins.

For a manufacturer, integrating forward may mean building a chain of closely supervised dealer franchises or establishing company-owned and -operated retail outlets. Alternatively, it could entail simply staffing regional and district sales offices instead of selling through manufacturer's agents or independent distributors.

The Strategic Disadvantages of Vertical Integration

Vertical integration has some potential weaknesses, however. It boosts capital requirements and can drain needed financial resources from more worthwhile investments. Second, integration introduces additional risks, since it extends the enterprise's scope of activity across the industry chain. Third, vertical integration can so increase a firm's vested interests in technology, production facilities, and procedures that it becomes reluctant to abandon heavy fixed investments even though they are becoming obsolete. Because of this inflexibility, fully integrated firms are more vulnerable to new technologies and new products than partially integrated or nonintegrated firms.

Fourth, vertical integration can pose problems of balancing capacity at each stage in the activity-chain. The most efficient scale of operation at each step in the activity-chain can vary substantially. Exact self-sufficiency at each interface is the exception not the rule. Where internal capacity is deficient to supply the next stage, the difference has to be bought externally. Where internal capacity is excessive, customers need to be found for the surplus. And if by-products are generated, they require arrangements for disposal.

All in all, therefore, a strategy of vertical integration can have both important strengths and weaknesses. Which direction the scales tip on vertical integration depends on (1) how compatible it is with the organization's long-term strategic interests and performance objectives, (2) how much it strengthens an organization's position in the overall industry, and (3) the extent to which it creates competitive advantage. Unless these considerations yield solid benefits, vertical integration is not likely to be an attractive business strategy option.[21]

FIRST-MOVER ADVANTAGES AND DISADVANTAGES

When to make a strategic move is often as crucial as *what* move to make. Timing is especially important when *first-mover advantages* or *disadvantages* exist.[22] Being first to initiate a particular move can have a high payoff when (1) pioneering helps build a firm's image and reputation with buyers, (2) early commitments to supplies of raw materials, new technologies, distribution channels, and so on can produce an absolute cost advantage over rivals, (3) customer loyalty is high so long-term benefits accrue to the firm that wins first-time buyers, and (4) moving first can be a preemptive strike, making imitation extra hard or unlikely. The stronger any first-mover advantages are, the more attractive a pioneering move becomes.

However, being late or following a "wait and see" approach is wise if first-mover disadvantages exist. Pioneering is risky when (1) the costs of opening up a new market are great but customer loyalty is weak, (2) technological change is so rapid that early investments can be rendered obsolete (thus allowing following firms to have the advantage of the newest products and processes), and (3) the industry is developing so rapidly that skills and know-how built up during the early competitive phase are easily bypassed and overcome by late movers. Good timing, therefore, is an important ingredient in deciding whether to be aggressive or cautious in pursuing a particular move.

KEY POINTS

The challenge of competitive strategy—whether it be a low-cost, differentiation, or focus strategy—is to create a competitive advantage for the firm. Competitive advantage comes from positioning a firm in the marketplace so it has an edge in coping with competitive forces and in attracting buyers.

A strategy of trying to be the low-cost producer works well in situations where:

---

[21] For an extensive, well-researched, and fresh look at the whole family of approaches to vertical integration, see Kathryn R. Harrigan, "Formulating Vertical Integration Strategies," *Academy of Management Review* 9, no. 4 (October 1984), pp. 638–52.

[22] Porter, *Competitive Strategy*, pp. 232–33.

- The industry's product is pretty much the same from seller to seller.
- The marketplace is dominated by price competition (buyers are prone to shop for the best price).
- There are few ways to achieve product differentiation that have much value to buyers.
- Most buyers use the product in the same ways and thus have common user requirements.
- Buyers' costs in switching from one seller or brand to another are low (or even zero).
- Buyers are large and have significant bargaining power.

To achieve a low-cost advantage, a company must become more skilled than rivals in controlling cost drivers and/or it must find innovative cost-saving ways to revamp the activity-cost chain.

Differentiation strategies can produce a competitive edge based on technical superiority, quality, service, or more value for the money. Differentiation strategies work *best* when:

- There are many ways to differentiate the product/service that buyers think have value.
- Buyer needs or uses of the product/service are diverse.
- Not many rivals are following a similar differentiation strategy.

Anything a firm can do to create buyer value represents a potential basis for differentiation. Successful differentiation is usually keyed to lowering the buyer's cost of using the item, raising the performance the buyer gets, or giving buyer utility a psychological boost.

The competitive advantage of focusing is earned either by achieving lower costs in serving the target market niche or by developing an ability to offer niche buyers something different from rival competitors—in other words, it is either *cost-based* or *differentiation-based*. Focusing works best when:

- Buyer needs or uses of the item are diverse.
- No other rival is attempting to *specialize* in the same target segment.
- A firm lacks the capability to go after a wider part of the total market.
- Buyer segments differ widely in size, growth rate, profitability, and intensity in the five competitive forces, making some segments more attractive than others.

A variety of offensive strategic moves can help secure a competitive advantage. Strategic offensives can be aimed at either competitors' strengths or weaknesses; they can involve end-runs or grand offensives on many fronts; they can be designed as guerrilla actions or as preemptive strikes; and the target of the offensive can be a market leader, a runner-up firm, or the smallest and/or weakest firms in the industry.

The strategic approaches to defending a company's position usually take the form of (1) making moves that fortify the company's present position, (2) presenting competitors with a moving target to avoid "out-of-date" vulnerability, and (3) dissuading rivals from trying to attack.

Vertically integrating forward or backward makes strategic sense if it strengthens a company's position via either cost reduction or creation of a competitive advantage.

The timing of strategic moves is important. First-movers sometimes gain strategic advantage; however, sometimes it is cheaper and easier to be a follower than a leader.

Illustration Capsule 11 presents 10 of the most common strategic mistakes.

ILLUSTRATION CAPSULE   11

TEN COMMON STRATEGIC MISTAKES

Experience has shown that some strategic actions fail more often than they succeed. Ten examples of strategic moves that usually produce poor results are presented below:

1. Imitating the moves of leading or successful competitors when the market has no more room for copycat products and look-alike competitors.
2. Spending more money on marketing and sales promotion to try to get around problems with product quality and product performance.
3. Establishing many weak market positions instead of a few strong ones.
4. Using debt to finance cost-saving investments in new facilities and equipment, then getting trapped with high fixed costs when demand turns down, excess capacity appears, and cash flows are too small to cover interest costs and debt repayment.
5. Allocating R&D efforts to weak products instead of strong products.
6. Attacking the market leaders head-on without having either a good competitive advantage or adequate financial strength.
7. Making such aggressive attempts to take market share that rivals are provoked into strong retaliation and a costly "arm-race" struggle ensues (such battles seldom produce a substantial change in market shares; the usual outcome is higher costs and profitless sales growth).

(continued)

8. Initiating price cuts to win added market share without having a cost advantage.

9. Going after the high end of the market without having the reputation to attract buyers looking for name-brand, prestige goods.

10. Depending on cosmetic product improvements to serve as a substitute for real innovation and extra customer value.

These mistakes usually are born out of acts of desperation, poor analysis of industry and competitive conditions, and/or misjudgments.

SUGGESTED READINGS

Aaker, David A. "Managing Assets and Skills: The Key to a Sustainable Competitive Advantage." *California Management Review* 31, no. 2 (Winter 1989), pp. 91–106.

Cohen, William A. "War in the Marketplace." *Business Horizons* 29, no. 2 (March–April 1986), pp. 10–20.

Coyne, Kevin P. "Sustainable Competitive Advantage—What It Is, What It Isn't." *Business Horizons* 29, no. 1 (January–February 1986), pp. 54–61.

Harrigan, Kathryn. "Guerrilla Strategies of Underdog Competitors." *Planning Review* 14, no. 16 (November 1986), pp. 4–11.

————. "Formulating Vertical Integration Strategies." *Academy of Management Review* 9, no. 4 (October 1984), pp. 638–52.

Hout, Thomas; Michael E. Porter; and Eileen Rudden. "How Global Companies Win Out." *Harvard Business Review* 60, no. 5 (September–October 1982), pp. 98–108.

MacMillan, Ian C. "Preemptive Strategies." *Journal of Business Strategy* 4, no. 2 (Fall 1983), pp. 16–26.

————. "Controlling Competitive Dynamics by Taking Strategic Initiative." *The Academy of Management Executive* 2, no. 2 (May 1988), pp. 111–18.

Porter, Michael E. *Competitive Advantage* (New York: Free Press, 1985), chaps. 3, 4, 5, 7, 14, and 15.

Rothschild, William E. "Surprise and the Competitive Advantage." *Journal of Business Strategy* 4, no. 3 (Winter 1984), pp. 10–18.

Thompson, Arthur A. "Strategies for Staying Cost Competitive." *Harvard Business Review* 62, no. 1 (January–February 1984), pp. 110–17.

6 Matching Strategy to the Situation

Strategy isn't something you can nail together in a slap-dash fashion by sitting around a conference table . . .
Terry Haller

The essence of formulating competitive strategy is relating a company to its environment . . . the best strategy for a given firm is ultimately a unique construction reflecting its particular circumstances.
Michael E. Porter

Which available strategy alternative best suits a company's business is conditioned partly by the industry environment in which it competes and partly by the company's situation. To demonstrate the kinds of considerations involved in matching strategy to the situation, this chapter surveys eight classic types of generic industry environments and company situations:

1. Competing in a young, emerging industry.
2. Competing during the transition to industry maturity.
3. Competing in mature or declining industries.
4. Competing in fragmented industries.
5. Competing in international markets.
6. Strategies for industry leaders.
7. Strategies for runner-up firms.
8. Strategies for weak and crisis-ridden firms.

STRATEGIES FOR COMPETING IN EMERGING INDUSTRIES

An emerging industry is one in the early, formative stage. Most companies are in a grow-and-build mode, adding people, acquiring or constructing facilities, gearing up production, trying to broaden distribution and gain buyer acceptance. Often, there are important product design problems and technological problems to be worked out as well. In addition, the market environments of emerging industries have several strategy-shaping features:[1]

- There are no "rules of the game"; the issue of how the market will function is open-ended.
- Much of the technological know-how tends to be proprietary and closely guarded, having been developed in-house by pioneering firms; patent protection is sought where possible, for whatever competitive advantage it may yield.
- There is uncertainty over which production technology will prove to be most efficient and which product attributes buyers will prefer. The result is erratic product quality, industrywide absence of product and technological standardization, and a situation where each firm is, at least until a broader consensus develops, committed to pioneering its own approach to technology, product design, marketing, and distribution.
- Firms have little hard information about competitors, uses for the product, whether demand will materialize as envisioned, how fast the market will grow, and how big it will get.
- Entry barriers tend to be relatively low; both new start-up companies and large outsiders will enter if the industry's future is promising.
- Experience curve effects permit significant cost reductions as volume builds.
- Since all buyers are first-time users, the marketing task is one of inducing initial purchase and overcoming customer confusion over the multiplicity of product attributes, technologies, and claims of rival firms. Many potential buyers may perceive that second- or third-generation technologies will make current products obsolete; hence, they may delay purchase until the product "matures" and a consensus emerges regarding design and technology.
- Firms may have difficulty securing ample supplies of raw materials and components (until suppliers gear up to meet the industry's needs).
- Because of the above conditions, firms in an emerging industry often find themselves short of funds to "get over the hump" of industry start-up.

The two critical strategic issues confronting firms in an emerging industry are (1) how to obtain the resources needed to support new product development and

---

[1] Michael E. Porter, *Competitive Strategy: Techniques for Analyzing Industries and Competitors* (New York: Free Press, 1980), pp. 216–23.

rapid company expansion and (2) what market segments and competitive advantage to go after in trying to secure a strong position among the industry leaders.[2] Competitive strategies keyed to low-cost or differentiation are usually viable. Focusing is necessary when financial resources are limited and when the industry has too many technological frontiers to pursue at once. Dealing with all the risks and opportunities of an emerging industry is one of the most challenging business strategy problems. The past experiences of firms in emerging industries have produced the following growth-stage strategy guidelines:[3]

1. Manage the business in an entrepreneurial mode with the aim of positioning the firm for future growth. In an emerging industry there are no established "rules of the game," and industry participants often try a wide variety of strategic approaches. Because firms enjoy wide strategic freedom, a pioneering firm that makes a good strategic choice can shape the rules, gain first-mover advantages, and achieve leadership recognition.

2. Push hard to perfect the technology, improve product quality, and develop attractive performance features.

3. Try to capture any first-mover advantages associated with more models, better styling, early commitments to technologies and raw materials suppliers, experience curve effects, and new distribution channels.

4. Search out new customer groups, new geographical areas to enter, and new user applications. Make it easier and cheaper for first-time buyers to try the industry's new product.

5. Gradually shift the advertising focus from building product awareness to increasing frequency of use and creating brand loyalty.

6. Move quickly when technological uncertainty clears and a "dominant" technology emerges; try to pioneer the "dominant design" approach (but be cautious when technology is moving so rapidly that early investments are likely to be rendered obsolete).

7. Use price cuts to attract the next layer of price-sensitive buyers into the market.

8. Expect large, established firms looking for growth opportunities to enter the industry as the perceived risk of investing in the industry lessens. Try to prepare for the entry of powerful competitors by forecasting (*a*) who the probable entrants will be (based on present and future entry barriers) and (*b*) the types of strategies they are likely to employ.

The short-term value of winning the early race for growth and market share leadership has to be balanced against the longer-range need to build a durable

---

[2] Charles W. Hofer and Dan Schendel, *Strategy Formulation: Analytical Concepts* (St. Paul, Minn.: West Publishing, 1978), pp. 164–65.

[3] Philip Kotler, *Marketing Management: Analysis, Planning, Control,* 5th ed. (Englewood Cliffs, N.J.: Prentice-Hall, 1984), p. 366; and Porter, *Competitive Strategy,* chap. 10.

competitive edge and a defendable market position.[4] New entrants, attracted by the profit potential, may crowd the market. Aggressive newcomers, aspiring for industry leadership, can trigger a battle for market share that forces out weaker competitors. A young, single-business enterprise in a fast-developing industry can help its cause by selecting knowledgeable members to its board of directors, hiring entrepreneurially oriented managers with experience in guiding young businesses through the developmental and takeoff stages, or gaining added expertise and a stronger resource base by merging with other firms in the industry.

STRATEGIES FOR COMPETING DURING THE TRANSITION TO INDUSTRY MATURITY

Rapid industry growth cannot go on forever. The transition to a slower-growth, maturing industry environment does not occur after any fixed period of time, and it can be forestalled by a steady stream of new products innovations or other driving forces that keep rejuvenating rapid growth. Nonetheless, as growth rates slack off, the transition usually produces fundamental changes in the industry's competitive environment:[5]

1. *Slowing growth in buyer demand generates more head-to-head competition for market share.* Since firms are unable to maintain their historical growth rates by holding the same market share, rivalry shifts to trying to take customers away from other firms. Outbreaks of price-cutting, increased advertising, and other aggressive tactics are common.

2. *Buyers become more sophisticated, often driving a harder bargain on repeat purchases.* Since the product is no longer new, buyers can concentrate on which brand to buy the next time.

3. *Competition often produces a greater emphasis on cost and service.* As all sellers begin to offer the product attributes buyers prefer, buyer choice among competing brands hinges more on which seller offers the best combination of price and service.

4. *Firms have a "topping out" problem in adding production capacity.* Slower rates of industry growth mean slowdowns in capacity expansion— or industry overcapacity results. Each firm has to monitor rivals' expansion plans carefully and time its own capacity additions to minimize excess capacity. Rapid industry growth no longer can cover the mistake of adding too much capacity too soon.

5. *Product innovation and new end-use applications are harder to come by.* The ability to continue generating marketable innovations tends to drop off. Firms run out of big new ideas and ways to stimulate product excitement.

---

[4] Hofer and Schendel, *Strategy Formulation*, pp. 164–65.

[5] Porter, *Competitive Strategy*, pp. 238–40.

6. *International competition increases.* Technological maturity, product standardization, and increased emphasis on low-cost production often generate a more globally competitive industry. Growth-minded domestic firms seek out new foreign markets and begin locating plants in countries with lower production costs; domestic and foreign firms are drawn into head-to-head competition, creating political issues over trade barriers and protectionism. Industry leadership passes to companies intent on winning the biggest global market shares with strategies designed to build strong competitive positions in most of the world's major geographic markets.

7. *Industry profitability falls, sometimes temporarily and sometimes permanently.* Slower growth, increased competition, more sophisticated buyers, and the erosion of competitive advantages frequently shrink industry profits. The profits of weaker, less-efficient firms are usually more adversely affected than are those of strong competitors.

8. *The resulting competitive shakeout induces a number of mergers and acquisitions among former competitors, drives some firms out of the industry, and, in general, produces industry consolidation.* Even inefficient firms and firms with weak competitive strategies can survive in a rapid growth industry; but the stiffer competition accompanying industry maturity generally exposes competitive weakness and opens the door for a survival-of-the-fittest contest to unfold.

These characteristics usually force firms to reexamine their business strategies. A refashioned competitive approach can sometimes be a matter of survival. Several strategic moves are well-suited to competing in maturing industries.[6]

Pruning the Product Line.   Although numerous models, sizes, and product options are competitively useful in a rapidly growing market, product-line proliferation can be costly in a slow-growth environment characterized by price competition and battles for market share. Average costing for groups of products and arbitrary allocations of overhead become inadequate for evaluating the product line and deciding what new items to add. Unwittingly subsidizing losses on one item with above-average profits on another hides items whose demand does not support their true costs and invites price-cutting or new product introductions by rivals. Pruning the slowest-selling items from the line and concentrating resources on items whose margins are highest and/or where the firm has a comparative advantage helps keep strategy matched to company strengths. In general, firms need enhanced "profit consciousness" to be successful in intensely competitive markets.

More Emphasis on Process Innovation.   The intensifying price competition that accompanies market maturity gives greater relative importance to process-oriented technological innovation. Cost-saving manufacturing innovations have high

---

[6] The following discussion draws from Porter, *Competitive Strategy*, pp. 241–46.

competitive value in markets where buyers are increasingly price conscious. Japanese firms have been successful emphasizing technological process strategies aimed at becoming the low-cost producer of a quality product.

A Stronger Focus on Cost Reduction. Stiffening price competition gives firms extra incentive to reduce unit costs. Such efforts can cover a broad front: pushing suppliers for better prices, switching to lower-priced components, adopting more economical product designs, emphasizing manufacturing and distribution efficiency, retrenching sales efforts (to concentrate on the best types of buyers), and trimming administrative overhead.

Increasing Sales to Present Customers. In a mature market, growing by taking customers away from rivals may not be as appealing as expanding sales to existing customers. Strategies to increase the purchases of existing customers can involve broadening the lines offered to include complementary products and ancillary services, finding more ways for customers to use the product, and performing more functions for the buyers (assembling components prior to shipment). Convenience food stores, for example, have boosted average sales per customer by adding video rentals, automatic bank tellers, and deli counters.

Purchasing Rival Firms at Bargain Prices. Sometimes the facilities and assets of distressed rivals can be acquired cheaply. Bargain-priced acquisitions can improve margins and help create a low-cost position if these facilities are not unduly inefficient or on the verge of being rendered obsolete by technological change. Heileman Brewing Company rose from relative obscurity to become the fourth largest beer company by acquiring small regional brewers and used equipment at bargain prices.

Expanding Internationally. As its domestic market matures, a firm may seek to enter foreign markets where attractive growth potential still exists and competitive pressures are not so strong. Foreign expansion is particularly attractive if equipment no longer suitable for domestic operations is usable for export production or for plants in less-developed foreign markets (a condition that lowers entry costs). Such possibilities arise when (1) foreign buyers have less sophisticated needs and have simpler, old-fashioned end-use applications, and (2) foreign competitors are smaller, less formidable, and do not employ the latest production technology. International strategies make particular sense when a domestic firm's skills and reputation are readily transferable to foreign markets.

Strategic Pitfalls

Perhaps the biggest pitfall during the transition to industry maturity is not making a clear strategic choice and, instead, steering a middle course between low-cost, differentiation, and focus. Such strategies give the firm an average image with buyers and no solid competitive advantage. Other pitfalls include sacrificing long-term position for short-term profit, waiting too long to respond to price-cutting, not getting rid of excess capacity as growth slows, and overinvesting in efforts to boost sales growth.

STRATEGIES FOR FIRMS IN MATURE OR DECLINING INDUSTRIES

Many firms operate in industries where demand is growing slower than the economywide average or even declining. Although cash-flow maximization, selling out, and closing down are obvious strategies for uncommitted competitors with dim long-term prospects, strong competitors may be able to achieve good performance in a stagnant market environment.[7] Stagnant demand by itself is not enough to make an industry unattractive. Selling out may or may not be practical, and closing operations is always a last resort.

Businesses competing in slow-growth/declining industries have to accept the difficult realities of continuing stagnancy and resign themselves to performance goals consistent with available market opportunities. Cash flow and return on investment criteria are more appropriate than growth-oriented performance measures, but sales and market share growth are by no means ruled out. Strong competitors may be able to take sales from weaker rivals, and either the acquisition or exit of weaker firms creates opportunities for the remaining companies to boost their sales and market shares significantly.

In general, the strategies of firms that have succeeded in stagnant industries have three themes:[8]

1. *Pursue a focus strategy by identifying, creating, and exploiting the growth segments within the industry.* Slow-growth or declining markets, like other markets, are composed of numerous segments and subsegments. Frequently, one or more of these segments is growing rapidly, despite a lack of growth in the industry as a whole. An astute competitor who is first to concentrate on the most attractive segments can escape stagnating sales and profits and possibly achieve competitive advantage in the target segments.

2. *Pursue differentiation based on quality improvement and product innovation.* Either enhanced quality or innovation can rejuvenate demand by creating important new growth segments or inducing buyers to trade up. Successful product innovation opens up an avenue for competing besides meeting or beating rivals' prices. Differentiation based on successful innovation has the additional advantage of being difficult and expensive for rival firms to imitate.

3. *Work diligently and persistently to drive costs down.* When increases in sales cannot be counted on to generate increases in earnings, an alternative strategy is to improve profit margins and return on investment by continuously reducing operating costs and increasing efficiency year after year.

---

[7] R. G. Hamermesh and S. B. Silk, "How to Compete in Stagnant Industries," *Harvard Business Review* 57, no. 5 (September–October 1979), p. 161.

[8] Ibid., p. 162.

Ways to achieve lower-cost position include (1) improving the manufacturing process via automation and increased specialization, (2) consolidating underutilized production facilities, (3) adding more distribution channels to ensure the unit volume needed for low-cost production, and (4) closing low-volume, high-cost distribution outlets.

These three strategic themes are not mutually exclusive.[9] Attempts to introduce new innovative versions of a product can *create* a fast-growing market segment. Similarly, relentless pursuit of operating efficiencies paves the way to price reductions that create price-conscious growth segments. Note, also, that all three themes are based on the three generic competitive strategies—all we indicate here is how to apply them to fit opportunities and conditions in an otherwise tough industry environment.

The most attractive declining industries are those in which decline is reasonably slow, there is a big built-in demand base, and some profitable niches remain. The pitfalls of continuing to compete in a stagnating market are: (1) firms may get trapped in a profitless war of attrition, (2) weakly positioned companies can drain their cash flow (thus accelerating their demise), and (3) firms can be overly optimistic about the industry's future and wait complacently for things to get better.

Illustration Capsule 12 describes the creative approach taken by Yamaha to reverse declining market demand for pianos.

ILLUSTRATION CAPSULE 12

YAMAHA'S STRATEGY IN THE PIANO INDUSTRY

For some years now, worldwide demand for pianos has been declining—in the mid-1980s the decline was 10 percent annually. Modern-day parents have not put the same stress on music lessons for their children as prior generations of parents did. In an effort to see if it could revitalize its piano business, Yamaha conducted a market research survey to learn what use was being made of pianos in households that owned one. The survey revealed that the overwhelming majority of the 40 million pianos in American, European, and Japanese households were seldom used. In most cases, the reasons the piano had been purchased no longer applied. Children had either stopped taking piano lessons or were grown and had left the household; adult household members played their pianos sparingly, if at all—only a small percentage were accomplished piano players. Most pianos were serving as a piece of fine furniture and were in good

(continued)

---

[9] Ibid., p. 165.

condition despite not being tuned regularly. The survey also confirmed that the income levels of piano owners were well above average.

Yamaha's piano strategists saw the idle pianos in these upscale households as a potential market opportunity. The strategy that emerged entailed marketing an attachment that would convert the piano into an old-fashioned automatic player piano capable of playing a wide number of selections recorded on 3½-inch floppy disks (the same kind used to store computer data). The player piano conversion attachment carried a $2,500 price tag. Concurrently, Yamaha introduced Disklavier, an upright acoustic player piano model that could play *and record* performances up to 90 minutes long; the Disklavier retailed for $8,000. At year-end 1988 Yamaha offered 30 prerecorded disks for $29.95 each. Another 30 selections were scheduled for release in 1989. Yamaha believed that these new high-tech products held potential to reverse the downtrend in piano sales.

STRATEGIES FOR COMPETING IN FRAGMENTED INDUSTRIES

A number of industries are made up of numerous small and medium-sized companies, many privately held and none with a king-sized share of total industry sales.[10] The key competitive feature of a fragmented industry is the absence of highly visible, well-known market leaders with the power to "dominate" the industry and set the tone of competition. Examples of fragmented industries include book publishing, landscaping and plant nurseries, kitchen cabinets, oil tanker shipping, auto repair, restaurants, public accounting, women's dresses, poultry processing, metal foundries, meat packing, paperboard boxes, log homes, hotels and motels, and furniture.

An industry can be populated with a host of small competitors for many reasons, some historical and some economic:

- Low entry barriers.
- An absence of scale economies.
- Diverse market needs in different geographic areas so demand for any particular product version is small and there is not enough volume to support producing, distributing, or marketing on a scale advantageous to larger firms.
- The need of buyers for relatively small quantities of customized products (as in business forms, advertising, and interior design).
- High degrees of product differentiation based on image.
- High transportation costs (which limit the radius a plant can economically service—as in concrete blocks, mobile homes, milk, and gravel).

---

[10] This section is summarized from Porter, *Competitive Strategy,* chap. 9.

- Local regulatory requirements that make each geographic area somewhat unique.
- Newness of the industry such that no firms have yet developed the skills and resources to command a significant market share.

Some fragmented industries consolidate naturally as they mature. The stiffer competition in a slow-growth industry produces a shakeout of weak, inefficient firms and a greater concentration of large, visible sellers. Other fragmented industries remain atomistically competitive because it is inherent to the nature of their business. And still others remain "stuck" in a fragmented state because existing firms lack the resources or ingenuity to employ a strategy that might promote industry consolidation.

Firms in fragmented industries usually are in a weak bargaining position with buyers and with suppliers. Entry is usually easy. Competition from substitutes may or may not be a major factor. In such an environment, the best a firm can hope for is a loyal customer base and a big enough sales volume to be successful. Competitive strategies based on low-cost, on some kind of differentiation theme, or on focus approaches are all viable except when the industry's product is highly standardized; then competitors are relegated to a strategy based on low cost or on focused specialization. Specific competitive strategy options include:

- *Constructing and operating "formula" facilities*—This is an attractive approach to achieving low cost when the firm must operate facilities at multiple locations. It involves designing a standard facility, constructing outlets in optimum locations at minimum cost, and operating them in a super-efficient manner. McDonald's and 7-Eleven have pursued this strategy to perfection, earning excellent profits in their respective industries.
- *A bare bones no-frills posture*—When price competition is intense and profit margins are constantly under pressure, a lean operation based on low overhead, use of high-productivity/low-cost labor, tight budget control, and rigid adherence to a no-frills expenditure policy can place a firm in the best position to play the price-cutting game and still earn profits above the industry average.
- *Increasing customer value through integration*—Backward or forward integration may lower costs or enhance the value given to customers (like cutting to size, assembling components before shipment to customers, or providing technical advice to customers).
- *Specializing by product type*—When a fragmented industry produces a broad product line with many models and styles, a focus strategy based on specialization in a particular area of the whole line can be very effective. Some firms in the furniture industry specialize in only one furniture type such as brass beds, rattan and wicker, lawn and garden, and early American. In auto repair, some firms specialize in transmission repair, body work, and mufflers, brakes, and shocks.
- *Specializing by customer type*—A firm can cope with the intense competition of a fragmented industry by catering to customers with the least bargaining leverage (because they are small in size or because they pur-

chase small annual volumes); by specializing in serving customers who are the least price sensitive; by going after buyers interested in additional services, attributes, or other ''extras''; by serving customers who place custom orders; or by targeting buyers who have special needs or tastes.

• *Focusing on a limited geographic area*—Even though a firm in a fragmented industry is blocked from winning a big industrywide market share, it can still realize significant internal operating economies by blanketing a local/regional geographic area. Concentrating facilities and marketing activities on a limited territory can produce greater sales force efficiency, speed delivery and customer services, and permit saturation advertising, while avoiding the diseconomies of trying to duplicate the strategy on a national scale. Convenience food stores, dry cleaning establishments, savings and loan associations, and department store retailers have been successful in operating multiple locations within a limited geographic area.

In fragmented industries, firms have a wide degree of strategic freedom—many different strategic approaches can exist side-by-side.

STRATEGIES FOR COMPETING IN INTERNATIONAL MARKETS

The motivations for ''going international'' center around any of three factors: a desire to seek out new markets, a desire to achieve lower costs, or a desire to access natural resource deposits in other countries. Whichever the reason, crafting a successful strategy has to be situation-driven and requires careful analysis of the global nature of the business. Special attention has to be paid to how national markets differ as to buyer needs and habits, distribution channels, long-run growth potential, technological requirements, driving forces, and competitive pressures. In addition to market differences from country to country, there are three other situational considerations unique to international operations: cost variations among countries, fluctuating exchange rates, and host government trade policies.

Manufacturing Cost Variations. Differences in wage rates, worker productivity, inflation rates, energy costs, tax rates, and the like create sizable variations in manufacturing costs from country to country. Some countries have major manufacturing cost advantages over other countries because of their lower input costs (especially labor) or their unique natural resources. Such countries become principal production sites and export their products all over the world. Companies with facilities in these locations (or which source their products from contract manufacturers in these countries) have a competitive advantage over those that do not. The importance of this consideration is most evident in low-wage countries like Taiwan, South Korea, Mexico, and Brazil, which have become production havens for goods with high labor content.

Fluctuating Exchange Rates. The volatility of exchange rates greatly complicates the issue of locational cost advantages. Exchange rate fluctuations of 20 to 40 percent annually are not unusual. Changes of this magnitude can totally wipe out historical cost advantages and make once unattractive manufacturing locations much more viable. The strong dollar during 1984–85 made it more attractive for U.S. companies to manufacture in Europe. The fall of the dollar against the Japanese yen in 1987–88 eliminated much of the cost advantage Japanese manufacturers had over U.S. manufacturers and prompted many Japanese firms to establish U.S. production plants.

Host Government Trade Policies.   National governments have enacted all kinds of measures affecting international trade and the operation of foreign companies in their markets. Host governments may impose import tariffs and quotas, set local content requirements on goods made inside their borders by foreign-based companies, and set a floor on prices of imported goods. In addition, foreign firms can face a web of regulations regarding technical standards, product certification, prior approval of capital spending projects, withdrawal of funds from the country, and minority (sometimes majority) ownership by local citizens. Some governments also provide subsidies and low-interest loans to domestic companies to help them compete against foreign-based companies. Other governments, anxious to obtain new plants and jobs, offer foreign companies a helping hand in the form of subsidies, privileged market access, and technical assistance.

All these situational considerations, along with the obvious cultural and political differences, shape the kind of strategic approach needed to pursue international markets.

Types of International Strategies

There are six generic strategic options for participating in international markets:

1. *Licensing foreign firms to produce and distribute one's products* (in which case revenues from international sales will equal only the royalty income from sales made by licensees).
2. *Maintaining a national (one-country) production base and exporting goods to foreign markets* utilizing either company-owned or foreign-controlled forward distribution channels.
3. *A multicountry strategy* where a firm tries to outcompete all rivals by excelling in being responsive to buyer needs and other relevant conditions in each target national market. This approach works well when buyer needs are sufficiently different from country to country that all international competitors are impeded in trying to use a uniform global strategy. Country-specific strategic opportunities emerge when buyers in a country insist on special-order or highly customized products and when host countries enact codes or statutes requiring unusually strict manufacturing specifications and performance attributes.
4. *A global low-cost strategy* where strategy is based on the company being a low-cost supplier to buyers in most or all major markets of the world.

5. *A global differentiation strategy* where a firm concentrates on developing several differentiating attributes that will appeal to buyers in most of the world's critical markets.

6. *A global focus strategy* where company strategy is aimed at serving the same identifiable niche in each of many critical markets worldwide.

Licensing makes sense when a firm with valuable technical know-how has neither the internal organizational capability nor the resources to compete in foreign markets. By licensing the technology to foreign-based firms, it at least realizes income from fees and royalties.

Using domestic plants as a production base for exporting goods to foreign markets is an excellent initial strategy for achieving international sales growth. It minimizes both risk and capital requirements, and it is a sensible way to test the international waters. Whether such a strategy can be pursued successfully over the long run hinges on the relative cost competitiveness of the one-country production base. In some industries, firms gain additional scale economies and experience curve benefits from centralizing production in one or several giant-scale plants whose output capability exceeds demand in any one national market; to capture such economies a company must export to markets in other countries.

The pros and cons of a multicountry strategy versus a global strategy are a bit more complex.

A Multicountry Strategy or a Global Strategy?

The logic and appeal of a multicountry strategy derives from the variability of cultural, economic, political, and competitive conditions in countries across the globe. The more diverse national market conditions are, the stronger the appeal for a *multicountry strategy* where the company tailors its strategic approach to fit each host country's market situation. In such cases, the company's international strategy is chiefly a collection of country strategies. However, in industries like automobiles, computers, motorcycles, sewing machines, heavy construction equipment, and commercial aircraft, products and buyer requirements are quite similar, allowing for a uniform worldwide or *global strategy*. Table 6–1 provides a point-by-point comparison of multicountry versus global strategies. The question of which to pursue is the foremost strategic issue firms face when they compete in international markets.

The strength of a multicountry strategy is that it provides an excellent way to match strategy to host country circumstances. A strategy of national responsiveness is essential when there are significant country-to-country differences in customers' needs and buying habits, when buyer demand for the product exists in a comparatively few national markets, when different technologies and specifications are required in different countries, and when the trade restrictions of host governments are so diverse and complicated as to virtually preclude a worldwide market approach. The problem, however, is that a multicountry strategy entails

Table 6-1 DIFFERENCES BETWEEN MULTICOUNTRY AND GLOBAL STRATEGIES

	Multicountry strategy	Global strategy
Strategic arena	Selected target countries and trading areas	Most countries which constitute *critical markets* for the product (at least North America, the European Community, and the Pacific Rim [Australia, Japan, South Korea, and Southeast Asia])
Business strategy	Custom strategies to fit the circumstances of each host country situation; little or no strategy coordination across countries	Same basic strategy worldwide; minor country-by-country variations where essential
Product-line strategy	Adapted to local needs	Mostly standardized products sold worldwide
Production strategy	Plants scattered across many host countries	Plants located on the basis of maximum competitive advantage (in low-cost countries, close to major markets, geographically scattered to minimize shipping costs, or use of a few world-scale plants to maximize economies of scale—as most appropriate)
Sources of supply for raw materials and components	Suppliers in host country preferred (local facilities meeting local buyer needs; some local sourcing may be required by host government)	Attractive suppliers from anywhere in the world
Marketing and distribution	Adapted to practices and culture of each host country	Much more worldwide coordination; minor adaptation to host country situations if required
Company organization	Form subsidiary companies to handle operations in each host country; each subsidiary operates more or less autonomously to fit host country conditions	All major strategic decisions are closely coordinated at global headquarters; a global organizational structure is used to unify the operations in each country

very little strategic coordination across country boundaries nor is it tied tightly to competitive advantage considerations. The primary orientation of a multicountry strategy is responsiveness to local country conditions, not building a multinational-based competitive advantage over other international competitors and the domestic companies of host countries.

A global strategy, because it is more uniform from country to country, can concentrate on securing a sustainable competitive advantage over both international and domestic rivals. Whenever national differences are small enough to be accommodated within a global strategy, a global strategy is preferable because of its competitive advantage potential.

The Benefits of Being a Global Competitor

In international markets there are three principal types of competitors:[11]

- Firms whose long-term strategic intent is *global dominance* or, at least, a high rank among global market leaders.
- Firms whose overriding strategic intent is *defending domestic dominance* in their home market, even though they participate in many foreign markets.
- Firms whose primary strategic orientation is *host country responsiveness*— this includes companies with a multicountry strategy and companies that operate only in their home country.

The three types of firms are *not* equally well-positioned to participate profitably in international markets. Consider the case of a purely domestic U.S. company in competition with a globally competitive Japanese company. The Japanese company can cut its prices in the U.S. market to gain market share at the expense of the U.S. company, subsidizing any losses with profits earned in its home sanctuary and in other foreign markets. The purely domestic U.S. company has no effective way to retaliate. It is vulnerable even if it is the dominant domestic company. However, if the U.S. company is a multinational competitor and operates in Japan as well as elsewhere, it can counter Japanese pricing in the United States with retaliatory price-cuts in its competitor's main profit sanctuary, Japan, and in other countries where it competes against the same Japanese company. To defend against aggressive international competitors intent on global dominance, a company almost has to be a multinational competitor.

The Concept of Critical Markets.   Building a defense against global competitors does not require competing in all or even most foreign markets, but it does mean competing in all critical markets. *Critical markets* are markets in countries that:

- Are the profit sanctuaries of key competitors.
- Provide big volume sales and customers who insist on state-of-the-art products and services.
- Offer exceptionally good profit margins due to weak competitive pressures.[12]

The more critical markets a company participates in, the greater capability it has to use cross-subsidization as a defense against aggressive price-cuts by competitors intent on global dominance.

The Concept of Manufacturing Share.   Another important consideration in international competition is the concept of *manufacturing share* as distinct from brand share or market share. For example, although less than 40 percent of all the video

---

[11] C. K. Prahalad and Yves L. Doz, *The Multinational Mission* (New York: Free Press, 1987), p. 52.

[12] Ibid., p. 61.

recorders sold in the United States carry a Japanese brand, Japanese companies do 100 percent of the manufacturing—all sellers source their video recorders from Japanese manufacturers.[13] In microwave ovens, Japanese brands have less than a 50 percent share of the U.S. market, but the Japanese manufacturing share is over 85 percent. *Manufacturing share is significant because it is a better indicator than market share of the industry's low-cost producer.* In a globally competitive industry where some competitors are intent on global dominance, being the worldwide low-cost producer is a powerful competitive advantage. Achieving such status usually requires a company to have the largest worldwide manufacturing share, with production centralized in one or a few state-of-the-art plants capable of the greatest economies of scale. However, important marketing and distribution economies associated with multinational operations can also yield low-cost leadership.

Winners and Losers in International Markets.   The preceding discussion highlights why both a purely domestic company and a multicountry competitor with no strategic coordination between its country strategies are vulnerable to competition from rivals intent on global dominance. A global strategy can defeat a domestic-only strategy because a one-country company cannot effectively defend its market share over the long-term against a global company with cross-subsidization capability. The global company can use lower prices to siphon the domestic company's customers, all the while gaining market share, building market strength, and covering losses with profits earned in other critical markets. A domestic company's best short-term hope is to seek protection from its government in the form of tariff barriers, import quotas, and antidumping penalties. In the long-term, the domestic company must find ways to compete on a more equal footing—a difficult task when it must charge a price to cover average costs while the global competitor can charge a price only high enough to cover the incremental costs of selling in the domestic company's profit sanctuary.

While a multicountry strategist has some cross-subsidy defense against a global strategist, its vulnerability comes from a lack of competitive advantage and a probable cost disadvantage. A global competitor with a big manufacturing share and state-of-the-art plants is almost certain to be a lower-cost producer than a multicountry strategist with many small plants and short production runs turning out specialized products country-by-country. Companies pursuing a multicountry strategy thus have to develop focusing and differentiation advantages keyed to local responsiveness to defend against a global competitor. Such a defense is adequate in industries with significant national differences to impede use of a global strategy. But if an international rival can accommodate the necessary local responsiveness within a global strategy approach and still retain a cost edge, then a global strategy can defeat a multicountry strategy. Illustration Capsule 13, which discusses how Nestlé became the world's number one food company, shows the power of a global strategy in today's markets.

---

[13] Ibid., p. 60.

ILLUSTRATION CAPSULE 13

NESTLÉ'S GLOBAL STRATEGY IN FOODS

Once a stodgy Swiss manufacturer of chocolate, Nestlé became one of the first multinational companies and then embarked on a global strategy during the 1980s. The themes of the Nestlé strategy were: acquire a wider lineup of name brands, achieve the economies of worldwide distribution and marketing, accept short-term losses to build a more profitable market share over the long term, and adapt products to local cultures when needed. In 1989 Nestlé ranked as the world's largest food company with nearly $28 billion in revenues, market penetration on all major continents, and plants in over 60 countries:

Continent	1988 sales	Major products
Europe	$10.2 billion	Nescafé instant coffee, Vittel mineral water, Chambourcy yogurt, Findus and Lean Cuisine frozen foods, Herta cold cuts, Sundy cereal bars, chocolate candy, Buitoni pasta
North America	$ 6.7 billion	Nescafé instant coffee, Carnation Coffee-Mate, Friskies pet foods, Stouffer frozen foods, Nestlé Crunch chocolate bars, Hills Bros. coffee
Asia	$ 3.1 billion	Nescafé instant coffee, Nido powdered milk, Maggi chili powder, infant cereals, and formulas
Latin America	$ 2.4 billion	Nescafé instant coffee, Nido powdered milk, infant cereal, Milo malt-flavored beverages
Africa	$ 0.7 billion	Nescafé instant coffee, Maggi bouillon cubes, Nespray powdered milk, Nestlé chocolates, Milo malt-flavored beverages
Oceania (Australia, New Zealand)	$ 0.6 billion	Nescafé instant coffee, Findus frozen foods, Lean Cuisine frozen foods

The Nestlé strategy was a response to two driving forces affecting the food industry in more and more nations around the globe: (1) changing consumer demographics, tastes, and cooking habits and (2) the new cost-volume economics of increasingly "high-tech" food products like gourmet dinners, refrigerated foods, packaged mixes, and even coffee. In both industrialized and developing nations, the 1980s were characterized by growing numbers of relatively affluent single professionals and two-income couples with more cosmopolitan food tastes and less price-sensitive grocery budgets. Moreover, microwave ovens were fast becoming a

(continued)

Source: The information in this capsule was drawn from Shawn Tully, "Nestlé Shows How to Gobble Markets," *Fortune,* January 16, 1989, pp. 74–78.

standard household item, a development that not only affected week-night and weekend food preparation methods but also changed the kinds of at-home food products people were buying. Products that appealed to this segment had tremendous growth potential. However, bringing such items to market was quickly turned into a high-risk, capital-intensive, R&D-oriented business that required millions of dollars of up-front capital for new product development and market testing, and millions more for advertising and promotional support to win shelf space in grocery chains. To get maximum mileage out of such investments, make up for the cost of product failures, and keep retail prices affordable began to take a larger and larger volume of sales, often more than could be generated from a single national market.

Nestlé management grasped early on that these driving forces would act to globalize the food industry and that companies with worldwide distribution capability, strong brand names, and the flexibility to adapt versions of the basic product to local tastes would gain significant competitive advantages. A series of acquisitions gave Nestlé a strong lineup of brands, some important new food products to push through its distribution channels, and a bigger presence in some key country markets. In 1985 Nestlé bought Carnation (Pet evaporated milk, Friskies pet foods, and Coffee-Mate nondairy creamer) and Hills Bros. coffee (the number three coffee brand in the United States) to strengthen its North American presence. In 1988, Nestlé acquired Rountree, a British chocolate company whose leading candy bar is Kit Kat, and Buitoni, an Italian pastamaker. Shortly after the Rountree acquisition, Nestlé management shifted worldwide responsibility for mapping chocolate strategy and developing new candy products from Nestlé headquarters in Vevey, Switzerland, to Rountree's headquarters in York, England. Nestlé management believed this decentralization put the company's candy business in the hands of people "who think about chocolate 24 hours a day." As of 1989, almost everything Nestle' sold involved food products, and the company was the world's largest producer of coffee, powdered milk, candy, and frozen dinners.

The star performer in Nestlé's lineup was coffee, with 1988 sales of $4.7 billion and operating profits of $600 million. Nestlé's Nescafé brand was the leader in virtually every national market except the United States (Philip Morris's Maxwell House brand was the U.S. leader, but Nescafé was number two and Hills Bros., purchased by Nestlé in 1985, was number three). Nestlé produced 200 types of instant coffee, from lighter blends for the U.S. market to dark espressos for Latin America. Four coffee research labs spent a combined $50 million annually to experiment with new blends in aroma, flavor, and color. Although instant coffee sales were

(continued)

declining worldwide due to the comeback of new-style automatic coffeemakers, they were rising in two tea-drinking countries, Britain and Japan. As the cultural shift from tea to coffee took hold during the 1970s in Britain, Nestlé pushed its Nescafé brand hard, coming out with a market share of about 50 percent. In Japan, Nescafé was considered a luxury item; the company made it available in fancy containers suitable for gift-giving.

Another star performer has been the company's Lean Cuisine line of low-calorie frozen dinners produced by Stouffer, a company Nestlé acquired in the 1970s. Introduced in 1981 in the United States, the Lean Cuisine line has boosted Stouffer's U.S. market share in frozen dinners to 38 percent. To follow up on its U.S. success, Nestlé introduced Lean Cuisine into the British market. At the time, Nestlé products in British supermarkets were mostly low-margin items, from fish sticks to frozen hamburger patties. British managers proposed a bold upgrading to a line of more expensive, high-margin items led by Lean Cuisine. Nestlé headquarters endorsed the plan and indicated a willingness to absorb four years of losses to build market share and make Lean Cuisine a transatlantic hit. The Lean Cuisine line was introduced in Britain in 1985. By 1988 the Lean Cuisine line in Britain included 12 entrées tailored to British tastes, from cod with wine sauce to Kashmiri chicken curry. By 1989 Nestlé had a 33 percent share of the British market for frozen dinners. Sales were expected to top $100 million in 1989, putting the Lean Cuisine brand into the black in Britain for the first time since its introduction to the British market. Lean Cuisine has recently been introduced in France.

Western Europe is Nestlé's top target for the early 1990s. The 1992 shift to free trade among the 12 member countries in the European Community will sweep away trade barriers which, according to a recent study, cost food companies over $1 billion in added distribution and marketing costs. With market unification in the 12-country EC, Nestlé sees major opportunities to gain wider distribution of its products, achieve economies, and exploit its skills in transferring products and marketing methods from one country and culture to another.

In summary, international strategies are grounded in competitive advantage— a technological edge, unique ability to serve certain national markets, transferable marketing or manufacturing skills, a low-cost advantage, a product differentiation advantage, or the ability to subsidize the building of market share in one national market with profits earned in others. Low-cost advantages can derive from (1) low-cost plant locations, (2) scale economies and experience curve benefits that exceed those realizable from competing in just one national market, (3) opportunities to transfer skills and business expertise from one country to another at little incremental cost, and (4) marketing and distribution economies associated with multinational operations. Competing internationally can give a company a differentiation edge in image, reputation, and credibility when it comes to serving customers whose own business is international. Customers with multinational operations often have needs that are best served by a company with personnel and facilities in the same countries. International competitors with cross-subsidization capabilities have an important competitive advantage over domestic-only companies. Thus the problem of matching company strategy to international markets is framed by two questions:[14]

1. Can strategic advantage be gained from competing on a multicountry or global basis?
2. How threatened is the company by international competitors—will it face strategic disadvantages if it does *not* compete on an international basis?

International competition is very much a game of offense *and* defense.

STRATEGIES FOR INDUSTRY LEADERS

The competitive positions of industry leaders normally range from stronger than average to powerful. Leaders typically enjoy a well-known reputation, and strongly entrenched leaders have proven strategies (keyed either to low-cost leadership or differentiation). Some of the best-known industry leaders are Anheuser-Busch (beer), IBM (computers), McDonald's (fast food), Gillette (razor blades), Campbell Soup (canned soups), Gerber (baby food), Xerox (copying machines), AT&T (long-distance telephone service) and Levi Strauss (jeanswear). The main strategic concern for a leader revolves around how to sustain a leadership position, perhaps becoming *the dominant leader* as opposed to *a leader*. However, the pursuit of industry leadership and large market share per se is primarily important because of the competitive advantage and profitability that accrues to leadership.

Three contrasting strategic postures are open to industry leaders and dominant firms:[15]

1. *Stay-on-the-offensive strategy*—This strategy rests on the principle that the best defense is a good offense. Offensive-minded leaders try to be "first-movers" to translate "being first" into a sustainable competitive advantage and solidify their reputation as *the* leader. The key to staying on the offensive is relentless pursuit of innovation and launching initiatives that keep rivals guessing, off-balance, and scrambling to respond. Using innovation to become *the* source of new products, better performance features, quality enhancements, improved customer services, and ways to cut production costs helps a leader avoid becoming complacent and keeps management trained on a goal of continuous improvement. The array of offensive options also includes initiatives to expand overall

[14] Porter, *Competitive Strategy,* p. 276.

[15] Kotler, *Marketing Management,* chap. 23; Porter, *Competitive Advantage* (New York: Free Press, 1985), chap. 14; and Ian C. MacMillan, "Seizing Competitive Initiative," *Journal of Business Strategy* 2, no. 4 (Spring 1982), pp. 43–57.

industry demand—discovering new uses for the product, attracting new users, and promoting more frequent use. In addition, a clever offensive leader stays alert for ways to make it easier and less costly for potential customers to switch their purchases from runner-up firms. Unless a leader's market share is already so dominant that it presents a threat of antitrust action (a market share under 60 percent is usually "safe"), it should stay on the offensive by trying to grow *faster* than the industry as a whole and to wrest market share from rivals. A leader whose growth does not equal or outpace the industry average is losing ground to competitors.

2. *Fortify-and-defend strategy*—The essence of "fortify and defend" is to make it harder for new firms to enter and challengers to gain ground. The goals of a strong defense are to hold onto present market share, strengthen current market position, and protect whatever competitive advantage the firm has. Specific defensive actions can include:

- Attempting to raise the competitive ante for challengers and new entrants via increased spending for advertising, higher levels of customer service, and bigger R&D outlays.
- Introducing more of the company's own brands to match the product attributes challenger brands have or could employ.
- Figuring out ways to make it harder or more costly for customers to switch to rival products.
- Broadening the product line to close off possible vacant niches for competitors to slip into.
- Keeping prices reasonable and quality attractive.
- Building new capacity ahead of market demand to try to block the market expansion potential of smaller competitors.
- Investing enough to remain cost competitive and technologically progressive.
- Patenting feasible alternative technologies (as Xerox did early in the development of the copier industry).
- Signing exclusive contracts with the best suppliers and dealer/distributors.

A fortify-and-defend strategy is appealing to firms that have already achieved industry dominance and don't wish to risk antitrust action. It is also well-suited to situations where a firm wishes to milk its present position for profits and cash flow because the industry's prospects for growth are low or because further gains in market share do not appear profitable enough to go after. But the fortify-and-defend theme always entails trying to grow as fast as the market as a whole (to stave off market share slippage) and reinvesting enough capital in the business to protect the leader's ability to compete.

3. *Competitive harassment strategy*—With this strategy the leader sends a clear message to rivals that any moves to cut into the leader's business will be "bloody" and will provoke heavy-handed retaliation. The strategic themes include being quick to meet all competitive price-cuts (with even larger cuts if necessary), being ready to counter with large-scale promotional campaigns if

smaller firms boost their advertising budgets in an attempt to increase their market share, offering better deals to the major customers of next-in-line or "maverick" firms, and using "hardball" measures to signal aggressive-minded small firms regarding who should lead and who should follow. (Possible signaling options include pressuring distributors not to carry rivals' products, having salespersons bad-mouth the products of aggressive small firms, or hiring the better executives of firms that "get out of line.") The objective of a harassment/confrontation type of competitive strategy is to enforce an unwritten tradition that smaller firms play follow the leader. Assuming the role of industry policeman gives the leader added strategic flexibility and "raises the ante" for would-be challengers.

STRATEGIES FOR RUNNER-UP FIRMS

Runner-up firms occupy weaker market positions than the industry leader(s). Some runner-up firms are *market challengers;* they are willing to fight one another and the leader(s) for a bigger market share and a stronger market position. Other runner-up firms play the role of *content followers;* they have no desire to rock the boat and are willing to coast along in their current position because profits are still adequate. Follower firms have no urgent strategic issue to confront beyond that of "What kinds of strategic changes do the leaders have in mind, and what do we need to do to follow along?"

A challenger firm interested in improving its market standing needs a strategy aimed at building a competitive advantage of its own. *Rarely can a runner-up firm improve its competitive position by imitating the leading firms; indeed, a cardinal rule in offensive strategy is to avoid attacking a leader head-on with an imitative strategy, regardless of the resources and staying power an underdog may have.*[16] Moreover, if a challenger has a 5 percent market share and needs a 20 percent share to earn attractive returns, it needs a more creative approach to competing than just "try harder."

In cases where large-size yields significantly lower unit costs and give large-share firms an important cost advantage, small-share firms have only two viable strategic options: move to increase their market share or withdraw from the business (gradually or quickly). The competitive strategies most used to build market share are based on (1) becoming a lower-cost producer and using lower price to win customers away from weak, higher-cost rivals and (2) using differentiation strategies based on quality, technological superiority, better customer service, or innovation. Achieving low-cost leadership is usually open to an underdog only when one of the market leaders is not already solidly positioned as the industry's low-cost producer. But a small-share firm may still be able to reduce its cost disadvantage by merging with or acquiring smaller firms; the combined market shares may provide the needed access to size-related economies. Other options include revamping its activity-cost chain to produce the needed cost-savings and finding ways to better control the cost drivers.

---

[16] Porter, *Competitive Advantage*, p. 514.

In situations where scale economies or experience curve effects are small and a large market share produces no cost advantage, runner-up companies have more strategic flexibility and can consider any of the following six approaches:[17]

1. *Vacant niche strategy*—The principle underlying this competitive positioning approach is to concentrate on customer or end-use applications that major firms have bypassed or neglected. An "ideal" vacant niche is of sufficient size and scope to be profitable, has some growth potential, is well-suited to a firm's own capabilities and skills, and is outside the interest of leading firms. Two examples of a successful vacant niche focus strategy are regional commuter airlines serving small and medium-sized population centers with too few passengers to attract the interest of major airlines, and small "no-name" tire manufacturers (like Armstrong Tire and Cooper Tire) that have managed to find enough holes in the market to survive alongside Goodyear, Michelin, Bridgestone, Uniroyal-Goodrich, and Firestone.

2. *Specialist strategy*—A specialist firm trains its competitive efforts on a few carefully chosen product-customer-use segments and does not try to compete for all types of customers with a full product line appealing to all different needs and functions. The strategic emphasis here is on differentiating attributes where the company has or can develop special expertise and where such expertise will be highly valued by customers. Smaller companies that have successfully used a specialist type of focus strategy include Formby's (stains and finishes for wood furniture, especially refinishing); Liquid Paper Co. (correction fluid for use by typists); Canada Dry (ginger ale, tonic water, and carbonated soda water); and American Tobacco (chewing tobacco and snuff).

3. *"Ours-is-better-than-theirs" strategy*—The approach here is to use a combination focus-differentiation strategy keyed to product quality. Sales and marketing efforts are aimed at quality-conscious and performance-oriented buyers. Fine craftsmanship, prestige quality, frequent product innovations and/or close contact with customers to develop a better product usually undergrid this "superior product" type of approach. Some examples include Beefeater and Tanqueray in gin, Tiffany in diamonds and jewelry, Chicago Cutlery in premium-quality kitchen knives, Baccarat in fine crystal, Mazola in cooking oil and margarine, Bally in shoes, and Pennzoil and Havoline in motor oil.

4. *Content follower strategy*—Follower firms deliberately refrain from initiating trend-setting strategic moves and from aggressive attempts to steal customers away from the leaders. Followers prefer approaches that will not provoke competitive retaliation, often opting for focus and differentiation strategies that keep them out of the leaders' paths. They react and respond rather than initiate and attack. They prefer defense to offense. And they rarely get out of line with the leaders on price. Burroughs (in computers) and Union Camp (in paper products) have been successful market followers by consciously concentrating on selected

[17] For more details, see Kotler, *Marketing Management*, pp. 397–412; R. G. Hamermesh, M. J. Anderson, Jr., and J. E. Harris, "Strategies for Low Market Share Businesses," *Harvard Business Review* 56, no. 3 (May–June 1978), pp. 95–102; and Porter, *Competitive Advantage*, chap. 15.

product uses and applications for specific customer groups, focused R&D, profits rather than market share, and cautious but efficient management.

5. *Growth via acquisition strategy*—One way to strengthen a company's position is to merge with or acquire weaker rivals to form an enterprise that has more competitive strength and a larger share of the market. Such beer manufacturers as Heileman, Stroh's, and Pabst owe their market share growth in the early 1980s to acquisition of smaller brewers. Likewise, a number of public accounting firms have achieved rapid growth and broader geographic coverage by acquiring or merging with smaller CPA firms.

6. *Distinctive image strategy*—Some runner-up companies build their strategies around ways to make themselves stand out from competitors. A variety of strategic approaches have been used: creating a reputation for charging the lowest prices, providing prestige quality at a good price, going all out to give superior customer service, designing unique product attributes, being a leader in new product introduction, or devising unusually creative advertising. Examples include Dr Pepper's strategy of calling attention to its distinctive taste, Apple Computer's approach to making it easier and interesting for people to use a personal computer, and Hyatt's use of architecture and luxurious hotel accommodations to appeal to upscale travelers and conventions.

In industries where big size is definitely a key success factor, firms with low market shares have some obstacles to overcome: (1) less access to economies of scale in manufacturing, distribution, or sales promotion; (2) difficulty gaining customer recognition; (3) an inability to afford mass media advertising on a grand scale; and (4) difficulty in funding capital requirements.[18] But *it is erroneous to view runner-up firms as less profitable or unable to hold their own against the biggest firms*. Many smaller firms earn healthy profits and enjoy good reputations with customers. Often the handicaps of smaller size can be surmounted and a profitable competitive position established by: (1) focusing on carefully chosen market segments where particular strengths can be developed and not attacking dominant firms head-on with price-cuts and increased promotional expenditure; (2) developing a distinctive competence in new-product development or technical capabilities, but only for the target market segments; and (3) using innovative/"dare-to-be-different"/"beat-the-odds" entrepreneurial approaches to outmanage stodgy, slow-to-change market leaders. Runner-up companies have a golden opportunity to gain market share if they make a leapfrog technological breakthrough, if the leaders stumble or become complacent, or if they have patience to nibble away at the leaders and build up their customer base over a long period of time.

STRATEGIES FOR WEAK BUSINESSES

A firm in an also-ran or declining competitive position has four basic strategic options. If it has the financial resources, it can launch a modest *strategic offensive*

---

[18] Hamermesh, Anderson, and Harris, "Strategies for Low Market Share Businesses," p. 102.

keyed either to low-cost production or to "new" differentiation themes, pouring enough money and talent into the effort to move up a notch or two in the industry rankings and become a respectable market contender within five years or so. It can pursue *aggressive defense,* using variations of the present strategy and fighting hard to keep sales, market share, profitability, and competitive position at current levels. It can opt for an *immediate abandonment* strategy and get out of the business, either by selling out to another firm or by closing down operations if a buyer cannot be found. Or it can employ a *harvest strategy* whereby reinvestment in the business is held to a bare-bones minimum and management's overriding objective is to generate the largest feasible short-term cash flow; the long-term objective of harvesting is orderly market exit. The gist of the first three options is self-explanatory. The fourth deserves more explanation.

A *harvest strategy* steers a middle course between maintenance and abandonment. Harvesting entails resource commitments in between those required to maintain the company's market position or get out as soon as possible. Harvesting is a phasing down or endgame approach in which strategy aims at an orderly market pullback and surrendering of market share, but in the process reaping a harvest of cash to deploy to other business endeavors.

The actions to harvest are fairly standard. The operating budget is reduced to a bare-bones level; stringent internal cost control is pursued. Capital investment in new equipment is given little if any financial priority depending on the current condition of fixed assets and on whether the harvest is to be fast or slow. Price may be raised, promotional expenses cut, quality reduced in not so visible ways, nonessential customer services curtailed, equipment maintenance decreased, and the like. The harvest objective is to *maximize short-term cash flow,* withdraw the funds from the business, and shift them into activities where the returns are more promising. It is understood that sales will shrink, but if costs can be cut proportionately then profits will erode slowly rather than rapidly.

Professor Kotler has suggested seven indicators of when a business should be harvested:[19]

1. When the industry's long-term prospects are unattractive.
2. When building up the business would be too costly or not profitable enough.
3. When the firm's market share is becoming increasingly costly to maintain or defend.
4. When reduced levels of competitive effort will not trigger an immediate falloff in sales.
5. When the enterprise can redeploy the freed resources in higher opportunity areas.
6. When the business is *not* a major component in a diversified corporation's portfolio of existing business interests.

---

[19] Philip Kotler, "Harvesting Strategies for Weak Products," *Business Horizons* 21, no. 5 (August 1978), pp. 17–18.

7. When the business does not contribute other desired features (sales stability, prestige, a well-rounded product line) to a company's overall business portfolio.

The more of these seven conditions present, the more ideal the business is for harvesting.

Harvesting strategies make the most sense in diversified companies whose business units have respectable market shares in unattractive industries. In such situations, cash flows from harvesting unattractive business units can be reallocated to business units with greater profit potential and better long-term industry attractiveness.

Crisis Turnarounds

Turnaround strategies come into play when a business worth rescuing goes into crisis. The objective is to arrest and reverse the sources of competitive and financial weakness as quickly as possible. The first task of rescue is diagnosis. What lies at the root of poor performance? Is it bad competitive strategy or poor implementation and execution of an otherwise workable strategy? Are the causes of distress beyond management control? Can the business be saved? Discerning what is wrong and how serious the firm's strategic problems are is a prerequisite to formulating a turnaround strategy.

Some of the most common causes of business trouble are ignoring the profit-depressing effects of an overly aggressive effort to "buy" market share with deep price-cuts, being burdened with heavy fixed costs because of an inability to utilize plant capacity, betting on R&D efforts to boost competitive position and profitability and failing to come up with effective innovations, betting on technological long-shots, being too optimistic about the ability to penetrate new markets, making frequent changes in strategy (because the previous strategy didn't work out), and being overpowered by the competitive advantages of more successful rivals. There are five generic approaches to achieving a business turnaround:[20]

- Revamping the existing strategy.
- Revenue-increasing strategies.
- Cost-reduction strategies.
- Asset reduction/retrenchment strategies.
- A combination of these.

Strategy Revision. When the cause of weak performance is diagnosed as "bad" strategy, the task of strategy overhaul can proceed along any of several paths: (1)

---

[20] For excellent discussions of the ins and outs of rescuing distressed firms, see Charles W. Hofer, "Turnaround Strategies," *Journal of Business Strategy* 1, no. 1 (Summer 1980), pp. 19–31; Donald F. Heany, "Businesses in Profit Trouble," *Journal of Business Strategy* 5, no. 4 (Spring 1985), pp. 4–13; and Eugene F. Finkin, "Company Turnaround," *Journal of Business Strategy* 5, no. 4 (Spring 1985), pp. 14–25.

shifting to a new competitive approach to rebuild the firm's market position, (2) overhauling internal operations and functional area strategies to better support the same overall business strategy, (3) merging with another firm in the industry and forging a new strategy keyed to the new firm's strengths, and (4) retrenching into a reduced core of products and customers more closely matched to the firm's strengths. The most appealing path depends on prevailing industry conditions, the firm s particular strengths and weaknesses vis-á-vis rival firms, and the severity of the crisis. "Situation analysis" of the industry, major competitors, the firm's own competitive position, and its skills and resources are prerequisites to action. As a rule, successful rescue of an ailing business needs to be predicated on a firm's strengths and its best opportunities.

Boosting Revenues. Revenue-increasing turnaround efforts aim at generating increases in sales volume. There are a number of revenue-building options: price-cuts, increased promotion, a bigger sales force, added customer services, and quickly achieved product improvements. If demand is price inelastic, revenues can be boosted by instituting a price increase instead of a price-cut. Attempts to increase sales revenues are necessary (1) when there is little or no room in the operating budget to cut expenses and still break even and (2) when the key to restoring profitability is increased utilization of existing capacity.

Cutting Costs. Cost-reducing turnaround strategies work best when an ailing firm's cost structure is flexible enough to permit radical surgery, when operating inefficiencies are identifiable and readily correctable, and when the firm is relatively close to its break-even point. Accompanying a general belt-tightening can be an increased emphasis on budgeting and cost control, elimination of jobs and hirings, modernization of existing plant and equipment to gain greater productivity, or postponement of capital expenditures.

Selling off Assets. Asset reduction/retrenchment strategies are essential when cash flow is a critical consideration and when the most practical way to generate cash is (1) through sale of some of the firm's assets (plant and equipment, land, patents, inventories, or profitable subsidiaries) and (2) through retrenchment (pruning marginal products from the product line, closing or selling older plants, reducing the work force, withdrawing from outlying markets, cutting back customer service, and the like). Sometimes, selling some of a firm's assets is done not so much to unload and stem cash drains as it is to raise funds to strengthen the remaining activities.

Combination Efforts. Combination turnaround strategies are usually essential in grim situations where fast action on a broad front is required. Likewise, combination actions frequently come into play when the rescue effort entails bringing in new managers and giving them a free hand to make whatever changes they see fit. The tougher the problems, the more likely the solutions will involve a multi-pronged approach.

Turnaround efforts tend to be high-risk undertakings and often fail. A recent study of 64 companies found no successful turnarounds among the most troubled companies in eight basic industries.[21] Many waited too long to begin a turn-around. Others found themselves short of both cash and entrepreneurial talent to compete in a slow-growth industry characterized by a fierce battle for market share; better positioned rivals simply proved too strong to defeat in head-to-head combat.

KEY POINTS

Successful strategies fit a firm's *external* situation (industry and competitive conditions) and *internal* situation (strengths, weaknesses, opportunities, and threats). Table 6–2 provides a summary checklist of the most important situational considerations and strategic options. Matching strategy to the situation starts with an overview of the industry environment and the firm's competitive standing in the industry (columns 1 and 2 in Table 6–2):

1. What basic type of industry environment does the company operate in (emerging, rapid growth, mature, fragmented, global, commodity product)? What strategic options and strategic postures are best suited for this environment?
2. What position does the firm have in the industry (strong vs. weak vs. crisis-ridden; leader vs. runner-up vs. also-ran)? How does the firm's standing influence its strategic options, given the stage of the industry's development—in particular, which options have to be ruled out?

Next, the strategist needs to factor in the primary external and internal situational considerations (column 3) and judge how all the factors add up. This should narrow the firm's basic market share and investment options (column 4) and strategic options (column 5).

The final step is to custom-tailor the chosen generic strategic approaches (columns 4 and 5) to fit *both* the industry environment *and* the firm's standing vis-à-vis competitors. Here, it is important to be sure that (1) the customized aspects of the proposed strategy are well-matched to the firm's skills and capabilities and (2) the strategy addresses all of the strategic issues the firm confronts.

In singling out stronger strategies from weaker ones and weighing the pros and cons of the most attractive strategic options, the answers to the following questions often indicate the way to go:

*   What kind of competitive edge can the company realistically hope to have, and what strategic moves/approaches will it take to secure this edge?
*   Does the company have the skills and resources it needs to be successful in pursuing these moves and approaches? If not, can they be gotten?
*   Once built, how can the competitive advantage be protected? What defensive strategies need to be employed? Will rivals counterattack? What will it take to blunt their efforts?

---

[21] William K. Hall, "Survival Strategies in a Hostile Environment," *Harvard Business Review* 58, no. 5 (September–October 1980), pp. 75–85.

Table 6–2 MATCHING STRATEGY TO THE SITUATION: A CHECKLIST OF OPTIONAL STRATEGIES AND GENERIC SITUATIONS

Industry environments	Company positions/situations	Situational considerations	Market share and investment options	Strategy options

• Young, emerging industry
• Rapid growth
• Consolidating to a smaller group of competitors
• Mature/slow growth
• Aging/declining
• Fragmented
• International/global
• Commodity product orientation
• High technology/rapid changes
	• Dominant leader
	  —Global
	  —National
	  —Regional
	  —Local
	• Leader
	• Aggressive challenger
	• Content follower
	• Weak/distressed candidate for turn-around or exit
	• "Stuck in the middle"/no clear strategy or market image
		• External
		  —Driving forces
		  —Competitive pressures
		  —Anticipated moves of key rivals
		  —Key success factors
		  —Industry attractiveness
		• Internal
		  —Current company performance
		  —Strengths and weaknesses
		  —Opportunities and threats
		  —Cost position
		  —Competitive strength
		  —Strategic issues and problems
			• Grow and build
			  —Capture a bigger market share by growing *faster* than industry as a whole
			  —Invest heavily to capture growth potential
			• Fortify and defend
			  —Protect market share; grow at least as fast as whole industry
			  —Invest enough resources to maintain competitive strength and market position
			• Retrench and retreat
			  —Surrender weakly held positions when forced to, but fight hard to defend core markets/customer base
			  —Maximize short-term cash flow
			  —Minimize reinvestment of capital in the business
			• Overhaul and reposition
			  —Try to turn around
			• Abandon/liquidate
			  —Sell out
			  —Close down
				• Competitive approach
				  —Overall low-cost leadership
				  —Differentiation
				  —Focus/ specialization
				• Offensive initiatives
				  —Attack
				  —End run
				  —Guerrilla warfare
				  —Preemptive strikes
				• Defensive initiatives
				  —Fortify/protect
				  —Retaliatory
				  —Harvest
				• International initiatives
				  —Licensing
				  —Export
				  —Multicountry
				  —Global
				• Vertical integration initiatives
				  —Forward
				  —Backward

- Are any rivals particularly vulnerable? Should the firm mount an offensive to capitalize on these vulnerabilities? What offensive moves need to be employed?
- What additional strategic moves are needed to deal with driving forces in the industry, specific threats and weaknesses, and any other issues/ problems unique to the firm?

As the choice of strategic initiatives is developed, there are some specific pitfalls to watch for:

- Underestimating the reactions of rival firms.
- Designing an overly ambitious strategic plan—one that calls for a lot of different strategic moves and/or overtaxes the company's resources and capabilities.
- Selecting a strategy that represents a radical departure from or abandonment of the cornerstones of the company's prior success—a radical strategy change need not be rejected automatically, but it should be undertaken only after careful analysis.
- Choosing a strategy that is capable of succeeding only under the best of circumstances.
- Choosing a strategy that goes against the grain of the organization's culture or that conflicts with the values and philosophies of senior executives.

Table 6–3 SAMPLE FORMAT FOR A STRATEGIC ACTION PLAN

1. Key assumptions	4. Approaches/moves to gain competitive edge
2. Basic strategic direction • Strategic mission	5. Specific functional area support strategies • Production
• Key strategic objectives/performance targets	• Marketing/sales
	• Finance
3. Overall business strategy	• Personnel/human resources
	• Other

- Forming a strategy that leaves the firm "stuck in the middle" with no clearly defined strategic theme and no basis on which to distinguish itself from rivals, thus causing it to be regarded as "average."

Table 6–3 presents a generic format of a strategic action plan for a single-business enterprise.

SUGGESTED READINGS

Bolt, James F. "Global Competitors: Some Criteria for Success." *Business Horizons* 31, no. 1 (January–February 1988), pp. 34–41.

Carroll, Glenn R. "The Specialist Strategy." In *Strategy and Organization: A West Coast Perspective,* ed. Glenn Carroll and David Vogel. Boston: Pitman Publishing, 1984, pp. 117–28.

Feldman, Lawrence P., and Albert L. Page. "Harvesting: The Misunderstood Market Exit Strategy." *Journal of Business Strategy* 5, no. 4 (Spring 1985), pp. 79–85.

Finkin, Eugene F. "Company Turnaround." *Journal of Business Strategy* 5, no. 4 (Spring 1985), pp. 14–25.

Hall, William K. "Survival Strategies in a Hostile Environment." *Harvard Business Review* 58, no. 5 (September–October 1980), pp. 75–85.

Hamermesh, R. G., and S. B. Silk. "How to Compete in Stagnant Industries." *Harvard Business Review* 57, no. 5 (September–October 1979), pp. 161–68.

Harrigan, Kathryn R. *Strategic Flexibility.* Lexington, Mass.: Lexington Books, 1985, chaps. 6 and 8.

Heany, Donald F. "Businesses in Profit Trouble." *Journal of Business Strategy* 5, no. 4 (Spring 1985), pp. 4–13.

Hofer, Charles W. "Turnaround Strategies." *Journal of Business Strategy* 1, no. 1 (Summer 1980), pp. 19–31.

Hout, Thomas; Michael E. Porter; and Eileen Rudden. "How Global Companies Win Out." *Harvard Business Review* 60, no. 5 (September–October 1982), pp. 98–108.

Kotler, Philip. *Marketing Management: Analysis, Planning, Control.* 5th ed. Englewood Cliffs, N.J.: Prentice-Hall, 1984, chap. 11.

Lei, David. "Strategies for Global Competition." *Long-Range Planning* 22, no. 1 (February 1989), pp. 102–9.

Mayer, Robert J. "Winning Strategies for Manufacturers in Mature Industries." *Journal of Business Strategy* 8, no. 2 (Fall 1987), pp. 23–31.

Ohmae, Kenichi. *The Mind of the Strategist.* New York: Penguin Books, 1983, chaps. 8, 9, and 11.

Porter, Michael E. *Competitive Strategy: Techniques for Analyzing Industries and Competitors.* New York: Free Press, 1980, chaps. 9–13.

7 Corporate Diversification Strategies

. . . .

To acquire or not to acquire: that is the question.
Robert J. Terry

. . . .

Doing too many things isn't always a good idea—no matter how much better you think you can do them than someone else.
Dan Ciampi

In this chapter and the next, we move up one level in the strategy-making hierarchy. We examine how to go from formulating strategy for a single business to formulating an overall corporate strategy for a diversified company. A diversified company is a collection of individual businesses. Diversification makes corporate strategy-making a bigger-picture exercise than crafting line-of-business strategy. With business strategy, management's attention can be restricted to one industry environment and how to compete successfully in it. But diversification turns corporate strategy into a multibusiness, multi-industry strategic plan where corporate managers strive to elevate corporate performance via actions taken across a number of different business divisions competing in distinctly different industries. The task of building and then managing a multibusiness portfolio is so taxing that corporate executives spend far more time on corporate strategy issues than business strategy issues. Core responsibility for business-level strategy-making is normally delegated to the head of each business unit.

As explained in Chapter 2, corporate strategy in a diversified company is focused primarily on:

1. Making moves to position the company in the industries chosen for diversification (the basic strategic options here are to acquire a company in the target industry, form a joint venture with another company to enter the target industry, or start a new company internally and try to grow it from the ground up).

2. Taking actions to improve the long-term performance of the corporation's portfolio of businesses once diversification has been achieved (helping to strengthen the competitive positions of existing businesses, divesting businesses that no longer fit into management's long-range plans, and adding new businesses to the portfolio).

3. Trying to capture whatever strategic fit benefits exist within the portfolio of businesses and turn them into competitive advantage.

4. Evaluating the profit prospects of each business unit and steering corporate resources into the most attractive strategic opportunities.

In this chapter we survey the generic approaches to building and managing a diversified company. In Chapter 7 we will examine the techniques for analyzing a multibusiness corporate portfolio and for creating competitive advantage using various diversification approaches.

FROM SINGLE-BUSINESS CONCENTRATION TO DIVERSIFICATION

Most companies begin as small single-business enterprises serving a local or regional market. During a company's early years, the product line tends to be limited, the capital base thin, and the company's competitive position tenuous to weak. Usually the initial strategic theme is "grow and build," with chief strategic thrusts aimed at increasing sales volume, boosting market share, cultivating a loyal clientele, and building a stronger competitive position vis-á-vis rival firms. Price, quality, service, and promotion are fine-tuned to respond more precisely to a detailed market need. The product line is broadened to meet variations in customer wants and end-use applications. The company's cash flow and debt capacity are used to finance investments in new facilities and equipment needed to serve the growing customer base.

Opportunities for geographical market expansion customarily are pursued next. Usually the sequence of geographic expansion proceeds from local to regional to national to international markets, though the degree of penetration may be uneven in each area because of varying profit potentials. Geographic expansion may, of course, stop well short of global or even national proportions because of intense competition, lack of resources, or the unattractiveness of further market coverage.

Somewhere along the way the potential of vertical integration, either backward to sources of supply or forward to the ultimate consumer, has to be looked into. Whether and when vertical integration becomes a part of business strategy depends on how much it enhances a company's overall competitive strength.

So long as the company has its hands full trying to capitalize on all the expansion opportunities in its present industry, there is no urgency to explore diversification. But when company growth potential starts to wane, the strategic options are either to attempt a more intensive implementation of the current line-of-business strategy or begin focusing on diversification opportunities and expanding the kind of businesses the company is in. The strategy of building a diversified business portfolio raises the issue of what new businesses to get into. There are many ways to answer the question "What kind and how much diversification?" An almost infinite number of diversified business portfolios can be created; the businesses can be closely related with a high degree of strategic fit or they can be unrelated with little strategic fit. The portfolio can consist of several business units or dozens. And after a diversified portfolio has been put together, the time will come when management has to consider divesting or liquidating businesses that are no longer attractive or that fail to perform up to expectations.

Why a Single-Business Strategy Is Attractive

The power of single-business concentration is testified to by the market prominence of such familiar companies as McDonald's, Holiday Inn, Coca-Cola, BIC Pen, Apple Computer, Timex, Campbell Soup, Anheuser-Busch, Xerox, Gerber, and Polaroid, all of which gained their reputations in a single business. In the nonprofit sector, single-activity emphasis has proved successful for the Red Cross, Salvation Army, Christian Children's Fund, Girl Scouts, Phi Beta Kappa, and American Civil Liberties Union.

Concentrating on a single line of business (totally or with a small dose of diversification) offers some impressive competitive strengths and advantages. First, single-business concentration entails less ambiguity about "who we are and what we do." The efforts of the *total* organization can be directed down the *same* business path. All entrepreneurial eyes can be trained on keeping the firm's business strategy and competitive approach responsive to industry change and fine-tuned to customer needs. There is less chance that senior management's time or limited organizational resources will be stretched thinly over too many diverse activities. All the firm's managers, especially top executives, can have hands-on contact with the core business and in-depth knowledge of operations. (Most senior officers will probably have come up through the ranks and possess first-hand experience in field operations—something hard to expect of corporate managers in broadly diversified enterprises.) Furthermore, concentrating on one business carries a heftier built-in incentive for managers to direct the company toward capturing a stronger long-term competitive position in the industry as opposed to wringing out higher short-term profits. The full force of organizational resources can be used to become better at what the company does. A distinctive competence is more likely to emerge. And with management's attention focused on the business 24 hours a day, the probability is higher that ideas will emerge on how to improve production technology, better meet customer needs with innovative new product features, or enhance efficiencies anywhere in the activity-cost chains. Many single-business enterprises have parlayed their accumulated experience and distinctive expertise into a sustainable competitive advantage and a prominent leadership position in their industry.

The Risk of a Single-Business Strategy

The big risk of single-business concentration is putting all of a firm's eggs in one industry basket. If the industry stagnates, declines, or otherwise becomes unattractive, the future outlook dims, the company's growth rate becomes tougher to sustain, and superior profit performance is much harder to achieve. At times, changing customer needs, technological innovation, or new substitute products can undermine or wipe out a single-business firm—recall what plastic bottles and paper cartons did to the market for glass milk bottles, what word processing has done to the electric typewriter business, and what compact disc players and cassette tapes are doing to the record business. For this reason most single-business companies turn their attention to diversification when their business peaks out.

When Diversification Starts to Make Sense

To analyze when diversification makes the most strategic sense, consider Figure 7–1 where the variable of competitive position is plotted against various rates of market growth to create four distinct strategic situations that might be occupied by an undiversified company.[1] Firms that fall into the rapid market growth/strong competitive position box have several logical strategy options, the strongest of which in the near term may be continuing to pursue single-business concentration. Given the industry's high growth rate (and implicit long-term attractiveness), it makes sense for firms in this position to push hard to maintain or increase their market shares, to further develop their distinctive competences, and to make whatever capital investments are necessary to continue in a strong industry position. At some juncture, a company in this box may find it desirable to consider vertical integration to undergird its competitive strength. Later, when market growth starts to slow, prudence dictates looking into diversification as a means of spreading business risks and transferring the skills or expertise the company has built up into closely *related* businesses.

Firms falling into the rapid growth/weak position category should first consider what options they have for reformulating their present competitive strategy (given the high rate of market growth) and address the questions of (1) why their current approach to the market has resulted in a weak competitive position and (2) what it will take to become an effective competitor. In a rapidly expanding market, even weak firms should be able to improve their performance and become stronger competitors. If the firm is young and struggling to develop, it usually has a better chance for survival in a growing market where plenty of new business is up for grabs than it does in a stable or declining industry. However, if a weakly positioned company in a rapid-growth market lacks the resources and skills to hold its own, then either merger with another company in the industry that has the missing pieces or merger with an outsider having the cash and resources to support the company's development may be the best strategic alternative. Ver-

---

[1] C. Roland Christensen, Norman A. Berg, and Malcolm S. Salter, *Policy Formulation and Administration*, 7th ed. (Homewood, Ill.: Richard D. Irwin, 1976), pp. 16–18.

Figure 7–1 MATCHING CORPORATE STRATEGY ALTERNATIVES TO FIT AN UNDIVERSIFIED FIRM'S SITUATION

Competitive position

	Weak	Strong
Rapid	STRATEGY OPTIONS (in probable order of attractiveness) • Reformulate single-business concentration strategy (to achieve turnaround). • Acquire another firm in the same business (to strengthen competitive position). • Vertical integration (forward or backward if it strengthens competitive position). • Diversification. • Be acquired by/sell out to a stronger rival. • Abandonment (a last resort in the event all else fails).	STRATEGY OPTIONS (in probable order of attractiveness) • Continue single-business concentration —international expansion (if market opportunities exist). • Vertical integration (if it strengthens the firm's competitive position). • Related diversification (to transfer skills and expertise built up in the company's core business to adjacent businesses).
Slow	STRATEGY OPTIONS (in probable order of attractiveness) • Reformulate single-business concentration strategy (to achieve turnaround). • Merger with a rival firm (to strengthen competitive position). • Vertical integration (only if it strengthens competitive position substantially). • Diversification. • Harvest/divest. • Liquidation (a last resort in the event all else fails).	STRATEGY OPTIONS (in probable order of attractiveness) • International expansion (if market opportunities exist). • Related diversification. • Unrelated diversification. • Joint ventures into new areas. • Vertical integration (if it strengthens competitive position). • Continue single-business concentration (achieve growth by taking market share from weaker rivals.)

Market growth rate (vertical axis label on left)

tical integration, either forward or backward or both, becomes a necessary consideration for weakly positioned firms whenever such a move can materially strengthen the firm's competitive position. A third option is diversification into related or unrelated areas (if adequate financing can be found). If all else fails, abandonment—divestiture in the case of a multibusiness firm or liquidation in the case of a single-business firm—has to become an active strategic option. While abandonment may seem extreme because of the high growth potential, a company unable to make a profit in a booming market probably does not have the ability to make a profit at all—particularly if competition stiffens or industry conditions sour.

Companies with a weak competitive position in a relatively slow-growth market should look at (1) reformulating their present competitive strategy—to turn the firm's situation around and create a more attractive competitive position, (2) integrating forward or backward provided good profit improvement and competitive positioning opportunities exist, (3) diversifying into related or unrelated areas, (4) merging with another firm, (5) employing a harvest, then divest strategy, and (6) liquidating their position in the business by either selling out to another firm or closing down operations.

Companies that are strongly positioned in a slow-growth industry should consider using the excess cash flow from their existing business to begin a program of diversification. One good approach is related diversification keyed to the distinctive competence that gave the company its dominant position. But unrelated diversification is an option when there is no related business opportunity that appears especially attractive. Joint ventures with other organizations into new fields of endeavor are another logical possibility, and vertical integration could be attractive if solid profit improvement opportunities exist. A company so positioned usually puts a damper on new investment in its present facilities (unless important growth *segments* within the industry merit grow-and-build approaches) to free up the maximum amount of cash to deploy in new endeavors.

This discussion should make it clearer that *when to diversify* is partly a function of a firm's competitive position and partly a function of the remaining opportunities in its home-base industry. There really is no well-defined point at which companies in the same industry should diversify. Indeed, companies in the same industry can rationally choose different diversification approaches and launch them at different times.

BUILDING SHAREHOLDER VALUE: THE ULTIMATE JUSTIFICATION FOR DIVERSIFYING

The underlying purpose of corporate diversification is to build shareholder value. For diversification to enhance shareholder value, corporate strategy must do more than simply diversify the company's business risk by investing in more than one industry. Shareholders can achieve this sort of risk diversification on their own by purchasing stock in companies in different industries. Conceptually, shareholder value is not enhanced by diversification unless the performance of the group of businesses operating under the corporate umbrella is superior to what their performance would be as independent, stand-alone units. In reality, this test is hard to apply because it is a matter of speculation how the business units of a diversified company would have performed on their own. However, three tangible benefits of diversification, if present, are capable of increasing shareholder value. (1) The industries chosen for diversification must be attractive enough to produce a high average return on investment. (2) The cost to enter each target industry must not erode the potential for good profitability. (3) The corporation must bring some competitive advantage to the new business it enters or else the new business must offer added competitive advantage potential to the corporation's other businesses.[2] We refer to these three conditions as *the attractiveness test, the cost of entry test,* and *the better-off test,* respectively. The most successful diversification moves satisfy all three.

In using diversification to build shareholder value, managers can proceed along many different paths and employ a variety of corporate strategy approaches. To get a better understanding of the options corporate managers have in creating and managing a diversified group of businesses, we look at six types of diversification strategies:

1. Strategies for entering new industries—acquisition, start-up, and joint ventures.
2. Related diversification strategies.
3. Unrelated diversification strategies.
4. Divestiture and liquidation strategies.
5. Corporate turnaround, retrenchment, and restructuring strategies.
6. Multinational diversification strategies.

Strategies for Entering New Businesses

Entry into new businesses can take any of three forms: acquisition, internal start-up, and joint ventures. *Acquisition of an existing business* is probably the most popular approach to corporate diversification.[3] Acquiring an established organization has the advantage of much quicker entry into the target market. At the same time, it helps companies hurdle such entry barriers as technological inexperience, gaining access to reliable sources of supplies, being big enough to match rivals in efficiency and unit cost, having to spend enough on introductory promotions to gain market visibility and brand recognition, and getting adequate distribution access. In many industries, going the internal start-up route and trying to develop the knowledge, resources, scale of operation, and market reputation necessary to become an effective competitor can take years and entail all the problems of getting a brand new company off the ground and operating. However, finding the right kind of company to acquire sometimes presents a challenge.[4] The big dilemma an acquisition-minded firm faces is whether to buy a successful company at a high price or a struggling company at a "bargain" price. If the buying firm has little knowledge of the industry it is seeking to enter but ample capital, it is often better off purchasing a capable firm—unless the acquisition price is unreasonably high. The cost-of-entry test requires that the expected profit

---

[2] Michael E. Porter, "From Competitive Advantage to Corporate Strategy," *Harvard Business Review* 65, no. 3 (May–June 1987), pp. 46–49.

[3] In recent years, takeovers have become an increasingly used approach to acquisition. The term *takeover* refers to the attempt (often sprung as a surprise) of one firm to acquire ownership or control over another firm against the wishes of the latter's management (and perhaps some of its stockholders).

[4] Michael E. Porter, *Competitive Strategy: Techniques for Analyzing Industries and Competitors* (New York: Free Press, 1980), pp. 354–55.

stream of the acquired business provide an attractive return on the total acquisition cost. On the other hand, when the acquirer sees promising ways to transform a weak firm into a strong one and has the money, the know-how, and the patience to grow it, the struggling company may be the better investment.

Achieving diversification through *internal development* involves creating a new business entity in the desired industry and, starting from scratch, establishing new production capacity, developing sources of supply, building channels of distribution, growing a customer base, and so on. Generally internal entry is more attractive when (1) there is ample time to launch the business from the ground up, (2) incumbent firms are likely to be slow or ineffective in responding to new entry, (3) internal entry has lower costs than entry via acquisition, (4) the company already has in-house most or all of the skills needed to compete effectively in the business, (5) the additional capacity will not adversely impact the supply-demand balance in the industry, and (6) the targeted industry is populated with many relatively small firms so that the new start-up business does not have to go head-to-head against larger, more powerful competitors.[5]

Joint ventures are a useful way to gain access to a new business in at least three types of situations.[6] First, a joint venture is a good way to do something that is uneconomical or risky for an organization to do alone. Second, joint ventures make sense when pooling the resources and competences of two or more independent organizations produces an organization with more of the skills needed to be a strong competitor. In such cases, each partner brings to the deal special talents or resources that the other doesn't have and that are important enough to spell the difference between success and near-success. Third, joint ventures with foreign partners are sometimes the only or best way to surmount import quotas, tariffs, nationalistic political interests, and cultural roadblocks. The economic, competitive, and political realities of nationalism often require a foreign company to team up with a domestic partner in order to gain access to the national market in which the domestic partner is located. Domestic partners offer outside companies the benefits of local knowledge, managerial and marketing personnel, and access to distribution channels. The drawback to joint ventures is that they create complicated questions about how to divide efforts among the partners and who has effective control.[7] Potential conflicts between foreign and domestic partners usually relate to sourcing of components, exporting, differences of opinion over whether operating procedures should conform to the foreign company's standards or to local preferences, and control over cash flows and the disposition of profits.

RELATED DIVERSIFICATION STRATEGIES

In choosing which industries to diversify into, the basic options are to pick industries *related* to the organization's core business or *unrelated* to what the organization already does. In related diversification, a firm's several lines of

---

[5] Ibid., pp. 344–45.

[6] Peter Drucker, *Management: Tasks, Responsibilities, Practices* (New York: Harper & Row, 1974), pp. 720–24.

[7] Porter, *Competitive Strategy*, p. 340.

business, although distinct, still possess some kind of "fit." The nature of the fit can be based on any of several factors: shared technology, common labor skills and requirements, common distribution channels, common suppliers and raw material sources, similar operating methods, similar kinds of managerial know-how, complementary marketing-distribution channels, or customer overlap—virtually any aspect where meaningful relatedness or sharing opportunities exist in the businesses' respective activity-cost chains. In contrast, with unrelated diversification there is no common linkage or element of fit among a firm's lines of business; in this sense unrelated diversification is *pure* diversification.

Some of the most commonly used approaches to related diversification are:

- Entering businesses where sales force, advertising, and distribution activities can be shared (a bread bakery buying a maker of crackers and salty snack foods).
- Exploiting closely related technologies (a maker of agricultural seeds and fertilizers diversifying into chemicals for insect and plant disease control).
- Sharing manufacturing facilities (an aluminum window manufacturer with idle equipment and unused plant space deciding to add aluminum lawn furniture to its product lineup).
- Acquiring a firm where the buyer can transfer its know-how and expertise to improve the seller's operations (a successful mass marketer of women's cosmetics buying a chain of retail stores specializing in women's jewelry and accessories).
- Transferring the organization's brand name and reputation with consumers to a new product/service (a tire manufacturer diversifying into automotive repair centers).
- Acquiring new businesses that will uniquely help the firm's position in its existing businesses (a cable TV company purchasing a sports team and a movie production company to provide more original programming).

Examples of related diversification abound. BIC Pen, which pioneered inexpensive throwaway ballpoint pens, used the distinctive low-cost production and mass merchandising competences it built in writing instruments to diversify into disposable cigarette lighters, disposable razors, and pantyhose; all three of these businesses rely heavily on low-cost production know-how and skilled consumer marketing for competitive success. Tandy Corp. practiced related diversification when its chain of Radio Shack outlets, which originally handled mostly radio and stereo equipment, added telephones, intercoms, calculators, clocks, electronic and scientific toys, personal computers, and peripheral computer equipment. The Tandy strategy was to use the marketing access provided by its thousands of Radio Shack locations to become one of the world's leading retailers of electronic technology to individual consumers. Philip Morris, a leading cigarette manufacturer, employed a marketing-related diversification strategy when it purchased Miller Brewing, General Foods, and Kraft and transferred many of its cigarette marketing skills to the marketing of beer and consumer foods. Lockheed pursued a customer needs-based diversification strategy in creating business units to supply the Department of Defense with missiles, rocket engines, aircraft, electronic equipment, ships, and contract R&D for weapons. Procter & Gamble's lineup of products includes Jif peanut butter, Duncan Hines cake mixes, Folger's coffee, Tide laundry detergent, Crisco vegetable oil, Crest toothpaste, Ivory soap, Charmin toilet tissue, and Head and Shoulders shampoo—all different businesses with different competitors and different manufacturing approaches. But what ties P&G's products together into a related diversification package is that they can all be marketed through a common distribution system to be sold in retail food outlets to customers everywhere; much the same core marketing and merchandising skills come into play for all of P&G's products. Illustration Capsule 14 shows the business portfolios of several companies that have pursued a strategy of related diversification.

ILLUSTRATION CAPSULE   14

EXAMPLES OF COMPANIES WITH RELATED BUSINESS PORTFOLIOS

Presented below are the business portfolios of four companies that have pursued some form of related diversification:

Gillette

- Blades and razors
- Toiletries (Right Guard, Silkience, Foamy, Dry Idea, Soft & Dri, Oral-B toothbrushes, White Rain, Toni)
- Writing instruments and stationery products (Paper Mate pens, Liquid Paper correction fluids, Waterman pens)
- Braun shavers, cordless curlers, coffeemakers, alarm clocks, and electric toothbrushes

PepsiCo

- Soft drinks (Pepsi, Mountain Dew, Slice)
- Kentucky Fried Chicken
- Pizza Hut
- Taco Bell
- Frito Lay
- 7 Up International (non-U.S. sales of 7 Up)

Philip Morris Companies

- Cigarettes (Marlboro, Virginia Slims, Benson & Hedges, and Merit)
- Miller Brewing Company
- General Foods (Maxwell House, Sanka, Oscar Mayer, Kool-Aid, Jell-O, Post cereals, Birds-Eye frozen foods)
- Mission Viejo Realty
- Kraft (cheeses, Sealtest dairy products, Breyer's ice cream)

Johnson & Johnson

- Baby products (powder, shampoo, oil, lotion)
- Disposable diapers
- Bandaids and wound care products
- Stayfree, Carefree, Sure & Natural, and Modess feminine hygiene products
- Tylenol
- Prescription drugs
- Surgical and hospital products
- Dental products
- Oral contraceptives
- Veterinary and animal health products

Related diversification has considerable appeal as a portfolio-building strategy. It allows a firm to maintain a degree of unity in its business activities and benefit from skills transfer or cost sharing while spreading the risks of enterprise over a broader base. When a firm has been able to build a distinctive competence in its original business, related diversification offers a way to exploit what a company does best and *transfer* a distinctive-competence-based competitive advantage to another business. Diversifying in ways that *extend a firm's skills and expertise to related businesses* is a principal way to build corporate-level competitive advantage in a diversified firm and permit the diversifier to earn greater profits than each business could earn by operating independently. The competitive advantage of diversifying into businesses where technology, facilities, or functional activities can be *shared* is *lower costs*.

The Benefits of Strategic Fit

What makes related diversification so attractive compared to unrelated diversification is the opportunity to capitalize on "strategic fit." *Strategic fit* exists when different businesses have sufficiently related activity-cost chains that there are important opportunities for activity sharing across businesses or for skills and expertise in one business to be transferred to another.[8] *A diversified firm that exploits these activity-cost chain interrelationships and captures the benefits of strategic fit achieves a consolidated performance greater than the sum of what the businesses can earn pursuing independent strategies.* The presence of strategic fit within a diversified firm's business portfolio, together with corporate management's skill in capturing the benefits of the interrelationships, makes related diversification capable of being a $2 + 2 = 5$ phenomenon. There are three broad categories of strategic fit.

Market-related Fits. When the activity-cost chains of different businesses overlap such that the products are used by the same customers, and/or are sold through essentially the same marketing and sales methods in the same geographic market, and/or are distributed through common dealers and retailers, then the businesses exhibit market-related strategic fit. A variety of opportunities for cost sharing spring from market-related strategic fit: use of a common sales force to call on customers, advertising the related products in the same ads and brochures, use of the same brand names, coordinated delivery and shipping, combined after-sale service and repair organizations, coordinated order processing and billing, use of common promotional tie-ins (cents-off couponing, free samples and trial offers, seasonal specials, and the like), and combined dealer networks. Such market-related strategic fits usually allow a firm to economize on its marketing, selling, and distribution costs. In addition to the cost-sharing potential, market-related fit can generate opportunities for skills transfer in selling techniques,

---

[8] Michael E. Porter, *Competitive Advantage* (New York: Free Press, 1985), pp. 318–19 and pp. 337–53; Kenichi Ohmae, *The Mind of the Strategist* (New York: Penguin Books, 1983), pp. 121–24; and Porter, "From Competitive Advantage to Corporate Strategy," pp. 53–57.

promotional tactics and advertising, and product differentiation. Where diversification creates a related family of products and brand-name associations, the enhanced customer appeal of the combined product lines can also yield a stronger differentiation-based competitive advantage.

Operating Fit.   Cost-sharing or skills transfer potential in procuring inputs, R&D and technology, manufacture and assembly, and administrative support functions give rise to *operating fit*. Sharing-related operating fits usually present cost saving opportunities; some derive from the potential to tap into more scale economies, and some derive from ways to boost operating efficiency through sharing of related activities. The bigger the proportion of cost that a shared activity represents, the more significant the shared cost savings become and the bigger the competitive advantage that accrues. The most important skills transfer opportunities usually are technology-related; i.e., technical expertise gained in one business is highly beneficial in another. The same technology often has applications in different industries.

Management Fit.   This type of fit emerges when different business units have comparable types of entrepreneurial, administrative, or operating problems, thereby allowing the managerial know-how associated with one line of business to be useful in managing another line. Transfers of managerial expertise can occur anywhere in the activity-cost chain. Ford Motor Co. transferred its automobile financing and credit management know-how to the savings and loan industry when it acquired some failing savings and loan associations during the 1989 bailout of the crisis-ridden S&L industry. Emerson Electric transferred its skills in being a low-cost producer to its newly acquired Beaird-Poulan chain saw business division. The transfer of management know-how drove Beaird-Poulan's new strategy, changed the way its chain saws were designed and manufactured, and paved the way for new pricing and distribution emphasis.

Capturing the Benefits.   It is one thing to diversify into industries with strategic fit and another to actually capture the benefits. To realize the benefits of sharing, the businesses must be reorganized so that the activities to be shared are merged into a single functional unit and coordinated; then the cost-savings (or differentiation advantages) must be squeezed out. Merger and coordination have a price, and management must determine that the benefit of *some* centralized strategic control is great enough to sacrifice business-unit autonomy. Likewise, where skills transfer is the cornerstone of strategic fit, a way must be found to make the transfer effective without stripping too many skilled personnel from the business with the expertise.

UNRELATED DIVERSIFICATION STRATEGIES

While many company managers prefer related diversification because of the benefits of strategic fit, managers of some firms are more attracted to unrelated diversification. A simple criterion of venturing into "any industry in which we think we can make a profit" captures the essence of the corporate strategy of the most broadly diversified firms. Illustration Capsule 15 shows the business port-folios of several companies that have pursued unrelated diversification. Such companies are often referred to as *conglomerates* because there is no strategic theme in their diversification makeup.

ILLUSTRATION CAPSULE 15

DIVERSIFIED COMPANIES WITH UNRELATED BUSINESS PORTFOLIOS

Union Pacific Corporation

- Railroad operations (Union Pacific Rail-road Company)
- Oil and gas exploration
- Mining
- Microwave and fiber optic transportation information and control systems
- Hazardous waste management disposal
- Trucking (Overnite Transportation Company)
- Oil refining
- Real estate

United Technologies

- Pratt & Whitney aircraft engines
- Carrier heating and air-conditioning equipment
- Otis elevators
- Sikorsky helicopters
- Essex wire and cable products
- Norden defense systems
- Hamilton Standard controls
- Space transportation systems
- Automotive components

Westinghouse Electric Corp.

- Electric utility power generation equipment
- Nuclear fuel
- Electric transmission and distribution products
- Commercial and residential real estate financing
- Equipment leasing
- Receivables and fixed asset financing
- Radio and television broadcasting
- Longines-Wittnauer Watch Co.
- Beverage bottling
- Elevators and escalators
- Defense electronics (radar systems, space electronic systems, missile launch equipment, marine propulsion)
- Commercial furniture
- Community land development

Textron, Inc.

- Bell helicopters
- Paul Revere Insurance
- Missile reentry systems
- Lycoming gas turbine engines and jet propulsion systems
- E-Z-Go golf carts
- Homelite chain saws and lawn and gar-den equipment
- Davidson automotive parts and trims
- Specialty fastners
- Avco Financial Services
- Jacobsen turf care equipment
- Tanks and armored vehicles

Unrelated or conglomerate diversification offers several kinds of appeal:

1. Business risk is scattered over a variety of industries, making the company less dependent on any one business.
2. Capital resources can be invested in whatever industries offer the best profit prospects; cash flows from businesses with lower profit prospects can be diverted to those with higher profit potential.
3. Company profitability is somewhat more stable because hard times in one industry may be offset by good times in another—that is, the ups and downs of various industries can even one another out.
4. Shareholder wealth can be enhanced to the extent that corporate managers are exceptionally astute at choosing industries to get into and companies to acquire in these industries.

While unrelated diversification can sometimes pass the attractiveness test, the cost-of-entry test, and the better-off test, such a strategy has three big drawbacks. First, the Achilles' heel of conglomerate diversification is the big demand it places on corporate-level management. The greater the number of diverse businesses that corporate managers must oversee and the more diverse they are, the harder it is for managers to stay on top of what is really going on in the divisions, to have in-depth familiarity with the strategic issues facing each business unit, and to probe deeply into the strategic actions and plans of business-level managers. As one president of a diversified firm expressed it:

> We've got to make sure that our core businesses are properly managed for solid, long-term earnings. We can't just sit back and watch the numbers. We've got to know what the real issues are out there in the profit centers. Otherwise, we're not even in a position to check out our managers on the big decisions. And considering the pressures they're under, that's pretty dangerous for all concerned.[9]

With broad diversification, corporate managers have to be shrewd and talented enough (1) to select capable managers to run each of many different businesses, (2) to discern when the major strategic proposals of business-unit managers are sound, and (3) to know what to do if a business unit stumbles into difficulty. Because every business eventually encounters rough sledding, a good way to measure the risk of diversifying into new unrelated areas is to ask, "If the new business got into trouble, would we know how to bail it out?" When the answer is no, the risk of unrelated diversification rises and the business's profit prospects are more chancy.[10] As the former chairman of a Fortune 500 company advised, "Never acquire a business you don't know how to run."

---

[9] Carter F. Bales, "Strategic Control: The President's Paradox," *Business Horizons* 20, no. 4 (August 1977), p. 17.

[10] Of course, management may assume the risk that trouble will not strike before it has had time to learn the business well enough to bail it out of almost any difficulty. See Peter Drucker, *Management,* p. 709.

Second, without some kind of strategic fit, consolidated performance of an unrelated multibusiness portfolio tends to be no better than the sum of what the individual business units could achieve if they were independent, and it may be worse to the extent that corporate managers meddle unwisely in business unit operations or hamstring them with corporate policies. Except, perhaps, for the added financial backing that a cash-rich corporate parent can provide, a strategy of unrelated diversification adds little to the competitive strength of the individual business units. In a widely diversified firm, the value added by corporate managers depends primarily on how good they are at portfolio management—deciding what new businesses to add, which ones to get rid of, and how best to deploy available financial resources to build a higher-performing portfolio.

Third, although in theory unrelated diversification offers the potential of greater sales-profit stability over the course of the business cycle, in practice attempts at countercyclical diversification fall short. The consolidated profits of broadly diversified firms are no more stable or less subject to reversal in periods of recession and economic stress than the profits of firms in general.[11]

Despite these drawbacks, though, unrelated diversification cannot be ruled out as a sometimes desirable corporate strategy alternative. Pure diversification makes the most sense when a firm needs to diversify away from an unattractive industry and has no particular skills it can transfer to an adjacent industry. Otherwise, the case for unrelated diversification hinges on management's preference to be in several unrelated businesses instead of a family of related ones. Financially attractive opportunities to acquire unrelated businesses often arise, in which case the attractiveness test and the cost-of-entry test can be passed successfully even if the better-off test is not. Because unrelated diversification turns corporate-level strategists into portfolio managers, the rationale for pure diversification is more financial than strategic. The only way unrelated diversification can pass the better-off test is for corporate managers to be exceptionally good at spotting undervalued acquisition candidates and steering corporate resources into businesses with above-average profit potential.

A key issue in unrelated diversification is how broad a net to cast in building the business portfolio. In other words, should the corporate portfolio contain few or many unrelated businesses? How much unrelated diversification can corporate executives successfully manage? A reasonable way to tackle the issue of how much diversification is best is by answering two questions: "What is the least diversification we need to attain our objectives and remain a healthy, viable entity capable of competing successfully?" and "What is the most diversification we can manage given the complexity it adds?"[12] In all likelihood, the optimal answer lies between these two extremes.

---

[11] Ibid., p. 767. Research studies in the interval since 1974, when Drucker made his observation, uphold his conclusion—on the whole, broadly diversified firms do not outperform less-diversified firms over the course of the business cycle.

[12] Ibid., pp. 692–93.

DIVESTITURE AND LIQUIDATION STRATEGIES

Even a shrewd corporate diversification strategy can result in the acquisition of business units that, down the road, just do not work out. Misfits or partial fits cannot be completely avoided because it is impossible to predict precisely how getting into a new line of business will actually work out. In addition, long-term industry attractiveness changes with the times; what was once a good diversification move into an attractive industry may later turn sour. Subpar performance by some business units is bound to occur, thereby raising questions of whether to continue. Other business units may not mesh as well with the rest of the firm as was originally thought.

Sometimes, a diversification move that seems sensible from the standpoint of common markets, technologies, or channels turns out to lack the compatibility of values essential to a *cultural fit*.[13] Several pharmaceutical companies had just this experience. When they diversified into cosmetics and perfume, they discovered their personnel had little respect for the "frivolous" nature of such products compared to the far nobler task of developing miracle drugs to cure the ill. The absence of shared values and cultural compatibility between the chemical and compounding expertise of the pharmaceutical companies and the fashion-marketing orientation of the cosmetics business was the undoing of what otherwise was diversification into a business with related technology and logical product fit.

When a particular line of business loses its appeal, the most attractive solution usually is to abandon it. Normally such businesses should be divested as fast as is practical. To drag things out merely drains valuable organization resources. The more business units in a firm's portfolio, the more likely that the need will arise to divest poor performers, "dogs," and misfits. A useful guide for determining if and when to divest a particular line of business is to ask the question, "If we were not in this business today, would we want to get into it now?"[14] When the answer is no or probably not, divestiture becomes a priority consideration.

Divestiture can take either of two forms. In some cases, the parent can divest a business by spinning it off as a financially and managerially independent company; the parent company may or may not retain partial ownership. In other cases, divestiture is best accomplished by selling the unit outright, in which case a buyer needs to be found. As a rule, divestiture should not be approached from the angle of "Who can we pawn this business off on and what is the most we can get for it?"[15] Instead, it is wiser to proceed by addressing "For what sort of organization would this business be a good fit, and under what conditions would it be viewed as a good deal?" By identifying organizations for whom the business is a good fit, the parent can also find buyers who will pay the highest price.

Of all the strategic alternatives, liquidation is the most unpleasant and painful, especially for a single-business enterprise where it means terminating the organi-

---

13 Ibid., p. 709.

14 Ibid., p. 94.

15 Ibid., p. 719.

zation's existence. For a multi-industry, multibusiness firm to liquidate one of its lines of business is less traumatic. The hardships of layoffs, plant closings, and so on, while not to be minimized, still leave an ongoing organization, perhaps one that is healthier after its pruning. In hopeless situations, an early liquidation effort usually serves owner-stockholder interests better than an inevitable bankruptcy. Prolonging the pursuit of a lost cause exhausts an organization's resources and leaves less to liquidate; it can also mar reputations and ruin management careers. Unfortunately, it is seldom simple for management to differentiate between when a cause is lost and when a turnaround is achievable. This is particularly true when emotions and pride get mixed with sound managerial judgment—as often they do.

CORPORATE TURNAROUND, RETRENCHMENT, AND PORTFOLIO RESTRUCTURING STRATEGIES

Corporate turnaround, retrenchment, and portfolio restructuring strategies come into play when senior management tries to restore an ailing corporate business portfolio to good health. The first task is always diagnosis of the underlying reasons for poor corporate performance. Formulation of curative strategies then follows. Poor performance can be caused by large losses in one or more business units that pull overall performance down, a disproportionate number of businesses in unattractive industries, a bad economy adversely impacting many of the firm's business units, or weak management at either the corporate or business levels.

How to attempt a *turnaround* necessarily depends on the roots of poor profitability and the urgency of any crisis. Depending on the causes, six action approaches can be used singly or in combination to turn around a diversified enterprise: (1) concentrate on restoring profitability in the money-losing units, (2) implement harvest strategies in the poorly performing units and divert cash flows to opportunities in better-performing units, (3) institute across-the-board economies in all business units, (4) revamp the composition of the business portfolio by selling weak businesses and replacing them with new acquisitions in more attractive industries, (5) replace key management personnel at the corporate and/or business levels, and (6) launch sales and profit improvement programs in all business units.

Retrenchment differs from turnaround in that retrenchment is a pullback and leaning up in the face of adverse conditions. The strategic posture of retrenchment is defensive—"battening down the hatches and weathering out the storm," withdrawing from activities where return on investment is subpar. General economic recessions, sharp increases in interest rates, periods of economic uncertainty, sudden downturns in market demand, harsh regulations, and/or internal financial crises can all make retrenchment wise or necessary. Retrenchment strategies in diversified companies are usually triggered by unsuccessful forays into industries where diversification did not turn out as well as expected; a retreat to the organization's core businesses is then instituted.

Retrenchment can be approached in either of two ways: (1) pursuing stringent across-the-board internal economies to eliminate waste and improve efficiency, and (2) singling out the weakest performing businesses in the corporate portfolio for divestiture, thus *narrowing* the diversification base. In the first instance, a firm in a defensive or overextended position elects to remain in most or all of its current businesses and ride out the bad times with various internal economy measures. Ordinarily this type of corporate retrenchment strategy is highlighted by directives to reduce operating expenses, boost productivity, and increase profit margins. It can involve curtailing the hiring of new personnel, trimming the size of corporate staff, postponing capital expenditure projects, stretching the use of equipment and delaying replacement purchases, retiring obsolete equipment, dropping marginally profitable products, closing older and less efficient plants, reorganizing internal work flows, reducing inventories, and the like.

The second variation of corporate retrenchment entails selling some parts of the corporate business portfolio and reducing the scope of diversification to a smaller number of core businesses. Retrenchment is usually a by-product of poor overall corporate performance and a conclusion by corporate management that the company is in too many businesses. Sometimes diversified firms retrench because they can't make certain businesses profitable after several frustrating years of trying or because they lack funds to support the investment needs of all the businesses in their corporate portfolios. More commonly, however, corporate management concludes that some businesses do not figure in the corporation's long-term future and have not performed up to expectations. Divesting such businesses frees resources that can be used to reduce debt or pursue opportunities in the remaining business units.

Portfolio restructuring strategies involve radical surgery on the mix and percentage makeup of the types of businesses in the portfolio. For instance, one company over a two-year period divested four business units, closed down four others, and added 25 new lines of businesses to its portfolio—16 through acquisition and 9 through internal start-up. Restructuring can be prompted by any of several conditions: (1) when a strategy review reveals that the long-term performance prospects for the corporation have become unattractive because the portfolio contains too many slow-growth, declining, or competitively weak business units, (2) when one or more of the firm's core businesses fall prey to hard times, (3) when a new CEO takes over and decides to redirect where the company is headed, (4) when "wave-of-the-future" technologies or products emerge and a major shakeup of the portfolio is needed to build a position in a potentially big new industry, (5) when the corporation has a "unique opportunity" to make an acquisition so big that it has to sell several existing business units to finance the new acquisition, or (6) when major businesses in the portfolio have become more and more unattractive, forcing a shakeup in the portfolio in order to produce satisfactory long-term corporate performance.

Portfolio restructuring frequently involves both divestitures and new acquisitions. Candidates for divestiture include not only those business units that are competitively weak or up-and-down performers or in unattractive industries, but also those that no longer "fit" (even though they may be profitable and in attractive enough industries). Indeed, many broadly diversified corporations, disenchanted with how some of their acquisitions perform and beset with the thorny problems of making successes out of so many unrelated business units, have restructured their business portfolios. Business units incompatible with newly established related diversification criteria have been divested and the remaining units regrouped and aligned to capture more strategic fit benefits. Illustration Capsule 16 provides an example of corporate restructuring at Times Mirror Company.

ILLUSTRATION CAPSULE 16

CORPORATE RESTRUCTURING AT TIMES MIRROR COMPANY

Times Mirror is a $3.3 billion media and information company principally engaged in newspaper publishing, broadcast and cable television, and book and magazine publishing. During the 1980s the company engaged in corporate restructuring activities to revamp the content of its business portfolio. The table below summarizes the company's acquisition and divestiture moves:

		Dispositions	Acquisitions
1983	Dec.	New American Library	
1984	Feb.	Spotlight satellite programming	
	Dec.	Commerce Clearing House stock	*The Morning Call*
1985	June	Art and graphic products companies (3)	Learning International, Inc.
	August		Wolfe Publishing Limited
	Sept.	Hartford, Connecticut, Cable Television	
	Oct.	Long Beach, California, Cable Television	
1986	Feb.	80 percent of Publishers Paper Co.	
	May		*National Journal*
	June	Times Mirror Microwave Communications Co.	
		Television stations in Syracuse and Elmira, New York, and Harrisburg, Pennsylvania	
		Las Vegas, Nevada, Cable Television	
	July		*Bottlang Airfield Manual*
	Sept.	*Dallas Times Herald*	
	Oct.		The *Baltimore Sun* newspapers
	Dec.	Times Mirror Magazines book clubs	*Broadcasting* magazine
		Graphic Controls Corporation	60 percent of Rhode Island CATV (cable)
		The H.M. Goushā Company	CRC Press, Inc.

(continued)

		Dispositions	Acquisitions
1987	Feb.		*Government Executive*
	Dec.	*The Denver Post*	*Field & Stream, Home Mechanix, Skiing, Yachting* magazines
	Throughout	Continuing timberland sales	
1988	Jan.	Times Mirror Press	
	Feb.		Richard D. Irwin, Inc.
	Throughout	Continuing timberland sales	
	Total	Approximately $1 billion	Approximately $1 billion

This series of moves left Times Mirror with the following business portfolio as of early 1988:

Newspaper publishing:
Los Angeles Times, Newsday, the *Baltimore Sun* newspapers, *The Hartford Courant, The Morning Call, The (Stamford) Advocate,* and *Greenwich Time.*

Book publishing:
Abrams art books; Matthew Bender law books; Year Book medical books; CRC Press scientific books; Wolfe medical color atlases; C. V. Mosby medical books, journals and college texts; and college texts by Richard D. Irwin, Inc.

Broadcast television:
CBS network affiliates KDFW-TV, Dallas, Texas, and KTBC-TV, Austin, Texas; ABC affiliate KTVI, St. Louis, Missouri; and NBC affiliate WVTM-TV, Birmingham, Alabama.

Magazine publishing:
Popular Science, Outdoor Life, Golf Magazine, Ski Magazine, The Sporting News, The Sporting Goods DEALER, National Journal, Government Executive, Broadcasting, Sports inc., The Sports Business Weekly, Field & Stream, Home Mechanix, Skiing, and *Yachting.*

Other businesses/properties:
Timberland, Jepperson Sanderson (producer of aeronautical charts and pilot training material), and Learning International (professional training).

Source: Company annual reports.

The trend to demerge and deconglomerate has been driven by a growing preference to gear diversification around creating strong competitive positions in a few, well-selected industries. Indeed, in response to growing investor disenchantment with the conglomerate approach to diversification (evident in the fact that conglomerates often have *lower* price-earnings ratios than companies built on related diversification), strategists at some conglomerates have undertaken portfolio restructuring and retrenchment in a deliberate effort to escape the dreaded C-word label.

MULTINATIONAL DIVERSIFICATION STRATEGIES

The distinguishing characteristic of a multinational diversification strategy is a *diversity of businesses* and a *diversity of national markets*.[16] Here, corporate strategists must delve deeply into the strategic characteristics of a variety of businesses along with the differences and similarities of the national markets in which those businesses compete. Diversified multinational corporations (DMNCs) are challenged to conceive and execute a substantial number of strategies—at least one for each industry, with as many multinational variations as is appropriate for the situation. At the same time, though, such corporations need strategic coordination across industries and countries. The goal of strategic coordination at the headquarter's level is to recognize, build, and defend long-term competitive advantages.[17]

The Emergence of Multinational Diversification

Until the 1960s, multinational companies (MNCs) operated fairly autonomous subsidiaries in each host country, each catering to the special requirements of its own national market.[18] Management tasks at company headquarters primarily revolved around finance functions, technology transfer, and export coordination. In pursuing a national responsiveness strategy, the primary competitive advantage of an MNC was grounded in its ability to transfer technology, manufacturing know-how, brand name identification, and marketing and management skills from country to country at costs lower than could be achieved by host country competitors. Standardized administrative procedures helped minimize overhead costs, and once an initial organization for managing foreign subsidiaries was put in place, entry into additional national markets could be accomplished at low marginal costs. Frequently, an MNC's presence and market position in a country was negotiated with the host government rather than driven by international competition.

During the 1970s, however, multicountry strategies based on national responsiveness began to lose their effectiveness. Competition became international in more and more industries as Japanese, European, and U.S. companies pursued international expansion in the wake of trade liberalization and the opening up of

---

[16] C. K. Prahalad and Yves L. Doz, *The Multinational Mission* (New York: Free Press, 1987), p. 2.

[17] Ibid., p. 15.

[18] Yves L. Doz, *Strategic Management in Multinational Companies* (New York: Pergamon Press, 1985), p. 1.

market opportunities in both industrial and less-developed countries.[19] The relevant market arena in many industries shifted from national to global principally because the strategies of global competitors, most notably the Japanese companies, involved gaining a market foothold in host country markets via lower-priced, higher-quality offerings than established companies. To fend off global competitors, traditional MNCs were driven to integrate their operations across national borders in a quest for better efficiencies and lower manufacturing costs. Instead of separately manufacturing a complete product range in each country, plants became more specialized in their production operations to gain the economies of longer production runs, the use of more automated equipment, and experience curve effects. Country subsidiaries obtained the rest of the product range they needed from sister plants in other countries. Gains in manufacturing efficiencies from converting to state-of-the-art, world-scale manufacturing plants more than offset increased international shipping costs, especially in light of globalization's other advantages. With a global strategy an MNC could take advantage of plant locations in countries with low labor costs—a key consideration in industries whose products had high labor content. With a global strategy an MNC could also exploit differences in tax rates, setting transfer prices in its integrated operations to produce higher profits in low-tax countries and lower profits in high-tax countries. Global strategic coordination also gave MNCs increased ability to take advantage of country-to-country differences in interest rates, exchange rates, credit terms, government subsidies, and export guarantees. Consequently, it became increasingly difficult for a company that produced and sold its product in only one country to succeed in a global industry.

During the 1980s another source of competitive advantage began to emerge: using the strategic fit advantages of related diversification to build a stronger competitive position in global industries. Being a DMNC became competitively superior to being an MNC—at least in some cases. Diversification is most capable of producing competitive advantage for a multinational company where expertise in a core technology can be applied in different industries (at least one of which is global) and where there are important distribution or brand name advantages to being in a family of related businesses.[20] Illustration Capsule 17 explains Honda's ability to exploit the technology of engines and its well-known name via its diversification into a variety of products with engines.

Sources of Competitive Advantage for a DMNC

When a multinational company has expertise in a core technology and has diversified into a series of product markets to exploit that core, a centralized R&D effort coordinated at the headquarters level holds real potential for competitive advantage. By channeling corporate resources directly into a strategically coordinated R&D/technology effort, as opposed to letting each business unit perform its own

---

[19] Ibid., pp. 2–3.

[20] Prahalad and Doz, *The Multinational Mission*, pp. 62–63.

ILLUSTRATION CAPSULE   17

HONDA'S COMPETITIVE ADVANTAGE: THE TECHNOLOGY OF ENGINES

At first blush anyone looking at Honda's lineup of products—cars, motorcycles, lawnmowers, power generators, outboard motors, snowmobiles, snowblowers, and garden tillers—might conclude that Honda has pursued unrelated diversification. But underlying the obvious product diversity is a common core: the technology of engines.

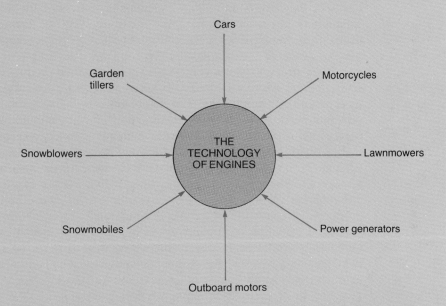

The basic Honda strategy is to exploit the company's expertise in engine technology and manufacturing and to capitalize on its brand recognition. One Honda ad teases consumers with the question, "How do you put six Honda's in a two-car garage?" It then shows a garage containing a Honda car, a Honda motorcycle, a Honda snowmobile, a Honda lawnmower, a Honda power generator, and a Honda outboard motor.

Source: Adapted from C. K. Prahalad and Yves L. Doz, *The Multinational Mission* (New York: Free Press, 1987), p. 62.

R&D function, the DMNC can launch a world-class, global-scale assault to advance the core technology, generate technology-based manufacturing economies within and across product/business lines, make across-the-board product improvements, and develop complementary products—all significant advantages in a globally competitive marketplace. In the absence of centralized coordination,

R&D/technology investments are likely to be scaled down to match each business's product-market perspective, allowing the strategic fit benefits of coordinated technology management to slip through the cracks.[21]

The second source of competitive advantage for a DMNC concerns the distribution and brand name advantages that can accrue to related diversification in global industries. Consider, for instance, the competitive strength of Japanese companies like Sanyo and Matsushita, both DMNCs, which over the years have diversified into a range of globally competitive consumer goods industries—TVs, stereo equipment, radios, VCRs, small domestic appliances (microwave ovens, for example), and personal computers. By widening their scope of operations in products marketed through similar distribution channels, Sanyo and Matsushita have not only exploited related technologies but also built stronger distribution capabilities, captured logistical and distribution-related economies, and established greater brand awareness for their products.[22] Such competitive advantages are not available to a domestic-only company pursuing a single-business concentration strategy. Moreover, with a well-diversified product line and a multinational market base, a DMNC can enter new country markets or new product markets and gain market share via below-market pricing (and below-average-cost-pricing if need be), subsidizing the entry with profits earned in other markets or businesses. A one-business domestic company is weakly positioned to defend its market share against a determined DMNC willing to forgo short-term profits to win long-term competitive position. DMNCs have the patience and resources year after year to hammer away at competitors with lower prices, all the while winning more market visibility and increased customer confidence in its whole family of products. A Sanyo, for example, by pursuing related diversification keyed to product-distribution-technology types of strategic fit and managing its product families on a global scale, can eventually encircle domestic companies like Zenith (which manufactures TVs and small computer systems) and Maytag (which manufactures only large home appliances) and put them under serious competitive pressure. In Zenith's case, Sanyo can peck away at Zenith's market share in TVs and in the process weaken the loyalty of TV retailers to the Zenith brand. In Maytag's case, Sanyo could elect to diversify into large home appliances (by acquiring an established appliance maker or by launching manufacture on its own) and cross-subsidize a low-priced market entry against Maytag and other less-diversified home appliance firms with cash flows from its other operations. If Sanyo chooses, it can keep its prices low for several years to gain market share at the expense of domestic rivals, turning its attention to profits after the battle for market share and competitive position is won.[23]

The point is clear. A DMNC has a strategic arsenal capable of defeating both a single-business MNC and a single-business domestic company over the long-term. The competitive advantages of a DMNC, however, hinge on employing a related strategy in industries that are already globally competitive or are on the verge of

---

[21] Ibid.

[22] Ibid., p. 64.

[23] Ibid.

becoming so. Then the related businesses have to be managed to capture the strategic fit potential. The most powerful competitive advantage potential of a DMNC arises in industries with technology-sharing and technology-transfer opportunities or with important product-market-distribution-brand name benefits from competing in related product families.

A DMNC also has important cross-subsidization potential for winning its way into attractive new markets. However, such powers cannot be deployed in the extreme. It is one thing to use a *portion* of the profits and cash flows from existing businesses to cover "reasonable" short-term losses associated with entering a new business or a new country market; it is quite another to drain corporate profits indiscriminately (and thus impair overall company performance) to support either deep price discounting and quick market penetration in the short term or continuing losses over a longer term. At some juncture, every business and every market entered has to make a profit contribution or become a candidate for abandonment. Moreover, the company has to wring consistently acceptable performance from the whole business portfolio. So there are limits to cross-subsidization. As a general rule, cross-subsidization is justified only if (a) managers judge there is a good chance that short-term losses can be amply recouped in one way or another over the long-term or (b) strategists place higher priority on building long-term competitive position than on profitability.

Illustration Capsule 18 provides examples of the business portfolios and global scope of several DMNCs.

ILLUSTRATION CAPSULE 18

THE GLOBAL SCOPE OF PROMINENT DIVERSIFIED MULTINATIONAL CORPORATIONS

Company (headquarters base)	Major lines of business	Number of employees	1987 Global sales	Global plant locations
Unilever (Netherlands, Britain)	Vaseline products, Cutex, Prince Matchabelli products, Ragu sauces, Lipton teas and soups, laundry detergents, soaps, toothpaste and other personal care products, margarine, frozen foods, agribusiness, and chemicals	300,000	$27 billion in 75 different countries • Europe, 61% • North America, 18% • Rest of world, 21%	340 subsidiary companies in 30 different countries
Siemens (West Germany)	Electrical equipment, lighting, power plants, security systems, medical engineering, communications and information systems, telecommunications networks	359,000	$27 billion • Europe, 73% • North America, 10% • Asia and Australia, 9% • Latin America, 4% • Africa, 4%	28 countries

(continued)

Company (headquarters base)	Major lines of business	Number of employees	1987 Global sales	Global plant locations
Philips (Netherlands)	Lighting, consumer electronics, domestic appliances, and telecommunications and data systems	337,000	$26 billion • Europe, 53% • North America, 29% • Asia and Australia, 10% • Latin America, 6% • Africa, 2%	60 countries
Nissan Motor Co. (Japan)	Automobiles, trucks, rockets, forklifts, boats, and textile machinery	51,200	$34 billion in 150 countries	15 countries
Toyota Motor Corp. (Japan)	Automobiles, trucks, buses, forklifts, power shovels, residential and commercial construction	66,300	$41.5 billion in 150 countries	11 plants in Japan 30 plants in 21 other countries
Hitachi (Japan)	Power plants, turbines, boilers, TV sets, VCRs, kitchen appliances, lighting fixtures, computers, word processors, fax machines, cranes, locomotives, machinery, wire and cable, chemicals, and steel products	164,000	$29 billion in 30 countries	7 countries
Dow Chemical Co. (United States)	Chemicals, plastics, hydrocarbons, pharmaceuticals, consumer products (1,800 different products in all)	55,000	$16.6 billion • Europe, 31% • U.S., 45% • Rest of world, 24%	120-plus plant locations in 32 countries
CPC International (United States)	Consumer foods (Hellman's, Mazola, Skippy, Knorr soups and sauces, margarine, English muffins, pasta) and corn refining products (corn starches, corn syrups, dextrose, animal feed ingredients)	31,400	$4.7 billion in 50 countries • North America, 46% • Europe, 36% • Latin America, 13% • Asia and Africa, 5%	28 countries

KEY POINTS

The six corporate diversification approaches are not mutually exclusive. They can be pursued in combination and in varying sequences, allowing ample room for companies to customize their diversification strategies to fit their own particular circumstances. The most common business portfolios created by corporate diversification strategies are:

- A "dominant-business" enterprise with sales concentrated in one major core business but with a modestly diversified portfolio of either related or unrelated businesses (amounting to one third or less of total corporatewide sales).

- A narrowly diversified enterprise having a *few* (two to five) *related core* business units.

Figure 7–2 CHECKLIST OF MAJOR CORPORATE STRATEGY ALTERNATIVES

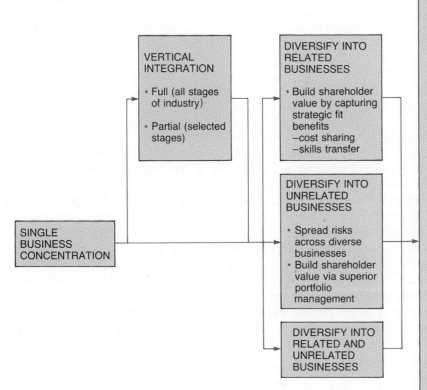

POST-DIVERSIFICATION STRATEGIC MOVE ALTERNATIVES

- Make new acquisitions (or seek merger partnerships)
  - to build positions in new related/unrelated industries
  - to strengthen the position of business units in industries where the firm already has a stake

- Divest some business units
  - to eliminate weak-performing businesses from portfolio
  - to eliminate businesses that no longer fit

- Restructure makeup of whole portfolio if many business units are performing poorly
  - by selling selected business units
  - by using cash from divestitures plus unused debt capacity to make new acquisitions

- Retrench/narrow the diversification base
  - by pruning weak businesses
  - by shedding all noncore businesses
  - by divesting one or more core businesses

- Become a multinational, multi-industry enterprise (DMNC)
  - to succeed in globally competitive core businesses against international rivals
  - to capture strategic fit benefits and win a competitive advantage via multinational diversification

- Liquidate/close-down money-losing businesses that cannot be sold

VERTICAL INTEGRATION
- Full (all stages of industry)
- Partial (selected stages)

DIVERSIFY INTO RELATED BUSINESSES
- Build shareholder value by capturing strategic fit benefits
  - cost sharing
  - skills transfer

DIVERSIFY INTO UNRELATED BUSINESSES
- Spread risks across diverse businesses
- Build shareholder value via superior portfolio management

DIVERSIFY INTO RELATED AND UNRELATED BUSINESSES

SINGLE BUSINESS CONCENTRATION

Moves to accomplish diversification can involve one or more of following:
- Acquisition/merger
- Start-up of own new businesses from scratch
- Joint venture partnerships

- A broadly diversified enterprise made up of *many* mostly *related* business units.
- A narrowly diversified enterprise comprised of a *few* (two to five) *core* business units in *unrelated* industries.
- A broadly diversified enterprise having *many* business units in mostly *unrelated* industries.
- A multibusiness enterprise that has diversified into unrelated areas but that has a portfolio of related businesses within each area—thus giving it *several unrelated groups of related businesses*.

In each case, the geographic markets of individual businesses within the portfolio can range from local to regional to national to multinational to global. Thus, a company can be competing in a local arena in some businesses, a national arena in others, and a global arena in still others.

Figure 7–2 presents a summary of the paths an undiversified company can take on the road to managing a diversified business portfolio. Most companies have their strategic roots in single-business concentration. Vertical integration strategies may or may not enter the picture depending on the extent to which forward or backward integration strengthens a firm's competitive position or helps it secure a competitive advantage. When diversification becomes a serious strategic option, a choice must be made whether to pursue related diversification, unrelated diversification, or some mix of both. There are advantages and disadvantages to all three options. Once diversification has been accomplished, management must figure out how to manage the existing business portfolio. The six primary postdiversification alternatives are (1) make new acquisitions, (2) divest weak business units or those that no longer fit, (3) restructure the makeup of the portfolio if overall performance is poor, (4) retrench to a narrower diversification base, (5) pursue multinational diversification, and (6) close down/liquidate money-losing business units that cannot be sold.

SUGGESTED READINGS

Ansoff, H. Igor. *The New Corporate Strategy.* New York: John Wiley, 1988, chap. 7.

Bright, William M. "Alternative Strategies for Diversification." *Research Management* 12, no. 4 (July 1969), pp. 247–53.

Buzzell, Robert D. "Is Vertical Integration Profitable." *Harvard Business Review* 61, no. 1 (January–February 1983), pp. 92–102.

Chandler, Alfred D. "The Evolution of Modern Global Competition." In *Competition in Global Industries,* ed. Michael E. Porter. Boston: Harvard Business School Press, 1986, pp. 405–48.

Drucker, Peter. *Management: Tasks, Responsibilities, Practices.* New York: Harper & Row, 1974, chaps. 55, 56, 57, 58, 60, and 61.

Harrigan, Kathryn R. "Matching Vertical Integration Strategies to Competitive Conditions." *Strategic Management Journal* 7, no. 6 (November–December 1986), pp. 535–56.

———. *Strategic Flexibility.* Lexington, Mass.: Lexington Books, 1985, chap. 4 and Table A–8, p. 162.

Kumpe, Ted, and Piet T. Bolwijn. "Manufacturing: The New Case for Vertical Integration." *Harvard Business Review* 88, no. 2 (March–April 1988), pp. 75–82.

Lauenstein, Milton, and Wickham Skinner. "Formulating a Strategy of Superior Resources." *Journal of Business Strategy* 1, no. 1 (Summer 1980), pp. 4–10.

Ohmae, Kenichi. "Planting for a Global Harvest." *Harvard Business Review* 67, no. 4 (July–August 1989), pp. 136–45.

Porter, Michael E. "From Competitive Advantage to Corporate Strategy." *Harvard Business Review* 65, no. 3 (May–June 1987), pp. 43–59.

Prahalad, C. K., and Yves L. Doz. *The Multinational Mission*. New York: Free Press, 1987, chaps. 1 and 2.

8 Techniques for Analyzing Diversified Companies

....

*If we can know where we are and something about how we got there, we might
see where we are trending—and if the outcomes which lie naturally in our course
are unacceptable, to make timely change.*
Abraham Lincoln

....

*No company can afford everything it would like to do. Resources have to be
allocated. The essence of strategic planning is to allocate resources to those
areas that have the greatest future potential.*
Reginald Jones

Corporate managers of a diversified enterprise build shareholder value by
acting effectively on the answers to three strategy-related questions:

* How strong is the firm's business portfolio?
* Assuming the company sticks with the present business lineup, how good
  is the overall performance outlook over the next five years?
* If the previous two answers are not satisfactory, what moves need to be
  considered to get out of some existing businesses, strengthen the positions
  of the remaining businesses, and get into new businesses?

The task of formulating and implementing action plans to improve the mix and
strength of a company's business-unit portfolio is the heart of what corporate-
level strategic management is all about. The procedure for evaluating the strategy
of a diversified company and deciding what corporate strategy moves to make
next entails a logical, straightforward eight-step process:

1. Identifying the present corporate strategy.
2. Constructing one or more business portfolio matrixes to analyze the makeup of the company's business portfolio.
3. Comparing the long-term attractiveness of each industry the company has diversified into.
4. Comparing the competitive strength of the company's business units to see which ones are strong contenders in their respective industries.
5. Rating the different business units on the basis of their historical performance and their prospects for the future.
6. Assessing each business unit's compatibility with corporate strategy and determining the value of any strategic fit relationships among existing business units.
7. Ranking the business units in terms of priority for new capital investment and deciding whether the general strategic posture and direction for each business unit should be aggressive expansion, fortify and defend, overhaul and reposition, or harvest/divest. (The task of initiating *specific* business-unit strategies to improve the business unit's competitive position is usually delegated to business-level managers, with corporate-level managers offering suggestions and having authority for final approval.)
8. Crafting new strategic moves to improve overall corporate performance— changing the makeup of the portfolio via acquisitions and divestitures, coordinating the activities of related business units to achieve cost-sharing and skills-transfer benefits, and steering corporate resources into the areas of greatest opportunity.

The rest of this chapter is devoted to exploring each of these eight steps.

IDENTIFYING THE PRESENT CORPORATE STRATEGY

Strategic analysis of a diversified company starts by probing the organization's present strategy and business makeup. Recall from Figure 2–2 in Chapter 2 that a good overall perspective of corporate strategy in a diversified company comes from looking at:

*   The extent to which the firm is diversified (as measured by the proportion of total sales and operating profits contributed by each business unit and by whether the diversification base is broad or narrow).
*   Whether the firm's portfolio is keyed to related or unrelated diversification, or a mixture of both.
*   Whether the scope of company operations is mostly domestic or increasingly multinational or global.
*   The nature of recent moves to boost performance of key business units in the portfolio and/or strengthen existing business positions.

- Moves to add new businesses to the portfolio and to build positions in new industries.
- Moves to divest weak or unattractive business units.
- The internal efforts of corporate management to realize the benefits of strategic fit relationships and to use diversification to create competitive advantage.
- The proportion of capital expenditures going to each of the different business units.

Identifying the current corporate strategy lays the foundation for conducting a thorough strategy analysis and, subsequently, for reformulating the strategy as it "should be."

MATRIX TECHNIQUES FOR EVALUATING DIVERSIFIED PORTFOLIOS

The most popular technique for analyzing the *overall makeup* of a diversified group of business units involves constructing a business portfolio matrix. A *business portfolio matrix* is a two-dimensional portrayal of the comparative strategic positions of different businesses. Matrixes can be constructed using any pair of strategically relevant variables, but in practice the most revealing variables are industry growth rate, market share, long-term industry attractiveness, competitive strength, and stage of product/market evolution. Two-dimensional business portfolio matrixes are relatively simple to construct and give a clear overall picture. Three types of business portfolio matrixes are used most frequently—the growth-share matrix developed by the Boston Consulting Group, the industry attractiveness-business strength matrix pioneered at General Electric, and the Hofer-A.D. Little industry life-cycle matrix.

The Four-Cell BCG Growth-Share Matrix

The first business portfolio matrix to receive widespread usage was a four-square grid devised by the Boston Consulting Group (BCG), a leading management consulting firm.[1] Figure 8–1 illustrates a BCG-type matrix. The matrix is formed using *industry growth rate* and *relative market share* as the axes. Each business unit in the corporate portfolio appears as a "bubble" on the four-cell matrix, with the size of each bubble or circle scaled to the percent of revenues it represents in the overall corporate portfolio.

Early BCG methodology arbitrarily placed the dividing line between "high" and "low" industry growth rates at around twice the real GNP growth rate plus

---

[1] The original presentation is Bruce D. Henderson, "The Experience Curve—Reviewed. IV. The Growth Share Matrix of the Product Portfolio," (Boston: The Boston Consulting Group, 1973), Perspectives No. 135. For an excellent chapter-length treatment of the use of the BCG growth-share matrix in strategic portfolio analysis, see Arnoldo C. Hax and Nicolas S. Majluf, *Strategic Management: An Integrative Perspective* (Englewood Cliffs, N.J.: Prentice-Hall, 1984), chap. 7.

Figure 8–1 THE BCG GROWTH-SHARE BUSINESS PORTFOLIO MATRIX

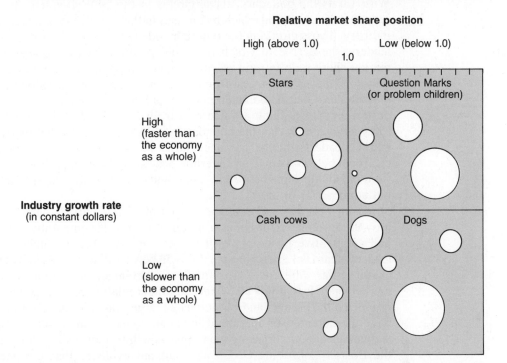

Note: Relative market share is defined by the ratio of one's own market share to the market share held by the largest *rival* firm. When the vertical dividing line is set at 1.0, the only way a firm can achieve a star or cash cow position in the growth-share matrix is to have the largest market share in the industry. Since this is a very stringent criterion, it may be "fairer" and more revealing to locate the vertical dividing line in the matrix at about 0.75 or 0.80.

inflation, but the boundary percentage can be raised or lowered to suit individual preferences. The essential criterion is to place the line so that business units in industries growing faster than the economy as a whole end up in the "high-growth" cells and those in industries growing slower than the economywide rate fall into the "low-growth" cells ("low-growth" industries usually merit labels like mature, aging, stagnant, or declining).

Relative market share is defined as the ratio of a business's market share to the market share held by the largest rival firm in the industry, with market share measured in unit volume, not dollars. For instance, if business A has a 15 percent share of the industry's total volume and the share held by the largest rival is 30 percent, then A's relative market share is 0.5. If business B has a market-leading share of 40 percent and its largest rival has a 30 percent share, B's relative market share is 1.33. Given this definition, only business units that are market share leaders in their respective units will have relative market share values greater than 1.0; business units that trail rival firms in market share will have ratios below 1.0.

The most stringent BCG standard calls for the border between "high" and "low" relative market share on the grid to be set at 1.0, as shown in Figure 8–1. With 1.0 as the boundary, those circles in the two left-side cells of the matrix identify how many and which businesses in the firm's portfolio are leaders in their industry. Those circles in the two right-side cells identify businesses that trail the leaders; the degree to which they trail is indicated by the size of the relative market share ratio (a ratio of .10 indicates that the business has a market share only 1/10 that of the largest firm in the market, whereas a ratio of .80 indicates a market share that is 4/5 or 80 percent as big as the leading firm's share). Many portfolio analysts think a value of 1.0 for the boundary is unreasonably large. They advocate placing the boundary so businesses to the left enjoy positions as market leaders (though not necessarily *the* leader) and those to the right are clearly in below-average or underdog positions. Applying this less-stringent criterion, the dividing line between "high" and "low" relative market share should be put at about .75 or .80.

Using *relative* market share instead of *actual* market share to construct the growth-share matrix provides a better indicator of comparative market strength and competitive position. A 10 percent market share is much stronger if the leader's share is 12 percent than if it is 50 percent; the use of relative market share captures this difference. An equally important consideration in using relative market share is that it is also likely to reflect relative cost based on experience in producing the product and economies of large-scale production. Large businesses have the potential to operate at lower unit costs than smaller firms because of technological and efficiency gains that attach to larger size. But personnel from the Boston Consulting Group accumulated evidence that the phenomenon of lower unit costs went beyond just the effects of scale economies; they found that as the cumulative volume of production increased, the resulting knowledge and experience gained often led to the discovery of additional efficiencies and ways to reduce costs even further. BCG labeled the relationship between *cumulative production experience* and lower unit costs *the experience curve effect* (for more details, see Figure 3–1 in Chapter 3). An important experience curve effect in the activity-cost chain of a particular business or industry places a strategic premium on market share: the firm that gains the largest market share tends to realize important cost advantages which, in turn, can be used to lower prices and gain still additional customers, sales, market share, and profit. The stronger the experience curve effect in a business, the more dominant its role in strategy-making.[2]

With these features of the BCG growth-share matrix in mind, we are ready to explore the portfolio implications for businesses falling into each cell of the matrix in Figure 8–1.

Question Marks and Problem Children.   Business units falling in the upper-right quadrant of the matrix have been tagged by BCG as "question marks" or "prob-

---

[2] For two recent discussions of the strategic importance of the experience curve, see Pankaj Ghemawat, "Building Strategy on the Experience Curve," *Harvard Business Review* 63, no. 2 (March–April 1985), pp. 143–49; and Bruce D. Henderson, "The Application and Misapplication of the Experience Curve," *Journal of Business Strategy* 4, no. 3 (Winter 1984), pp. 3–9.

lem children." Rapid market growth makes such business units attractive from an industry standpoint. But their low relative market share (and thus reduced access to experience curve effects) raises questions about whether the profit potential associated with market growth can realistically be captured—hence, the "question mark" or "problem child" designation. Question mark businesses, moreover, are typically "cash hogs"—so labeled because their cash needs are high (owing to the investment requirements of rapid growth and product development) and their internal cash generation is low (owing to low market share, less access to experience curve effects and scale economies, and consequently thinner profit margins). The corporate parent of a cash hog business has to decide whether it is worthwhile to invest corporate capital to support the needs of a question mark division.

BCG has argued that the two best strategic options for a question mark business are (1) an aggressive grow-and-build strategy to capitalize on the high-growth opportunity or (2) divestiture, in the event that the costs of strengthening its market share standing via a grow-and-build strategy outweigh the potential payoff and financial risk. Pursuit of a fast-growth strategy is imperative any time an attractive question mark business is characterized by strong experience curve effects, because it takes major gains in market share to begin to match the lower-cost position enjoyed by firms with greater cumulative production experience and their usually bigger market shares. The stronger the experience curve effect, the more powerful the competitive position enjoyed by the competitor that is the low-cost producer. Consequently, so the BCG thesis goes, unless a question mark/problem child business can successfully pursue a fast-growth strategy and win major market share gains, it cannot hope to ever become cost competitive with large-volume firms that are further down the experience curve—in which case divestiture becomes the only other viable long-run alternative. The corporate strategy prescriptions for managing question mark/problem child business units thus become straightforward: divest those that are weaker and have less chance to catch the leaders on the experience curve; invest heavily in the attractive question marks and groom them to become tomorrow's "stars."

Stars. Businesses with high relative market-share positions in high-growth markets rank as "stars" in the BCG grid because they offer both excellent profit and growth opportunities. They are the business units an enterprise depends on to boost overall performance of the total portfolio.

Given their dominant market-share position and rapid growth environment, stars typically require large cash investments to support expansion of production facilities and working capital needs. But they also tend to generate their own large internal cash flows due to the low-cost advantage of scale economies and cumulative production experience. Star-type businesses vary as to whether they can support their investment needs from self-generated cash flows or whether they require infusions of investment funds from corporate headquarters to support continued rapid growth and high performance. In the BCG model (based on experience with clients), some stars (usually those that are well-established and beginning to mature) are virtually self-sustaining in terms of cash flow and make little claim on the corporate parent's treasury. Young stars, however, often require substantial investment capital *beyond what they can generate on their own* and may thus be cash hogs.

Cash Cows.   Businesses with a high relative market share in a low-growth market are designated "cash cows" in the BCG scheme. A cash cow business generates substantial cash surpluses over what is needed for reinvestment and growth in the business. The reason businesses in this box tend to be cash cows is straightforward: because of the business's high relative market share and industry leadership position, it should be earning attractive profits; because of the slow-growth character of the industry, it typically needs less capital reinvestment to sustain its present market position than the cash flows generated from current operations.

Many of today's cash cows are yesterday's stars, having dropped into the bottom cell from the top cell as industry demand matured. Cash cows, though less attractive from a growth standpoint, are valuable to a corporate portfolio. They can be "milked" for the cash to pay corporate dividends and headquarters' overhead, they provide cash for financing new acquisitions, and they provide funds for investing in young stars and problem children being groomed as the next round of stars (cash cows provide the dollars to "feed" the cash hogs). Strong cash cows should never be harvested but rather should be maintained in a healthy status to sustain long-term cash flow. The goal is to fortify and defend a cash cow's market position while efficiently generating dollars to reallocate to business investments elsewhere. Weakening cash cows, however, may become candidates for harvesting and eventual divestiture if industry maturity produces unattractive competitive conditions and dries up the cash flow surpluses.

Dogs.   Businesses with a low relative market share in slow-growth industries are called "dogs" because of their trailing market position and the presumption of lower profit margins due to their being behind the leaders on the experience curve. The industry's subpar growth outlook adds further justification for the dog label. In the BCG analysis, dog businesses are usually seen as being unable to generate attractive cash flows on a long-term basis. Sometimes they cannot produce enough cash to support a rearguard fortify-and-defend strategy—especially if competition is brutal and profit margins are chronically thin. Consequently, except in unusual cases, the BCG corporate strategy prescription is that dogs be harvested, divested, or liquidated, depending on which alternative yields the most cash.

Implications for Corporate Strategy.   The chief contribution of the BCG growth-share matrix is the attention it draws to the cash flow and investment characteristics of various types of businesses and how corporate financial resources can be shifted between business units to optimize the long-term strategic position and performance of the whole corporate portfolio. According to BCG analysis, the foundation of a sound, long-term corporate strategy is to utilize the excess cash generated by cash cow business units to finance market-share increases for cash hog businesses—the young stars still unable to finance their own growth internally and those problem children singled out as having the best potential to grow into stars. If successful, the cash hogs eventually become self-supporting stars. Then, when the markets of the star businesses begin to mature and their growth slows, the stars will become the cash cows of the future. The "success sequence" is thus problem child/question mark to young star (but perhaps still a cash hog) to self-supporting star to cash cow.

The weaker, less attractive question mark businesses deemed unworthy of the financial investment necessary to fund a long-term grow-and-build strategy are often a portfolio liability because of the high-cost economics associated with a low relative market share and because they do not generate enough cash on their own to keep abreast of fast-paced market growth. According to BCG prescriptions, these question marks should be prime divestiture candidates *unless* they can be kept profitable and viable with their own internally generated funds. All problem child businesses are not untenable cash hogs, however; those in industries with small capital requirements and weak experience curve effects may be able to hang on against the industry leaders and contribute enough to corporate earnings and return on investment to justify retention in the portfolio. Clearly, though, weaker question marks still have a low-priority claim on corporate resources and a dim future in the portfolio. Question mark businesses unable to move leftward and become stars are destined to drift vertically downward in the matrix, becoming dogs, as their industry growth drops and market demand matures.

Dogs should be retained only as long as they contribute adequately to overall company performance. Strong dogs may produce a positive cash flow and show average profitability. But the further right and down a dog business is positioned in the BCG matrix, the more likely it is tying up assets that could be redeployed in a more profitable endeavor. The BCG recommendation for managing a weakening or already weak dog is to employ a harvesting strategy. If and when a harvesting strategy is no longer attractive, a weak dog should be eliminated from the portfolio.

There are two "disaster sequences" in the BCG scheme of things: (1) when a star's position in the matrix erodes over time to that of a problem child and then falls to become a dog and (2) when a cash cow loses market leadership to the point where it becomes a dog on the decline. Other strategic mistakes include overinvesting in a safe cash cow; underinvesting in a question mark so that instead of moving into the star category it tumbles into a dog; and shotgunning resources thinly over many question marks rather than concentrating on the best question marks to boost their chances of becoming stars.

Strengths and Weaknesses in the Growth-Share Matrix Approach.   The BCG business portfolio matrix makes a definite contribution to the strategist's toolkit when it comes to diagnosing the portfolio makeup and reaching broad prescriptions regarding the strategy and direction for each business unit in the portfolio. Viewing a diversified corporation as a collection of cash flows and cash requirements (present and future) is a major step forward in understanding the financial aspects of corporate strategy. The BCG matrix highlights the financial "interaction" within a corporate portfolio, shows the kinds of financial considerations that must be dealt with, and explains why priorities for corporate resource allocation can differ from business to business. It also provides good rationalizations for both grow-and-build strategies and divestiture. Yet it has several legitimate shortcomings:

1. A four-cell matrix based on high-low classifications hides the fact that many businesses (the majority?) are in markets with an "average" growth rate and have relative market shares that are neither high nor low but in between or intermediate. In which cells do these average businesses belong?

2. While viewing all businesses as stars, cash cows, dogs, or question marks does indeed add flavor and communicative appeal, it is a misleading simplification to categorize the members of a corporate portfolio into just four types. Some market leaders may be getting stronger while others are getting weaker—a few one-time stars or cash cows encounter hard times, and some end up bankrupt as dogs. Some market-share leaders never really were stars in terms of profitability. All businesses with low relative market shares are not dogs or question marks—in many cases, runner-up firms have proven track records in terms of growth, profitability, and competitive ability, even gaining on the so-called leaders. Hence, a key characteristic to assess is the *trend* in a firm's relative market share—is it gaining ground or losing ground and why? This weakness can be solved by placing directional arrows on each of the circles in the matrix—see Figure 8–2.

3. The BCG matrix is not a reliable indicator of relative investment opportunities across business units.[3] For example, investing in a star is not necessarily more attractive than investing in a lucrative cash cow. The matrix doesn't indicate if a question mark business is a potential winner or a likely loser. It says nothing about whether shrewd investment can turn a strong dog into a star or a cash cow.

4. Being a market leader in a slow-growth industry is not a surefire guarantee of cash cow status because (*a*) the investment requirements of a fortify-and-defend strategy, given the impact of inflation on the costs of replacing worn-out facilities and equipment, can soak up much or all of the available internal cash flows and (*b*) as markets mature, competitive forces often stiffen and the ensuing vigorous battle for volume and market share can shrink profit margins and wipe out any surplus cash flows.

5. A thorough assessment of the relative long-term attractiveness of business units in the portfolio requires an examination of more than just industry growth and relative market-share variables—as was shown in our discussion in Chapter 3.

6. The connection between relative market share and profitability is not as tight as the experience curve effect implies. The importance of cumulative production experience in lowering unit costs varies from industry to indus-

---

[3] Derek F. Abell and John S. Hammond, *Strategic Market Planning* (Englewood Cliffs, N.J.: Prentice-Hall, 1979), p. 212.

Figure 8–2 PRESENT VERSUS FUTURE POSITIONS IN THE PORTFOLIO MATRIX

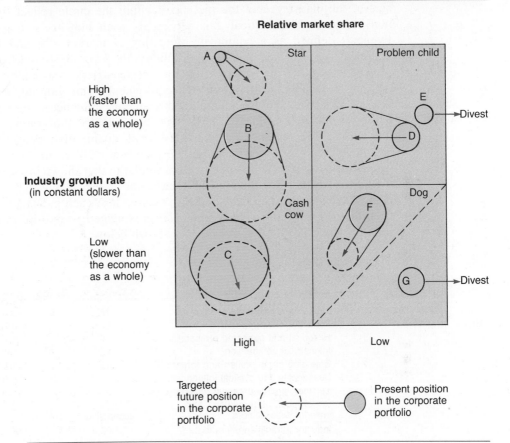

try. In some cases, a larger market share can be translated into a unit-cost advantage; in others, it cannot. Hence, it is wise to be cautious in basing strategy prescriptions on the assumption that experience curve effects are strong enough and cost differences among competitors big enough to totally drive competitive advantage (in Chapter 5 we demonstrated that competitive advantage springs from far more than just experience curve economics).

The Industry Attractiveness/Business Strength Matrix

An alternative matrix approach that avoids some of the shortcomings of the BCG growth-share matrix has been pioneered by General Electric with help from the consulting firm of McKinsey and Company. GE's effort to analyze its broadly diversified portfolio produced a nine-cell matrix based on the two dimensions of long-term industry attractiveness and business strength/competitive position.[4] In this matrix, depicted in Figure 8–3, the area of the circles is proportional to the size of the industry, and the pie slices within the circle reflect the business's market share. The vertical axis represents each industry's long-term attractiveness, defined as a composite weighting of market size and growth rate, historical and projected industry profitability, the favorable or unfavorable impact of driving forces, competitive intensity, entry barriers, seasonality and cyclical influences, technological and capital requirements, emerging threats and opportunities, and social, environmental, and regulatory influences—essentially a summation of all the considerations that go into industry and competitive analysis (covered in Chapter 3). To arrive at a formal, quantitative measure of industry attractiveness, as opposed to a simple judgment of high, medium, or low, GE developed a list of attractiveness factors similar to that shown in the box in Figure 8–3. Each industry attractiveness factor was assigned a weight based on its importance to GE. Then management assessed how each industry stacked up on each factor (using a 1 to 5 rating scale); a weighted composite rating for each industry was calculated in the manner shown below:

Industry attractiveness factor	Weight	Rating	Value
Market size and projected growth	.15	5	0.75
Impact of driving forces	.20	1	0.20
Historical and projected profitability	.10	1	0.10
Intensity of competition	.25	4	1.00
Emerging opportunities and threats	.15	1	0.15
Seasonality and cyclical influences	.05	2	0.10
Technological and capital requirements	.10	3	0.30
Social, political, regulatory, and environmental factors	Must be acceptable	—	—
Industry attractiveness rating	1.00		2.60

Each industry's attractiveness rating determines its position on the vertical scale in Figure 8–3.

To arrive at a quantitative measure of business strength/competitive position, each business was rated, using the basic approach shown above, on a series of indicators GE devised to reflect business strength/competitive position—relative market share, success in increasing market share and profitability, ability to match rival firms on cost and product quality, knowledge of customers and markets, how well the firm's skills and competence in the business matched the industry's key success factors, adequacy of production capacity, and caliber of

---

[4] For an expanded treatment, see Michael G. Allen, "Diagraming G.E.'s Planning for What's WATT," in *Corporate Planning: Techniques and Applications,* ed. Robert J. Allio and Malcolm W. Pennington (New York: AMACOM, 1979); and Hax and Majluf, *Strategic Management: An Integrative Perspective,* chap. 8.

Figure 8–3 GENERAL ELECTRIC'S INDUSTRY ATTRACTIVENESS/BUSINESS STRENGTH MATRIX

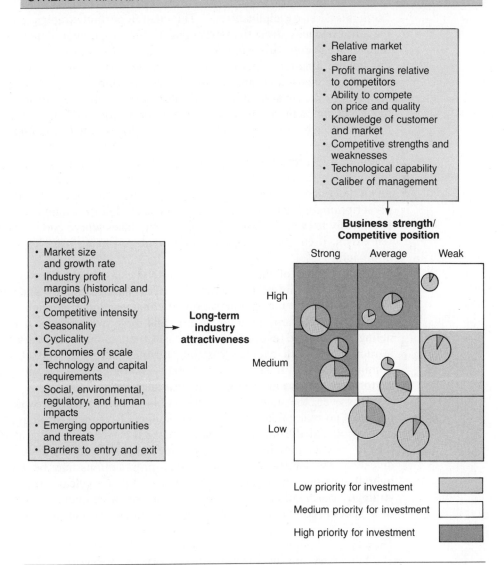

management (as specified in the box in Figure 8–3). The analytical issue here is whether to rate each business unit on the very same generic factors (which strengthens the basis for interindustry comparisons) or whether to rate each business unit's strength on the particular factors relative to its own industry (which gives a sharper measure of competitive position than a generic set of factors). Each business's strength/position rating determines its horizontal location in the matrix—that is, whether it ends up with a strong, average, or weak designation.[5]

Corporate Strategy Implications. The most important strategic implications from the attractiveness-strength matrix concern the assignment of investment priorities to each of the company's business units. Businesses in the three cells at the upper left, where long-term industry attractiveness and business strength/competitive position are favorable, are accorded top investment priority. The strategic prescription is "grow and build," with businesses in the high-strong cell having the highest claim on investment funds. Next in priority come businesses positioned in the three diagonal cells stretching from the lower left to the upper right. These businesses are usually given medium priority. They merit steady reinvestment to maintain and protect their industry positions; however, if one of them has an unusually attractive opportunity, it can win a higher investment priority and be given the go-ahead to employ a more aggressive strategic approach. The strategy prescription for businesses in the three cells in the lower right corner of the matrix is typically harvest or divest (in exceptional cases where good turnaround potential exists, it can be "overhaul and reposition" using some type of turnaround approach).[6]

The strength of the nine-cell attractiveness-strength approach is threefold. One, it allows for intermediate rankings between high and low and between strong and weak. Two, it incorporates explicit consideration of a much wider variety of strategically relevant variables. Three, and most important, it stresses the channeling of corporate resources to businesses that combine medium-to-high industry attractiveness with average-to-strong business strength/competitive position—combinations with the greatest probability of competitive advantage and superior performance. It is hard to argue against such logic.

However, the nine-cell GE matrix, like the four-cell growth-share matrix, provides no real guidance as to the specifics of business strategy; the most that can be concluded from the GE matrix analysis is what *general* strategic posture to take in managing the business: aggressive expansion, fortify-and-defend, harvest-divest, or overhaul-and-reposition. Such prescriptions may be valuable from an overall portfolio management perspective, but they leave the whole issue of strategic coordination across related businesses wide open, as well as the issue of what specific competitive approaches and strategic actions to take at the business-

---

[5] Essentially the same procedure is used in company situation analysis to do a competitive strength assessment (see Table 4–3 in Chapter 4). The only difference is that in the GE methodology the same set of competitive strength factors are used for every industry to provide a common benchmark for making comparisons across industries. In strategic analysis at the business level, the strength measures are *always* industry specific, never generic generalizations.

[6] At General Electric, each business actually ended up in one of five types of categories: (1) *high-growth potential* businesses deserving top investment priority, (2) *stable base* businesses deserving steady reinvestment to maintain position, (3) *support* businesses deserving periodic investment funding, (4) *selective pruning or rejuvenation* businesses deserving reduced investment funding, and (5) *venture* businesses deserving heavy R&D investment.

unit level. Another weakness has been pointed out by Professors Hofer and Schendel: the GE methodology tends to obscure businesses that are about to emerge as winners because the product/market is entering the takeoff stage.[7]

The Life-Cycle Matrix

To better identify a *developing-winner* type of business, Hofer developed a 15–cell matrix in which businesses are plotted in terms of stage of industry evolution and competitive position, as shown in Figure 8–4.[8] Again, the circles represent the sizes of the industries involved, and pie wedges denote the business's market share. In Figure 8–4, business A appears to be a *developing winner;* business C might be classified as a *potential loser,* business E as an *established winner,* business F as a cash cow, and business G as a loser or a dog. The power of the life-cycle matrix is the story it tells about the distribution of the firm's businesses across the stages of industry evolution.

Deciding What Type of Matrix to Construct

There is no need to use just one type of portfolio matrix. Provided adequate data is available, all three can be constructed to gain insights from different perspectives, and each matrix type has its pros and cons. The important thing is to try to capture the overall character of the firm's business makeup in a way that provides insight into the portfolio as a whole and how to best allocate corporate resources across the portfolio.

COMPARING INDUSTRY ATTRACTIVENESS

To determine the strategic roles of various business units and to what extent the company should invest additional funds in each one, corporate strategists must compare the long-term attractiveness of each industry represented in the corporate portfolio. Some business units will be situated in more attractive industries than others. The question to be explored in this third analytical step is "How good an *industry* is this for the company to be in?" All the methods for appraising industry attractiveness discussed in Chapter 3 come into play—the industry's economic characteristics, driving forces analysis, competition analysis, and identification of key success factors. If the nine-cell industry attractiveness-business strength matrix has already been constructed in the preceding analytical step, managers have a strong basis for comparing which business units are in the most

---

[7] Charles W. Hofer and Dan Schendel, *Strategy Formulation: Analytical Concepts* (St. Paul, Minn.: West Publishing, 1978), p. 33.

[8] Ibid., p. 34. This approach to business portfolio analysis was reportedly first used in actual practice by consultants at Arthur D. Little, Inc. For a full-scale review of this portfolio matrix approach, see Hax and Majluf, *Strategic Management: An Integrative Perspective,* chap. 9.

Figure 8–4   THE LIFE-CYCLE PORTFOLIO MATRIX

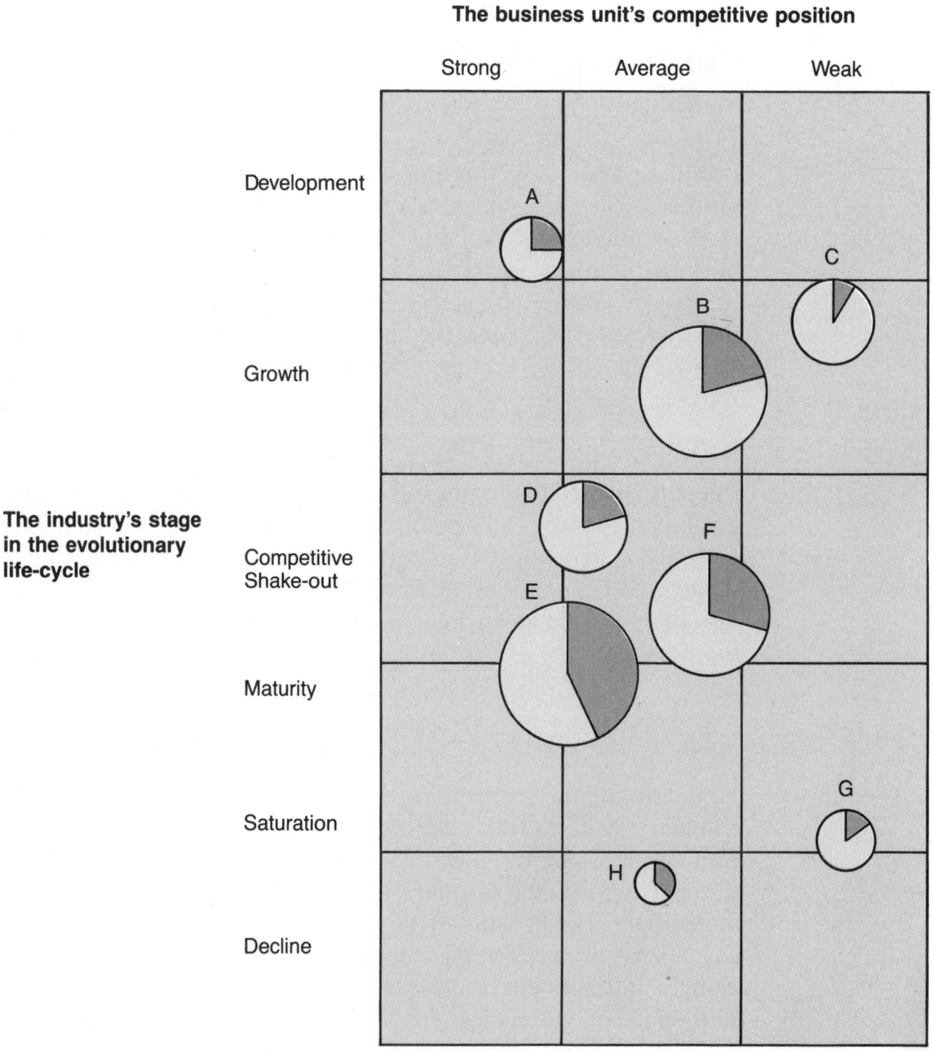

The business unit's competitive position

attractive industries. A quantitative ranking of industry attractiveness can be obtained using the nine-cell GE portfolio matrix. A qualitative or subjective ranking from most attractive to least attractive may suffice, however, if managers have done sufficient industry and competitive analysis to make dependable judgments.

For a diversified company to be a strong performer, a substantial portion of its revenues and profits must come from business units judged to be in attractive industries. It is particularly important for core businesses to be in industries where the outlook for growth and above-average profitability is good. Business units in the least attractive industries may be divestiture candidates, unless they are well enough positioned to overcome the adverse industry environment or they are a critical component of the portfolio.

COMPARING BUSINESS-UNIT STRENGTH

Doing an appraisal of each business unit's strength and competitive position in its industry helps corporate managers judge the business unit's chances for success in its industry. The task here is to evaluate whether the company's business unit is well-positioned in its industry and the extent to which it already is or can become a strong market contender. The two most revealing techniques for evaluating a business's position in its industry are SWOT analysis and competitive strength assessment. Quantitative rankings of the strength/position of the various business units in the corporate portfolio can be calculated using either the GE-style attractiveness-strength matrix or the procedure presented in Chapter 4. Subjective rankings from strongest to weakest may prove just as functional so long as the judgments are trustworthy.

The evaluations of which businesses in the portfolio enjoy the strongest competitive positions add further rationale and justification for corporate resource allocation. The long-term profit payoff from investing in a business with a strong position in a moderately attractive industry can be bigger than from investing in a weak business in a glamour industry. This is why a diversified company needs to consider *both* industry attractiveness *and* business strength in deciding where to steer resources.

Many diversified companies concentrate their resources on industries where they can be strong market contenders and divest businesses they don't think have the potential to be leaders in their respective industries. At General Electric, the whole thrust of corporate strategy and corporate resource allocation is to put GE's businesses into a number one or two position in both the United States and globally—see Illustration Capsule 19.

ILLUSTRATION CAPSULE 19

PORTFOLIO MANAGEMENT AT GENERAL ELECTRIC

When Jack Welch became CEO of General Electric in 1981, he launched a corporate strategy effort to reshape the company's diversified business portfolio. Early on he issued a challenge to GE's business-unit managers to become number one or number two in their industry; failing that, the business units either had to capture a decided technological advantage translatable into a competitive edge or face possible divestiture.

By 1989, GE was a different company. Under Welch's prodding, GE divested operations worth $9 billion—TV operations, small appliances, a mining business, and computer chips. It spent a total of $24 billion

(continued)

acquiring new businesses, most notably RCA, Roper (a maker of major appliances whose biggest customer was Sears), and Kidder Peabody (a Wall Street investment banking firm). Internally, many of the company's smaller business operations were put under the direction of larger "strategic business units." But, most significantly, in 1989, 12 of GE's 14 strategic business units were market leaders in the United States and globally (the company's financial services and communications units served markets too fragmented to rank):

	Market standing in the United States	Market standing in the world
Aircraft engines	First	First
Broadcasting (NBC)	First	Not applicable
Circuit breakers	Tied for first with 2 others	Tied for first with 3 others
Defense electronics	Second	Second
Electric motors	First	First
Engineering plastics	First	First
Factory automation	Second	Third
Industrial and power systems	First	First
Lighting	First	Second
Locomotives	First	Tied for first
Major home appliances	First	Tied for second
Medical diagnostic imaging	First	First

In 1989, having divested most of the weak businesses and having built existing businesses into leading contenders, Welch launched a new initiative within GE to dramatically boost productivity and reduce the size of GE's bureaucracy. Welch argued that for GE to continue to be successful in a global marketplace, the company had to press hard for continuous cost reduction in each of its businesses and cut through bureaucratic procedures to shorten response times to changing market conditions.

Source: Developed from information in Stratford P. Sherman, "Inside the Mind of Jack Welch," *Fortune*, March 27, 1989, pp. 39–50.

COMPARING BUSINESS-UNIT PERFORMANCE

Having rated business units on the basis of industry attractiveness and competitive strength, the next step is to compare their *actual historical performance* and their *future performance prospects*. Information regarding a business unit's past performance can be gleaned from the company's financial records. The industry attractiveness/business strength evaluations provide a basis for judging future prospects. The most important performance yardsticks tend to be sales growth, profit growth, contribution to company earnings, and return on assets employed in the business; however, cash flow generation can also be a big consideration, especially for cash cow businesses or for businesses with potential for harvesting.

The profits the company's core businesses generate determine whether the portfolio as a whole will turn in a strong or weak performance. Noncore businesses with subpar track records and little expectation for improvement generally become candidates for divestiture. Business units with the brightest profit and growth outlook generally head the list for capital investment.

STRATEGIC FIT ANALYSIS

The next step is to determine how well each business unit fits in the portfolio. Fit needs to be looked at from two angles: (1) whether the business unit has valuable strategic fit with other business units in the portfolio and (2) whether the business unit meshes well with corporate strategy or adds a useful dimension to the corporate portfolio. A business is more attractive as a portfolio holding when it presents cost-sharing or skills transfer opportunities that can be translated into stronger competitive advantage and/or added profitability. Likewise, a business unit is more valuable when it is capable of contributing heavily to corporate performance objectives (sales growth, profit growth, above-average return on investment, and so on), when it fits in with the corporation's strategic direction, when it has characteristics that senior management wants to build into the portfolio, and when it enhances the value of the corporation's portfolio.

RANKING THE BUSINESS UNITS ON INVESTMENT PRIORITY

Using the information and results of the preceding evaluation steps, managers can easily rank the business units in terms of priority for new capital investment and develop a general strategic direction for each business unit. The task is to draw conclusions about where the corporation should be investing its financial resources. Which business units should have top priority for new capital investment and financial support? Which business units should carry the lowest priority for new investment? Out of this ranking comes a clearer idea of what the basic strategic approach for each business unit should be—grow and build (aggressive expansion), fortify and defend (protect current position with new investments as needed), overhaul and reposition (try to move the business into a more desirable industry position and to a better spot in the business portfolio matrix), or harvest/divest. In deciding whether to divest a business unit, one needs to use a number of evaluating criteria: industry attractiveness, competitive strength, strategic fit with other businesses, performance potential (profit, return on capital employed, contribution to cash flow), compatibility with corporate priorities, capital requirements, and value to the overall portfolio.

As part of this evaluation step, consideration needs to be given to whether and how corporate resources and skills can be used to enhance the competitive standing of particular business units.[9] The potential for skills transfer and infusion of new capital becomes especially important when the firm has business units in less-than-desirable competitive positions and/or where improvement in some key success area could make a big difference to the business unit's performance. It is also important when corporate strategy is predicated on strategic fit and the managerial game plan calls for transferring corporate skills and strengths to recently acquired business units in an effort to give them a competitive edge and bolster their market position.[10]

CRAFTING A CORPORATE STRATEGY

The preceding analysis sets the stage for crafting strategic moves to improve the company's overall performance. The basic issue of "what to do" hinges on the conclusions drawn about the overall *mix* of businesses in the portfolio.[11] The key considerations here are: Does the portfolio contain enough businesses in very attractive industries? Does the portfolio contain too many marginal businesses or question marks? Is the proportion of mature or declining businesses so great that corporate growth will be sluggish? Does the firm have enough "cash cows" to finance the stars and emerging winners? Do the company's core businesses generate dependable profits and/or cash flow? Is the portfolio overly vulnerable to seasonal or recessionary influences? Does the firm have too many businesses it really doesn't need or should divest? Does the firm have its share of industry leaders, or is it burdened with too many businesses in average-to-weak competitive positions? Does the makeup of the business portfolio put the corporation in good position for the future? Answers to these questions point to the need for divestitures, acquisitions, and restructuring of the portfolio.

The Performance Test

The best test of the business portfolio's overall attractiveness is whether the combined growth and profitability of each business in the portfolio will allow the company to attain its performance objectives. If so, no major corporate strategy changes are indicated. However, if a performance shortfall is probable, top management can take any of several actions to close the gap:[12]

1. *Alter the strategic plans for some (or all) of the businesses in the portfolio.* This option essentially involves renewed corporate efforts to get better performance out of its present business units. Corporate managers can push business-level managers for better performance. However, pursuing better short-term

---

[9] Hofer and Schendel, *Strategy Formulation*, p. 80.

[10] Michael E. Porter, *Competitive Advantage: Creating & Sustaining Superior Performance* (New York: Free Press, 1985), chap. 9.

[11] Barry Hedley, "Strategy and the Business Portfolio," *Long Range Planning* 10, no. 1 (February 1977), p. 13; and Hofer and Schendel, *Strategy Formulation*, pp. 82–86.

[12] Hofer and Schendel, *Strategy Formulation*, pp. 93–100.

performance, if done too zealously, can impair long-term performance of the adversely affected business units. In any case there are limits as to how much extra performance can be achieved to reach established targets.

2. *Add new business units to the corporate portfolio.* Making new acquisitions and/or internal start-up of new businesses to boost overall performance, however, raises some new strategy issues. Expanding the corporate portfolio means taking a close look at (*a*) whether to acquire related or unrelated businesses, (*b*) what size acquisition(s) to make, (*c*) how the new units will fit into the present corporate structure, (*d*) what specific features to look for in an acquisition candidate, and (*e*) if acquisitions can be financed without shortchanging present business units on their new investment requirements. Nonetheless, adding new businesses is a major strategic option, one frequently used by diversified companies needing to escape sluggish earnings performance.

3. *Delete weak-performing or money-losing businesses from the corporate portfolio.* The most likely candidates for divestiture are businesses in a weak competitive position, in a relatively unattractive industry, or in an industry that does not "fit". Funds from divestitures can, of course, be used to finance new acquisitions, pay down corporate debt, or fund new strategic thrusts in the remaining businesses.

4. *Form alliances to try to alter conditions responsible for subpar performance potentials.* In some situations, alliances with domestic or foreign firms, trade associations, suppliers, unions, customers, or special interest groups may help ameliorate adverse performance prospects.[13] Forming or supporting a political action group may be an effective way of lobbying for solutions to import-export problems, tax disincentives, and onerous regulatory requirements.

5. *Reduce corporate performance objectives.* Adverse market circumstances or declining fortunes in one or more core business units can render companywide performance targets unreachable. So can overly ambitious objective-setting. Closing the gap between actual and desired performance may then require downward revision of corporate objectives to bring them more in line with reality. As a practical matter, though, this tends to be a "last-resort" option; it is used only after other options have come up short.

Translating Strategic Fit into Competitive Advantage

A second major corporate strategy-making category concerns what to do about strategic fit opportunities. Creating and capturing strategic fit benefits is what makes the corporate strategists in diversified companies *more than portfolio managers* and the firm itself *more than a holding company.*[14] Indeed, building

---

[13] For an excellent discussion of the benefits of alliances among competitors in global industries, see Kenichi Ohmae, "The Global Logic of Strategic Alliances," *Harvard Business Review* 67, no. 2 (March–April 1989), pp. 143–54.

[14] Porter, *Competitive Advantage*, p. 364. This point is also emphasized in Kenichi Ohmae, *The Mind of the Strategist* (New York: Penguin Books, 1983), pp. 137–40.

competitive advantage out of diversification is perhaps the chief way corporate executives really *add value* to a diversified enterprise.[15] If diversification produces no strategic fit opportunities of consequence, corporate strategists must try to build shareholder value in some or all of the following ways:

- Doing an especially good job of portfolio management (selecting new businesses to get into that will prove to be outstanding performers, selling business units at their peak and getting premium prices, and so on) so the enterprise consistently outperforms other firms in generating dividends and capital gains for stockholders.

- Doing such a good job helping to manage the various business units (by providing expert problem-solving skills, innovative ideas, and improved decision-making acumen to the business-level managers) that the business units perform at a higher level than they would otherwise be able to do.

- Providing such inspirational leadership that business-unit managers and employees are motivated to perform ''over their heads'' on a sustained basis, thereby adding an ''extra'' measure of performance.

All three of these ways amount to ''better management.'' For corporate management to add value to a diversified firm in some way other than capturing strategic fit benefits and creating competitive advantage, corporate executives must be ''managerially superior'' and produce results that business-level managers cannot. There is no credible evidence that the managers of diversified companies have turned in exceptional records of portfolio management.[16]

It is difficult to build shareholder value in a diversified enterprise unless the diversification involves a deliberate effort to pursue the competitive advantage opportunities to strategic fit. Unrelated or conglomerate diversification is, for the most part, a *financial approach to diversification* where shareholder value accrues from spreading investment risks across more businesses and from astute portfolio management. Related diversification, however, is clearly a *strategic approach to diversification* because it is predicated on exploiting the linkages between the activity-cost chains of different businesses in order to build competitive advantage and strengthen the company's overall long-term competitive position.

Taking Actions to Achieve Strategic Coordination. Building competitive advantage out of diversification at the corporate level is grounded in coordinating and managing the interrelationships in the activity-cost chains of a firm's business units. Strategic fit analysis begins with analyzing the activity-cost chains of each

---

[15] The term *add value* is used here to mean that performance of the *corporate-level* management functions is done in a manner that causes the profit performance of a diversified firm to be *more* than the total of what its business units would earn operating as independent companies. To put it another way, unless a diversified firm turns in a better performance than its business units could earn in the aggregate on their own, corporate management adds no pecuniary value to the enterprise.

[16] See Michael E. Porter, ''From Competitive Advantage to Corporate Strategy,'' *Harvard Business Review* 65, no. 3 (May–June 1987), pp. 43–46.

business unit to identify opportunities for cost sharing, skills transfer, and/or differentiation enhancement.[17] In searching for business unit interrelationships to capitalize on, care has to be taken to distinguish between opportunities where real sharing benefits can be achieved and those where the degree of relatedness is insignificant or else disappears when subject to scrutiny. Moreover, there are many sources of business-unit linkages: (1) supplier and/or component parts interrelationships, (2) technology and production process overlaps, (3) distribution channel interrelationships, (4) customer overlaps, (5) common managerial know-how requirements, and (6) competitor interrelationships (different business units may have common competitors and often two or more business units of one diversified firm may compete with two or more business units of another—a condition that makes them *multipoint competitors*).

Once the interrelationships among business units already in the corporate portfolio are identified, the next step is to identify important interrelationships between a firm's present business units and other industries not represented in its portfolio.[18] Looking for sharing potentials in industries outside the portfolio can turn up interesting acquisition candidates and is a fruitful way of developing stronger strategic fits. Studying the portfolios of other firms with related portfolios can yield clues about which industries may offer attractive cost sharing, skills transfer, and differentiation possibilities.

Once the strategic fit opportunities inside and outside the portfolio are identified, corporate strategists have to assess how much the opportunities can contribute to building an attractive corporate-based competitive advantage.[19] The size of the competitive advantage depends directly on whether the strategic benefit potential is competitively significant, the cost of capturing the benefits, and the difficulty of matching and coordinating the business unit interrelationships. Analysis usually reveals that while there are many actual and potential business unit interrelationships and linkages, only a few have enough strategic importance to generate meaningful competitive advantage.

The final step is to develop a corporate action plan to coordinate those targeted business unit interrelationships where an attractive net competitive potential exists.[20] Corporate coordination of these interrelationships can be pursued in several different ways:[21]

1. Implementing sharing of the related activities in the cost chain—examples include centralizing the procurement of raw materials, combining R&D and design activities in one unit, integrating manufacturing facilities wholly or partially, combining dealer networks and sales force organizations, and combining order processing and shipping.

---

[17] Porter, *Competitive Advantage*, p. 368; see also Ohmae, *The Mind of the Strategist*, pp. 137–38.

[18] Porter, *Competitive Advantage*, pp. 370–71.

[19] Ibid., pp. 371–72.

[20] Ibid., p. 372.

[21] Ibid., pp. 372–75; and Ohmae, *The Mind of the Strategist*, pp. 142–62.

2. Coordinating the strategies of the related business units to unify and strengthen the firm's overall approach to customers, suppliers, and/or distribution channels and to present a stronger offensive or defensive front against the actions of competitors.

3. Formulating a corporate-level game plan for attacking and/or defending against multipoint competitors, the thrust of which is to strengthen the firm's overall position and put multipoint rivals under added competitive pressure.

4. Setting up interbusiness task forces, standing committees, or project teams to transfer generic know-how, proprietary technology, and skills from one business unit to another and/or to implement sharing.

5. Diversifying into new businesses that enhance or extend strategic fit relationships in the activity-cost chains of existing businesses.

6. Divesting units that do not have strategic fit relationships or that make sharing and coordination more difficult.

7. Establishing incentives for business-unit managers to work together in realizing strategic fit potentials.

Deploying Corporate Resources

Getting ever-higher levels of performance out of the company's business portfolio also depends on doing an effective job of corporate resource allocation. The strategy-making task is to steer resources out of low opportunity areas into high opportunity areas. Divesting marginal businesses serves this purpose by freeing unproductive assets for redeployment. Added to the corporate treasury are the surplus funds from cash cow businesses and businesses being harvested. Options for allocating such funds include (1) investing in the maintenance and expansion of existing businesses, starting with those given the highest priority, until expected ROI hits the minimum acceptable level, (2) making acquisitions if needed, (3) funding long-range R&D ventures, (4) paying off existing long-term debt, (5) increasing dividends, and (6) repurchasing the company's stock. The first three represent *strategic* actions; the last three are *financial* moves. Ideally, funds are available to serve both strategic and financial purposes; if not, strategic uses should take precedence over financial uses except in unusual and compelling circumstances.

GUIDELINES FOR MANAGING THE CORPORATE STRATEGY FORMATION PROCESS

Although formal analysis and entrepreneurial brainstorming are important to corporate strategy selection, there is more. The process used to make major strategic decisions is typically fragmented, incremental, and the product of a consensus among senior management.[22] Rarely is there an all-inclusive grand

---

[22] James Brian Quinn, *Strategies for Change: Logical Incrementalism* (Homewood, Ill.: Richard D. Irwin, 1980), p. 15.

formulation of the total corporate strategy. Instead, corporate strategy in major enterprises emerges incrementally from the unfolding of many different internal and external events, the result of probing the future, experimenting, gathering more information, sensing problems, building awareness of the various options, developing ad hoc responses to unexpected "crises," communicating partial consensus as it emerges, and acquiring a "feel" for all the strategically relevant factors, their importance, and their interrelationships.[23]

Strategic analysis in diversified companies is not a time that executives set aside to undertake a single comprehensive review. Such big reviews may be scheduled, but evidence suggests that major strategic decisions emerge gradually rather than from periodic, full-scale analysis followed by prompt decision. Typically, top executives approach major strategic decisions a step at a time, often starting from broad, intuitive conceptions and then embellishing, fine-tuning, and modifying their original thinking as more information is gathered, as formal analysis confirms or modifies emerging judgments about the situation, and as confidence and consensus build for what strategic moves need to be made. Often attention and resources are concentrated on a few critical strategic thrusts that illuminate and integrate corporate direction, objectives, and strategies.

KEY POINTS

Strategic analysis in diversified companies is an eight-step process. Step one is to identify the present corporate strategy. Step two is to construct business portfolio matrixes as needed to see what the overall composition of the present portfolio looks like. Step three is to profile the industry and competitive environment of each business unit and draw conclusions about how attractive each industry in the portfolio is. Step four is to probe the competitive strength of the individual businesses and how well situated each is in its respective industry. Step five is to compare the different business units on the basis of their performance track record and their future performance prospects. Step six is to determine how well each business unit fits in with corporate direction and strategy and whether it has important strategic fit relationships with other businesses in the portfolio. Step seven is to rank the business units from highest to lowest in investment priority, drawing conclusions about where the firm should be putting its money and what the general strategic direction of each business unit should be (grow and build, hold and maintain, overhaul and reposition, harvest, or divest). Step eight is to use the preceding analysis to craft a series of moves to improve overall corporate performance. The primary corporate strategy moves involve:

- Making acquisitions, starting new businesses from within, and divesting marginal businesses or businesses that no longer match the corporate direction and strategy.
- Devising moves to strengthen the long-term competitive positions of the company's core businesses.

---

[23] Ibid., pp. 58 and 196.

- Acting to create strategic fit opportunities and turn them into long-term competitive advantage.
- Steering corporate resources out of low-opportunity areas into high-opportunity areas.

SUGGESTED READINGS

Bettis, Richard A., and William K. Hall. "Strategic Portfolio Management in the Multibusiness Firm." *California Management Review* 24 (Fall 1981), pp. 23–38.

————. "The Business Portfolio Approach—Where It Falls Down in Practice." *Long Range Planning* 16, no. 2 (April 1983), pp. 95–104.

Christensen, H. Kurt; Arnold C. Cooper; and Cornelis A. Dekluyer. "The Dog Business: A Reexamination." *Business Horizons* 25, no. 6 (November–December 1982), pp. 12–18.

Hamermesh, Richard G. *Making Strategy Work*. New York: John Wiley & Sons, 1986, chaps. 1, 4, and 7.

Haspeslagh, Phillippe. "Portfolio Planning: Uses and Limits." *Harvard Business Review* 60, no. 1 (January–February 1982), pp. 58–73.

Hax, Arnoldo, and Nicolas S. Majluf. *Strategic Management: An Integrative Perspective*. Englewood Cliffs, N.J.: Prentice-Hall, 1984, chaps. 7–9.

Henderson, Bruce D. "The Application and Misapplication of the Experience Curve." *Journal of Business Strategy* 4, no. 3 (Winter 1984), pp. 3–9.

Naugle, David G., and Garret A. Davies. "Strategic-Skill Pools and Competitive Advantage." *Business Horizons* 30, no. 6 (November–December 1987), pp. 35–42.

Porter, Michael E. *Competitive Advantage: Creating & Sustaining Superior Performance*. New York: Free Press, 1985, chaps. 9–11.

————. "From Competitive Advantage to Corporate Strategy." *Harvard Business Review* 65, no. 3 (May–June 1987), pp. 43–59.

9 Implementing Strategy: Organization-Building, Budgets, and Support Systems

Just being able to conceive bold new strategies is not enough. The general manager must also be able to translate his or her strategic vision into concrete steps that "get things done."
Richard G. Hamermesh

Organizing is what you do before you do something, so that when you do it, it is not all mixed up.
A. A. Milne

Once the course of strategy has been charted, the manager's priorities swing to converting the strategic plan into actions and good results. Putting the strategy into effect and getting the organization moving in the chosen direction calls for a fundamentally different set of managerial actions and skills. Whereas crafting strategy is largely an *entrepreneurial* activity, implementing strategy is primarily an internal *administrative* activity. Whereas strategy formulation entails heavy doses of vision, analysis, and entrepreneurial judgment, successful strategy implementation depends on the skills of working through others, organizing, motivating, culture-building, and creating strong fits between strategy and how the organization does things. Ingrained behavior does not change just because a new strategy has been announced.

Strategy implementation poses the tougher, more time-consuming management challenge. Practitioners are emphatic in saying that it is a whole lot easier to develop a sound strategic plan than it is to "make it happen." To see why, let's look at what strategy implementation involves.

THE STRATEGY IMPLEMENTATION FRAMEWORK

Strategy implementation entails *converting the strategic plan into action and then into results.* Implementation is successful if it produces the intended results and levels of performance. What makes the process so demanding is the wide sweep of managerial activities that have to be attended to, the many ways managers can proceed in tackling each activity, the skill it takes to get a variety of initiatives launched and moving, and the resistance to change that has to be overcome. In addition, each strategy implementation situation is unique enough to require its own specific *action agenda.* The manner in which strategy is implemented has to fit the organization's situation. In addition, it has to take into account the nature of the strategy (implementing a strategy to become the low-cost producer is different from implementing a differentiation strategy keyed to superior quality and premium prices). And it has to take into account the amount of strategic change involved (shifting to a bold new strategy poses different implementation problems than making minor changes in a strategy already in place).

The Key Tasks

But, while the details of strategy implementation are specific to the situation, certain administrative bases have to be covered in one way or another during implementation, no matter what the organization's situation. Figure 9–1 shows the principal administrative tasks that crop up repeatedly in the strategy implementation process. Depending on the organization's circumstances, some of these tasks are likely to prove more significant and time-consuming than others. To arrive at an agenda for what needs to be done to put the chosen strategy into place, managers have to thoroughly evaluate what internal conditions are needed to execute the organization's strategy successfully and then create these conditions as rapidly as practical.

The implementation goal is to unite the total organization behind strategy accomplishment and to fit the organization's conduct of its operations to the requirements for successful strategy execution. The motivational and inspirational challenge is to build such determined commitment up and down the ranks that an enthusiastic organizationwide crusade emerges to carry out the strategy and meet performance targets. Along with enthusiasm and strategic commitment, however, must come a concerted managerial effort to create a series of strategy-supportive "fits." The internal organization structure must be matched to the strategy. The necessary organizational skills and capabilities must be developed. Resource and budget allocations have to be made strategy-supportive; departments have to be given the positions and the budgets needed to carry out their assigned strategic role. The reward structure, key policies, the information system, and operating practices all need to help enforce a push for effective strategy execution, as opposed to having a passive role or, even worse, acting as obstacles. Equally important, managers must do things in a manner and style that creates and nurtures a strategy-supportive work environment and corporate culture. The

Figure 9–1 IMPLEMENTING STRATEGY: THE KEY TASKS

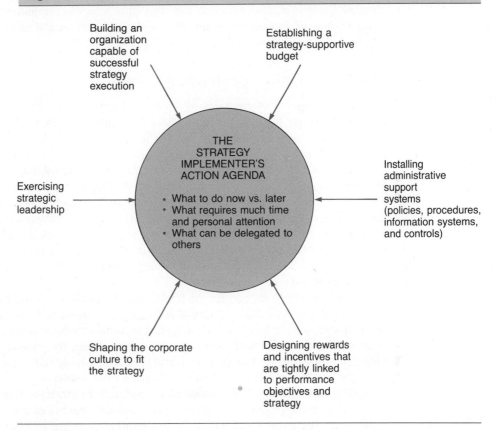

stronger the strategy-supportive fits management is able to create in various internal areas, the greater the chances of successful strategy implementation.

Who Are the Strategy Implementers?

An organization's chief executive officer and the heads of major organizational units are the persons most responsible for implementation. However, implementing strategy is not a job just for senior managers; it is a job for the whole management team. Strategy implementation involves every organization unit, from the head office down to each operating department, asking "What is required for us to implement our part of the overall strategic plan, and how can we best get it done?" In this sense, all managers become strategy implementers in their respective areas of authority and responsibility. Although big initiatives on the strategy implementation agenda pretty much have to be orchestrated by the CEO and other senior officers, top-level managers need to rely upon the active support and cooperation of lower-level managers to get things done and achieve the intended results. Lower-level managers are always active participants in the strategy implementation process; they not only lead the implementation process in their areas of responsibility but they also are instrumental in carrying out the day-to-day requirements mandated from above.

Leading the Implementation Process

One of the biggest determinants of successful implementation is how well strategy-implementers lead the process. There are many ways to go about the job. For instance, a strategy implementer can opt for an active, visible role or a low-key, behind-the scenes one. He/she can make decisions authoritatively or on the basis of consensus, delegate much or little, be personally involved in the details of implementation or stand on the sidelines and coach others carrying the day-to-day burden. The strategy implementer can decide whether to proceed swiftly (launching implementation initiatives on many fronts) or move deliberately, content with gradual progress over a long time frame. Moreover, work on all six strategy-implementing tasks (Figure 9–1) has to be launched and supervised and decisions made regarding which of the several strategy-supportive fits to work on first and what steps to take to create the fits.

How a manager goes about the implementation task is, in addition, a function of his/her experience and accumulated knowledge about the business—whether the manager is new to the job or a secure incumbent; the manager's network of personal relationships with others in the organization; the manager's own diagnostic, administrative, interpersonal, and problem-solving skills; the authority the manager has been given; and the manager's own leadership preferences. The remaining determinant of the manager's approach to strategy implementation is the context of the organization's situation—the seriousness of the firm's strategic difficulties, the nature and extent of the strategic change involved, the type of strategy being implemented, the strength of any ingrained behavior patterns, the financial and organizational resources available to work with, the configuration of personal and organizational relationships in the firm's history, the pressures for short-term performance, and other factors that make up the firm's "culture" and circumstances.

Each company's internal situation is unique enough so the strategy implementer has to custom-tailor his/her action agenda to fit the specific organizational environment at hand. This forces the manager to carefully consider all that strategy implementation involves and carefully diagnose action priorities and their sequence. The strategy implementer's role is thus all important. His/her agenda for action and his/her conclusions as to how hard and how fast to push for change are decisive in shaping the character of implementation and moving the process along.

In the remainder of this chapter and in Chapter 10, we survey the ins and outs of the manager's role as chief strategy implementer. For convenience, the discussion will be organized around the six administrative components of the strategy implementation process and the recurring administrative issues associated with each (see Figure 9–2). This chapter explores the management tasks of organiza-

Figure 9-2 THE ADMINISTRATIVE COMPONENTS OF STRATEGY IMPLEMENTATION

BUILDING AN ORGANIZATION CAPABLE OF EXECUTING THE STRATEGY	ESTABLISHING A STRATEGY-SUPPORTIVE BUDGET	INSTALLING INTERNAL ADMINISTRATIVE SUPPORT SYSTEMS	DEVISING REWARDS AND INCENTIVES THAT ARE TIGHTLY LINKED TO OBJECTIVES AND STRATEGY	SHAPING THE CORPORATE CULTURE TO FIT THE STRATEGY	EXERCISING STRATEGIC LEADERSHIP
Specific Tasks:	*Specific Tasks:*	*Specific Tasks:*	*Specific Tasks:*	*Specific Tasks:*	*Specific Tasks:*
• Creating a strategy-supportive organization structure.	• Seeing that each organizational unit has the budget to carry out its part of the strategic plan.	• Establishing and administering strategy-facilitating policies and procedures.	• Motivating organizational units and individuals to accomplish strategy.	• Establishing shared values.	• Leading the process of shaping values, molding culture, and energizing strategy accomplishment.
• Developing the skills and distinctive competence upon which strategy is grounded.	• Ensuring that resources are used efficiently to get "the biggest bang for the buck."	• Developing administrative and operating systems to give the organization strategy-critical capabilities.	• Designing rewards and incentives that induce the desired employee performance.	• Setting ethical standards.	• Keeping the organization innovative, responsive, and opportunistic.
• Selecting people for key positions.		• Generating the right strategic information on a timely basis.	• Promoting a results orientation.	• Creating a strategy-supportive work environment.	• Dealing with the politics of strategy, coping with power struggles, and building consensus.
				• Building a spirit of high performance into the culture.	• Enforcing ethical standards and behavior.
					• Initiating corrective actions to improve strategy execution.

tion building, budgetary allocation, and installing administrative support systems. Chapter 10 deals with linking rewards and incentives to performance objectives and strategy, building a strategy-supportive corporate culture, and exercising strategic leadership.

BUILDING A CAPABLE ORGANIZATION

Successful strategy execution depends greatly on good internal organization and competent personnel. Building a capable organization is thus always a top strategy implementation priority. Three organizational issues dominate:

1. Developing an internal organization structure that is responsive to the needs of strategy.
2. Building and nurturing the skills and distinctive competences in which the strategy is grounded and seeing that the organization has the managerial talents, technical know-how, and competitive capabilities it needs.
3. Selecting people for key positions.

Matching Organization Structure to Strategy

There are very few hard-and-fast rules for designing a strategy-supportive organization structure. Every firm's internal organization is partly idiosyncratic, the result of many organizational decisions and historical circumstances. Moreover, every strategy is grounded in its own set of key success factors and critical tasks. The only real ironclad imperative is to design the internal organization structure around the key success factors and critical tasks inherent in the firm's strategy. The following five-sequence procedure serves as a useful guideline for fitting structure to strategy:[1]

1. Pinpoint the key functions and tasks requisite for successful strategy execution.
2. Reflect on how the strategy-critical functions and organizational units relate to those that are routine and to those that provide staff support.
3. Make strategy-critical business units and functions the main organizational building blocks.
4. Determine the degrees of authority needed to manage each organizational unit, bearing in mind both the benefits and costs of decentralized decision-making.
5. Provide for coordination among the various organizational units.

Pinpointing the Strategy-Critical Activities.   In any organization, some activities and skills are always more critical to strategic success than others. From a strategy perspective, much of an organization's total work effort is routine and

---

[1] LaRue T. Hosmer, *Strategic Management: Text and Cases on Business Policy* (Englewood Cliffs, N.J.: Prentice-Hall, 1982), chap. 10; and J. Thomas Cannon, *Business Strategy and Policy* (New York: Harcourt Brace Jovanovich, 1968), p. 316.

falls under the rubric of administrative good housekeeping and necessary detail (handling payrolls, managing cash flows, controlling inventories, processing grievances, taking care of warehousing and shipping, processing customer orders, and complying with regulations). Other activities are primarily support functions (data processing, accounting, training, public relations, market research, and purchasing). Yet there are usually certain crucial tasks and functions that have to be exceedingly well done for the strategy to be successful. For instance, tight cost control is essential for a firm trying to be the low-cost producer in a commodity business where margins are low and price-cutting is a widely used competitive weapon. For a luxury goods manufacturer, the critical skills may be quality craftsmanship, distinctive design, and sophisticated promotional appeal. The strategy-critical activities vary according to the particulars of a firm's strategy and competitive requirements.

Two questions help identify what an organization's strategy-critical activities are: "What functions have to be performed extra well and on time for strategy to succeed?" and "In what areas would malperformance seriously endanger strategic success?"[2] The answers generally point squarely at what activities and skills are crucial and indicate where to concentrate organization-building efforts.

Understanding the Relationships among Activities.   Before the various critical, supportive, and routine activities are grouped into organizational units, the strategic relationships prevailing among them need to be scrutinized thoughtfully. Activities can be related by the flow of material through the production process, by the type of customer served, by the distribution channels used, by the technical skills and know-how needed to perform them, by a strong need to centralize authority over them for purposes of coordination, by the sequence in which tasks must be performed, and by geographic location, to mention some of the most obvious. Such relationships are important because one (or more) of the interrelationships usually become the basis for grouping activities into organizational units. If the needs of strategy are to drive organization design, then the relationships to look for are those that link one piece of the strategy to another.

Grouping Activities into Organization Units.   The chief guideline here is to make strategy-critical activities the main building blocks in the organization structure. The rationale is compelling: if activities crucial to strategic success are to get the attention and visibility they merit, they have to be a prominent part of the organizational scheme. When key functions and critical tasks take a backseat to less important activities, the politics of organizational budgetmaking usually leads to them being given fewer resources and accorded less significance than they have. On the other hand, when they form the core of the whole organization structure, their role and power in the overall scheme of things is highlighted and institutionalized. Senior managers seldom give a stronger signal as to what is strategically important than by making key functions and critical skills the most

---

[2] Peter F. Drucker, *Management: Tasks, Responsibilities, Practices* (New York: Harper & Row, 1974), pp. 530, 535.

prominent organizational building blocks and, further, assigning them a high position in the organizational pecking order.

Determining the Degree of Authority and Independence to Give Each Unit.   How much authority and decision-making latitude to give each organization unit, especially line-of-business units, is important. In the case of line-of-business units, one polar alternative is to centralize authority for the big strategy and policy decisions at the corporate level and delegate only operating decisions to business-level managers. At the other extreme, line-of-business units can be delegated enough autonomy to function independently, with little direct authority exerted by corporate headquarters staff.

Several guidelines for parcelling out authority across the various units can be offered. Activities and organizational units with a key role in strategy execution should not be subordinated to routine and nonkey activities. Revenue-producing and results-producing activities should not be subordinated to internal support or staff functions. With few exceptions, decisions should be delegated to managers closest to the scene of the action. Corporate-level authority over operating decisions at the business-unit level and below should be held to a minimum. The crucial administrative skill is selecting "strong" managers to head each unit and delegating them enough authority to formulate and execute an appropriate strategy for their unit; if the results such managers produce prove unsatisfactory, those with a poor track record should be weeded out.

Providing for Coordination among the Units.   Coordinating the activities of organizational units is accomplished mainly through positioning them in the hierarchy of authority. Managers higher up in the pecking order generally have authority over more organizational units and thus the clout to coordinate, integrate, and arrange for the cooperation of units under their supervision. The chief executive officer, the chief operating officer, and business-level managers are central points of coordination because of their position of authority over the whole unit. Besides positioning organizational units along the vertical scale of managerial authority, strategic efforts can also be coordinated through informal meetings, project teams, special task forces, standing committees, formal strategy reviews, and annual strategic planning and budgeting cycles. Additionally, the formulation of the strategic plan itself serves a coordinating role. The whole process of negotiating and deciding on objectives and strategies of each organizational unit and making sure related activities mesh helps coordinate operations across organizational units.

The Structure-Follows-Strategy Thesis

The practice of *consciously* matching organization design and structure to the particular needs and requirements of strategy is a fairly recent management development, and it springs from research evidence about firms' actual experiences. A landmark study by Alfred Chandler found that changes in an organization's strategy bring about new administrative problems which, in turn, require a new or refashioned structure for the new strategy to be successfully implemented.[3] His study of 70 large corporations revealed that structure tends to follow the growth strategy of the firm—but often not until inefficiency and internal operating problems provoke a structural adjustment. The experience of these firms followed a consistent sequential pattern: new strategy creation, emergence of new administrative problems, a decline in profitability and performance, a shift to a more appropriate organizational structure, and recovery to more profitable levels and improved strategy execution. Chandler found this sequence to be oft-repeated as firms grew and modified their corporate strategies. The lesson of Chandler's research is that the choice of organization structure *does make a difference* in how an organization performs. A company's internal organization merits reassessment whenever strategy changes.[4] A new strategy is likely to entail new or different skills and key activities. When these go unrecognized in the formal structure, the resulting mismatch between strategy and structure opens the door for implementation and performance problems.

The *structure-follows-strategy* thesis is undergirded with powerful logic: how an organization's work is structured is just a means to an end—not an end in itself. Structure is no more than a managerial device for facilitating execution of the organization's strategy and helping to achieve performance targets. An organization's structural design should be looked at as a tool for "harnessing" individual efforts and coordinating the performance of diverse tasks. In addition, it needs to promote getting things done efficiently. Without *deliberately* organizing responsibilities and activities to produce linkages between structure and strategy, the outcomes are likely to be disorder, friction, and inefficiency.[5]

How Structure Evolves as Strategy Evolves. As firms progress from small, entrepreneurial enterprises following a basic concentration strategy to more complex strategic phases of volume expansion, vertical integration, geographic expansion, and line-of-business diversification, their organizational structures tend to evolve from one-person management to functional departments to divisions to decentralized line-of-business units. Single-business companies almost always have some variant of a centralized functional structure. Vertically integrated firms and companies with broad geographic coverage typically are organized into operating divisions. The basic building blocks of a diversified company are the various individual businesses; decision-making is decentralized and each

---

[3] Alfred Chandler, *Strategy and Structure* (Cambridge, Mass.: MIT Press, 1962). Although the stress here is on matching structure to strategy, it is worth noting that structure can and does influence the choice of strategy. A "good" strategy must be doable. When an organization's present structure is so far out of line with the requirements of a particular strategy that the organization would have to be turned upside down and inside out to implement it, the strategy may not be doable and should not be given further consideration. In such cases, structure shapes the choice of strategy. The point here, however, is that once strategy is chosen, structure must be made to fit the strategy if, in fact, an approximate fit does not already exist. Any influences of structure on strategy should, logically, come before the point of strategy selection rather than after it.

[4] For an excellent study documenting how companies have revised their internal organization to accommodate strategic change, see Raymond Corey and Steven H. Star, *Organization Strategy: A Marketing Approach* (Boston: Harvard Business School, 1971), chap. 3.

[5] Drucker, *Management,* p. 523.

business is staffed to operate as an independent, stand-alone unit, with corporate headquarters performing only minimal functions for the business.

The Strategic Advantages and Disadvantages of Different Organizational Structures

There are five strategy-driven approaches to organization: (1) functional specialization, (2) geographic organization, (3) decentralized business divisions, (4) strategic business units, and (5) matrix structures featuring dual lines of authority and strategic priority. Each form has its own set of strategic advantages and disadvantages.

The Functional Organization Structure.   A functional organization structure tends to be effective in single-business units where key activities revolve around well-defined skills and areas of specialization. In such cases, in-depth specialization and focused concentration on performing functional area tasks and activities can enhance both operating efficiency and the development of a distinctive competence. Generally speaking, organizing by functional specialities promotes full utilization of the most up-to-date technical skills and helps a business capitalize on efficiency gains from using specialized manpower, facilities, and equipment. These are strategically important considerations for single-business organizations, dominant-product enterprises, and vertically integrated firms and account for why they usually have some kind of centralized, functionally specialized structure.

However, just what form the functional specialization takes varies according to customer-product-technology considerations. For instance, a technical instruments manufacturer may be organized around research and development, engineering, production, technical services, quality control, marketing, personnel, and finance and accounting. A municipal government, on the other hand, may be departmentalized according to function—fire, public safety, health services, water and sewer, streets, parks and recreation, and education. A university may divide its organizational units into academic affairs, student services, alumni relations, athletics, buildings and grounds, institutional services, and budget control. Two types of functional organizational approaches are diagrammed in Figure 9–3.

The Achilles' heel of a functional structure is getting and keeping tight strategic coordination across separated functional units. Functional specialists, partly because of how they were trained and the technical "mystique" of their jobs, tend to develop their own mind-set and ways of doing things. The more functional specialists differ in their perspectives and approaches, the more difficult it becomes to achieve strategic and operating coordination. They don't "talk the same language" and they don't have adequate appreciation for one another's strategic roles and problems. Each functional group tends to be more interested in its own "empire" and promoting its own strategic interest and importance (despite the lip service given to cooperation and "what's best for the company"). Functional politics and narrow perspectives can impose a time-consuming administrative burden on a business-level manager in terms of resolving cross-functional differ-

Figure 9–3 FUNCTIONAL ORGANIZATIONAL STRUCTURES

A. The building blocks of a "typical" functional organizational structure

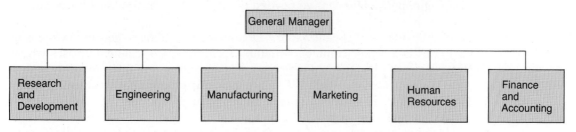

B. The building blocks of a process-oriented functional structure

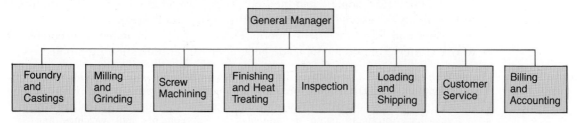

Strategic Advantages

- Permits centralized control of strategic results.
- Very well suited for structuring a single business.
- Structure is linked tightly to strategy by designating key activities as functional departments.
- Promotes in-depth functional expertise.
- Well suited to developing a functional-based distinctive competence.
- Conducive to exploiting learning/experience curve effects associated with functional specialization.
- Enhances operating efficiency where tasks are routine and repetitive.

Strategic Disadvantages

- Poses problems of functional coordination.
- Can lead to interfunctional rivalry and conflict, rather than cooperation—GM must referee functional politics.
- May promote overspecialization and narrow management viewpoints.
- Hinders development of managers with cross-functional experience because the ladder of advancement is up the ranks within the same functional area.
- Forces profit responsibility to the top.
- Functional specialists often attach more importance to what's best for the functional area than to what's best for the whole business—can lead to functional empire-building.
- Functional myopia often works against creative entrepreneurship, adapting to change, and attempts to restructure the activity-cost chain.

ences, enforcing joint cooperation, and opening lines of communication across departments. In addition, a functionally dominated organization tends to have tunnel vision when it comes to promoting entrepreneurial venturesomeness, developing creative responses to major customer-market technological changes, and pursuing opportunities that go beyond the industry's conventional boundaries.

Geographic Forms of Organization.   Organizing according to geographic areas or territories is a rather common structural form for large-scale enterprises whose strategies need to be tailored to fit the needs and features of different geographical areas. As indicated in Figure 9–4, geographic organization has its advantages and disadvantages, but the chief reason for its popularity is that, for one reason or another, it promotes improved performance.

In the private sector, a territorial structure is typically utilized by chain store retailers, power companies, cement firms, restaurant chains, and dairy products enterprises. In the public sector, such organizations as the Internal Revenue Service, the Social Security Administration, the federal courts, the U.S. Postal Service, the state troopers, and the Red Cross have adopted territorial structures to be directly accessible to geographically dispersed clientele.

Corey and Star cite Pfizer International as a good example of a company whose strategic requirements made geographic decentralization propitious:

> With sales of $223 million in 1964, Pfizer International operated plants in 27 countries and marketed in more than 100 countries. Its product lines included pharmaceuticals (antibiotics and other ethical prescription drugs), agriculture and veterinary products (such as animal feed supplements and vaccines and pesticides), chemicals (fine chemicals, bulk pharmaceuticals, petrochemicals, and plastics), and consumer products (cosmetics and toiletries).
>
> Ten geographic area managers reported directly to the president of Pfizer International and exercised line supervision over country managers. According to a company position description, it was "the responsibility of each area manager to plan, develop, and carry out Pfizer International's business in the assigned foreign area in keeping with company policies and goals."
>
> Country managers had profit responsibility. In most cases a single country manager managed all Pfizer activities in his country. In some of the larger, well-developed countries of Europe there were separate country managers for pharmaceutical and agricultural products and for consumer lines.
>
> Except for the fact that New York headquarters exercised control over the to-the-market prices of certain products, especially prices of widely used pharmaceuticals, area and country managers had considerable autonomy in their respective geographic areas. This was appropriate because each area, and some countries within areas, provided unique market and regulatory environments. In the case of pharmaceuticals and agriculture and veterinary products (Pfizer International's most important lines), national laws affected formulations, dosages, labeling, distribution, and often price. Trade restrictions affected the flow of bulk pharmaceuticals and chemicals and packaged products, and might in effect require the establishment of manufacturing plants to supply local markets. Competition, too, varied significantly from area to area.[6]

---

[6] Corey and Star, *Organization Strategy*, pp. 23–24.

Figure 9–4 A GEOGRAPHIC ORGANIZATIONAL STRUCTURE

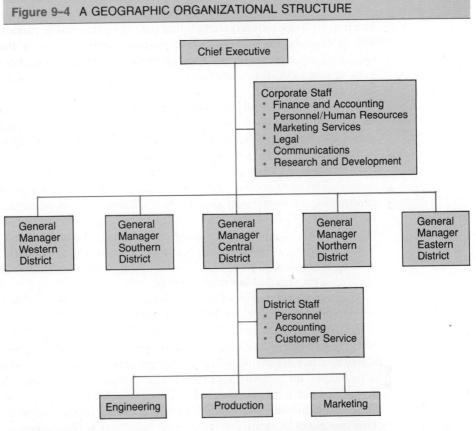

Strategic Advantages

- Allows tailoring of strategy to needs of each geographical market.
- Delegates profit/loss responsibility to lowest strategic level.
- Improves functional coordination within the target market.
- Takes advantage of economies of local operations.
- Area units make an excellent training ground for higher-level general managers.

Strategic Disadvantages

- Poses a problem of how much geographic uniformity headquarters should impose versus how much geographic diversity should be allowed.
- Greater difficulty in maintaining consistent company image/reputation from area to area when area managers exercise much strategic freedom.
- Adds another layer of management to run the geographic units.
- Can result in duplication of staff services at headquarters and district levels, creating a relative-cost disadvantage.

Decentralized Business Units.   Grouping activities along business and product lines has been a clear-cut trend among diversified enterprises for the past half century, beginning with the pioneering efforts of DuPont and General Motors in the 1920s. Separate business/product divisions emerged because diversification made a functionally specialized manager's job incredibly complex. Imagine the problems a manufacturing executive and his/her staff would have if put in charge of, say, 50 different plants using 20 different technologies to produce 30 different products in 8 different businesses/industries. In a multibusiness enterprise, the needs of strategy virtually dictate that the organizational sequence be corporate to line of business to functional area within a business rather than corporate to functional area (aggregated for all businesses). The latter produces a nightmare in making sense out of business strategy and achieving functional area coordination for a given business.

Strategy implementation is facilitated by grouping key activities belonging to the same business under one organizational roof, thereby creating line-of-business units (which then can be subdivided into whatever functional subunits suit the key activities/critical tasks makeup of the business.) The outcome not only is a structure that fits strategy but also a structure that makes the managers' jobs more doable. The creation of separate business units is then accomplished by decentralizing authority over the unit to the business-level manager. The approach, very simply, is to put entrepreneurially oriented general managers in charge of the business unit, giving them enough authority to formulate and implement the business strategy they deem appropriate, motivating them with incentives, and holding them accountable for the results they produce. Each business unit then operates as a stand-alone profit center.

Decentralized business units, however, pose a big problem to companies pursuing related diversification: *there is no mechanism for strategic coordination of related activities across business units*. It can be tough to get autonomy-conscious business-unit managers to cooperate in coordinating and sharing related activities; they are prone to argue long and hard about "turf" and about being held accountable for activities outside their control. To capture strategic fit in a diversified company, corporate headquarters must create an organizational mechanism for achieving strategic coordination across related business-unit activities. This can entail centralizing the related functions at the corporate level (having a corporate R&D department if there are technology and product development fits to be managed; creating a special corporate sales force to call on customers who purchase from several of the company's business units). Alternatively, corporate officers can develop bonus arrangements that give business-units managers the incentive to cooperate. If the strategic fit relationships involve skills or technology transfers across businesses, corporate headquarters can initiate the movement of skilled personnel from one business to another to effect the transfer of expertise.

A typical line-of-business organizational structure is shown in Figure 9–5, along with the strategy-related pros and cons of this type of organizational form.

Strategic Business Units.   In broadly diversified companies, the number of decentralized business units can be so great that the span of control is too much for a single chief executive. Then it may be useful to group related units and delegate authority over them to a senior executive who reports directly to the chief executive officer. While this imposes a layer of management between business-level managers and the chief executive, it may nonetheless improve strategic planning and top-management coordination of diverse business interests. This explains both the popularity of the group vice president concept among multi-

Figure 9–5 A DECENTRALIZED LINE-OF-BUSINESS TYPE OF ORGANIZATION STRUCTURE

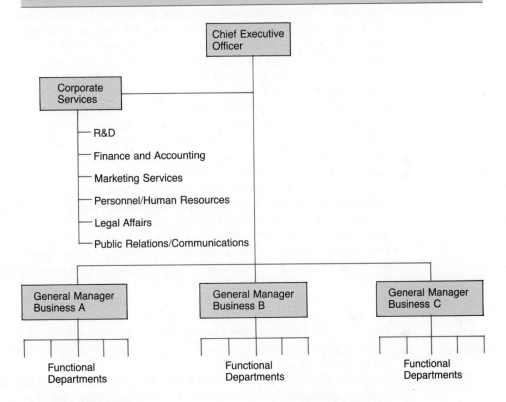

Strategic Advantages

- Offers a logical and workable means of decentralizing responsibility and delegating authority in diversified organizations.
- Puts responsibility for business strategy in closer proximity to each business's unique environment.
- Allows each business unit to organize around its own set of key activities and functional requirements.
- Frees CEO to handle corporate strategy issues.
- Puts clear profit/loss accountability on shoulders of business unit managers.

Strategic Disadvantages

- May lead to costly duplication of staff functions at corporate and business unit levels, thus raising administrative overhead costs.
- Poses a problem of what decisions to centralize and what decisions to decentralize (business managers need enough authority to get the job done, but not so much that corporate management loses control of key business level decisions).
- May lead to excessive division rivalry for corporate resources and attention.
- Business/division autonomy works against achieving coordination of related activities in different business units, thus blocking to some extent the capture of strategic fit benefits.
- Corporate management becomes heavily dependent on business unit managers.
- Corporate managers can lose touch with business unit situations, end up surprised when problems arise, and not know much about how to fix such problems.

business companies and the recent trend toward the formation of strategic business units.

A *strategic business unit* (SBU) is a grouping of business units based on some important strategic elements common to each. Possible elements include an overlapping set of competitors, a closely related strategic mission, a common need to compete globally, an ability to accomplish integrated strategic planning, common key success factors, and technologically related growth opportunities. At General Electric, a pioneer in the concept of SBUs, 190 units were grouped into 43 SBUs and then aggregated further into six "sectors."[7] At Union Carbide, 15 groups and divisions were decomposed into 150 "strategic planning units" and then regrouped and combined into 9 new "aggregate planning units." At General Foods (now a division of Philip Morris), SBUs were originally defined on a product-line basis but were later redefined according to menu segments (breakfast foods, beverages, main meal products, desserts, and pet foods).

The managerial value of the SBU concept is that it provides diversified companies with a way to rationalize the organization of many different businesses and an organizational arrangement for capturing strategic fit benefits. The strategic function of the group vice president is to provide the SBU with some cohesive direction and enforce strategic coordination across related businesses. Indeed, the group vice president, as strategic coordinator for all businesses in the SBU, is in a position to organize the SBU in ways that facilitate sharing and skills transfers where appropriate and to centralize "big" strategic decisions at the SBU level. The SBU, in effect, becomes a decision-making unit with broader strategic perspective than a single business unit, serving chiefly as the organizational mechanism for capturing strategic benefits and thereby creating competitive advantage for all businesses in the SBU.

SBUs are also helpful in reducing the complexity of dovetailing corporate strategy and business strategy and in "cross-pollinating" the growth opportunities in different industries, perhaps to create altogether new industries. SBUs make headquarters' reviews of the strategies of lower-level units less imposing (there is no practical way for a CEO to conduct in-depth reviews of a hundred or more different businesses). Figure 9–6 illustrates the SBU form of organization, along with its strategy related pros and cons.

Matrix Forms of Organization.   A matrix organization is a structure with two (or more) channels of command, two lines of budget authority, and two sources of performance and reward. The key feature of the matrix is that business (or product, project, or venture) and functional lines of authority are overlaid (to form a matrix or grid), and managerial authority over the activities in each unit/cell of the matrix is shared between the business/project/venture team manager and the functional manager—as shown in Figure 9–7. In a matrix structure, subordinates

---

[7] William K. Hall, "SBUs: Hot, New Topic in the Management of Diversification," *Business Horizons* 21, no. 1 (February 1978), p. 19. For an excellent discussion of the problems of implementing the SBU concept at 13 companies, see Richard A. Bettis and William K. Hall, "The Business Portfolio Approach—Where It Falls Down in Practice," *Long Range Planning* 16, no. 2 (April 1983), pp. 95–104.

Figure 9–6 AN SBU TYPE OF ORGANIZATION STRUCTURE

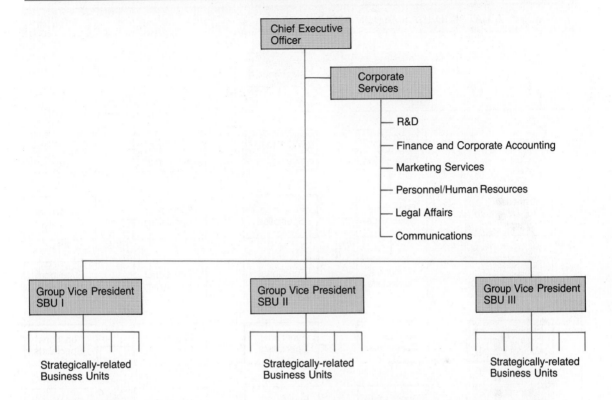

Strategic Advantages

- Provides a strategically relevant way to organize the business unit portfolio of a broadly diversified company

- Facilitates the coordination of related activities *within* an SBU, thus helping to capture the benefits of strategic fits in the SBU.

- Promotes more cohesiveness among the new initiatives of separate but related businesses.

- Allows strategic planning to be done at the most relevant level within the total enterprise.

- Makes the task of strategic review by top executives more objective and more effective.

- Helps allocate corporate resources to areas with greatest growth opportunities.

Strategic Disadvantages

- It is easy for the definition and grouping of businesses into SBUs to be so arbitrary that the SBU serves no other purpose than administrative convenience. If the criteria for defining SBUs are rationalizations and have little to do with the nitty-gritty of strategy coordination, then the groupings lose real strategic significance.

- The SBUs can still be myopic in charting their future direction.

- Adds another layer to top management.

- The roles and authority of the CEO, the group vice president, and the business-unit manager have to be carefully worked out or the group vice president gets trapped in the middle with ill-defined authority.

- Unless the SBU head is strong willed, very little strategy coordination is likely to occur across business units in the SBU.

- Performance recognition gets blurred; credit for successful business units tends to go to corporate CEO, then to business-unit head, last to group vice president.

Figure 9-7   A MATRIX ORGANIZATION STRUCTURE*

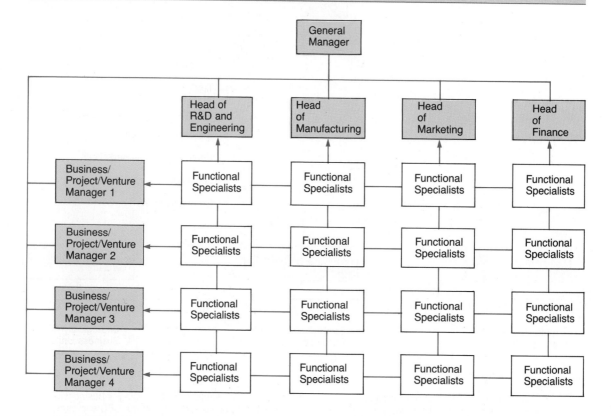

Strategic Advantages

- Gives formal attention to each dimension of strategic priority.

- Creates checks and balances among competing viewpoints.

- Facilitates capture of functionally-based strategic fits in diversified companies.

- Promotes making trade-off decisions on the basis of "what's best for the organization as a whole."

- Encourages cooperation, consensus-building, conflict resolution, and coordination of related activities.

Strategic Disadvantages

- Very complex to manage.

- Hard to maintain "balance" between the two lines of authority.

- So much shared authority can result in a transactions logjam and disproportionate amounts of time being spent on communications.

- It is hard to move quickly and decisively without getting clearance from many other people.

- Promotes an organizational bureaucracy and hamstrings creative entrepreneurship.

* Arrows indicate reporting channels.

have a continuing dual assignment: to the business/product/project and to their home-base function.[8] The outcome is a compromise between functional specialization (engineering, R&D, manufacturing, marketing, finance) and product-line, project, line-of-business, or special venture divisions (where all of the specialized talent needed for the product line/project/line-of-business/venture are assigned to the same divisional unit).

A matrix-type organization is a genuinely different and new structural form. One reason is that the unity-of-command principle is broken; two reporting channels, two bosses, and shared authority create a new kind of organizational climate. In essence, the matrix is a conflict resolution system through which strategic and operating priorities are negotiated, power is shared, and resources are allocated internally on the basis of "strongest case for what is best overall for the unit."[9]

The impetus for matrix organizations stems from growing use of strategies that add new sources of diversity (products, customer groups, technology, lines of business) to a firm's range of activities. Out of this diversity are coming product managers, functional managers, geographic area managers, new venture managers, and business-level managers—all of whom have important strategic responsibilities. When at least two of several variables (product, customer, technology, geography, functional area, and market segment) have roughly equal strategic priorities, a matrix organization can be an effective structural form. A matrix arrangement promotes internal checks and balances among competing viewpoints and perspectives, with separate managers for different dimensions of strategic initiative. A matrix approach thus allows each of several strategic considerations to be managed directly and to be formally represented in the organization structure. In this sense, it helps middle managers make trade-off decisions from an organizationwide perspective.[10] The other big advantage of matrix organization is as a mechanism for capturing strategic fit. When the strategic fits in a diversified company are related to a specific functional area (R&D, technology, marketing), matrix organization can be a reasonable structural arrangement for coordinating sharing and skills transfer.

Companies using matrix structures include General Electric, Texas Instruments, Citibank, Shell Oil, TRW, Bechtel, Boeing, and Dow Chemical. However, most applications of matrix organization are limited to a portion of what the firm does (certain important functions) rather than spanning the whole of a large-scale diversified enterprise.

---

[8] A more thorough treatment of matrix organizational forms can be found in Jay R. Galbraith, "Matrix Organizational Designs," *Business Horizons* 15, no. 1 (February 1971), pp. 29–40.

[9] For two excellent critiques of matrix organizations, see Stanley M. Davis and Paul R. Lawrence, "Problems of Matrix Organizations," *Harvard Business Review* 56, no. 3 (May–June 1978), pp. 131–42; and Erik W. Larson and David H. Gobeli, "Matrix Management: Contradictions and Insights," *California Management Review* 29, no. 4 (Summer 1987), pp. 126–38.

[10] Ibid., p. 132.

A number of companies shun matrix organization because of its chief weaknesses.[11] It is a complex structure to manage; people often end up confused over who to report to for what. Moreover, because the matrix signals that everything is important and, further, that everybody needs to communicate with everybody else, a "transactions logjam" can emerge. Action turns into paralysis since, with shared authority, it is hard to move decisively without first considering many points of view and getting clearance from many other people. Sizable transactions costs, communication inefficiencies, and delays in responding can result. Even so, in some situations the benefits of conflict resolution and consensus building outweigh these weaknesses.

Combination and Supplemental Methods of Organization. A single type of structural design is not always sufficient to meet the requirements of strategy. When this occurs, one option is to mix and blend the basic organization forms, matching structure to strategy requirement by requirement and unit by unit. Another is to supplement a basic organization design with special-situation devices. Three of the most frequently used ones are:

1. The *project manager* or *project staff approach,* where a separate, largely self-sufficient subunit is created to oversee the completion of a special activity (setting up a new technological process, bringing out a new product, starting up a new venture, consummating a merger with another company, seeing through the completion of a government contract, supervising the construction of a new plant). Project management is a relatively popular means of handling one-of-a-kind situations having a finite life expectancy when the normal organization is ill-equipped to achieve the same results in addition to regular duties.

2. The *task force approach,* where a number of top-level executives and/or specialists are brought together to work on unusual assignments of a problem-solving or innovative nature. Special task forces provide increased opportunity for creativity, open communication across lines of authority, tight integration of specialized talents, expeditious conflict resolution, and common identification for coping with the problem at hand. One study showed that task forces were most effective when they had less than 10 members, membership was voluntary, the seniority of the members was proportional to the importance of the problem, the task force moved swiftly to deal with its assignment, the task force was pulled together only on an as-needed basis, no staff was assigned, and documentation was scant.[12] In these companies, the prevailing philosophy about task forces is to use them to solve real problems, produce some solution efficiently, and then disband them. At the other extreme, Peters and Waterman report one

---

[11] Thomas J. Peters and Robert H. Waterman, Jr., *In Search of Excellence* (New York: Harper & Row, 1982), pp. 306–7.

[12] Ibid., pp. 127–32.

instance where a company had formed 325 task forces, none of which had completed its charge in three years and none of which had been disbanded.

3. The *venture team approach,* whereby a group of individuals is formed for the purpose of bringing a specific product to market or a specific new business into being. Dow, General Mills, Westinghouse, General Electric, and Monsanto have used the venture team approach to regenerate an entrepreneurial spirit. The difficulties with venture teams include deciding who the venture manager should report to; whether funding for ventures should come from corporate, business, or departmental budgets; how to keep the venture clear of bureaucratic and vested interests; and how to coordinate large numbers of different ventures.

Perspectives on the Methods of Organizing

The foregoing discussion brings out two points: (1) there is no such thing as a perfect or ideal organization design, and (2) there are no universally applicable rules for matching strategy and structure. All of the basic organizational forms have their strategy-related strengths and weaknesses. Moreover, use of one of the basic organizational forms does not preclude simultaneous use of others; many organizations are large enough and diverse enough to have subunits organized by functional specialty, geographical area, market segment, line of business, SBU, and matrix principles. There is no need to adhere slavishly to one basic organization type. In a very real sense, *the best organizational arrangement is the one that best fits the firm's situation at the moment.* Experience shows that firms have a habit of outgrowing their prevailing organizational arrangement—either an internal shakeup is deemed periodically desirable or changes in the size and scope of customer-product-technology relationships make the firm's structure strategically obsolete. An organization's structure thus is dynamic; changes are not only inevitable but typical.

There is room to quibble over whether organization design should commence with a strategy-structure framework or with a pragmatic consideration of the realities of the situation at hand—the corporate culture, the constraints imposed by the personalities involved, and the way things have been done before. By and large, agonizing over where to begin is unnecessary; both considerations have to be taken into account. However, strategy-structure factors usually have to take precedence if structure is to be built around the organization's strategy-critical tasks, key success factors, and high-priority business units. Adapting structure to the peculiar circumstances of the organization's internal situation and personalities is usually done to modify the strategy-structure match in "minor" ways.

Drucker sums up the intricacies of organization design thusly:

> The simplest organization structure that will do the job is the best one. What makes an organization structure "good" are the problems it does not create. The simpler the structure, the less that can go wrong.
>
> Some design principles are more difficult and problematic than others. But none is without difficulties and problems. None is primarily people-focused rather than task-focused; none is more "creative," "free," or "more democratic."

Design principles are tools; and tools are neither good nor bad in themselves. They can be used properly or improperly; and that is all. To obtain both the greatest possible simplicity and the greatest "fit," organization design has to start out with a clear focus on *key activities* needed to produce *key results*. They have to be structured and positioned in the simplest possible design. Above all, the architect of organization needs to keep in mind the purpose of the structure he is designing.[13]

Peters and Waterman, in their study of excellently managed companies, confirm what Drucker says; their organization prescription is "simple form, lean staff."[14] Illustration Capsule 20 explains some of the organizational principles and approaches being used at these companies.

ILLUSTRATION CAPSULE 20

ORGANIZATION LESSONS FROM THE "EXCELLENTLY MANAGED" COMPANIES

Peters and Waterman's study of America's best-managed corporations provides some important lessons in building a strategically capable organization:

- The organizational underpinning of most of the excellently managed companies is a fairly stable, unchanging form—usually a decentralized business/product division—that provides the structural building block which everyone in the enterprise understands and that serves as the base for approaching day-to-day issues and complexities.

- Beyond the crystal-clear primacy of this basic and simple organizational building block, the rest of the organization structure is deliberately kept fluid and flexible to permit response to changing environmental conditions. Much use is made of task forces, project teams, and the creation of new, small divisions to address emerging issues and opportunities.

- New divisions are created to pursue budding business opportunities, as opposed to letting them remain a part of the originating division. Often, there are established guidelines when a new product or product line automatically becomes an independent division.

(continued)

---

[13] Drucker, *Management,* pp. 601–2.

[14] Peters and Waterman, *In Search of Excellence,* chap. 11.

- People and even products and product lines are frequently shifted from one division to another—to improve efficiency, promote shared costs, enhance competitive strength, and adapt to changing market conditions.

- Many excellently managed companies have comparatively few people at the corporate level, and many of these are out in the field frequently, rather than in the home office all the time. Emerson Electric with 54,000 employees had a headquarters staff of fewer than 100 people. Dana Corporation employed 35,000 people and had a corporate staff numbering about 100. Schlumberger Ltd., a $56 billion diversified oil service company, ran its worldwide organization with a corporate staff of 90 people. At Intel (sales of over $1 billion), all staff assignments were temporary ones given to line officers. Rolm managed a $200 million business with about 15 people in corporate headquarters. In addition, corporate planners were few and far between. Hewlett-Packard Company, Johnson & Johnson, and 3M had no planners at the corporate level; Fluor Corporation ran a $6 billion operation with three corporate planners. At IBM, management rotated staff assignments every three years. Few IBM staff jobs were manned by "career staffers"; most were manned temporarily by managers with line jobs in the divisions who eventually rotate back to line jobs.

- Functional organization forms are efficient and get the basic activities performed well; yet they are not particularly creative or entrepreneurial, they do not adapt quickly, and they are apt to ignore important changes.

- The key to maintaining an entrepreneurial, adaptive organization is *small size*—and the way to keep units small is to spin off new or expanded activities into independent units. Division sizes often run no bigger than $50 to $100 million in sales, with a maximum of 1,000 or so employees. At Emerson Electric, plants rarely employed more than 600 workers, so that management could maintain personal contact with employees. (Emerson, by the way, has a good track record on efficiency; its strategy of being the low-cost producer has worked beautifully in chain saws and several other products.) At Blue Bell, a leading apparel firm, manufacturing units usually employ under 300 people. The lesson seems to be that small units are both more cost-effective and more innovative.

- To prevent "calcification" and stodginess, it helps to rely on such "habitbreaking" techniques as (*a*) reorganizing regularly; (*b*) putting top talent on project teams and giving them a "charter" to move quickly to solve a key problem or execute a central strategic

(continued)

thrust (i.e., the creation of the General Motors Project Center to lead the downsizing effort); (*c*) shifting products or product lines among divisions to take advantage of special management talents or the need for market realignments; (*d*) breaking up big, bureaucratic divisions into several new, smaller divisions; and (*e*) being flexible enough to try experimental organization approaches and support the pursuit of new opportunities.

- It is useful to adopt a simultaneous "loose-tight" structure that on the one hand fosters autonomy, entrepreneurship, and innovation from rank-and-file managers yet, on the other hand, allows for strong central direction from the top. Such things as regular reorganization, flexible form (the use of teams and task forces), lots of decentralized autonomy for lower-level general managers, and extensive experimentation all focus on the excitement of trying things out in a slightly "loose" fashion. Yet, regular communication, quick feedback, concise paperwork, strong adherence to a few core values, and self-discipline can impose "tight" central control so that nothing gets far out of line.

Application of these "principles" in the best-managed companies tends to produce an environment that fosters entrepreneurial pursuit of new opportunities and adaptation to change. A fluid, flexible structure is the norm—the basic form is stable, but there is frequent reorganization "around the edges." The aim is to keep structure matched to the changing needs of an evolving strategy and to avoid letting the current organization structure become so ingrained and political that it becomes a major obstacle to be hurdled.

Source: Drawn from Thomas J. Peters and Robert H. Waterman, Jr., *In Search of Excellence* (New York: Harper & Row, 1982), especially chaps. 11 and 12.

Building a Distinctive Competence

A good match between structure and strategy is plainly one key facet of a strategically capable organization. But an equally dominant organization-building concern is that of staffing the chosen structure with the requisite managerial talent and technical skills—and, most particularly, staffing in a manner calculated to give the firm a distinctive competence in performing one or more critical tasks. The strategic importance of deliberately trying to develop a distinctive competence stems from the extra contribution special expertise and a competitive edge make to both performance and strategic success. To the extent an organization can build an astutely conceived distinctive competence in its chosen business, it creates a golden opportunity for achieving a competitive advantage and posting a superior record of performance. As indicated in prior chapters, a distinctive competence can take the form of greater proficiency in product development, quality of manufacture, caliber of technical services offered to customers, speed of response to changing customer requirements, being the low-cost producer, or any other strategically relevant factor.

However, distinctive competences don't just naturally appear. They have to be consciously developed and nurtured. Consequently, for a distinctive competence to emerge from organization-building actions, strategy implementers have to push aggressively to establish top-notch technical skills and capabilities in select subunits where superior performance of strategically critical tasks can make a real difference to greater strategic success. Usually, this means (1) giving above-average operating budget support to strategy-critical tasks and activities, (2) seeing that these tasks and activities are staffed with high-caliber managerial and technical talent, and (3) insisting on high performance standards from the subunits backed up with a policy of rewarding superior performance. In effect, strategy implementers must take premeditated actions to see that the organization is staffed with enough of the right kinds of people and that these people have the budgetary and administrative support needed to generate the desired distinctive competence.

Once developed, the strengths and capabilities that attach to distinctive competences become logical cornerstones for successful strategy implementation as well as for the actual strategy itself. Moreover, really distinctive internal skills and capabilities are not easily duplicated by other firms; this means that any advantage is likely to have a lasting strategic impact and help pave the way for above-average performance over the long term. Conscious management attention to the task of building strategically relevant internal skills and strengths into the overall organizational scheme is therefore one of the central tasks of organizational building and effective strategy implementation.

Employee Training. Training and retraining of people become important when a company shifts to a strategy requiring different skills, managerial approaches, and operating practices. The training function also takes on strategic importance in organizational efforts to build a skills-based distinctive competence. And it is a key activity in businesses where technical know-how is changing or advancing so rapidly that a company loses its ability to compete unless its skilled people are kept updated and have cutting-edge expertise. Successful strategy implementers see that the training function is adequately funded and that effective training programs are put in place. Normally, training is placed near the top of the action agenda because it needs to be done early in the strategy implementation process.

Selecting People for Key Positions

Assembling a capable management team is an obvious part of the strategy implementation task. The recurring administrative issues here center around deciding what kind of core management team is needed to carry out the strategy and finding the people to fill each slot. Sometimes the existing management team is suitable; sometimes the core executive group needs to be strengthened and/or expanded by promoting qualified people from within or by bringing in skilled managerial talent from the outside to help infuse fresh ideas and fresh approaches into the organization's management. In turnaround or rapid-growth situations, and when a company doesn't have the right kinds of managerial experience and skills, recruiting outsiders to fill key management slots is a fairly standard part of the organization-building process.

The important dimension of assembling a core executive group is discerning what mix of backgrounds, experiences, know-how, values, beliefs, styles of managing, and personalities will reinforce and contribute to successful strategy execution. As with any kind of team-building exercise, it is important to put together a compatible group of managers who possess a full set of skills to get things done—the personal "chemistry" needs to be right and the talent base needs to match the managerial requirements of the chosen strategy. Picking good lieutenants and consciously molding a solid management team is always an essential organization-building function—often it is the first strategy implementation step to take.[15] Until all the key slots are filled with the right people, it is hard for strategy implementation to proceed at full speed.

LINKING THE BUDGET WITH STRATEGY

Keeping an organization on the strategy implementation path thrusts a manager squarely into the budgeting process. Not only must a strategy implementer oversee "who gets how much" but the budget must also be put together with an equal concern for "getting the biggest bang for the buck."

Organizational units need the resources to carry out their part of the strategic plan, including enough of the right kinds of people and enough operating funds. Moreover, each subunit must program its activities to meet its objectives, establish schedules and deadlines for accomplishment, and designate who is responsible for what by when. Budgets and programs go hand in hand. Programs lay out detailed, step-by-step action plans, and budgets specify the costs of the planned activities.

How well a strategy implementer ties the organization's budget to the needs of strategy can either promote or impede the process of strategy implementation and execution. Too little funding deprives subunits of the ability to carry out their piece of the strategic plan. Too much funding is a waste of organizational resources and reduces financial performance. Both outcomes argue for the strategy implementer to be deeply involved in the budgeting process, closely reviewing the programs and proposals of strategy-critical subunits within the organization.

A willingness to shift resources from one area to another in support of strategic change is especially critical. A change in strategy nearly always calls for budget reallocation. Units that carried a big role in the old strategy may now be oversized and overfunded. Units that now have a bigger and more critical strate-

[15] For an analytical framework in top management team analysis, see Donald C. Hambrick, "The Top Management Team: Key to Strategic Success," *California Management Review* 30, no. 1 (Fall 1987), pp. 88–108.

gic role may need more people, new equipment, additional facilities, and above-average increases in their operating budgets. The strategy implementer's task is to engineer budget reallocations, downsizing some departments and functions, up-sizing others, and steering ample resources into parts of the organization's activities that can make or break success. *Strategy must become the driver of how budget allocations are made.* Denying funds to the organizational units on which strategic success or failure ultimately depends can defeat the whole implementation process.

Successful strategy implementers are good resource reallocators. For example, at Harris Corporation, where one element of strategy is to diffuse research ideas into areas that are commercially viable, top management regularly shifts groups of engineers out of government projects and (as a group) into new commercial venture divisions. Boeing has a similar approach to reallocating ideas and talent; according to one Boeing officer, "We can do it (create a big new unit) in two weeks. We couldn't do it in two years at International Harvester."[16] A fluid, flexible approach to reorganization and reallocation of people and budgets is characteristic of implementing strategic change successfully.

Fine-tuning existing strategy usually involves less reallocation and more of an extrapolation approach. Big movements of people and money from one area to another are seldom necessary. Fine-tuning can usually be accomplished by incrementally increasing or decreasing the budgets and staffing of existing organization units. The chief exception occurs where a prime ingredient of corporate/business strategy is to generate fresh, new products and business opportunities from within. Then, as attractive ventures "bubble up" from below, major decisions have to be made regarding budgets and staffing. Companies like 3M, GE, Boeing, IBM, and Digital Equipment shift resources and people from area to area on an "as-needed" basis to support budding ideas and ventures. They empower "product champions" and small bands of would-be entrepreneurs by giving them financial and technical support and by setting up organizational units and programs to facilitate moving things along.

PUTTING INTERNAL ADMINISTRATIVE SUPPORT SYSTEMS IN PLACE

A third key task of strategy implementation concerns installing internal administrative support systems that fit the needs of strategy. The specific strategy-implementing considerations here are:

1. What kinds of strategy-facilitating policies and procedures to establish.
2. How to enhance organizational capabilities via the installation of new or enhanced administrative and operating systems.
3. How to get the right strategy-critical information on a timely basis.

---

[16] Peters and Waterman, *In Search of Excellence,* p. 125.

Implementing Strategy-Supportive Policies and Procedures

Changes in strategy generally call for some changes in how internal activities are conducted and administered. The process of changing from old ways to new has to be initiated and managed. Asking people to alter actions and practices always "upsets" the internal order of things. It is normal for pockets of resistance to emerge and questions will be raised about the *hows* as well as the whys of change. The role of new and revised policies is to promulgate "standard operating procedures" that will (1) facilitate strategy implementation and (2) counteract any tendencies for parts of the organization to resist or reject the chosen strategy. Policies and procedures help enforce strategy implementation in several noteworthy respects:

1. Policy acts as a lever for institutionalizing strategy-supportive practices and operating procedures on an organizationwide basis, thus pushing day-to-day activities in the direction of efficient strategy execution.

2. Policy places limits on independent action and sets boundaries on the directions and kinds of action that can be taken. By stating how things are to be done now, policy communicates what is expected, guides strategy-related activities in particular directions, and places bounds on unwanted variations.

3. Policy acts to align actions and behavior with strategy throughout the organization, thereby minimizing zigzag decisions and conflicting practices and establishing some degree of regularity, stability, and dependability in how the organization is attempting to make the strategy work.

4. Policy helps to shape the character of the internal work climate and translate the corporate philosophy into how things are done, how people are treated, and what the corporate beliefs and attitudes mean in terms of everyday activities. Policy operationalizes the corporate philosophy, thus potentially playing a key role in establishing a fit between corporate culture and strategy.

From a strategy implementation perspective, managers need to be inventive in establishing policies that can provide vital support to an organization's strategic plan. McDonald's policy manual, in an attempt to channel "crew members" into stronger quality and service behavior patterns, spells out such detailed procedures as: "Cooks must turn, never flip, hamburgers. If they haven't been purchased, Big Macs must be discarded in 10 minutes after being cooked and french fries in 7 minutes. Cashiers must make eye contact with and smile at every customer." At Delta Airlines, it is corporate policy to check all stewardess applicants thoroughly regarding their aptitudes for friendliness, cooperativeness, and teamwork. Caterpillar Tractor has a policy of giving its customers 48-hour guaranteed parts delivery anywhere in the world; if it fails to fulfill the promise, the part is supplied free of charge. Hewlett-Packard has a policy requiring R&D people to make regular visits to customers' premises to learn about their problems, talk about new product applications, and, in general, keep the company's R&D programs customer-oriented.

Thus there is a definite role for policies and procedures in the strategy implementation process. Wisely constructed policies and procedures help enforce strategy implementation by channeling actions, behavior, decisions, and practices in directions that promote strategy accomplishment. If management fails to check the alignment between existing policies and strategy, some existing policies may act as obstacles and people who disagree with the strategy may use certain policies to thwart the strategic plan. On the other hand, consciously instituting policies and procedures that promote strategy-supportive behavior builds organization commitment to the strategic plan and creates a tighter fit between corporate culture and strategy.

However, companies don't need policy manuals. Too much policy can be as stifling as wrong policy or as chaotic as no policy. Sometimes, the best policy for implementing strategy is a willingness to let subordinates "do it any way they want if it makes sense and works." A little "structured chaos" can be a good thing if individual creativity is more essential to strategy than standardization and strict conformity. When Rene McPherson became CEO at Dana Corp., he dramatically threw out 22½ inches of policy manuals and replaced them with a one-page statement of philosophy focusing on "productive people."[17] Creating a strong supportive fit between strategy and policy can mean more policies, less policies, or different policies. It can mean policies that require things to be done a certain way or policies that give the person performing a job the autonomy to do it the way he/she thinks best.

Installing Support Systems

Effective strategy execution requires an organization to develop a number of support systems. An airline, for example, cannot function without a computerized reservation system, a baggage handling system at every airport it serves, and a strong maintenance program. A supermarket that stocks about 17,000 different items has to have systems for tracking inventories, maintaining shelf freshness, and allocating shelf space. A company that manufacturers many models and sizes of its product must have a sophisticated cost accounting system to price each item intelligently and know which items generate the biggest profits. In businesses where large numbers of employees have to be kept on the cutting-edge of technical know-how, companies have to install systems to train and retrain employees regularly and keep them supplied with up-to-date information. Fast-growing companies have to develop employee recruiting systems to attract and hire qualified employees in large numbers.

Strategy implementers must be alert to what specific support systems their organization needs to execute strategy successfully. If the present administrative support and operating systems are inadequate, resources must be allocated to put the needed systems capabilities into place. Illustration Capsule 21 describes the administrative support systems put in place at Mrs. Fields Cookies.

---

[17] Ibid., p. 65.

ILLUSTRATION CAPSULE   21

STRATEGY IMPLEMENTATION AT MRS. FIELDS COOKIES, INC.

In 1988 Mrs. Fields Cookies was one of the fastest growing specialty foods companies in the United States. Sales in 1987 were $150 million, up from $87 million in 1986. The company had over 400 Mrs. Fields outlets in operation and over 250 outlets retailing other bakery and cookie products. Debbi Fields, age 31, was the company's founder and CEO. Her business concept for Mrs. Fields Cookies was "to serve absolutely fresh, warm cookies as though you'd stopped by my house and caught me just taking a batch from the oven." Cookies not sold within two hours were removed from the case and given to charity. The company's major form of advertising was sampling; store employees walked around the shopping mall giving away cookie samples. People were hired for store crews on the basis of warmth, friendliness, and the ability to have a good time giving away samples, baking fresh batches, and talking to customers during the course of a sale.

To implement its strategy, the company developed several novel practices and a customized computer support system. One key practice was giving each store an *hourly* sales quota. Another was for Fields to make unannounced visits to her stores, where she masqueraded as a casual shopper to test the enthusiasm and sales techniques of store crews, sample the quality of the cookies they were baking, and observe customer reactions; she visited each outlet once or twice annually.

Debbi's husband Randy developed a software program that kept headquarters and stores in close contact. Via the computer network, each store manager receives a daily sales goal (broken down by the hour) based on the store's recent performance history and on such special factors as special promotions, mall activities, weekdays vs. weekends, holiday shopping patterns, and the weather forecast. With the hourly sales quotas also comes a schedule of the number of cookies to bake and when to bake them. As the day progresses, store managers type in actual hourly sales figures and customer counts. If customer counts are up but sales are lagging, the computer is programmed to recommend more aggressive sampling or more suggestive selling. If it becomes obvious the day is going to be a bust for the store, the computer automatically revises the sales projections for the day, reducing hourly quotas and instructing how much to cut back cookie baking. To facilitate crew scheduling by the store manager, sales projections are also provided for two weeks in advance. All job applicants must sit at the store's terminal and answer a computerized set of questions as part of the interview process.

(continued)

In addition, the computer software contains a menu giving store staff immediate access to company personnel policies, maintenance schedules for store equipment, and repair instructions. If a store manager has a specific problem, it can be entered on the system and routed to the appropriate person. Messages can be sent directly to Debbi Fields via the computer; even if she is on a store inspection trip, her promise is to respond to all inquiries within 48 hours.

The computerized information support system serves several objectives: (1) it gives store managers more time to work with their crews and achieve sales quotas as opposed to handling administrative chores and (2) it gives headquarters instantaneous information on store performance and a means of controlling store operations. Debbi Fields sees the system as a tool for projecting her influence and enthusiasm into more stores more frequently than she could otherwise reach.

Source: Developed from information in Mike Korologos, "Debbi Fields," *Sky Magazine,* July 1988, pp. 42–50.

Instituting Formal Reporting of Strategic Information

Accurate information is an essential guide to action. Every organization must develop a system to gather and report strategy-critical information. Information is always needed *before* actions are fully completed to steer them to a successful conclusion in case the early steps taken don't produce the intended outcomes and need to be modified. Monitoring the outcomes of the first round of implementation actions serves two purposes: (1) early detection of the need to adjust either the strategy or how it is being implemented and (2) assuring that things are moving ahead as planned.[18] Early experiences are sometimes difficult to assess, but they yield the first hard data from the action front and thus merit close scrutiny as a basis for corrective action.

But the information system needs to be more comprehensive than just monitoring the first signs of progress. All key strategic performance indicators have to be tracked as often as practical. Many retail companies generate daily sales reports for each store and maintain up-to-the-minute inventory and sales records on each item. Manufacturing operations typically generate daily production reports and track labor productivity on every shift. Monthly profit-and-loss statements are common, as are monthly statistical summaries.

In designing formal reports to monitor strategic progress, five guidelines are recommended:[19]

---

[18] Boris Yavitz and William H. Newman, *Strategy in Action* (New York: Free Press, 1982), pp. 209–10.

[19] Drucker, *Management,* pp. 498–504; Harold Koontz, "Management Control: A Suggested Formulation of Principles," *California Management Review* 2, no. 2 (Winter 1959), pp. 50–55; and William H. Sihler, "Toward Better Management Control Systems," *California Management Review* 14, no. 2 (Winter 1971), pp. 33–39.

1. Information and reporting systems should involve no more data and reporting than is really needed to give a reliable picture of what is going on. The information gathered should emphasize strategically meaningful variables and symptoms of potentially significant developments. Temptations to supplement "what managers need to know" with other "interesting" but marginally useful information should be avoided.

2. Reports and statistical data-gathering have to be timely—not come too late to take corrective action or generated so often as to overburden.

3. The flow of information and statistics should be kept simple. Complicated reports are likely to confound and obscure because of the attention that has to be paid to mechanics, procedures, and interpretive guidelines instead of measuring and reporting the really critical variables.

4. Information and reporting systems should aim at "no surprises" and generating "early-warnings signs" rather than just producing information. It is debatable whether reports should receive wide distribution ("for your information"), but they should, without fail, be put directly in the hands of managers who are in a position to act when trouble signs appear.

5. Statistical reports should make it easy to flag big or unusual variances from plan and the "exceptions," thus directing management attention to significant departures from targeted performance.

Statistical information gives the strategy implementer a feel for the numbers, reports and meetings provide a feel for new developments and the problems that exist, and personal contacts and conversations add a feel for the people dimension. All are good barometers of the overall tempo of performance and indicate which things are on and off track. Identifying deviations from plan and problem areas to be addressed are prerequisites for initiating actions to either improve implementation or fine-tune strategy.

KEY POINTS

The job of strategy implementation is to translate plans into actions and to achieve the intended results. The test of successful strategy implementation is whether actual organization performance matches or exceeds the targets spelled out in the strategic plan. Shortfalls in performance signal weak strategy, weak implementation, or both.

In deciding how to implement strategy, managers have to determine what internal conditions are needed to execute the chosen strategic plan successfully and then initiate actions to create these conditions as rapidly as practical. The process involves creating a series of tight fits:

- Between strategy and organization structure.
- Between strategy and what the organization's skills and competences give it the ability to do.
- Between strategy and budget allocations.
- Between strategy and internal policies, procedures, and support systems.

- Between strategy and the reward structure.
- Between strategy and the corporate culture.

The tighter the fits, the more powerful strategy execution becomes and the more likely targeted performance can actually be achieved.

Implementing strategy is not just a top management function; it is a job for the whole management team. All managers function as strategy implementers in their respective areas of authority and responsibility. All managers have to consider what actions to take in their areas to achieve the intended results—they each need an *action agenda*.

The three major components of organization-building are (1) deciding how to organize and what the organization chart should look like, (2) developing the skills and competences needed to execute the strategy successfully, and (3) filling key positions with the right people. All organization structures have strategic advantages and disadvantages; there is no one best way to organize. In choosing a structure, the guiding principles are to make strategy-critical activities the major building blocks, keep the design simple, and put decision-making authority in the hands of managers closest to the scene of the action. Functional and geographic organization structures are well-suited to single-business companies. SBU structures are well-suited to companies pursuing related diversification. Decentralized business-unit structures are well-suited to companies pursuing unrelated diversification. Project teams, task forces, and new venture teams can also be useful organizational mechanisms to handle temporary or one-time strategic initiatives.

The other two aspects of organization-building—skills development and filling key positions—are just as important as matching structure to strategy. Taking deliberate action to develop strategy-supportive skills and to create a distinctive competence not only strengthens execution but also helps build competitive advantage. Selecting the right people for key positions tends to be one of the earliest strategy implementation steps because it takes a full complement of capable managers to put the strategy into operation and make it work.

Reworking the budget to make it more strategy-supportive is a crucial part of the implementation process because every organization unit needs to have the people, equipment, facilities, and other resources to carry out its part of the strategic plan (but no *more* than what it really needs!). Strategy implementation often entails shifting resources from one area to another—downsizing units that are overstaffed and overfunded, and upsizing the budgets and staffs of units more critical to strategic success.

A third key implementation task is to install some necessary support systems—policies and procedures to establish desired types of behavior, information systems to provide strategy-critical information on a timely basis, and whatever inventory, materials management, customer service, cost accounting, and other administrative systems are needed to give the organization important strategy-executing capability.

In the next chapter, we examine the remaining three key tasks of the strategy implementation process: designing the reward system, creating a strategy-supportive corporate culture, and exercising strategic leadership.

SUGGESTED READINGS

Bartlett, Christopher A. "Building and Managing the Transnational: The New Organizational Challenge," in *Competition in Global Industries,* ed. Michael E. Porter (Boston: Harvard Business School Press, 1986), pp. 367–401.

Bettis, Richard A., and William K. Hall. "The Business Portfolio Approach—Where It Falls Down in Practice." *Long Range Planning* 16, no. 2 (April 1983), pp. 95–104.

Chandler, Alfred D. *Strategy and Structure.* Cambridge, Mass.: MIT Press, 1962.

Hall, William K. "SBUs: Hot, New Topic in the Management of Diversification." *Business Horizons* 21, no. 1 (February 1978), pp. 17–25.

Hambrick, Donald C. "The Top Management Team: Key to Strategic Success." *California Management Review* 30, no. 1 (Fall 1987), pp. 88–108.

Larson, Erik W., and David H. Gobeli. "Matrix Management: Contradictions and Insights." *California Management Review* 29, no. 4 (Summer 1987), pp. 126–27.

Leontiades, Milton. "Choosing the Right Manager to Fit the Strategy." *Journal of Business Strategy* 3, no. 2 (Fall 1981), pp. 58–69.

Mintzberg, Henry. "Organization Design: Fashion or Fit." *Harvard Business Review* 59, no. 1 (January–February 1981), pp. 103–16.

Paulson, Robert D. "Making It Happen: The Real Strategic Challenge." *The McKinsey Quarterly,* Winter 1982, pp. 58–66.

Peters, Thomas J., and Robert H. Waterman, Jr. *In Search of Excellence.* New York: Harper & Row, 1982.

Powell, Walter W. "Hybrid Organizational Arrangements: New Form or Transitional Development?" *California Management Review* 30, no. 1 (Fall 1987), pp. 67–87.

Waterman, Robert H.; Thomas J. Peters; and Julien R. Phillips. "Structure Is Not Organization." *Business Horizons* 23, no. 3 (June 1980), pp. 14–26.

10 Implementing Strategy: Commitment, Culture, and Leadership

Weak leadership can wreck the soundest strategy; forceful execution of even a poor plan can often bring victory.
Sun Zi

Ethics is the moral courage to do what we know is right, and not to do what we know is wrong.
C. J. Silas
CEO, Philips Petroleum

A leader lives in the field with his troops.
H. Ross Perot

In the previous chapter we examined three of the strategy implementer's tasks—building a capable organization, steering resources into strategy-critical programs and activities, and creating a series of internal supports to enable better execution. In this chapter we explore the three remaining implementation tasks: designing rewards and incentives that induce stronger commitment to carrying out the strategy, creating a strategy-supportive corporate culture, and exercising strategic leadership.

DEVELOPING AN EFFECTIVE REWARD STRUCTURE

It is important for organizational subunits and individuals to be committed to implementing and accomplishing strategy. Solidifying organizationwide commitment to putting the strategic plan in place is typically achieved through motivation, incentives, and reward for good performance. The range of options involves creative use of the standard reward-punishment mechanisms—salary raises, bonuses, stock options, fringe benefits, promotions, the fear of being "sidelined" and ignored, praise, recognition, constructive criticism, tension, peer pressure, more (or less) responsibility, increased (or decreased) job control and decision-making autonomy, the promise of attractive locational assignments, and the bonds of group acceptance.

Motivational Practices

Successful strategy implementers inspire employees to do their best, getting them to buy in to the strategy and commit to making it work. They are good at thinking up and implementing effective strategy-supportive motivational approaches. Consider some actual examples:[1]

- At Mars Inc. (best known for its candy bars), every employee, including the president, gets a weekly 10 percent bonus by coming to work on time each day that week. This on-time incentive is based on minimizing absenteeism and tardiness to boost worker productivity and to produce the greatest number of candy bars during each available minute of machine time.

- In a number of Japanese companies, employees meet regularly to hear inspirational speeches, sing company songs, and chant the corporate litany. In the United States, Tupperware conducts a weekly Monday night rally to honor, applaud, and fire up its salespeople who conduct Tupperware parties. Amway and Mary Kay Cosmetics hold similar inspirational get-togethers for their sales force organizations.

- A San Diego area company assembles its 2,000 employees at its six plants the first thing every workday to listen to a management talk about the state of the company. Then they engage in brisk calisthenics. This company's management believes "that by doing one thing together each day, it reinforces the unity of the company. It's also fun. It gets the blood up." Managers take turns making the presentations. Many of the speeches "are very personal and emotional, not approved beforehand or screened by anybody."

- Texas Instruments and Dana Corp. insist that teams and divisions set their own goals and have regular peer reviews.

- Procter & Gamble's brand managers are asked to compete fiercely against each other; the official policy is "a free-for-all among brands with no holds

---

[1] The list that follows is abstracted from Thomas J. Peters and Robert H. Waterman, Jr., *In Search of Excellence* (New York: Harper & Row, 1982), pp. xx, 213–14, 276, and 285.

barred.'' P&G's system of purposeful internal competition breeds people who love to compete and excel. Those who ''win'' become corporate ''heroes,'' and around them emerges a folklore of ''war stories'' of valiant brand managers who waged uphill struggles against great odds and made a market success out of their assigned brands.

These motivational approaches accentuate the positive; others blend positive and negative features. Consider the way Harold Geneen, former president and chief executive officer of ITT, allegedly combined the use of money, tension, and fear:

> Geneen provides his managers with enough incentives to make them tolerate the system. Salaries all the way through ITT are higher than average—Geneen reckons 10 percent higher—so that few people can leave without taking a drop. As one employee put it: ''We're all paid just a bit more than we think we're worth.'' At the very top, where the demands are greatest, the salaries and stock options are sufficient to compensate for the rigors. As some said, ''He's got them by their limousines.''
>
> Having bound his men to him with chains of gold, Geneen can induce the tension that drives the machine. ''The key to the system,'' one of his men explains, ''is the profit forecast. Once the forecast has been gone over, revised, and agreed on, the managing director has a personal commitment to Geneen to carry it out. That's how he produces the tension on which the success depends.'' The tension goes through the company, inducing ambition, perhaps exhilaration, but always with some sense of fear: what happens if the target is missed?[2]

If a strategy implementer's use of rewards and punishments induces too much tension, anxiety, and job insecurity, the results can be counter-productive. Yet, it is doubtful whether it is ever useful to completely eliminate tension, pressure for performance, and anxiety from the strategy implementation process. There is, for example, no evidence that ''the quiet life'' is highly correlated with superior strategy implementation. On the contrary, high-performing organizations need a cadre of ambitious people who relish the opportunity to climb the ladder of success, love a challenge, thrive in a performance-oriented environment, and find some competition and pressure useful to satisfy their own drives for personal recognition, accomplishment, and self-satisfaction. There has to be some meaningful incentive and career consequence associated with implementation or few people will attach much significance to the strategic plan.

Rewards and Incentives

The conventional view is that a manager's push for strategy implementation should incorporate more positive than negative motivational elements because when cooperation is positively enlisted and rewarded, rather than negatively strong-armed, people tend to respond with more enthusiasm and more effort. Nevertheless, how much of which incentives to use depends on how hard the task of strategy implementation will be in light of all the obstacles to be overcome. A

---

2 Anthony Sampson, *The Sovereign State of ITT* (New York: Stein and Day, 1973), p. 132.

manager has to do more than just talk to everyone about how important strategy implementation is to the organization's future well-being. Talk, no matter how inspiring, seldom commands people's best efforts for long. Sustained, energetic commitment to strategy virtually always requires resourceful use of individual incentives. The more a manager understands what motivates subordinates and the more motivational incentives are relied on to implement and execute strategy, the greater will be the commitment to carrying out the strategic plan.

Linking Work Assignment to Performance Targets.   The first step in creating a strategy-supportive system of rewards and incentives is to define jobs and assignments in terms of the *results to be accomplished,* not the duties and functions to be performed. Training the job holder's attention and energy on *what to achieve* as opposed to what activities to engage in makes the chances of reaching the agreed-on objectives greater. It is flawed thinking to stress duties and activities in job descriptions in hopes that the by-products will be the desired kinds of accomplishment. In any job, doing an assigned activity is not equivalent to achieving the intended objectives. Working hard, staying busy, and diligently attending to assigned duties do not guarantee results. Stressing "what to accomplish" instead of "what to do" is an important difference. As any student knows, just because an instructor teaches doesn't mean students are learning. Teaching and learning are different things—the first is an activity and the second is a result.

Emphasizing what to accomplish and the performance targets to be reached for individual jobs, work groups, departments, businesses, and the company as a whole has the larger purpose of making the work environment results-oriented. Without target objectives it is easy for people and organizations to become so engrossed in doing their duties and performing assigned functions on schedule that they lose sight of what the work tasks were intended to accomplish in the first place. By keeping the spotlight on achievement and targeted performance, strategy implementers are taking proactive steps to make the right things happen rather than passively hoping they will happen (this, of course, is what "managing by objectives" is all about).

Creating a tight fit between work assignments and accomplishing the strategic plan thus goes straight to the objectives and performance targets spelled out in the strategic plan. If the details of strategy have been fleshed out thoroughly from the corporate level down to the operating level, performance targets exist for the whole company, for each business unit, for each functional department, and for each operating unit. These become the targets that strategy implementers aim at achieving and the basis for deciding how many jobs and what skills, expertise, funding, and time frame it will take to achieve them.

Usually a number of performance measures are needed at each level; rarely does a single measure suffice. At the corporate and line-of-business levels, the typical performance measures include profitability (measured in terms of total profit, return on equity investment, return on total assets, return on sales, operating profit, and so on), market share, growth rates in sales and profits, and hard evidence that competitive position and future prospects have improved. In the manufacturing area, the strategy-relevant performance measures may focus on unit manufacturing costs, productivity increases, meeting production and shipping schedules, quality control, the number and extent of work stoppages due to labor disagreements and equipment breakdowns, and so on. In the marketing area, measures may include unit selling costs, increases in dollar sales and unit volume, increased sales penetration of each target customer group, increases in market share, the success of newly introduced products, the severity of customer complaints, advertising effectiveness, and the number of new accounts acquired. While most performance measures are quantitative, several have elements of subjectivity—improvements in labor-management relations, employee morale, customer satisfaction, advertising success, and whether the firm is ahead or behind rivals on quality, service, technological capability, and other key success factors.

Rewarding Performance. The only dependable way to keep people's eyes trained on the objectives laid out in the strategic plan and to make achieving them "a way of life" up and down the organization is to provide adequate rewards to individuals who achieve their strategic targets and deny rewards to those who don't. Strategy implementers cannot waver far from the standard that "doing a good job" *equals* "achieving the agreed-on performance targets. Any other standard undermines implementation of the strategic plan and condones the diversion of time and energy into activities that don't matter much (if such activities are really important, they deserve a place in the strategic plan). The pressure to achieve the targeted strategic performance should be unrelenting. A "no excuses" standard has to prevail.[3]

But with the pressure to perform must come ample rewards. Without a payoff, the system breaks down, and the strategy implementer is left with the unworkable option of barking orders and pleading for compliance. Some of the most successful companies—Wal-Mart Stores, Nucor Steel, Lincoln Electric, Electronic Data Systems, Remington Products, and Mary Kay Cosmetics—owe much of their success to having designed a set of incentives and rewards that induce people to do the very things needed to hit performance targets and execute strategy well enough to become leaders in their industries. Nucor's strategy was (and is) to be *the* low-cost producer of steel products. Because labor costs are a significant fraction of total cost in the steel business, successful implementation of Nucor's low-cost strategy required achieving lower labor costs per ton of steel than competitors. To drive its labor costs per ton below rivals, Nucor management introduced production incentives that gave workers a bonus roughly equal to their regular wages provided their production teams met or exceeded weekly production targets; the regular wage scale was set at levels comparable to other manufacturing jobs in the local areas where Nucor had plants. Bonuses were paid every two weeks based on the prior weeks' actual production levels measured against the target. The results of Nucor's piece-rate incentive plan were impressive. By paying workers about twice what they could make in other jobs in their community, Nucor's labor productivity (in output per worker) rose to eight

---

[3] Tom Peters and Nancy Austin, *A Passion for Excellence* (New York: Random House, 1985), p. xix.

times the average of the unionized work forces of the industry's major producers; Nucor enjoyed about a $100 per ton cost advantage over large, integrated steel producers like U.S. Steel and Bethlehem Steel (a substantial part of which came from its labor cost advantage); and Nucor workers were the highest-paid workers in the steel industry (with incomes of $35,000 to $40,000 annually in the mid-1980s). At Remington Products, 65 percent of factory workers' paychecks is salary and the rest is based on piece-work incentives. The company conducts 100 percent inspections of products, and rejected items are counted against incentive pay for the responsible worker. Top-level managers get more from their bonuses than from their salary. Over the four years the incentive program has been in place, productivity has risen 17 percent.

The important lessons about designing rewards and incentives from these and other experiences are as follows:

1. *The performance payoff must be a major, not a minor, piece of the total compensation package*—incentives that amount to 20 percent or more of total compensation are big attention-getters and are capable of driving individual effort.

2. *The incentive plan should ideally extend to all managers and all workers,* not just be restricted to the top levels of management (after all, why should all workers and managers work their tails off and hit performance targets just so a few senior executives can get lucrative rewards?).

3. *The system must be administered with scrupulous care and fairness*—if performance standards are set unrealistically high or if individual performance evaluations are not accurate and well-documented, dissatisfaction and disgruntlement with the system will overcome any positive benefits that still emerge.

4. *The incentives must be linked tightly to achieving only performance targets spelled out in the strategic plan* and not to any other factors that get thrown in because they are thought to be nice occurrences. Performance evaluations based on factors not related to carrying out the strategy are a sign that either the strategic plan is incomplete (because important performance targets were left out) or the real managerial action agenda is something other than what was stated in the strategic plan.

5. *The performance targets which each individual is expected to achieve should involve outcomes that the individual has personal ability to affect,* as opposed to something beyond the individual's ability to control or manage. The role of incentives is to enhance individual commitment and channel behavior in beneficial directions; this role is not well-served when the performance measures an individual is judged by are outside his/her arena of influence.

Aside from these general guidelines it is hard to prescribe what kinds of incentives and rewards to develop, except to say that the payoff must be directly attached to performance measures that indicate the strategy is working and implementation is on track. If the company's strategy is to be a low-cost producer, then the incentive system needs to reward performance that lowers costs. If the company has a differentiation strategy predicated on superior quality and service, the incentive system needs to reward such targets as zero defects, infrequent need for product repair, low numbers of customer complaints, and speedy order fulfillment and delivery. If a company's growth is predicated on a strategy of new product innovation, incentives must be based on the percentages of revenues and profits coming from new product introduction.

Why the Performance-Reward Link Is Important

The use of incentives and rewards is the single most powerful tool management has to win strong employee commitment to carrying out the strategic plan. Failure to use this tool wisely and powerfully weakens the entire implementation process. *Decisions on salary increases, incentive compensation, promotions, key assignments, and ways and means to award praise and recognition are the strategy implementer's foremost attention-getting, commitment-generating devices.* How a manager structures incentives and parcels out the rewards signals what sort of behavior and performance management wants and who is doing a good job. Such matters seldom escape the closest scrutiny of every member of the organization. The system of incentives and rewards thus ends up as the vehicle by which strategy is emotionally ratified in the form of real commitment. Incentives are what makes it in employees' self-interest to go all out trying to make the strategy work and to achieve strategic objectives.

Using Performance Contracts

Creating a tight fit between strategy and the reward structure is generally best accomplished by agreeing on strategic objectives, fixing responsibility and deadlines for achieving them, and treating their achievement as a *contract*. Next, the contracted-for strategic performance has to be the *real* basis for designing incentives, evaluating individual efforts, and handing out rewards. To prevent undermining and undoing the whole "managing-with-objectives" approach to strategy implementation, a manager must insist that actual performance be judiciously compared against the contracted-for target objectives. The reasons for any deviations have to be explored fully to determine whether the causes are attributable to "poor" individual performance or to circumstances beyond the individual's control. All managers need to understand clearly how their rewards have been calculated. In short, managers at all levels have to be held accountable for carrying out their assigned part of the strategic plan, and they have to know their rewards are based on the caliber of their strategic accomplishments (allowing for both the favorable and unfavorable impacts of uncontrollable, unforeseeable, and unknowable circumstances).

BUILDING A STRATEGY-SUPPORTIVE CORPORATE CULTURE

Every organization is a unique culture. It has its own special history, its own ways of approaching problems and conducting activities, its own mix of managerial personalities and styles, its own established patterns of "how we do things around here,'' its own set of war stories and heroes, its own experiences of how changes have been instituted—in other words, its own atmosphere, folklore, and organization personality. This says something important about the leadership task of orchestrating strategy implementation: *anything so fundamental as implementing and executing a strategic plan involves moving the whole organizational culture into alignment with strategy.* The optimal condition is a work environment so in tune with strategy that execution of the game plan can be truly powerful. As one observer noted:

> It has not been just strategy that led to big Japanese wins in the American auto market. It is a culture that enspirits workers to excel at fits and finishes, to produce moldings that match and doors that don't sag. It is a culture in which Toyota can use that most sophisticated of management tools, the suggestion box, and in two years increase the number of worker suggestions from under 10,000 to over 1 million with resultant savings of $250 million.[4]

What Is Corporate Culture?

The taproot of corporate culture is the organization's beliefs and philosophy about how its affairs ought to be conducted—the reasons why it does things the way it does. The philosophy and beliefs underlying a company's activities can be hard to pin down, even harder to characterize accurately. In a sense they are intangible and ''soft.'' They are manifest in the values and beliefs that senior managers espouse, in the ethical standards they demand, in the policies that are set, in the style with which things are done, in the traditions the organization maintains, in people's attitudes and feelings, in the stories that are repeatedly told about happenings in the organization, and in the ''chemistry'' and the ''vibrations'' that surround the work environment and give definition to the organization's culture. What we are beginning to learn and appreciate is that an organization's culture is an important contributor (or obstacle) to successful strategy execution.

Illustration Capsule 22 looks at some of the traits and characteristics of ''strong-culture'' companies to provide more insight into why the culture-strategy fit makes such a big difference. While Illustration Capsule 22 helps demonstrate the contribution culture can have on ''keeping the herd moving roughly West'' (as Professor Terry Deal puts it), the strategy implementer is concerned with what actions to take to create a culture that facilitates strategy execution.

Establishing Ethical Standards and Values

A strong corporate culture founded on ethical principles and sound values is a vital strategic key to long-term success. Many executives are convinced that a company must care about *how* it does business; otherwise it puts its reputation at risk and ultimately its performance. Corporate ethics and corporate values programs are not window-dressing. They create an environment of strongly held

---

[4] Robert H. Waterman, Jr., ''The Seven Elements of Strategic Fit,'' *Journal of Business Strategy* 2, no. 3 (Winter 1982), p. 70.

ILLUSTRATION CAPSULE   22

**TRAITS AND CHARACTERISTICS OF
"STRONG-CULTURE" COMPANIES**

To illustrate what corporate culture is and why it plays a role in successful strategy execution, let's examine the distinctive traits and themes of companies with strong cultures:

- At Frito-Lay, stories abound about potato chip route salesmen slogging through sleet, mud, hail, snow, and rain to uphold the 99.5 percent service level to customers in which the entire organization takes such great pride. At McDonald's the constant message from management is the overriding importance of quality, service, cleanliness, and value; employees are drilled over and over on the need for attention to detail and perfecting every fundamental of the business. At Delta Airlines, the culture is driven by "Delta's family feeling" that builds a team spirit and nurtures each employee's cooperative attitude toward others, cheerful outlook toward life, and pride in a job well done. At Johnson & Johnson, the credo is that customers come first, employees second, the community third, and shareholders fourth and last. At DuPont, there is a fixation on safety—a report of every accident must be on the chairman's desk within 24 hours (DuPont's safety record is 17 times better than the chemical industry average and 68 times better than the all-manufacturing average).

- Companies with strong cultures are unashamed collectors and tellers of stories, anecdotes, and legends in support of basic beliefs. L. L. Bean tells customer service stories. 3M tells innovation stories. P&G, Johnson & Johnson, Perdue Farms, and Maytag tell quality stories. From an organizational standpoint, such tales are very important because people in the organization take pride in identifying strongly with the stories, and they start to share in the traditions and values which the stories relate.

- The most typical values and beliefs that shape culture include (1) a belief in being the best (or at GE "better than the best"), (2) a belief in superior quality and service, (3) a belief in the importance of people as individuals and a faith in their ability to make a strong, positive contribution, (4) a belief in the importance of the details of execution, the nuts and bolts of doing the job well, (5) a belief that customers should reign supreme, (6) a belief in inspiring people,

(continued)

whatever their ability, (7) a belief in the importance of informality to enhance communication, and (8) a recognition that growth and profits are essential to a company's well-being. While the themes are common, however, every company implements them differently (to fit their particular situations), and every company's values are the articulated handiwork of one or two legendary figures in leadership positions. Accordingly, each company has its own distinct culture which, they believe, no one can copy successfully.

- In companies with strong cultures, managers and workers either "buy in" to the culture and accept its norms or they opt out and leave the company.

- The stronger the corporate culture and the more it is directed toward customers and markets, the less a company uses policy manuals, organization charts, and detailed rules and procedures to enforce discipline and norms. The reason is that the guiding values inherent in the culture convey in crystal-clear fashion what everybody is supposed to do in most situations. Often, poorly performing companies have strong cultures too. The difference is that their cultures are dysfunctional, being focused on internal politics or operating by the numbers as opposed to emphasizing customers and the people who make and sell the product.

Companies with strong cultures are clear on what they stand for, and they are serious about the tasks of establishing company values, winning employees over to these values, and causing employees to observe cultural norms religiously.

Source: Compiled from Thomas J. Peters and Robert H. Waterman, Jr., *In Search of Excellence* (New York: Harper & Row, 1982), pp. xxi, 75–77, and 280–85; and Thomas J. Peters and Nancy Austin, *A Passion for Excellence* (New York: Random House, 1985), pp. 282–83 and 334.

values and convictions and make ethical conduct a way of life. Strong values and high ethical standards nurture the corporate culture in a very positive way.

Companies take different approaches to establishing values and ethical standards.[5] Companies steeped in tradition with a rich folklore to draw on rely on word-of-mouth indoctrination and the power of tradition to instill values into employees and to enforce ethical conduct. But the general and growing approach is to set forth value statements and codes of ethics in the form of written documents. Table 10–1 indicates the kinds of topics covered in such statements. Written statements have the advantage of explicitly stating what the company intends and expects; and they serve as benchmarks for judging both company policies and actions and individual conduct. They put a stake in the ground and

---

[5] The Business Roundtable, "Corporate Ethics: A Prime Asset," February 1988, pp. 4–10.

Table 10–1	TOPICS GENERALLY COVERED IN VALUES STATEMENTS AND CODES OF ETHICS

Topics covered in values statements	Topics covered in codes of ethics
• Importance of customers and customer service	• Honesty and observance of the law
• Commitment to quality	• Conflicts of interest
• Commitment to innovation	• Fairness in selling and marketing practices
• Respect for the individual employee and the duty the company has to employees	• Using inside information and securities trading
• Importance of honesty, integrity, and ethical standards	• Supplier relationships and purchasing practices
• Duty to stockholders	• Payments to obtain business/Foreign Corrupt Practices Act
• Duty to suppliers	• Acquiring and using information about others
• Corporate citizenship	• Political activities
• Importance of protecting the environment	• Use of company assets, resources, and property
	• Protection of proprietary information
	• Pricing, contracting, and billing

define the company's position. Value statements serve as a cornerstone for culture-building; a code of ethics serves as a cornerstone for developing a corporate conscience. Illustration Capsule 23 presents the Johnson & Johnson Credo; it is the most publicized and celebrated code of ethics and values among U.S. companies. J&J's CEO calls the credo "the unifying force for our corporation."

Once values and ethical standards have been formally set forth, they must be institutionalized and ingrained into policies, practices, and actual conduct. Implementing the values and code of ethics entails several actions:

- Incorporating the statement of values and the code of ethics into employee training and educational programs.

- Giving explicit attention to values and ethics in recruiting and hiring people, the objective being to screen out applicants who do not exhibit compatible character traits.

- Communicating the values and ethics code to all employees and explaining compliance procedures.

- Management involvement and oversight, from the CEO to first-line supervisors.

- Strong endorsements by the CEO.

- Word-of-mouth indoctrination.

In the case of codes of ethics, special attention must be given to sections of the company that are particularly sensitive and vulnerable—purchasing, sales, and political lobbying.[6] Employees who deal with external parties are in ethically sensitive positions and often are drawn into compromising situations. Procedures for enforcing ethical standards and handling violations have to be developed.

---

[6] Ibid., p. 7.

ILLUSTRATION CAPSULE 23

THE JOHNSON & JOHNSON CREDO

—We believe our first responsibility is to the doctors, nurses and patients, to mothers and all others who use our products and services.

—In meeting their needs everything we do must be of high quality.

—We must constantly strive to reduce our costs in order to maintain reasonable prices.

—Customers' orders must be serviced promptly and accurately.

—Our suppliers and distributors must have an opportunity to make a fair profit.

—We are responsible to our employees, the men and women who work with us throughout the world.

—Everyone must be considered as an individual.

—We must respect their dignity and recognize their merit.

—They must have a sense of security in their jobs.

—Compensation must be fair and adequate, and working conditions clean, orderly and safe.

—Employees must feel free to make suggestions and complaints.

—There must be equal opportunity for employment, development and advancement for those qualified.

—We must provide competent management, and their actions must be just and ethical.

—We are responsible to the communities in which we live and work and to the world community as well.

—We must be good citizens—support good works and charities and bear our fair share of taxes.

—We must encourage civic improvements and better health and education.

—We must maintain in good order the property we are privileged to use, protecting the environment and natural resources.

—Our final responsibility is to our stockholders.

—Business must make a sound profit.

—We must experiment with new ideas.

—Research must be carried on, innovative programs developed and mistakes paid for.

—New equipment must be purchased, new facilities provided and new products launched.

—Reserves must be created to provide for adverse times.

—When we operate according to these principles, the stockholders should realize a fair return.

Source: 1982 Annual Report.

The effort to implement values and ethical behavior must permeate all parts of the company and extend down through all organizational levels. The attitudes, character, and work history of prospective employees must be scrutinized. Every employee must receive adequate training. Line managers at all levels must give serious and continuous attention to the task of explaining how the values and ethical conduct are applicable in their assigned areas. In addition, they must insist that company values and ethical standards become a way of life. In general, instilling values and insisting on ethical conduct must be looked on as a continuous culture-building, culture-nurturing exercise. Whether the effort succeeds or fails depends largely on how well corporate values and ethical standards are visibly integrated into company policies and managerial practices and actions at all levels.

Creating the Fit between Strategy and Culture

It is the *strategy-maker's* responsibility to select a strategy compatible with the "sacred" or unchangeable parts of prevailing corporate culture. It is the *strategy implementer's* task, once strategy is chosen, to bring the corporate culture into alignment with strategy and keep it there.

Aligning culture with strategy presents a strong challenge. The first step is to diagnose which facets of the present culture are strategy-supportive and which are not. Then, there must be some innovative thinking about concrete actions management can take to modify the cultural environment and create a stronger fit with the strategy.

Symbolic Actions and Substantive Actions. Normally, managerial actions to tighten the culture-strategy fit are both symbolic and substantive. Symbolic actions are valuable for the signals they send about the kinds of behavior and performance strategy implementers wish to encourage. The most common symbolic actions are the events organizations hold to designate and honor new kinds of heroes—people whose actions and performance serve as role models. Many universities give outstanding teacher awards each year to symbolize their commitment to and esteem for instructors who display exceptional classroom talents. Numerous businesses have employee-of-the-month awards. The military has a long-standing custom of awarding ribbons and medals for exemplary actions. Some football coaches award emblems to players to wear on their helmets as symbols of their exceptional performance.

Successful strategy implementers are experts in the use of symbols to build and nurture the culture. They personally conduct ceremonial events, and they go out of their way to personally and publicly congratulate individuals who exhibit the desired traits. Individuals and groups that "get with the program" are singled out for special praise and visibly rewarded. They use every ceremonial function and every conversation to implant values, send reinforcing signals, and praise good deeds.

In addition to being out front, personally leading the push for new attitudes and communicating the reasons for new approaches, the manager has to convince all those concerned that the effort is more than cosmetic. Talk and symbols have to be complemented by substance and real movement. The actions taken have to be credible, highly visible, and unmistakably indicative of the seriousness of management's commitment to a new culture and new ways of doing business. There are several ways to accomplish this. One is to engineer some quick successes in reorienting the way some things are done to highlight the value of the new order, thus making enthusiasm for the changes contagious. However, figuring out how to get some instant results is usually not as important as having the will and patience to mold the parts of the organization into a solid, competent team psychologically committed to carrying out the strategy in a superior fashion. The strongest signs that management is truly committed to creating a new culture come from actions to replace traditional managers with "new breed" managers, changes in long-standing policies and operating practices, major reorganizational moves, big shifts in how raises and promotions are granted, and reallocations in the budget.

At the same time, chief strategy implementers must be careful to *lead by example.* For instance, if the organization's strategy involves a drive to become the industry's low-cost producer, senior managers must display frugality in their own actions and decisions: utilizing Spartan decorations in the executive suite, establishing policies that forbid lavish use of expense accounts and entertainment allowances, keeping a lean staff in the corporate office, and not resorting to personal use of limousines, private jets, and other executive privileges.

Implanting the needed culture-building values and behavior depends on a sincere, sustained commitment by the chief executive coupled with extraordinary persistence in reinforcing the culture at every opportunity through both word and deed. Neither charisma nor personal magnetism are essential. However, being highly visible around the organization is essential; culture-building cannot be done from an office through written pronouncements and the filtering of information about executive decisions. Moreover, creating and sustaining a strategy-supportive culture is a job for the whole management team. Senior officers have to keynote the values and shape the organization's philosophy. But for the culture-building effort to be successful, strategy implementers must enlist the support of subordinate managers, getting them to do things in their areas of responsibility to instill values and establish culture norms at the lowest levels in the organization. Until a big majority of employees have really joined the culture and share an emotional commitment to its basic values and beliefs, there's considerably more work to be done in both installing the culture and tightening the culture-strategy fit.

The task of making culture supportive of strategy is not a short-term exercise. It takes time for a new culture to emerge and dominate. Culture-building, culture-changing initiatives can't be expected to take hold immediately and effect an overnight transformation. The bigger the organization and the greater the cultural shift needed to produce the desired culture-strategy fit, the longer the time it takes. In large companies, changing the corporate culture in significant ways is a three- to five-year exercise at minimum. In fact it is usually a more tedious task to reshape a deeply ingrained culture that is not strategy-supportive than it is to instill a strategy-supportive culture from scratch in a brand new organization.

Building a Spirit of High Performance into the Culture

An ability to instill strong individual commitment to strategic success and create an atmosphere where there is constructive pressure to perform is one of the most valuable strategy-implementing skills. When an organization performs consistently at or near peak capability, the outcome is not only improved strategic success but also an organizational culture permeated with a spirit of high performance. Such a spirit of performance should not be confused with whether employees are "happy" or "satisfied" or whether they "get along well together." The test of whether an organization exemplifies a spirit of performance is the emphasis placed on achievement and on excellence. The organization's culture must be results-oriented, and management must deliberately pursue policies and practices that inspire people to do their best.

The successful approaches to creating a spirit of high performance typically involve an intense people orientation, reinforced at every conceivable occasion in every conceivable way and mirrored to down-the-line people in every activity. Some of the important managerial do's include treating employees with dignity and respect, training each employee thoroughly, encouraging employees to use their own initiative and creativity in performing their work, setting reasonable and clear performance expectations, utilizing the full range of rewards and punishment to enforce high performance standards, holding managers at every level responsible for developing the people who report to them, and granting employees enough autonomy to stand out, excel, and contribute. An important aspect of creating a results-oriented organizational culture is making champions out of the people who turn in winning performances; examples of how this is done are cited below:[7]

- At Boeing, IBM, General Electric, and 3M Company, top executives deliberately make "champions" out of individuals who believe so strongly in their ideas that they take it on themselves to hurdle the bureaucracy, maneuver their projects through the system, and turn them into improved services, new products, or even new businesses. In these companies, "product champions" are given high visibility, room to push their ideas, and strong executive support. Champions whose ideas prove out are usually handsomely rewarded; those whose ideas don't pan out still have secure jobs and are given chances to try again.

- The manager of a New York area sales office rented the Meadowlands Stadium (home field of the New York Giants) for an evening. After work, the salesmen were all assembled at the stadium and asked to run one at a time through the player's tunnel onto the field. As each one emerged, the electronic scoreboard flashed his name to those gathered in the stands— executives from corporate headquarters, employees from the office, family, and friends. Their role was to cheer loudly in honor of the individual's sales accomplishments. The company involved was IBM. The occasion for

---

[7] Peters and Waterman, *In Search of Excellence,* pp. xviii, 240, and 269; and Peters and Austin, *A Passion for Excellence,* pp. 304–7.

this action was to reaffirm IBM's commitment to satisfy an individual's need to be part of something great and to reiterate IBM's concern for championing individual accomplishment.

- Some companies upgrade the importance and status of individual employees by referring to them as cast members (Disney), crew members (McDonald's), or associates (Wal-Mart and J. C. Penney). Companies like IBM, Tupperware, and McDonald's actively seek out reasons and opportunities to give pins, buttons, badges, and medals to good showings by average performers—the idea being to express appreciation and help give a boost to the "middle 60 percent" of the work force.

- McDonald's has a contest to determine the best hamburger cooker in its entire chain. It begins with a competition to determine the best hamburger cooker in each store. Store winners go on to compete in regional championships, and regional winners go on to the "All-American" contest. The winners get trophies and an All-American patch to wear on their shirts.

- Milliken & Co. holds corporate sharing rallies once every three months; teams come from all over the company to swap success stories and ideas. A hundred or more teams make five-minute presentations over a two-day period. Each rally has a major theme—quality, cost reduction, and so on. No criticisms and negatives are allowed, and there is no such thing as a big idea or a small one. Quantitative measures of success are used to gauge improvement. All those present vote on the best presentation, and several ascending grades of awards are handed out. Everyone, however, receives a framed certificate for participating.

What makes a spirit of high performance come alive is more than a belief, statement, philosophy or program. It is a complex network of practices, words, symbols, styles, values, and policies pulling together that produces extraordinary results with ordinary people. The drivers of the system are a belief in the worth of the individual, strong company commitment to job security and promotion from within, managerial practices that encourage employees to exercise individual initiative and creativity in doing their jobs, and pride in doing the "itty-bitty, teeny-tiny things" right. A company that treats its employees well tends to reap benefits in the form of increased teamwork, higher morale, and greater employee loyalty.

While emphasizing a spirit of high performance nearly always accentuates the positive, there are negative aspects too. Managers whose units consistently perform poorly have to be removed. Aside from the organizational benefits, weak performing managers should be reassigned for their own good—people who find themselves in a job they cannot handle are usually frustrated, anxiety ridden, harassed, and unhappy.[8] Moreover, subordinates have a right to be managed with competence, dedication, and achievement; unless their boss performs well, they themselves cannot perform well. In addition, weak-performing workers and peo-

---

[8] Peter Drucker, *Management: Tasks, Responsibilities, Practices* (New York: Harper & Row, 1974), p. 457.

ple who reject the cultural emphasis on dedication and high performance have to be weeded out. Recruitment practices need to aim at selecting highly motivated, ambitious applicants whose attitudes and work habits mesh well with a results-oriented corporate culture.

Illustration Capsule 24 presents an example of how one major company has endeavored to link its values and culture with its performance objectives.

ILLUSTRATION CAPSULE 24

SQUARE D COMPANY: VISION, MISSION, PRINCIPLES, OBJECTIVES, PERFORMANCE

Square D Company is a $1.7 billion producer of electrical equipment and electronic products. Below is the company's presentation of its vision, mission, principles, objectives, and actual performance against its long-term financial goals.

Vision

Dedicated to Growth
Committed to Quality

Mission

We are dedicated to growth for our customers, shareholders and employees through quality, innovation and profitable reinvestment.

Principles

As a company responsible to our customers, shareholders and employees, we will:

- Provide our customers with innovative, functional and reliable products and services at a cost and quality level consistent with their needs.
- Concentrate on enhancing long-term shareholder value.
- Actively pursue equal opportunity for all individuals and provide an environment which encourages open communications, personal growth and creativity.
- Expect integrity and professional conduct from our employees in every aspect of our business.
- Conduct our operations ethically and well within the framework of the law.
- Actively contribute to the communities and industries in which we participate.

(continued)

Financial Objectives

We are committed to providing our shareholders with an attractive return on their investment, and our specific goals for doing so are to:

- Achieve a minimum after-tax return on capital of 14%.
- Leverage return on shareholders' equity through a capital structure which includes 25 to 35% debt.
- Achieve a minimum return on equity of 18%.
- Pay dividends equal to approximately 40% of earnings.
- Achieve average annual growth in earnings of at least 10%.

Operating Objectives

Market Leadership

- Have a leading market share position in our major markets.
- Be recognized as a leader in the application of technology to meet customer requirements.
- Be a "best-value" supplier throughout the world.
- Expand our international business to a level equalling 20 to 25% of company sales.
- Invest in research and development at a rate of 4% of sales as a means of achieving our market leadership objectives.

Employee Development

- Encourage initiative, innovation and productivity by appropriately recognizing and rewarding employee performance.
- Invest in employee training and development at a rate of 2% of payroll.
- Honestly and accurately appraise and evaluate the performance of each employee on at least an annual basis.
- Provide for the orderly succession of management.
- Maintain a positive affirmative action program and provide employees with the opportunity for advancement commensurate with their abilities.

Social/Community Responsibility

- Maintain a safe, clean and healthy environment for our employees and the communities in which we operate.

(continued)

- Invest 1.5% of net income in social, cultural, educational and charitable activities.
- Encourage appropriate employee involvement in community activities.

Performance against Financial Goals

Year ended December 31	Long-term financial goals	1988	1987	1986	1985	1984
After-tax return from continuing operations on average capital	14.0%	14.8%	13.5%	12.5%	13.9%	16.4%
Average total debt as a percentage of average capital	25.0–35.0%	28.2%	23.7%	29.9%	30.5%	29.5%
Return from continuing operations on average equity	18.0%	18.1%	15.7%	15.5%	17.7%	20.6%
Dividend payout percentage	40.0%	45.7%	48.6%	53.9%	60.9%	49.7%
Annual growth in earnings from continuing operations	10.0%	8.1%	11.2%	(3.4)%	(6.7)%	65.0%

Source: 1988 Annual Report.

Bonding the Fits: The Role of Shared Values

As emphasized earlier, "fits" with strategy need to be created internally as concerns structure, organizational skills and distinctive competence, budgets, support systems, rewards and incentives, policies and procedures, and culture. The better the "goodness of fit" among these administrative activities and characteristics, the more powerful strategy execution is likely to be.

McKinsey & Co., a leading consulting firm with wide-ranging experiences in strategic analysis, has developed a framework for examining the fits in seven broad areas: (1) strategy, (2) structure, (3) shared values, attitudes, and philosophy, (4) approach to staffing the organization and its overall "people orientation," (5) administrative systems, practices, and procedures used to run the organization on a day-to-day basis, including the reward structure, formal and informal policies, budgeting and programs, training, cost accounting, and financial controls, (6) the organization's skills, capabilities and distinctive competence, and (7) style of top management (how they allocate their time and attention, symbolic actions, their leadership skills, the way the top management team comes across to the rest of the organization).[9] McKinsey has diagramed these seven elements into what it calls the McKinsey 7-S Framework (the seven S's are strategy, structure, shared values, staff, systems, skills, and style—so labeled to promote recall) shown in Figure 10–1.

Shared values are the core of the 7-S framework because they are the heart-and-soul themes around which an organization rallies. They define its main beliefs and aspirations, its guiding concepts of "who we are, what we do, where we are headed, and what principles we will stand for in getting there." They drive the corporate culture.

The virtue of the McKinsey 7-S Framework is that it draws attention to some important organizational interconnections and why these interconnections are relevant in trying to effect change. In orchestrating a major shift in strategy and gathering full momentum for implementation, the pace of real change will be governed by all seven S's. The 7-S framework is a simple way to illustrate that the job of implementing strategy is one of creating fits and harmonizing the seven S's.

EXERTING STRATEGIC LEADERSHIP

The litany of good strategic management is simple enough: formulate a sound strategic plan, implement it, execute it to the fullest, win! But it's easier said than done. Exerting take-charge leadership, being a "spark plug," ramrodding things through, and getting things done by coaching others to do them are not simple tasks to execute. Moreover, a strategy manager has many different leadership roles to play: chief entrepreneur, chief administrator, crisis solver, taskmaster, figurehead, spokesman, resource allocator, negotiator, motivator, adviser, inspirationist, consensus builder, policymaker, mentor, and head cheerleader. Sometimes it is useful to be authoritarian and hardnosed; other times being a perceptive listener and a compromising decision-maker works best; and still other times call for a strongly participative, collegial approach. Many occasions call for a highly visible role and extensive time commitments, while others entail a brief ceremonial performance with the details being delegated to subordinates.

In general, the problem of strategic leadership is one of diagnosing the situation and choosing from any of several ways to handle it. Six leadership tasks dominate the strategy implementer's action agenda:

1. Staying on top of what is happening and how well things are going.
2. Promoting a culture in which the organization is "energized" to accomplish strategy and perform at a high level.
3. Keeping the organization responsive to changing conditions, alert for new opportunities, and bubbling with innovative ideas.
4. Building consensus, dealing with the politics of strategy formulation and implementation, and containing "power struggles."

---

[9] For a more extended discussion, see Robert H. Waterman, Jr., Thomas J. Peters, and Julien R. Phillips, "Structure Is Not Organization," *Business Horizons* 23, no. 3 (June 1980), pp. 14–26; and Waterman, Jr., "The Seven Elements of Strategic Fit," pp. 68–72.

Figure 10–1   BONDING THE ADMINISTRATIVE FITS: THE McKINSEY 7-S FRAMEWORK

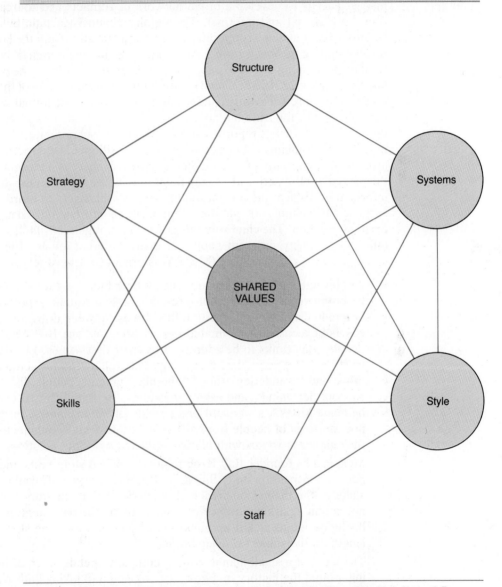

Source: Thomas J. Peters and Robert H. Waterman, Jr., *In Search of Excellence* (New York: Harper & Row, 1982), p. 10.

5. Enforcing ethical standards.
6. Pushing corrective actions to improve strategy execution and overall strategic performance.

Managing by Walking Around

To stay on top of how well the strategy implementation process is going, a manager needs to develop a broad network of contacts and sources of information, both formal and informal. The regular channels include talking with key subordinates, reading written reports, gleaning statistics from the latest operating results, getting feedback from customers, watching the competitive reactions of rival firms, tapping into the grapevine, listening to what is on the minds of rank-and-file employees, and firsthand observation. However, some of this information tends to be more trustworthy than others. The content of formal written reports may represent "the truth but not the whole truth." "Bad news" may be covered up, minimized, or not reported at all. Sometimes subordinates delay conveying failures and problems in hopes that more time will give them room to turn things around. As information flows up an organization, there is a tendency for it to get "censored" and "sterilized" to the point that it may fail to reveal strategy-critical information. Hence, there is reason for strategy managers to guard against major surprises by making sure that they have accurate information and a "feel" for the existing situation. The chief way this is done is by regular visits "to the field" and talking with many different people at many different levels. The technique of *managing by walking around* (MBWA) is practiced in a variety of styles.[10]

- At Hewlett-Packard, there are weekly beer busts in each division, attended by both executives and employees, to create a regular opportunity to keep in touch. Tidbits of information flow freely between down-the-line employees and executives—facilitated in part because "the H-P Way" is for people at all ranks to be addressed by their first names. Bill Hewlett, one of HP's co-founders, had a companywide reputation for getting out of his office and "wandering around" the plant greeting people, listening to what was on their minds, and asking questions. He found this so valuable that he made MBWA a standard practice for all HP managers. Furthermore, ad hoc meetings of people from different departments spontaneously arise; they gather in rooms with blackboards and work out solutions informally.

- McDonald's founder Ray Kroc regularly visited store units and did his own personal inspection on Q.S.C.& V. (Quality, Service, Cleanliness, and Value)—the themes he preached regularly. There are stories of him pulling into a unit's parking lot, seeing litter lying on the pavement, getting out of his limousine to pick it up himself, and then lecturing the store staff at length on the subject of cleanliness.

- The CEO of a small manufacturing company spends much of his time riding around the factory in a golf cart, waving and joking with workers, listening to them, and calling all 2,000 employees by their first names. In addition, he spends a lot of time with union officials, inviting them to meetings and keeping them well informed about what is going on.

---

[10] Ibid., pp. xx, 15, 120–23, 191, 242–43, 246–47, 287–90. For an extensive report on the benefits of MBWA, see Peters and Austin, *A Passion for Excellence,* chaps. 2, 3, and 19.

- Sam Walton, Wal-Mart's founder, insists "The key is to get out into the store and listen to what the associates have to say. Our best ideas come from clerks and stockboys." Walton himself has had a longstanding practice of visiting Wal-Mart's stores regularly. On one occasion he flew the company plane to a Texas town, got out, and instructed the copilot to meet him 100 miles down the road. Then he flagged a Wal-Mart truck and rode the rest of way to "chat with the driver—it seemed like so much fun." Walton makes a practice of greeting store managers and their spouses by name at annual meetings and has been known to go to the company's distribution centers at 2:00 A.M. (carrying boxes of doughnuts to share with all those on duty) to have a chance to find out what was on their minds.

- When Ed Carlson became CEO at United Airlines, he traveled about 200,000 miles a year talking with United's employees. He observed, "I wanted these people to identify me and to feel sufficiently comfortable to make suggestions or even argue with me if that's what they felt like doing. . . . Whenever I picked up some information, I would call the senior officer of the division and say that I had just gotten back from visiting Oakland, Reno, and Las Vegas, and here is what I found."

- At Marriott Corp. Bill Marriott not only personally inspects all Marriott hotels at least once a year but he also invites all Marriott guests to send him their evaluations of Marriott's facilities and services. He personally reads every customer complaint and has been known to telephone hotel managers about them.

Managers at many companies attach great importance to informal communications. They report that it is essential to have a "feel" for situations and to gain quick, easy access to information. When executives stay in their offices, they tend to become isolated and often surround themselves with people who are not likely to offer criticism and different perspectives; prompt, flexible, timely solutions to problems then tend to go by the wayside.

Fostering a Strategy-Supportive Climate and Culture

Strategy implementers have to be "out front" in promoting a strategy-supportive organizational climate. When major strategic changes are being implemented, the manager's time is best spent personally leading the changes needed to institute a more strategy-supportive work environment. When only strategic fine-tuning is being implemented, less generally needs to be done, but there is still a lead role for the manager to play in pushing ahead and prodding for continuous improvements. Successful strategy leaders recognize it is their responsibility to convince people that the chosen strategy is right and that implementing it to the best of the organization's ability is "top priority."

Both words and deeds play a part. Words are needed to inspire accomplishment of the strategy, to infuse spirit and drive, to define strategy-supportive cultural norms and values, to articulate the reasons for strategic and organizational change, to legitimize new viewpoints and new priorities, to urge and reinforce commitment to the course being charted, and to arouse confidence in the new strategy being implemented. Deeds are essential to add credibility to the words, to create strategy-supportive symbols, to set examples, to give meaning and content to the language, and to teach the organization what sort of behavior is needed and expected.

Highly visible symbols and imagery are needed to complement substantive actions. As an example of the value of symbolic actions, consider the explanation one General Motors manager gave for the striking difference in performance between two large plants:[11]

> At the poorly performing plant, the plant manager probably ventured out on the floor once a week, always in a suit. His comments were distant and perfunctory. At South Gate, the better plant, the plant manager was on the floor all the time. He wore a baseball cap and a UAW jacket. By the way, whose plant do you think was spotless? Whose looked like a junkyard?

As a rule, the greater the degree of strategic change being implemented and/or the greater the shift in cultural norms needed to accommodate a new strategy, the more visible the strategy implementer's words and deeds need to be. The lesson from well-managed companies is that what the strategy-leader says and does has a significant bearing on down-the-line strategy implementation and execution.[12] According to one view, "It is not so much the articulation . . . about what an [organization] should be doing that creates new practice. It's the imagery that creates the understanding, the compelling moral necessity that the new way is right."[13] Moreover, the actions and images, both substantive and symbolic, have to be hammered out regularly, not just restricted to ceremonial speeches and special occasions. This is where a high profile and "managing by walking around" comes heavily into play. As a Hewlett-Packard official expresses it in the company publication *The HP Way:*

> Once a division or department has developed a plan of its own—a set of working objectives—it's important for managers and supervisors to keep it in operating condition. This is where observation, measurement, feedback, and guidance come in. It's our "management by wandering around." That's how you find out whether you're ontrack and heading at the right speed and in the right direction. If you don't constantly monitor how people are operating, not only will they tend to wander off track but also they will begin to believe you weren't serious about the plan in the first place. It has the extra benefit of getting you off your chair and moving around your area. By wandering around, I literally mean moving around and talking to people. It's all done on a very informal and spontaneous basis, but it's important in the course of time to cover the whole territory. You start out by being accessible and approachable, but the main thing is to realize you're there to listen. The second reason for MBWA is that it is vital to keep people informed

---

[11] As quoted in Peters and Waterman, *In Search of Excellence,* p. 262.

[12] Peters and Waterman, *In Search of Excellence,* chap. 9.

[13] Warren Bennis, *The Unconscious Conspiracy: Why Leaders Can't Lead* (New York: AMACOM, 1987), p. 93.

about what's going on in the company, especially those things that are important to them. The third reason for doing this is because it is just plain fun.

Such contacts give the manager a feel for how things are progressing, and they provide opportunity to speak with encouragement, lift spirits, shift attention from the old to the new priorities, create some excitement, and project an atmosphere of informality and fun—all of which drive implementation in a positive fashion and intensify the organizational energy behind strategy execution. John Welch of General Electric sums up the hands-on role and motivational approach well: "I'm here every day, or out into a factory, smelling it, feeling it, touching it, challenging the people."[14]

Keeping the Internal Organization Responsive and Innovative

While formulating and implementing strategy is a manager's responsibility, the task of generating fresh ideas, identifying new opportunities, and being responsive to changing conditions cannot be accomplished by a single person. It is an organizationwide task, particularly in large corporations. One of the toughest parts of exerting strategic leadership is generating a dependable supply of fresh ideas from the rank and file, managers and employees alike, and promoting an entrepreneurial, opportunistic spirit that permits continuous adaptation to changing conditions. A flexible, responsive, innovative internal environment is critical in fast-moving high-technology industries, in businesses where products have short life cycles and growth depends on new product innovation, in managing widely diversified business portfolios (where opportunities are varied and scattered), in industries where successful product differentiation is key, and in businesses where the strategy of being the low-cost producer hinges on productivity improvement and cost reduction. Managers cannot mandate such an environment by simply exhorting people to be "creative."

One useful leadership approach is to take special pains to foster, nourish, and support people who are willing to champion new ideas, better services, new products and product applications, and are eager for a chance to try turning their ideas into new divisions, new businesses, and even new industries. When Texas Instruments recently reviewed its last 50 or so successful and unsuccessful new product introductions, one factor marked every failure: "Without exception we found we hadn't had a volunteer champion. There was someone we had cajoled into taking on the task. When we take a look at a product and decide whether to push it or not these days, we've got a new set of criteria. Number one is the presence of a zealous, volunteer champion. After that comes market potential and project economics in a distant second and third."[15] The rule seems to be that the idea of something new or something better either finds a champion or it dies. And

---

[14] As quoted in Ann M. Morrison, "Trying to Bring GE to Life," *Fortune*, January 25, 1982, p. 52.

[15] As quoted in Peters and Waterman, *In Search of Excellence*, pp. 203–4.

the champion is usually persistent, competitive, tenacious, committed, and fanatic about the idea and seeing it through to success.

Empowering Champions.   In order to promote an organizational climate where champion innovators can blossom and thrive, strategy managers need to do several things. First, individuals and groups have to be encouraged to bring their ideas forward, be creative, and exercise initiative. Second, the maverick style of the champion has to be tolerated and given room to operate. People's imaginations need to be encouraged to "fly in all directions." Autonomy to experiment and informal brainstorming sessions need to become ingrained behavior. Above all, people with creative ideas must not be looked on as disruptive or troublesome. Third, managers have to induce and promote lots of "tries" and be willing to tolerate mistakes and failures. Most ideas don't pan out, but a good attempt results in learning even when it fails. Fourth, strategy managers should demonstrate a willingness to use all kinds of ad hoc organizational forms to support ideas and experimentation—venture teams, task forces, internal competition among different groups working on the same project (IBM calls the showdown between the competing approaches a "performance shootout"), informal "bootlegged" projects composed of volunteers, and so on. Five, strategy managers have to see that the rewards for a successful champion are large and visible and that people who champion an unsuccessful idea are encouraged to try again rather than punished or shunted aside. In effect, the leadership task here is one of putting internal support systems for entrepreneurial innovation into place.

Dealing with Company Politics

A manager can't effectively formulate and implement strategy without being perceptive about company politics and being adept at political maneuvering.[16] Politics virtually always comes into play in formulating the strategic plan. Inevitably, key individuals and groups form coalitions, and each group presses the benefits and potential of its own ideas and vested interests. Political considerations enter into which strategic objectives take precedence and which lines of business in the corporate portfolio have top priority in resource allocation. Internal politics is a factor in building a consensus for which business strategy to employ and in settling on the role and contribution of each functional area in supporting line-of-business strategy.

Likewise, there is politics in implementing strategy. Typically, internal political considerations enter into decisions affecting organization structure (whose areas of responsibility need to be reorganized, who reports to who, who has how much authority over subunits), what individuals will fill key positions and head strategy-critical activities, and which organizational units will get the biggest

---

[16] For further discussion of this point see Abraham Zaleznik, "Power and Politics in Organizational Life," *Harvard Business Review* 48, no. 3 (May–June 1970), pp. 47–60; R. M. Cyert, H. A. Simon, and D. B. Trow, "Observation of a Business Decision," *Journal of Business,* October 1956, pp. 237–48; and James Brian Quinn, *Strategies for Change: Logical Incrementalism* (Homewood, Ill.: Richard D. Irwin, 1980).

budget increases. As a case in point, Quinn cites a situation where three strong managers who fought each other constantly formed a potent coalition to resist a reorganization scheme that would have coordinated the very things that caused their friction.[17]

In short, political considerations and the forming of alliances are an integral part of building organizationwide support for the strategic plan and gaining consensus on the various mechanics of how to implement strategy. Indeed, having astute political skills is a definite, and maybe even a necessary, asset for managers in orchestrating the whole strategic process.

There is a clear-cut imperative for a strategy manager to understand how an organization's power structure works, who wields influence in the executive ranks, which groups and individuals are "activists" and which are "defenders of the status quo," who can be helpful in a "showdown" on key decisions, and which direction the political winds are blowing on a given issue. On those occasions where major decisions have to be made, strategy managers need to be especially sensitive to the politics of managing coalitions and reaching consensus. As the chairman of a major British corporation expressed it:

> I've never taken a major decision without consulting my colleagues. It would be unimaginable to me, unimaginable. First, they help me make a better decision in most cases. Second, if they know about it and agree with it, they'll back it. Otherwise, they might challenge it, not openly, but subconsciously.[18]

The politics of strategy centers chiefly around stimulating options, nurturing support for strong proposals and killing weak ones, guiding the formation of coalitions on particular issues, and achieving consensus and commitment. A recent study of strategy management in nine large corporations showed that the political tactics of successful executives included:[19]

- Letting weakly supported ideas and proposals die through inaction.
- Establishing additional hurdles or tests for strongly supported ideas that the manager views as unacceptable but that are best not opposed openly.
- Keeping a low political profile on unacceptable proposals by getting subordinate managers to say no.
- Letting most negative decisions come from a group consensus that the manager merely confirms, thereby reserving his/her personal veto for big issues and crucial moments.
- Leading the strategy but not dictating it—giving few orders, announcing few decisions, depending heavily on informal questioning and seeking to probe and clarify until a consensus emerges.
- Staying alert to the symbolic impact of one's actions and statements lest a false signal stimulates proposals and movements in unwanted directions.

---

[17] Quinn, *Strategies for Change,* p. 68.

[18] This statement was made by Sir Alastair Pilkington, Chairman, Pilkington Brothers, Ltd.; the quote appears in Quinn, *Strategies for Change,* p. 65.

[19] Ibid., pp. 128–45.

- Ensuring that all major power bases within the organization have representation in or access to top management.
- Injecting new faces and new views into considerations of major changes to preclude those involved from coming to see the world the same way and then acting as systematic screens against other views.
- Minimizing the executive's own political exposure on issues that are highly controversial and that involve circumstances where opposition from major power centers can trigger a "shootout."

The politics of strategy implementation is especially critical in attempting to introduce a new strategy. Except for crisis situations where the old strategy is plainly revealed as out-of-date, it is usually bad politics to push the new strategy via attacks on the old one.[20] Bad-mouthing old strategy can easily be interpreted as an attack on those who formulated it and those who supported it in the enterprise's climb to its present success. In addition, the former strategy and the judgments behind it may have been well suited to the organization's earlier circumstances, and the people who made these judgments may still be in positions where support for the new strategy is important.

In addition, it is wise to recognize that the new strategy and/or the plans for implementing it may not have been the first choices of others and lingering doubts may remain. Good arguments may exist for pursuing other action approaches. Consequently, in trying to surmount resistance, nothing is gained by "knocking" the arguments for alternative approaches. Such attacks are likely to produce alienation instead of cooperation.

In short, to bring the full force of an organization behind a strategic plan, the strategy manager must assess and deal with the most important centers of potential support and opposition to new strategic thrusts.[21] He or she needs to secure the support of key people, co-opt or neutralize serious opposition and resistance when and where necessary, learn where the zones of indifference are, and build as much consensus as possible.

Enforcing Ethical Behavior

For an organization to display consistently high ethical standards, the CEO and those around the CEO must be openly and unequivocally committed to ethical conduct.[22] In companies that strive hard to make high ethical standards a reality, top management communicates its commitment in a code of ethics, in speeches and company publications, in policies concerning the consequences of unethical behavior, in the deeds of senior executives, and in the actions taken to ensure compliance. Senior management iterates and reiterates to employees that it is not only their *duty* to observe ethical codes but also to report ethical violations. While such companies have provisions for disciplining violators, the main purpose of

---

[20] Ibid., pp. 118–19.

[21] Ibid., p. 205.

[22] The Business Roundtable, "Corporate Ethics," p. 4–10.

enforcement is to encourage compliance rather than administer punishment. Although the CEO leads the enforcement process, all managers are expected to make a personal contribution by stressing ethical conduct with their subordinates and by involving themselves in the process of monitoring compliance with the code of ethics. "Gray area" issues are identified, openly discussed with employees, and mechanisms for providing guidance and resolution put in place. The lesson from these companies is that it is never enough to assume activities are being conducted ethically, nor can it be assumed that employees understand they are expected to act with integrity.

There are several concrete things managers can do to exercise ethics leadership.[23] First and foremost, they must set an excellent ethical example in their own behavior and establish a tradition of integrity. Company decisions have to be seen as ethical—"actions speak louder than words." Second, managers and employees have to be educated about what is ethical and what is not; ethics training programs may have to be established and "gray areas" pointed out and discussed. Everyone must be encouraged to raise issues with ethical dimensions, and such discussions should be treated as a legitimate topic. Third, top management should explicitly refer to the company's ethical code and take a strong stand on ethical issues. Fourth, top management must be prepared to act as the final arbiter on hard calls; this means removing people from a key position or terminating them when they are guilty of a violation. It also means reprimanding those who have been lax in monitoring and enforcing ethical compliance. Failure to act swiftly and decisively in pursuing ethical misconduct is interpreted as a lack of real commitment.

A well-developed program to ensure compliance with ethical standards typically includes (1) an oversight committee of the board of directors, usually made up of outside directors, (2) a committee of senior managers to direct the ongoing training, implementation, and compliance effort, (3) an annual audit of each manager's efforts to uphold ethical standards and formal reports on the actions taken by managers to remedy deficient conduct, and (4) periodically requiring people to sign documents certifying compliance with ethical standards.[24]

Leading the Process of Making Corrective Adjustments

No strategic plan and no scheme for strategy implementation can foresee all the events and problems that will arise. Making adjustments and "mid-course" corrections are therefore a normal and necessary part of strategic management.

Consider, first, the case of reacting and responding to new conditions involving either the strategy or its implementation. The process of what to do starts with an evaluation of whether immediate action needs to be taken or whether time permits a more deliberate response. In a crisis, the approach typically is to push key subordinates to gather information and formulate recommendations, personally preside over extended discussions of the pros and cons of proposed re-

---

[23] Ibid.

[24] Ibid.

sponses, and try to build a quick consensus among members of the executive "inner circle." If no consensus emerges or if several key subordinates remain divided, the burden falls on the strategy manager to choose the response and urge its support.

When time permits a full-fledged evaluation, strategy managers seem to prefer a process of incrementally solidifying commitment to a response.[25] The approach seems to be one of consciously:

1. Staying flexible and keeping a number of options open.
2. Asking a lot of questions.
3. Gaining in-depth information from specialists.
4. Encouraging subordinates to participate in developing alternatives and proposing solutions.
5. Getting the reactions of many different people to proposed solutions to test their potential and political acceptability.
6. Seeking to build commitment to a response by gradually moving toward a consensus solution.

The governing principle seems to be to make a final decision as late as possible to (1) bring as much information to bear as needed, (2) let the situation clarify enough to know what to do, and (3) allow the various political constituencies and power bases within the organization to move toward a consensus solution. Executives are often wary of committing themselves to a major change too soon because it discourages others from asking questions that need to be raised.

Corrective adjustments to strategy need not be just reactive, however. Proactive adjustments constitute a second approach to improving strategy or its implementation. The distinctive feature of a proactive posture is that adjusting actions arise out of management's own drives and initiatives for better performance as opposed to forced reactions. Successful strategy managers employ a variety of proactive tactics.[26]

1. Commissioning studies to explore and amplify areas where they have a "gut feeling" or sense a need exists.
2. Shopping ideas among trusted colleagues and putting forth trial concepts.
3. Teaming people with different skills, interests, and experiences and letting them push and tug on interesting ideas to expand the variety of approaches considered.
4. Contacting a variety of people inside and outside the organization to sample viewpoints, probe, and listen, thereby trying to get early warning signals of impending problems/issues and deliberating short-circuiting all the careful screens of information flowing up from below.
5. Stimulating proposals for improvement from lower levels, encouraging the development of competing ideas and approaches, and letting the momen-

---

[25] Quinn, *Strategies for Change,* pp. 20–22.

[26] Ibid., chap. 4.

tum for change come from below, with final choices postponed until it is apparent which option best matches the organization's situation.

6. Seeking options and solutions that go beyond extrapolations from the status quo.

7. Accepting and committing to partial steps forward as a way of building comfort levels before going on ahead.

8. Managing the politics of change to promote managerial consensus and solidify management's commitment to whatever course of action is chosen.

Both the reactive and proactive approaches are similar in the process of deciding what adjusting actions to take; the leadership sequence seems to be sensing needs, gathering information, amplifying understanding and awareness, putting forth trial concepts, developing options, exploring the pros and cons, testing proposals, generating partial solutions, empowering champions, building a managerial consensus, and formally adopting an agreed-on course of action.[27] The ultimate managerial prescription may have been given by Rene McPherson, former CEO at Dana Corporation. In speaking to a class of students at Stanford, he said, "You just keep pushing. You just keep pushing. I made every mistake that could be made. But I just kept pushing."[28]

This points to a key feature of strategic management: the job of formulating and implementing strategy is not one of steering a clear-cut, linear course of carrying out the original strategy intact according to some preconceived and highly detailed implementation plan. Rather, it is one of creatively (1) adapting and reshaping strategy to unfolding events and (2) employing analytical-behavioral-political techniques to bring internal activities and attitudes into alignment with strategy. The process is iterative, with much looping and recycling to fine-tune and adjust in a continuously evolving process where the conceptually separate acts of strategy formulation and strategy implementation blur and join.

KEY POINTS

The managerial tasks of designing rewards and incentives, creating a strategy-supportive corporate culture, and exercising strategic leadership are key facets of successful strategy implementation. The use of incentives is the single most powerful tool at management's disposal in gaining employee "buy-in" and energetic commitment to carrying out the strategy. For incentives to work well, (1) the monetary payoff must be a major percentage of the compensation package, (2) the incentive plan must extend to all managers and workers, (3) the system must be administered with scrupulous care and fairness, (4) the incentives need to be linked tightly to performance targets spelled out in the strategic plan, and (5) each individual's performance targets should involve outcomes the person is able to affect personally.

---

[27] Ibid., p. 146.

[28] As quoted in Peters and Waterman, *In Search of Excellence*, p. 319.

Building a strategy-supportive corporate culture is important to successful implementation because it produces a work climate and organizational *espirit de corps* that thrives on meeting performance targets and being part of a winning effort. An organization's culture emerges from why and how it does things the way it does, the values and beliefs that senior managers espouse, the ethical standards expected, the tone and philosophy underlying key policies, and the traditions the organization maintains—culture, thus, concerns the "atmosphere" and "feeling" a company has and the style in which things get done. Companies with strong cultures are clear on what they stand for, and they take the process of getting people to "buy-in" to the cultural norms very seriously. The stronger the fit between culture and strategy, the less managers have to depend on policies, rules, procedures, and close supervision to enforce what people should and should not do: rather, cultural norms are so well observed that they automatically guide behavior.

Successful strategy implementers also exercise an important leadership role. They stay on top of how well things are going by spending considerable time outside their offices, wandering around the organization, listening, coaching, cheerleading, picking up important tidbits of information, and keeping their fingers on the organization's pulse. They take pains to reinforce the corporate culture through the things they say and do. They encourage people to be creative and innovative in order to keep the organization responsive to changing conditions, alert for new opportunities, and anxious to pursue fresh initiatives. They provide support to "champions" who are willing to stick their necks out and try something new. They work hard at building consensus on how to proceed, on what to change and what not to change. They enforce high ethical standards. And they push corrective action to improve strategy execution and overall strategic performance.

The action menu for implementing strategy is thus expansive. Virtually every aspect of administrative and managerial work comes into play. However, each strategy implementation situation is somewhat unique to the organization and to its own circumstances. The strategy implementer's action agenda, therefore, is always a function of the specific situation at hand. Diagnosing the situation and coming up with a series of action steps to put strategy into place and achieve the desired results is a major managerial challenge.

SUGGESTED READINGS

Bettinger, Cass, "Use Corporate Culture to Trigger High Performance." *Journal of Business Strategy* 10, no. 2 (March–April 1989), pp. 38–42.

Bower, Joseph L., and Martha W. Weinberg, "Statecraft, Strategy, and Corporate Leadership." *California Management Review* 30, no. 2 (Winter 1988), pp. 39–56.

Deal, Terence E., and Allen A. Kennedy, *Corporate Cultures*. Reading, Mass.: Addison-Wesley, 1982, especially chaps. 1 and 2.

Drucker, Peter F. *Management: Tasks, Responsibilities, Practices*. New York: Harper & Row, 1974, chaps. 16–19 and 33–39.

Freeman, R. Edward, and Daniel R. Gilbert, Jr. *Corporate Strategy and the Search for Ethics*. Englewood Cliffs, N.J.: Prentice-Hall, 1988.

Gabarro, J. J. "When a New Manager Takes Charge." *Harvard Business Review* 64, no. 3 (May–June 1985), pp. 110–23.

Green, Sebastian. "Strategy, Organizational Culture, and Symbolism." *Long Range Planning* 21, no. 4 (August 1988), pp. 121–29.

Herzberg, Frederick. "One More Time: How Do You Motivate Employees." *Harvard Business Review* 65, no. 4 (September–October 1987), pp. 109–20.

Oliver, Alex R., and Joseph R. Garber. "Implementing Strategic Planning: Ten Sure-Fire Ways To Do It Wrong." *Business Horizons* 16, no. 2 (March–April 1983), pp. 49–51.

O'Toole, James. "Employee Practices at the Best-Managed Companies." *California Management Review* 28, no. 1 (Fall 1985), pp. 35–66.

Pascale, Richard. "The Paradox of 'Corporate Culture': Reconciling Ourselves to Socialization." *California Management Review* 27, no. 2 (Winter 1985), pp. 26–41.

Peters, Thomas J., and Nancy Austin. *A Passion for Excellence.* New York: Random House, 1985, especially chaps. 11, 12, and 15–19.

Peters, Thomas J., and Robert H. Waterman, Jr. *In Search of Excellence.* New York: Harper & Row, 1982, chaps. 4, 5, and 9.

Quinn, James Brian. *Strategies for Change: Logical Incrementalism.* Homewood, Ill.: Richard D. Irwin, 1980, chap. 4.

————. "Managing Innovation: Controlled Chaos." *Harvard Business Review* 64, no. 3 (May–June 1985), pp. 73–84.

Reimann, Bernard C., and Yoash Wiener. "Corporate Culture: Avoiding the Elitest Trap." *Business Horizons* 31, no. 2 (March–April 1988), pp. 36–44.

Scholz, Christian. "Corporate Culture and Strategy—The Problem of Strategic Fit." *Long Range Planning* 20 (August 1987), pp. 78–87.

Vancil, Richard F. *Implementing Strategy: The Role of Top Management.* Boston: Division of Research, Harvard Business School, 1985.

Cases in Strategic Management

A Guide to Case Analysis

*I keep six honest serving men
(They taught me all I knew);
Their names are What and Why and When;
And How and Where and Who.*
Rudyard Kipling

In most courses in strategic management, students practice at being strategy managers via case analysis. A case sets forth, in a factual manner, the events and organizational circumstances surrounding a particular managerial situation. It puts readers at the scene of the action and familiarizes them with all the relevant circumstances. A case on strategic management can concern a whole industry, a single organization, or some part of an organization; the organization involved can be either profit seeking or not-for-profit. The essence of the student's role in case analysis is to *diagnose* and *size up* the situation described in the case and then to *recommend* which, if any, actions need to be taken.

WHY USE CASES TO PRACTICE STRATEGIC MANAGEMENT

*A student of business with tact
Absorbed many answers he lacked.
But acquiring a job,
He said with a sob,
"How does one fit answer to fact?"*

The foregoing limerick was used some years ago by Professor Charles Gragg to characterize the plight of business students who had no exposure to cases.[1] Gragg observed that the mere act of listening to lectures and sound advice about managing does little for anyone's management skills and that the accumulated managerial wisdom cannot effectively be passed on by lectures and assigned readings alone. Gragg suggested that if anything had been learned about the practice of management, it is that a storehouse of ready-made textbook answers does not exist. Each managerial situation has unique aspects, requiring its own diagnosis, judgment, and tailor-made actions. Cases provide would-be managers with a valuable way to practice wrestling with the actual problems of actual managers in actual companies.

The case approach to strategic analysis is, first and foremost, an exercise in learning by doing. Because cases provide you with detailed information about conditions and problems of different industries and companies, your task of analyzing company after company and situation after situation has the twin benefit of boosting your analytical skills and exposing you to the ways companies and managers actually do things. Few college students have much direct personal contact with different companies and real-life strategic situations. Cases offer a viable substitute for actual on-the-job experience by (1) bringing you into close contact with a variety of industries, organizations, and strategic problems; (2) forcing you to assume a managerial role (as opposed to that of just an onlooker); (3) providing a test of how to apply the tools and techniques of strategic management; and (4) asking you to come up with pragmatic managerial action plans to deal with the issues at hand.

OBJECTIVES OF CASE ANALYSIS

Using cases to learn about the practice of strategic management is a powerful way for you to accomplish five things:[2]

1. Increase your understanding of what managers must and must not do to make a business succeed over the long haul.

2. Build your skills in conducting strategic analysis in a variety of industries, competitive situations, and company circumstances.

3. Get valuable practice in diagnosing strategic issues, evaluating strategic alternatives, and formulating workable plans of action.

4. Enhance your sense of business judgment, as opposed to uncritically accepting the authoritative crutch of the professor or "back-of-the-book" answers.

---

[1] Charles I. Gragg, "Because Wisdom Can't Be Told," in *The Case Method at the Harvard Business School,* ed. M. P. McNair (New York: McGraw-Hill, 1954), p. 11.

[2] Ibid., pp. 12–14; and D. R. Schoen and Philip A. Sprague, "What Is the Case Method?" in *The Case Method at the Harvard Business School,* ed. M. P. McNair, pp. 78–79.

5. Gain in-depth exposure to the conditions and problems of different industries and companies in ways that provide something close to actual business experience.

If you understand that these are the objectives of case analysis, you are less likely to be consumed with curiosity about "the answer to the case." Students who have grown comfortable with and accustomed to textbook statements of fact and definitive lecture notes are often frustrated when discussions about a case do not produce concrete answers. Usually, case discussions produce good arguments for more than one course of action. Differences of opinion nearly always exist. Thus, should a class discussion conclude without a strong, unambiguous consensus on what to do, don't grumble too much when you are *not* told what the answer is or what the company actually did. Just remember that in the business world answers don't come in conclusive black-and-white terms. There are nearly always several feasible courses of action and approaches, each of which may work out satisfactorily. Moreover, in the business world, when one elects a particular course of action, there is no peeking at the back of a book to see if you have chosen the best thing to do and no one to turn to for a provably correct answer. The only valid test of management action is *results*. If the results of an action turn out to be "good," the decision to take it may be presumed "right." If not, then the action chosen was "wrong" in the sense that it didn't work out.

Hence, the important thing for a student to understand in case analysis is that the managerial exercise of identifying, diagnosing, and recommending builds your skills; discovering the right answer or finding out what actually happened is no more than frosting on the cake. Even if you learn what the company did, you can't conclude that it was necessarily right or best. All that can be said is "here is what they did. . . ."

The point is this: *The purpose of giving you a case assignment is not to cause you to run to the library to look up what the company actually did but, rather, to enhance your skills in sizing up situations and developing your managerial judgment about what needs to be done and how to do it.* The aim of case analysis is for *you* to bear the strains of thinking actively, of offering your analysis, of proposing action plans, and of explaining and defending your assessments—this is how cases provide you with meaningful practice at being a manager.

PREPARING A CASE FOR CLASS DISCUSSION

If this is your first experience with the case method, you may have to reorient your study habits. Unlike lecture courses where you can get by without preparing intensively for each class and where you have latitude to work assigned readings and reviews of lecture notes into your schedule, *a case assignment requires conscientious preparation before class*. You will not get much out of hearing the class discuss a case you haven't read, and you certainly won't be able to contribute anything yourself to the discussion. What you have got to do to get ready for class discussion of a case is to study the case, reflect carefully on the situation presented, and develop some reasoned thoughts. Your goal in preparing the case should be to end up with what you think is a sound, well-supported analysis of the situation and a sound, defensible set of recommendations about which managerial actions need to be taken.

To prepare a case for class discussion, we suggest the following approach:

1. *Read the case through rather quickly for familiarity.* The initial reading should give you the general flavor of the situation and indicate which issue or issues are involved. If your instructor has provided you with study questions for the case, now is the time to read them carefully.

2. *Read the case a second time.* On this reading, try to gain full command of the facts. Begin to develop some tentative answers to the study questions your instructor has provided. If your instructor has elected not to give you assignment questions, then now is the time to start forming a clear picture of the overall situation being described and to think about how to tackle the issues posed in the case.

3. *Study all the exhibits carefully.* Often, the real story is in the numbers contained in the exhibits. Expect the information in the case exhibits to be crucial enough to materially affect your diagnosis of the situation.

4. *Decide what the strategic issues are.* Until you have identified the strategic issues and problems in the case, you don't know what to analyze, which tools and analytical techniques are called for, or otherwise how to proceed. At times the strategic issues are clear—either being stated in the case or else obvious from reading the case. At other times you will have to dig them out from all the information given.

5. *Start your analysis of the issues with some number crunching.* A big majority of strategy cases call for some kind of number crunching on your part. This means calculating assorted financial ratios to check out the company's financial condition and recent performance, calculating growth rates of sales or profits or unit volume, checking out profit margins and the makeup of the cost structure, and understanding whatever revenue-cost-profit relationships are present. See Table 1 for a summary of key financial ratios, how they are calculated, and what they show.

6. *Use whichever tools and techniques of strategic analysis are called for.* Strategic analysis is not just a collection of opinions; rather, it entails application of a growing number of powerful tools and techniques that cut beneath the surface and produce important insight and understanding of strategic situations. Every case assigned is strategy related and contains an opportunity to usefully apply the weapons of strategic analysis. Your instructor is looking for you to demonstrate that you know *how* and *when* to use the strategic management concepts presented earlier in the course. Furthermore, expect to have to draw regularly on what you have learned in your finance, economics, production, marketing, and human resources management courses.

7. *Check out conflicting opinions and make some judgments about the validity of all the data and information provided.* Many times cases report views and

Table 1 A SUMMARY OF KEY FINANCIAL RATIOS, HOW THEY ARE CALCULATED, AND WHAT THEY SHOW

Ratio	How calculated	What it shows
Profitability ratios:		
1. Gross profit margin	$$\frac{\text{Sales} - \text{Cost of goods sold}}{\text{Sales}}$$	An indication of the total margin available to cover operating expenses and yield a profit.
2. Operating profit margin (or return on sales)	$$\frac{\text{Profits before taxes and before interest}}{\text{Sales}}$$	An indication of the firm's profitability from current operations without regard to the interest charges accruing from the capital structure.
3. Net profit margin (or net return on sales)	$$\frac{\text{Profits after taxes}}{\text{Sales}}$$	Shows aftertax profits per dollar of sales. Subpar-profit margins indicate that the firm's sales prices are relatively low or that its costs are relatively high, or both.
4. Return on total assets	$$\frac{\text{Profits after taxes}}{\text{Total assets}}$$ or $$\frac{\text{Profits after taxes} + \text{Interest}}{\text{Total assets}}$$	A measure of the return on total investment in the enterprise. It is sometimes desirable to add interest to aftertax profits to form the numerator of the ratio since total assets are financed by creditors as well as by stockholders; hence, it is accurate to measure the productivity of assets by the returns provided to both classes of investors.
5. Return on stockholders' equity (or return on net worth)	$$\frac{\text{Profits after taxes}}{\text{Total stockholders' equity}}$$	A measure of the rate of return on stockholders' investment in the enterprise.
6. Return on common equity	$$\frac{\text{Profits after taxes} - \text{Preferred stock dividends}}{\text{Total stockholders' equity} - \text{Par value of preferred stock}}$$	A measure of the rate of return on the investment which the owners of the common stock have made in the enterprise.
7. Earnings per share	$$\frac{\text{Profits after taxes} - \text{Preferred stock dividends}}{\text{Number of shares of common stock outstanding}}$$	Shows the earnings available to the owners of each share of common stock.
Liquidity ratios:		
1. Current ratio	$$\frac{\text{Current assets}}{\text{Current liabilities}}$$	Indicates the extent to which the claims of short-term creditors are covered by assets that are expected to be converted to cash in a period roughly corresponding to the maturity of the liabilities.
2. Quick ratio (or acid-test ratio)	$$\frac{\text{Current assets} - \text{Inventory}}{\text{Current liabilities}}$$	A measure of the firm's ability to pay off short-term obligations without relying on the sale of its inventories.
3. Inventory to net working capital	$$\frac{\text{Inventory}}{\text{Current assets} - \text{Current liabilities}}$$	A measure of the extent to which the firm's working capital is tied up in inventory.
Leverage ratios:		
1. Debt-to-assets ratio	$$\frac{\text{Total debt}}{\text{Total assets}}$$	Measures the extent to which borrowed funds have been used to finance the firm's operations.
2. Debt-to-equity ratio	$$\frac{\text{Total debt}}{\text{Total stockholders' equity}}$$	Provides another measure of the funds provided by creditors versus the funds provided by owners.
3. Long-term debt-to-equity ratio	$$\frac{\text{Long-term debt}}{\text{Total stockholders' equity}}$$	A widely used measure of the balance between debt and equity in the firm's long-term capital structure.
4. Times-interest-earned (or coverage) ratio	$$\frac{\text{Profits before interest and taxes}}{\text{Total interest charges}}$$	Measures the extent to which earnings can decline without the firm becoming unable to meet its annual interest costs.
5. Fixed-charge coverage	$$\frac{\text{Profits before taxes and interest} + \text{Lease obligations}}{\text{Total interest charges} + \text{Lease obligations}}$$	A more inclusive indication of the firm's ability to meet all of its fixed-charge obligations.

Table 1   (concluded)

Ratio	How calculated	What it shows
Activity ratios:		
1. Inventory turnover	$\dfrac{\text{Sales}}{\text{Inventory of finished goods}}$	When compared to industry averages, it provides an indication of whether a company has excessive or perhaps inadequate finished goods inventory.
2. Fixed assets turnover	$\dfrac{\text{Sales}}{\text{Fixed assets}}$	A measure of the sales productivity and utilization of plant and equipment.
3. Total assets turnover	$\dfrac{\text{Sales}}{\text{Total assets}}$	A measure of the utilization of all the firm's assets; a ratio below the industry average indicates the company is not generating a sufficient volume of business, given the size of its asset investment.
4. Accounts receivable turnover	$\dfrac{\text{Annual credit sales}}{\text{Accounts receivable}}$	A measure of the average length of time it takes the firm to collect the sales made on credit.
5. Average collection period	$\dfrac{\text{Accounts receivable}}{\text{Total sales} \div 365}$ or $\dfrac{\text{Accounts receivable}}{\text{Average daily sales}}$	Indicates the average length of time the firm must wait after making a sale before it receives payment.
Other ratios:		
1. Dividend yield on common stock	$\dfrac{\text{Annual dividends per share}}{\text{Current market price per share}}$	A measure of the return to owners received in the form of dividends.
2. Price-earnings ratio	$\dfrac{\text{Current market price per share}}{\text{Aftertax earnings per share}}$	Faster growing or less risky firms tend to have higher price-earnings ratios than slower growing or more risky firms.
3. Dividend payout ratio	$\dfrac{\text{Annual dividends per share}}{\text{Aftertax earnings per share}}$	Indicates the percentage of profits paid out as dividends.
4. Cash flow per share	$\dfrac{\text{Aftertax profits} + \text{Depreciation}}{\text{Number of common shares outstanding}}$	A measure of the discretionary funds over and above expenses that are available for use by the firm.

Note: Industry-average ratios against which a particular company's ratios may be judged are available in *Modern Industry* and *Dun's Reviews* published by Dun & Bradstreet (14 ratios for 125 lines of business activities), Robert Morris Associates' *Annual Statement Studies* (11 ratios for 156 lines of business), and the FTC–SEC's *Quarterly Financial Report* for manufacturing corporations.

contradictory opinions (after all, people don't always agree on things, and different people see the same things in different ways). Forcing you to evaluate the validity of the data and information presented in the case helps you develop your powers of inference and judgment. Asking you to resolve conflicting information "comes with the territory" because a great many managerial situations entail opposing points of view, conflicting trends, and inaccurate information.

8. *Support your diagnosis and opinions with reasons and evidence.* The most important things to prepare for are your answers to the question "Why?" For instance, if after studying the case you are of the opinion that the company's managers are doing a poor job, then it is your answer to "Why?" that establishes just how good your analysis of the situation is. If your instructor has provided you with specific study questions for the case, by all means prepare answers that

include all the reasons and number-crunching evidence you can muster to support your diagnosis. *Generate at least two pages of notes!*

9. *Develop an appropriate action plan and set of recommendations.* Diagnosis divorced from corrective action is sterile. The test of a manager is always to convert sound analysis into sound actions—actions that will produce the desired results. Hence, the final and most telling step in preparing a case is to develop an action agenda for management that lays out a set of specific recommendations on what to do. Bear in mind that proposing realistic, workable solutions is far preferable to casually tossing out off-the-top-of-your-head suggestions. Be prepared to argue why your recommendations are more attractive than other courses of action that are open.

As long as you are conscientious in preparing your analysis and recommendations, and as long as you have ample reasons, evidence, and arguments to support your views, you shouldn't fret unduly about whether what you've prepared is the right answer to the case. In case analysis there is rarely just one right approach or one right set of recommendations. Managing companies and devising and implementing strategies are not such exact sciences that there exists a single provably correct analysis and action plan for each strategic situation. Of course, some analyses and action plans are better than others; but, in truth, there's nearly always more than one good way to analyze a situation and more than one good plan of action So, if you have done a careful and thoughtful job of preparing the case, don't lose confidence in the correctness of your work and judgment.

PARTICIPATING IN CLASS DISCUSSION OF A CASE

Classroom discussions of cases are sharply different from attending a lecture class. In a case class students do most of the talking. The instructor's role is to solicit student participation, keep the discussion on track, ask "Why?" often, offer alternative views, play the devil's advocate (if no students jump in to offer opposing views), and otherwise lead the discussion. The students in the class carry the burden for analyzing the situation and for being prepared to present and defend their diagnoses and recommendations. Expect a classroom environment, therefore, that calls for *your* size up of the situation, *your* analysis, what actions *you* would take, and why *you* would take them. Do not be dismayed if, as the class discussion unfolds, some insightful things are said by your fellow classmates that you did not think of. It is normal for views and analyses to differ and for the comments of others in the class to expand your own thinking about the case. As the old adage goes, "Two heads are better than one." So it is to be expected that the class as a whole will do a more penetrating and searching job of case analysis than will any one person working alone. This is the power of group effort, and its virtues are that it will help you see more analytical applications, let you test your analyses and judgments against those of your peers, and force you to wrestle with differences of opinion and approaches.

To orient you to the classroom environment on the days a case discussion is scheduled, we compiled the following list of things to expect:

1. Expect students to dominate the discussion and do most of the talking. The case method enlists a maximum of individual participation in class discussion. It is not enough to be present as a silent observer; if every student took this approach, there would be no discussion. (Thus, expect a portion of your grade to be based on your participation in case discussions.)

2. Expect the instructor to assume the role of extensive questioner and listener.

3. Be prepared for the instructor to probe for reasons and supporting analysis.

4. Expect and tolerate challenges to the views expressed. All students have to be willing to submit their conclusions for scrutiny and rebuttal. Each student needs to learn to state his or her views without fear of disapproval and to overcome the hesitation of speaking out. Learning respect for the views and approaches of others is an integral part of case analysis exercises. But there are times when it is OK to swim against the tide of majority opinion. In the practice of management, there is always room for originality and unorthodox approaches. So while discussion of a case is a group process, there is no compulsion for you or anyone else to cave in and conform to group opinions and group consensus.

5. Don't be surprised if you change your mind about some things as the discussion unfolds. Be alert to how these changes affect your analysis and recommendations (in case you get called on).

6. Expect to learn a lot from each case discussion; use what you learn to be better prepared for the next case discussion.

There are several things you can do on your own to be good and look good as a participant in class discussions:

- Although you should do your own independent work and independent thinking, don't hesitate before (and after) class to discuss the case with other students. In real life, managers often discuss the company's problems and situation with other people to refine their own thinking.

- In participating in the discussion, make a conscious effort to contribute, rather than just talk. There is a big difference between saying something that builds the discussion and offering a long-winded, off-the-cuff remark that leaves the class wondering what the point was.

- Avoid the use of "I think," "I believe," and "I feel"; instead, say, "My analysis shows . . ." and "The company should do . . . because. . . ." Always give supporting reasons and evidence for your views; then your instructor won't have to ask you "Why?" every time you make a comment.

- In making your points, assume that everyone has read the case and knows what it says; avoid reciting and rehashing information in the case—instead, use the data and information to explain your assessment of the situation and to support your position.

- Always prepare good notes (usually two or three pages worth) for each case and use them extensively when you speak. There's no way you can remember everything off the top of your head—especially the results of your number crunching. To reel off the numbers or to present all five reasons why, instead of one, you will need good notes. When you have prepared good notes to the study questions and use them as the basis for your comments, *everybody* in the room will know you are well prepared, and your contribution to the case discussion will stand out.

PREPARING A WRITTEN CASE ANALYSIS

Preparing a written case analysis is much like preparing a case for class discussion, except that your analysis must be more complete and reduced to writing. Unfortunately, though, *there is no ironclad procedure for doing a written case analysis.* All we can offer are some general guidelines and words of wisdom—this is because company situations and management problems are so diverse that no one mechanical way to approach a written case assignment always works.

Your instructor may assign you a specific topic around which to prepare your written report. Or, alternatively, you may be asked to do a comprehensive written case analysis, where the expectation is that you will (1) *identify* all the pertinent issues that management needs to address, (2) perform whatever *analysis* and *evaluation* is appropriate, and (3) propose an *action plan* and set of *recommendations* addressing the issues you have identified. In going through the exercise of identify, evaluate, and recommend, keep the following pointers in mind.[3]

Identification. It is essential early on in your paper that you provide a sharply focused diagnosis of strategic issues and key problems and that you demonstrate a good grasp of the company's present situation. Make sure you can identify the firm's strategy (use the concepts and tools in Chapters 1–8 as diagnostic aids) and that you can pinpoint whatever strategy implementation issues may exist (again, consult the material in Chapters 9 and 10 for diagnostic help). Consult the key points we have provided at the end of each chapter for further diagnostic suggestions. Consider beginning your paper by sizing up the company's situation, its strategy, and the significant problems and issues that confront management. State problems/issues as clearly and precisely as you can. Unless it is necessary to do so for emphasis, avoid recounting facts and history about the company (assume your professor has read the case and is familiar with the organization).

---

[3] For some additional ideas and viewpoints, you may wish to consult Thomas J. Raymond, "Written Analysis of Cases," in *The Case Method at the Harvard Business School,* ed. M.P. McNair, pp. 139–63. Raymond's article includes an actual case, a sample analysis of the case, and a sample of a student's written report on the case.

Analysis and Evaluation.   This is usually the hardest part of the report. Analysis is hard work! Check out the firm's financial ratios, its profit margins and rates of return, and its capital structure, and decide how strong the firm is financially. Table 1 contains a summary of various financial ratios and how they are calculated. Use it to assist in your financial diagnosis. Similarly, look at marketing, production, managerial competence, and other factors underlying the organization's strategic successes and failures. Decide whether the firm has a distinctive competence and, if so, whether it is capitalizing on it.

Check to see if the firm's strategy is working and determine the reasons why or why not. Probe the nature and strength of the competitive forces confronting the company. Decide whether and why the firm's competitive position is getting stronger or weaker. Use the tools and concepts you have learned about to perform whatever analysis and evaluation is appropriate.

In writing your analysis and evaluation, bear in mind four things:

1. You are obliged to offer analysis and evidence to back up your conclusions. Do not rely on unsupported opinions, overgeneralizations, and platitudes as a substitute for tight, logical argument backed up with facts and figures.

2. If your analysis involves some important quantitative calculations, use tables and charts to present the calculations clearly and efficiently. Don't just tack the exhibits on at the end of your report and let the reader figure out what they mean and why they were included. Instead, in the body of your report cite some of the key numbers, highlight the conclusions to be drawn from the exhibits, and refer the reader to your charts and exhibits for more details.

3. Demonstrate that you have command of the strategic concepts and analytical tools to which you have been exposed. Use them in your report.

4. Your interpretation of the evidence should be reasonable and objective. Be wary of preparing a one-sided argument that omits all aspects not favorable to your conclusions. Likewise, try not to exaggerate or overdramatize. Endeavor to inject balance into your analysis and to avoid emotional rhetoric. Strike phrases such as "I think," "I feel," and "I believe" when you edit your first draft and write in "My analysis shows," instead.

Recommendations.   The final section of the written case analysis should consist of a set of definite recommendations and a plan of action. Your set of recommendations should address all of the problems/issues you identified and analyzed. If the recommendations come as a surprise or do not follow logically from the analysis, the effect is to weaken greatly your suggestions of what to do. Obviously, your recommendations for actions should offer a reasonable prospect of success. High-risk, bet-the-company recommendations should be made with caution. State how your recommendations will solve the problems you identified. Be sure the company is financially able to carry out what your recommend; also check to see if your recommendations are workable in terms of acceptance by the persons involved, the organization's competence to implement them, and prevailing market and environmental constraints. Try not to hedge or weasel on the actions you believe should be taken.

By all means state your recommendations in sufficient detail to be meaningful—get down to some definite nitty-gritty specifics. Avoid such unhelpful statements as "the organization should do more planning" or "the company should be more aggressive in marketing its product." For instance, do not simply say "the firm should improve its market position" but state exactly how you think this should be done. Offer a definite agenda for action, stipulating a timetable and sequence for initiating actions, indicating priorities, and suggesting who should be responsible for doing what.

In proposing an action plan, remember there is a great deal of difference between being responsible, on the one hand, for a decision that may be costly if it proves in error and, on the other hand, casually suggesting courses of action that might be taken when you do not have to bear the responsibility for any of the consequences. A good rule to follow in making your recommendations is: *Avoid recommending anything you would not yourself be willing to do if you were in management's shoes.* The importance of learning to develop good judgment in a managerial situation is indicated by the fact that, even though the same information and operating data may be available to every manager or executive in an organization, the quality of the judgments about what the information means and which actions need to be taken do vary from person to person.[4]

It goes without saying that your report should be well organized and well written. Great ideas amount to little unless others can be convinced of their merit—this takes tight logic, the presentation of convincing evidence, and persuasively written arguments.

THE TEN COMMANDMENTS OF CASE ANALYSIS

As a way of summarizing our suggestions about how to approach the task of case analysis, we have compiled what we like to call "The Ten Commandments of Case Analysis." They are shown in Table 2. If you observe all or even most of these commandments faithfully as you prepare a case either for class discussion or for a written report, your chances of doing a good job on the assigned cases will be much improved. Hang in there, give it your best shot, and have some fun exploring what the real world of strategic management is all about.

---

[4] Gragg, "Because Wisdom Can't Be Told," p. 10.

Table 2 THE TEN COMMANDMENTS OF CASE ANALYSIS

To be observed in written reports and oral presentations, and while participating in class discussions.

1. Read the case twice, once for an overview and once to gain full command of the facts; then take care to explore every one of the exhibits.
2. Make a list of the problems and issues that have to be confronted.
3. Do enough number crunching to discover the story told by the data presented in the case. (To help you comply with this commandment, consult Table 1 to guide your probing of a company's financial condition and financial performance.)
4. Look for opportunities to use the concepts and analytical tools you have learned earlier.
5. Be thorough in your diagnosis of the situation and make at least a one- or two-page outline of your assessment.
6. Support any and all opinions with well-reasoned arguments and numerical evidence; don't stop until you can purge "I think" and "I feel" from your assessment and, instead, are able to reply completely on "My analysis shows."
7. Develop charts, tables, and graphs to expose more clearly the main points of your analysis.
8. Prioritize your recommendations and make sure they can be carried out in an acceptable time frame with the available skills and financial resources.
9. Review your recommended action plan to see if it addresses all of the problems and issues you identified.
10. Avoid recommending any course of action that could have disastrous consequences if it doesn't work out as planned; therefore, be as alert to the downside risks of your recommendations as you are to their upside potential and appeal.

A The Manager as Chief Strategy-Maker and Strategy-Implementer

TURNER BROADCASTING SYSTEM IN 1988*

In this, the heyday of the large corporation that follows the morally and socially neutral judgments of committees of lawyers and accountants, Ted Turner is a character—in the best sense of that much misused word. He is in the great tradition of the individual entrepreneur who had a dream and backed it with his money and his sweat.

George N. Allen
Washington Journalism Review

Robert E. (Ted) Turner III was born in 1938 in Cincinnati, where his father, Ed, was in the outdoor advertising business. In the early 1940s, Ed Turner purchased a billboard firm in Savannah, Georgia, and moved his family there, where Ted got his first taste of the sea and sailing. Ted Turner's father was a stern, tough, self-made man who came from a poor, farm background in Mississippi. As a youngster, Ted was told to read a book every two days.[1] He was disciplined with a wire coat hanger. At 11, Ted was sent to McCallie Military School in Chattanooga, Tennessee; even though he professed dislike of the school, he completed six years at McCallie and graduated in the top 15 percent of his class as a company commander. (Later, he sent his own son, Robert Edward Turner IV, to McCallie.) At 17, he won the Tennessee State Debate Championship by redefining the basic question and taking an approach no one was prepared to debate.

During the summers of his high school years, he worked in the family business digging postholes and doing other manual labor tasks; one summer Turner worked a 40-hour week, was paid $50, and then was charged $25 a week to live at home. As Turner viewed it, "My father put the screws to me early. If he hadn't, I never would have survived. My father made me a man."

On graduation from McCallie, it was agreed by Turner and his father that he would enroll at Brown University in Providence, Rhode Island. When Turner informed his businessman father that he was planning to major in classics, his father wrote him a letter (which Ted had published in the school newspaper) describing Plato and Aristotle as "old bastards" and ending with the observation that "you are rapidly becoming a jackass, and the sooner you get out of that filthy atmosphere, the better. . . . You are in the hands of the Philistines, and dammit, I sent you there. I am sorry, Devotedly, Dad." Later, Turner switched his major to economics.

---

* Prepared by Professor Arthur A. Thompson, Jr., The University of Alabama, with the research assistance of Miriam Aiken.

[1] Curry Kirkpatrick, "Going Real Strawwng," *Sports Illustrated,* October 14, 1977.

Turner's college years at Brown were eventful. He shot a rifle from his dorm window and was thrown out of his fraternity for burning down its homecoming display. During his sophomore year, when his father refused to let him take a summer job at a Connecticut yacht club, he broke his agreement to refrain from drinking until he was 21 (for which he was to get a $5,000 reward), got drunk, and then got caught in a dorm room at Wheaton, a girl's college in nearby Norton, Massachusetts; Brown University officials expelled him. Turner joined the Coast Guard for a short stint and then was readmitted to Brown. He became vice president of the debating union and commodore of the yacht club. But in his senior year he was expelled again when a Wheaton girl was caught in his dorm room.

Without a degree, Turner returned in 1960 to Georgia, where he went to work for his father and learned the business from the bottom up. His assigned tasks included posting the books and cutting weeds around billboards. A short time later, his father sent him to Macon to run the firm's branch office. In 1962 the elder Turner arranged to more than triple the size of his company and, with borrowed funds, he purchased billboard operations in Atlanta; Richmond, Virginia; and Roanoke, Virginia. Within a year Turner's father had a breakdown and committed suicide.

THE FIRST CHALLENGE

Turner at age 24, found himself in charge of a struggling business that was short of cash and $6 million in debt. The company's bankers advised Turner that they didn't believe the business could survive under his unseasoned management and expressed reluctance at financing further operations. Turner was given an opportunity to sell out but refused and ended up persuading the lenders to stick with him a while longer. He then sold off some assets to improve the company's cash position, arranged for some innovative financing, reworked contracts with customers, hired a sales force, and proceeded to turn things around. Within two years the company was making its loan payments on time, and by 1969 the debt was paid off.

THE SECOND CHALLENGE

With the company now secure, Turner began to prospect for new growth opportunities. He felt that the billboard business had only limited growth potential and was not challenging enough (it took only about half of his time to run things), so he elected to diversify into something more exciting. The first acquisitions were two radio stations in Chattanooga, a move which prompted Ted Turner to rename his company Turner Communications Corporation. Turner wanted to buy a radio outlet in Atlanta, but nothing attractive was available at the right price. In 1970 he settled for acquiring financially strapped WTCG-TV, Channel 17, a two-year-old, independent UHF station that was losing $50,000 per month trying to compete with Atlanta's three network affiliates, WSB-TV, WAGA-TV, and WXIA-TV. To finance the acquisition of Channel 17, Turner Communications Corporation went public, and its stock was traded in local over-the-counter markets; Ted Turner retained about 47 percent of the stock.

Turner's biggest problem in turning Channel 17's operations around was how to get Atlanta TV viewers to watch Channel 17 programs instead of the programs carried on the three major network stations. Writer Roger Vaughn, who knew Turner in college, has written two books about him, and has sailed with him, described Turner's efforts:

> When Turner bought Channel 17, there was another independent in the Atlanta market. It belonged to United States Communications and was one of five stations in the country owned by that company, a subsidiary of the American Viscose conglomerate. It was a fact that the Atlanta market could not support two independents. "Ted knew this," one of the early Channel 17 employees says, "but I doubt if he realized how serious the situation was." Only one of the stations was going to survive, and it didn't look like it would be Channel 17, which was running a solid fifth out of five Atlanta stations.
>
> The instability of the situation was reflected in the fact that in the first 22 months of Turner's ownership, the personnel of the station turned over twice. By the spring of 1971, every spare dollar Turner could find had been poured into the station. As Will Sanders recalls, the whole show was about to sink. Then overnight, without warning, the U.S. Communications station folded. It was a high stroke of luck for Turner, a lifeline for a drowning man.
>
> In one day, Channel 17 went from fifth of five stations to fourth of four. As the only independent in Atlanta, the way ahead was clear for development, but the problems were still immense. UHF reception was terrible, for one thing. . . .
>
> "I can remember going into an advertiser's office and asking him to buy time on Channel 17," Turner says. "The answer would be 'We don't buy UHF.' And I would tell them, 'Why not? It's coming, like FM radio. We're not asking you to pay for the future. We're just asking you to buy our audience at the same cost per thousand. Our audience isn't very big, but our viewers are way above the average viewers' mentality.'
>
> "And they would say, 'How do you know that? How come!' and I would tell them, 'Because you have got to be smart to figure out how to tune in a UHF antenna in the first place. Dumb guys can't do it. Can you get Channel 17? No? Well, neither can I. We aren't smart enough. But my viewers are.'
>
> "Then I would ask them if their commercials were in color. And they would say, 'Of course.' And I would tell them their commercials would stand out better on my station. Why? Because most of the programs were in black and white and when the commercial came on, it would have more shock value, it would catch the viewers' attention. They fell over. They hadn't thought of that.
>
> "And finally I told them my audience was richer. Every set with UHF capability was color, which costs more. Don't you think that was a pretty good sales pitch?"
>
> With the competition gone, Turner put more money into strengthening his signal. Then he got his second break. The Atlanta ABC affiliate was forced by the network to pick up the 6 P.M. news, which they had not been running. It is a television fact of life that roughly 25 percent of an audience will actively avoid the

news. So Turner scheduled "Star Trek" at 6 P.M. and not only increased his rating at that hour but got a few more people acquainted with Channel 17's presence. In Turner's mind, a philosophy was beginning to take shape. As he told *Television/Radio Age* in 1974, "All three stations had big group-ownership money behind them. They all programmed pretty much alike. I felt the people of Atlanta were entitled to something different than a whole lot of police and crime shows with murders and rapes going on all over the place. I believe that people are tired of violence and psychological problems and all the negative things they see on TV every night."

Turner concentrated his energies on buying films, the titles of which he selected himself, and on composing a lineup of old shows that sounded like the sitcom hall of fame: "I Love Lucy," "Gilligan's Island," "Leave It to Beaver," "Petticoat Junction," "Father Knows Best," "Gomer Pyle," and "Andy Griffith." "We're essentially an escapist station," Turner announced to those who hadn't noticed. "As far as our news is concerned, we run the FCC minimum of forty minutes a day."

Having moved into the entertainment void left by ABC's commitment to news, Turner attacked the NBC affiliate (WSB-TV), Atlanta's number-one station. WSB had chosen not to air five network shows, which meant that those shows could be picked up by an independent in the area. Turner grabbed all five, and soon billboards (Turner's, of course) around Atlanta were announcing. "The NBC network moves to Channel 17," and listing the five shows.

"We didn't think we could take over as the number-one station in the market," Turner said at the time. "But we felt we could shake 'em up a bit, get 'em to think about us, let 'em know we were in the race." They were shook and started thinking. The move was splashed all over the newspapers, and if success could be measured in phone calls from NBC lawyers, it was a hit.

While WSB-TV was still fuming over their public embarrassment, Turner grabbed their rights to telecast Atlanta Braves games. At the time, the Braves were paying WSB to run 25 games a year. Turner made the Braves an offer they couldn't refuse, paying them $2.5 million for the TV rights to games for five years.

"The Braves games were the top-rated locally produced program in the Atlanta market," Gerry Hogan says. Hogan is general sales manager of Channel 17. He is a dapper, precise fellow with styled red hair and the office manner of a Park Avenue physician discussing a social disease of moderate seriousness. He left Chicago advertising in 1971 to take a chance with Turner.

"Signing the Braves did a lot for our image," Hogan says, "It changed our image from that of a kiddie station. It forced people to tune us in. We became a factor. Atlanta went from a three-station market plus WTCG to a four-station market. We were in it after the Braves signed with us."[2]

Atlanta-area residents were attracted by the new style of programming and began to tune in to Channel 17's programs more regularly. Viewers and advertising revenues increased steadily, and by 1972 Channel 17 had positive operating profits:

[2] Roger Vaughn, "Ted Turner's True Talent," *Esquire,* October 10, 1978, pp. 35–36. Quoted with permission.

Year	Channel 17's Operating Profits
1970	$ (550,707)
1971	(531,584)
1972	181,406
1973	1,043,316
1974	732,340
1975	1,707,987
1976	3,687,447
1977	3,714,648

While Channel 17 was still in the red, Turner acquired a second UHF station at a bankruptcy sale in Charlotte, North Carolina. It was purchased with Turner's personal funds because the directors of Turner Communications were not willing to risk corporate funds on the deal, given Channel 17's still unprofitable status and the high risk of trying to turn the Charlotte operation around. To help get the Charlotte station on track, Turner appeared on a series of televised "beg-a-thons" asking Charlotte viewers for financial support; he received more than 36,000 contributions ranging from 25 cents to $80. Turner collected $25,000 and used the proceeds to help finance the same movie-sports-rerun programming emphasis that he had pioneered in Atlanta. By 1975 the Charlotte station was breaking even, and Turner sold a controlling interest in the station to Turner Communications; later the station became an NBC affiliate.

THE EMERGENCE OF TURNER BROADCASTING SYSTEM

In 1975 the billboard advertising operations were spun off from Turner Communications and made a separate company, Turner Advertising, with Ted Turner as majority stockholder. Turner Advertising succeeded in becoming the largest billboard firm in the Atlanta and Chattanooga markets; the remaining branches were sold. Meanwhile, Turner Communications began repurchasing its stock on the open market, increasing Ted Turner's ownership percentage to about 85 percent of the shares outstanding.

Turner's 1972 bid to televise the Atlanta Braves baseball games on Channel 17 not only was the first step in the company's major sports involvement, but it also established a business relationship with the Braves owners, Chicago-based Atlanta LaSalle Corporation. In 1975 Atlanta LaSalle's management approached Ted Turner about buying the Braves club. Turner moved quickly, and in January 1976 Turner Communications acquired the Braves through a newly formed, wholly owned subsidiary, Atlanta National League Baseball Club (ANLBC); the purchase price was $9.65 million, to be paid over 12 years at 6 percent interest.

In 1977 the Company acquired, through Atlanta Hawks, Inc., a 95 percent limited partnership interest in Hawks, Ltd., owner of the Atlanta Hawks professional basketball team, which competed in the National Basketball Association. In 1978 Turner Communications acquired a limited partnership interest in Soccer, Ltd., the owner of the Atlanta Chiefs professional soccer team. Also in 1978 the company sold its radio stations in Chattanooga for $1,050,000 cash, realizing a pretax gain of $395,000.

Three important developments occurred in 1979. The company launched plans for the first 24-hour news programming network for cable television operators (to be called CNN); by the end of 1979 the company had invested $6.7 million in the CNN venture, acquired and begun renovations of a headquarters facility, hired key personnel, and obtained purchase commitments to provide the programming. The second development was to change the name of Turner Communications Corporation to Turner Broadcasting System, Inc. (TBS) and the letters of WTCG (Channel 17) to WTBS. The third involved an agreement to sell the Charlotte TV station for $20 million cash to help finance CNN's start-up.

DEVELOPMENTS DURING 1980–1988

Much managerial time and considerable company resources were invested in making a success out of CNN. The challenge of this project was so big that Turner and TBS were unable to make any major new strategic moves between 1980 and 1985. But by early 1985 CNN was well on its way to earning its first profit and the cash drain of CNN had eased considerably.

In April 1985, Turner announced that he intended to purchase CBS, an organization 17 times the size of TBS. When his initial attempts to gain control of CBS by friendly means failed, Turner made a public tender offer to CBS shareholders. Turner planned to acquire 73 percent of the network's 30 million outstanding shares of stock. CBS's net worth was about $7.6 billion, or $254 per share; the face value of Turner's offer (composed of TBS stock, interest-bearing "junk bonds," and zero coupon bonds) was $175 a share, with estimates of the market value of the offer ranging between $130 and $155 a share.

CBS fought Turner's takeover attempt vigorously with a series of moves involving increased debt and the repurchase of 6.4 million shares (21 percent of the outstanding shares) at a cost of $960 million. To make the company unattractive for future takeover attempts, CBS engineered a provision to place a ceiling on the amount of debt that CBS could carry. Turner's court suit to halt the repurchase plan was denied; his lack of cash to compete with CBS's repurchase offer and lack of ability to wage a proxy battle ended the takeover attempt. Turner's abortive efforts to win control of CBS cost TBS $18.2 million in fees and expenses.

One week after his failed bid for CBS, Turner reached an agreement with MGM/United Artists Entertainment Company to purchase the movie company for $1.5 billion, about $29 a share. MGM's stock was trading at $24 at the time and had traded in the $13–$15 range in 1984. The 2,200-film library of MGM was the primary motivation for Turner's acquisition move. The acquisition was financed by the issue of $1.4 billion of high-yield, high-risk junk bonds that were viewed with skepticism by many institutions. The acquisition was completed officially in March 1986.

A series of very complicated financing moves ensued to ease the extremely high debt burden which TBS took on in the $1.5 billion buyout of MGM. MGM's moviemaking operations and various other assets were sold off to pay down some of the debt; all that was kept was the 2,200-film library. To ease the debt burden, in June 1986 TBS and Turner sold $568 million in TBS stock to a consortium of cable industry investors; these investors got 7 of the 15 seats on the company's board of directors. Proceeds of the stock sale went to pay down the debt.

In December 1987 TBS purchased rights to the RKO film and television library for approximately $30 million. The rights acquired included cable television rights and limited domestic free television rights not previously acquired when TBS purchased MGM/UA. Included in the RKO film library were approximately 750 feature-length theatrical motion pictures, 80 television productions, 50 short subjects, and in excess of 150 episodes of Abbott and Costello cartoons.

In October 1988 the company launched a new cable channel called TNT, or Turner Network Television, as a basic cable service for cable operators. Programming consisted principally of movies and other programming from the MGM library. Future programming plans included major sports and special events and original programming. Revenues were derived from the sale of advertising time and, beginning in 1989, the subscription sale of the service to cable operators. As an incentive to carry its programming, TNT provided four minutes per hour for local cable systems to sell their own advertising time.

As of late 1988 Turner Broadcasting System was engaged in television broadcasting, cable television productions, program syndication and licensing, professional sports, and real estate operations. The television broadcasting segment consisted of the operations of WTBS and TNT. The cable television productions business was composed of two 24-hour cable news services, the Cable News Network (CNN) and CNN Headline News, which were available to subscribing television systems. The company's program syndication and licensing business was made up of Turner Entertainment Co. (TEC), a wholly owned subsidiary that handled the syndication and licensing of the MGM/UA and RKO film libraries. In sports, the company owned the Atlanta Braves baseball club and was the principal partner in a limited partnership owning the Atlanta Hawks basketball team. The real estate segment consisted of company interests in multiuse properties in downtown Atlanta (the Omni Hotel and office/shopping complex, CNN Center, and activities associated with the Omni Coliseum).

The company's revenues had exhibited exceptionally strong growth since 1976 but profits were sporadic and huge losses were incurred in 1986 and 1987 because of the MGM/UA purchase:

Year	Revenues ($000)	Net Income ($000)
1976	$ 25,345	$ 648
1977	28,799	(1,232)
1978	33,843	1,203
1979	37,721	(1,496)
1980	54,610	(3,775)
1981	95,047	(13,423)
1982	165,641	(3,350)
1983	224,532	7,012

Year	Revenues ($000)	Net Income ($000)
1984	$281,732	$ 10,062
1985	351,891	1,157
1986	556,917	(238,903)
1987	652,419	(191,732)

Exhibits 1, 2, and 3 present more extensive financial data for TBS.

Exhibit 1 FINANCIAL INFORMATION FOR TBS BY BUSINESS SEGMENT, 1978–1987 (in thousands)

	1978	1980	1983	1985	1986	1987
Revenues from unaffiliated customers:						
Broadcasting	$23,434	$35,495	$136,217	$186,217	$ 204,378	$ 222,273
Cable productions	—	7,201	65,169	122,947	167,210	208,646
Program syndication and licensing	—	—	—	10,073	134,944	158,980
Professional sports	8,181	9,211	21,401	21,764	23,921	22,796
Real estate operations	—	—	—	8,072	23,479	38,026
Other	2,228	2,703	1,745	2,818	2,985	1,698
	$33,843	$54,610	$224,532	$351,891	$ 556,917	$ 652,419
Operating profit (loss):						
Broadcasting	$ 6,089	$10,166	$ 43,335	$ 60,165	$ 12,532	$ 61,769
Cable productions	—	(16,024)	(14,162)	12,510	38,648	55,274
Program syndication and licensing	—	—	—	1,852	(6,652)	(10,014)
Professional sports	(1,688)	(4,461)	(1,829)	(6,480)	(12,158)	(6,699)
Equity in losses of limited partnership owning professional sports team	(1,225)	(2,905)	(3,350)	(2,707)	(1,675)	(21)
Real estate operations/other	418	15,689	—	(138)	(1,193)	1,552
Operating profit before interest and general corporate expenses	3,594	2,465	23,994	65,202	29,502	101,861
Interest expense	1,323	4,437	14,383	37,567	203,321	211,891
General corporate expenses	743	1,603	2,599	7,472	11,523	17,513
(Loss) profit before income taxes and extraordinary items	$ 1,528	$(3,575)	$ 7,012	$ 20,163	($185,342)	($127,543)
Identifiable assets at end of year:						
Broadcasting	$19,942	$22,196	$ 84,646	$125,480	$ 141,703	$ 160,793
Cable productions	—	12,257	58,023	57,638	58,549	73,821
Program syndication and licensing	—	—	—	10,226	1,439,211	1,367,855
Professional sports	6,974	5,894	4,538	17,808	28,354	24,599
Investment in limited partnership interest of professional sports team	2,578	2,027	1,633	1,181	981	917
Real estate operations	—	—	—	52,565	115,966	117,754
Corporate assets	904	11,644	56,998	91,660	119,219	92,612
	$30,398	$54,018	$205,838	$356,558	$1,903,983	$1,838,351
Capital expenditures:						
Broadcasting	$ 2,532	$ 3,828	$ 1,062	$ 2,123	$ 3,377	$ 2,090
Cable productions	—	9,731	4,509	6,168	3,237	8,274
Program syndication and licensing	—	—	—	—	3,520	1,176
Professional sports	77	180	237	273	172	231
Real estate operations	—	—	—	48,069	37,011	7,871
Other	—	—	2,981	1,021	6,233	7,001
	$ 2,609	$13,739	$ 8,789	$ 57,654	$ 53,550	$ 26,643

Sources: 1980 Annual Report, 1985 10-K Report, and 1987 10-K Report.

Exhibit 2 CONSOLIDATED STATEMENTS OF INCOME, TURNER BROADCASTING SYSTEM, INC., 1985, 1986, AND 1987 (in thousands)

	Year ended December 31		
	1987	**1986**	**1985**
Revenues	$ 652,419	$ 556,917	$351,891
Cost and expenses:			
Cost of operations, exclusive of depreciation and amortization shown below . .	263,913	277,855	158,161
Selling, general, and administrative	171,064	150,654	108,771
Amortization of film costs and other intangible assets	115,740	94,936	16,331
Depreciation of property, plant, and equipment	17,354	15,493	10,898
Interest expense, net of interest income	211,891	203,321	37,567
	779,962	742,259	331,728
(Loss) income before provision for income taxes and extraordinary items . . .	(127,543)	(185,342)	20,163
Provision for income taxes	3,665	1,972	2,862
(Loss) income before extraordinary items	(131,208)	(187,314)	17,301
Extraordinary items:			
Costs of proposed exchange offer, net of income tax benefits of $2,325	—	—	(16,326)
Realization of operating loss carryforwards	—	—	182
Net (loss) income	($131,208)	($187,314)	$ 1,157
Preferred stock dividends and accretion of discount on preferred stock	(60,524)	(51,589)	—
Net (loss) income applicable to common stock	($191,732)	($238,903)	$ 1,157

Source: 1987 10-K Report.

SUPERSTATION WTBS-TV

Turner Broadcasting System's principal revenue and profit source was WTBS-TV. Although WTBS-TV operated as an independent UHF station broadcasting free to the Atlanta market on Channel 17, its signal reached a far greater number of homes via cable-TV systems in 48 states and was transmitted via telecommunications satellite.

From the time Turner purchased WTBS-TV in 1970 to the fall of 1976, only 462,000 cable TV customers were added to the station's viewing audience. But two key events drastically changed the market potential for WTBS's signal. In 1975 the Federal Communications Commission determined that cable growth in many areas had been held back by FCC regulations forbidding cable operators from bringing in a more desirable distant signal over that of a local independent; the FCC lifted its restrictions on "leapfrogging." Then, in December 1975, RCA launched its first communications satellite into orbit some 22,000 miles above the equator; a television signal could be beamed to the orbiting satellite and retransmitted to a receiving earth station antenna anywhere in the United States. Turner took full note of both changes. He quickly joined the cable-operators' association and got to know the operators personally. And on seeing Home Box Office (a rival subscriber offering movies for home viewing on pay TV) unveil the first satellite broadcast to cable operators, Turner moved quickly. Satellite transmission of the WTBS signal began in December 1976, after being delayed six months by FCC proceedings.

Exhibit 3 CONSOLIDATED BALANCE SHEETS, TURNER BROADCASTING SYSTEM, INC., 1986 AND 1987 (in thousands)

	December 31	
	1987	**1986**
Assets		
Current assets:		
Cash, including short-term investments of $20,094 in 1987 and $47,078 in 1986	$ 27,701	$ 62,715
Accounts receivable, less allowance for doubtful accounts of $11,090 in 1987 and $11,751 in 1986	134,205	127,277
Film costs	79,836	79,426
Installment contracts receivable, less reserves of $16,134 in 1987 and $14,304 in 1986	38,090	58,160
Prepaid expenses and other assets	15,182	12,899
Total current assets	295,014	340,477
Property, plant, and equipment, less accumulated depreciation	165,485	156,866
Film costs and related intangibles, less current portion	1,236,838	1,272,797
Installment contracts receivable, less unamortized discount of $4,864 in 1987 and $4,269 in 1986	27,408	23,774
Other assets	113,606	110,069
Total assets	$1,838,351	$1,903,983
Liabilities and Stockholders' Deficit		
Current liabilities:		
Accounts payable and accrued expenses	$ 70,527	$ 98,467
Accrued interest	41,841	34,335
Accrued taxes	—	64,517
Participants' share and royalties payable	20,691	18,388
Current portion of long-term debt	12,464	4,516
Film contracts payable	19,521	12,659
Other	27,975	21,371
Total current liabilities	193,019	254,253
Long-term debt, less current portion	1,418,211	1,366,217
Accrued taxes	63,249	—
Other liabilities	124,075	96,492
Total liabilities	1,798,554	1,716,962
Commitments and contingencies:		
Series A Cumulative Preferred Stock, par value $.10; authorized 500,000 and 150,000,000 shares; issued and outstanding—0—and 52,571,000 shares; aggregate redemption value of $543,059	—	396,099
Class B Cumulative Preferred Stock, par value $.125; authorized 12,600,000 and—0— shares; issued and outstanding 12,396,976 and—0—shares; aggregate redemption value of $382,240	309,993	—
Stockholders' deficit:		
Class C Convertible Preferred Stock, par value $.125; authorized 12,600,000 and—0— shares; issued and outstanding 12,396,976 and—0—shares	260,438	—
Class D Serial Preferred Stock, par value $.0625; authorized 100,000,000 shares	—	—
Class A Common Stock, par value $.0625; authorized 25,000,000 shares; issued 22,708,000 shares; outstanding 21,780,000 and 21,775,000 shares	1,419	1,419
Class B Common Stock, par value $.0625; authorized 150,000,000 shares; issued 22,708,000 shares; outstanding 21,780,000 and 21,775,000 shares	1,419	1,419
Capital in excess of par value	29,772	29,750
Accumulated deficit	(562,003)	(240,418)
	(268,955)	207,830)
Less—1,856,000 and 1,866,000 shares of common stock in treasury	(1,241)	(1,248)
Total stockholders' deficit	(270,196)	(209,078)
Total liabilities and stockholders' deficit	$1,838,351	$1,903,983

Source: 1987 10-K Report.

To reflect the size of the station's geographic coverage and its availability to more and more households, the company began in 1979 to refer to WTBS as Superstation. Meanwhile, the number of full-time, cable TV subscribers receiving the WTBS signal soared:

Year	Subscribers
1977	1,350,000
1983	28,492,000
1984	33,111,000
1985	36,100,000
1986	39,300,000
1987	43,100,000

At year-end 1987, WTBS could be seen in 92 percent of U.S. homes with cable service and in 49 percent of U.S. homes with television. Much of the growth in WTBS's viewing audience was due to Turner's own entrepreneurial vision of the potential of cable and the personal sales job he did promoting WTBS to cable operators. A rival executive observed, "You have to hand it to Turner. He surrounded himself with people who new the cable industry, and he made friends. He had the timing, the ambition, the foresight, and the will to put his money where his mouth was."[3]

Programming.   To fill the time slots for its 24-hour, seven-day-a-week broadcast schedule (8,760 hours per year) WTBS relied on sports events (especially games of its sports affiliates), television feature film suppliers, program syndicators, and a limited amount of internal programming. Movies contributed the most-viewed segment of WTBS programming; more than 40 movies were featured weekly from a library of 4,500 feature films (not including the recently acquired MGM library of 2,200 films). Responding to critics who complained about using so many reruns and old movies instead of new programming, Turner quipped, "At least our shows were successful once."

WTBS obtained a significant portion of its sports programming from its sports affiliates. Beginning in 1981, the hours of scheduled sports programming were increased; the most significant change was upping the number of televised Braves baseball games from 100 to 150. TBS paid the National Basketball Association $95 million for rights to televise up to 75 NBA games each basketball season from 1984 through 1990. TBS also televised college football games.

In July 1985 TBS entered an agreement with the All-Union Association Soyuzsport and the U.S.S.R. State Committee for Television and Radio to organize a major international sports competition, known as the "Goodwill Games," to be held during 1986 in Moscow and during 1990 in the United States. TBS agreed to pay $7.5 million in participation fees to Soyuzsport for each set of games (which were to feature 18 of the most popular Olympic sports), $5.4 million

---

[3] Quoted in Vaughn, "Ted Turner's True Talent," p. 46.

to The Athletic Congress of the U.S.A., Inc. for assembling the 1986 team, transportation fees for the U.S. team to and from Moscow, and all the costs of the 1990 Goodwill Games. These games added a planned 129 hours to WTBS's sports broadcasting. The 1986 Goodwill Games attracted fewer advertisers than expected, resulting in a net loss of $25.7 million. Plans for the 1990 games were proceeding full steam.

Beginning in July 1981, programming at WTBS was shifted to begin five minutes past the hour and at five minutes past the half hour. The rationale was explained by a WTBS executive:

> Ever since TV programming began, it has been scheduled on the hour and half hour. Since all stations program in this format, millions of viewers have to suffer through commercial clutter on all channels at the same time. Our trademark has been and continues to be innovation, and we're going to give viewers a chance to see something other than ads on those half-hour breaks. We're going to run programs when all other stations are running commercials. When dials are being flipped, we're going to provide an alternative for viewers. Once we have these viewers, we're going to keep them.

According to a TBS vice president, "the development of our own uniquely original programming, both on CNN and WTBS, has brought us into a potential new source of income, the syndication of Turner-created programs." To follow up on this opportunity, a new unit called Turner Program Sales was established in late 1980 to syndicate TBS programming. Approximately 24 percent of the programming broadcast on WTBS in 1987 was produced specifically for the station, either internally or by others under contract. The production facilities of WTBS included two fully equipped studios and two mobile remote units.

Advertising.   Advertising revenues of WTBS-TV were largely a function of audience size. Because of its sizable, rapidly growing viewing audience, WTBS was able to compete for national spot advertising and network advertising which otherwise would not be available to an independent station. In January 1979 WTBS instituted substantially higher "Superstation rates" for ads as a result of its greatly increased audience size. Even so, WTBS ad rates were not up to what might be justified by its 1 percent share of the national viewing audience. TBS management offered three reasons why this was so: (1) the Superstation concept was still new to the advertising community and did not conveniently fit into the long-established budgeting practices of major firms for network and national spot ads; (2) some national advertisers did not consider WTBS coverage and audience size large enough to shift some of their allocation of TV advertising away from the major networks; and (3) there was a significant time lag between documenting audience size and being able to establish rates on that basis. Still, scores of national advertisers ran ads on the Superstation; total advertising revenues for WTBS were $206 million in 1987, up from $185 million in 1986. Advertising time for WTBS as well as for CNN and CNN Headline News was marketed by TBS's own advertising sales force of about 100 persons.

Competition.   In the Atlanta market, WTBS competed with affiliates of the three major television networks, three independent TV stations, and two affiliates of the

Public Broadcasting System. The PBS affiliates offered programming for educational or intellectual appeal; the three independents generally geared their programs to appeal to a variety of special audiences.

Competition for cable TV viewers came from several other large, independent stations which, like WTBS, were trying to go national and offer an alternative to traditional network programming. Two of the biggest independents were WPIX-TV in New York and WGN-TV in Chicago. In 1981 the parent firm of WGN-TV in Chicago bought into the Chicago Cubs National League baseball team. Major competition also came from ESPN, a 24-hour sports network, and from pay TV operators, such as Home Box Office, Showtime, Cinemax, and the Movie Channel, which offered cable subscribers regular showing of movies, some of which were relatively new first- and second-run films. In addition, there were over 30 other cable channels, including the Disney Channel, the Nashville Network, USA, Playboy, CNN, and CBN. As of 1987, most cable TV subscribers could choose between 5 and 25 channels in addition to the three major networks (ABC, NBC, and CBS), a PBS channel, and local independent TV stations (at least one independent TV station served virtually every metropolitan area). In mid-1985 the top choices of cable TV watchers were:

ESPN	36.5 million subscribers
WTBS	34.8
CNN	34.0
USA	31.0
CBN	29.7

THE ATLANTA BRAVES BASEBALL CLUB

Turner's purchase of the Atlanta Braves had several entrepreneurial pluses. Sports programming was a key feature of Channel 17, and Braves games had high audience ratings. By owning the Braves, Turner avoided contract disputes and renegotiations over broadcast rights and TV schedules, and the certainty of baseball programming enhanced Channel 17's appeal—especially to cable operators. Moreover, there was "fit" in another respect: Channel 17 could be used locally to promote attendance at Braves games; higher attendance meant more gate receipts, an ability to sign better players, and a better win-loss record. The improved record would attract more viewers to Channel 17. And with more viewers Channel 17 could command higher advertising rates. These considerations, in conjunction with the acquisition terms (a purchase price of $9.65 million, payable $1 million in cash and the balance in quarterly installments over 12 years at 6 percent interest), were attractive to Turner in spite of the fact that (1) there was little likelihood that the Braves club would ever make much profit and (2) at the time of purchase the Braves were doing poorly (some sportswriters labeled them a disaster).

Turner wasted little time in involving himself in the Braves activities. For the first time, he became widely known and highly visible in Atlanta, but he did not move in Atlanta's social circles. Bruce Galphin, in a feature article in a 1977 issue of *Atlanta* magazine, described some of what transpired:

> The Braves ended their first Turner season 32 games off the pennant pace, but attendance rose some 300,000 (to a still miserably unprofitable 830,000). Andy Messersmith was the new $1.5 million star on the field, but Ted Turner made the headlines. Before the season was out, everybody knew his name (and quite a few took it in vain).
>
> He turned somersaults for the fans. He vaulted his box-seat rail to congratulate home run-hitting Braves. (Cincinnati Reds' President Bob Howsam threatened to have him arrested if Turner pulled that trick on his turf.) He put Channel 17 promotion on the back of Messersmith's uniform. He played poker with the players. Such varied maverick behavior drew rebukes from National League President Chub Feeney.
>
> The Atlanta sports press was critical of the Braves in general and especially such deals as trading five players for Texas Ranger Jeff Burroughs. Turner retaliated by cutting off the press box's traditional free beer and sandwiches.
>
> Bowie Kuhn fined the Braves $10,000 for making overtures to outfielder Gary Matthews, then a San Francisco Giant, though soon to be a free agent. Blame that one not on Turner but on a now departed employee. But Turner did fly Matthews to Atlanta during the season for a cocktail bash and welcomed him with a Turner billboard at the airport.
>
> That turned into one of Kuhn's charges in suspending Turner. Another was a drunken boasting match at the World Series with Bob Lurie, part owner of the Giants, about who would bid the most for Matthews. (Turner did: $1.75 million for a five-year contract. Kuhn at least left him that.)
>
> "It's only my first year in baseball, OK?" says Turner. "I don't know that much about it, all right. I mean it's all complicated. When you get into a new kind of thing, there's a power structure that you're not really sure of, and there are unwritten rules as well as written rules. There's no book on how to be an owner."
>
> Turner is proud, too, of bringing home run king Hank Aaron back to the Braves to take charge of the minor league teams and new-talent search. "His main thing is to go around and to fire up the young players and teach them how to hit the baseball."
>
> He enjoys the company of his players. If he's forbidden to play poker with them, then he takes them hunting and generally treats them "like people." There are other owners who don't like this.
>
> "They'd rather treat them like—well, like an owner-race horse relationship. My ballplayers aren't horses. They're my friends. I want them to be happy here."

In 1976 Ted Turner was suspended from all baseball activities for a year by Commissioner Bowie Kuhn for "conduct unbecoming to baseball." The Braves finished last in the Western Division of the National League the first four seasons under Turner's ownership. Early in the fifth season Turner remarked to a reporter, "I promised Atlanta that the Braves would be winners in five years; I still have one year to do it. Maybe there'll be a miracle. Besides, the Russians never make their five-year programs. They start new ones."[4] (The fifth year the Braves moved up to 4th place in their division, with a win-loss record of 81–80.)

---

[4] As quoted in Kim Chapin, "The Man Who Makes Waves," *United Mainliner*, May 1980, p. 86.

The Atlanta Braves baseball team and associated activities made up the entire professional sports segment of Turner Broadcasting's business (Exhibit 1) and accounted for 9 percent of TBS's revenue in 1983, 6 percent in 1985, and 5 percent in 1987. Operating losses were incurred every year of Turner's ownership, and a continuation of the trend of increasing operating losses was expected. Increased ticket prices were not expected to boost gate receipts substantially; management believed that it would be necessary for the team to contend for its divisional championship to achieve a significant revenue increase.

During 1978–87 period, the operating expenses of the Braves increased rapidly as a result of escalating player salaries, travel costs, and preseason training costs. Record losses for the segment in 1986 resulted from higher salary costs and dwindling attendance.

The National League's baseball schedule called for 162 regular-season games—81 home games and 81 road, or away, games. The Braves home games were played in the Atlanta–Fulton County Stadium, seating capacity 52,194. Each season 150 of the Braves games were telecast by WTBS. Exhibit 4 presents selected statistics on the Braves' performance during Turner's ownership.

THE ATLANTA HAWKS BASKETBALL TEAM

In 1976 Tom Cousins, an Atlanta real-estate developer and principal owner of the Atlanta Hawks, approached Turner about buying the team. The Hawks team was in about the same condition as the Braves; the team had a poor win-loss record, attendance was falling, and financial losses were sizable. The owners wanted out, even if it meant that the franchise would be moved out of Atlanta. When Turner's board of directors balked at the company acquiring the Hawks, Turner acquired a 95 percent limited partnership interest himself. Turner's investment was financed

Exhibit 4 SELECTED STATISTICS OF ATLANTA BRAVES BASEBALL TEAM UNDER TURNER OWNERSHIP, 1976–1987

	Win-loss record/division standing				Season attendance		
Year	Games won	Games lost	Games behind division leader	Final rank in division (six teams)	Atlanta Braves	All major league teams	Braves' attendance ranking (out of 26 teams)
1976	70	92	32	6th	818,179	31,300,000	26th
1977	61	101	37	6th	872,464	38,700,000	26th
1978	69	93	26	6th	904,494	40,800,000	26th
1979	66	94	23½	6th	769,465	43,600,000	24th
1980	81	80	11½	4th	1,048,412	43,000,000	20th
1981†	50	56	8½	4th	535,418	26,450,000†	25th
1982	89	73	0	1st*	1,801,985	44,587,000	10th
1983	88	74	3	2nd	2,119,935	45,557,000	9th
1984	80	82	12	2nd (tie)	1,724,892	44,735,000	14th
1985	66	96	NA	5th	1,350,127	46,864,000	19th
1986	72	82	23½	6th	1,387,137	47,506,203	20th
1987	69	92	20½	5th	1,217,402	52,011,506	22nd

* Lost National League playoffs to St. Louis, three games to zero in a best-of-five series.
† Shortened season due to player's strike.

entirely by the company, however, through a $1 million secured note receivable from Atlanta Hawks, Ltd., (AHL), and a $400,000 advance to Turner. In addition, for a 2 percent partnership interest, Turner Advertising advanced $742,000 to the Hawks on an unsecured basis. In 1977 the directors of TBS agreed to let Turner transfer his 95 percent interest in the Hawks to the company, at cost plus accrued interest. In 1979 the new general managing partner of AHL was granted a 1 percent ownership interest; in 1980 TBS acquired the 2 percent limited partnership interest of Cousins for $41,000, bringing TBS's share in AHL to 96 percent.

The Atlanta Hawks competed in the Central Division of the 23-team National Basketball Association (NBA). The NBA was recognized as the top professional basketball league in the world, and its champion each year was accorded the world championship in professional basketball. Like baseball team owners, basketball team owners received a pro rata distribution of television revenues from telecasts by the national networks, but unlike baseball team owners, they received none of the gate receipts from away games (the home team retained the net gate receipts). Teams were subject to rules and regulations promulgated by the NBA's commissioner of basketball. Employment relationships with players were governed by a contract between the NBA and the National Basketball Players Association.

During Turner's first year as owner of the Hawks, Curry Kirkpatrick wrote:

> Turner's ignorance about both baseball and basketball is a matter of public record as well as the basis of many jokes he tells on himself. After two years as owner of the Braves, he thinks he finally knows what a balk is. But much of pro basketball has him stumped.
>
> He is forever calling NBA coaches managers and officials umpires. Although Turner knows his Hawks are "not too shabby" but rather "strawwwnnng" (two of the more annoying expressions in the terrific Turner lexicon someone once called "Southern bebop"), he does not seem to know their names or what positions they play. For instance, former Hawk Ron Behagen was always "Berhagen" to Turner. When the hulking 6'7" forward, John Brown—whose name Turner appears to have less difficulty pronouncing—fouled out of a game, the owner jumped and yelped, "Golly! Now we've got only three guards left." Later in the same game, after the Hawks were warned for using the illegal zone defense, Turner was bewildered.
>
> "What the hell was that?" he said.
>
> "A zone warning," he was told.
>
> "Awww for Chrissakes, forget it," he concluded, angrily giving up.[5]

But what Turner lacked in knowledge, he substituted with energy, enthusiasm, and a flair for promotion. In the 1979–80 season, the Hawks won the NBA Central Division Championship and compiled the best record of any Hawks team since Atlanta obtained the franchise; the team set a new attendance record, drawing a total of 449,843 persons—an average of 10,792 fans per home game. The next five seasons were disappointing however, and attendance fell off substantially. (See

---

[5] Kirkpatrick, "Going Real Strawwng," p. 76.

Exhibit 5 SELECTED STATISTICS OF ATLANTA HAWKS BASKETBALL TEAM, 1975–1988

	Win-loss record/division standing				Season attendance		
Season	Games won	Games lost	Games behind division leader	Final rank in division*	Atlanta Hawks	All NBA teams	Hawks' attendance ranking (out of 22 teams)
1975–76	29	53	20	5th	n.a.	n.a.	n.a.
1976–77	31	51	18	6th	214,775	9,898,521	22nd
1977–78	41	41	11	4th	304,482	9,874,155	19th
1978–79	46	36	2	3rd	329,064	9,761,377	20th
1979–80	50	32	0	1st†	449,843	9,937,975	11th
1980–81	31	51	29	4th	362,702	9,449,340	16th
1981–82	42	40	13	2nd	308,899	9,964,919	20th
1982–83	43	39	8	2nd	292,673	9,637,614	20th
1983–84	40	42	10	3rd	292,690	10,014,543	20th
1984–85	34	48	25	5th	299,514	10,506,355	22nd
1985–86	50	32	7	2nd	377,678	11,214,888	19th
1986–87	57	25	0	1st	549,652	12,000,000	8th
1987–88	50	32	4	2nd	583,042	12,500,000	8th

n.a. = Not available.
* There were six teams competing in the Hawks' division each year, except for 1975–1976 when there were five teams.
† Hawks lost in first round of NBA playoffs.

Exhibit 5.) In 1985–86 and again in 1986–87, the team performed well. Attendance rose and in 1987 operations were essentially at a breakeven level (see Exhibit 1). Attendance during the 1987–88 season set an all-time record for the team, averaging 14,219 per home game. The Hawks games were played at the Omni in downtown Atlanta (seating capacity 16,181); the lease agreement required payments to the Omni of 15 percent of gate receipts from each home game. The Atlanta Hawks routinely purchased TV advertising from WTBS.

Ted Turner, using personal funds, and TBS routinely advanced the Hawks partnership the necessary funds to cover the losses and negative cash flows incurred. During 1985 CBS and the NBA entered into an agreement to televise NBA games through 1990; the Hawks pro rata share of the TV rights fees from CBS was $1.7 million in 1987, $1.8 million in 1988, $1.95 million in 1989, and $2.06 million in 1990. Rights to televise the Hawks home games were sold to an independent Atlanta station.

THE ATLANTA CHIEFS PROFESSIONAL SOCCER TEAM

In October 1978 Turner Broadcasting formed a limited partnership, Atlanta Professional Soccer, Ltd. (APSL), to acquire the assets of the Colorado Caribous professional soccer team. The team was moved to Atlanta and its name changed to the Atlanta Chiefs. In 1979 the Chiefs won 12 games, lost 18, and finished last in its four-team division; in 1980 the Chiefs won only 7 games, lost 25 games, and again finished last in its division.

The partners of APSL included Turner Broadcasting (the sole limited partner with a 1 percent equity interest) and Atlanta Professional Soccer, Inc. (the general partner with 99 percent equity interest). TBS paid $1,554,000 cash for its partnership interest. The partnership agreement provided that the operating losses of APSL were to be allocated 99 percent to the limited partner and 1 percent to the general partner. As the sole limited partner, TBS provided all necessary operating funds to the Chiefs' operations. The Chiefs lost money in 1978 ($115,000), 1979 ($1,224,000), and 1980 ($2,128,000). During the early 1980s, Ted Turner concluded that the popularity of soccer was not growing fast enough to warrant continued financing of this investment; the venture was abandoned.

CABLE NEWS NETWORK

One of the most expensive ventures of Turner Broadcasting was the Cable News Network. After a 19-month development period, CNN began operations on June 1, 1980, as a comprehensive, continuous, 24-hour-a-day programming service, consisting of world, national, and sports news; analysis; commentary; and special features. CNN sold this service by subscription to cable television systems nationwide and distributed it by telecommunication satellite using the transmission services of a satellite common carrier. Like WTBS, CNN also derived revenues from advertising.

At the June 1, 1980, sign-on date, CNN's signal was available to 1.7 million households; seven months later, CNN was providing programming to 663 cable systems having a total of 4.3 million households—a growth rate of 10,000 subscribers per day. At the end of 1987, CNN could be seen on cable in more than 43 million television households; CNN was also broadcast in the Caribbean, Australia, Japan, Germany, Ireland, Italy, Korea, Central America, and the Philippines—a total of 57 countries on six continents.

The first national telephone survey for CNN, conducted by a nationally known research firm in the early 1980s, showed that 77 percent of the respondents rated CNN's performance as above average or better relative to all services carried on their cable system; 31 percent ranked CNN as the best or one of the best channels offered. Management said that "a significant number" of viewers who regularly viewed CNN considered it their primary source of national news. Ted Turner saw CNN as a no-frills network concerned with communicating the news, not exploiting it; according to Turner, "At CNN the news, not the anchor, is the star."

CNN Programming and Personnel.   The original CNN staff consisted of more than 400 journalists, reporters, executives, and technical personnel. The first president hired by Ted Turner to run CNN was Reese Schonfield, a 25-year veteran of television news. Schonfield had been founder and managing director of the Independent Television News Association (ITNA), which supplied a daily 90-minute news package to major independent television stations; prior to running ITNA, Schonfield was with the United Press International Television News service for 17 years.

CNN operations were headquartered at Turner Broadcasting System facilities in Atlanta. Other domestic news bureaus were located in Washington, New York City, Chicago, Dallas, Los Angeles, and San Francisco. CNN foreign bureaus were located in Rome and London, with traveling correspondents based in the

Middle East and Bangkok. CNN's own news coverage capability was amplified by the services of United Press International Television News and the wires of United Press International, the Associated Press, and Reuters. CNN management felt that its resource base gave it an unprecedented capability to go "live" anywhere in the world to cover major news breaking at any hour of the day or night. The aim at CNN was to report the news as it broke, not at midday, 6 P.M., or 11 P.M. as the network stations did.

CNN management saw an all-news channel as having several advantages in covering a breaking news story. First, interrupting normal programming for coverage of breaking news would enhance program content for most of the audience; for the network, the result would be an annoyed audience and a loss of revenue from commercials not aired. Second, CNN could stay with a developing news story without any time restraints. Third, when a network went live on a long-lasting event, it could not easily switch back to entertainment during the dull segments and then break off an entertainment program when the live action picked up; an all-news operation, however, could switch in and out of its normal programming, returning to the live event the moment it became more interesting. Fourth, CNN had the capability to go live whenever and wherever a good news story developed. Turner declared, "The majority of people now depend on TV for their basic news, and I don't think they're getting a straight story, only a few headlines about what bad has happened. That's pretty scary."[6]

The main weakness in CNN's "narrowcasting" approach was that its all-news format was not very appealing to viewers who watched TV for long stretches of time. Many of CNN's news events and stories were reported as many as 25 to 50 times each day. During normal viewing hours, CNN rewrote the script for the news every half hour to update and freshen its stories, but much of the film footage was still identical. Between 2 A.M. and 6 A.M., nearly everything shown was a repeat of material telecast earlier.

Advertising and Subscription Revenues.   CNN sold 10 minutes of national advertising each hour, with an additional two minutes an hour to be sold by the local operators. Advertising revenues totaled about $87 million during 1987, up from $73 million in 1986. Over 100 national advertisers had chosen to use CNN, including American Express, Bristol-Myers, General Motors, Campbell Soup, Eastern Airlines, Exxon, General Mills, General Foods, Goodyear, Holiday Inns, K mart, Kraft Foods, Merrill Lynch, Nestlé, Procter & Gamble, Quaker Oats, RCA, Schlitz, Sears, Toyota, and Xerox. Bristol-Myers' strategy in electing to advertise on CNN was to get TV exposure for some of its lesser-known brands (Ammens powder and Congespirin cold remedy) whose sales were not large enough to justify paying the much higher ad rates charged by the three major networks. Joining the major advertisers on CNN were numerous mail-order houses, all using the same 800 toll-free number and Atlanta post office box; the mail-order products included records, jewelry, books and magazines, household items, and health and nutrition products. CNN received a commission on these

---

[6] As quoted in Allen, "Ted Turner's Dream," p. 32.

sales of mail-order products bought by CNN viewers. CNN also had cable subscription revenues of $85 million in 1987, up from $69 million in 1986.

As had become a tradition in Turner ventures, during the start-up period at CNN, Turner himself appeared live and on tape on both CNN and WTBS to try to raise money for CNN. His ads promoting CNN urged people to send in their orders for bumper stickers, at $5 for a set of five, proclaiming "I Love CNN." Turner also donated a disk antenna to make CNN available to members of Congress at their Capitol offices.

CNN Headline News. TBS launched CNN Headline News at the beginning of 1982. The goal of Headline News was to give viewers a concise, fast-paced update on current news headlines, business, weather, and sports every half hour. Headline News utilized the news-gathering resources of CNN. Carried by 2,000-plus cable systems in 1987, Headline News was seen in 30 million households. Total advertising revenues in 1987 for Headline News were $24 million, up from $18 million during the previous year. Subscription revenues in 1987 were an additional $2.9 million.

PROGRAM SYNDICATION AND LICENSING

In March 1986 TBS completed the acquisition of MGM/UA and subsequently sold essentially all of the nonfilm assets that had been acquired. Turner Entertainment Co., a wholly owned subsidiary of TBS, was formed for the purpose of handling TBS's interests in the rental, licensing, and distribution of the 3,700 feature-length films and entertainment products in the MGM library. TEC was pursuing a variety of worldwide revenue sources, including the theatrical, home video, pay television, and syndication markets.

The MGM Film Library. MGM's film holdings represented one of the largest feature film libraries in the world and included approximately 2,200 MGM pictures, 750 pre-1950 Warner Bros. pictures and 750 RKO pictures. Among the MGM pictures were such classics as *Gone with the Wind, Ben Hur, Gigi, 2001: A Space Odyssey, Mutiny on the Bounty, Dr. Zhivago,* and *The Wizard of Oz,* as well as more recent releases such as *Poltergeist, Victor/Victoria,* and *2010.* The Warner Bros. films included *Casablanca, The Maltese Falcon, The Adventures of Robin Hood,* and *Yankee Doodle Dandy.* The RKO film holdings (to which the company acquired additional rights in December 1987) included *Citizen Kane, Gunga Din, Hunchback of Notre Dame,* and *King Kong.*

Many of the pictures in the MGM film library were licensed for home video and to pay television and had had substantial exposure on network and local television stations. Certain pictures were subject to contractual restrictions in designated markets and were not available for home video distribution and/or for pay television licensing until the restrictions expired.

Licensing of motion pictures and television programs from the MGM film library for showings on television stations around the world (called syndication) was an important source of current and expected future revenues. TBS expected that use of MGM films on WTBS and on TNT would adversely affect the fees it could charge other commercial television stations for rights to broadcast the same films. To promote and handle licensing of films to commercial television markets, the company had sales offices in Atlanta, Chicago, Los Angeles, New York, Brazil, Mexico, Australia, Puerto Rico, Great Britain, France, and the Netherlands.

Colorization of Films.   During 1986 TBS initiated action to colorize some of the black-and-white films in the MGM library. An agreement was entered with Color Systems Technology to colorize up to 100 motion pictures. Thirteen were completed and shown on WTBS in 1987; another 20 were scheduled for completion and showing in 1988. Turner believed that colorization would significantly enhance the potential revenues that could be derived from older films. Colorizing a black-and-white film cost anywhere from $225,000 to $300,000 per film, depending on its length. The colorization effect was considered a success, despite objections from numerous old-movie fans who believed colorization destroyed some of the artistic content of black-and-white pictures. A second company was engaged in 1988 to colorize an additional 12 films.

REAL ESTATE OPERATIONS

The company got into real estate operations in a big way in 1985 when it acquired a 75 percent interest in a general partnership which owned the Omni International hotel and office complex in downtown Atlanta. The hotel contained 470 rooms and the complex had 775,000 square feet of office and retail shopping space. In 1986 the company acquired the remaining 25 percent ownership interest and renamed the office and shopping complex CNN Center; the corporate offices and operations of CNN and CNN Headline News were located in CNN Center. In late 1986 TBS created a wholly owned subsidiary called Turner Arena Production and Sales, Inc. to acquire and operate interests involving the Omni Coliseum. The subsidiary had contracts to operate the Omni Coliseum adjacent to CNN Center, was authorized to contract for major events held in the coliseum, and operated a computerized ticket sales agency specializing in sporting and entertainment events.

TED TURNER'S STYLE OF ENTREPRENEURSHIP AND MANAGEMENT

Turner's approach to business and to dealing with people was both colorful and controversial. He was frequently interviewed by the media and seldom hesitated to say exactly what he thought. This, of course, delighted reporters, and when they printed his quotes a swirl of discussion often ensued. During the 1981 baseball strike, it was rumored and reported in the *Atlanta Constitution* that Turner, at one of the owner's meetings to discuss the strike situation, remarked that all the players should be drowned and the teams restaffed from scratch.

Over the years, writers and journalists had used many labels to describe the personality and characteristics of Ted Turner: Captain Courageous, Captain Outrageous, Terrible Ted, the Mouth of the South, honest, petulant, childlike, loud, raucous, profane, impulsive, sentimental, egotistical, rebellious, ruthless, cold, money-grubbing, engrossing, multifaceted, flirtatious, hyperactive, sincere, outspoken, antiestablishment, likable, enjoyable, and chauvinistic. He had been called a humanist, a romantic, and the world's best-known sailor and had been accused of having basic racist tendencies, an elitist view of society, and a fascist ideology. Among his incongruous interests and activities, he had attended a state dinner at the White House, ridden in an ostrich race at Atlanta Stadium, read the Bible twice from cover to cover, permitted the screening of pornographic movies for his baseball players and their wives on a bus ride from Plains, Georgia, to Atlanta, nudged a baseball around the base paths with his nose, arrived drunk at a news conference following his victory in the world-famous America's Cup race, been named Yachtsman of the Year four times, appeared in ads for Cutty Sark Scotch, acquired a taste for Beechnut chewing tobacco, and quoted classical literature. In 1976 Turner was suspended from baseball, and in 1980 he was presented the Private Enterprise Exemplar Medal by the Freedom Foundation at Valley Forge.

Turner was highly motivated, energetic, and willing to do what it took to achieve his goals. He told one interviewer, "I have such a distaste for people who can't roll up their sleeves and get the job done. . . . My father always said to never set goals you can reach in your lifetime. After you accomplished them, there would be nothing left."[7] He valued and appreciated money—"Life is a game, but the way you keep score is money."[8] And he sought out success—"I've always been encouraged since I was a little kid to be a top competitor, and to be a worker, not a shirker."[9] Turner was known for being candid and honest with everyone. Honor, truth, and sincerity were his bywords.

Close associates described Turner as having a strong sense of what to do and when to do it. As one of his vice presidents expressed it, "He's a good concept man. He's got a good eye for where profitable growth lies, where growth potential is. He has ability to put things together that make sense."[10]

Complementing Turner's sense of direction and sense of timing was a knack for picking capable managers to work under him. He delegated authority readily. Administrative matters and day-to-day operating details were left to his vice presidents and lower-echelon managers. He did not, as a general rule, supervise them closely, preferring instead to let them do their jobs with a minimum of interference as long as things seemed to be progressing satisfactorily. The executives under Turner were regarded as devoted to him and seemed motivated by his leadership. A friend and sailing partner observed, "He is always winning, never losing, and he gives that same feeling to people sailing or working with him."

---

[7] As quoted in Kirkpatrick, "Going Real Strawwng," p. 78.

[8] Ibid., p. 75.

[9] As quoted in Bruce Galphin, "Other Things to Do," *Atlanta,* Spring 1977, p. 40.

[10] As quoted in Wayne Minshew and DeWitt Rogers, "A Winner," *Atlanta Constitution,* January 8, 1977.

Turner's approach was to throw 100 percent of his energies into a project until he felt he could go on to something else. He got bored sitting still doing the same things over and over and handling routine matters. As one writer described it:

> When he approaches a project, he demonstrates great powers of positive thinking and an even greater innocence. ("It can't be done? Let's find out.") If things aren't going particularly well, Turner is capable of short temper tantrums and brief flurries of petulance. When a project bores him, Turner is quick to turn his back on it and move to something fresh, leaving to his corporate subalterns the job of seeing the project through—as well as the task of pouring oil on the inevitable troubled waters he has left in his wake.[11]

By Turner's own admission, the thing that turned him on was trying to win, the playing of the game, the competition, the matching of wits. He liked to turn losers into winners, in sports and in business. The general manager of WTBS-TV described his perception of Turner:

> He has a tremendous desire to win. He doesn't like to lose. If he does, he is one of the few people I know who benefits from the loss. He asks himself, "Why did I lose?" I don't know why he has to win so. It's a compulsion with him.
>
> One of my responsibilities is, if I know he is doing something wrong, to try and stop him. But did you ever try and stop a speeding train?
>
> If he wants something, he is going to get it. The problem is, he will pay more than it's worth. And the other guy knows it.[12]

However, Turner did not look at himself as a "win at all costs" practitioner:

> I don't think winning is everything. It's a big mistake when you say that. I think *trying* to win is what counts. Be kind and fair, and make the world a better place to live, that's what important. . . .
>
> I think the saddest people I've ever met were people with a lot of wealth. If you polled 90 percent of the people and asked them what they want most, most would want to be millionaires. I'll tell you, you've got to be one to know how unimportant it is.
>
> I'm blessed with some talents. I've made a lot of money, more than I ever thought I would. . . . But if I continue to be successful, I would like to serve my fellow man in some way other than doing a flip at third base. . . .
>
> People want leadership, somebody to rally around, and I want to be a leader.[13]

FUTURE OUTLOOK

In 1981, replying to questions from the casewriter, Ted Turner was confident and optimistic about the prospects for TBS:

> The future outlook is excellent. We have not peaked and I feel competition is always good; you continue to do better with competition.

---

[11] As quoted in Chapin, "The Man Who Makes Waves," p. 85.

[12] As quoted in Minshew and Rogers, "A Winner."

[13] Ibid.

CNN's future is solid. . . .

Moreover, we are currently doing well in competing both against the major networks and the other emerging alternatives.

Five years from now, I expect TBS to be five times stronger.

Turner's 1981 assessment of TBS's prospects were pretty much on target. In 1981 TBS was a $95 million company; in 1988 it was a $650 million company, with seemingly ample room for further growth. The two big questions facing the company in 1988 were: (1) Could the company overcome its huge 1986 and 1987 losses and improve its very, very grim balance sheet picture? and (2) What new strategic moves did the company need to make? To maintain the company's financial viability over the long term, Turner needed to get revenues up quickly, boost cash flows, generate some profits, and eliminate the negative net worth position on the balance sheet. Investor confidence in the company was running higher in 1988; shares were trading in the high 20s and low 30s, after hitting a low of $8 per share in late 1987. Assuming investors were correct and that Turner had TBS on the road to financial recovery, the issue of the company's future hinged on whether Ted Turner would launch another bold entrepreneurial initiative and in which direction he might take the company. Turner himself characterized the company's opportunity for growth as "numerous, exciting, and sizable."

WEST SHORES REALTY*

West Shores Realty, Inc., was a small real estate firm primarily engaged in facilitating the sale of residential properties. Located in the small city of Bremerton in Kitsap County, Washington, West Shores had enjoyed the advantage of a rapidly growing market for homes from its first days until recently.

Over the past two years Larry Proctor, a part owner of West Shores, developed an uneasiness concerning the way he and his partners were managing the company. In an effort to confirm or disconfirm his uneasiness, Proctor asked a long-standing friend, George Watkins, a professor of management at a nearby university, to assess the company and make recommendations for improvement. As Proctor explained to Watkins, "We just don't seem to be getting anywhere. Although we are selling more than when we started six years ago, our competitors seem to be larger now and growing. I wonder if we should be more aggressive and make changes to go after the market as it changes."

BUSINESS ENVIRONMENT

Real estate sales fall into one of three categories: residential, commercial, or land. Residential sales involve facilitating the transfer of ownership of previously occupied and new housing units. Commercial sales include the sale of nonresidential buildings and businesses. Land sales are concerned with the transfer of unimproved and improved ready-to-build land for residential, commercial, or other use. Real estate sales companies tend to specialize and concentrate on one or another of these three market segments. However, firms often sell outside of their primary concentration to the extent that they possess requisite competencies and have good contacts with potential buyers and sellers. It is common for residential specialist firms to handle transactions involving land and two- to four-family multiple dwellings. In Kitsap County the majority of real estate firms specialized in residential sales, with some product line diversification into land and light commercial sales or even into property management.

Key Factors

The demand for real estate is highly sensitive to interest rates and availability of mortgage loans. High interest rates or tight money place a significant constraint on demand. The high interest rates of the early 1980s, ranging up to 15 or 16 percent at the worst, seriously reduced potential buyers' ability and interest in

---

* Prepared by Professor Stephen E. Barndt of Pacific Lutheran University.

buying. With a decline in rates to less than 10 percent for a 30-year conventional mortgage loan early in 1987, demand rebounded. Current interest rates were at 1 to 1.5 percentage points above the March 1987 lows and mortgage money was plentiful.

The general state of the local economy was also important. A strong demand for goods and services, with attendant high levels of employment and optimism, was associated with high levels of real estate sales activity. Recessions or fear of recession had the opposite effect. Business and employment conditions in Kitsap County were favorable through the 1980s, because of a rapidly growing population base and the general business prosperity in the Northwest region and the nation as a whole.

Local Market

Geographically, Kitsap County is nearly an island, bordered on the west by Hood Canal and on the north and east by the Puget Sound (Exhibit 1). Its population of approximately 170,000 was fairly widely distributed, with the greatest density in the corridor from Poulsbo (population 3,800) through Bremerton (population 38,000) to Port Orchard (population 4,900). The county's rate of population growth in the early 1980s was one of the highest in the state. Most of this growth had been in the area north of Bremerton and centered around the unincorporated town of Silverdale. A major factor in population growth was an increase in activity and employment at the county's three U.S. Navy installations: Puget Sound Naval Shipyard at Bremerton, a submarine base six miles northwest of Silverdale at Bangor, and an undersea warfare center at Keyport, six miles northeast of Silverdale. Enlargement of the submarine base to service Trident nuclear submarines was the most important contributor to growth, boosting population to support construction and increasing civil service, military, and support service contractor employment at the base.

Completion of the county's first enclosed shopping mall at Silverdale and a general upgrading of shopping and business activity facilities, coupled with the fact that Seattle was less than an hour away via passenger ferry, all helped to increase quality-of-life. Recognition of the county as a good place to live was expected to ensure a moderate growth in population even though employment at the naval installations had stabilized.

The economy of Bremerton and Kitsap County was, however, highly dependent on its largest employer, the U.S. Navy. A cutback in defense programs or transfer of functions elsewhere would have a multiple effect throughout the county and leave an economic void. The land transportation barriers presented by the deep water that nearly surrounds the county made it an unattractive location for any kind of industry that relied on ease of access to a transportation network. On the other hand, the three navy installations had survived budget cuts and base closings and had actually enlarged their missions in submarine use, thus reducing the probability of personnel and budgetary cutbacks.

Exhibit 1 KITSAP COUNTY GEOGRAPHICAL SETTING

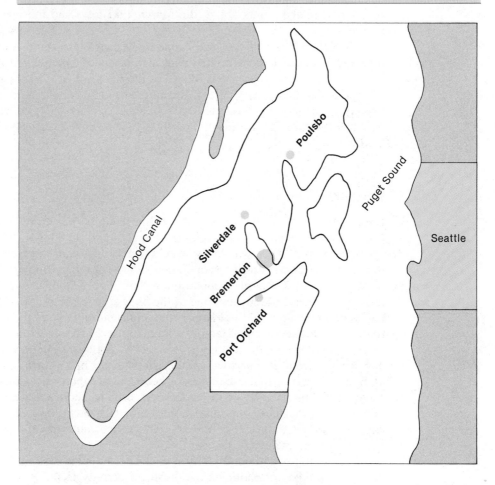

	Distances (in miles)			
	Silverdale	**Poulsbo**	**Port Orchard**	**Bremerton**
Silverdale	X	8	12	6
Poulsbo	8	X	20	14
Port Orchard	12	20	X	6
Bremerton	6	14	6	X

Competition

The real estate sales market industrywide was highly fragmented and had traditionally been served by small single proprietorships, partnerships, or corporations operating out of one office or a limited number of branch offices catering to a localized market. Low capital investment requirements and relatively easy and fast licensing requirements for brokers and salespersons created low entry and exit barriers. The functions performed by real estate firms were basically the same from firm to firm. Companies differentiated themselves largely on the basis of the caliber of their salespeople and their reputations and images. Attempts at differentiation through providing better service were generally doomed because of the ease with which firms could match each other. Some firms were able to achieve a distinctive image based on the type of property (price range, neighborhood, or end use) they specialized in or on the lower sales commission rates they charged.

There was a high degree of cooperation and interchange among competing firms. A major reason for this was the widespread use of multiple listings. Under this system, the firm that obtains a contract to sell a property shares information about the real estate with other firms and allows—or even helps—another firm to sell the property. When this happens, typically the listing firm retains 50 percent of the sales commission for listing the property, with the other 50 percent going to the selling firm. Another reason for cooperation is the personal interaction of individuals from different firms on local real estate boards that are aimed at furthering their common good. Finally, movement of salespeople, many of whom work only part time or seasonally, from one firm to another means that salespeople know one another and what is happening in their respective firms.

Several trends in the real estate sales industry were evident: First was the trend to establish branch offices in locations that make firms more accessible and visible. A second trend was the addition of ancillary services as revenue generators and the provision of a full spectrum of services. Such ancillary services included escrow management, appraisals, insurance, and finding tenants for rentals. A third trend involved affiliation with nationwide franchisors (e.g., Century 21, Better Homes and Gardens, The Gallery of Homes, and ERA), and chains such as Coldwell Banker (Sears) in order to gain greater market visibility by blanketing a local area with offices and to gain economies of scale through centralization or consolidation of such functions as sales training, advertising, and relocation referrals.

More than 70 real estate firms operated in Kitsap County. Over 70 percent concentrated basically on residential sales, while more than 20 percent targeted residential, commercial, and land sales. Nationwide franchise operations were represented by firms affiliated with Century 21 and The Gallery of Homes. In addition, there were two strong multi-office firms—John L. Scott, Inc., and Spot Realty.

COMPANY SITUATION

West Shores Realty was founded in 1981 by five real estate salespeople to provide themselves with more opportunity to capitalize on their individual talents and success in the business. The company was incorporated in the state of Washington with an initial investment of $2,600 per owner. All of the founders were residents of Bremerton and familiar with the residential real estate market in that city and surrounding area.

A favorable and growing housing market supported a substantial growth in total sales. This growth in sales was attained through an increase in the sales force. At present the firm has five owner-salespeople and eight nonowner sales-people. With the expansion of its sales force, West Shores recently enlarged its sales office by expanding into an adjoining office in the same downtown building.

Objectives

Long-range objectives at West Shores Realty were not consciously and formally developed. Although profitability is an implied objective, standards or specific targets had not been established. As a consequence, assessment of profitability is largely a personal matter with each owner-salesperson deciding whether or not his or her profitability expectations have been met. Similarly, diversification and expansion—shared objectives in a general sense—have not yet been opera-tionalized with specific targets.

Short-range projects, such as installing a data terminal and remodeling the office interior, have been discussed verbally. The owners intuitively believe that these projects support the company's longer-term objectives; however, the rela-tionship is unclear.

West Shores' Competitive Posture

Obtaining contracts to sell, that is, listings from people who want to sell property, was pursued as a major source of revenue by West Shores Realty. This was because the listing firm receives 50 percent of the sales commission even when another real estate firm finds the buyer.

People who wish to sell tend to place their listings with a particular firm because of its convenient location or because they are familiar with its reputation or because they know and trust a salesperson associated with that firm. Buyers choose certain real estate agents for many of the same reasons plus the fact that they might see the firm's name tied to an advertisement of a property in which they are interested. In the latter case, because the advertising firm is the same as the listing firm, listing provides an added advantage of keeping the company's name visible in the marketplace.

At present, West Shores has strong competition for listings and sales from Spot Realty and other well-established firms that advertise extensively. Competi-tion is increasing from franchised real estate companies that have nationwide referral services and the advantages of national advertising to put their names in peoples' minds.

In the face of this strong competition, West Shores' strategy is to create a competitive niche as a highly reputable, service-oriented firm. The owners believe the key to a reputation for service is having a staff of highly motivated, well-trained, professionally capable salespeople. Through careful selection of sales-people and better than average commission splits, the five West Shores owners had assembled a quality sales force. The company's name was well established in the area, and both the owners and sales force were well known in the community, knowledgeable about the market, and respected for fair dealing and extra service.

The whole sales force seemed to possess an air of professionalism and satisfaction in their work.

Commissions paid by sellers of residential properties are a uniform 6 percent of the sales price among the area's full service real estate sales companies. The commissions charged for the sale of commercial property and land are variable and negotiable depending on the nature and value of the property. In the case of unimproved land, commissions vary between approximately 7.5 and 10 percent, with the rates usually declining with increasing sales prices. Even though commissions on commercial properties and land are negotiable, the final rates tend to be generally competitive among firms. The 50/50 split of a sales commission between listing and selling is an informal but well-established standard in the industry. West Shores is more generous in splitting earned commissions between the company and salespeople. A salesperson who obtains a listing is paid 25 percent of the sales commission after the sale. The company retains the other 25 percent. A salesperson who sells a property receives 35 percent of the commission, with 15 percent going to the company. Thus a West Shores' salesperson who both lists and sells the same piece of property earns 60 percent of the total commission. This compares to less than 50 percent at most other firms. Owner-salespeople do even better, earning a full 50 percent of the commission for either listing or selling. Such liberal sharing of commissions is used as a means of motivating personnel toward obtaining listings and buyers.

West Shores does not actively advertise to get its name before the public. Last year approximately 6.9 percent of revenue was spent on advertising. Ninety-nine percent of this went for classified advertisements of its listed residential and other properties. Only 1 percent of advertising expenditures was used to inform potential buyers and sellers of West Shores' existence and services—through a Yellow Pages ad. Major reliance is on word of mouth and personal contacts for locating both sellers and people seeking property.

WEST SHORES' SALES OFFICE

West Shores' downtown sales office is in an area of Bremerton that is declining. Many businesses have moved to retail business strips and shopping malls on the outskirts of Bremerton and in the Silverdale, Poulsbo, and Port Orchard areas. The office is in a nondescript single-story building and is identified by a small, difficult-to-see sign. There is no off-street parking in the immediate area; on-street parking is limited and often difficult to find within West Shore's block.

A visitor to the West Shores office enters a small waiting area. At the far end is a receptionist/secretary who is near a multiple listing service computer terminal that she and sales personnel use for inputting and obtaining information on listings. On the wall opposite the visitors' seating is a small unattractive display of Polaroid snapshots of West Shores listings. Also visible to a visitor is the sales area. This open area is filled with an assortment of desks. At any given time, these desks could all be occupied (very unlikely) or unoccupied (a common occurrence). Private meetings are held in the broker's office or conference area, neither of which is visible from the visitors area.

MANAGEMENT AND ORGANIZATION

West Shores Realty is equally owned by Howard Daley, Anne Peterson, Larry Proctor, Barbara Scott, and Martha West. All five owners are directors of the company and at the same time salespeople. The company has four officer positions: president, vice president, secretary, and broker. The first three of these are essentially ceremonial offices established to comply with state corporate law and do not have any special roles in the strategic or operational management of the firm.

At the time the firm was founded, the owners agreed that each would act as the real estate broker for one year on a rotating basis, a condition that forced each owner to pass a state-administered examination and to be licensed as a broker. Preparation for and passing the broker examination usually requires extra study and taking short courses on real estate law, regulations, and procedures, but it is not difficult. None of the owners had any trouble qualifying as a broker.

The broker is responsible for the care, custody, and correct processing of all real estate transactions. This person is the only one who can close a sale and handle funds received in escrow for disbursement on closing. The broker assumes responsibility for the actions of sales personnel and, therefore, performs the final quality control checks on procedures and paperwork involved in a sale. At West Shores, the broker also acts as office manager. Howard Daley is the current broker/office manager.

The owners—including the designated broker—are associated with the firm as independent contractors rather than employees, earning commissions from obtaining listings and selling property. All nonowner salespeople are also affiliated with West Shores as independent contractors and carry the title of sales associates. The use of independent contractor status leaves the secretary/receptionist as the only person in the firm who is strictly an employee.

The relationship between an independent contractor and West Shores Realty is relatively straightforward. The independent contractor works for himself or herself—not West Shores. The company provides clerical support, office space, supplies, telephones, access to real estate listings, forms, broker services, advertising, and an affiliation. The independent contractor salesperson, in turn, is the active contact between prospective buyers and sellers, obtains listings, and consummates sales. The use of independent contractors has both advantages and disadvantages. On the advantage side are reduced paperwork and little company fringe benefit expense. In addition, virtually everyone other than the secretary/receptionist and, to some extent, the broker, can devote full time to the primary mission of selling real estate. The principal disadvantage is the limited power of the broker over the sales force. Basically this means that neither the broker nor any other owner can dictate work schedules or anything else not spelled out in the contract. To exercise employer-employee directions and supervision would open the firm to an Internal Revenue Service claim that salespeople are really employees subject to federal income tax withholding and employer social security contributions.

Within the parameters of certain rules and conventions (such as sales commissions, fees, and state laws governing sales), individual sales associates were free to let their common sense guide their actions. Working hours, telephone use, and so forth were pretty much left to the individual. The broker and other owners had little direct authority over another owner or nonowner salesperson. No one at West Shores had the responsibility, authority, and resources to develop and implement standing office procedures to determine performance in such basic areas as costs of sales by type of property, location, and salesperson; profit performance of salespeople; and advertising effectiveness. On occasion, uneconomical purchasing, uncoordinated advertising, and failure to have salespeople on the floor to handle inquiries resulted in higher than necessary costs and lost sales. These shortcomings were not the subject of special concern by the group of owners.

OWNERS' REWARDS

West Shores was formed to provide each of the owners a place to sell real estate independently, free from the constraints and controls they had experienced when selling for other firms. The commissions they earned were regarded as the principal reward for participation as owners. In return for their investment and contributions to the costs of operating the company, owners gross 100 percent of the commissions they generate for listing and selling property.

According to the terms of their original agreement, each owner was to maintain a minimum balance of $1,500 in a director's account for the corporation's use. Because the corporation did not share in commissions, the directors' accounts provided the working capital base from which corporate overhead and operating expenses were paid. Owners were to deposit money in their directors' accounts from commission income or other sources on a monthly basis to replace funds expended for rent, salaries, taxes, advertising, utilities, and other company-paid expenses. These expenses were to be shared equally by the owners. In addition to corporate expenses, directors' accounts provided the individual owner with a fund from which the corporation would pay personal expenses and client-reimbursable expenses associated with listing a property on his or her behalf. Thus, the required monthly restitution to maintain each director's account at $1,500 consists of an equal amount to pay back office expenses and a variable amount to cover personal business expenses. The requirement to maintain a director's account effectively increased each owner's investment in the firm to $4,100 ($2,600 for stock plus a $1,500 director's account). However, as can be seen in Exhibit 2, no director maintains an account at $1,500 and there is considerable variability in the level to which the owners do share in providing working capital.

The addition of nonowner independent contractors to the West Shores sales force provided a new, significant source of funds to pay corporate overhead and operating expenses. The corporation received 15 percent of gross commissions for selling and 25 percent for listing by nonowner independent salespeople. Although

Exhibit 2 DIRECTORS' ACCOUNTS—1987

	(1) Beginning balance	(2)* Additions to account	(3)† Charges against account	(4)†† Ending balance (1) + (2) − (3)	(5)†† Average account balance
Daley	$ (210)	$8,967	$9,929	$(1,172)	$(1,918)
Peterson	176	4,546	4,633	89	961
Proctor	765	4,599	4,999	365	674
Scott	329	5,698	5,148	879	816
West	1,170	4,547	4,858	859	507

Notes:
* Includes reimbursement from sellers for appraisals, cleanup, repairs, utilities payments, and so forth.
† Includes payments on clients' behalf for appraisals, cleanup, repairs, utilities payments, and so forth.
†† By agreement, each director is to maintain a minimum of $1,500 in his or her account.

Exhibit 3 OWNERS' COMMISSION EARNINGS—1987

	(1) Gross commissions generated	(2) Contribution toward operating expenses	(3) Earned commissions after expenses
Daley	$23,640	$4,470	$19,170
Peterson	12,566	4,470	8,096
Proctor	15,705	4,470	11,235
Scott	18,800	4,470	14,330
West	29,873	4,470	25,403

nonowner-generated revenue was not sufficient to cover all overhead and operating expenses, it did cover most. In 1987 each owner paid only $4,470 from his or her director's account to cover the year's deficit. Exhibit 3 shows the owners' earnings assuming that each director's account had adequate funds to fully pay a pro rata share of corporate expenses. Actual net income to the individual would be less because each independent contractor was responsible for his or her personal business expenses such as memberships, automobile expenses, entertainment, educational and training expense, licenses, travel, and donations. The substantial variation in commission income among owners reflected differences in sales ability and commitment to sales work. Not all of the five owners worked full time at real estate sales. Two of the owners were semiretired and one had other business interests.

FINANCIAL STATUS

The fiscal year 1987 balance sheet (Exhibit 4) shows an improvement in sales activity over 1986 evidenced by increased trust accounts and earnest money deposits. The value of buildings and equipment has also grown significantly,

Exhibit 4   WEST SHORES' BALANCE SHEETS, 1986 and 1987

	1986	1987
Assets		
Current assets:		
Cash	$ 1,603	$ 4,681
Inventory	12,462	
Trust accounts	7,840	8,226
Earnest money deposits	0	6,100
Advances to sales personnel	0	2,620
Total current assets	$21,905	$21,627
Fixed assets:		
Buildings and equipment	9,644	23,326
Less: depreciation	3,453	5,729
	6,191	17,597
Intangible assets	710	710
Less: amortization	604	710
	106	0
Total fixed assets	6,297	17,597
Total assets	$28,202	$39,224
Liabilities and Stockholders' Equity		
Current liabilities:		
Notes payable	$ 0	$ 8,708
Trust accounts	7,840	8,226
Other current liabilities	75	0
Total current liabilities	$ 7,915	$16,934
Long-term notes	15,783	11,979
Total liabilities	$23,698	$28,913
Stockholders' equity:		
Common stock	5,390	5,390
Retained earnings	(886)	4,921
Total stockholders' equity	4,504	10,311
Total liabilities and stockholders' equity	$28,202	$39,224

reflecting recent costs of expanding and remodeling the office interior. There is no separate accounting classification for directors' accounts. These balances are included in cash and retained earnings. Total equity ownership is relatively low and has eroded since the start-up when each owner invested $2,600 in common stock plus $1,500 in a director's account.

As noted earlier, profit taking by the owners is provided through commission income based on their individual abilities as salespeople, with only minimal contributions toward coverage of expenses. Nevertheless, West Shores has shown a profit in two of the last five years. In FY 1987, net income before federal taxes reached $8,277, for a 21 percent return on total assets (see Exhibit 5). The company experiences below-industry average costs relative to income for rent, maintenance and operation of the office, salaries, advertising, telephone, and legal and accounting expense. If West Shores' outlays in these categories were at industry averages as a percent of revenue, 1987 would not have been profitable.

Bookkeeping was essentially limited to keeping track of cash receipts and disbursements. The secretary maintained a check register and transferred data on

Exhibit 5 WEST SHORES' INCOME STATEMENT—1987	
Commissions and fees	$295,635
Rents	1,224
Total receipts	$296,859
Commissions paid	191,535
Advertising	20,321
Selling costs	14,721
Referral fees	2,981
Cost of goods sold	$229,558
Salaries	12,448
Repairs	1,278
Rent	8,442
Taxes	6,782
Interest	2,896
Contributions	408
Depreciation and amortization	3,351
Office expense	3,392
Janitorial expense	962
Dues and subscriptions	4,576
Phone	5,997
Utilities	2,315
Computer lease	1,684
Legal and accounting expense	3,268
Miscellaneous expense	1,225
General and administrative expense	$ 59,024
Net taxable income	$ 8,277

deposits and checks written to a worksheet at the end of each month for reconciliation. A CPA prepared the federal income tax returns at the end of each fiscal year. Budgets were not used. Decisions to expend additional funds or to cut back on expenses were made by the broker or other owners.

GROWTH OPTIONS

Individually, several owners have given informal consideration to avenues of growth. Although expansion is talked about from time to time, there is no consensus on the direction it should take or even that the company should grow at all.

The means of expansion that have been suggested are opening offices at other county locations, offering appraisal service, selling insurance to buyers, and providing an escrow service. All are tied to real estate sales, although in the case of residential and commercial property insurance, the only connection is that insurance coverage is needed on newly acquired properties.

Opening additional offices has been advocated because it would allow West Shores to capitalize on its expertise at listing and selling real estate. Appraisal and escrow services were seen as providing an advantage of a wider line of services to sellers and buyers. Similarly, insurance for the property buyer would widen the line of services available. The dollar investment, an important consideration to the owners, is low for all four options. The two most costly options would be branch offices (due to the cost of rent, improvements, computer, and phone) and escrow services (due to bonding and licensing fees). Appraisal, escrow, and insurance would each require the acquisition of new skills and, in the case of escrow and insurance services, on-premise availability of the qualified personnel during business hours.

THE CHALLENGE

Having completed his review of the local real estate market environment, West Shores' operations, and the company's financial performance, George Watkins was contemplating how he should go about recommending a course of action. He recognized that some owners appeared satisfied with the status quo while others were less satisfied. He was also concerned that several of the owners seemed to have already made up their minds about what should be done. For instance, Watkins was sure that Larry Proctor favored expanding into a branch office while Howard Daley, the broker, favored offering escrow and appraisal services.

With these thoughts in mind, Watkins posed the question to himself, "Which changes can I recommend that will make a meaningful improvement and be acceptable to this group of owners, and how can I sell them?"

CARMIKE CINEMAS, INC.*

In 1982 Fuqua Industries, Inc., sold Martin Theaters for $25 million. The new owners were Carmike, Inc., a private Georgia company owned by the Patrick family and a New York investment company. At the time of the divestiture Martin was the seventh largest U.S. theater circuit and had been a Fuqua subsidiary for over 12 years.

In early 1986 Martin Theaters, now renamed Carmike Cinemas, was headed by Chairman of the Board Carl Patrick and his son Mike Patrick, president. The company faced numerous challenges including difficult industry conditions and continuing capital requirements. In addition, the Patricks were considering taking the company public.

HISTORY OF THE COMPANY

Originally Carmike Cinemas was the Martin Theaters circuit founded in 1912. C. L. Patrick, the company's chairman of the board, joined Martin Theaters in 1945, and became a director and its general manager in 1948. Martin Theaters was acquired by Fuqua Industries, Inc., in 1969. Patrick served as president of Fuqua from 1970 to 1978 and as vice chairman of the board of directors of Fuqua from 1978 to 1982. The Patrick family and a limited number of investors acquired Martin Theaters in April 1982 in a leveraged buy-out for $20 million in cash and a 10 percent note in the principal amount of $5 million.

In 1986 the company was the fifth largest motion picture exhibitor in the United States and, in the South, the leading exhibitor in the number of theaters and screens operated. The company operated 156 theaters with an aggregate of 436 screens located in 94 cities in 11 southern states with a total seating capacity of 125,758. (See Exhibits 1 and 2.) All but 22 theaters were multiscreen. Most of Carmike's screens were located in smaller communities, typically with populations of 40,000 to 100,000 people, where the company was the sole or leading exhibitor. The company was the sole operator of motion picture theaters in 55 percent of the cities in which it operated, including Montgomery, Alabama; Albany, Georgia; and Longview, Texas. The company's screens constituted a majority of the screens operated in another 22 percent of such cities, including Nashville and Chattanooga in Tennessee and Columbus, Georgia.

Approximately 95 percent of the company's screens were in multiscreen theaters, with over 62 percent in theaters having three or more screens. The company had an average of 2.79 screens per theater. The company's strategy was

* Prepared by Professor Marilyn L. Taylor, University of Kansas. The research for the case was partially supported by the University of Kansas, School of Business Research Fund provided by the Fourth National Bank and Trust Company, Wichita, Kansas.

Exhibit 1 CARMIKE CINEMAS, INC.

	Screens per theater							Percent of total screens
	1	2	3	4	5	6–8	Total	
Alabama	1	16	9	12	0	15	53	12.2%
Florida	1	0	3	0	0	0	4	0.9
Georgia	3	12	15	4	10	16	60	13.8
Kentucky	0	2	0	4	5	6	17	3.9
New Mexico	0	2	0	0	0	0	2	0.4
North Carolina	0	28	9	4	0	0	41	9.4
Oklahoma	9	24	3	12	10	18	76	17.4
South Carolina	0	10	6	0	0	0	16	3.7
Tennessee	6	24	12	32	0	18	92	21.1
Texas	2	16	3	28	0	18	67	15.4
Virginia	0	8	0	0	0	0	4	1.8
Total	22	142	60	96	25	91	436	100.0%
Percent of total screens	5.0%	32.6%	13.8%	22.0%	5.7%	20.9%	100.0%	

Exhibit 2 CARMIKE CINEMAS, INC. THEATER LOCATIONS

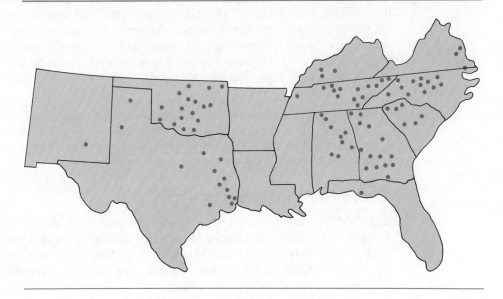

designed to maximize utilization of theater facilities and enhance operating effi-ciencies. In the fiscal year ending March 27, 1986, aggregate attendance at the company's theaters was approximately 15.3 million people.

The company owned 37 of its 156 theaters and leased 78. The land under 30 of its theaters was also leased. In addition, Carmike shared an ownership or lease-hold interest in 11 of its theaters with various unrelated third parties.

At the time of Carmike's acquisition of Martin Theaters, the circuit had 265 screens (excluding 26 drive-in theater screens) in 128 theaters. The company acquired or constructed an additional 215 screens and closed or disposed of 44 screens. The following table describes the scope of the company's theater opera-tions at the indicated dates:

Date	Theaters	Screens
March 25, 1982	128	265
March 31, 1983	126	283
March 29, 1984	158	375
March 28, 1985	160	407
March 27, 1986	156	415

The locations of the company's theaters are indicated in Exhibit 2.

THE POST-DIVESTITURE PERIOD

Even though financing arrangements for purchasing Martin Theaters were very favorable, the purchase of the theaters was highly leveraged, as can be seen from the financial statements in Exhibit 3. Early efforts were directed toward improv-ing the company's cash flow to reduce the debt. At the same time the company had significant capital improvement requirements. To make the venture viable, the Patricks undertook a number of changes in operations. Success was by no means assured, as Mike Patrick explained:

> When we bought Martin, Martin was going downhill. It looked bad. And I want you to know that it looked pretty bad for us for a while. I mean it really did. For a while there we were asking ourselves, "Why are we in this mess?" Not only were we leveraged 100 percent, but we realized that we had to spend somewhere in the neighborhood of $25 million more to renew the company.

Streamlining the Organization

Mike Patrick had first worked in Martin Theaters as a high school student in Columbus, Georgia, and later in Atlanta as a student at Georgia State. Still later, back in Columbus, he worked at Martin while he finished his studies in economics at Columbus College. He explained these time periods in his life and how he became acquainted with the company:

Exhibit 3 CARMIKE CINEMAS, INC. (in thousands, except per share data)

	Fiscal years ended				
	March 25, 1982	March 31, 1983	March 29, 1984	March 28, 1985	March 27, 1986
Income Statement Data					
Revenues:					
Admissions	$33,622	$40,077	$43,778	$49,040	$42,828
Concessions and other	13,595	15,490	16,886	19,917	18,150
	47,217	55,567	60,664	68,957	60,978
Costs and expenses:					
Cost of operations (exclusive of concession merchandise)	36,436	39,981	44,760	50,267	45,902
Cost of concession merchandise	2,695	2,703	3,117	3,566	3,004
General and administrative	2,522	2,878	3,008	2,702	2,760
Depreciation and amortization	2,348	1,964	2,868	3,140	3,385
	44,001	47,526	53,753	59,675	55,051
Operating income	3,216	8,041	6,911	9,282	5,927
Interest expense	380	2,569	2,703	2,337	2,018
Income before income taxes	2,836	5,472	4,208	6,945	3,909
Income taxes	1,323	2,702	1,615	3,054	1,745
Net income	$ 1,513	$ 2,770	$ 2,593	$ 3,891	$ 2,164
Earnings per common share	—	$ .65	$ .61	$ .92	$ .51
Weighted average common shares outstanding	—	4,200	4,200	4,200	4,200
Balance Sheet Data (at end of period)					
Cash and cash equivalents	$(1,317)	$ 433	$ 767	$ 770	$ 786
Total assets	34,742	27,754	35,324	34,953	40,665
Total long-term debt	3,656	18,853	22,125	16,969	18,843
Redeemable preferred stock	—	405	405	405	405
Common shareholders' equity	27,752	2,829	5,382	9,233	11,357

Movie theaters was the only business in which I really wanted to work . . . it's a fun business. If you are in construction, no one cares about your business. But if you tell someone that you are in the theater business, then everybody has seen a movie. Everyone has something they want to talk about. So it's an entertaining industry. Plus when I got into it, I was in the night end of it. I wasn't into administrative. So I got captured, as I called it. If you have never worked at night, then you don't understand. I really went to work at 8 AM and got off at 10 AM and then went back at 2 PM and got off at 11 PM at night. So your whole group of friends is a total flip-flop. You have nighttime friends. Before you know it, you are trapped into this life. All your friends work at night. So your job becomes a little more important to you because that's where you spend all your time. Working in a theater . . . is a lot of fun. It really is, especially when you are 19 and you get to handle the cash. A theater is a cash business.

My father was president of Martin. In 1970 he became president of Fuqua and moved to Atlanta. My father wanted to sell the house in Columbus and my mother did not want to. I was very homesick for Columbus. . . . So I said, "I will go to Columbus College and I will live in the house." I moved back here in the summer of 1970 and worked in the accounting department because I wanted to understand the reports, why I filled out all these forms, and where they went. I learned then that the treasurer of the accounting department did not understand the paper flow at all.

The treasurer had been "sort of in the right place at the right time . . . when the previous treasurer, a brilliant man" had a stroke in 1969. When Carl Patrick moved to Atlanta in 1970 as president of the parent company Fuqua, the newly appointed Martin president was "good in real estate but very poor in accounting."

When Carmike purchased Martin Theaters in early 1982, Mike Patrick became president. He explained the advantage of working so long in the company:

> I had done every job in this company except that of Marion Jones, our attorney. But my brother is an attorney, so I have someone in the family to talk to if I have a question. No one can put one over on me . . . I've fired them too, and I want to tell you something—I do my own firing . . . and firing a man who is incompetent when he doesn't know it is hard. He breaks down because he thinks he's good. When I first became president there was a family member who had to go. The other management noticed that.

In considering the purchase of Martin, Mike Patrick had described the firm to his father as "fat." Mike Patrick described what he did after purchase of the firm:

> It appeared that each layer of management got rid of their responsibilities to the next echelon down. For example, I could not figure out what the president, Sam Fowler (Ron Baldwin's successor) did . . . I kept looking at management trying to figure out what they did. I sort of took an approach like you call zero budgeting. Instead of saying my budget was $40,000 last year and I need 10 percent more this year, I required that an individual had to justify everything he did. For example, there is now only one person in our financial department. The young man in there makes less than the guy that had the job as vice president of finance three years ago and the current guy does not have a subordinate. The advertising department went from a senior vice president level to a clerk. You are talking about the difference between $80,000 and a $19,000 salary.
>
> When we got hold of the company, we let the president, the financial vice president, and the senior vice president go. At the same time film people retired because they were over 65. All I know is, everyone must answer and be responsible for everything they spend. They can't come to me and say "Well, we've done it every year this way." Since the purchase we have become more and more efficient each year.
>
> So I have streamlined the organization tremendously. When we got Martin, Martin had 2,100 employees. Since then we bought a circuit called Video out in Oklahoma. They had 900 employees. Today I have 1,600 employees. Let me double check that number. As of October 31, I had 1,687 and the year before I had 1,607. So I actually have 80 more employees than I had last year. But when I got the company, it had 2,100 and the other company had 900.

Approximately 75 percent of the employees were paid minimum wage. About 8 percent of the employees were in a managerial capacity and the company was totally nonunion. Employee relationships were generally good. Initially, however, there were difficulties. Mike Patrick recalled the initial time period:

Management was not well disciplined when we came into Martin. I had to almost totally clean house: I eliminated all of top management but it took about six months to get second-level management to where it felt secure and had a more aggressive attitude. I call it a predator attitude. But that first year we had some great hits, such as *E.T.* We did so well that first year breaking all previous records so that the management team, even though it was new, became really confident— maybe too confident. Today they don't believe we can lose. Here's a list of the directors and key employees. (See Exhibit 4.)

The company also implemented improved technology to trim the number of employees. Mike Patrick explained what happened in one city when the firm switched to totally automated projection booths:

Exhibit 4 CARMIKE CINEMAS, INC. (backgrounds of directors, officers, and key employees)

C. L. Patrick (61) has served as chairman of the board of directors since April 1982. He joined the company in 1945, became its general manager in 1948, and served as president of the company from 1969 to 1970. He served as president of Fuqua from 1970 to 1978, and as vice chairman of the board of directors of Fuqua from 1978 to 1982. Patrick is a director of Columbus (Georgia) Bank & Trust Company and Burnham Service Corporation.

Michael W. Patrick (36) has served as president of the company since October 1981 and as a director of the company since April 1982. He joined the company in 1970 and served in operational, film booking, and buying capacities prior to becoming president.

Carl L. Patrick, Jr. (39) has served as a director of the company since April 1982. He was the director of taxes for the Atlanta, Georgia, office of Arthur Young & Co. from October 1984 to September 1986, and is currently self-employed. Previously, he was a certified public accountant with Arthur Andersen & Co. from 1976 to October 1984.

John W. Jordan II (38) has been a director of the company since April 1982. He is a cofounder and managing partner of The Jordan Company, which was founded in 1982, and a managing partner of Jordan/Zalaznick Capital Company. From 1973 until 1982, he was vice president at Carl Marks & Company, a New York investment banking company. Jordan is a director of Bench Craft, Inc., and Leucadia National Corporation, as well as the companies in which The Jordan Company holds investments. Jordan is a director and executive officer of a privately held company which in November 1985 filed for protection under Chapter 11 of the Federal Bankruptcy Code.

Carl E. Sanders (60) has been a director of the company since April 1982. He is engaged in the private practice of law as chief partner of Troutman, Sanders, Lockerman & Ashmore, an Atlanta, Georgia, law firm. Sanders is a director and chairman of the board of First Georgia Bank, and a director of First Railroad & Banking Company of Georgia, Fuqua Industries, Inc., Advanced Telecommunications, Inc., and Healthdyne, Inc.

David W. Zalaznick (32) has served as a director of the company since April 1982. He is a cofounder and general partner of The Jordan Company, and a managing partner of Jordan/Zalaznick Capital Company. From 1978 to 1980, he worked as an investment banker with Merrill Lynch White Weld Capital Markets Group, and from 1980 until the formation of The Jordan Company in 1982, Zalaznick was a vice president of Carl Marks & Company, a New York investment banking company. Zalaznick is a director of Bench Craft, Inc. as well as the companies in which The Jordan Company holds investments. He is a director and executive officer of a privately held company which in November 1985 filed for protection under Chapter 11 of the Federal Bankruptcy Code.

John O. Barwick III (36) joined the company as controller in July 1977 and was elected treasurer in August 1981. In August 1982 he became vice president-finance of the company. Prior to joining the company, Barwick was an accountant with the accounting firm of Ernst & Whinney from 1973 to 1977.

Anthony J. Rhead (45) joined the company in June 1981 as manager of the film office in Charlotte, North Carolina. Since July 1983, Rhead has been vice president-film of the company. Prior to joining the company he worked as a film booker for Plitt Theatres from 1973 to 1981.

Lloyd E. Reddish (58) has been employed by the company since 1948. He served as a district manager from 1971 to 1982 and as eastern division manager from 1982 to 1984, when he was elected to his present position as vice president-general manager.

Marion Nelson Jones (39) joined the company as its general counsel in December 1984 and was elected secretary of the company in March 1985. Prior to joining the company, Jones was a partner in the law firm of Evert & Jones in Columbus, Georgia, from 1979 to 1984.

I called our attorney in and I asked him, "What is the recourse?" He said, "You must reinstate them and pay them the back pay." I said, "You mean there is no million dollar fine?" He replied "No, you just got to worry about that." He went on to ask, "Well, why are you going to get rid of them?" I said, "There is equipment for showing movies that will work very similar to an eight-track tape player." And he says, "Well, you can do it."

The city had a code which said to be a projectionist you must take a test from the electrical board to be certified. That law was put in about 1913 because back in the old days, they didn't have light bulbs. You used two carbon arcs and it was a safety issue because back then film was made out of something that burned. That was before my time that film burned like that and you had a fire in the lamp house. Now we have Zenith bulbs. The projectionists hadn't gone and gotten their cards from the electrical board for years. But the rule was on the books. So I figured the only problem we had was the city. As soon as we fired projectionists, they went to the council and had the police raid my theater. I sued the City of Nashville. . . . In the meantime we sent an engineer from Columbus up and started teaching all our managers how to pass the test. As they began to pass the board's test, it became a moot question.

Martin had already leased and installed all the needed equipment except an automatic lens turn. Its cost of $15,000 per projector was not justified since it took only a few seconds to change the lens. The new equipment made it possible to eliminate the position of projectionist. Patrick explained how he was able to get the theater managers to cooperate:

I told our managers that I would give them a raise consisting of 40 percent of whatever the projectionist had made. So all of a sudden the manager went from being against the program to where I got a flood of letters from managers saying, "I'm now trained. Fire my projectionist."

Improving Theater Profitability

At the time they purchased the Martin Theater circuit, the Patricks were well aware that some of the theaters were losing money and that many of Martin's facilities were quickly being outmoded. A 1981 consulting report on Martin underscored that during the 1970s Martin had not aggressively moved to multiplexing. In addition, one of the previous presidents had put a number of theaters into "B-locations" where there were "great leases . . . but the theaters were off the beaten track." Mike Patrick explained his approach for handling the situation:

I looked at all the markets we were in, the big markets where the money was to be made, and I said, "Here's what we will do. First, let's take the losers and make them profitable." At the time the losing theaters were a $1.2 million deficit on the bottom line. So I decided to experiment . . . Phenix City is a perfect example. I took the admission price from $3.75 to $0.99. Everybody said I was a fool. The first year it made $70,000 which I thought was a great increase over the $26,000 it had been making. The next year what happened was—the people in Phenix City are poor, very poor, blue-collar workers, but the theater is as nice as anything I have over here in Columbus—so as word of mouth got going, it kept getting better and better. Now it almost sells out every Friday, Saturday, and Sunday. And I still charge $0.99. That theater will make over $200,000 this year.

As Patrick put it, the conversion to dollar theaters was "a new concept. No one else is doing that." By 1986 Carmike had twenty 99¢ theaters. The company also offered a discount in admission prices on Tuesdays and discount ticket plans to groups. Two facilities called "Flick 'n' Foam" had restaurants and bar services in the theater. Mike Patrick commented on a theater chain he was considering buying and converting to 99¢ theaters with multiplex screens:

> I'm looking at a circuit of theaters in a major metropolitan area. Now the owner hasn't told me that it is for sale yet. He wants me to make him an offer and I won't do it. I want him to make me the first offer. He has no new facilities. All his theaters are twins except one and that's a triple. He's getting killed. A large chain is coming against him with a twelve-plex. He's located all around the metro area and he's getting killed. He had that town for years and now he's almost knocked out of it. His circuit is going to be worthless. I've been up there. There are no 99¢ or dollar theaters anywhere. His locations are good for that.

Facility Upgrading

When Martin Theaters was originally purchased, its facilities were quickly becoming outmoded. As Mike Patrick put it, "We were basically noncompetitive . . . we were just getting hit left and right in our big markets . . . the biggest thing we had was a twin and we had competitors dropping four and six-plexes on us." One reason for the earlier reticence was the tendency to put emphasis on the number of theaters rather than screens. In addition, management of the theater company, although not so required by the parent company, had managed the circuit for its cash flow. Patrick explained, "Ron [Baldwin] really never understood working for a $2 billion company. He still managed the firm as though it were privately owned."

By the early 80s the lack of capital replacement began to tell on the firm. Mike Patrick explained:

> Oh, we were just outclassed everywhere you went. Ron Baldwin told me that Columbus Square was doomed. I made it an eight-plex. With our nice theater, the Peachtree, I added one screen but I didn't have any more room. But I took the theater no one liked and made it an eight-plex. It is one of the most profitable theaters we have today.

New theaters, either replacements or additions, were undertaken usually through build, sale, and leaseback arrangements. Carl Patrick explained that in 1985 the theaters were about 75 percent leased and about 25 percent company owned. Carmike gave close attention to cost control in construction as Mike Patrick explained:

> Under Fuqua, Martin usually owned the theater. In some instances the land was also owned; in others the company had a ground lease. Since theaters were basically the same from one site to another, the cost of construction of the building was fairly standardized once the site, or pad, was ready.

Mike Patrick built his first theater in 1982 at a cost of $26 per square foot. At the time the usual price was $31. He explained that even his insurance company had questioned him when he turned in his replacement cost estimate. To reduce his costs Mike Patrick had examined every element of cost. Initially the Patricks worked with the E&W architectural firm as Martin Theaters had done for years. Mike Patrick explained that their costs were so favorable that other theater companies began to use E&W. Eventually costs went up. In 1985 Mike employed a firm of recent University of Alabama graduates to be the architects on a new theater in Georgia.

Costs were also carefully controlled when a shopping center firm built a theater for Carmike to lease. The lease specified that if construction costs exceeded a certain amount, Carmike had the option of building the theater. Without that specification there was, as Mike Patrick explained, no incentive for the development firm to contain costs. Carmike's lease payment was based on a return on investment to the development firm. On a recent theater the estimated costs came in at $39 per square foot versus the $41 per square foot that the lease specified. Mike Patrick convinced the development company to use one of his experienced contractors to reduce the $39 per square foot cost.

Zone Strategy

Considering the totality of activity in a zone is critical. Mike Patrick explained what happened over a period of two years in one major metropolitan area.[1]

> This city has a river which divides it in two. There is only one main bridge and so there are automatically two zones. There is a third zone which is somewhat isolated. When we first bought Martin there were seven theaters and 14 screens. They were as follows:

	Martin	Competition
Singles	1	1
Twins	3	
Triples	1	1

> A strong competitor came into Zone 1 and built a six-plex against me. Let me tell you what happened in that zone. I leased land, built a six-plex theater, and did a sale leaseback. I built the six-plex here right off one of the two shopping centers. I leased the equipment and I leased the building. I actually have no investment. Last year that theater made $79,000. Think about the return you have with no investment.
>
> I took one of the single theaters and put a wall down the middle of it. That cost me $30,000. I added an auditorium to a triple. Both of these theaters are near the competitor's six-plex. Now it's six—four here and two here. So that is six against his six. So now I have 12 screens in Zone 1. No one else can come in. My competitor has no advantage over me in negotiations with Warner Brothers and Paramount. In fact, I have an advantage over him. He's only here in one location and I am in three.

[1] A zone was considered a natural geographic division within a city.

In the other zone I took a twin and added three auditoriums. Then I took a triple theater and made it a dollar house, 99¢ discount. . . . It was way off the beaten track, way off. So I had eight screens against the competitor theaters. There was an opposition single screen, but he closed. We basically had 20 screens in the two zones.

If you are playing *Rocky,* you can sell three prints to this town. If you carefully choose your theaters where you show it, you can make a lot more money. That's something the previous president [of Martin] never understood.

EXPANSION

In May 1983 Carmike acquired the outstanding stock of Video Independent Theaters, Inc. The purchase price included $1.1 million cash and $2.7 million in a note. The note was at 11 percent, payable in three equal installments. Mike Patrick talked about the acquisition:

During the 1970s Martin had not been aggressive. In our industry if you are not on the attack you are being attacked. Then you are subject to what the industry does. We believe in making things happen.

Video was owned by a company which had bought Video for its cable rights. In the mid 1970s the management was killed in an air crash. I went up and talked to the guy in charge. He told me the parent company wasn't interested in theaters.

The circuit had a lot of singles and a lot of profitable drive-ins. We borrowed $1 million as a down payment and the parent accepted a note for the remainder due in three equal yearly installments.

We immediately looked at all the drive-ins and sold two drive-ins for about $1.5 million. So immediately we paid back the down payment. We planned to use the cash flow to meet the installment payments and the depreciation to rebuild the circuit. Today Video is completely paid for.

In some of the towns we went into a tremendous aggressive buying program for film which was very successful. In another we bought out an independent who was building a five-plex. In others we converted twins into four-plexes. We closed singles and in some instances overbuilt with four, five, or six-plexes. As a result, our revenue per screen is low.

In one town we went in with a new six-plex which cost $620,000. We had used basic cement block construction and furnished the facility beautifully. An independent had put in a four-plex, about the same size facility, which had cost $1.1 million. A large circuit also had a twin. I attacked with a six-plex during a time when the state economy was down. In addition, there were a lot of bad pictures. The two companies really beat each other up during the period bidding up what pictures were available. The independent went under. The circuit was bought by a larger company which wants to concentrate on larger cities. They've offered us their twin. We'll pick up the other theater from the bank.

Control Systems

The company also put considerable emphasis on budgeting and cost control. As Mike Patrick explained, "I was brought up on theater P&L's." The systems he set in place for Carmike theaters were straightforward. Every theater had what Patrick called "a PL . . . I call them a Profit or Loss Statement." Results came across Patrick's desk monthly; results for the theaters were printed out in descending order of amount of profit generated for that month. No overhead was charged to the theaters. As Patrick explained, "if you can charge something to an overhead (account), then no one cares, no one is responsible." Rather, a monthly statement of expenses was generated for each administrative department. Mike Patrick explained his approach:

> I used something like zero budgeting on every department. For example, here's the Martin Building. It cost me $18,700 for the month. The report for the Martin Building even has every person's name . . . What they made last year, what they made this year, what they made current month, every expense they have . . . I know what my dad's office cost me each month and mine also.

Every department head received a recap each week. Patrick noted that in a recent weekly report he had a charge for $2,000 for new theater passes reading Carmike instead of Martin. Charges for business lunches appeared on the statement of the person who signed the bill. Patrick checked the reports and required explanations for anything out of line. Theater expenses also received close scrutiny, as he explained:

> Then I go a step beyond that. All district managers have a pet peeve. They all want their facilities to look brand new. You can write them letters, you can swear, you can cuss. It makes no difference. They are in that theater and that's the only thing they see. It's their world. They want new carpet every week. They want a new roof every week. They want a new projector and a new ticket machine every week . . . the government says you have to capitalize (but) I hate to capitalize on expense. If the air conditioning breaks, you capitalize it. Horse feathers. I wrote the check for $18,000. The money is gone. Now I give every district manager a repair report. It shows anything charged to repairs. Yes, I could probably accomplish the same thing with a cash flow statement, but they wouldn't understand it.

Managing the Theaters

The company did not have a policy discouraging nepotism. Indeed, Mike Patrick encouraged the hiring of family. Especially in smaller towns where there might be several family members in visible positions, hiring family was a deterrent to theft. As Mike Patrick explained:

> I will let them hire family for two reasons: One, they don't want to quit me. They're married to me as much as they are the family. Second, you get people who just would not steal. They have more to lose than just the job. None of the family will steal from me because it would have a direct bearing on the father, the uncle, the whole family. I am in a lot of little towns and in a small town a son is either going to work on a farm, a grocery store, a filling station, or a theater, cause there is no industry there. The cleanest job in town is the theater manager. Also, in a small town we allow the manager to look like he owns the theater. Cause I don't go in and act like "Here's the boss," and all that.
>
> Theater managers are paid straight salary. Under Fuqua ownership the manager's salary was linked to theater performance. But, we changed that. Theater managers don't make the theater profit; the movie does. Theater managers used to

select the movies. But now they don't have anything to do with it. I am the only theater chain in the United States in which the booking and buying for the circuit is done by computer from right here. This computer on my desk is hooked to Atlanta and Dallas which are my two booking offices.

Mike Patrick had hired both of the present booking managers after the previous incumbents retired. He explained how one came to work for Carmike:

Let me tell you how I got Tony Rhead. Tony Rhead was the biggest SOB I went against. He was the booker for Chattanooga. He booked the circuit that was the best in town. He used to give me fits. And I used to spend more time trying to figure out how to get prints away from him than anybody else. So what did I do? I hired him. Rhead made $19,000 a year working for a competitor and he makes $65,000 working for me. That's a lot of difference.

Planning

The orientation under Martin management in the 1970s had been a systemwide operations approach. Mike Patrick's approach to theater location and number of screens was zone by zone and theater by theater.

The planning system for booking films was set up so that past, current, and future bookings could be called up by theater, zone, or film. In addition, competitor's bookings were also available. The system allowed interaction between home office and the two booking offices.

The Outlook in 1986

As the 1985 fiscal year came to a close, Carmike, like much of the industry, faced disappointing year-end results. Part of the problem was attributed to the number of executive turnovers in the movie production companies. Patrick explained:

A number of production executives changed jobs within a 90-day period. That meant that production stopped. Production is like developing a shopping center. It takes 18 months from the time you decide to do it to the time it opens. This year is off because there were no pictures out there. I believe that it will get better. . . . (however) *Rocky IV* has just come out so we will end the year on an upbeat.

The industry faced a number of challenges that affected the company. Lack of films was a negative factor. However, the increase in ancillary markets (movies shown on TV and home VCRs) was viewed as a positive factor; as Patrick explained:

By 1979–80 the ancillary market became very big. I understand the ancillary market is now about $3 billion and our side is $4 billion . . . (but) I talked to a man in Home Box Office when he first started. He told me that they could not figure a way to sell a movie on its first run at all. If it was a bad movie, he couldn't give it away. If it was a good movie, he had all the attendance watching it he needed. He told me, "Mike, I want you to do better every year. The more blockbusters you get, the more demand I have. And if you get, *Who Shot Mary?* and it dies in your theater, no one will watch it on Home Box Office.'' The theater is where you go to preview a movie. That establishes the value. I realized then that CBS will pay more for a big movie than they will a lousy one, so anything that comes through the tube is no problem with me. I love it because . . . (the revenues) help create more new movies.

A setback caused by the Justice Department's decision on the right of first sale threatened loss of expected revenue to producers and distributors. In addition, an increase in films might be offset by the unabated increase in the number of screens. However, the Patricks did not, as did others, foresee the demise of the movie theater. Moreover, Mike Patrick especially felt that the difficult times offered opportunities to those who were prepared:

There is more opportunity in bad times than in good times. The reason is that no one wants to sell when business is good and if they do the multiples are too high. So you want to buy when business is bad (and). . . . You got to plan for those times.

I have to know where my capital is. I run this company through this book. This is every financial thing you want to know about Carmike Cinemas—construction coming up, everything we are going to spend, source of cash, where it's going to go, everything. One of the critical things we are thinking about is how to expand. I know that if business goes bad, within 90 days, three or four more circuits are going to come up for sale. I must be in a position to buy them and I must have the knowledge to do it with. I will not bet the store on any deal.

One of those opportunities was outside the theater industry:

Our new office building is 100 percent financed with an Industrial Revenue 20-year bond issue. In case the theater business goes bad, I want to own an asset that is not a theater.

NATIONAL WESTMINSTER BANK USA*

When Bill Knowles, then an executive vice president at Bankers Trust in New York, was first called by a corporate headhunter in 1981 with an offer to become the chief executive officer (CEO) of National Bank of North America (NBNA), Knowles said he wasn't interested. Two years earlier, NBNA had been acquired by National Westminster Bank Group, a London-based international financial institution with assets of more than $110 billion. NBNA was the result of more than 20 mergers and acquisitions in the 1950s and 60s, structured around Meadow Brook National Bank, a well-run bank that had built a strong presence on Long Island and expanded into New York City and Westchester. However, over a period of many years, NBNA was reputed to have become bureaucratic, depersonalized, and lacking in direction.

Knowles' initial response had no doubt been influenced by the fact that NBNA had been known to be a marginal bank in the very competitive New York marketplace. No doubt his hesitation was reinforced by his strong roots in Bankers Trust, where he was well compensated, recognized as successful, and had as secure a career position as one could ask for. Still, Knowles was intrigued by NBNA's need for strategic planning and cultural redirection, and understood that its new parent bank would be willing to give him a relatively free hand and the space he needed to run things as he saw fit.

Eventually he reconsidered the offer and accepted the job, later confessing that he was also excited by the challenge of a David-and-Goliath situation: NBNA being 11th in size among New York City banks and heading for direct competition in some markets with Chase, Chemical Bank, and Citibank—the industry's giants. He had a hope, which has since become a conviction, that the bank could become a dynamic organization, a good place to work, and that it would outperform its competitors in target markets.

THE EARLY DAYS: SYSTEMS IN PLACE AND INITIAL CHANGES

In his first few months at NBNA, Knowles listened and observed. For one thing, he found himself with a lot of good people and saw some changes already under way. He also found that the bank badly needed a clear mission and a strong corporate culture. Its market needed to be defined more clearly; and from the customer's perspective, working with the bank needed to become simpler and more straightforward. The bank was run through a complex set of checks and balances, and most decisions were made by committees that met almost continuously. Its bureaucratic system allowed for little risk-taking and encouraged political behavior, while control was in the hands of the auditors and staff

---

* Prepared by Professor Charles Smith, Hofstra University.

functionaries. NatWest USA President Bob Wallace recalled some of the early problems:

> Our good officers were frustrated by rules that seemed designed to guard the bank against its own customers. Endless procedural crosschecks made it difficult to put a loan on the books. The emphasis had been on control, rather than on service, and line officers couldn't present the bank nor themselves in a positive manner. There were attitude problems. In one instance, a senior officer held up approval of a floor plan for the relocation of his division until he succeeded in adding three feet to his own office. Little kingdoms flourished. There was poor communication between groups, even when it was necessary for the conduct of business. Information was viewed as a source of power and wasn't shared freely.
>
> Clerical employees got no consideration at all. Several of us were shown the site of a processing operation. It was a room without windows, with inadequate lighting, and the paint was peeling off the walls. The officer in charge took pride that it had a low occupancy expense, and was shocked when we told him it would have to be corrected immediately. . . .
>
> Coming in late and leaving early were not causes for reprimand and counseling. Arriving late for meetings had become the standard because they never started on time anyway. There was no sense of urgency. . . .
>
> In some areas, form was more important than substance. The best example was a system purchased to track officer calls on customers. It offered many features, including grouping customers by geographic area, sales size, and the success of the calling effort. However, the bank had only bought the module that accounted for the actual number of calls made, using information from the system for employee performance reviews. It didn't take a genius to realize that what mattered was the number of calls made, rather than the results [of the calls]. The system, needless to say, got an early burial. . . .
>
> All of our contacts with the calling officers convinced us that they did not have a winning mentality. They questioned the value of bringing in new business. They assumed that if we had won the business away from another bank, it had to be tainted. There were no rewards for introducing a new relationship to the bank. . . but there were certainly penalties if something went wrong.

Nevertheless, Knowles did find some positive elements with which to work. The new ownership held to its hands-off policy and provided support and encouragement. Also, there were talented people in the organization who knew how to get things done despite the rules, and who later became valued contributors to the new culture.

Bill Knowles' first task was to describe the values and direction he felt should be operative. He prepared a detailed statement of mission and strategy he hoped would be understandable and relevant at every level in the organization. The statement identified a two-phase transition strategy, intended to first install a solid infrastructure, then build a consistently profitable and competitive bank. In a departure from the past, the bank would concentrate on clearly defined markets, rather than endeavor to be a full-service operation. The present Statement of Values and Mission is presented in Exhibit 1.

Knowles also set goals for return on assets (ROA) and return on equity (ROE) at levels that would make NatWest USA's performance comparable to its com-

Exhibit 1   NATWEST'S STATEMENT OF VALUES AND MISSION

THE NATWEST WAY:
Our Values, Mission, and Commitment to Quality

The Statement of Values

The Statement of Values provides the philosophical foundation for all we do. It is our credo, our system of fundamental beliefs.

As National Westminster Bank USA we share values that both support our Mission Statement and commit us to excellence in fulfilling the needs of our customers, the communities we serve, our parent organization, and ourselves.

Customers

Our customers are the foundation of our business. We listen to their needs and respond in a manner that is timely, straightforward, and courteous. We earn our future with them through leadership in quality and service.

Communities

The prosperity and well-being of the communities in which we live and work are fundamental to our long-term success. Therefore, we commit to serve them by providing leadership and support that enrich the overall quality of life.

Parent

The National Westminster Bank Group has entrusted us with capital and its good name. We commit to invest these resources prudently, to earn a superior return, and to work in partnership with our parent to enhance its worldwide stature.

Ourselves

We, the employees, are the strength of the bank and the source of its character. We work together to foster an open environment where trust and caring prevail. Pride and enjoyment come from commitment, leadership by example, and accomplishment. We encourage personal growth and ensure opportunity based on performance.

We recognize our individual responsibility to uphold these values, and in turn, to enhance the bank's reputation rooted in integrity, achievement, and quality.

The Mission Statement

The Mission Statement is the strategic translation of the Statement of Values. It is more specific, converting the value system into goals and programs.

Mission

As the principal banking vehicle of the NatWest Group in the United States, our mission is to serve the overall marketing and operational requirements of the group in this country. In doing so, we achieve profitable growth and an enhanced reputation.

To fulfill this mission we must continue to see ourselves not as a full-service, across-the-board competitor of the largest money-center banks in every market, but rather as a significant competitor in what we regard as our core businesses. In addition, we must continue to develop the considerable potential for synergy that exists with our parent, in international markets as well as in this country.

Customers

We are in four core businesses. In each of these core markets two fundamental precepts apply: our commitment to relationship banking and the essential responsibility of our support units to provide high-quality, low-cost service.

Consumer

In this market, an area of traditional strength, we seek a stable and increasing source of core deposits that can be invested at an acceptable spread. We are relatively well-positioned for this with a sizable branch network, including offices in some key locations in New York City and substantial coverage in the desirable suburban counties surrounding it.

We will compete not by attempting to gain market share through the introduction of product breakthroughs, but by offering superior personal service, coupled with a competitive line of both deposit and consumer credit products introduced in a timely manner.

Commercial lending and deposit responsibility for companies with sales of up to $10 million is an important element of our consumer business. Commercial business adds a significant dimension to what was formerly a purely retail approach, and is aimed at enabling us to use our branch system more efficiently.

Middle Market

The middle market continues to be one of the natural markets for NatWest USA. By our definition, it consists of companies with annual sales ranging between $10 million and $250 million, located primarily within a 100-mile radius of New York City, as well as companies on a selective basis throughout the country wherever we can serve them effectively. We compete by meeting the credit needs of customers in a responsive and flexible manner, and by bringing specialty services—particularly trust, treasury, cash management, and trade finance—to middle-market companies in a more effective way than do other major banks.

Exhibit 1 *(continued)*

Customers *(continued)*

Corporate

Together with our parent, we have developed a rational and effective way for the group to approach the enormous corporate market on a national basis. NatWest PLC is responsible for multinational companies and for servicing certain specialized-industry customers on behalf of London. Other than these, NatWest USA is responsible for the national market. We address this on a niche basis, both as to industry and geography, through our network of regional offices. Here again, our specialized support services—cash management, trust, treasury, and trade finance—play a key role in our ability to compete effectively against money-center as well as regional banks.

International

Although we will continue to service the well-established and profitable public and quasi-public sectors, our mission in international is to increasingly concentrate on activities that more directly serve the offshore needs of our domestic customer base. These are principally credit and noncredit transactions that facilitate foreign trade.

Further, we will continue to built on our strengths in correspondent banking, and from that base expand selectively into private sector lending if margins are acceptable. Our areas of particular expertise are Latin America and the Far East. In Europe, we utilize the capabilities of our parent to a greater extent. Our international strategy reflects, ir. a complementary way, our role within the worldwide coverage of the NatWest Group.

Communities

We derive business and our profits from the communities in which we operate. Therefore, we acknowledge a responsibility to invest in those communities to keep them vigorous and attractive. This goes beyond mere compliance with the Community Reinvestment Act. It involves active participation by our staff, as well as direct financial support.

Parent

Because we have been entrusted with our parent's name, we have a responsibility to enhance its reputation in all we do, as well as to achieve a superior financial return.

We expect to achieve this year—two years ahead of schedule—the 60-basis-point return on assets (ROA) goal set forth in the original 1981 Mission Statement. Our new goal is 70 basis points by 1988. In comparing our performance, we continue to regard Bank of New York, Marine Midland, and European American Bank as our peers.

Our quality effort is directly related both to achieving our new ROA goal and to enhancing the reputation of our parent.

Ourselves

The internal environment we seek, as outlined in the Statement of Values, rests on a set of strategies, policies, and programs that are fundamental in our bank:

- An upcompromising insistence on quality people.
- A pay-for-performance policy which has application bankwide as well as individually.
- A standard of excellence in communications.
- A lean organizational structure, free of redundant staff layers, to encourage individual initiative and decision making.
- A willingness by supervisors and managers to be judged on how well they foster the desired environment in their areas.

Quality Program

Quality represents the everyday expression of our value system. It is the means by which we carry out the strategies and goals set forth in the Mission Statement.

The bank's commitment to quality is thoroughgoing and long term. It is how we intend to differentiate ourselves and, at the same time, achieve a cost advantage over our competitors. In addition, customers are willing to pay a premium for high-quality services.

Customers

The everyday things we do to better serve customers are obvious, but they bear repeating. These actions apply to everyone because, even where there is not direct customer contact, everything we do is related to serving customers:

- We listen to our customers to determine their needs and then attempt to fill those needs.
- We respond in a thoughtful, professional, and timely manner.
- We deliver our products and services error free and in a consistent manner.
- We price our products and services fairly.
- We are always respectful and courteous.
- We do our work in essential staff areas as cost effectively as possible, because we invest our principal resources in customer-driven activities.

Exhibit 1 *(concluded)*

Quality Program *(continued)*

Communities

In all our community activities we seek to reflect the bank's commitment to quality and excellence while helping others.

This is a dimension of our job that goes beyond day-to-day duties. It involves community services: giving generously to United Way, donating blood, and taking leadership roles in significant community organizations.

We furnish substantial community support on the corporate level as well. Our contributions budget has grown each year and provides major funding for education, health care, community welfare, and the arts. In addition, we have chosen to direct significant portions of our corporate communications budget to sponsorship of quality arts projects.

Parent

Superior quality in everything we do is the only way to meet the dual responsibility we have to our parent of enhancing its reputation and meeting our financial goals.

High-quality work is key to enhancing the NatWest name. But it is also critical to achieving our new financial goal, because we must do this by improving margins rather than by expanding assets. Quality banking involves several things:

- Wider lending and investing spreads.
- Increased fee and service-charge income, which can be expected if we deliver quality products consistently.
- Expanded demand deposits.
- Higher credit quality, resulting in lower credit costs and fewer nonperforming loans and charge-offs.
- Reduced tax liability.

An additional element that enhances our reputation as a quality institution and ensures that we achieve our goals is consistent prudence both in the extension of credit and in our asset/liability management activities.

Ourselves

The competence, dedication, and hard work of our staff are the essential ingredients in our success. We need quality people. Therefore, we are very selective in hiring, and take training and promotion from within very seriously.

We closely monitor salary and benefit trends and seek to be fully competitive, increasing compensation levels in relation to those of our peers as the performance of the bank improves. On an individual level, we reward according to the contribution.

We have developed a variety of programs to improve communication: an expanded NewsBeam, staff and management bulletins, staff meetings, special surveys, and the like. We constantly seek new ways to increase communication at all levels of the bank.

We encourage leadership by example, creating an environment that is caring, trusting, fair, and enjoyable.

By doing quality work, each of us contributes directly to achieving the bank's goals. In the process, we also foster a stimulating work environment and enhance our individual well-being.

petitors—Irving Trust, The Bank of New York, Marine Midland, and European American Bank.

In the mission statement, Knowles emphasized the need to gain respect in the financial community; to develop first-class talent; to become more efficient and cost-conscious; to push decision making downward; and to develop group effectiveness, cooperation, and team spirit.

By identifying core businesses and setting financial goals, Knowles had set a standard by which success could be measured, and established a time frame within which the goals could be reached. These goals would put NatWest at the high end of New York banks.

Some thought the new CEO appeared overly optimistic. At a time when the only earnings on the bank's income statement were coming from tax credits, Knowles was calling for a benchmark ROA of .60 percent by 1987. The benchmark for ROA was reached in 1985—two years ahead of target—and surpassed in 1986. A comparison to 1981 when Knowles accepted the CEO post

Exhibit 2 FINANCIAL HIGHLIGHTS, NATIONAL WESTMINSTER BANK USA, 1983–1987
(in thousands)

	1987	1986	1985	1984	1983
For the year					
Net interest income	$394,125	$371,104	$336,175	$283,699	$234,878
Provision for loan losses	349,400	57,400	51,500	44,400	31,000
Noninterest income	130,109	110,020	96,187	81,494	61,745
Operating expenses	352,574	322,638	292,978	255,276	222,808
Net income (loss)	(212,008)	67,673	54,575	40,062	25,332
At year-end					
Assets	$11,539,277	$11,080,016	$9,796,328	$8,726,726	$7,470,847
Loans	8,216,356	7,363,751	6,415,038	5,679,582	4,631,661
Deposits:					
Core	6,372,288	6,174,877	5,145,869	4,642,772	3,578,957
Other	3,166,725	2,609,434	2,764,292	2,376,446	2,167,288
Equity capital	409,036	621,044	554,443	504,534	498,067

Source: 1987 Annual Report.

indicates the extent of the change—return on assets then was .22 percent.[1] A five-year financial summary is presented in Exhibit 2.

With markets well defined and staff functions altered and reduced, the bank set forth strategies to achieve new objectives. The major changes focused on two areas: developing a high-quality management team and developing a customer orientation emphasizing profitability rather than growth.

Knowles felt that a complete transformation of NatWest's internal culture was crucial to building a more customer-oriented bank. In his 1981 mission statement, he called for synergy, a less parochial focus on profit-center earnings, and the willingness of management to lead by example.

He communicated a sense of urgency, stressing that changes in corporate culture had to start at the top. Decision making was to be pushed down the line, and pleasing customers, instead of bank examiners, was underscored as paramount.

MANAGEMENT TRANSITIONS

In the 1981 statement, Knowles also tackled the sensitive issue of management personnel changes—changes necessary for more effective functioning and instilling a new culture. He felt senior management needed more qualified people, and recognized the need to go outside to find new managers. He recalls:

> I was very open with the staff about this. I said we were going to have to go outside because we were just too big a bank to be competitive without introducing additional talent. I said I would try to get it over with as quickly as possible, but

---

[1] Due to an increase in loan reserves of $295 million in 1987 (against loans to developing countries who are experiencing debt servicing problems) NatWest suffered a loss in 1987 of $212 million. Without the extraordinary item, the 1987 ROA would have been approximately .70 percent.

that I needed a window of about a year to accomplish it. At the end of the year, we were able to limit outside hires to primarily specialists, tax lawyers, and so forth.

The following was part of his public statement, excerpted from the August 1981 Statement of Mission and Strategy:

> The single most important element that will enable us to compete more effectively in the future than we have in the past is people. We have to be uncompromising in insisting on first-class talent, because if we don't have it, or grow it, we cannot move up. Neither our name nor our ownership can compensate for less than top-flight personnel who perform in a superior way. . . .
>
> As a first step, therefore, we are identifying the 50 to 60 key jobs in the organization and determining if the incumbent either is or can operate at a superior performance level. If not, changes will be made. This does not imply a cold or heavy-handed approach to people. On the contrary, we should always conduct ourselves so as to demonstrate respect and compassion in our dealings with our staff. It does mean, however, that we will be rigorous in setting goals and measuring results, and rewarding those who can do the job or making changes where results are not satisfactory. . . .
>
> Once the 50 to 60 key jobs are filled by people who meet high standards of performance as professionals and/or managers, they will serve as role models, and we will then attempt to build the organization by recruiting trainees and advancing people already here. We want to move away from the habit of going outside to fill our senior and even semisenior positions. This will have to be done for a while longer, but our goal is to "grow on our own" in time.

Building from the Top Down

The grooming of the management team became the main focus of the transition. Knowles chose to bring in outsiders for two top-level positions: one to be the bank's chief operating officer (COO), the other to be the liaison with the NatWest parent organization. As COO, he brought in Bob Wallace, who had been CEO of an Oregon bank owned by a holding company. John Gale was brought in as the liaison, and the three formed a partnership under the heading Office of the Chairman, that, according to Knowles, "is based on trust, informality and candor. . . . We've developed into a team that represents the values we wanted to see projected throughout the bank."

Knowles, Wallace, and Gale meet every Monday before their individual sector meetings and off-site at dinner every few weeks to discuss what is going on in their respective sectors.

The Office of the Chairman saw the selection of people as the key to success. They agreed that all outside hires, as well as internal promotions, had to buy into the new value system, and they have held firmly to their standards.

Wallace recalled that, in their internal process, they found outstanding people a couple of levels down in the organization, people who'd gone unrecognized before, but who were able to flourish in the changing environment.

Some jobs did have to be filled from outside, and all three members of the Office of the Chairman interviewed candidates for positions at levels of vice presidents and above. In each case, they looked for people with compatible values. Wallace describes the selection and promotion criteria:

> We want people who are team players who want to work in an atmosphere of openness and caring. We may have made some mistakes with the professional skills of people brought in, but never on their values.
>
> At every opportunity, we promoted people who would be seen by their peers as apolitical. One of the first tasks was to pick four division heads for our United States Group. We reviewed the candidates, their qualifications, and chose the candidates who hadn't run a "campaign" for the job. This and other promotions gave a clear signal that politics were out.

Developing a Customer Orientation

Selection of the management team took place simultaneously with the bank's development of competitive strategies based on customer service. Wallace was instrumental in setting the tone for this aspect of the transition:

> First, we had to get a good grip on the bank's strengths and weaknesses. We quickly concluded that the bank's senior officers should get out in the marketplace to sample our customer's attitudes, and evaluate the skill-level of our lending officers. While what follows may seem a litany of what was wrong with the bank, let me assure you that we were encouraged by the good things we found, including some excellent talent among our line officers.
>
> We found product deficiencies that put us at a competitive disadvantage. . . . And we were troubled by the lack of value placed on the contact with customers.
>
> For example, I once asked the head of one division to coordinate his calling with mine. He told me that would be easy, because he didn't call on customers. He viewed himself purely as an administrator, and he added that the bank knew that when he was hired. Unfortunately, while his statement was extreme, it was not inconsistent with the feelings of others. We had to show by example that customer contact was the most important job at the bank.
>
> The three members of the Office of the Chairman emphasized their desire to make calls on customers. At first, we would be taken on safe calls where the customer wouldn't embarrass the officer or the bank by telling stories of inadequate levels of services. But before long, there was less screening of the names we called on. We are still calling on customers wherever it will do the most good in marketing the bank. More to the point, it is (now) recognized throughout the bank that you don't graduate from customer contact. It's the most important thing we do.
>
> When we became serious about developing a customer-oriented atmosphere, changes were dramatic. It was like a dam breaking. We were literally flooded with information on why customers found us a difficult bank to deal with. On some of my early calls, I had found a key symptom of disregard for service. Officers simply did not listen to customers. Therefore, they never found out what customers wanted from the bank. Some of our officers acted as if they'd been sent in on a mission, and the customers better not get in their way. Today, one of the primary thrusts of our sales training is learning to listen. In addition, we have worked hard to change how people think about customer service. We emphasized that every-

one in the bank has customers to serve; the support people's customers are the line people, and the line people, in turn, have external customers. It took repeated emphasis, but I think today most people have their priorities in order.

Changes Slow in Coming

Somewhat ironically, a lack of products had forced the bank's officers to develop extraordinary skills in the only area they had available to them: lending. Several parts of the bank were successful, driven by the ability to outperform competitors and to structure difficult credit transactions. In the area of lending, NatWest could function effectively because it was one area where officers did not have to depend on the performance of others in the organization.

In spite of an initial euphoria, some officers thought change was slow to come. Ed McDougal, formerly a line head and now executive vice president for Human Resources, recalled that his initial enthusiasm was dampened when he saw how attempts at action and decision making were continually swamped in bureaucracy. McDougal recalls:

> I found basically four types of people in the bank at that time. There were the cynics who said, "This, too, shall pass." There were the skeptics who said, "I'm all for it, but it will never work." Both of these groups suffered from a genuine inferiority complex about NBNA. The third group was a small corps of leaders who said, "Believe it." And finally we had a bunch of supporters who said, "Why not?" Many were young, and lacked experience. But they were smart, energetic, and ambitious, and had a real can-do attitude. In my opinion, we needed to convert the skeptics and develop the can-do people.

McDougal also recalled an informal talk with Knowles that kept him from becoming too discouraged. McDougal was then at a midmanager's level, five levels down in the organization. When Knowles would drop in once in a while at NatWest's midtown headquarters, he'd ask how things were going. McDougal would express his frustrations, and Knowles would encourage him and also share his own frustrations. Once he told McDougal, "You keep pushing from the bottom, and I'll keep pushing from the top. Someday, we'll meet in the middle."

When McDougal was finally promoted to department head, he began his push. One particular frustration for him was the lack of credit approval authority at the line level. The charter for his department said that the minimum loan the department could make was $250,000, yet the largest loan anyone could approve, himself included, was $250,000. In effect, despite being solely accountable for growing a loan portfolio, McDougal or his staff couldn't make any loans without someone else's approval.

It was clear the time had come to stop focusing on just the problems and get on with the job at hand. As McDougal said:

> I was tired of hearing about our limited product line and our cumbersome credit approval process. The time had come to do business and to celebrate some victories. It was September (1982). We were in our budgeting cycle, and we put together a budget for 1983 that showed a 15 percent loan growth despite a three-

year history of no growth. Also in September, as a tangible demonstration of our confidence and resolve, we scheduled a party for November, to celebrate the victories we would have over the next two-and-a-half months. There were some skeptics, but we did have our victory party, and we had something to celebrate. In fact, our portfolio grew by over 25 percent in 1983 without sacrificing quality or profitability standards. . . .

My function at that time was to be a teacher of credit and marketing, and we tried to use mistakes as a springboard to learn, and not an excuse to punish. I saw myself as a role model, confidence builder, cheerleader, and facilitator. I learned how to use the bureaucracy to slow down the imposition of new rules, regulations, and controls, and how to avoid it to get the job done.

As slow as the process was, changes were clearly happening. Success stories began to replace complaints and the bank began to openly celebrate these successes. When a deal was completed, a senior person would make a point of saying, "Good job!" Wallace noted that people in the bank responded immediately to the much-needed praise.

A good example that change for the better was manifesting itself was seen in the way NatWest USA handled a new problem. In an effort to build volume, the bank had accepted greater domestic risks than it should have. This, on top of an emerging international debt crisis, resulted in an overall asset quality in 1983 that was not as good as had been expected. Bob Wallace noted:

> The bank had good enough credit people to deal with the situation quickly. We evaluated the problem loans, devised strategies and set out to make corrections. The plan worked, and today our asset quality is among the best of the New York banks. Best of all, it was accomplished without enormous write-offs. But solving the asset quality problem had an additional benefit. It demonstrated clearly that we were working as a team. It showed that we were more interested in solutions than in pointing the finger. It proved that we were becoming a different bank.

Exhibits 3, 4, and 5 present changes in the makeup of NWB's loan portfolio.

Flexibility was enhanced at NatWest when the authority for lending was pushed down in the organization, allowing lending departments to make loans of up to $2 million without outside approval. McDougal noted the significance of this event and some of the critical events that followed:

> No one ever believed it could happen. This was the first significant sign to the line units that the bureaucracy was in retreat. The symbolism went well beyond the actual impact. A new core of leaders had made it happen. But the biggest signpost was yet to come. The bank had waited until September 1983—until it was reasonably sure that it would show its third consecutive year of increased earnings—before taking on a name which would identify it with our parent. To celebrate the new name and our success to date, the bank held a party for the entire staff—a party complete with excellent food, music, and a 15-minute sound-and-slide show that actually had people cheering. This was not NBNA, it was NatWest USA. There was a euphoria throughout the whole bank that lasted for weeks. Even when it finally wore away, morale was at a new, higher plateau. The bank has been permanently lifted by this one gala celebration.

Anecdotes about successes increasingly replaced jokes about failure. Stories of teamwork replaced some of the legends about the idiosyncrasies of individuals.

Exhibit 3 COMPOSITION OF NATIONAL WESTMINSTER BANK'S LOAN PORTFOLIO, 1983–1987
(in thousands)

	December 31				
	1987	**1986**	**1985**	**1984**	**1983**
Domestic					
Commercial, financial, and agricultural	$5,377,938	$4,415,500	$3,630,686	$2,749,054	$1,758,653
Real estate construction	125,672	110,102	164,578	168,586	131,689
Real estate mortgage and warehouse	816,102	967,586	691,940	715,493	718,044
Installment loans to individuals	696,797	587,973	541,440	446,149	362,115
Other loans to individuals	177,576	162,174	205,899	135,214	79,793
Lease financing	29,581	21,345	23,676	23,561	4,106
Other	114,257	96,210	39,424	96,014	31,499
Total domestic . . . . : . . .	7,337,923	6,360,890	5,297,643	4,334,071	3,085,899
Foreign					
Governments and official institutions	472,009	464,163	435,079	440,823	485,695
Banks and other financial institutions	284,859	348,768	368,934	438,525	508,451
Commercial and industrial	206,477	249,645	358,018	506,332	580,391
Other	436	749	1,624	811	1,090
Total foreign	963,781	1,063,325	1,163,655	1,386,491	1,575,627
Less: Unearned income	85,348	60,464	46,260	40,980	29,865
Total loans, foreign and domestic	$8,216,356	$7,363,751	$6,415,038	$5,679,582	$4,631,661

Source: 1987 Annual Report.

Exhibit 4 CROSS-BORDER LOANS OUTSTANDING, NATIONAL WESTMINSTER BANK USA,
1985–1987 (in thousands)

	Governments and official institutions	Banks and other financial institutions	Commercial and industrial	Total
December 31, 1987				
Argentina	$ 96,313	$ 23,997	$ 13,553	$133,863
Brazil	87,579	120,901	250	208,730
Mexico	102,608	9,303	16,858	128,769
December 31, 1986				
Argentina	$ 83,976	$ 30,350	$ 12,823	$127,149
Brazil	88,167	115,799	267	204,233
Mexico	93,623	9,280	18,727	121,630
December 31, 1985				
Argentina	$ 69,223	$ 40,936	$ 10,500	$120,659
Brazil	73,827	125,706	767	200,300
France		104,771		104,771
Mexico	96,464	4,131	20,466	121,061
South Korea	40,265	63,459	22,730	126,454

The above schedule discloses cross-border outstandings (loans, acceptances, interest bearing deposits with banks, accrued interest receivable, and other interest bearing investments) due from borrowers in each foreign country where such outstandings exceed 1.00 percent of total assets.

At December 31, 1987, 1986, and 1985, countries whose total outstandings were individually between .75 and 1.00 percent of total assets are as follows.

1987—France and Japan, totaling $197.7 million.
1986—Chile, France, South Korea, and Venezuela, totaling $362.4 million.
1985—Canada, Chile, and Venezuela, totaling $267.3 million.

Source: 1987 Annual Report.

Exhibit 5 LOAN MATURITIES, NATIONAL WESTMINSTER BANK USA, 1987 (in thousands)				
		December 31, 1987		
	Total	**Due before one year**	**Due in one to five years**	**Due after five years**
Commercial, financial, agricultural and other	$5,492,195	$3,006,427	$1,887,733	$598,035
Real estate construction	125,672	33,931	85,797	5,944
Foreign	963,781	577,506	166,249	220,026
Total	6,581,648	3,617,864	2,139,779	824,005
Loans with interest-sensitive rates	6,131,510	3,518,861	1,870,741	741,908
Loans with fixed rates	450,138	99,003	269,038	82,097
Total	$6,581,648	$3,617,864	$2,139,779	$824,005

Excludes real estate mortgage and warehouse loans, loans to individuals, and lease financing loans.
Source: 1987 Annual Report.

At our victory party, we invited all branch managers to attend. Now, understand, our business customers were primarily medium-sized companies scattered over the five boroughs of New York. They used our branches to make deposits, cash checks, and bring documents. Many saw the local branch manager more often than they saw the account officer. But the branch managers were rarely thanked for their efforts. They felt that they were not appreciated. The only time they ever heard from us was when the customers felt they didn't receive the service they were entitled to. Inviting the managers to our party to thank them for their help in serving our customers seemed like a little thing at the time, but it created a bond which enhanced our ability to serve our customers.

(In addition), my predecessor had started a tradition of a quarterly profit improvement award. We (in middle-market lending) decided to give the award to an assistant branch manager who had referred us a large piece of business. The branch people were ecstatic. It was unheard of that a branch person would receive an award from another group.

The Human Resource Function

Ed McDougal was promoted in 1984 to executive vice president and head of Human Resources. With the fervor of a crusader, he took responsibility for the staff meetings, audiovisual presentations, and gala celebrations that continue to repeat over and over again the desire for change as stated in the original mission statement. McDougal's recollection of this period indicates the importance of the Human Resources Group and his role in the transition:

My first priority as head of Human Resources was to have a team. We had many people who were competent from a professional/technical point of view, but effectiveness was hampered by a lack of teamwork. It wasn't a fun place to work. I told the department heads at our first group management meeting that I had never worked in a place for very long where I didn't have a good time, and I didn't expect to start here. That was the only threat I ever issued. From then on we met regularly to discuss all issues.

One of the first major tasks of the group management was to create a strategic plan for Human Resources. In effect, we needed to create a vision of our future—a vision we all shared, and would work cooperatively to reach. We launched this planning process not through some technical preparation, but rather by spending three days together, off site, learning how to work together. Our next step was to create a statement of values and beliefs for the Human Resources Group. And it was only at this point that we began the process of creating a strategic plan. That plan served as a basis for providing increasingly higher levels of service to our customers, the employees, and managers of the bank.

From the bank's perspective, we went through the process in the spring of 1985 of creating a statement of values for the overall organization. This involved a series of meetings with teams composed of members of the Office of the Chairman, executive vice presidents, all senior vice presidents, and a representative group of eight people, male and female, black and white, vice president to secretary. The final result is a statement of values [see Exhibit 1] which spells out how it is appropriate to act within the bank. This statement of values was presented to all the employees of the organization during a series of 11 breakfasts, conducted in Westchester, New York, and Long Island. The presenters were all the senior and executive officers of the bank.

The final event which stands out in my mind is the bank's second victory celebration. Shortly after I became the head of Human Resources, Bill Knowles said we needed an occasion to have another employee party. The occasion became the launching of the bank's new quality effort. This, along with our success to date, suggested the name "Just the Beginning" parties throughout the bank. Once again, they were a rousing success and lifted the morale of almost everyone in the organization. But there is one anecdote about the "Just the Beginning" parties which I think is a fitting story to close with.

One of our division heads who managed people on off-shifts asked if we could have one of the parties other than at night when many of her people could not attend. These were employees who often felt ignored. So we held a sit-down luncheon with music and dancing, and concluded with the unveiling of a lavish dessert table. An older woman, whom I had never met before, grabbed my elbow as we walked up to the dessert table and said this reminded her of a wedding reception. Kiddingly I said, "Well, you're really our bride today." She looked at me and said, almost with tears in her eyes, "I feel like royalty." Nothing in my entire time in the bank has ever brought home to me more how people can be made to feel special.

At a conference on organizational development, in the fall of 1986, NatWest USA presented a history of its transformation process since the 1981 changeover. In closing remarks Ed McDougal and Bob Wallace expressed their perceptions of how far the bank had come. McDougal noted:

We are a successful organization. We have done it by acting in a way that is consistent with values originally outlined in our mission statement, now codified in a statement of values. The challenges ahead of us are greater than the challenges behind. But we are prepared to meet them with a formula for success. There may still be some cynics, but most of the skeptics have been converted, and the core of believers is much larger. The younger people are still mostly here, four years older, and when they see our success to date, still say, "Why not?" I report directly to Bill [Knowles], which says something about the role Human Resources plays in the organization. Bill and Bob [Wallace] had both talked to me at the time of the change. They said they were looking for someone who was practical, yet sensitive. They wanted the function to have credibility within the bank and to have a customer orientation. I also took it as the ultimate confirmation of a management style.

McDougal's views are consistent with Wallace's:

We now have an organization whose strengths are apparent. We have a marketing organization based on customer requirements and input from our own officers. Systems and operations areas now work in partnerships with line areas, because of the leadership provided by those who head these groups.

When something we put in place didn't work, it was changed. We were able to prove by example that there was not pride of authorship or a penalty for an innovation that didn't work. And people began to realize that there was more fun in accomplishing an objective than in trying to find out who to blame. We in the Office of the Chairman continue to walk around, to meet with customers and seek information wherever we can. People realize that there is no penalty for speaking their minds.

My own experience . . . [illustrates] the atmosphere. . . . When Bill [Knowles] and I were looking at whether I could make a contribution, he said he was looking for a full partner. I knew he meant that, but I also know that somebody has to run the store. Well, after five years, I can honestly say that the three of us in the Office of the Chairman have a partnership. We trust, respect, and like each other and, maybe more importantly, we feel free to disagree with each other. It's worked for us, and I think it has worked for the whole bank. We are all proud to be part of a winning team.

Summary: Some Candid Observations by the CEO

With changes apparent and financial statements that tell a story of success in many areas, there are still problems and challenges in NatWest's efforts to differentiate itself and to reach its goals. In an interview with the casewriter, Bill Knowles frankly expressed his concerns and hopes:

We're now finding that we have got to work through, but also around, the system to try to enrich the environment down below, to unleash the energies that are there. There are still supervisors who grew up in the old school, who use knowledge as power, who feel threatened, who will not permit their people to advance their careers by seeking positions elsewhere in the bank.

About bureaucracy:

What did disappear, fairly quickly, were the committees. There were committees for everything. All the executive vice presidents met to decide the salaries, the computer systems questions, real estate questions, loan questions. It was like the knights would consider everything, whether they had expertise or not in the particular thing.

What didn't go away, and what we had a couple of false starts on, was the clutter in the system. This was because of the mergers, sticking 23 banks together so quickly, and the self-protective mentality that had grown up here. It was very hierarchical.

The clutter was incredibly hard to disassemble. Those vines had grown around all the pipes and wires and furniture, and it was just impossible to pull out. We established a clutter committee to monitor the process. It's like weeding a garden; you cannot do it in 10 minutes. It takes a long time, and you have to pick the weeds out one at a time. We are still doing it, and we still have a six-part-form mentality in some places where we still cannot think simply.

The people in our organization are intelligent and honest. If you catch a dishonest person you deal with that, but you don't set up a whole mechanism to protect yourself from the odd, random event.

We tried to change the whole fundamental philosophical basis of the organization, and say, "Hey, wait a minute, why in God's name do I have to sign a form that I received a report? If I received it, I received it, and if I didn't receive it, I didn't receive it."

There are still vestiges, and they stick out more now, and we can laugh at them a little.

Dealing with the isolation of the CEO:

I deal with the isolation just by being informal and walking around; I have breakfast with the officers on all levels. We also have an endless series of excuses to get together for meetings and parties here. I mean, I have been to eight events here in the last three weeks with 50 or 60 officers, and it's rare if I don't know who they are. I walk around and try to see everybody in the nonbranch staff at Christmas, to wish them a good holiday. I probably see 2,500 to 3,000, out of the 4,500, and the executive vice presidents do, too.

On basic strategy:

This has really been the story of trying to make a bank competitive by narrowing its mission, its focus, and trying to achieve superiority in the area of commodity services by working through people. Because all services are the same in the businesses we are in. It's like insurance companies. If I asked you to identify the differences among them, you can't. Nobody could name the difference between banks either. So what we've got to do is to work very hard to take a representative sample of our society, which is our employees, and somehow to work with them in delivery of faceless services and try to do something special.

What we're doing now is having the "Executive Vice President of the Week." For a week, on a rotating basis, an executive vice president takes all the complaint calls that come into the bank, the "let-me-speak-to-the-president" calls. This means the EVP's are getting calls about their peers and about the organizations of other EVP's, and it saves complainers from being battered around by a dozen or so people before they get an answer.

The CEO's personal philosophy:

In our society, in the business sector of our society and, I'm sure, in other sectors as well, people are driven by the attractiveness, the appeal, of putting their stamp on something, or effecting a change that will be identified with them, putting their imprimatur on something. People go to work to do that—they don't go to work to earn a paycheck. There is a self-pride that says, "I did that, I was associated with that, I was on the team that installed this.'' Just so that they are a part of something that is significant. I think that's what really motivates me, but I also think it's what motivates others. And for me, putting my stamp on something, not just in profit terms but in human terms as well. I have a feeling that there is a power in the ability of a staff to produce when they are committed to doing something that makes sense to them—if they can see [the mission] is productive in terms of profit and the environment is conducive to letting them put their stamp on something worthwhile.

Then what you do is make it fun. Make it enjoyable to be in that environment. That's part of the compensation and part of the benefits. It's more style.

Work should be fun. . . . If you go out and sample 6 out of 10 people here, they'll tell you work is tough, it's not fun, but 4 will tell you yes, it's fun. There is that slice. If we can make that five next year and six the next year, we're on our way.

Whether it's NatWest or some other organization, it's important to keep in mind what that organization is there for, what you are there to do. An organization left on its own will run off in different directions, because of the natural desire to experiment and grow and change. Unless that is properly channeled all the time, it will grow in a lot of directions; all those energies need to be focused on something that you and they really want. The biggest change around here is not so much what I have done, or anyone has done. The biggest turnaround here is to see what the people are doing translated into something the marketplace values—and that is profit. Can you imagine how disheartening, how debilitating it is to work very hard and to end up in a losing enterprise? That is how this organization once was—good people working hard, and it was coming out all wrong.

When most people ask, ''What's wrong with this place?'' the answer is usually communication, teamwork. But have you ever heard of any place, any organizational system that was perfect? I think we have to work hard to keep on the track we are on now, keep at it all the time.

Exhibits 6 and 7 present NatWest's financial statements. Exhibit 8 profiles NatWest's operations as of 1988. Exhibit 9 presents a summary of recent market research done by NatWest to determine its success in differentiating its customer service and quality of banking operations from competitors'.

Exhibit 6 CONSOLIDATED STATEMENT OF OPERATIONS, NATIONAL WESTMINSTER BANK USA, 1985–1987 (in thousands)

	Year ended December 31		
	1987	**1986**	**1985**
Interest income			
Loans	$740,775	$680,964	$665,170
Investment securities			
U.S. Treasury and federal agencies	71,683	69,622	66,339
State and municipal	52,346	55,940	29,426
Other	4,464	1,247	1,100
Trading account	1,553	6,220	4,588
Deposits with banks, federal funds sold and securities purchased under agreements to resell	53,867	52,484	68,177
Total interest income	924,688	866,477	834,800
Interest expense			
Deposits	435,424	399,530	438,027
Borrowed funds	94,842	95,459	60,131
Long-term debt	297	384	467
Total interest expense	530,563	495,373	498,625
Net interest income	394,125	371,104	336,175
Provision for loan losses	349,400	57,400	51,500
Net interest income after provision for loan losses	44,725	313,704	284,675
Non interest income			
Service charges on deposit accounts	37,049	33,027	30,469
Letter of credit and acceptance fees	19,583	16,394	13,659
Credit card fees	14,897	14,933	14,252
Syndication and other loan related fees	13,740	5,481	2,715
Investment securities gains	4,926	7,890	8,762
Other	39,914	32,295	26,330
Total noninterest income	130,109	110,020	96,187
Operating expenses			
Salaries and benefits	205,074	190,390	173,725
Supplies and services	48,677	43,811	40,833
Net occupancy	33,839	30,618	26,659
Business development	24,472	18,386	17,154
Equipment	24,447	21,735	18,816
Other	16,065	17,698	15,791
Total operating expenses	352,574	322,638	292,978
Income (loss) before income taxes	(177,740)	101,086	87,884
Provision for income taxes	34,268	33,413	33,309
Net income (loss)	$(212,088)	$ 67,673	$ 54,575

Source: 1987 Annual Report.

Exhibit 7 CONSOLIDATED STATEMENT OF CONDITION, NATIONAL WESTMINSTER BANK USA, 1986–1987 (in thousands)

	December 31 1987	1986
Assets		
Cash and due from banks	$ 582,220	$ 677,574
Interest bearing deposits with banks	646,618	578,026
Investment securities		
U.S. Treasury and federal agencies	919,395	813,760
State and municipal	734,693	837,811
Other	155,648	25,867
Total (approximate market value of $1,787,723 and $1,724,036)	1,809,736	1,677,438
Trading account	44,560	95,791
Federal funds sold and securities purchased under agreements to resell	6,936	23,213
Loans, less unearned income of $85,348 and $60,464	8,216,356	7,363,751
Allowance for loan losses	(407,790)	(112,299)
Loans—net	7,808,566	7,251,452
Premises and equipment—net	236,606	235,276
Due from customers on acceptances	249,752	365,935
Other assets	154,283	175,311
Total assets	$11,539,277	$11,080,016
Liabilities and Equity Capital		
Deposits		
Demand	$ 2,114,470	$ 2,427,387
Retail savings and time	4,257,818	3,747,490
Other domestic time	1,335,644	983,570
Foreign office	1,831,081	1,625,864
Total	9,539,013	8,784,311
Borrowed funds		
Federal funds purchased	618,140	677,957
Securities sold under agreements to repurchase	263,220	177,103
Other	312,740	313,569
Total	1,194,100	1,168,629
Acceptances outstanding	252,668	372,399
Accounts payable and accrued liabilities	139,733	126,983
Long-term debt	4,727	6,650
Total liabilities	11,130,241	10,458,972
Equity capital		
Common stock, $5 par value	38,376	38,376
Authorized 7,773,867 shares; issued and outstanding 7,675,138 shares		
Surplus	238,657	238,657
Undivided profits	132,003	344,011
Total equity capital	409,036	621,044
Total liabilities and equity capital	$11,539,277	$11,080,016

Source: 1987 Annual Report.

Exhibit 8   A PROFILE OF NATWEST USA IN 1988

In early 1988, once regulatory approvals have been obtained, First Jersey will join the National Westminster Bank Group as an affiliate of a newly formed holding company, to be named National Westminster Bancorp. The other banking subsidiary will be National Westminster Bank USA, headquartered across the Hudson River in New York City.

NatWest USA: In Perspective

National Westminster Bank USA traces its origins to the charter of The First National Bank of Freeport, established in 1905, under which NatWest USA operates today. After a series of mergers, the bank became known as National Bank of North America (NBNA). In 1979 NBNA was acquired by the National Westminster Bank Group. In September 1983 the bank changed its name to National Westminster Bank USA, and in June 1984 dedicated National Westminster Bank Center, the 30-story corporate headquarters at 175 Water Street near Manhattan's South Street Seaport.

Customer Service

These operations include four lending areas (the Community Banking, New York City, Regional, and United States groups), and five support areas (the Technology & Processing, Financial & Planning, Credit Policy & Administration, Human Resources, and Administration groups). The bank's Treasury group supports the line areas and is responsible for asset and liability management, brokerage sales and services, and trading. The bank also has Marketing and Corporate Trust divisions.

NatWest USA serves its retail customers through a 135-branch network and a network of automated teller machines, called Teller Beam, in New York City, Westchester County, and Long Island. Teller Beam is part of the NYCE (New York Cash Exchange) network of automated teller machines and the nationwide CIRRUS network. NatWest USA is a founding member of NYCE, which was established in 1984.

Retail customers are also served by the bank's Consumer Credit division, which offers VISA, MasterCard and Gold MasterCard, as well as a full line of consumer credit products. Individuals whose net worth is $1 million or more may also take advantage of the personalized financial services offered by the bank's private Banking department, through offices in Manhattan and Great Neck, Long Island. This department offers opportunities for cross-selling bank products, an important aspect of doing business at NatWest USA.

NatWest USA's other specialties include lending to middle-market corporate customers in the printing, textile and apparel, diamond and jewelry, publishing and real estate industries, particularly in New York City. Nationwide, NatWest USA specializes in meeting the financial needs of the health services, media, utilities and leasing industries.

The bank also concentrates on geographic niches, lending to middle-market corporate customers in the tristate area outside of New York City. Large corporate and middle-market customers outside the tristate area are served by representative offices and an Edge Act Office in Miami. NatWest USA's international division serves the international needs of the bank's domestic customers.

Two major staff areas provide key support to the bank's lending groups. They are the Administration and Technology & Processing groups. Administration encompasses the Legal, Auditing, Loan Review, Consulting Services, and General Services divisions.

Two separate groups, Systems and Operations, were recently combined to form Technology & Processing. This restructuring was done to open the door to new opportunities and to further enhance customer service.

Community Involvement

NatWest USA encourages voluntarism, is a leading supporter of United Way and has a substantial corporate contributions program. Also, the bank has developed a far-reaching "Arts in the Community" program which, this summer, won a Presidential Citation as part of the White House Program on Private Sector Initiatives, and awards in 1985 and 1987 from Business Committee for the Arts.

Major "Arts in the Community" events have included concerts by Luciano Pavarotti and Placido Domingo, and numerous concerts in Carnegie Hall. The bank also sponsors a wide range of arts events in local communities, such as concerts by Long Island Concert Pops, American Concert Band, New Orchestra of Westchester and Brooklyn Philharmonic.

In addition to "Arts in the Community" sponsorships, other community involvement includes employee participation in walk-a-thons and other civic functions, as well as bank sponsorship of events to benefit organizations such as the American Heart Association and Special Olympics. In all, NatWest USA was involved in 107 community events in the past year.

Exhibit 8 *(concluded)*

Among the community events sponsored by the bank are several concerned with education. Through its "Outstanding Young Achiever" award program, the bank recognized and gave financial awards to outstanding seniors at 22 New York metropolitan area high schools. And, in connection with its sponsorships of PBS broadcasts, NatWest USA develops and sends teaching kits to music teachers to encourage interest in the arts among students.

During the past four quarters, as part of the NatWest USA "Speakers in Your Community" program, bank representatives have given 102 speeches on financial topics—an average of one every three working days—to business, civic and service organizations important to the bank.

The National Westminster Bank Group, headquartered in London, is among the largest, most profitable financial institutions in the world, with total assets of more than $120 billion and more than 90,000 employees worldwide. Including subsidiary companies, the group has operations in 36 countries.

Exhibit 9 THE RESULTS OF NATWEST'S MARKETING RESEARCH

The Marketing Department at NatWest USA provided research indicative of the degree to which the firm has been able to achieve its goal of differentiation via quality programs and other strategic and cultural changes. Representatives noted that the true test for NatWest USA is the degree to which any organizational changes translated into changing perceptions by customers. That is, whether customers feel that they are receiving more valuable products and information, and whether they feel confident about the bank and positive about the treatment received from it. It was observed that the types of changes that NatWest USA is seeking are very long term, and the full effects of programs implemented will have to be evaluated over a number of years into the future.

The following summaries describe the conclusions of three major studies:

The Middle Market Study

The Middle Market Study, concluded in March 1986, examined the financial behavior, needs and attitudes of middle-market companies operating nationwide, and also examined NatWest USA's competitive position within the tristate region of New York, New Jersey, and Connecticut. The middle-market study covered firms with sales between $50 and $250 million.

The middle market was dominated by manufacturing (50 percent) and wholesale trade (27 percent) businesses. The manufacturing industry was described as a "huge, attractive market, but also the most competitive market segment." The wholesale trade industry, while less competitive for banking services, also used fewer banks and fewer services. Yet the companies in the wholesale trade had the greatest demand for borrowing, both in the percentage of firms in the industry that borrow as well as the amounts that they seek.

The intense competition in the middle market was evidenced by the fact that most companies used four banks and were, on the average, actively solicited by four new banks as well. The research concluded that the intense competition "underscores the importance of staying actively involved in customer relationships, of having targeted calling programs, and of making effective calls on companies." It was observed that customers are becoming increasingly involved in their bank relationships and that this trend will continue. More companies want to know exactly where they stand with their banks and want the details of their agreements in writing. There were three areas of changes that middle-market customers consistently reported:

1. More calls are being made by bank representatives.

2. More is being asked of the banks.

3. A greater participation of company's treasury staff is present in initiating and maintaining a relationship with a bank.

The study indicated that the vice president of finance was the officer most often responsible for selection of a bank as a service provider. The key selection criterion was described as "the company's overall relationship with the bank," an overall relationship seen as more important than specifics such as loan terms and conditions. For firms dealing internationally, the study indicated that the key criteria for selection of a bank for international services were the presence of an existing domestic relationship and a bank's international service capabilities.

Exhibit 9 *(continued)*

The financial strength of the bank was a very important concern to the middle-market companies. Utilizing annual reports, accounting and financial officers of the middle-market companies evaluate the financial condition of the banks they use and the banks that solicit them.

Banks were found to increase in importance to middle-market companies to the degree they are willing to lend, provide account officer service and have competitive loan pricing. The bank's relationship with the company was found to improve with the introduction of new ideas and new services, the interest of the servicing bank in company information, the improvement of quality, and frequency of the bank's visits. The most serious mistake, from the point of view of the customers, was when the bank was not thoroughly familiar with the company being serviced.

The Middle Market Study concluded that in the tristate region NatWest USA was an important competitor, with a 12 percent market share and positioned similarly to Marine Midland, Bank of New York, and Irving Trust. Most customers consider NatWest USA to be a principal bank (i.e., one of the banks they used most for domestic banking services) and one third used NatWest USA as their overall lead bank.

With regard to customer calling, the study indicated that 78 percent of NatWest USA's prospects were called on more frequently by at least one or more competitors than they were called on by NatWest USA. However, NatWest USA's customer calls were found to be highly effective in gaining new business, and more effective overall when compared to the competition.

The Commercial Banking Study

The Commercial Banking Study was concluded in August 1986 and examined companies with annual sales of between $5 and $50 million.

The Commercial Banking Study focused on the nine-county New York area where NatWest USA's principal commercial market was located (Bronx, Kings, Nassau, New York, Queens, Richmond, Rockland, Suffolk, and Westchester). This study indicated that NatWest USA was a major competitor in the commercial banking market. The bank was tied with Chase Manhattan in market share—in fourth position behind Chemical Bank, Manufacturers Hanover, and Citibank.

Interviews with the commercial market customers indicated that NatWest USA's account officers and top management were doing an excellent job of visiting and serving the commercial market customers. A high proportion of customers were called on regularly and interactions were perceived as highly effective.

NatWest USA was viewed as a credit provider to the commercial banking market, having a higher proportion of borrowing customers than most of the competition and a credit policy that was viewed more favorably than that of its competition.

The Branch Shopping Study

The Branch Shopping Study, concluded in January 1987, was undertaken to determine how the customer was treated and how the customer perceived a NatWest USA branch when they came in to open an account or inquire about the bank's services.

In this study, a researcher approached the NatWest USA branch representative as a shopper and recorded opinions and experiences resulting from the contact. The shopper either came into a branch to open a checking account or to cash a check and inquire about high-interest-bearing checking accounts.

In the case where a checking account was opened, shoppers were instructed not to specify the type of checking account they wanted to open, in an effort to see if branch representatives mentioned or discussed and explained the types of accounts available, explained about service charges and types of checks available, and counseled shoppers about appropriate accounts for them.

In the case where the customers came in to cash a check, they proceeded to the teller lines. They were instructed not to endorse the check prior to seeing the teller. They took note of any inappropriate behavior displayed by the tellers as well as the procedures followed by them. After the check was cashed, shoppers asked if the bank offered high-interest checking accounts. This procedure was designed to measure the ability of the tellers to service customers and provide information about products and services offered by the institution.

Approximately 200 account opening and check cashing transactions were evaluated, two thirds of which were with NatWest USA branches and the remaining third with the branches of competitors. The study was completed over a two-month period in late 1986.

Exhibit 9 *(concluded)*

The Branch Shopping Study's main conclusions were as follows:

1. Overall, NatWest USA branch personnel are performing equal to, and at times, better than the personnel of competitors in the quality of service they are providing. The study found that 66 percent of the shoppers were either extremely or very satisfied with NatWest USA, while only 59 percent were satisfied with competitor branch personnel.

2. NatWest USA representatives scored at least as high as competitors on courtesy and friendliness and higher on attitude and the initial establishment of rapport.

3. For the personal attributes of tellers and branch representatives, NatWest USA rated equal to or higher than competitors in terms of efficiency, professional appearance, promptness, organization, and businesslike attitudes.

4. Service at NatWest USA branches was found to be slightly better during the busy hours.

5. Concerning branch environments, the study indicated that the interior and exterior environments for both NatWest USA and its competition are in excellent condition. The average waiting time in NatWest USA branches was found to be lower than the average for other banks.

THE GRAND THEATRE COMPANY*

....

"There is no better director than me. Some may be as good, but none better."
Robin Phillips

In December 1982 the board of directors of Theatre London in London, Ontario, (see Exhibit 1) were considering a proposal to hire Robin Phillips as artistic director, to replace Bernard Hopkins. The hiring decision was complicated by Phillips's ambitious plans for the theatre, which included a change from a subscription theatre to repertory, an increase in budget from $1.9 million to $4.4 million, and even changing the organization's name. The board had to act quickly as plans had to be made, and actors hired, for the next season.

THEATRE IN ONTARIO

Theatre is big business in Ontario. In Toronto alone (including cabaret, dinner theatre and opera) some 3.5 million people attended 120 productions in 1982, in 28 locations. There are 24 nonprofit professional theatres in Toronto, and 18 in the rest of Ontario.

Virtually all theatre organizations in Ontario and the rest of Canada are nonprofit and are subsidized by local, provincial, and federal grants. Thus theatres compete for funds with charities, educational, and health care organizations. As shown in Exhibit 2, a third of revenue typically comes from government sources and half of this comes from The Canada Council. Another 10 percent comes from individual and corporate donors, and the balance from the box office. Because of the pressing need for box office revenues, most theatre companies sell subscriptions of five or so plays from October to May.

In 1982–83, audience size was 570,000 for the Stratford Festival, the largest art organization in Canada, and 268,000 for The Shaw Festival, the second largest theatre company. According to a Stratford audience study, audiences break down into: (1) committed theatregoers (27 percent) who see a number of plays each year, and who tend to be older and more educated and live in Ontario; (2) casual theatregoers (53 percent) who attend a theatre every year or two to see plays of particular interest; and (3) first-timers (20 percent). The challenge for these theatres is to develop these first-timers to be the audience of the future.

* Prepared by Dr. Larry M. Agranove with the assistance of Dr. J. Peter Killing from published sources and interviews with numerous people in theatre, government, and arts organizations. Copyright © 1985, Wilfrid Laurier University. Reprinted with permission.

Exhibit 1 THE GRAND THEATRE COMPANY, BOARD OF DIRECTORS, DECEMBER 1982

J. Noreen De Shane	President, and president of a stationery firm
Peter J. Ashby	Partner, major consulting firm
W. C. P. Baldwin, Jr.	President, linen supply firm
Bob Beccarea	Alderman and civic representative
Art Ender	Life insurance representative
Ed Escaf	Hotel and restaurant owner
Dr. John Girvin	Surgeon
Stephanie Goble	Representative of London Labour Council
Elaine Hagarty	Former alderman, active in arts community
Barbara Ivey	Active board member of various theatre groups
Alan G. Leyland	Entrepreneur
John F. McGarry	Partner, major law firm
C. Agnew Meek	Corporate marketing executive
Robert Mepham	Retired civic leader and businessman
Elizabeth Murray	Board member of theatre groups and Ontario Arts Council
John H. Porter	Vice president and partner, major accounting firm
Peter Schwartz	Partner, major law firm
Dr. Tom F. Siess	University professor
Dr. Shiel Warma	Surgeon

Exhibit 2 THE MAJOR ARTS ORGANIZATIONS IN CANADA—RANKED BY SIZE OF TOTAL REVENUE FOR 1982-1983

Arts organizations	Total revenue 1982–1983	Box office and earned	Government grants	Private donations	Accumulated surplus (deficit) end of 1982–1983
1. Stratford Festival	$12,314,300	$9,678,285	$1,405,939	$1,230,076	$(1,731,492)
2. Toronto Symphony	9,480,503	6,020,112	1,893,100	1,567,291	(149,391)
3. National Ballet	7,271,616	3,233,810	2,943,856	1,093,950	(675,096)
4. Orchestre Symphonique de Montreal	7,071,886	4,048,749	2,164,350	858,787	(857,662)
5. Canadian Opera Company	5,969,077	2,668,698	2,029,100	1,271,279	(290,168)
6. Vancouver Symphony	5,189,041	2,488,690	1,784,315	916,036	(818,951)
7. Shaw Festival	4,801,700	3,848,200	586,000	367,500	(45,167)
8. Royal Winnipeg Ballet	4,021,263	1,884,339	1,611,463	525,461	343,639
9. Centre Stage	3,483,020	1,923,312	1,316,000	243,708	(212,108)
10. Citadel Theatre	3,541,911	2,097,096	1,117,733	327,082	177,821
18. Grand Theatre	1,990,707	1,277,625	390,000	323,082	0*

* Reduced by Wintario Challenge Fund.
Source: Council for Business and the Arts in Canada.

Theatre audiences tend to be well educated, with most having university education, and slightly over 50 percent having attended a graduate or professional school. Those aged 36 through 50 make up 35 percent of the Stratford audience, and the 21-to-35 and 51-to-64 age groups each make up 25 percent. Visitors from the United States account for 35 percent of box office receipts at the Stratford Festival; Toronto accounts for 25 percent, and the remaining 40 percent come from elsewhere in Ontario. Twice as many women attend as men. It is understood that Shaw's market is similar, with slightly fewer coming from the United States.

A recent study showed that while 42 percent of Ontario residents attended live plays and musicals in 1974, this number grew to 55 percent by 1984.[1] Some 24 percent of the Ontario population are "frequent attenders" (at least six times a year). They come from all age groups, but many are "singles," and many are university educated and affluent. In fact, while only 63 percent of Ontarians without a high school education attended live theatres, 94 percent with university degrees have attended live theatre.

There is some price sensitivity: 73 percent said they would attend more often if tickets were less expensive. However, 77 percent (which included young adults and lower-middle income families) said they would accept a tax increase of up to $25 to support the arts.

THE ORGANIZATION OF A THEATRE COMPANY

The Board of Directors. The board of directors is fiscally and legally responsible for the theatre. They may determine the theatre's artistic objectives, then delegate the fulfilling of these objectives to the artistic director. However, any artistic plan has financial objectives, and the board's responsibility is essentially financial. Artistic directors generally demand, and are generally granted, a great deal of autonomy in such matters as programming and casting; to a large extent the board "bets" on the artistic director's ability to put on a season of theatre, subject to his accountability in meeting budgets and providing an appropriate level of quality.

Board members are typically expected to assist in fund raising, and to set an example by contributing generously themselves.

Board members often have business backgrounds. As a result, they may be—and are certainly often perceived to be—insensitive to the unique needs of an artistic organization. Artistic boards often include lawyers and accountants, who are recruited to serve a specific function, but who tend to remain on long enough to achieve positions of power.

Busy businesspeople serve on boards for a number of reasons. They may perceive their serving as a civic responsibility. Others may see it as an opportunity to wield power at a board level, something they are not allowed to do in their own organizations. Membership on a board allows people to widen their social and

[1] Report to the Honorable Susan Fish, The Minister of Citizenship and Culture, by the Special Committee for the Arts, Spring 1984.

business contacts; this can be important to lawyers and accountants, who are limited in their freedom to advertise. One common motivation for businesspeople to join arts boards is the opportunity to mingle with luminaries in the arts. Here is one view of their performance:

> It has often been charged that many a hard-headed businessman loses his business sense on entering a meeting of an arts board. Lacking a profit motive to guide the affairs of the organization, businessmen who serve on arts boards sometimes feel unsure of themselves and their expertise. Compounding this problem is the inclination on the part of arts organizations to consider themselves a breed apart, outside the realm of normal business practice. But whether a company manufactures widgets or mounts exhibitions, the basic business concerns remain the same: strategic planning, good marketing, adequate financing, and competent management are essential to any enterprise.[2]

Theatre Management.   In addition to the artistic director, whose role and relationship with the board were described above, there is usually a general manager who is responsible for the business affairs of the organization. Since artistic directors strive for maximum quality, which is expensive, and since business managers have to find and account for the money to run the theatre, conflicts often occur. Not surprisingly, boards often side with the business manager because of their similarities of culture and values. Typically both artistic director and general manager report directly to the board.

MOUNTING A PRODUCTION

The theatre company selects "products" to suit its objectives and audiences. For example, a theatre might select a playbill of classics or children's plays. A regional theatre might select a Canadian play (to satisfy government grant-giving agencies), a classic (to satisfy the artistic aspirations of the artistic director), a resounding hit from Broadway or England (to help sell the series), and one or more plays that have been successful elsewhere.

Each production requires a producer (who may be the artistic director) to act as the "entrepreneur" to put the show together.[3] He acquires the rights to the play, if it is not in the public domain, for a fee of 7 to 10 percent of the box office revenue. He also retains a director, who may be on staff or who may be a freelance director retained for the run of the play. In the latter case, minimum scale would be $6,174.80 for a run of three weeks of rehearsal and three to four weeks of performance.

Casting is done, beginning with the major parts, on the basis of a uniform contract, which sets out fees (minimum of $416.27 per week for a major com-

---

[2] "Developing Effective Arts Boards," undated publication of The Council for Business and the Arts in Canada, pp. 28, 29.

[3] Harry Chartrand, Research Director, "An Economic Impact Assessment of the Canadian Fine Arts," The Canada Council, February 1, 1984, p. 77.

pany), starting date, billing, working time, and "perks" (e.g., dressing room, accommodation).

Finally, a stage manager is contracted, as are designers for sets, costumes, and lighting. It is essential, of course, that all these people work well together.

The above describes the typical stock, or subscription, company. However, Stratford and Shaw operate as repertory companies, hiring a group of actors for one or more seasons, and allocating roles among the members of the company. Repertory companies typically sell tickets for individual plays, while subscription companies sell their series at the beginning of the season, with few single tickets.

Lead times are considerable; in Stratford, for example, plays that open in May are firmly cast by the previous December, and the entire season is planned by March, when rehearsals begin.

THEATRE LONDON

Background

The Grand Opera House was opened in London, Ontario on September 9, 1901, by Ambrose J. Small, a Toronto theatrical entrepreneur and frustrated producer. It quickly became the showcase of Small's theatrical chain, opening with such attractions as the Russian Symphony Orchestra, and later offering such performers as Barry Fitzgerald, Bela Lugosi, Clifton Webb, Sidney Poitier, and Hume Cronyn. Small sold his theatre chain in 1919, deposited a million dollars in his bank, and disappeared. There has been no explanation to this day; however, Small's ghost is said to haunt the Grand.

Famous Plays bought the theatre in 1924, tore out the second balcony, and converted the theatre to a cinema. They sold to The London Little Theatre for a token amount in 1945, and the building housed an amateur community theatre until the spring of 1971. The theatre employed professional business management and a professional artistic director, but the actors were all amateur. Some of London's leading citizens acted in plays, and some even displayed a high level of competence. The theatre was prominent in the social life of the city and attracted one of the largest subscription sales in North America, both as a percentage of available seats and in absolute terms. It also achieved a reputation for a very high level of quality, given that it was essentially an amateur theatre. Articles about the theatre appeared in such magazines as *Life*. However, there was some concern in the theatre that the level of quality was as high as it was going to get as a company of amateurs, and that the community deserved, and was ready to support, a professional theatre. Another local organization, the London Symphony, had engaged a conductor with an international reputation and was changing from an amateur to a professional orchestra. An active art gallery association was formed to work toward providing London with a major art gallery. Although strong objections were raised against the proposal for a professional theatre, particularly because of the increased financial burden, the risk, and the denial to many of the theatre's supporters of an opportunity to participate in their hobby of acting, London Little Theatre changed to Theatre London in 1971 under artistic director

Heinar Piller. The progressives were vindicated, as theatregoers in London and the area were treated to a decade of artistically and financially successful theatres.

Piller was succeeded, at the end of the 1975 season, by William Hutt, who had achieved great success as an actor at Stratford and was well known to Londoners. He served from 1976 to 1978. Bernard Hopkins arrived in 1979 and was artistic director until May 1983.

The Grand was attractively and authentically renovated at a cost of $5.5

Exhibit 3   THEATRE LONDON, CONDENSED FIVE-YEAR OPERATING RESULTS

	June 30				
	1979	**1980**	**1981**	**1982**	**1983***
Revenue					
Productions					
Ticket sales	$ 551,650	$ 585,938	$ 620,313	$ 664,058	$1,100,000
Sponsored programs	26,000	25,000	26,500	9,000	9,000
Program advertising	17,283	17,270	19,652	24,241	24,000
	594,933	628,208	666,465	697,299	1,133,000
Grants					
Canada Council	145,000	163,000	173,000	185,000	210,000
Ontario Arts Council	145,000	152,000	160,000	170,000	180,000
Wintario	89,254	—	—	—	—
City of London	12,500	—	—	—	—
Cultural Initiative Program	—	—	25,000	—	—
	391,754	315,000	358,000	355,000	390,000
Other					
Operating fund drive	41,222	27,462	182,559	183,188	160,000
Special projects	36,811	36,525	43,881	41,281	65,000
Interest	34,553	50,608	62,128	86,106	80,000
Concessions	33,500	75,073	69,581	62,065	78,000
Theatre school	8,720	17,687	19,481	—	—
Box office commissions	3,319	3,721	651	6,142	3,000
Theatre rental and miscellaneous	3,170	—	—	4,704	2,000
	161,295	211,076	378,281	383,486	388,000
Total revenue	$1,147,982	$1,154,284	$1,402,946	$1,435,785	$1,911,000
Expenses					
Public relations	$ 179,880	$ 128,502	$ 139,907	$ 177,267	$ 270,000
Administration	91,973	115,798	162,723	167,749	330,000
Production overhead	190,911	237,606	282,270	339,474	350,000
Productions	466,906	414,644	416,440	421,161	780,000
Front of house, box office, and concessions	75,563	123,910	107,617	126,673	140,000
Facility operation	131,445	139,215	152,153	142,061	140,000
Theatre school	9,742	20,832	34,804	—	—
Total expenses	1,146,420	1,180,507	1,295,914	1,374,375	2,010,000
Excess of revenue over expense	$ 1,562	$ (26,223)	$ 107,032	$ 61,410	$ (99,000)
Alternate expense compilation					
Salaries, fees, and benefits	$ 658,507	$ 754,109	$ 791,954	$ 823,260	$1,100,000†
Supplies and expenses	487,913	426,398	503,960	551,115	910,000
	$1,146,420	$1,180,507	$1,295,914	$1,374,375	$2,010,000

* Estimate.
† In addition, development costs for the establishment of a repertory company in the 1983–1984 season could be incurred which could be largely offset by federal and provincial grants.

Exhibit 4 CONDENSED BALANCE SHEETS, THEATRE LONDON, 1979–1982

| | June 30 | | | |
	1979	1980	1981	1982
Assets				
Current assets:				
Cash and term deposits	$351,010	$372,868	$325,631	$316,939
Accounts receivable	3,908	13,957	35,208	10,916
Inventory	7,463	7,146	6,050	—
Prepaid expenses	20,257	32,788	46,938	72,471
Total assets	$382,638	$426,759	$413,827	$400,326
Liabilities and Surplus				
Current liabilities:				
Bank loan	—	$ 25,000	—	—
Accounts payable	$ 26,253	24,041	$ 30,112	$ 67,198
Advance ticket sales	280,431	324,524	319,843	302,983
Advance grants	1,060	—	15,201	14,805
Payable to Theatre London Foundation	—	4,523	—	15,340
	307,744	378,088	365,156	400,326
Surplus	74,894	48,671	48,671*	—
Total liabilities and surplus	$382,638	$426,759	$413,827	$400,326

* In addition, there was equity of $453,080 from the Wintario Challenge Fund Program in 1981 and $807,289 in 1982. Under the terms of the program, Wintario will match two dollars for every eligible contributed dollar raised (during the three-year period ending June 30, 1983) in excess of 5.9 percent of the current year's operating expenses. All these matching contributions are placed in a separate investment fund for at least five years, although interest earned on the fund may be used for current operations.

million, reopening in the fall of 1978, after being closed for a full season. (The company had a reduced season during that time in small, rented accommodations.) During the renovation, seating capacity was reduced from 1,100 to 845, but the Grand emerged from the renovations as one of the finest theatres in Canada.

Theatre London ran successful stock seasons from 1979 to 1982. The 1981–82 season was particularly successful, operating at 85 percent of capacity. Eighty percent of its tickets were sold through subscription to some 13,431 subscribers. Financial statements are shown in Exhibits 3 and 4.

THE LONDON ENVIRONMENT

London was founded at the forks of the Thames River in 1793 by Governor Simcoe with the intention of making it the capital of Upper Canada. Instead, it became the cultural and commercial center of southwestern Ontario. Located on three railroad lines and on Highway 401, which serves the Quebec-Windsor corridor, London also has a major airport served by two airlines. London is two hours away from Detroit or Toronto; however, it is in a major snow belt. London is a major retail center, with the second highest per capita retail capacity in North America. However, it serves as a trading area of almost a million people, although

Exhibit 5 SELECTED DEMOGRAPHIC STATISTICS FOR CANADIAN METROPOLITAN AREAS

	Income rating		1983 per capita personal disposable income	
	Index	Rank	Dollar amounts	Rank
Toronto	117	6	$12,693	7
Montreal	103	11	11,212	14
Vancouver	118	5	12,793	6
Ottawa-Hull	118	5	12,796	5
Edmonton	126	4	13,668	4
Calgary	132	1	14,324	1
Winnipeg	111	8	11,997	9
Quebec	98	14	10,623	18
Hamilton	112	7	12,114	8
St. Catharines	103	11	11,223	13
Kitchener	101	13	10,974	16
London	106	10	11,462	11
Halifax	101	13	10,923	17
Windsor	107	9	11,602	10
Regina	130	2	14,056	2
Saskatoon	129	3	14,021	3
Oshawa	106	10	11,450	12
Thunder Bay	102	12	11,089	15
Canadian average	100		$10,851	

Note: This list shows all 18 census metropolitan areas in which the principal city had a population of at least 100,000 in the 1981 Census.

LONDON-CENTERED SEVEN-COUNTY MARKET AREA DATA

	Seven counties	Canada
Population, June 1, 1983	838,500	24,886,600
Ten-year growth rate	5.7%	12.0%
Households (June 1, 1983)	293.7	8,335.0
Wage earner average income (1981)	$14,522	$15,141
Per capita disposable income (1983)	$10,669	$10,851
Per capita retail sales (1983)	$ 4,238	$ 4,153

Source: *Canadian Markets,* 1984, and 1981 income tax returns.

its own population is only 259,000—see Exhibit 5. There are four hotels near the core area and motels in outlying areas. Many interesting restaurants had opened with a great deal of excess capacity; a few restaurants closed or changed hands.

There is little heavy industry in London, but there is a major university, a community college, a teacher's college, and two small church-affiliated colleges. Four major hospitals serve a wide area and provide teaching facilities for the university medical school and dental school. In addition to being a retail center, London is the home of major financial institutions and agribusiness firms, as well as a major brewery.

London is also a major cultural center. In addition to Theatre London, London has a professional symphony orchestra and a couple of significant choral groups. The university has an active program of theatre and music, and the community is a center for visual artists. There are various commercial art galleries, an art gallery connected with the university, and a major public art gallery located in the city center. There are several museums, including a unique children's museum and a museum of Indian Archaeology. The latter two attract visitors from a wide area.

THE GRAND THEATRE COMPANY

In late 1981, a decade after the company had become professional, concern was again raised in the theatre that the level of quality had stagnated, and the theatre would have to move in new directions. Bernard Hopkins was a superb actor and a competent artistic director. He had directed a few plays, rather than have to pay for a free-lance director, with some success. However, some members of the board believed that he had taken the theatre as far as he was able, and there was no initiative on either side to extend Hopkins' contract beyond its expiration in May 1983.

A planning committee, under one of the board members, addressed the issue of continuing the growth in quality. They conducted a number of retreats and interviewed experts in professional theatre as well as officers of The Canada Council and The Ontario Arts Council. During the course of the investigation, they interviewed Robin Phillips. Phillips had been artistic director at The Stratford Festival and was well known to Barbara Ivey (who served on both the Stratford and Theatre London boards) and to other Theatre London directors. He also had directed, with considerable artistic success, two productions for Theatre London: *The Lady of the Camellias* and *Long Day's Journey into Night*.

Robin Phillips.   Robin Phillips is a highly talented artistic director and a person of incredible charm. (In *all* of the interviews conducted by the casewriter, words like *charm, charisma,* and *talent* abounded). Actress Martha Henry said, "Once you've worked with Robin, it's almost impossible to work for anyone else."

He came to Canada from England in 1974 to plan the 1975 Stratford season, although he would not direct any specific plays until 1976. His tenure at Stratford has been described as successful but stormy. When he was contracting to direct a production for The Canadian Opera Company in 1976, he said he would not renew his Stratford contract unless he had more evidence of support for his ambition to make Stratford the focus of Canadian theatre, with film and television productions as well as live theatre. He received a five-year contract to run from November 1, 1976; the contract could be terminated with four months' notice.

There was a series of resignations from, and returns to, Stratford starting in July 1978, until Phillips' departure in 1981. In addition to his Stratford activities, Phillips was involved with theatre in Calgary, New York, Toronto's Harbourfront, and Vancouver. He also filmed *The Wars,* a novel by Timothy Findley. It was generally understood that he was seeking a theatre in Toronto to serve as a base for his stage, film, and television ambitions. However, none was available.

The Phillips Plan.   Robin Phillips had a plan for Theatre London and would only come if he had a budget to fulfill his plan and complete artistic autonomy. His plan called for raising Theatre London from 18th place in Canadian theatre to 3rd.

The plan required a budget of $4.7 million, up from $1.9 million. This included $400,000 of capital cost to improve the Grand's facilities. Box office and concessions would provide 73 percent of the budget, 18 percent would come from donations, 5 percent from the Canada Council, and 4 percent from the Ontario Arts Council. Revenue projections were based on playing to 80 percent of capacity; this was considered feasible because Phillips had surpassed that performance at Stratford, and Theatre London had been operating at 85 percent. The theatre requested a permanent tax exemption from the city of London; the deputy mayor described this request as "cavalier."

Three of the stage productions would be adapted for television and filmed by Primedia Productions of Toronto. This would provide some $100,000 of additional revenue for each production, as well as audience exposure.

Robin Phillips strongly favored a repertory company over a subscription policy. He believed, and often stated, that subscriptions denied audiences a choice, and audiences must learn to discriminate. A change had to be made to make the theatre different, special, and exciting. A repertory company would provide a company of salaried actors who could not be lured away during the season, and who would be attracted by steady employment.

Another advantage of the repertory concept is the flexibility afforded patrons, who may choose the dates they see a play and their seat locations.

In a subscription series, patrons are restricted to the same seat location on the same night for each performance. In repertory theatre several productions are typically run simultaneously.

The Playbill.   Phillips proposed to offer nine plays from October to May on the main stage (in addition to a children's program in a small, secondary theatre):

- *Godspell,* by John-Michael Tebelak—A rousing rock musical with audience appeal, especially for younger audiences.
- *The Doctor's Dilemma,* by George Bernard Shaw—An established, classical hit.
- *Waiting for the Parade,* by John Murrell—A Canadian play, with an all female cast, showing what women did while their men were fighting World War II.
- *Timon of Athens,* by William Shakespeare—A little-performed, little-known Shakespearean play, ignored by Stratford.
- *The Club,* by Eve Merrian—A musical spoof of men's clubs, with a female cast playing the part of men.
- *Arsenic and Old Lace,* by Joseph Kesselring—A well-known classic comedy of American theatre.
- *The Prisoner of Zenda,* adapted by Warren Graves—A comedy of political intrigue and romance, set in a mythical Eastern European kingdom.
- *Hamlet,* by William Shakespeare—One of his best-known plays.

- *Dear Antoine,* by Jean Anouilh—A comedy by a leading contemporary French playwright.

Casting for these plays was not a problem, as leading actors from Canada, the United States, and England were eager to work with Phillips.

Pricing.   Since the plan envisioned a box office yield of $3.2 million, up from the $1.2 million planned for the 1982–83 season, revenue would have to be increased in two ways. The number of productions would be increased, with nine productions in the season instead of the previous six. There would be a record 399 performances, instead of the 230 performances in the 1982–83 season. Thus the plan projected an audience of 270,000, compared with the 137,000 planned for the 1982–83 season. In addition, prices would be increased.

A subscriber in the 1982–83 season could see five plays for $55 on weekends or $45 on weekdays. The pricing schedule proposed for the 1983–84 repertory season was:

	Price	
Seats	**Weekdays**	**Weekends**
178	$20.00	$22.50
245	14.50	15.50
422	10.50	12.50

Promotion.   Since the theater would require an expanded audience from a wider area, the plan envisioned a program of investment spending in major area newspapers: *The Toronto Star* and *Globe and Mail,* the *Kitchener–Waterloo Record,* and the *Detroit Free Press,* as well as the *London Free Press.* The advertising would be directed at a first-time audience.

Group sales would be stressed, particularly to schools. Hotel-restaurant-transportation-theatre ticket packages were planned to attract theatregoers from neighboring areas.

THE DECISION

The directors were impressed by the charm and the reputation of Robin Phillips. The proposal to hire Phillips—and to accept his plan—was supported by some board members who had sound business backgrounds and who had worked in theatre for some years. They had a comfortable, modern theatre, with a recently acquired computer to issue tickets. They had a proven record in selling tickets, as did Robin Phillips.

On the other hand, if Phillips were hired, his artistic strengths might not be matched administratively. There was an administrative director who had been there for only two years, and a chief accountant, but no controller. And Stratford, Canada's leading summer theatre, was less than an hour's drive down the road.

B Strategic Analysis in Single Business Companies

COMPETITION IN OUTDOOR POWER EQUIPMENT: BRIGGS & STRATTON VERSUS HONDA*

In early 1984 Briggs & Stratton President and Chief Executive Officer Frederick P. Stratton told the company's shareholders:

> The most significant development in our industry in recent years has been the increased activity of Japanese manufacturers. The strength of the U.S. dollar . . . combined with the perennial artificial weakness of the Japanese yen has given Japanese manufacturers an unearned price advantage. Their [Japanese] stated interest in engine-powered equipment and the continued strengths of the dollar and weakness of the yen make them a continuing threat.

Briggs & Stratton had long been the industry leader in manufacturing small gasoline engines for such outdoor power equipment as lawn mowers, rotary tillers, snow throwers, and lawn vacuums (see Exhibit 1). Now Honda, the largest Japanese manufacturer of small engines, was in the process of challenging Briggs & Stratton's leadership position in the U.S. market.

COMPANY HISTORY

Briggs & Stratton (B&S) began conducting business in Milwaukee in 1908. The company's first product was a six-cylinder, two-cycle engine that Stephen F. Briggs had developed during his engineering courses at South Dakota State College. After he graduated in 1907 he was eager to produce his engine and enter the rapidly expanding automobile industry. Through a mutual friend, Briggs, the inventor, met Harold M. Stratton, the successful businessman. With that introduction, the Briggs & Stratton Corporation was born. Unfortunately, the engine cost too much to produce as did their second product, an automobile called the

---

Exhibit 1 OUTDOOR POWER EQUIPMENT PRODUCTS

Lawn mowers	Lawn edger-trimmers
Garden tractors	Shredder-grinders
Rotary tillers	Lawn vacuums
Snow throwers	Leaf blowers

Source: "Facts about OPEI."

---

* Prepared by Professor Richard C. Hoffman with the assistance of graduate researchers John Couch and David Monti, School of Business Administration, College of William and Mary.

Superior. The partners were soon out of money and out of the automobile assembly business.

However, they were not out of the automobile industry. In 1909 Briggs filed a patent for a gas engine igniter to replace the existing magneto ignition system in automobiles. This product set the stage for the company to later become the largest U.S. producer of switch and lock apparatuses used in automobiles. By 1920 the company was widely recognized as a major producer of electrical specialties.

In 1920 Briggs & Stratton acquired the patents and manufacturing rights to the Smith motor wheel and the Flyer, a buckboard-like motor vehicle powered by the Smith motor wheel. The Smith motor wheel was a wheel with a small engine attached for propulsion. It could also be used on bicycles. The price for the two-passenger Flyer was $150, but it still could not compete with Ford's Model T. The Model T was higher priced but was more technologically advanced.

As sales of the motor wheel slowed, the company found that a stationary version, the model PB, provided a good power source for washing machines, garden tractors, and lawn mowers. By 1936 engines were being mass-produced at the rate of 120 units per hour. During World War II, Briggs & Stratton produced bomb fuses and aircraft ignitions.

After the war, Briggs & Stratton set out to capture a larger share of the growing lawn and garden equipment market. Recognizing the lawn mower market as a potential growth area, the company set out to make a lighter weight, low-cost engine. Briggs developed and introduced the aluminum alloy engine in 1953, which achieved both a 40 percent weight and price reduction. The aluminum engine was a huge success, with initial demand outstripping supply. In response to demand, the company opened a new engine plant in Wauwatosa, Wisconsin, on an 85-acre site.

In November 1975, some 56 years after the motor wheel opened the way into the small engine business, the 100 millionth Briggs & Stratton engine came off the assembly line. In 1983 B&S ranked 392nd in sales and 75th in ROI on the Fortune 500 list of the largest U.S. industrial corporations. Over 90 percent of the company's revenues came from the sale of small gasoline-powered engines.

OUTDOOR POWER EQUIPMENT INDUSTRY

In 1984 the outdoor power equipment industry (OPE) was a divergent group of various-sized manufacturers of finished goods, attachments, and components. Composed of 87 major manufacturers located in 31 states, the industry produced over 8 million pieces of equipment having an annual retail value of over $3 billion. Seven companies produced some 65 percent of the output of four key products: rotary lawn mowers, riding mowers, lawn tractors, and tillers. Six companies produced 70 percent of the walk-behind power mowers.

Approximately 75 percent of lawn mower purchases were for replacement demand, and 25 percent were first-time purchases. First-time purchases closely tracked the number of new single-family housing starts. In 1983 1.61 million new single and multiple dwellings were constructed; forecasts called for new housing starts in 1984 and 1985 of 1.74 million and 1.59 million, respectively. The number of housing starts was highly dependent on interest rates. Most lawn mowers had a life of six to eight years, making replacement demand dependent on housing starts and related demographics.

Industry Trends

The power equipment industry had been consolidating since 1974. The number of manufacturers had declined from 145 competitors in 1974 (about half of which were power mower manufacturers) to under 90 in 1984. The 10 largest companies in 1984 accounted for nearly 70 percent of total production.

In 1983 power equipment manufacturers employed 13,000 people, with component manufacturing affiliates adding some 22,000–27,000 more jobs. An additional 45,000 people worked for distributors and suppliers. More than 50 percent of the industry's workers were union members. A total of 33 manufacturing plants existed nationwide. In recent years most new plant openings had been in the South and Southwest where unions were not as strong.

Outdoor power equipment manufacturing was not vertically integrated to any significant extent. Industry members manufactured components, attachments, or finished goods (see Exhibit 2). Component manufacturers comprised 30 percent of the industry and produced one or more of the following: engines, transmissions, gear assemblies, and other parts for use in fully assembled outdoor power equipment. Attachment manufacturers produced optional equipment that could be used with the power equipment to supplement its basic operation or to add new capabilities such as lawn dethatching, leaf or snow blowing, and garden tilling. The finished goods manufacturers produced consumer end-use products such as

Exhibit 2 SELECTED U.S. OUTDOOR POWER EQUIPMENT MANUFACTURERS (sales in millions of dollars)

Company	1983 sales	Main product(s)*	Company	1983 sales	Main product(s)*
Ariens Corp.	N/A	FG	Magna American Corp.	$ 9	FG
Auburn Consolidated Industries	$ 4	A	MTD Products Co.	400†	FG
			Murray Ohio Mfg. Co.	386	FG
Bolens Corp.	55	FG	Roper Corporation	256	FG
Briggs & Stratton Corp.	572	E	Snapper (division of Fuqua		
Brinly-Hardy Co.	20	A	Industries)	190	FG
Engineering Products Co.	12	A	Southland Mower Co., Inc.	26	FG
Excel Industries, Inc.	20	A	Tecumseh Products Co.	232	E
J. B. Foote Foundry Co.	14	FG	Teledyne Wisconsin Motor Co.	N/A	E
Jacobsen/Homelite (division			Toro Company, Inc.	241	FG
of Textron)	372	FG	Wheel Horse Products, Inc.	78†	FG
John Deere & Co.	400†	FG	Yazoo Mfg. Co., Inc.	19	FG
Kohler Co.	N/A	E			
Lawn-Boy (division of Outdoor Marine)	129	FG			

N/A = not available (usually because firm was privately held).
* A = attachments, E = engines, FG = finished goods (mowers, tractors, tillers, and so forth).
† Estimate.

lawn mowers, tillers, and tractors. Lawn-Boy was the only finished goods manufacturer that had vertically integrated backward into the manufacture of major components, particularly engines, in producing its outdoor power equipment. All other domestic power equipment manufacturers had chosen not to integrate backward to any significant degree, opting instead to assemble their products from parts supplied by the components and attachments manufacturers. The assemblers of power equipment did do some of their own metal fabrication such as producing the frame and housing for lawn mowers.

Largely because the power equipment manufacturers had not engaged in much backward integration, the industry was a big purchaser of basic raw materials (see Exhibit 3). In 1974 purchases of both materials and components were $720 million, with raw materials amounting to $200 million; engines, $360 million; and components, $160 million. By 1983 purchases were $712 million, equal to 54 percent of total finished goods sales.

Distribution in the industry was fragmented among independent, factory-direct, and company-owned distributors. Independent distributors handled 48 percent of total manufacturing output, with factory-direct sales accounting for 35 percent of manufacturers' sales. At the retail level, sales through national department stores comprised 22 percent of total sales, whereas hardware stores, farm equipment dealers, and home improvement and building suppliers handled 35 percent of total retail sales. The remaining sales were through lawn mower stores (17 percent), discount department stores (8 percent), and other types of retail outlets (18 percent).

In 1983 outdoor power equipment manufacturers spent $60 million on advertising and promotion, $35 million on R&D, $11 million on new product development, and $67 million for new facilities and equipment. During the 1970s sales in the industry had grown rapidly, and many companies prospered. Shipments of walk-behind rotary lawn mowers had peaked at 5.7 million units in 1980 and then tumbled to 4.4 million by 1983. Much of this decline in sales was caused by a

Exhibit 3   RAW MATERIALS PURCHASED FROM SUPPLIERS BY THE OUTDOOR POWER EQUIPMENT INDUSTRY (in millions)

	1983		1974	
Material	**Amount**	**Percent of total**	**Amount**	**Percent of total**
Steel	$186	52%	$123	61%
Cartons	18	5	31	15
Aluminum	39	11	16	8
Plastics	72	21	8	4
Magnesium	2	1	10	5
Paint	8	2	6	3
Other	26	8	6	4
Total	$351	100%	$200	100%

Source: *Profile of the Consumer Outdoor Power Equipment Industry,* 1984.

Exhibit 4 SHIPMENTS OF OUTDOOR POWER EQUIPMENT, 1980–1983, WITH FORECASTS FOR 1984–1989 (units in thousands and dollars in millions)

| | Equipment | | | | | |
| | Walk-Behind | | | Riding | | |
Year	Rotary mowers	Rotary tillers	Snow throwers	Rear-engine mowers	Front-engine mowers	Garden tractors
1980:						
Units	5,700	667	1,577	314	494	220
Dollar value*	$701	$159	$397	$185	$345	$351
1981:						
Units	4,600	501	345	250	370	151
Dollar value*	$606	$138	$98	$162	$291	$266
1982:						
Units	4,600	497	95	261	393	146
Dollar value*	$674	$143	$27	$190	$359	$280
1983:						
Units	4,400	408	264	276	415	129
Dollar value*	$695	$132	$91	$205	$395	$275
Near-term forecasts:						
1984:						
Units	5,000	416	340	314	467	151
Dollar value*	$750	$205	$120	$246	$448	$309
1985:						
Units	5,015	430	258	322	479	153
Dollar value*	$617	$215	$88	$260	$467	$315

Extended forecasts (units only):	**Walk-behind mowers and tillers**	**Riding units**
1986	5,700	945
1987	5,500	900
1988	5,700	920
1989	5,900	1,000

* F.O.B. factory shipment value. Not available for extended forecast.

recession and a drop-off in housing starts. Industry shipments are presented in Exhibit 4.

Foreign Exports and Imports

In 1974 U.S. exports amounted to $85 million, with imports amounting to a meager $2 million. By 1983 exports were $52 million, and imports into the United States were $30 million. In 1981 exports accounted for 8 percent of total shipments. This number was expected to decline to 3 percent by 1985. Industry experts believed that exports and imports were closely tied to exchange rates. Exports went mainly to Canada, while Japan accounted for over 70 percent of the imports to the United States in 1983. Exchange rates from 1979 to 1983 are displayed in Exhibit 5.

Exhibit 5 EXCHANGE RATES FOR CANADA AND JAPAN, 1979 TO 1983 (units per U.S. dollar)					
	1979	**1980**	**1981**	**1982**	**1983**
Canadian dollar	1.16	1.17	1.19	1.23	1.23
Japanese yen	219	227	221	249	237

Source: "International Statistics," *Federal Reserve Bulletin,* August 1985.

Industry Regulation

Prior to 1982 manufacturers of OPE were not regulated by the Consumer Products Safety Commission (CPSC); compliance was voluntary. Voluntary standards were promulgated by the American National Standards Institute and had been supported by the industry trade association since the mid-1950s. The standards were primarily concerned with improved product performance and safety. Safety standards involved both the protection from thrown objects and noise level. About 90 percent of the industry's products were in compliance with these voluntary standards. Products complying with the standards were affixed with a triangular seal.

Since 1973 the industry had been working with the CPSC for mandatory power mower safety standards. At that time, mowers ranked third on the commission's most hazardous products list. Improvements in voluntary standards had reduced mowers to 20th place on the hazardous products list by the end of the decade.

However, in 1982 a number of new CPSC regulations were put into effect calling for increased safety restrictions for walk-behind power mowers, including performance and labeling requirements. The standards included the use of shields to protect people from thrown objects, deflectors and drain holes to prevent fuel ignition, and the deadman blade control system. The most controversial regulation was the deadman blade control system. Mowers built after July 1, 1982, had to have blades that stopped within 3 seconds after the operator released a deadman control at the handle of the mower. Meeting this standard involved either installing a blade brake or the addition of a rechargeable, battery-powered electric starter. Both of these alternatives were very expensive. The CPSC estimated that the cost of compliance would be approximately $35 per unit.

By 1981 many companies, including Briggs & Stratton, had successfully developed the technology to make manual starting of engines much easier. The lawn mower industry asked Congress to amend the safety standard to allow engine stop with manual restart as a third method of compliance with the blade control requirement. President Reagan signed the amendment despite the CPSC's strong opposition.

The industry also had to comply with the Magnuson-Moss Act of 1975 requiring that all products with a written warranty, and costing the consumer $15 or more, come with either a statement concerning the duration of the warranty or a limited warranty. The industry also had to comply with an assortment of state and local regulations concerning noise and pollution levels for outdoor power equipment. In 1983 OPE product liability expenses amounted to $21 million ($18 million on warranty claims plus $3 million on insurance premiums).

The Outdoor Power Equipment Institute (OPEI)

The trade association for outdoor power equipment was the Outdoor Power Equipment Institute (OPEI). OPEI's membership represented over 90 percent of the industry's annual volume. Founded in 1952 as a nonprofit organization, the OPEI represented the outdoor power equipment industry before governmental bodies on the state and national level. OPEI compiled industry statistics for its members and was active in promoting safety of equipment through voluntary industry activities and in conjunction with the federal government. The institute also monitored tariff and freight rates to reduce shipping costs for the industry's products.

In recent years OPEI had worked closely to help develop international safety standards for power mowers. Recently, OPEI had confronted whether foreign importers should be allowed membership. Foreign manufacturers with plants in the United States were automatically admitted. Several U.S. manufacturers did not want to admit foreign importers, but OPEI's executive director felt that one good way of learning what foreign competitors were doing was by admitting them as members.

Competition: Domestic

Competition within the industry occurred mainly within two broad strategic groups—finished goods producers and components producers. The finished goods manufacturers, which represented the largest group of competitors, could be further subdivided by market segment. The major producers of premium-priced lawn mowers included Lawn-Boy, Toro, Snapper, Jacobsen, and Deere and Co. MTD Products, Murray, and Roper Corporation were the chief producers of outdoor power equipment for the medium-priced and discount markets; they were also the major suppliers of equipment for the private-label segment of the market.

Lawn-Boy, a subsidiary of Outboard Marine Corporation, achieved sales of $128.9 million and earnings of $11.1 million in 1983. By designing and making all the components needed to assemble its final products, Lawn-Boy was able to give its products a distinctive integrated look (that is, its engines didn't look bolted on). This was appealing to some consumers in the premium-priced segment. Lawn-Boy was the only leading U.S. brand-name manufacturer to produce its own engines. All of its engines were of two-cycle design (meaning that they ran on a mixture of gasoline and oil) while the other major engine manufacturers in the industry produced four-cycle engines (engines running on gasoline only).

The largest assembler of finished goods for the premium-priced segment was the Toro Company, Inc., headquartered in Minneapolis. Toro sold $241 million of OPE in 1983. Toro was also the leading manufacturer of snow-throwing equipment.

The Snapper Division of Fuqua Industries was also a major producer of OPE in 1983 and competed in the premium-priced market. Snapper marketed a full line of lawn mowers, tillers, and snow blowers. The division sold $190 million of OPE in 1983 and accounted for 26 percent of Fuqua's total sales.

The Jacobsen/Homelite Division of Textron, Inc., also produced high-quality lawn mowers, power appliances, and chain saws. In 1983 this division had sales totaling $372 million, a significant portion of which involved chain saws (which used two-cycle engines).

Deere and Company was the remaining leading producer of premium-priced OPE products. Its OPE sales in 1983 amounted to $400 million, but a significant portion of this figure was for farm and industrial equipment. In recent years, Deere, Toro, and Snapper had chosen B&S engines to power their mowers.

MTD Products, Inc., of Valley City, Ohio, was closely held and had estimated annual sales of about $400 million. MTD bought its engines from Briggs & Stratton, manufactured its own OPE frames and bodies, and assembled the units for sale. MTD sold to private-label distributors and marketed nationally under the brand name Yardman. MTD was the nation's largest producer of walk-behind lawn mowers and competed in the lower-priced end of the market.

Roper Corporation was the nation's second largest producer of lawn mowers with total OPE sales in 1983 of $256 million. Seventy-three percent of Roper's 1983 output was purchased by Sears and sold under the Sears Craftsman label. Roper was also a private-label supplier to other discount chains. Roper primarily used Tecumseh engines on its equipment.

The Murray Ohio Manufacturing Co., located in Brentwood, Tennessee, was a major producer of both OPE and bicycles for the medium-priced and discount segments. Total corporate sales amounted to $386 million in 1983. The company sold mowers under its own Murray brand and also supplied a variety of private-label retailers.

The major cost component of lawn mowers was the engine. The four largest producers of mower engines were Briggs & Stratton, Tecumseh Products, Kohler, and Teledyne Wisconsin. Tecumseh posed the only real domestic competitive threat to Briggs & Stratton; its strongest product category was air-cooled aluminum alloy engines ranging from 2 to 18 horsepower. Tecumseh Products was the largest U.S. producer of refrigerator compressors and the second largest producer of small, gasoline-powered engines. The company also produced gear assemblies and related transmission parts. In 1983 Tecumseh's net income from engine sales was $41 million. Eleven percent of its total sales and 39 percent of its engine output went to Sears or Sears's suppliers such as Roper. Tecumseh's next three engine customers bought only 6.3 percent, 5.7 percent, and 5.6 percent of the company's total volume, respectively. Exhibit 2 lists some of the key industry competitors and their sales.

Competition: Foreign

Japan was the primary source of imported OPE products into the United States, and in 1983 Japanese products made up 76 percent of the total value of OPE goods imported into the United States. Most foreign imports of OPE products into the United States were garden tractors and rotary walk-behind lawn mowers. Garden tractors were imported as agricultural machinery and were exempted from paying U.S. tariffs. The three leading import brands of garden tractors were all Japanese: Kubota, Yanmar, and Satoh. The leading Japanese importers of riding and walk-behind lawn mowers were Honda, Kawasaki, Suzuki, and Yamaha, all of whom also produced motorcycles for the U.S. market.

In lawn mowers, Honda was the only foreign brand considered to be a factor in the U.S. market. Japanese competition was not a new problem for the industry, but it had become much more severe since the early 1980s. Japanese firms manufactured both engines and finished products. The value of Japanese imports of lawn mowers and parts increased from less than $3 million in 1978 to $22.7 million in 1983. This increase in Japanese competition was attributed to the extraordinary strength of the dollar against the yen and the worldwide weakness of the motorcycle business.

Global recession in general and the softening of the motorcycle business in particular had forced Japanese motorcycle manufacturers to look to other product markets in order to maintain full use of their production facilities. All four Japanese motorcycle manufacturers (Honda, Kawasaki, Suzuki, and Yamaha) had identified power products as appropriate new business opportunities. Honda had stated publicly that it intended to become a leader in the powered products field and had transferred resources from its motorcycle division to its powered products division. Honda had achieved the greatest penetration in the United States. Its small engine production was about 1.3 million units in 1982. Honda also expanded capacity in that year, giving the firm a combined capacity of over 4 million units per year. The company sold its mowers through established OPE distributors and not its own auto or motorcycle dealers.

Although Honda sold small gasoline-powered engines, it preferred to sell finished goods. The company marketed a broad line of outdoor power equipment including garden tillers, snow throwers, walk-behind power mowers, and lawn tractors. This product line represented approximately 6 percent of total sales. Honda and other Japanese manufacturers were also strong OPE competitors in other parts of the world.

Honda's strategy in the OPE industry focused on the high-priced segment as a manufacturer of finished goods for the consumer market. Similar to Lawn-Boy, it manufactured both the lawn mower engine and body, which resulted in equipment having an integrated look. Honda engines were noted for being lightweight and dependable. Professional users of OPE had casually dubbed Honda's engines "Briggs-Hondas" because of their dependability. They often replaced worn-out Briggs & Stratton engines with new Honda engines on still-serviceable used equipment. Honda's product strength was based on heavy R&D expenditures, which ensured that the firm's products would remain technologically advanced. Honda marketed its products by making extensive use of advertising and promotion. It also priced its products competitively, setting prices below rivals in order to gain market share. Honda had been extremely successful in both the U.S. motorcycle and automobile markets using similar strategies and possessed exten-

Exhibit 6	SELECTED FINANCIAL AND STATISTICAL DATA FOR HONDA MOTOR CO. (in thousands)			
	For years ended February 28			
	1983	**1982**	**1981**	**1980**
Sales	$8,771,902	$8,254,192	$7,545,423	$5,703,204
Net income	289,215	292,297	422,151	122,986
Assets	5,558,243	4,940,944	4,655,544	3,546,191
Stockholders' equity	2,020,151	1,607,435	1,608,444	894,576
Number of employees	46,238	42,415	38,481	33,405

Compiled from: "The International 500," *Fortune.*

sive resources to support its strategy in the OPE market (see Exhibit 6). The company had considerable expertise in gasoline engine technology and produced a wide line of products incorporating gasoline engines: automobiles and trucks, motorcycles, power generators, snowmobiles, outboard motors, garden tillers, pumps, snow throwers, and lawn tractors, as well as lawn mowers.

In 1983 Honda sold approximately 10,000 high-priced lawn mowers in the United States. Honda also sold replacement engines compatible with many makes of mowers. Until 1983 Honda lawn mowers bound for the United States had been manufactured in Japan. Apparently satisfied that it could gain significant market share, Honda decided, in August 1983, to build a manufacturing plant for lawn mowers in Alamance County, North Carolina. Honda planned to produce 10,000 units in the first year and employ 80 workers. The engines would still be produced at the Hamamatsu plant in Japan. Labor costs in Japan were, on average, 30 percent lower than in the United States and 50 percent lower than at Briggs & Stratton. Labor costs were typically around 40 percent of the total cost of outdoor power equipment.

Honda's products had been well received in the United States, getting excellent ratings from consumer magazines. Comparisons with domestic models revealed that there were no disadvantages associated with Honda mowers themselves. The few disadvantages had to do with distribution, parts, and service. Honda mowers received high marks for convenience, performance, and safety. The starting controls were simple, easy to reach, and had an automatic choke which eliminated the need for a choke control on the throttle. The cutting performance of Honda mowers was usually rated excellent; they provided a level cut, even in tall heavy grass, and efficiently bagged clippings. Honda's mowers met or exceeded safety standards including a deadman clutch that stopped the blade one second after the control was released, well within the three-second requirement. In 1983 Honda had an estimated 1 percent of the U.S. walk-behind lawn mower market.

Other Japanese manufacturers were actively calling on B&S's OEM customers. By the end of 1983 Toro and John Deere had switched from B&S to Suzuki and Kawasaki engines, respectively, for their consumer walk-behind lawn mowers.

In February 1983 Frederick Stratton said in an interview with *Business Week,* "The real battle over the next five years is with the Japanese. I hate to admit it, but Japan has set a new standard of quality."

THE BRIGGS & STRATTON CORPORATION

Briggs & Stratton (B&S), headquartered in Wauwatosa, Wisconsin, was the world's largest producer of small, gas-powered engines used primarily for outdoor power equipment. The company operated in a mature market with growth averaging 2 percent per year. B&S had an estimated 70 to 80 percent share of the small engine market in the United States and over 50 percent of the worldwide market in 1983. Engines and parts accounted for 93 percent of Briggs's total revenues in 1983 (see Exhibit 7). The other 7 percent was from the sale of automotive lock and key sets. B&S was the largest producer of automobile ignition systems and door and trunk locks in the United States with over a 90 percent market share. B&S sales are summarized in Exhibit 7.

Briggs's number one customer for small engines was MTD which bought about 10 percent of B&S's total output in 1983. Toro also used B&S engines on some of its mowers. Kendrik B. Melrose, president of Toro, referred to B&S as "The General Motors of the small lawn mower engine business." Snapper was another heavy user of B&S engines.

In 1980 export sales were a record 26 percent of Briggs & Stratton's engine sales; in June close to half of the company's engine shipments were to customers outside of North America. Foreign customers received longer payment terms than domestic customers in recognition of longer shipping times. In addition, many of B&S's domestic customers exported products powered by B&S engines. B&S estimated that 30 percent of its total engine business was derived from markets outside the United States. Frederick P. Stratton, the company's CEO observed:

> The markets for products powered by our engines is increasingly international. The flow of material around the world is truly amazing. For example, we know of cases where engines we ship to customers in Australia are mounted on equipment

Exhibit 7 BRIGGS & STRATTON'S SALES OF OEM AND AIR-COOLED ENGINES BY END USE, 1978–1983

	Engine sales as a percent of total B&S revenues					
End uses	1978	1979	1980	1981	1982	1983
Lawn and garden equipment	77%	80%	84%	83%	85%	88%
Industrial, agricultural	23	20	16	17	15	12
All exports	20	23	26	23	21	16
Total engine sales as a % of total B&S revenues	91%	91%	94%	93%	94%	93%

Source: Company annual reports.

destined for Europe, and engines we ship to customers in Europe are mounted on equipment destined for the United States.

In 1981 B&S's engine sales declined 31 percent, the largest year-to-year percentage decline since 1932. Because of the slow demand and dry weather, B&S customers' inventories were at a high level. By late December, when the prime rate reached 21 percent, most B&S customers had made inventory reduction a major objective.

In March 1982 B&S made its first shipments from a new distribution center in Lambertheim, West Germany. This new facility was the stocking point for service parts and replacement engines bound for central service distributors in Europe. Later the same year B&S opened a sales office in Manila, Philippines, to promote sales and service to lesser developed nations in the Pacific Basin. These nations primarily used larger cast iron engines for agriculture, marine, and industrial use. During 1983 B&S again expanded its sales network to developed countries having markets for lawn and garden equipment by opening sales offices in Oslo, Norway, and Auckland, New Zealand. B&S's international operations were coordinated by Michael Hamilton.

Economic conditions in export markets remained depressed in 1983, and the continued strength of the dollar made B&S prices less competitive in those markets. Export sales fell to the lowest level in 10 years.

Current Management

The president of Briggs & Stratton, Frederick P. Stratton, Jr., was the grandson of the cofounder of Briggs & Stratton. A graduate of Stanford's MBA program, he formerly had worked for a brokerage house. He joined B&S in 1973 and was named president in 1977. Other officers and their areas of responsibility included:

L. William Dewey, Jr.—Executive Vice President
Laverne J. Socks—Executive Vice President
Roger E. De Meritt—Manufacturing Development
J. Byron Smith—Production
Bernard O. Davis—Controller
James F. Sullivan—Sales
Charles L. Fricke—Service
Walter O. Schneider—Procurement
James L. Bunda—Quality Assurance
Robert K. Catterson—Research & Engineering
Richard E. Marceau—Administration
David G. Morton—Manufacturing Operations
Michael D. Hamilton—International

Products

B&S made a wide line of engines. All were 4-cycle engines that ran on straight gas (not mixed with oil). More than 95 percent of the engines sold by B&S were air-

Exhibit 8 SMALL-ENGINE INNOVATIONS DEVELOPED BY BRIGGS & STRATTON

1953: Aluminum alloy gasoline engine: Reduced weight and cost of small engines.

1961: Easy spin starting: Engine starting effort cut in half by a simple cam-controlled, fault-proof compression release.

1962: Oil foam air cleaner: Dirt banned from the engine for its life by an easy-to-clean polyurethane foam filter.

1966: Synchro balance design: Engine and riding equipment vibrations smoothed out by a synchronized counterweight system.

1968: Automatic vacuum controlled choke: Replaced manual choke, providing extra power when needed for heavy loads.

1971: 12 volt gear-type starter with dual circuit alternator: Provided for quick starting at low temperatures. Alternator provided both D/C battery charging and A/C for lights or external loads.

1977: Quiet power: The 16 HP twin-cylinder engine prompted by the noise abatement guidelines provided quiet running and low vibration levels.

1982: Magnetron ignition: A self-contained transistor with no moving parts. Provided more consistent spark for dependable starting. Could be installed on existing engines.

1983: The electric engine was introduced for power mowers.

Source: Compiled from company pamphlets.

cooled, aluminum alloy gasoline engines ranging from 2 to 18 horsepower. Less than 5 percent of the engines were the air-cooled, cast iron variety ranging from 9 to 16 horsepower. B&S also produced air- and water-cooled diesel engines ranging from 3 to 28.5 horsepower. Walk-behind power mowers generally had a 3 to 4 horsepower engine. B&S engines were of high quality and had many innovative features. Some of B&S's successful innovations are listed in Exhibit 8.

B&S emphasized continuing product improvements. In addition to the introduction of electronic ignition in 1982 (see Exhibit 8), the company had, in recent years, designed new features to reduce noise levels such as better mufflers and synchro-balanced engines. In 1983 the company introduced a small electric engine for use on lawn and garden equipment. The new 120 volt, 1,000 watt motor was quiet, light (11 pounds), had a 10-year life, and met the government's standards for deadman blade control.

B&S's major form of distribution was through contractual arrangements with finished goods manufacturers, which were generally negotiated on a yearly basis. Contracts with finished goods manufacturers of lawn mowers accounted for 75 percent of B&S's sales.

Marketing and Promotion

Traditionally B&S sold engines directly to finished goods manufacturers. B&S engines were functional and did not have fancy decals or paint jobs. B&S relied heavily on its quality image and reputation to gain sales. B&S was well known among older consumers, many of whom were accustomed to seeing B&S engines on their equipment. Younger consumers, many of whom were starting to buy their first homes, were not as familiar with the Briggs & Stratton name.

B&S had recently put together a six-member marketing staff under the direction of L. William Dewey. One of its roles was to market engines to end-use consumers and retailers. B&S wanted consumers to ask for their engines by name when buying a lawn mower. In 1983 the company began a television advertising campaign for the first time. The campaign slogan was "Briggs & Stratton: the power in power equipment." The commercial employed trick photography to show B&S engines floating above invisible tillers and lawn mowers, emphasizing the fact that B&S engines were responsible for providing the power. The company quadrupled its 1982 advertising expenditures, spending $4 million in 1983. Company engineers had also taken steps to improve the appearance of B&S engines.

B&S assured service for its engines (even though they became components of other manufacturer's products) via a network of over 25,000 authorized service centers worldwide. To shore up relations with its OEM customers, B&S assured them that it would not enter the end-use product market and compete with them. No customer enjoyed a special price.

Production

Briggs & Stratton manufactured almost all of the components used in assembling its engines except for piston rings, spark plugs, and valves. All gasoline engine manufacturing facilities were located in the Milwaukee area; diesel engines were manufactured in the company-owned plant in West Germany. During 1983, 20 percent of each revenue dollar went for direct materials, 48 percent for wages and benefits, 5 percent for taxes, 8 percent for new machinery, and 8 percent for all other expenses; profit margins on sales were 5 percent. The compounded growth rate in net plant investment over the last 10 years was 13 percent. Production was highly seasonal and was heaviest from December to March. B&S manufactured engines to individual customer specifications and, as a result, did not build finished goods for its own inventory. To try to even out seasonal demand, B&S offered incentive discounts to customers who would accept delivery in the off season; however, payment terms on these orders were very short. Growth in year-end order backlogs had averaged 13 percent over the last five years.

Labor costs represented the largest proportion of the total cost of a B&S mower engine in 1983. Company wages and benefits in Wisconsin averaged $17.70 per hour, higher than both domestic and foreign competitors. Growth in the number of employees had been near zero for the past 10 years. In an effort to hold down labor costs, the company in 1983 proposed a three-year wage freeze and work rule concessions in return for a profit-sharing plan and an improved pension. Local 232 of the Allied Industrial Workers' Union (AIW) rejected the proposal, and over 7,000 employees went on strike when their labor contract expired on August 1, 1983. The strike occurred during the slowest point in the production season but, nonetheless, caused concern from customers about the dependability of their supplies. The AIW agreed three months later to a new contract which did not reduce labor costs for B&S but did reduce the rate of increase of such costs in the future.

The ready acceptance of Japanese products by American consumers had created new production challenges for B&S. The company had committed large capital expenditures to new technologies such as robotics. Over $20 million was scheduled to be spent on cost-reducing machinery in 1984. This figure was expected to double in 1985.

Improved production management techniques were implemented in 1983 and included installation of materials requirements planning (MRP), an inventory reduction program (EOQ), and statistical process control. The purpose of the MRP system was to provide the correct parts in the right quantities when they were needed in the manufacturing process. This system took advantage of information stored in a computer for timely response and scheduling. The goal of the new inventory reduction program was to cut inventory in half with no loss of response to customer needs. Quality centers were being created to ensure a constant flow of ideas from the bottom up on how to improve inventory and other production management activities.

The statistical process control system was intended to provide detection of any trend toward making bad parts before such parts were even produced. On a regular basis, sample parts were taken from inventory and measured in terms of allowable tolerances, and the average measure for each sample was plotted on a chart. Should the measures fall outside of accepted limits, corrective action would be taken immediately. Management believed the system would produce two benefits: (1) the elimination of shipments of poorly made products and (2) a reduction in safety stock held by the firm.

Exhibit 9 BRIGGS & STRATTON'S PERFORMANCE BY BUSINESS SEGMENT, 1980–1983 (in thousands)

	Year ended June 30			
	1983	**1982**	**1981**	**1980**
Sales:				
Engines and parts	$571,736	$597,669	$527,954	$669,305
Locks	42,071	37,997	41,032	39,257
Total	$613,807	$635,666	$568,986	$708,562
Operating income:				
Engines and parts	$ 52,447	$ 66,566	$ 38,623	$ 85,375
Locks	1,875	574	646	1,903
Total	$ 54,233	$ 67,140	$ 39,269	$ 87,278
Assets:				
Engines and parts	$298,463	$271,454	$253,835	$281,491
Locks	33,445	24,518	25,798	30,007
Unallocated	55,872	70,684	53,534	29,986
Total	$387,780	$366,656	$333,167	$341,484
Depreciation expense:				
Engines and parts	$ 14,537	$ 13,074	$ 11,645	$ 9,866
Locks	1,189	964	896	818
Total	$ 15,726	$ 14,038	$ 12,541	$ 10,684
Expenditures for plant and equipment:				
Engines and parts	$ 31,037	$ 20,089	$ 26,094	$ 52,443
Locks	1,073	1,186	2,478	2,672
Total	$ 32,110	$ 21,275	$ 28,572	$ 55,115

Source: Company annual reports.

Finance

Briggs & Stratton reported declining earnings and sales in fiscal 1983. Growth in sales for the last five years was almost zero (0.9 percent). Sales of most types of OPE in 1983 were flat or declining. However, the market for automobile locks was quite strong; B&S was gaining a larger share of the market by becoming the exclusive supplier to GM. Despite the poor sales and earnings, the company raised the yearly dividend to $1.58 from $1.54; B&S tried to maintain a constant dividend payout ratio of 50 percent of earnings to shareholders. However, in low-profit years, dividends were not reduced to meet the 50 percent payout target.

B&S was continuing its long-standing policy of financing capital expenditures entirely out of retained earnings. The company had no long-term debt. The *Value Line* survey gave B&S its highest rating of A+ for its financial strength. B&S's financial statements are presented in Exhibits 9–11.

Exhibit 10   BRIGGS & STRATTON'S SALES, EARNINGS, AND STATISTICAL DATA, 1974–1983 (in thousands of dollars except per share data)

	For the years ended June 30		
	1983	**1982**	**1981**
Summary of operations:			
Net sales	$613,807	$635,666	$568,986
Gross profit on sales*	97,491	105,295	77,533
Provision for income taxes	27,020	34,250	19,470
Net income*	31,762	39,353	23,495
Average number of shares of common stock outstanding (in thousands)†	14,464	14,464	14,464
Per share of common stock:†			
Net income	$2.20	$2.70	$1.62
Cash dividends	1.58	1.54	1.52
Shareholders' investment	18.05	17.44	16.31
Other data:			
Shareholders' investment	$261,054	$252,240	$235,923
Total assets	$387,780	$366,656	$333,167
Plant and equipment	$310,449	$283,147	$265,644
Plant and equipment, net of reserves	$179,436	$165,689	$160,902
Provision for depreciation	$ 15,726	$ 14,038	$ 12,541
Expenditures for plant and equipment	$ 32,110	$ 21,275	$ 28,572
Working capital	$108,836	$111,008	$ 95,476
Current ratio	2.1 to 1	2.2 to 1	2.2 to 1
Number of employees at year-end	9,254	8,138	8,179
Number of shareholders at year-end	10,006	11,140	11,865
Quoted market price:			
High	$37¼	$26⅝	$28¼
Low	23⅞	22	22

* Years prior to 1977 reflect the first-in, first-out (FIFO) method for pricing inventory while 1977 and years after reflect the last-in, first-out (LIFO) method.
† Number of shares of common stock and per share data have been adjusted for the 2-for-1 stock split in 1976.
Source: Company annual reports.

Outlook

Frederick Stratton commented on the challenge from Honda: "We are determined to build customer awareness of our product and maintain our leadership position. We are not going to let the Japanese take this market from us." Some skeptics doubted that a component manufacturer could effectively advertise directly to a consumer. But Stratton argued that the company's advertising, combined with its clean balance sheet, modern plant, and new product commitment, would carry the day.

Exhibit 10 *(concluded)*

1980	1979	1978	1977	1976	1975	1974
$708,562	$590,964	$456,960	$388,852	$326,959	$316,286	$317,852
126,771	118,838	96,501	86,389	72,024	51,439	65,801
42,370	44,770	36,570	32,140	26,690	17,050	26,630
49,098	48,455	37,466	33,360	27,572	18,269	25,873
14,464	14,464	14,464	14,464	14,464	14,464	14,464
$3.39	$3.35	$2.59	$2.31	$1.91	$1.26	$1.79
1.46	1.35	1.22	1.12	.93	.80	.88
16.17	14.24	12.24	10.87	9.68	8.70	8.24
$233,915	$205,934	$177,005	$157,185	$140,025	$125,832	$119,134
$341,484	$290,047	$241,922	$213,303	$191,524	$153,183	$155,830
$240,435	$190,277	$168,320	$150,839	$137,508	$127,359	$107,609
$148,303	$107,659	$ 93,862	$ 83,803	$ 77,218	$ 72,911	$ 59,219
$ 10,684	$ 8,901	$ 8,092	$ 7,585	$ 6,708	$ 5,856	$ 4,999
$ 55,115	$ 24,782	$ 19,300	$ 15,252	$ 12,302	$ 20,760	$ 24,771
$102,082	$111,206	$ 94,010	$ 82,410	$ 69,379	$ 57,148	$ 62,026
2.1 to 1	2.6 to 1	2.7 to 1	2.8 to 1	2.5 to 1	3.5 to 1	2.8 to 1
10,873	10,605	8,931	7,936	6,950	6,378	8,601
12,893	13,185	13,388	12,973	12,634	13,037	13,535
$29⅛	$31¼	$30⅜	$33⅜	$32¾	$25	$31¼
20¾	25	23½	25⅛	20⅞	14¾	17½

Exhibit 11 CONSOLIDATED BALANCE SHEETS, BRIGGS & STRATTON, 1980–1983 (in thousands)

	Fiscal year ending June 30			
	1983	**1982**	**1981**	**1980**
Assets				
Current assets:				
Cash	$ 4,255	$ 3,666	$ 3,081	$ 4,099
Certificates of deposit	41,223	52,428	35,224	11,626
U.S. government securities	0	1,990	4,062	2,046
Receivables, net	59,273	53,064	44,484	75,241
Inventories:				
Finished products	60,359	39,968	33,351	34,444
Work in process	23,224	27,683	31,674	37,824
Raw materials	8,015	8,965	7,814	15,285
Total inventories	91,598	76,616	72,839	87,553
Future income tax benefits	5,878	8,294	7,751	7,797
Prepaid expense	6,117	4,909	4,854	4,819
Total current assets	208,344	200,967	172,295	193,181
Plant and equipment:				
Land and land improvements	8,779	8,757	8,599	6,255
Buildings	83,275	82,473	79,249	56,523
Machinery and equipment	193,342	175,593	159,245	136,953
Construction in progress	25,053	16,324	18,551	40,704
	310,449	283,147	265,644	240,435
Less accumulated depreciation and unamortized investment tax credit . . .	131,013	117,458	104,736	92,132
Total plant and equipment, net . . .	179,436	165,689	160,908	148,303
Total assets	$387,780	$366,656	$333,167	$341,484
Liabilities and Shareholders' Equity				
Current liabilities:				
Accounts payable	$ 23,925	$ 16,069	$ 16,486	$ 29,065
Foreign loans	9,987	8,229	9,891	
Accrued liabilities:				
Wages and salaries	14,245	14,502	12,675	12,048
Retirement plan	17,879	18,186	18,779	18,756
Taxes, non-income	3,973	3,201	2,498	2,345
Other	21,189	20,268	16,608	17,461
Total accrued liabilities	57,286	56,157	50,560	50,610
Federal and state income taxes	8,310	9,504	1,882	11,424
Total current liabilities	99,508	89,959	78,819	91,099
Deferred income taxes	18,202	16,145	10,373	8,702
Accrued employment benefits	9,016	8,312	8,052	7,768
Shareholders' equity:				
Common stock:				
Authorized 15,000,000 shares, $3.00 par value; issued and outstanding, 14,463,500 shares in 1983 and 1982	43,391	43,391	43,391	43,391
Retained earnings	218,021	209,111	192,032	190,524
Cumulative translation adjustments	(358)	(262)	500	
Total shareholders' equity	261,054	252,240	235,923	233,925
Total liabilities and shareholders' equity . . .	$387,780	$366,656	$333,167	$341,484

Source: Company annual reports.

MONTICELLO POTTERY, INC.*

Quincy Adams, president of Old-South Management, met the case writer on Thursday, July 7, to discuss the history and future of Monticello Pottery, Inc. Adams is evaluating alternative plans of action to rectify the current situation at Monticello Pottery, Inc. Time is of the essence, as Monticello Pottery, Inc.'s $3.5 million line of credit with its lead bank is up for renewal. "The bank insists that we inject more equity into the business," states Adams. The request for more equity could not have come at a worse time.

Sales at the Lynchburg, Virginia, Monticello Pottery retail outlet are down from 1987 levels, and the newly opened Savannah, Georgia, store is not performing as anticipated. Combine these two unforeseen events with several erroneous Christmas purchasing decisions and one can envision Monticello Pottery, Inc., heavily loaded with inventory and financially strapped. In the midst of this financial crisis Adams faces an additional challenge: removing his parents' names from the company books.

When asked to describe Monticello Pottery, Inc., Adams replied, "We are a small company in some respects and a large one in others." Monticello Pottery, Inc. has 350 employees, three retail outlets, and has been operational for five years. The first store, in Charlottesville, Virginia, opened its doors in November of 1983. In 1986 a second store opened in Lynchburg, Virginia. Recently a third location opened in Savannah, Georgia. Monticello Pottery, Inc. is currently experiencing problems typical of many start-up ventures that survive the transformation from the development stage of the business cycle to the growth stage. Many of the management strategies that were successful when the company had a single location with sales of $3 million no longer work now that sales have exceeded $17 million and stores are spread over a wider geographic area. In the early stages of the business, family members played the roles of generalists. As the business grew, specialization was needed. Lack of specialization led to many of the current problems.

Background.   For many years, the Adams family maintained a comfortable existence by operating three Bed and Breakfast motels and actively investing in real estate. In the mid-1970s John Adams (Quincy's father) was looking for a way to expand the family business. Quincy comments that his father "has tremendous vision. He is not one to write down business plans. He knows what he wants to do and does it. He is an entrepreneur who has the ability to relate to others and can work with and through others." John Adams decided to become more aggressive

---

* Prepared by Sandy Miller under the direction of Professor Richard I. Levin, The University of North Carolina at Chapel Hill. Names and locations have been disguised; all other information is actual.

in land development. After discovering the outlet shopping concept, he wanted to construct an outlet mall in Charlottesville. In 1978 John Adams began to seriously investigate the outlet shopping concept. He traveled extensively, getting a first-hand view of this new shopping phenomenon.

In their purest sense, outlet stores are usually located near manufacturing facilities and offer prices substantially below discount merchandisers. These stores provide an outlet for manufacturers' excess, damaged, and returned goods. Originally these outlets were open only to employees of the manufacturing plants, but popularity with shoppers encouraged manufacturers to open their outlet doors to the public. Several manufacturers in the Freeport, Maine, area decided to locate their outlet stores near one another, and thus the outlet shopping center concept was born.

John Adams solicited a number of manufacturing companies to locate stores in Charlottesville on a plot of land he intended to develop by a major highway. It is an important north/south artery on the East Coast, and a major route to popular tourist areas; Myrtle Beach, South Carolina, and Florida. All companies contacted rejected the idea. Most stated they would prefer to locate a store at a final destination, not in route to a destination. John Adams continued to pursue the retailing idea when a well-known businessman suggested that if the Adams family was going to pursue this outlet mall concept they should have an anchor store to attract other tenants.

"We originally planned to develop an outlet mall; the pottery store idea arose because of a need to have an anchor tenant to attract manufacturers," continued Quincy Adams. On a visit to Little Squaw Pottery, Quincy's mother Martha suggested that a pottery store would be an ideal anchor tenant for their mall. In 1982 John Adams approached his local bank to inquire how much he could borrow on an unsecured loan to establish a retail store. The original line of credit extended by the bank was $250,000.

John Adams had 25 years of experience in land development and motel management but lacked retail experience. Therefore, he contacted a recently departed buyer and a manager of Little Squaw Pottery and asked the two to serve as consultants to Monticello Pottery, Inc. These consultants established contact with vendors, placed the original orders, and helped determine the sales budgets and forecasts. First year projected sales were $2.5 million. Revenues exceeded $3 million. "Things were always upbeat. There was never a time when we wondered if we were going to make it or not in the retail business," commented Quincy Adams.

Corporate Structure and Affiliation. Monticello Pottery, Inc., the holding company that owns 100 percent of the stock in the three retail locations, is owned solely by members of the Adams family (see Exhibit 1). John and Martha Adams each own 18.97 percent of the stock in Monticello Pottery, Inc. Their four children—Quincy; Sam; John, Jr.; and Betsy—each own slightly over 13.5 percent of the company. The remaining almost 8 percent is owned by George King III. (Betsy Adams Martin's stock is owned by her husband Paul.)

Old-South Management, a consulting company owned by the four children, oversees and directs the operations of Monticello Pottery, Inc. Each store pays a

Exhibit 1   MONTICELLO POTTERY, INC., SCHEDULE OF OWNERSHIP

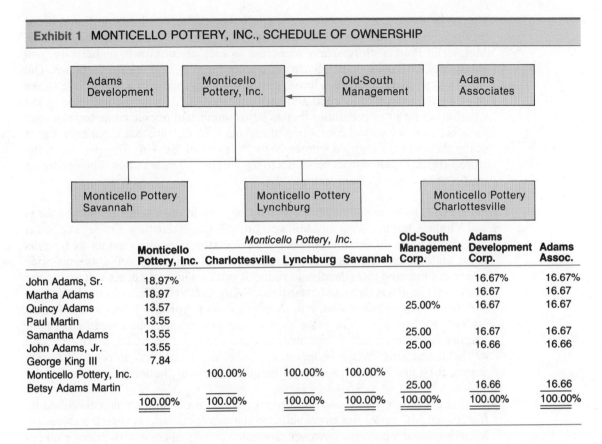

	Monticello Pottery, Inc.	Monticello Pottery, Inc.			Old-South Management Corp.	Adams Development Corp.	Adams Assoc.
		Charlottesville	Lynchburg	Savannah			
John Adams, Sr.	18.97%					16.67%	16.67%
Martha Adams	18.97					16.67	16.67
Quincy Adams	13.57				25.00%	16.67	16.67
Paul Martin	13.55						
Samantha Adams	13.55				25.00	16.67	16.67
John Adams, Jr.	13.55				25.00	16.66	16.66
George King III	7.84						
Monticello Pottery, Inc.		100.00%	100.00%	100.00%			
Betsy Adams Martin					25.00	16.66	16.66
	100.00%	100.00%	100.00%	100.00%	100.00%	100.00%	100.00%

consulting fee to Old-South Management for services. In 1987 the Charlottesville store paid a consulting fee equal to 8 percent of its net sales, Lynchburg paid 5.5 percent, and Savannah paid 3 percent. No individual in the Adams family works directly for Monticello Pottery, Inc. or is on its payroll. The Adams family members are paid for their contributions to Monticello Pottery, Inc. through the consulting fees Old-South Management draws from the stores.

Adams Development Corporation, a third and separate company, developed and owns the land and buildings in Savannah and Lynchburg. John and Martha Adams and their four children each own 16.6 percent of this company. In Savannah, Adams Development purchased land, modified an existing building, and then leased the location to Monticello Pottery of Savannah. In Lynchburg, Adams Development purchased land, constructed a building, and then leased the location to Monticello Pottery of Lynchburg.

Adams Associates, the fourth separately owned family enterprise, developed the outlet mall in Charlottesville on a parcel of property long owned by the family. (This mall celebrated its grand opening in July 1988. There was an earlier store, but it has since been converted to a warehouse.) At this location Adams Associates leases space not only to Monticello Pottery of Charlottesville for its store, but also to 24 manufacturer-owned outlet stores.

Monticello Pottery, Inc.   "We are a specialty retailer emphasizing home decor products, housewares, specialty gifts, and handicrafts," explains Quincy Adams. Monticello Pottery stores carry numerous brands of cookware, dinnerware, and glassware. All stores stock silk flowers, straw baskets, and wicker furniture. The selection of giftware includes brass, pewter, and ceramics. In addition, the stores offer an abundance of kitchen and bath accessories. A survey conducted at the Charlottesville store concludes that an equal number of people come to browse at the store as come with the intention of making specific purchases. Ninety percent of the shoppers are married women 26 to 55 years old. Seventy-five percent of the store's traffic is pulled from residents living within a 50-mile radius. The remaining traffic comes mostly from tourists.

Industry.   Outlet malls are fast approaching a saturation point in the Carolinas and Virginia, but the West and Midwest are still virgin territory. Quincy Adams is quick to draw a distinction between off-price stores, or discounters as he calls them, and true manufacturer-owned and -operated stores. By definition, off-price stores sell branded merchandise at reduced prices. Quincy Adams states that the term *outlet mall* has become bastardized. "Any mall that offers discount prices or perceives itself as being a bargain shopping center typically refers to itself as an outlet," he explains. "Off-price stores have low prices, but much of their inventory is imported and of low quality. Consumers are becoming more educated to the distinctions. When shoppers compare manufacturers' stores to off-price stores, they find higher quality and better bargains at the manufacturers' outlet stores."

Pottery stores are considered neither outlet nor off-price. When classified by the federal SIC code, the stores fall into the wholesale and superstore category. Retail prices at a pottery, however, are more closely aligned with prices charged at an outlet than with prices charged at a discount store. When asked to compare his stores to discount stores such as Wal-Mart or K mart, Quincy Adams acknowledges a few cross mixes of inventory, but says even those giant discounters cannot compete with prices or depth of merchandise on specific items in his stores.

Studies indicate that manufacturers' outlets attract many more shoppers than off-price malls. In addition, outlet shoppers travel greater distances to shop. A recent article in *Value Retail News* argues that outlet centers should continue to proliferate and their tenants profit because of value-oriented retailing.

The following quote is taken from a recent article published in a trade paper about one of Monticello Pottery, Inc.'s competitors:

> The name pottery, as a retail entity, is somewhat misleading, since we carry pottery and thousands of other related items. Pottery stores are one of the newest and hottest retail concepts in the country. We enjoy tremendous customer appeal and are destination points in the centers we anchor. Pottery stores make an ideal anchor tenant because we are compatible with any type of retailer, national or local. We have little competition from the discount or full-line department stores, because the particular merchandise assortments and sizes of each of our departments is larger and more competitive than those similar departments of the more traditional retailers.

Little Squaw Pottery, the company considered to be the closest competition and a company where many of the concepts and ideas for Monticello Pottery, Inc. originated, is moving more upscale. "This leaves a niche for us," says Quincy Adams. Monticello Pottery, Inc. operates out of large warehouses with unfinished ceilings, no carpet, and no fancy fixtures. Little Squaw on the other hand is expanding—upgrading its facilities and merchandise. It is starting to carry soft goods (sheets, drapes, towels, and clothes which normally offer lower margins) and is planning to discontinue using the word *pottery*. Little Squaw is also pioneering the expansion of the pottery concept by departing from its traditional southern roots. It recently constructed stores in Illinois and Washington, D.C. megacenters (several anchor tenants) that draw heavily from surrounding areas. This leaves plenty of smaller surrounding areas for Monticello Pottery, Inc. Quincy Adams is optimistic about the future of manufacturers' outlets. He again emphasizes that the goal of Monticello Pottery, Inc. and Old-South Management is to locate future stores in manufacturers' centers.

Expansion. Growth for Monticello Pottery, Inc., in both dollar sales and number of retail locations, has been driven thus far by real estate transactions owned and managed by Adams Development and Adams Associates.

The expansion to Lynchburg was somewhat of a fluke. The developer of the Lynchburg off-price mall was looking for an anchor tenant and offered a contract to Little Squaw Pottery, who rejected the proposal. On the way back to his office this developer noticed the Charlottesville Monticello Pottery store and approached Quincy Adams about being the anchor tenant. Monticello Pottery, Inc. agreed to locate a store in Lynchburg but only if Adams Development was permitted to own the land and building that was to house the store. Adams Development purchased land next to the mall and built its own store. Quincy Adams adds, "We are the anchor tenant, but our store is at the end of the mall in our own building."

The location in Savannah came about in a similar fashion. The leasing agent for the new larger outlet mall under construction by Adams Associates in Charlottesville led Quincy Adams to nine acres of property, including a free standing warehouse located directly on I–95 in Savannah. Adams Development decided to develop the Savannah property; they spent $1.7 million to renovate the store which opened in July 1987. A J.C. Penney outlet store and a Pace Wholesale Club are located near this store.

From a property development point of view, the Savannah store has been a good investment. "Land next to our Savannah property that was selling for $70,000 an acre when we bought ours recently sold for $160,000 per acre," says Quincy Adams. In Lynchburg real estate originally purchased for $1.6 million was appraised in 1988 at $3.5 million (land and building). In Charlottesville, Adams Associates owns 60 acres of land, 30 of which are currently developed. The land has a book value of $6,000 per acre. The most recent appraisal valued the entire tract of land at $2.1 million.

Quincy Adams smiles and points to a cardboard box behind his desk which is overflowing with manila envelopes and exclaims, "I have proposals from all over the country wanting Monticello Pottery, Inc. to be anchor tenants at malls!"

Adams makes it clear that if he pursues this line of expansion, he could grow faster than with his current plans. If he agrees to be the anchor tenant in malls or buildings that his family does not build, he can gain concessions from developers for being the anchor. In some cases, these concessions could be large enough to inventory the store.

Forecast. Quincy Adams states that Monticello Pottery, Inc. intends to continue to expand by one to two stores per year. Projections show sales of $100 million by 1992 with 12 to 15 stores. He estimates that gross profits should reach 35 to 37 percent. The bottom line profit should be about 4 or 5 percent. Adams admits that when Monticello Pottery, Inc. reaches a sales volume of $100 million, "We will begin looking for investors!" For fiscal year 1988 projected sales were $25 million. Consistent regional growth and the development of the Monticello Pottery name to make it a big draw are the objectives of Old-South Management. To achieve long-term goals Adams realizes that the company needs additional sources of capital. The land development aspect has been lucrative to date and has considerably increased the family's net worth, but the financial requirements are prohibitive and Monticello Pottery, Inc. cannot achieve long-term goals if development of all future stores is to be done by the family. The company's current financial statements are presented in Exhibits 2 through 5.

Adams's short-term goals are: (1) Remove his parents' names from the loan agreements. Their names are on the loan agreements at the bank; because they are at retirement age they want their names removed. (2) Establish banking relations that will supply needed capital so that Monticello Pottery, Inc. can expand and achieve its long-term growth goals. As are most retail establishments, this company is highly leveraged. Quincy Adams acknowledges that the debt-to-equity level must be brought down to acceptable levels. The lead bank is requesting that Monticello Pottery, Inc. reduce the current 18 to 1 debt-to-equity ratio to 6 to 1. Adams conceded that equity may have to come from an outside source, but this is a last alternative as far as he is concerned. He would rather see the equity come from growth. This may take years, but he is willing to exert the needed effort to keep Monticello Pottery, Inc., a family business as long as possible.

The company is currently negotiating with three banks. Previously, Monticello Pottery, Inc. has dealt with several banks, but presentations were made to attract one bank to service all of the company's needs. Adams does not hesitate to say that the lead bank has made it difficult to operate efficiently. "They gained the upper hand and set overly restrictive covenants on us," he insists. For example, one covenant of the loan agreement says that Monticello Pottery, Inc. is not allowed to transfer inventory from one store to another. Monticello Pottery, Inc. usually purchases inventory by container or truck load with the intention of distributing it among the three locations.

Problems. A repeated theme at the Old-South Management offices is the organization's lack of expertise in operations, finance, and human resource management. Adams is quick to point out that his company's main weaknesses at the present time are in operations and finance. Bobby Lee, a retired vice president of operations from a leading national retail chain, was hired temporarily as a consultant. Many new systems of inventory and internal control have been implemented, but Lee concedes that much work is still needed. Lee believes that Monticello Pottery is headed in the right direction and when it gets the planned systems in place, it will be more advanced than any other company in the pottery retail business. Adams concedes that the weakest link in the Monticello Pottery chain is its financial expertise.

A bank executive from the lead bank handling the Monticello Pottery, Inc., account is very enthusiastic. He assures Adams that the capital needed to fund further growth is available; but the trick, he emphasizes, is knowing the avenues to travel to obtain the money. Adams confides that the banker has already assisted three companies that have successfully gone public. According to Adams, this bank executive has shown interest in joining Monticello Pottery as CFO. "By letting this individual buy into our company, we would have to give up some control, but he would bring much needed financial expertise and bargaining power."

Monticello Pottery, Inc.'s third problem is management related and stems directly from the organization's lack of retail experience. Store managers who claimed they sought autonomy and who wanted responsibility for making store decisions were hired from major retail chains. Old-South learned that although these store managers sought to be independent, they were actually accustomed to the road map type of store management. Quincy confesses, "We thought these people would know how to run their stores and know how to merchandise inventory. We were wrong. We also lack proper training programs for our people at the store level." One of the problems singular to the Savannah store was that the hired managers did not understand the pottery concept. When Old-South Management fired these managers, it hurt morale.

Asked to elaborate on what caused Monticello Pottery's current problems, Adams replies that two main events brought the company to where it is now: (1) the expansion to the Savannah market, and (2) the unforeseen occurrences in Lynchburg.

Pointing out the errors in Savannah, he says, "We were undercapitalized and overly optimistic from the start in Savannah." Old-South Management projected the Savannah store would do in excess of $9 million in its first year. They'll be lucky to do $7 million because Monticello Pottery, Inc., suffers from lack of exposure in Savannah. The store in Savannah, unlike the successful Charlottesville location, is not in a mall. This free-standing store cannot justify or afford to advertise extensively. Furthermore, inventory and management problems are pervasive. Adams believes that to break even on advertising in Savannah, Monticello Pottery, Inc., would need four retail units in the Savannah market.

As for the Lynchburg fiasco, no one foresaw that the closing of a theme park would impact tourism so negatively in the surrounding area. This store seems much more dependent on tourists than the Charlottesville location. Like the Charlottesville store, the Lynchburg store is in a mall, not an outlet mall but an off-price mall. Furthermore, Little Squaw opened a store in the vicinity. Old-South Management had not anticipated Little Squaw's arrival.

Exhibit 2 COMPARATIVE BALANCE SHEET AND INCOME STATEMENT, MONTICELLO POTTERY, INC., 1985–1987

| | Charlottesville | | | Lynchburg | | Savannah* |
	1987	1986	1985	1987	1986	1987
BALANCE SHEET DATA						
Assets						
Cash	$ 14,698	$ (90,506)	$ 44,717	$ 27,288	$ (60,992)	$ 81,536
Accounts receivable	5,563	9,117	290	8,102	8,433	5,840
Other receivables	304,399	1,030	18,168	455,440	101,894	21,219
Refunded income taxes	54,772	—	24,987	42,068	—	—
Inventory	1,259,612	850,347	907,307	1,950,241	1,112,193	1,834,683
Prepaid expenses	28,408	3,845	2,891	20,832	2,224	57,199
Property, plant, and equipment	414,556	383,693	272,305	269,678	233,061	497,361
Accumulated depreciation	130,456	189,524	88,897	46,629	38,268	12,754
Other assets	3,760	8,772	14,209	83	110	220
Total assets	$1,955,311	$ 976,776	$1,195,976	$2,727,103	$1,358,655	$2,485,304
Liabilities						
Bank overdraft	15,812	—	—	128,829	—	45,585
Notes payable—Bank	680,000	460,243	694,183	997,399	1,095,693	1,860,071
Notes payable—Other	163,594	79,162	—	330,386	14,644	390,785
Accounts payable	344,982	89,393	190,840	618,500	89,204	399,688
Accrued expenses	29,375	15,900	8,849	114,026	26,657	18,215
Taxes payable	20,232	49,848	32,421	16,571	45,684	9,619
Long-term notes payable	77,243	—	—	500,000	—	—
Deferred income taxes	43,608	—	—	18,297	—	—
Total liabilities	$1,374,847	$ 694,546	$ 926,292	$2,724,008	$1,271,882	$2,723,963

Stockholders' Equity

Common stock	16,200	10,200	10,200	4,000	4,000	1,000
Retained earnings	564,263	272,030	259,484	(905)	82,774	(239,659)
Total equity	$ 580,463	$ 282,230	$ 269,684	$ 3,095	$ 86,774	$(238,659)
Total liabilities and stockholders' equity	$1,955,311	$ 976,776	$1,195,976	$2,727,103	$1,358,655	$2,485,304

INCOME STATEMENT DATA

Revenues	$6,532,540	$5,437,957	$4,302,388	$8,033,737	$6,686,275	$3,429,978
Cost of goods sold	4,272,308	3,291,242	2,691,268	5,386,041	4,124,745	2,321,840
Gross profit	2,260,232	2,146,715	1,611,120	2,647,696	2,561,530	1,108,138
Operating expenses	1,980,174	1,897,939	1,373,578	2,581,944	2,417,931	1,274,268
Profit from operations	280,058	248,777	237,542	65,752	143,599	(166,130)
Other income	54,347	27,528	13,885	5,654	10,715	3,523
Other expenses (interest)	77,249	79,059	37,805	129,800	42,184	77,052
Income tax expense	19,105	63,481	—	(1,470)	27,637	—
Cumulative accounting change	40,720	—	—	1,641	—	—
Net income	$ 278,771	$ 133,765	$ 213,622	$(55,283)	$ 84,493	$(239,659)

Fiscal Year—January to January.
* Savannah figures are from July 1987 to January 1988.

Exhibit 3   1987 OPERATING EXPENSES, MONTICELLO POTTERY, INC.

	Office	Charlottesville store	Lynchburg store	Savannah store	Eliminations	Consolidated balances
Payroll		$ 553,836	$ 754,778	$ 377,609		$1,686,222
Utilities		74,390	113,792	75,175		263,357
Security		3,312	8,066	3,381		14,759
Telephone		25,737	24,703	6,327		56,768
Repairs and maintenance		21,989	12,602	13,913		48,504
Common area maintenance			104,745			104,745
Office expenses	166	29,461	28,688	13,815		72,130
Operating supplies		26,602	46,329	43,329		116,260
Travel		28,565	26,526	49,124		104,216
Legal and accounting	315	31,076	38,257	18,974	$16,000	72,621
Advertising		274,008	364,156	234,621		872,785
Laundry and linen		4,283	1,967	1,507		7,757
Uniforms		676	676			1,352
Cleaning services		4,210				4,210
Miscellaneous		4,394	887	164		5,445
Management fees*		519,546	434,190	102,919		1,056,655
Rent on buildings**		150,167	300,000	150,000		600,167
Credit card commissions		26,352	46,603	12,065		85,020
Waste disposal		6,228	13,700	15,565		35,493
Payroll taxes	631	47,374	77,374	37,662		163,040
Other taxes and licenses	40	12,454	18,499	19,683		50,676
Bad debts		3,111	6,936	1,789		11,835
Dues and subscriptions		718	905	565		2,188
Insurance		71,676	77,380	18,798		167,854
Contributions		2,067				2,067
Equipment rental		4,114	14,537	4,968	10,852	12,767
Warehouse expense		8,024	11,164	6,273		25,461
Depreciation	1,104	46,430	26,974	12,754		87,262
Amortization		5,012	26	20		5,058
Contract services		67	273	22,807	12,254	10,893
Bank charges	24	408	10,436	21		10,889
Loss from theft		2,483	13,161	1,990		17,634
Cash short		33	4,203	5,555		9,791
Annual loan fee to bank				10,000		10,000
Loan commitment fee				12,896		12,896
Loan fee to officer			1,393			1,393
Total operating expenses	$2,280	$1,988,801	$2,583,924	$1,274,268	$39,106	$5,810,168

* Retail stores pay a management consulting fee to Old-South Management for services. Nonfamily employees of Old-South Management account for approximately $100,000 of consulting fees.
** Rent paid to Adams Development and Adams Associates for rental of retail locations.

STRENGTHS, WEAKNESSES, OPPORTUNITIES, AND THREATS

Family members saw Monticello Pottery's situation as follows:

Strengths: The unique concept. The market is so new and undefined that Monticello Pottery, Inc., is one of the pioneers in this type of retailing. The entire family is committed to this concept—we all work for the good of the company. All family members have equal ownership in the business.

Weaknesses: Capitalization. Internal systems and automation. Retail experience. We lack proper structure, proper employee training, and good employee relations. Marketing is another weakness.

Exhibit 4 1987 CONSOLIDATED BALANCE SHEET, MONTICELLO POTTERY, INC. (unaudited)

Assets		Liabilities	
Current assets:		**Current liabilities:**	
Cash	$ 124,419	Bank overdraft	$ 193,064
Accounts receivable	19,504	Notes payable—Bank	3,537,470
Other receivables	20,792	Notes payable—Other	135,000
Refundable income taxes	96,840	Accounts payable	1,363,170
Inventory	5,044,536	Accrued expenses	162,702
Prepaid expenses	106,439	Taxes payable	50,137
Total current assets	$5,412,530	Total current liabilities	$5,441,542
Fixed assets:		**Long-term liabilities:**	
Signs	160,262	Notes payable	577,243
Vehicles	39,624	Deferred income taxes	61,905
Equipment	406,295	Total liabilities	$6,080,690
Shelving and fixtures	421,170	**Stockholders' equity**	
Office furniture and equipment	62,240	Common stock ($1 par, 100,000 shares	
Leasehold improvements	108,568	authorized, 10,850 outstanding)	10,850
Accumulated depreciation	(190,944)	Paid-in capital	325,344
Other	4,063	Retained earnings	6,925
Total fixed assets	$1,011,279	Total stockholders' equity	343,119
Total assets	$6,423,809	Total liabilities and stockholders' equity	$6,423,809

* Notes payable consisted of the following loans and credit arrangements:

Banks	Current	Long Term	Total
Note, bearing interest at the prime rate, due June 26, 1988, collateralized by all inventory and all fixtures now owned or hereafter acquired wherever located.	$ 680,000		$ 680,000
Revolving line of credit bearing interest at the rate of prime plus 1½, due June 10, 1988, unless extended by the bank by written agreement, collateralized by all debtors' inventory and fixtures owned or hereafter acquired.	$2,857,466		2,857,466
Total			$3,537,470
Officers			
Notes bearing interest at prime plus 1, due after January 31, 1989, payable to family members.		$ 77,243	$ 77,243
Note bearing interest at prime plus 1, due after January 31, 1989, payable to John Adams.		500,000	500,000
Total			$ 577,243
Other			
Note bearing interest at prime due January 29, 1989, to Old-South Management Corporation.	135,000		135,000
Total			$ 135,000

Threats: As with any business, economic trends. If interest rates go up, the carrying cost of inventory goes through the ceiling. Also there is the threat that a retailer with deep pockets will challenge us.

Opportunities: The opportunities are limitless.

Solutions. Old-South realizes that before the banks can be approached about removing John and Martha Adams' names from the loans, the stores must be in sound financial condition and have a positive cash flow.

Exhibit 5 CONSOLIDATED INCOME STATEMENT, MONTICELLO POTTERY, INC. (year ending January 1988)

Sales		$17,996,256
Cost of goods sold		
Beginning inventory	$ 1,874,547	
Purchases	15,148,178	
Ending inventory	(5,044,536)	
Cost of goods sold		11,978,189
Gross profit		6,018,067
Operating expenses		5,810,165
Income from operations		207,902
Other income		22,419
Other expenses (interest)		(284,101)
Net income before taxes		(53,780)
Income taxes		13,390
Cumulative effect of		
accounting change		74,095
Net income		$ 6,925

Solutions available range from selling the entire Monticello Pottery business to taking the company public—see Exhibit 6. Quincy Adams believes he can rectify the problems of Monticello Pottery if he straightens out his problem in Savannah.

To remedy its current problems, Monticello Pottery has five options: (1) Sell equity in the business. As stated earlier, the lead banker has demonstrated interest in joining forces with Monticello Pottery. In addition, investors could be sought in the open markets. (2) Refinance the real estate owned by Adams Associates and Adams Development; this land has increased significantly in value and the proceeds could be invested in the retail business. (3) Raise capital by issuing debt. (4) Persuade the banks to increase the line of credit to Monticello Pottery. (5) Locate a partner interested in developing the Monticello Pottery name through joint venture. These strategies give the business needed working capital. With sufficient working capital, Monticello Pottery, Inc., can expand. Rapid expansion to outlet malls not owned by the family would allow Monticello Pottery to outgrow its troubles by operating on larger economies of scale.

Suggestions on how to handle Savannah include: (1) Franchise the Monticello Pottery name in the Savannah market only. A party with substantial resources is interested in negotiating this deal in Savannah. (2) Create a joint venture in Savannah and continue expansion in this market through partnership. These two suggestions would help make the Monticello Pottery name more visible in Savannah and make advertising in this market more feasible. (3) Sell the store in Savannah. This would supply equity, allowing the company to lower its debt-to-equity ratio, thereby gaining more bargaining power with the banks. Quincy Adams realizes that he may have to relinquish control of the Savannah store to achieve the desired long-term goals. Adams's final statement on Savannah is, "Maybe we entered the Savannah market too soon."

Exhibit 6 DECISION TREE FOR MONTICELLO POTTERY, INC.

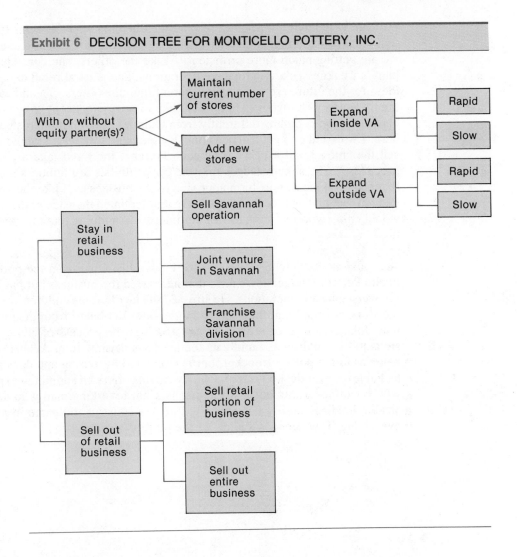

A feasible but rarely mentioned solution is for the Adams family to sell the entire retail operation and concentrate solely on land development.

Family Views. Different opinions on how to handle the current situation at Monticello Pottery were expressed by family members. Although they all want to see the business succeed, Quincy, Sam, and John have different ideas on what they would like to see happen to the business.

Samantha Adams. Sam is the head buyer. She travels extensively hunting for bargains and close-outs on merchandise. She points out that cost of goods might be cut by several percentage points because of the newly installed internal control systems and the expanded buying power that comes with size. Sam states, "The problem with buying for our stores and the dilemma we face stems from the fact that we buy six months in advance, and we are still new to this game. However, we are getting much more proficient.'' Like the others, she conceded this company's weaknesses are in finance, operations, and general retail experience. Her ideas for the future are somewhat different than the others. She indicates that the family works well together. She would like to see the concept grow but she views her role in the company differently from Quincy. "I am not interested in a career here. I would like to get married someday and start a family. I would just as soon sell the entire retail aspect (Monticello Pottery, Inc.) and take my share of the proceeds." She acknowledges that the opportunities are limitless and confesses that she is taking a short-term approach to the business. "I like the land development aspect and believe that there is great potential in that side of the business and would enjoy working on that. I'm not interested in doing retail for the rest of my life."

John Adams, Sr.   John is anxious to remove his name from the books of Monticello Pottery. He acknowledges that he started the business but has since given up overseeing the operations. He stressed the fact that the children are doing all of the work now and that they should be the ones to benefit from their efforts—not him. John Adams is at retirement age and is in the process of giving his possessions to his children as rapidly as the tax laws permit. John Adams says that he believes in the pottery concept, but is interested in retiring and does not want to be liable for Monticello Pottery. Quincy Adams offers an additional explanation of why his father wants out. "My father is a hard-working man who has amassed sizable holdings and is not interested at this stage of the game in jeopardizing everything. Dad seems skeptical of the pottery business!"

FOOD LION, INC.*

In 1957 three former Winn-Dixie employees opened their first supermarket in Salisbury, North Carolina, under the name Food Town. Cofounders Ralph Ketner, Brown Ketner, and Wilson Smith all had considerable retail experience in the grocery industry; however, Food Town struggled in its early years. Various marketing gimmicks were implemented (the company gave away trading stamps and even free automobiles), but the stores failed to win the loyalty of customers. In fact, Ralph Ketner had to close 9 of the 16 stores during the first 10 years of operation. He blamed much of this failure on the underpricing techniques of Winn-Dixie. By 1966, only seven Food Town stores remained.

In response to the problem, Ketner decided to slash prices on all items sold in the stores. He realized that a drastic increase in volume would be necessary to make this approach work and keep the company afloat. The company theme of LFPINC or "Lowest Food Prices in North Carolina" became popular as both customers and sales increased greatly. Sales rose 54 percent to $8.9 million, and profits rose 165 percent to $95,000 in the first year under the new pricing strategy.[1]

In 1970 the company went public. Etablissements Delhaize Freres et Cie, a Belgium grocery chain, purchased 47.6 percent of the stock in 1974. Today, Delhaize controls 50.6 percent of the voting stock and has 5 of the 10 seats on the board of directors.[2] The company changed its name to Food Lion in 1983 to avoid confusion with another similarly named chain. Also, the company began implementing its expansion program.

Today, Food Lion operates in eight states, from Delaware to Florida, and is considered to be one of the fastest growing retail grocers in the country. (See Exhibit 1.) Food Lion President and CEO Tom E. Smith explains, "Our goal is to bring extra low grocery prices to as many people in the Southeast as possible."[3]

Food Lion has 27,000 employees, and continues to operate conventional size stores (21,000–29,000 square feet) and to offer discount prices. The company remains committed to expansion throughout the Southeast and has avoided moving into the sales of general merchandise in its stores. A food consultant's comments highlight the company's success in the aforementioned areas. He states that Food Lion is "probably the best example of commitment to a format and operating style in the industry today. And although it is a conventional store

---

* Prepared by Janet L. Caswell under the direction of Professor Neil H. Snyder, both of the University of Virginia. © 1988 by Neil H. Snyder.

[1] Richard Anderson, "That Roar You Hear Is Food Lion," *Business Week*, August 24, 1987, p. 66.

[2] Ibid.

[3] *1987 Food Lion, Inc. Annual Report*, p. 1.

Exhibit 1 STORE DISTRIBUTION		
Location	Stores	Percent of total
North Carolina	233	49.1%
Virginia	112	23.5
South Carolina	74	15.6
Tennessee	29	6.1
Georgia	19	4.0
Florida	6	1.3
Delaware	1	0.2
Maryland	1	0.2
Total	475	100.0%

Source: *Standard & Poor's Stock Report*, p. 3905.

operator, it also stands as an excellent practitioner of niche marketing. The stores aren't fancy, but beat everyone on price, and the company doesn't make many mistakes."[4]

Ralph Ketner

Since cofounding Food Lion, Ralph Ketner has continued to be a force behind its success. In 1968 it was his idea to adopt the strategy of discount pricing and his LFPINC theme which promoted the company. He acted as chief executive officer until 1986, when he passed the reins to President Tom Smith. Despite giving up his CEO title, Ketner still exerts considerable influence over the operation of Food Lion. He remains chairman of the board of directors, and plans to retain this position until 1991. In addition, Delhaize signed an agreement in 1974 to vote with Ketner for 10 years. This agreement was later extended and was in effect until 1989.[5]

Tom E. Smith

President and CEO Tom E. Smith is very much responsible for Food Lion's growth and success. This is largely attributed to his involvement with the company since his youth. At age 17, Smith began as a bag boy at Food Lion's first store. He attended night school at Catawba College and graduated in 1964 with a degree in business administration. He spent the next six years working for Del Monte, when he was hired as Food Lion's sole buyer. Smith developed the successful strategy of stocking fewer brands and sizes than his competitors. He also took advantage of wholesaler specials by purchasing large volumes at discount prices. He was named vice president for distribution in 1974, and later

[4] Richard DeSanta, "Formats: Growing Apart, Coming Together," *Progressive Grocer*, January 1987, p. 37.

[5] "Ketner Gives Up Food Lion Reins," *Supermarket News*, January 6, 1986, p. 18.

became executive vice president in 1977. His continued success in these areas led to his promotion to president in 1981, at the age of 39. In 1986 he was named CEO.

Smith views himself as a planner who carefully molds the company's growth while keeping a close eye on the operations. This style has enabled him to react to and resolve any problems quickly and effectively. He has been a primary reason for Food Lion's constant commitment to its overall strategy of discount pricing and cost reduction. Smith has also become well-known through his participation in over 50 percent of the Food Lion commercials. This media exposure has brought him recognition not only in the Southeast, but as far away as San Francisco and even Scotland from visiting customers.[6] These commercials portray Smith as a hard-working and very trustworthy manager.

FOOD LION'S ATTITUDE TOWARD SOCIAL RESPONSIBILITY

Food Lion is recognized as a corporate neighbor, and it takes pride in performing charitable acts. In 1986 the company received the Martin Luther King, Jr., Award in recognition of its humanitarian efforts. Food Lion received the award for its role in donating trucks to aid southeastern farmers during a prolonged drought; the trucks enabled the farmers to transport hay from Indiana. Also, the company was cited for providing equal opportunity employment and establishing express lanes for handicapped customers.[7]

THE SUPERMARKET INDUSTRY

Several trends in the supermarket industry were of concern to many retail grocers. During 1987 there was a decline in the percentage of disposable income spent for food at home. After discounting inflation, real sales did not increase from 1986. As Exhibit 2 shows, food-at-home spending accounted for more retail sales than any other category in 1983. However, slow growth has caused a reduction in this percentage, leaving food stores in second place behind auto dealers. The percentage of retail sales for eating and drinking establishments during this same period has trended upward.

The grocery industry is also experiencing competition from other types of stores. Discount department and drug stores are starting to sell more packaged foods. Many fast-food restaurants continue to sell a larger variety of prepared foods for takeout. Sales from specialty shops, which concentrate on one particular type of food, have increased as well. Wholesale clubs have also been of concern to retail grocers. These clubs have been effective at luring many customers away from conventional supermarkets. Those supermarkets stressing discount prices have been hurt most by the emergence of the wholesale clubs.

In response to the trends, most grocery chains are stressing the idea of one-stop shopping. New store formats and product offerings are abundant. These

---

[6] Anderson, "That Roar You Hear Is Food Lion," p. 65.

[7] *1986 Food Lion, Inc. Annual Report,* p. 4.

Type of establishment	1983	1984	1985	1986	1987*
Exhibit 2 PERCENTAGE OF U.S. RETAIL SALES BY TYPE OF ESTABLISHMENT					
Food stores	22.0%	21.1%	20.6%	20.4%	20.3%
Eating and drinking	9.9	9.6	9.7	10.0	10.1
Drug and proprietary	3.5	3.4	3.4	3.4	3.6
General merchandise	11.1	11.0	10.9	10.7	11.0
Furniture and appliance	4.6	4.8	5.0	5.4	5.5
Auto dealers	19.8	21.6	22.6	22.9	22.2
Hardware and lumber	4.4	4.7	4.8	5.2	4.7
Clothing	5.3	5.3	5.4	5.5	5.8
Gas stations	8.5	7.8	7.3	6.1	5.7
All others	10.9	10.7	10.4	10.4	11.2

* First six months.
Source: Bureau of the Census (Revised) 1987.

ideas are an attempt to obtain a product mix that stresses higher margin items and services, as well as creating an atmosphere causing consumers to view the supermarket as more than a place to buy groceries. Items such as flowers, greeting cards, videocassettes, and pharmacy items are appearing more frequently in many supermarkets. There has also been a greater emphasis on stocking perishables.

However, the biggest trend in the industry is the shift to bigger stores. Several experts believe that increased size is necessary to provide the variety that many consumers desire. One chain president expressed this sentiment: "Customer satisfaction starts with the store design: one-stop shopping, complete service departments, and integrating a drugstore and pharmacy into the store."[8] Much of the one-stop shopping trend is a result of increases in the numbers of working women, dual-income families, single parents, and singles living alone. Time and convenience are two characteristics that consumers fitting into these groups often desire.

The one-stop shopping concept has resulted in several new store formats. Combination stores offer consumers a variety of nonfood items. These stores can be as large as 35,000 square feet, and 25 percent of the space is devoted to nonfood and pharmacy items. Superstores are similar to the combination stores in that they offer a wide selection of general merchandise items. These stores are all greater than 40,000 square feet, and are thought to be the strongest format for the near future. Exhibit 3 shows chain executives' views on the prospects for the various formats that exist today.

The newest and largest of the formats it the hypermarket. Currently, 55 of these stores exist in the United States. The typical hypermarket ranges in size from 125,000 to 330,000 square feet and requires $25 to $50 million in sales per

---

[8] "Retail Operations: The New Basics," *Progressive Grocer*, September 1987, p. 56.

| Exhibit 3 | CHAIN EXECUTIVES' OPINIONS ON PROSPECTS FOR NEW FORMATS |

	Percent		
	Excellent	**Good**	**Fair/Poor**
Superstores	56%	36%	8%
Combination	38	53	9
Convenience stores	26	39	35
Super warehouse	22	39	39
Hypermarkets	10	33	57
Specialty	8	37	55
Wholesale clubs	6	30	62
Conventional	4	35	59
Warehouse stores	1	17	79

Source: *Progressive Grocer,* April 1988.

year just to break even.[9] Normally, 40 percent of the floor space in hypermarkets is devoted to grocery items and the remaining 60 percent is used for general merchandise. Freeway access, population density, and visibility are all key variables contributing to a hypermarket's success. A majority of the stores are run by companies which are not U.S. food retailers. For example, Wal-Mart has opened several stores under the Hypermarket USA name. Also, Bruno's, a retail grocery chain, is teaming up with K mart to build a store in Atlanta.[10]

Because of the trend to expand store size, the number of stores declined for the first time in years. However, the larger store sizes resulted in an increase in actual square footage. Many small units have been closed due to the openings of larger stores. In many market areas, there continue to be too many stores and too few customers to support them. This is going to be an even bigger concern given the advent of the combination stores and hypermarkets, since they tend to attract customers from a wider area than the conventional stores.

Although the majority of retailers believe that the bigger stores are necessary to be successful in the future, there is a large group that believes the industry is going overboard in its attempt to provide one-stop shopping. Chain executive Carole Bitter believes that the emphasis on size is unfounded. "There has been an ego problem in the industry that has led to overbuilding and has driven up store sizes and has increased the number of formats."[11] Proponents of conventionals claim that the larger stores are too impersonal to be attractive to everyone. They also believe that many consumers desire the conventional type of store, and that

---

[9] David Rogers, "Hypermarkets Need Something Special to Succeed," *Supermarket Business,* May 1988, p. 26.

[10] Ibid.

[11] "Retail Operations: The New Basics," p. 62.

Exhibit 4	STORE ATTRIBUTES DESIRED BY CONSUMERS

Rank	Characteristic
1	Cleanliness
2	All prices labeled
3	Low prices
4	Good produce department
5	Accurate, pleasant clerks
6	Freshness date marked on products
7	Good meat department
8	Shelves kept well stocked
9	Short wait for checkout
10	Convenient store location

Source: *Progressive Grocer,* April 1988.

this format will continue to be successful. Although many consumers claim that they want more service departments, studies have shown that the shoppers are not willing to pay enough for such departments to make them profitable. Exhibit 4 reveals what the average shopper desires. One-stop shopping capabilities rates only 26th on the list.

COMPETITION

In recent years, competition in the Southeast has become quite intense. Previously, this area was characterized by predominantly conventional stores. Combination and superstores were scarce. However, many retailers realized that the Southeast was a prime location for the newer formats. In 1984 Cub Foods opened three large, modern stores in the Atlanta area in an attempt to challenge Kroger's dominance in the Southeast. This move marked the beginning of several competitive shakeups in the South.

Kroger

Kroger operates 1,317 supermarkets and 889 convenience stores in the South and Midwest. In 1987 sales were nearly $18 billion. More than 95 percent of the floor space is either new or has been remodeled during the past 10 years.[12] This is a result of the chain's move to larger combination and superstore formats. Kroger has not been as successful as it would like. The company realizes a net profit margin of approximately 1 percent. This is partly due to its new outlets cannibalizing its existing stores and has caused same-store sales comparisons to be relatively flat.[13]

---

[12] *Standard & Poor's Standard Stock Reports,* p. 1318.

[13] *Value Line Investment Survey,* 1987, p. 1511.

In response to the disappointing profit margins, Kroger is planning to decrease its capital spending plans by about $300 million. It is hoped that this will reduce interest costs as well as keep start-up expenses down. Also, the firm is cutting corporate overhead 20 percent. As for future store designs, Kroger is considering the curtailment of the new super-warehouse stores. These stores combine low grocery prices with high-priced service departments and have not appealed to a large segment of the market. Furthermore, the company is planning to reduce store remodeling in mature market areas.[14]

Winn-Dixie

Winn-Dixie is the fourth largest food retailer in the country with sales of nearly $9 billion. The chain operates 1,271 stores in the Sunbelt area, with the heaviest concentration of stores located in Florida, North Carolina, and Georgia. During the past few years, Winn-Dixie has been hurt by the influx of competition in the Southeast. As a result, profit margins have dipped to just over 1 percent. Net income also declined in 1987. Management points to a lack of investment in new stores and a rather slow response to competitors' underpricing methods as the main reasons for the decline in profits.[15]

Management has adopted several new strategies to combat the competition. Foremost is the move to larger store formats. In the past, the chain operated mostly conventional stores and depended on operating efficiencies to realize sizable profits. However, management believes that it is now necessary to alter the stores in response to changing consumer needs. At the end of 1987, the average supermarket was 27,700 square feet. There are approximately 250 new stores in the 35,000–45,000-square-feet range, and they are expected to account for nearly half of all sales in the next five years.[16] The units in the 35,000-square-feet category are combination stores operated under the Winn-Dixie name. The 45,000-square-feet stores employ the superstore format and use the name Marketplace. Emphasis is being placed on service departments as well as price-sensitivity.

Other changes involve management. Last year, the company eliminated a layer of management that resulted in 60 layoffs. The firm is also adopting a decentralized strategy which divides the company into 12 operating units. Each division is allowed to develop its own procedures and image. It is hoped that this will help the stores cater to the consumers in each market area more effectively.

Lucky Stores

Lucky operates nearly 500 supermarkets throughout the country. The majority of these are located in California; however, the chain does operate 90 stores in

---

[14] Ibid.

[15] *Standard & Poor's*, p. 2491.

[16] "Winn-Dixie Strategy," *Supermarket News*, March 3, 1987, p. 12.

Florida. In 1986 Lucky began a major restructuring. This resulted in the sale of all the nonfood businesses. Also, the company has concentrated on increasing the store size to enable the sale of more service and nonfood items. The average size of the stores at the end of 1986 was 31,000 square feet.[17]

At the end of the year, there was much speculation that American Stores Company would begin to pursue an unsolicited tender offer for all outstanding shares of Lucky common stock. American is a leading retailer in the country and operates mostly combination food and drug stores.

Bruno's

Bruno's operates approximately 100 supermarkets and combination food and drug stores in the Southeast. This chain pursues a strategy of high-volume sales at low prices. Another strategy involves the use of four different formats under various names. Consumer Warehouse Foods stores are relatively small warehouse stores which emphasize lower prices and reduced operating costs. Food World stores are large supermarkets which offer a variety of supermarket items at low prices. Bruno's Food and Pharmacy stores promote the idea of one-stop shopping through the combination store format. Finally, FoodMax stores are super-warehouses which offer generic and bulk foods in addition to the national labels.[18]

The company is also well-known for its innovative forward buying program. Bruno's is able to purchase goods at low prices because of its 900,000-square-feet distribution center which houses excess inventory. This strategy has been very successful as the company boasts high operating and net profit margins.[19] Exhibit 5 presents comparative statistics for Food Lion and its four major competitors.

EXPANSION AT FOOD LION

Food Lion has continued to grow and expand in the Southeast. During 1987 the chain opened 95 new stores while closing only 8, bringing the total to 475. With the exception of four supermarkets, Food Lion operates its stores under various leasing arrangements. The number of stores has grown at a 10-year compound rate of 24.1 percent.[20] With this expansion has come a 29.7 percent compound growth rate in sales and a 30.9 percent compound growth rate in earnings—see Exhibit 6.[21]

The existence and further development of distribution centers serve as the core for continued expansion. At the end of 1987, four such centers had been completed. These are located in Salisbury and Dunn, North Carolina; Orangeburg County, South Carolina; and Prince George County, Virginia. Two additional centers are planned for Tennessee and Jacksonville, Florida. These distribution

---

[17] *Standard & Poor's*, p. 1387.

[18] Ibid., p. 3358M.

[19] John Liscio, "Beefing Up Profits," *Barron's*, May 25, 1987, p. 18.

[20] *1987 Food Lion, Inc. Annual Report*, p. 9.

[21] Ibid.

Exhibit 5   SELECTED STATISTICS FOR MAJOR SOUTHEASTERN SUPERMARKET CHAINS, 1987

	Kroger	Lucky	Winn-Dixie	Bruno's	Food Lion
Stores	2,206	481	1,271	111	475
Employees	170,000	44,000	80,000	10,655	27,033
Sales ($ million)	$17,660	$6,925	$8,804	$1,143	$2,954
Sales/employee	103,881	157,386	110,049	107,265	109,267
Net profit ($ million)	$246.6	$151	$105.4	$31	$85.8
Net profit margin	1.4%	2.2%	1.2%	2.7%	2.9%
Gross margin	22.4	25	22	20.8	19.2
Current ratio	1.1	.83	1.65	1.63	1.41
Return on equity	24.5	46.3	15.2	15.4	25.3
Return on assets	5.5	11.8	7.9	10.3	10.6
Long-term debt/equity	.69	.38	.03	.04	.26
Earnings per share	$3.14	$3.92	$2.72	$.79	$.27
Average price/earnings ratio	15.1	10.2	13.9	23.1	35.3

Source: Standard and Poor's

Exhibit 6   FOOD LION'S GROWTH AND EXPANSION (in thousands)

Year	Stores	Sales	Net income
1987	475	$2,953,807	$85,802
1986	388	2,406,582	61,823
1985	317	1,865,632	47,585
1984	251	1,469,564	37,305
1983	226	1,172,459	27,718
1982	182	947,074	21,855
1981	141	666,848	19,317
1980	106	543,883	15,287
1979	85	415,974	13,171
1978	69	299,267	9,481

Source: Food Lion annual reports.

centers enable Food Lion to pursue expansion using its "ink blot" formula. Using this strategy, new stores are added to an existing market area in order to saturate the market. "If anyone wants to go to a competitor, they'll have to drive by one of our stores," explains CFO Brian Woolf.[22] Despite the emergence of new stores, cannibalization has not been a problem. In fact, same-store sales increase approximately 8 percent annually. When Food Lion enters a new area, the strategy of underpricing the competitors is employed. Such a strategy has caused average food prices to decline 10–20 percent in some parts of the country.[23] Every new store is constructed no further than 200 miles from a distribution center. With

---

[22] Liscio, "Beefing Up Profits," p. 19.

[23] "Food Lion's Roar Changes Marketplace," *Tampa Tribune*, April 5, 1988, p. 1.

continued expansion, new distribution centers whose radiuses overlap an existing distribution territory are erected to keep warehouse and transportation costs down.

Moreover, Food Lion continues to employ a cookie-cutter approach to its new stores. Rather than purchase existing stores, the firm much prefers to build new ones from scratch. All the stores fall into the conventional store category. The majority are 25,000 square feet and cost only $650,000 to complete. These stores emphasize the fruit and vegetable departments. Approximately 40 percent of the new stores are 29,000 square feet and contain a bakery/delicatessen. These are placed after careful consideration is given to the demographics and psychographics of the area. Normally, new stores turn a profit within the first six months of operation. In comparison, most competitors construct slightly larger stores which cost over $1 million to complete.[24]

The standard size of the stores has allowed the company to keep costs down while sticking to basics. Aside from the bakery departments, Food Lion has stayed away from service departments such as seafood counters and flower shops. Such departments are often costly due to the increase in required labor. Also, Food Lion has remained a retail grocery chain, shunning the idea of moving into the general merchandise area.

With the steady increase in stores over the past 10 years comes an increase in the need for quality employees. In an interview last March, Smith expressed concern over the high dropout rate of high school students.[25] Food Lion relies heavily on recent graduates, and the current trend may signal a decline in the quality of the average worker. Food Lion has responded to the labor problem by setting up an extensive training program for its 27,000 employees. These programs range from in-store training at the operational level to comprehensive training programs for potential managers. In addition, the firm continues to offer programs at headquarters to upgrade the work of the upper staff. Management is also attempting to increase the use of computers within the company. More specifically, Smith is hoping to utilize computer systems to handle much of the financial reporting aspects in the individual stores in an attempt to lessen the need for more employees.

ADVERTISING

Rather than employ costly advertising gimmicks, such as double coupon offers, Food Lion's advertising strategy combines cost-saving techniques with an awareness of consumer sentiment. Smith is the company's main spokesman, appearing in over half of the television commercials. Not only has this method kept advertising expenses down, but it has also made the public aware of both Smith and his discount pricing policy. By producing most of the ads in-house and using only a few paid actors, the cost of an average TV spot is only $6,000. Also, the company policy of keeping newspaper ads relatively small results in annual

---

[24] Anderson, "That Roar You Hear Is Food Lion," p. 65.

[25] "Food Lion, Inc.," *The Wall Street Transcript,* March 28, 1988, p. 88890.

savings of $8 million. Food Lion's advertising costs are a mere 0.5 percent of sales, one fourth of the industry average.[26]

The content of the ads is another reason for Food Lion's success. Many of the TV spots feature some of the cost-cutting techniques used by the firm. One often-mentioned theme at the end of ads in "When we save, you save." Another commonly used theme states, "Food Lion is coming to town, and food prices will be coming down." Before moving into the Jacksonville, Florida, area, Food Lion launched a nine-month advertising campaign. Many of these ads focused on innovative management methods which permit lower prices to be offered in the stores. For example, one ad demonstrates how a central computer is used to help control freezer temperatures. Other ads attempt to characterize Food Lion as a responsible community member. One such spot describes the importance that management places on preventive maintenance for its forklifts and tractor trailers.

Smith has also used the media to react to potential problems. For instance, Winn-Dixie launched an advertising attack against Food Lion reminding customers how competitors have come and gone. The company countered with an ad featuring Tom Smith in his office reassuring consumers. "Winn-Dixie would have you believe that Food Lion's low prices are going to crumble and blow away. Let me assure you that as long as you keep shopping at Food Lion, our lower prices are going to stay right where they belong—in Jacksonville."[27] Smith also reacted quickly to a possible conflict in eastern Tennessee in 1984. Several rumors circulated which linked the Food Lion logo to Satanic worship. In response, Smith hired Grand Ole Opry star Minnie Pearl to appear in the Tennessee advertisements until the stories disappeared.[28]

INNOVATIONS

The grocery industry is characterized by razor-thin margins. While most retail grocery chains have failed to introduce new innovations in the industry, Food Lion has employed several techniques which enable the firm to offer greater discounts on nearly all its products. These innovations help Food Lion to realize a profit margin of nearly 2.9 percent, twice the industry average. The company's credo is doing "1,000 things 1 percent better."[29] Such a philosophy has resulted in keeping expenses at 14 percent of sales as compared to the industry average of 20 percent.

Examples of the company's cost-cutting ideas are abundant. Rather than purchase expensive plastic bins to store cosmetics, Food Lion recycles old banana crates. These banana boxes are also used for storing groceries in warehouses. These innovations save the company approximately $200,000 a year.[30]

---

[26] Anderson, "That Roar You Hear Is Food Lion," p. 65.

[27] "Food Lion, Winn-Dixie in Animated Squabble," *Supermarket News,* September 14, 1987, p. 9.

[28] Anderson, "That Roar You Hear Is Food Lion," p. 66.

[29] Ibid., p. 65.

[30] "Ad Series Heralds First Florida Food Lion," *Supermarket News,* March 2, 1987, p. 12.

Furthermore, the firm utilizes waste heat from the refrigerator units to warm part of the stores. Also, motion sensors automatically turn off lights in unoccupied rooms. Costs are further reduced by Food Lion's practice of repairing old grocery carts rather than purchasing newer, more expensive models. Perhaps the greatest savings can be attributed to the carefully planned distribution system. This system allows management to take advantage of wholesalers' specials. The centralized buyout-and-distribution technique allows products for all stores to be purchased at one volume price.

Moreover, labor costs remain lower than those of many competitors. Smith is vehemently opposed to the use of unionized labor. Despite protests from the United Food and Commercial Workers International Union claiming that Food Lion's wages are well below union standards, management has continued to please its workers and avoid unionization. In fact, Smith believes its employee-benefit package is unequaled in the industry. A profit-sharing plan linking an employee's efforts in making Food Lion profitable with wealth accumulation for the future is already in use. Plans to improve long-term disability insurance benefits are underway.[31] In contrast, several other chains have experienced problems solving labor union problems. For example, a month-long strike by Kroger's Denver-area employees resulted in concessions on wages, benefits, and work rules. Safeway employees were also given quick concessions after threatening to close down several stores.[32]

Other innovations are designed to increase sales. Food Lion often sells popular items such as pet food and cereal at cost in an attempt to draw more customers into the stores. The company makes $1 million a year selling fertilizer made from discarded ground-up bones and fat. Lower prices are also feasible due to the policy of offering fewer brands and sizes than competitors. The company has increased its private label stock, which now includes at least one unit in every category. These two methods allow the company to price its national brand products below many competitors' private brands. As mentioned earlier, the smaller store size and sale of mostly food items have contributed to the high profit margin realized by the company.

FINANCE

Food Lion has been able to expand without becoming overextended or burdened with heavy debt repayments. The firm's capital structure consists of 26 percent long-term debt and 74 percent equity. The majority of growth has been financed through internally generated funds. The company does not want to grow at the expense of profits. Exhibit 7 presents selected financial ratios for the company.

The growth in Food Lion's stock price also reflects the sound financial position of the company. This growth illustrates the continued confidence of investors in the future productivity of the firm. In response to the rapid rise of

[31] *1986 Food Lion, Inc. Annual Report.*

[32] *Value Line Investment Survey,* August 28, 1987, p. 1501.

Exhibit 7   SELECTED FINANCIAL RATIOS FOR FOOD LION, 1978–1987

Year	Operating margin	Net profit margin	Return on assets	Return on equity	Long-term debt as a percent of capital
1987	6.8%	2.9%	14.2%	32.4%	26.0%
1986	6.9	2.6	14.1	29.8	24.0
1985	6.3	2.6	14.4	29.1	20.5
1984	6.3	2.5	13.6	30.2	22.8
1983	5.9	2.4	13.0	28.3	25.9
1982	5.6	2.3	15.7	28.1	18.0
1981	6.7	2.9	18.1	32.3	12.4
1980	5.9	2.8	17.7	33.4	15.5
1979	6.7	3.2	20.0	39.0	19.0
1978	6.9	3.2	19.5	38.3	22.8

Source: *1987 Food Lion Inc. Annual Report.*

Exhibit 8   TRADING RANGE OF FOOD LION'S STOCK PRICES, 1983–1987

Quarters	Class A Shares		Class B Shares	
	High	Low	High	Low
1983				
4	2⅛	1⅝	2⅛	2
1984				
1	1⅝	1⅜	1¾	1⅜
2	1⅝	1⅜	1⅝	1½
3	1⅞	1⅜	1⅞	1½
4	2¼	1⅞	2⅜	1⅞
1985				
1	2⅝	2⅛	2⅞	2¼
2	3⅛	2¼	3⅛	2¾
3	3	2¾	3	2⅞
4	3¾	2¾	3¾	2⅞
1986				
1	4½	3⅜	4⅞	3⅜
2	6⅛	4⅛	7⅛	4⅝
3	7¼	5½	9	6⅞
4	6⅛	5	7⅜	5⅞
1987				
1	7⅝	6⅛	8½	6⅜
2	8⅛	6⅞	8½	7
3	12¼	7¾	13	8¼
4	13⅜	7¾	14¼	8

Source: Food Lion annual reports.

Exhibit 9 PER SHARE DATA FOR FOOD LION, 1978–1987

Year	Earnings per share	Price/Earnings range	Dividends	Payout ratio
1986	.19	4/-1/	.01⅛	9
1985	.15	25-15	.01¼	8
1984	.12	20-12	.00¾	6
1983	.09	28-19	.00¾	8
1982	.07	32-12	.00¾	9
1981	.06	17-10	.00⅝	9
1980	.05	13-9	.00½	9
1979	.05	17-8	.00½	9
1978	.03	11-5	.00⅛	4

Source: *1988 Standard & Poor's Corp.,* p. 3906.

Food Lion's stock price, management has declared two stock splits since late 1983, when the two separate classes of stock were formed from the previous single class. These splits are designed to keep the price of the stock low enough to be attractive and affordable to all investors. Exhibit 8 shows the adjusted stock prices beginning in 1983, when the two classes were formed.

Furthermore, the per share data reveals the success Food Lion has achieved over the past decade. (See Exhibit 9.) These figures also illustrate investors' desire for Food Lion stock. More specifically, the price/earnings ratio indicates how much investors are willing to pay for a dollar of the company's earnings. In 1987 Food Lion's P/E ratio was the 83rd highest of all the companies listed in the Value Line Investment Survey.

FUTURE

Next week, Tom Smith is meeting with the board of directors to discuss and present his ideas for the next few years. Given the recent troublesome trends in the grocery industry as well as the increasing competition in the Southeast, he is reviewing the future strategy of Food Lion. Foremost in his mind is the extent to which Food Lion should continue to expand operations of its conventional stores in this area. He is also pondering movement into other market areas. Smith wants to be sure that the company will be able to finance future growth without greatly changing its current capital structure. Although the current success of Food Lion is quite impressive, Smith realizes that other grocery chains have experienced problems by not responding to the changing environment. He wants to be certain that this does not happen to Food Lion.

BIODEL, INC. (A)*

Dr. Oscar Feldman, founder and president of Biodel, Inc., sat back for a moment and reflected. The year 1979 had recently ended. It had been a constructive 12 months for his small biotechnology company, yet Feldman knew that several difficult strategic choices loomed before him in 1980.

Biodel stood at an enviable crossroad. Feldman was confident that Biodel had distinct competencies in its current biotechnologies. These competencies currently provided the company with competitive advantages on which the president had resolved to capitalize. Should the company pursue the significant growth prospects in these current technologies—cell biology, molecular biology, and immunodiagnostics? Or should the company expand its technological focus to include genetic engineering, a field poised at the threshold of exciting advances? If Biodel were to pursue genetic engineering, how should it do so?

Finally, Feldman wondered if Biodel had sufficient personnel and funds to pursue an aggressive strategy.

COMPANY BACKGROUND

Oscar Feldman was originally from Scotland, where his father had been a successful businessman. After receiving a Ph.D. in chemistry from McGill University and doing postdoctoral work at Harvard Medical School, Dr. Feldman taught at Stanford University. His work there centered on applying chemistry to biological and medical problems, including cancer research. During his 11 years at Stanford, Dr. Feldman published almost 100 papers, enjoyed widespread popularity, and established a base of contacts in the academic community which he valued highly.

Biodel was founded in 1962 shortly after Dr. Feldman obtained a contract for research which he felt could be executed more effectively in a commercial setting. The contract required the combination of several disciplines, including chemistry, biochemistry, biology, and enzymology, in order to obtain the best results. In an effort to cover initial working capital and facilities requirements for the start-up, Dr. Feldman raised $50,000 from local businessmen. He considered seeking a larger sum but decided that he would rather remain the principal shareholder of a smaller enterprise.

Dr. Feldman's initial business objective for Biodel was simply to establish a position of technological leadership in the biomedical industry. A key to his

---

* Prepared by Jeffrey Crowe under the supervision of Modesto A. Maidique, associate professor of engineering management, Stanford University. The case is based in part on an earlier ICCH (now HCS) case (Biodel, Inc. #9-681-004, Rev. 7/82) prepared by Mason Drew Haupt under the same supervisor. Reprinted from *Stanford Business Cases 1983* with permission of the Publishers, Stanford University Graduate School of Business, © 1983 by the Board of Trustees of the Leland Stanford Junior University.

strategy was the leveraging of his academic contacts. Dr. Feldman relied on his contacts at Stanford, for example, to bring on scientists to commence work on Biodel's first contract. He also planned to obtain additional government research contracts. Such contracts would provide Biodel with the financial support necessary to build technological leadership through the development of high-quality facilities and staff. Finally, Dr. Feldman began to assemble a small group of leading academics to advise Biodel. He stated at the time: "It is important to associate with none but the very best minds in the field."

During the start-up phase, Dr. Feldman held several views about his company's long-term strategy. Once Biodel had established itself in the contract research marketplace, he expected that the company would expand its focus. Dr. Feldman's exposure to his father's lumber business had convinced him that earning contract revenues and royalties would not be a sufficient long-term business base for Biodel. He envisioned a time when his company would manufacture and market biomedical products developed through its own research. Dr. Feldman was also wary of Biodel depending only on a few government agencies for its revenues. Marketing a product, he believed, would endow his company with a broad base of customers.

Despite slow but steady growth throughout the 1960s, Dr. Feldman's fears about dependence on government contracts were eventually realized. (See Exhibit 1.) In the early 1970s government cutbacks resulted in the loss of Biodel contracts with the Surgeon General, the Quartermaster Corps, and other agencies. At the time, the government had been responsible for 85 percent of Biodel's revenues. Biodel was forced into its first layoff, which troubled Dr. Feldman greatly. He considered the technological expertise of his employees to be one of Biodel's significant assets and regarded layoffs as damaging to the company's long-term potential.

This period of cutbacks and layoffs was a crucial point in the company's history. Biodel faced the threat of bankruptcy. Dr. Feldman later claimed that "It

Exhibit 1   BIODEL'S FINANCIAL HISTORY

Fiscal year	Revenues	Net income	Net income as a percent of revenues
1962	$ 250,000	$ 5,000	2%
1965	510,000	45,000	9
1968	619,000	31,000	5
1969	647,000	59,000	9
1970	352,000	(32,000)	−8
1971	289,000	(44,000)	−11
1972	394,000	26,000	7
1973	460,000	15,000	3
1974	583,000	49,000	8
1975	748,000	62,000	8
1976	1,011,000	88,000	9

was a good thing I wasn't such a good businessman, otherwise I would have realized that Biodel was insolvent.''

Concerns with its long-term survival caused Biodel in the early 1970s to move into the business of scientific research products, an area which Dr. Feldman had not originally anticipated. Biodel's scientific research products, numbering approximately 500, were initially items which the company produced to utilize in its own research efforts. Biodel discovered, however, that biochemists and molecular biologists in other organizations also needed such research products, yet often lacked the technical expertise to make them. Biodel found a ready market for various reagents and synthetic nucleic acids which it had been using internally. Relying on word of mouth as its basic marketing tool, Biodel generated enough demand for its research products to reverse the sharp decline in revenues from lost contracts. The company was so successful in commercializing research products throughout the 1970s that research products constituted approximately 60 percent of the company's revenues by 1980.

In January 1980, Biodel conducted all of its research and development at a 14,000-square-foot, leased location in Menlo Park, California. Due to the rapid growth of the late 1970s, quarters in the aging building were becoming cramped and Dr. Feldman knew that he had to start looking for additional space soon.

TECHNOLOGIES AND PRODUCTS

By the end of the 1970s, Biodel had developed special expertise in three areas of biotechnology: molecular biology, cell biology, and immunology. The company conducted research and sold research products to scientists working in each of the three areas.

All of Biodel's researchers were in some way studying cells, which are the basic biological units of life. Each cell possesses the biochemical machinery to grow and reproduce. An important component of this machinery is nucleic acid, a form of which is deoxyribonucleic acid (DNA). DNA is a relatively large molecule which consists of small building blocks called nucleotides. Specific arrangements of nucleotides, called genes, determine the production of specific proteins through a sequence of steps aided by biocatalysts called enzymes. Proteins provide the machinery by which cells utilize nutrients to grow and reproduce.

The techniques of *molecular biology* have played a leading role in determining the molecular structure and function of DNA and relating this structure to the production of proteins. In 1980 Biodel was using the techniques of molecular biology to isolate and prepare biologically active substances, such as nucleic acids and enzymes. The company then marketed the products to other researchers in molecular biology and genetic engineering.

Cell culture technology, a technique of *cell biology,* concerns itself with the growth of mammalian cells. Such cells have stringent nutrition requirements normally supplied by serum, the fluid portion of the blood. In this area, Biodel was primarily involved in manufacturing and marketing cell growth factors, products which could be used, either partially or completely, to replace serum in helping cells to grow. Adequate quantities of uniformly high-quality serum (usually derived from horses, pigs, and calves) were proving difficult for researchers to obtain. Thus, Biodel had enjoyed increasing success in the late 1970s in selling its cell growth factors to scientists who could not locate serum for use in their cell proliferation research. By 1980 Biodel's pioneering efforts had paid off. The company dominated the growth factor market with about a 60 percent share.

Biodel's third area of special expertise was *immunodiagnostics*. Immunodiagnostics is one field within immunology, which is the study of how organisms protect themselves against infection. When foreign substances (antigens) are introduced into an organism, the organism responds by producing antibodies which bond themselves to the antigens. The presence of a specific antigen in a sample may be measured by adding to the sample a known level of antigen which has been radioactively tagged. The radioactive antigen competes with the sample's antigen for the antibodies in the sample. By measuring the residual radioactive antigen not attached to the antibodies, the level of antigen in the sample can be accurately estimated. Biodel had research expertise and a small product line in radioactive immunodiagnostic products.

CURRENT ORGANIZATION

Contract Research

During the 1970s, Biodel reported its revenues in two lines: contract research and research products. (See Exhibit 2.) The contract research activities were projected to generate $1 million in revenues in fiscal 1980. Seventy percent of those revenues related to industrial research, the two prime customers being a large pharmaceutical company and a large chemical company. The government accounted for the remaining 30 percent of the contract research.

The scope of Biodel's contract research included work in the company's three primary areas of expertise (molecular biology, cell biology, and immunology) as well as in fields such as cancer chemotherapy, and enzymology. Within those areas the company offered its customers high-quality technical advice, numerous links to the scientific community, and a highly sophisticated contract research and development service with a record of many successes.

Dr. Feldman marketed Biodel's contract research efforts. He personally secured the contracts through his relationships with scientists in government and industry. Dr. Feldman also supervised the ongoing contract research activities. He managed the activities informally, preferring not to set exceedingly detailed milestones and budgets. He commented: "I considered my researchers to be professionals. I see no need for me to continually monitor them. Scientists are motivated by new technical challenges, not by heavy-handed supervision."

Research Products

Dr. Feldman expected sales of research products to reach $1.5 million in fiscal 1980. Research products consisted of three interrelated product lines corresponding to the company's three areas of scientific expertise: molecular biological products, cell biological products, and immunodiagnostic products. The product

Exhibit 2   SELECTED FINANCIAL DATA FOR BIODEL, INC., 1977–1980

| | For fiscal years ending August 31 | | | |
	1977	**1978**	**1979**	**1980***
Revenues:				
Product sales	$ 598,941	738,732	$1,153,749	$1,450,000
Contract revenue	754,207	836,385	730,942	1,000,000
Royalty and license income	—	—	—	50,000
Total revenue	1,353,148	1,575,117	1,884,691	2,500,000
Cost of revenue:				
Cost of product sales	271,225	324,781	489,091	750,000
Cost of contract revenue	550,652	659,480	667,548	800,000
Total cost of revenue	821,877	984,261	1,156,639	1,550,000
Gross profit	531,271	590,856	728,052	950,000
Operating expenses:				
Research and development	146,228	193,285	274,224	200,000
Selling, general, and administrative	205,592	245,475	436,057	650,000
Total operating expenses	351,820	438,760	710,281	850,000
Net interest income	—	—	2,000	—
Income before income taxes	179,451	152,096	19,771	110,000
Income taxes	81,400	56,200	2,000	10,000
Net income	$ 98,051	$ 95,896	$ 17,771	$ 100,000
Net income per common share	$.08	$.08	$.01	$.07
Common shares outstanding	1,351,875	1,351,875	1,351,875	1,351,875
Working capital	$ 449,209	$ 485,587	$ 476,698	$ 325,000
Total assets	$ 803,238	$1,875,063	$ 965,559	$1,400,000
Long-term debt, including capital lease obligations	$ 127,095	$ 108,414	$ 114,732	$ 30,000
Stockholders' investment	$ 433,233	$1,529,129	$1,546,900	$ 650,000

* Estimated.

lines were generally sold to researchers in universities, private laboratories, and industrial firms. Despite a limited marketing effort, sales had been growing at a 35 percent clip over the last several years.

In the area of molecular biology, Biodel prepared and stocked the largest commercially available selection of synthetic nucleotides. Researchers used nucleotides as substitutes and primers for nucleic acid enzymes, as reference compounds for sequence analysis in studies of nucleic acids, for the development of new separation techniques, and as tools in recombinant DNA research. Nucleotides accounted for 50 percent of the sales of all research products (Exhibit 3).

Cell growth factors, Biodel's primary product offspring in the cell biology field, generated 40 percent of the research product revenues. Sales of cell growth factors had risen rapidly over the past several years, and Dr. Feldman believed that they represented a fertile area for future growth. There did exist disagreement within the company's management team, however, over the company's current competitive position in cell growth factors. Dr. Feldman considered Biodel to be the technological leader, yet several top employees believed that this assessment might be too optimistic. All did agree, however, that they lacked the necessary market research data to back their conclusions with confidence.

Biodel had been a major factor in the immunodiagnostics market for several years until several large firms aggressively entered the field and slashed the

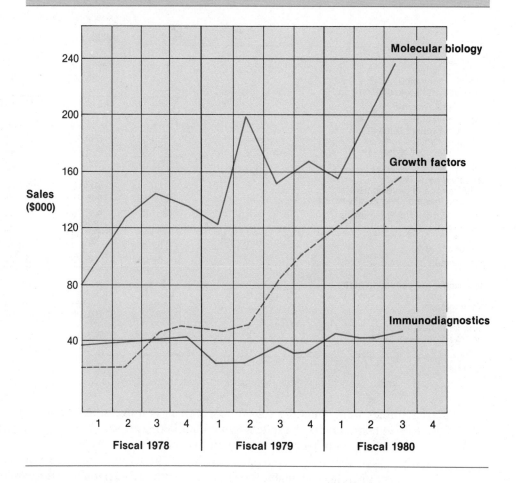

Exhibit 3 BIODEL'S RESEARCH PRODUCT SALES

company's market share. The product line had not expanded since that time and constituted 10 percent of the sales of research products in 1980. Further significant growth in radioactive diagnostic products was not considered likely.

Profitability for these research products varied, depending upon the intensity of the product's research and development. Operating profit margins, after charges for product cost, research and development, and marketing, were estimated at 20 percent in the aggregate. Biodel's current accounting system, however, did not provide product-by-product profitability data and aggregate data was clouded by overhead allocations that in the opinion of some managers were "arbitrary."

Personnel

Biodel was organized along lines of scientific expertise (Exhibit 4). The three operating groups—molecular biology, cell biology, and immunodiagnostics—

Exhibit 4 BIODEL'S ORGANIZATION CHART

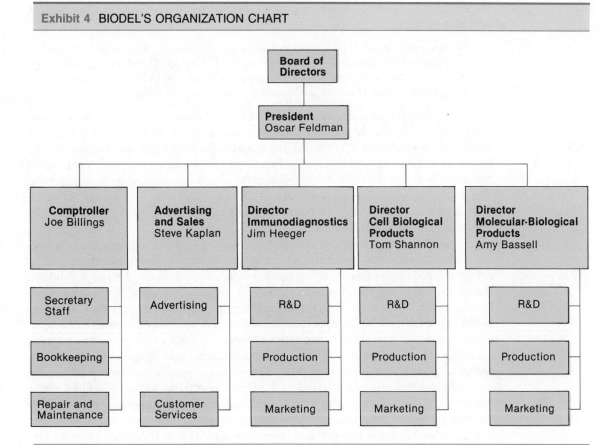

were each under the control of a manager who reported directly to Dr. Feldman. All three managers were experienced scientists who were longtime employees of the company. Each manager supervised R&D and production and held some marketing responsibility. The organization within each operating group was highly fluid. Generally, those scientists who completed research on a particular product would then turn to manufacturing the product in small quantities and would also determine which scientists in other organizations would be likely customers for that product.

From the standpoint of staff, Dr. Feldman had kept Biodel a lean organization. Biodel had 55 employees, most of whom were scientists or technicians. The company employed neither a marketing manager nor a research director. Dr. Feldman filled both roles due to his widespread contacts and scientific expertise. All of Biodel's financial functions were handled by an accountant who was also a longtime employee. Insofar as Dr. Feldman perceived major strategic, financial, or administrative issues, he invariably made the decisions himself. He rarely convened staff meetings and did not require regular reports from his subordinates.

Dr. Feldman considered his management style well-fitted to Biodel's organization and atmosphere:

> We are a paternalistic company. I believe in management by walking around and talking to people. That's the best way for me to stay on top of what is happening. I don't want our employees tied up in paper shuffling. And anyway, professional management, goals, budgets, and meetings are not my "schtik."

One employee characterized Biodel's board of directors as "Dr. Feldman and his friends." The board consisted of four members, including Dr. Feldman. A corporate lawyer, age 79, sat on the board. He had been involved with the company since its founding. Dr. Feldman had also wanted scientific expertise on the board and had persuaded a gifted Stanford scientist, now retired, to join him. The fourth member was an associate of Dr. Feldman who was an officer of an investment banking firm. The board was convened infrequently, whenever Dr. Feldman felt a need to discuss the company's affairs.

From the standpoint of the researchers, Biodel was an exciting place to work. Dr. Feldman believed that he placed heavy pressure on his researchers and in return offered them projects at the cutting edge of technology. Although Biodel's equipment was not the most sophisticated and the company's quarters were Spartan, the work itself was more challenging and fruitful than that of many commercial labs. In fact, employees likened the company's atmosphere to one of an academic facility. They considered the combination of informality and high challenge to be attractive. Turnover among employees, especially the senior technical people, was extremely low. The technical staff expressed pride in the company's work, and one referred to the firm's reputation as the "Cadillac of the industry." Dr. Feldman, who had distinct automotive preferences, preferred to refer to it as the "Mercedes of the industry."

A second reason for the low turnover was Oscar Feldman himself. Dr. Feldman was generally regarded as the hub of Biodel's universe. The senior employees were unanimous in their affection for the president. One of the senior scientists explained the phenomenon as follows:

> Simply put, Oscar is an attractive man. His warmth and effusiveness is infectious. He is so naturally witty and charming that you can't help but enjoy working with him. Oscar gets so enthusiastic about the work that it's contagious.

A senior manager added:

> Oscar is unique. Irrespective of the situation, he never fails to appear distinguished. He wears perfectly tailored suits, drives a stately old convertible, and has impeccable manners. He also looks remarkably trim and healthy for his age. There are not too many people still skiing avidly at age 65. True, sometimes he'll forget a fact or two, but he can also be extraordinarily articulate.

Marketing

Throughout the 1970s Biodel's marketing effort was an informal mixture of different activities. Research products were sold by mail, with customers typically having heard of the company through word of mouth. Trade shows, advertising, direct mail, and phone solicitation were also employed from time to time. Order processing and shipping were handled informally, without much emphasis on control. Dr. Feldman cited Biodel's customer service as "almost laughable."

In 1979 Dr. Feldman determined that the company needed to market its research products more aggressively and systematically. He decided that he needed someone who had familiarity both with the sales function and with biotechnology. In May 1979, he hired Steve Kaplan, who had been marketing manager at a large pharmaceutical company.

Tension eventually developed between Dr. Feldman and his new manager. Dr. Feldman wanted Kaplan only to organize a sales effort and gather information on customers and competitors. He still felt that he should direct Biodel's marketing strategy himself. Kaplan, on the other hand, perceived a need for focus in the company's marketing strategy. In addition, he concluded that Biodel was understaffed and proceeded to hire additional salespeople, an administrative assistant, an order clerk, and a secretary.

The results were mixed. Sales of research products increased 65 percent in the first quarter of fiscal 1980, an achievement for which Kaplan took credit. In addition, the customer service function began to respond more systematically to shipment delays and other problems. On the other hand, marketing costs increased 500 percent, resulting in sharply reduced profits despite the jump in sales. Dr. Feldman began to wonder if its marketing group was too large for Biodel, given its size and stage of development. He also began to question Steve Kaplan's tendency to make solo decisions regarding the company's marketing direction.

GROWTH OPPORTUNITIES

While Dr. Feldman was satisfied with the course Biodel had taken over the past 10 years, he knew that important choices remained to be made. Several of his top scientists were excited about two of the company's new product developments in cell biology and immunodiagnostics. At the same time, interest was building rapidly in scientific and financial circles in genetic engineering. The new genetic engineering technology was closely related to Biodel's expertise in molecular biology and could be a natural extension of the company's scientific focus. Each of the growth opportunities looked attractive, and Dr. Feldman wondered how he should decide which path to pursue.

Cell Biology

Based on its experience and expertise in using cell growth factors as components of serum substitutes, Biodel had under development several synthetic serums which were formulated to satisfy the growth requirements of a variety of cell lines in tissue culture. The synthetic serum substitutes would replace natural fetal calf serum, which was currently the most widely used source of growth for cells. Horse serum was second in market importance. The price and quality of fetal calf serum had been unstable over time because the availability of the product depended upon the slaughter of cattle, which tended to be cyclical. Biodel's researchers projected the market for fetal calf serum at about $50 million domestically in 1980 and $80 million worldwide and growing at 15 percent a year. Biodel believed that the market for synthetic serums of uniformly high quality and reliable supply would be even larger. However, these numbers were somewhat speculative, for the firm had not conducted a systematic analysis of the serum market.

Dr. Feldman believed that the company would have a competitive edge in synthetic serums which would be difficult for other firms to overcome. This advantage would allow Biodel to achieve a market share of up to 20 percent of the current market. The serums would be produced by adding to distilled water certain combinations of cell growth factors which would not be easy to break down and analyze. Even if a competitor could break the combinations down, Dr. Feldman believed that developments in this scientific discipline could not be quickly duplicated. It might require several years between the time a firm initially studied an area and the time it commercialized a product. Dr. Feldman was not certain whether other firms were currently pursuing the same course as his company. Finally, Biodel planned to cement its advantage by applying for patent protection, although it was by no means certain that a patent could be obtained.

Tom Shannon, the cell biology manager, felt that Biodel could eventually produce the synthetic serums at costs which would allow it to price the products competitively with fetal calf serum. At this point, Shannon guessed that a $1–2 million investment would be needed in manufacturing facilities. Dr. Feldman thought that the company would also need additional management personnel to oversee the venture. Both he and Tom Shannon were unsure as to just how best to market the product and what product introduction and marketing costs would likely be.

Immunodiagnostics

Within immunodiagnostics lay another opportunity for Biodel to enter markets vastly larger than its current customer base in research organizations. The company had under development a new testing technology based on enzyme membranes rather than radioactivity. Jim Heeger, the immunodiagnostics manager, expected that the new product (called DEMA) would have many applications in clinical, medical, environmental and industrial testing. The product could determine the presence and level of many substances, including hormones, enzymes, drugs, viruses, and bacteria. The tests could include, among others, those for pregnancy, syphilis, hepatitis, cancer, toxins in food, and carcinogens in the environment.

Heeger considered DEMA an alternative to tests based on radioactivity. It appeared to share the high sensitivity of radioactive tests without the drawbacks and hazards associated with radioactivity. In addition, Heeger believed that DEMA tests would be simpler, faster, and less expensive than radioactive tests. Other enzyme-linked immunodiagnostic technologies, such as EMIT and ELISA, were already in existence, but Heeger judged them to be less sensitive and applicable to fewer substances than DEMA. The company had filed for patent protection and had been encouraged to believe by its patent attorneys that a patent for the technology would be forthcoming.

As with synthetic serums, the market for DEMA tests appeared to be vast, perhaps in excess of $100 million. One analyst's estimate placed the potential home market at over $1 billion. Again, however, Dr. Feldman and his subordinates were unsure how to bring the product to the marketplace. Investments in the necessary manufacturing and marketing facilities and personnel could easily total in the millions. Further R&D costs would range from $1 to $3 million. On the other hand, several large drug companies had expressed an interest in exploring a joint venture or licensing agreement. Under such conditions license percentages ranged from 4 percent to 7 percent, depending on the fraction of R&D costs funded by the sponsoring firm. Dr. Feldman wanted Biodel to have some manufacturing and marketing capability, but he did not know how much of the marketplace his company could feasibly pursue on its own. One possibility was to have Biodel target the clinical diagnostics market, which was limited and well defined. Medical clinics would be a logical place to introduce the new DEMA technology. On the other hand, drugstore sales of DEMA potentially could generate enormous revenues and would be best pursued in conjunction with a partner that had an established distribution system and brand name. Pharmacies greatly outnumbered clinics, and DEMA would easily have numerous applications in the vast consumer markets.

Genetic Engineering

Dr. Feldman saw genetic engineering as a third opportunity for Biodel's expansion. The company currently had no direct expertise in the the field, although it was closely associated with genetic engineering laboratories by virtue of its work as a supplier of molecular biology products. The nucleotides and synthetic genes which Biodel produced and sold were used as support products by genetic engineers. In some cases, Biodel was the sole supplier.

The opportunity for Biodel to move into genetic engineering itself arose through Dr. Feldman's contacts. Dr. Daniel Ballantine, a University of California, Berkeley, Nobel Laureate and a pioneer in genetic engineering, was a longtime friend of Dr. Feldman and a consultant to Biodel. He had risen to prominence in the 1970s, and for the last two years he had been suggesting to Dr. Feldman that genetic engineering offered Biodel explosive opportunities for growth. Dr. Feldman began to consider seriously his associate's recommendations when he noticed an intensive interest developing in financial circles in the concept of genetic engineering.

The technology of genetic engineering is not complex in theory. To "engineer" a cell to produce a specific product, DNA containing the desired sequence must be isolated. The desired gene is either obtained from a biological source or is synthesized chemically. The gene is then spliced into a carrier molecule, called a vector, to form a recombinant DNA molecule. Control sequences which program the cell to produce the product coded by the gene are introduced into the vector, which itself could be a virus or a plasmid. The vector carries the new gene into the host cell, thereby programming the host cell to manufacture the desired product. The most widely used host cell has been Escherichia coli, or E. coli. More is known about E. coli than about any other bacteria.

While the theory of genetic engineering may be easy to understand, the techniques have been difficult to perform. Procedures for isolating DNA and for utilizing vectors were not discovered until the early 1970s. By the mid-1970s, however, the academic world realized the future of gene splicing and many major universities launched DNA research programs. A critical breakthrough came in 1973 when Stanley Cohen of Stanford and Herb Boyer of the nearby University of California in San Francisco first chemically translated DNA from one species to another by gene splicing. In contrast, the commercialization of the technology began slowly. In 1971 Cetus was the only genetic research firm. Genentech and Bethesda Research Labs were founded in 1976, followed by Genex in 1977, and Biogen in 1978 (Exhibit 5). Venture capitalists and large pharmaceutical, chemical, and energy companies provided the financing for the start-up phases of the fledgling firms. The large corporate investors had two goals: (1) to establish a technological window in a potentially revolutionary technology and (2) to make a profitable investment.

The early investments were already generating large capital gains by 1979. In 1976 Inco purchased $400,000 of Genentech's stock, only to sell it to Lubrizol four years later for $5.2 million. In early 1980 Genentech estimated that the market value of its privately held stock exceeded $100 million—one half of which was owned by the company's officers, directors, and employees. A frenzy was enveloping the whole field of genetic engineering. Investors seemed willing to stake significant sums of money on almost any company who employed well-known

---

Exhibit 5 THE FOUR PACESETTING GENETIC ENGINEERING FIRMS

Genentech, Inc.

Headquarters: South San Francisco. Founded in 1976; 110 employees. Has announced more DNA-made products than competitors. Joint ventures with Eli Lilly for human insulin; with A. B. Kabi of Sweden for human growth hormone; with Hoffmann-La Roche for interferon. Half-owned by employees. Lubrizol, a lubricating oil company, holds 20 percent; venture capitalists own the rest.

Cetus Corporation

Headquarters: Berkeley, California. Founded in 1971; 250 employees. Concentrates on industrial and agricultural chemicals, also interferon. Joint ventures with Standard of California for chemicals and fruit sugar; with National Distillers for fuel alcohol. Founders, employees, and private investors own almost 40 percent; Standard California, 24 percent; National Distillers, 16 percent; Standard Indiana, 21 percent.

Genex Corporation

Headquarters: Rockville, Maryland. Founded in 1977; 50 employees. Concentrates on industrial chemicals. Has interferon research contract with Bristol-Myers; another contract with Koppers, a mining and chemicals company. Management owns about 45 percent; Koppers, 30 percent; InnoVen, a venture capital company backed by Monsanto and Emerson Electric, about 25 percent.

Biogen S. A.

Headquarters: Geneva, Switzerland. Founded in 1978; about a dozen employees, plus others under contract. First to make interferon. Schering-Plough, a New Jersey pharmaceutical company that owns 16 percent, plans to begin pilot production of the antiviral drug using Biogen's process. Inco, formerly International Nickel, owns 24 percent. Remainder held by management and various outside investors.

Source: *New York Times*, June 29, 1980. Section 3, p. 1. Reprinted by permission.

scientists with connections to gene splicing. Financial journals continually touted genetic engineering's revolutionary potential to impact the manufacturing processes of products in the chemical, pharmaceutical, and petrochemical industries. The *New York Times* editorialized, "Recombinant DNA technology seems poised at the threshold of advances as important as antibiotics or electronic semiconductors." (January 19, 1980.)

Despite the euphoria surrounding genetic engineering, no firm had yet sold a genetically engineered product in mass quantities. Investors were lured by the prospects of production of a host of recombinant products, including pharmaceuticals, biologicals, chemicals, and fuels. Several firms had announced product capability—Biogen was making interferon; Genetech, interferon and insulin—but observers believed that years would transpire before any genetically engineered product generated significant revenues. The major pharmaceutical and chemical companies had set up their own gene splicing departments, but they, as well as the small firms, had yet to understand the intricacies of production on a mass scale.

Amidst the mounting excitement over gene splicing's long-run potential, Dr. Feldman pondered Biodel's role. While the business of selling support products to the genetic engineering firms was expected to grow at a 30 to 50 percent clip over the next several years, it held neither the glamour nor the potential for explosive expansion associated with genetic engineering. One of Biodel's competitors in the molecular biology products industry was quoted as saying: "Our market won't ever compare to the markets for genetically engineered products. After all, it only takes one dollar of our stuff to make a thousand or a million dollars of their stuff." Cetus was the world's biggest user of enzymes in its genetic engineering research, yet it could have bought one year's supply for $12,000. The market for synthetic nucleotides, enzymes, and the like seemed limited.

What Dr. Ballantine offered Biodel was a route to expand into genetic engineering itself. He proposed a novel approach to the problem of growing cells by using yeast organisms as hosts in place of the E. coli predominantly used by other genetic engineering firms. For the past two years, Dr. Ballantine had been collaborating with three other renowned scientists on the development of yeast as the host cell in the genetic engineering process. The four men believed that yeast cells would ultimately prove more attractive than E. coli for industrial applications of genetic engineering. Yeast cells were easier and less costly to grow and it was believed by Biodel scientists that they could be grown to higher yields and thus with lower costs than E. coli. In addition, yeast cells contained biochemical machinery, absent in E. coli, which allowed for the possibility of programming the yeast cells to produce glycoproteins (proteins which contained carbohydrates).

Interferon and urokinase were two examples of glycoproteins which, although currently produced by conventional extraction processes, could potentially be manufactured by yeast cells through genetic engineering techniques. Interferon was a protein which performed a regulatory function in the body; it appeared to inhibit the multiplication of viruses and cancerous tissue cells. Because of the extraordinary difficulty of producing it in large quantities through conventional techniques, interferon was highly valued in medical circles. In 1980 its price exceeded $1 billion per pound. Urokinase was an enzyme produced in the human body as an agent to dissolve blood clots. Sales of urokinase up to 1980 had been limited due to the complication and high cost of conventional extraction processes. Biodel had already had some experience producing urokinase through a tissue culture process and knew that several drug companies were interested in securing a large, stable supply of the enzyme if it could be genetically engineered. In short, Biodel scientists believed that genetic engineers using yeast might have an advantage over researchers using E. coli in producing both interferon and urokinase.

Dr. Ballantine indicated his willingness to convene his three colleagues with Dr. Feldman to discuss a possible association with Biodel. Dr. Ballantine and his friends were all experts in yeast genetics. Full professors at the nation's most distinguished university laboratories, the four had been elected to the National Academy of Sciences and had jointly won all of the coveted biochemistry and molecular genetics prizes in American science. Dr. Feldman was excited at the possibility of attracting them to Biodel. He commented:

> As a group, they have talents unsurpassed in genetic engineering. James Finney, Columbia's leading biochemist, possesses one of the most penetrating intellects I've come across. He is a mature scientist with unimpeachable integrity. He's the type of person you'd want at your side when the going gets tough. Ralph Davidson is noted among the scientists at Cal Tech for his brilliant creativity. Despite his quiet nature, he could make invaluable intellectual contributions to our activities. Dennis Bernstein generates more ideas than 10 scientists combined. His work at University of Wisconsin has earned acclaim throughout scientific circles. And of course, we have my good friend Daniel Ballantine. He is simply the best there is. If the four of them worked with us, it would give our company a tremendous edge. If even one of them joined us, we'd have an advantage over Genentech, Cetus, and the rest. However, if we plan to land any or all of them, we will have to make an extraordinary offer.

Indeed, all four individuals were in high demand. They had offers from large chemical and pharmaceutical companies for positions as senior scientists with salaries ranging from $75,000 to $100,000. Smaller biotechnology firms were luring them with stock option packages which included 1 percent to 4 percent of the companies' outstanding stock. Leading universities were proposing prestigious endowed chairs with unparalleled academic freedom and clout. Even venture capital firms had approached them, exploring the possibilities of a start-up. One venture capitalist had asserted that he could raise $5 million on the strength of Dr. Ballantine's reputation alone.

Biodel, however, was not without its attraction. The company could offer the scientists both the freedom to start up their own gene-splicing R&D operation and the expertise in key related areas. Biodel had placed itself at the leading edge of technology and had earned a position of respect in science. The scientists' ideas could be further developed and enhanced through an association with the company. Despite the intangible benefits, however, Dr. Feldman knew that he would also have to structure a lucrative financial package to lure them away, even on a consulting basis, from their well-established academic environments.

Although there was much uncertainty surrounding genetic engineering—estimates varied widely on market sizes and on the time required for successful refinement of production processes—Dr. Feldman hoped that Biodel would be able to quickly generate revenue if it secured the services of the four scientists. He felt that the company could land a gene-splicing research contract from one of several large corporations for $5 to $10 million over a period of five years. From such an arrangement Biodel could earn as much as a 25 percent margin after deduction for salaries, capital expenditures, and other associated costs. More important, the company would retain licensing rights at agreed-upon rates for potential products. In effect, Biodel would be conducting research at the expense of a commercial sponsor who sought to participate in genetic breakthroughs but who lacked the necessary technical capability.

Actions to Be Taken

Several routes lay open to Biodel at this point. Shannon was pushing to develop synthetic serums. He thought the company would lose any competitive edge it might have in cell biology if it did not bring the serum to market as soon as possible. Heeger, in contrast, pressed for more investment in DEMA. The immunodiagnostics manager argued that DEMA could reach the marketplace in a year if his group could obtain substantial additions in people and facilities. Both managers believed that Biodel could within reason meet whatever goals Dr. Feldman might set simply by pursuing the company's present product opportunities. They saw little reason to look elsewhere. Genetic engineering, on the other hand, represented a potentially lucrative expansion of Biodel's focus and a considerable boost to the company's prestige. Dr. Feldman was fascinated by the idea of having world-famous scientists officially and intimately associated with his firm.

No matter what course Biodel chose, tough financial decisions needed to be made. Development of synthetic serums was projected to cost more than $500,000; development of DEMA was estimated to be several times more expensive. On the advice of a finance professor at the Graduate School of Business at Stanford, Dr. Feldman held informal conversations with local bankers and venture capitalists. He discovered from the bankers that a loan above $500,000 would require his personal guarantee. One bank was willing to supply Biodel with as much as $1 million. In exchange, it wanted two points over the prime rate (currently 17 percent) and covenants restricting further debt, dividend payments, equity issues, and mergers and acquisitions. Venture capitalists generally expressed reluctance to invest in Biodel unless it strengthened its management team. One venture capital firm, however, tentatively offered Dr. Feldman $2 million for 40 percent of the company's equity. On January 1, 1980, Biodel had 1 million shares of common stock outstanding. Upon hearing the proposal, Dr. Feldman exclaimed that his company was worth many times more, prompting the investor to dryly remark that the financial community would not commit large sums of money simply for the potential of developing synthetic serums.

Another issue was the financial package that Biodel might offer to Dr. Ballantine and his cohorts. One alternative was to set up a separate subsidiary of Biodel, with all transactions between the parent and the subsidiary at arm's length. The four scientists would not work directly for the subsidiary, but they would act as an advisory board and recruit other top scientists to work for it. In return, they would receive a consulting fee and restricted stock in the subsidiary, which would vest over a four-year period at 25 percent per year. In this way the four could maintain their affiliation with their respective universities. The finance professor guessed that a per diem of $500 to $1,000 and ownership of 2 percent to 10 percent of the subsidiary for each of the scientists would be a reasonable range within which Dr. Feldman could make an offer.[1]

A second possibility was to hire one or more of the geneticists as employees of the company itself. Dr. Feldman knew that to employ the scientists directly he would have to match any salary and equity combination that another company might offer. This would pose a commitment larger than Dr. Feldman was used to for his own employees. Biodel's three managers currently earned salaries under $35,000, and their ownership of the company's stock jointly totaled less than 2 percent. Dr. Feldman owned over 80 percent of the outstanding stock. Friends, business associates, and relatives of Dr. Feldman owned another 10 percent. On the other hand, by hiring directly, Biodel would get at least one top scientist solely committed to the company's efforts and an immediate boost to its reputation. Dr. Feldman believed that one of the geneticists ought to be employed full-time if Biodel planned to set up and operate a significant genetic engineering operation. He was not certain, however, of how difficult it would be to entice one of the scientists away from his academic research on a full-time basis.

A third alternative was to retain the scientists as technical consultants. Biodel would pay them a per diem fee of $800–$1,200 in exchange for guidance on the company's current projects, proposals for new avenues of research, and recruitment of geneticists. In addition, the company would offer incentive agreements which would allot the scientists stock options on the basis of the company's performance. One possible measure of performance was revenue earned from genetic engineering contracts and products. The Stanford finance professor suggested the following proposal: Biodel would grant the scientists, as a group, options to purchase 50,000 shares at $.10 per share for each incremental $1 million in annual revenues related to genetic engineering. The grants would be made yearly for the next four years, based on Biodel's genetic engineering revenues in the particular year. Dr. Feldman estimated that over a four-year period genetic engineering contract revenue could rise to about $5 to $10 million. The options would be exercisable starting one year from the date of grant if, and only if, the scientists were still consulting for the company. In this way, the Stanford professor noted, the scientists would have an incentive to remain with Biodel. They would also be motivated to help the company grow enough to go public, a development which would greatly increase the value of their options. A final advantage of this alternative was that Biodel would be able to avoid a drain on its cash flow stemming from large salaries.

Dr. Feldman felt that he had to make a move. Shannon and Heeger were pressing for more money, more people, and more facilities. Dr. Ballantine warned that his colleagues were being pressured to accept individual offers. It was a time for decisions.

---

[1] Maximum allowed consulting time at major universities was one day per week.

WTD INDUSTRIES, INC.*

Portland, Oregon-based WTD Industries is the sixth largest lumber producing company in the United States. The company is recognized as the fastest-growing forest products company. WTD started with 3 sawmills in 1983 and by late 1988 had grown to own and operate 27 sawmills and plants in Oregon, Washington, Montana, and New York; they produce softwood lumber, hardwood lumber, plywood, and veneer. In addition, WTD owns approximately 26,000 acres of timberlands in Oregon.

Founder and president, Bruce Engel has directed WTD's successful growth through a consistent strategy that aims at (1) maintaining a capital investment level that is low relative to competitors with comparable capacity, and (2) substituting variable for fixed costs. The company has received widespread recognition as a maverick among forest products companies through its unorthodox strategies, including:

1. Use of leverage for acquisitions.
2. Acquisition of new production capacity only when it is underpriced relative to its production potential.
3. Improving employee productivity through nontraditional production incentives (rather than through facility/equipment technology changes).
4. Buying logs rather than harvesting its own and timing purchases so that inventories are kept very low and conversion into products occurs very quickly, before swings in either log prices or lumber prices squeeze profit margins.

WOOD PRODUCTS INDUSTRY

Forest products companies compete in one or both of two basic industry segments. One of these, the pulp, paper, and paper products segment is largely restricted to larger companies because of the high capital investment required for mills and plants. The other segment, wood products, has varying capital requirements depending on the technology employed, size of facilities, and level of timberlands' self-sufficiency. The size of firms engaging in the wood products segment varies from very large to very small.

Wood Products and Services

Firms engaging in the wood products business produce one or more of a number of products including dimension lumber; beams; siding; hardwoods for furniture,

---

* Prepared by Stephen E. Barndt of Pacific Lutheran University. Copyright 1989 Stephen E. Barndt.

cabinet, and other industrial uses; railroad ties; poles; plywood; decorative panel-ing; and composite panels for construction and industrial uses. Products used in residential and commercial construction are essentially undifferentiated and com-pete as commodities. Industrial products and special dimension or proprietary products for the construction market are less vulnerable to direct competition from substitutes and can command a premium price. Special services to buyers, even among producers of commodity products can also allow those producers to command a higher price and/or a preferred supplier relationship. Services such as technical assistance on selecting the best type of product for particular applica-tions, rapid order processing, assured delivery, shipments of assorted products, and split shipments are being offered increasingly, especially by larger firms attempting to gain a competitive advantage.

Factors Affecting Profitability

Demand, prices, and profits in the wood products industry are tied to the national and international economy. During economic downcycles, commercial construc-tion and home building slackens, resulting in depressed demand and competitive downward pressure on prices. In addition, demand for exports to and imports from foreign nations is directly impacted by the strength of the dollar relative to other currencies. A strong dollar adversely affects the domestic industry by both lowering demand for exports and encouraging imports of wood products, particu-larly from Canada.

The wood products industry is mature with many firms producing and selling reasonably standardized products. Exit barriers are significant. Most owned timberlands can only yield a satisfactory return on investment through conversion of timber assets into lumber and other wood products. In addition, specialized mills located in sparsely populated areas have few if any alternative uses. As a consequence, production does not decrease proportionately with demand during downturns. Often mills continue in operation as long as variable costs are cov-ered. Independent mill operators tend to continue producing until insolvency forces them to close down. The overcapacity that results during periods of decreased demand intensifies price competition. On the other hand, increases in demand are readily matched with increased production through the addition of shifts, restarting closed facilities, and the addition of new mills.

In addition to price, cost is a major determinant of profit at the individual producing mill. Raw materials—that is, logs—are the largest single cost item. Therefore, the availability of a low-cost source of logs is critical to profitable operation. Some firms buy logs on the open market at competitive prices or purchase timber harvesting contracts from the state or federal government through competitive bidding. Others harvest timber on their own timberlands. When open-market log prices are high, companies that harvest their own timber tend to have a cost advantage because of the typically lower costs of timber assets acquired in the past. On the other hand, when log prices are depressed, buying on the open market can provide an advantage over harvesting timber from owned land.

Transportation cost is another important factor in the ability to profitably serve markets. Most wood products are bulky and costly to transport. As a result, marketing tends to be limited to the regional markets closest to a mill or plant, especially for commodity products. If there are many competing mills all vying for the same markets, competitive forces tend to reduce prices and profits. An exception to this dependence on immediate regional markets exists for firms with access to bulk ocean shipping. Firms with access to ocean-going shipping and with production sufficient to fill a ship or barge are able to serve other regions. For example, some Oregon and Washington coastal mills are able to compete cost effectively in the Southern California and Gulf Coast markets.

The availability of substitutes is an additional factor that can impact on the profitability of wood products. Lower cost (and price) particleboard is, for many uses, a direct substitute for plywood. Over a period of years, particleboard has been gaining user acceptance and making competitive inroads against plywood. Nonwood substitutes have also reduced demand for wood; for example, aluminum siding for wood siding, steel posts and beams for wood, and asphalt shingles for wood shingles.

Competitors

The wood products industry in the United States is comprised of approximately 15 large and midsized firms and a large number of small, localized companies. Many of the larger firms have advantages in financial resources, research and engineering capabilities, and marketing. A mill sees its competition as other local mills, whether operated by a large company or independently owned, that compete with it directly for logs, labor, and sales.

International competition in the U.S. market comes primarily from Canada which accounts for nearly 30 percent of U.S. sales. Significant competition in foreign markets comes from northern European, Asian, and Australian firms.

Virtually all the major U.S. competitors are involved in producing commodity products such as lumber. In addition, all are striving to lower their costs of production. Owning or controlling timberlands for self-sufficiency and developing differentiated, higher value-added products are other strategies being pursued by a majority of the larger firms. Two of the largest, Georgia-Pacific Corporation and Weyerhaeuser Company, are seeking improved customer service and market penetration through use of extensive multiproduct sales and distribution systems.

Market segmentation strategies are being followed by several of the major competitors in an effort to better identify and respond to customer needs and shift production and marketing emphasis to capitalize on profit potential. The major movement has been to de-emphasize the building contractor segment and shift resources toward serving the do-it-yourself and industrial segments. The do-it-yourself segment is seen as particularly attractive because it is not directly tied to the housing cycle. The aging of residential structures indicates repair and remodeling demand will continue to be strong. It even tends to increase during housing downcycles as owners try to make do with older structures by improving them. While the industrial segment demand is dependent on business conditions, it is not as sensitive to interest (mortgage) rates as are the residential and commercial construction segments. Thus, developing do-it-yourself and industrial markets is seen as a way of stabilizing revenues.

Typical major competitors include Boise Cascade Corporation; Champion International Corporation; Georgia-Pacific; International Paper Company; Louisiana Pacific Corporation; Pope and Talbot Inc.; and Weyerhaeuser Company. These companies vary considerably with respect to their strategic thrust but all produce and sell commodity products that are similar to WTD's.

Boise Cascade.   Boise Cascade is a large, integrated forest products company with significant operations in the Pacific Northwest, the Northeast, the South, and upper Midwest/Ontario. The company owns over 3 million acres of timberland that provides half its wood needs. Additional timber resources are controlled through long-term leases. It engages in the production and marketing of pulp, paper, paper products, office products, lumber, plywood, hardboard, particleboard, and veneer. Wood products account for about one fourth of the company's sales. The company has nine wholesale distribution centers for building materials in six western states. Exhibit 1 contains selected financial statistics.

Boise Cascade has indicated its desire to grow in paper, paperboard, containerboard, and timberland ownership through acquisition; to grow its office products distribution business internally; and to maintain its position in pulp and wood products. The company has indicated it aims to:

1. Be a low-cost producer, stressing modernization, improved processes, and cost reduction.
2. Continue as a producer and marketer of commodity products but move into higher value-added products and services. In the building products business, industrial particleboard, Ponderosa pine boards, and premium studs will be emphasized.
3. Pursue the remodeling (do-it-yourself) market.

Exhibit 1   FINANCIAL SUMMARY, BOISE CASCADE, 1983–1987 (in millions)

	1983	1984	1985	1986	1987
Net sales	$1,268	$1,278	$957	$985	$1,031
Operating costs and expenses	$1,215	$1,342	$882	$867	$903
Depreciation	$38	$38	$34	$32	$32
Operating income	$15	$ –102	$41	$86	$96
Capital expenditures	$31	$183	$41	$37	$37
Average assets*	$826	$907	$892	$805	$782
Profit margin	1.2%	–8.0%	4.3%	8.7%	9.3%
Asset turnover	1.5	1.4	1.1	1.2	1.3
Return on net assets	1.8%	–11.2%	4.6%	10.7%	12.3%
Capital expenditures as a percent of sales	2.4%	14.3%	4.3%	3.8%	3.6%
Working capital	$362	$278	$244	$313	$262
Debt + equity/equity	2.2	2.6	2.4	2.4	2.2
Ratio of long-term debt to equity	0.5	0.8	0.8	0.8	0.6

* Note: Includes timber and timberlands assets.

4. Maximize the use of company-owned timber for higher margins.
5. Concentrate marketing in the Northwest, Intermountain West, South Central, and Midwest regions.
6. Focus growth in paper and paper-related businesses with high, long-term growth potential and maintain position in building materials.

Champion International. Champion, with over 6 million acres of timberland, some 18 lumber mills, 7 plywood plants, and numerous timber plants, is one of the largest integrated forest products companies. Its major business is the paper business which commands a leading market position. The lumber and plywood business which produces softwood plywood, lumber, particleboard, hardboard, and logs, accounts for roughly 25 percent of sales revenue. Champion also owns 74 percent of a Canadian forest products company.

Recent growth has been in paper with the latest acquisition being the St. Regis Company. Recent divestitures or liquidations have affected the lumber and plywood business. These include the closing of sawmills that converted purchased timber and dismantling the company's building products distribution centers. Other thrusts in recent years have aimed at improving mill efficiency, reducing costs (mainly overhead), increasing employee responsibility for production, and paring down the product line.

Champion's principal strategy is to increase its pulp and paper businesses through acquisition and expansion of present facilities. The lumber, plywood, and building products business has the role of supporting growth in paper by generating cash. The basic strategy for the lumber and plywood business to meet cash generation objectives is to:

1. Produce commodity lumber, plywood, and other building products from company-owned or -controlled forests.
2. Supply building materials in bulk, keeping costs down by processing large orders and turning inventory over fast.

Exhibit 2 contains recent financial data on Champion's performance.

Exhibit 2 FINANCIAL SUMMARY, CHAMPION INTERNATIONAL, 1983–1987 (in millions)

	1983	1984	1985	1986	1987
Net sales	$1,730	$1,818	$1,503	$1,042	$1,185
Operating costs and expenses	$1,576	$1,723	$1,330	$879	$953
Depreciation	$76	$72	$86	$60	$67
Operating income	$78	$23	$87	$103	$165
Capital expenditures	$19	$43	$10	$23	$50
Average assets*	$1,189	$1,780	$2,186	$2,000	$2,017
Profit margin	4.5%	1.3%	5.8%	9.9%	13.9%
Asset turnover	1.5	1.0	0.7	0.5	0.6
Return on net assets	6.6%	1.3%	4.0%	5.2%	8.2%
Capital expenditures as a percent of sales	1.1%	2.4%	0.7%	2.2%	4.2%
Working capital	$443	$−223	$−77	$71	$232
Debt + equity/equity	2.2	2.9	2.5	2.3	2.1
Ratio of long-term debt to equity	0.6	0.8	0.7	0.8	0.6

* Note: Includes timber and timberlands assets.

Georgia-Pacific.   Georgia-Pacific is a leading integrated forest products company producing a full line of building materials and paper products to serve markets throughout the United States. Over 5 million acres are under company control in the West, South, Northeast, and Eastern Canada. The company supplies 45 percent of its wood needs from its own timberlands.

Georgia-Pacific has been moving toward developing its pulp and paper business to a size equal to building products. At the same time, the building products business has been growing. This growth has been internal through market penetration and external through acquisition of U.S. Plywood Corporation in 1987. The company is a leader in structural panels and lumber. Within the panels segment, Georgia-Pacific has been moving toward developing markets for higher value-added specialty products, especially in the remodel and replace and industrial segments.

Georgia-Pacific has a strong distribution business that serves as a ready market for manufacturing operations. This has allowed plants and mills to run at or near capacity. The company has 141 distribution centers, the largest number in the industry. It adapts its overall distribution organization to fit emerging needs. For example, it has recently created a new division in charge of manufacturing, marketing, and sales of prefinished panels to focus on and provide better customer service. In addition, it has opened a new pilot program distribution center to handle specialty products and has installed a computer network in its distribution division to speed up order processing and improve credit control, inventory control, and profitability analysis. A new sales group has been formed to market do-it-yourself products to major home center chains. Exhibit 3 presents recent financial performance data.

In wood products, Georgia-Pacific's strategic emphasis is on:

1. Continued backward integration from distribution to products and production capability in growing remodel and replace markets, along with promising sectors of commercial and industrial markets while maintaining its position in residential construction markets.

Exhibit 3   FINANCIAL SUMMARY, GEORGIA-PACIFIC, 1983–1987 (in millions)

	1983	1984	1985	1986	1987
Net sales	$4,180	$4,641	$4,658	$5,088	$6,029
Operating costs and expenses	$3,658	$4,118	$4,122	$4,435	$5,308
Depreciation	$168	$144	$145	$153	$188
Operating income	$354	$379	$391	$500	$533
Capital expenditures	$122	$272	$187	$248	$409
Average assets*	$2,264	$2,298	$2,401	$2,483	$2,794
Profit margin	8.5%	8.2%	8.4%	9.8%	8.8%
Asset turnover	1.8	2.0	1.9	2.0	2.2
Return on net assets	15.6%	16.5%	16.3%	20.1%	19.1%
Capital expenditures as a percent of sales	2.9%	5.9%	4.0%	4.9%	6.8%
Working capital	$771	$733	$591	$583	$733
Debt + equity/equity	2.5	2.4	2.3	2.1	2.2
Ratio of long-term debt to equity	0.7	0.7	0.6	0.4	0.5

* Note: Includes timber and timberlands assets.

2. Adding value to its lumber resource in general and its low-grade lumber in particular by producing specialty products. Specialty product lines will be expanded through internal growth and acquisition.

3. Capitalize on its strong distribution system. Wide breath of coverage, personal selling, or single point of contact selling, and a motivated sales force are key strengths to secure sales. Thorough planning, measurable and realistic sales objectives, constant communication of objectives, and pay incentives are supportive of sales productivity. Selling purchased as well as manufactured products helps to more fully use the distribution system and better serve customers.

4. Marketing emphasis on low price and fast delivery.

5. Running facilities at capacity with efficient processes to achieve low production costs.

International Paper.   International Paper (IP) is the largest producer of paper products. It controls some 6.7 million acres of timber through its 95 percent ownership of International Paper Timberlands, Ltd. With such extensive holdings, the company engages in significant production of lumber and building products to extract the highest value from the timber and at the same time provide lower value wood chips from the residual portions of logs for use in making pulp. About 20 percent of total sales is accounted for by lumber, plywood, and other building materials—see Exhibit 4 for additional financial data on IP's performance.

Since the early 1980s, the company has committed to substantial investments for production rationalization, facility updating, and modernization to get costs down and improve productivity. Within the company's wood products businesses, notable investment has been made in southern lumber and plywood mills, opening four composite panel plants, and in developing a network of distribution centers.

Exhibit 4   FINANCIAL SUMMARY, INTERNATIONAL PAPER, 1983–1987 (in millions)

	1983	1984	1985	1986	1987
Net sales	$892	$829	$719	$825	$1,069
Operating costs and expenses	$597	$652	$565	$637	$857
Depreciation	$80	$84	$74	$67	$67
Operating income	$215	$93	$80	$121	$145
Capital expenditures	$97	$110	$60	$76	$66
Average assets*	$1,449	$1,411	$1,275	$1,248	$1,275
Profit margin	24.1%	11.2%	11.1%	14.7%	13.6%
Asset turnover	0.6	0.6	0.6	0.7	0.8
Return on net assets	14.8%	6.6%	6.3%	9.7%	11.4%
Capital expenditures as a percent of sales	10.9%	13.3%	8.3%	9.2%	6.2%
Working capital	$652	$574	$350	$296	$657
Debt + equity/equity	1.7	1.8	1.9	2.1	2.1
Ratio of long-term debt to equity	0.3	0.3	0.4	0.5	0.5

* Note: Includes timber and timberlands assets.

Improvements in International Paper lumber and building products are sought through:

1. Improving utilization of owned forests. This involves increasing the yield from timberlands by extending the harvest cycle and replanting with improved seedlings.
2. Modernizing mills to reduce labor content and waste.
3. Limited product line reshaping, (e.g., a shift to higher value-added products such as laminates).
4. Improving customer responsiveness through quality, reliability, and product tailoring improvements, and the development of distribution systems that support this responsiveness.

Louisiana Pacific.   Louisiana Pacific is primarily a commodity-oriented firm that uses price and volume to its competitive advantage in markets where logistics are favorable. Most of its sales revenue is from lumber and structural panels. Its emphasis in product development has been on waferboard and other fiber composite panel products. However, the company does own and operate three pulp or paper product mills, marketing domestically and abroad. Major capital investments in recent years have increased waferboard capacity, southern lumber production capacity, and the southern lumber production base. The company has been generally shifting from the West to the South.

Marketing and sales are primarily aimed at construction (residential and commercial) and, to a lesser extent, repair and remodeling uses with waferboard, lumber, and some specialty products. The company is increasing its efforts to sell industrial particleboard and medium density fiberboard to industrial cabinet and furniture manufacturers. Geographically, Louisiana Pacific has moved to strengthen international sales via investment in a mill in Alaska to produce lumber for Japan. However, U.S. domestic markets are clearly emphasized, particularly in the South, West, and Northeast, in that order.

Exhibit 5   FINANCIAL SUMMARY, LOUISIANA PACIFIC, 1983–1987 (in millions)

	1983	1984	1985	1986	1987
Net sales	$944	$1,028	$1,075	$1,288	$1,630
Operating costs and expenses	$789	$906	$894	$1,058	$1,286
Depreciation	$74	$80	$93	$100	$124
Operating income	$81	$42	$88	$130	$220
Capital expenditures	$100	$147	$138	$534	$189
Average assets*	$771	$849	$910	$1,169	$1,437
Profit margin	8.6%	4.1%	8.2%	10.1%	13.5%
Asset turnover	1.2	1.2	1.2	1.1	1.1
Return on net assets	10.5%	4.9%	9.7%	11.1%	15.3%
Capital expenditures as a percent of sales	10.6%	14.3%	12.8%	41.5%	11.6%
Working capital	$113	$87	$106	$99	$119
Debt + equity/equity	1.7	1.8	1.8	2	1.9
Ratio of long-term debt to equity	0.3	0.2	0.3	0.6	0.5

* Note: Includes timber and timberlands assets.

Louisiana Pacific has invested in modern physical and process technology to be a lowest-cost producer. These investments have included developing and operating small mills with lower depreciation expenses, higher capacity use rates, and lower raw material transportation costs. See Exhibit 5 for a summary of the company's recent financial performance.

Pope and Talbot. Pope and Talbot is a medium-sized forest products company that produces building materials, along with pulp and paper products. Its building materials are mostly commodity-type products. Five sawmills produce lumber, veneer, and chips. The pulp and paper businesses specialize in the production of private-label tissues and disposable diapers plus market pulp. The wood products and paper segments of its business each contribute roughly half of its sales revenue—see Exhibit 6 for a financial performance summary.

Building materials operations are located in Washington, Oregon, South Dakota, and Canada. The company has spun off most of its timberlands to an independent limited partnership because of top management's view that owning and operating timberlands offers low returns. Virtually all required logs are purchased on the open market or through competitive bidding for the right to harvest government timberlands.

An overall objective of Pope and Talbot is to be a balanced forest products company. Highest priority goes to continued diversification and growth in pulp and paper businesses. In the wood products business, the company seeks to:

1. Maintain present size.
2. Be a low-cost producer. This is accomplished by reducing costs through modernization of old mills and reducing personnel. Low labor costs and low production costs resulting from modernization have made Pope and Talbot's mills some of the most competitive in the industry.
3. Conduct sales by phone out of a central office, with shipments direct from mill to customer.

Exhibit 6 FINANCIAL SUMMARY, POPE AND TALBOT, 1983–1987 (in millions)

	1983	1984	1985	1986	1987
Net sales	$160	$179	$185	$163	$207
Operating costs and expenses	$133	$169	$162	$136	$172
Depreciation	$11	$11	$12	$9	$9
Operating income	$16	$−1	$11	$18	$26
Capital expenditures	$7	$6	$7	$7	$8
Average assets*	$109	$109	$97	$92	$98
Profit margin	10.0%	−0.6%	5.9%	11.0%	12.6%
Asset turnover	1.5	1.6	1.9	1.8	2.1
Return on net assets	14.7%	−0.9%	11.3%	19.6%	26.5%
Capital expenditures as a percent of sales	4.4%	3.4%	3.8%	4.3%	3.9%
Working capital	$34	$33	$29	$38	$45
Debt + equity/equity	2	2.1	2.1	1.8	1.8
Ratio of long-term debt to equity	0.6	0.6	0.4	0.3	0.4

* Note: Includes timber and timberlands assets.

Weyerhaeuser.   Weyerhaeuser is a large, integrated forest resource company. Its nearly 6 million acres of owned timber in the Northwest and southern states, along with control over double that acreage in Canada, provides a continuous presence near major markets and a substantial profit advantage during periods of high timber prices. Operations are conducted in every U.S. region, Canada, and the Far East. North America, Europe, the Middle East, and the Far East provide major markets for the company.

Weyerhaeuser's businesses fall into three groups: forest products, pulp and paper, and other diversified businesses. The forest products and paper companies are roughly equal in sales and earnings. The forest products company produces and sells a wide range of tree-derived products including logs, dimension lumber, plywood, composite fiber panels, and specialty cuts of lumber for industrial markets. The company has been moving toward higher-priced specialty application products at the expense of its traditional undifferentiated commoditylike lumber and panel products. It operates approximately 150 wholesale distribution centers and two regional sales centers; there are sales personnel assigned to both the centers and the individual mills and plants to handle customer orders and provide customer service.

The Weyerhaeuser strategy is firmly anchored on managing its timberland yield and finding the best match between timber resources and market needs; specific actions include:

1. Expanding its line of specialized products designed to meet customer needs in form, fit, strength, appearance, or other desired attributes.

2. Differentiating itself through superior sales service and quality of products.

3. Targeting sales growth in remodel and repair, industrial, and specialized markets with special-application and high-quality products and dedicated, service-oriented sales forces.

Exhibit 7   FINANCIAL SUMMARY, WEYERHAEUSER, 1983–1987 (in millions)

	1983	1984	1985	1986	1987
Net sales	$2,608	$2,634	$2,357	$2,434	$3,003
Operating costs and expenses	$2,121	$2,351	$2,022	$2,017	$2,491
Depreciation	$188	$217	$172	$181	$173
Operating income	$299	$66	$163	$236	$339
Capital expenditures	$166	$170	$178	$191	$223
Average assets*	$2,239	$2,165	$2,048	$2,006	$2,089
Profit margin	11.5%	2.5%	6.9%	9.7%	11.3%
Asset turnover	1.2	1.2	1.2	1.2	1.4
Return on net assets	13.4%	3.0%	8.0%	11.8%	16.2%
Capital expenditures as a percent of sales	6.4%	6.5%	7.6%	7.8%	7.4%
Working capital			$491	$482	$808
Debt + equity/equity	1.8	1.8	1.8	2	1.9
Ratio of long-term debt to equity	0.4	0.3	0.3	0.4	0.4

* Note: Includes timber and timberlands assets.
Source: Company annual reports.

4. Pricing specialized products and services at a premium relative to competitors.

5. Developing export markets with offshore-based sales and distribution organizations.

6. Defensively investing at a level sufficient to maintain or slightly grow in market position and presence in commodity and most composite-fiber products. Invest to update mills and plants for efficiency. Limit offensive growth in capacity or capability to selected specialty products targeted at growing markets or unfilled niches.

Exhibit 7 contains selected statistics indicating Weyerhaeuser's financial performance over the most recent five-year period.

COMPANY HISTORY

WTD Industries is the creation of Bruce L. Engel, a Portland, Oregon, lawyer educated at Reed College and the University of Chicago School of Law. In the early 1980s, Engel became involved in an effort to save a client's financially troubled sawmill business. Ultimately, Engel and a partner acquired the bankrupt mill in exchange for assuming $2 million in debts. His original idea was to make changes necessary to achieve profitability, operating it until industry conditions improved, and then sell it. Subsequently, success with the first sawmill and other opportunities for bargain acquisitions in a depressed industry caused Engel to shift to objectives of growth and profitable operation of wood products converting facilities. In pursuing these new objectives, using a consistent but unusual strategy, in seven years Bruce Engel built an original $3,000 investment into a company with $146 million in assets and $294 million in sales in fiscal year 1988.

The growth and profitability of WTD are anchored on a low fixed cost—high variable cost structure with constant pressure to keep variable costs per unit of output low. There were six key elements in the WTD strategy:

1. Low acquisition cost. This has been achieved by buying mills and plants, most of which were financially distressed, at bargain prices. A result is that WTD's investment is at a level considerably below replacement cost. Increasing output to capacity or near capacity allows WTD to operate at a fixed cost per unit of output well below many of its major competitors. In addition to concentrating on acquiring undervalued mills, the company generally avoids investing in owned timberlands, preferring to buy its logs on the open market.

2. Substantial increase in production at mills relative to levels achieved under prior ownership.

3. High labor productivity. Using bankruptcy and high unemployment in the depressed lumber industry as leverage points, hourly wages at newly acquired mills are lowered. However, workers are given the opportunity to earn compensation as high as or higher than paid by competing companies through the use of production bonuses. As a consequence, output per worker is high. None of WTD's mills are unionized.

4. Aggressive use of debt leverage.

5. Aggressive management to keep working capital low compared to the rest of the industry. The major thrust is aimed at avoiding excessive inventories of logs.

6. Centralized financial controls and marketing that keeps overhead low and provides advantages of scale and customer service.[1]

Following acquisition of the original sawmill at Glide, Oregon, in 1981, a second mill at Silverton, Oregon, was acquired in 1982. In 1983 sawmills located at Philomath, Oregon, were acquired and the business was incorporated as WTD Industries.

In 1984 the company added another softwood sawmill operation, this one near Corvallis, Oregon, and its first hardwood sawmill at Philomath, Oregon. The next year, 1985, WTD started operations in Washington with newly acquired softwood and hardwood mills at Sedro Woolley, Olympia, and South Bend. Three more mills were added in 1986—Valley and Aberdeen in Washington and Tillamook in Oregon. Late in 1986, WTD went public with 1.85 million shares of common stock. Net proceeds in excess of $15 million fueled a major expansion in 1987.

Thirteen companies were acquired in 1987—seven in Oregon, five in Washington, and one in Montana. In addition to WTD's first geographic expansion outside of the Pacific Northwest, 1987 also marked the company's growth into nonsawmill production operations. Five of the 1987 acquisitions were plants producing veneer and one was a plywood plant. Growth in 1988 was modest by comparison with only three acquisitions—sawmills in Washington and Oregon and a plywood plant in New York. Exhibit 8 shows the company's 27 operating locations.

Although it is contrary to company strategy to invest in timberlands, 25,000 acres were obtained in 1987. Part of this (8,000 acres) was included with the Union, Oregon, sawmill deal. The remaining 17,000 acres are located near the Philomath mills and were acquired because open-market log prices in that area were considered too high.

OPERATIONS

The forest products industry leaders are moving toward increased emphasis on specialized, differentiated wood products. In addition, extensive capital investment in technologies that help extract maximum value from a log and investing in owned timberlands to assure a supply of known-cost logs are widely accepted as competitive necessities. WTD has rejected all of these as elements of its strategy.

Products and Product Strategy

The company produces and sells a variety of wood products, principally falling in the following categories: softwood lumber, hardwood lumber, softwood veneer,

---

[1] Chad E. Brown, "WTD Industries," Company Analysis, Kidder, Peabody & Co., August 18, 1987, p. 4.

| Exhibit 8 | WTD MILLS, PRODUCTS, AND 1988 CAPACITY UTILIZATION |

		Capacity/FY1988 production* (in thousands)			
Mill/Plant location	**Start-up**	**Softwood lumber**	**Hardwood lumber**	**Veneer**	**Plywood**
Glide, Oregon	5/82	120/114.2			
Silverton, Oregon	5/82	80/51.9			
Philomath, Oregon	3/83	185/175.8			
Philomath, Oregon	6/84		17/13.9‡		
Corvallis-Philomath, Oregon	3/85	65/64.7			
Sedro Woolley, Washington	6/85	100/92.2			
Olympia, Washington	8/85	75/36.1			
South Bend, Washington	11/85		14/13.6		
Tillamook, Oregon	5/86		12/5.3		
Aberdeen, Washington	1/87		14/7.6		
Eugene, Oregon	1/87	50/24.6			
Halsey, Oregon	2/87			60/43.3	
Crater Lake, Oregon	3/87	150/63.2§			
Tumwater, Washington	3/87	60/50.3			
Union, Oregon	3/87	55/44.2			
Spanaway, Washington	5/87	50/30.6			
Columbia Falls, Montana	6/87	70/50.2			
Goshen, Oregon	7/87			72/43.5	
Morton, Washington	7/87	90/46.5		150/75.8	
Valley, Washington	8/87	75/36.5			
Lake Cle Elum, Washington	8/87			120/31.2	
Graham, Washington	9/87				150/40.6
North Powder, Oregon	9/87	75/16.2			
Modoc Point, Oregon	12/87			75/11.6	
Whitehall, New York	1/88				75/11.9†
Junction City, Oregon	8/88	50/†			
Orient, Washington	9/88	50/†			

Notes: * Lumber capacity measured in thousand board feet; veneer and plywood capacity measured in thousand square feet (3/8″ basis).

† Production of mills started up in FY1988 only reflects output while under WTD ownership.

‡ Philomath hardwood sawmill output includes 15,200 thousand board feet of softwood lumber.

§ Crater Lake mill destroyed by fire in late 1987 was out of production while rebuilding.

plywood, and chips. Softwood lumber is the major product and consists of studs and other dimension lumber in a wide range of widths, lengths, and thicknesses. The predominant species that are converted into softwood lumber are Douglas fir, hemlock, white pine, lodgepole pine, red pine, spruce, and larch. Although softwood lumber, along with all other products, is branded with the name of WTD's marketing organization and its logs, these products are basically commodities competing against similar, substitute products.

The second highest source of 1988 sales was chips, a residual product made from the parts of logs not suitable for conversion into lumber or veneer. Chips are used to make pulp for later conversion into paper products. The product with third highest sales revenue in 1988 was veneer, a thin layer of wood peeled from logs and used in the lay-up of plywood. Hardwood is the fourth highest revenue generator and is produced in sizes appropriate for cabinet and furniture manufacturers. The major species is alder although some maple is also cut. Plywood plants, using veneers to produce sheathing, underlayment, sanded, and marine plywood in standard sizes, were the fifth highest source of sales revenue.

With the minor exception of a few specialty or highly finished products such as marine plywood, some sanded plywood, and special cuts of wood for furniture, WTD is a producer of undifferentiated products. The company aims to produce and move these commoditylike products in volume, relying on high per-worker output. In fact, labor productivity improvements in the company's existing mills have boosted aggregate lumber production by about 50 percent.

Raw Materials Inventory Strategy

Inventories of raw materials, that is, logs, impact profitability in two ways. The first is that assured and continuous availability is necessary for an efficient conversion process and the satisfaction of customers' order delivery requirements. The second is that logs are a costly resource and can represent a substantial tie up of working capital as well as a major factor in determining the profit margin. While lumber prices tend to slightly lead log prices, moving in the same direction, and maintaining a more or less constant relationship over the long term, short-term variations can and do occur. For example, increased foreign demand for logs, environmentalist special-interest group activities to restrict sale of government timber, and weather conditions unfavorable for logging have all decreased log supply and raised prices independent of domestic demand for lumber. With the cost of purchased logs at delivery accounting for over 50 percent of total costs, such a rise in log prices not accompanied by a rise in lumber prices can turn a profitable operation into an unprofitable one.

WTD's larger competitors tried to lessen risks associated with uncertain availability and the potential of high open-market log prices by lining up inventories of standing timber sufficient for two years or more of production and stockpiling substantial inventories of logs at the mills. They typically secured control over timberlands either through ownership or harvest rights. WTD's timber-owning competitors were in a position to either (1) buy on the open market or through harvest contracts when log prices are low and harvest owned timber (presumably on the books at a lower, historical cost) when log prices are high, or (2) give priority to filling their needs from owned timber on a continuing basis. In either strategy, there is a potential to sustain higher operating margins. Competitors without timberlands usually contract with timberland owners or the government for the right to harvest timber over a number of years. Such contracts are subject to competitive bidding and bid prices reflect the near-term profit potential of lumber manufacturing operations. Companies that rely on timber contracts can be expected to do well during periods of rising lumber prices and poorly when lumber prices fall. In fact, WTD owes its start to the fact that in the late 1970s many sawmill owners committed themselves to high-priced timber contracts prior to an industry downturn. When lumber prices fell, they found themselves faced with bankruptcy because they were unable to operate profitably or break their contracts.

WTD purposely avoids holding large inventories of logs. The company does not want to speculate in logs, preferring to buy in the open market at prices that closely follow lumber market prices. WTD's intent is to buy its logs and convert them into lumber within a matter of weeks. The ability to follow this strategy provides consistent, although modest, margins between materials costs and sales revenues.

In support of its low inventory strategy, WTD aims to maintain log inventories equal to approximately three weeks' operating requirements. Larger inventories are carried only when it is necessary to collect selected materials for specialty orders, weather or seasonal factors prevent regular deliveries, or open-market buying is not possible, necessitating purchasing timber-cutting contracts. The latter are primarily sold by government agencies and ordinarily require the cutting and removal of public timber within three years. WTD attempts to harvest timber under these contracts within one year and preferably within three to four months to minimize the risk of a reduced margin from falling lumber prices. In keeping with WTD's acceptance of variable costs in place of fixed costs, all forest operations are contracted to logging companies. This includes road building, cutting, and delivery to the mills.

Reliance on a supply of reasonably priced logs has left the company vulnerable to imbalances between log supply and demand. In late 1987, two of WTD's softwood sawmills, both of which normally rely on timber harvesting contracts with government agencies, were faced with a shortage of logs and unprofitably high prices created by foreign demand and forest fires. The company was forced to shut the two mills down temporarily until a supply of acceptably priced logs could be assured. The acquisition of 17,000 acres of timberland near Philomath was a direct response to the problem of overdependence on public timber and the corresponding shortage of private open-market logs in the Philomath area. Reflecting its desire to minimize reliance on public timber contracts, the company used that source for only 20 percent of its logs in FY 1988, down from 23 percent in FY 1987. In 1988, 73 percent of WTD's logs were acquired on the open market and 7 percent were supplied by cutting fee-based (owned) timber.[2]

Technology Strategy

Many major competitors such as Weyerhaeuser have been investing in new technologies, some using computers and lasers, that increase the yield of higher value products by optimizing the way each log is cut. Other technologies are commonly being incorporated to reduce the labor content and increase capacity.

WTD relies on employee productivity incentives rather than investing in expensive automated machinery to increase production. As stated in the company's 1987 report: "We strive to avoid the capital costs of expensive high

---

[2] WTD Industries, *1987* and *1988 Annual Reports.*

technology equipment that purports to eliminate production employees. We prefer to rely on the flexibility and productivity of our workers."[3]

Although the company purposely avoids investing in costly automated plants and machinery, it does invest in projects offering major savings or immediate production improvements that have paybacks of three years or less. For the most part, this has meant modest capital expenditures, approximating annual depreciation costs, to replace and upgrade worn and inefficient equipment. As an example of the difference in WTD's approach to investment in technology, WTD invested $1 million to replace old parts at its Glide, Oregon, mill while International Paper invested $90 million in a computer-driven mill process at its competing Gardiner, Oregon, mill.[4] Another example of WTD's modest, selective investment is its acquisition of a 2.1 mile spur railroad connecting its Union, Oregon, mill to a Union Pacific mainline.[5] This investment cost only $107,000 and eliminates one load-unload cycle.

SALES AND MARKETING

All marketing, sales, and distribution of WTD's products are the responsibility of Treesource, Inc., a wholly owned subsidiary. Treesource, with approximately 50 sales, managerial, and clerical employees, is located in Portland, Oregon. Through this centralized sales and marketing unit, WTD gains economies of scale not available to independent mills. Treesource is able to coordinate production at various mills to satisfy customer orders, arrange lowest production location–transportation cost alternatives, and fill orders for an assortment of products beyond the capability of any single mill. In addition, centralized credit management offers economies in credit checking, monitoring, and collecting. Since each salesperson is responsible for the marketing and sales for one or two of the company's mills, fewer salespeople are needed than if each mill handled its own sales.

Treesource has targeted the construction, industrial, and remodel and replace (do-it-yourself) segments. Of these, the construction segment is the most active. In fiscal year 1988, most sales were to distributors and wholesalers, industrial users, and retailers.[6] Products sold to approximately 700 distributors and wholesalers, amounting to 68 percent of FY 1988 sales, included softwood lumber for the residential construction, commercial construction, and remodel and replace segments; hardwood boards for the construction and remodel and replace segments; and plywood for both construction and remodel and replace markets. Major customers include Georgia-Pacific, Weyerhaeuser, and Boise Cascade Corporation. Sales to about 250 industrial buyers accounted for 16 percent of 1988 sales and included hardwood for furniture and cabinet manufacturers as well as plywood for industrial uses. Sales to retailers, including chain merchandisers,

[3] WTD Industries, *1987 Annual Report,* p. 12.

[4] David Arnold, "Risky Business," *The Sunday Oregonian Magazine,* August 21, 1988.

[5] WTD Industries, Inc., Form 10K, fiscal year ended April 30, 1987.

[6] WTD Industries, *1988 Annual Report,* p. 15; and 1988 Form 10K, p. 6.

provide a market for softwood and hardwood lumber for the remodel and replace user and, in FY 1988 provided 11 percent of sales. Direct sales of intermediate materials (veneer) plus products that are immediately usable by the customer (railroad ties) provided 5 percent of FY 1988 sales. Ninety-five percent of WTD's sales were to buyers in the United States and the remaining 5 percent were to Canadian buyers.

Most sales are arranged through telephone contact between salesperson and buyer. The company offers competitive delivered prices, a variety of products, availability of products, and reliability as competitive advantages. In fact, Weyerhaeuser, a major customer, named WTD as its "supplier of the year" in 1987 for its reliability, cooperation, and quality. The company also offers a 1 percent discount if an account is paid within 10 days, providing an effective incentive for prompt payment. In addition, WTD attempts to create a name familiarity by identifying all product lots with the Treesource trademark and name of the producing mill after they are packaged or strapped.

Transportation is the third highest cost component of a delivered product, exceeded only by logs and labor. Treesource arranges for the transportation of products from all WTD mills and, as a result, is able to secure volume discounts that help WTD to be both profitable and price competitive. Shipments of products are normally made direct from the mill to the buyer's destination via rail, truck, or barge.

HUMAN RESOURCES

WTD considers people to be the most important factor determining company profitability. This importance is operationalized in the human resource strategy and policies that support objectives of efficiency in the use of the total work force and high levels of individual and work team productivity. High productivity is motivated by programs that highlight the importance of individual contributions to the company through incentives based on those contributions.

Functional Specialization

Activities that benefit or apply to more than one mill are performed at a centralized location in order to gain advantages of functional specialization and scale. Sales, market development, engineering, finance, and legal services are the key activities that are centralized. Log buying specialists are located at the individual mills because of their need to be familiar with and responsive to local conditions, suppliers, and mill needs. With most support functions performed elsewhere by others, local mill managers can concentrate on what is most important to them— effective and efficient production.

Specialization and centralization have allowed WTD to operate with a relatively lean support structure. Out of approximately 2,500 employees, fully 84 percent are directly engaged in mill production. Marketing and sales (Treesource) account for only 2 percent of the employees, while WTD corporate management and support involve 3 percent, and mill management and administrative support involve the remaining 11 percent.

Incentive Pay

To encourage flexibility and productivity, WTD has nonunion labor in all its mills and has substituted pay based partly on productivity for straight wages. As a nonunion employer, WTD has greater freedom in assigning duties and can require time lost from breakdowns to be made up on Saturday at weekday pay rates.

The industry norm is a straight hourly wage, often established in union-company labor contracts. Many firms in the industry recognize that under such a compensation system labor is essentially a fixed cost and their profits will be high or low depending solely on demand and price in the marketplace. However, some companies are incorporating some form of incentive pay schemes tied to profitability.

WTD has two incentive pay systems. One, applicable to salaried employees, is a profit-sharing plan computed and paid monthly. Bonuses are based on monthly pretax profits at the mill, region, or entire corporation depending on the employee's level of involvement and are allocated as a percent of base salary. In recent years the bonus portion of total salary compensation has ranged from about 40 to 50 percent.[7]

The incentive pay system for hourly employees is based on production, safety, and attendance. Each mill sets weekly production goals. Each week a bonus is paid to all members of a work shift if the shift has met its production goals and minimum safety standards, with no worker losing more than three hours due to an on-the-job injury. In addition, an individual shift member is eligible for the weekly bonus if he or she has not been absent or late for work during the week. Although base wage levels are typically lower than prevailing wages in the local area, the addition of production bonuses makes overall compensation comparable or better. In 1988 WTD mill workers averaged $8.40 per hour in base wages and $3 per hour in bonuses.[8] In addition to the regular bonus system, when a shift sets a new production record, every member of the shift receives a cash bonus—a $50 bill handed out by Bruce Engel.

The bonus systems are significant contributors to the company's competitive advantage in low manufacturing costs. Profit-based bonuses for managers foster constant attention to cost control while the production bonus system motivates teamwork, innovation, high levels of individual effort, improved safety, and attendance. By the time a new mill has completed implementation of WTD's operations and human resource strategies, production increases per shift typically have reached 50 percent. The result is a lower than average labor cost per thousand board feet. WTD's higher than average labor productivity may account for a 4 to 5 percent profit margin on sales (out of its total 7 percent profit margin).[9] In addition, improvements in safety have allowed the company to self-insure in Oregon and Washington, substantially reducing workers' compensation insurance costs.

---

[7] Brown, "WTD Industries," p. 14.

[8] Arnold, "Risky Business."

[9] Brown, "WTD Industries," p. 6.

WTD does not have retirement or pension plans, but does provide health insurance. Vacation policies are in line with the industry and require a shorter period of employment for eligibility.

FINANCING GROWTH

The company has followed a two-step process of external growth through acquisition followed by internal growth of acquired mills. Capital required to support these two types of growth has been provided from three sources: debt, new stock issues, and reinvestment of profits.

Acquisitions, modernizations, and working capital growth have been largely financed through assumption of existing debt and creation of new debt. The company's rapid growth in the last four years through the use of debt leverage is reflected in $75,721,000 in long-term debt on April 30, 1988. This debt includes $35 million in unsecured notes, due 1994 and 1997; various secured mortgage notes totaling $7,624,000; other secured notes totaling $5,426,000; $27 million in sinking fund senior subordinated debentures, due 1997; and $3 million in tax-exempt economic development revenue bonds, granted for use on the company's Graham Plywood Company. In addition, WTD has a $21.7 million line of credit, secured by accounts receivable and inventories, of which approximately $11 million is outstanding. As a result of significant increases in debt in FY 1988, fixed-interest payment obligations increased and income before interest and taxes ($7.7 million) was only 2.7 times interest, down from 6.0 in FY 1987 and 3.3 in FY 1986. Changes in the company's assets and debt liabilities from 1986 through 1988 are shown in Exhibit 9.

The one-time 1986 public stock offering that netted over $15 million provided for working capital expansion and fueled much of the acquisition activity in 1987. A consistent and growing source of funds for capital projects has been current operations. The company has a policy of not paying cash dividends, leaving all net cash flow available for capital investment, working capital improvement, or long-term debt payment. In FY 1988 company operations provided nearly $15 million in cash to support such needs.

Acquisition criteria have been adapted to reflect greater availability of funds and changes in the industry environment. Initially the company targeted mills that were underproducing their potential and that were priced well below replacement cost. The idea was to buy troubled mills with a minimum outlay of cash, fix them up, and implement the WTD system of human resource and operations management. A two-year start-up before reaching profit potential was not unexpected.

MANAGEMENT

WTD manages its 27 operating locations using a decentralized-centralized structure. Individual production units (mills or plants) are profit centers under a manager who has overall responsibility for the profitability of that unit. Each production unit is incorporated as a wholly owned subsidiary under a name that identifies it as a local company; for example, Silverton Forest Products Co., Sedro Woolley Lumber Co., and Whitehall Plywood, Inc.

Exhibit 9 WTD'S CONSOLIDATED BALANCE SHEET (in thousands)

	April 30		
	1988	**1987**	**1986**
Assets			
Current assets			
Cash and near cash	$ 2,019	$ 1,418	$ 371
Receivable from underwriter	18,764		
Accounts receivable, net	20,181	15,530	11,431
Inventories	21,100	17,345	8,238
Prepaid expenses	2,285	905	380
Timber and timber related assets	10,885	4,595	3,992
Total current assets	56,470	58,557	24,412
Notes and accounts receivable	1,346	264	
Timber and timberlands	11,624	2,458	258
Property, plant, and equipment	79,132	47,578	16,902
Less: accumulated depreciation	16,749	10,196	6,861
	62,383	37,382	10,041
Construction in progress	11,349	1,972	652
	73,732	39,354	10,693
Other assets	2,910	2,800	267
Total assets	$146,082	$103,433	$35,630
Liabilities and Stockholders' Equity			
Current liabilities			
Notes and acceptances payable	$ 11,025	$ 14,193	$ 9,179
Accounts payable	10,962	9,586	5,790
Accrued expenses	8,517	5,418	3,013
Income taxes payable	182	974	610
Timber contracts payable	5,132	3,049	4,391
Current maturities of long-term debt	2,329	2,904	2,213
Total current liabilities	38,147	36,124	25,196
Deferred income taxes payable	320	591	442
Long-term debt, less current maturities	48,721	13,679	6,868
Senior subordinated debentures	27,000	30,000	
Stockholders' equity			
Common stock	15,835	15,380	166
Paid-in capital	15	15	15
Retained earnings	16,044	7,644	2,943
Total equity	31,894	23,039	3,124
Total liabilities and stockholders' equity	$146,082	$103,433	$35,630

Source: WTD annual reports.

The company feels its use of a decentralized local mill management team concept provides operating flexibility to be responsive to local competitive conditions while maintaining tight control over costs. The local mill management team has responsibility for log procurement, log and chip sales, by-product sales, log recovery projects, safety programs, workers' compensation claims, and accounts payable as well as production scheduling and control. However, where larger size, greater volume, or other conditions favoring scale economies exist, activities are centralized. WTD currently centralizes marketing, sales, credit, mill-to-market transportation, and financing.

With growth, administrative and specialist support employment has increased. Mill management and clerical staff are added for the administration of each new acquisition. Growth of WTD's centralized management and staff has occurred in spurts. The most recent such growth occurred in FY 1988 coincident with the surge in acquisitions in that year. Division managers were interposed between mill managers and WTD headquarters. The divisional differentiation is based on geography and/or product. Thus the Oregon, Washington, and Inland Softwood divisions reflect a geographical grouping of mills that use the same general kind of material. The hardwood division is a grouping of those mills producing hardwood products. The eastern division is geographical and, at present, consists of only one plant—the Whitehall plywood plant. Other key additions to top management were experienced vice presidents of operations, acquisitions, and pulp, the latter to be responsible for developing and implementing a proposed pulp mill. Overall, additions to nondirect labor increased selling, general, and administrative expenses to nearly double the FY 1987 level.

Bruce Engel, the president, along with his wife Teri, owns approximately 56 percent of the WTD common stock and, thus, is in a controlling position.[10] He has been and continues to be the chief architect of WTD's growth. As WTD has grown, he has added managers and staff capable of performing or assisting him perform most of the executive functions that he has assumed. This has not diminished his involvement. He is deeply involved in performing the duties of chief executive, including public relations, choosing and effecting acquisitions, integrating new units into the company, and guiding ongoing operations. Other Engel enterprises have been estimated to take only 5 to 10 percent of his time.[11] These include bowling alleys in three cities, three radio stations, a weekly newspaper, three light manufacturing firms, and a clothing alteration and tailoring service. Other outside interests may be added—recently he lost in a bid to buy the Seattle Mariners major league baseball club.

PROFIT PERFORMANCE

WTD has shown a steady growth in net sales, operating income, and net income, reflecting both the addition of mills and plants and an increase in production in mills, once acquired. In terms of efficiency and profit ratios, as can be seen in Exhibit 10, it has been a consistent performer without major variations from year to year. The only measure of profit performance that has shown significant change is the net income return on average equity which was affected by the shift from private to public ownership in late 1986 (FY 1987).

Exhibit 11 shows the return on assets, and underlying profit margins and asset turnover, earned by WTD and selected competitors for a five-year period.

---

[10] WTD Industries, Inc., Form 10K, p. 35.

[11] Brown, "WTD Industries," p. 9.

Exhibit 10   FINANCIAL STATISTICS FOR WTD INDUSTRIES, 1983–1988 (in millions)

	April 30					
	1983	**1984**	**1985**	**1986**	**1987**	**1988**
Net sales	$14.0	$36.6	$48.6	$99.0	$176.2	$293.7
Cost of goods sold	$12.4	$30.9	$41.4	$85.2	$152.7	$246.5
Selling, general, and administrative expense . . .	$0.9	$2.6	$3.1	$6.6	$10.0	$20.0
Depreciation	NA	$1.2	$1.6	$2.6	$3.3	$6.5
Operating income	$0.7	$1.9	$2.5	$4.6	$10.2	$20.7
Interest expense	$0.8	$1.6	$1.4	$1.5	$1.7	$7.7
Other, including taxes	$0.1	$0.3	$−0.2	$−1.1	$−3.8	$−4.6
Net income	$0.0	$0.6	$0.9	$2.0	$4.7	$8.4
Capital expenditures	NA	$2.1	$2.1	$4.5	$14.4	$16.8
Working capital	NA	NA	$−2.1	$−0.8	$22.5	$18.3
Average assets	NA	$15.0	$20.0	$29.0	$70.0	$125.0
Owners' equity	NA	$0.3	$1.1	$2.4	$13.1	$27.5
Gross margin	11.4%	15.6%	14.8%	13.9%	13.3%	16.1%
Profit margin	5.0%	5.2%	5.1%	4.6%	5.8%	7.0%
Asset turnover	NA	2.4	2.4	3.4	2.5	2.3
Operating ROA	NA	12.7%	12.5%	15.9%	14.6%	16.6%
After-tax return on equity	NA	221.0%	78.7%	85.0%	35.9%	30.6%
Debt + equity/equity	NA	NA	13.8	11.5	4.5	4.6
Ratio of long-term debt to equity	NA	NA	3.8	2.2	1.9	2.4
Capital expenditures as a percent of sales	NA	5.7%	4.3%	4.5%	8.2%	5.7%

NA: not applicable.
Source: WTD Industries, Inc., 1988 and 1987 annual reports; 1987 Form 10K.

THE FUTURE

WTD is committed to fast growth. The announced intent is to grow both internally and externally. Internal growth in production at existing mills is a continuing goal that requires focused application of the company's human resource strategy. One thrust of external growth is the ongoing acquisition of new lumber mills using cash generated from operations and debt. Acquisitions are sought that:

1. Require reasonably low capital investment.
2. Are capable of increased productivity through incentive plans.
3. Are located in areas with an adequate supply of open-market logs.
4. In view of the preceding, offer an acceptable ROI.
5. Provide cash flow sufficient to service debt.

In addition, Bruce Engel has indicated his intent to add to WTD's production capacity in new geographical regions.

The company's second external growth thrust is a departure from the past. WTD has announced its intent to enter the pulp and paper industry with the construction and operation of a market-pulp mill. Building a mill to produce pulp, although costly, is generally seen as an unusual opportunity for the company because of favorable foreign market conditions and synergy with WTD sawmill

Exhibit 11 PROFITABILITY COMPARISONS

	Year*				
	1983	**1984**	**1985**	**1986**	**1987**
Operating Profit Margins					
Boise Cascade	1.2%	−8.0%	4.3%	8.7%	9.3%
Champion International	4.5	1.3	5.8	9.9	13.9
Georgia-Pacific	8.5	8.2	8.4	9.8	8.8
International Paper	24.1	11.2	11.1	14.7	13.6
Louisiana Pacific	8.6	4.1	8.2	10.1	13.5
Pope and Talbot	10.0	−0.6	5.9	11.1	12.6
Weyerhaeuser	11.5	2.5	6.9	9.7	11.3
WTD	5.2	5.1	4.6	5.8	7.0
Asset Turnover					
Boise Cascade	1.5	1.4	1.1	1.2	1.3
Champion International	1.5	1.0	0.7	0.5	0.6
Georgia-Pacific	1.8	2.0	1.9	2.0	2.2
International Paper	0.6	0.6	0.6	0.7	0.8
Louisiana Pacific	1.2	1.2	1.2	1.1	1.1
Pope and Talbot	1.5	1.6	1.9	1.8	2.1
Weyerhaeuser	1.2	1.2	1.2	1.2	1.4
WTD	2.4	2.4	3.4	2.5	2.3
Return on Assets					
Boise Cascade	1.8%	−11.2%	4.6%	10.7%	12.3%
Champion International	6.6	1.3	4.0	5.2	8.2
Georgia-Pacific	15.6	16.5	16.3	20.1	19.1
International Paper	14.8	6.6	6.3	9.7	11.4
Louisiana Pacific	10.5	4.9	9.7	11.1	15.3
Pope and Talbot	14.7	−0.9	11.3	19.6	26.5
Weyerhaeuser	13.4	3.0	8.0	11.8	16.2
WTD	12.7	12.5	15.9	14.6	16.6

* Note: WTD figures are based on eight months in the listed year plus the first four months of the following year.
Source: Author's calculations using each company's annual report and 10K data.

operations that provide the wood chips used in making pulp. Conditions favoring the project include:

1. A current short supply of pulp.
2. Expectations that the United States will be a low-cost producer of pulp in the foreseeable future.
3. Japanese (and other) market-pulp buyers prefer to own capacity to assure supply in a tight market.
4. WTD's mills produce the largest single supply of wood chips not controlled by an existing paper company in the Northwest. Demand for a new pulp mill can be expected to raise chip prices in the region. WTD expects the mill to provide a market for about half the wood chips it produces. WTD's revenue is expected to rise on the order of $10 million as a result of wood chip price rises alone.[12]

---

[12] Chad E. Brown, "WTD Industries," Company Comment, Kidder, Peabody & Co., March 18, 1988, p. 2.

WTD's plan is to build a $425 million mill with a capacity of 300,000 metric tons per year of bleached softwood kraft market pulp. This type of market pulp is used in paper mills to produce newsprint. The mill will operate as Port Westwood Pulp Company, and will export 95 percent of its production—75 percent of its exports going to Pacific Rim markets and 25 percent to Europe. The estimated annual market value of the output of this mill is $180 million.[13]

WTD plans to joint venture the mill with foreign investors. Japanese, Chinese, and Korean firms have indicated interest in the project and WTD does not anticipate trouble in finding partners. However, WTD plans to operate the mill and control the venture with majority ownership. Thus the company may need to raise substantial capital for its share, possibly more than $200 million. Possible sources of funds mentioned by the company include a public stock offering, senior debentures, industrial revenue bonds, and bank loans, alone or in combination.

In summer 1988, WTD subleased 250 acres of land owned by the Port of St. Helens, on the Columbia River, west of Portland, Oregon, from Portland General Electric Company. The location offers economical transportation from a large number of WTD mills and loading facilities for ocean-going ships. The lease option is for a two-year period during which time WTD plans to arrange financing, secure permits, finalize engineering studies, and start construction. Production is expected to start in mid-1992.

---

[13] "Pulp Mills Proposed for Oregon," *The Oregonian,* August 25, 1988; and "Questions Asked about WTD's Funding of Mill," *Business Journal* (Portland, Oregon), September 11, 1988.

THE GOLDEN GATE BREWING COMPANY*

At a booth in Harry's, a local bar overlooking the San Francisco Bay, James Cook poured a fresh glass of amber-colored Golden Gate Lager and dropped a bottle cap onto the beer's head. The cap floated like a lily pad on the foam. "That's what you get from using all malt, no rices or corn—a very firm head," he said. "It looks like whipped cream and acts like egg whites, as my father used to say." When Cook's glass was finished, the inside was coated with strips of foam, "Belgian lace" in brewer's jargon, and a sign of a beer's purity. "People usually think of a local beer as crummy, cheap beer. I plan to change the way they think," Cook said.

James Cook, age 36, was president of the fledgling Golden Gate Brewing Company, the brewer of Golden Gate Lager, and sixth consecutive eldest son in the Cook family to become a brewer. Cook was a former high-paid, high-powered management consultant with the Boston Consulting Group. He held a Harvard BA, MBA, and JD. The Golden Gate Brewing Company was incorporated in 1984 and Golden Gate Lager was introduced in San Francisco on July 4, an appropriate day, but accidental timing according to Cook. Cook's goal was to establish Golden Gate Lager as a superpremium beer with a distinctive taste:

> I intend to go head-to-head against imported beers. Nowhere in the world but America do they drink so much imported beer. Here, imported beer is popular because our domestic beer is so bad. My work is to give Americans an alternative to drinking foreign beers. I want to start a revolution in the way people think about American beer. There is nothing wrong with standard domestic beers, for what they are. They are clean, consistent, and cheap. But they are also bland and mediocre. They are mass market products. People can recall, off the top of their heads, the advertising, the slogans, and the music for most beers, but they can't remember the taste.

THE SITUATION

For years, small local breweries had either closed down or been acquired by one of the industry leaders. The advent of small boutique breweries, in California, Colorado, and New York, making limited quantities of quality beer, had opposed this trend. Cook acknowledged the odds and history were against small regional breweries. But Cook was betting on a combination of his family's brewing background, management training, and a limited target market to create long-term Golden Gate Lager drinkers.

---

* Prepared by Brent Callinicos, research assistant, under the direction of Professor Richard I. Levin, University of North Carolina at Chapel Hill. Copyright © 1988 by the authors.

Golden Gate Lager is currently sold in two locations, San Francisco and Munich. As of November 1985, the current sales volume of 6,000 cases per month represents less than one minute of production for Anheuser-Busch, the long-standing industry leader. Cook reports that he has sold as much beer in the past six months as Anheuser-Busch makes in about six minutes. "They spill more beer every hour than I make in a month." In six months, the Golden Gate Brewing Company has sold 25,000 cases in California. His more than 200 accounts range

---

Exhibit 1   BEER INDUSTRY FACTS AND TERMS

Dimensions of the industry

The annual wholesale value of the brewing industry's products in 1985 was $13.7 billion.

Total employment in the industry was close to 40,000 people.

The average hourly earnings of a brewing industry employee was $18.27 in 1985, a 3.2 percent increase over 1984.

In a recent typical year, the industry's gross assets amounted to $6,639,979,000. Its net worth, computed from income tax returns, was $3,377,780,000.

What the industry buys

Agricultural commodities, the output of more than 4 million acres of farm land, worth $700 million plus are used annually by the brewing industry. These include:

- 4.9 billion pounds or 143.8 million bushels of choice malt—worth $380 million.
- Other select grains, chiefly corn and rice—worth $221 million.
- Hops—value to the grower of $80 million.

Some 86.9 percent of all beer sold is packaged in cans or bottles. In one year, the brewing industry uses more than:

- 33.1 billion steel and aluminum cans.
- 19.2 billion bottles in returnable and nonreturnable form.
- $525 million for interest, rentals, repairs, and maintenance.

The industry's annual bill for containers—cans, bottles, kegs, and related packaging materials purchased from other American industries, is close to $4.5 billion. Supplies and services of numerous kinds are also required in brewing and distributing malt beverages. Annual average outlays for these include:

- Fuel, power and water—$420 million.
- Wholesale payroll—$1.8 billion.
- Brewery equipment and improvements—$550 million.

The industry's products and terminology

Beers fall into two broad categories—those that are top-fermented and those that are bottom-fermented.

Bottom-fermented

Pilsner/Pilsener. The world's most famous beer style, it was named after the excellent beer brewed in Pilsen, Czechoslovakia, for the past 700 years. It is a pale, golden-colored, distinctly hoppy beer.

Lager. All bottom-fermented beers are lagers. This is a generic term, though it is sometimes applied to the most basic bottom-fermented brew produced by a brewery. In Britain and the United States, the majority of lagers are very loose, local interpretations of the Pilsner style.

Top-fermented

Ale. Generic term for English-style top-fermented beers. Usually copper-colored, but sometimes darker. It is usually paler in color and differs in flavor from lager beer.

Stout. Darker in color and sweeter or maltier than ale. The darkest, richest, maltiest of all regularly produced beers.

"Malt Liquor." This is a term conjured up to describe beers that exceed a country's legal alcohol levels—5 percent in the United States. They are most often made as lagers, but the American version can be sweetish or more bitter than the traditional lagers.

Barrel. This refers to a full barrel, which has a volume of 31 gallons.

from liquor stores to exclusive hotels to neighborhood bars, such as Harry's. Exhibits 1 through 3 provide industry background, population demographics of the San Francisco/Oakland area, and general demographics of U.S. beer drinkers.

"By my standards I have been very successful," said Cook. While demand has been strong, he wondered if it would last. "People who drink imports will try it because it's new, but will Golden Gate Lager be just a flash?" Cook is hoping there are enough beer aficionados in San Francisco, but he is wondering if he should try to expand in Europe, or if he should concentrate on the West Coast, the East Coast, or selected cities throughout the country. How fast should he expand? With several comparable local brews being sold in the area, will his marketing strategy have to change? What are the risks involved? Cook realized he needed to make some strategic decisions.

Exhibit 2   POPULATION CHARACTERISTICS OF THE SAN FRANCISCO/OAKLAND AREA, 1980

Year	Population	Percentage change
1960	2,649,000	N/A
1970	3,109,000	17.37%
1980	3,251,000	4.5

Age composition

Age	Population	Percentage of total
Under 18	1,296,000	25.02%
18–24	666,000	12.86
25–34	989,000	19.10
35–44	668,000	12.90
45–54	536,000	10.35
55–64	491,000	9.48
65–Over	533,000	10.29
Under 21	1,571,000	30.33

Ethnic composition

Race	Percentage of total
White	62.37%
Black	10.71
Spanish	9.64
Indian	10.93
Eskimo	0.47
Other*	5.88

Education (persons 25 years old and over)

Years of education	Percentage of total
Less than five	3%
High school only	71
Four years college or more	26
Median school years completed	13

Occupational profile

Group	Percentage of total
Managerial and professional	28.28%
Technical and sales-related	35.43
Service occupations	11.84
Farming/forestry/fishing	1.15
Craft/repair group	11.12
Operators/laborers	12.18

Income breakdown

Income	Households	Percentage of total
Under $5,000	199,763	10.12%
$5,000–$9,999	243,278	12.32
$10,000–$19,999	511,225	25.90
$20,000–$34,999	611,279	30.97
$35,000–$49,999	258,758	13.11
$50,000–Over	149,577	7.58
Total households	1,973,880	
Median income	$20,607	

* Includes Japanese, Chinese, Filipino, Korean, Asian Indian, Vietnamese, Hawaiian, and Samoan.
Source: U.S. Bureau of the Census, *Census of Population*, 1980.

| Exhibit 3 | 1983 U.S. BEER DRINKER DEMOGRAPHICS |

Percentage of the population drinking

	Domestic	Light	Imported	Malt	Ale	Draft
All Adults	39.6%	24.4%	15.8%	8.3%	8.6%	26.2%
Males	54.0	28.6	22.0	11.0	12.0	35.6
Females	26.6	20.6	10.3	5.9	5.5	17.7
Age						
18–24	51.2	29.1	26.6	14.8	14.0	36.5
25–34	49.0	30.8	20.8	10.9	10.9	36.1
35–44	39.3	27.8	15.8	7.3	7.8	26.8
45–54	35.5	23.5	13.5	5.6	7.0	22.8
55–64	30.9	16.7	8.5	4.1	5.6	16.9
65 or older	23.4	13.0	4.6	4.3	3.8	9.8
College graduate	47.5	32.2	28.0	6.0	12.4	36.3
Attended college	45.3	30.0	22.0	8.9	11.9	33.5
High school graduate	38.4	23.9	13.6	8.4	7.8	25.8
Not high school graduate	23.6	17.4	8.5	9.2	5.6	16.7
Employed full time	46.2	30.2	20.4	9.0	10.5	33.2
Part time	36.7	24.9	17.7	8.0	9.0	26.5
Not employed	32.1	17.3	10.1	7.6	6.2	17.7
Professional	48.2	32.8	27.1	7.4	12.8	37.0
Clerical/sales	38.6	29.8	17.6	7.3	9.2	29.2
Craftsperson/supervisor	52.9	30.7	17.7	9.1	8.4	36.3
Other employed	44.3	25.5	16.2	11.5	9.6	28.9
Single	50.8	28.5	29.0	14.9	14.5	36.5
Married	38.3	24.1	12.9	6.1	7.1	24.6
Divorced	30.7	20.2	11.0	8.7	6.7	19.6
Parents	41.0	26.5	14.5	8.8	7.7	27.9
White	39.8	24.9	15.8	6.1	8.4	27.4
Black	36.8	19.3	14.4	25.4	9.8	16.4
Other	42.0	27.6	25.6	12.7	7.5	27.6
Geographic location						
Northeast	42.9	22.0	22.3	7.2	13.5	27.7
East Central	39.1	24.2	11.6	7.5	9.3	27.2
West Central	42.3	29.0	13.1	7.4	5.6	30.3
South	32.7	22.8	11.1	9.6	6.4	21.0
Pacific	45.1	26.1	22.3	9.5	7.8	28.4
Household Income						
$40,000 +	45.6	29.7	24.1	6.0	11.8	32.7
$30,000 +	44.2	28.8	22.5	6.0	10.7	32.0
$25,000 +	44.1	28.4	21.3	6.4	10.3	31.4
$20–24,999	38.1	26.0	14.0	6.8	7.7	27.5
$15–19,999	42.5	26.7	14.5	10.9	8.7	28.8
$10–14,999	36.0	20.9	11.2	9.1	7.1	21.7
under $10,000	32.3	16.5	9.5	11.3	6.5	16.6

INDUSTRY OVERVIEW

Historically, the U.S. beer industry had many small local producers, but now it is dominated by the six largest brewers (see Exhibits 5 and 6). In 1876 there were 2,685 breweries; in 1952 there were only 350; and in 1982 there were 79. (Exhibit 4). Major firms were more willing to purchase struggling regional producers or construct new facilities in the South and West so as to establish nationwide distribution of their brands.

Exhibit 4   OPERATING BREWERIES BY CENSUS REGION

Region	1952	1960	1970	1982	Percentage of total	
					1952	1982
Northeast	100	62	45	18	28.0%	22.8%
North Central	164	99	61	25	45.9	31.6
South	42	33	26	20	11.8	25.3
West	51	35	22	16	14.3	20.3
Total United States	357	229	154	79	100.0%	100.0%

Exhibit 5   LEADING U.S. BREWERS' DOMESTIC BEER MARKET SHARE

Brewer	1970	1975	1980	1982	1983	1984
Anheuser-Busch	18.2%	23.7%	28.9%	33.5%	34.1%	34.6%
Miller	4.2	8.7	21.5	22.3	21.1	22.1
Stroh	2.7	3.5	3.6	13.0	13.7	13.5
G. Heileman	2.5	3.1	7.7	8.2	9.9	9.3
Adolph Coors	6.0	8.0	8.0	6.8	7.7	7.2
Pabst	8.6	10.5	8.7	6.8	7.2	6.8
Genesee	1.2	1.5	2.1	1.9	1.8	1.9
C. Schmidt	2.5	2.2	2.1	1.8	1.8	1.7
Falstaff	5.4	5.0	2.3	1.8	1.5	1.8
Pittsburgh			0.6	0.6	0.6	0.5
Other	48.7	33.8	14.5	3.3	0.6	0.6
Total	100.0%	100.0%	100.0%	100.0%	100.0%	100.0%

Exhibit 6   BARRELAGE OF TOP 10 BREWERS—1984 COMPARED TO 1983

	1983	1984	Gain/Loss	
			Barrels*	Percent
Anheuser-Busch	60,500,000	64,000,000	3,500,000	5.8%
Miller	37,470,000	37,520,000	50,000	0.1
Stroh	24,300,000	23,900,000	(400,000)	−1.6
G. Heileman	17,549,000	16,760,000	(789,000)	−4.5
Adolphs Coors	13,719,000	13,187,000	(532,000)	−3.9
Pabst	12,804,000	11,562,000	(1,242,000)	−9.7
Genesee	3,200,000	3,000,000	(200,000)	−6.3
C. Schmidt	2,800,000	2,500,000	(300,000)	−10.7
Falstaff	2,705,000	2,338,000	(367,000)	−13.6
Pittsburgh	1,000,000	950,000	(50,000)	−5.0
All Others	3,597,000	2,134,000	(1,463,000)	−40.7
Total	179,644,000	177,851,000	(1,793,000)	−1.0%

* In 31-gallon barrels.

Exhibit 7 U.S. BEER SALES—DOMESTIC BRANDS AND IMPORTED BRANDS, 1983–1984

	31-Gallon barrels (millions)		Percent of total		Percent change
	1983	1984	1983	1984	
Domestic beer	177.5	175.3	96.6%	96.1%	−1.2%
Imported beer	6.3	7.2	3.4	3.9	14.3
Total sales	183.8	182.5	100.0	100.0	−0.7

Exhibit 8 PRODUCTION OF MALT BEVERAGES IN THE UNITED STATES FOR SELECTED YEARS (thousands)

Year	Barrels	Year	Barrels
1904	48,265	1977	172,229
1914	66,189	1978	171,639
1924	4,891	1979	183,515
1934	37,679	1980	188,374
1944	81,726	1981	194,542
1954	92,561	1982	193,984
1964	103,018	1983	195,664
1974	153,053	1984	193,416

Exhibit 9 PER CAPITA U.S. CONSUMPTION OF MALT BEVERAGES, 1974–1984

Year	Gallons	Year	Gallons
1974	20.9	1980	24.3
1975	21.3	1981	24.6
1976	21.5	1982	24.4
1977	22.4	1983	24.2
1978	23.1	1984	24.0
1979	23.8		

Following several years of flat or nearly flat sales, beer consumption declined about 0.7 percent in 1984 (Exhibit 7), the first decline in 27 years; production declined approximately 1.2 percent (Exhibit 8). Per capita consumption of beer also declined (Exhibit 9), and for 1985, per capita consumption is estimated to remain at the 1984 level of 24 gallons. The long-term outlook for the industry is less encouraging. Chris Lole of the Stroh Brewery Company believes beer sales will remain flat for the next 10, possibly 20, years.

However, there is one segment of growth in this troubled industry—imports. Imported brands have grown from 0.7 percent of total consumption in 1970 to 3.4 percent in 1983 (aided somewhat over the years by a strong U.S. dollar). Imports occupy the high ground in terms of quality in consumers' perception; and trading up continues to benefit imports. As import volume has grown, an increasing number of brands have appeared, and many more are now being advertised. The continued growth in this segment, coupled with the decline in domestic sales, meant an increase in import's share to almost 4 percent in 1984.

For regional and smaller brewers, it is becoming increasingly difficult to move a product which is falling in demand and cannot be backed by the advertising revenues of the large national breweries. Interestingly, the microbrewer/brew pub trend continues. More and more entrepreneurs are allured by the prospects of concocting their own distinctive beer and operating their own business.

EXTERNAL THREATS

Several external threats were affecting the beer industry: First, the U.S. population is more concerned about healthier lifestyles, which potentially reduces beer consumption. Consumption and the purchase-pattern preference of 25- to 40-year-olds have changed dramatically in recent years. This group, because of interests in appearance, exercise, and career advancement, exhibits a preference for drinks with fewer calories and lower alcohol content. Over-40 drinkers are also increasingly health and diet conscious.

An important negative factor for future beer sales is demographics. Growth of the 18-to-34 age group is winding down. Beer sales have closely tracked the baby boom age bulge in the population. The teenage population (the source of most new drinkers) has been decreasing and is forecast to continue its decline. Brewers, therefore, confront a decline in potential new users. In addition, the young adult population (20 to 29 years) is also declining. The beer industry relies on this segment to replace sales lost due to attrition in the drinking population. Finally, people between the ages of 30 and 49 will increase substantially and by 1990 will constitute 30 percent of the population. Historically, this group has been an important beer-drinking group. However, industry analysts say this group is the one most concerned about alcohol abuse and drunk driving.

The beer industry faces another demographic change that will create problems. Blue-collar workers have traditionally been the heaviest consumers of beer. Today, the economy is shifting toward the service sector and the blue-collar work force is declining.

The emergence of wine coolers is also taking a toll on the beer industry. Wine coolers appeal to beer drinkers and to nonbeer drinkers. Coolers are, to some extent, a beer substitute. Introduced five years ago, there are about 50 cooler brands now available which contain 6 percent alcohol. Retail sales in 1984 were $360 million and in 1985 approached $700 million. However, cooler sales for 1986 are projected at 35 million cases, versus the 2.5 billion cases of the beer market. Some analysts believe that wine coolers are firmly established, while others contend that coolers are just a fad.

The market will shrink further due to stiffer penalties for drunk driving and the rise of the national legal drinking age to 21. The growing awareness of the need for responsible drinking habits has been fostered by groups such as Mothers Against Drunk Drivers (MADD). According to MADD, about 55 percent of all highway fatalities in 1983 were alcohol related; 1984 figures indicated a small decline to 54 percent.

In July 1984, President Ronald Reagan signed into law the National Minimum Drinking Age Act, which grants the federal government the authority to withhold federal highway funds from states that fail to raise their legal drinking age to 21 by 1987. When the law was enacted there were 27 states and the District of Columbia with a minimum age below 21, but many have introduced legislation to raise the age, or are expected to. Some 360 new laws regarding drunk driving have been passed nationwide since 1981. Many states and municipalities have banned "happy hours," which encourage increased alcohol consumption through discount prices. Also, there are 37 states with statutes holding the establishments and hosts liable for the subsequent behavior of intoxicated patrons or guests. These could also serve to reduce beer consumption.

INDUSTRY REACTION

Faced with these problems, many other industries would retrench, concentrate on keeping primary profit-making brands afloat, and try to ride out the storm. The brewery industry's response has been almost the opposite. New brands and extensions have appeared on retailers' shelves at a record pace. Beers that had been available only regionally are being moved into broader distribution. New light beers, low-alcohol beers, low-priced beers, superpremium beers and malt liquors have emerged. Exhibit 10 lists the brands introduced in 1984 by both national and regional brewers.

The major U.S. brewers introduced 26 new products or line extensions in 1984. Two-thirds of these new product introductions were low-alcohol or low-calorie products. Anheuser-Busch (A-B) was the first major brewer to unveil its low-alcohol entry, LA; and regional brewers soon got into the act. To date, however, the low- and no-alcohol products have not worked out well. They are viewed as weak with no zing. They seem to appeal to the drinker who does not drink very much beer to begin with, in contrast to light beers which appeal to the heavy beer drinker.

While new product introductions slowed in 1985, the beer industry is doing everything possible to attract new customers. A shrinking market means brewers must steal share from competitors. Lower-priced brands have been introduced and major firms, particularly Anheuser-Busch and Miller, have expanded their advertising budgets.

TAXES

The brewing industry confronts another problem, the ever-present threat of increased taxation. Beer is one of the most highly taxed consumer products. Taxes constitute the largest individual item in the price of beer. The federal excise

Exhibit 10   DOMESTIC BEER BRANDS INTRODUCED IN 1984

Brand	Brewer
Black Label 11–11 Malt Liquor	Heileman
Black Label LA*	Heileman
Blatz LA *	Heileman
Big Man Malt Liquor	Eastern Brewing
Choice *	F.X. Malt
Golden Hawk	Schmidt
Ice Man Malt Liquor	Pabst
I. C. Golden Lager	Pittsburgh
King Cobra Malt Liquor	Anheuser-Busch
LA†	Anheuser-Busch
Light-N-Lo*	Latrobe
Little Kings Premium	Schoenling
Lone Star LA*	Heileman
Low Alcohol Gold* †	Pabst
Low Alcohol Pabst Extra Light* †	Pabst
Meister Brau Light	Miller
Milwaukee's Best	Miller
Old Style LA*	Heileman
Oscar Wildes's	Pearl
Plank Road Original Draft	Miller
Rainier LA*	Heileman
Schaefer Low Alcohol*	Stroh
Schmidt LA*	Heileman
Select Special 50 Low Alcohol*	Pearl
Sharpe's LA*	Miller
Silver Thunder Malt Liquor	Stroh

* Low in alcohol.
† Repositioned brand.

tax is $9 a barrel, and state taxes average approximately $5.41 a barrel. Combined annual federal, state, and local taxes equal almost $3 billion. While the government earns over $14 for each barrel of beer or ale sold, the brewing industry's average profit rate per barrel after taxes is estimated between $2 and $3. The federal government was debating the merits of increased excise taxes on beer as part of a plan to reduce the federal deficit. It was common for state and local governments to raise taxes on beer periodically. In California, where Golden Gate was headquartered, brewers paid taxes equal to $1.24 per barrel.

INTERNAL/INDUSTRY FACTORS

The major causes of consolidation in the beer industry were economies of scale and product differentiation. Economies of scale, which occur when large plants produce at lower unit costs than smaller ones, existed in both the brewing and bottling processes. The increased capacity attained by many individual breweries over the past 20 years has forced the closing or sale of numerous regional producers. Industry experts contend that the wave of consolidation has not ended. Currently there is excess capacity and certain plants are inefficient (Exhibit 11). Except for A-B, the industry is operating between 75 percent and 85 percent of capacity.

Exhibit 11 U.S. BREWING INDUSTRY CAPACITY AND USAGE—1983

Brewer	Plants	Total capacity (million)	Shipments	Percent of capacity
Anheuser-Busch	11	66.5	60.5	91.0%
Miller	7	54.0	37.5	69.4
Stroh	7	32.6	24.3	74.5
G. Heileman	12	25.5	17.5	68.6
Adolph Coors	1	15.5	13.7	88.4
Pabst	4	15.0	12.8	85.3
Genesee	1	4.0	3.2	80.0
C. Schmidt	2	5.0	3.2	64.0
Falstaff	5	5.0	2.7	54.0
Pittsburgh	1	1.2	1.0	83.3
All Others	34	7.4	3.7	50.0
Domestic total	85	231.7	180.1	77.7%

Even though the U.S. beer industry is suffering from overcapacity, two brewers announced expansion plans during 1985. Adolph Coors Company intends to build a $70 million beer packaging plant in Virginia, and, if sales justify it, the facility will be expanded to include full brewing facilities. G. Heileman Brewing Company plans to construct a new brewery in Milwaukee. The facility will specialize in more costly imported-style beers. The industry's overcapacity was accentuated by Miller Brewing's decision to write-down $140 million of its $450 million new plant and Stroh Brewery Company's decision to close its older, underutilized Detroit plant.

Successful product differentiation occurs when a firm convinces customers that real or imagined differences in its beer render it preferable to that of the competitors. Larger brewers, with national sales and multiplant operations, can often more easily attain this high-quality image than local or regional brewers. There also appear to be economies of scale in brand proliferation and product extensions. Large brewers can more easily (and cost-effectively) segment all price and product categories. The high fixed costs associated with advertising new brands can be spread over a large sales volume that smaller brewers do not have. Large firms can realize lower advertising costs on each barrel than small firms.

Advertising has grown considerably in importance and in expense. In 1984 brewers spent an estimated $780 million. Advertising expenditures in 1983 averaged $2.74 per barrel. The evidence that high advertising expenditures and high-profit levels are positively correlated is, however, somewhat mixed. At Schlitz, for example, advertising expenditures on each barrel rose dramatically at a time when sales and operating profit per barrel both fell. Similarly, Coors had higher profit figures when advertising expenditure levels were extremely low and lower profits when advertising outlays accelerated. However, A-B and Miller have increased both profit on each barrel and market share, at a time when advertising expenditures increased.

IMPORTS

Imports are expected to perform well throughout the remainder of the 1980s. Between 1980 and 1984, the quantity of beer imported increased about 12 percent annually. Five countries, the Netherlands, Canada, West Germany, Mexico, and the United Kingdom, account for about 90 percent of all U.S. imports, but over 40 other countries ship beer to the United States. The imports' share of the U.S. beer market has grown from 1.1 percent in 1975 to 3.9 percent in 1984. Many beer wholesalers felt imports would capture at least 10 percent of the total U.S. beer market by 1990.

Ten years ago, imported beers were esoteric products consumed by a small elite, in a handful of markets. Since then, the industry has exploded with beer drinkers' desire, taste, and imagery fueling this growth. According to industry analyst Emanuel Goldman, "The imports have image. We live in a self-indulgent age that's getting more and more self-indulgent, and people want something different. They can get something different, upscale, and feel good about it with imports. There is a tremendous selection, too. The consumer seems to feel that imports are superior beers."

The top 10 imported brands dominate about 87 percent of the sales (Exhibit 12). Heineken maintains the lead with an estimated 34 percent of the market, while Molson holds second place with 13.4 percent. Fortifying the Canadian segment is Moosehead in the number four spot and Labatt in the fifth place with 6 percent and 4.5 percent of the market, respectively. Beck's is in third place with 8.9 percent of the market and its closest German competitor, St. Pauli Girl, ranks sixth.

Favorable demographics and an improving economy have aided this segment. The rise of the Hispanic population and the popularity of Mexican cuisine has fared well for Mexican beers, while the growing Oriental population has given rise to a host of Chinese and Japanese brews. Most significant has been the appeal of imported beer to status-conscious consumers. A prime market eager for imported beers has been the young urban professionals, with a desire for unusual and different products, especially those of a foreign bent.

Exhibit 12   TOP IMPORTED BEER BRANDS

Top ten	Second ten (alphabetically)
1. Heineken (Netherlands)	11. Carta Blanca (Mexico)
2. Molson (Canada)	12. Dinkelacker (Germany)
3. Beck's (Germany)	13. Dortmunder (Germany)
4. Moosehead (Canada)	14. Grolsch (Netherlands)
5. Labatt (Canada)	15. Guiness (United Kingdom)
6. St. Pauli Girl (Germany)	16. Kirin (Japan)
7. Dos Equis (Mexico)	17. Kronenbourg (France)
8. Foster's Lager (Australia)	18. O'Keefe (Canada)
9. Amstel Light (Netherlands)	19. San Miquel (Philippines)
10. Corona (Mexico)	20. Tecate (Mexico)

Exhibit 13   IMPORTED BEER BRANDS INTRODUCED IN 1984

Brand	Country	Brand	Country
ABC Stout	Singapore	Hombre	Mexico
Affligem	Belgium	John Peel Export	Britain
Alfa Beer	Holland	Jever Pilsner	West Germany
Anchor Pilsener	Singapore	Kaiser	Germany
Bamburger Hofbrau	Germany	Koff Stout	Finland
Brador	Canada	Kronenhaler*	Austria
Broken Hill	Australia	Lindener	West Germany
Castillio Beer	Italy	Lorimer	Britain
Castle St.	Britain	Maes Pils	Belgium
China Beer	Taiwan	Oktober Beer	West Germany
China Clipper	China	Orangebloom	Holland
Danish Light	Denmark	Pacifico	Mexico
De Koninck	Belgium	Rolland Light	Germany
Dempseys	Ireland	Scandia Gold	Denmark
Elan*	Switzerland	Tientan	China
Feingold Pils	Austria	Vaux	Britain
Felinfoel	Britain	Vienna Lager	Austria
Festive Ale	Britain	Warteck*	Switzerland
Glacier*	Sweden	Wolfbrau	Germany
Golden Ox	Germany	Yuchan Beer	China
Grizzly Beer	Canada	Zero*	Germany

* Denotes low or nonalcoholic brand.

An estimated 10 new imported beers entered the United States every month in 1984. Exhibit 13 provides a partial list of the imported brands introduced in 1984.

There are two major obstacles in trying to capture American market share. The first is Van Munching & Company, which distributes Heineken. Heineken, with its commanding market share, essentially sets the benchmark pricing level for much of the import category. Many feel you cannot enter the U.S. market if you are above Heineken in price. The second major problem is a paradox created by the very success of the category, namely brand proliferation and the resulting market dilution.

Success hinges on the ability to come up with a unique selling proposition to cut through the multitude of brands competing for available market share. One technique used by imports is a unique packaging profile. The theory behind this is that the consumer knows none of the beers, but will try the one that looks a little different. This is supported by the number of American beer drinkers who first bought Grolsch, if for no other reason than to see what sort of brew was in its distinctive bottle with the old-fashioned wire closure and ceramic stopper. More imports are also moving to green bottles for their products. Consumer research shows that Americans feel green glass is more appealing for a light-colored beer.

Even though beer tasting and tavern promotion nights are the most cost-effective ways to promote public awareness, reliance on heavy advertising is increasing. In 1985 Van Munching spent an estimated $22 million advertising and promoting Heineken. For Molson $15 million was spent. St. Pauli Girl had a $14 million budget, and Mexican Tecate plans regional advertising at $4 million in 1986. Although imports account for less than 4 percent of the beer market, the category held 10 percent of all beer advertising in 1984. About five imported beers represent 78.9 percent of all imported beer advertising. Heineken leads the list of import advertisers with 33.9 percent, Molson has 20.5 percent, Amstel Light follows with 15.8 percent, Moosehead and St. Pauli Girl trail with 4.5 percent and 4.2 percent, respectively. However, some importers are not marketing at all and some import companies have 10 to 20 restaurants and delicatessens to whom they sell beer.

EXPORTS

Confronted with a static-to-declining domestic market, beer producers are being forced to seek new markets abroad. A-B sees the international market, which is more than twice as large as the U.S. market, as critical to U.S. brewers' long-term success. Miller Vice President Alan Easton echoes this view, "Anybody who is really serious about being in the beer industry is going to have to consider participating in non-U.S. markets." Because substantial foreign opposition exists, brewers are seeking to expand government efforts to negotiate for trade barrier reductions.

Currently, the United States is Canada's major export customer for beer. In contrast, the United States is a residual supplier of beer to Canada. Canadian provinces protect local producers by severely limiting beer imports. But some provinces, particularly in western Canada, are insisting that foreign beers be imported freely. The new Liberal government in Ontario (37 percent of Canada's beer drinkers reside in Ontario) is promising to break up the Ontario brewers' retail monopoly.

Anheuser-Busch is relying on licensees to brew regular Budweiser for its overseas production, marketing, and distribution. To meet A-B standards, the licensees import ingredients from the United States and their production must be approved by Anheuser's four international brewmasters, as well as Chairman August A. Busch III. Licensees are brewing Bud in Britain, Japan, and Israel. Negotiations are being conducted in Australia, Korea, and the Philippines. Anheuser is also considering the purchase of foreign breweries and exports to about 10 other countries. Budweiser has failed, however, to crack the West German market, and Bud sales in France have been a disappointment.

NATIONAL BREWERS

Anheuser-Busch, Inc.

The St. Louis-based "King of Beers" has the most profitable product mix in the industry and is least in need of price increases. The key to its growth has been the world's best-selling beer, Budweiser. Bud has taken a big part of the youth market from Miller High Life and now commands a 24 percent market share (Exhibits 14 and 15). A good product reputation and a powerful distribution network of virtually exclusive distributors contributes to A-B's success. A-B has marketing muscle; its average wholesaler does a 50 percent greater volume than a Miller

---

Exhibit 14 TOP FIVE NATIONAL BREWERS

1984 Rank	Company name	Principal brands
1.	Anheuser-Busch, Inc. St. Louis, Missouri	Budweiser, Bud Light, Michelob, Michelob Light, Busch, Natural Light, LA, King Cobra Malt Liquor
2.	Miller Brewing Co. Milwaukee, Wisconsin	Miller High Life, Miller Lite, Plank Road, Milwaukee's Best, Meister Brau, Sharpe's LA, Lowenbrau, Genuine Draft
3.	The Stroh Brewery Co. Detroit, Michigan	Stroh's, Stroh's Light, Old Milwaukee, Piels, Schlitz, Signature, Schaefer, Goebel, Silver Thunder Malt Liquor
4.	G. Heileman Brewing Co. La Crosse, Wisconsin	Old Style, Old Style LA, Special Export, Blatz, Rainer, Black Label, Lone Star, 11-11 Malt Liquor
5.	Adolph Coors Company Golden, Colorado	Coors, Coors Light, Herman Josephs, George Killian's Irish Red

---

Exhibit 15 TOP 10 BRANDS FOR 1984

Rank	Brand	Market share	Brand growth
1	Budweiser	24.0%	5.0%
2	Miller Lite	10.0	2.0
3	Miller High Life	7.8	−18.0
4	Coors	5.0	−5.0
5	Old Milwaukee	3.8	1.5
6	Michelob	3.8	−3.5
7	Pabst	3.4	−20.0
8	Stroh	3.2	2.0
9	Old Style	2.9	−5.0
10	Bud Light	2.3	10.5
Top 10		66.2%	−30.5%

---

counterpart. A-B also has exposure; advertising expenditures in 1985 were $440 million. A-B has created the ability to outspend its competitors, because its gross margin and gross profits are growing while others are not. Moreover, A-B is in the driver's seat as far as pricing goes.

Miller Brewing Company

Acquired in 1970 by Philip Morris, Inc., Miller surged during the 70s and continues to be in the number two position. The premium-priced High Life brand has been losing momentum and its luster as sales erode. However, the Lite brand is doing well, but faces more competition. Miller's strategy of introducing two low-priced, low-profit beers, Meister Brau and Milwaukee's Best, is questioned by analysts. They believe this maneuver, coupled with a large advertising budget, cannot succeed. Miller is innovating at the higher segment with Plank Road and Miller High Life Genuine Draft. It is trying to reposition Lowenbrau as a brand with worldwide image. Since the Lowenbrau which Miller sells in the United

States is brewed in Milwaukee, not Munich, this campaign has failed in the past. Miller remains hopeful about its future.

The Stroh Brewery Company

Until 1981 this family-owned brewery, founded in 1849, was primarily a regional brewer. Since acquiring F&M Schaefer Brewing Company in 1981 and Jos. Schlitz Brewing Company in 1982, Stroh has carved a comfortable lead over its nearest competitor, G. Heileman. The acquisition of Schlitz gave Stroh a strong national wholesalers' network to distribute the rest of its products. Stroh's national rollout had some bad introductions in the Northeast, but it has a solid product line—Stroh's, Old Milwaukee, Schaefer, and superpremium Signature. A company with good management, Stroh will be a difficult force to contend with since it has minimized unit costs and is operating at full capacity. Moreover, since it is a private company, it does not have to show good quarterly returns; it just has to generate enough cash flow to cover the family's needs.

G. Heileman Brewing Company

The G. Heileman Brewing Company entered 1984 leading the industry in five-year profitability and growth. It's return on equity averaged 31.7 percent. It has 11 breweries—five in the Midwest and two each in the South, Southwest, and Northwest. Heileman's growth is a result of acquisition, and it has expanded its own distribution network by acquiring companies with well-established distribution systems. Despite excellent, street fighting management and good marketing, Heileman lacks a national image for its 50-plus brands. This makes competing with A-B difficult. Heileman is, however, competing with the imports by building a new small plant exclusively for the production of a specialty beer. It does not want to mix the new beer with its domestic brands.

Adolph Coors Company

Famous for using Rocky Mountain spring water in its flagship Coors brands, Coors is expanding its distribution eastward. The rollout has worked very well, especially in New England, where it ran ads at the rate of one TV commercial per second to introduce its brands. Also, Coors seems to have stemmed the market share erosion in its core territories out West and hopes to regain the lost ground. Coors Light is doing very well, and in 1985 accounted for 40 percent of Coors' total barrelage. The success of Coors Light is helping to elevate the confidence that both the consumers and the wholesalers have in the Coors brand name. The imported superpremium George Killian's Irish Red is also making strong headway.

THE REGIONAL/SMALL BREWERS

In an industry increasingly dominated by a few firms, several regional brewers have endured and continue to flourish. Some have 150-year histories and others have only recently emerged. All stand as evidence that hometown loyalties and the strength of the regional market can be cornerstones of success.

Some of the strategies for survival being used include: (1) the specialty brewer serving the moderate beer drinker and catering to the growing market of image-enhanced goods in select markets; (2) the dual-purpose brewer who wants to serve his loyal home market while developing more prestigious and distinctive beers for select markets; and (3) the more traditional regional brewer whose markets are blue collar and whose customers are more loyal than those in the more transient metropolitan areas.

The Genesee Brewing Company, Rochester, New York

Founded just after Prohibition's demise, Genesee is now the seventh largest brewery in America. Genesee's territory has been expanding and now includes all of the East Coast, Ohio, Indiana, Kentucky, West Virginia, and the province of Ontario. Genesee has implemented major advertising campaigns and has had an impressive growth rate throughout the 1970s, with sales increasing at an average annual rate of 10.3 percent.

The F. X. Matt Brewing Company, Utica, New York

The F. X. Matt Brewing Company reflects the tradition of family involvement that characterizes the industry. Besides a strategy of capital improvements, three other factors have been keys to success: consistent quality, loyal personnel, and a hands-on management philosophy. The extensive product line includes: Utica Club; Utica Club Light; Utica Club Cream Ale; Matt's Premium; Matt's Premium Light Choice, a low-alcohol beer; Maximus Super Beer, with a 6.5 percent alcohol content; and Saranac 1888, the newest product. Approximately 125 distributors carry Matt products throughout New York, Pennsylvania, parts of New England, and north-central Colorado. Distributors must have a good game plan, ability to cover the market, competence, and a certain way of doing business.

Anchor Brewing Company, San Francisco, California

In 1965 Fritz Maytag, heir to part of the Maytag appliance fortune, bought this bankrupt brewery. Using his personal finances, he embarked on an extensive capital investment plan to renovate and replace equipment. Anchor, operating at a loss for 10 years, went into the black in 1975. Anchor's initial annual capacity of 600 barrels has been expanded to 50,000 barrels. In 1984 Anchor produced over 37,000 barrels. The brewery's flagship, Anchor Steam Beer, accounts for 80 percent of sales and Anchor Porter and Anchor Liberty constitute 7 percent of total sales. The remaining sales volume is made up by a barley ale, wheat beer, and its Christmas ale.

While the brewery initially self-distributed its products, it now uses two distributors on the West Coast. With over 100 total distributors, Anchor is available on the West Coast; in parts of Maryland; Delaware; Virginia; Washington, D.C.; New Jersey; Connecticut; and Massachusetts. The company has done almost no advertising, but relies instead on distinctive packaging.

A quasimarket research study provided the following buyer profile: The buyers are young adults, upscale, predominately college-educated, and very knowledgeable about beer. Many drink a variety of beers and consider themselves aficionados. They drink primarily imported brands and enjoy a rich, distinctive taste in the beer they consume.

Maytag explains Anchor's success as follows: "We start with a respect for the brewing tradition and a reputation for integrity. It's a concept that starts with the product. Our brew is low key, high quality, and nonestablishment. We actually try to make a beer that most people don't like—heavy, hoppy, and flavorful. It's traditional and distinctive, not designed for high volume, but for rapid growth, with relatively high margins, on a small scale."

THE MICROBREWERS

The American brewing industry has one small, dedicated group of mavericks. These are the microbrewers, defined as brewers with annual production under 15,000 barrels. Microbreweries are as individual as the personalities of their owners, yet all share an attitude of respect and enthusiasm for the brewer's art.

Jack McAuliffe, an unemployed sailor who started the first microbrewery in 1976 in Sonoma, California, reintroduced top-fermented English-type ale in the United States. His New Albion Brewery survived only a few years, but others have followed. Today there are about 25 micros and another 30 are set to begin production in 1986. Exhibit 16 provides a comprehensive list of American microbreweries.

Real ale is not the only style produced by microbreweries. A new American-style nouveau lager has emerged on the market. This bottom-fermented beer is decidedly more hoppy and brewed in the German Reinheitsgebot tradition.

Reinheitsgebot dates from 1516, when the Bavarian ruler of that day, Wilhelm IV, limited the ingredients in beer to water, malted barley, hops, and yeast. In West Germany, Norway, and a few other countries, all beer produced for local consumption must be Reinheitsgebot pure, with only those four ingredients, no cereals, no additives, and no enzymes. The new wave of micro-beers in the United States nearly all are made to these specifications.

The West Coast is a hotbed of microbrewery activity. The area is an ideal geographic market for these niche beers, because of the generally high personal incomes, coupled with a widespread awareness and appreciation of small wineries. The classic flavor and quality these breweries achieve, combined with their antiestablishment stance, has resulted in attractive alternatives for the price-inelastic, high-end beer drinker.

Microbrewing, however, is a risky business, even on the West Coast. In 1982 in the San Francisco Bay area, there were five micros in business. Only two are still brewing. With a failure rate of more than 40 percent, this business is not for amateurs. Micro success is often unattainable, because of competition from imported labels and a high-cost production set-up that requires super-premium

Exhibit 16 AMERICAN MICROBREWERIES AND BREW PUBS	
Name	**Location**
Riley-Lyon Brewing Company	Little Rock, Arkansas
Palo Alto Brewing Company	Mountain View, California
Sierra Nevada Brewing Company	Chico, California
Stanislaus Brewing Company	Modesto, California
Thousand Oaks Brewing Company	Berkeley, California
Golden Gate Brewing Company	Berkeley, California
Boulder Brewing Company	Boulder, Colorado
Snake River Brewing Company	Caldwell, Idaho
Millstream Brewing Company	Amana, Iowa
Boston Beer Company	Boston, Massachusetts
Montana Beverage Company	Helena, Montana
The Manhattan Brewing Company	New York, New York
Old New York Brewing Company	New York, New York
Wm. S. Newman Brewing Company	Albany, New York
Columbia River Brewing Company	Portland, Oregon
Widmer Brewing Company	Portland, Oregon
Reinheitsgebot Brewing Company	Plano, Texas
Chesapeake Bay Brewing Company	Virginia Beach, Virginia
Hart Brewing Company	Kalama, Washington
Hales Ales Ltd.	Coleville, Washington
Independent Ale Brewing, Inc.	Seattle, Washington
Kemper Brewing Company	Rolling Bay, Washington
Kuefner Brewing Company	Monroe, Washington
Yakima Brewing and Malt Company	Yakima, Washington
Brew Pubs:	
Buffalo Bill's Microbrewery & Pub	Hayward, California
Mendocino Brewing Co.	Hopeland, California
Hopeland Brewery	Hopeland, California

pricing to eke out a profit margin. Microbreweries are faced with the dilemma of needing to increase production to build market share and trim unit costs, yet having to contend with a mature and oversaturated market that simply does not justify scaling up.

Because of their low volume sales, it is also difficult to find distributors willing to carry the brands of microbrewers. The few that are receptive are normally attracted by label graphics and by superlative quality. Most distributors cannot, or will not, distribute a label that sells in such small numbers. Therefore, most microbrewers rely on personalized preselling of their brew to retailers, supplemented with point-of-purchase displays to generate buyer interest.

The strategy of the micros involves charging a little more, maintaining a rigorous quality-conscious image, and providing more and more beer drinkers with the joys of fresh, wholesome, handmade brews. Their market goal is to make premium an adjective that means something in the beer business.

Sierra Nevada Brewing Company, Chico, California

Located in a farming and college town near Sacramento, this ale brewery has a current sales volume of 3,000 barrels. Started in 1979, the first brew was sold in 1981. Sierra Nevada produces pale ale, porter, and stout, which all retail for about $18 a case. The firm also sells full and half kegs of draft ale and a Christmas ale. Operating efficiency and a steadily growing reputation among serious beer lovers have proven to be keys for survival. But owner/brewer, Camusi, predicts a shakeout among microbrewers, a direct result of an overcrowded specialty market.

The critical areas of size and capacity may be the deciding factors in its long-term success. Sierra Nevada has added to its capacity every year and now approaches an annual capacity of 7,500 barrels. Its draft beer, accounting for a large percentage of its volume, enables the brewery to avoid the crowded single bottle market. Camusi believes growth is essential for survival. According to Camusi, "The really small brewery is just not a viable business anymore."

Mendocino Brewing Company, Hopeland, California

Situated 100 miles north of San Francisco, this brewery was formed from the equipment and staff of the defunct New Albion Brewery. Mendocino has overcome many of the economic viability issues of distribution and scale by operating a "brew pub." Approximately 660 barrels a year of ale, porter, and stout are sold through the pub under the name of the Hopeland Brewery. Mendocino produces a wide variety of products, with Red Tail Ale its mainstay.

This amber, heavy bodied, English-style brew sells in a one-and-a-half-liter magnum bottle for $6. Its Black Hawk Stout, pale ale, and Christmas, summer, and spring ales sell on draft at the pub. The owners describe Mendocino as a domestic alternative which provides a small group of beer drinkers with a fresh, premium product. By selling exclusively to a local market, Mendocino has overcome the problem of finding distributors.

Boulder Brewing Company, Boulder, Colorado

Founded in 1979 by a small group of home brewers, this brewery sold its first beer on July 3, 1980. Boulder's products are unpasteurized, English-type brews. The two products, Boulder Extra Pale Ale and Boulder Stout, are sold in 12-ounce nonreturnable bottles. No draft is produced. Accounts are served by wholesale distributors who approached the company. Distribution is confined to the state of Colorado, with a network of 12 outlets currently handling the brewery's products. Although the company enjoys considerable free publicity, word-of-mouth advertising serves as its primary source of demand. Marketing resources are focused on upgrading packaging graphics. A public stock offering in September 1983 financed the company's capitalization and construction of its recently completed $1.1 million brewery. Forty million common shares were issued at 5 cents a share, raising a total of $2 million. The new facility covers about 14,000 square feet and annual capacity now stands at 15,000 barrels.

The Old New York Beer Company, New York, New York

The first of the nouveau lagers came from New York in 1982, when Matthew Reich introduced New Amsterdam Amber, a rich, hoppy, full-bodied, all malt lager beer. Reich invested his life's savings, $10,000, and hired Dr. Joseph Owades, an international brewing consultant and director of the Center for Brewing Studies in San Francisco, to design a lager beer similar to Anchor Steam.

Reich had always dreamed of being a brewer. While working as the director of operations at Hearst Magazine, he often wished he was out creating his own beer. He believed there was room for a connoisseur's beer, the kind poured from kegs, without rice or corn—a pure beer. For two years Reich and Owades slaved over the beer's body, color, and taste, during which time Reich still worked at Hearst.

Based on a 15-page business plan, 22 private investors invested $255,000 to form a limited partnership. In the summer of 1982 Reich left Hearst, and that August he began buying brewing time at F. X. Matt Brewing Company in Utica, New York. New Amsterdam Amber ferments for one week and ages for 26 days before being bottled or kegged and shipped to Manhattan.

In 1983, Old New York Beer Company sold 44,000 cases for $600,000. Sales doubled to $1.2 million in 1984, with earnings of $50,000 (after taxes). Reich expects to reach a sales level of $1.8 million in 1985 on 100,000 cases. The average retail price for a six-pack is $6.

Like other micros, Reich personally sold his brew, first approaching trendy restaurants and bars in Manhattan. While he originally intended to target only New York, his beer is now available in 21 states, including the West Coast. Reich's initial success has enabled him to raise an additional $2.2 million from two venture capital firms. He is using the money to construct a new brewery in Manhattan that will also have a restaurant, a tap room, and a visitors' center. Although this action dilutes Reich's holding in the company to 25 percent, it improved Old New York's image and increased its annual production capacity to 30,000 barrels. When the brewery is completed late in 1986, he will be able to triple 1985's expected production.

THE GOLDEN GATE BREWING COMPANY

James Cook, christened Charles James, attended Harvard College, where he majored in government and graduated with honors in 1971. For the next three years, he was a mountaineering instructor with Outward Bound. In 1974 he returned to Harvard to study law and business administration. In 1977 Cook climbed to the snow-covered peak of Alaska's 20,320 foot Mount McKinley. "After traveling for weeks and seeing nothing but white," he recalls, "I wondered what magic sight awaited me at the summit. And when I got to the top, there it was, glowing in the light, an empty beer can, planted like somebody's flag. Ah," he exclaims, "the power of beer is transcendent!"

With a JD and MBA, Cook joined the Boston Consulting Group (BCG). He spent seven years honing his management skills and advising industrial, primarily international, managers. After six years he got tired of telling other people how to run their companies and decided to start his own. "I wanted to create something, I wanted to make something of my own," said Cook. Cook's choices boiled down to either brewing beer or building a chain of for-profit medical clinics in Seattle. The consultant in Cook voted for the doc-in-the-box setup. But as the eldest son of a fifth generation brewer, he figured he really did not have a choice.

Cook vividly remembers the smell of fermenting beer on days he visited his father at work. "I liked it. I never liked hard liquor and never understood wine. Even now I drink two-three beers a day, rarely less, rarely more. Breweries are neat places and the brewmaster has the best job. He walks around, tastes beer and makes changes. It's almost like playing God," notes Cook. Cook believes he was put on earth for one thing—"to make the greatest beer in the United States." He recalled:

> On the surface it was an insane thing to do, but I was convinced there was a small emerging market for what I wanted to do. It was the time for microbreweries and hand-crafted beers, and it seemed tragic that I was ending a line of five generations of brewers. I realized Americans had begun to appreciate premium beers in recent years, especially on the West Coast, but I felt they relied too heavily on imported beers, which are inherently inferior. I think that the American appreciation of beer is very much in its infancy. We're in the Blue Nun stage of beer drinking. There was a time when people thought that Blue Nun was a great wine, just as now there are people who think Heineken and Beck's are great beers. In fact, they're the Schlitz of Europe. They have a certain mystique, but it's a phony mystique. These beers aren't fresh. Beer has a shelf life that's not a whole lot longer than orange juice. And you'd never think of buying orange juice from Germany.
>
> In Germany, they don't drink Beck's. They drink the local beer. Americans have this notion that the further away a beer is made, the better is is. But the imports we get in America not only have preservatives, which are illegal in Germany, but by the time they arrive here, they are almost always spoiled, stale and/or skunked. Beer must be fresh. It deteriorates the instant you put it in a bottle. The day it leaves the brewery, it goes downhill. The travel time in importing beer and use of green bottles that expose beer to damaging light can often mean the expensive imported beer is not what it claims to be.

The Start-Up

Although Cook had no formal education in brewing, he studied notes and material his father had saved from the Siebel Institute of Brewing in Chicago where he learned to be a brewmaster. Although American tastes in mass-marketed beers favor light, paler versions, Cook decided to buck the tide, go with family tradition and brew a full-bodied lager. He wanted a connoisseur's beer, brewed in an old-world tradition.

His father suggested he revive the old family formula. After searching his father's attic in Cincinnati, Cook found his great-great-grandfather's original recipe, first developed by his ancestor in the 1870s. With his family's formula, Cook hired biochemist and brewery consultant, Joseph L. Owades to aid in devising the final formula. In the summer of 1984, Cook traveled to the fermentation lab at the University of California at Davis and worked with Owades on translating Louis Cook's Midwestern American lager into a 1980s West Coast superpremium beer.

The formula is water, malt, hops and a special yeast strain developed by Owades. The hops is the best in the world, Tettnang and Hallertau Mittlelfreuh hops, imported from Bavaria at a cost of $4.50 a pound. A pound of ordinary hops costs 55 cents. The hops, according to Cook, is key as it gives the beer its flavor. Two-row summer malted barley and some caramel malt are used for color and body. While many people think water is the most important ingredient that goes into beer, it is, in fact, the least important. The quality of the yeast strain is much more important, but seldom talked about as it lacks advertising appeal. Cook points out, "When you listen to what people advertise about their beers, it's things that have real macho appeal—fire brewing, beechwood aging, mountain spring water. What matters are things like hops, malt, and yeast. Unfortunately, they don't have the advertising appeal of cool mountain streams."

To make this beer formula a reality Cook needed to raise capital. He tossed in all his personal savings, $100,000, and raised an additional $300,000 from friends, business associates, clients, and even his father. "While you can start a small boutique brewery with $400,000, a good lager is difficult to produce in a micro-brewery. A lager requires more sophisticated brewing equipment and more careful handling than the ale produced by most micros. I was forced to find an existing brewery, and luckily, I was able to find a brewery in Berkeley that was perfect for my purposes," relates Cook.

The Brewing Process

Golden Gate's hundred-year-old recipe requires a craft brewing process not used by American brewers in this century. The sweetness is drawn from the malt through a process traditional in Germany, but rarely used anymore by American brewers. Fresh hops are added in six stages during the brewing process to give the beer its complex hop character. (The usual process is to add hops only during the cooking stage of production, when boiling extracts the greatest amount of bitterness and, therefore, is more economical.) Cook's beer then goes through a second fermentation that carbonates the beer and also removes some of its impurities for a smoother taste. A final addition of fresh hops is made to the beer as it ages to impart the striking aroma. This is a labor-intensive technique. Golden Gate takes 40-45 days to make—one day to cook, seven days to ferment, and about two weeks to ferment the second time. The rest of the time is lagering, or aging. These efforts in the brewing process create the full-bodied flavor, rich with coppery color.

The beer is produced in batches, between 250-300 barrels a batch. Cook currently travels to the brewery every one to two weeks to oversee the brewing of a new batch. He follows the process step-by-step to ensure his recipe is followed precisely.

Packaging

Golden Gate is currently only bottled; no draft beer is produced. The classic American beer bottle, the 12-ounce longneck, or bar bottle, that requires an opener is used. This shape and the cap offer the most protection from light and oxidation. The bottle is also a dark brown, because a dark bottle protects beer from light, a deadly enemy of beer. Beer left in light for more than ten minutes begins to spoil.

After being bottled in Berkeley, the beer arrives in San Francisco four hours later. Cook has hired two truck drivers and leases trucks. Each trip to San Francisco costs about $800 per truck. Initially, 500 cases per week were delivered, but this has grown to about 1,500 cases per week. (Each truck has a maximum capacity of 2,500 cases.) The beer is delivered to an old San Francisco brewery, where Cook rents office and warehouse space, prior to distribution.

Organization

The employment roster of the Golden Gate Brewing Company numbers five people including James Cook—the brewer and chief salesman. In addition to two truck drivers, there is a part-time bookkeeper and an accounts manager, Rhonda Kallman, who was Cook's secretary at BCG. Her numerous and varied duties include selling and even delivering when necessary. To keep overhead as low as possible, the business has no secretary, no typewriter, and no computer. Cook also took a 75 percent pay cut from his BCG salary.

Financial Information

According to Cook, the Golden Gate Brewing Company, "Is still in the red, but we're getting back toward recovering our losses. The business after six months is doing remarkably well." Exhibit 17 shows the Golden Gate Brewing Company's income statement for the first six months of operations. Golden Gate sells for about 25 cents more per bottle than Heineken, between $1.75 and $3.50 per bottle retail.

A six-pack retails for about $6.50 and a case varies from $20 to $24. Asked if he thought the high price might limit sales, Cook said, "I don't drink wine, but I understand a good bottle of wine costs about $30. Well, for the price of a mediocre bottle of wine, you can go out and buy a six-pack of the best beer in America." Golden Gate wholesales for about $16 a case.

Golden Gate Lager costs two to three times what it costs to brew imported beers. The delivered cost into San Francisco was initially listed at $12 a case, but, because of increased volume, it is now down to $10.50 a case. Other expenses include salaries, office/warehouse rent, truck leasing, marketing and promotion, public relations, general administrative expenses, and taxes.

	1985
Exhibit 17 1985 INCOME STATEMENT FOR GOLDEN GATE BREWING CO.	
Sales	$408,000[1]
Cost of goods sold	273,000[2]
Gross margin	135,000
Less:	
Shipping	840[3]
Salaries and wages	101,003[4]
Office/warehouse rent	4,800[5]
Truck leasing	20,800[6]
Marketing and promotion	55,000[7]
Repairs	1,000[8]
Depreciation	7,500[9]
General selling, administrative, and other expenses	9,057[10]
Net income (loss) before taxes	($65,000)

[1] Includes 25,000 cases sold in California and 500 in Munich.
[2] The first 3,500 cases cost $12/case, the rest cost $10.50/case.
[3] Includes shipping costs of $0.07/bottle for 500 cases shipped. (Larger shipments would decrease the per bottle cost.)
[4] Includes Cook's salary of $25,000 for July–December and average hourly earnings of his four employees of $18.27/hr. (Another 4 percent increase is expected in 1986.)
[5] Office and warehouse rent totals $800 per month.
[6] Twenty-six truck trips were made into San Francisco in the first six months.
[7] Includes $35,000 for booklet and $10,000 for placards used in July and August.
[8] Cost of incidental repairs, including labor and supplies, which do not add materially to the value of the property.
[9] Depreciation is on the straight-line basis, assuming a 20-year useful life, no salvage value, one half year's depreciation taken in the first year and $300,000 of assets acquired.
[10] Included are salaries and wages not deducted elsewhere, amounts not otherwise reported, such as administrative, general and office expenses, bonuses and commissions, delivery charges, research expenses, sales discounts, and travel expenses.

Advertising and Marketing

Golden Gate Lager spends no money advertising its beer. The main marketing element is quality and freshness, and the main marketing tool is personal selling and word-of-mouth. Tabletop display cards are also placed in bars and restaurants in and around San Francisco. In addition, a little blue miniature booklet, each hand-applied, dangles from each long-stem bottle. The booklet is entitled "Why Is This Special Beer Different?" and describes the beer, brewing process, and flavor. The first order alone cost $35,000.

During the summer of 1985 Cook experimented with advertising. Placards were placed on the sides of San Francisco's tour buses. While it was relatively cheap advertising at $5,000 per month, Cook is not sure it was worth it. "I don't think we generated enough sales to pay for it." This experience confirmed his gut feeling that small, specialized companies do better relying on word-of-mouth advertising and publicity. "The first thing you must have in business is a solid, substantial advantage over the alternatives. Somehow you've got to have a reason for people to buy your product, and it's got to be more solid than anything advertising can create. There are very few products that have really lasted long-term on marketing alone," says Cook. "However, nothing is so good that it automatically sells itself. You have to go out and hustle."

While he links the logistics of introducing this beer to those of a fine wine, with the best advertising being word-of-mouth, Cook was fortunate to gain a credible third-party endorsement. Less than two months after the introduction of Golden Gate Lager, it was crowned the Best Beer in America at the annual Great American Beer Festival in Denver. The 4,000 plus attendees selected one beer as best from over 102 entries. The resulting publicity played a major role in boosting sales. Cook, thrilled by the victory, said, "For a family that has been making beer for 150 years to suddenly get recognized as making the best beer in the country— that is the ultimate accolade."

James Cook also conducts his own market research and studies. Three nights a week he visits local pubs and restaurants. He questions patrons as to why they drink imports when they can have Golden Gate. He asks what they like about imported brands. He asks beer drinkers for their opinion of Golden Gate. If they have not tasted Golden Gate, he describes the flavor and suggests they try it. After a short conversation, he identifies himself as the brewer. Aside from polling patrons, Cook chats with bartenders and questions waitresses and waiters about sales. According to Cook, "The neatest thing is to come into a bar and see people drinking my beer. The second neatest thing is to take the empty cases out."

Distribution

"Getting the beer on the market boils down to a door-to-door campaign with restaurants, bar managers, and liquor store owners," says Cook. Cook wins new accounts by asking potential carriers to taste the beer. "The response is incredible," boasts Cook. "Bar managers and owners like the personal attention. It shows them how much you believe in your product."

Since Golden Gate requires an amount of personal attention and credibility that the normal beer sales and distribution channels cannot give, Cook has set up his own distribution company. He even goes as far as making deliveries, pinstriped suit and all, out of his station wagon when regular drivers can't get to a particular account on time. Cook realizes all this costs money, probably twice what traditional distributors pay. Cook is currently negotiating with a major regional beer distributor. Affiliation with a large distributor provides access to numerous, established accounts that Cook would otherwise have to pursue one by one. He wonders if this is a sound strategy.

Target Market

The Golden Gate Co.'s target is the beer drinker who knows how to distinguish a well-made beer from an average to below-average one and cares more about quality and taste than advertising appeal. Cook believes the typical Golden Gate drinker could be anyone, from gourmets to yuppies to construction workers, who likes a good beer. The current diverse cross section of drinkers cuts across traditional demographics.

Export Plunge

In October 1985, Cook shipped 12,000 bottles (500 cases) of Golden Gate Lager to Munich, West Germany, a city with the most finicky beer drinkers in the world, becoming the first U.S. brewed beer to be sold in West Germany outside U.S. military bases. It took four weeks before the Wiehenstathan, or beer institute, gave Cook's beer its seal of approval. Obtaining an import license was the next task.

The 500 cases were sent to George Thaler, a business consultant friend and now part-time beer distributor, who attempts to get Germans to try, and then order, Golden Gate. Thaler explains his sales techniques as follows, "I bring three cold bottles with me, then I tell them what has happened to beer in America and then discuss the brewing process. Then we taste." Thaler says Germans like the beer, which helps both sales of Golden Gate and the image American products have. "It's a quality image for a U.S. product."

The Munich market is not without problems. In Munich, six breweries own 90 percent of all pubs and they will only serve their brand of beer. Therefore, Golden Gate is locked out of all but a few of Munich's restaurants, delicatessens, and hotels (the so-called free bars). In addition, while shipping costs add only 7 cents to the price of a bottle of Golden Gate, the beer costs 30-50 percent more than German draft beers, or about 5½ marks more per beer. But Thaler explains that this is consistent with the product positioning. "We don't want student beer drinkers to get drunk on Golden Gate. We want the beer connoisseur to drink Golden Gate." Thaler presently has five accounts taking 70 cases per week which he delivers in the trunk of his Mercedes-Benz. The accounts range from a high-class delicatessen to a New York-style bar.

While Cook's plunge into West Germany is primarily to demonstrate his product's quality, he is now considering expansion. Thaler hopes to soon expand to Düsseldorf and Austria. Cook wonders what other markets he should pursue, how fast he should expand and how much time he should devote to export possibilities. He is confident that his time-consuming brewing process and choice ingredients make Golden Gate competitive with the best of European brews.

Capital Needs

The Golden Gate Brewing Co. currently rents office and warehouse space at an old San Francisco brewery. This brewery with three-foot thick walls was abandoned in 1965. It was cheaper to abandon than to tear down. It is now owned by the nonprofit Neighborhood Development Corporation, but Cook has an option on about one fourth of the building's 170,000 square feet. He hopes to be able to buy the building, renovate it and brew Golden Gate in 40,000 square feet following funding completion. Cook estimates his needs at $3.75 million, with $1.1 million going for renovations and $2.1 million for new tanks and bottling gear. His goal is an annual capacity of 30,000 barrels. Initially, the project is expected to create 12 to 15 new jobs and potentially 55 to 60. Actual renovation and equipment installation is estimated to take 4 to 10 months.

Cooks says it would be cheaper to build a brewery in the suburbs, but "romance" led him to the old San Francisco brewery. "I could save $800,000 if I moved to a suburban industrial park, but I don't want to make California, or West Coast Lager Beer. I want to make Golden Gate Lager."

Cook has explored several financing possibilities—industrial revenue financing, Urban Development Action Grants, and market rate financing.

Industrial Revenue Financing. Industrial Revenue Bonds (IRB) are vehicles that developers and corporations use to raise low-interest financing for construction projects. They are issued by a municipality only to achieve tax-exempt status, and are not guaranteed by the full faith and credit of the government. IRB's are backed by the future revenue of the project. IRB's were originally designed to attract industry into communities for employment and economic benefits through the use of tax-exempt financing. IRB loans in San Francisco generally carry interest rates of 70 percent of prime with a 15-year balloon and a 30-year amortization.

The San Francisco Industrial Development Financing Authority (SFIDFA) must give initial approval to an application by Cook's Golden Gate Brewing Company. The revenue bonds must then gain City Council and mayoral approval. Cook is confident that the mayor will bestow enthusiastic support, since he campaigned on revitalizing San Francisco neighborhoods. Once the IRB's are approved, a bank must agree to loan the funds. Most banks require IRB loans to be secured by the personal guarantees of the principals.

Urban Development Action Grants. The Urban Development Action Grant (UDAG) is another possibility. The UDAG is a flexible program which offers a source of cheap money. The maturity and interest rate are negotiated between the city and the borrower. The collateral is normally limited to the assets being financed (and personal guarantees). The UDAG can be used for fixed assets whose life expectancy exceeds seven years. The terms and conditions negotiated between the city and the borrower must be approved by the City Council and the U.S. Department of Housing and Urban Development. The UDAG process averages three to four months. Another important advantage of this subsidy is that the UDAG can be mixed with IRB's and other federal programs.

The UDAG subsidy does have one drawback. To raise money for future projects, the local program shares in the profits of the subsidized projects. This can restrict profit potential. Cook was not excited about sharing profits and/or giving up control or ownership.

Market Rate Financing. Another option for capital, explored by Cook, is market rate financing from local commercial banks. San Francisco has five major banks, one of which, the Bank of San Francisco, has already solicited the Golden Gate Brewing Co. Cook has yet to supply necessary financial statements or projections, however. The loan would be a mortgage, used to cover all the expenses associated with the completed property. The interest rate would be based on the prime rate. Cook feels that the rate on a commercial mortgage would be prime plus 1 percent for a 15-year balloon with a 30-year amortization.

Expansion/Growth Strategy

Winning the America's Best Beer Award, and the resulting publicity, caused many distributors from other states to solicit the Golden Gate Brewing Company and Golden Gate Lager. Cook has put several possible new accounts temporarily on hold and has turned down requests from distributors in Washington, Colorado, Kentucky, and Alaska. Cook's current agreement with the Berkeley Brewery to brew Golden Gate Lager limits production and Cook felt it was important to penetrate and service San Francisco first. Renovating the old San Francisco brewery, however, would provide a much higher production capacity level. Cook also realized that beer is regulated in 50 different ways in the United States. The bureaucratic red tape is complicated and time-consuming. Cook sometimes thinks it is easier to sell Golden Gate in Munich than in the United States. Germany requires only that the beer be pure.

Regardless, Cook wonders if he should expand, how quickly he should expand and where he should expand. Cook concedes that he will never slay the major domestic giants. "I don't compete with them. I make a different product and sell it for a different price. I compete with foreign beers." But he is uncertain of the strategy he should use.

COMPETITION IN THE U.S. ICE CREAM INDUSTRY*

Production of ice cream in the United States remained essentially flat throughout the 1970–85 period. As of 1985 sales in gallons were below the 1975 production peak. Underneath this calm surface of leveling sales volume, however, was a highly competitive, very lucrative superpremium ice cream segment averaging over 15 percent annual growth. Trying to capitalize on the trail blazed by Häagen-Dazs, many local and national ice cream companies had launched new superpremium brands, aggressively pursued ways to gain wider distribution, and tried to capture the interest of consumers with a stream of new ice cream-related products. A number of major developments highlighted the 1980–85 period:

1980:
  • Two superpremium ice cream brands with foreign names, Frusen Glädjé and Alpen Zauber, were introduced and positioned as direct competitors to Häagen-Dazs; distribution of these brands was mainly in the northeastern states.

  • A superpremium brand, Rich and Creamy, was introduced by Flavorich in southeastern markets; consumers in the Southeast had not taken to brands with foreign names as had consumers in the Northeast.

  • Ben & Jerry's Homemade Ice Cream began distributing pint cartons of its superpremium ice cream through supermarkets in Vermont.

1981:
  • The use of the "mix-in" at Steve's Ice Cream in Somerville, Massachusetts, became a widely recognized success. (A mix-in was crushed candy or cookies, nuts, fruit, or granola, blended with ice cream to create new flavor combinations.) Steve's already unique flavors developed a reputation that spread to New York.

  • Alpen Zauber brought legal action against Häagen-Dazs for threatening to withhold its ice cream from distributors who also sold Alpen Zauber.

1982:
  • Swensen's (a 290-store ice cream parlor chain) began testing an "ultra-premium" ice cream and announced plans to open 50 to 60 new stores in the following year.

  • Häagen-Dazs opened 90 dipping stores in 18 months (late 1981 to early 1983) for a total of 210 franchises nationwide; 55 more were under construction.

---

* Prepared by graduate researcher Miriam Aiken and Professor Arthur A. Thompson, Jr., The University of Alabama. Copyright © 1986 by Arthur A. Thompson, Jr.

1983:
- Frusen Glädjé launched a national franchise effort and opened more than 50 stores.
- Häagen-Dazs was purchased by the Pillsbury Company for $75 million. The company introduced six ice cream liqueur desserts using Hiram Walker liqueurs such as cognac and amaretto.
- Integrated Resources purchased Steve's Ice Cream for $4.5 million and announced plans to expand from 25 outlets to 525 over the next four years.
- Dreyer's Grand Ice Cream (Oakland, California), a long-time competitor in the premium ice cream market, launched a line of superpremium chocolate ice creams flavored after European candies.
- Campbell Soup began testing a superpremium line under its Pepperidge Farms brand name and introduced an even richer ice cream through its Godiva Chocolatier subsidiary.
- Pet, Inc.'s Dairy Division introduced three premium ice cream lines—Great Ice Creams of the South, Cellini (an Italian type of ice cream), and Creams of England.
- Popsicle Industries paired with Nabisco to introduce a line of Oreo ice cream products.
- Zack's Famous Frozen Yogurt (New Orleans) and I Can't Believe It's Yogurt (Dallas) initiated rapid regional franchising campaigns.

1984:
- Land O'Lakes began distributing its Country Creamery brand ice cream in Minnesota and Wisconsin.
- Häagen-Dazs began distribution of Le Sorbet, a low-calorie frozen fruit dessert similar to sherbet. Castle & Cooke's Dole Fruit Sorbet was test-marketed in several states.
- Larry's Ice Cream headquartered in Florida began interstate franchising with hopes of opening stores throughout the Southeast.
- Swensen's purchased two ice cream plants from Foremost Dairies in exchange for 2.4 million shares of Swensen's stock, which gave Foremost a controlling interest in Swensen's. Foremost was named the exclusive distributor of Swensen's new line of ice cream packaged for retail sale in supermarkets.

1985:
- Kraft acquired Frusen Glädjé and also started to introduce its Breyer's premium ice cream line in western and midwestern markets.
- Swensen's reversed its deal of 1984 with Foremost Dairies and reacquired the 2.4 million shares of stock, saying that it had decided to focus its resources on its parlor and package ice cream business. Foremost, however, continued in its role as the sole supplier of packaged ice cream for supermarket sales under the Swensen's brand.
- Baskin-Robbins (B-R) announced a $20 million renovation program for its 3,000 franchised ice cream parlors and a $3 million advertising campaign to boost its image with consumers. B-R also filed a suit

against Pillsbury and Häagen-Dazs, alleging trademark infringement on its "Pralines 'N Cream" flavor name.

HISTORY OF THE ICE CREAM INDUSTRY

Ice cream evolved from chilled wines and other iced beverages. The earliest known commercial venture was in 1660 in Paris where water ices and possibly cream ices were manufactured and sold. The date of ice cream's arrival in America is uncertain, but in 1700, guests of Maryland's governor were treated to an ice creamlike delicacy. George Washington and Thomas Jefferson both enjoyed ice cream; Dolley Madison greatly increased the popularity of ice cream, serving it as a dessert at her husband's second inauguration in 1812. An American, Nancy Johnson, invented the hand-cranked rock salt-and-ice freezer in 1846. The first commercial ice cream plant in this country was established in 1851, and Bassett's Ice Cream, introduced in 1861 in Philadelphia, ranked as the oldest brand still on the U.S. market in 1985. The first ice cream sodas were created by a Philadelphia businessman who added carbonated beverages to ice cream. When these concoctions were banned from sale on Sunday, a syrup was substituted for the carbonation, and the "sundae" came into being. The ice cream cone was first made and sold at the St. Louis World's Fair in 1904 when rolled waffles were used as "dishes" for ice cream.

The commercial production of ice cream was facilitated by a number of mechanical and technical advances: the homogenizer (which gave ice cream its smooth texture), freezers, mechanical refrigeration, electric motors, sophisticated test equipment, packaging machines, insulation methods, and the motorized delivery van. Dramatic boosts in production resulted—from 5 million gallons in 1899 to 30 million gallons in 1909 to 150 million gallons in 1919.

Other products such as ice cream on sticks, bars, and other forms of ice cream, ice milk, and sherbet (known as novelties) originated in the 1920s. By 1922 a million Eskimo Pie ice cream bars were being sold each day. The Good Humor bar on a stick followed, and in 1924, the Individual Drinking Cup Company began manufacturing its Dixie Cup containers for individual servings of ice cream. The banana split also came into popularity. By the 1920s, ice cream was a typical American food, sold everywhere from corner drugstores to the best restaurants. Ice cream gained in popularity during the Prohibition era as people joked that the "cold stuff" was a substitute for the "hard stuff."

Rationing of milk and sugar during World War II greatly curtailed ice cream production, but production snapped back quickly in 1946, and sales of all kinds of ice cream products averaged over 16 quarts per capita by 1950. Consumption of ice cream alone remained around the 15-quart per capita level from 1955 to 1985 (see Exhibit 1), with total production tracking population growth. When drugstores began replacing their soda fountains with more profitable drug and cosmetic products in the 1950s, the bulk of ice cream sales shifted to custard stands, mom-and-pop stores, fast-food outlets, and supermarkets. By 1960 half of all ice cream sales were through supermarkets. Most supermarket chains wasted little

Exhibit 1 TOTAL U.S. PRODUCTION OF ICE CREAM AND RELATED PRODUCTS FOR SELECTED YEARS, 1909–1984

	All ice cream and related products		Ice cream only	
	Total gallons (in thousands)	Per capita production (in quarts)	Total gallons (in thousands)	Per capita production (in quarts)
1909	29,637	1.31	29,637	1.31
1919	152,982	5.86	152,982	5.86
1920	171,248	6.43	171,248	6.43
1930	255,439	8.30	255,439	8.30
1940	339,544	10.29	318,088	9.64
1950	634,768	16.79	554,351	14.66
1955	819,934	19.96	628,525	15.30
1960	969,004	21.54	699,605	15.55
1965	1,130,215	23.36	757,000	15.65
1970	1,193,144	23.42	761,732	14.95
1975	1,263,213	23.45	836,552	15.53
1980	1,225,223	21.58	829,798	14.61
1981	1,238,712	21.61	832,450	14.52
1982	1,248,552	21.54	852,072	14.70
1983	1,295,294	22.14	881,543	15.07
1984	1,303,031	22.07	883,525	14.96

Source: *The Latest Scoop,* 1985 edition, International Association of Ice Cream Manufacturers, p. 9.

time in introducing their own private label brands of ice cream, most of which were lower in butterfat, artificially flavored, higher in air content, and cheaper in price.

MARKET SIZE AND GROWTH

The retail value of ice cream and related products in 1984 was about $6 billion. Production of ice cream alone in 1984 was estimated at 884 million gallons. Increases in ice cream production had slowed significantly over the past four decades:

Period	Average annual growth rate
1940–49	7.4%
1950–59	2.6
1960–69	.9
1970–80	.9
1981	.3
1982	2.4
1983	3.5
1984	.2

The slowdown was attributed mainly to the fact that consumers were already eating as much ice cream as often as they wanted. Total consumption was not expected to fluctuate greatly for the remainder of the decade.

INDUSTRY STRUCTURE

The ice cream industry in the United States had historically been comprised of a multitude of regional and local producers. For a century commercial ice cream was made in local dairies, neighborhood stores, or restaurants for limited distribution in the immediate area. As improvements in refrigeration techniques made it possible to transport the product long distances, larger dairy corporations and bigger ice cream producers began squeezing out or absorbing the smaller companies; about 1,700 ice cream plants closed between 1957 and 1970. Most dairy producers viewed ice cream as a sideline of selling milk.

In 1970 there were 1,628 plants producing ice cream in the United States; by 1985 this number had declined to 853 (see Exhibit 2). Many of these were small local operations, but major producers operated large fully equipped plants. In early 1983 Dreyer's Grand Ice Cream installed $2.5 million worth of new equipment in its Los Angeles plant, making this facility capable of producing more than 5 million gallons of ice cream per year. Ben & Jerry's had a 23,000 square-foot facility which could process up to 820 gallons of ice cream an hour. Some manufacturers preferred to operate relatively small, geographically scattered plants, feeling that it allowed stricter quality control and delivery of a fresher product to surrounding localities. It was not uncommon for a major ice cream marketer to contract with local dairy producers to make and distribute its brand locally so as to cut down on steep transportation charges from its own more distant plants.

Exhibit 2 EMPLOYEES, PLANTS, AND CAPITAL EXPENDITURES IN THE FROZEN DESSERTS INDUSTRY, 1972–1982

Year	Employees	Plants producing ice cream and related products	Capital expenditures for new plant and equipment (in thousands)
1972	21,100	1,451	$35,800
1973	21,300	1,330	29,200
1974	21,300	1,239	27,800
1975	20,200	1,167	37,200
1976	20,300	1,124	43,200
1977	19,100	1,095	56,800
1978	18,500	1,062	56,400
1979	19,900	990	46,300
1980	19,600	949	46,800
1981	20,100	895	41,800
1982	17,800	884	79,900

Source: *The Latest Scoop,* 1985 edition, International Association of Ice Cream Manufacturers, pp. 6, 7.

Häagen-Dazs and the Superpremium Phenomenon

Reuben Mattus of the Senator Ice Cream Company in the Bronx, New York, viewed the increasing market share of the best-selling brands with alarm as he watched his company's products being edged out in the supermarkets. In response, he developed a rich, high butterfat ice cream with all natural ingredients and began to market it in 1961 under the brand name Häagen-Dazs. Although Mattus was soon able to sell all the ice cream he could make, the initial success of the Häagen-Dazs brand produced no overnight move to superpremium quality on the part of either consumer or producers. However, the 1960s did bring a proliferation of ice cream shops featuring high-quality products. Many were local businesses, while others, such as Baskin-Robbins, expanded across the nation.

Consumer enthusiasm for superpremium ice cream products spurted dramatically in the 1980s. By 1985 superpremium brands accounted for about 20 percent of the $6 billion in annual retail sales of ice cream. Despite the market penetration efforts of such major manufacturers as Kraft and Borden, no brand of ice cream commanded more than 14 percent of the market in 1984. Regional manufacturers

Exhibit 3 MAJOR ICE CREAM PRODUCERS, BRANDS PRODUCED, AND GEOGRAPHIC AREAS OF SALES STRENGTH

Company	Brand of ice cream	Areas of sales strength
Kraft	Frusen Glädjé	New York, New England, California
	Breyers	Eastern United States
	Sealtest	Eastern United States
Borden	Lady Borden	Southeast, Southwest
	Borden	Southeast, Southwest
(distributor for)	Gelare	West Coast, New York
Ben & Jerry's Homemade, Inc.	Ben & Jerry's Homemade	New England
Integrated Resources	Steve's	Massachusetts, New England, Mid-Atlantic
Pillsbury	Häagen-Dazs	New England, Mid-Atlantic, California
Friendly Restaurants	Friendly's	New England, Mid-Atlantic, Midwest
Bluebell Dairies	Bluebell	Texas
Dreyer's Grand Ice Cream	Dreyer's/Edy's	Midwest, western United States
Schrafft's Ice Cream Company	Schrafft's	New York
Larry's Ice Cream	Larry's	Florida, Georgia, South Carolina, California
Swensen's	Swensen's	South Florida, Texas, Arizona, California, New England
Baskin-Robbins	Baskin-Robbins	Nationwide
Pet, Inc.	Great Ice Creams of the South	Florida, Georgia, North Carolina, South Carolina, Tennessee, Virginia, West Virginia
Mayfield Dairies	Mayfield's	Georgia, Tennessee
Bassett's Ice Cream Company	Bassett's	Pennsylvania, New York

were still a prominent factor, and many had established very respectable niches in local and regional markets (see Exhibit 3).

THE MANUFACTURING PROCESS

Ice cream consisted largely of cream and milk combined with sweeteners and flavoring. Depending on the variety and brand, ice cream ingredients could include fresh or frozen cream, whole milk, skim milk, buttermilk, butter, powdered milk products, sugar, honey, corn sweeteners, sucrose, dextrose, fructose, fresh eggs, frozen or powdered eggs, salt, colorings, and flavorings; fruit and nuts were added to some varieties. Many manufacturers included additives such as stabilizers and emulsifiers. Stabilizers were used to prevent the formation of ice crystals in the product; emulsifiers produced a smooth, creamy texture. Many types and brands of ice cream were made with all natural ingredients, however.

The ingredients were blended in proper proportions in a mixing tank. The mix then went to a pasteurizer where it was heated and held at a predetermined temperature for a specified period of time. Homogenization was the next step in the process; under pressure of 2,000 to 2,500 pounds per square inch, the milk fat globules were broken into still smaller particles to make the ice cream smooth. The mix was then quickly cooled to a temperature of about 40° F.

The actual freezing of the mix could be done in a continuous freezer, which used a steady flow of mix, or in a batch freezer, which made a single quantity of ice cream at a time. While it was being frozen, the ice cream was whipped and aerated by blades (called dashers) in the freezers. The aeration, known as overrun, was controlled in all states by requirements regarding the weight and content of total food solids of all products labeled as ice cream. Overrun, stated as a percentage of two times the actual air content, could be as great as 100 percent, meaning that the product would actually be 50 percent air. Too little overrun resulted in a rock-hard frozen mass, while too much made ice cream thin and foamy.

Federal standards required that ice cream contain a minimum of 10 percent milk fat and weigh not less than 4.5 pounds per gallon. Ice cream that contained at least 1.4 percent egg yolks could be labeled as french ice cream or frozen custard.

If a continuous freezer were used, ingredients such as fruit and nuts could be added after the freezing stage by a mechanical flavor feeder. Otherwise they were added along with the liquid flavors to the mix before freezing. In the filling operation the ice cream was packaged in gallon, half-gallon, quart, or pint containers or was used to fill molds to make ice cream bars or other novelties. Ice cream was stored at subzero temperatures to further harden the product. From the hardening room it was loaded into refrigerated trucks for distribution. Production levels varied throughout the year, with May, June, July, and August being peak production months.

The costs of manufacturing ice cream varied greatly according to the quality of ingredients, the amount of air incorporated, and the size and efficiency of facilities. On the average, ingredients cost the ice cream processor 52.5 percent of revenues; processing and packaging, 30.9 percent; distribution expense, 9.5 percent; administrative expense, 2.8 percent; and pretax profit margins averaged 4.3 percent of revenue.

TYPES OF ICE CREAM

The difference between ice creams was directly related to the quality, richness, and freshness of the ingredients and the way they were blended and treated. The economy brands used a higher proportion of dried products, air, stabilizers, and emulsifiers and had a lower milk fat content. High-quality ice creams contained fresh whole products, less air, as much as 20 percent milk fat, and a minimum of additives.

Butterfat and overrun were commonly used as criteria to classify ice creams as ordinary, premium, or superpremium. Typical supermarket brands contained the minimum 10 to 12 percent of butterfat and 80 to 100 percent overrun. Premium brands had 12 to 16 percent butterfat and 40 to 60 percent overrun, while the superpremium varieties included 16 to 20 percent butterfat and less than 40 percent overrun. Many premium and superpremium brands used no additives or artificial flavors or colors. A four-ounce scoop of superpremium vanilla contained about 260 calories; the same scoop of premium had only 180, while an economy brand had 150 or fewer calories. However, as of 1985, there was little industry standardization in the classification and labeling of various types of ice cream; producers who wanted to promote their brands as premium or superpremium could ignore the butterfat and overrun criteria observed by most sellers.

Ice milk was similar to ice cream except that it contained 2 to 7 percent milk fat. Sherbet had to include 1 to 2 percent milk fat and weigh not less than six pounds per gallon. The best-known sherbets were those flavored with fruit, but other flavors of sherbet appeared in the 1970s. Frozen yogurt and tofu desserts were similar to ice milk, but the milk fat was replaced, in part or in whole, with vegetable fat. The minimum fat content for these products was 6 percent. Gelato had less butterfat and overrun than ice cream and carried a much stronger flavor impact. Exhibit 4 shows total and per capita production figures for ice cream and related products for 1984.

About 4 percent of ice cream was produced in a soft-serve form; in 1984 this amounted to 38,586,000 gallons. The vast majority of soft-serve desserts were actually ice milk; Dairy Queen and Tastee Freeze were the leading dispensers of soft-serve products.

From a pricing perspective, the ice creams available in the United States in 1985 could be characterized as luxury-priced, superpremium, premium, standard-priced, and economy-priced. The luxury-priced ice creams included such specialty brands as Godiva ($3.75 per pint) and Borden's Gelare ($2.49 per pint). In the superpremium group (the leaders being Häagen-Dazs, Frusen Glädjé, Ben & Jerry's Homemade) prices ranged from $1.69 per pint to $2.19. Most of the best selling ice creams (Breyers, Dreyer's/Edy's, Sealtest) fit into the premium category and retailed from $2.59 up to $3.49 per half-gallon in 1985. Luxury and superpremium priced ice creams were almost always sold in round pint cartons, while premium and lower priced types were usually sold by half-gallons; 65 percent of all packaged ice cream sold was in half-gallon containers. Standard-

Exhibit 4   TOTAL AND PER CAPITA PRODUCTION OF ICE CREAM
PRODUCTS, 1984

	1984	Percent change from 1983
Total—ice cream and related products	1,303,031,000 gallons	+0.60
Per capita production	22.07 quarts	−0.32
Ice cream (hard and soft)	883,525,000 gallons	+0.22
Per capita production	14.96 quarts	−0.73
Ice milk (hard and soft)	299,624,000 gallons	+1.60
Per capita production	5.08 quarts	+0.79
Sherbet (hard and soft)	47,292,000 gallons	−0.92
Per capita production	0.80 quarts	−1.84
Water ices (hard)	41,613,000 gallons	+5.55
Per capita production	0.70 quarts	+4.60
Frozen yogurt and tofu desserts (hard and soft)	8,236,000 gallons	−18.34
Per capita production	0.14 quarts	−19.03

Source: *The Latest Scoop,* 1985, p. 4.

priced ice creams (usually produced by local dairies) carried prices of $1.99 to $2.59 and included some premium-quality products at the lower price. The economy-priced category consisted of store brands and inexpensive local ice creams and were priced from $.99 to $1.99. It was not uncommon though for some premium-quality products (based on butterfat and overrun criteria) to be sold at superpremium prices; a few premium ice creams were marketed at popular prices.

DISTRIBUTION

While the majority of ice cream was sold in supermarkets, consumer desires for elaborate ice cream desserts and a variety of unusual flavors spawned numerous parlor franchise outlets, and dipping stores that featured cones, sundaes, sodas, milk shakes, ice cream dessert specialties, and hand-packed ice cream. As of 1985 there were 31 different franchisors operating almost 6,200 retail ice cream outlets. The number of stores, as well as store sales, had increased steadily since 1980:

Year	Retail outlets	Total sales	Average sales per retail outlet
1981	5,427	$793,518,000	$146,217
1982	5,547	856,466,000	154,402
1983	5,847	917,326,000	156,888
1984	6,193	998,714,000	161,265

Source: *Restaurant Business.*

Most ice cream companies who contracted out the manufacture of their brands to local dairies also relied on them to deliver their products to supermarkets and keep the freezer cases stocked with the most popular flavors. Other companies who produced their own ice cream, such as Ben & Jerry's and Häagen-Dazs, maintained a network of regional distributors to deliver their products to supermarkets. However, Dreyer's Grand Ice Cream operated its own plant-to-store delivery system in an effort to attain better control over product freshness and to secure better space in supermarket freezer displays.

INDUSTRY COST STRUCTURE

Raw materials comprised over half of the ice cream processor's costs. Cartons and labels were generally purchased from outside suppliers. The manufacturing cost of goods sold ran about 80 percent of the processor's selling price, although this varied according to product category (superpremium, premium, and so on). Producers tried to achieve about a 10 percent operating profit margin overall. Exhibit 5 shows the chain of costs from the manufacturer through to the price paid by shoppers in supermarkets.

For private-label ice cream the markups at the distributor levels were between 25 and 30 percent; distributors received much higher margins (up to 70 percent) on premium and superpremium brands. Margins at retail were similar for all types of ice cream, usually about 28 percent.

ICE CREAM CONSUMERS

Nine out of 10 households purchased ice cream, and 83 percent of the country's households bought it for home consumption. New Englanders consumed 23.1 quarts of ice cream and related products per person in 1984, while the rest of the nation averaged about 15 quarts per capita.

Exhibit 5   ESTIMATED COST STRUCTURE FOR THE ICE CREAM INDUSTRY, 1985

	Estimated cost composition for half-gallons	
	Private label	**Premium ice cream**
1. Manufacturing costs:		
Raw materials	$0.71	$0.86
Processing and packing	.42	.51
Distribution expense	.13	.15
Administrative expense	.03	.06
Total manufacturing costs	1.29	1.58
2. Manufacturer's operating profit	.06	.07
3. Manufacturer's price to distributor	1.35	1.65
4. Average distributor mark-up over manufacturer's price	.35	1.17
5. Average distributor price to retailer	1.70	2.82
6. Average retail markup over cost	.49	.77
7. Average price to consumer at retail	$2.19	$3.59

Source: Compiled by the case researchers from a variety of documents and field interviews.

The maturation of the baby boom generation resulted in a large adult population for whom ice cream seemed to be the perfect snack or dessert. Adults ate three times as much ice cream as children, and men consumed more than women. Adults were more prone to purchase premium and superpremium brands, frequently equating price with quality and taking the superiority of higher-priced items for granted. The pint and single-serving containers were very popular with one- and two-person households.

Despite the apparent contradiction, many health-conscious people did not exclude rich ice cream from their diets. People might exercise more and eat more nutritiously, but they also tended to splurge more. With desserts, instant gratification was often the goal; calories and cholesterol didn't count. Also, because of ice cream's wholesome image, some people viewed it as an appropriate reward for exercise or dieting. This was especially true for frozen yogurt and tofu desserts (which might contain little or no sugar, butterfat, or cholesterol) and for ice cream brands which contained no artificial ingredients.

It was also hypothesized that an ailing economy made people turn to small luxuries like ice cream. Purchases of premium and superpremium ice cream crossed economic and cultural lines, and there was little data on the makeup of these buyers or on brand loyalty. Foreign mystique was readily available by purchasing Frusen Glädjé (Swedish for "frozen delight"), Alpen Zauber (German for "alpine magic") or Häagen-Dazs (meaningless words in English or Danish), all of which were headquartered in New York.

Consumer willingness to try new flavors and ice cream creations often seemed unlimited. However, vanilla was still the preferred flavor of more than 30 percent of consumers. The most popular flavors are shown in Exhibit 6. Pralines 'N Cream (vanilla laced with praline-covered pecans and caramel) was voted the all-time favorite among Baskin-Robbins's more than 500 flavors. Variations of

Exhibit 6 MOST POPULAR ICE CREAM FLAVORS IN THE UNITED STATES

Flavors	Percent of total sales
1. Vanilla	31.02%
2. Chocolate	8.81
3. Neopolitan	6.19
4. Vanilla Fudge	4.16
5. Cookies 'n Cream	3.89
6. Butter Pecan	3.83
7. Chocolate Chip	3.60
8. Strawberry	3.53
9. Rocky Road	1.31
10. Tin Roof Sundae	1.26
11. Cherry	1.26
12. French Vanilla	1.21
13. Praline Pecan	0.91
14. Heavenly Hash	0.91
15. Chocolate Almond	0.85

Source: *The Latest Scoop*, 1985, p. 28.

chocolate were in the 2nd through 10th positions. Several companies, including Dreyer's and Baskin-Robbins, had developed new lines of chocolate and chocolate-combination flavors.

Foods critics proclaimed various brands of ice cream as best. Howard Johnson's ice cream, Swensen's, Häagen-Dazs, and Baskin-Robbins all had won assorted taste tests. In 1981 a test of 28 brands of vanilla was conducted by nine food experts. Häagen-Dazs received a second-place rating, while Alpen Zauber, Baskin-Robbins, Louis Sherry, and Dreyer's were far down the list. First place went to the Giant Food chain's economy vanilla "Kiss," which sold for $1.29 a half-gallon and contained preservatives, stabilizers, fillers, artificial color, and the legal minimum of 10 percent butterfat. Several guides for ice cream gourmets had appeared on the market; one was titled *The Very Best Ice Cream and Where to Find It.*

Consumer Reports rated Schrafft's, a superpremium ice cream made in Pelham, New York, number 1 out of about 30 brands tested. Expert tasters judged the ice cream against standards of excellence used by the American Dairy Science Association. Various brands of chocolate and vanilla ice cream were evaluated for firm body and a smooth velvety texture free from graininess or perceptible ice crystals. Appearance and flavor balance were other criteria. The vanilla ice creams produced by Schrafft's, Friendly, and Howard Johnson's were all rated "excellent." Judged "very good" were Baskin-Robbins, Louis Sherry, Sealtest, Dreyer's, and Breyers. Häagen-Dazs, Borden, and the house brand products of Safeway, A&P, and Kroger supermarkets received "good" ratings. None of the chocolate ice creams were rated excellent by *Consumer Reports;* Schrafft's, Friendly, Baskin-Robbins, Howard Johnson's, Dreyer's, Häagen-Dazs, and several others received a very good ranking. Lack of flavor, lack of flavor balance, and icy texture were among the defects noted. The panel of tasters asserted that the all-natural compositions of Breyers and Häagen-Dazs could account for many of the defects of these products; the lack of additives contributed to a deterioration of flavor and texture.

SUBSTITUTES

Ice milk and sherbet were relatively well-established substitutes for ice cream and had stable consumption patterns. Frozen yogurt and tofu-based dessert products gained more recognition in the early 1980s. Several regional chains emerged to sell the low-calorie, low-fat, frozen yogurt creations: I Can't Believe It's Yogurt of Dallas, Zack's Famous Frozen Yogurt of New Orleans, and The Country's Best Yogurt (TCBY) of Little Rock. The products were usually produced as soft-serve and in a wide range of flavors. Frozen yogurt outlets were usually patterned after ice cream parlors and dipping stores and often sold a tofu-based dessert as well. Zack's had 40 stores while The Country's Best Yogurt sold 224 franchises in less than two years after the company's formation. Independent yogurt stores appeared in many areas of the country, and many restaurants and delicatessens installed frozen yogurt machines.

Of the large yogurt producers, only TCBY was publicly owned. Many of the other producers did not report their sales volumes, so the total market for frozen yogurt could not be exactly determined. 1985 sales in California alone were 3.5 million gallons. Total sales for 1984 were estimated at 8 million gallons, worth about $125 million at retail. There were 57 plants producing mix for frozen yogurt and tofu products.

Development of the market for frozen yogurt varied according to geographic regions. Frozen yogurt was a familiar treat in California, Texas, and New York. Annual growth rates in these states ranged from 20 to 30 percent. More dramatic growth was witnessed in the rapidly developing markets in the southeastern states. One industry source estimated annual growth in the region at more than 30 percent. In other areas of the United States, frozen yogurt was not popular at all. The markets in the Midwest and plains states were essentially undeveloped.

The best known of the tofu mixtures was Tofutti, a nondairy, bean curd-based dessert made by the Brooklyn-based company Tofu Time. Tofu Time experienced more than 600 percent growth in sales from 1983 to 1984; its 1985 sales were expected to top $4 million, an increase of 68 percent over the previous year. Tofutti had no butterfat or cholesterol, contained no dairy products, (which made it suitable for the 30 million lactose-intolerant Americans), and had only half the calories of ice cream. To gain acceptance in supermarkets for Tofutti, Tofu Time had entered into an agreement for Häagen-Dazs to act as distributor for its hard-serve product in the grocery segment. Tofutti retailed for about $2.50 per pint, and its packaging cultivated the same superpremium image as Häagen-Dazs. Tofu Time had opened its own dipping stores in New York, and Tofutti was also sold soft-serve through more than 300 Häagen-Dazs franchise stores.

A relative newcomer to the ice cream market was sorbet, a low-calorie frozen dessert with an intense fruit flavor and a creamier texture than regular sherbet. Castle & Cooke's Dole Fruit Sorbet and Häagen-Dazs's Le Sorbet were both introduced in 1984. Both companies emphasized the French origins of sorbet and the all natural compositions of their products. The round pint containers were similar to those for superpremium ice cream, and each pint sold for about $1.99. Sorbet contained no dairy products; Le Sorbet contained only fruit, water, and sugar and was available in such flavors as raspberry, mango, lemon, strawberry, cantelope, and passion fruit.

A multitude of new pudding and juice bars from companies such as General Foods, Castle & Cooke, and Welch's had appeared in the 1980s to compete with Eskimo Pies, Good Humor bars, and Popsicles. Many of the new products bore labels proclaiming "all natural" and describing the nutrients contained in the bars. Popsicle, Good Humor, and other companies known for ice cream novelties responded with new shapes and flavors of their own. The pudding bars and juice bars typically carried a higher price than traditional ice-cream-on-a-stick products.

Ice Cream Novelties

The ice cream novelty category included bars, sticks, cones, sandwiches, and parfaits made from ice cream, ice milk, and sherbet. Novelties typically accounted for between 20 and 25 percent of total ice cream sales.

In trying to capture more of the adult market, many manufacturers had begun to make high-quality, richer novelties. Often targeted at one- or two-person households, the premium or superpremium novelties were made larger and were sold in packages of fewer units. Typical of this trend was the Chipwich (ice cream sandwiched between two chocolate chip cookies and rimmed in chocolate morsels), which sold for about $1. Dove Bar International had a single product: a six-ounce ice cream bar with four ounces of superpremium ice cream hand-dipped in dark bittersweet chocolate; a single bar sold for $1.75 to $2, and a grocery store two-pack retailed for $2.99. Created by a candy maker, the Dove Bar was described by one ice cream expert as two ounces of "very fine candy—the ice cream is really the chaser."

COMPETITIVE RIVALRY

Rivalry among the ice cream processors revolved mainly around price, quality (or at least the image of quality), and variety. There was no clear price leader in any of the categories, although prices on the premium-priced, standard-priced, and economy-priced brands were usually fairly close within their respective categories. Regional brands in these categories tended to be priced slightly below national brands. Price was seldom featured in the marketing of superpremium and luxury-priced ice creams, but supermarkets did run shopper discount specials on ice cream.

Most manufacturers chose to emphasize the natural, fine quality ingredients used and the superiority of the product that resulted. Quality claims based on low overrun and high butterfat seemed to reach an ultimate with Borden's Gelare; the product had no air and 18 percent butterfat, making it so hard that it had to sit out of the freezer for 15 minutes before it could be spooned from the carton. Foreign names or names that already carried prestige, such as Godiva, were used to further enhance the image of superpremium and luxury ice cream. New exotic flavors appeared frequently, and many dipping stores featured a variety of mix-ins or add-ons to differentiate their frozen creations.

With the proliferation of brands and flavors, the distribution battle became more heated. Competition for limited shelf space in the supermarket meant that advertising played an increasingly important role in attracting distributors as well as consumers. Traditionally ice cream marketers shunned advertising. Reuben Mattus was very proud of the fact that Häagen-Dazs's early success was due to word-of-mouth advertising. In 1981 the ice cream industry spent a total of $5 million on national advertising. This had risen to $14 million by 1983, but on the average, ice cream manufacturers spent less than 1 percent of sales on advertising.

In 1984 Häagen-Dazs's ads appeared in *Essence* and *Ebony* to reach the black market, while Spanish language advertising was used in New York and Miami. A 1984 Frusen Glädjé campaign challenged: "You'll like Frusen Glädjé ice cream better than Häagen-Dazs or we'll refund your money." Borden's Gelare targeted Häagen-Dazs with print ads that showed Gelare outweighing its competitor on a scale. Schrafft's offered incentives to retailers on a regular basis and also helped supermarkets with their product displays. Some sellers used newspaper ads and couponing to attract consumers.

Fancier cartons appeared as manufacturers sought to catch the consumer's eye. Kraft chose a round black carton for its introduction of Breyers ice cream into new western and midwestern markets.

Profiles of seven large ice cream manufacturers and of TCBY Enterprises follow. Exhibit 7 contains comparative financial data for these companies.

FRIENDLY ICE CREAM/HERSHEY FOODS CORP.

In 1985 Hershey Foods was a major producer of chocolate and confectionery products and pasta products. The company was best known for its Hershey candy bars. The company's management sometimes used a quote by founder Milton S. Hershey to summarize the approach to consumers: "Give them quality and value—that's the best kind of advertising there is."

Hershey purchased the Friendly Ice Cream Corporation in 1979. Friendly's was founded in 1935 in Springfield, Massachusetts, as one small store with a single ice cream freezer. At the end of 1984 there were 707 Friendly Restaurants in 16 states, primarily in the Northeast and Midwest. Friendly's sales in 1984 were $427 million; the Friendly division accounted for 23 percent of Hershey Foods' total revenues and for 17 percent of consolidated operating profits. Friendly's had both a strong mealtime menu and a strong ice cream specialty menu and was one of the largest nonfranchised chains. Most of the units were freestanding, but since about 1980, the company had begun opening units in shopping malls. During this time many of the older units were refurbished, and menu offerings were standardized.

Friendly increased advertising and promotional activities significantly in 1983 in response to greater competition in the fast-food industry. New ice cream desserts, such as pies and rolls, had recently been introduced, and Hershey candy had been incorporated into sundaes and parfait selections. Modest price increases were instituted in 1984. Ice cream represented about 40 percent of Friendly's business; 8 to 10 percent of ice cream was sold on a take-home basis. Friendly did not discuss its ice cream's content of butterfat or other ingredients, stating only that the company made an ice cream that appealed to a broad range of tastes and that was affordable by the average family.

Friendly's expansion had taken it as far west as Illinois and as far south as Virginia. By the end of 1986, however, Friendly hoped to have 15 to 20 sites in the Orlando, Florida, area. Plans called for continued development of stores in the mid-Atlantic area and in the Midwest, but management viewed the Southeast region as a prime area for consideration. Friendly had recently acquired more than 30 properties from Sambo's, Howard Johnson Restaurants, and Roy Rogers Family Restaurants and converted them to Friendly restaurants; company plans included more such acquisitions. Friendly's also operated a small number of franchised ice cream shops called O'goodies, where customers created their own ice cream desserts.

DART & KRAFT, INC.

Dart & Kraft, Inc., in 1984 had consolidated net sales of $9.8 billion and net income of $456 million. The company was structured into four main divisions: (1)

Exhibit 7 COMPARATIVE FINANCIAL PERFORMANCE OF SELECTED PRODUCERS OF ICE CREAM AND YOGURT, 1979–1984 (dollars in thousands)

Company	1979	1980	1981	1982	1983	1984
Swensen's, Inc.						
Franchising revenues and royalties	$ 4,963	$ 4,587	$ 8,313	$ 12,377	$ 14,929	$ 11,415
Net loss	(226)	(2,788)	(3,013)	(1,680)	(285)	(1,790)
Total assets	2,229	4,969	6,816	11,282	11,529	18,932
Shareholders' equity	11	404	149	1,585	5,481	7,491
Total sales at retail	51,904	64,615	79,615	88,575	92,050	99,600
Number of stores open	255	292	316	340	357	387
Hershey Foods Corp.						
Net sales	$1,161,295	$1,335,289	$4,451,151	$1,565,736	$1,706,105	$1,892,506
Operating profit	125,177	143,154	173,012	186,566	207,069	229,804
Net after-tax income	53,504	62,055	80,362	94,168	100,166	108,682
Total assets	607,199	684,472	829,447	904,754	983,944	1,122,567
Shareholders' equity	320,730	361,550	469,664	532,495	596,037	660,928
Friendly Restaurants division only						
Net sales		$ 272,297	$ 302,908	$ 335,836	$ 383,543	$ 427,122
Income from operations		25,567	29,309	34,279	39,428	41,770
Assets		219,196	223,265	234,860	251,781	273,356
Baskin-Robbins Ice Cream Co.*						
Revenues					$ 125,173	$ 145,978
Operating profit					19,589	25,046
Net after-tax income					10,446	13,396
Total assets					58,607	69,362
Shareholders' equity					36,502	43,164
Borden, Inc.						
Net sales	$4,312,533	$4,595,795	$ 4,415,174	$4,111,277	$4,264,771	$4,568,018
Operating profit	274,924	300,043	305,043	319,860	403,620	416,662
Net after-tax income	134,015	147,485	159,939	165,855	189,069	191,407
Total assets	2,468,860	2,649,644	2,508,816	2,589,702	2,720,471	2,884,127
Shareholders' equity	1,177,940	1,227,284	1,318,755	134,333	1,391,039	1,367,944

Dart & Kraft, Inc.

Net sales	$9,411,000	$10,211,000	$9,974,000	$9,714,000	$9,759,000
Operating profit	694,000	752,000	748,000	817,000	848,000
Net after-tax income	383,000	348,000	350,000	435,000	456,000
Total assets	4,650,000	5,054,000	5,134,000	5,418,000	5,285,000
Shareholders' equity	2,621,000	2,718,000	2,774,000	2,923,000	2,598,000

Food products division (Kraft) only

Net sales			$7,041,100	$6,660,400	$6,837,000
Operating profit			488,500	553,500	615,400
Assets			2,364,800	2,131,800	2,316,500

Pillsbury Company†

Net sales	$2,166,000	$ 3,301,700	$3,385,100	$3,685,900	$4,172,300
Operating profit	186,800	267,500	267,300	269,600	347,900
Net after-tax income	104,700	119,600	136,300	138,900	169,800
Total assets	1,804,500	2,174,500	2,428,300	2,366,600	2,608,300
Shareholders' equity	577,700	747,200	890,000	956,400	1,046,200

TCBY Enterprises

Franchising revenue			$ 406	$ 622	$ 1,989
Sales revenue			1,122	1,711	5,419
Operating profit			N/A	265	2,124
Net after-tax income			226	161	1,011
Total assets			845	4,594	8,136
Shareholders' equity			N/A	469	5,635
Systemwide sales			1,775	5,219	11,462
Number of stores open			18	41	102

Ben & Jerry's Homemade, Inc.

Net sales	$ 374	$ 615	$ 968	$ 1,815	$ 4,010
Operating profit	40	33	16	97	297
Net after-tax income (loss)	33	29	(56)	57	213
Total assets	92	193	295	509	3,894
Shareholders' equity	48	77	21	154	1,068

* Privately held company; financial data from 1984, 1979–82 not available.
† Pillsbury's fiscal year ends May 31.
Source: Annual reports and 10-K reports.

Kraft, Inc., the sole component of the Food Products Division; (2) Direct Selling—Tupperware; (3) Consumer Products—Duracell (batteries), West Bend (appliances), Health Care, and Kitchenaid; and (4) Commercial Products—Hobart commercial equipment and Wilsonart brand decorative laminates. Food products accounted for 70 percent of 1984 corporate sales; the division's operating profit was $615.4 million, an 11 percent increase from 1983.

Kraft's mission was to become the world's leading food company. It marketed more than 3,300 food products under some 850 trademarks to consumers in about 130 nations. Most of the products fit into five broad categories:

1. Natural and process cheese.
2. Ice cream and other frozen desserts.
3. Cultured dairy products including cottage cheese, sour cream, and yogurt.
4. Vegetable oil-based products including salad dressings, mayonnaise, margarine, edible oils, and shortening.
5. Other grocery products including frozen foods, confections, condiments, juices, and other foods.

Ice cream accounted for less than 5 percent of the sales of Kraft's Food Products Division. Kraft's ice cream products were marketed under the brand names Sealtest, Breyers, and the newly acquired (1985) Frusen Glädjé brand. Sealtest and Breyers were widely available in states east of the Mississippi River. Although sales of Sealtest ice cream were down somewhat in 1984, Breyers continued to perform well, and Kraft held its position as the market share leader of ice cream in supermarkets. Breyers was one of the best selling premium ice creams in the country, and Kraft continued to extend the market coverage for this brand by initiating distribution in some western and midwestern areas. New packaging and extensive ad campaigns were developed for Breyers' market expansion. Breyers was promoted as all natural and was positioned as a top-of-the-line brand in the premium ice cream segment. In the 1980s Breyers began to replace the Sealtest brand in many supermarket freezers.

Frusen Glädjé was the number-two-selling superpremium ice cream brand in the United States behind Häagen-Dazs at the time of its acquisition. Kraft management anticipated that the addition of Frusen Glädjé would help the dairy group achieve nationwide distribution of its ice cream and provide Kraft the means to gain a solid position in the superpremium segment. Kraft acquired the company's trademark, product formula, and pint retail business (90 percent of Frusen Glädjé's sales).

In its 1984 advertising, Frusen Glädjé did direct comparisons with Häagen-Dazs, urging consumers to compare the two brands. Kraft continued this approach with an advertising blitz including TV spots. Taste samples of Frusen Glädjé were offered in supermarkets as Kraft continued to expand distribution of the brand. Frusen Glädjé subsequently joined forces with Sunshine Biscuits to produce a line of cookies-and-cream products featuring Hydrox cookies. Frusen Glädjé also manufactured and marketed Gloria Vanderbilt's Glace Tofu frozen dessert. This product was sold through Frusen Glädjé's 50 or so dipping stores as well as through supermarkets. Frusen Glädjé also introduced a sorbet dessert in 1985.

PILLSBURY/HÄAGEN-DAZS ICE CREAM

The Pillsbury Company was a diversified international food and restaurant organization with 1984 sales of $4.6 billion. The company's first flour mill was built in 1869, and since then Pillsbury had grown through internal development and acquisitions to be a leading manufacturer of consumer packaged goods including dessert mixes, canned and frozen vegetables, refrigerated bread products, frozen pizza, frozen fish, and superpremium ice cream. The company was the largest diversified restaurant operator in the world in 1984, owning the Burger King Corporation, Steak & Ale Restaurants, and Bennigan's. Over the past 10 years its major acquisitions included Totino's Fine Foods, Green Giant Company, Häagen-Dazs, Van de Kamp's, and Diversifoods, Inc.

Pillsbury's Restaurants Group had sales of $2.05 billion (up 16 percent) and operating profit equal to $220 million (up 17 percent) in 1985. Included in the Restaurants Group were the more than 300 Häagen-Dazs Shoppes. Some of these shops were dipping stores, while others were larger dessert shop operations. Pillsbury purchased Häagen-Dazs in mid-1983 for $75 million. A family-held company for 23 years, Häagen-Dazs had annual sales of $115 million (excluding revenues from its franchised shops) at the time of the purchase. The annual growth rate for Häagen-Dazs then was between 25 and 35 percent, and the company held a 25 percent share of the superpremium ice cream market. During its first year with Pillsbury, physical volume for Häagen-Dazs increased 22 percent. Volume rose another 20 percent in fiscal 1985, despite a slight decline in total U.S. ice cream consumption. Häagen-Dazs sales were $130 million in 1985, up 34 percent over 1984. The opening of a second plant in 1985 increased capacity by 50 percent, allowing greater penetration of the markets in the western United States.

In 1984 Häagen-Dazs became the national distributor of Tofutti and Le Sorbet, as well as launching a line of Sorbet and Cream products. Sorbet and Cream combined fruit ices with Häagen-Dazs vanilla ice cream. Through a joint venture with Suntory of Japan, Häagen-Dazs ice cream became available through some Tokyo supermarkets, and Häagen-Dazs had dipping stores in Japan, Singapore, Hong Kong, and Korea. Häagen-Dazs planned to continue with rapid geographic and product expansion.

BORDEN, INC.

Borden, Inc., operated in two major industry segments: foods and chemicals. Net sales in 1984 were $4.6 billion; its Consumer Products Division accounted for 64 percent of sales and 53 percent of operating income in 1984.

Borden's food segment included a wide variety of dairy products, instant beverages, snack foods, confections, jams and jellies, pasta, and seafood. Lady Borden was the company's premium brand of ice cream. Lady Borden had been a market leader in the premium category for many years and showed strong sales gains in 1982 due to richer formulas, new flavors, and new packaging. Pudding bars and fruit bars were first introduced in 1982 under the Borden label.

In 1983 Borden expanded its ice cream line by signing an agreement to produce and distribute Gelare, a superpremium all natural ice cream with 18 percent butterfat content and no overrun. The product had Italian origins and had become popular on the West Coast two and a half years before the licensing agreement. Borden hoped to capitalize on the "ice cream awareness" created by other superpremium brands and to entice some customers away from Häagen-Dazs and Frusen Glädjé.

BASKIN-ROBBINS ICE CREAM COMPANY

The Baskin-Robbins ice cream business was founded in 1946 by Burton Baskin and Irvine Robbins and was engaged in the development and manufacture of ice cream products, operation of retail ice cream stores, and granting of franchises for such stores. Allied-Lyons North America Corporation owned 100 percent of the shares of stock of Baskin-Robbins.

Retail sales for all 3,300 Baskin-Robbins stores were $470 million in 1984, $455 million in 1983, and $423 million in 1982. About one third of Baskin-Robbins 3,300 stores were company-owned, and two thirds were franchised. Baskin-Robbins's revenue from product sales to its 3,300 retail stores in 1984 were $152 million; 1983 sales were $146 million, up from $125.1 million in 1982. The parent derived revenue from product sales to its retail franchises and by charging each of its franchised factories a license fee. Baskin-Robbins charged its franchisees a royalty on ice cream rather than on gross sales. For many years Baskin-Robbins had viewed the interest in super-rich ice cream as a passing fad; their own product was classified as premium because of its butterfat content and 50 percent overrun. In 1982 the company chose to market a low-fat frozen dessert in hopes of appealing to health-conscious consumers. Management also decided against expanding its take-out stores into the higher-cost, sit-down parlors as some competitors had done.

A 1984 Tastes of America survey voted Baskin-Robbins the favorite fast-food chain for the second consecutive year. In 1985 the company implemented a multiphase program to update its image with consumers. The program included a $20 million renovation of its more than 3,000 franchised ice cream parlors, a $3 million advertising program that included network TV, and increased investment in new products. Baskin-Robbins president Robert Marley explained, "There is so much excitement in the ice cream industry today, and we are not getting our fair share. We've been silent too long. We have excellent product awareness and product preference. We just have to capitalize on it."

To entice more adults and professionals into its stores, Baskin-Robbins replaced its pink, white, and brown decor with new store graphics, new furniture, increased seating capacity, and softer color tones. For the first time Baskin-Robbins stores differed in appearance as the company allowed franchise owners to tailor their store decors to fit in with shopping centers or malls.

Advertising, sales promotions, and local publicity efforts reminded consumers that Baskin-Robbins offered more flavors and styles of ice cream to "families of all ages.'' Baskin-Robbins had a rotating lineup of 31 flavors with a repertoire of more than 500 flavors.

In 1985 Baskin-Robbins filed suit against Pillsbury and Häagen-Dazs for trademark infringement of its ''Pralines ' N Cream'' flavor name. Häagen-Dazs ads had stated that ''Pralines & Cream'' was exclusively available at its shops. In keeping with its new aggressive stance, Baskin-Robbins had plans to file suit against other companies for similar infringements. The company also planned capacity expansions and additional efforts in new product development.

SWENSEN'S, INC.

Swensen's, Inc., through its wholly owned subsidiaries Swensen's Manufacturing Company, Swensen's Distributing Company, and Swensen's Ice Cream Company (Australia) Pty. Ltd., operated and franchised more than 380 ice cream parlors and dip shoppes through the United States and 14 foreign countries. In 1984 the company had entered into the packaged ice cream business and marketed its Swensen's Old Fashioned ice cream products to supermarkets and convenience stores in Arizona. Plans for national distribution through supermarkets were contingent on consumer response.

Unlike many of its competitors, Swensen's ice cream was made in 20- or 40-quart batches by the operator of each store, either on the premises or in a nearby location. This method allowed each store to make small quantities of a wide variety of flavors, thus ensuring freshness. The company had recipes for 175 flavors with each store offering between 16 and 45 flavors at any one time. A new menu format was developed in 1983, and in the following year Swensen's Supreme, a superpremium ice cream, was offered. Swensen's stores ranged from ice-cream-only shops with no seats, to ice-cream-only stores with 25 to 30 seats, to limited-menu restaurants with 80 to 100 seats. These restaurants served sandwiches, soups, salads, and a full complement of ice cream and fountain items. Swensen's planned to have 390 stores in operation by the end of 1984. Sixteen new stores were to be located in other countries. Total sales for all Swensen's stores in 1984 were $99.6 million, up from $92 million in 1983 and $88.6 million in 1982. Management estimated that about 60 percent of Swensen's system sales were from the retail sales of its superpremium ice cream.

In August 1984 Swensen's acquired two ice cream manufacturing facilities from Foremost Dairies, Inc. Swensen's planned to maintain close control over its pints and half-gallons of ice cream for supermarket sale by owning and staffing these dairies. The ''theme song'' for introducing the packaged ice cream was ''You Made Me Love You.''

In late 1984 Swensen's president, E. C. Schoenleb, resigned following a dispute with the company's directors who viewed his plans to revamp Swensen's menus and decor as overaggressive. Schoenleb had joined the company in 1981 and was credited with helping to reverse the company's loss record. Losses in 1980 were $2.8 million and $3 million the following year. By February of 1985 Swensen's had reached an agreement to transfer ownership of the manufacturing facilities back to Foremost Dairies. The company stated that it decided to focus its resources on its parlor and packaged ice cream business. Foremost would continue to manufacture the pints and half-gallons of ice cream sold under Swensen's name in the supermarkets.

Over the past several years Swensen's new ice cream and food items had included the richer ice cream called Swensen's Supreme (16–18 percent butterfat), a "walkaway" sundae in a freshly baked, waffle batter cone, croissant sandwiches, new soups, and gourmet salads.

TCBY ENTERPRISES (THE COUNTRY'S BEST YOGURT)

TCBY franchised and owned soft-serve frozen yogurt stores. A majority of the company-owned and franchised stores operated under the name "This Can't Be Yogurt!!" until December 1985, when the settlement of a trademark infringement lawsuit with "I Can't Believe It's Yogurt" of Dallas required TCBY to change its name. Afterward known as "TCBY Yogurt!!" and "The Country's Best Yogurt," the stores sold more than 20 flavors of yogurt in various ways as a dessert, snack, or light meal item. As of March 1985 there were 142 franchise stores and 19 company stores open or under construction with 72 more planned. TCBY intended to open 200 more shops each year in 1986 and 1987. TCBY was the only publicly owned franchisor of yogurt shops. Average annual net income per store was $22,500, about 15 percent of the average annual store sales of $150,000.

The yogurt was served in cones, sundaes, shakes, and cups and sometimes included cookies, crepes, or waffles, as well as a variety of toppings. The stores were patterned after ice cream shops, and TCBY operated under the slogan "All of the pleasure and none of the guilt." TCBY owned its yogurt supplier, Arthur's Food. The company began offering frozen tofu desserts in its shops in mid-1985, hoping to capitalize further on the public's concern with health and weight maintenance. Marketing programs were aimed at increasing the acceptance of the product and creating loyalty to the TCBY name.

BEN & JERRY'S HOMEMADE, INC.

Ben & Jerry's Homemade, Inc., manufactured and marketed Ben & Jerry's superpremium ice cream to supermarkets, convenience stores, and restaurants, as well as franchising ice cream parlors in New England and upstate New York. Thirty flavors were available in bulk and 10 flavors in pints at retail food outlets. In 1984 about two thirds of company revenues resulted from the sale of the packaged pints. Bulk sales to restaurants and franchises accounted for one fourth of the revenues, while the remaining 8 percent came from sales at company-owned ice cream parlors.

In 1978 Ben Cohen and Jerry Greenfield opened a retail store featuring homemade ice cream in a renovated gas station in Burlington, Vermont. They learned to make the ice cream from a $5 correspondence course and experimentation with a rock-salt freezer. In the beginning their ingredients were mostly free samples from suppliers, resulting in flavors like lemon-peppermint carob chip. Demand was such that by 1979 Ben & Jerry's began a wholesale operation selling ice cream to local restaurants. Cohen drove around the state delivering ice cream from a cooler in the back of his Volkswagen.

More than 300 restaurants and supermarkets in New England, in addition to eight franchised stores, carried the product by the end of 1984. *Dairy Record* named the company its "Ice Cream Retailer of the Year" in 1984, and *Time* magazine called Ben & Jerry's "The best ice cream in the world." To meet the growing demand, in early 1985 the company built a plant capable of processing 820 gallons an hour. The factory was financed by a Vermont-only public stock offering of which hundreds of people purchased one or two shares.

Ben & Jerry's marketing emphasized the ice cream's high quality and natural ingredients and projected a "down home" Vermont image. Packaging and advertising carried pictures of Cohen and Greenfield, paintings of cows, and hand lettering. The company relied heavily on promotional events, free sampling, and word-of-mouth advertising to market its product. Four percent of total sales were put into radio, print, and TV advertising. Ben & Jerry's also sponsored community celebrations and contributed cash and merchandise equal to about 4 percent of its income before taxes to charitable events and enterprises.

The ice cream was primarily distributed through independent regional ice cream distributors. When Ben & Jerry's learned in 1984 that Häagen-Dazs had told some distributors that they would lose access to Häagen-Dazs products if they carried any other superpremium ice cream brands, Ben & Jerry's initiated an antitrust suit against Häagen-Dazs and Pillsbury. In fear of being shut out of new markets, Ben & Jerry's also instituted a "What's the Pillsbury Doughboy Afraid of?" campaign including bumper stickers, t-shirts and a toll-free information number. The litigation was settled in March 1985 when Ben & Jerry's agreed to discontinue this campaign and Häagen-Dazs agreed not to interfere with the distribution of Ben & Jerry's ice cream. The company planned to begin distribution in Washington, D.C.; Virginia; and Florida during 1985. Management projected that at least 23 franchised dipping stores would be operating by the end of 1985.

COMPETITION IN THE WORLD TIRE INDUSTRY*

Tire manufacturing became an important industry in the first half of the 20th century as motor vehicles increasingly became the dominant mode of transportation. The demand for original equipment tires was directly related to the number of new motor vehicles currently produced, while the demand for replacement tires depended on such factors as the number of vehicles in service, the average number of miles driven per vehicle, and tire tread durability. In 1986 the replacement market was roughly three times as big as the original equipment segment; a vehicle during its useful life could require anywhere between two and six sets of replacement tires. Replacement tire sales generated much bigger profit margins for the manufacturers than original equipment sales because tiremakers could command higher prices on their replacement sales through wholesale and retail channels than they could on selling tires in mass quantities to the hard-bargaining automobile and truck manufacturers.

World tire production in 1986 was approximately 715 million tires, with the following geographic breakdown:

Geographic origin	Units shipped (in millions)	Percent of total
United States	245	34%
Canada and Mexico	35	5
Central and South America	45	6
Western Europe	160	22
Africa and Asia, except China	140	20
Eastern Europe and China	90	13
Total	715	100%

U.S. tire consumption as a percentage of worldwide demand peaked in the 1950s at around 60 percent; growing use of automobiles and trucks in the rest of the world coupled with maturing U.S. usage had made the U.S. tire market a steadily declining percentage of the total world market. Ten major producers accounted for around 84 percent of production in 1986; the world leaders in tire sales were:

---

* Prepared by Professor Arthur A. Thompson, Jr., with the research assistance of Ken Tucker and Jennifer Lowry, The University of Alabama. Copyright © 1987 by Arthur A. Thompson, Jr.

Company (headquarters country)	World tire sales (billions)	
	1983	1986
Goodyear Tire & Rubber Co. (United States)	$6.0	$6.2
Michelin (France)	4.9	5.5
Bridgestone Tire (Japan)	2.4	2.7
Firestone Tire & Rubber Co. (United States)	2.6	2.5
Uniroyal Goodrich Tire Co. (United States)	2.1	2.0
Pirelli (Italy)	1.6	1.7
Continental Gummi-Werke (West Germany)	.9	1.3
General Tire (United States)	.8	1.2
Sumitomo Rubber Co. (Japan)	.8	1.2
Yokohama Rubber Co. (Japan)	.8	1.0

Exhibit 1 shows the market share trends for each of the current leaders. In addition to the major producers, there were perhaps as many as 50 other producers of tires, each with one or more plants serving mainly a national or continental market.

For the past decade tire companies had been plagued with chronic overcapacity problems caused by a shift in demand from low-mileage, bias-ply tires to much longer lasting radial tires. All the tire companies had invested in R&D and technological advances to improve performance, traction, and tread wear under a variety of road conditions, resulting in increases in the number of miles driven before tires had to be replaced. This, coupled with a leveling off in the production of new motor vehicles, had caused the sales of both original equipment and replacement tires to flatten over the past decades. The industry became both mature and cyclical. Increased competition for market share brought falling prices, stimulated efforts to cut costs to preserve profit margins, and forced the

Exhibit 1 MARKET SHARES OF THE WORLD'S LEADING TIRE MANUFACTURERS, 1971–1985

Company (home country)	1971	1979	1983	1985
Goodyear (United States)	24%	23%	22%	21%
Michelin (France)	11	16	18	18
Bridgestone (Japan)	3	7	9	9
Firestone (United States)	17	14	10	8
Uniroyal Goodrich (United States)	14	9	7	7
Pirelli (Italy)	10	10	6	6
Continental (West Germany)	2	3	3	4
Sumitomo (Japan)	n.a.	n.a.	3	4
General Tire (United States)	4	4	3	4
Yokohama (Japan)	n.a.	n.a.	3	3
Others	15	14	16	16
Total	100%	100%	100%	100%

Sources: *Rubber and Plastics News;* company estimates; and Arnhold and S. Bleichroeder, Inc.

Exhibit 2 ANNUAL WORLD VEHICLE PRODUCTION, 1975–1986 (in millions)

Year	Australia	Belgium	Brazil	Canada	France	Italy	Japan	Korea
1975	.46	.22	.93	1.45	2.86	1.46	6.94	.04
1976	.46	.33	.99	1.64	3.40	1.60	7.84	.05
1977	.45	.34	.92	1.70	3.51	1.58	8.51	.08
1978	.38	.30	1.06	1.81	3.51	1.66	9.27	.16
1979	.46	.31	1.13	1.60	3.61	1.63	9.64	.20
1980	.36	.26	1.17	1.37	3.38	1.61	11.04	.12
1981	.39	.24	.78	1.20	3.02	1.43	11.18	.13
1982	.41	.28	.86	1.27	3.15	1.45	10.73	.16
1983	.34	.29	.90	1.52	3.34	1.58	11.06	.22
1984	.40	.25	.86	1.88	3.06	1.60	11.39	.27
1985	.41	.27	.97	1.94	3.02	1.57	12.27	.38
1986	.36	n.a.	1.06	1.86	3.19	1.83	12.26	.60

closing of marginally efficient, relatively high-cost plants. A number of distressed companies had in recent years merged or been acquired in an attempt to revamp operations and meet competitive threats.

THE ORIGINAL EQUIPMENT MARKET SEGMENT

All original equipment (OE) tires were sold by the tire manufacturers factory-direct to the automobile and truck manufacturers. Vehicle manufacturers bought all of their tires from the tire manufacturers; none had integrated backward into tire manufacturing as they had into other component vehicle parts. As a consequence, OE tire demand was rigidly fixed by the number of vehicles being produced—each new automobile, for example, was equipped with five tires (four on the ground and a spare). In the highly industrialized nations of the world, the motor vehicle industry was seen as being mature as of 1986, and the demand for vehicles was cyclical. Exhibit 2 shows world production of motor vehicles.

Since tires were such a small cost item in the overall price of a new vehicle, changes in OE tire prices had virtually zero effect on total OE tire demand. However, while overall OE tire demand was highly price inelastic, the demand facing an individual tire manufacturer was considered highly elastic due to the ease with which vehicle manufacturers could switch to other manufacturers' brands.

Competition among the tire manufacturers to supply tires to the automobile and truck manufacturers was especially fierce. Most every major tiremaker was anxious to have new vehicles equipped with its brand of tires to enhance replacement sales, the belief being that vehicle owners satisfied with their OE tires would be more likely to choose the same brand when time came for replacement. The sale of OE tires was thus seen as strategically important, not only as a way to strengthen sales in the more profitable replacement segment but also to achieve volume-related scale economies in manufacturing. At the same time, the car and

Exhibit 2 *(concluded)*

Mexico	Spain	Sweden	United Kingdom	United States	USSR	W. Germany	World Total
.36	.81	.37	1.65	8.99	1.96	3.19	33.00
.32	.87	.37	1.71	11.48	2.02	3.87	38.34
.28	1.13	.29	1.71	12.73	2.09	4.10	40.95
.38	1.14	.31	1.61	12.83	2.15	4.19	42.30
.44	1.12	.35	1.48	11.39	2.17	4.25	41.52
.49	1.18	.30	1.31	8.01	2.20	3.88	38.51
.60	.99	.31	1.18	7.98	2.20	3.90	37.23
.47	1.07	.35	1.16	6.88	2.17	4.06	36.11
.29	1.29	.41	1.29	9.51	2.18	4.15	39.78
.34	1.31	.43	1.13	10.92	2.21	4.06	41.74
.40	1.42	.46	1.31	11.67	2.20	4.45	44.28
.27	1.53	.49	1.25	11.37	n.a.	4.60	n.a.

Note: World totals include all other countries in addition to those countries listed.
Source: *Automotive News,* 1987 Market Data Book Issue, April 29, 1987, p. 3.

truck manufacturers were sophisticated buyers and devoted considerable time and effort to tire purchasing and to their relationships with tire manufacturers. The tire purchasing strategies of the Japanese and U.S. automakers were in sharp contrast.

Tire Purchasing Practices of the U.S. Automakers

All the U.S. auto and truck manufacturers set strict, detailed tire specifications for each of their car and truck models that would-be tire suppliers had to meet in order for their tires to be considered. It was typical for the auto/truck manufacturers to establish higher quality standards and more rigid specifications for their OE tires than was the case for the usually available kinds of replacement tires. Some of the automobile manufacturers regularly inspected the plants of their tire suppliers to make sure quality standards were being met, and it was not unusual for them to ask for data on costs to compare against their own independently made estimates of what it cost their tire suppliers to make tires to their specifications. Different size cars and trucks were equipped with different size tires. The smallest cars had 13-inch wheelbases and required narrower tires; large luxury cars had 14-inch and 15-inch wheelbases and required wider treads. Heavy-duty trucks and tractor-trailer rigs were equipped with still bigger and stronger tires, capable of withstanding heavier loads.

Vehicle manufacturers typically contracted out their tire requirements annually on a model-by-model basis, normally using several different tire suppliers to equip their full lineup of models. General Motors and Ford each bought tires for their U.S. automobile models from five tiremakers—Goodyear, Firestone, Uniroyal, General Tire, and Michelin (see Exhibits 3 and 4). Using their bargaining leverage, U. S. automobile manufacturers had over the years negotiated an

Exhibit 3   ESTIMATED MARKET SHARES OF TIRE COMPANIES FOR ORIGINAL EQUIPMENT PASSENGER TIRES IN THE UNITED STATES, 1986

Original equipment buyer	Tire company							
	Goodyear	**Firestone**	**Uniroyal Goodrich**	**General Tire**	**Michelin**	**Pirelli**	**Dunlop**	**Continental**
General Motors	22.5%	21.5%	34.5%	17.5%	4.0%	0.0%	0.0%	0.0%
Ford	23.5	39.0	6.0	10.0	21.5	0.0	0.0	0.0
Chrysler	85.0	1.0	0.0	0.0	14.0	0.0	0.0	0.0
AMC	55.0	0.0	0.0	0.0	45.0	0.0	0.0	0.0
VW of U.S.	34.0	0.0	0.0	0.0	24.0	22.0	0.0	20.0
Honda of US.	43.0	0.0	0.0	0.0	56.0	0.0	1.0	0.0
Nissan	38.0	18.0	0.0	44.0	0.0	0.0	0.0	0.0
NUMMI (GM-Toyota)	50.0	50.0	0.0	0.0	0.0	0.0	0.0	0.0
Overall OE market share	33.0%	21.0%	21.0%	13.0%	11.4%	0.1%	0.1%	0.4%

Source: *Modern Tire Dealer,* January 1987, p. 38.

Exhibit 4   TRENDS IN TIRE COMPANY MARKET SHARES FOR OE PASSENGER CAR TIRES, 1978–1986

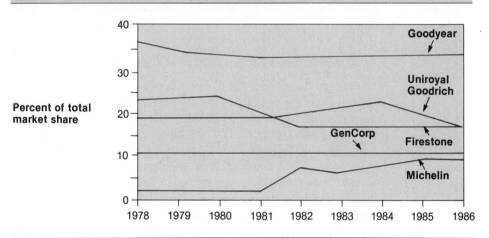

Source: *Modern Tire Dealer,* January 1987, p. 38.

average price for OE tires that was several dollars per tire below what wholesale distributors ended up paying the tiremakers for somewhat lower quality replacement tires. In effect, the automobile companies bought OE tires for roughly half the retail price commanded by replacement tires; in 1986, for example, U.S. automobile manufacturers paid under $35 for an average-size radial tire of superior quality whereas an auto owner paid about $70 for a perhaps lesser quality replacement tire of the same brand and size bought from a local tire dealer.

Tire Purchasing Practices of the Japanese Automakers

The Japanese vehicle manufacturers, principally Honda, Toyota, and Nissan, usually single-sourced their tires under long-term contracts. They worked very closely with their tire suppliers, emphasizing the importance of a mutually beneficial long-term relationship. There were few requests for price bids from rival tiremakers. The Japanese automakers placed less stress on explicit tire specifications and were less price-oriented in comparison to the U.S. automakers. They did, however, work diligently with their tire suppliers on ways to hold down tire costs, and they placed great importance on timely delivery, minimal shipping and inventories, and other facets of the "just-in-time" inventory and logistic systems that they used extensively with all auto components suppliers to control purchasing, materials handling, and warehousing costs. In Japan all of the Japanese tire manufacturing plants were located within a few miles of the assembly plants of the Japanese automakers.

THE REPLACEMENT TIRE MARKET

Replacement tires accounted for 70 to 75 percent of tire production. Unit shipments had been flat since the 1970s—see Exhibit 5 for volume trends in the United States by segment. Weak demand was partly a function of the adverse effect that sharply higher gasoline prices had had on the average number of miles driven annually per vehicle. In the United States the average had dropped to 9,500 miles in 1983 versus about 10,800 prior to the gasoline-shortage era. Every 100-mile change in the average number of miles traveled per vehicle produced a 1 million unit change in the size of the replacement market, given current tread wear life.

Tire manufacturers produced a large variety of grades and lines of tires for distribution under both manufacturers' brand names and private labels. Branded replacement tires were made to the tiremaker's own specifications, usually less rigid than required by vehicle manufacturers for OE tires. Some private-label tires supplied to wholesale distributors and large chain retailers were made to the buyer's specifications rather than to the manufacturer's standards. To those untrained in tire-making techniques or unfamiliar with tire-making practices, replacement tires appeared to be quite comparable if not exactly similar to OE tires. But there were often subtle differences in tread depth, grades of rubber, and component construction such that the vast majority of replacements on the market were not strictly equal to the quality and durability of OE tires. As a consequence, replacement tires tended to have a somewhat shorter life cycle than did OE tires. Low-grade replacement tires had a tread life of 10,000 to 20,000 miles compared to 30,000 to 40,000 miles (or longer) for OE tires. In 1986 only a few manufacturers provided guaranteed mileage warranties to the buyers of replacement tires; however, nearly all branded replacement tires carried lifetime warranties against manufacturing defects, and all tires met certain specified safety standards regarding traction and resistance against heat buildup.

The major brand-name tire producers had gained an early marketing advantage in selling replacement tires through their position as suppliers of OE tires to

Exhibit 5	SHIPMENTS OF TIRES IN THE UNITED STATES, 1976–1985 (in thousands)						

		Passenger car tires			Truck and bus tires		
Year	Passenger car, truck, and bus production	Original equipment	Replacement	Total*	Original equipment	Replacement	Total*
1985	195,972	54,838	141,455	200,918	7,698	32,098	41,131
1984	209,375	50,993	144,580	201,637	7,777	31,707	40,817
1983	186,923	43,845	133,964	182,015	5,519	30,301	36,850
1982	178,500	33,981	130,539	167,469	4,652	28,149	33,767
1981	181,762	35,979	125,263	165,259	5,732	28,453	35,846
1980	159,263	34,933	106,912	145,919	5,294	24,359	31,144
1979	206,687	48,188	121,922	174,019	9,884	28,859	39,910
1978	223,406	54,963	135,211	193,927	11,922	29,982	42,713
1977	231,638	55,668	129,283	189,552	10,330	25,912	37,031
1976	185,950	49,905	123,000	177,009	8,668	22,282	31,529

* Including exports.
Source: Rubber Manufacturers Association.

the automobile companies. As the new car and truck business developed into a major industry worldwide, the tiremakers were able to trade on the reputation and experience gained as original equipment suppliers to build strong wholesale distributor and retail dealer networks through which to access replacement tire buyers. The major manufacturers often used network TV campaigns to promote their brands and to introduce new types of tires. Their network TV ad budgets commonly ran in the $10 million–$30 million range, and their budgets for co-op ads with dealers were in the $20 million–$100 million range. Several tire companies sponsored auto racing events as a way of promoting the performance capabilities of their tires.

Distribution Channels

Replacement tires were marketed to vehicle owners through a variety of distribution channels: independent tire dealers, service stations, manufacturer-owned retail tire stores, major department stores with auto centers, retail chains (such as Sears, K mart, and Montgomery Ward), automobile dealerships, and assorted other outlets. In the United States alone there were approximately 40,000 tire, battery, and accessory dealers in 1986. Independent tire dealers, tiremaker retail stores, and service station outlets were the main sources of replacement tires for passenger cars (see Exhibit 6). Independent tire dealers usually carried the brands of two or three different manufacturers and perhaps a private-label brand so as to give replacement buyers a full assortment of qualities, brands, and price ranges to choose from. Service stations affiliated with Exxon, Chevron, and Amoco marketed Atlas brand tires; other service stations, especially those that really pushed tire sales, stocked one or two manufacturers' brand tires and maybe a private-label brand. Retail tire outlets that were owned or franchised by the manufacturers (that is, Goodyear Tire Stores and Firestone Auto Centers) carried only the

Exhibit 5   *(concluded)*

Tractor-implement tires			Total tire shipments		
Original equipment	**Replacement**	**Total***	**Original equipment**	**Replacement**	**Total***
598	2,395	3,169	63,134	175,948	245,218
920	2,592	3,694	59,690	178,879	246,148
912	2,191	3,238	50,276	166,456	222,103
1,003	2,108	3,226	39,636	160,796	204,462
1,597	2,427	4,197	43,308	156,143	205,302
1,569	2,560	4,334	41,796	133,831	181,397
2,107	3,139	5,445	60,179	153,920	219,374
1,693	2,985	4,804	68,578	168,178	241,444
1,887	2,972	5,048	67,885	158,167	231,631
2,066	3,173	5,376	60,639	148,455	213,914

manufacturers' brands and perhaps a private-label line made by the manufacturer. Department stores and the major retail chains occasionally carried manufacturers-label tires but more usually marketed only their own private-label brand. Exhibit 7 shows the 1986 market shares of the various brands in the U.S. replacement market.

Typically, retail tire outlets carried a wide selection of grades and qualities of tires, ranging in price from retreaded tires selling for under $20 to top-of-the-line tires listing for $125 and $175 each. To provide tires suitable for so many different types of vehicles driven under a variety of road and weather conditions, manufacturers found it advantageous to have a product line broad enough to appeal to

Exhibit 6   WHOLESALE AND RETAIL CHANNELS FOR REPLACEMENT TIRES, UNITED STATES, 1981–1986

	1986	1985	1984	1983	1982	1981
How passenger car replacement tires reach U.S. retail outlets:						
Independent tire distributors	68%	68%	68%	67%	67%	65%
Oil companies (acting as wholesalers)	3	3	4	4	4	5
Tire company stores (factory-direct)	13	12	11	11	10	10
Chain stores, department stores, and discount stores (factory-direct sales)	16	17	17	18	19	20
Percentage sales of U.S. passenger car replacement tires by retail outlet:						
Tire dealerships	56	55	55	54	53	51
Service stations	8	9	9	9	10	11
Tire company stores	11	10	10	10	9	9
Miscellaneous outlets	3	3	3	3	3	3
Auto dealerships	2	2	2	2	2	2
Chain stores, department stores*	17 }	21	21	22	23	24
Warehouse and discount clubs*	3 }					

Note: The types of channel outlets were similar in the rest of the world, although the percentages varied from country to country.
* In previous years, figures for these two categories were combined.
Source: *Modern Tire Dealer*, January 1987, p. 42.

Exhibit 7 ESTIMATED BRAND SHARES OF REPLACEMENT MARKET FOR PASSENGER CAR TIRES, UNITED STATES, 1986

Goodyear	15.5%	Montgomery Ward	1.5%
Firestone	9.0	Atlas	1.5
Michelin	8.5	Remington	1.5
Sears	8.0	Stratton	1.5
BF Goodrich	4.5	Hercules	1.5
Uniroyal	3.0	Western Auto	1.5
Multi-Mile	2.5	Monarch	1.5
Kelly-Springfield	2.5	K mart	1.0
Cooper	2.5	Centennial	1.0
Dunlop	2.5	Pirelli	1.0
General	2.5	EMPCO	1.0
Armstrong	2.0	Summit	1.0
Cordovan	2.0	Winston	1.0
Dayton	2.0	Regul	1.0
Jetzon-Laramie	2.0	Pep Boys	1.0
Bridgestone	2.0	Others	10.5

Source: *Modern Tire Dealer*, January 1987, p. 38.

most every buyer segment and end use. Thus, when vehicle owners went to a tire dealer to shop for replacement tires, they had a range of tread designs, tread widths, tread durabilities, performance characteristics, and price categories to choose from. Car and light truck owners were often confused by the host of choices they had; few buyers were really knowledgeable about tires. Many ended up choosing on the basis of price, while others followed the recommendation of the local dealer whom they regularly patronized. Tire dealers ran frequent price promotion ads in the local newspapers, making it easy for price-sensitive buyers to watch for sales and buy at off-list prices. However, it was hard for car owners to comparison shop on the basis of tire quality and tread durability because of the proliferation of brands, lines, grades, and performance features. Manufacturers had resisted the development of standardized specifications for replacement tires, and there was a general lack of common terminology in describing tire grades and construction features to the public.

Dealer Competition for Replacement Tire Buyers

In most communities the retail tire market was intensely competitive. Sellers advertised extensively in newspapers, on outdoor billboards, and occasionally on local TV to establish and maintain their market shares. Price was the dominant competitive variable. Many dealers featured and pushed private-label and off-brand tires because they carried higher margins than the name brands of the major manufacturers. Dealer-sponsored private-label tires accounted for 15 percent of total replacement tire sales in the United States in 1985. Surveys showed that dealers were able to influence a car owner's choice of replacement tires, both as to brand and type of tire, especially when prices were comparable. Most replacement tire buyers did not have strong tire brand preferences, making it fairly easy for tire salesmen to switch customers to tire brands and grades with the highest dealer margins. Normal dealer margins on replacement tires were in the 35 to 40 percent range, but many dealers shaved margins to win incremental sales.

Since the mid-1970s tire retailers' profit margins had been under competitive pressure. Profitability problems had been compounded by declining retail prices since 1980 (see Exhibit 8). To bolster profitability, dealers began to expand into auto repair services (engine tune-ups, shock absorber and muffler replacement, and brake repair), retreading, and automobile accessories. Some tire retailers were experimenting with becoming "total car care centers." Auto service work was very attractive because gross profit margins were well above the margins earned on replacement tire sales. A survey of the 25 largest U.S. dealers revealed significant changes in the revenue makeup of their businesses:

	Revenue distribution		
Product Lines	**1976**	**1981**	**1986**
Sales of new replacement tires	80%	49%	58%
Retread tire sales	10	19	12
Auto services	6	15	23
Other	4	16	7
	100%	100%	100%

Exhibit 8 MEDIAN RETAIL PRICES OF PASSENGER CAR TIRES IN THE U.S. MARKET, 1971–1986

	Median retail prices			
Year	**Bias-ply**	**Bias-belted**	**Radial**	**Overall**
1986	$35.00	$38.00	$53.80	$50.84
1985	36.63	39.95	54.60	51.81
1984	37.15	39.00	55.50	51.74
1983	39.93	43.66	60.00	55.03
1982	39.00	44.00	65.00	58.93
1981	37.95	44.41	72.13	59.50
1980				60.59
1979				54.05
1978				49.31
1977				45.13
1976				42.26
1975				40.95
1974				37.28
1973				34.22
1972				31.93
1971				31.34

Source: National Tire Dealers and Retreaders Association.

Several aggressive dealers were turning to the strategy of opening multiple locations, providing quick tire change turnaround, employing relatively heavy advertising, buying large quantities of tires from wholesale distributors at favorable prices, and using a high volume/low margin pricing strategy based on high inventory turnover, fuller utilization of facilities and tire-changing/mounting personnel, and related volume-based economies.

TYPES OF TIRES

In 1986 there were three basic tire construction types: bias-ply, bias-belted, and radial. Bias-ply tires were the cheapest to manufacture and utilized conventional tire-making technology that had been in place for several decades. In bias-ply tires the tire casing consisted of many thin sheets of rubberized fabric, called plies, which were alternately layered crisscross with their grains diagonal or on a bias. Except for retreads, bias-ply tires were the cheapest and lowest-grade replacement tires on the market. Bias-belted tires represented an improvement in bias-ply tire construction and offered better mileage, strength, and safety; they were produced with technology and equipment well known by all tire manufacturers. In bias-belted tires the casing was formed using thicker, diagonal layers of belted rubberized fabric plies, reinforced with steel in the case of steel-belted tires. In 1986 bias-belted tires were considered medium grade and were medium priced.

Radial tires were by far the hardest and most expensive to manufacture; as of 1986 only Michelin, Goodyear, the Japanese, and a few other tiremakers had mastered radial tire technology to the point where they could manufacture a radial tire of superior quality for larger size cars and trucks. All the remaining manufacturers were struggling to improve their radial tire-making skills in an effort to match the quality of the industry leaders. Just recently had Goodyear reached the point where its radial tire quality approached Michelin's—Michelin had pioneered radial tire technology, and its steel-belted radial tires were generally regarded by European and U.S. consumers as the best on the market.

Michelin's strength as a competitor stemmed from its development of radial tire technology. The company began marketing radial tires in 1948 and was the only European radial tire manufacturer until 1963. Radial tires were first marketed in Japan in the early 1950s. Radial tires became so popular in Europe and Japan that by the mid-1960s they were the dominant-selling tire. In 1972 Michelin became the first foreign manufacturer to build a tire plant in the U.S. market; it had sought to avoid locating a plant in the United States because of the higher wage rates, but European market saturation coupled with U.S. tariffs on tire imports made a U.S. plant location the most feasible way to penetrate the U.S. tire market. In its first year, Michelin sold 35 percent of all radials sold in the United States.

Michelin's dramatic success in steel-belted radial tires started a pronounced market trend away from bias tires during the 1960s in Europe and during the 1970s in the United States. Radial tires emerged as the fastest-growing segment of the industry. Radials appealed to consumers because of their improved safety and puncture resistance, better skid and traction performance, contribution to better gas mileage (due to less friction with road surfaces), and longer service life—a set of high-quality radials could last 40,000 to 60,000 miles, and even the 25,000 to 35,000 mileage life for lower grade radials represented a big improvement over the 10,000 to 20,000 mileage life of bias tires. Although more expensive than bias-ply and bias-belted tires (see Exhibit 8), radial tires still delivered substantially more miles of service per dollar of cost than conventional bias tires.

A conscious decision by U.S. tiremakers to go slow on radial tire manufacturing opened the door for foreign firms to enter American tire markets. U.S tiremakers saw the U.S. market eventually converting over to radials, but a number of obstacles turned them away from a strategy of promoting rapid conversion during the late 1960s and early 1970s. Use of radial tires as original equipment first required motor vehicle manufacturers to modify vehicle suspension systems at a small but not insignificant cost. Meanwhile tiremakers ran up against an array of quality-control problems and technical difficulties in making radials for large-sized American cars. Radial manufacturing required different-style production equipment; the cost of industrywide conversion to radial production in 1965 was estimated at over $700 million. In light of these barriers, U.S. tiremakers chose to introduce a bias-belted "transition" tire in the United States that allowed the industry to pursue a slower, phased-in conversion to radials that would be completed in the 1980s.

Demand for radials in the United States took off quicker than expected, however, and U.S. makers were caught with too much bias tire capacity, too little radial tire capacity, and radial tire production problems. All this coincided with the major European and Japanese markets for radials beginning to level off. Moreover, the earlier conversion to radials had forced Michelin and the Japanese producers to confront the technical difficulties of larger-sized radial tire construction sooner, providing them with a technological lead and a quality differential over U.S. producers. Despite a price disadvantage, foreign tiremakers—especially Michelin—made inroads into the U.S. market, then used this foothold to build their U.S. market shares steadily over the next decade. Until price competition intensified in the 1980s, Michelin sold its radials at a 30 percent premium over rival brands.

During the 1980s radial tires virtually took over the world tire market. By 1982 all new automobiles in the United States came with radial tires as standard equipment; and by 1986, 83 percent of the tires sold in the passenger tire replacement market were radials. Radial tire penetration of the replacement market was expected to expand further. The market swing to radial tires was the driving force behind the tire industry's overcapacity problems (nearly all of which involved bias tire production) and had prompted the tire manufacturers to make heavy investments in radial tiremaking.

High-Performance Tires

In 1980 Goodyear introduced high-performance radial tires and created one of the industry's fastest-growing segments. High-performance tires were of superior construction, providing more safety under a variety of hazardous road conditions, and were designed for sportier high-horsepower cars that had rack-and-pinion steering; they retailed for $30 to $40 per tire more than other premium-quality tires. By 1986 high-performance radials accounted for about 15 percent of the OE market and 15 to 20 percent of replacement purchases; industry estimates were that 25 percent of the new vehicles produced in 1987 would be equipped with high-performance radials. While other tiremakers had recently begun offering their versions of high-performance radials, Goodyear in 1986 was the clear leader with 90 percent of OE sales; Goodyear's share of replacement sales of high-performance radials was much smaller, however. The high-performance tire segment was the only piece of the tire market that was expected to grow over the 1987–1991 period; overall tire demand was expected to be flat at best, with good chances for a 1–2 percent decline.

All-Season Tires

Another popular category of tires in 1986 was referred to as the all-season tire. All-season tires were of radial construction and were designed to deliver superior traction in both rain and snow—a popular feature with drivers in the snow belt, many of whom were used to putting snow tires on their vehicles for the winter months. Sales of all-season passenger tires in the United States had grown from 1 million units in 1977 to 21.5 million units in 1982 to almost 70 million units in 1986. All-season tread designs were on about 47 percent of the replacement tires sold in the U.S. market in 1986 (versus 17 percent in 1982). Insofar as all-season tread designs were concerned, the makeup of the U.S. replacement market in 1986, including retreaded tires, was 73 million all-season tires, 13 million snow tires, and 75 million conventional tires.

Private-Label Tires

Private-label tires were usually manufactured to specifications below those carrying manufacturers' brands. The leading manufacturers made tires for private-labeling to utilize otherwise idle excess capacity; lesser-known manufacturers were often big private-label producers. Some private-label production was sold directly to major chain retailers; these were typically made to the retailer's own specifications and carried a private-label brand specified by the retailer. Other private-label brands were sold in mass quantities to wholesale distributors who, in turn, marketed them to retailers. The largest distributors of private-label tires contracted to purchase big enough volumes (sometimes as many as several million tires annually) to win a significant price break from manufacturers and passed through some of the savings to retailers. Private-label tires sold at a discount to name-brand tires and were mainly attractive to the most price-conscious buyers.

Truck Tires

Truck tires and tires for specialty vehicles (motor homes, boat trailers, motorcycles, tractors, farm implements, buses, and off-the-road construction vehicles) represented a relatively small portion of industry volume (under 15 percent) but accounted for over one fourth of industry revenues. The median price of truck tires in 1986 ranged from a low of $69 for a bias tire to a high of $533 for a steel-belted radial. Tires for tractors and for heavy-duty earthmoving equipment ranged in price from several hundred dollars to over $5,000 per tire. Tires for earthmoving equipment had large ribbed treads for added traction and often were 6 to 10 feet in diameter. Truck tire prices were falling as much as 5 percent annually in some categories. Only a limited number of tiremakers made tires for heavy trucks and other specialty vehicles. Goodyear produced tires for virtually every type of vehicle; in the United States and Europe Michelin dominated heavy-duty truck tire replacement with market shares in excess of 40 percent.

Retreaded Tires

Retreaded tires were made from tires with worn-out treads. New treads, suitable for retreading, could be obtained from tire manufacturers or from tread manufacturers who specialized in retreading. Retreading equipment was available from several suppliers, and a small retread shop could be set up by a local dealer for an investment of under $250,000. Most cities of 50,000 or more had at least one retread shop that served the local market for passenger car and light truck retreads in competition with retreads available from wholesalers and manufacturers. Tire retreading for heavy-duty trucks was usually done by a manufacturer of retreads rather than by a local retread shop; in the United States the leading maker of truck retreads was Bandag with a 70 percent market share. Virtually all retailers sold replacement tires at trade-in prices; those worn-out tires suitable for retreading were collected and sold to retreaders.

In 1986 the retreaded tire segment was small and on the decline, principally due to safety concerns. There were instances when the tread on a retreaded tire separated from the tire casing; the hazards of retreads increased with speed, heat, and rough road conditions. In 1986 U.S. truck retread sales were 20 million units, equal to $1.46 billion in sales revenues; the outlook for truck tire retreads was optimistic, with unit sales expected to be steady or even increase slightly. Radial truck tires were retreaded an average of three times, and truckers were retreading over 80 percent of their radial tires. The U.S. passenger car retread market was 18 million units, accounting for $431 million in sales; projections were that unit volume would decline steadily. Radials were 65 percent of the retread market, and the percentage was increasing. Retread buyers were very price conscious. The median price for passenger car retreads in 1986 was around $29, compared to a median price of $51 for new passenger car tires. Radial retreads were more expensive than bias tire retreads. Dealer margins or retreads were in the 40–45 percent range, compared to margins of 35 to 40 percent on new tires.

Tire-Grading Practices

An article in the April 1983 issue of *Consumer Reports* began with the observation:

There are few products more mystifying to buy than a tire for your car. How can you judge which tire will last longer? Are you really getting a better tire by paying a premium price?[1]

To help U.S. consumers answer such questions, in 1980 the National Highway Traffic Safety Administration (NHTSA) acting under a Congressional mandate instituted a comparative grading system for all tires sold in the United States; tiremakers were ordered to test their tires and report the grades assigned to them in three performance areas—traction, heat resistance, and tread life. The *Consumer Reports* article commented on the value of the grading system to consumers:

> Traction and heat resistance are important safety factors, but their labeling has not provided consumers with a meaningful way to choose among tires. For traction, almost all tires are rated either A or B, the two top grades. The difference between the two grades has little practical meaning. As for heat resistance, every tire sold in the U.S. must pass a Department of Transportation heat-resistance test, so even a tire carrying the lowest heat-resistance grade, a C, is safe.
>
> The tread-life factor, on the other hand, is an indicator of how long the tire will last before becoming hazardously bald. It thus has significant economic as well as safety relevance. The grade is represented by a number, each point of which represents 300 miles of life. Thus, a grade of 150 means a tread life of 45,000 miles under the ideal test-track conditions. (In real-world driving, you might achieve considerably less, depending on how you drive and on the materials used in your state's highways.)[2]

In February 1983 NHTSA suspended indefinitely the requirement for grading tires on the basis of tread wear, citing as its reason the statistical variability in tread-life test results and the potential for disseminating "potentially misleading information." Much of the statistical variability stemmed from giving tiremakers the latitude to set different confidence intervals in their testing procedures; inexactness in manufacturing resulted in not all samples of a particular tire performing the same in road-track tests. Some manufacturers assigned tread-wear grades based on a 95 percent confidence interval (95 percent of all tires sold would meet the assigned grade) whereas others adopted a more stringent 99 percent confidence interval in assigning grades.

Manufacturers were well aware that tread-life grading had begun to affect the purchases of replacement tire buyers. In fall 1982 Kelly-Springfield Tire Company, a subsidiary of Goodyear, made improvements in three lines of its tires that boosted tread-wear grades by 20 points (the equivalent of 6,000 extra miles under ideal test-track conditions) in order to make its tread-wear grades more competitive with those of rival tire makers. Uniroyal was advertising how well its tires had done in tread-wear life tests—several Uniroyal tires had graded between 170 and 240. Both Michelin and Goodyear vigorously opposed the tread-life grades. A Goodyear official said the standard served only to "confuse customers" and that

---

[1] "U.S. Punctures Tire Grading," *Consumer Reports*, April 1983, p. 166.

[2] Ibid.

it "led to misuse and misinterpretation." Michelin opposed tread-wear grading on grounds that it would trigger a "grading war" among tire manufacturers, arguing that "designing tires merely to achieve high tread-wear grades may result in tires of inferior quality because of the compromises that will have to be made in safety-related performance characteristics." At the time Michelin rated all its tires with a tread-wear grade of 140. As of 1986 the NHTSA had not reinstituted requirements for tread-wear grading, but some manufacturers were voluntarily making tread-wear tests and furnishing tread-wear grades to consumers.

Insofar as the world market was concerned, the recent improvements in tiremaking and tread life had been driven more by competitive pressures than by government regulations. Motor vehicle manufacturers in the United States and Europe had increased their demands on tiremakers for improved mileage and performance on OE tires (and at the same time they shopped hard on price). The battle for market share in the replacement tire market, given slack demand and an excess of tire-making capacity, was forcing rival tire manufacturers to attract replacement tire purchasers on the basis of quality and performance as well as on price.

MANUFACTURING

Tires consisted of four basic components: (1) the casing or carcass that formed the skeleton of the tire; (2) the tread—made of compounded rubber; (3) the sidewall, also made of compounded rubber, that sheathed the casing and protected it from damage; and (4) high-tensile steel bead wire that was formed into stiff loops and then embedded in parts of the sidewall and casing to give the tire added strength and to prevent the edges of the tire from stretching. Tire manufacturing was a three-stage process that included materials processing, fabrication of the component tire parts, and tire assembly.

Materials Processing

Over 200 different raw materials were used in manufacturing tires, the most important of which were natural rubber, synthetic rubber, fabric and fabric cord (nylon, rayon, polyester, and/or fiberglass), polyvinyl alcohol, sulfur, crude oil, carbon black, and high-carbon steel bead wire. Crude oil was the single largest raw material cost; about 10 gallons of crude oil were consumed in making an average-size passenger car radial tire. Raw material costs for a typical passenger car radial tire were about $16 in 1986, down about $2 from the previous year due to declining crude oil prices. Virtually all of the raw materials were commodities available in bulk form from a variety of sources. Several manufacturers had, however, in years past integrated backward into rubber plantations, rubber manufacturing, and tire textiles (fabrics used in tire-making) and supplied all or part of their production needs for these materials. The principal functions during materials processing involved cutting the rubber, mixing the needed rubber compounds and making sheet rubber, and putting adhesive on the cord and then heat-setting the fabric.

Fabrication of Components

During this phase several activities took place. The bead wire was rubber coated and formed into loops. Rolls of cord fabric were treated to facilitate bonding, then cut on an angle and spliced into a continuous sheet in preparation for making the casing. Some sheet rubber stock was milled to the desired width and thickness, forced through an extruder to form tread slabs of exact dimensions and design, cooled, and the "green" treads stored until time for assembly. Other sheet rubber stock was warmed and rolled into thin sheets. Sheeted gum stock, used for tubeless interliner and special reinforcement, was cut to various widths in readiness for tire assembly. Belts of fabric, or steel reinforced fabric, were rubber coated, cut into appropriate shapes, and then spliced into rolls.

Tire Assembly

This multistage process first involved assembling tire casing and sidewall components on a rotating collapsible drum called a building drum. At the next step several workers using a tire-building machine added belts and the tread to produce a green tire. Green tires were sprayed with mold-release lubricants, painted, inspected, and moved to the curing press. Tires assumed their final shape through the use of high pressure and high temperature in the molding press (referred to as the vulcanization process). Cured or vulcanized tires were next moved to the buffing and trimming areas where excess molding material was trimmed off and white raised letters or whitewall stripes buffed out. The completed tire was electronically tested, visually inspected, and stacked for shipment.

The materials processing and tire component fabrication stages were very similar for both bias-tire and radial-tire production, though there was more labor time involved for radials. The tire-building stage for radials required substantially more labor time than did bias production. A tire builder could only build 100 radials in the time required to build 150 bias-ply tires. In addition, quality control and inspection of radials was more labor-intensive than for bias-ply tires. It was not unusual for U.S. tiremakers to have the percentage of scrap or defective radial tires run two to three times higher than for conventional tire production.

Most of the tire plants operated by U.S. and European companies were laid out according to process, with each process having its own section of the plant and each separate activity having its own assigned area. The manufacturing flow was from materials processing to component fabrication to tire assembly with items stocked and stored at each end of the three processes as they awaited the next stage. There was considerable materials handling, and components could travel long distances between steps.

Japanese tire plants, in contrast, were organized with much more of an emphasis on integrating the process and creating a series of production lines, with each line doing some of its materials processing and all of its own component fabrication and tire assembly. Materials processing was centralized for those few functions where economies of scale were sizable and it was too expensive to have separate pieces of equipment for each workstation. The effect was to make the production process continuous within each workstation and to minimize materials handling and the distance traveled by each part. Such arrangements utilized one third less space, reduced changeover costs from tire model to tire model, and shortened the lead times for production scheduling from 12 weeks to 1 week. The Japanese arranged for just-in-time shipments of raw materials from suppliers to cut back sharply on storage space requirements for inventory as well as working capital for inventory stocks. They also worked closely with suppliers on raw materials specifications to eliminate the need for materials checking and testing when raw materials arrived. Insofar as possible, incoming raw materials were moved directly into the manufacturing flow and stocked at the workstation where they were needed.

Labor Costs

Although tire manufacturing was relatively capital-intensive (a new plant of minimum efficient size could cost as much as $150 million), there was significant labor content in the tire manufacturing process. Labor costs ran from a low of about 15 percent to a high of about 40 percent, depending on the wage rate and the efficiency of labor; the U.S. average was about 25 percent. Some parts of the radial tire manufacturing process required 25 percent more labor time than for bias tire assembly. In 1986 hourly wage and fringe benefit costs varied widely from country to country of manufacture:

Country	Average wage and fringe benefit costs per hour
United States (as per contracts with United Rubber Workers Union)	$20.00
Europe	15.00
Japan	15.00
Canada	15.00
Taiwan	3.00
Mexico	2.60
Korea	2.00
Brazil	1.80

Industry observers were predicting increased worldwide sourcing of tires from countries having the lowest labor costs, with Korea and Brazil becoming major players in the world market. Several major tire manufacturers were said to be considering plant locations in low-wage countries. Shipping costs for tires made in foreign countries and then marketed in the United States were approximately $1 per tire in 1986.

Virtually all of the manufacturers with tire plants in high-wage locations were working hard to reduce the labor-cost content of their tires to enable them to be more cost competitive with tires manufactured in low-wage locations. The average manufacturing costs of passenger car tires made in Korea and Brazil were estimated to be in the $20–$25 range in 1986; Japanese-made tires were thought to entail manufacturing costs for an average size tire in the $25–$30 range.

For the most part, the high-cost producers of tires in 1986 were U.S. manufacturers; their manufacturing costs averaged $32–$40 for passenger car radials. Uniroyal Goodrich and Firestone were reportedly the highest-cost producers; labor costs were an estimated 40 percent of total production costs at some Goodrich tire plants. The Korean producers were thought to be the overall low-cost leaders in 1986, but their tires did not carry the manufacturer's brand name, and Korean-made tires had not yet won buyer recognition for quality as had the tires of Michelin, Goodyear, several of the Japanese firms, and the other leading producers.

Efforts to reduce labor costs in the United States focused mainly on unionized plants and generally took the form of bargaining with the United Rubber Workers (URW) for wage concessions and for the elimination of costly work rules. Tiremakers' relations with the URW had historically been stormy; the URW over the years had won, sometimes only after long strikes, an excellent wage and fringe benefit package—one very comparable to what the United Automobile Workers union had negotiated with the major automakers. Each local union had also negotiated plant work rules that in many cases held down labor productivity. Labor militancy was a fact of life in unionized plants; grievance filings and arbitration of disputes were frequent occurrences.

By 1986 the pressure to reduce labor costs had built to the point where industrywide pattern bargaining had given way to bargaining on a plant-by-plant basis, even within the same company. "Distressed plants" often had special contract provisions that resulted in cost savings big enough to stave off a plant closedown. In a few cases companies thrust their plant managers into a survival-of-the-fittest contest to see who could achieve the biggest overall cost reductions (but with emphasis on winning the biggest labor cost concessions since these represented a major variable cost item); the winner's plant was kept open, and the loser's was either closed or scheduled for layoffs and production scale-downs. There were many instances where tire production had been shifted from unionized plants with high labor costs to nonunion plants with lower labor costs. Eight of the nine tire plants built in the United States since 1970 were nonunion and had been located in states and communities where the threat of union organization was weak. All U.S. tire plants closed since 1970 had been unionized plants. None of the U.S. tire plants of foreign manufacturers were unionized. Exhibit 9 shows the U.S. plants of the various tiremakers, their unionized status, and their tire-making capacities.

COST-CUTTING EFFORTS

Falling tire prices, mature demand conditions, and overcapacity conditions industrywide during the 1980s had given a clear competitive edge to the low-cost tiremakers. Manufacturers, especially those with the highest production costs, were scrambling hard to cut costs across-the-board and to eliminate inefficient production. No part of the cost structure was being ignored. Efforts were underway to try to automate more of the radial tire-building process, particularly those activities with high-labor content. Most manufacturers were investing heavily in new equipment to boost productivity levels; aging equipment was being scheduled

Exhibit 9 ESTIMATED PRODUCTION CAPABILITIES OF U.S. TIRE PLANTS AS OF JANUARY 1, 1987 (in thousands)

Company	Location	Unionized		Passenger tires per day	All other tires per day	Total tires per day
Armstrong	Des Moines, Iowa	Yes		7.0	7.6	14.6
	Hanford, California	Yes		10.0	1.9	11.9
	Natchez, Mississippi[a]	Yes		6.0	3.1	9.1
	Nashville, Tennessee	Yes		13.0	0.0	13.0
			Total	36.0	12.6	48.6
Bridgestone	LaVergne, Tennessee	Yes		—	3.5	3.5
Cooper	Findlay, Ohio	Yes		11.4	6.0	17.4
	Texarkana, Arkansas	Yes		21.3	4.6	25.9
	Tupelo, Mississippi	Yes		9.8	—	9.8
			Total	42.5	10.6	53.1
Denman	Warren, Ohio	Yes		0.4	2.5	2.9
Dunlop	Buffalo, New York	Yes		5.0	7.0	12.0
	Huntsville, Alabama	Yes		23.0	—	23.0
			Total	28.0	7.0	35.0
Firestone	Bloomington, Illinois*	Yes		—	0.1	0.1
	Decatur, Illinois	Yes		20.0	5.5	25.5
	Des Moines, Iowa*	Yes		6.0	3.0	9.0
	Wilson, North Carolina	No		20.0	—	20.0
	Oklahoma City, Oklahoma*	Yes		24.0	3.8	27.8
			Total	70.0	12.4	82.4
General	Bryan, Ohio	Yes		—	0.1	0.1
	Charlotte, North Carolina	Yes		18.5	—	18.5
	Mayfield, Kentucky	Yes		29.0	7.2	36.2
	Waco, Texas[b]	Yes		3.0	—	3.0
	Mt. Vernon, Illinois	No		15.0	2.7	17.7
			Total	65.5	10.0	75.5
Goodyear	Danville, Virginia	Yes		—	10.6	10.6
	Gadsden, Alabama	Yes		48.0	13.1	61.1
	Topeka, Kansas	Yes		—	5.5	5.5
	Union City, Tennessee	Yes		44.0	—	44.0
	Lawton, Oklahoma	No		40.0	—	40.0
			Subtotal	132.0	29.2	161.2
Kelly-Springfield (a Goodyear subsidiary)	Cumberland, Maryland[c]	Yes		8.0	3.0	11.0
	Freeport, Illinois	Yes		2.0	17.0	19.0
	Tyler, Texas	Yes		25.0	—	25.0
	Fayetteville, North Carolina	Yes		40.0	8.0	48.0
			Subtotal	75.0	28.0	103.0
			Goodyear total	207.0	57.2	264.2
McCreary	Indiana, Pennsylvania	Yes		.3	2.7	3.0
Michelin	Greenville, South Carolina	No		23.0	—	23.0
	Spartanburg, South Carolina	No		—	4.5	4.5
	Dothan, Alabama	No		—	4.0	4.0
	Lexington, South Carolina	No		12.0	—	12.0
			Total	35.0	8.5	43.5
Mohawk	Salem, Virginia	Yes		12.5	0.5	13.0
Uniroyal Goodrich	Tuscaloosa, Alabama	Yes		32.5	1.5	34.0
	Eau Clair, Wisconsin	Yes		22.8	4.0	26.8
	Ft. Wayne, Indiana	Yes		18.5	11.5	30.0
	Opelika, Alabama	Yes		22.0	4.0	26.0
	Ardmore, Oklahoma	No		33.0	—	33.0
			Total	128.8	21.0	149.8
Grand total				626.0	148.5	774.5

[a] Armstrong to dispose of plant this year, possibly by selling it to investment group. [b] Plant to close this spring. [c] Plant to close about mid-year. * Plants placed on "distressed" list by Firestone and in danger of cutbacks or closing.
Source: *Modern Tire Dealer*, January 1987, pp. 44–45.

for earlier than usual replacement; and in some plants the layouts of production activities were being reconfigured to achieve a more economical manufacturing flow. The costs of plant renovation efforts commonly ran into the tens of millions of dollars per plant, particularly in the case of plants more than 10 years old. Companies were also spending heavily to convert production lines from bias tire production to radial tire production and, at the same time, to improve their radial tire-making practices. Radial tire quality was a big factor with both OE and replacement buyers since the worst-made radial tires provided a harder and bumpier ride, tended to wear unevenly, got out of balance easier, sometimes did not maintain the proper inflation and tire pressure for long periods, and consequently, had a shorter tread life—characteristics that created owner dissatisfaction and complaints. Virtually all of the radial tire manufacturers were under competitive pressure to improve the performance of their radial tires at the same time they were struggling to reduce production costs.

The closing of nearly 30 tire plants in North America since 1975 had eliminated about 23 percent of North American tire-making capacity; most of these plants were outmoded facilities that made bias-ply and bias-belted tires. Still it was estimated that bias-ply tire excess capacity was about 10 million tires annually and there was an estimated 23 million units of excess radial tire capacity. Total U.S. tire-making capacity had fallen from a high of just over 1 million tires per day in 1975 to a 20-year low of 775,000 per day in 1986—see Exhibit 9; over 81 percent of this capacity was in passenger car tires. There were only 9 U.S. tiremakers in business in 1986, down from 14 in 1965, 23 in 1945, and 178 in 1921.

COMPETITION AMONG THE TIRE MANUFACTURERS

In 1986 competition in tires centered around the variables of price and tire performance. The retail prices of tires of all types were trending downward (see Exhibit 8 for the price trends in the United States). Overall tire quality and tire performance was on the upswing. Increased tread life on OE and replacement tires threatened to cut deeply into the number of sets of replacement tires needed per vehicle in service. Moreover, competition among the tiremakers was increasingly global in nature.

In the U.S. market, imports of foreign-made tires were on the rise (see Exhibit 10). In 1986, 28 percent of all the new passenger cars sold in the United States were foreign imports; virtually all came equipped with foreign-made tires. Bridgestone and Michelin were the leading foreign manufacturers—many European car imports came equipped with Michelin or Pirelli tires, and most Japanese car imports were equipped with Bridgestone tires.

Bridgestone had recently begun manufacturing truck tires in the United States, acquiring a truck tire plant from Firestone in 1984, and was expected to build a passenger car tire plant as soon as its replacement tire volume rose from its present 2 million level to 4 million. Bridgestone was working hard to expand its network of retail dealers to provide better access to replacement tire buyers.

Michelin had built a nationwide network of U.S. dealers years earlier and was represented by dealers in all cities and most towns—a substantial number of dealers carried the Michelin brand as their primary line. The Michelin name was

Exhibit 10 TIRE IMPORTS INTO THE UNITED STATES, BY COUNTRY OF ORIGIN, 1982–1985 (in millions)

Year	Country of origin	Passenger tires		Truck tires	
		Total imports	Percent of total	Total imports	Percent of total
1985	Japan	8.0	24.5%	2.5	32.1%
	Canada	7.6	23.1	1.7	21.7
	Korea	4.0	12.4	1.5	19.2
	All others	13.1	39.9	2.1	27.0
	Total	32.7	99.9%	7.8	100.0%
1984	Canada	7.4	24.5%	2.1	31.8%
	Japan	6.4	21.4	1.8	27.3
	Korea	4.2	13.9	0.8	12.1
	All others	12.1	40.2	1.9	28.8
	Total	30.1	100.0%	6.6	100.0%
1983	Canada	6.2	26.7%	1.8	40.0%
	Japan	4.5	19.4	1.0	22.2
	Korea	3.5	15.2	0.6	13.3
	All others	8.9	38.7	1.1	24.4
	Total	23.1	100.0%	4.5	99.9%
1982	Canada	6.3	37.5%	1.7	44.7%
	Japan	2.9	17.3	0.7	18.4
	France	1.6	9.5	0.6	15.8
	All others	6.0	35.7	0.8	21.1
	Total	16.8	100.0%	3.8	100.0%

Notes: 1. In each year 90 percent or more of the passenger tire imports were radial tires.
2. Approximately 60 percent of the truck tire imports were radials.
3. Imports as a percent of the U.S. tire market were: 1975— 7.6%
                1982—12.8%
                1985—23.2%
                1986—23.8% (estimated).

Source: Rubber Manufacturers Association.

well known and widely advertised in both the United States and Europe. Michelin's market share in replacement tires was much lower than for OE tires because of its premium pricing strategy. The top-dollar prices charged by Michelin dealers scared off some would-be buyers and usually resulted in the dealer switching the buyer over to another brand in the store, often a brand carrying as big or bigger dealer percentage margin as the Michelin brand. The name-brand replacement tires of the leading U.S. manufacturers typically carried lower dealer margins than most Asian and European brands.

Michelin, Bridgestone, Sumitomo, Yokohama, and the Korean tire producers were all trying to increase their shares of the U.S. market. Recent declines in the value of the dollar against the Japanese yen were said to be forcing the Japanese to consider acquiring or building tire plants in the United States to support their increasing U.S. sales. The Japanese and Korean tiremakers dominated the tire market in countries in the Pacific and Southeast Asia, except for New Zealand and Australia; Goodyear and Firestone both had a strong presence in New Zealand and Australia.

Japanese efforts to penetrate the European market had not met with as much success as in the United States. Japanese cars accounted for between 10 and 12 percent of new car sales in Europe and for just under 10 percent of total car registrations, making it harder for the Japanese tiremakers to enter the replacement tire segment just on the basis of selling Japanese-made replacement tires for Japanese-made cars. In terms of overall new car-truck production in Europe, U.S. manufacturers (Ford and GM) had about a 20 percent market share, the Japanese about a 11 percent share, and the European manufacturers a 69 percent share. In Europe the market leaders in tires were Michelin, Goodyear, Continental, Pirelli, and Dunlop (a British brand tire that had recently been acquired by Sumitomo). Sumitomo's acquisition of Dunlop's troubled and unprofitable European operations was seen as a signal of Japanese intent to use the well-known Dunlop brand name to increase their penetration of the European tire market. Distribution channels for replacement tires in Europe functioned in much the same manner as in the United States, with the competitive focus on price, performance, and strong dealer networks.

RESTRUCTURING AND DIVERSIFICATION

Fierce competition and declining profit prospects in tires had prompted the leading U.S. tire manufacturers to take a hard look at their dependence on tires and to consider just what their future course should be. Goodyear, Firestone, Goodrich, General Tire, and Uniroyal all concluded during the 1970s that maturity in tires called for diversification into other businesses to open up new avenues for growth and profitability. Each began to make acquisitions. By the early 1980s their business portfolios included investments in plastics, aerospace, flooring, footwear, rubberized roofing, petroleum production and transportation, chemicals, packaging film, and a variety of industrial products. By late 1986, however, most U.S. tire manufacturers were retreating from their forays into diversification and were in a restructuring/retrenchment mode in an effort to improve their corporate profitability as well as their position in tires. In many instances diversification had not proved to be as profitable as the tire business. GenCorp, Inc. (the parent of General Tire) had announced the sale of certain of its television stations, the closing of a bias-ply tire plant, and a significant stock repurchase program. Firestone's diversified businesses, which accounted for 25 percent of sales in 1979, made up less than 5 percent by year-end 1986; businesses that were divested included plastic resins, beer kegs, automotive seat belts, polyurethane foam, and wheels for trucks, tractors, and construction machinery. Uniroyal had divested all of its nontire operations and then merged its tire business with the tire division of B. F. Goodrich to form Uniroyal Goodrich Tire Company, a venture that was owned 50–50 by Uniroyal Holding Co. and B. F. Goodrich.

PROFILES OF THE LEADING COMPETITORS

In 1986 all of the world's leading tiremakers were trying to strengthen their market positions and achieve low enough manufacturing costs to meet increased price competition. Exhibit 11 provides comparative financial data for the major competitors. Profiles for the various tire companies follow.

Exhibit 11   COMPARATIVE STATISTICS ON THE 10 LARGEST TIRE MANUFACTURERS, 1984–1986 (dollars in millions)

Company	Year	Sales	Net income (loss)	Assets	Stockholders' equity	Number of employees
Goodyear	1984	$10,241	$411.0	$6,194	$3,171	133,271
	1985	9,897	412.4	6,954	3,507	134,115
	1986	10,328	124.1	8,610	3,003	121,586
Michelin	1984	5,076	(256.5)	6,111	801	120,000
	1985	5,191	110.1	7,041	968	120,000
	1986	6,689	274.6	8,132	1,501	119,300
Bridgestone	1984	3,375	65.1	2,849	1,030	32,577
	1985	3,624	87.6	3,781	1,387	32,834
	1986	4,705	123.5	4,763	1,962	33,425
Uniroyal Goodrich	1984	5,626*	137.7*	4,075*	1,809*	48,770*
	1985	5,366*	(320.6)*	3,812*	782*	45,191*
	1986	Comparable data for 1986 is not available.				
Firestone	1984	4,161	102.0	2,571	1,236	59,900
	1985	3,836	3.0	2,528	1,163	54,700
	1986	3,712	85.0	2,593	1,167	55,000
Pirelli	1984	3,498	72.2	3,639	n.a.	62,000
	1985	3,650	101.0	3,200	1,500	61,500
	1986	4,714	127.0	4,880	1,736	68,000
Continental	1984	1,241	14.4	623	162	26,401
	1985	1,699	26.2	1,159	229	31,673
	1986	2,288	52.6	1,643	378	32,012
GenCorp (General Tire)	1984	2,727	7.2	2,037	910	27,800
	1985	3,021	75.2	2,073	951	27,000
	1986	3,099	130.0	2,119	1,048	26,700
Sumitomo	1984	978	7.0	815	66	6,900
	1985	975	8.6	1,052	89	6,900
	1986	1,325	17.1	1,683	128	10,000
Yokohama	1984	1,180	4.2	961	77	10,675
	1985	1,264	17.9	1,319	119	10,775
	1986	1,677	12.6	1,715	166	10,814

* In 1986 Uniroyal and B. F. Goodrich merged the tire business parts of their two companies. The figures shown for 1984 and 1985 represent the combined performances of Uniroyal, Inc., and B. F. Goodrich, Inc.
Sources: Compiled by the case researchers from *Fortune,* various issues, and company annual reports.

Goodyear Tire & Rubber Company

Goodyear's principal business was the development, manufacture, distribution, and sale of tires throughout the world. Tires and tubes represented 61 percent of Goodyear's corporate sales of $10.3 billion in 1986; other products and businesses included an oil and gas production and pipeline subsidiary and the manufacture of nontire automotive products, synthetic rubber, chemicals, and high-technology items for aerospace, defense, and other applications. Goodyear was both the world's largest tire producer and the world's largest rubber manufacturer and had held this ranking since the 1920s. The company operated 5 U.S. tire plants (see Exhibit 9) and 5 foreign tire plants (Sweden, Australia, Brazil, Argentina, and

Chile) as well as operating 7 rubber plantations and 30 domestic and foreign tire-related subsidiaries. In addition to Goodyear tires, the company owned Kelly-Springfield Tire Company and Lee Tire and Rubber Company; both Kelly-Springfield and Lee made private-label tires in addition to their own branded tires. Goodyear/Kelly-Springfield in 1986 had about one third of the tire-making capacity in the United States and about one fourth of the world's tire-making capacity. Foreign sales accounted for about 36 percent of revenues and 56 percent of earnings.

During the 1980s Goodyear had made significant strides in reducing the labor content in its tire operations. Its Goodyear tire plant in Lawton, Oklahoma, and Kelly-Springfield tire plant in Tyler, Texas, were state-of-the-art operations and were very cost competitive; the Lawton plant was nonunion. In January 1986 Goodyear acquired worldwide rights for a new tire-making technology that integrated tire-making into a single continuous process and had the potential to cut manufacturing costs by 15 to 25 percent. Goodyear was endeavoring to accelerate development of the process and bring it to the point of being ready for commercialization; some Goodyear officials believed the process could be in place in some of its tire plants by 1990 or shortly thereafter. In addition, Goodyear was aggressively pursuing cost-reduction programs at all of its tire plants—major modernization projects were underway at its Lincoln, Nebraska, and Mount Pleasant, Iowa, plants. On the average, Goodyear's production costs for tires were near the middle of the range between high and low worldwide. Goodyear's goal was to become a low-cost producer. Goodyear's corporatewide budget for R&D was in the $250 million–$300 million range. Its reputation for tire quality was good to excellent, generally in the top three with Michelin and Bridgestone—although during 1985 and 1986 the quality differentials in tires had narrowed significantly. In the United States Goodyear was the clear leader in high-performance radial tires, with an 80 percent-plus market share in 1986; the expected tread-wear life of high-performance radials was significantly shorter than for standard radials.

Goodyear was active in purchasing multi-outlet retailers, and its sales force was striving to convert independent tire dealers over to the Goodyear brand and, to a lesser extent, to win new accounts for Kelly-Springfield and Lee tires. Goodyear's strategy in acquiring large-volume independent dealers who typically carried three or four brands was to increase the share of Goodyear tires being sold in these outlets; over 275 retail dealer outlets had been acquired in the past two years. Goodyear saw the replacement market as holding the biggest potential for increasing its market share. Goodyear's share of the U.S. replacement market was only 15.5 percent, well below its 33 percent share of the U.S. OE segment. The company in 1986 had a $150 million advertising budget and was among the top 50 leading national advertisers. It had had a high profile in auto racing for over 20 years in an effort to stress the high-performance capabilities of its tires.

Within the past year Goodyear had purchased Long Mile Rubber, a tread rubber producer, and AMF Tire Equipment in moves to increases its share of the truck retreading business. Outside of tires, the Celeron division was the only one of Goodyear's diversification moves that was currently soaking up much capital investment and top management attention. Celeron was rapidly increasing its crude oil production capabilities and was completing a $1 billion, 1,750-mile California-to-Texas pipeline. The Celeron project was expected to have a big impact on corporate earnings—up or down, depending on its success and on crude oil prices. In comparison with other tire and rubber companies, Goodyear had over the past 10 years showed a bigger earnings boost for the capital expenditures the company had invested than any other tiremaker.

Michelin

Michelin was a French company with about $6.7 billion in worldwide tire sales in 1986. Michelin's worldwide market share was strongly upbeat, and the company was close to challenging Goodyear as the industry leader. The company operated tire plants on six continents. Michelin was strongest in Europe (it was the market-share leader) and in the United States (where its overall market share was about 10 percent—behind Goodyear, Uniroyal Goodrich, and Firestone). Michelin's market share in heavy-duty truck tires was much bigger than its share of the passenger tire market. In the United States Michelin had four tire plants, all nonunion, representing about 6 percent of the passenger tire-making capacity and 5 percent of all other tire-making capacity. Substantial numbers of Michelin tires were imported into the United States from Michelin's Canadian tire plant.

Michelin was the acknowledged leader in radial-tire technology, and its reputation for radial-tire quality was the best in the industry. The company was extremely secretive about its tire-making practices, but its plants were reputed to be among the most highly automated in the industry. Michelin tires were generally premium priced and appealed mainly to quality-sensitive buyers who drove relatively expensive cars. Truck owners were attracted to Michelin-brand tires because of their perceived tread wear and longer life cycle (in terms of being retreadable). Michelin drummed the theme to OE and replacement tire buyers that its tires deserved a price premium because they were unmatched in terms of quality and performance.

Michelin was the second-largest supplier of private-label tires to Sears, behind Armstrong Tire and Rubber. Michelin's market share in the United States was viewed as having plateaued. The company's U.S. tire operation essentially broke even in 1985 and was estimated to earn 1986 profits of about $20 million. Michelin was pushing aggressively to capture a bigger share of the high-performance radial-tire market from Goodyear; its strategy was to position the company to be a major player in the high-performance segment worldwide. Michelin was second to Pirelli in the high-performance segment in Europe. Even though Michelin's U.S. plants were relatively new and nonunion, its tire production costs were relatively high, forcing it into the premium-quality, premium-price niche. Michelin's Canadian plant was its lowest cost North American plant. Industry observers expected that Michelin would soon expand its U.S. tire-making capacity. Michelin had excess capacity in its European tire plants.

Bridgestone Tire

Bridgestone was the Goodyear of Japan, with a dominant 50 percent share of the Japanese passenger tire market and strength in truck tires as well. It was the third-largest producer worldwide, and it was the most profitable of the four leading Japanese tiremakers. Bridgestone had become the dominant Japanese producer following World War II using technology licensed from Goodyear. The company had made substantial technology investments of its own in recent years and was an accomplished manufacturer of radial tires.

One of Bridgestone's current strategic thrusts was to increase its share of the U.S. replacement market. Efforts were underway to expand the number of independent tire dealers handling Bridgestone tires and to use advertising to establish the Bridgestone name. Bridgestone's replacement sales for passenger tires in the United States in 1986 were an estimated 2 million units. Bridgestone was said to have a short-term goal of selling 4 million units in the United States, at which time it was expected to either build a passenger tire plant (probably near Nashville, Tennessee) or acquire a plant from another manufacturer. Bridgestone had recently acquired a small truck tire plant located near Nashville from Firestone; production from this plant was supporting Bridgestone's market-share penetration of the truck tire segment. So far, Bridgestone was not a big factor in the European market, though its European sales were growing along with the sales of Japanese cars in Europe. Bridgestone's areas of greatest market strength outside Japan and the United States were mainly in Asia, the Pacific, and South America, where Japanese cars and trucks were being heavily marketed. The company had strong momentum, was spending heavily on innovation and improved facilities, and was viewed as the only company in the industry capable of challenging Goodyear and Michelin on a global scale.

Uniroyal Goodrich Tire Company

This company was the product of a 1986 merger of the tire businesses of Uniroyal, Inc., and B. F. Goodrich, Inc., and was a 50-50 joint venture of the two parent companies. Uniroyal's strength was as an OE supplier, primarily to General Motors and, to a much lesser extent, to Ford. Goodrich tires were marketed only in the replacement segment; the company had withdrawn from the OE segment in 1981. The product line consisted mainly of passenger tires and light truck tires. Geographically, sales were heavily concentrated in the United States; Uniroyal had recently sold all of its European operations to Continental, the leading West German manufacturer and a major competitor in the European market. Uniroyal Goodrich was a relatively high-cost producer and was striving hard to cut labor costs. Just prior to their merger, both Uniroyal and Goodrich had divested their company-owned retail tire stores. In 1986 about one third of the company's tire production was for original equipment, one third was for replacement tires sold under the Uniroyal and Goodrich brands, and one third was for the private-label market. Uniroyal Goodrich was said to be on the verge of developing a new tire-building machine that had the potential to cut its labor costs by $2 to $4 per tire. Management had not yet announced how far it would go in trying to consolidate and integrate the operations of the newly merged companies.

Firestone Tire & Rubber Company

Firestone, under the leadership of a new chief executive officer, had just completed a restructuring program in which most nontire businesses had been sold. High priority was being placed on strengthening Firestone's position in tires—tires and related products accounted for 95 percent of revenue. Firestone's most successful nontire business was in rubberized roofing where it was a close second to the market-share leader. As of 1986 the company operated five U.S. tire plants; one of these was nonunion, and three of the remaining four plants were on its "distressed plants" list and in danger of cutbacks or being closed. Firestone had foreign tire and related products facilities in Argentina, Brazil, Canada, France, Italy, Portugal, Spain, Venezuela, and New Zealand and had minority interests in tire operations in Mexico, South Africa, Thailand, Kenya, and the Philippines; the plant in Spain was the largest of Firestone's foreign operations. Additionally, Firestone owned a rubber plantation in Liberia and manufactured a major part of its requirements for synthetic rubber, rayon polyester, and nylon cord. The company produced and marketed a broad line of tires for automobiles, trucks, trailers, buses, construction vehicles, agricultural machinery, off-the-road vehicles, and other vehicles for both the OE and replacement markets. Besides Firestone brand tires, the company marketed tires under the Dayton and Road King names. The company promoted itself as a full-line, full-service supplier.

In 1983 Firestone acquired J. C. Penney automotive centers. As of 1986 Firestone owned and operated approximately 1,500 retail automotive centers that offered a wide range of maintenance and repair services under the "MasterCare by Firestone" program and that doubled as retail tire outlets. Firestone tires were also sold through independent dealers and some service stations. The company had just entered the high-performance segment with its Firehawk Performance Tire. Firestone was weak in medium and heavy truck tires, having sold both its truck tire plant to Bridgestone and its retread truck tire centers. Several years previously, Firestone had encountered major quality problems with its Firestone 500 radial tire, damaging its quality image severely. The company was in the middle of the pack relative to competitors on manufacturing costs, and its tires were perceived as being of average quality.

According to one Wall Street investment analyst:

> To invest in Firestone, one has to believe that the company will succeed in its venture to increase the penetration and the profitability of its automotive service operation, which it calls its MasterCare business. Firestone is trying to change the profile of its former tire stores to be more automotive repair oriented. That's a tough business to make money in, characterized by extremely intense competition. A key question will be, can Firestone become what amounts to the

McDonald's or the franchise leader of the fragmented automotive repair marketplace.[3]

Pirelli

Pirelli was seen as astute at picking good niches to concentrate on. Pirelli had beat out Michelin for the leadership position in the European high-performance tire segment. Substantial numbers of European sports cars came equipped with Pirelli tires made at its Italian plants. About 80 percent of the tires sold by Pirelli in the United States were imported from its Brazilian plant. Pirelli was said to be interested in boosting its share of the U.S. replacement market.

Continental Gummi-Werke

Continental was Germany's largest tire producer and the number two company, behind Michelin, in Europe. Worldwide, Continental was the fourth-largest manufacturer of radial truck tires and the fifth-largest maker of radial passenger tires. Overall, it was the world's sixth-largest producer. Continental supplied OE tires to Mercedes-Benz, BMW, Volvo, Audi, and Volkswagen. Continental was committed to product development and research. Its tires were viewed as premium quality, and it offered independent tire dealers attractive profit margins. Continental's production facilities were concentrated in Europe.

Sumitomo

Sumitomo was the third-largest Japanese tiremaker. Following World War II Sumitomo had acquired tire-making technology under an ongoing licensing agreement with Uniroyal. Sumitomo had recently acquired the British and European tire business of Dunlop Tire, making it the first Japanese producer to establish a major European base. In 1983 Dunlop had $1.4 billion in tire sales (including its U.S. operations) and a 5 percent global market share. Sumitomo was viewed as a likely purchaser of Dunlop's two U.S. tire operations in Buffalo, New York, and Huntsville, Alabama; in the United States Dunlop supplied some OE tires and had a 2.5 percent share of the replacement market.

Sumitomo was trying to increase its U.S. share in replacement tires. It sold replacement tires through wholesale distributors in the United States, who in turn marketed them to independent tire dealers as a second or third line. In 1986 Sumitomo radials retailed for a price virtually equal to name-brand U.S. radials but cost the dealer $5 to $15 less per tire, depending on size. Sumitomo provided buyers of its replacement tires with a written 40,000-mile guarantee, something very few other tiremakers were willing to do.

---

[3] As quoted in *The Wall Street Transcript*, October 6, 1986, pp. 83, 317.

Yokohama Tire Corporation

Yokohama was the second largest tire company in Japan and the 10th largest in the world. Years ago, Yokohama had entered into a technology licensing agreement with B. F. Goodrich; in exchange for its technology BFG received a minority ownership position in Yokohama Tire. Yokohama's strategic objectives were to double its share of the U.S. market and to become the world's fifth-largest manufacturer. Yokohama was concentrating its efforts on advanced designs, better engineering, and innovation. It had just introduced a new style asymmetrical tire for the high performance tire segment, and it offered truck tires that delivered proven fuel savings, retreadability, and long tread life.

In the United States, Yokohama was one of the suppliers of tires to the newly emerging "price clubs" and "warehouse clubs" retail outlets. These outlets were estimated to sell about 4 million passenger tires in 1986 (about 3 percent of the replacement market). Observers were predicting fast growth for price clubs and warehouse clubs, mainly at the expense of mass-merchandise chains. The clubs sold Michelin tires, Yokohama tires, Armstrong tires, and several other brands.

Korean Tire Producers

The leading Korean tire manufacturer was Kumho (selling under the Trisun brand); Kumho had one of the world's 10 largest tire manufacturing plants, and it was outfitted with the most advanced equipment and systems available. Kumho supplied over 100 countries with a full line of bias and steel radial tires for everything from small passenger cars to off-the-road earthmoving equipment. The company was diversified into petrochemicals, rubber, electrical products, lubricants, and finance.

There were several other Korean tire manufacturers, all of whom had built capacity aggressively on the expectation that the Korean car export business would grow rapidly. However, U.S. sales of the Hyundai (the leading Korean car), Daewoo's joint venture with General Motors, and Kia's relationship with Ford had not as yet produced a boom in Korean car exports to the United States. The Korean tire producers had excess capacity in 1986 and were using their low-cost producer position to gain volume on the basis of the low prices at which they were willing to supply wholesale distributors and dealers.

THE FUTURE OUTLOOK

Most observers saw the world tire industry as having more negative than positive forces on the horizon. As one person expressed it:

> On the whole it is a stale industry with substandard returns. It is a battlefield of attrition.
> The surprises in this industry are mostly on the negative side. Goodyear, Michelin, and Bridgestone from time to time sort of tantalize you with saying that a new technological revolution might be in the wings. We certainly have within the

industry the possibility of a tire which would last as long as the car itself. Of course, that is the kiss of death of the industry. Contrary to technological evolution in the computer industry, where the price elasticity generally leads to an even higher demand by the market, in the tire industry, technological revolution works against the innovators. In essence, if you are delivering more miles per tire without a commensurate increase in tire demand, whoever initiates that revolution initially will gain market share over the remainder of the pack. But I suspect that there are several companies who could quickly follow suit.[4]

Another analyst predicted that not all the current companies would survive:

I believe that you'll see Goodyear, Michelin, and Bridgestone increase their domination of the worldwide tire markets by improving their respective domestic market shares in the United States, Europe, and Japan. These market-share gains will result from successfully competing against the smaller tire manufacturers on a tire versus tire basis rather than on a consumer brand-name perception basis. Such an approach will enable them to showcase their technological superiority, rather than just showcase their names. You'll still see the "second tier" tire manufacturers remaining competitive in certain market segments simply because allowing their tire operations to deteriorate would be economically unjustifiable to them.[5]

---

[4] Ibid., pp. 83, 319.

[5] *The Wall Street Transcript,* November 19, 1984, pp. 75, 941.

UNIROYAL GOODRICH TIRE COMPANY*

On August 1, 1986, Uniroyal, Inc., and the B. F. Goodrich Company formed a joint venture to merge their worldwide tire businesses. The new company, called Uniroyal Goodrich Tire Company (UGTC), was a New York general partnership equally owned by the two parents, Uniroyal, Inc., and the B. F. Goodrich Company. With expected sales of $2 billion annually, the joint venture was expected to jump ahead of Firestone into second place in the North American market, behind the industry leader Goodyear. UGTC, with nine tire plants in the United States, Canada, and Mexico, planned to manufacture and sell automobile and light truck tires in North America.

Prior to the merger, both parents were considered as candidates for abandoning the tire business due to stagnant tire sales, the 25 percent (and still rising) share of the U.S. replacement market held by foreign imports, industry overcapacity (despite 29 plant closings from 1975 to 1985), and their own weak profit prospects and competitive positions. Uniroyal went private in a leveraged buyout in 1985 and had put all its businesses up for sale, including its tire business, to pay off the $1 billion debt incurred in the buyout. Goodrich had recently closed two of its plants, sold or closed all of its company-owned retail tire stores in 1985, and tried unsuccessfully to sell its remaining tire operations. The company's tire operations were saddled with a $240 million unfunded pension liability that it could not walk away from. Goodrich Chairman John D. Ong said, "We saw an inevitable contraction of the tire industry. Only really large competitors . . . would be survivors."

The formation of UGTC represented an effort to combine the strengths of both tire operations in their respective niches. Commenting on the merger, Uniroyal's Chairman Joseph P. Flannery said, "The proven strengths of Uniroyal in the original equipment market, combined with B. F. Goodrich's excellent replacement tire capabilities, make for a perfect fit, creating a new well-balanced company with an excellent future." Ong added, "This sort of combination is a strategic necessity. We are convinced that efficient, high-volume operations can make money in the face of imports and other obstacles."

UGTC was headed by executives from both Uniroyal and Goodrich. Patrick C. Ross, president and chief operating officer of Goodrich prior to the merger, became chairman and chief executive officer of the joint venture. Sheldon R. Salzman, group vice president–Tires Worldwide for Uniroyal, became vice chairman and chief operating officer of UGTC. Robert A. Eisentrout, president of Goodrich's tire group, was appointed president, and Stuart M. Smith, vice presi-

---

*Prepared by Professor Arthur A. Thompson, Jr., and graduate MBA researchers Pete Clark and Jeff Ingram, The University of Alabama. Copyright © 1987 by Arthur A. Thompson, Jr.

dent of sales and marketing for Uniroyal's tire business became executive vice president. Ross described the new company as follows:

> The important advantage of this venture is that our customers and suppliers will be dealing with a strong company, one whose management is entirely focused on the tire business and the customer's demand for innovative quality products. We will put our money behind the uniformity and quality of the tires and production efficiencies. Tires are—and will be—our only business. We intend to focus all our combined talents, experience, and dedication on being one of the premier tire companies in the world.

UNIROYAL, INC.: HISTORY AND BACKGROUND

Uniroyal, Inc., was founded in 1882 by Charles R. Flint and was originally known as United States Rubber Company. The company was originally organized as a holding company to acquire rubber footwear manufacturers in an attempt to consolidate the industry; by 1917 U.S. Rubber owned 15 of the 17 rubber footwear manufacturers that were in existence in 1890. U.S. Rubber got into the sulfuric acid business in 1904 (diluted sulfuric acid was used in reclaiming old rubber), purchased its first rubber plantation in Malaysia in 1910, and became the first tire and rubber company to make its own textiles when it acquired the controlling interest in Winnsboro (South Carolina) Mills in 1917.

U.S. Rubber entered the tire business in 1896 when it began to manufacture solid rubber bicycle tires but abandoned this market in 1901 due to low sales volume. The company reentered the tire business in 1905 when it acquired a small tiremaker. By 1912 U.S. Rubber was the largest tire manufacturer in the United States with a 25 percent share of the total U.S. market. Most of its sales during this early period consisted of clincher-type tires which were difficult to handle and to mount on the wheel. Meanwhile Goodyear, Goodrich, and Firestone had introduced a straight-sided tire that was easier to handle and mount and that was gaining in acceptance by the auto manufacturers. U.S. Rubber introduced its brand of straight-sided tires in 1913, 10 years after acquiring the technology. In 1917 Goodyear overtook U.S. Rubber as the industry leader.

Through close associations with Du Pont and General Motors, U.S. Rubber maintained its number two position in the industry for the next 50 years. The company changed its name to Uniroyal in 1967. Between 1970 and 1973 Uniroyal lost its number two position in the United States to Firestone; in 1980 Goodrich overtook Uniroyal to become the number three U.S. tiremaker; and in 1985 General Tire moved past Uniroyal to become the fourth-largest U.S. tiremaker. Uniroyal's fifth-place ranking rode on its long-standing relationship as a supplier of original equipment tires to General Motors.

Uniroyal's Turnaround Efforts during the 1970s

Uniroyal struggled throughout the 1970s; profits were up and down, and long-term debt increased by $300 million. In 1973 Uniroyal announced a restructuring plan to make the company profitable in two to three years. The first step in the plan was to begin a 30-year program to finance over $500 million in unfunded pension liabilities that had been accruing since the pension's inception in the 1940s. The second step involved selling off unprofitable businesses and placing greater emphasis on radial tires. By 1976 Uniroyal had exited the polyvinyl chloride business, reduced production of bias-ply tires, and upped radial tire production to 60 percent of total tire output. In 1973 Uniroyal began efforts to prune out its unprofitable retail tire stores. By 1978 management had reduced the number of company-owned stores from 475 to 200.

During 1978 it became clear that the restructuring efforts of the past five years had failed to produce significant improvements. Unfunded pension liabilities were $515 million; Uniroyal's pension charge for 1977 was $82.2 million, equal to 3.2 percent of sales and twice the pension-to-sales burdens of Goodyear and Firestone. Funding these liabilities had curtailed Uniroyal's ability to invest in much-needed plant improvements. Even though Uniroyal invested an average of $100 million per year in plant and equipment during the 1973–78 period, the company's investments were only about one half of Firestone's capital expenditures and one third of Goodyear's. Sixty percent of Uniroyal's capital spending was allocated to the tire business. To raise more cash, management decided to divest more unprofitable businesses; the Ked's and Sperry Top-Sider divisions, the Royal golf equipment division, and the William Heller knit fabric business were sold in 1978. Uniroyal also closed out an outmoded bias-ply tire facility in Los Angeles. But despite the renewed emphasis on tires, which accounted for between 35 percent and 50 percent of sales, Uniroyal's tire business continued to be only marginally profitable (see Exhibit 1).

In 1979 Uniroyal lost $120 million and appeared on the verge of bankruptcy. Despite spending an average of $80 million per year for pension expense, Uniroyal still had over $500 million in unfunded pension liabilities. Total debt and capitalized lease obligations, including the debt of its financing arm, Uniroyal Credit

Exhibit 1 UNIROYAL'S PERFORMANCE IN TIRES AND RELATED PRODUCTS, 1970–1985 (in millions)

Year	Sales of tires and related products	Operating profits from tire sales	Tire business assets	Capital expenditures in tire business
1970	$ 869	$48	—	—
1971	970	72	—	—
1972	1,028	66	—	—
1973	1,216	62	—	—
1974	1,269	64	—	—
1975	1,265	66	$829	$31
1976	1,323	58	845	37
1977	1,489	77	912	54
1978	1,575	55	922	47
1979	1,359	(99)	630	36
1980	1,117	4	559	20
1981	1,048	69	493	34
1982	939	57	478	27
1983	933	78	476	28
1984	1,018	85	503	43
1985	1,039	70	558	55

Source: Company annual reports.

Corporation, were $861 million—an amount that precluded Uniroyal from using long-term debt to finance any growth initiatives. A Uniroyal director observed, "We were in too many kinds of businesses that required too much management time, and it was a tremendous financial strain."

Uniroyal's Second Turnaround Effort

In 1979 Uniroyal began a more drastic restructuring plan. Joseph Flannery, Uniroyal's newly appointed CEO, sold Uniroyal's remaining footwear operations in Spain, its ABS resin production facility in Baton Rouge, its 49 percent interest in a Japanese tire-making firm (Sumitomo Naugatuck Co. Ltd.), and its Computeristics division, a company formed in 1969 to sell and lease computers. Several other minor businesses that "did not fit in" were likewise sold off. Uniroyal Credit Corporation was liquidated.

The tire business was overhauled in a number of significant ways. Two inefficient tire production plants were closed. All of Uniroyal's tire production facilities outside of North America were sold, including five plants in Europe to Continental Gummi-Werke of West Germany. This left Uniroyal with five domestic tire plants, three of which had been operating since the 1920s. The company also began to divest the remaining 200 company-owned tire stores; by 1985 all 200 had been sold or closed. Uniroyal's tire lines were pruned back to only passenger car and light truck tires. In the capital spending area, Uniroyal shifted emphasis away from tires to chemicals and plastics, devoting about 60 percent of its annual capital budget on nontire businesses. As these restructuring efforts were completed, management reorganized the company into four business groups (reduced to three in 1982): (1) tires and related products; (2) chemicals, rubber, and plastic materials; (3) engineered products; and (4) other (dropped in 1982). Exhibits 2 and 3 summarize Uniroyal's financial performance during the 1980s.

Exhibit 2 FINANCIAL PERFORMANCE SUMMARY FOR UNIROYAL, INC., 1980–1985 (in millions, except per share amounts)

	1980	1981	1982	1983	1984	1985
Operations:						
Sales	$2,299	$2,260	$1,967	$2,040	$2,122	$2,072
Cost of goods sold	1,897	1,820	1,619	1,651	1,700	1,671
Interest expense	86	73	55	45	39	62
Net income	(8)	52	26	67	77	34
Earnings per share	(0.30)	1.62	0.76	1.89	2.02	0.29
Financial Position:						
Current assets	851	826	773	877	847	848
Fixed assets	537	518	526	508	493	614
Total assets	1,537	1,458	1,381	1,486	1,453	1,552
Current liabilities	426	352	310	385	419	461
Long-term liabilities	582	533	490	377	285	999
Total liabilities	1,043	936	848	814	726	1,460
Stockholders' equity	494	521	533	672	727	92

Source: Company annual reports.

Exhibit 3 UNIROYAL'S FINANCIAL PERFORMANCE BY BUSINESS SEGMENT, 1980–1985 (in millions)

	1980	1981	1982	1983	1984	1985
Sales:						
Tires and related products	$1,117	$1,084	$ 939	$ 933	$1,018	$1,039
Chemical, rubber, and plastic materials	488	573	515	593	672	682
Engineered products	476	436	382	410	432	351
Other products	219	203	—	—	—	—
Total	$2,300	$2,260	$1,836	$1,936	$2,122	$2,072
Operating profits:						
Tires and related products	$ 4	$ 69	$ 57	$ 78	$ 85	$ 70
Chemical, rubber, and plastic materials	103	79	43	65	110	97
Engineered products	20	22	18	35	37	34
Other products	(26)	(14)	—	—	—	—
Total	$ 101	$ 156	$ 118	$ 178	$ 232	$ 201
Identifiable assets:						
Tires and related products	$ 559	$ 493	$ 478	$ 476	$ 503	$ 558
Chemical, rubber, and plastic materials	402	415	418	460	443	451
Engineered products	246	230	175	183	190	214
Other products	111	98	—	—	—	—
Total	$1,318	$1,236	$1,071	$1,119	$1,136	$1,223
Capital expenditures:						
Tires and related products	$ 20	$ 34	$ 27	$ 28	$ 43	$ 55
Chemical, rubber, and plastic materials	41	27	36	25	35	31
Engineered products	11	10	13	12	17	16
Other products	4	2	—	—	—	—
Total	$ 76	$ 73	$ 76	$ 65	$ 95	$ 102

Source: Company annual reports.

Tires and Related Products. During the 1980s this business group was Uniroyal's largest, accounting for between 45 percent and 50 percent of total sales (see Exhibit 3 for segment financial data for 1980–1985). Uniroyal manufactured several tire lines (Steeler, Royal Seal, Tiger Paw, Tiger Paw Plus, and Fastrak) under the Uniroyal name and was also the maker of Rallye, Fisk, and Laredo tires. In addition, Uniroyal produced private brands for wholesale distributors and retail chains. Uniroyal brand tires were sold factory direct to the car and truck manufacturers, primarily General Motors. In the replacement segment Uniroyal sold through a network of about 55 distributors who, in turn, marketed to several thousand retailers. Factory-direct sales were made to such large replacement buyers as government agencies and vehicle fleet operators. The company produced its own tire cording at its textile mill in Winnsboro, South Carolina.

Chemical, Rubber, and Plastic Materials. During the 1980s, this group was Uniroyal's next largest and its fastest-growing segment with sales between 21 percent and 32 percent of corporate revenues. The unit produced rubber chemicals, specialty chemicals, agricultural chemicals, synthetic and natural rubbers, and plastic materials. Uniroyal was one of the largest producers of natural rubber, both dry grades and liquid latex. Uniroyal used part of the natural and synthetic rubbers it produced to supply its tire manufacturing plants and sold the remainder in the open market. Plastic materials were produced by Uniroyal for its own use and for sale to others. All of these products, except agricultural chemicals, were sold through district sales offices to manufacturers; agricultural chemicals were sold through independent distributors and dealers. The rubber plantations and related properties were divested during the 1980s.

Engineered Products.   After businesses in the "other" group were divested in 1982, this division became the smallest of the three business groups, accounting for 11 to 22 percent of total sales between 1980 and 1985. The operating units comprising Engineered Products made such items as plastic-coated fabrics sold under the trademark Naugahyde for automotive, furniture, clothing, and luggage applications; thermoplastic sheets; fabricated plastic parts for automotive interiors; rigid cellular materials for recreational vehicles and boats; flexible cellular materials for sound and thermal insulation, flotation, and shock absorption applications; foam rubber for automotive and furniture cushioning; and automotive and hydraulic hoses, conveyor belts, and power transmission belts.

The Leveraged Buyout of Uniroyal, Inc.

Uniroyal's second restructuring plan succeeded in reducing Uniroyal's debt load from a high of $861 million in 1979 to $256 million at the beginning of 1985 and in reducing unfunded pension liabilities to $307 million by early 1985. The company's improved financial position attracted the attention of corporate raider Carl Icahn; Icahn initiated a hostile takeover of Uniroyal in April 1985 via a tender offer of $18 per share for 53 percent of Uniroyal's outstanding shares. To thwart Icahn's bid, Uniroyal's Board of Directors agreed to a leveraged buyout by a company formed by Clayton & Dubilier, an investment banking firm specializing in leveraged buyouts, and a Uniroyal management group. The agreement called for the buying firm, called CDU Holding, Inc., to pay stockholders $22 per share for 93 percent of the outstanding stock. To finance the buyout, CDU borrowed approximately $1 billion from a group of banks, agreeing to repay $750 million by September 20, 1987. The leveraged buyout was handled as a merger of Uniroyal, Inc., and CDU Holding, with Uniroyal, Inc., being the surviving company.

In order to repay the loan as agreed, Uniroyal's new owners decided that the quickest and best way to raise the cash needed to meet its debt requirement was to liquidate the company. Uniroyal, Inc., then reorganized as a holding company to accomplish the liquidation in an orderly manner. Four subsidiary companies were formed by the reorganization and their assets disposed of:

1. Uniroyal Chemical Co., made up of all of Uniroyal's chemical operations, was sold for $710 million.
2. Uniroyal Power Transmission Co., Inc., made up of rubber hose and belt production facilities and sealed tank divisions, was sold to Gates Rubber for $125 million.

3. Uniroyal Plastics Co., composed of all of Uniroyal's plastics operations, was sold for $100 million.

4. Uniroyal Tire Co., made up of tire production facilities, textile (tire cord) production facilities, and synthetic rubber production facilities, was merged into UGTC for a 50 percent interest and $225 million in cash (paid by B. F. Goodrich).

All of these transactions were completed by the end of 1986. Uniroyal, Inc., then repaid all of its obligations, retired its preferred stock for $100 per share ($87 million), and retired all of its common stock by distributing the remaining cash and stock in Uniroyal Holding, Inc. By 1987 Uniroyal Holding, Inc., with 50 percent ownership of UGTC, was all that remained of what once was a $2.7 billion operation.

B. F. GOODRICH CO.: HISTORY AND BACKGROUND

The B. F. Goodrich Co. (BFG) was founded in 1870 by Dr. Benjamin Franklin Goodrich; initial operations consisted of a small fire-hose factory in Akron on the Ohio canal. By 1900 BFG was a major force in the infant automotive industry, supplying tires and other rubber parts to eager inventors who were pinning their hopes on the "horseless carriage." In 1895 the company set up the industry's first experimental laboratory. Dr. Goodrich's emphasis on scientific inquiry and technological innovation allowed the company to establish itself as the source of solutions for rubber-related problems. The company began making tires for aircraft as early as 1910; it became a part of aviation history when the *Spirit of St. Louis* piloted by Charles Lindbergh landed in Paris on B. F. Goodrich tires.

In 1926 a Goodrich scientist discovered how to plasticize polyvinyl chloride. This was the first step in turning PVC into the second most used plastic—vinyl. In 1937, after 11 years of research, BFG built a pilot plant to produce man-made rubber, and in 1940 BFG introduced the first passenger car tire containing man-made rubber.

After World War II BFG continued its technological leadership. In 1947 the company introduced the tubeless tire. In the 1950s BFG developed a high-impact rigid PVC, making vinyl a viable building product; not long thereafter the company introduced two engineered plastic materials, thermoplastic polyurethane and chlorinated polyvinyl to the market. In 1965 BFG became the first company to market radial tires produced in the United States, and during the 1970s and 1980s BFG supplied wheels and brakes for the space shuttle program.

BFG: The 1970–1986 Years

Despite its technological accomplishments, B. F. Goodrich did not have a strong track record in tires insofar as profit and market-share performance were concerned. Only recently had it reached third place in the U.S. market; during most of its history the company ranked a weak fourth or fifth to industry leader Goodyear. The company had begun a diversification program outside of tires following World War II and by the 1970s had a considerable number of companies in its portfolio. From 1971 on up through 1986 the company went from one restructuring program into another trying to find a revenue and product mix that would produce sustained growth and profits.

As of 1970 it was apparent that B. F. Goodrich was a poorly managed company living on past laurels. The company was described as the Chrysler of the tire industry and was seen as weakly positioned to deal with changing conditions in its primary markets. BFG was fourth in tire production and had weak marketing, high labor costs, and spotty international representation. At $1 billion in sales, tires were "the guts" of the company, yet tire operations were netting less than 10 cents in profits per tire. When O. Pendleton Thomas took over as chairman and CEO in 1971, he launched the first in a series of attempts to revamp BFG's operations. During the next three years, BFG sold its trucking subsidiary and discontinued production of footwear, most molded rubber products, sponge rubber products, and surgical gloves. In 1975 and 1976 the company sold its Australian tire manufacturing plant, closed its Los Angeles tire manufacturing facilities, sold its Dutch tire and industrial products subsidiary, and consolidated the number of tire distribution warehouses from 33 to 6. Thomas felt that tires should be downplayed in the company's growth plans and that cash flows from tires should be diverted to fund expansion efforts in BFG's other businesses. The strategy was to reinvest just enough in the tire business to give BFG a modest capability for participating in the fast-emerging radial tire segment.

In 1979 John Ong took over as BFG's chief executive. Ong made several moves to enhance BFG's nontire revenues and earnings, the most important of which was to develop stronger business positions in chemicals and particularly in polyvinyl chloride production. Over the next several years approximately $1 billion was invested to build up BFG's market share in PVC from 20 to 30 percent; management wanted to boost the company's leadership in PVC even though PVC demand was cyclical. John Ong stated, "BFG's salvation lies in the commodity chemicals business of polyvinyl chloride. BFG is pushing the industry where it is a leader instead of an also-ran."

Ong's stated rationale for deemphasizing tires and emphasizing PVC was that "the [tire] industry peaked in 1973 and will never again enjoy good growth rates. Returns will improve, but I am skeptical profits will ever be satisfactory." Under Ong's strategy, another $500 million was invested in the acquisition of new nontire businesses—conveyor equipment, construction sealants, adhesives and coatings, aircraft and off-highway vehicle braking systems, chemicals for water desalination, and specialty polymers. Meanwhile the company abandoned efforts to market tires as original equipment (electing to concentrate solely on the replacement segment), reduced its holdings in Yokohama Rubber Co. (Japan's third largest tire-maker) to under 20 percent of the outstanding shares, sold its tire-manufacturing facility in the Philippines, sold most of its ownership in tire-production facilities in Colombia, South America, phased out the manufacture of certain industrial rubber products at its Akron plant, and sold its tire interests in Liberia and Ireland.

In 1981 when the decision was made to withdraw from the OE market, BFG was selling about 4 million OE tires and generating $120 million in OE revenues;

its share of the OE market in the United States was about 8 percent—fifth among the OE tire suppliers. However, BFG's profit margins on OE sales were only about five cents per tire. BFG's withdrawal from OE competition meant the loss of 25 percent of the company's passenger tire volume; to make up for production inefficiencies created by so much excess capacity, BFG's management hoped to be able to increase its sales of passenger car replacement tires from 12 million units to 14 million units. Margins on replacement tires were expected to average $2–$3 per tire, if not more. Exhibit 4 shows the BFG tire group's performance over the 1977–1985 period; Exhibits 5, 6, and 7 provide financial performance data for the company as a whole.

By late 1983 Ong concluded that the corporate strategy BFG had been pursuing since 1977 was a failure. The assumptions top management had made about the long-run attractiveness of the PVC market were off-target. PVC prices had dropped unexpectedly, and BFG, whose costs were among the highest in the industry, got caught in the squeeze. BFG's strengths in PVCs were in special resins for bottling and food wrapping, neither of which were fast-growing niches. Another restructuring effort was launched.

In 1985 BFG management decided to close two of the company's tire manufacturing plants in a move to exit production of farm equipment tires, off-the-road vehicle tires, and radial heavy-duty truck tires. Late in 1985 BFG sold 137 of its 166 retail tire stores, closed 22 stores, and kept the remaining 7; the 137 stores were purchased by a former BFG executive who formed a new company known as Tire Centers, Inc., to operate the chain and who agreed to carry BFG tires as the primary tire line for a number of years. Management also closed a small tire cord mill and then made the decision to sell the Convent, Louisiana, chlor-alkali and ethylene dichloride complex which had been a centerpiece in the company's earlier investment program to boost its market leadership in PVC production. A company that produced lightweight, nonmetallic composite materials for aerospace applications was acquired. In 1986 BFG sold its Continental Conveyor and Equipment division (acquired in 1978 as an attempt to broaden the company's

---

Exhibit 4 PERFORMANCE OF BFG'S TIRE GROUP, 1977–1985 (in millions)

Year	Sales	Operating income	Assets	Capital expenditures
1977	$1,137	$91	—	—
1978	1,234	84	—	—
1979	1,296	48	$785	$44
1980	1,294	65	749	41
1981	1,352	79	696	32
1982	1,339	84	624	45
1983	1,400	79	681	45
1984	1,500	93	718	53
1985	1,399	68	686	46

Source: Company annual reports and records.

Exhibit 5   FINANCIAL PERFORMANCE SUMMARY, B. F. GOODRICH CO., 1975–1985
(dollars in millions, except per share amounts)

	1975	1980	1981	1982	1983	1984	1985
Statement of income data:							
Sales	$2,041.4	$3,079.6	$3,085.4	$2,871.6	$3,099.3	$3,340.8	$3,200.5
Cost of sales	1,528.9	2,367.1	2,363.7	2,193.8	2,356.1	2,502.1	2,416.8
Gross profit	512.5	712.5	721.7	677.8	743.2	838.7	783.7
Selling and administrative expenses	435.2	587.3	618.8	629.0	642.7	662.7	658.8
Operating income	77.3	129.9	102.9	48.8	100.5	176.0	124.9
Interest expense (net)	51.2	56.3	60.7	83.8	82.7	90.9	96.5
Net income (loss)	22.1	61.7	109.5	(32.8)	18.4	60.6	(354.6)
Per share of common stock	$1.40	$3.57	$5.75	$2.43	$0.68	$2.52	($15.79)
Balance sheet data:							
Current assets	$ 791.7	$1,043.6	$1,153.5	$ 782.9	$ 950.4	$ 976.6	$ 998.9
Current liabilities	347.7	540.0	626.4	549.8	602.0	662.8	833.8
Net property	762.3	925.1	1,310.4	1,313.8	1,289.1	1,307.4	1,043.9
Total assets	1,666.4	2,224.7	2,712.1	2,378.2	2,535.1	2,577.9	2,260.3
Noncurrent long-term debt and capital lease obligations	494.9	553.7	742.5	599.8	652.3	675.9	536.5
Total shareholders' equity	709.6	947.8	1,091.6	1,013.2	1,108.3	1,081.1	690.1
Other data:							
Capital expenditures	$108.3	$184.0	$553.3	$143.6	$115.1	$153.2	$202.3
Research and development expenses	$ 36.3	$ 49.4	$ 54.3	$ 58.1	$ 61.9	$558.7	$ 64.1
Dividends per share of common stock	$ 1.12	$ 1.56	$ 1.56	$ 1.56	$ 1.56	$ 1.56	$ 1.56
Book value per share of common stock	$49.61	$55.42	$58.16	$53.76	$47.05	$48.25	$30.43
Number of employees at end of year	44,898	40,232	33,705	30,042	29,427	28,770	26,191

Source: Company annual reports.

diversification beyond tires and chemicals), reached an agreement to sell its industrial hose and belt business, and was trying to sell its Off-Highway Braking Systems Division.

Throughout all of this restructuring, the tire business group continued to be BFG's most profitable business. Although top management's emphasis was on expanding PVC production and sales, profits in PVC proved meager. The company's aerospace and specialty chemicals businesses, though producing only 20 percent of revenues, generated 46 percent of operating profit in 1984; the aerospace unit was the leading maker of airplane de-icing systems. Exhibit 6 shows the recent performance of the company's business divisions.

At year-end 1985 BFG's continuing operations were classified into five business segments: polyvinyl chloride and intermediate compounds (27 percent of revenues), specialty chemicals (16 percent of revenues), aerospace and defense products (7 percent of revenues), industrial products (6 percent of revenues), and tires and related products (44 percent of revenues). The tire division had sales of $1.5 billion in 1984 and $1.4 billion in 1985 (see Exhibit 4). BFG competed only in the replacement tire segment (except for supplying a small number of light truck

Exhibit 6 PERFORMANCE OF B. F. GOODRICH'S BUSINESS DIVISIONS, 1980–1985 (in millions)

	1980	1981	1982	1983	1984	1985
Trade sales:						
Net sales to unaffiliated customers:						
PVC and intermediates	$ 579.5	$ 620.3	$ 704.7	$ 851.7	$ 920.5	$ 865.8
Specialty chemicals	403.8	439.6	407.0	468.3	503.3	517.8
Aerospace and defense products	161.4	176.0	175.1	173.9	182.8	223.3
Industrial products	355.0	362.3	379.6	204.9	234.7	194.3
Tires and related products	1,320.8	1,397.8	1,338.9	1,400.5	1,499.5	1,399.3
Other	259.9	186.6	—	—	—	—
Total	$3,079.6	$3,184.6	$3,005.3	$3,099.3	$3,340.8	$3,200.5
Segment operating income (loss):						
PVC and intermediates	$ 37.3	$(12.0)	$(18.7)	$ 6.8	$ 39.2	$ 24.1
Specialty chemicals	28.0	40.3	31.6	59.3	75.0	55.2
Aerospace and defense products	15.0	10.1	7.6	4.9	14.6	23.8
Industrial products	4.8	(3.0)	(21.8)	(25.3)	(18.5)	(15.8)
Tires and related products	65.9	84.2	75.6	78.9	93.1	67.5
Other	(4.2)	(1.1)	—	—	—	—
Adjustments and eliminations— change in intersegment profit in inventories	.3	.4	2.8	.3	—	.4
Corporate expenses	(21.9)	(20.5)	(26.6)	(24.4)	(27.4)	(30.3)
Total operating income	$125.2	$ 98.4	$ 50.5	$100.5	$176.0	$124.9
Identifiable assets:						
PVC and intermediates	$ 446.0	$ 943.8	$ 943.0	$ 995.9	$ 979.4	$ 744.8
Specialty chemicals	337.8	367.3	353.3	364.7	386.6	409.4
Aerospace and defense products	82.1	84.0	77.6	73.0	85.7	111.3
Industrial products	238.5	250.3	255.6	151.9	161.6	112.3
Tires and related products	740.3	670.8	624.0	680.7	718.1	685.8
Other	168.7	108.1	—	—	—	—
Adjustments and eliminations	(4.4)	(4.0)	(3.1)	(2.8)	(2.8)	(2.4)
Corporate assets	215.7	300.6	172.0	271.7	249.3	199.1
Total	$2,224.7	$2,720.9	$2,422.4	$2,535.1	$2,577.9	$2,260.3
Capital expenditures:						
PVC and intermediates	$ 67.9	$477.9	$ 59.4	$ 31.2	$ 49.6	$ 90.9
Specialty chemicals	34.3	29.9	26.5	14.9	23.8	39.4
Aerospace and defense products	8.7	3.2	3.4	4.0	6.4	15.6
Industrial products	22.8	17.9	10.3	11.2	15.9	5.7
Tires and related products	41.8	32.3	44.8	44.9	52.6	45.7
Other	7.6	2.9	—	—	—	—
Corporate	.9	1.5	4.3	8.9	4.9	5.0
Total	$184.0	$565.6	$148.7	$115.1	$153.2	$202.3
Depreciation and amortization expense:						
PVC and intermediates	$25.1	$31.4	$ 51.6	$ 55.4	$ 57.4	$ 51.3
Specialty chemicals	10.6	10.4	12.7	13.4	16.0	17.0
Aerospace and defense products	2.5	3.2	2.7	3.3	3.5	3.5
Industrial products	8.4	9.0	12.0	8.1	7.5	7.0
Tires and related products	33.0	31.8	36.0	37.2	38.0	34.5
Other	10.0	6.8	—	—	—	—
Corporate	1.7	1.7	2.0	1.9	3.8	4.8
Total	$91.3	$94.3	$117.0	$119.3	$126.2	$118.1

Source: 1985 annual report.

Exhibit 7 SELECTED FINANCIAL STATISTICS FOR B. F. GOODRICH, BY GEOGRAPHICAL AREA, 1980–1985 (in millions)

	1980	1981	1982	1983	1984	1985
Sales to unaffiliated customers:						
United States	$2,432	$2,579	$2,503	$2,598	$2,826	$2,707
Canada	648	302	375	318	317	308
Other		304	227	183	198	185
Total	$3,080	$3,185	$3,105	$3,099	$3,341	$3,200
Segment operating income:						
United States	$ 94	$ 79	$25	$ 76	$145	$106
Canada	58	31	10	36	40	33
Other		21	15	13	18	17
Total*	$152	$131	$50	$125	$203	$156
Identifiable assets:						
United States	$1,593	$2,085	$1,923	$1,944	$1,999	$1,721
Canada	418	199	198	215	222	233
Other		136	129	104	108	107
Total	$2,011	$2,420	$2,250	$2,263	$2,329	$2,061

* Note: Segment operating income totals do not reconcile with the operating income totals in Exhibits 5 and 6 because corporate expenses and certain other items were not allocated by geographic area.
Source: Company annual reports.

Exhibit 8 B. F. GOODRICH'S PRODUCT LINES IN TIRES, 1985

Major product lines	Description	Distribution channel
T/A® Radials: • Comp T/A • Euro-Radial T/A • Radial T/A • Advantage T/A • Radial All-Terrain T/A • Radial Mud-Terrain T/A • Radial Sport Truck T/A	A line of premium, high-performance radial tires. Specific products for luxury and sports cars, light trucks, and four-wheel-drive vehicles.	Replacement sales through dealers and export sales.
Broadline radial passenger tires: • XLM H/T® • Lifesaver® GT-4 • XLM®	Durable, dependable steel-belted radial tires, including all-season products, for all domestic and imported cars.	Replacement sales through dealers; export.
Broadline radial light truck tires: • The Edge® • Trail Edge® • The Trac Edge®	A line of reliable steel-belted radials, including all-season and mud-and-snow applications.	Replacement sales through dealers; export; original equipment sales to truck manufacturers.
Heavy-duty truck tires	An extensive line of bias tires for all types of large trucks and trailers.	Replacement sales through dealers; export; original equipment sales to truck and trailer manufacturers.
Private-brand products	Radial and nonradial passenger and light truck tires.	Independent tire retailers and wholesalers.

Source: 1985 annual report.

tires to GM as original equipment) and had a fifth-place market share of 4.5 percent in replacement tires, behind Goodyear, Firestone, Sears, and Michelin. The company also manufactured tires for the private-label segment. Exhibit 8 shows BFG's product line; the T/A radial line was the most profitable.

BFG's T/A tire line had good brand recognition among buyers and was viewed as a high-quality tire that delivered good performance. In 1985 the company introduced a new generation Comp T/A—BFG's ultra-high-performance radial tire with improved handling, traction, and treadwear characteristics. The company also came out with a third generation Radial T/A tire and a 50 series Euro-Radial T/A. Together, these new tires represented the most additions and improvements made to the T/A line in its 15-year history. T/A brand radial tires were produced at the BFG plant in Tuscaloosa, Alabama. At the time the joint venture with Uniroyal was formed, BFG was following a two-pronged niche strategy in tires that involved:

1. Identifying profitable performance-oriented markets where technology and brand identification were important and where the company could build an "umbrella" image for all BFG brand tires.

2. Focusing on high-volume private-brand accounts that administered their own marketing and distribution programs.

BFG's Relationship with the URW

B. F. Goodrich's hourly employees in the tire division were represented by the United Rubber Workers union; all of the company's U.S. tire-producing facilities were unionized. In 1985 when new contract negotiations between the URW and the four largest tiremakers were all underway, the URW initially concentrated on reaching an agreement with Goodyear first but later shifted its efforts to BFG. When the URW and BFG reached agreement on a wage-fringe benefit package, the other three tiremakers ended up agreeing to essentially the same terms. The URW reported that the average compensation for BFG workers was $13.50 per hour, with fringe benefits equal to an additional 41 percent of the average hourly wage. The agreement between the URW and the tire companies, however, provided leeway for negotiations at specific plants, especially older high-cost plants, to deviate from some of the terms of broader agreement.

At BFG each tire plant negotiated local agreements on work rules and certain other issues that were included as supplements to the company contract. In recent years the relationship between the URW and BFG had improved in some significant ways as it became apparent that BFG was one of the high-cost producers and as rumors persisted that the company was a logical candidate for exit from the tire business altogether. As of 1985 it had become apparent to both management and union officials that a more cooperative posture was needed if BFG was to survive increased competition. At BFG's Tuscaloosa, Alabama, tire plant, labor and management were working together on the development of a new tire-building machine that had the potential to cut labor costs some 15 to 25 percent. The tire-building machine was still in the experimental stage in early 1987. Estimated costs to build and install these machines (if they proved workable) were $250,000 each; at current production levels BFG would need roughly 200 of the new machines for its plants.

Uniroyal Goodrich Tire Company after the Merger

Under the joint venture agreement UGTC borrowed approximately $500 million from a group of banks. The company then gave each parent about one half of the cash and a 50 percent equity interest in the joint venture in return for $1.6 billion in assets. Prior to the merger Goodrich sold $26 million of its accounts receivable to Uniroyal in order to equalize the value of the business contributed by each parent. The two parent companies both used the cash received from UGTC to pay down some of their own debts. In addition to receiving the assets from both Uniroyal's and Goodrich's tire operations, UGTC also assumed substantially all of the liabilities of their tire operations, including approximately $240 million in unfunded pension liabilities. Exhibit 9 gives some limited financial information on UGTC four months after the merger. Projections were that UGTC might have earnings of $150 million in 1987, $80 million of which was to be realized from consolidating operations and reducing overhead expenses.

Organization.   UGTC was organized into two divisions, the Uniroyal division and the Goodrich division. The Uniroyal division consisted of the plants and other assets that were contributed by Uniroyal. This division manufactured and sold passenger car and light truck tires under the Uniroyal brand. UGTC planned to continue to supply the OE segment with Uniroyal brand tires, the strength that Uniroyal brought to the joint venture; Uniroyal's share of OE sales in the United States had been roughly one fifth of the OE market for almost a decade:

Exhibit 9 PERFORMANCE SUMMARY, UNIROYAL GOODRICH TIRE COMPANY, AUGUST 1–NOVEMBER 30, 1986 (in millions)

Statement of income data (for the period August 1 to November 30, 1986):

Sales	$ 725.4
Gross income	193.4
Provision for rationalization costs	19.6
Net earnings	16.8

Balance sheet data (at November 30, 1986):

Current assets	$ 725.0
Noncurrent assets	756.6
Total assets	1,481.6
Current liabilities	370.6
Long-term debt	368.9
Other noncurrent liabilities	240.6
Total liabilities	980.1
Net assets	$ 501.5

Source: B. F. Goodrich Company.

Year	Uniroyal's OE market share
1986	21%
1985	22
1984	23
1983	22
1982	21
1981	20
1980	20
1979	19
1978	19

Source: *Modern Tire Dealer.*

In years past, General Motors had purchased approximately 35 percent of its tire needs from Uniroyal, representing between 15 and 25 percent of Uniroyal's total tire volume during the 1970 to 1985 period. However, some analysts believed that GM might well curtail its Uniroyal tire purchases in the years to come because UGTC was no longer so dependent on GM's contract. According to one Wall Street analyst, the new joint venture gave GM more flexibility and relieved GM of "any obligation to artificially prop them [Uniroyal] up. If anything, GM will try to reduce its purchases from UGTC." UGTC supplied 6 percent of Ford's tire needs with Uniroyal brand tires in 1986. Uniroyal brand tires had about a 3 percent share of the replacement tire market.

The Goodrich division was made up of the plant and other assets that were contributed by BFG. About 5 percent of the Goodrich division sales were OE sales, all of which were light truck tires to GM. All of Goodrich's remaining production consisted of B. F. Goodrich brand passenger car and light truck tires sold in the replacement market and tires made for the private-label segment. In 1986 B. F. Goodrich brand tires had 4.5 percent of the replacement market. Exhibit 10 shows the U.S. market shares of the various sellers of replacement tires in 1985 and 1986; UGTC was not a major factor in the replacement market outside North America.

Combined, the two divisions had an 18 percent share of the total U.S. market and a 7.5 percent share of the world market. UGTC was the second largest U.S. tiremaker, though well behind industry leader Goodyear's 31 percent market share. UGTC was the fourth largest worldwide tiremaker, behind Goodyear, Michelin, and Bridgestone. The vast majority of UGTC's sales were in the U.S. market.

During 1986 UGTC continued to operate the two divisions as if they had never merged. Each division continued to use the same channels of distribution they had used prior to the merger. The Uniroyal division sold tires factory-direct to the motor vehicle manufacturers and went through independent distributors to access the replacement segment. The Goodrich division sold its brand of tires directly to independent retailers. Both sales forces were retained. Replacement sales made up one third of total sales, OE sales made up another one third, and private-label

Exhibit 10 ESTIMATED BRAND SHARES OF REPLACEMENT PASSENGER TIRE MARKET, 1985 and 1986

	1985	1986		1985	1986
Goodyear	15.5%	15.5%	Montgomery Ward	2.0%	1.5%
Firestone	9.5	9.0	Atlas	1.5	1.5
Michelin	8.0	8.5	Remington	1.5	1.5
Sears	9.0	8.0	Stratton	1.5	1.5
BF Goodrich	4.5	4.5	Hercules	1.5	1.5
Uniroyal	3.0	3.0	Western Auto	1.0	1.5
Multi-Mile	3.0	2.5	Monarch	1.0	1.5
Kelly-Springfield	3.0	2.5	K mart	1.5	1.0
Cooper	2.5	2.5	Centennial	1.0	1.0
Dunlop	2.5	2.5	Pirelli	1.0	1.0
General	2.5	2.5	EMPCO	1.0	1.0
Armstrong	2.0	2.0	Summit	1.0	1.0
Cordovan	2.0	2.0	Winston	1.0	1.0
Dayton	2.0	2.0	Regul	1.0	1.0
Jetzon-Laramie	2.0	2.0	Pep Boys	.9	1.0
Bridgestone	2.0	2.0	Others	9.6	10.5

Source: *Modern Tire Dealer*, January 1986 and January 1987.

sales made up the final one third. First-year sales were estimated to be about 50 million units.

Manufacturing.   UGTC produced passenger car and light truck tires at nine plants in the United States, Canada, and Mexico. It was also backward vertically integrated, making its own tire textiles at four plants and synthetic rubber at two others. Uniroyal contributed three tire manufacturing facilities in the United States, one in Canada, and two in Mexico, along with two textile plants and one synthetic rubber plant. BFG contributed two tire production plants in the United States, one in Canada, and a 35 percent interest in a Mexican production facility, along with one textile plant and one synthetic rubber plant. Exhibit 11 shows the location, capacity, and percentage of radial production for the five U.S. plants. Four of the U.S. plants were unionized, and one was nonunion. The Goodrich plants were operating at 100 percent capacity in 1987, while the Uniroyal plants were operating at 85 percent capacity. In 1987 the company began to produce some Goodrich brand tires in Uniroyal plants. There were no announced plans to close any of the manufacturing facilities.

On the average, UGTC's plants were older and less efficient than the plants of many of its competitors. Another disadvantage was in the length of the production runs. UGTC production runs were shorter due to a wider variety of tires being produced, resulting in above-average changeover costs. UGTC's costs per tire were estimated to average about $40; the cost makeup was estimated as follows:

Exhibit 11   UGTC's TIRE PLANT LOCATIONS IN THE UNITED STATES, 1986

Plant location	Passenger tires	All other tires	Total	Percent radial tire production
	Daily capacity			
Uniroyal Division:				
Ardmore, Oklahoma*	33,000	0	33,000	100%
Opelika, Alabama	22,000	4,000	26,000	100
Eau Claire, Wisconsin	22,800	4,000	27,800	5
Uniroyal total	77,800	8,000	86,800	
Goodrich Division:				
Tuscaloosa, Alabama	32,500	1,500	34,000	76
Fort Wayne, Indiana	18,500	11,500	30,000	90
Goodrich total	51,000	13,000	64,000	
UGTC total	128,800	21,000	150,800	

* Nonunion plant.
Source: *Modern Tire Dealer,* January 1987.

Raw materials	$16	40%
Direct labor	16	40
Overhead	8	20
Total	$40	100%

Average profit margins varied by market segment:

Segment	Profit margin	Percent of manufacturer's selling price
OE	$ .04– .05	.1%
Replacement	1.20–1.30	3.1
Private label	1.50–1.60	3.9

Labor.   UGTC employed about 21,000 people at an average wage of $13.50 per hour with benefits averaging 41 percent of wages. After the merger UGTC honored both the Uniroyal and BFG contracts with the URW. These contracts were due to expire in 1988. The URW approved of the merger from the beginning because the members working for both parents realized that the companies might well not survive without the merger. Recently, UGTC workers had begun taking responsibility for product quality by monitoring production output through a statistical process control system; the SPC system involved teams of workers checking on the quality of tires as they were produced. UGTC had increased the level of employee involvement in its plants, a move that both parties said reduced the level of friction between labor and management.

Capital Expenditures and R&D.   UGTC had plans to spend approximately $100 million annually on plant equipment improvements. Most of these expenditures were expected to be made for the new tire-building machine (called the VMI machine) that was under development. The VMI tire machine could be operated by two people and could make 800 tires per day during three shifts; with existing equipment, tire building took four people and four machines working three shifts to achieve the same output. UGTC also planned to spend $150 million on research and development, an amount about 50 percent more than Uniroyal and Goodrich together would have spent prior to the merger.

Worldwide Sales.   In 1986 UGTC exported 5 percent to 10 percent of its production to foreign countries (excluding Canada and Mexico). Instead of building plants outside of North America, UGTC had licensed companies worldwide to use its processes and tradenames. Goodrich for many years had licensed Yokohama Tire in Japan to use Goodrich technology and had also licensed Yokohama to sell tires under the Goodrich names.

UGTC's FUTURE

There was skepticism about whether UGTC would really prove to be a strong competitor. As one securities analyst expressed it:

> I am not sure that the new joint venture company will be able to turn around their combined tire business. Can you take two losing operations, join them together, and come up with a winner? I don't know. I believe it will be difficult.

Another analyst stated:

> The challenges are for Goodrich to get back into the OE business without diluting any of the Uniroyal OE volume. If Goodrich can get back in, that's a plus for them. One of their problems will be the synergy of the people. As you form a new company, I think there will be redundancies. Also, it will take a year or so for all the people to function in a very smooth operative way.

The merger had implications for the industry as well. Prior to their merger, Uniroyal and Goodrich were viewed as the two major firms in the industry that were most likely to exit the business in the early 1990s or sooner. Their merger signified that the industry's overcapacity problem might take longer to solve; had Uniroyal or Goodrich or both exited the business, the demand and supply of tires in the United States (and to some extent worldwide) would have come into balance quickly and boosted overall industry profitability.

NORTHERN TELECOM, INC.*

Hall Miller, vice president of marketing for the Central Office Switching Division of Northern Telecom, Inc., looked up from the reports on his desk to a picture on the wall of his office that reminded him of his childhood in British Columbia. It was of a single snow-covered log cabin, with stately mountains rising in the background. His eyes moved from the picture to the window, where he could see traffic already starting to pile up on Interstate 40 running through Research Triangle Park, North Carolina, between Durham, Chapel Hill, and Raleigh. It was midafternoon in March 1988, and the traffic would be bumper-to-bumper in another hour.

Miller had been reviewing the results of a survey conducted by *Communications Week* in the fourth quarter of 1987. The purpose of the study was to identify purchase trends and priorities in the selection of central office telephone switching equipment and manufacturers. The respondents were primarily telephone company planners, and as such they were directly involved with selecting and purchasing central office switches. It was obvious that Miller was extremely interested in the results.

While Miller had also been reviewing the company's 1987 performance, his thoughts were on the future—if and how the telecommunications market was changing and how to best position the division in response to these changes. Miller smiled as he realized that the picture on the wall represented his perception of Northern's performance in the United States to this point, while the impending traffic jam reminded him of the changing market conditions he felt the company would soon be facing.

HISTORY

Northern Telecom, Inc. (NTI), the U.S. subsidiary of Canadian-based Northern Telecom, Ltd. (NTL), was originally part of the Bell System. Bell Canada, the parent company of NTL, was a subsidiary of AT&T until the late 1950s when AT&T was ordered to divest its foreign subsidiaries. Prior to divestiture, Northern Telecom was known as Northern Electric, serving as the Canadian counterpart to Western Electric, the U.S. manufacturing arm of AT&T.

Northern Telecom established its presence in the U.S. in the 1960s and 1970s as a private branch exchange supplier (customer-owned telephone switches that reside at customer sites) and a vendor of terminals (telephone sets). (A switch is a device that routes individual calls from the calling party (point of origin) to the telephone network. Once in the network, the call is routed from switch to switch

---

* Prepared by Professor Lew G. Brown, University of North Carolina at Greensboro, and Richard Sharpe, MBA candidate at The University of Tennessee, Knoxville.

until reaching the party being called.) Manufacturing and support facilities were established in West Palm Beach, Florida; Atlanta, Georgia; Richardson, Texas; Minnetonka, Minnesota; San Ramon, California; and Nashville, Tennessee, the U.S. headquarters of NTI. Northern's first facility in North Carolina opened in the early 1970s in Creedmoor, a small community north of Durham. It still amazed Miller to think that Northern had grown from 300 people at Creedmoor to 10,000 employees in the Raleigh area in less than a decade.

DEVELOPMENT OF THE DIGITAL SWITCH

Throughout the 1970s, Northern Telecom, in conjunction with Bell-Northern Research (BNR), Northern's R&D equivalent to Bell Labs, developed a process known as *digital* switching. Unlike *analog* signals—continuous electrical signals varying in amplitude and frequency in response to changes in sound—*digital* signals involve sampling the human voice at a rate of 8,000 times per second, breaking it into a stream of thousands of bits of electrical impulses in a binary code. As calls are routed through the network, they are multiplexed, which involves coding and sending the digital bits together in streams, allowing transmission of multiple conversations simultaneously on the same line. At the next switching office, the bits are either routed to another destination or are multiplexed back into voice signals and sent to the appropriate terminating parties for the cells. Digital technology offers a number of advantages over analog switching, including faster and cleaner transmission, lower costs per line, and decreased floor space requirements for switching equipment (a digital switch required less than 50 percent the space of an analog switch).

THE BREAKUP OF AT&T AND EQUAL ACCESS

Northern installed its first digital central office switch in 1979. AT&T still had a monopoly in the U.S. telephone market at the time, providing local and long-distance telephone service through the Bell System to more than 85 percent of the United States with Western Electric as the only supplier of telecommunications equipment. The remaining 15 percent of the U.S. market was served by 1,200 independent telephone companies. Northern, along with other vendors, sold its products only to the independents until the early 1980s.

In 1982 through the provisions of the Modification of Final Judgment which ordered the breakup of AT&T, AT&T divested the 22 local operating companies comprising the Bell System. Although the new AT&T retained the long-distance portion of the business (called AT&T Communications), the newly formed Bell operating companies providing local service became distinct entities and were no longer tied to AT&T. As such, the Bell operating companies were free to buy telecommunications equipment from suppliers other than Western Electric (renamed AT&T Technologies). For Northern Telecom and other vendors, divestiture was the end of a monopoly and the beginning of a highly competitive marketplace. Exhibit 1 shows the territories of the new regional Bell operating companies.

Exhibit 1 REGIONAL BELL OPERATING COMPANIES

The Modification of Final Judgment also included the provision that the local telephone companies must provide exchange access to all long-distance carriers (such as MCI and US Sprint) "equal in type, quality, and price to that provided to AT&T and its affiliates." To provide equal access many telephone exchanges (central office switches) had to be replaced with digital technology switches. Northern Telecom was well positioned for success in the U.S. central office switching market, having a product lead in digital switching and now being able to compete in an open market driven by equal access. Thus began an era for Northern known to some observers in the industry as "one of the great marketing successes of recent times."

NORTHERN'S PRODUCTS

Hardware

Northern Telecom's digital central office switching components fell into four categories: systems, remotes, extensions, and lines. Systems equated to digital central-office switches. Northern had three versions collectively known as the DMS-100 Family—the DMS (Digital Multiplex System)-100, the DMS-100/200, and the DMS-200. The DMS-100 handled local lines only, the DMS-100/200 handled both local lines and toll trunks (trunks were lines between offices carrying long-distance traffic), and the DMS-200 handled toll trunks only. Each DMS system had a maximum capacity of 100,000 lines. Exhibits 2 and 3 show Northern Telecom's U.S. installed equipment base by customer type, by service type, and sales by year.

Remotes were digital switching units that extended central office features to remote areas. Northern's remotes ranged in size from 600 to 5,000 lines. Unlike central office systems which were housed in buildings, remotes were usually constructed in environmentally controlled cabinets and placed outside on concrete platforms in areas away from central offices. In addition to extending central office features and services, most remotes had some stand-alone capability (i.e., if the host central office switch went out of service for some reason, calls could still be made between customers being served by the same remote). Remotes also provided a cost savings in lines by performing a line concentrating function since all the subscribers who were served by a remote in a particular location were wired to the remote rather than to the central office. All the customers on the

---

Exhibit 2 NORTHERN TELECOM'S DMS-100 FAMILY INSTALLED BASE BY CUSTOMER TYPE AS OF YEAR-END 1987

Customer	Systems	Remotes	Extensions	Lines (thousands)
Bell operating companies	658	248	1,106	9,841
Independent operating companies	434	1,303	1,120	5,686
Total United States	1,092	1,551	2,226	15,527

				Lines
Year	Systems	Remotes	Extensions	(thousands)
1979	5			2
1980	13			75
1981	69	31	19	453
1982	51	86	41	492
1983	83	130	58	798
1984	116	210	152	1,379
1985	266	304	332	3,665
1986	235	359	604	3,962
1987	254	431	1,015	4,701
Total	1,092	1,551	2,226	15,527

Exhibit 3 DMS-100 FAMILY U.S. SALES BY YEAR

Source: Northern Telecom Data.

remote were served by a single pair of wires extending from the remote to the central office. Remotes could be located up to 150 miles away from their hosts.

Extensions represented hardware additions and software upgrades to existing Northern switches. Lines are reported in thousands; thus, as of year-end 1987, NTI had over 15.5 million lines in service.

Software

In addition to hardware, an important portion of Northern Telecom's product line was software. Northern Telecom's DMS switches were driven by both operating software (similar to DOS in a PC environment) and applications software performing specific functions. Originally an AT&T brand name, centrex had become a generic term describing any central-office based applications software package combining business-oriented voice, data networking, and control features bundled with intercom calling and offered to end-users as a package. As a shared central-office-based service, centrex was designed to replace applications served by equipment located at the customer's premises, such as key telephone systems and private branch exchanges. As opposed to investing in telephone switching equipment, the customer simply paid the telephone company a monthly fee per centrex line for access to a multitude of sophisticated business voice and high-speed data features. Call Forwarding and Call Waiting are examples of centrex basic voice features that have been offered to the residential market. Centrex (as an AT&T brand offering) was widespread throughout the 22 local Bell System telephone companies prior to divestiture; as a generic product, centrex was a major source of revenue for the telephone operating companies.

In the late 1970s AT&T began what was known as a migration strategy, urging business customers to switch over to a private branch exchange (on-site) solution as opposed to a central-office-based solution for business service features. Implementation of this strategy, which was designed to bypass the local telephone companies, intensified during and following divestiture. Telephone companies were directly affected by this strategy, for end-users began purchasing their own

Exhibit 4 MERIDIAN DIGITAL CENTREX USE IN THE UNITED STATES AS OF MARCH 26, 1988

	In-service		Shipped and in-service		In-service, shipped, and firm orders		
	Systems	**Lines**	**Systems**	**Lines**	**Systems**	**Lines**	**SRs***
Bell operating companies	594	1,610,166	696	1,956,973	757	2,087,921	44
Independent operating companies	265	292,633	280	387,810	288	401,299	6
Total United States	859	1,902,799	976	2,344,783	1,045	2,489,220	50

* Schedule requests are jobs that are not yet firm orders.
Source: Northern Telecom data.

private branch exchanges directly from AT&T and other vendors, rather than paying the telephone company's monthly per-line fees for central office-based business service features. The telephone companies did not like this migration strategy.

Northern Telecom introduced its digital centrex applications software and was able to capitalize on the resentment telephone companies felt toward AT&T. Meridian Digital Centrex (MDC), Northern's centrex software offering, was introduced in 1982, and sales grew significantly from 1985 to 1987. Exhibit 4 shows NTI's MDC statistics by customer type.

Telephone companies purchased MDC software for their DMS switches from NTI for the purpose of reselling to end-users the business service features the applications software provided. They often renamed the service for the purpose of developing brand identity and loyalty (much as in the same way Sears bought appliances made by Whirlpool and sold them under the Kenmore label). Bell-South, for example, used John Naismith to advertise centrex as ESSX service.

Exhibit 5 MAJOR END-USERS OF NTI'S MERIDIAN DIGITAL CENTREX

Vertical markets	Major MDC end-users	Example
Universities	35	Indiana University
Government offices		
Municipal	30	City of Las Vegas
State	20	Suncom (Florida)
Federal	11	Senate/White House
Major businesses	50	Ford Motor Company
Airports	15	Los Angeles (LAX)
Banks	27	Citicorp
Hospitals	16	Marquette Hospital
Telephone companies	11	NYNEX headquarters

Source: Northern Telecom data.

Exhibit 6 MERIDIAN DIGITAL CENTREX LINE SIZE DISTRIBUTION

MDC lines	Systems
1–1,999	658
2,000–9,999	241
10,000 +	71
MDC software, no lines	75
Total in-service, shipped, and on order through 1Q88	1,045

Source: Northern Telecom data.

Exhibit 5 provides a profile of some of the major Meridian Digital Centrex end-users by vertical markets served; Exhibit 6 provides a breakdown by line size of the Northern Telecom DMS systems that have Meridian Digital Centrex software.

FINANCIAL PERFORMANCE

Exhibit 7 is a consolidated review of the financial performance of Northern Telecom Limited and its subsidiaries during the period 1979–1987. As indicated, revenues for 1987 were $4.8 billion, up 11 percent from 1986. Net earnings for 1987 rose 15 percent to $329 million; up from $287 million in 1986. Central office switching accounted for $2.6 billion or 53 percent of total revenues in 1987. NTL had 48,778 employees as of year-end 1987, and 1987 earnings per share were $1.39.

Miller felt that Northern's success through the 1980s had been driven by five major factors:

- A sustained product development lead in digital central office switching technology (AT&T did not introduce a digital central office switch until 1983).
- Access to a huge market which had previously been restricted due to monopolistic constraints.
- A willingness by the regional Bell operating companies to be served by a vendor other than AT&T (AT&T had moved from the position of supplier and parent organization to that of a competitor).
- Equal access legislation requiring product replacement of old technology exchanges with new digital switches.
- The ability to dilute the effect of AT&T's migration strategy on the Bell operating companies by providing them with revenue-generating features in MDC applications software for the DMS.

AT&T'S 5ESS

Hall Miller believed that the marketplace was changing in a number of ways, in spite of Northern's continued success. Demand for digital switches had exceeded supply in the early 1980s. AT&T did not enter the digital switching marketplace

Exhibit 7 CONSOLIDATED 11-YEAR STATISTICAL REVIEW, NORTHERN TELECOM, INC., 1977–1987 (dollars in millions, except per share figures)

	1977	1979	1981	1983	1984	1985	1986	1987
Earnings and related data:								
Revenues	$1,149.7	$1,625.5	$2,146.1	$2,680.2	$3,374.0	$4,262.9	$4,383.6	$4,853.5
Cost of revenues	821.4	1,117.0	1,542.5	1,713.3	2,074.1	2,495.6	2,730.5	2,895.8
Selling, general, and administrative expense	149.1	234.9	300.1	454.8	603.2	701.9	764.6	917.8
Research and development expense	64.2	117.6	151.8	263.2	333.1	430.0	474.5	587.5
Depreciation on plant and equipment	29.1	77.9	100.8	126.6	162.8	203.3	247.3	264.1
Provision for income taxes	45.5	30.3	29.8	79.3	120.3	132.8	127.9	141.5
Earnings before extraordinary items	76.3	97.4	92.1	183.2	255.8	299.2	313.2	347.2
Net earnings applicable to common shares	80.2	97.4	105.4	216.7	243.2	273.8	286.6	328.8
Earnings per revenue dollar (cents)	7.0	6.0	4.9	8.1	7.2	6.4	6.5	6.8
Earnings per common share (dollars)								
Before extraordinary items	0.48	0.53	0.45	0.83	1.06	1.18	1.23	1.39
After extraordinary items	0.51	0.53	0.50	0.98	1.06	1.18	1.23	1.39
Dividends per share (dollars)	0.11	0.12	0.14	0.16	0.16	0.18	0.20	0.23
Financial position at December 31:								
Working capital	307.3	477.4	421.6	563.4	$1,570.7	859.0	933.9	1,188.7
Plant and equipment (at cost)	356.9	602.4	829.8	1,152.2	1,458.0	1,737.5	1,975.2	2,345.6
Accumulated depreciation	184.3	237.8	355.0	506.4	591.5	672.4	877.3	1,084.2
Total assets	698.8	1,620.8	1,809.4	2,309.4	3,072.9	3,490.0	3,961.1	4,869.0
Long-term debt	48.0	165.0	207.5	102.3	100.2	107.6	101.1	224.8
Redeemable retractable preferred shares	—	—	—	—	293.6	277.5	281.0	153.9
Redeemable preferred shares	—	—	—	—	—	73.3	73.3	73.3
Common shareholders' equity	431.0	793.5	719.5	1,178.3	1,379.8	1,614.6	1,894.9	2,333.3
Return on common shareholders' equity	19.4%	14.6%	15.7%	21.7%	19.0%	18.3%	16.3%	15.6%
Capital expenditures	42.1	148.4	174.9	305.7	437.3	457.3	303.8	416.7
Employees at December 31	24,962	33,301	35,444	39,318	46,993	46,549	46,202	48,778

Exhibit 7 (concluded)

	1st Quarter		2nd Quarter		3rd Quarter		4th Quarter	
	1986	1987	1986	1987	1986	1987	1986	1987
Quarterly financial data (unaudited)								
Revenues	$969.6	$1,143.3	$1,067.4	$1,253.0	$1,032.2	$1,158.1	$1,314.4	$1,299.1
Gross profit	323.1	403.8	389.4	489.9	404.5	479.1	536.1	584.9
Net earnings	50.1	60.1	64.9	77.6	66.0	69.5	132.2	140.0
Net earnings applicable to common shares	43.3	53.7	58.0	72.9	59.4	66.2	125.9	136.0
Earnings per common share	0.19	0.23	0.25	0.31	0.25	0.28	0.54	0.57
Weighted average number of common								
shares outstanding (thousands) . . .	233,154	235,237	223,650	235,573	234,199	236,024	234,767	236,444

	1983	1984	1985	1986	1987				
Revenues by principal product lines									
Central office switching	$981.9	$1,452.9	$2,141.3	$2,230.9	$2,577.2				
Integrated business systems and terminals	985.8	1,162.9	1,256.6	1,284.7	1,302.0				
Transmission	376.3	385.1	431.2	468.1	498.6				
Cable and outside plant	275.5	314.9	373.4	348.4	408.2				
Other telecommunications	60.7	58.9	60.4	51.5	67.5				
Total	$2,680.2	$3,374.0	$4,262.9	$4,383.6	$4,853.5				

Exhibit 8 NORTHERN DMS AND AT&T 5ESS SYSTEM SHIPMENTS BY HALF YEAR		
	Northern	**AT&T**
1985		
First half	144	169
Second half	145	141
1986		
First half	108	152
Second half	139	144
1987		
First half	128	135
Second half	127	130

Sources: Northern Telecom data; AT&T estimates.

until 1983 with the 5ESS switch; as a result, Northern Telecom had a substantial competitive lead in both product and feature development and in marketing its products to the telephone companies. AT&T found itself in the unusual position of being an industry technology follower rather than the industry leader. Moreover, AT&T had not been concerned previously with having to market its products.

Exhibit 8 compares Northern's DMS and AT&T's 5ESS shipments in half-year increments starting in 1985. Although only 13 of AT&T's 5ESSs were in service by the end of 1983, with an additional 72 being placed in service in 1984, pent-up demand in the telephone companies for additional products and suppliers to help satisfy equal access requirements helped sales of the 5ESS to grow. Moreover, Northern experienced delivery problems in 1985 with its Remote Switching Center (RSC), one of its remote products, as well as performance issues with a particular release of operating system software. Combined with the strong market demand for digital technology, these events helped to assure that AT&T's 5ESS would be a successful product. The U.S. telephone digital switching market became a two-supplier arena. AT&T claimed to have 800 5ESS systems, 660 remotes, and 15 million lines in service as of September 1987.

PRICING

Due to equal access, demand for digital switches exceeded supply from 1982 to 1986. During this period, delivery time determined which vendor a telephone company would choose to buy digital switches from. Volume sales agreements negotiated with each regional or local telephone company for multiple changeouts of old technology switches were the norm rather than the exception; price was not a key selection criteria. However, with supply exceeding the demand for digital switches from 1986 onward, the situation had become one of competitive bidding for each switch replacement, with bidding parties offering aggressive discounts. The objective was to win the initial system even at the sake of short-term profits, for winning the switch meant additional opportunities for revenue through software and hardware upgrades and extensions.

As in many companies, Northern Telecom's marketing organization had a competitive intelligence group. A major emphasis of this group was tracking competitive positioning in the marketplace. Hall Miller had developed a great deal of confidence in the reliability of the models used by this group to support the competitive bidding process. Pricing had become an extremely sensitive issue. Miller had concerns that the discounts the vendors were offering often resulted in the winner leaving large sums of money on the table (e.g., coming in with a bid at $500,000 less than the next lowest competitor, when all that would have been necessary to win the switch was a $100,000 discount). Moreover, Miller did not want bids to be so low that the telephone companies would refuse to accept higher bids.

In addition to increased competition and pricing pressures from AT&T, other factors were affecting the market. With the completion of the equal access process, telephone company construction budgets were declining 3-4 percent annually. Along with the decline in capital budgets was a corresponding increase in the expense budgets. As a result of this shift, telephone companies were expected to allocate more budget dollars toward upgrading equipment and less toward the purchase of new switches.

THE ANALOG SWITCH REPLACEMENT MARKET

Following equal access, the next major determinant of growth in the U. S. telecommunications market was replacement of analog switches. These switches were analog stored program control (software driven) AT&T switches that were installed throughout the late 1960s and the 1970s. Exhibit 9 shows historical information and projections of the central office switch market by technology through 1991. As indicated in Exhibit 9, the analog switches accounted for 57 million lines of the total installed base, or 46 percent of the market, compared to a total of 36 million digital lines. The analog replacement market was said to be a $30 billion market for switch manufacturers over the next 20 years.

Numerous factors were involved in analog replacement. Unlike other switches that had to be replaced, analog switches had been upgraded to support equal access requirements because they were software driven. With depreciation service lives of 15–20 years, they would remain in the network until the early 1990s, assuming that the depreciation rates and regulatory positions continued (switch replacement required approval from the appropriate Public Utility Commission). The latest versions of these switches offered a comprehensive set of centrex features, and they traditionally were large in terms of line size (30,000–55,000 lines). As such, a digital replacement switch would require both sufficient capacity and an equivalent set of centrex features.

These analog switches were traditionally located in wire centers, which were simply buildings that housed more than one type of central office switch. Northern had a number of strategies to establish a presence in these wire centers (which were typically located in high-growth metropolitan areas) in the hope that this initial presence would provide a competitive advantage when an analog switch became available for digital replacement. Other vendors were marketing adjuncts for the analog switches, which were enhancements designed to prolong their lives,

Exhibit 9   CENTRAL OFFICE EQUIPMENT MARKET BY TECHNOLOGY (lines in thousands)

	1986	1987	1988	1989	1990	1991
TOTAL MARKET						
Installed Base:						
Digital	27,048	36,560	45,230	54,072	62,693	72,057
Analog	56,143	57,022	57,426	57,854	56,750	54,800
Other	38,175	31,322	25,613	19,826	15,933	12,293
Total	121,366	124,904	128,269	131,752	135,376	139,150
Percent:						
Digital	22.3	29.3	35.3	41.0	46.3	51.8
Analog	46.3	45.6	44.8	43.9	41.9	39.4
Other	31.4	25.1	19.9	15.1	11.8	8.8
Demand:						
Digital	10,066	9,508	8,670	8,844	8,620	9,365
Analog	1,591	881	417	429	36	0
Total	11,657	10,389	9,087	9,273	8,656	9,365
REGIONAL BELL OPERATING COMPANIES						
Installed Base:						
Digital	14,509	21,341	27,389	33,553	39,997	46,966
Analog	53,899	54,729	55,114	55,451	54,317	52,379
Other	25,246	20,114	15,998	11,891	9,077	6,648
Total	93,654	96,184	98,501	100,895	103,391	105,993
Percent:						
Digital	15.5	22.2	27.8	33.3	38.7	44.3
Analog	57.6	56.9	56.0	55.0	52.5	49.4
Other	27.0	20.9	17.2	11.8	8.8	6.2
Demand:						
Digital	6,904	6,832	6,048	6,165	6,443	6,969
Analog	1,53	830	385	338	0	0
Total	8,434	7,662	6,432	6,502	6,443	6,969
INDEPENDENT OPERATING COMPANIES						
Installed Base:						
Digital	12,539	15,219	17,841	20,519	22,696	25,091
Analog	2,244	2,293	2,312	2,403	2,433	2,421
Other	12,929	11,208	9,615	7,935	6,856	5,645
Total	27,712	28,720	29,768	30,857	31,895	33,157
Percent:						
Digital	45.2	53.0	59.9	66.5	71.0	75.7
Analog	8.1	7.9	7.8	7.8	7.6	7.3
Other	46.7	39.1	32.3	25.7	21.4	17.0
Demand:						
Digital	3,162	2,676	2,622	2,679	2,177	2,396
Analog	61	51	32	91	36	0
Total	3,223	2,727	2,654	2,770	2,213	2,396

Source: Northern Business Information, *Central Office Equipment Market: 1987 Edition.*

while these same vendors worked to develop competitive replacement digital switches. As such, adjuncts were basically stopgap measures designed to meet a particular need and to buy additional R&D switch development time.

INTEGRATED SERVICES DIGITAL NETWORKS

Beyond the replacement of analog switches, the next phase of telecommunications technology was called ISDN (Integrated Services Digital Network). ISDN would allow standard interfaces between different pieces of equipment, such as computers, and it would free end-users from concerns as to whether new equipment from one vendor would interface with existing equipment made by another vendor which an end-user might already own. ISDN would also allow the transmission of voice, data, and video simultaneously over the same facilities (with existing technology, voice, high-speed data, and video must be transmitted separately or over separate lines).

Although universal standards for ISDN had yet to be resolved, useful applications were already apparent. Since ISDN phones were designed to display the calling number and the name assigned to the number on a small screen simultaneous with ringing, the party being called would be able to know where the call was coming from prior to answering. This call screening ability would severely limit the ability of prank callers to remain anonymous, and could provide opportunities to greatly enhance 911 services (police, fire department, and rescue squad) by immediately identifying the calling party's location and other useful information (such as a known medical condition or the location of the nearest fire hydrant) and efficiently routing both the call and the information to all parties involved.

Northern was positioning ISDN as its premier Meridian Digital Centrex offering, as it offered both business voice features and high-speed data capabilities over a single line. Northern's strategy was to move end-users from MDC to ISDN, stressing that existing MDC feature capabilities could serve customer needs today while ISDN standards and applications were being developed by industry regulatory organizations and other telecommunications equipment and computer vendors. In addition, MDC was fully integrated with ISDN, with ISDN combining existing voice and data services while adding additional new features and sophisticated applications.

AT&T, on the other hand, had been advertising ISDN heavily to end-users and was attempting to position it as a technologically superior *replacement* to centrex, rather than as a centrex enhancement. AT&T was pursuing this strategy since BRCS, its digital centrex offering, was perceived as being much less "feature-rich" than its analog centrex systems or Northern's Meridian Digital Centrex.

Northern Telecom placed the first successful ISDN phone call in the United States in November 1987, and had a number of DMS sites in service offering ISDN capabilities. In addition, both Northern Telecom and AT&T had numerous ISDN field trials and commercial applications scheduled with telephone companies and business end-users throughout the country at specific sites during the 1988–1990 time frame.

OTHER COMPETITORS

Replacement of analog switches and ISDN were two potential markets attracting other companies into the U.S. digital central office telecommunications market. Another potential opportunity/threat for Northern was that the seven regional Bell operating companies (RBOCs) had petitioned Judge Green to lift the restrictions barring them from providing information services, going into the long-distance business, and manufacturing terminals and central office switches through direct subsidiaries and/or joint ventures. Most of the telephone companies were interested in having a third supplier in addition to AT&T and Northern Telecom to ensure that pricing and product development remained highly competitive. Following is a discussion of some of these potential competitors and the inroads each had made into the RBOCs.

Siemens

Siemens, a West German conglomerate, had sales of DM 8 billion for its telecommunications segment in 1987 (sales for the entire company in 1987 were $20 billion U.S.). Seventy-three percent of Siemens's total sales for the year were from Germany and Europe, with 10 percent from North America.

The headquarters for Siemens's U.S. telecommunications division was in Boca Raton, Florida. Also located at Boca Raton was an R&D facility, while manufacturing sites were located at Cherry Hill, New Jersey, and Hauppauge, New York. Siemens had 25,000 employees in the United States.

Siemens's digital central office offering was available in three versions: DE3, with a maximum capacity of 7,500 lines; DE4, with a maximum capacity of 30,000 lines; and DE5, with a maximum capacity of 100,000 lines.

Siemens had announced ambitious feature rollout plans for its offerings, promising both centrex and ISDN feature parity with both AT&T and Northern Telecom. However, whether it could effectively leapfrog the software development intervals incurred by the industry leaders remained to be seen.

Siemens had made inroads with five of the seven RBOCs: Ameritech, Bell-South, Bell Atlantic, NYNEX, and Southwestern Bell. Siemens's progress to this point had been based primarily on both competitive pricing and the desire of the Bell Operating Companies to increase competition in the central office switch market.

In spite of Siemens's recent success, industry consultants cited operational and maintenance problems with the company's digital products regarding system reliability, architecture, and compliance to Bellcore standards. (Bell Communications Research, or "Bellcore," was a standards organization jointly owned by the seven RBOCs.) However, heavy R&D efforts were underway to resolve these issues at Boca Raton, and Siemens was fully committed to adapting its products to U.S. market specifications.

Siemens had a $2.1 million contract with West Virginia University to develop computer-based training courses in operating its digital central office equipment. To strengthen its international position in telecommunications, the company purchased 80 percent of GTE's foreign transmissions operations in 1986.

Ericsson

Ericsson, a Swedish-based telecommunications company, had consolidated international sales of $5.5 billion in 1987. Europe and Sweden accounted for 84 percent of the geographic distribution of total sales for the year, with the United States and Canada contributing 7 percent. Like Siemens, Ericsson was attempting to crack the hold that Northern Telecom and AT&T shared on the U.S. central office switch market. Ericsson had targeted BellSouth, NYNEX, Southwestern Bell, and US West as key accounts it wanted to go after.

Ericsson's digital central office offering was the AXE 10. Ericsson had already installed the AXE in 64 countries and had a worldwide installed base of over 11 million lines. Like Siemens, Ericsson had announced aggressive feature rollout plans (bypassing years of software development by AT&T Technologies and Bell-Northern Research) which it might not be able to deliver.

The AXE was manufactured in 16 countries and was being made available by Ericsson's Network Systems Division in Richardson, Texas. No plans were underway to construct manufacturing facilities for the AXE in the United States.

Ericsson had made a number of recent strategic moves intended to strengthen its position in the U.S. marketplace. The company had reorganized by regions to serve more effectively the RBOC markets; moreover, it had reorganized marketing for the division into the functional areas of market development, marketing communications, systems engineering, and marketing systems. Plans had been announced for a technical training center at the company's U.S. headquarters in Richardson, Texas. In addition, Ericsson had announced that it would be working with IBM to develop private networking capabilities.

NEC

NEC had $13 billion in worldwide sales for 1987, $4 billion of which was from its communications segment. NEC was the leading telecommunications company in Japan; 67 percent of sales were to Japanese customers and 33 percent were in overseas markets.

NEC's digital central office offering was the NEAX61E. The switch was primarily an ISDN adjunct that interfaced analog systems and grew into a full central office. As such, it was basically an interim offering designed to extend the life of analog switches while buying time to improve the product in the hopes of having a competitive offering ready when analog replacement began.

NEC claimed that the NEAX61E was serving 4.8 million lines in over 250 sites in 40 countries. The U.S. headquarters was located in Irving, Texas, where production of the system was scheduled to begin by mid-1988. NEC had made inroads with four of the seven RBOCs—Bell Atlantic, NYNEX, Pacific Telesis, and US West.

The company had recently announced plans for a switching technology center in Irving, Texas, dedicated to developing software for central office switches and customer premises equipment. A second facility in San Jose, California, would develop software for intelligent transport networks, transmission systems, data communications, and network management systems. NEC claimed that it was moving its software development closer to its customers.

A major problem that NEC had to overcome was one of perception. NEC's first attempt to enter the U.S. market with the NEAX61E in the early 1980s met with little success. The product was highly-touted, launched, and subsequently withdrawn due to numerous performance issues. Many industry experts felt that NEC was again entering the U.S. market prematurely with a product that was not powerful enough to provide advanced business features or large capacities.

Stromberg-Carlson

Stromberg-Carlson was a division of Plessy, a British telecommunications corporation. Reliable data on Plessy and Stromberg's 1987 financial performance was not available. Stromberg-Carlson's offering, the DCO (Digital Central Office), was available in three versions: the DCO-CS, which was a toll version of the DCO (7,000 trunks maximum); the DCO-SE (a 1,080 line switch designed to serve as a rural central office); and the DCO (32,000 lines maximum). In addition, Stromberg-Carlson offered a full line of remotes, ranging in size from 90 lines to 10,000 lines.

Unlike Siemens, Ericsson, and NEC, Stromberg-Carlson had been a player in the U.S. telecommunications marketplace for a number of years. Stromberg was a primary supplier to the independent operating companies; however, it was now trying to crack the RBOC market as well.

Although owned by Britain's Plessy Telecommunications, Stromberg-Carlson's U.S. headquarters and DCO manufacturing were located in Lake Mary, Florida, a suburb of Orlando. Stromberg's manufacturing capacity was 1 million lines per year at the Lake Mary facility; however, less than half of this capability was being used.

Stromberg-Carlson was committed to maintaining strong ties with its independent operating company customers. In addition, the company had made inroads with BellSouth and Pacific Telesis. Stromberg had recently signed a volume supply agreement with South Central Bell over the 1989–1990 time frame.

Stromberg's strategy was to target small-to-mid-size central offices (5,000–12,000 lines), focusing on rural applications. Stromberg's lack of a large switch limited the market it could address; however, its niche strategy had served it well over the years in that it could economically provide digital central office capabilities in small line sizes.

In response to its agreement with South Central Bell, Stromberg-Carlson had recently opened a sales office in Birmingham, Alabama. The company had a small installation force and was negotiating with AT&T to arrange to install some of its switches in South Central Bell.

Stromberg-Carlson shipped its 1,000th remote in December 1987 and placed its 2 millionth line in service in January 1988; 200 switches, 400 remotes, and 400,000 lines were shipped by Stromberg-Carlson to the U.S. market in 1987.

HALL MILLER'S STRATEGIC PROBLEM

Musing over the status of Northern's potential competitors, Hall Miller's gaze returned to the report on his desk. Overall, the *Communications Week* study had given Northern high marks relative to most of the competitors. However, there were shortcomings in particular areas he wanted to address (Exhibits 10 and 11

Exhibit 10 SUMMARY OF VENDOR PERFORMANCE RANKINGS BY BELL OPERATING COMPANY RESPONDENTS (n = 497; scale of 1 to 5, where 1 = Poor and 5 = Excellent)

	AT&T	Ericsson	NEC	Northern Telecom	Siemens	Stromberg-Carlson
Initial cost	3.12	3.37	3.42	3.83	3.51	3.76
Life cycle cost	3.55	3.26	3.29	3.53	3.48	3.26
Strength of financial backing	4.66	3.48	3.74	4.24	4.05	3.05
Availability	3.90	3.36	3.29	4.17	3.40	3.56
Service/support	4.07	3.21	2.97	3.39	3.22	3.50
Reliability	4.06	3.31	3.08	3.52	3.47	3.24
Delivery	3.76	3.18	2.80	3.71	3.21	3.39
Experience in industry	4.88	3.97	3.34	4.29	3.78	3.91
High technology company	4.63	3.77	3.69	4.28	4.08	3.23
Sound technical documentation	4.32	3.24	2.67	3.50	3.37	3.10
Breadth of product line	4.07	3.24	3.14	3.90	3.33	2.80
International experience	3.19	4.08	3.83	3.58	4.20	2.64
Long-term commitment to R&D	4.44	3.81	3.83	3.99	3.91	3.04

Source: *Communications Week.*

Exhibit 11 SUMMARY OF VENDOR PERFORMANCE RANKINGS BY INDEPENDENT OPERATING COMPANY RESPONDENTS (n = 1,047; scale of 1 to 5, where 1 = Poor and 5 = Excellent)

	AT&T	Ericsson	NEC	Northern Telecom	Siemens	Stromberg-Carlson
Initial cost	2.40	2.67	3.70	3.67	3.12	3.96
Life cycle cost	3.24	2.74	3.17	3.71	3.04	3.61
Strength of financial backing	4.65	3.31	3.69	4.34	3.65	3.50
Availability	3.56	2.61	3.22	4.06	2.93	4.03
Service/support	3.79	2.81	2.98	3.81	3.02	3.75
Reliability	4.23	2.80	3.41	4.08	3.25	3.63
Delivery	3.46	2.61	3.16	3.83	2.91	3.80
Experience in industry	4.74	3.27	3.55	4.58	3.62	4.19
High technology company	4.72	3.35	3.93	4.45	3.84	3.72
Sound technical documentation	4.47	2.78	2.95	4.08	3.32	3.63
Breadth of product line	4.16	2.83	3.43	4.12	3.27	3.47
International experience	3.84	3.48	4.04	3.84	4.03	3.27
Long-term commitment to R&D	4.67	3.21	3.80	4.29	3.69	3.57

Source: *Communications Week.*

contain the results of the study, segmented by Bell and independent operating company respondents).

In terms of the changing market and increased competition, Miller felt Northern had a competitive advantage in that the company had the largest installed base of digital switches of any vendor. This would help generate revenue through hardware and software extensions and new features prior to the replacement of analog switches. However, Hall had seen AT&T's 5ESS shipments reach parity in a relatively short period of time, and it seemed that competitors were popping up everywhere. In addition, 1988 MDC sales had been sluggish; Hall felt this was largely due to customer misperception resulting from AT&T's hype of ISDN.

Miller glanced out the window toward the Raleigh-Durham Airport. It was 5:20 PM, and the highway was packed with traffic. He knew that he faced a number of strategic decisions if Northern Telecom were to maintain its leadership position in the digital central office switch market.

NUCOR CORPORATION*

"It's the closest thing to a perfect company in the steel industry."
Daniel Roling, analyst for Merrill Lynch

With earnings growth over the past decade averaging better than 23 percent per year, Nucor prospered in the steel industry while giant companies barely survived. Few high-tech companies could match Nucor's record (see Exhibit 1). But in 1986, Nucor was moving into an era where the easy pickings were over. One securities analyst believed that Nucor would not be able to find alluring new opportunities, stating: "Their rapid growth of the last 10 years is simply not repeatable."

BACKGROUND

Nuclear Corporation. Nuclear Corporation of America was formed in 1955 by a merger of Nuclear Consultants, Inc., and parts of REO Motors. Between 1955 and 1964 various managements tried unsuccessfully to make a profit by way of acquisitions and divestitures. One of the acquisitions was Vulcraft, a steel joist manufacturer. By 1965 Nuclear Corporation was losing $2 million on sales of $22 million. A new group got control of the company in 1965 and installed Vulcraft general manager Ken Iverson (who headed the only profitable division) as president. "I got the job by default," Iverson said.

Entry into the Steel Industry. Iverson decided that Vulcraft—a manufacturer of steel joists for buildings—ought to make its own steel. His goal was to achieve a low-cost position so as to match or beat the low prices of imported steel: "We had some vision that if we were successful, we could expand and create another business by selling steel in the general marketplace." In 1968 Nucor built its first steel mill in Darlington, South Carolina. By 1985 Nucor operated four steel mills, six joist plants, two cold finishing plants, three steel deck plants, and a grinding ball plant throughout the South, Southwest, and West. About 65 percent of Nucor's steel was sold in open markets, while 35 percent went to Vulcraft and other Nucor products. Until the recession of 1982–83 sales and earnings grew at an astonishing clip. Even during the recession Nucor managed to eke out a profit while other integrated steel companies lost billions.

* Prepared by Professors Charles I. Stubbart and Dean Schroeder, the University of Massachusetts.

Exhibit 1   SIX-YEAR FINANCIAL REVIEW, NUCOR CORPORATION, 1980–1985

	1980	1981	1982	1983	1984	1985
Net sales	$482,420,363	$544,820,621	$486,018,162	$542,531,431	$660,259,922	$758,495,374
Costs and expenses:						
Cost of products sold	369,415,571	456,210,289	408,606,641	461,727,688	539,731,252	600,797,865
Marketing and administrative expenses	38,164,559	33,524,820	31,720,315	33,988,054	45,939,311	59,079,802
Interest expense (income)	(1,219,965)	10,256,546	7,899,110	(748,619)	(3,959,092)	(7,560,645)
	406,360,165	499,991,655	448,226,128	494,967,123	581,711,471	652,317,022
Earnings before taxes	76,060,198	44,828,966	37,792,034	47,564,308	78,548,451	106,178,352
Federal income taxes	31,000,000	10,100,000	15,600,000	19,700,000	34,000,000	47,700,000
Net earnings	$ 45,060,198	$ 34,728,966	$ 22,192,034	$ 27,864,308	$ 44,548,451	$ 58,478,352
Net earnings per share	$3.31	$2.51	$1.59	$1.98	$3.16	$4.11
Dividends declared per share	$.22	$.24	$.26	$.30	$.36	$.40
Percentage of earnings to sales	9.3%	6.4%	4.6%	5.1%	6.7%	7.7%
Return on average equity	29.0%	17.8%	10.0%	11.4%	16.0%	17.8%
Return on average assets	16.9%	10.3%	5.9%	7.0%	9.8%	11.2%
Capital expenditures	$ 62,440,354	$101,519,282	$ 14,788,707	$ 19,617,147	$ 26,074,653	$ 29,066,398
Depreciation	13,296,218	21,599,951	26,286,671	27,109,582	28,899,421	31,105,788
Sales per employee	150,756	155,663	133,156	148,639	176,069	197,011
Current assets	$115,365,727	$131,382,292	$132,542,648	$193,889,162	$253,453,373	$334,769,147
Current liabilities	66,493,445	73,032,313	66,102,706	88,486,795	100,533,684	121,255,828
Working capital	$ 48,872,282	$ 58,349,979	$ 66,439,942	$105,402,367	$152,919,689	$213,513,319
Property, plant, and equipment	$173,074,273	$252,616,074	$239,071,390	$231,304,817	$228,102,790	$225,274,674
Total assets	$291,221,867	$384,782,127	$371,632,941	$425,567,052	$482,188,465	$560,311,188
Long-term debt	$ 39,605,169	$ 83,754,231	$ 48,229,615	$ 45,731,000	$ 43,232,384	$ 40,233,769
Percentage of debt to capital	18.2%	28.3%	17.2%	15.0%	12.6%	10.1%
Stockholders' equity	$177,603,690	$212,376,020	$232,281,057	$258,129,694	$299,602,834	$357,502,028
Per share	$12.96	$15.25	$16.60	$18.32	$21.16	$24.97
Shares outstanding	13,699,994	13,927,014	13,991,882	14,090,181	14,161,079	14,315,005
Stockholders	22,000	22,000	22,000	21,000	22,000	22,000
Employees	3,300	3,700	3,600	3,700	3,800	3,900

STEEL INDUSTRY CONDITIONS, 1985

Companies competing in the U.S. steel industry in 1985 were of four distinct types: integrated U.S. companies, foreign manufacturers, minimills, and specialty steel producers. The large integrated domestic companies (see Exhibit 2) got their start at the turn of the century. Integrated companies held about 45 to 55 percent of the market. Specialty steel producers manufactured relatively low volumes of steel with varying degrees of hardness, purity, and strength. Imports of steel into the United States accounted for about 20 to 25 percent of domestic sales. (Imports probably held a larger share, taking into account the steel in imported automobiles and other products.) Minimills, which transformed scrap metal into steel using electric furnaces, had a market share of about 20 to 25 percent of the domestic market.

Recent History.   Since the early 1970s integrated steel producers had suffered a painful decline. During 1965–74 steel demand was strong, and industry officials expected major growth after 1974. But they were wrong. Steel production in the United States had fallen from its 1974 level, and many analysts believed that the 1974 levels would never be reached again (Exhibit 3). Much of this decline was traceable to the long-term trends toward smaller lighter cars, the inroads of competing materials (such as aluminum and plastics), a shift in emphasis away from smokestack industries to service industries, and greater use of imported steel in U.S. products.

Between 1960 and 1985 foreign competitors and domestic minimills invested heavily in building all-new facilities with the latest technology. Major integrated companies spent their investment capital on trying to spruce up existing plants and correct gross inefficiencies. Facing weak demand, having less efficient facili-

---

Exhibit 2   PRODUCTION CAPACITY OF LARGEST U.S. INTEGRATED STEEL COMPANIES, 1984

Firm	Raw steel capacity (millions of tons per year)
1. U.S. Steel	26.2
2. LTV	19.1
3. Bethlehem	18.0
4. Inland	9.4
5. Armco	6.8
6. National	5.6
7. Wheeling-Pittsburgh	4.5
8. Weirton	4.0
9. Ford Motor Co. (Rouge Steel)	3.6
10. McLouth	2.0
11. CF&I	2.0 (partially closed)
12. Interlake	1.4
13. Sharon	1.0
14. California	2.1 (closed)
Total	105.7

Source: Company reports; Oppenheimer & Co., *Metal Bulletin*; *Iron and Steel Works of the World*, 8th edition.

Exhibit 3 U.S. RAW STEEL PRODUCTION, FINISHED STEEL SHIPMENTS, AND STEEL IMPORTS, 1956–1984

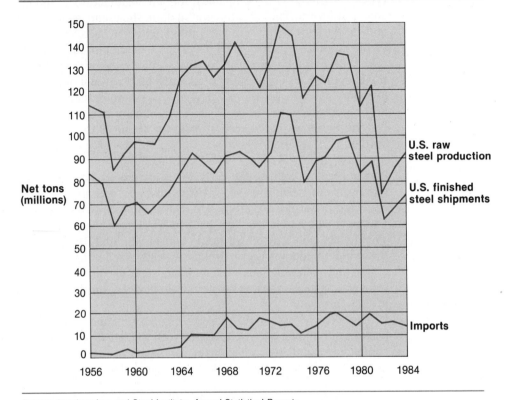

Source: American Iron and Steel Institute, *Annual Statistical Reports.*

ties, and with an appreciating U.S. dollar making the price of foreign-made steel cheaper and cheaper, the biggest domestic integrated companies suffered huge losses in the late 1970s and early 1980s (Exhibit 4).

Other problems also contributed to the rapid slide. The steelworkers union was able to negotiate large wage increases in 1968 and 1971, and union work rules hampered steel company efforts to increase productivity in their plants. Only in 1983 did the steelworkers union reluctantly agree to wage concessions and work rule modifications under the pressure of plant closings.

Poor Investments. Expecting major increases in demand for 1975–85, integrated companies made large investments in ore mines and iron pelletizing facilities. An important share of their investment dollars went into meeting environmental regulations. Integrated companies' financial calculations persuaded them to stick with modifications of existing plants instead of building new "greenfield" plants. As a result, not one all-new integrated steel plant had been built for over 20 years in the United States. Given the high cost of capital, the complex environmental constraints, weak demand, and intense foreign/domestic competition, it was

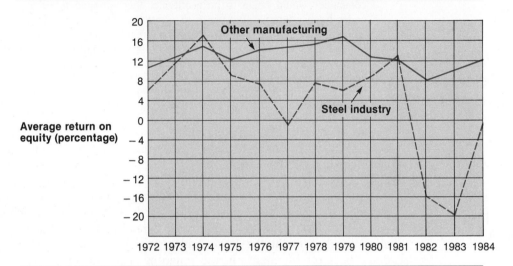

Exhibit 4   PROFITABILITY OF U.S. DOMESTIC STEEL INDUSTRY RELATIVE TO ALL OTHER MANUFACTURING INDUSTRIES, 1972–1984

Source: *Forbes,* May 1986.

unlikely that any new integrated plants would be built in the United States in the foreseeable future.

Imports and Protection.   The steel strike of 1959 provided the first opportunity for foreign steel firms to make inroads into the U.S. market. By the 1980s—despite several attempts to limit imports via voluntary restraints and trigger pricing (a minimum pricing rule)—the integrated companies found themselves with 140 million tons of excess capacity, much of it in old, inefficient plants. They had no choice but to face the music, close many plants, and sell unproductive assets—a protracted and painful process for the companies, the steelworkers, and many local communities. Within one four-year period steelmakers wrote off $4.4 billion in assets and took $7 billion in losses. Steel companies, steelworkers, and endangered communities struggled mightily to persuade the Reagan administration and the Congress to limit steel imports. A reluctant Reagan administration agreed to negotiate voluntary restraints in 1985. Even so, to the integrated companies, the rust bowl communities, and to over 200,000 permanently laid-off steelworkers, it seemed that too little had been done too late.

Foreign steel imports in 1985 accounted for about 25 percent of the U.S. market in spite of the Reagan administration's negotiating bilateral voluntary restraints with foreign governments. These restraint agreements aimed at limiting imports to about 21 percent of the market. Sentiment was growing in Congress to stem the tidal wave of foreign imports in the face of a $130 billion trade deficit during 1985. Ken Iverson, Nucor's CEO, steadfastly argued against protecting the domestic steel industry:

We've had this "temporary" relief for a long time. We had a voluntary quota system in the early 1970s. We had trigger prices in the late 1970s. And what happened during these periods? As soon as prices began to rise so that steel companies would begin to be profitable, they stopped modernizing. It's only under intense competitive pressure—both internally from minimills and externally from the Japanese and the Koreans—that the big steel companies have been forced to modernize. . . . In 1980 the industry still had rolling mills dating from the Civil War. . . . Out of all this turmoil will come a lot of things which are beneficial: more of an orientation toward technology, greater productivity, certainly a lot of changes in management structure.

Future Prospects. Speculating about 1986, steel producers expected another year like 1985: declining tonnage, stable prices, slightly declining import shares, and overall profitability near zero for the industry. Their forecasts hinged on a GNP growth of approximately 3 percent. Industry analysts foresaw that a reduction in imports (traced to the falling value of the U.S. dollar) would offset an expected decline in steel consumption. Demand for steel in machinery, railroad equipment, farm equipment, and other capital items was falling. Analysts were also uncertain about the 1986 demand for autos. Some estimates placed 1986 domestic steel shipments in the range of 70 to 75 million tons (not counting imports). The prospect of labor negotiations beginning in the second half of 1986 represented a major uncertainty for steel producers and customers.

Exhibit 5 UTILIZATION RATES OF U.S. STEELMAKING CAPACITY, 1975–1985

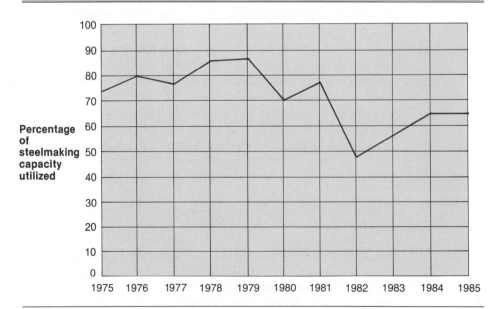

Source: AISI statistics.

Exhibit 6 STEEL INDUSTRY PROJECTIONS FOR 1985, 1990, AND 2000						
				Projected Ranges		
			1990		*2000*	
	1980 actual	**1985 (projected)**	**Low**	**High**	**Low**	**High**
Import share of U.S. market (percent)	17.0%	24.0%	28.0	28.0%	32.0%	32.0%
Domestic shipments (millions of tons)	83.9	76.0	73.1	75.6	71.4	78.2
Imports (millions of tons)	17.2	24.0	28.4	29.4	33.6	36.8
Total shipments (millions of tons)	86.7	77.0	74.1	76.6	72.4	79.2
Minimill shipments (millions of tons)	12.0	14.4	20.5	20.5	29.0	29.0
Minimill capacity (millions of tons)	16.0	22.0	27.0	27.0	35.0	35.0
Minimill productivity (work hours per ton)	4.0	2.8	2.2	2.2	1.5	1.5
Integrated shipments (millions of ton)	74.7	62.6	53.6	56.1	43.4	50.2
Integrated raw steel production (millions of tons)	102.3	82.3	67.8	71.0	49.9	57.7
Integrated capacity (millions of tons)	138.4	108.3	80.0	81.6	55.4	64.1
Integrated productivity (work hours per ton)	9.5	7.2	6.0	6.0	4.5	4.5
Capacity utilization rate (percent)	75.3%	76.0%	85.0%	87.0%	90.0%	90.0%
Total employment (in thousands)	401.6	247.9	195.0	201.6	129.6	141.7

Source: Barnett, *Minimills.*

But there was a bright side too. Steel companies entered the year determined to extract concessions from the United Steelworkers Union. Companies had eliminated most of their grossly inefficient facilities. Prices were edging up. Capacity utilization approached 70 percent, compared to a low of 48 percent in 1982 (Exhibit 5). A weakening dollar made imports less attractive.

Analysts estimated that worldwide demand had stabilized. From 1979 to 1985 steel output in the industrial nations dropped precipitously from 442 million tons to 331 million tons. Capacity had been cut back 28 million tons in Europe, 23 million tons in the United States, and 17 million tons in Japan. One U.S. steel producer predicted that an additional 20 million tons in U.S. capacity would have to go. Exhibit 6 offers some industry projections for steel.

STEEL MINIMILLS: AN INDUSTRY WITHIN AN INDUSTRY

The United States had about 50 minimills. As U.S. Steel, Bethlehem, Republic, National, and LTV surrendered market share and lost billions, new entrants into the domestic market such as North Star, Nucor, Co-Steel, Florida Steel, and others prospered—and even displaced imports. Contrary to typical relationships between scale and efficiency, minimills manufactured high-quality steel inexpensively, with plants of 200,000 to 1 million tons of annual electric-furnace capacity; integrated plants producing 2 million to 10 million tons using open-hearth and basic oxygen furnace equipment were the high-cost producers.

Technology.   The electric-furnace technology of minimills was first developed by Northwestern Steel and Wire in the 1930s. Exhibit 7 shows a comparison of the two processes, integrated versus minimill; the comparative simplicity of minimills is apparent. First, minimills use electric arc furnaces compared to integrated plants that use open-hearth (about 10 percent) or basic oxygen furnaces (about 90 percent), as shown in Exhibit 8. Minimills simply charge scrap into an electric arc furnace to produce molten steel, then continuously cast the molten metal into semifinished shapes. Continuous casters eliminated reheating and increased the yield from molten metal to finished product. Unlike integrated mills, minimills were expressly designed for rebuilding and technical updating. Many integrated plants used obsolete ingot-casting technologies.

Product Specialization.   Early on, minimills fashioned small specialized steel products like reinforcing rods for use in concrete work, rather than making huge beams, slabs, or sheets. Product specialization increased their efficiency. Steel

Exhibit 7   COMPARATIVE STEELMAKING METHODS

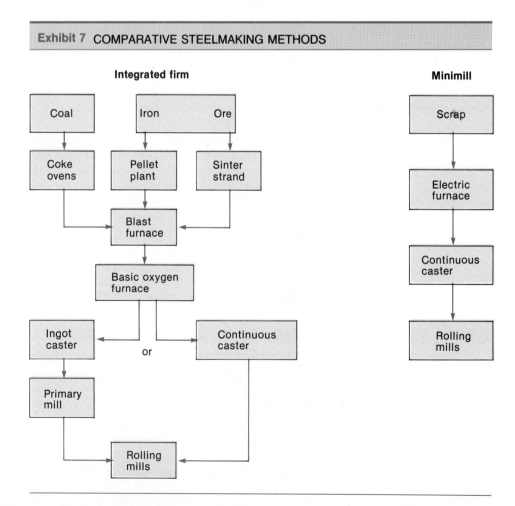

Exhibit 8   U.S. STEEL PRODUCTION BY PROCESS, 1975–1985

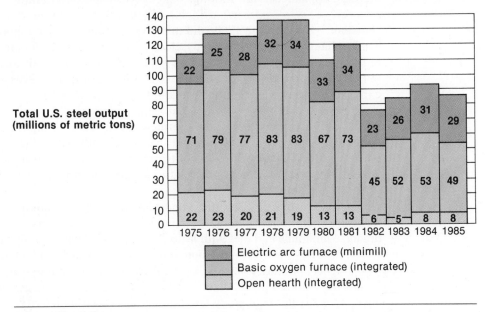

**Total U.S. steel output
(millions of metric tons)**

Source: AISI statistics.

slabs were still predominantly the private preserve of the integrated companies. But, as time passed, minimill companies expanded their product lines. Exhibit 9 compares minimill product lines to integrated mill product lines. Nucor in 1985 produced cold-finished bars and was devoting a major innovative effort to the challenge of adapting minimill technology to sheet steel production. If Nucor

Exhibit 9   PRODUCT CATEGORIES OF INTEGRATED MILLS AND MINIMILLS

Products of integrated mills	Capable of being made with present minimill production technology?
Slabs:	
Hot-rolled sheets	No
Cold-rolled sheets	No
Coated sheets	No
Plates	Yes
Welded pipe and tube	Limited
Blooms and Billets:	
Wire rods	Yes
Bars	Yes
Reinforcing bars	Yes
Small structural shapes	Yes
Large structural shapes	Limited
Rails	No
Seamless tube	Yes
Axles	No

could perfect this new technology, the company would be able to challenge integrated companies on their home ground—the flat-rolled steel used in automobiles, appliances, and roofing.

Location.   Only by the 1960s did minimills become a force within the industry. Their strategy was to utilize only electric furnaces and to locate their plants in regions near customer markets and scrap supplies but more distant from integrated plants (steel was expensive to ship). During the 1970s minimills grew explosively, capturing significant market shares (Exhibit 8).

Input Costs.   Scrap steel was the principal raw material input for minimill production. While the cost of iron ore had constantly risen (as rich high-quality sources in the United States ran out), scrap remained plentiful. Over the last 10 years scrap prices had declined relative to iron ore prices.

Work Force Flexibility.   Another important advantage of minimills was their work force flexibility. Most minimills employed nonunion workers. Union attempts to organize minimills had met with little success. Although nonunion minimill wages were not always lower than union wages, their worker productivity was always much higher, primarily because of the flexibility and latitude management had in organizing work. Without union work rule restrictions, management could introduce labor-saving technology and link earnings to productivity.

Productivity.   Electric furnace technology, work force flexibility, and constant efforts to operate facilities more efficiently added up to a significant cost advantage (that translated into a price advantage) for minimills. The advantage in 1985 was about $100 per ton ($375 for integrated firms versus $275 for minimills). Much of the advantage stemmed from the fact that output per worker at minimills ran about double the 350 tons per employee at integrated companies. Because minimill wages were comparable (some lower but not much) to workers' earnings in the unionized plants of bigger, integrated producers, minimills had about half the labor costs per ton of integrated companies.

Developmental Sequence.   Minimills did not win their market niche overnight. Some minimills failed. While minimills had advantages in low-cost labor and low-cost scrap, they faced scale disadvantages and began with an untested technology and no customer base. The initial market penetration successes came in low-grade steel products. Then, as they learned and made operating improvements, they moved gradually and selectively to challenge integrated mills and imports in an ever-broadening array of products but always where their relative cost position was strongest. The largest, and generally most successful, minimill companies in 1985 are shown in Exhibit 10.

Intensified Competition.   Contrary to popular impressions about imported steel, minimills' production accounted for more of the displacement of integrated companies' share than had imports. The relationship between the minimills and the

Exhibit 10 LEADING MINIMILL COMPANIES IN UNITED STATES, 1985			
Firm	Plants	Capacity (tons)	Products
Nucor	4	2,100,000	Bars, small structurals
North Star	4	2,050,000	Bars, rods, small structural steel
Northwestern	1	1,800,000	Bars, rods, small and large structural steel
Co-Steel	2	1,750,000	Bars, rods, small and large structural steel
Florida Steel	5	1,560,000	Bars, small structurals

Note: The minimill segment consisted of 50 firms and 65 plants. Of total minimill production, 55 percent came from plants with less than 600,000 tons of annual capacity.

integrated companies resembled a successful guerilla war. In 1985, however, the competitive scene was changing. Having used their lower costs to force integrated companies and imports out of many markets, minimills were beginning to compete against each other. An official at an integrated company noted: "Minimills have passed the stage of taking tonnage from integrated producers. We are concentrating on more sophisticated products where they can't compete. Let them have the inefficient products." Iverson observed: "We are now head to head against much tougher competition. It was no contest when we were up against the integrated companies. Now we are facing minimills who have the same scrap prices, the same electrical costs, and who use the same technologies.

Minimills coveted the bigger market for flat-rolled steel where profit margins were higher. But they were shut out of this segment by technological limitations. In technological capabilities, productivity, work force practices, and expanding products, Nucor was viewed as the leader among minimill producers. Nucor operated steel minimills in South Carolina, Nebraska, Texas, and Utah with a total capacity of about 2 million tons; this made Nucor about the 10th largest steel company in the United States.

VULCRAFT: THE OTHER HALF OF NUCOR

Ken Iverson said:

> Most people think of us as a steel company, but we are a lot more than a steel company. The business is really composed of two different factors. One is manufacturing steel and the other is steel products. We like it if in an average year each factor contributes about 50 percent of our sales and 50 percent of our earnings. It is important for the company in the long run that we keep this balance. If one of them began to dominate the company it would cause problems we wouldn't like to see.

Products.   Vulcraft was the nation's largest producer of steel joists and joist girders. Steel joists and girders served as support systems in industrial buildings, shopping centers, warehouses, high rise buildings, and to a lesser extent in small office buildings, apartments, and single-family dwellings. Vulcraft had six joist

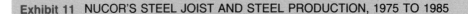

Exhibit 11 NUCOR'S STEEL JOIST AND STEEL PRODUCTION, 1975 TO 1985

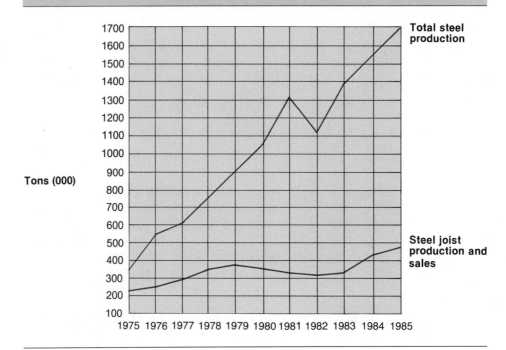

plants and four deck plants. Steel deck was used for floor and roof systems. In 1985 Vulcraft produced 471,000 tons of joists and girders and 169,000 tons of steel deck (Exhibits 11 and 12).

Manufacturing Process.   Joists were manufactured on assembly lines. The steel moved on rolling conveyors from station to station. Teams of workers at each station cut and bent the steel to shape, welded joists together and drilled holes in them, and painted the completed product.

Competition.   Many competitors participated in the joist segment, and a large number and variety of customers bought joists. Competition centered around timely delivery and price. Joist manufacturing was not capital intensive like basic steel-making, but was more of an engineering business. Vulcraft bid on a very high percentage of all new buildings which needed joists. Sophisticated computer software was used to design the joists needed on a job and to develop bid estimates. Success also depended on marketing and advertising. Vulcraft had a 40 percent national market share in joists in 1985, making it the largest joist manufacturer in the United States. In 1985 Vulcraft manufactured joists for about 15,000 buildings. Vulcraft management pursued a strategy of being the low-cost supplier of joists.

Exhibit 12 NUCOR'S STEEL DECK AND COLD FINISHED STEEL SALES, 1977–1985

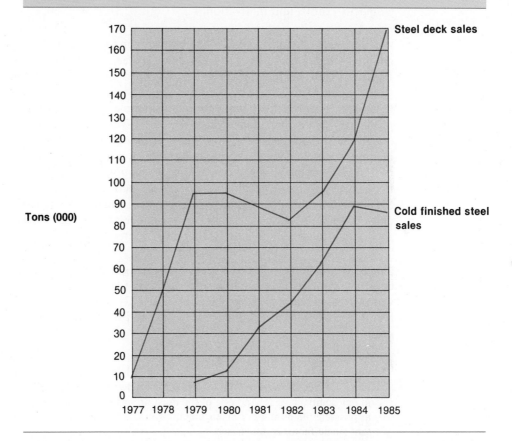

Tons (000)

Steel deck sales

Cold finished steel sales

1977 1978 1979 1980 1981 1982 1983 1984 1985

Organization. Each Vulcraft plant was managed by a general manager who reported directly to Dave Aycock, president of Nucor. Each Vulcraft general manager had spent many years in the joist business. In general, the Vulcraft division's relationships with corporate headquarters paralleled those of the steel division.

OTHER NUCOR BUSINESSES

In addition to steel and joists, Nucor operated three cold finish plants which produced steel bars used in shafting and machining precision parts; a plant which produced grinding balls used by the mining industry; and a research chemicals unit which produced rare earth oxides, metals, and salts. Exhibits 11 and 12 show Nucor's sales by business.

KEN IVERSON AND THE NUCOR CULTURE

Iverson had consciously modeled Nucor on certain bedrock values: productivity, simplicity, thrift, and innovation.

Productivity.   Iverson liked to contrast Nucor to integrated companies. He recounted a field trip he took to an integrated steel plant when he was a student at Purdue: "This was the late afternoon. We were touring through the plant, and we actually had to step over workers who were sleeping there. I decided right then that I didn't ever want to work for a big steel plant." The average Nucor worker produced 700 to 800 tons of steel per year versus 350 tons per employee at integrated companies; total labor costs at Nucor averaged less than half that at integrated producers. At the production level, people were arranged into groups of 25 to 35 people. Each group had a production standard to meet and a steep bonus schedule for exceeding its standard. Nucor production workers could earn $30,000 or more in a good year. Producing steel and joists entailed hard, hot, dirty, and occasionally dangerous jobs. Performance at all levels of the company was rigidly tied to efficiency and profitability criteria.

Simplicity and Thrift.   Iverson and other managers at Nucor had developed practices and symbols which conveyed simplicity. One of their notable achievements was a streamlined organizational structure. Only four levels separated the official hierarchy: workers, department managers, division managers, corporate. Iverson said:

> You can tell a lot about a company by looking at its organization charts. . . . If you see a lot of staff, you can bet that it is not a very efficient organization. . . . Secondly, don't have assistants. We do not have that title and prohibit it in our company. . . . And one of the most important things is to restrict as much as possible the number of management layers. . . . It is probably the most important single factor in business.

Iverson's pioneering approach in steel was beginning to be copied by the bigger companies:

> I spent two days as a lecturer at a business school not long ago. One of the students heard me talk about getting rid of management layers. He spoke up and said that when he visited U.S. Steel's new pipe mill near Birmingham, Alabama, the thing they were most proud of wasn't the technology but that they had only 4 management layers instead of the usual 10.

Nucor's spartan values were most evident at its corporate headquarters. Instead of having a handsome, expensive showcase building sited on landscaped grounds, Nucor rented a few thousand square feet of the fourth floor of a nondescript office building with an insurance company's name on it. The only cue that Nucor was there was its name (listed in ordinary size letters) in the building directory. The office decor was spartan, simple, and functional. Only 16 people worked in the headquarters—no financial analysts, no engineering staff, no marketing staff, no research staff. The company assiduously avoided the normal paraphenalia of bureaucracy. No one had a formal job description. The company had no written mission statement, no strategic plan, and no MBO system. There was little paperwork, few regular reports, and fewer meetings. Iverson commented on his staff and how it functioned.

> They are all very sharp people. We don't centralize anything. We have a financial vice president, a president, a manager of personnel, a planner, internal auditing, and accounting. . . . With such a small staff there are opportunities you miss and things you don't do well because you don't have time . . . but the advantages so far outweigh the disadvantages. . . . We focus on what can really benefit the business. . . . We don't have job descriptions, we just kind of divide up the work.

Innovation.   Nucor was a leading innovator among steel minimills and in the joist business as well. Plant designs, organizational structure, incentives, and work force allocations synchronized with cultural pressure for constant innovative advancements. Iverson projected that minimills could eventually capture as much as 35 to 40 percent of the steel business if they succeeded in developing technological advances which enabled them to produce a wider variety of steel products very economically. The breakthroughs hinged on revamping continuous casting technology. Currently, a minimill couldn't produce certain shapes. Iverson thought the key to unlock the door was the "thin-slab caster":

> We are trying to develop a thin slab. Then we could produce plate and other flat-rolled products. Right now the thinnest slab that can be produced is 6 inches thick. If we can get down to 1½ inches with the thin slab caster, then we can map out the growth for another 10 years. We could build those all over the country. We're trying to develop this new technology in our Darlington mill. The investment will probably run $10 to $20 million. Now, if we could do it, the new mills would probably cost about $150 million.

Many analysts doubted that such a breakthrough was really in the offing, but Iverson believed it would come within three years and was monitoring seven experimental programs.

Ken Iverson: Public Figure.   Nucor's success had made Iverson a public figure. He had been interviewed by newspapers, magazines, radio, and TV; he spoke to industry groups and business schools; and he had been called to testify before Congress. He explained why he was willing to devote his time to these extracurricular activities.

> Generally, our policy is to stay as far away as we can from government . . . except that I felt so strongly about protectionism that I thought I should make my views known—especially because our view is so different from the other steel mills. . . . Talking to investors is an important part of the company's relationship with the marketplace . . . the company gets a direct benefit and it makes good sense. . . . I do some talks at business schools just from the standpoint that I get pleasure out of that. . . . We do occasionally hire MBAs, but we haven't had much success with them.

Iverson had a casual, informal, and unaffected style. His office was neither large nor furnished with expensive decorations. For lunch he took visitors across the street to a delicatessen—their "executive dining room"—for a quick sandwich. Nucor had no executive parking spaces, no executive restrooms, no company cars. Everyone, including Iverson, flew coach class. When Iverson went to New York he rode the subway instead of taking a limousine or taxi. Other Nucor managers followed Iverson's example, shunning ostentation, luxury, and status symbols common among other successful companies.

Managers at Nucor described Iverson's management style:

Ken is straightforward. If he says something you can pretty well count on it. He sets the tone and the direction and everybody pitches in. That's the way he acts and approaches things—directly.

Ken is one of the greatest leaders the steel industry has ever had.

Ken is liberal with people and conservative with money.

ORGANIZATION

Organization Structure.   Following Iverson's lean-management philosophy, only four levels of management separated Iverson from the hourly employees. At corporate headquarters they joked that with four promotions, a janitor could become CEO! Exhibit 13 depicts Nucor's organization chart. Below the corporate level the company was organized into divisions. These divisions roughly correspond to plant locations.

Recently, under the pressure of the growing size of the company and Iverson's busy public role, the jobs of president and CEO were separated. By trying to be "everything to everyone," Iverson was spreading himself a little thin. Dave Aycock was promoted from a plant manager's job to president, responsible for day-to-day operations of Nucor; Aycock talked about his new role:

I worked at Vulcraft when it was acquired by Nucor in 1955. . . . I've been in this new job for about a year. . . . It's very exciting. . . . If I had actually known roughly half of what I thought I knew, I would probably have been more valuable. . . . Most of my time has been spent learning the personalities, the reactions, and philosophies of the operating personnel. . . . Many of them were glad to see the change because they thought Ken was overworked.

Division Management.   Because Nucor had no headquarters staff and because of top management's great confidence in operating personnel, division managers played a key role in decision making. Iverson said of the division managers: "They are all vice presidents, and they are behind our success. They make the policies of this company. Most of them have been with Nucor at least 10 years. But a vice president's pay is based on how this company does—not on how well the vice president's division does—it's the group concept again."

Corporate-Division Interaction.   Contact between divisions and corporate headquarters was limited to a report of production volume, costs, sales, and margin—the Monthly Operations Analysis. Each month every division received the "smiling face" report, comparing all the divisions across about a dozen categories of efficiency and performance. One division manager described how Iverson delegated and supervised:

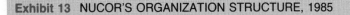

Exhibit 13 NUCOR'S ORGANIZATION STRUCTURE, 1985

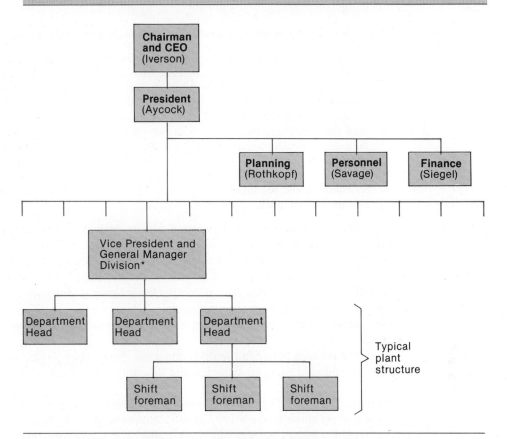

Note: Nucor has four steel mills (divisions), six joist plants, three cold-finished steel plants, a grinding ball plant, and a research chemicals division—each is headed by a vice president and general manager.

Mr. Iverson's style of management is to allow the manager all the latitude in the world. His involvement with managers is quite limited. As we have grown, he no longer has the time to visit with division managers more than once or twice a year. . . . In a way I feel like I run my own company because I don't get marching orders from Mr. Iverson. He lets you run the division the way you see fit, and the only way he will step in is if he sees something he doesn't like, particularly bad profits, high costs, or whatever. But in the four years I've worked with him I don't recall a single instance where he issued an instruction to me to do something differently.

The casewriters asked a division manager how the corporate officers would handle a division which wasn't performing as it should:

I imagine he (Aycock) would call first and come out later, but it would be appropriate to the situation. Ken and Dave are great psychologists. Right now, for instance, the steel business is showing a very poor return on assets, but I don't feel any pressure on me because the market is not there. I do feel pressure to keep my costs down, and that is appropriate. If something went wrong Dave would know.

How does Nucor respond to problems in management performance?

We had a situation where we were concerned about the performance of a particular employee . . . a department manager. Ken, Dave, and I sat down with the general manager to let him know where we were coming from. So now the ball is in his court. We will offer support and help that the general manager wants. Later I spent a long evening with the general manager and the department manager. Now the department manager understands the corporate concern. Ken will allow the general manager to resolve this issue. To do otherwise would take the trust out of the system. . . . We are not going to just call someone in and say "We're not satisfied. You're gone.". . . But, eventually, the string may run out. Ken will terminate people. He takes a long time to do it. I respect that. Ken would rather give people too much time than too little.

Important issues merited a phone call or perhaps a visit from a corporate officer. A division manager told the casewriters that he talked to headquarters about once a week. Divisions made their own decisions about hiring, purchasing, processes, and equipment. There was no formal limit on a division manager's spending authority. Sales policy and personnel policy were set at the corporate level. Divisions didn't produce a plan, but: "People in this company have real firm ideas about what is going on and what will be happening . . . mostly by word of mouth."

Relationships between the divisions were close. They shared ideas and information, and sold each other significant amounts of product.

Decision Making. Division managers met formally in a group with corporate management three times a year at the "Roundtable." Sessions began at 7 A.M. and ended at 8 P.M. At these meetings, budgets, capital expenditures, and changes in wages or benefits were agreed on, and department managers were reviewed. Iverson waited for a consensus to emerge about an alternative before going ahead with a decision. He did not impose decisions. Corporate officers described Nucor's decision making processes:

Over a long period of time, decisions in this company have been made at the lowest level that they can—subject to staying within the philosophy of the company. We get a lot of work done without too many managers. Ken has the business courage to stay out of the small things. It takes a lot of courage for general managers to resist the temptation to control every event.

I can walk into Ken's office anytime and talk about anything I want to talk about. Agree or disagree with anything he has done. I don't agree with every decision that is made. I have the right to disagree. Sometimes I disagree strongly. Ken hears me out. Ken listens to other people. He does not feel that he is always right. Sometimes he will change his mind.

I remember when I first started to work for Nucor and I was sitting down with Ken Iverson. He told me, "John, you are going to make at least three mistakes with this company in the first few years that you are with us. Each one of these mistakes will cost us $50,000. I want you to be aggressive, and I want you to make decisions. One word of caution. We don't mind you making the mistakes, but please don't make them all in one year."

Ken defers a decision when the executives are strongly divided to give people a chance to consider it more. Ken is a superb negotiator. He might look at the various positions and say "I have a compromise," and lay that out. Many times he can see a compromise that everyone is comfortable with.

FINANCIAL POSITION

The theme of simplicity also extended to financial matters. Sam Siegel, Nucor's vice president of finance, did not use a computer. He told the casewriters: "When you make too many calculations they get in the way of business. Each of the divisions uses computers for many purposes, including financial analysis. You could make an economic case for centralizing some of that here at corporate headquarters. We could save money and create all kinds of information, but then we would have to hire more people to study that information."

Investments.   No financial analysts worked at corporate headquarters. Nucor did not use sophisticated models of discounted cash flow or complicated formulas to govern capital expenditures, preferring an eclectic capital investment policy. Iverson commented: "Priority? No. We don't even do that with capital expenditures. Sometimes we'll say . . . we won't put up any buildings this year. . . . But in recent years we've been able to fund anything we felt we needed. We don't do it by priorities." Responding to a query about whether the company used an internal hurdle rate of return, Iverson said:

> We look at it from the standpoint of whether it's replacement and if it's modernization, what the payback period is, or if it is a new facility. In many cases the payback on a new steel mill is longer than you would like, but you can't afford not to do it. I think maybe that is where other manufacturing companies go wrong— where they have these rigid ideas about investments. If you don't put some of these investments in, after four or five years you are behind. . . . You can't afford to fall behind, even if you don't get the payback. That's why the integrated steel companies didn't put in continuous casters, because they couldn't get the payback they wanted. . . . Now they have got to do it. . . . From an economic point of view they didn't do anything wrong, they didn't make a mistake.

Financial Reporting.   Each division had a controller who reported directly to the division manager and indirectly to Siegel. Siegel saw the role of his controllers as being broad: "Controllers who merely do financial work are not doing a good job. A controller should become involved with key plant operations . . . should learn the whole operation." Siegel spent only about one half of his own time on strictly financial matters, contributing the other half toward "problems, issues, and projects" of importance to the company.

Financial Condition.   According to Siegel, the company was in good financial condition except for having too much invested in short-term assets (Exhibits 14 and 15). Wall Street analysts had speculated about what Nucor might decide to do with its excess short-term assets.

Exhibit 14 BALANCE SHEETS, NUCOR CORP., 1984 AND 1985		
	1984	**1985**
Assets		
Current assets:		
Cash	$ 2,863,680	$ 8,028.519
Short-term investments	109,846,810	177,115,854
Accounts receivable	58,408,244	60,390,448
Contracts in process	8,462,815	10,478,296
Inventories	73,797,302	78,641,805
Other current assets	74,522	114,125
Total current assets	253,453,373	334,769,147
Property, plant, and equipment	228,102,790	225,274,674
Other assets	632,302	267,367
Total assets	$482,188,465	$560,311,188
Liabilities and Stockholders' Equity		
Current liabilities:		
Long-term debt due within one year	$ 2,402,462	$ 2,402,462
Accounts payable	32,691,249	35,473,011
Federal income taxes	23,705,195	27,597,464
Accrued expenses and other current liabilities	41,734,778	55,782,891
Total current liabilities	100,533,684	121,255,828
Other liabilities:		
Long-term debt due after one year	43,232,384	40,233,769
Deferred federal income taxes	38,819,563	41,319,563
	82,051,947	81,553,332
Stockholders' equity:		
Common stock	5,669,757	5,732,382
Additional paid-in capital	18,991,334	24,299,195
Retailed earnings	275,035,788	327,816,850
	299,696,879	357,848,427
Treasury stock	(94,045)	(346,399)
Total stockholders' equity	299,602,834	357,502,028
Total liabilities and stockholders' equity	$482,188,465	$560,311,188

HUMAN RESOURCES

Besides being known for its stunning success in joists and steel, Nucor was also known for its remarkable human resources practices. The casewriters visited a Vulcraft plant and talked with a department manager who had worked at Vulcraft for 16 years about what made Nucor different:

> Our plants are located strategically. The company puts them in rural areas, where we can find a good supply of quality labor—people who believe in hard work. We have beaten back three unionizing campaigns in the last 10 years. These employees are very loyal. In fact, we had to hire a guard to protect the union organizers from some of our workers. We see about 3 percent turnover and very little absenteeism. They are proud of working with us. It's fun when they come to you and ask for work.

Why did Nucor do so well with employees?

> Most companies want to take their profits out of their employees. We treat employees right. They are the ones who make the profits. Other companies aren't

Exhibit 15   STATEMENT OF CHANGES IN FINANCIAL POSITION, NUCOR CORP., 1983–1985

	1983	1984	1985
Funds provided:			
Operations:			
Net earnings	$27,864,308	$44,548,451	$58,478,352
Depreciation of plant and equipment	27,109,582	28,899,421	31,105,788
Deferred federal income taxes	8,200,000	5,600,000	2,500,000
Total funds provided by operations	63,173,890	79,047,872	92,084,140
Disposition of plant and equipment	274,138	377,259	788,726
Decrease in other assets	—	—	364,935
Issuance of common stock	2,201,183	2,006,460	5,387,182
Total funds provided	$65,649,211	$81,431,591	$98,624,983
Funds applied:			
Purchase of property, plant, and equipment	$19,617,147	$26,074,653	$29,066,398
Increase in other assets	354,170	259,229	—
Reduction in long-term debt	2,498,615	2,498,616	2,998,615
Cash dividends	4,216,854	5,081,771	5,697,290
Acquisition of treasury stock	—	—	269,050
Increase in working capital	38,962,425	47,517,322	60,593,630
Total funds applied	$65,649,211	$81,431,591	$98,624,983
Analysis of change in working capital:			
Increase (decrease) in current assets:			
Cash	$ (4,283,370)	$ (3,521,115)	$ 5,164,839
Short-term investments	38,445,234	37,177,195	67,269,144
Accounts receivable	16,424,874	7,297,872	1,982,204
Contracts in process	8,402,160	1,404,012	2,015,481
Inventories	7,723,168	·17,242,200	4,844,503
Other current assets	(366,052)	(35,593)	39,603
Net increase (decrease)	61,346,514	59,564,211	81,315,774
Increase (decrease) in current liabilities:			
Long-term debt due within one year	799,000	—	—
Accounts payable	14,186,217	(4,443,835)	2,781,762
Federal income taxes	2,278,813	8,891,286	3,892,269
Accrued expenses and other current liabilities	5,120,059	7,599,438	14,048,113
Net increase (decrease)	22,384,089	12,046,889	20,722,144
Increase in working capital	$38,962,425	$47,517,322	$60,593,630

willing to offer what is needed to allow people to work. They can't see the dollar down the road for the nickel in their hand. Nucor's people make it strong.

Nucor's incentive systems had been a subject of much discussion and comment. *Fortune* estimated in 1981 that Nucor's workers earned an average of $5,000 more than union steelworkers. Moreover, Nucor workers were the highest paid manufacturing, blue-collar workforce in the United States.

Casewriter: But doesn't that prove the point—that American steelworkers earning $30,000 per year have priced the industry out of business?

Iverson: They earn every bit of it! Sure, it's generous. . . . There's a reason for it. It's hot, hard, dirty, dangerous, skilled work. We have melters who earn more than $40,000, and I'm glad they earn it. It's not what a person earns in an absolute sense, it's what he earns in relation to what he produces that matters.

The incentive system at Nucor had several key elements. John Savage, manager of personnel services, explained the company's personnel philosophy:

> Our employee relations philosophy has four primary components. . . . Management's first and foremost obligation to employees is to provide them the opportunity to earn according to their productivity. . . . Next, we are obligated to manage the company in such a way that employees can feel that if they are doing their job properly, they will have a job tomorrow. . . . Third, employees must believe that they are treated fairly. . . . Lastly, employees must have an avenue of appeal if they believe they are being treated unfairly, to Mr. Iverson himself if necessary.

Everyone at Nucor participated in incentive plans. These incentives took several different forms depending on the type of work involved.

Production Incentives.   Production groups of 25 to 30 employees were given clearly measurable production tasks. About 3,000 Nucor employees made joists and steel under production incentives based on historical time standards. If, for example, a group produced a joist in 50 percent less than standard time, they got a 50 percent bonus. Bonuses were paid at the end of the following week. When equipment sat idle, no bonus accrued. If an employee was absent for a day, he or she lost a week's bonus—a difference amounting to as much as $7 per hour. The system was very tough:

> If you work real hard and you get performance, the payment is there next week. . . . You worked like a dog and here is the money. . . . There are lots of people who don't like to work that hard, and they don't last for long. We have had groups get so mad at a guy who wasn't carrying his weight that they chased him around a joist plant with a piece of angle iron and were gonna kill him. . . . Don't get the idea that we're paternalistic. If you are late even five minutes you lose your bonus for the day. If you are late by more than 30 minutes because of sickness or anything else, you lose your bonus for the week. We do grant four "forgiveness" days a year. We have a melter, Phil Johnson, down in Darlington. One day a worker arrived at the plant and said that Phil had been in an auto accident and was sitting by his car on Route 52 holding his head. The foreman asked, "Why didn't you stop to help him?" The guy said, "And lose my bonus?"

Many Nucor workers earned between $30,000 and $40,000 per year. Nucor's monetary incentives made the company attractive to jobseekers (see Exhibit 14). Iverson told a story about hiring new workers:

> We needed a couple new employees for Darlington, so we put out a sign and put a small ad in the local paper. The ads told people to show up Saturday morning at the employment office at the plant. When Saturday rolled around, the first person to arrive at the personnel office was greeted by 1,200 anxious jobseekers. There were so many of them that the size of the crowd began to interfere with access into and out of the plant. So the plant manager called the state police to send some officers over to control the crowd. But, the sergeant at the state police barracks told the plant manager that he couldn't spare any officers. You see, he was short-handed himself because three of his officers were at the plant applying for jobs!

Managerial Compensation. Department managers received a bonus based on a percentage of their division's contribution to corporate earnings. In an operating division such bonuses could run as high as 50 percent of a person's base pay. In the corporate office the bonus could reach 30 percent of base pay. Employees such as accountants, secretaries, clerks, and others who didn't work in production got a bonus based on either their division's profit contribution or corporate return on assets.

Senior officers had no employment contracts or pension plan. More than half of their compensation was based on company earnings. Their base salaries were set at about 70 percent of market rates for similar jobs. Ten percent of pretax earnings were set aside and allocated to senior officers according to their base salary. The base level was tied to a 12 percent return on shareholder's equity. Half the bonus was paid in cash, and half was deferred in the form of Nucor stock. In a profitable year officers could earn as much as 190 percent of their base salary as bonus and 115 percent on top of that in stock.

Other Compensation Incentives. Nucor also operated a profit sharing trust. The plan called for 10 percent of pretax earnings to be assigned to profit sharing each year. Of that amount, 20 percent was paid to employees in the following year, and the remainder was held to fund the worker retirement program. Vesting in the trust was 20 percent after one year and 10 percent each following year. The arrangement had the effect of making the retirement income of Nucor employees depend on the company's success. Additionally, Nucor paid 10 percent of whatever amount an employee was willing to invest in Nucor stock, gave employees five shares of stock for each five years of employment, and occasionally paid extraordinary bonuses.

Lastly, Nucor ran a scholarship program for children of full-time employees. In 1985 over 300 were enrolled in universities, colleges, and vocational schools. Since the program's inception over 900 students had participated. One family had educated eight children on Nucor's plan.

No Layoffs. Nucor had never laid off or fired an employee for lack of work. Iverson explained how the company handled the need to make production cutbacks:

> When we have a difficult period, we don't lay anybody off. . . . We operate the plants four days a week or even three days. We call it our "share the pain program.". . . . The bonus system remains in place, but it's based on four days' production instead of five. The production workers' compensation drops about 25 percent, the department managers' drops 35 to 40 percent, and the division manager's can drop as much as 60 to 80 percent. Nobody complains. They understand. And they still push to get that bonus on the days they work.

The Downside. Nucor's flat structure and steep incentives also had certain negative side effects. First, the incentive system was strictly oriented toward the short term. If a general manager was thinking about a major capital investment project, he was also thinking about reducing his short-term income. Iverson described how the ups and downs of the incentive plans affected officers: "If the company can hit about 24 percent return on equity, the officers' salary can reach 300 percent of the base amount. It maxed out in 1979 and 1980. In 1980 and 1981 total officers' compensation dropped way off. In 1980 I earned about $400,000, but in 1981 I earned $108,000. So officers have to watch their lifestyle!" Iverson's 1981 pay made him, according to *Fortune,* the lowest paid CEO in the *Fortune 500* industrial ranking. Iverson commented that it was "Something I was really a little proud of."

Second, promotions came very slowly. Many managers had occupied their current jobs for a very long time. Additionally, Nucor experienced problems in developing the skills of its first-line supervisors.

Many other companies studied Nucor's compensation plans. The casewriters asked John Savage about the visits other companies made to study Nucor's system:

> Many companies visit us. We had managers and union people from General Motors' Saturn project come in and spend a couple of days. They were oriented

---

Exhibit 16   EXCERPTS OF INTERVIEWS WITH HOURLY EMPLOYEES AT NUCOR

Jim
Jim is 32 years old, did not finish school, and has worked at Vulcraft for 10 years. He works at a job that requires heavy lifting. Last year he earned about $38,500.

> This is hard physical work. Getting used to it is tough, too. After I started working as a spliceman my upper body was sore for about a month. . . . Before I came to work here I worked as a farmer and cut timber. . . . I got this job through a friend who was already working here. . . . I reckon I was very nervous when I started here but people showed me how to work. . . . The bonuses and the benefits are mighty good here . . . and I have never been laid off. . . . I enjoy this work. . . . This company is good to you. They might let employees go if they had problems, but first they'd give him a chance to straighten out. . . . In 1981 things were slow and we only worked three or four days a week. Sometimes we would spend a day doing maintenance, painting, sweeping. . . . and there wasn't no incentive. I was glad I was working . . . I was against the union.

Kerry
Kerry is 31 years old, married, and about to become a parent. He has worked on the production line for about three years.

> I was laid off from my last job after working there five years, I went without work for three months. I got this job through a friend. My brother works as a supervisor for Nucor in Texas. . . . This is good, hard work. You get dirty, too hot in the summer and too cold in the winter. They should air-condition the entire plant (laughs). On this joist line we have to work fast. Right now I'm working 8½ hours a day, six days a week. . . . I get good pay and benefits. Vulcraft is one of the better companies in Florence (South Carolina). . . . Everyone does not always get along, but we work as a team. Our supervisor has his off days. . . . I want to get ahead in life, but I don't see openings for promotion here. Most of the foremen have had their jobs for a long time, and most people are senior to me in line. . . . This place is very efficient. If I see a way to improve the work, I tell somebody. They will listen to you.

Other comments from hourly workers
> I am running all day long. It gets hot and you get tired. My wife doesn't like it because sometimes I come home and fall asleep right away.

> When something goes down, people ask how they can help. Nobody sits around. Every minute you are down it's like dollars out of your pocket. So everybody really hustles.

toward a bureaucratic style. . . . You could tell it from their questions. I was more impressed with the union people than with the management people. The union people wanted to talk dirty, nitty-gritty issues. But the management people thought it was too simple, they didn't think it would work. Maybe their business is too complex for our system. . . . We never hear from these visitors after they leave. . . . I believe it would take five to seven years of working at this system before you could detect a measurable change.

High wages and employment stability got Nucor listed in the book *The 100 Best Companies to Work for in America*. A division manager summed up the Nucor human relations philosophy this way: "It's amazing what people can do if you let them. Nucor gives people responsibility and then stands behind them." Exhibit 16 presents selected excerpts from interviews with hourly employees about their jobs at Nucor.

STRATEGIC PLANNING

Nucor followed no written strategic plan, had no written objectives (except those stated in the incentive programs), and had no mission statement. Divisions promulgated no strategic plans. We asked Sam Siegel about long-range strategic planning. He confided: "You can't predict the future. . . . No matter how great you may think your decisions are, the future is unknown. You don't know what will happen. . . . Nucor concentrates on the here-and-now. We do make five-year projections, and they are good for about three months. Five to 10 years out is philosophy." We also asked Bob Rothkopf (planning director) about planning at Nucor:

I work on the strategic plan with Ken twice a year. It's formulated out of the projects we are looking at. He and I talk about the direction we feel the company is going. . . . The elements of the most recent plan are that we take the basic level of the company today and project it out for five years. We look at net sales, net income, under different likely scenarios. In this last plan I looked at the potential effects of a mild recession in 1986. . . . We add new products or projects to that baseline.

Rothkopf had responsibility for generating most of the information he used in his forecasts. He often used consultants or other companies to get the information he needed. None of the other senior executives or division managers got deeply involved in this planning process.

Nucor didn't rely on its strategic planning system to make strategic decisions. Rothkopf described how strategic decisions were reached:

Projects come from all over. Some come from our general managers, or from our suppliers, our customers . . . or come walking in the door here. Iverson is like a magnet for ideas, because of who he is and what Nucor is. . . . We evaluate each project on its own, as it comes up. As each opportunity arises, we go in and investigate it. Some investigations are short; we throw out quite a few of them. We don't make any systematic search for these ideas.

Exhibit 17 A SUMMARY REVIEW OF NUCOR'S STRATEGIC OPTIONS

Strategic considerations	Option 1 Build a seamless tube mill	Option 2 Get into preengineered buildings
Market	About $2.5 billion Oilfield equipment companies Commodity Mature, competitive, low growth Integrated companies sell here	$350 million Small growth Numerous competitors, all sizes Regional, fragmented Not a commodity
Investment	$150–180 million	$5–7 million plant generates $15–20 million sales in four years. Want about 20 percent market share in five to six years
Time period needed	About two years	8–12 months
Fit to present activities	Could sell some product to joist division increase efficiency	Already manufacturing parts for such buildings
Revenues/profits	Sales $240–270 million 20–25 percent profit before taxes	About same as present earning power
Support among executives	Some active support Analyses in process	Joist division favors it Corporate execs divided
Skills and resources	Know market Have most skills, others not too hard to learn	Selling to whole new market Manufacturing skills help
Downside risk	Risky, uncertain market	New market to understand Can do gradually Not very risky

Strategic considerations	Option 3 Build bar minimill	Option 4 Acquire bar minimills
Market	Same as current	Same as current
Investment	$50–75 million for a 250,000 ton mill	A six- to seven-year-old, 175,000-ton mill costs $50 million to build Earns $10–15/ton before tax
Time period needed	18 months	± 1989, 1987 earliest
Fit to present activities	Perfect fit	Obvious, yes
Revenues/profits	$65–75 million sales. Lose money years one and two. Over long term make $4–10 million before taxes.	$45 million sales, earns ± $1 million Under Nucor, such a mill can see sales of $60 million, earn ± $5 million
Support among executives	Quite a bit	Unknown
Skills and resources	In place, no problems	OK, in place
Downside risk	No growth in market. Must take business from entrenched competitors	Antitrust? Company culture might not fit; exposure to union problems

Rothkopf compared Nucor's planning to formal strategic planning done by other companies:

> I think there might be some advantages for us to do that sort of thing. However, our business has been pretty simple. Our businesses are all related and easy to keep track of. When a big decision comes up we discuss it. That's easy because of the simple structure of the company. . . . Planning has disadvantages . . . time-consuming . . . expensive . . . hard to get the information for it . . . tends to get bureaucratic.

Exhibit 17 *(concluded)*

Strategic considerations	Option 5 Innovative flat-rolled minimill	Option 6 Build bolt plant
Market	25–30 million tons Stable, a commodity Integrated mills dominant	$800 million Mature, stable Commodity dominated by four companies
Investment	$125–$175 million for 400,000, to 600,000 ton mill	$25 million/plant
Time period needed	Could build four plants in 5–10 years	
Fit to present activities	Extends product range Sales to joist division Keeps steel/joist "balance"	Steel currently produced goes into product
Revenues/profits	Must project 25 percent profit before tax to justify Lower cost $100/ton?	$28–32 million sales per plant
Support among executives	High company support; spending $10 million to develop process at Darlington	Agreed to build one plant
Skills and resources	Don't know marketing of flat-rolled products Must learn flat-rolling of steel	Need marketing skills
Downside risk	Must invest $10–15 million in any case Hard to invest new technology Competitors leap-frog with new processes Estimate 50–75 percent chance it will work	If foreign steel is barred in United States, bolts get "dumped" here. International prices of bolts unstable.

Strategic considerations	Option 7 Increase dividends	Option 8 Purchase Nucor stock for treasury
Market	Stockholder reaction uncertain Number of shares × increase	14,000,000 shares at $45 currently Number of shares × price
Time period needed	Anytime	One to two years
Fit to present activities	Change in philosophy	Underlines management confidence
Revenues/profits	N/A	Sell shares for profit? Enrich remaining stockholders?
Support among executives	Iverson thinking about it	At the right price/earnings ratio
Skills and resources	N/A	N/A
Downside risk	If earnings slip, could pressure ability to invest	Price of stock could decline

Strategic considerations	Option 9 Diversification outside steel products or joists
Market	Faster growing markets open
Investment	Nucor has $100–150 million Could borrow more
Time period needed	One to two years
Fit to present activities	Depends on business
Revenues/profits	Greater profitability?
Support among executives	Very little
Skills and resources	Nucor understands heavy manufacturing Nucor has skills in streamlined management Employee-relations philosophy
Downside risk	Company has to learn new things? Might require different organizational set-up.

Although Nucor had no formal planning system, important strategic decisions loomed on the company horizon. Exhibit 17 provides information on Nucor's strategic options.

NUCOR'S FUTURE: WHAT NEXT?

In spite of Nucor's remarkable successes, Iverson stated a modest, cautious view of the company's capabilities:

> We are not great marketers or financial manipulators. . . . We do two things well. We build plants economically and we run them efficiently. We stick to those two things. . . . Basically, that's all we do. We are getting better at marketing, but I wouldn't say we are strong marketers . . . that is not the base of the company. . . . We're certainly not financial manipulators. We recognized a long time ago how important it was for us to hold down overhead and management layers.

Iverson talked about the future of Nucor:

> The company's position is much different than it was in past years. In the 60s we nearly went bankrupt. It was a miniconglomerate, so I got rid of half the company. We started all over again. We built steel mills. From the late 60s to the 80s our constraints were financial. We decided that we wanted debt to be less than 30 percent of capital. That restricted the number of mills we could finance. But then in the 1980s things changed. Our restraints are not financial now. We no longer see the opportunities in minimills which we saw in the 60s and 70s. So, what direction should the company go? We have about $120 million in cash and short-term securities.
>
> Since we don't see much opportunity for building additional minimills, we have been looking at various alternatives . . . merger or acquisition, internal growth . . . buying back our own stock . . . and other things. It goes forward by project. We looked at buying another steel company that had problems. Dave visited their plant. Bob (the planner) did some projections on what it would cost us to put that mill in shape. We also have an outside consultant working on it. That is what we have done so far (Iverson points to a report). . . . We are looking at the bolt business too. About 95 percent of bolts used in the United States are made outside of the United States. We are studying whether we should spend $25 million to build a plant. . . . Maybe we ought to buy our own stock. It reduces the number of shares and increases the per share earnings. I feel comfortable with that, given the price/earnings ratio we are at.
>
> We are thinking about a seamless tube mill. That business seems to meet many of our requirements. Also, the Vulcraft people believe that we could easily enter the business of preengineered buildings. Although that is a new market for us, it's not very risky, and it is a logical extension of the joist business.
>
> We are also talking to the Japanese about a joint venture to produce large and medium structural steel shapes. That's a 6 million ton market worth about $2 billion per year. It's cyclical because it's tied to the construction industry. Imports have about 32 percent of that. We might invest $200 million. We know this market, but we lack some technology which the Japanese can supply. We would be 51 percent partners and run the plant.

Was he worried about a takeover?

I really don't expect someone to try to take us over. We have a staggered board. So if someone tries to do it they will have to wait for quite a while to control enough directors. We have other provisions in the bylaws which would make a takeover difficult. Besides, we're in a lousy business—steel.

What about an acquisition by Nucor?

We have some problems with going that route. We don't have any experience with acquisitions; all our growth has been internally generated. The second thing, we would never acquire outside our business, which is the manufacture of steel and steel products. We might be able to go into some nonferrous metals. But if we went into, say, textiles or something else like that . . . it's not . . . If stockholders want to invest in those businesses, let them do it themselves. Conglomeration is a lot of nonsense.

CAMBRIDGE PRODUCTS, LTD. (A)*

Seated in his Waterloo, Ontario, office one morning in June 1982, Bill Spencer picked up one of his recently printed business cards. On one side, above his name, address, title (Vice President, Corporate Relations) and the "Cambridge Products, Ltd." logo, a bright red Canadian Maple leaf stood out prominently against a silver background; on the other side the same information was printed in Japanese characters. The cards and the company brochures printed in Japanese were just the latest (and relatively minor) expense item in CPL's bid to export its conventional top of the range cookware products to Japan.

A week earlier, in Tokyo, Spencer had met with Jiro Hattori, president of the Kuwahara Co., one of the largest manufacturers of cookware in Japan. Hattori had proposed that Kuwahara would distribute 1,500 sets of CPL cookware a month in the Japanese market starting in October, if CPL could produce an exclusive cookware product, with whistling knobs and specially designed handles. In a few hours' time, Bill would be meeting with Jack Nolin, executive vice president, to discuss whether CPL should begin a crash development program to modify CPL's existing product at an anticipated cost of over $140,000, and place orders for steel and other raw materials worth over $100,000 by the end of the week, to prepare for the expected October delivery. For CPL, with 1981 sales of $6.3 million and net profits of $500,000, this represented a substantial investment.

As he gazed at the Japanese print on his business card, Bill Spencer wondered what he should recommend to Jack Nolin. Should CPL make the investment? There appeared to be considerable potential in the Japanese market but the risks were enormous. Would CPL be better off concentrating on familiar markets in which it was already quite successful, rather than attempting to penetrate that notoriously difficult market in a far corner of the world?

THE COMPANY

CPL's origins can be traced back to 1944, when Brian Wilson, a young entrepreneur, started up a small metal finishing plant that polished "anything in metal." Sales in that first year were $4,000. The company specialized in custom metal-working jobs that included polishing of cookware for other manufacturers. In 1952 Wear Ever, one of CPL's U.S. customers, went bankrupt and left CPL

* Prepared by Ken Coelho under the direction of Professor Donald Lecraw, The University of Western Ontario. The case was developed with the cooperation of a company which prefers to remain anonymous. Names, locations, and figures have been disguised, but essential relationships have been preserved. Copyright © 1986, The University of Western Ontario.

holding a substantial quantity of cookware; CPL inadvertently entered the cookware business.

Initially, CPL marketed aluminum cookware manufactured for the company by others. By the early 1960s, the company brought in new equipment and began to manufacture its own cookware products. Cookware sales in the early 1960s reached $1 million. CPL, which until then sold only aluminum cookware, began to experiment with stainless steel, and by 1963, introduced stainless steel cookware in the market. It soon discovered that stainless steel cookware was a market whose time had come. By 1967 CPL was completely out of aluminum and sold only stainless steel cookware.

By the late 1960s, CPL had acquired major department store accounts and sales had risen to $200,000 a month. Throughout this period the company maintained its original industrial sales business, which provided a fall-back position when problems arose in the cookware industry. In the 1970s, the Canadian market for cookware began to mature, and over the decade, the number of distributors declined. Competition was strong and included Canadian companies such as Supreme Aluminum Ltd., Soren, and Paderno and foreign competitors such as Regal, Culinaire, Westbend, Ekco, and Lagostina.

Yet CPL performed well in this market, managing to capture a market share of approximately 50 percent in the segments in which it competed. It had managed to accomplish this by constant product innovation and efficient, low-cost production. In fact, CPL had, at one time or another, supplied parts directly to its competitors at prices lower than the competitors could produce for themselves, while still making a profit. In 1981 CPL operated an 80,000-square-foot manufacturing facility in Waterloo, Ontario (where it also conducted its R&D activities) and a sales office in Newark, New Jersey.

PRODUCT DEVELOPMENT

In the late 1960s, CPL was the first developer (at a cost of $1 million) in five-ply cookware, which it marketed under the brand name Ultraware. Five-ply construction bonded a three-layered aluminum core between two layers of stainless steel. Because of aluminum's exceptionally good capacity to store and conduct heat, the multilayered construction resulted in quick and even heat distribution across the bottom and sides of the utensil, reducing cooking time and saving energy. CPL also experimented and designed specially weighted covers, knobs, and handles—innovations that paid off well in sales.

In the 1980s CPL began experimenting with seven-ply cookware and magnetic steel which, in the future, could be used with magnetic stoves then being developed in Japan. The use of magnetic stoves and utensils would result in energy savings of up to 30 percent, which was of far greater significance in energy-poor Japan than in North America. (Three-ply cookware sold better in Canada and the United States than the five-ply variety, which, although more expensive, was more energy efficient.)

EXPORTS

When CPL first started in the cookware business in the early 1950s, it realized (as had other cookware manufacturers who had set up plants for the British Commonwealth Preference rather than just the Canadian market) that the Canadian market was not large enough to support an efficient scale operation. CPL found it convenient to do business through Wear Ever distributors in the United States, and to promote its products through trade shows. CPL's industrial sales division also sold its products in the United States. (The industrial sales product list included fire extinguisher shells, nonpressure brake housings, heat lamp reflectors, lamp bases, barbecue bowls, ashtrays, hospital equipment, kettle bodies, motor housings, meat hooks, venturi collars, and animal feeding and stainless steel dishes. The company had, at one time, even supplied missile launching shell casings to the U.S. government.)

By 1979 exports constituted $2 million of $4.8 million in total sales. U.S. exports made up 40–49 percent of total exports. The other countries to which CPL exported included Italy, Australia, and South Africa. Exports to EEC countries were especially difficult, since the EEC had imposed tariffs of up to 22.5 percent on cookware. In the 1980s CPL put sales to the United States on the back burner, while it concentrated on markets in Japan, Australia, and Europe.

In 1981 CPL exports were $3.5 million of total company sales of $6.3 million (Exhibit 1). Of total exports, $1 million were to the United States, $800,000 to Australia, and the remainder ($1.7 million) to Europe, Hong Kong, Singapore, and Japan. Sales to Japan, however, were very small and sporadic. Every once in a while CPL received an order, but there was little on-going business.

ENTRY INTO THE JAPANESE MARKET

CPL's entry into the Japanese market was almost accidental. An earlier routine introductory letter to the Canadian embassy in Japan had elicited the reply that

---

Exhibit 1   CAMBRIDGE PRODUCTS, LTD. (A), 1982 FINANCIAL SUMMARY

Income data

Total sales	$6,300,000
Total exports	$3,500,000
Profit before taxes	$ 800,000
Net profit	$ 500,000

Financial data*	Net book value	Realizable value
Inventory	$3,000,000	$3,000,000
Building	500,000	2,000,000
Machinery and equipment (10 percent, straight line depreciation)	800,000	2,500,000
Dies, tools	0	500,000
Retained earnings	1,400,000	

* As of September 1982.

the Japanese market was too difficult for CPL to successfully penetrate—they should not even try, the Canadian embassy advised. CPL did have one customer in Japan prior to 1981, who had seen CPL cookware at a trade show and ordered about 100 sets (worth approximately $20,000) sporadically every two or three months.

In early 1981, David Taylor, vice president of CPL's U.S. subsidiary, showed samples of CPL cookware to an acquaintance, Izu Tsukamoto. Tsukamoto, born of Japanese parents in China, had moved to Japan with his parents as a child. Shortly after World War II, the Tsukamotos migrated to the United States. Izu Tsukamoto spoke Japanese, and was familiar with Japanese customs. In 1981 Izu Tsukamoto worked as a California-based distributor of cookware (for among others, Ecko) on a 5 percent commission basis. Tsukamoto felt that CPL's product would sell well in Japan, and sent samples by Federal Express to distributors in Japan.

Tsukamoto's first contact was Jiro Hattori, president of Kuwahara Company, a Japanese import-export firm specializing in cookware and related items such as china and cutlery. Kuwahara was 50 percent owned by Hattori, and 50 percent by Ohto Overseas Corp., one of the largest pen manufacturers in the world, with assets of over 2 billion yen ($100 million U.S). Kuwahara in 1981 distributed approximately 100,000 sets of Regal and Westbend cookware imported from the United States and one product line of Japanese make, to six or seven direct sales organizations.

CPL's five-ply cookware, relatively new to Japan, was so well received by Jiro Hattori, that Tsukamoto decided to travel personally to Japan. Thus began a series of trips to Japan by Tsukamoto, Taylor, Nolin, and Spencer which culminated in Jiro Hattori's proposal to CPL in June 1981.

Hattori's Proposal

Jiro Hattori expressed an interest in distributing 3 of CPL's 20 styles of cookware. However, he wanted exclusive products and two major modifications—a whistling knob and specially designed wraparound flameguards. These flameguards around the handles were desirable, said Hattori, because most Japanese consumers used liquid propane gas (LPG) for cooking (even though the existing cookware did have heat resistant handles). If CPL could have satisfactory samples of the redesigned cookware ready by the end of August, Hattori would accept deliveries of 1,500 sets a month for four months and more thereafter. The exact price would be negotiated later, but Hattori and Spencer tentatively agreed on a price of (U.S.) $125 a set.

Bill Spencer gathered all the notes on the Japanese market that he had made during his trips—the useful information provided by the Ontario government trade office in Japan (the Canadian government office in Japan, in contrast was useless, Bill felt), and his analysis of the development costs. There were several factors he would have to consider before making his recommendations to Jack Nolin.

The Market

The Japanese consumed more cookware per capita than any other country in the world. The market for cookware in Japan was estimated to be about $100 million. It was (as the market for more consumer goods in Japan appeared to be) very competitive. The high end in which CPL would be competing was approximately $60 million and was dominated by imports (97 percent).

Regal, which had just introduced five-ply cookware, had developed a whistle knob (which was probably the reason for Hattori's haste). Westbend, and Ekco, which produced bonded bottom cookware, were already well entrenched in the market. Two local Japanese manufacturers served the low end of the market.

The Japanese Consumer

The cliches about a Japanese consumer—"very knowledgeable, extremely quality conscious, and willing to pay high prices for exclusive, prestigious products," appeared to be quite true, Bill Spencer reflected. He recalled conversations with other executives doing business in Japan:

"The Japanese market is the toughest in the world. I would prefer to deal in Taiwan or South Korea."

"The Japanese customer is very knowledgeable, very demanding, and the market is extremely competitive. Understanding Japanese customs and preferences is a necessary prerequisite for doing business in Japan."

"The Japanese are very thrifty—as individuals they are among the highest savers in the world. They are willing to spend money only on high-quality goods. In Canada there are three criteria by which consumers select cookware: (1) Price, (2) Quality, (3) Appearance. In Japan it is (1) Quality, (2) Quality, (3) Quality! They are so quality conscious, it is almost revolting; there are customers who check cookware handles using a screwdriver! It is not unusual to see a car buyer *underneath* a car in a showroom, checking it out."

"Japanese consumers are very knowledgeable. They read every word in a brochure (you must have literature in Japanese) and ask pointed questions. The distributors are also extremely knowledgeable—the typical distributor knows as much about a product's characteristics as a manufacturer in North America."

"The Japanese are also very fond of exclusivity—and designer names—this appears to be the only exception to the quality rule. We know this from experience. A line of cheap yellow-colored pans sold a million sets in an extremely short time—because they bore the designer name—Pierre Cardin!"

"It is important to understand Japanese customs—because the islands are so crowded and houses are so small (it is common for a family of four to occupy a one-bedroom apartment), cookware is hung on the wall—it is therefore important for the cookware to look good (and to be exclusive)."

"Understanding Japanese customs is also important when negotiating—they use a lot of euphemisms—if they say they will 'think about it' more than three times, most likely they are politely saying 'no.' If they do say 'no' directly—you had better leave quickly."

"They can take very long to make decisions. When negotiating with a team it is difficult to identify the decision maker—he is usually silent. The person you do most of your talking to is not usually the decision maker. When negotiating with the Japanese, you have to be very well prepared—know precisely what your costs are, and what potential modifications will cost you."

Method of Entry

Given the potential in the Japanese market, there were other possible means of entry besides sales through the Kuwahara Company. CPL had ruled out a wholly owned subsidiary or a joint venture in Japan, since CPL did not have the necessary resources. Even a sales office would be too expensive to maintain, for a company with sales of $6 million, and net profits of $500,000. Bill estimated that it would cost (U.S.) $50,000 in salary and $150,000 in expenses for a one-person operation. Licensing was a poor option—patents were, for all practical purposes, ineffective in protecting cookware design; and in addition, the prestige associated with imported goods was an important buying criterion for the Japanese consumer.

The choice of the appropriate distribution system in Japan often posed a serious problem to many companies trying to penetrate the Japanese market. There were three broad patterns of distribution for consumer goods (Exhibit 2). Distribution varied depending on the type of product. (Distinction is made between the three routes for illustrative purposes only; in actual fact, the distribution routes could be very complex.)

1. *The Open Distribution Route,* used for distributing merchandise over extremely broad areas and involving many intermediate distributors, such as primary and secondary wholesalers. Manufacturers who sold products through this route, usually entrusted ensuing sales to the wholesaler, not knowing clearly where or how their merchandise would be sold from then on, and having little direct contact with the secondary wholesalers or retailers. This form of distribution was adopted primarily for basic essential products with a wide demand, such as fresh and processed foods.

2. *The Restricted Distribution Route* in which distribution was restricted to certain licensed retail stores, with the products going through specialized distribution channels. This form of distribution was common for specialty items such as pharmaceuticals and cosmetics.

3. *The Direct Distribution Route* involved direct transactions between the producer and retailer, or the producer and consumers via door-to-door salespersons. The Kuwahara Company employed a form of this method of direct sales, which was common for imported products in the cookware category, where the originality and specific features of the foreign merchandise had to be directly conveyed to consumers.

While in Japan, the CPL executives had contacted several distributors besides Kuwahara—Basic Japan, Silverware, Noah, Zeny, Prima, Magry Systems,

Exhibit 2 DISTRIBUTION ROUTES FOR CONSUMER GOODS IN JAPAN

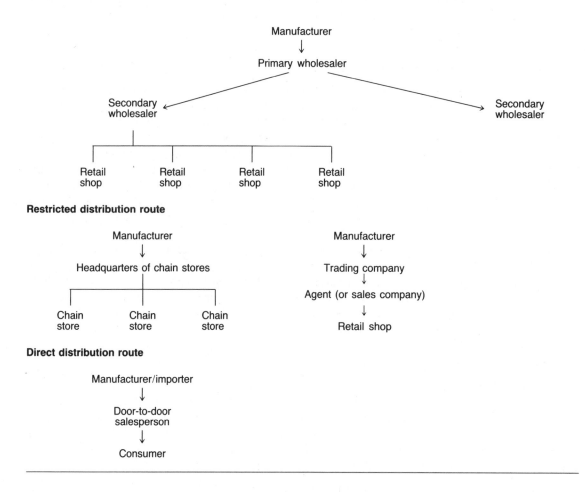

Open distribution route

Restricted distribution route

Direct distribution route

Royal Cookware, and Sunware. These were operations similar to the Kuwahara Co., which was one of the largest and most established (distributing 8,000 cookware sets a month, besides other kitchenware products).

The direct sales organizations that Kuwahara had connections with comprised several hundred door-to-door salespersons, who underwent a six- to-eight week training program organized by Kuwahara. Each sales organization serviced a certain region, such as Osaka. The selling techniques emphasized getting in the door—once that was accomplished, there was usually an 80 percent chance of getting a sale. Part of the selling job included lessons on how to use the cookware. Some distributors had even set up test kitchens to teach women how to cook, and to display cookware. This tactic proved very effective. It was estimated that approximately 80 percent of Japanese women learned to cook outside their homes. The average salesperson sold two to three cookware sets a week, in addition to related items such as china and cutlery.

Pricing

The tentative price that CPL and Hattori agreed on ($125 U.S.) would enable CPL to earn a margin of 15 percent, which was normal for a volume of 1,500 to 2,000 sets a month. CPL would charge up to 35 percent more for smaller volumes. Izu Tsukamoto would earn a 5 percent commission and David Taylor would get 5 percent after Tsukamoto's commission. The cookware would be subjected to a 20 percent tariff, and Kuwahara would usually sell at a 30 percent markup over landed costs. The door-to-door salesperson would sell at a 75 percent markup over the Kuwahara price. Payment would be made by letters of credit. Table 1 illustrates the margins involved.

Development Costs

The modifications that Jiro Hattori requested would, under normal circumstances, take CPL above five months to develop; but Hattori wanted samples by the end of August, and that left CPL only 10 weeks in which to redesign the handles and knobs. Bill Spencer was confident it could be done. The costs involved would be as follows:

Whistle knob development	$100,000
Two molds for new handles at $20,000 each	40,000
	$140,000

In addition, at $5,000 per trip to Japan for travel and the traditional Japanese after-hours business entertainment, CPL had already spent $25,000 on exploring the market; and travel costs could be expected to total at least $50,000 more if the decision to begin product development was made.

Table 1 PROJECTED COSTS AND MARGINS ON THE JAPANESE DEAL	
CPL cost	$100.00
CPL price (from factory)	115.00
Freight and insurance	15.00
	130.00
Tsukamoto's commission	5.75
Taylor's commission	5.45
CPL's price to Kuwahara (cost, insurance, freight)	141.20
Tariffs	28.24
Kuwahara's landed costs	169.44
Kuwahara's price to sales organization	220.27
Price to final consumer	$385.50

Capacity

1981 and 1982 were boom years for the cookware industry. Manufacturers in the industry were usually affected by downturns in the economy with a six-month lag, being cushioned by retailer's preplanned orders. CPL was working at full normal capacity, which involved 10-hour shifts, four days a week, producing approximately 3,125 sets a month. The machines could be worked up to 18 hours a day (one 8-hour shift five days a week, and one 10-hour shift four days a week) or the work week could be extended to accommodate extra sales to Japan if necessary, but such a pace could not be maintained in the long run (over a year) without adversely affecting machine maintenance. Also, CPL's planned four-year $2 million machine upgrading program might have to be speeded up, should capacity utilization be increased.

CPL currently employed approximately 60 production workers, and an increase in capacity utilization would necessitate hiring about 30 to 40 new employees. To begin deliveries in October, CPL would have to begin hiring and training workers by July. In addition, because of the long lead times involved, steel and other raw materials worth over $100,000 would have to be ordered by the end of the week. By the end of August, orders for a further $200,000 in steel (which constituted 50 percent of the direct cost of sales) would have to be placed, for a total investment of $300,000 in raw materials, $140,000 in product development and $75,000 in travel costs, before a firm order could be obtained. Because of CPL's good relationship with its banks, Bill Spencer foresaw no problem in obtaining an extension in its line of credit to cover the increased working capital.

As he reviewed his notes, Bill Spencer wondered what recommendations he should make to Jack Nolin. Could CPL compete in the Japanese market? The risks were enormous. As yet CPL had no written contract with Jiro Hattori, and once the product development was started and the steel was ordered, these costs were sunk. The decision that the CPL managers would make that day would indeed be critical to CPL's future operations.

CAMBRIDGE PRODUCTS, LTD. (B)*

Bill Spencer shook his head in exasperation as he gathered up his papers at the end of a long day of negotiations. Outside the Cambridge Products, Ltd. (CPL) office in Waterloo, Ontario, in late September 1982, the first snowflakes of what promised to be a cold winter were drifting to the ground; but inside, no one even noticed. Present at the meeting which had just ended were Jiro Hattori, president of the Kuwahara Company, one of the largest wholesalers of cookware in Japan; Jack Nolin, executive vice president of CPL, Canada's leading manufacturer of conventional, top of the range cookware; David Taylor, vice president, CPL U.S.; Izu Tsukamoto, CPL's California-based distributor; and Bill Spencer, vice president, corporate relations.

The CPL executives had entered the meeting expecting to reach a final agreement with Jiro Hattori to commence shipping 2,000 sets of cookware a month at (U.S.) $125 per set in late October. Three weeks earlier, after a 10-week crash development program, CPL had sent Hattori 150 sample sets of high quality, 3- and 5-ply cookware that sported whistling knobs and handles with wraparound flameguards (ferrules)—modifications that Hattori had specifically requested. CPL had spent nearly $225,000 on product development and travel to date on this project. Taylor and Tsukamoto had verbally negotiated price and delivery terms with Hattori in Japan, although no written contract had been drawn. Steel and other components had been ordered, at a cost of $400,000, and 40 new employees hired to prepare for the expected October delivery.

Therefore, CPL executives were flabbergasted when Jiro Hattori, on this first day's meeting, announced that more modifications were required—a higher gloss on the outside and more polish on the inside. Doing a quick calculation, Bill Spencer figured it would cost CPL $3.00 more per set, lowering CPL's 15 percent margin. But even more disturbing was the possibility that this new demand by Hattori was just the tip of the iceberg—would more demands follow? Bill wondered if the Japanese would ever be satisfied. Had CPL miscalculated in investing nearly a quarter of a million dollars developing a product for the Japanese market without a written contract? And what should CPL do now—cancel the deal? Or try to negotiate more favorable price and volume terms? The CPL executives knew they would have to consider their options carefully and come up with some answers before negotiations resumed the next day.

---

* Prepared by Ken Coelho under the direction of Professor Donald Lecraw, The University of Western Ontario. The case was developed with the cooperation of a company which prefers to remain anonymous. Names, locations and figures have been disguised, but essential relationships have been preserved. Copyright © 1986, The University of Western Ontario.

Bill Spencer thought back to that warm summer day in June, when he and Jack Nolin had discussed Jiro Hattori's proposal to distribute 1,500 sets a month if CPL could come up with a satisfactory product by August. The two executives had considered several factors—the development costs, capacity expansion, and pricing; had analyzed the information they had available on the Japanese market; and finally decided to go ahead with the product development.

A crash program was instituted and the modifications were developed in 10 weeks instead of the normal five months required for such a job. And they were heartened by Hattori's subsequent offer to take 2,000 sets a month instead of the 1,500 he had proposed earlier—the increased production would not add to overhead significantly. In early September, Tsukamoto and Taylor took 150 sample sets to Japan. The product was superior to anything on the market, the CPL executives felt; although no formal contract had been signed, preparations were made for deliveries of 2,000 sets a month by late October. Steel and other components worth $400,000 were ordered. Hiring and training of new employees began in July and, by September, employees totaled 100, up from 60 in June.

With price and delivery terms already settled in principle, CPL executives had looked forward to Jiro Hattori's first trip to Canada. The Japanese executive came alone, Izu Tsukamoto acted as translator. The CPL executives expected the meeting to end with a formal ratification of the earlier agreement, and the discussions began amicably. Hattori's latest demand for more polish and a "sungloss" finish therefore took them by surprise, especially since they believed they had achieved the ultimate in quality.

They had few options:

1. *Drop Hattori and switch to another distributor.* On their trips to Japan, Bill Spencer had talked to other distributors besides Hattori. They had all appeared to be willing, even eager, to carry CPL's cookware line. In the end, however, CPL had decided to go with Hattori, one of the largest and most powerful distributors in Japan, and their agent Izu Tsukamoto's initial contact there. Spencer was uncertain about the implications of switching agents at this late date in terms of credibility, volume, price, redesign, and delays. But at least there were other distributors besides Hattori. Spencer was also uncertain of whether CPL should try to raise this option with Jiro Hattori to try to gain leverage in the negotiations.

2. *Forget the Japanese market.* CPL could not cancel its steel orders without facing price penalties in the future. If steel was stored for use in normal production for the North American market, it could take well over a year to use up since cookware manufacturers were now beginning to feel the effects of the recession. Bill Spencer calculated that it would cost CPL roughly $150,000 in inventory costs and penalties if such a course of action were followed. Also, 40 of the new employees would probably have to be terminated, with at least two weeks' notice.

3. *Accept Hattori's terms and try to negotiate a better price/volume.* CPL had no written contract. Acceding to Hattori's request would lower margins by $3 per set, and a further investment of $20,000 in equipment and $25,000 in buffs and compounds. And even more worrying was the thought—was this the final de-

mand, or were there more to follow? An increase in volume from 2,000 to 3,000 would lower direct costs by $5 per set, just covering the added costs of the modifications and additional investment. At this volume, sales to Japan would represent almost 50 percent of total sales.

As he politely shook hands with Jiro Hattori, Bill Spencer wondered what was in store for CPL.

NEC CORPORATION'S ENTRY INTO EUROPEAN MICROCOMPUTERS*

In April 1985, nearly five years after the introduction of its first personal computer to the European market, NEC Corporation (formerly Nippon Electric Company, Ltd.) had not yet established a significant presence in Europe. Despite the vast commercial potential of microcomputers, and despite NEC's widely recognized technological leadership and considerable financial resources, the company had not transferred its phenomenal success in Japan, where it had captured 55 percent of the personal computer market, to Europe. The time had come for NEC to reevaluate its strategy for entry into the rapidly evolving European microcomputer market, to review its current position, and to consider its options for the future.

EVOLUTION OF NEC CORPORATION

From its modest beginnings in 1899 as an importer and then manufacturer of telephone equipment, NEC, with 1984 sales of $8 billion, and net income of nearly $200 million, had become a leading international force in telecommunications, the world's third largest vendor of microchips, and Japan's number two computer maker (behind Fujitsu). Expanding from a single plant in Tokyo, NEC became a multinational corporation, manufacturing 15,000 products in 71 plants scattered throughout Japan and 11 other countries, supplying these products to over 140 nations through its 21 marketing and service organizations in 13 countries, and employing 78,000 people worldwide. Expertise in the three major areas of the information industry—telecommunications, semiconductors, and computers—placed NEC in a unique and enviable position to challenge its rivals both at home and abroad. Claimed Tadahiro Sekimoto, NEC's president, "IBM may be ahead in computers, AT&T has good capacity in communications, and Texas Instruments is strong in semiconductors. But no company has such a combination of businesses in all three areas."

Until only 25 years ago, however, NEC's primary line of business was making telecommunications equipment for the domestic market. Set up in 1899 by American Telephone and Telegraph's (AT&T) Western Electric subsidiary, NEC became Japan's first joint venture company. During these early years, Western Electric furnished all the product designs for its minority partner. In 1925 NEC passed into the hands of International Telephone and Telegraph (ITT), which sold off the last of its shares in 1978.

Natural disasters and human catastrophes played a major role in shaping the course of NEC's evolution. A major earthquake in 1923 destroyed a large propor-

---

* Prepared by Michael Hergert and Robin Hergert, San Diego State University.

tion of Japan's wired communications system, prompting the Ministry of Communications not only to rebuild the network, but also to supplement it with a radio broadcasting system, which would not be as vulnerable to seismological activity. NEC thus moved into the field of radio, borrowing Western Electric technology to produce its first vacuum tubes in 1928. World War II precipitated the destruction of nearly 80 percent of the telephone installations in Japan. Japanese authorities once again sought desperately to replace the communications infrastructure, and this time it appeared that microwave technology would provide the answer. NEC thus entered the field of microwave communications. In 1985 it claimed world leadership in microwave, with over 30 percent of "uncommitted" (those that do not favor local suppliers) world markets. Ironically, NEC also licensed its technology for microwave devices made of gallium arsenide to its former joint venture partner, Western Electric.

The postwar years also witnessed the creation of a climate favorable to NEC's development in other directions. Reconstruction of the telecommunications system stimulated the demand for equipment, and the network was to be administered by the newly created Nippon Telegraph and Telephone Public Corporation (NTT). NEC, whose former president became first president of NTT, was NTT's largest supplier, although NTT had not been increasing investment levels and was beginning to bow to strong political pressure to purchase some equipment from the United States.

During the years immediately following the war, Japanese authorities eased restrictions on consumer radio use, thus accelerating the growth of a consumer segment. In response, NEC created a wholly owned subsidiary in 1953, New Nippon Electric, Ltd. (NNE), to take responsibility for the production and sales of electric household appliances. At one time NEC's second most important business after communications, accounting for 20 percent of NEC's sales, consumer products dwindled to 8 percent of sales in the early 1970s.

It was also during the postwar period that NEC began researching solid-state technology. In 1949 the company turned its investigative efforts toward semiconductors, a more reliable and higher-quality alternative to vacuum tubes. Soon after transistors became commercially available in the early 1950s, NEC launched an all-out campaign to catch up with the United States. It began volume production of transistors in 1958, and in 1964 its efforts were rewarded by a major contract in Australia. More recently, NEC's rapid growth in computer sales had provided a large in-house market for its semiconductor division. Rather than depend exclusively on its captive market, however, the company had spent heavily to expand into the merchant market, becoming Japan's largest chip maker in the process. NEC boasted that its Kumamoto plant on Kyushu—Japan's "silicon island"—was the largest factory in the world producing memory chips. According to an industry expert, "NEC is the leader because it was the first Japanese company to understand that semiconductors are big business in itself (sic)."

Although "buy domestic" policies currently represented an ever-increasing threat to NEC's penetration of American and European markets, protectionist attitudes at home during the 1930s provided the catalyst for research that would eventually lead NEC into such advanced technologies as fiber optics. At that time, most of the patents, parts, and materials for telecommunications equipment originated outside Japan, eliciting a wave of sentiment for domestic technology. The search began for an alternative to Bell Laboratories' "loaded" cable for long-distance transmission. The solution was found in 1937 with the completion of a "nonloaded" cable carrier transmission system. One of the engineers working on this all-Japanese project was Dr. Koji Kobayashi, NEC's chairman and chief executive officer. Short, stocky, and still domineering enough at the age of 78 to frighten his colleagues, Kobayashi had been the principal architect of NEC's success in the last 20 years. NEC's continued involvement in transmission technology led to the development of a system capable of carrying digital signals in 1962. Six years later, following investigation into the possibility of using light to transmit information, NEC produced SELFOC, its first optical fiber.

NEC's pioneering role in microwave transmission enabled the company to carve a distinctive international niche and to apply its expertise to the field of satellite communications. After watching the first television show to be relayed by Telestar 1, Dr. Kobayashi personally orchestrated NEC's entry into this emerging industry. Traveling to Hughes Aircraft Company headquarters in Los Angeles, he arranged a joint venture with Hughes to develop a synchronous communications satellite. The successful product of this collaborative effort was Relay I, whose first transmission was the shocking announcement of President John F. Kennedy's assassination. By 1985 NEC had established a dominant position in satellite communications and was the only company to supply the entire system, including the satellite itself.

It was also telecommunications research that provided NEC's springboard into data processing. Company engineers, seeking a faster way to design filters for transmission lines, developed the world's first solid-state computer. NEC licensed Honeywell technology from 1962 to 1979, and, following a suggestion from MITI in 1971, elected to produce mainframe computers that were not compatible with those of IBM. This decision contributed to NEC's limited presence in world data-processing markets; meanwhile archrivals Fujitsu and Hitachi, also under MITI's direction, built up a significant international business in the so-called IBM plug-compatible computers, designed to be plugged into IBM installations as replacements for IBM machines. Nevertheless, at home NEC had captured 16 percent of the thriving mainframe market, and it dominated the markets for printers, displays, and other peripherals. NEC's personal computers had raced to the front of the pack in Japan since their introduction in 1979.

To its competitors outside Japan, NEC was known and respected primarily as a supplier of microchips and telecommunications equipment. Although the company had been involved in several ventures in the Far East during the first 20 years of its existence, it was not until the early 1960s, an era of falling trade restrictions and resultant growth in world trade, that NEC emerged as a multinational corporation. Its first overseas manufacturing facility, a joint venture in telecommunications, was set up in Taiwan in 1958. Other plants followed in

Table 1 NEC INCOME STATEMENT AND BALANCE SHEET DATA, 1984

	1984	Percent change 1983–1984
Income Statement Data (in thousands, except per share figures):		
Sales and other income	$8,017,862	23%
Net sales	7,830,489	22
Communications	2,546,031	9
Computers and industrial electronic systems	2,391,107	34
Electron devices	1,889,231	35
Home electronics	754,693	14
Other	249,427	1
Income before income taxes	384,578	36
Income taxes	213,671	29
Net income	198,089	35
Per share of common stock		
Net income	0.166	30
Cash dividends	0.034	19
Balance Sheet Data (in millions):		
Assets:		
Cash and securities	$1,894	
Accounts receivable	3,299	
Inventories	1,572	
Gross fixed assets	3,773	
Accumulated depreciation (loss)	(1,780)	
Other assets	485	
Total assets	$9,243	
Liabilities and net worth:		
Short-term debt	$2,091	
Accounts payable	2,010	
Other current liabilities	1,089	
Long-term debt	1,579	
Other long-term liabilities	639	
Stockholders' equity	1,171	
Retained earnings	646	
Total liabilities and net worth	$9,243	

Source: NEC annual report.

neighboring Asian countries, Latin America, and the United States, where NEC incorporated its first North American subsidiary, Nippon Electric New York, Inc., in 1963. Its first European plant, for assembly of microchips, was opened in Ireland in 1975. A second, bigger chip factory in Scotland became operational in late 1982. Representing only 10 percent of sales in 1965, international sales accounted for 35 percent of NEC's revenues in 1984. Over half of these overseas sales were attributable to communications, a market NEC had exploited particularly successfully in the United States and Brazil. The corporation supplied equipment to five of the seven regional Bell operating companies formed after the breakup of AT&T and held 80 percent of the Brazilian microwave market. NEC's stock is currently listed on the Amsterdam, Frankfurt, London, Basel, Zurich, and Geneva exchanges. Financial data for NEC appears in Table 1.

PRODUCT AREAS

NEC is divided into four separate divisions for its main businesses: communications, computers and industrial electronic systems, electric components, and home electronics. Summaries of the company's performance by product area follow with analyses of the major factors that characterize the respective markets and a list of NEC's major products.

Communications

Sales of communications systems and equipment in fiscal 1984 rose to $2.55 billion and had been growing at a compounded annual rate of 15.3 percent since 1980. NEC is the largest Japanese telecommunications company and has had considerable success in export markets, including selling its digital public telephone exchange in 28 countries. The company is also the world's largest supplier of satellite earth stations and microwave communications equipment, having captured 50 percent and 33 percent, respectively, of these world markets.

NEC's product offerings in this area are very broad. The major products are electronic telephone-switching systems, digital data-switching systems, telephone sets, teleconference systems, facsimile equipment, carrier-transmission equipment, submarine cable repeaters, fiber-optic communication systems, microwave and satellite communications systems, laser communications equipment, mobile radio equipment, pagers, broadcast equipment, satellites, radio application equipment, and defense electronic systems.

Although just under one third of NEC's sales are in communications, profit margins in this area have been squeezed as the company makes the transfer from analog to digital communications. International markets for telecommunications have become intensely competitive as companies struggle to maintain a presence in an overcrowded market. Sustained growth in computer sales has helped to reduce NEC's dependence on communications from 44 percent of sales in 1974 to 32 percent in 1984.

As the volume of NEC's business with its major customer, NNT, did not grow significantly in 1984, NEC is looking to the private sector and overseas markets for future growth. The company projects that the world telecommunications market will grow more rapidly in the latter half of the decade than it has over the past five years. NEC is keen to enter the newly liberalized U.K. market; it intends to build a plant in the United Kingdom and has recently won a major order to supply Brith Telecom and Securicor with mobile radios for their joint cellular radio mobile telephone network.

Computers and Industrial Electronic Systems

Computer and industrial electronic systems recorded sales of $2.39 billion in fiscal 1984, sustaining a compounded annual growth rate of 26.7 percent since 1980. The division has an extensive product list. The major products are super computers, general-purpose ACOS series computers, minicomputers, control computers, personal computers and software, data communications equipment and software, peripheral and terminal equipment, magnetic memory equipment, distributed data-processing systems, office-automation systems, word processors, industrial telemetering systems, postal automation systems, numerical control equipment, medical electronic equipment, speech recognizers, industrial and communications control systems, robots, and CAD/CAM systems.

Although within Japan, NEC still lags behind Fujitsu and IBM in overall computer sales, the company leads the Japanese market in sales of personal computers with a 55 percent share. It was also the only major computer maker between 1974 and 1981 to increase its share of the Japanese market, both in cumulative value and number of machines installed. As a result, computers now account for 31 percent of revenues, up from 20 percent in 1974. According to Takeshi Kawashi, head of radio communications, the major reason for this success lies in NEC's strength in semiconductors.

Although NEC is looking to overseas data-processing markets for growth, its penetration of international markets for computers is very limited. The Japanese company has garnered only a tiny share of the personal computer market in the United States, the single largest of NEC's foreign markets. The 16-bit Advanced Personal Computer (APC) made its marketing debut in Europe in fiscal 1984, following its introduction in Australia and the United States the year before. In March 1984, NEC entered into an agreement with the United States-based Honeywell Information Systems, Inc., granting Honeywell distribution and manufacturing rights for NEC's large computers. The link with Honeywell gives NEC a strong marketing arm and access to a customer base in the United States. It also gives Honeywell an extension to its range of computers it could not have afforded to develop itself. In years past NEC had licensed technology from Honeywell.

Industry analysts attribute NEC's lack of significant international presence in computers in foreign markets to the company's refusal to produce IBM-compatible mainframes. Observers note that IBM's more aggressive stance and its dominance of the mainframe market has made it very hard for other companies to succeed with different systems. NEC counters that companies that seek to poach IBM's customers by offering technically compatible machines expose themselves to the threat of crippling retaliation by IBM. Yukio Mizuno, senior vice president in charge of the computer division, intimates that the battle with the U.S. giant is undergoing a shift in emphasis: "IBM's profits will come increasingly from software, maintenance, and system communications rather than from the computer hardware itself. So we have to compete with IBM in software rather than hardware."

Though NEC is putting huge resources into improving the production of its software—it has 13 wholly owned software subsidiaries and employs some 8,500 programmers—senior vice president Tomihiro Matsumura believes that Japan's social and educational system may be a handicap. By emphasizing highly organized group activity, he thinks it discourages the individualism that often sparks off innovation. The company aims to fill the gap by tapping outside talent. It has already commissioned American software houses to write programs for it, notably for its personal computers. It plans to set up its own software centers in the United States and recruit American programmers to staff them.

Although NEC management predicts that demand for computers and industrial electronic systems will continue to rise as harsh conditions force companies to rationalize and upgrade their operations, it also admits that competition is certain to mount as computer manufacturers around the world move to capitalize on the wealth of opportunity at hand. Industry observers are less than completely enthusiastic about NEC's ability to capitalize on these international opportunities. Says Frederic G. Withington, vice president for information systems at Arthur D. Little, "While they've done fine with the Spinwriter [high-quality printer] and [semiconductor] components, in computers they aren't strong enough."

Electronic Components

NEC's sales of electronic devices reached $1.89 billion in fiscal 1984 and had been growing at a compounded annual rate of 23.1 percent since 1980. The company leads the increasingly successful Japanese assault on the world's semiconductor markets, and it ranks among the globe's top four microchip suppliers, along with Texas Instruments, National Semiconductor, and Motorola of the United States. A sustained global shortage of memory and other devices has contributed heavily to this performance. NEC's chip business currently accounts for 24 percent of revenues, up from 16 percent in 1975, and it is the most profitable of its product lines.

The company produces a wide range of electronic devices. The major products are integrated circuits (ICs), circuits for large-scale integration (LSIs), circuits for very-large-scale integration (VLSIs), microprocessors, transistors, diodes, gallium arsenide field-effect transistors, gate arrays, electron tubes, color picture tubes, display tubes, plasma display panels, lasers, laser application devices, circuit components, rectifiers, bubble memories, and vacuum equipment.

While Texas Instruments, the world's biggest chip maker, is laying off workers in anticipation of a weaker semiconductor market, NEC is pressing ahead with the construction of new plants and the expansion of existing facilities, both at home and abroad. The Japanese multinational insists that demand for its chips still outstrips supply, and it is vying for top position in the chip-makers' league by year's end. According to preliminary estimates by the California market research firm Dataquest, NEC's semiconductor sales will grow by about 60 percent in 1985, allowing it to overtake Motorola and to close the gap on TI.

NEC can apparently withstand the slower market growth more easily than its American rivals because Japanese demand for chips has been less volatile than demand across the Pacific. The four top Japanese chip makers—NEC, Fujitsu, Hitachi, and Toshiba—are also four of the biggest chip consumers. This makes demand easier to forecast and moderates the industry's boom-bust cycles. There is thus no need for chip users to overbook to ensure deliveries when demand is rising.

Another factor in NEC's favor is its strength in both memory chips and microprocessors. Prices for the latter tend to be more stable than prices for memory chips. The firm has also invested heavily in the mass production of cheap memory chips. NEC's main microchip plant in Kumamoto, southern Japan, is the largest and most efficient in the world.

Home Electronics

The fourth main area of NEC's business is home electronics. This division posted sales of $755 million in fiscal 1984 and has grown at a compounded annual rate of 11 percent since 1980. It is an area of NEC's activities that is easily overlooked because it only represents 10 percent of revenues, down from 14 percent in 1981, and is fairly insignificant alongside the leading producers of consumer electronics in Japan such as Matsushita, Sony, Sanyo, JVC, and Hitachi.

The NEC-brand product line is extensive, and the major products include television sets, video recorders, portable video cameras, television projectors, radio receivers, transceivers, tape recorders, hi-fi audio systems, compact disk digital audio systems, personal computers, lighting products, refrigerators, microwave ovens, kitchen appliances and air conditioners. NEC does not manufacture the whole range, but concentrates on producing consumer electronic products while rebranding the nonelectronic appliances.

Despite the firm's modest showing in consumer electronics, NEC believes that the division, and particularly the personal computer, is potentially highly important. NEC's president explains, "In 10 or 20 years' time, consumer products will be the largest single part of [our strategy]."

NEC STRATEGY

NEC sees itself as a tree whose roots are firmly embedded in high technology. One product recently developed by the Tokyo-based company is an automatic software-development system that makes productivity 5 to 50 times more efficient than previous manual work. Known as SEA/I, the system is designed for automation of software development, which was chiefly a manual process until now. SEA/I is among the most advanced systems of its kind in the world. Yet management thinks it could do better, committing over 10 percent of consolidated sales to research, development, and engineering activities.

NEC's competitors are beginning to run out of adjectives to describe such relentless striving for higher performance. The Japanese multinational, however, harbors still bolder ambitions. It has set its sights on the twin goals of increasing sales at an annual pace of 18–20 percent for the rest of the decade and of becoming a world leader in the creation of the high-technology information society of tomorrow. To reach these overall growth objectives, NEC plans to raise overseas contribution to sales from 35 percent to 40 percent, half of it manufactured outside Japan.

If NEC's targets are bold, its operational style is even riskier. While archrivals Fujitsu Ltd. and Hitachi Ltd. have set up partnerships with computer manufacturers in the United States and Europe to assure a sizable penetration of the information-processing markets, NEC has generally shunned such shortcuts in favor of developing its brand name. Explains Dr. Kobayashi, NEC's chairman,

"Our intention is simple: walking on our own feet." The company's president, Dr. Tadahiro Sekimoto, elaborates on this point: "We aim to establish real companies abroad that can design, make, and maintain the products that they sell on their own." He is convinced that this policy of decentralization is the most effective way to secure NEC's future in an increasingly volatile and treacherous business climate. Indeed, growing fears of a trade war with the United States and the European Economic Community (EEC) have heightened the sense of urgency.

As a result of this go-it-alone approach, coupled with the decision not to make computers that are compatible with those made by IBM, NEC's machines have not yet achieved significant penetration in the West. To compensate, NEC has resorted to aggressive marketing and ruthless price cutting. "NEC uses its profits in other areas to allow it to cut prices in computers," says Tamizo Kimura, an analyst at Yamaichi Research Institute. A strategy based on price competition, however, is not totally without risk. In a suit brought by U.S. rivals Aydin Corporation and MCL, Inc., the Commerce Department in 1982 found Nippon Electric guilty of dumping $3 million worth of microwave communications components on the U.S. market.

As NEC has also discovered, establishing offshore manufacturing operations can cause other kinds of headaches as well. Neither Electronic Arrays, a small California chip maker bought in 1978, nor its telecommunications plant opened the same year in Dallas, Texas, was judged to be up to Japanese quality standards in 1982. Executives were appalled by the conditions they found when they took over Electronic Arrays. Workers at NEC's Kumamoto plant must change into special protective garments and pass through a forced-air "shower" before entering the ultra-clean section where the most delicate part of the chipmaking process is performed. "But in California, people were wandering in wearing street clothes," according to one NEC manager. A good deal of management effort has been devoted to bringing the plants up to snuff.

Although NEC departed from the firm's policy of developing largely through internal growth when it acquired Electronic Arrays, executives say there are no plans to bolster international marketing operations through the purchase of other companies with strong marketing organizations. However, Dr. Sekimoto does not rule out this possibility categorically. An enthusiast of American futurologist Alvin Toffler, the president quips, "After all, this is the Age of Drastic Change."

NEC's second driving ambition is symbolized in its slogan "C&C," standing for the convergence of computer and communications technologies that lies at the heart of the revolution in electronic information handling. Since Dr. Kobayashi first publicly coined the term at the International Telecommunications Exposition in Atlanta in 1977, NEC's patriarch has been actively promoting C&C within his entire organization. This theme dominates NEC management and activities to an almost obsessive degree. No document, no conversation—whether formal or informal—is complete without some reference to C&C.

This convergence of computer and communications technologies is, of course, widely recognized by electronics companies throughout the world, bringing computer companies such as IBM into telecommunications and communications companies such as AT&T into data processing. Few companies, however, have made this convergence into such a pervasive management theme, and fewer still actually straddle these worlds quite as comprehensively as NEC. The concept is made tangible in the so-called decision room at corporate headquarters in Tokyo, where top management regularly meets. An elegant wood-paneled chamber, it is equipped with a panoply of sophisticated systems permitting two-way video communications with distant offices and instantaneous retrieval and display of massive amounts of information.

Despite NEC's technical achievements and strongly held belief in the convergence of computers and communications, the company has a long way to go in coordinating its communications, computer, semiconductor, and consumer electronics divisions. Says Dr. Sekimoto, "I think they will remain separate forever. For instance, the communications business will always be there . . . the telephone will never disappear. In the same way the stand-alone computer will never disappear. However, C&C will create new fields and will become very much bigger."

To enhance cooperation, the company has set up occasional project teams that span the different divisions, such as for automatic broadcasting equipment and some defense projects. In addition, the marketing and sales organization, which is separate from the manufacturing divisions, has a team devoted to the promotion of C&C products such as office and factory automation.

THE EUROPEAN MICROCOMPUTER INDUSTRY

In 1985 the microcomputer industry in Europe displayed many features typical of emerging markets. Great technological uncertainty, buyer confusion, and unclear market segments created an environment where strategy formulation was difficult at best. Current events left many industry observers puzzled; spectacular successes and failures were the norm, and some of the world's mightiest multinationals had proven unable to establish viable competitive positions. Among this group was NEC, whose European microcomputers had failed to capture a significant market share, even after five years of attempts.

In this market, even a precise product description is controversial. Microcomputers span the range from simple machines costing a few hundred dollars and primarily used for playing games to sophisticated desktop units capable of supporting several hundred users simultaneously. For the following discussion, the main emphasis is on products selling for $1,000 to $10,000 and designed for individual use. A typical microcomputer setup has the components described below.

System Unit

The system unit is the heart of a microcomputer. It contains the microprocessor, which is the semiconductor chip where numerical operations actually take place. The microprocessor size is an important determinant of the speed and power of the computer. First-generation microcomputers, such as the Apple II, relied on an 8-bit microprocessor, meaning that information is processed for computations in blocks of 8 units. An 8-bit microprocessor is quite adequate for many applications, and is still used in a large number of products.

IBM ushered in the second generation of microcomputers in August 1981 when it introduced the PC. The PC uses the Intel 8088 microprocessor, which processes 16 bits of information at a time. This permits the IBM PC and other second-generation products to run more powerful software and handle larger problems. It also creates the possibility of making the microcomputer a multitasking machine (i.e., capable of handling more than one job at a time) and a multiuser machine (i.e., capable of handling more than one user at a time).

More recently, even larger microprocessors have become common. The IBM AT, introduced in August 1984, is a 16–24-bit product, and the Apple Macintosh, also introduced in 1984, has a 32-bit processor. Although the technology of large microprocessors was well established by 1985, limited availability and high costs have made many microcomputer producers wary of committing to advanced technology.

In addition to a central processing unit, a microcomputer must have internal memory. Internal memory consists of RAM (Random Access Memory) and ROM (Read Only Memory). Both RAM and ROM are made up of memory chips installed inside the system unit. ROM consists of instructions permanently stored in the machine that cannot be modified by the user. ROM memory often contains essential software to control the operation of the machine and increasingly is used to provide applications packages, such as word processing or spreadsheet software. RAM memory is addressable by the user, meaning that he can write his own data and programs to memory for temporary storage and can modify the contents at will. The amount of internal memory in a microcomputer plays a large role in determining the size of the problem that can be handled. Memory is measured in kilobytes (K). Most microcomputers have at least 64K of RAM. Larger machines may be expanded to 640K or more.

External Memory

In addition to internal memory, microcomputers generally provide some form of external storage medium for permanent storage. Early microcomputers stored data on audio cassettes, but this proved to be slow and unreliable. In 1978 Apple began using floppy diskettes for external storage, which quickly became adopted as the standard system. Floppy diskettes are inexpensive disks of magnetic storage film that are capable of recording 160–2400K of data. Individual diskettes sell for under $2.50. The disk drive used to store data onto diskettes sells for $150 to $500, depending on size and storage capacity. A typical microcomputer system will have one or two disk drives, which can be mounted inside the system unit or in separate expansion cabinets. During 1984 and 1985, the use of hard disks as a storage medium increased dramatically. Hard disks, also known as Winchester disks or fixed disks, are similar in size to floppy disks, but are capable of holding far greater amounts of information. Hard disks for microcomputers typically hold 10–20 megabytes of data (1 megabyte = 1000 kilobytes), and are available up to 100 megabytes or more. Prices for hard disks have fallen drastically during the last two years, and they are now available for as little as $500. Exotic mass storage devices of even greater capacity should be available in the near future. In 1985,

3M announced a laser optical disk capable of holding 450 megabytes of information on a 5.25-inch disk. Industry analysts expect the disk drive to sell for under $1,500 within a few years.

Video Display

Microcomputers display information on several forms of video devices. Early microcomputers were often hooked into television sets for display. Current computers typically have a dedicated cathode ray tube (CRT) device, which can display output in multiple colors and screen formats. In order to increase the portability of microcomputers, extensive research is being done on LCD, plasma, and other flat-screen technologies. In late 1984, Data General announced a notebook-sized computer with a fold-up, full-sized (25 lines by 80 characters) display.

Printers

To create a physical record of microcomputer output, it is necessary to use some form of printing device. The most popular printer technology is the dot matrix. Dot-matrix printers are inexpensive ($200 and up) and relatively fast (as many as 400 characters per second). The main drawback of dot-matrix printers is that they are unable to provide high-quality output and are viewed by many people as unsuitable for business correspondence. For letter-quality printing, daisy wheel printers are more common. Daisy wheel printers work on the same principle as many office typewriters and are able to provide very high-quality output. A daisy wheel printer intended for office use will usually sell for at least $1,000.

New printing technologies are also emerging. In 1984 Hewlett Packard introduced its LaserJet printer, which is based on the xerographic process used in copier machines. Laser printers are fast, very high quality, capable of producing any form of graphics output (unlike daisy wheel printers), and are extremely quiet. Similar printers had been available previously from Xerox and others, but at prices of $25,000 to $400,000. The HP LaserJet sells for approximately $3,000.

Modems

Modems (or modulator-demodulators) are devices that allow a microcomputer to access another computer over telephone lines. This is very useful for accessing data provided by an outside information vendor, or for accessing data stored in a central location within a company. Modems also allow microcomputers to function as computer terminals for use with a larger computer to run jobs beyond the capability of the microcomputer. This linkage is viewed as an important first step in office automation.

Software

Most microcomputer users view their machines as a black box capable of running specific applications. Software is the complementary product that makes this possible. The two main categories of software are operating system software and applications software.

Operating systems software does the housekeeping of a microcomputer. It manages files and controls the operations of other programs, such as applications software. Because this function is central to the operation of a microcomputer, the operating system determines the extent to which data and programs can be shared between two microcomputers. Generally, two microcomputers that share the same operating system are compatible, although different versions of the same system can lead to problems. Because the operating system controls the microprocessor, the software is somewhat specific to the chip and architecture of the individual product.

For the first generation of 8-bit microcomputers, CP/M, developed by Digital Research Corporation, was the most widely used operating system. However, since the advent of 16-bit microprocessors, the operating system used by IBM, MS DOS, has emerged as the de facto industry standard. The choice of which operating system to employ is a crucial one to the strategy of a firm. The choice of operating system will determine which applications programs will run on a given computer. If a firm chooses to follow IBM's lead and uses MS DOS, this provides the advantage of immediate access to a large number of software programs available in the market. Unfortunately, it also creates a stigma of copying IBM's product and being viewed as a "me-too" producer. Alternatively, a firm can choose to provide a proprietary operating system. This has the advantage of allowing a firm to differentiate itself and provide the only applications software capable of being used on the machine. It also creates the risk that the new operating system and software will not be viewed as sufficiently superior to the industry standard products to warrant switching systems. Apple has followed this

Table 2 POPULAR MICROCOMPUTER SOFTWARE PACKAGES

Product	Retail price	Mail-order price	Application
dBase III	$695	$339	Database
Framework	695	339	Integrated multifunction
Multiplan	195	115	Spreadsheet
Sidekick	55	35	Utility
1-2-3	495	289	Integrated multifunction
Symphony	695	409	Integrated multifunction
Wordstar 2000	495	239	Word processing
VisiCalc 4	250	159	Spreadsheet
Volkswriter Deluxe	395	149	Word processing
rBase: 4000	495	269	Database
Microsoft Word	375	235	Word processing
TK Solver!	399	265	Modeling/simulation
SuperCalc III	395	245	Spreadsheet
Perfect Writer	349	179	Word processing
Crosstalk XVI	195	99	Communications
Prokey	130	79	Utility

Source: *PC World,* March 1985.

latter approach in developing specialized software for its Macintosh line of products.

Applications software provides functional capability to a microcomputer. The main uses for applications software are word processing, spreadsheet analysis, database management, graphics, communications between computers, and games. In addition, language compilers, such as BASIC and FORTRAN, allow users to run specific programs written in those languages. Some of the most popular software packages and their prices are shown in Table 2.

A cottage industry supplying software for microcomputers has emerged in the United States and Europe. For example, the DataPro Directory of Microcomputer Software lists over 1,000 firms in the United States in which PC software is included in their principal line of business. Early analysts of the microcomputer industry predicted that a typical user would spend at least as much on software as on hardware. Recent events have led these analysts to reconsider their positions. Many microcomputer producers have adopted the practice of bundling software with their hardware and pricing the package very aggressively. For example, in early 1985, the Sanyo MBC 555, an IBM-compatible microcomputer with 128K of RAM and two floppy disk drives, was available for under $1,000. This price included several popular software packages, such as MS DOS, Easywriter, Wordstar, Calcstar, Spellstar, Mailmerge, and Infostar, which if bought separately would cost over $1,000. For many users, this is all the software they would ever need.

MARKET SIZE AND SEGMENTATION

The European microcomputer industry is not a unified market of standard products or users. Rather, it is composed of many national markets, each with different requirements, levels of sophistication, and distribution channels. As a result, it is dangerous to generalize about competitive requirements for success using the whole of Europe as a reference point.

Many industry observers believe that the evolution of the European market will parallel the development of the American market. In the 1970s, this seemed to be the case, as European markets were dominated by American multinationals exporting products they were already selling in the United States. A brief summary of key events in the evolution of the microcomputer industry appears in Table 3.

The largest market in Europe is the United Kingdom, with approximately 24 percent of the $2 billion industry in 1983. As shown in Table 4, Germany is a close second, and the four largest markets (United Kingdom, Germany, France, and Italy) account for 76 percent of European sales.

The major market segments are as follows:

- The home user/hobbyist whose demand is oriented toward smaller micros and leisure applications. This segment was especially well developed in England by Sinclair. A strong position in the home market is thought to provide a basis for creating customer loyalty that can be exploited in trade-ups to larger products.

Table 3	EVOLUTION OF MICROCOMPUTER INDUSTRY

1974	Intel announces the 8080 microprocessor Motorola announces the 6800 microprocessor
1975	Early microcomputer kits appear on market Dick Heiser opens first retail computer store in Santa Monica
1976	Zilog announces Z80 microprocessor Steve Wozniak designs Apple 1; Apple founded by Wozniak and Steve Jobs Steve Leninger joins Radio Shack to design a computer 100 companies active in field by year-end 132 computer clubs in existence by year-end
1977	Apple II announced Radio Shack TRS-80 announced Microsoft begins to market BASIC and FORTRAN for microcomputers First Computerland franchise store opened in Morristown, New Jersey; 24 stores open by year-end Over 200 active manufacturers by year-end
1978	Atari announces the 400 and 800 computers Apple and Radio Shack begin using 5¼" disk drives Dan Bricklin and Bob Frankston write VisiCalc
1979	Texas Instruments introduces 99/4 home computer Radio Shack announces Model II business computer Micropro announces Wordstar NEC demonstrates the 8000 computer at Hannover, West Germany, trade show
1980	Sinclair ZX80 introduced first computer under $200 Apple introduces the Apple III Epson announces the MX-80 printer Microsoft agrees to work with IBM to design software Xerox, DEC, and Intel announce Ethernet Local Area Network
1981	Osborne introduces the first transportable computer IBM announces the PC Microsoft products MS-DOS (PC-DOS) for IBM PC
1982	Commodore 64 announced DEC announces Rainbow 100 Apple begins selling "user friendly" LISA in United States Franklin introduces Apple-compatible Ace 100 NEC announces 16-bit Advanced Personal Computer NEC introduces the 8800 series in Europe Seven IBM-compatible computers appear on the market
1983	IBM introduces PCjr and PC XT Radio Shack announces Model 100 notebook computer; NEC announces 8201 Timex introduces Timex/Sinclair 2000, but withdraws from market eight months later Texas Instruments withdraws 99/4A Osborne Computer files for bankruptcy NEC begins selling 8201 notebook computer in Europe IBM lookalikes flood the market

1984	Apple announces Macintosh, Apple IIc
	Hewlett-Packard introduces Model 110 notebook portable, similar in power to desktop
	    machines
	Mattel, Timex, Specta-Video, Victor, Actrix, and Computer Devices leave market or sell out
	Warner sells Atari to Jack Tramiel after losses of $539 million
	NEC sells over 1 million personal computers in Japan
	First national TV advertising for software (Lotus Symphony and Ashton-Tate Framework);
	    number of software manufacturers tops 500

Source: *Creative Computing*, November 1984.

Table 4 EUROPEAN NATIONAL MARKETS, 1983

	Revenues	Percentage of European market
United Kingdom	$480 million	24%
Germany	460	23
France	360	18
Italy	220	11
Scandinavia	160	8
Benelux countries	140	7
Spain/Portugal	100	5
Switzerland/Austria	80	4
Total (approximately 300,000 units)	$2 billion	100%

European user segments by size:

	Percentage of total market	
	Units	Value
Home	61%	12%
Business	26	63
Education	7	3
Scientific	6	22

Source: International Data Corporation.

- The educational institution that purchases microcomputers to teach computer literacy. This segment has not proven very lucrative for producers because government purchasers are price sensitive and may use their purchasing power to promote a national champion. This segment has been used as a loss leader by some manufacturers to create brand visibility and preferences. For example, Apple has created an educational consortium of major universities that receive Macintosh computers at deep discounts.
- The scientist who uses the microcomputer instead of a mainframe to perform very specific applications. Scientific applications typically require powerful microcomputers with specialized software.
- The business user who relies on a microcomputer for word processing, data analysis, terminal emulation, or a variety of other administrative tasks. As shown in Table 4, this is the largest segment in Europe, accounting for nearly two thirds of all microcomputer revenues.

DISTRIBUTION

Microcomputers in Europe are sold through a variety of channels. Although distribution networks differ somewhat across countries, the following channels generally exist to some extent in all European nations. A summary of the distribution channels for Europe appears in Table 5.

Table 5 EUROPEAN DISTRIBUTION NETWORKS FOR MICROCOMPUTERS PRICED $1,000 AND ABOVE

	Retail outlets	System houses	Total network
United Kingdom	832	350	1,182
Germany	672	250	922
France	620	250	870
Italy	580	100	680
Belgium	144	100	244
Netherlands	145	70	215
Spain	130	70	200

Distribution network by type of outlet
(percentages based on 1983 volumes)

	Mass outlets	Computer stores	Office equipment stores	System houses	Direct sales
United Kingdom	7–10%	42–45%	2–4%	23–25%	20–22%
Germany	3–4	26–29	22–24	24–26	20–22
France	<1	38–40	4–5	32–34	22–25
Italy	—	31–35	19–21	28–32	16–18
Spain	4–6	33–35	16–18	29–31	13–15
Belgium	3–5	38–40	8–10	24–28	21–23
Netherlands	2–4	33–35	12–14	18–20	30–32
USA	28	33	6	13	15

Source: *Electronics Business and Electronics Intelligence.*

Direct Sales Force

For large accounts, direct sales calls are common. Companies with an existing position in a related field, such as telecommunications, large computers, or office products, are most likely to emphasize this channel. This provides the advantage of being able to sell a bundle of related products as a customized system to corporate clients. The ability to provide such systems is thought to be a crucial capability for future success in large accounts.

Retail Stores

Retail computer stores are the single most important channel of distribution, accounting for over one third of all sales in Europe, and as much as 45 percent in the United Kingdom. This category includes company-owned stores, such as those used by Tandy as its exclusive form of distribution, mass merchandisers who sell a wide variety of consumer products in addition to microcomputers, independent retailers, and franchise chains, of which Computerland and Entre are the largest. As of 1984, Computerland operated 791 stores worldwide and generated sales of $1.4 billion. Computer franchise stores, which originally appeared in the United States and are well established in that market, have yet to make a similar impact in Europe. Nonetheless, both Computerland and Entre have announced aggressive plans to expand their European networks.

PRODUCTION

Manufacturing microcomputers is a relatively easy task. Components and sub-assemblies are readily available on world markets, and many producers have adopted policies of purchasing nearly all inputs externally and simply assembling the product and attaching their brand name. Even IBM, with its great potential for vertical integration, has chosen to rely on outside vendors for nearly all of the components of the PC. As shown in Table 6, approximately 73 percent of the manufacturing cost of the IBM PC comes from components purchased from Asian producers. Table 7 summarizes the manufacturing strategies of several major microcomputer producers.

BASES FOR COMPETITIVE ADVANTAGE

In choosing a competitive strategy in microcomputers, there are numerous bases for competitive advantage. The strategies of many competitors are derived from

Table 6   IBM PC MANUFACTURING SOURCES

Element	IBM	Other	
Video display	—	Korea	$ 85
Printer	—	Japan	160
Floppy disks	$ 25	Singapore	165
Keyboard	—	Japan	50
Semiconductors	105	Japan	105
Power supply	—	Japan	60
Case and final assembly	105		—
Total cost	$235		$625

Source: *Business Week,* March 11, 1985.

Table 7   MICROCOMPUTER MANUFACTURING STRATEGIES

Company	Major models	Main unit	Keyboard	Monitor	Disk drive	Printer	Software
Apple	IIe, Lisa	MF	OS	OS	OS	OS	MF
Atari	400, 800	MF	OS	N/A	OS	OS	MF
Commodore	VIC-20, 64	MF	OS	OS	OS	OS	MF
DEC	Rainbow	MF	MF	MF	MF	MF	OS/MF
Hewlett-Packard	75C, HP-86, 87, 150	MF	OS	MF	MF	MF	MF
IBM	PC, XT	OS/MF	OS	OS	OS	OS	OS/MF
Tandy	Model III, Model XVI, Color Computer	MF	OS	MF	OS	OS	MF
Texas instruments	Professional	MF	MF	OS	MF	MF	MF

Abbreviations: MF = manufactured in-house; OS = bought from outside supplier

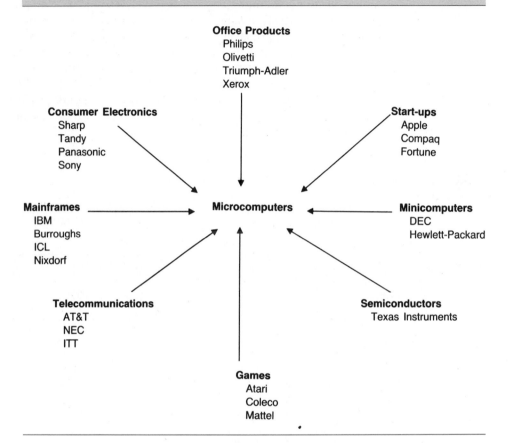

Table 8   MICROCOMPUTER ENTRY GATEWAYS

Office Products
Philips
Olivetti
Triumph-Adler
Xerox

Consumer Electronics
Sharp
Tandy
Panasonic
Sony

Start-ups
Apple
Compaq
Fortune

Mainframes
IBM
Burroughs
ICL
Nixdorf

Microcomputers

Minicomputers
DEC
Hewlett-Packard

Telecommunications
AT&T
NEC
ITT

Semiconductors
Texas Instruments

Games
Atari
Coleco
Mattel

their strategies in related markets. Because the microcomputer is at the intersection of several technologies, firms have been attracted to the industry from many directions. This pattern of gateways is summarized in Table 8. For example, as producers of typewriters, such as Olivetti and Triumph-Adler, saw their products increasingly being replaced by word processors, they were induced into offering their own microcomputers. Similarly, as microcomputers became more powerful and better substitutes for larger computers, integrated computer companies were motivated to introduce their own products. On the technology side, the trend toward a convergence of data processing and telecommunications brought the entry of AT&T, ITT, and NEC. Similarly, consumer electronics companies (Panasonic, Sharp, Tandy), toy producers (Atari, Mattel, Coleco), and start-ups (Apple, Fortune) all entered the market with distinctive motivations, resources, and ways of doing business.

This variety of perspectives has manifested itself in different competitive postures. It is possible to strive for competitive advantage in any of the following (not necessarily mutually exclusive) ways.

Cost Leadership

In its announcements and in its actions IBM has indicated that it intends to be the low-cost producer of microcomputers. It has even deviated substantially from corporate tradition to attain this goal. For example, despite its strong existing capabilities in many aspects of microcomputer technology, IBM has declined to vertically integrate for fear of increasing its costs. In the case of printers, which IBM purchases from Epson, the IBM printer-manufacturing division was invited to submit a bid for supplying dot-matrix printers. The bid was higher than Epson's, and thus was refused, despite tremendous internal politicking to push it through. IBM's large market share allows it to receive volume purchasing discounts and scale economies in assembly and marketing. Although it has yet to occur, industry analysts look to Asia for significant future challengers to IBM's cost position.

Full-Line Complementarity

Another strategic approach is to view the microcomputer not as a stand-alone product but as a part of an office system. Producers who sell a full line of office products, such as PABXs, local area networks, telex machines, terminals, large computers, and word processors, can sell their microcomputers as part of an integrated system. This overcomes the problems of incompatibility between individual products supplied by different vendors. DEC and Xerox have been leaders in pursuing this strategy.

Proprietary Closed System

As an alternative to conforming to industry standards in hardware and software, a microcomputer producer may elect to introduce its own unique computer architecture and operating system. As mentioned earlier, the benefits of differentiation must be weighed against the risk of the market not accepting the new system.

Microcomputers exist in multiple configurations of processor speed, memory size, machine size, and other special features. It is possible for a manufacturer to specialize in one hardware segment of the market and attempt to build an image as the industry leader. For example, Compaq recorded the all-time largest volume of sales in the first year of operation for a company (over $100 million) by dominating the market for "transportable" microcomputers. These products weigh approximately 30 pounds and are self-contained for relatively easy movement.

"Me-Too"

The single most common competitive strategy in microcomputers is to offer a clone or look-alike product that emulates the industry standard (generally IBM). There are currently hundreds of companies that produce microcomputers that are physical and electronic copies of IBM's PC. Such products generally sell for discounts of 15–40 percent off the IBM price. This strategy is not limited to small firms: ITT, Siemens, Ericsson, Olivetti, and Tandy have joined ranks with the many start-up firms that offer products with little or no enhancement to the basic IBM model. Indeed, this has led many observers to speculate that the microcomputer may be entering a stage of evolution resembling a commodity.

National Market Segmentation

European national markets for microcomputers demonstrate some differentiating characteristics that create the possibility of national market segmentation. Local governments have a long history of preferential purchasing of large computers, and this has continued into the realm of microcomputers as well. Different languages and cultures also create possible advantages for a local supplier. For example, no foreign producer has succeeded in capturing any significant share of the Japanese market. IBM failed to reach the company target of 120,000 PCs sold in Japan in 1984 despite a reorganization and new product design to push the microcomputer. Attempts by Sinclair, Tandy, Commodore, and Apple have been similarly frustrated. Early product offerings by all these companies were simply exports of existing machines and were unable to use kana and kanji characters. Today, NEC has over 50 percent of the Japanese microcomputer market, and its chief rivals are all Japanese firms.

Technological Leadership

Another method for strategic differentiation is to strive for leadership in the underlying technology of microcomputers. The current standard microcomputer, as exemplified by the IBM PC, is a modest machine relative to state-of-the-art possibilities. Faster microprocessors, higher density storage, more advanced memory chips, better fundamental architecture, and more sophisticated operating systems are all currently possible. However, packaging these components into a high-powered microcomputer creates significant risks: lack of software, high costs, risks of supply interruptions, and general lack of customer acceptance in the same way as a proprietary closed system.

Competitor Profiles

In 1985 the European microcomputer market was crowded with several hundred firms, ranging from small start-ups working out of a garage to some of the world's largest corporations. Table 9 provides a financial overview of some of the most significant competitors. Strategic profiles appear in the following paragraphs.

IBM

IBM is the world leader in microcomputers. IBM began selling microcomputers in the United States in August 1981 and started exports to Europe in January 1983. Today, IBM dominates both markets. In 1984 it is estimated that IBM sold over 2 million PCs in the United States alone. IBM's market share is especially high in the corporate market. In early 1985 it was estimated that 76 percent of all desktop computers in Fortune 500 companies are made by IBM. To serve this market,

Table 9 COMPETITOR PROFILES

Apple Computer (1983)

Income statement data	(millions)	Sales by activity	
Net sales	$983	Microcomputers	100%
COGS	484		
Depreciation	22		
R&D	60	Sales by area	
Marketing	230	United States	78%
G&A	57	Europe	13
EBIT	130	Other	9
Net income	77		
Dividends	0		

Balance sheet data			
Cash	$143	Accounts payable	$ 53
Accounts receivable	136	Notes payable	0
Inventory	142	Other current liabilities	76
Other current assets	48	Long-term debt	0
Fixed assets	67	Other liabilities	50
Other noncurrent assets	21	Shareholders' equity	378
		Preferred stock	0

IBM (1983)

Income statement data	(millions)	Sales by activity	
Net sales	$23,274	Processors	23%
Other income	16,906	Peripherals	15
COGS	13,033	Office systems	14
Depreciation	3,362	Program products	6
R&D	2,514	Other sales	6
Engineering expense	1,068	Rentals	23
SG&A	10,614	Maintenance	11
Operating profit	9,589	Other services	2
Other income	741		
EBIT	10,330	Sales by area	
Net income	5,485	United States	58%
Dividends	2,251	Europe	27
		Americas/Far East	15

Balance sheet data			
Cash	$ 5,336	Accounts payable	$ 1,253
Accounts receivable	6,380	Notes payable	532
Inventory	4,381	Other current liabilities	7,722
Other current assets	973	Long-term debt	2,674
Net fixed assets	16,142	Other liabilities	1,843
Other noncurrent assets	3,831	Shareholders' equity	23,219
		Preferred stock	0

Commodore International (1983)

Income statement data	(millions)	Sales by activity	
Net sales	$681	Home computers	45%
COGS	346	Business and educational systems	23
Depreciation	14	Peripherals	19
R&D	37	Software	9
Marketing	139	Office equipment	4
SG&A	24		
EBIT	121	Sales by area	
Extraordinary item	4	United States	58%
Net income	92	Canada	16
Dividends	0	Europe	23
		Other	3

Balance sheet data			
Cash	$ 23	Accounts payable	$246
Accounts receivable	180	Notes payable	21
Inventory	327	Other current liabilities	61
Fixed assets	81	Long-term debt	92
Other noncurrent assets	4	Other liabilities	4
		Shareholders' equity	191
		Preferred stock	0

Table 9   *(continued)*

Tandy Corporation (1983)

Income statement data	(millions)	*Sales by activity*	
Net sales	$2,475	Microcomputers	35%
Other income	38	Stereos	18
COGS	1,008	Radios and TVs	14
Depreciation	39	Components	13
R&D	N/A	Calculators and toys	12
SG&A	930	Telephones	8
EBIT	536		
Net income	279	*Sales by area*	
Dividends	0	United States	84%
		Canada	8
		Europe	5
		Other	3

Balance sheet data			
Cash	$280	Accounts payble	$ 65
Accounts receivable	107	Notes payable	56
Inventory	844	Other current liabilities	165
Other current assets	32	Long-term debt	138
Fixed assets	258	Other liabilities	37
Other noncurrent assets	61	Shareholders' equity	1,121
		Preferred stock	0

Olivetti (1983)

Income statement data	(billions of lire)	*Sales by activity*	
Net sales	L3,736	Typewriters and word processors	23%
COGS	1,824	Terminals	24
Depreciation	226	Computers	21
R&D	187	Telecommunications	5
SG&A	1,031	Other office equipment	27
Operating profit	468		
Other expenses	173		
Net income	295	*Sales by area*	
Dividends	84	United States	7%
		Europe	76
		Latin America	5
		Other	12

Balance sheet data			
Cash	L1,381	Accounts payable	L 797
Accounts receivable	1,546	Notes payable	715
Inventory	808	Other current liabilities	603
Other current assets	105	Long-term debt	1,391
Fixed assets	1,034	Other liabilities	373
Other noncurrent assets	247	Shareholders' equity	1,242

Hewlett Packard (1983)

Income statement data	(millions)	*Sales by activity*	
Net sales	$4,710	Computers	60%
COGS	2,195	Test equipment	26
R&D	493	Medical instruments	9
Marketing	771	Analytical	5
SG&A	523		
Taxes	296	*Sales by area*	
Net income	432	United States	59%
Dividends	0	Europe	29
		Other	12

Balance sheet data			
Cash	$ 880	Accounts payable	$ 351
Accounts receivable	951	Other current liabilities	569
Inventory	798	Long-term debt	71
Other current assets	151	Other liabilities	283
Fixed assets	1,431	Shareholders' equity	2,887

IBM relies on its direct selling staff of 6,000 to 7,000 people, compared to 60 for Apple, the second largest supplier.

In the European market, IBM attained a market share of 16 percent in its first year. This figure would have been higher if not for chronic parts shortages at its Greenock, Scotland, plant. By 1984 IBM had captured over 30 percent of the market and seemed destined to replay its American success.

IBM's strategy was based on several key elements. As mentioned earlier, IBM is dedicated to low-cost production, even if this implies reliance on outside vendors. Low costs have been translated into aggressive pricing. As shown in Figure 1, IBM has cut the price of the PC by over 62 percent since its introduction. This has kept tremendous pressure on "me-too" producers to keep their prices low.

IBM has also blanketed the microcomputer market with a full line of products. At the low end, IBM introduced the PCjr in late 1983 at a price of $699. The PCjr was targeted at the home user and was capable of running much of the software written for the PC. IBM's first venture into the home market was backed up with extensive advertising. According to IBM sources, during the period from August 1 to December 31, 1984, 98 percent of the American public saw at least 30 PCjr advertising messages. At the high end, IBM announced the PC AT in August 1984 as the flagship of its microcomputer line. The AT is based on a sophisticated microprocessor that facilitates multitasking and multiuser systems. Along with the

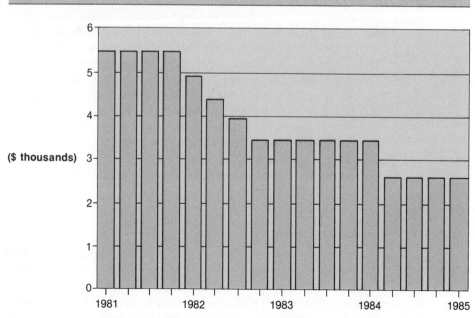

Figure 1 IBM PRICING STRATEGY FOR THE PC

($ thousands)

Source: *Business Week,* March 25, 1985.

AT, IBM introduced a local area network capable of supporting up to 72 users simultaneously.

IBM's strategy has also capitalized on its strengths in related markets. As the world's largest computer maker, IBM has a worldwide distribution network and an unequaled reputation for service. In 1982 the U.S. Justice Department dropped a 13-year antitrust suit against IBM, and since that date IBM has moved aggressively into new markets and technologies. IBM has acquired Rolm Corporation, a leading producer of telecommunications products, and has purchased a minority interest in Intel, the supplier of microprocessors for the PC. IBM has also experienced antitrust problems in Europe. The European Commission of the European Economic Community filed suit against IBM in late 1980 accusing the company of abusing its leadership position and restricting competition. For IBM, the stakes in Europe are high. IBM operates 15 factories and nine research laboratories in Europe, employing over 100,000 people.

Apple Computer

Apple is one of the legends of microcomputing. In 1976 Steve Jobs and Steve Wozniak quit their jobs in Silicon Valley and began experimenting with the use of microprocessors. After designing a crude computer system, Jobs and Wozniak sold their van and calculator to raise $1,300 in seed money. The machine was an instant success, and Apple began to grow explosively. From these humble beginnings, Apple Computer grew to $1.9 billion in annual sales by 1985 and took its place in the Fortune 500.

Apple's early success was based on its ability to innovate and to make computers less threatening to large segments of the population, many of whom had never used a computer before. Apple's early leadership gave it extensive distribution in hobby and specialist shops and a large market share in small businesses and the home. Apple entered the European market in 1978 and proceeded to attain a very strong position. However, increased competition has led to an erosion in Apple's position in both the United States and Europe. In 1984 Apple pinned its hopes on the Macintosh, a machine designed to make computers as friendly and as easy to use as possible. Apple claimed that a new user could begin to perform productive work within 30 minutes of using the Macintosh for the first time. This is in stark contrast to the esoteric and complex languages associated with most microcomputer applications. Priced at $2,495, the Macintosh was placed in direct competition with IBM's PC.

Tandy

One of Apple's earliest competitors in microcomputers was Tandy Corporation. Tandy built a strong position in the early stages of market development on the basis of its strong retail store network. In 1985 Tandy sold computers out of approximately 1,350 Radio Shack stores worldwide. Until 1984 Tandy had maintained a proprietary operating system. However, more recent products are IBM compatible. Tandy is particularly strong in the "notebook" (under 10 pounds) segment, where it has the largest share of any producer.

Commodore

Commodore was another early entrant into the microcomputer business. In the United States, Commodore focused on the low end of the market and built a strong position in inexpensive machines used for game playing and computer literacy. Commodore entered the European market in 1977 and was somewhat more successful in penetrating the small-business segment. By 1983 Commodore had the largest installed base of microcomputers (in terms of units) of any manufacturer in Europe. In 1984 Commodore introduced a line of IBM-compatible machines targeted at the corporate market.

European Competitors

The leading European producers of microcomputers were Olivetti of Italy, Triumph-Adler of Germany, Applied Computer Technologies of the United Kingdom, Bull-Micral and SMT-Goupil of France, and L. M. Ericsson of Sweden. Although each of these firms had captured roughly 10 percent of their home markets, none had succeeded in developing significant exports. In addition to the leading firms in each national market, many small companies had emerged. For example, in France alone, there were over 90 small firms offering 170 different machines. These small competitors were joined by nearly every large European firm that had previously sold large computers, telecommunications equipment, consumer electronics, office products, or other related goods. The list of competitors includes such firms as Rank Xerox, Siemens, Philips, ICL, Nixdorf, and Thomson. In 1984 AT&T bought 25 percent of Olivetti and began a program of reciprocal product distribution. This exchange was intended to strengthen Olivetti's position in telecommunications products and AT&T's position in small computers. Like most of the competitors mentioned, Olivetti's strategy was to offer an IBM compatible machine at a lower price.

Japanese Competitors

Although often discussed, the Japanese threat in microcomputers had failed to materialize in either America or Europe. As shown in Table 10, many Japanese firms exported their products. However, none had attained an overall share of 5 percent or more outside of Japan. The failure of the Japanese to penetrate the United States or Europe was attributed to the following factors:

Inadequate Distribution. The landslide of entrants into microcomputers left many firms scrambling for distribution. Japanese firms generally lacked established channels of their own and were slow to break into other means of distribution. The problem was particularly severe in Europe, where most dealers would handle only three brands at a time. This meant that available shelf space was often captured by IBM, Apple, and a local producer.

Poor Software. Early Japanese products were offered with little software for applications. The first generation of Japanese products were late to adopt the popular CP/M operating system, thus leaving users confused as to what software was available. More recently, the Japanese products have usually followed the

Table 10 JAPANESE MICROCOMPUTERS FOR EXPORT

Company		Product	RAM	Microprocessor	Format	Software bundle
Canon		X-07	8K–24K	8 bit	P	No
		AS-100	64K–512K	16 bit	D	No
Casio		FP-200	8K	8 bit	P	Yes
Epson		HX-20	16K–32K	8 bit	P	No
		QX-10	16K–256K	8 bit	D	Yes
Fujitsu		16s	128K–1Mb	8 bit	D	No
NEC		APC	128K–640K	16 bit	D	No
		APC III	128K–640K	16 bit	D	No
		PC-6000	16K–32K	8 bit	D	No
		PC-8800	128K	8 bit	D	No
		PC-8200	16K	8 bit	P	Yes
		PC-8401	64K	8 bit	P	Yes
Panasonic		Sr. Partner	128K–512K	16 bit	T	Yes
Ricoh	(OEM)	Monroe 2000	128K–640K	16 bit	D	No
Sanyo	MBC	550/555	128K–256K	16 bit	D	Yes
	MBC	1100/1150	64K	8 bit	D	Yes
	MBC	4000/4050	128K–512K	16 bit	D	Yes
Seiko		8600 XP	256K	16 bit	D	Yes
Sharp		PC-5000	128K–256K	16 bit	P	Yes
Sony		SMC-70	64K	8 bit	D	No
Sord		IS-11	32K–64K	8 bit	P	Yes
		M23P	128K	8 bit	D	Yes
		M68	256K–1Mb	16/32 bit	D	No
Toshiba		T300	192K–512K	16 bit	D	No

Abbreviations: P = portable; D = desk top; T = transportable.
Source: *Creative Computing,* Aug., 1984.

IBM standard and have access to the large published base of programs. However, critics often complain that the Japanese products do not offer any advantages over the IBM machine or its look-alikes.

Poor Documentation. In the rush to bring products to the market, many user guides were translated quickly and were poorly produced. This gave the Japanese products a reputation for being hard to use.

Despite the poor start by Japanese firms, the presence of these companies gave many competitors cause for concern. Memories of the Japanese success in televisions, VCRs, stereo equipment, cameras, and other similar products were painfully fresh for microcomputer firms who had competed with the Japanese in these markets previously.

NEC'S ENTRY INTO THE EUROPEAN MICROCOMPUTER MARKET

In 1985 NEC was struggling to find a way to transfer its success in the Japanese microcomputer market to Europe. At home, NEC enjoyed a market share of over 55 percent in personal computers. In addition to systems, NEC offered a full line of peripherals such as printers, screens, and modems. NEC's position in the Japanese market was similar to the role of IBM in America and Europe. A majority of personal computer software developed in Japan was written for NEC machines.

NEC first tested the European market in 1979 when it displayed the PC 8000 at the annual industrial fair in Hannover, West Germany. The PC 8000 was an 8-bit machine with 32K of RAM, expandable to 64K. As a result of a mediocre response at Hannover, NEC delayed the entry of the PC 8000 until the following year. By 1981 NEC was selling microcomputers in Germany, the Netherlands, France, Spain, and Italy. Sales grew slowly, but steadily, and in late 1982 NEC launched the PC 8800, an upgraded machine with an 8-bit processor, 64K memory, and excellent color graphics. These two machines were the mainstays of NEC's product line for the next two years.

NEC continued to expand into both smaller and larger machines. In 1983 NEC introduced the 8201, a notebook computer weighing only 4 pounds. Despite its small size, the 8201 featured an 8-bit processor and 16–64K of RAM, with three software packages built in. In 1985 the 8401 was introduced and offered more memory, a bigger screen, more software, and a built-in modem, all for under $1,000. As they have done in mainframes, NEC has declined to conform to the IBM standard in microcomputers.

During this period, NEC began to develop distribution channels throughout Europe. Some observers felt that this process was inhibited by NEC's complex organizational structure. Small computers were administered through two independent divisions: NEC Home Electronics, headquartered in Neuss, West Germany, and NEC Business Systems, headquartered in London, England. NEC Home Electronics was responsible for distributing 8-bit computers, such as the 8000 and 8800 series, and the supporting peripherals. NEC Business Systems handled 16-bit computers, such as the APC and APC III, introduced in 1984, as well as office-automation equipment. The two divisions operated independently and were responsible for developing their own marketing strategy and distribution channels. For most countries, NEC worked through an exclusive national distributor who specialized in NEC products and sought retail distributors. For example, in France, NEC worked through Omnium Promotion, who had secured retail distribution for NEC in 80 stores throughout France.

NEC was best known in Europe for its computer peripherals. Obtaining distribution for microcomputers was extremely difficult as a result of the practice of handling only three brands in each store. For peripherals, however, distribution was far easier for NEC to obtain. NEC's Spinwriter series of printers was extremely popular and in great demand by retail store operators. In France, the Spinwriters are sold through over 350 outlets. In addition, competition in peripherals was less intense. Although it was widely suspected that few microcomputer companies were making a profit on their computers, NEC acknowledged that the peripherals business was very lucrative.

NEC produced all of its microcomputers in Japan. The freight to Europe was approximately 10 percent of the product's cost, and an additional 5.4 percent duty was paid on entry. NEC stated that it would continue to produce exclusively in Japan as long as delivered costs were minimized. If volume in Europe became sufficient, or EEC policy dictated import penalties, NEC would consider local production.

RECENT EVENTS

As NEC contemplated its strategy for the European market in early 1985, recent events gave the company cause for concern. Persistent rumors of an imminent shake-out made NEC executives wonder if the time for a major commitment to this market had already passed. Several smaller firms, such as Osborne and Gavilan, had already gone bankrupt, and even the industry leaders were beginning to feel the pinch. In March 1985 IBM announced that the PCjr had not met expectations and would be discontinued. Similarly, Apple suffered a number of setbacks. Sales for the Macintosh dropped 45 percent in the first quarter of 1985, and Apple was forced to shut down four factories to work off unsold inventories. Continued sluggish sales of the higher-priced LISA finally led Apple to discontinue the product. Meanwhile, DEC stopped production of its Rainbow, and Xerox was rumored to be getting out of the microcomputer business entirely. NEC management felt that its outstanding technological skills in microcomputers and related markets and its competitive cost structure should provide the basis for success. However, making the concept of C&C a reality was proving far more elusive than NEC had anticipated.

C Strategic Analysis in Diversified Companies

CAMPBELL SOUP COMPANY*

In mid-1985, five years after he had been appointed president and chief executive officer of Campbell Soup Company, Gordon McGovern decided it was time to review the key strategic theme he had initiated—new-product development. Shortly after he became Campbell's CEO, McGovern reorganized the company into autonomous business units to foster entrepreneurial attitudes; his ultimate objective was to transform Campbell from a conservative manufacturing company into a consumer-driven, new-product-oriented company. As a result of McGovern's push, Campbell had introduced 334 new products in the past five years—more than any other company in the food processing industry.

During the 1970s Campbell's earnings had increased at an annual rate just under 9 percent—a dull performance compared to the 12 percent average growth for the food industry as a whole. With prior management's eyes fixed mainly on production aspects, gradual shifts in consumer buying habits caused Campbell's unit volume growth to flatten. McGovern's five-year campaign for renewed growth via new-product introduction had produced good results so far. By year-end 1984 sales were up 31 percent—to $3.7 billion—and earnings had risen by 47 percent—to $191 million. But now it appeared that Campbell's brand managers may have become so involved in new-product development that they had neglected the old stand-by products, as well as not meeting cost control and profit margin targets. Campbell's growth in operating earnings for fiscal year 1985 fell far short of McGovern's 15 percent target rate. Failure to control costs and meet earnings targets threatened to leave Campbell without the internal cash flows to fund its new-product strategy. Exhibit 1 summarizes Campbell Soup's recent financial performance.

THE FOOD PROCESSING INDUSTRY

In the early 19th century small incomes and low urban population greatly limited the demand for packaged food. In 1859 one industry—grain mills—accounted for over three-fifths of the total U.S. food processing. Several industries were in their infancy: evaporated milk, canning, candy, natural extracts, and coffee roasting. From 1860 to 1900 the industry entered a period of development and growth that made food processing the leading manufacturing industry in the United States. The driving forces behind this growth were increased urbanization, cheaper rail transport, and the advent of refrigeration and tin can manufacturing.

At the beginning of the 20th century, the food processing industry was highly fragmented; the thousands of local and regional firms were too small to capture

---

* Prepared by graduate researcher Sharon Henson under the supervision of Professor Arthur A. Thompson, The University of Alabama. Copyright © 1986 by Sharon Henson and Arthur A. Thompson.

Exhibit 1 FINANCIAL SUMMARY, CAMPBELL SOUP COMPANY, 1979–1985 (in thousands of dollars)

	1979	1980	1981	1982	1983	1984	1985
Total sales (includes interdivisional)	n.a.	$2,566,100	$2,865,600	$2,995,800	$3,359,300	$3,744,600	$4,060,800
Net sales (excludes interdivisional)	$2,248,692	2,560,569	2,797,663	2,955,649	3,292,433	3,657,440	3,988,705
Cost of products sold	1,719,134	1,976,754	2,172,806	2,214,214	2,444,213	2,700,751	2,950,204
Marketing and sales expenses	181,229	213,703	256,726	305,700	367,053	428,062	478,341
Administrative and research expenses	94,716	102,445	93,462	136,933	135,855	169,614	194,319
Operating earnings	253,613	267,667	274,669	298,802	345,312	359,013	365,841
Interest—net	1,169	10,135	30,302	21,939	39,307	26,611	32,117
Earnings before taxes	252,444	257,532	244,367	276,863	306,005	332,402	333,724
Taxes on earnings	119,700	122,950	114,650	127,250	141,000	141,200	135,800
Net earnings, after taxes	119,817	134,582	129,717	149,613	165,005	191,202	197,824
Percent of sales	5.3%	5.3%	4.6%	5.1%	5.0%	5.2%	5.0%
Percent of stockholders' equity	13.8%	14.6%	13.2%	14.6%	15.0%	15.9%	15.0%
Per share of common stock	1.80	2.04	2.00	2.32	2.56	2.96	3.06
Dividends declared per share	.86	.93	1.02	1.05	1.09	1.14	1.22
Average shares outstanding	66,720	65,946	64,824	64,495	64,467	64,514	64,572
Salaries, wages, pensions, etc.	$ 543,984	$ 609,979	$ 680,946	$ 700,940	$ 755,073	$ 889,450	$ 950,143
Current assets	680,955	861,845	845,343	921,501	932,099	1,063,330	1,152,761
Working capital	362,187	405,628	368,246	434,627	478,899	541,515	579,490
Plant assets—gross	1,134,571	1,248,735	1,368,663	1,472,693	1,607,634	1,744,866	1,856,122
Accumulated depreciation	520,603	560,730	613,643	657,315	718,478	774,004	828,662
Plant assets purchased and acquired	159,603	155,796	155,275	175,928	178,773	201,864	222,321
Total assets	1,325,823	1,627,565	1,722,876	1,865,519	1,991,526	2,210,115	2,437,525
Long-term debt	36,298	137,879	150,587	236,160	267,465	283,034	297,146
Stockholders' equity	900,017	958,443	1,000,510	1,055,762	1,149,404	1,259,908	1,382,487
Depreciation	60,360	67,958	75,118	83,813	93,189	101,417	119,044

Source: Annual reports of Campbell Soup Company.

scale economies in mass production and distribution as was occurring in other industries. During the 1920s industry consolidation via acquisition and merger began; the process was evolutionary not revolutionary and continued on into the 1960s and 1970s. Companies such as Del Monte and Kraft, whose names have since become household words, were established, as were the first two multiline food companies—General Foods and Standard Brands (later part of Nabisco Brands). With consolidation came greater production cost efficiency and national market coverages. Following World War II, the bigger food companies moved toward more product differentiation and increased emphasis on advertising. Some became multinational in scope, establishing subsidiaries in many other countries. Starting in the 1960s and continuing into the 1980s, the industry went through more consolidation; this time the emphasis was on brand diversification and product-line expansion. Acquisition-minded companies shopped for smaller companies with products having strong brand recognition and brand loyalty.

Exhibit 2 THE TOP 15 COMPANIES IN THE FOOD PROCESSING INDUSTRY, 1985 (millions of dollars)

Company		Sales	Profits	Assets	Return on common equity	Example brands
1. RJR Nabisco	1985	$ 16,595	$2,163	$16,930	20.3%	Nabisco, Del Monte
	1984	12,974	1,619	9,272	22.1	
2. Dart & Kraft	1985	9,942	466	5,502	17.0	Velveeta, Parkay,
	1984	9,759	456	5,285	16.5	Miracle Whip
3. Beatrice	1985	12,595	479	10,379	21.8	Swiss Miss, Wesson,
	1984	9,327	433	4,464	20.4	Tropicana
4. Kellogg	1985	2,930.1	281.1	1,726.1	48.0	Mrs. Smith's, Eggo,
	1984	2,602.4	250.5	1,667.1	27.0	Rice Krispies
5. H. J. Heinz	1985	4,047.9	266	2,473.8	22.6	Star-Kist Tuna,
	1984	3,953.8	237.5	2,343	21.0	Heinz Ketchup
6. Ralston Purina	1985	5,863.9	256.4	2,637.3	26.7	Hostess Twinkies,
	1984	4,980.1	242.7	2,004.2	23.1	Meow Mix
7. Campbell Soup	1985	3,988.7	197.8	2,437.5	15.0	Prego, Le Menu,
	1984	3,657.4	191.2	2,210.1	15.9	Vlasic pickles
8. General Mills	1985	4,285.2	(72.9)	2,662.6	(6.5)	Cheerios, Betty
	1984	5,600.8	233.4	2,858.1	19.0	Crocker
9. Sara Lee	1985	8,117	206	3,216	20.5	Popsicle, Bryan,
	1984	7,000	188	2,822	19.4	Rudy's Farm
10. CPC International	1985	4,209.9	142.0	3,016.6	10.5	Mazola, Skippy,
	1984	4,373.3	193.4	2,683.4	14.7	Hellmann's
11. Borden	1985	4,716.2	193.8	2,932.2	14.3	Wyler's, Bama,
	1984	4,568	182.1	2,767.1	13.7	Cracker Jack
12. Pillsbury	1985	4,670.6	191.8	2,778.5	17.3	Green Giant,
	1984	4,172.3	169.8	2,608.3	17.0	Häagen-Dazs
13. Archer Daniels	1985	4,738.8	163.9	2,967.1	10.8	LaRosa,
	1984	4,907	117.7	2,592.7	NA	Fleischmann's
14. Quaker Oats	1985	3,520.1	156.6	2,662.6	20.3	Gatorade, Van-
	1984	3,334.1	138.7	1,806.8	19.8	Camp's
15. Hershey Foods	1985	1,996.2	112.2	1,197.4	16.6	Delmonico, Hershey's
	1984	1,848.5	108.7	1,122.6	17.3	Chocolate
Industry composite	1985	$101,669.0	$4,004.0	$58,294.0	16.5%	

Ranking by market value of common stock according to *Business Week*, April 18, 1986.
Financial data from annual reports.
NA = Not available.

Then, in the 1980s, giants began acquiring other giants. In 1984 Nestlé acquired Carnation for $3 billion. In 1985 R. J. Reynolds purchased Nabisco Brands for $4.9 billion (and then changed its corporate name to RJR Nabisco), and Philip Morris acquired General Foods Corporation for $5.7 billion—the biggest nonoil deal in U.S. industry. In 1985 the U.S. food processing industry had sales over $100 billion and combined net profits of over $4 billion. Exhibit 2 shows data for leading companies in the industry in 1985.

COMPANY BACKGROUND

Campbell Soup Company was one of the world's leading manufacturers and marketers of branded consumer food products. In 1985 the company had approximately 44,000 employees and 80 manufacturing plants in 12 nations, with over 1,000 products on the market. Its major products were Prego spaghetti sauces, Le Menu frozen dinners, Pepperidge Farm baked goods, Mrs. Paul's frozen foods, Franco-American canned spaghettis, Vlasic pickles, and its flagship red-and-white-label canned soups.

Founded in 1869 by Joseph Campbell, a fruit merchant, and Abram Anderson, an ice box maker, the company was originally known for its jams and jellies. In 1891 it was incorporated as the Joseph Campbell Co. in Camden, New Jersey. In 1899 John T. Dorrance, a brilliant 24-year-old with a Ph.D. from MIT, developed a process for canning soup in condensed form. He was also a master salesman who came up with the idea of attaching snappy placards to the sides of New York City streetcars as a way of promoting the company's products.

From 1900 to 1954 the company was owned by the Dorrance family. It was incorporated as the Campbell Soup Company in 1922. When Dorrance died in 1930 after running the company for 16 years, he left an estate of over $115 million, the third largest up to that time. He also left a company devoted to engineering, committed to supplying value (in recessions it would rather shave margins than lower quality or raise prices), and obsessed with secrecy. John T. Dorrance, Jr., ran the company for the next 24 years (1930–54) and few, if any, important decisions were made at Campbell without his approval. In 1954 the company went public, with the Dorrance family retaining majority control. In 1985 the Dorrance family still held about 60 percent of Campbell's stock and picked the top executives of the company. In 1984 John Dorrance III became a member of the board. The more than eight decades of family dominance contributed to what some insiders described as a conservative and paternalistic company culture at Campbell.

Over the years Campbell had diversified into a number of food and food-related businesses—Swanson frozen dinners, Pepperidge Farm bakery products, Franco-American spaghetti products, Recipe pet food, fast-food restaurant chains, Godiva chocolates, and even retail garden centers. Still, about half the company's revenues came from the sale of its original stock-in-trade: canned soup. Throughout most of its history, the company picked its top executives from among those with a production background in the soup division—most had engineering training and good track records in furthering better manufacturing efficiency. One such person, Harold A. Shaub, a 30-year veteran of the company, was named president in 1972. An industrial engineer, Shaub placed a premium on controlling production cost while maintaining acceptable product quality. There were occasions when Shaub, during unannounced inspection tours, shut down a complete plant that didn't measure up to the strict standards he demanded.

During his tenure Shaub began to set the stage for change at Campbell, acknowledging that "The company needed changes for the changing times."[1] He restructured the company into divisions built around major product lines. Then in 1978, realizing that Campbell's marketing skills were too weak, he hired aggressive outsiders to revitalize the company's marketing efforts. That same year Campbell purchased Vlasic Foods, Inc., the largest producer of pickles in the United States.

Also in 1978 Campbell launched Prego spaghetti sauce products, the first major new food items introduced by Campbell in 10 years. The former Campbell policy required that a new product had to show a profit within a year and the pay-out on Prego was expected to be three years. But because the policy held back new-product development, Shaub changed it and set a goal of introducing two additional products each year.

In 1980 Campbell broke a 111-year-old debt-free tradition, issuing $100 million in 10-year notes. Until then the company had relied primarily on internally generated funds to meet long-term capital requirements.

Because of company tradition, everyone expected Shaub's successor to come from production. Thus it came as a surprise to Gordon McGovern, president of Connecticut-based Pepperidge Farm and a marketing man, when Shaub called him into his office and said, "I'd like you to come down here and take my place."[2] When McGovern became Campbell's president and CEO on December 1, 1980, Shaub remained on the board of directors.

McGovern was at Pepperidge Farm when the company was bought by Campbell in 1961. He was in business school when Margaret Rudkin, founder of Pepperidge Farm, spoke to his class. She told how she had built her bread company from scratch in an industry dominated by giants. McGovern was impressed. He wrote to Rudkin for a job, received it in 1956, and began his climb through the ranks. When Campbell acquired Pepperidge Farm in 1961, it had sales of $40 million. When McGovern became its president in 1968, sales had reached $60 million. When he left to become president of Campbell in 1980, Pepperidge Farm's sales had climbed to $300 million. McGovern brought some of what he considered Pepperidge's success strategy with him to Campbell; experimentation, new-product development, marketing savvy, and creativity.

MANAGEMENT UNDER McGOVERN

Every Saturday morning McGovern did his family's grocery shopping, stopping to straighten Campbell's displays and inspect those of competitors, studying packaging and reading labels, and trying to learn all he could about how and what people

---

[1] *The Wall Street Journal,* September 17, 1984, p. 1.

[2] *Forbes,* December 7, 1981, p. 44.

were eating. He encouraged his managers to do the same. Several board meetings were held in the backrooms of supermarkets so that afterward directors could roam the store aisles interviewing customers about Campbell products.

McGovern's style of management was innovative to a company known as much for its stodginess as for its red-and-white soup can. For decades, Campbell Soup operated under strict rules of decorum. Eating, smoking, and drinking coffee were not permitted in the office. Managers had to share their offices with their secretaries, and an unwritten rule required executives to keep their suitcoats on in the office. When McGovern joined Campbell, he drove to work in a yellow Volkswagen that stuck out in his parking space so much that the garagemen quietly arranged to have it painted. Finding the atmosphere at headquarters stifling, he promised a change.

He began wandering through the corridors every day, mingling easily among the employees. McGovern's voluble personality and memory for names made him popular with many employees. But not everyone was impressed by McGovern's style. Some production people were suspicious of his marketing background. Others believed that his grocery trips and hobnobbing with employees were ploys calculated to win him support and a reputation. But McGovern pressed forward with several internal changes: (1) a day-care center for the children of employees (complete with Campbell Kids posters on the wall), (2) a health program including workouts in a gymnasium, and (3) an unusual new benefit program that covered adoption expenses up to $1,000 and gave time off to employees who adopted children—in the same way that women were given maternity leave. He appointed the first two women vice presidents in the company's history; one of these, a former director of the Good Housekeeping Institute, was hired to identify consumers' food preferences and needs.

McGovern decentralized Campbell management to facilitate entrepreneurial risktaking and new-product development, devising a new compensation program to reward these traits. He restructured the company into some 50 autonomous units and divided the U.S. division into eight strategic profit centers: soups, beverages, pet foods, frozen foods, fresh produce, main meals, grocery, and food service. Units were encouraged to develop new products even if another unit would actually produce the products. Thus, the Prego spaghetti sauce unit—not the frozen food group—initiated frozen Mexican dinners. And although it wasn't his job, the director of market research created "Today's Taste," a line of refrigerated entrees and side dishes. "It's like things are in constant motion," the director said. "We are overloaded, but it's fun."[3]

The new structure encouraged managers, who had to compete for corporate funding, to be more aggressive in developing promising products. According to McGovern:

> These integral units allow the company to really get its arms around chunks of the business. The managers are answerable to the bottom line—to their investments, their hiring, their products—and it's a great motivation for performance.[4]

---

[3] *The Wall Street Journal*, September 17, 1984, p. 10.

[4] *Advertising Age*, January 3, 1983, p. 38.

As part of this motivation, Campbell began annually allotting around $30 million to $40 million to support new ventures, each requiring a minimum of $10 million. This strategy was intended to encourage star performers while enabling management to weed out laggards. McGovern felt that this was much easier to determine when everyone knew where the responsibilities lay—but that it was no disgrace to fail if the effort was a good one. An employee noted that McGovern was endorsing "the right to fail," adding that "it makes the atmosphere so much more positive."[5]

Every Friday McGovern held meetings to discuss new products. The fact-finding sessions were attended by financial, marketing, engineering, and sales personnel. Typical McGovern questions included: "Would you eat something like that?" "Why not?" "Have you tried the competition's product?" "Is there a consumer niche?" The marketing research director noted that in Shaub's meetings the question was "Can we make such a product cost-effectively?"[6]

Under Shaub the chain of command was inviolable, but McGovern was not hesitant about circumventing the chain when he felt it was warranted. He criticized one manager's product to another manager, expecting word to get back to the one with the problem. Although this often motivated some to prove McGovern wrong, others were unnerved by such tactics. When he became aware of this, McGovern eased up a bit.

Under prior CEOs, cost-cutters got promoted; in McGovern's more creative atmosphere, the rules weren't so well defined. As one insider put it, "There's a great deal of uncertainty. No one really knows what it takes to get ahead. But that makes us all work harder."[7]

When hiring managers McGovern, himself a college baseball player, tended to favor people with a competitive sports background. "There's teamwork and determination, but also the idea that you know how to lose and get back up again. 'Try, try, try' is what I say. I can't stress how important that is."[8]

STRATEGY

The strategic focus was on the consumer—considered to be the key to Campbell's growth and success in the 1980s. The consumer's "hot buttons" were identified as nutrition, convenience, low sodium, price, quality, and uniqueness—and managers were urged to "press those buttons." General managers were advised to take into account the consumer's perceptions, needs, and demands regarding nutrition, safety, flavor, and convenience. Key strategies were: (1) improving operating efficiency, (2) developing new products for the modern consumer, (3) updating advertising for new and established products, and (4) high quality.

When he took over, McGovern developed a five-year plan that included four financial performance objectives: a 15 percent annual increase in earnings, a 5

---

[5] Ibid.

[6] *The Wall Street Journal*, September 17, 1984, p. 10.

[7] Ibid.

[8] *Advertising Age*, January 3, 1983, p. 38.

percent increase in volume, a 5 percent increase in sales (plus inflation), and an 18 percent return on equity by 1986. His long-range strategy included making acquisitions every two years that would bring in $200 million in annual sales. Campbell's acquisition strategy was to look for small, fast-growing food companies strong in product areas where Campbell was not and companies on the fast track that were in rapidly growing parts of their industries. Under McGovern Campbell made a number of acquisitions:

1982
- Mrs. Paul's Kitchens, Inc., a processor and marketer of frozen prepared seafood and vegetable products, with annual sales of approximately $125 million (acquired at a cost of $55 million).
- Snow King Frozen Foods, Inc., engaged in the production and marketing of a line of uncooked frozen specialty meat products, with annual sales of $32 million.
- Juice Bowl Products, Inc., a Florida producer of fruit juices.
- Win Schuler Foods, Inc., a Michigan-based producer and distributor of specialty cheese spreads, flavored melba rounds, food service salad dressings, party dips and sauces, with annual sales of $6.5 million.
- Costa Apple Products, Inc., a producer of apple juice retailed primarily in the Eastern United States, with annual sales of $6 million.

1983
- Several small domestic operations at a cost of $26 million, including Annabelle's restaurant chain of 12 units in the southeastern United States.

  Triangle Manufacturing Corp., a manufacturer of physical fitness and sports medicine products.

1984
- Mendelson-Zeller Co., Inc., a California distributor of fresh produce.

1985
- Continental Foods Company S.A. and affiliated companies that produced sauces, confectioneries, and other food products in Belgium and France; the cost of the acquisition was $17 million.

Campbell was by no means alone in adding companies to its portfolio; many major mergers in the food industry were taking place (see Exhibit 3). Several factors were at work:

- Many food companies had been stung by ill-fated diversification forays outside food. In the 1960s when industry growth had slowed, it was fashionable to diversify into nonfoods. Many of the acquired companies turned out to be duds, draining earnings and soaking up too much top management attention. Now food companies were refocusing their efforts on food—the business they knew best.
- Even though the food industry was regarded as a slow-growth/low-margin business, the fact remained that stable demand, moderate capital costs, and high cash flows had boosted returns on equity to almost 20 percent for some companies. Food processors discovered that they were earning better returns on their food products than they were earning in the nonfood businesses they had earlier diversified into.

Exhibit 3 EXAMPLES OF MAJOR ACQUISITIONS IN THE FOOD PROCESSING INDUSTRY, 1982–1985

Buyer	Acquired company	Year	Price (millions of dollars)	Products/brands acquired
Beatrice	Esmark	1984	$2,800	Swift, Hunt-Wesson brands
CPC	C. F. Mueller	1983	122	Makes CPC biggest U.S. pasta maker
ConAgra	Peavey	1982	NA	Jams & syrups
	ACLI Seafood	1983	NA	
	Armour Food	1983	166	Processed meats
	Imperial Foods' Country Poultry	1984	18	
Dart & Kraft	Celestial Seasonings	1984	25	Herbal teas
Esmark	Norton Simon	1983	1,100	Hunt-Wesson
General Foods	Entenmann's	1982	315	Baked goods
	Otto Roth	1983	NA	Specialty cheeses
	Monterey	1983	NA	
	Peacock Foods	1983	NA	
	Ronzoni	1984	NA	Pasta
	Oroweat	1984	60	Bread
McCormick	Patterson Jenks	1984	53	Major British spice and food distributor
Nestle	Carnation	1984	3,000	Evaporated milk, Friskies pet food
Philip Morris	General Foods	1985	5,750	Jell-O, Maxwell House
Pillsbury	Häagen-Dazs	1983	75	Ice cream
	Sedutto	1984	5	
Quaker Oats	Stokely-Van Camp	1983	238	Baked beans, canned goods
Ralston Purina	Continental Baking	1984	475	Hostess Twinkies, Wonder Bread
R. J. Reynolds	Nabisco Foods	1984	4,900	Oreo cookies, Ritz crackers, ginger ale, soda, tonic
	Canada Dry	1984	175	

NA = Not available.
Data compiled from various sources.

While companies such as Beatrice, the nation's largest food company, and Nestle, the world's largest, paid substantial sums to buy out large established companies with extensive brand stables, others—such as Campbell—followed the route of concentrating on internal product development and smaller, selective acquisitions to complement their existing product lines. In fact, Campbell was considered the leader among the food processors that were striving to limit acquisitions in favor of heavy, in-house product development. Campbell's emphasis on new-product development was not without risk. It took $10 million to $15 million in advertising and couponing to launch a brand. Because of the hit-or-miss nature of new products, only about one out of eight products reaching the test market stage were successful. Moreover, industry analysts predicted the continuing introduction of new products would lead to increased competition for shelf space and for the consumer's food dollar.

MARKETING

The outsiders Shaub had hired to revitalize Campbell's marketing included a vice president for marketing who was an eight-year veteran of a New York advertising firm and a soup general manager who was a former Wharton business school professor. In addition to those hired by Shaub, the rest of McGovern's marketing-oriented executive team included: a frozen foods manager (a former marketing manager with General Foods), the head of the Pepperidge Farm division, and the head of the Vlasic Foods division (both marketing men from Borden). This team boosted Campbell's marketing budget to $428 million by 1984 (up 57 percent from 1982). Advertising spending grew from $67 million in 1980 to $179 million in 1985. Prior to McGovern, Campbell used to cut ad spending at the end of a quarter to boost earnings. Besides hurting the brands, it gave the company an unfavorable reputation among the media. In 1985, the marketing expenditures (including advertising and promotion) of some of the leading food companies were: Campbell—approximately $488 million, Quaker—$619 million, Heinz—$303 million, Pillsbury—$365 million, and Sara Lee—$594 million.

In 1982 McGovern was named *Advertising Age's* Adman of the year for his efforts in transforming Campbell into "one of the most aggressive market-driven companies in the food industry today."[9] *Advertising Age* noted that McGovern had almost doubled the advertising budget and had replaced the company's longtime ad agency for its soups, leading to a new ad campaign that helped reverse eight years of flat or lower sales. The new campaign emphasized nutrition and fitness, as opposed to the former "mmm,mmm,good" emphasis on taste. Print ads included long copy that referred to major government research studies citing soup's nutritional values. The new slogan was: "Soup is good food." New products and advertising were aimed at shoppers who were dieting, health conscious, and usually in a hurry. In keeping with the new fitness image, the 80-year-old Campbell Kids, although still cherubic, acquired a leaner look. Campbell's marketing strategy under McGovern was based on several important market research findings and projections:

- Women now comprised 43 percent of the work force and a level of 50 percent was projected by 1990.
- Two-income marriages represented 60 percent of all U.S. families. These would take in $3 out of every $5 earned.
- Upper-income households would grow 3.5 times faster than total household formations.
- More than half of all households consisted of only one or two members.
- There were 18 million singles, and 23 percent of all households contained only one person.
- The average age of the population was advancing, with the number of senior citizens totaling 25 million-plus and increasing.
- The percentage of meals eaten at home was declining.
- Nearly half of the adult meal-planners in the United States were watching their weight.
- Poultry consumption had increased 26 percent since 1973.
- Ethnic food preparation at home was increasing, with 40 percent, 21 per-

---

[9] *Advertising Age,* January 3, 1983, p. 38.

cent, and 14 percent of households preparing Italian, Mexican, and Oriental foods, respectively, at home from scratch.

- There was growing consumer concern with food avoidance: sugar, salt, calories, chemicals, cholesterol, and additives.
- The "I am what I eat" philosophy had tied food in to life-styles along with Nautilus machines, hot tubs, jogging, racquet ball, backpacking, cross-country skiing, and aerobic dancing.

In response to growing ethnic food demand, Campbell began marketing ethnic selections in regions where interests were highest for particular food types. For instance, it marketed spicy Ranchero Beans only in the south and southwest and planned to market newly acquired Puerto Rican foods in New York City.

The product development priorities were aimed at the themes of convenience, taste, flavor, and texture. The guidelines were:

- Prepare and market products that represent superior value to consumers and constantly strive to improve those values.
- Develop products that help build markets.
- Develop products that return a fair profit to Campbell and to customers.

In support of these guidelines, Campbell adopted several tactics:

- Use ongoing consumer research to determine eating habits by checking home menus, recipe preparation, and foods that are served together. Study meal and snack eating occasions to determine which household members participate so volume potential can be determined for possible new products and product improvement ideas.
- Develop new products and produce them in small quantities that stimulate actual plant production capabilities.
- Test new or improved products in a large enough number of households that are so distributed throughout the United States that results can be projected nationally. Once the product meets pretest standards, recommend it for market testing.
- Once packaging and labels have been considered, design the pretest introductory promotion and advertising.
- Introduce a new product in selected test markets to determine actual store sales that can be projected nationally.
- If test marketing proves successful, roll out the new product on a regional or national plan using test market data as a rationale for expansion.

A key part of the strategy was the "Campbell in the Kitchen" project, consisting of some 75 homemakers across the country. Three to five times a year Campbell asked this "focus group" to try different products and give opinions. McGovern regularly dispatched company executives to the kitchens of these homemakers to observe eating patterns and see how meals were prepared. He sent Campbell's home economists into some of the households to work with the cooks on a one-to-one basis.

Exhibit 4 CAMPBELL'S LEADING NEW PRODUCTS (total $600 million in sales for fiscal 1985)

1985 ranking	Year introduced
Le Menu Frozen Dinner	1982
Prego Spaghetti Sauce	1982
Chunky New England Clam Chowder	1984
Great Starts Breakfasts	1984
Prego Plus	1985

Source: *The Wall Street Journal*, August 14, 1985.

All this was in sharp contrast to the pre-McGovern era. Campbell averaged about 18 new-product entries a year through the late 1970s. Many of these were really line extensions rather than new products. Substantial numbers flopped, partly because they had often been subjected to only the most rudimentary and inexpensive tests. Sometimes the testing had consisted only of a panel of the company's advertising and business executives sipping from teaspoons.

In 1983 Campbell was the biggest new products generator in the combined food and health and beauty aids categories with a total of 42 new products. Second was Esmark, 36; followed by Lever/Lipton, 33; Nabisco Brands, 25; Beatrice and General Foods, 24 each; American Home Products, 23; Quaker Oats, 21; Borden, 19; and General Mills and Noxell, 17 each. Exhibit 4 shows Campbell's leading new products from 1982 to 1985.

PRODUCTION

McGovern summarized Campbell's philosophy on quality: "I want zero defects. If we can't produce quality, we'll get out of the business."[10] In 1984 Campbell held its first Worldwide Corporate Conference dedicated to quality. Hundreds of Campbell managers from all levels and most company locations spent three days at this conference. Campbell believed that the ultimate test of quality was consumer satisfaction and its goal was to maintain a quality-conscious organization at every employee level in every single operation.

Before McGovern took over, Campbell used to emphasize new products compatible with existing production facilities. For example, a square omelet was designed for Swanson's frozen breakfasts because it was what the machine would make. After McGovern's appointment, although low-cost production was still a strategic factor, consumer trends—and not existing machinery—were the deciding factors for new-product development. Other important factors considered in the production process included:

---

[10] *Savvy*, June 1984, p. 39.

- The growing move toward consumption of refrigerated and fresh produce in contrast to canned or frozen products.
- The emerging perception that private label and/or generic label merchandise would drive out weak national and secondary brands unless there was a clear product superiority and excellent price/value on the part of the brands supported by consumer advertising.
- The polarization of food preparation time with long preparation on weekends and special occasions, but fast preparation in between via microwaves, quick foods, and instant breakfasts.
- The cost of the package—especially metal packaging—which was outrunning the cost of the product it contained.
- Energy and distribution costs—these were big targets for efficiency with regional production, aseptic packaging, and packages designed for automatic warehouse handling and lightweight containers becoming standard.

The bulk of $154 million in capital expenditures in 1983 went into improvement of production equipment, expenditures for additional production capacity, the completion of the $100 million canned foods plant in North Carolina, and the start of a mushroom-producing facility at Dublin, Georgia. In 1984 construction began on a $9 million Le Menu production line in Sumter, South Carolina. Capital expenditures in 1985 totaled $213 million. Most of this went into improvements of production equipment, packaging technology, and expenditures for additional production capacity.

Campbell was considered a model of manufacturing efficiency. Production was fully integrated from the tomato patch to the canmaking factory. Campbell was the nation's third-largest can manufacturer behind American Can Company and Continental Group. Yet Campbell, which made the red-and-white soup can with the gold medallion an American institution, had recently concluded that food packaging was headed in the direction of snazzier and more convenient containers. McGovern compared sticking with the can to the refusal of U.S. automobile makers to change their ways in the face of the Japanese challenge:

> There's a tremendous feeling of urgency because an overseas company could come in here with innovative packaging and technology and just take us to the cleaners on basic lines we've taken for granted for years.[11]

Other soup companies—including Libby, McNeill & Libby, a Nestlé Enterprises, Inc., unit that made Crosse & Blackwell gourmet soup—had already started experimenting with can alternatives. Campbell's testing was considered the most advanced, but a mistake could mean revamping production facilities at a cost of $100 million or more.

Researchers at the Campbell Soup Company's DNA Plant Technology unit were working toward the development of the "perfect tomato." They were seeking ways to grow tasty, high solids tomatoes under high-temperature conditions that would cause normal plants to droop and wither. They also hoped to

---

[11] *Business Week*, November 21, 1983, p. 102.

crossbreed high quality domestic tomatoes with tough, hardy, wild tomatoes that could withstand cold weather. A breakthrough in this area could result in two harvests a year. Campbell researchers estimated that they were four to five years ahead of Heinz. (Heinz began similar research several years after Campbell.)

Campbell believed its key strengths were: (1) a worldwide system for obtaining ingredients, (2) a broad range of food products that could be used as a launching pad for further innovation, and (3) an emphasis on low-cost production.

CAMPBELL'S OPERATING DIVISIONS

Campbell Soup Company was divided into six operating units—Campbell U.S., Pepperidge Farm, Vlasic Foods, Mrs. Paul's Kitchens, Other United States, and International. Sales and profit performance by division are shown in Exhibit 5.

CAMPBELL U.S.

In 1985 the Campbell U.S. Division was Campbell's largest operating unit, accounting for almost 62 percent of the company's total consolidated sales. Operating earnings increased 5 percent over 1984. Unit volume rose 7 percent in 1983, 9 percent in 1984, and 4 percent in 1985. The Campbell U.S. division was divided into eight profit centers: soup, frozen foods, grocery business, beverage business, food service business, poultry business, fresh produce business, and pet

Exhibit 5 SALES AND EARNINGS OF CAMPBELL SOUP, BY DIVISION, 1980–1985 (millions of dollars)

	1980	1981	1982	1983	1984	1985
Campbell U.S.:						
Sales	$1,608	$1,678	$1,773	$1,987	$2,282	$2,500
Operating earnings	205	190	211	250	278	292
Pepperidge Farm:						
Sales	283	329	392	433	435	426
Operating earnings	29	35	41	43	35	39
Vlasic Foods:						
Sales	130	137	149	168	193	199
Operating earnings	8	10	12	13	14	16
Mrs. Paul's Kitchens:						
Sales				108	126	138
Operating earnings				10	14	11
Other United States:						
Sales	35	27	56	64	84	81
Operating earnings	1	(1)	(1)	(1)	(2)	(3)
International:						
Sales	512	694	643	599	624	716
Operating earnings	33	46	46	33	34	35

Source: Campbell's annual reports.

foods business. Exhibit 6 shows the brands Campbell had in this division and the major competitors each brand faced.

The soup business group alone accounted for more than 25 percent of the company's consolidated sales (as compared to around 50 percent in the 1970s). Campbell's flagship brands of soups accounted for 80 percent of the $1 billion-plus annual canned soup market; in 1985 Campbell offered grocery shoppers over 50 varieties of canned soups. Heinz was second with 10 percent of the market. Heinz had earlier withdrawn from producing Heinz-label soup and shifted its production over to making soups for sale under the private labels of grocery chains; Heinz was the leading private-label producer of canned soup, holding almost an 80 percent share of the private-label segment. See Exhibit 6 for information on competitors and their brands.

Although the soup business was relatively mature (McGovern preferred to call it underworked), Campbell's most ambitious consumer research took place in this unit. McGovern planned to speed up soup sales by turning out a steady flow of new varieties in convenient packages: "Ethnic, dried, refrigerated, frozen, microwave—you name it, we're going to try it."[12]

In 1985 Campbell began an assault on the $290 million dry-soup mix market dominated by Thomas J. Lipton Inc., a unit of the Anglo-Dutch Unilever Group. This move was made because dry-soup sales in the United States were growing faster than sales of canned soup. Lipton's aggressive response to test marketing of an early Cambell dry-soup product resulted in Campbell's rushing a six-flavor line into national distribution ahead of schedule.

In 1982 McGovern caused a stir when he announced publicly that Campbell's Swanson TV-dinner line was "junk food": "It was great in 1950, but in today's world it didn't go into the microwave; it didn't represent variety or a good eating experience to my palate."[13] He maintained that consumers had discovered high-quality options to the TV-dinner concept. The market niche for more exotic, better quality entrees was being exploited by Nestlé's Stouffer subsidiary and Pillsbury's Green Giant division (Exhibit 6).

Campbell's frozen foods group answered the challenge by producing its own frozen gourmet line, Le Menu. Campbell committed about $50 million in manufacturing, marketing, and trade promotion costs on the basis of encouraging marketing tests. In the five years prior to Le menu, Swanson's sales volume had slipped 16 percent, its biggest volume decline (23 percent) was in the area that had been its stronghold: sales of dinners and entrees. Overall industry sales in dinners and entrees grew to $2 billion during 1982. The single-dish entree market had increased 58 percent since 1978 with sales being dominated by Stouffer's Lean Cuisine selections.

Le Menu—served on round heatable plates and consisting of such delicacies as chicken cordon bleu, al dente vegetables, and sophisticated wine sauces—produced 20 percent growth in the frozen-meal unit with sales of $150 million

---

[12] *Business Week,* December 24, 1983, p. 67.

[13] Ibid.

Exhibit 6 THE CAMPBELL U.S. DIVISION; PRODUCTS, RIVAL BRANDS, COMPETITORS

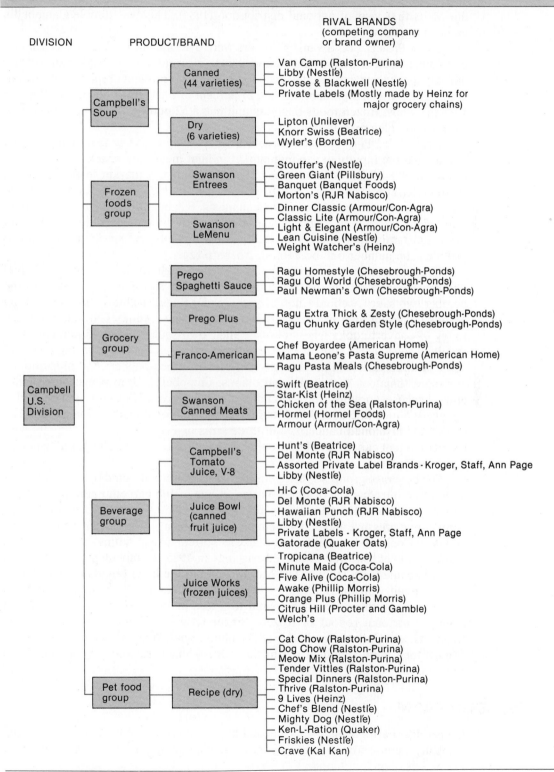

DIVISION   PRODUCT/BRAND   RIVAL BRANDS (competing company or brand owner)

Campbell U.S. Division

Campbell's Soup
- Canned (44 varieties)
  - Van Camp (Ralston-Purina)
  - Libby (Nestlé)
  - Crosse & Blackwell (Nestlé)
  - Private Labels (Mostly made by Heinz for major grocery chains)
- Dry (6 varieties)
  - Lipton (Unilever)
  - Knorr Swiss (Beatrice)
  - Wyler's (Borden)

Frozen foods group
- Swanson Entrees
  - Stouffer's (Nestlé)
  - Green Giant (Pillsbury)
  - Banquet (Banquet Foods)
  - Morton's (RJR Nabisco)
- Swanson LeMenu
  - Dinner Classic (Armour/Con-Agra)
  - Classic Lite (Armour/Con-Agra)
  - Light & Elegant (Armour/Con-Agra)
  - Lean Cuisine (Nestlé)
  - Weight Watcher's (Heinz)

Grocery group
- Prego Spaghetti Sauce
  - Ragu Homestyle (Chesebrough-Ponds)
  - Ragu Old World (Chesebrough-Ponds)
  - Paul Newman's Own (Chesebrough-Ponds)
- Prego Plus
  - Ragu Extra Thick & Zesty (Chesebrough-Ponds)
  - Ragu Chunky Garden Style (Chesebrough-Ponds)
- Franco-American
  - Chef Boyardee (American Home)
  - Mama Leone's Pasta Supreme (American Home)
  - Ragu Pasta Meals (Chesebrough-Ponds)
- Swanson Canned Meats
  - Swift (Beatrice)
  - Star-Kist (Heinz)
  - Chicken of the Sea (Ralston-Purina)
  - Hormel (Hormel Foods)
  - Armour (Armour/Con-Agra)

Beverage group
- Campbell's Tomato Juice, V-8
  - Hunt's (Beatrice)
  - Del Monte (RJR Nabisco)
  - Assorted Private Label Brands - Kroger, Staff, Ann Page
  - Libby (Nestlé)
- Juice Bowl (canned fruit juice)
  - Hi-C (Coca-Cola)
  - Del Monte (RJR Nabisco)
  - Hawaiian Punch (RJR Nabisco)
  - Libby (Nestlé)
  - Private Labels - Kroger, Staff, Ann Page
  - Gatorade (Quaker Oats)
- Juice Works (frozen juices)
  - Tropicana (Beatrice)
  - Minute Maid (Coca-Cola)
  - Five Alive (Coca-Cola)
  - Awake (Phillip Morris)
  - Orange Plus (Phillip Morris)
  - Citrus Hill (Procter and Gamble)
  - Welch's

Pet food group
- Recipe (dry)
  - Cat Chow (Ralston-Purina)
  - Dog Chow (Ralston-Purina)
  - Meow Mix (Ralston-Purina)
  - Tender Vittles (Ralston-Purina)
  - Special Dinners (Ralston-Purina)
  - Thrive (Ralston-Purina)
  - 9 Lives (Heinz)
  - Chef's Blend (Nestlé)
  - Mighty Dog (Nestlé)
  - Ken-L-Ration (Quaker)
  - Friskies (Nestlé)
  - Crave (Kal Kan)

during its first year of national distribution (1984). This was double Campbell's earlier projection of sales.

Under Project Fix, Swanson dinners were overhauled, putting in less salt and more meat stock in gravies and adding new deserts and sauces. The revamped line had new packaging and a redesigned logo. Swanson products reported an overall volume increase of 3 percent in 1983, 27 percent in 1984, and 2 percent in 1985. In 1985 the whole frozen foods business unit had a 52 percent increase in operating earnings as sales rose 10 percent.

Meanwhile, Pillsbury had targeted the $4 billion-a-year frozen main meal market and the rapidly expanding market in light meals and snacks as vital to its future. In 1984 Pillsbury purchased Van de Kamp's, a market leader in frozen seafood and ethnic entrees, for $102 million. During 1985 Van de Kamp's became the number one seller of frozen Mexican meals. Pillsbury also sold more than one-third of the 550 million frozen pizzas consumed in the United States in 1985 and made substantial investments in quality improvements and marketing support to maintain the number one position in frozen pizza.

The grocery business unit's star was Prego Spaghetti Sauce that in 1984 had obtained 25 percent of the still-growing spaghetti sauce market and was the number two sauce, behind Chesebrough-Pond's Ragu. (Exhibit 6 lists competing brands.) Chesebrough had recently introduced Ragu Chunky Gardenstyle sauce to try to convert cooks who still made their own sauce (about 45 percent of all spaghetti sauce users still cooked their own from scratch). The new Ragu product came in three varieties: mushrooms and onions, green peppers and mushrooms, and extra tomatoes with garlic and onions. Campbell had no plans for a similar entry because copying Ragu wouldn't be innovative. However, a Prego Plus Spaghetti Sauce line completed its first year of national distribution in 1985. To show "old-fashioned concern," all three sizes of Prego sauce came in jars with tamper-evident caps; Campbell would buy back from grocery shelves all jars that had been opened.

The beverage group's 1985 operating earnings were affected by a slower-than-anticipated introduction of Juice Works—a line of 100 percent natural, no-sugar-added, pure, blended fruit juices for children. This was attributed to intense competitive pressure and major technological problems. Campbell's Tomato Juice and V-8 Cocktail Vegetable Juice also reported disappointing earnings. Juice Bowl, however, showed improved earnings in 1985. Campbell's competition in this area came from Hunt's, Del Monte, and private label brands (Exhibit 6).

The poultry business unit sales were up 13 percent in 1985. Operating earnings for the year were positive, compared to a loss in 1984. These results stemmed from the national rollout of frozen "finger foods"—Plump & Juicy Dipsters, Drumlets, and Cutlets—and sales of Premium Chunk White Chicken. Some of the competitors were Banquet's Chicken Drum-Snackers and Tyson's Chick'n Dippers.

PEPPERIDGE FARM

Pepperidge Farm, Campbell's second-largest division with 12 percent of the company's consolidated sales, reported a decline in operating income and a sales gain of less than 1 percent between 1983 and 1984. In 1980 it was one of the fastest growing units; sales had risen 14 percent annually, compounded.

1984's disappointing results were largely blamed on losses incurred in the apple juice (Costa Apple Products, Inc., purchased in 1982) and "Star Wars" cookies businesses. When Pepperidge Farm introduced Star Wars cookies, McGovern called them a "travesty" because they were faddish and did not fit the brand's high-quality, upscale adult image. Plus, at $1.39 a bag, he maintained that it was a "lousy value." But he didn't veto them because, "I could be wrong."[14] As the popularity of the movie series waned, so did sales.

The frozen biscuit and bakery business unit volume was also down. New products such as Vegetables in Pastry and Deli's reportedly did not receive enough marketing support.

To remedy the division's growth decline, a number of steps were taken:

- Apple juice operations were transferred to the Campbell U.S. Division Beverage Unit.
- During the year Pepperidge divested itself of operations that no longer fit into its strategic plan, including Lexington Gardens, Inc., a garden center chain.
- Deli's went back into research and development to improve quality.
- By the start of the 1985 fiscal year, a new management team was in place and a comprehensive review of each product was being conducted in an effort to return emphasis to traditional product lines and quality standards that accounted for its success and growth in the past.

At the end of 1985 Pepperidge Farm showed an 11 percent increase in operating earnings over the previous year in spite of a 2 percent drop in sales. This was considered a result of the transfer of Pepperidge Farm beverage operations to the Campbell U.S. Beverage Group and the sale of the Lexington Gardens nursery chain. During 1985 sales in the confectionery business unit increased 22 percent and seven Godiva boutiques were added. Goldfish Crackers and Puff Pastry contributed to a volume increase in the food service business unit, while some varieties of Deli's and the Snack Bar products were discontinued.

One of Pepperidge Farm's major competitors in frozen bakery products was Sara Lee, which had 40 percent of the frozen sweet goods market and an ever-increasing 33 percent share of the specialty breads category. Pepperidge Farm's fresh breads and specialty items competed against a host of local, regional, and national brands. Exhibit 7 presents more details.

VLASIC FOODS

Campbell's third-largest domestic division enjoyed an 11 percent increase in operating earnings in 1985. Vlasic maintained its number one position with a 31

---

[14] *Business Week*, November 21, 1983, p. 102.

Exhibit 7 THE PEPPERIDGE FARM DIVISION: PRODUCTS, RIVAL BRANDS, COMPETITORS

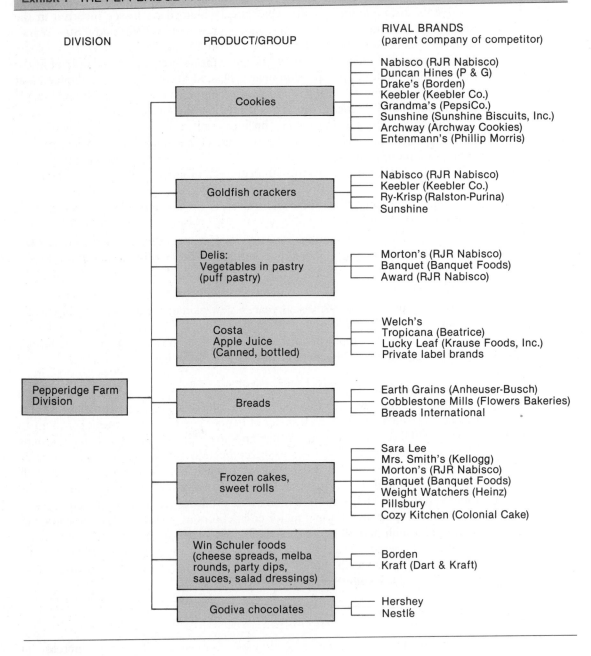

DIVISION   PRODUCT/GROUP   RIVAL BRANDS
                                                         (parent company of competitor)

Cookies
- Nabisco (RJR Nabisco)
- Duncan Hines (P & G)
- Drake's (Borden)
- Keebler (Keebler Co.)
- Grandma's (PepsiCo.)
- Sunshine (Sunshine Biscuits, Inc.)
- Archway (Archway Cookies)
- Entenmann's (Phillip Morris)

Goldfish crackers
- Nabisco (RJR Nabisco)
- Keebler (Keebler Co.)
- Ry-Krisp (Ralston-Purina)
- Sunshine

**Delis:
Vegetables in pastry
(puff pastry)**
- Morton's (RJR Nabisco)
- Banquet (Banquet Foods)
- Award (RJR Nabisco)

**Costa
Apple Juice
(Canned, bottled)**
- Welch's
- Tropicana (Beatrice)
- Lucky Leaf (Krause Foods, Inc.)
- Private label brands

**Pepperidge Farm
Division**

Breads
- Earth Grains (Anheuser-Busch)
- Cobblestone Mills (Flowers Bakeries)
- Breads International

**Frozen cakes,
sweet rolls**
- Sara Lee
- Mrs. Smith's (Kellogg)
- Morton's (RJR Nabisco)
- Banquet (Banquet Foods)
- Weight Watchers (Heinz)
- Pillsbury
- Cozy Kitchen (Colonial Cake)

**Win Schuler foods
(cheese spreads, melba
rounds, party dips,
sauces, salad dressings)**
- Borden
- Kraft (Dart & Kraft)

Godiva chocolates
- Hershey
- Nestlé

Exhibit 8 VLASIC DIVISION: PRODUCTS, RIVAL BRANDS, AND COMPETITORS

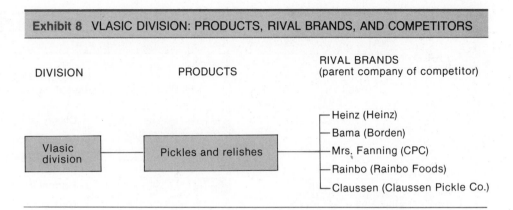

DIVISION   PRODUCTS   RIVAL BRANDS (parent company of competitor)

Vlasic division → Pickles and relishes →
- Heinz (Heinz)
- Bama (Borden)
- Mrs. Fanning (CPC)
- Rainbo (Rainbo Foods)
- Claussen (Claussen Pickle Co.)

percent share of the pickles market. Seventeen percent of Vlasic's sales were in the food service category.

In 1985 Vlasic implemented new labels that used color bands and a flavor rating scale to help consumers find their favorite tastes quickly on the supermarket shelf. Taking advantage of its marketing research, which indicated consumer desires for new and interesting flavors, Vlasic introduced "Zesty Dills" and "Bread & Butter Whole Pickle" lines in 1985. Heinz was Campbell's leading national competitor in this area (Exhibit 8), but there were a number of important regional and private label brands that competed with Heinz and Vlasic for shelf space.

Win Schuler, the Vlasic subsidiary purchased in 1982, reported flat sales in 1984 due to a general economic decline in the Michigan and upper midwest markets where its products were sold. In 1985 it was moved to Campbell's refrigerated foods business unit where there were plans to begin producing a wider range of food products under the Win Schuler brand name.

MRS. PAUL'S KITCHENS

Sales of this division for 1984 were up 16 percent over the previous year, operating earnings increased 36 percent, and unit volume increased 9 percent. Mrs. Paul's sales represented just over 3 percent of Campbell's total business; all results exceeded goals set for the year. However, strong competitive pressure on its traditional lines was blamed for the unit's drop in operating earnings for 1985. Competing brands included Hormel and Gorton's (Exhibit 9).

When Campbell acquired Mrs. Paul's in 1982, it was rumored that Heinz and Pillsbury, among others, were considering the same acquisition. Shortly after the acquisition, Campbell responded to consumer preferences for convenience seafood products that were nutritious, low in calories, microwavable, and coated more lightly, by introducing Light & Natural Fish Fillets in 1983. Quality improvements were made to existing products, and a promising new product, Light Seafood Entrees, was introduced in 1984. Market share increased about 25 per-

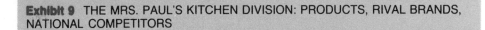

Exhibit 9 THE MRS. PAUL'S KITCHEN DIVISION: PRODUCTS, RIVAL BRANDS, NATIONAL COMPETITORS

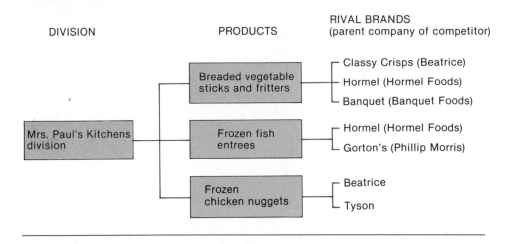

cent over 1983, and Light Seafood Entrees went national in 1985. This line, which featured seven varieties of low-calorie, microwavable, seafood dishes, accounted for 11 percent of 1985's volume. However, sales of the company's established product lines of breaded frozen seafood items dipped below the 1984 level.

CAMPBELL'S OTHER U.S. BUSINESSES

Beyond the base of Campbell's main operating groups, there were several additional small businesses: Triangle Manufacturing Corp., a health and fitness products manufacturer; Campbell Hospitality, the restaurant division; and Snow King Frozen Foods, Inc., a manufacturer of frozen meat specialty products.

In 1984 the Hospitality Division, encompassing 59 Pietro's restaurants, 15 Annabelle's, and 6 H. T. McDoogal's, reported an operating loss slightly less than 1983. During the year, the division added one H. T. McDoogal's, two Annabelle's, and nine Pietro's units.

In 1985 Annabelle's experienced a 14 percent increase in sales and a 43 percent rise in operating earnings. During the year, Campbell announced its intention to sell four H. T. McDoogal's restaurants. Snow King reported a sales decline of 19 percent and an operating loss of almost $1 million.

Competing food companies in the restaurant business included General Mills and Pillsbury. General Mills' Red Lobster unit was the nation's largest full-service dinnerhouse chain. Red Lobster had 1985 sales of $827 million—an all-time high—and its operating profits also set a record. Pillsbury's Restaurants Group was comprised of Burger King, Steak & Ale Restaurants, and Bennigan's; all three achieved record sales and earnings in 1985. Pillsbury opened 477 new restaurants in 1985—the most ever in a single year—bringing the total to 4,601.

Triangle, Campbell's physical fitness subsidiary, in its second full year of operation in 1985, reported that sales had more than tripled, but that increased marketing costs aimed at securing brand recognition resulted in an operating loss. Sales growth was a result of doubling the size of Triangle's distribution system. It's best known product line, "The Band" wrist and ankle weights, maintained the number two position in its category with a 14 percent market share. Triangle planned to build on its strengths by entering the exercise equipment category and by marketing its products internationally.

CAMPBELL'S INTERNATIONAL DIVISION

Campbell's International Division provided 18 percent of the company's consolidated sales in 1984. Campbell had subsidiaries in 11 foreign countries and was planning to expand further. Total restructuring of the International Division was in progress with goals of increasing sales and earnings and building a solid base for growth.

In 1985 steps were taken toward the division's goal of contributing 25 percent of Campbell's corporate sales and earnings. A number of operations were consolidated, and new businesses were added. Other international objectives were to improve Campbell's presence in all international markets and to make Campbell into a premier international company.

RECENT EVENTS

During 1985 the market price of Campbell's stock reached a new high of $80.50 a share. In July the stock was split two for one. At year-end 1985, the market price was $51.50 and the stock price was up $4 during one December week. Analysts were puzzled by this sudden rise in market price, and there were rumors of a takeover.

Analysts observed that the company had been hurt by fierce competition in 1985, an increasing softness in many of its markets, and mistakes on new-product introduction. In its *1985 Annual Report* Campbell acknowledged increased competition in the marketplace:

> The supermarket has become an arena of intense competitive activity as food companies introduce a steady stream of new consumer-oriented products and support them with massive marketing dollars in an attempt to carve out a first or second place position in the respective categories. That competitive activity is keeping the pressure on Campbell's operating results.

BOMBARDIER*

I want a company with a continuous flow that is not subject to the drastic fluctuations of being in just one business.

These were the words of Laurent Beaudoin, chairman of Bombardier, as he contemplated his company's dramatic rise to prominence during the 1960s and 1970s.[1] The Canadian company's name had been at one point synonymous with snowmobiles. Its pioneering efforts in the development and the launching of the Ski-Doo had been handsomely rewarded. By the late 1960s, Bombardier controlled close to 50 percent of the snowmobile market, about three times as much as its closest competitor (see Exhibit 1).

Laurent Beaudoin had long believed that the fortunes of his company were too closely tied to a single product. Thus, even before the demand for snowmobiles began to slow, Bombardier took steps to insulate itself from the uncertainties of the recreational market. Throughout the 1970s, Beaudoin led the company on an aggressive strategy of diversification into other areas of leisure and transportation. As the company moved into the 1980s, its revenues had grown considerably beyond the $165 million it had generated from snowmobiles at the start of the previous decade. But while Bombardier's revenues grew dramatically, it continued to experience wide swings in profits. In 1981 and 1982 Bombardier lost money (see Exhibit 2); the 1982 loss was the biggest in company history.

GROWING WITH SNOWMOBILES

Work on the snowmobile started in the mid-1920s by Joseph-Armand Bombardier in his father's garage at Valcourt, Quebec. But it took until 1935 before Joseph-Armand had built the first snowmobile. It consisted of a large plywood body set on caterpillar tracks and driven by a heavy, conventional internal combustion engine.

These early snowmobiles were hand-assembled in versions intended to accommodate from 5 to 25 passengers. In each case, the machine was individually adapted for a specific use according to the wishes of different customers. By 1942, Joseph-Armand had incorporated his garage to form Bombardier Snowmobile Limited and was producing snowmobiles to serve doctors, missionaries, woodmen, foresters, trappers, and farmers in outlying districts of Quebec.

With the advent of World War II, the basic snowmobile design was adapted to produce an amphitrack armored carrier called the "Penguin" for use by Canadian

---

Prepared by Joseph Lampel and Jamal Shamsie, McGill University. Copyright © 1988, by Joseph Lampel and Jamal Shamsie.

[1] "Bombardier: Making a Second Leap from Snowmobiles to Mass Transit," *Business Week,* February 23, 1981.

Exhibit 1 BOMBARDIER'S SNOWMOBILE SALES (1963–86)

Season	Industry	Bombardier	Bombardier's market share
1963–64	17,000	8,000	47%
1964–65	30,000	14,000	47
1965–66	60,000	26,000	43
1966–67	120,000	48,000	40
1967–68	170,000	78,000	46
1968–69	250,000	120,000	48
1969–70	415,000	170,000	41
1970–71	540,000	195,000	36
1971–72	530,000	190,000	36
1972–73	515,000	150,000	29
1973–74	400,000	110,000	28
1974–75	330,000	84,000	25
1975–76	245,000	67,000	27
1976–77	195,000	62,000	32
1977–78	225,000	68,000	30
1978–79	270,000	72,000	27
1979–80	200,000	55,000	28
1980–81	180,000	60,000	33
1981–82	145,000	55,000	38
1982–83	105,000	37,000	35
1983–84	115,000	38,000	33
1984–85	100,000	34,000	34
1985–86	110,000	39,000	35

Source: Bombardier Annual Reports.

Exhibit 2 BOMBARDIER'S CONSOLIDATED INCOME STATEMENTS, 1981–86 (in millions of Canadian dollars)

	For the year ended January 31					
	1981	1982	1983	1984	1985	1986
Net sales	$394.4	$448.8	$551.1	$491.0	$515.5	$656.6
Cost of sales	310.8	368.1	452.6	418.9	428.8	557.5
Selling and administrative	72.2	85.4	62.1	50.0	58.7	56.2
Depreciation and amortization	8.1	9.9	11.3	10.8	15.6	21.5
Other income	(1.0)	(0.5)	(2.7)	(7.5)	(11.2)	(12.2)
Interest on long-term debt	3.1	8.3	7.5	5.6	6.7	5.2
Other interest	9.4	11.5	10.1	2.8	0.1	1.6
Income taxes	(2.4)	(15.4)	4.1	4.1	6.7	10.7
Net income (loss)	($5.8)	($18.5)	$6.1	$6.3	$10.1	$16.1

Source: Bombardier Annual Reports.

troops. Subsequently, the demonstrated durability and ruggedness of the snow-mobile also led to the development and production of various forms of specialized industrial equipment. These consisted of machines that were especially suited for use in forestry, logging, oil exploration, and snow removal.

Eventually, Joseph-Armand and his son Germain tackled the challenge of developing and producing a smaller and lighter version of the basic snowmobile design intended to carry one or two persons. The key to the new design was the coupling of a recently introduced two-cycle motor-scooter engine with an all-rubber track that had internal steel rods built in for added strength. By 1959, the first snowmobile directed at the individual user was introduced. Initially, Joseph-Armand thought of calling his invention the Ski-Dog, but he decided in favor of a more bilingual name, the Ski-Doo.

Development of the Snowmobile

When he died in 1964, Joseph-Armand left behind a company that had 700 employees and a product that was enjoying increasing popularity. Some 16,500 Ski-Doos had been sold, and demand was clearly on the rise. Germain took over as president but shortly after relinquished his post for health reasons. The company passsed into the hands of son-in-law Laurent Beaudoin, a chartered accountant and one of the first management graduates of the University of Sherbrooke. Beaudoin realized certain factors were standing in the way of the development of the full potential of the snowmobile:

> There were two fundamental problems arising from the nature of the company's beginnings. First, there was no research and development department because it had all taken place in the mind of Joseph-Armand Bombardier. Second, the company which he created was, very naturally, a production-oriented company. It produced machines to fill a market need, which was mainly for large machines to do practical jobs, rather than creating and seeking out new markets.[2]

Beaudoin introduced an R&D section, set up an integrated marketing system, and geared up facilities for efficient mass production. Extensive research confirmed that an untapped snowmobile market existed not only for transport, but also for recreation and sport. Bombardier invested heavily in the development of this potential market. Over the next several years, massive advertising, combined with the establishment of a dealership network, culminated in the setting up of 18 regional sales groups covering Canada, the United States, and Europe. These efforts resulted in making Bombardier a leader in the snowmobile market and turned the Ski-Doo trademark into a generic term for snowmobiles.

But the success of Bombardier also brought about the entry of new producers of snowmobiles. Most of the new competition came from U.S. companies that had been closely watching the development of the snowmobile business. Beaudoin, however, was not fazed at the prospect of more competition. He was confident about the capabilities of his company to maintain its leadership:

---

[2] "Bombardier Skids to Success," *International Management*, January 1972.

It's an industry that looks very simple. Everybody looks and says: "Gee, we can get in tomorrow morning and grab everything." But it's not that simple. The advantage we have over all those companies is that we eat snow, we know snow, and are snowmobilers ourselves.[3]

In order to ensure that it could meet this growing competition, Beaudoin also decided to start acquiring almost all of his suppliers, most of which were situated within the province of Quebec. These acquisitions led to the development of a series of subsidiaries and affiliates that manufactured parts or accessories related to snowmobile production. This push for acquisitions eventually climaxed in the $30 million purchase of Rotax-Werk A. G. Located in Austria, Rotax-Werk manufactured the two-stroke engines used in the Ski-Doos. By 1970, Bombardier's own production facilities or those of its subsidiaries and affiliates were supplying over 90 percent of the 1,400 parts that went into the manufacturing of the Ski-Doo. Beaudoin saw these moves as a necessary precaution against an eventual intensification of competition, in particular the likely outbreak of price wars: "If there is any price war, we will be in a position to face it. This has been our first idea."[4]

Shortly after, Bombardier moved to buy out its largest competitor. In 1971, it finalized the acquisition of Moto-Ski from its U.S. parent, Giffin Industries. This acquisition consolidated Bombardier's domination of the snowmobile market. By this time, the achievements and stature of Bombardier were acclaimed as a product of Canadian imagination and entrepreneurial vigor. An article, published at the beginning of 1972, bestowed praise upon the company:

> Not many companies can claim to have started an entirely new industry—fewer still to have done so and stayed ahead of the pack. Bombardier Ltd. has done just that. . . . It is a company owned and managed by Canadians, which several foreign companies would dearly love to own. It is the largest Quebec-owned company operating in the province, and is one of the 200 most profitable public companies in Canada.[5]

The Crunch for Snowmobiles

The early 1970s saw an increasing number of companies competing in the snowmobile market. In addition to new American and Canadian firms, Bombardier saw the entry of Swedish, Italian, and Japanese manufacturers. Yet while the number of competitors was increasing, market growth in snowmobiles was slowing.

Several reasons were advanced for the softening of snowmobile sales. The main blame was put on the stagnant economy, which was seen as the principal cause of the decline in demand. Snowmobiles constituted a type of purchase that was often postponed by consumers during a downturn in the economy. Other reasons were more peculiar to the snowmobile market. Poor winters, with late

---

[3] "Snow Job?" *Forbes*, February 1, 1970.

[4] Ibid.

[5] "Bombardier Skids to Success."

snow and unusually low precipitation, reduced the recreational use of snow-mobiles. At the same time, newspaper stories of crashes and decapitated riders led to a mounting concern over the safety of snowmobiles. Finally, environmentalists were vocal in their criticism of the high noise levels generated by snow-mobiles, particularly in wilderness areas.

There was growing awareness that stricter legislation covering the design and use of snowmobiles was likely to be forthcoming. For its part, Bombardier attempted to meet these concerns by trying to design better safety features and special mufflers for their upcoming snowmobile models. It also produced films, slides, and brochures on safety measures and the proper use of the snowmobile. Furthermore, a newly created public relations department tried to involve the various levels of government and different types of businesses in the creation of a system comparable to the one found in the ski industry. This was to include the development of snowmobile trails, snowmobile weekends, and snowmobile resorts.

Early in 1973 it looked like demand would increase again. But the sudden fuel crisis dampened the hopes of Bombardier. Its sales of snowmobiles continued to decline sharply, down from the high of 195,000 units sold during the winter of 1970–1971 (see Exhibit 1). This was accompanied by consecutive losses of $5.8 million in 1973 and $7.3 million in 1974.

Beaudoin attributed the poor performance of Bombardier to the general state of the snowmobile industry. But eventually he acknowledged that Bombardier's position in the depressed snowmobile market had also been slipping. From a 40 percent share in 1970, based on the Ski-Doo alone, the company's share had declined to about 25 percent for the combined Ski-Doo and Motor-Ski brands. The competition had been closing in on Bombardier's leadership, causing it to have second thoughts about the merits of the industry it had pioneered.

MOVING AWAY FROM SNOWMOBILES

In 1974 Bombardier seized upon an opportunity to bid on a four-year $118 million contract to build 423 new cars for the proposed extension of the Montreal subway system. The bid represented a major departure from the core business of the company. It was not, however, the first time Bombardier had ventured away from snowmobiles.

Early Moves

Even before the snowmobile market was developed, Bombardier had been producing all-terrain tracked and wheeled vehicles for different kinds of industrial use. The company had continuously developed and marketed many basic types or sizes of vehicles for work in swamps, forests, and snow. The earliest of these were the Muskeg series of carriers, tractors, and brush cutters that were used in logging, construction, petroleum, and mining. Later developments included the SW series for urban snow removal, the Skidozer line for grooming snowmobile trails and ski slopes, and the Bombi carrier for transporting people over snowy or marshy terrain.

A further departure from snowmobiles came as a result of Bombardier's acquisition of suppliers. Originally, the acquisitions were undertaken to consolidate the company's position in the snowmobile market. Once made, they presented attractive opportunities. For example, Rotax-Werk was acquired in 1970 because it supplied the engines that were used on Ski-Doos. But it also manufactured engines for boats and motorcycles. Another acquired subsidiary proceeded to develop and introduce a new type of fiberglass sailboat, followed by a canoe and a catamaran.

In addition, the success of the snowmobile created other ancillary markets. For instance, traveling on snowmobiles at 40 miles per hour in subfreezing temperatures required specialized clothing. Beaudoin saw this new type of market as a promising opportunity:

> Someone was going to have to supply wet-proof clothing that was warm enough to prevent our customers from freezing to death on our machines. We decided it might as well be us.[6]

Consequently, Bombardier acquired an apparel manufacturer in order to introduce snowmobile clothing. This led the company into the sportswear market because the acquired manufacturer was already engaged in the production and marketing of several other types of sportswear. Said Beaudoin: "We are in the leisure business."[7]

In other instances, Bombardier sought to enter markets not directly related to its core snowmobile business. In 1970 the company introduced a new product called the Sea-Doo, which was a kind of snowmobile on water. This was marketed most heavily in Florida and California. Unfortunately, the Sea-Doo was found to rust in salt water, and production was suspended after a couple of years. A more technically successful product was the Can-Am motorcycle, which was test marketed by Bombardier in 1973. The idea for the motorcycle originated with the development of a new engine by Bombardier's new Rotax subsidiary in Austria. The result was a light, high-performance motorcycle that quickly gained recognition after it won several races in Canada, the United States, and Europe.

New Thrusts

It was around this time that Bombardier began to see mass transit as a potentially lucrative market. As Beaudoin put it some time later, the company had already entered into this line of business when it had purchased Rotax-Werk in 1970:

> We acquired Rotax-Werk . . . and its parent company, Lohnerwerke, which made tramways for the city of Vienna, came along with it. We didn't intend to stay in the mass transit business, but at first sign of the energy crisis, that changed.[8]

---

[6] Ibid.

[7] Ibid.

[8] "Snowmobiles to Subways: Bombardier Maps Out Its Route," *Financial Post,* September 13, 1980.

But the move was facilitated by overtures to Bombardier from the French-based Compagnie Industrielle de Matériel de Transport (CIMT). CIMT had been involved in a partnership with Canadian Vickers Limited on a previous subway car order. Charles Leblanc, who was vice president of administration for the company at the time stated:

> CIMT came to us. They said don't be afraid of it. They pointed out that the same manufacturing steps were needed for subway cars as for snowmobiles. So we went ahead and bid.[9]

Although Vickers had underbid it by $140,000, Bombardier won the contract. It was stated that Vickers had been disqualified because its bid did not include a specified Swedish coupling device.

The award of this substantial contract represented Bombardier's entry into the mass-transit market. The company moved to convert the Moto-Ski plant at La Pocatiere to handle production of subway cars. There were strong doubts about whether Bombardier had the necessary capabilities to complete the order. Up to this point, the company's involvement in mass transit products had been limited to trams and streetcars produced by its Austrian subsidiary. But trams and streetcars are classified as light rail vehicles and are substantially different in design from subway cars.

Bombardier did experience some problems in production, due in part to a labor strike in its newly converted plant. Nevertheless, the company began to make deliveries of subway cars to the city of Montreal late in 1976. By this time, Bombardier had also received its first order from outside Canada. This was for 36 electric-powered double-decker commuter cars that were to be built at a cost of $27 million for the South Chicago Transit Authority.

In the following years, Bombardier began to receive larger orders from all parts of North America (see Exhibit 3). It received an order for 117 push-pull commuter cars from the New Jersey Transit Corporation. This was followed by an even larger order for 180 subway cars for Mexico City. A senior marketing official subsequently described the manner in which Bombardier had been developing its mass transit business:

> We progress in terms of both regional expansion and product expansion in a logical, structured fashion. It's more a question of corporate policy or strategy. We started off in Canada in Montreal, then we went to the United States. Now, we've broadened it into Mexico. There are no wild leaps into blue sky and the glorious beyond because that's the way companies go out of business.[10]

Spreading Out

Shortly after its entry into mass transit, Bombardier was trying to find new acquisitions that would help it to become a significant competitor in the transpor-

---

[9] "Why Bombardier Is Trying out Mass Transit," *Business Week,* March 10, 1975.

[10] "Firm Looks to Commuter Vehicles as Gravy Train to Large Profits," *Financial Post,* December 12, 1981.

Exhibit 3 MASS TRANSIT ORDERS, 1974–85

Year	Type of vehicle	Quantity	Customer	Delivery
1974	Rubber-tired subway cars	423	Montreal Urban Community	1976–79
1976	Self-propelled commuter cars	36	Chicago South Suburban Transit	1978–79
1978	LRC coaches	50	Via Rail Canada	1981–82
1980	Push-pull commuter cars	117	New Jersey Transit	1982–83
1981	Rubber-tired subway cars	180	Mexico City	1982–83
1981	Light rail vehicles	26	Portland, Oregon	1984–85
1981	Push-pull commuter cars	9	Metropolitan Authority of New York	1983
1982	LRC coaches	50	VIA Rail Canada	1984
1982	Steel-wheeled subway cars	825	Metropolitan Authority of New York	1984–87
1983	Push-pull commuter cars	19	Metro-North Commuter of New York	1985
1984	Push-pull commuter cars	20	Connecticut Department of Transportation	1986
1985	Push-pull commuter cars	15	Metro-North Commuter of New York	1987

Source: Fred Schilling, Nesbitt Research, 1986.

tation business. In 1976, Bombardier eventually succeeded in purchasing the Montreal Locomotive Works (MLW) from its U.S. parent for a cash payment of $16.8 million. Bombardier was given much-needed financial help from the Quebec government in finalizing this deal. The province's holding company, Société Générale de Financement, contributed about 40 percent of the purchase price of MLW in exchange for a block of Bombardier's shares.

MLW had previously made subway cars for Toronto, but its main products were diesel-electric locomotives and diesel engines for locomotives, ships, and power plants. The locomotives produced by the MLW plant were mostly in the lighter category, ranging from 1,000 to 2,000 horsepower. Because of this, their appeal was largely restricted to railways in developing countries. Bombardier was subsequently able to generate sales of diesel-engine locomotives to customers in several of these countries, including Venezuela, Jamaica, Cuba, Mexico, Guatemala, Pakistan, Bangladesh, Cameroon, Tanzania, and Malawi.

However, Bombardier's purchase of MLW had been largely motivated by its growing interest in the design and development of a light, rapid, and comfortable (LRC) passenger train. Its partners in this project were Alcan and Dofasco. The Canadian government also contributed development grants through its program for the advancement of industrial technology. The new train was meant to run at constant high speeds on existing North American tracks. Bombardier Vice President Henry Valle, who had previously headed MLW, talked about the distinctive features of the LRC:

> We think the LRC is as good or better than anything comparable on the market anywhere. And we don't think anyone anywhere knows any more about high-speed trains than we do.[11]

One of the first LRC contracts Bombardier managed to obtain was a $10 million lease-purchase contract with Amtrak for two trains. The Amtrak contract was followed shortly thereafter by a $70 million order for 21 locomotives and 50 coaches for Via Rail in Canada (see Exhibit 3). The locomotives went into production at the MLW facility in Montreal, while the cars were slated for assembly at the La Pocatiere plant for mass transit products. Upon obtaining the contract from Via Rail, a senior marketing official at Bombardier declared: "Now that we have a home base, we can really begin to sell actively internationally."[12]

Thus far, according to Beaudoin, Bombardier's move into mass transit and rail products had done much to ameliorate the company's dependence on recreational products such as the snowmobile. He summed up his company's goals in the following terms:

> Our goal is to develop some equilibrium between transportation and recreation. The transportation and recreation cycles are different. Recreational products are strong when the economy is strong. It's the reverse for transportation because of energy problems.[13]

CURRENT SITUATION

The change in Bombardier during the 1970s was seen by Beaudoin as more than merely a shift in the company's products and markets. It represented a strong desire for an expansion of the company's scope of activities that would allow it to better spread out its risk. During the 1980s Bombardier was trying to push for the further development of its several different types of business. In addition to the original line of recreational and utility products, the company was now engaged in new lines of mass transit and rail and diesel products. Exhibits 4 through 7 present financial data for each of the company's primary business segments. Exhibit 8 presents Bombardier's balance sheets.

Recreational Products

The bulk of sales in recreational products continued to come from snowmobiles. Bombardier offered about 15 models of snowmobiles that were geared toward different uses. These included family models developed for better comfort and

---

[11] "Bombardier Looks to Amtrak to Open Doors to U.S. Inter-City Market," *Globe & Mail,* November 16, 1977.

[12] "LRC Sale Considered Key to Foreign Market," *Globe & Mail,* November 4, 1977.

[13] "Snowmobiles to Subways."

Exhibit 4   BOMBARDIER'S SALES BY CLASS OF BUSINESS, 1981–86 (in millions of Canadian dollars)

	For the year ended January 31					
	1981	1982	1983	1984	1985	1986
Recreational and utility products	$216.0	$215.4	$234.4	$260.2	$198.4	$252.3
Mass-transit products	34.0	67.6	178.4	134.2	202.3	296.4
Rail and diesel products	144.4	165.8	138.3	96.6	114.8	107.9
Total	$394.4	$448.8	$551.1	$491.0	$515.5	$656.6

Source: Bombardier Annual Reports.

Exhibit 5   BOMBARDIER'S PROFIT FROM OPERATIONS BY CLASS OF BUSINESS, 1981–86 (in millions of Canadian dollars)

	For the year ended January 31					
	1981	1982	1983	1984	1985	1986
Recreational and utility products	($5.5)	($24.2)	$ 0.1	$ 7.5	$16.2	$12.1
Mass-transit products	5.0	1.4	17.4	17.6	9.3	3.6
Rail and diesel products	4.2	8.6	7.6	(13.7)	(13.1)	5.7
Total	$3.7	($14.2)	$25.1	$11.4	$12.4	$21.4

Source: Bombardier Annual Reports.

Exhibit 6   BOMBARDIER'S CAPITAL EXPENDITURES BY CLASS OF BUSINESS, 1981–86 (in millions of Canadian dollars)

	For the year ended January 31					
	1981	1982	1983	1984	1985	1986
Recreational and utility products	$11.2	$14.3	$ 4.0	$ 9.0	$13.0	$ 8.4
Mass-transit products	5.5	8.0	4.4	8.7	5.4	1.0
Rail and diesel products	2.2	4.3	5.5	3.8	1.0	2.0
Total	$18.9	$26.6	$13.9	$21.5	$19.4	$11.4

Source: Financial Post Corporation Service.

Exhibit 7   BOMBARDIER'S CAPITAL EXPENDITURES BY GEOGRAPHIC AREA, 1981–86 (in millions of Canadian dollars)

	For the year ended January 31					
	1981	1982	1983	1984	1985	1986
Canada	$15.4	$18.6	$11.2	$17.9	$13.9	$ 4.1
United States	0.2	4.7	0.7	1.3	1.7	2.8
Europe	3.3	3.3	2.0	2.3	3.8	4.5
Total	$18.9	$26.6	$13.9	$21.5	$19.4	$11.4

Source: Financial Post Corporation Service.

Exhibit 8   BOMBARDIER'S CONSOLIDATED BALANCE SHEETS, 1981–86
(in millions of Canadian dollars)

	For the year ended January 31					
	1981	**1982**	**1983**	**1984**	**1985**	**1986**
Assets						
Current assets						
Cash	—	—	—	—	—	$ 6.9
Accounts receivable	$ 67.8	$ 73.2	$ 56.9	$ 77.3	$ 90.6	103.3
Inventories	158.6	121.4	149.0	117.2	167.5	152.3
Deficient income taxes	—	18.7	15.9	13.5	10.3	8.0
Prepaid expense	3.0	4.3	4.9	4.1	6.2	7.4
Investments	6.4	13.1	19.0	17.8	18.6	19.5
Fixed assets						
Buildings and equipment	153.6	177.8	171.7	186.9	234.6	234.9
Accumulated depreciation	81.0	87.8	84.0	88.1	110.3	123.1
Other assets	5.0	5.7	4.7	8.6	9.7	10.8
	$313.4	$326.4	$338.1	$337.3	$427.2	$420.0
Liabilities and shareholders' equity						
Current liabilities						
Bank loans	$ 19.5	$ 39.5	$ 13.7	$ 1.6	—	—
Accounts payable	80.6	91.1	95.9	73.3	$107.4	$134.7
Advances due	—	—	—	—	—	26.3
Income taxes	0.3	2.8	0.3	0.7	2.4	4.3
Mature long-term debt	11.0	4.4	6.1	6.0	4.6	5.3
Contract advances	—	—	32.6	77.0	132.5	39.5
Long-term debt	65.7	73.0	66.9	49.0	39.8	35.2
Provision for pensions	7.3	5.3	5.8	6.2	6.6	7.4
Shareholders' equity						
Capital stock	93.6	93.4	93.7	94.2	95.6	119.9
Retained earnings	35.4	16.9	23.1	29.3	38.3	47.4
	$313.4	$326.4	$338.1	$337.3	$427.2	$420.0

Source: Bombardier Annual Reports.

more safety as well as sporty models designed for higher speed and better performance.

The market for snowmobiles had picked up in the late 1970s, but declined again in the early 1980s. This resulted in lower profits for Bombardier from its lines of snowmobiles. Beaudoin, however, believed good snowfalls and an improving economy would bring about a growth in sales as well as greater profits. As he saw it, snowmobiles still had an important role to play in the future of Bombardier:

> We see it as a cash cow. The shakeout has taken place and, with around 40 percent of the market, it could be a very profitable business for us in the future even on lower volume.[14]

In order to adjust to these lower levels of sales, the company sold the various firms that were producing parts and accessories for snowmobiles. Now, apart

---

[14] "Making the 'A' Train," *Forbes*, September 27, 1982.

from assembling the snowmobiles, Bombardier's actual manufacture of the vehicle is limited to the engine, which is made by the Rotax division in Gunskirchen, Austria.

Bombardier was among the five remaining competitors in snowmobiles. Its share of the market had recently risen to as much as 35 percent (see Exhibit 1). But this position was under attack from Yamaha, a Japanese competitor with strong technological and manufacturing advantages. Other firms in the industry posed less of a threat since they were struggling with the downturn in snowmobile sales. In fact, Bombardier had at one point expressed interest in the purchase of Polaris, a U.S.-based firm that was experiencing some financial difficulties. But the negotiations were dropped when the U.S. Justice Department threatened to block the sale on antitrust grounds.

Apart from snowmobiles, the company had experienced limited success with its other recreational products. Its only other notable offering was its line of Can-Am off-road racing bikes. These appealed to specialized sectors of the market because of their technical performance attributes. Bombardier had received several orders for military versions of these motorcycles from certain NATO countries, such as Britain and Belgium. In 1981 a license was purchased from an Austrian company for the assembly and distribution of moped bicycles in Canada. "Our long term strategy is to develop other recreational products," said Beaudoin."[15]

Mass Transit Products

The greatest push for sales was being given to mass-transit products. Bombardier was able to offer a wide variety of heavy, conventional, and light-rail vehicles as a result of licensing to gain access to the different technologies (see Exhibit 9). Beaudoin was confident that this wide range of products placed his company in the best possible position to exploit the mass-transit business. He also felt that an energy-conserving society will in the future rely more heavily upon mass transit:

Exhibit 9 MASS TRANSIT TECHNOLOGY CAPABILITY

Heavy rail
Rubber-tired subway cars — License from CIMT France
Steel-wheeled subway cars — License from Kawasaki

Conventional rail
Commuter cars — License from Pullman
LRC cars — Developed with Alcan & Dofasco

Light rail
Light-rail vehicles — License from BN Belgium
Monorail — License from Disney
PeopleMover — License from Disney

Source: Tony Hine, McLeod Young Weir Equity Research, 1986.

[15] "Snowmobiles to Subways."

Exhibit 10   MASS TRANSIT CARS CURRENTLY IN USE IN NORTH AMERICA

Type of car	Units in operation	Exceeding normal useful life
Steel-wheeled subway cars	10,200	2,324
Rubber-tired subway cars	792	
Commuter cars	1,282	487
Light-rail vehicles	4,502	568
Intercity rail cars	2,589	837
Total	19,365	4,216

Source: Fred Schilling, Nesbitt Research, 1986.

> We're forecasting a North American mass transit market of $1 billion annually . . . and we aim to get a good part of it.[16]

Such a strong and sustained demand for mass-transit products did appear to be likely. It had recently been estimated that of the close to 20,000 cars currently in operation all over North America, over 20 percent had already exceeded their normal useful life (see Exhibit 10). These cars would have to be replaced or refurbished. Refurbishing is usually cheaper, costing only about a third or a half of the $1 million purchase price of a new car.

In 1982 Bombardier was able to win a large and prestigious order worth about $1 billion for subway cars from the Metropolitan Transportation Authority of New York (see Exhibit 3). The company had recently started to make its first deliveries of the 825 steel-wheeled subway cars that had been ordered. However, the company was still searching for other orders of significant size that would allow it to maintain sufficient production activity after the deliveries to New York were completed in 1987.

Bombardier was experiencing severe difficulties in trying to break into large Canadian markets outside of Quebec because of the declared commitment of various provincial governments to award mass-transit jobs to companies that are locally based. For example, Bombardier had just experienced a major setback when it lost out on a bid to acquire UDTC, a significant competitor located in Toronto with a $1.3 billion backlog of orders from the city.

It was also feared that cuts in mass-transit funding by the federal government would make future sales in the United States even harder to come by. In fact, several large U.S. firms, such as Pullman, Rohr, and General Electric had recently pulled out of the mass-transit business because of uncertainty of orders and problems with contracts. Furthermore, competition for mass-transit orders in the United States and in other export markets was coming from large firms that included Budd in the United States. Kawasaki in Japan, FrancoRail of France, Breda Ferroviaria of Italy, and Siemens-Duwag of West Germany.

Since 1981 Bombardier had begun to put much more emphasis on light-rail vehicles due to their cheaper construction and maintenance costs. Toward this end, the company had acquired the rights to build, market, and operate its own

---

[16] Ibid.

versions of elevated and automated monorail systems from the Disney organization. It had also just completed a $13.5 million acquisition of a 45 percent interest in a Belgian mass-transit company that had supplied the technology to develop and build the streetcars it had already delivered to Portland, Oregon. Nevertheless, Vice President Poitras stated recently: "We don't want to depend completely on mass transit, because transit could also have cycles of good and bad years."[17]

Rail and Diesel Products

Bombardier had made substantial investments to upgrade the MLW facilities for the production of diesel locomotives. Besides manufacturing the locomotives, the plant also produced diesel engines that were used in locomotives, ships, and turbines. In 1984 the company attempted to expand its capacity and to obtain new customers through the $30 million acquisition of Alco Power, located in Auburn, New York. Alco produced diesel locomotives and diesel engines similar to those offered by MLW.

But sales of locomotives had begun to drop in recent years, primarily due to a decline in orders from the various developing countries. Furthermore, the company began to increasingly believe there was little likelihood of substantial improvement in sales unless it could become more competitive in the development and production of locomotives with greater horsepower, such as those presently produced by General Electric and General Motors.

Bombardier did manage to secure orders for as many as 30 higher-powered diesel locomotives from Canadian National, but serious problems with their performance after production resulted in the eventual delivery of only four of the locomotives. Efforts were made to convince Canadian National to increase the size of its order in order to justify further development work on a higher-powered locomotive. The company also explored the possibility of linking up with existing large competitors such as General Electric or Kawasaki in order to gain better access to technology as well as markets.

Ultimately, Bombardier was forced to terminate the production of new locomotives in 1985 and to focus primarily upon the manufacturing of diesel engines and the servicing of existing locomotives. Most of this work was subsequently channelled into the Alco facility in New York state. Raymond Royer, soon to become the company's president, stated: "It has been very painful to us. It's a major decision to take, but if we can't make a profit, we have to act as good managers."[18]

At the same time, Bombardier was also being forced to reevaluate its potential orders for passenger locomotives that would result from the sales of its LRC train. The company had believed it would eventually make worldwide sales of 150 locomotives and 750 coaches. But by 1986, after the sale of only 31 locomotives and 100 coaches to Canadian-based Via Rail, there were no more orders on hand.

---

[17] "Bombardier's Formula for Growth," *Financial Times of Canada,* November 28, 1983.

[18] "Locomotives To Be Dropped," *Globe & Mail,* July 13, 1985.

Even Via Rail had declined to exercise its options for further orders because of mechanical and electrical problems it had experienced with equipment it had already received. Company officials had recently been trying to generate sales of the LRC outside North America. Said Poitras: "We've had discussions on the LRC in other countries, but it takes time. Up to now, we have not succeeded."[19]

Utility Products

The industrial products of the company were constantly being expanded to include new kinds of vehicles for different types of markets. In recent years, Bombardier had introduced a new hydrostatic-drive vehicle for ski slope maintenance. It had also started to offer wheeled carriers and skidders aimed at the forestry industry. These were being manufactured under license from companies in the United States and Finland.

Industrial products were currently experiencing a period of slow demand. In part, this was attributed by the company to poor snow conditions that had affected demand for vehicles designed for snow removal as well as for ski and snowmobile trail grooming. At the same time, depressed conditions in the construction and forestry industry were being blamed for decline in sales of other industrial products.

But this decline in demand for industrial products has been offset by Bombardier's recent push into the area of logistic support equipment for the military. The company had already been adapting some of its snowmobiles, motorcycles, and industrial tracked vehicles to the needs of the military. In 1981 this activity was given a considerable boost when Bombardier was awarded a $150 million contract to build 2,700 trucks for the Canadian Armed Forces. These two-and-a-half ton trucks were built using a design of AM General Corporation, a subsidiary of American Motors.

In 1982 Bombardier also acquired worldwide rights for the production of the Iltis, a four-wheel-drive military vehicle designed by Volkswagenwerk of West Germany. The license led to an initial order for 1,900 Iltis vehicles for the Canadian Armed Forces. This was followed by the sale of 2,500 vehicles to Belgium and 350 vehicles to West Germany. A senior official in the logistics division explained:

> Our principle in developing the logistic division is pretty similar to Bombardier's thinking with any other product—first sell into Canada, build a base in Canada, then go offshore.[20]

Bombardier is counting on the current worldwide shift away from traditional Jeeps as army vehicles to create a major potential market for the Iltis. More orders for these vehicles are expected not only from Canada, but also from the Netherlands, Turkey, and Saudi Arabia.

---

[19] "Bombardier's Formula for Growth."

[20] "Bombardier Has High Hopes in Military Vehicle Market," *Globe & Mail,* November 12, 1983.

Exhibit 11 BUSINESSES ACQUIRED AND DIVESTED BY BOMBARDIER, 1957–84

Year of acquisition	Name and location of company	Type of business
1957	Rockland Industries[e] Kingsbury, Quebec	Rubber parts
1968	La Salle Plastic[e] Richmond, Quebec	Plastic parts
1969	Roski[e] Roxton Falls, Quebec	Fiberglass products
1970	Lohnerwerke Vienna, Austria	Streetcars
1970	Rotax-Werk Gunskirchen, Austria	Engines
1970	Walker Manufacturing Company[e] Montreal, Quebec	Sportswear
1970	Drummond Automatic Plating[c] Drummondville, Quebec	Chrome plating
1970	Jarry Precision[a] Montreal, Quebec	Transmissions
1971	Moto-Ski[b] La Pocatiere, Quebec	Snowmobiles
1972	Ville Marie Upholstering[d] Beauport, Quebec	Foam seats
1976	Montreal Locomotive Works Montreal, Quebec	Locomotives Diesel engines
1980	Heroux[f] Longueuil, Quebec	Aeronautical parts
1984	Alco Power Auburn, N.Y.	Locomotives Diesel engines

[a] Closed in 1973. [d] Divested in 1979.
[b] Dissolved in 1975. [e] Divested in 1983.
[c] Divested in 1976. [f] Divested in 1985.

Source: Financial Post Corporation Service.

Finally, the company has just signed an agreement with Oshkosh Truck Corporation of Wisconsin to produce and sell an 8.5-ton military truck known as the Oshkosh. The Oshkosh is a six-wheel-drive vehicle designed to carry heavy equipment and ammunition in rough terrain and is already in use with the U.S. Army. Bombardier is hoping to sell 500 to 1,000 of these trucks to the Canadian Armed Forces. It has also obtained the rights to sell the vehicle in 28 countries aside from Canada.

Exhibit 11 presents a list of Bombardier's acquisitions and divestitures during the 1957–1984 period.

PROFILE OF OPERATIONS

Organization

Bombardier's rapid growth and diversification forced top management to seek a more formal and structured approach to the running of the business. Toward this end, the company had been engaged in a series of moves designed to better

Exhibit 12   ORGANIZATION OF BOMBARDIER'S BUSINESS DIVISIONS

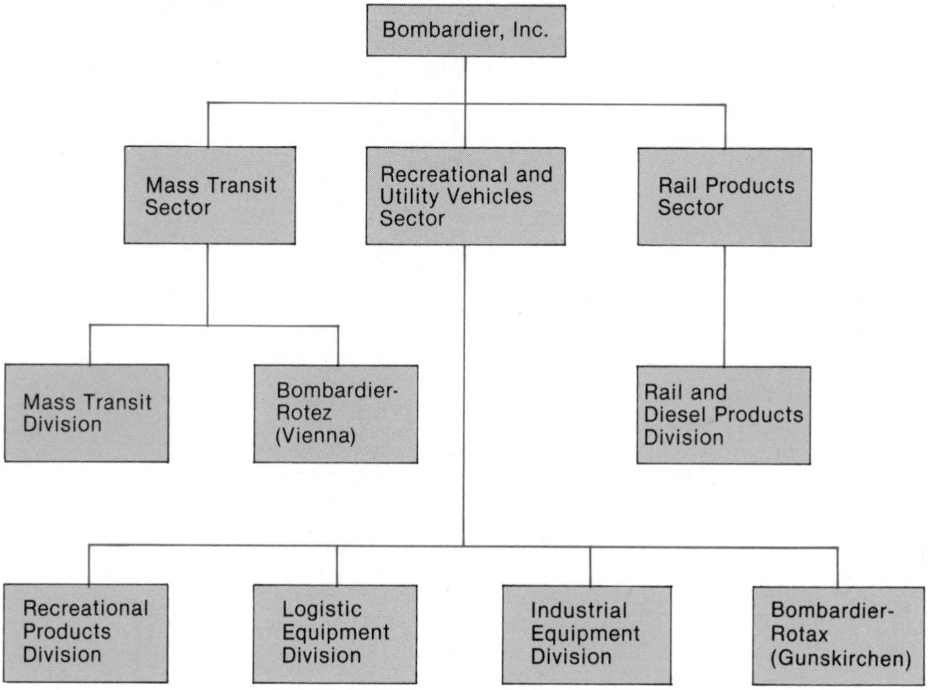

Source: Bombardier Annual Reports.

integrate its operations with those of its various acquisitions. Beaudoin had anticipated the need for this restructuring in the early 1970s:

> As we diversify more and more, we shall need to ensure central control of the overall operation. . . . Our management structure isn't finalized yet and will change with the needs of the business.[21]

By 1986 Bombardier was organized into seven different divisions or subsidiaries. These fell into three different sectors (see Exhibit 12). Total employment stood at between 5,000 and 6,000 employees. The largest number of divisions or subsidiaries was associated with the recreational and utility vehicles sector, which produced recreational products such as snowmobiles as well as certain types of industrial and logistic equipment. However, the main thrust of the company was oriented toward the mass-transit sector that manufactured several forms of subway cars, train cars, and streetcars. Finally, the rail and diesel products sector

---

[21] "Bombardier Skids to Success."

had concentrated upon the production of locomotives, but was now relying mainly upon diesel engines for various industrial uses.

Although Bombardier moved to bring its various divisions and subsidiaries under centralized control, they remained separate administrative and financial entities. Each division or subsidiary was headed by a chief executive who possessed a considerable degree of autonomy. These chief executives were expected to submit on an annual basis a formal draft of a three-to-five-year plan for their own divisions.

R&D

Bombardier's ability to produce and market such a diverse range of products hinged upon a policy of exploiting proven and tested technologies that were acquired through licensing agreements. As Vice President Poitras explained, it was a policy that made a virtue of necessity:

> The risk that has been taken on the various contracts we've bid for has been minimal. It takes years to develop a technology. It takes years to prove the technology. Bombardier can't afford to do that. What we are trying to find is new products just before they reach the market. Then we would be an ideal manufacturer and marketing organization for those products.[22]

The reliance on licensing was particularly heavy in mass transit (see Exhibit 9). For Beaudoin, product reliability was crucial to success in mass transit. He felt that this reliability could be enhanced through the purchase of proven technology:

> Mass transit technology may not be as sophisticated as aerospace, but it has to be very, very reliable. It has to be in operation for at least five years before you know that you have a good product. Technology in mass transit has been developed for many years in Europe and Japan, and it's available.[23]

The recent push into logistic equipment was also dependent upon the use of various licensing agreements with U.S. and European firms. But the company's moves in rail products were based upon working in partnership with other companies. The LRC project had been undertaken as a joint venture with Alcan and Dofasco, in which Bombardier invested more than $30 million.

The only products Bombardier had developed through its own extensive research and development were its original recreational products and industrial equipment. The company's primary research facilities had been established in Valcourt for the development of its early snowmobiles and all-terrain vehicles. They included various kinds of laboratories and several different test tracks and chambers. These facilities had been expanded and renovated in 1979 and continue to be used for the early testing of most of the company's extensive range of products.

---

[22] "Bombardier's Formula for Growth."

[23] "Making the 'A' Train."

Production

Bombardier's diverse production activities are carried out in 3 million square feet of plants and warehouses scattered over Canada, the United States, and in Austria. All of the company's recreational and utility products are manufactured in a large facility in Valcourt where the company started. An assembly line has been designed that is capable of producing several hundred snowmobiles and motorcycles daily. Snowmobiles are manufactured for eight months of the year, from April to November. Facilities have been expanded or adapted for the manufacturing of industrial and logistic equipment, with rates of production that can vary from three to six units per day.

The mass-transit products are primarily constructed at La Pocatiere, in what had formerly been a Moto-Ski plant. The facilities, originally used for the manufacturing of snowmobiles, were converted in 1974 for the construction of subway cars. The complexity of a subway car is several orders of magnitude greater than that of a snowmobile. A subway car has 8,000 parts and 14 kilometers of electric wiring, compared to only 2,000 parts in a snowmobile. The shift to subway cars required considerable retraining of the labor force. It was also costly in terms of physical facilities. The estimated cost of conversion was about $5 million, of which $1 million was provided by a grant from the Canadian government.

The converted facility is now geared toward production of a variety of mass-transit vehicles and contains about 65 workstations. Currently, the plant is capable of producing two to five cars per week based on a single daily eight-hour shift. Bombardier had also recently completed an assembly plant in Barre, Vermont, to handle U.S. orders. Partly assembled transit cars are now shipped from La Pocatiere to this facility, where U.S.-made components are added.

Production of the diesel-electric locomotives and diesel engines is spread out over the old MLW facility in Montreal and the Alco plant in Auburn, New York. However, the MLW facility has not been utilizing its capacity for producing 100 locomotives and 50 diesel engines per year since the decision was made to withdraw from the manufacturing of locomotives.

Sales

Each of the categories of products offered by Bombardier represents a different type of sale and requires its own marketing effort. Most of the company's products, with the exception of its recreational line, are typically sold in bulk orders to industrial or governmental clients.

Mass-transit equipment tends to require the most complex and extensive marketing effort. The average price for mass-transit vehicles is about $1 million per unit. Sales are generated through the company's submission of competitive bids as it vies for each potential order (see Appendix concerning the bidding process). In order to be successful, a bid must be low in price, yet fulfill stringent technical requirements. In many cases, orders for mass-transit equipment are accompanied by allegations that the choice was made on the basis of political and regional favoritism. The Montreal and New York orders were both legally contested by the companies that lost out to Bombardier.

Sales of logistic equipment and diesel products are similarly developed through competitive bidding based upon price, specifications, and performance. Most of the military vehicles offered by Bombardier range in price from $20,000 to $30,000 per unit. Export sales to the military may also depend upon the ability of Bombardier to collaborate with a local firm.

Finally, sales of the company's original lines of recreational products and industrial equipment continue to be separately developed. Its snowmobiles and motorcycles are sold through a network of about 2,000 distributors and dealers throughout North America, as well as in select foreign markets. The list price of snowmobiles typically ranges from $1,500 to $7,000, with a good basic machine selling for about $3,000.

On the other hand, most industrial equipment is marketed directly by the company through its service centers. The various types of all-terrain tracked or wheeled vehicles usually cost between $125,000 and $150,000 per unit. The bulk of sales continue to be made in North America, but the company is concentrating on building sales in overseas markets through its Rotax division in Austria.

Contracts

The sale and delivery of most of Bombardier's product lines, with the exclusion of snowmobiles, is highly dependent on the specific terms as laid out in carefully negotiated contracts. Though contracts tend to be very elaborate, they can not anticipate all contingencies. Disputes tend to arise over technical specifications associated with the design, unforeseen developments that may contribute to escalation of costs, and the rights of the customer to withdraw from the deal. These disputes are costly in the short run, but more importantly they can damage the reputation of the manufacturer in the long run.

Consequently, Beaudoin has frequently emphasized that care must be taken to avoid the problems that have forced other companies to drop out of the mass-transit business. To start with, Bombardier has tried to avoid technical problems with its designs by obtaining licenses on tried and tested technologies. This policy reduces the likelihood of expensive delays and repairs as well as the possibility of the customer moving to cancel a contract in midstream.

Additionally, Bombardier sought to negotiate contracts that stipulate precise conditions under which the customer can terminate a contract. In the event of disputes over quality or performance, the company attempted to avoid costly litigation by including provisions for specific arbitration procedures. The most serious problems were encountered with the early deliveries of subway cars to New York. Various mechanical and electrical problems led to the temporary suspension of production while the cars were tested. It was speculated that failure on these tests could have led to cancellation of the contract.

Finally, all contracts typically include a schedule for prepayments and progress payments to ensure sufficient financing for carrying out the order. Additional protection is provided through the specification of limits on penalties for delay in deliveries as well as through escalator clauses that index the price to the inflation rate. However, as Vice President Poitras pointed out: "There is no protection against cost overruns. That is our risk."[24]

Labor

Most of Bombardier's products are fairly labor intensive because of the company's dependence upon manual assembly lines. When the company was essentially engaged in the production of snowmobiles and all-terrain vehicles at its facilities in Valcourt, the employees were administered by committees that set salary levels based upon the average levels that prevailed in the area. Since then, the majority of the company's employees have become unionized and are covered by as many as 10 agreements.

Furthermore, some of the agreements with labor were concluded only after long strikes that disrupted production in various plants. Bombardier had to deal with its first strike in 1975. The strike occurred at the La Pocatiere plant during the conversion to mass-transit production. It lasted almost five months and resulted in considerable delays in the final delivery of subway cars to the City of Montreal. Recurrent and crippling strikes were also encountered at the MLW plant, which underwent a five-month lockout in 1977 and a six-month strike in 1979.

However, Beaudoin felt that the relationship between management and labor had improved considerably over the past few years. This was due to changes in management personnel within the divisions and the introduction of new working arrangements. At the end of 1979, Bombardier also offered to all of its Quebec employees the opportunity to subscribe to a share purchasing plan. This plan was designed to allow employees to benefit from tax advantages recently introduced by the Quebec government, as well as to participate more directly in the growth of the company.

Top Management

Bombardier shifted its headquarters from Valcourt to Montreal in 1975. The move brought together in one location the chairman and chief executive officer of the company and seven vice presidents responsible for different areas of the company's operations. Except for a brief period, the position of chairman and chief executive officer has been occupied by Laurent Beaudoin. Joseph-Armand's son, André Bombardier, and son-in-law, Jean-Louis Fontaine, are among the most senior of the group of vice presidents.

In 1975 Beaudoin tried to bring in an outsider to help with running the company. Sixty-one-year-old Jean-Claude Hébert was appointed chairman and chief executive officer, with Beaudoin keeping the post of president. Beaudoin stated the reasons behind this move: "We really needed someone on the management end to guide the organization going into diversification."[25] It was under

---

[24] "Bombardier's Formula for Growth."

[25] "Why Bombardier Is Trying Out Mass Transit."

Hébert's direction that Bombardier mounted its aggressive search for possible acquisitions. But the poor performance of MLW subsequent to its acquisition led the family to question Hébert's plans for other major acquisitions. He was subsequently forced out in 1978, with the position returning to Beaudoin.

In 1979 Beaudoin appointed Louis Hollander as the president and chief operating officer of the company. Hollander, who had previously been in charge of recreational and industrial products, remained in this position until the end of 1981. Recently, the position has been filled by Raymond Royer, who had been responsible for the company's mass-transit products.

Financing

In 1986 the capital stock of Bombardier stood at 6.9 million class A and 5.9 million class B shares. The shares represented close to $120 million of equity on the balance sheets of the company (see Exhibit 8). At the same time, long-term debt had dropped to $35 million, most of which was in the form of bonds, notes, and debentures.

Bombardier became a publicly owned organization in 1969. Its initial issue consisted of 2 million class A voting shares, representing about 15 percent of the company's equity. All of the 13 million class B nonvoting shares were kept by Les Enterprises de J. Armand Bombardier, a family-owned holding company. No dividends could be paid on the class B shares unless a dividend of a similar nature had been paid during the same fiscal year on the class A shares. But the class B shares were convertible at any time on a share-for-share basis into class A shares.

During 1976 all outstanding class A and B shares were exchanged for a total of 3.9 million class A shares. Since 1981, newly created class B shares have again been issued to the public. They have less voting rights but entitle their holders to dividends. As of early 1986, Les Enterprises de J. Armand Bombardier still held 71.9 percent of the class A shares, which gave it a 66.2 percent voting interest. Another 3 percent of the class A shares were held by directors, managers, and employees of the company.

DEVELOPING PROSPECTS

In the summer of 1986, Bombardier was taking steps to enter into two new areas of activity. One of these would move the company into aerospace, while the other would lead it into automobiles. Each of these would represent a major shift for the company, the first since its entry into mass transit. However, Laurent Beaudoin believed the company had the financial, technical, and management capability to handle both of these moves.

Aerospace

Bombardier was making a serious bid for Canadair, an aerospace company located in Montreal. Canadair employed more than 4,000 people and had reported a profit of $19.6 million on sales of $430 million in the previous year. However, the company had only recently begun to show profitability, and this had been largely based upon sales of its newly developed Challenger business jet.

The Challenger executive jet has earned a reputation for being spacious, quiet, and fuel efficient. It was conceived and developed by Canadair following the acquisition of the company from General Dynamics by the Canadian government in 1975. But the design of the aircraft had taken longer than anticipated, resulting in development costs in excess of $1 billion. As a result, the company found itself unable to sell enough of these jets to cover its expenses until the government absorbed the development costs.

Although it was now free of its debt, Canadair still has to contend with the inherent uncertainty of the business jet market. The total market for such aircraft is believed to be between 75 and 100 units per year. Canadair has already sold about 140 of its Challenger jets since it was introduced in 1980. But the company has not yet found buyers midway into the year for the 15 aircraft it needs to build this year in order to break even. In fact, there were no outstanding orders for the Challenger business jet on the books of the company.

Apart from the business jet, the only other substantial offering of Canadair was a recent version of the CL-215 water bomber. The CL-215 had been the main drawing card for the company through the 1970s while the Challenger was being developed. The water bomber continues to offer excellent fire-fighting capabilities and can also be adapted to other uses. Although annual production stands at only 10 units, demand for this type of aircraft is expected to pick up.

The recent decision to sell Canadair had been made by the newly elected Conservative government that was determined to privatize many of its business holdings. The book value of the company was estimated to be between $225 million and $250 million. But it is considered to be quite likely that the government would settle for a lower price in exchange for some assurance that the company would remain intact and continue its operations.

Beaudoin was optimistic about his company's chances of winning the bid to acquire Canadair. He also felt that if successful, the acquisition would provide Bombardier with a complementary business with a strong cash flow. At the same time, Bombardier would have to continue to make investments into its business jets and water bombers in the face of increasing competition from other U.S. and European firms. A greater push may also be needed to develop more subcontracting work with other aerospace companies and maintenance work for military aircraft.

Automobiles

Bombardier was also actively exploring the possibility of introducing into the North American market a small car designed to carry two people. The car would use a three-cylinder engine and would offer a maximum speed of about 55 to 65 miles per hour. It would be targeted as a second car that is mainly to be used for city driving.

The company has already concluded an agreement with Daihatsu Motor Company of Japan to obtain the technology that would be used in the design of the car. It was now negotiating a joint venture agreement with the Japanese company under which these cars would be produced. Daihatsu, which is partly owned by Toyota, is the smallest producer of cars in Japan.

The joint venture agreement could first result in the production of a new version of a Daihatsu three-cylinder car that is already being sold in Asia and Europe. Production on these could start as early as late 1987 or early 1988. A new front-wheel-drive version of this car being designed by Bombardier would not be expected before 1991.

The cars would be produced by Bombardier at Valcourt, where the company has spare factory space. The facilities are initially expected to be able to produce about 200,000 cars annually. It was believed that about 350 of Bombardier's snowmobile dealers in Canada and the United States could handle sales and service. The car was expected to retail for about $7,000.

The company was spending about $15 million, most of which was provided by various levels of government, to undertake feasibility studies. Testing of four prototype cars has been going well, leading to speculation that a positive decision is forthcoming. Beaudoin had recently provided his own assessment about the possible move into the production of small cars: "We have the technical experience and the management depth to handle the job."[26] At the same time, it is widely speculated that Bombardier will take the final plunge only if it is able to develop a joint venture to get strong technical and financial backing for the move.

···················

APPENDIX
Bidding Process*

Bids are very expensive to prepare. The cost of preparing a complex bid often reaches six figures. Each component of the order must be analyzed and costed, and labor overhead and tooling costs must also be evaluated. Working capital, maintenance, and warranty costs must all be factored in.

The process is further complicated by the customized nature of the work. Municipal transit authorities tend to retain consultants to define system and vehicle specifications in great detail. There are variations in tunnel construction and gauge that determine the width of the cars. Furthermore, there are differences in electrical voltages on which the different systems run.

The number of cars ordered is usually a key variable in costing as there are economies of scale and learning curve developments that must be correctly calculated. Frequently, however, scale economies are impeded by the tendency of the customers to require a certain amount of parts that have been locally manufactured.

Parts usually make up 50 to 60 percent of the final cost, while direct labor accounts for around 10 percent. There is greater profit potential on repeat orders because tooling and start-up expenses are substantially reduced.

---

[26] "Bombardier Plans Mini-Car, Eyes Canadair," *Globe & Mail*, June 17, 1986.

* Adapted from Tony Hine, McLeod Young Weir Equity Research, 1986.

EXXON CORPORATION, 1986*

Throughout the 20th century, Exxon Corporation ranked as the largest company in the international petroleum industry and as one of the largest corporations in the world. In 1985 Exxon reported revenues of $92.9 billion, net income of $4.9 billion, and total assets of $69.1 billion. These results gave Exxon a worldwide ranking among corporations of all types of number two in sales, number two in after-tax profits, and number one in assets.

Exxon Corporation and its affiliated companies operated in the United States and more than 80 other countries. The company's business interests included exploring for and producing crude oil and natural gas, operating marine and pipeline facilities for transporting both crude and refined products, refining and marketing petroleum-based products, manufacturing petrochemicals, fabricating nuclear fuel, mining coal and other minerals, producing electric motors and electrical equipment, and generating electric power in Hong Kong. Over 70 percent of invested capital and over 85 percent of revenues were tied to Exxon's oil and natural gas activities. Exhibit 1 provides a financial overview.

COMPANY HISTORY AND BACKGROUND

Exxon Corporation is the surviving parent company from the legendary breakup of the Standard Oil Company of New Jersey in 1911, then headed by John D. Rockefeller—the man who dominated the oil industry in its early years and who became a symbol for both the sins and the virtues of capitalism. When the Supreme Court ruled in 1911 that the Rockefeller-controlled Standard Oil of New Jersey constituted a monopoly in restraint of trade, the court-ordered remedy was a breakup; Standard Oil (New Jersey) continued on as the largest of 34 new downsized companies.

In 1960 Standard Oil (New Jersey) consolidated a number of divisions into one U.S. subsidiary, Humble Oil and Refining Company. Humble's trademark, Esso, was one of the best known in the world and was widely used by Standard Oil (New Jersey) in many foreign countries. However, since use of Esso as a trademark in the United States had been ruled by the courts as inappropriate owing to conflicts with other trademarks established during the Rockefeller era, Humble marketed its products under the Esso brand in some areas, under the Enco (from Energy Company) brand in others, and under Humble in Ohio; retail operations were conducted in 35 states. In 1972, frustrated by an inability to use any one of the existing trademarks under which to market and advertise nationwide, Standard Oil (New Jersey) and its domestic operating subsidiary, Humble

---

* Prepared by Professor Arthur A. Thompson, Jr., The University of Alabama, with the research assistance of Victor Gray and Miriam Aiken. Copyright © 1986 by Arthur A. Thompson, Jr.

Exhibit 1 FINANCIAL SUMMARY, EXXON CORPORATION, 1981–85 (dollar figures in millions, except per share amounts)

	1981	1982	1983	1984	1985
Sales and other operating revenue					
Petroleum and natural gas	$102,418	$ 92,570	$ 83,622	$ 85,415	$ 81,399
Chemicals	7,116	6,049	6,392	6,870	6,670
Coal	204	288	272	327	357
Minerals	83	80	115	97	108
Reliance Electric	1,673	1,561	1,397	1,538	1,667
Hong Kong power generation	604	584	566	608	586
Other and eliminations	1,122	927	1,083	1,018	833
Total sales and other operating revenue	113,220	102,059	93,447	95,873	91,620
Earnings from equity interests and other revenue	1,702	1,500	1,287	1,415	1,249
Revenue	$114,922	$103,559	$ 94,734	$ 97,288	$ 92,869
Earnings:					
Petroleum and natural gas					
Exploration and production	$ 4,117	$ 3,431	$ 4,079	$ 4,789	$ 4,937
Refining and marketing	1,132	1,141	1,156	408	872
International marine	29	(76)	(101)	(63)	(65)
Total petroleum and natural gas	5,278	4,496	5,134	5,134	5,744
Chemicals	238	93	270	430	249
Coal	13	23	37	43	39
Minerals	(97)	(95)	(57)	(52)	(21)
Reliance Electric	29	(32)	(33)	11	30
Hong Kong power generation	36	51	71	88	90
Other operations	(78)	14	44	47	(19)
Corporate and financing	(507)	(323)	(497)	(298)	(508)
Earnings before special items	4,912	4,227	4,969	5,403	5,604
Foreign exchange on debt	(32)	166	85	267	(2)
Facilities restructuring	(54)	(207)	(76)	(142)	(187)
Hawkins provision	—	—	—	—	(545)
Net income	$ 4,826	$ 4,186	$ 4,978	$ 5,528	$ 4,870
Net income per share	$ 5.58	$ 4.82	$ 5.78	$ 6.77	$ 6.46
Cash dividends per share	$ 3.00	$ 3.00	$ 3.10	$ 3.35	$ 3.45
Net income to average shareholders' equity (*percent*)	17.8	14.9	17.2	19.0	16.8
Net income to total revenue (*percent*)	4.2	4.0	5.3	5.7	5.2
Working capital	$ 5,500	$ 3,328	$ 3,556	$ 1,974	$ (1,734)
Total additions to property, plant, and equipment	$ 9,003	$ 9,040	$ 7,124	$ 7,842	$ 8,844
Exploration expenses, including dry holes	$ 1,650	$ 1,773	$ 1,408	$ 1,365	$ 1,495
Research and development costs	$ 630	$ 707	$ 692	$ 736	$ 681
Total assets	$ 61,575	$ 62,289	$ 62,963	$ 63,278	$ 69,160
Long-term debt	$ 5,153	$ 4,556	$ 4,669	$ 5,105	$ 4,820
Total debt	$ 8,186	$ 7,303	$ 5,536	$ 6,382	$ 7,909
Shareholders' equity	$ 27,743	$ 28,440	$ 29,443	$ 28,851	$ 29,096
Average number of shares outstanding (*thousands*)	864,926	867,959	861,399	816,169	754,093
Number of shareholders at year-end (*thousands*)	776	865	889	839	785
Wages, salaries, and employee benefits	$ 5,832	$ 5,993	$ 5,849	$ 5,550	$ 5,381
Average number of employees (*thousands*)	180	173	156	150	146

Source: *1985 Annual Report.*

Oil and Refining Company, announced that they would, henceforth, use Exxon as their single primary trademark on a nationwide basis. Subsequently, Standard Oil (New Jersey) became known as Exxon Corporation, and Humble Oil and Refining became known as Exxon Company, U.S.A.

One of the most important strategic decisions in the company's history unfolded in 1960 when Monroe J. Rathbone started a five-year stint as Exxon's CEO. Rathbone believed that the demand for oil, rising faster than new discoveries, would one day convert the presently abundant oil supplies into a scarcity and that the Middle East oil-producing countries would be able to charge much higher prices for their crude. Thus, even though Exxon then had more crude than its refined-products markets could absorb, Rathbone persuaded the company's board to approve major outlays for a search for oil outside the Middle East. Rathbone set up a new subsidiary called Esso Exploration and sent geologists and drilling crews into new areas of the world; Exxon's existing subsidiaries were ordered to begin combing their territories for more oil. In the period 1964–67 Exxon spent nearly $700 million on exploration, mostly in non-OPEC areas. Other major oil companies indicated their amusement at Exxon's move by declining to follow suit on any large scale. Mobil, for instance, with the greatest lack of crude oil reserves of any major U.S. company, spent just $267 million for exploration during the same period. Exxon's decision paid off; as of 1977 Exxon had more proven oil reserves outside the Middle East than any other major company. For his role and foresight in engineering Exxon's move, *Fortune* in 1975 named Monroe R. Rathbone to its Business Hall of Fame—he was one of four living executives so chosen (along with 15 other decreased laureates, one of whom was John D. Rockefeller).

ORGANIZATION AND MANAGEMENT

Exxon first adopted the principle of decentralized management of its operations in the late 1920s. Decentralized approaches were much in evidence in 1986. Generally speaking, strategy formulation, planning, and coordination were functions of Exxon Corporation's senior management and staff. Activities such as drilling wells, running refineries, and marketing products were delegated to local and division managements close to the scene of these activities. Management positions in Exxon's foreign affiliates and subsidiaries were, with few exceptions, staffed by personnel native to the countries where Exxon operated.

Prior to 1966 some 40 subsidiary companies were reporting directly to corporate headquarters in New York. Feeling that this system was becoming unwieldy and inefficient, Exxon reorganized into a smaller number of regional and operating units. The top official in each subunit was given broad responsibility and a sizable staff in an effort to permit quicker response to changing conditions and, further, to reduce the number of people reporting to corporate headquarters. Some subunits had geographic responsibilities for designated parts of the world—the United States, Europe and Africa, Latin America, and the Far East; others had worldwide responsibilities for particular segments of Exxon's business, such as chemicals or research. As of 1986 there were 14 such subunits, each headed by a senior executive: Exxon Company, U.S.A.; Esso Middle East; Exxon Chemical Company; Exxon International Company; Esso Eastern, Inc.; Esso Europe Inc.; Esso Exploration Inc.; Esso Inter-American, Inc.; Exxon Enterprises, Inc.; Exxon Research and Engineering Company; Imperial Oil Limited (70 percent owned by Exxon); Exxon Production Research Company; Reliance Electric Company; and Exxon Minerals Company.

In 1986 the principal link between Exxon and each regional or operating subunit was provided by one of seven senior management officials (either a senior vice president or the corporation president) who were on Exxon's board of directors. The officer-director was designated as the "contact executive" for at least one of the regional or operating subunits. The concept of "contact" responsibilities was, according to Exxon, a significant innovation when introduced in 1943. A contact executive's responsibilities were implicit rather than precisely defined, but the chief role was to provide strategic guidance over the assigned subunits. The contact executive endeavored to stay well informed about the plans of the regional or operating subunits and the problems they faced. On many matters, the contact executive had final review authority; on big issues, recommendations had to go before Exxon's management committee (composed of all seven officer-directors) or the compensation and executive development (COED) committee. From time to time the contact assignments of the officer-directors were rotated so as to provide new viewpoints and broaden their own experience.

In 1986 Exxon's board chairman was Clifton C. Garvin; he had been board chairman since August 1975 and director since 1968. Garvin began his career with Exxon in 1947. A graduate of Virginia Polytechnic Institute, he joined Exxon as a process engineer at Exxon's Baton Rouge refinery and became operating superintendent in 10 years. Later he moved through a series of positions in Exxon Company, U.S.A., gaining experience in other major functions of the oil business. In 1964 he went to New York as executive assistant to Exxon's president. During the three years prior to his election as a director, he headed Exxon Chemical, U.S.A., and Exxon's worldwide chemical organization. Garvin regularly consulted with the corporation's management committee composed of all eight employee directors; he was chairman of this committee and was also chairman of the COED committee, which was primarily concerned with the continuity and quality of Exxon's management. The COED committee directly concerned itself with about 200 senior management positions around the world and indirectly kept an eye on another 400 top management jobs in affiliated companies and subsidiary operations. The COED committee met weekly. Garvin had announced that he planned to retire at the end of 1986.

Exxon's president was Lawrence G. Rawl; he served as vice chairman of both the management committee and the COED committee. Rawl started with Exxon as an engineer in Texas in 1952, holding a variety of supervisory jobs in the southwest United States. Rawl eventually took on U.S. marketing operations and was the number two executive of Exxon's Esso Europe unit. In 1980 Rawl was appointed to the Exxon board; he played a critical role in boosting Exxon's oil production and profits during the 1980s. Rawl was named president in early 1985 and was expected to take over the chairman's position when Garvin retired.

Anthony Sampson, in a book largely critical of the seven biggest international oil companies, said the following about Exxon and its management:

In the middle of Manhattan, in the line of cliffs adjoining the Rockefeller Center, is the headquarters of the most famous and long-lived of them all: the company known in America as Exxon, and elsewhere as Esso, and for most of its hundred years' existence as Standard Oil of New Jersey or simply Standard Oil. It is a company which perhaps more than any other transformed the world in which we live. For much of its life it was automatically associated with the name of Rockefeller and some links still remain. The family still owns two percent of the stock; Nelson Rockefeller once worked for it in Venezuela; and the desk of the founder, John D. Rockefeller I, is still preserved as a showpiece at the top of the building. But Exxon has long ago outgrown the control of a single family.

The tranquil style of Exxon's international headquarters seems to have little in common with the passionate rhetoric of Arab politicians in Algiers. Beside a bubbling fountain and pool on Sixth Avenue, the fluted stone ribs soar up sheer for 53 storeys, and inside the high entrance hall is hung with moons and stars. On the 24th floor is the mechanical brain of the company, where the movements of its vast cargoes are recorded. A row of TV screens are linked with two giant computers and with other terminals in Houston, London, and Tokyo, in a system proudly named LOGICS (Logistics Information and Communications Systems). They record the movement of 500 Exxon ships from 115 loading ports to 270 destinations, carrying 160 different kinds of Exxon oil between 65 countries. . . .

Up on the 51st floor, where the directors are found, the atmosphere is still more rarefied. The visitor enters a high two-story lobby with a balcony looking down on high tapestries; the wide corridors are decorated with Middle East artifacts, persian carpets, palms, or a Coptic engraving. It is padded and silent except for a faint hum of air-conditioning, and the directors' offices are like fastidious drawing rooms, looking down on the vulgar bustle of Sixth Avenue. It all seems appropriate to Exxon's reputation as a "United Nations of Oil."

But in this elegant setting, the directors themselves are something of an anticlimax. They are clearly not diplomats or strategists or statesmen; they are chemical engineers from Texas, preoccupied with what they call "the Exxon incentive." Their route to the top has been through the "Texas pipeline"—up through the technical universities, the refineries, and tank farms. The Exxon Academy, as they call it, is not a university or a business school, but the giant refinery at Baton Rouge, Louisiana. . . . The core of the board was made up of the engineers, enclosed in their own specialized discipline. . . .

Once outside their own territory, their confidence easily evaporates. Confronting their shareholders they seem thoroughly nervous, sitting in a row, their fingers fidgeting and their cheekbones working, as they listen to questions about Exxon's African policy, Exxon's salary policy, Exxon's kidnap policy, Exxon's Middle East policy. They know well enough that their company, while one of the oldest, has also been the most hated.

It is in Texas, not New York, that the Exxon men feel more thoroughly at home; and it is the Exxon skyscraper in Houston, the headquarters of Exxon U.S.A., which seems to house the soul of the company. At the top is the Houston Petroleum Club with two entire storeys making up a single room where the oilmen can lunch off steaks and strawberries every day of the year. They like to show visitors the view of which they are justly proud. The flatlands stretch in every direction, broken only by the jagged man-made objects: the domes and tower-blocks in place of cliffs and hills; the curving freeways instead of rivers; the giant roadsigns instead of trees. The glaring gasoline signs stick up from the desolate landscapes like symbols leading to some distant shrine: Exxon, Texaco, Shell, Gulf, Exxon. The fluid which has wrought all these changes is concealed from the view: around Houston there are only a few little pumps nodding in the fields, a few piles of pipelines to indicate the underground riches. But no one needs reminding: it was all done by oil.[1]

SIZE AND STRUCTURE OF THE PETROLEUM INDUSTRY

The business of supplying crude oil and petroleum products in 1985 was not only economically crucial, but it was also the largest industry in the world. Worldwide sales of crude oil and petroleum products in 1985 approached $1 trillion, and worldwide petroleum consumption averaged over 50 million barrels per day. Billion-dollar oil companies were commonplace, and no nation was without at least one truly large-scale oil company. In 1985, 11 of the 20 largest U.S. industrial corporations were primarily petroleum companies.

The petroleum industry spanned a wide range of geographically separate and technically distant activities relating to getting oil from the ground to the final user. The main stages in the process were (1) finding and producing the crude oil, (2) transporting it to the point of processing, (3) refining it into marketable products, (4) transporting the products to regions of use, and (5) distributing them at retail. However, in the search for oil, producing companies were commonly involved in the production, use, and sales of natural gas; many of the major oil companies were suppliers of natural gas.

In the United States roughly 10,000 companies were involved in oil and gas exploration and production. No one firm accounted for more than 11 percent of oil and gas production. Over 80 percent of total U.S. crude oil output came from Texas, Louisiana, California, Alaska, and Oklahoma. It moved mainly through about 70,000 miles of gathering lines and 85,000 miles of trunk pipelines, as well as on oceangoing tankers, river barges, railroad tank cars, and trucks to some 200 operating refineries, with total 1984 capacity of about 15 million barrels per day. In 1984 the U.S. refining industry operated at about 80 percent of capacity. These refineries were operated by approximately 140 companies; in 1984 the top four companies accounted for under 35 percent of refining capacity. In 1985 over 75 pipeline companies were engaged in transporting crude oil and refined products on an interstate basis; additional companies operated intrastate. The top four pipeline companies accounted for less than 30 percent of total volume moved.

Most petroleum products moved from the refinery to the final customer via one or more intermediate storage facilities. Although residual fuel oil, for example, was delivered to large utility and industrial customers directly from the refinery, most products first went to large terminals, located generally at the outlet of a pipeline or on a river, lake, or coastal port, where they could take barge

---

[1] Anthony Sampson, *The Seven Sisters* (New York: The Viking Press, 1975), pp. 8–10. Quoted with permission.

or tanker delivery. By far most of these terminals were owned by refiners, although independent wholesaler-owned terminals took a substantial portion of the distillate and residual oils. Most gasoline and home heating oils were shipped next to local bulk storage facilities. From area bulk plants, the gasoline was transported to service stations and the heating oil to the storage tanks of homes and commercial establishments. However, in the case of gasoline, it was not uncommon for the marketing departments of the refinery companies to bypass local bulk plants and ship gasoline directly to their own service stations from large area terminals. This development was made possible by the construction of large-volume retail outlets and the use of increasingly efficient truck carriers.

In 1985 there were over 12,000 wholesale distributors and about 120,000 service stations retailers (down from a peak of 226,000 in 1972). Another 100,000 outlets (convenience food stores and car washes) retailed gasoline as a secondary activity. The large oil companies owned less than 10 percent of the retail outlets they supplied; most were owned (or leased) by wholesalers and retail resellers who established their own prices and operating practices.

EXXON'S PETROLEUM AND NATURAL GAS BUSINESS

Prior to the 1960s, the strategic emphasis at Exxon had always been focused on strengthening the company's position as a major, transnational, fully integrated petroleum enterprise. Its operating scope was worldwide. Even though diversification efforts were begun in the 1960s, in 1986 Exxon was predominantly still an oil company (see the revenue and earnings breakdowns in Exhibit 1). The company was a major factor in all phases of the oil business.

Exploration and Production. Exxon's worldwide production of crude oil and natural gas liquids from internally generated sources declined in 1985 to about 1.7 million barrels a day (one barrel = 42 gallons)—down from the 1976 record high of 5.6 million barrels per day and from 4.0 million barrels per day in 1980. This was due to three factors: (1) weak economic conditions in many of the large industrial nations, (2) stagnating demand for petroleum products stemming from the meteoric climb of prices for petroleum products over the past ten years and growing conservation efforts by users, and (3) the expiration of long-term and special agreements with foreign governments for fixed supply amounts. Exxon in 1985 filled much of its needs for crude oil with purchases on the open market. Exxon was struggling to keep its discoveries of new oil and gas deposits abreast of current production rates from its own wells so as to stabilize its net proved reserves position. Exxon's crude oil reserves totaled nearly 7.5 billion barrels worldwide, and its natural gas reserves were about 45 trillion cubic feet.

Exxon drilled more than 2,400 wells in 1985, versus about 2,100 in 1984, 1,500 in 1983, 1,725 in 1978, and 1,550 in 1970. At year-end 1981, Exxon had drilling and exploration rights to some 596 million acres, up from 443 million acres in 1970. In 1985 additional exploration acreage was acquired in 15 countries. The company has increased its worldwide oil and natural gas reserves for four consecutive years—only a select group of oil companies were accumulating new reserves at a rate that more than replaced volumes currently produced.

Exhibit 2 SUMMARY OF EXXON'S EXPLORATION AND PRODUCTION OPERATIONS (millions of dollars)

	1970	1978	1980	1983	1984	1985
Earnings from operations:						
United States	$ 517	$ 1,202	$ 2,131	$ 1,866	$ 2,012	$ 2,111
Foreign	579	1,282	1,869	2,213	2,777	2,826
Total	1,096	2,484	4,000	4,079	4,789	4,937
Average capital employed:						
United States	2,418	5,871	7,306	11,625	11,907	12,312
Foreign	2,374	4,987	5,095	4,724	4,428	4,812
Total	4,792	10,858	12,401	16,349	16,335	17,124
Capital and exploration expenditures:						
United States	368	1,523	2,395	3,564	4,224	4,638
Foreign	370	1,884	2,818	2,521	2,715	2,923
Total	$ 738	$ 3,407	$ 5,213	$ 6,085	$ 6,939	$ 7,561
Research and development costs	$ 18	$ 61	$ 78	$ 151	$ 174	$ 159

Source: *Annual Reports*, 1979, 1981, 1984, 1985.

Exxon's exploration teams were considered superior in selecting sites to drill for oil; in recent years, Exxon had compiled a 20 percent success rate in finding oil and/or gas on new tracts where it has obtained drilling leases—compared to an industry average of 10 percent. Exxon U.S.A.'s senior vice president of exploration indicated there was no real alternative to anteing up and accepting the drilling risks of dry holes: "You have nightmares going into these things, but an exploration man has to learn early that it's better to try and fail than not to try and have nothing."[2] To try to reduce the risk of choosing drill sites, Exxon, like other oil companies, sent out seismographic teams to assess the probability of discovery.

Operating and financial results for Exxon's exploration and production activities are highlighted in Exhibit 2.

Refining and Marketing. Exxon was the world's largest refiner with a capacity of roughly 5 million barrels a day. About 30 percent of Exxon's refining capacity was in the United States, and its domestic capacity advantage over other U.S. companies was much less than its size advantage elsewhere.

Total U.S. refining capacity in 1984 was 15.1 million barrels daily (down from 15.9 million barrels in 1983). Worldwide refining capacity was 74.5 million barrels in 1984 down from 76.4 million barrels in 1983. The declines reflected shutdowns of old inefficient refineries.

At Exxon, as well as at other integrated oil companies, the role of refining and marketing had shifted dramatically during the past decade. Prior to the 1973 Arab oil embargo, refining and marketing assets were considered a support conduit for transforming crude oil into profit-making capability. Most of the profit in the oil business was made at the wellhead, and refining and distribution operations were only marginally profitable. Beginning with the 1973 embargo, however, major oil

[2] Ibid., p. 120.

companies lost their influence over world crude oil prices and supplies; effective control shifted to the OPEC nations. This reduced the need to protect the profitabilty of crude oil production via forward integration into refining and distribution. At the same time, in the United States the oil and gas depletion allowance was phased out, and a windfall profit tax was imposed on the revenues from crude oil production, both of which limited profitability at the wellhead. In those foreign countries where oil companies were able to retain some ownership position in crude oil reserves, taxes imposed by government amounted to 80 percent or more of profits. The upshot was that the major integrated companies like Exxon came to regard refining and marketing investments as "stand alone" assets that were expected to generate returns on capital employed commensurate with alternative investment opportunities.

This "decoupling" of the investment/profitability links between production operations and refining/marketing operations came at a time when refining/marketing activities faced increased worldwide profit pressures. Chief among these were (1) the prospect of no long-range growth in demand for refined petroleum products in industrialized nations, (2) a need to alter refining capabilities to accommodate shifts in the demand mix for refined products and in the patterns of "light" and "heavy" (high-sulfur content) crude oil availability, (3) the possibilities that OPEC countries would acquire existing refinery capacity and integrate forward, and (4) a growing refinery overcapacity.

In the United States the demand for refined products topped out in 1978 at about 19.2 million barrels per day; declines were recorded each of the next six years—down to 16.0 million barrels in 1984; forecasts of U.S. demand to the year 2000 indicated very small amounts of demand growth (see Exhibit 3). The worldwide peak in refined product sales occurred in 1979 with declines registered the following five years. Over the longer term, prospects were for little if any growth in demand in the industrialized free-world nations, but small demand gains were projected to occur in lesser-developed countries. The stagnant demand prospects reflected the sharp run-up in the prices of all petroleum products and the conservation effect of more fuel-efficient automobiles, altered driving habits, greater industrial energy efficiency, shifts of electric utilities from fuel oil to coal and nuclear-powered generation, and growing efforts of homeowners to use less fuel

Exhibit 3 U.S. DEMAND FOR REFINED PETROLEUM PRODUCTS (millions of barrels per day)

	Actual		Projected	
	1980	**1984**	**1990**	**2000**
Total demand	17.0	16.0	16.5	17.0
Gasoline	6.9	6.5	6.2	5.9
Kerosene	1.2	1.0	1.1	1.4
Distillate	3.0	3.0	3.2	3.4
Residual	2.5	1.5	1.7	1.9
Other	3.4	4.0	4.3	4.4

Source: *World Oil.*

oil for space heating. Long-term demand was proving to be much more price elastic than short-term demand.

These trends had greatly affected Exxon's refinery capacity utilization. In 1981 Exxon's refinery utilization averaged about 74 percent in the United States, about 61 percent in foreign countries, and about 65 percent overall—well below the 85–93 percent rates typical of previous decades and the levels needed for maximum efficiency. Exxon reacted by closing its least efficient U.S. refining capacity, and eight refineries in Europe were sold or shut down between 1980 and 1986. In 1985 Exxon's U.S. refineries ran at 80 percent of capacity.

To improve the profitability of its refining and marketing operations. Exxon had undertaken several major cost reduction efforts. The energy efficiency of Exxon refineries had been improved over 25 percent since 1974. Computer automation and job content studies in plants and distribution terminals had been completed. Marginal service station outlets had been eliminated (over 66,000 were closed between 1969 and 1981). Self-service pumps had been installed in most stations. In 1985 the company introduced 120 Exxon Shops to the U.S. motoring public; the shops carried convenience goods, beverages, and automotive items and were entirely self-service outlets staffed only by a cashier. Credit card operations had been tightened, and 4 cents per gallon discounts for customers who paid cash at self-service pumps had been instituted to discourage credit card sales and thereby reduce working capital tied up in financing accounts receivable.

Exhibit 4   SUMMARY OF EXXON'S REFINING AND MARKETING OPERATIONS (millions of dollars)

	1970	1978	1980	1983	1984	1985
Earnings from operations:						
United States	$ 103	$ 294	$ 202	$ 456	$ 161	$ 229
Foreign	187	563	1,702	674	196	643
Total	290	857	1,904	1,130	357	872
Average capital employed:						
United States	2,372	2,741	2,546	2,535	2,380	2,547
Foreign	7,058	5,349	7,541	6,151	5,730	6,297
Total	7,430	8,090	10,087	8,686	8,110	8,844
Capital expenditures:						
United States	315	271	250	363	380	624
Foreign	577	606	947	818	1,003	1,309
Total	892	877	1,197	1,181	1,383	1,933
Research and development costs	33	56	93	113	111	104
	Thousands of barrels a day					
Petroleum product sales:						
United States	1,753	1,736	1,503	1,146	1,149	1,123
Foreign	3,931	3,654	3,450	2,939	3,055	2,959
Total	5,684	5,390	4,953	4,085	4,204	4,082
Refinery crude oil runs:						
United States	989	1,426	1,246	958	1,021	1,054
Foreign	4,281	3,001	2,903	2,308	2,199	1,849
Total	5,270	4,427	4,149	3,266	3,220	2,903

Source: *Annual Reports,* 1979, 1981, 1984, 1985.

Exhibit 4 presents selected statistics for Exxon's refining and marketing operations.

International Marine Transportation.   In recent years a world tanker surplus combined with slumping crude oil production had made a money loser of Exxon's international tanker operations:

	1970	1978	1980	1983	1984	1985
	Millions of dollars					
Earnings (losses) from operations	$112	$ (31)	$ 34	$ (126)	$(117)	$(65)
Average capital employed	581	1,676	1,438	1,031	828	640
Average expenditures	162	48	65	14	5	1
Research and development costs	3	4	5	3	2	2
	Millions of deadweight tons					
Average capacity, owned and chartered						
Owned vessels	8.1	17.3	16.8	13.3	12.0	11.2
Chartered vessels	10.6	8.9	8.6	2.2	1.5	1.5
Total	18.7	26.2	25.4	15.5	13.5	12.7

Responding to the marine division losses during 1985, Exxon sold or scrapped six large crude oil carriers and three smaller vessels, reducing the capacity of fleet tonnage almost 25 percent to 9.7 million tons; these efforts followed on the heels of major fleet reductions between 1981 and 1984.

CHEMICAL OPERATIONS

Exxon's chemical plants were primarily in the United States, Canada, and Europe. Products included plastics and polyethylene, solvents and specialty chemicals, petroleum resins, lubricant additives, agricultural fertilizers, and primary petrochemicals. Revenues totaled $6.7 billion in 1985, and earnings from operations amounted to $249 million. Although its petrochemical business was inherently cyclical, Exxon's management felt bullish on the long-term prospects for its petrochemical operations because of Exxons' strong feedstock position and the company's long-standing experience in managing the technologies involved. Several chemical plants in Europe were sold or closed in 1985 to enhance long-term profit prospects.

A profile of the performance of Exxon's chemical operations is shown in Exhibit 5.

EXXON'S STRATEGIC SHIFT TO BECOME AN ENERGY COMPANY

As far back as the 1960s Exxon management began to sense that oil and gas reserves would be inadequate to meet the world's need for energy. It was with this in mind that Exxon started laying the groundwork for a major strategic shift from being just a petroleum company to becoming an energy company.

Exhibit 5 SUMMARY OF EXXON'S CHEMICAL OPERATIONS (millions of dollars)

	1970	1978	1980	1983	1984	1985
Earnings from operations:						
United States	$ 22	$ 154	$ 129	$ 118	$ 204	$ 123
Foreign	23	114	273	152	226	126
Total	45	268	402	270	430	249
Average capital employed:						
United States	410	1,052	1,480	1,890	1,858	1,767
Foreign	865	1,160	1,331	1,889	1,875	1,862
Total	1,275	2,212	2,811	3,779	3,733	3,627
Capital expenditures:						
United States	47	359	260	207	109	146
Foreign	54	111	155	338	194	187
Total	101	470	415	545	303	333
Research and development costs	31	40	72	105	124	133

Source: *Annual Reports,* 1979, 1980, 1984, 1985.

Exxon's strategic move into nonpetroleum energy sources was motivated by two factors: (1) projections that all types of new and existing energy sources would be needed to meet a growing U.S. and world demand for energy and (2) the conviction that Exxon could meaningfully contribute to meeting these needs in a fashion that served both consumers and shareholders. Top management was convinced that the skills needed to develop these energy sources were similar to those Exxon had acquired in its existing business. A senior executive of Exxon described the desirability of diversifying thusly:

Over many years Exxon has regularly prepared energy supply/demand outlooks for both the United States and the world. In the early 1960s we were projecting that oil and gas demand would continue to grow at about the same rate as the total demand for energy; however, it was not clear just where in the long term these supplies would come from. It appeared to us at that time that domestic production of both oil and gas could peak during the 1970s. We were also aware that there were very substantial reserves of oil and gas located overseas; however, like others, we were becoming increasingly concerned over the national security aspects of increased imports. Thus, we concluded at this early date that there could be substantial future needs for synthetic oil and gas. It also appeared that since coal reserves are so plentiful in this country, a high percentage of the synthetic fuels would be made from coal. . . .

Another important conclusion reached by our appraisals during this period was that use of electricity was going to grow about twice as fast as the demand for total energy. The high projected growth rate for electricity led to our interest in uranium. Looking ahead it appeared to us that nuclear power would play a significant and increasingly important role in meeting the electric utility demand growth. . . .

Another important question which had to be answered before we made a decision to enter either the coal or uranium business was the availability of resources. . . . Our studies indicated that of this amount of potential reserves, approximately 65 percent were not owned or under lease by any company then producing coal. . . .

In the case of uranium, the reserves situation was quite different. Because uranium is difficult to find, it has a very high discovery value. This resource had been much more actively sought after than coal, and all known reserves were controlled by companies which were already active in the business. We believed, however, that the company's accumulated oil and gas exploration skills would offer a good start toward discovering new reserves . . . most of the known uranium deposits in the United States occur in sedimentary rocks. . . . Since oil and gas occur in a similar environment, we had a great deal of geological expertise which could be applied to uranium exploration. Also, Exxon U.S.A. had an extensive library of geological and geophysical information that had not yet been examined with the objective of locating uranium deposits. Many of the areas of the United States containing known or potential uranium deposits had been explored in the course of our oil and gas exploration efforts. It seemed possible that rock samples and detailed geological information could be reexamined for guides to locating uranium deposits. In addition, the company held mineral leases which covered not only oil and gas but also other minerals, including uranium. For all these reasons, we believed we could contribute to uranium discovery.

In addition to our exploration capabilities, we had other strengths which could be effectively used in establishing a position in the nuclear fuel and coal businesses. For example, we had developed over the years considerable expertise in processing hydrocarbons in our refineries. We believed that much of the research and development work we had done in refining would prove useful in developing processes for converting coal to gas or liquids.

It was determined at an early date that, to be successful, the coal and nuclear fuel business would require sizable amounts of front-end capital. Another important factor was that our company had considerable experience in the area of high-risk, capital-intensive, long-lead ventures. In short, we concluded that the needs to be met in these energy fuel areas were compatible with the capabilities of our company.[3]

Exxon's corporate strategy became one of using a sizable and growing fraction of the company's cash flow from oil and gas operations to diversify into other energy endeavors and gradually lessen the firm's total dependence on its petroleum-related operations. The strategy was to be implemented over a 10- to 20-year period with heavy investments in other energy sources coming during the 1980s; the strategic objective was to transform Exxon into a well-diversified, full-line energy supplier by sometime in the 1990s. Generally speaking the strategy called (1) for starting up the new energy activities internally rather than via acquisition so as to avoid any antitrust problems or adverse public reaction associated with acquiring existing companies and (2) for energy diversification to be financed by investing an increasing percentage of Exxon's $8 to $10 billion cash flows in developing new energy businesses. Meanwhile, in the near term, the bulk of Exxon's capital expenditures would be concentrated in protecting the company's long-term position as a leader in the worldwide petroleum industry.

---

[3] Testimony before Senate Committee on Interior and Insular Affairs, December 6, 1973.

EXXON'S ENTRY INTO COAL

Exxon's studies revealed that the economically recoverable domestic coal reserves in the United States were in the range of 200 billion tons. When compared to current annual coal production of about half a billion tons, these reserves represented more than a 400-year supply. Since coal was plentiful, it was expected to be a raw material for production of synthetic fuels. Synthetics were believed to be a likely future raw material for Exxon's refineries and chemical plants or to be substitutable as retail products.

Exxon's coal activities became the responsibility of a subsidiary, The Carter Oil Company. The purchase of undeveloped coal reserves began in 1965; bituminous coal reserves were purchased in Illinois, West Virginia, and Wyoming, and lignite reserves were obtained in Arkansas, Montana, North Dakota, and Texas. Coal marketing activities began in 1967. Initially coal from the Illinois reserves offered the best sales prospects because of its proximity to midwestern electric utilities—power companies with coal-fired generating plants used 80 percent of all the coal consumed in the United States (an average-sized coal-fired plant used 1 to 2 million tons of coal per year). In 1968 a sales contract was negotiated with Commonwealth Edison, a large electric utility based in Chicago, and Monterey Coal Company, a Carter subsidiary, was formed and began development of its first mine in southern Illinois; production commenced in mid-1970. The mine employed about 500 people, had a maximum capacity of about 3 million tons of coal per year, and was one of the largest and most modern underground mines in the country. A second mine was opened in 1977 to supply coal to Public Service Company of Indiana; its capacity was 3.6 million tons per year.

The Carter Mining Company, another subsidiary of the Carter Oil Company, developed Exxon's coal reserves in the West. By 1982 two large surface mines

Exhibit 6 SUMMARY OF EXXON'S COAL MINING AND DEVELOPMENT OPERATIONS (millions of dollars)

	1970	1978	1980	1983	1984	1985
Earnings from operations, after tax:						
Operating mines	$—	$ 42	$ 22	$ 60	$ 65	$ 59
New business and mine development costs	(1)	(22)	(19)	(23)	(22)	(20)
Total	(1)	(20)	3	37	43	39
Research and development costs	—	4	2	7	8	3
Average capital employed	24	271	358	792	1,057	1,333
Capital and exploration expenditures	13	87	52	336	397	367
			Millions of short tons			
Recoverable reserves	7,000	9,500	10,500	10,566	11,070	11,040
Production	.3	5.2	11.4	20.5	25.1	28.9
Design capacity						
Existing operations	3.0	26.6	36.0	37.9	37.9	37.9
Under construction	—	1.0	9.3	8.3	8.3	9.1
Mines						
In operation	1	4	4	5	5	5
Under construction	—	1	2	1	1	1

Sources: *Annual Reports,* 1978, 1980, 1984, 1985.

were in operation in Wyoming's coal-rich Powder River Basin. Outside the United States Exxon had coal mining properties in operation or under development in Columbia, Canada, and Australia; in Columbia, Exxon was one of the partners in a $3 billion project to construct and operate a coal mine, railroad, and port for coal exporting. The company's coal investments outside the United States were part of an ongoing strategy to establish Exxon as one of the major players in the global coal market.

As of 1985, Exxon had become the fifth-largest coal producer in the United States. Production at the company's U.S. mines was expected to be up in 1986 by as much as 20 percent over 1985 levels. The company's two mines in the Powder River Basin had low production costs—under $5 per ton on average—and were generating operating profits of between $2 and $3 per ton on the 20 million tons being produced at these two sites. Over the longer term Exxon had the potential to produce up to 48 million tons per year at its two Wyoming mines. The company had no plans to expand its U.S. production capacity of coal any further, believing the additional output capabilities in Wyoming were ample. The company's main strategic focus in coal was to obtain additional coal mining properties outside the United States and build up its capability to compete worldwide. Exhibit 6 presents recent statistics on Exxon's coal operations.

EXXON'S ENTRY INTO NUCLEAR ENERGY

As far back as the mid-1960s, Exxon's analysis of the energy situation indicated that use of electricity was to grow about twice as fast as the demand for total energy; Exxon believed that nuclear power would supply as much as 30 percent of the U.S. electric energy supply by the 1990s—an outcome that would greatly increase uranium demand and make diversification into uranium mining and nuclear fuels a profitable business opportunity.

As Exxon saw it, the nuclear fuel business consisted of several distinct activities—uranium exploration, mining, and milling; uranium enrichment; fabrication of enriched uranium into nuclear fuel assemblies; chemical reprocessing of the spent fuel assemblies to recover uranium and plutonium for recycling into the fuel cycle, thus reducing requirements for new uranium supply and enrichment services; and ultimate safe storage and disposal of nuclear wastes. Exxon elected to enter only the first three of these segments.

Exploration, Mining, and Milling.   Exxon initiated its uranium exploration program in the United States in 1966. By 1977 the company had made two uranium discoveries that had been brought into production and two others that were in varying stages of evaluation. Exxon's petroleum activities played a role in two of the four discoveries: one discovery was located on a lease originally obtained as a petroleum prospect and another resulted, in part, from information gained during geophysical exploration for hydrocarbons. Exxon estimated that in 1977 it had about 5 percent of the uranium reserves in the United States. The reserves that had been assessed as commercially viable were already committed under contract to the utility industry.

Nuclear Fuel Fabrication.   During the 1970s Exxon entered into uranium marketing and into the design, fabrication, and sale of nuclear fuel assemblies to electric utilities with nuclear-generating plants. The company also began to provide a range of fuel management and engineering services to electric utility firms. Responsibility for these activities was assigned to a newly created subsidiary, Exxon Nuclear, Inc. Exxon Nuclear competed only in the market segment for refueling nuclear reactors. Nuclear reactors were refueled every 12 to 18 months during their 30- to 40-year life. Exxon Nuclear's primary rivals in the replacement fuel market were Westinghouse, General Electric, Combustion Engineering, Inc., and Babcock & Wilcox Co. Exxon Nuclear was the only fuel fabricator not engaged in selling nuclear reactors and supplied about 6 percent of the domestic fuel fabrication market.

Even though Exxon's nuclear operation lost money every year during the 1970s, Exxon continued to be optimistic about the outlook for its budding nuclear fuels business because of continued construction of nuclear plants all over the world. Over 270 nuclear plants were either in operation or under construction at various sites worldwide. However, by early 1982, the outlook for nuclear fuel was reversed. Although Exxon Nuclear had signed contracts with seven utilities for the fabrication of nuclear fuel through 1990, reduced demand projections for nuclear fuel (owing to numerous cancellations in nuclear plant construction and stretchouts in the construction of others) had caused management to begin planning in 1983 for shutdowns of Exxon Nuclear's U.S. mining operations. Moreover, Exxon's uranium exploration had been stopped, developmental engineering work at one mineable deposit was deferred, and a joint venture to develop techniques for separating uranium isotopes with laser beams was ended. The company halted its research activities in nuclear enrichment and reprocessing because of uncertainties in the outlook for profitable investment opportunities.

Exhibit 7 SUMMARY OF EXXON'S URANIUM MINING AND NUCLEAR FUEL FABRICATION ACTIVITIES (millions of dollars)

	1970	1978	1980	1981	1982	1983	1984	1985
(Losses) from operations, after tax:								
Operating results	$(3)	$(33)	$(18)	$(41)	NA	NA	NA	NA
Exploration costs	(1)	(18)	(14)	(9)	NA	NA	NA	NA
Total	(4)	(51)	(32)	(50)	$(14)	$23	$20	$(19)
Research and development costs	1	25	17	14	NA	NA	NA	NA
Average capital employed	7	201	229	203	NA	NA	NA	NA
Capital and exploration expenditures	10	74	72	42	NA	NA	NA	NA
Revenue	1	142	183	273	NA	NA	NA	NA
				Millions of pounds				
Production of uranium concentrates	—	3.3	3.6	3.1	.8	1.4	.4	0
Mines:								
In operation	—	3	3	3	1	1	—	—
Under development	1	—	—	—	—	—	—	—

NA = not available.
Source: *Annual Reports,* 1979, 1980, 1983, 1984, 1985.

In mid-1984 the Wyoming uranium mine was closed due to low demand and depressed prices, terminating Exxon's uranium mining operations. In the meantime, both General Electric and Westinghouse had moved to divest their nuclear fuel businesses. So far Exxon had decided to remain in the nuclear fuel fabrication business; since 1969 Exxon Nuclear had provided fuel for more than 40 reactors in the United States, Europe, and the Far East. In the United States in 1985 there were 99 nuclear reactors in operation, and 32 more were under construction; outside the United States, there were an additional 244 nuclear units in operation and another 137 under construction. In 1985 Exxon's shipments of nuclear fuel assemblies were up 22 percent.

Exhibit 7 summarizes the recent operating results of Exxon's ventures into uranium mining and nuclear fuel fabrication.

EXXON'S OTHER DIVERSIFICATION EFFORTS IN ENERGY

Exxon's diversification into other energy areas was motivated by some of the same factors that motivated its diversification into coal and nuclear fuel. As late as 1977, Exxon's total expenditures on these other diversification efforts were small relative to coal and nuclear fuel expenditures. The company's efforts were designed to learn about emerging technologies, to contribute to their development, and to position the company so a competitive commercial contribution could be initiated when and if market demand led to profit opportunities that appeared to be commensurate with the risks involved.

Oil Shale. Oil shale from deposits in Colorado, Utah, and Wyoming represented a potential source of supplemental liquid and gaseous fuels many times that of the proved domestic reserves of crude petroleum. While considerable shale lands were held by oil companies, the vast majority—about 80 percent—of potential reserves were federally controlled.

Exxon's oil shale activities were relatively limited because of the high-cost economics and because of federal control of most oil shale lands. During the early 1960s Exxon acquired a number of small tracts of patented land and mining claims in the oil shale area of Colorado. These holdings, however, were widely scattered and would have to be consolidated to form mineable blocks. Exxon's expenditures in oil shale totaled more than $16 million as of 1977. Of this, $8.8 million went to acquire oil shale reserves in the early 1960s, $4.9 million was spent on research, and $2.8 million on core drilling, administrative expenses, and the like.

During the late 1970s Exxon became a 60 percent partner in the Colony oil shale project in northwestern Colorado. The project (scheduled to begin producing in 1986 with an ultimate production target of 47,000 barrels a day of upgraded synthetic oil) was halted in 1983 when a growing worldwide surplus of crude oil and declines in crude oil prices combined to make the production of synthetic fuel uneconomic; in 1983 Exxon wrote off losses of $106 million on the Colony project. An Australian oil shale project, in which Exxon was a joint venture partner, was halted for reappraisal in 1982.

Solar.   Exxon started investigating commercial uses of solar energy in 1970 when a research program was initiated to develop advanced low-cost photovoltaic devices. Throughout the 1970s Exxon and other companies worked at developing applications for photovoltaic devices for use in microwave transmitters and ocean buoys. In 1979 Exxon's Solar Power Corp. recorded a 33 percent increase in unit sales of its solar photovoltaic products. It also obtained government contracts for several major demonstration projects in amounts sufficient to assure that 1980 sales would more than double the 1979 total. In the mid-1980s, Exxon's efforts in solar energy were terminated, partly because the paths of solar technology that Exxon was pursuing were found to be less promising than those under development elsewhere; the solar activities were never profitable.

Batteries and Fuel Cells.   Recognizing the increasing electrification of energy and the need for efficiently storing solar-generated electricity, Exxon funded research in electrochemistry during the 1970s. Fuel cells (devices that convert special fuels such as hydrogen to electricity) had been under study in Exxon Research and Engineering since 1960. In 1970 Exxon Enterprises entered a joint development effort with a French electrical equipment manufacturer to develop a more efficient power supply for electric vehicles and to replace generators driven by engines or gas turbines. Program costs through 1975 exceeded $15 million, but technical progress as of 1985 had not met expectations. Fuel cell technology had progressed to the point in 1986 where many electric utilities were engaged in constructing and operating small-scale pilot projects utilizing fuel cell technology.

A battery development program was initiated at Exxon in 1972 based on concepts developed by Exxon Research and Engineering Company. Batteries with increased energy densities were viewed as being useful as storage devices to help utilities meet peak electricity demands and as potential power sources for electric vehicles. Company experts felt the technological challenge was to develop new batteries that would store from two to five times more energy per unit weight than conventional batteries and be rechargeable hundreds of times without deterioration. In 1978, Exxon's Advanced Battery Division began selling a titanium disulfide button battery for uses in watches, calculators, and similar products. As of 1986, however, Exxon had not become a major factor in pioneering significant breakthroughs in either batteries or fuel cells.

Laser Fusion.   Exxon Research and Engineering Company was one of the sponsors of a program at the University of Rochester begun in 1972 to study the feasibility of laser-ignited fusion of light atoms for the economical generation of power. Out of an estimated program cost of $5.8 million through August 1975, Exxon Research and Engineering Company had contributed about $917,000. This included the cost of Exxon scientists on direct loan to the university. In 1986 Exxon's laser fusion efforts were still in the long-range research and product development stage; the bulk of Exxon's activities were in monitoring results elsewhere.

HONG KONG POWER GENERATION

Exxon's biggest and most profitable nonoil energy venture was launched during the late 1970s and 1980s when Exxon became a 60 pecent partner in a $3 billion joint venture with China Light and Power Co. to build and operate two large multiunit coal-fired electric power generation plants in Hong Kong. In 1986, five out of the eight generating units were operational, and construction was continuing on three 677-megawatt units. All of the facilities were managed and operated by China Light and Power. Eight percent of China Light and Power's total sales of electricity were to the People's Republic of China. Operating statistics for Exxon's Hong Kong venture are summarized below:

	Millions of dollars				
	1981	**1982**	**1983**	**1984**	**1985**
Revenues	$604	$584	$566	$608	$ 586
Operating earnings	36	51	71	88	90
Average capital employed				839	1,002
Capital expenditures				328	346

MINERALS MINING AND DEVELOPMENT

For about 10 years Exxon participated in ventures to develop and operate several minerals projects. In 1986 these projects involved two copper mines in Chile, a gold mine in Australia, and a zinc/copper mine. The copper mines in Chile made their first profit from operations in 1985 after incurring losses of $500 million during the past decade. The gold mine in Australia also had a small profit for the year on production of about 35,000 ounces; mining began at midyear. Exxon was a 50 percent owner and was the operator of the gold mine. A profile of recent operating results for the Exxon Minerals division is shown in Exhibit 8.

EXXON'S ACQUISITION OF RELIANCE ELECTRIC COMPANY

During 1979 Exxon acquired 100 percent ownership of the Reliance Electric Company of Cleveland, Ohio, at a cost of $1.2 billion. With 31,000 employees and principal operations or subsidiaries in 16 states and 14 foreign countries, Reliance's primary domestic operating organizations were a rotating machinery group that made electric motors; a drives and systems group that made motor controls; a mechanical group that made mechanical power products and components; a weighing and controls group that was composed primarily of the Toledo Scale subsidiary; a telecommunications group, primarily a supplier to the telephone industry; and Federal Pacific Electric, a subsidiary that manufactured and marketed electric power distribution equipment.

Exxon's principal purpose in making the acquisition was to obtain the means for rapid development and marketing of a new energy-saving technology called

Exhibit 8   OPERATING RESULTS OF EXXON MINERALS DIVISION, 1982–85 (millions of dollars)

	1982	1983	1984	1985
Revenues	$ 80	$ 115	$ 97	$ 108
Earnings (losses):				
Operating results	(67)	(24)	(16)	1
Mine predevelopment & development costs	(23)	(10)	(17)	(9)
Exploration costs	(24)	(23)	(19)	(13)
Total earnings (losses)	$(114)	$(57)	$(52)	$(21)
Average capital employed	$325	$338	$352	$359
Capital and exploration expenditures	93	59	71	82
Research & development costs	7	5	4	2
	Thousands of metric tons			
Recoverable reserves with contained metal:				
Copper	12,716	12,530	12,819	12,752
Zinc	4,454	4,212	4,212	4,088
Lead	366	353	353	388
Molybdenum	231	212	214	213
Gold (thousands of troy ounces)			354	330
Production:				
Copper			67	77
Gold (thousands of troy ounces)			—	18

alternating current synthesis (ACS). The new technology, which grew out of Exxon's research efforts on an electric car, was thought to have the potential for cutting the energy required by a standard industrial electric motor as much as 50 percent (the equivalent of 1 million barrels of crude oil a day)—there were an estimated 20 million electric motors in industrial use. Exxon felt it needed to acquire a well-established electrical equipment manufacturer to manufacture and market the ACS device with a high probability of success. Reliance Electric in 1978 had sales of $966 million and profits of $65 million; about 12 percent of its sales were in electric motors.

Exxon was also interested in Reliance Electric because of Exxon's high-priority research into a new power system for automobiles. In 1979 Exxon had reached the prototype stage in its efforts and had come up with a hybrid car powered by both a battery-driven motor and a small gasoline engine. The electric motor, equipped with the new ACS device, provided the power for acceleration and steep grades; the gasoline engine took over on level stretches and served to recharge the batteries. Exxon felt the new system would be very fuel efficient even on larger cars.

The Reliance Electric acquisition did not produce spectacular results for Exxon. Shortly after Exxon made the acquisition, antitrust violations surfaced in Reliance Electric's Federal Pacific Division and settlement damages ran into the millions. More importantly, development work on the ACS project hit major snags and it was determined that the concept would not be cost effective. An alternative concept was explored, but did not offer a significant competitive advantage over existing products. In August 1981 the whole ACS project was canceled. In 1985 the Federal Pacific unit of Reliance was sold. Reliance's revenues in 1985 were $1.67 billion, up from $1.54 billion in 1984; several new products were introduced. A profile of Reliance's performance since its acquisition is shown below:

	Millions of dollars					
	1980	**1981**	**1982**	**1983**	**1984**	**1985**
Revenues	$1,595	$1,673	$1,561	$1,397	$1,538	$1,667
Operating results	1	39	(41)	(51)	15	NA
Business development costs	(7)	(8)	(9)	(7)	(4)	NA
Total operating earnings (loss)	(6)	31	(50)	(58)	11	30
Research and development costs	29	34	36	30	25	40
Average capital employed	1,586	1,566	1,451	1,307	1,230	1,085
Capital expenditures	83	102	98	56	51	49

NA = not available.
Reliance took $60 million of write-offs in 1984.

EXXON ENTERPRISES

A subsidiary, Exxon Enterprises, was started in the early 1970s. Its role was to develop nonenergy options for Exxon's future, mainly in case Exxon's diversification into other energy sources did not prove to be as successful as anticipated and also to take up slack from the eventual decline of the oil business. Unlike other oil companies such as Mobil and Atlantic Richfield that chose to diversify by acquiring well-established companies, Exxon opted for buying ownership interests in small entrepreneurial companies that were just getting started and appeared to have products capable of achieving $100 million in sales. The idea was to grow up with a new industry as opposed to entering an established industry.

By 1981 Exxon Enterprises had invested over $800 million in some two dozen new ventures. Only two involved the energy industry—Solar Power and Daystar, both of which made equipment for collecting solar energy and both of which were divested in 1981–82 because they were no longer felt to be attractive investments. Scan-Tron sold scholastic tests that were automatically graded by its own machine; Environmental Data produced instruments for measuring air pollution; Qyx marketed computer-controlled office typewriters; Graftek made graphite shafts for golf clubs and fishing rods; Delphi had developed a way to store voice messages in a computer; Zilog manufactured microprocessors to transmit and process data; Qume made high-speed printers; Vydec produced word-processing display terminals and text-editing systems; and Periphonics made switching computers. Other companies that were a part of Exxon Enterprises included Amtek, Xentex, Qwip, Micro-Bit Corporation, Magnex Corp., Intecom, and Optical Information Systems.

In 1980 Exxon Enterprises consolidated its several ventures in the office equipment and office systems field. Fifteen of the small "startup" companies were molded into a new unit called Exxon Information Systems; the combined sales of these companies totaled $200 million in 1979 and nearly all were experiencing rapid growth (though none were profitable). A drive was also launched to recruit senior executives away from other information processing companies—

IBM and Xerox in particular. A senior vice president of Exxon Enterprises said, "We intend to be *the* systems supplier to the office market." The strategy was to become a major factor in advanced office systems equipment within three to five years using a "supermarket approach"—offering customers a wide variety of products (typewriters, word processors, fast printers, electronic files, voice-input devices, message units, and so on) with the potential of computer-controlled coordination. Most industry observers predicted that Exxon would try to challenge IBM and Xerox head-on in the office automation market, which, by the end of the 1980s, was projected to be a $150 to $200 billion industry.

Exxon indicated that revenues would probably have to reach $1 billion before the Exxon Information Systems unit became profitable. Management stated that Exxon was prepared to be patient in integrating the 15 companies into a single systems company and in "growing" the unit into a profitable and high competitive market position. However, the prospects for making EIS profitable got gloomier between 1980 and 1984. By 1984 Exxon had invested more than $600 million in the office systems units, but losses continued to mount—the cumulative total exceeded $250 million. In early 1985 the foreign operations of the Office Systems Division were sold to Italy's Olivetti and the U.S. operations were sold to Harris Corporation's Lanier Business Products unit; the sales price was undisclosed, but Exxon did not come close to recovering its $600 million investment. The only company of significance from the original group of Exxon Enterprises companies still owned by Exxon in 1985 was Zilog. Several new companies had recently been added to Exxon Enterprise's business portfolio; the biggest of these was Gilbarco.

MAJOR NEW DEVELOPMENTS: 1981-86

Between 1981 and 1986 conditions in the worldwide oil and gas market swung sharply from shortage to surplus. Worldwide crude oil supplies were plentiful as end-use demand fell well short of earlier projections. Crude oil prices softened slowly during 1982–84, began a slide from the $34 to $38 range to the $25 to $30 range in 1985, and crashed temporarily to the $10 to $14 per barrel range in early 1986. In 1980–81 it had been widely predicted that crude oil prices would reach at least $50 per barrel by 1985 and perhaps $70 to $100 per barrel by 1990.

Efforts to conserve all types of petroleum products, brought on by the sharp runup of prices in the 1974–80 period and by expectations of further sharp increases to come, were the driving forces in the shift from shortages to surplus conditions. Energy-saving technology of all types was increasingly available and, in 1986, automobiles were delivering about double the miles per gallon of the early 1970s. Conditional upon developments in energy-saving technology, on energy prices, and on economic growth rates, it seemed probable that worldwide demand for crude oil in 1990 would not be substantially higher than the 1979 peak of 63 million barrels per day. Supplies of natural gas had also shifted from short to abundant; prices were declining and a surplus of natural gas was expected at least through 1988.

The jolt to enterprises tied to the oil and gas business as the sellers' market turned into a buyers' market was far reaching. The belief that oil and gas prices were destined to rise indefinitely and that investing in drilling and exploration for oil and natural gas were certain payoff propositions had prompted a rush in the late 1970s and early 1980s to invest in oil and gas exploration by all kinds of small companies as well as the major oil companies like Exxon. Banks were willing to finance speculative drilling projects and many independent operators borrowed heavily. Multimillion dollar limited partnerships were formed to drill for new supplies. Du Pont acquired Conoco Oil, and U.S. Steel bought Marathon Oil (both multibillion-dollar transactions) because of the lucrative long-term-profit prospects in oil. But in 1982 when the glut became highly visible and several OPEC countries turned to price cuts to help them maintain production volumes, the near-term outlook for companies dependent on rising oil prices became desperate. Many oil companies began major restructuring to avoid possible takeover attempts and there were several buy-outs among the oil giants: Occidental Petroleum acquired Cities Service; Texaco bought Getty Oil; Chevron acquired the Gulf Oil Corporation; and Mobil acquired Superior Oil. Capital investments in drilling, coal-based synthetic fuels, and oil shale were cut back drastically. Drilling activity fell off sharply. Financing dried up for the programs of many small independent operators. Long-term contracts to supply oil and natural gas, which buyers had rushed to sign in the shortage era, became unattractive. The budding synthetic fuel business virtually collapsed. Many coal-based synthetic fuels projects, always looked upon as marginally viable and longer range than oil shale, were canceled or downsized. The bulk of the major oil shale projects in the United States were slowed, reduced in size, or halted; two multibillion-dollar Canadian projects were canceled. A $40 billion pipeline to transport Alaskan North Slope gas to the lower 48 states was put on hold. Most oil company exploration and production programs were tailored to maximize cash generation rather than to find reserves that might be recoverable at a profit later if prices rose enough.

Long term, oil's share of total energy use was still expected to drop from 53 percent in 1980 to 40 percent by the year 2000; natural gas was expected to hold onto its roughly 18 percent share of the energy market. Coal, synthetic fuels, nuclear energy, and solar energy were expected to fill the gap. However, the potential for coal, oil shale, tar sands, coal liquefaction, and coal gasification really depended on (1) how much new oil and natural gas was discovered, (2) the extent to which energy-saving technologies were developed to permit conventional oil and gas to stretch further, (3) how much of the total energy demand would be supplied by nuclear power plants (the accident at Three Mile Island in the United States and the disaster at Chernobyl in Russia raised major safety questions), and (4) the speed with which developments in solar energy technology made solar power a cost effective and almost infinite energy source. Coal was coming under closer environmental scrutiny, and there was now a consensus that the use of high-sulfur coal contributed to "acid rain." Tougher, more costly pollution regulations concerning coal use were a virtual certainty before 1990.

Exxon's chairman, Clifton Garvin, reflected on both the successes of 1985 and uncertainty about the future.[4]

---

[4] *1985 Annual Report.*

That we were able to do as well as we did in 1985 is attributable to strategies set in motion some time ago. A major emphasis in our planning over the past several years has been to prepare for a more competitive future. We have done this in a variety of ways, all directed toward making Exxon a more productive organization. In refining and marketing, for instance, we have systematically phased out less efficient capacity when it became apparent that it could no longer compete. Current refining capacity, as a result, is down about a quarter from its 1981 level. At the same time, we have upgraded to higher levels of efficiency and productivity those facilities that we have retained. Average sales volume in Exxon service stations is an example. Over the same four-year period this has increased some 30 percent. Emphasis on higher-value products and greater selectivity in geographical market participation have been other elements in our downstream strategy.

In exploration and production our goal has been twofold: to develop and maximize recovery from existing oil and gas fields (about two thirds of our producing investments have gone for this purpose) and to strengthen our resource based through cost-effective additions to reserves. In 1985 we drilled a record number of development wells and the largest number of exploration wells in the last quarter of a century. The new discoveries and extensions to existing fields that resulted, along with purchases and revised recovery estimates, more than replaced volumes produced. For the fourth year running we increased our reserve base.

All in all, then, it was a good year for Exxon. But as we all know much has happened since the year ended. Early in 1986 spot crude oil prices experienced their most drastic drop in the modern history of the oil industry. How far this may go, how permanent it may be, and all that it implies for the future remains to be seen. But that there will be far reaching consequences for our industry seems certain. As a result, we are having to rethink our entire strategy. Exploration ventures, capital investments, the lines of business that we are in—all must be reexamined to make sure that they continue to make sense in a radically new environment.

In April 1986 Exxon offered 40,000 employees the opinion to retire early or resign with compensation, citing the poor outlook for the oil industry due to recent drastic declines in oil prices. The company planned a major reorganization with staff reductions extending to all levels of the corporations. Some divisions faced a 30 to 50 percent reduction in staff, as the company sought a method of coping with $15 per barrel oil.

The company was using portions of its $11 billion annual cash flow to (1) repurchase shares of its stock (a 125 million-share stock buyback campaign had helped boost earnings per share and keep Exxons' stock price in the $50 to $65 dollar range), (2) make small acquisitions of distressed U.S. oil properties (about $600 million had been spent since early 1984 to acquire at least 100 million barrels of oil reserves and an undisclosed amount of natural gas), (3) search for new oil reserves in altogether new fields (30 percent of exploration expenditures) and in fields where oil had already been discovered (70 percent of exploration expenditures), and (4) fund the expansion efforts of existing operations. Analysts estimated that Exxon could take on an additional $4 to $5 billion in long-term debt without jeopardizing its AAA bond ratings.

WALSH PETROLEUM*

John Walsh sighed as he looked again at the financial statements his accountant had delivered that morning (see Exhibits 1 and 2). When John's father died two years ago, his accountant had advised against selling the business. "It's a good business, John," he said, "and I think you could do a lot to improve it."

While Walsh Petroleum, Inc., had increased profits in 1985, John still considered them unacceptably low. Company sales had declined for the third straight year, and, while John realized that other oil distributors faced the same problems, he had to wonder what type of future he could expect if he stayed with the family business. Now 31 years ago and just married, maybe he should consider selling the business and starting another career before he got too old.

COMPANY HISTORY

Walsh Petroleum was founded in 1957 by John's mother and father as commission agents in the oil business. By 1976 the senior Walsh had converted the company to a conventional oil distributorship. Both the family and the company were well respected in the local community, and the company grew steadily. The 1970s and early 1980s were a period of relative prosperity for Walsh Petroleum. Dollar sales in 1982 were four times higher than sales in 1977 (although most of this increase was a result of increased unit sales prices). Nonetheless, profits were at their highest level in 1982. A year later, sales gallonage started a decline that had continued unabated. In 1984, John's father died, leaving John's mother and John to manage the firm.

COMPANY OPERATIONS

Walsh Petroleum distributed oil products throughout a seven-county area of the southeastern United States. The marketing area was semi-rural, but contained two county seats with populations of 15,000 and 25,000. The area's proximity to a growing, major city was expected to result in higher-than-average population growth over the next 10 years, but in no way was the area likely to become a suburb of the city. The firm represented a major branded oil company and carried a full line of petroleum products. There were three basic classes of customers for Walsh:

Reseller Accounts.   Walsh served as a distributor of oil products to 10 reseller locations, most of which were local gas stations. Gaining new reseller customers

---

* Prepared by Professors George Overstreet, Jr.; Stewart Malone; and Bernard Morin, McIntire School of Commerce, The University of Virginia.

Exhibit 1 WALSH PETROLEUM'S INCOME STATEMENTS, 1981–85

	1981	1982	1983	1984	1985
Gallons:					
Premium	386,144	687,087	584,076	617,420	593,777
Unleaded	1,193,536	1,236,757	830,002	898,065	841,184
Regular	1,930,719	2,656,736	1,660,004	1,290,969	1,039,110
Lube	24,847	17,793	18,184	16,660	15,725
Heating oil	491,583	409,267	327,845	373,609	335,054
Diesel	375,478	373,704	338,249	348,420	327,098
Kerosene	79,769	96,215	99,733	138,555	125,182
Other products	1,810	414	713	5,301	10,682
Total	4,483,886	5,477,973	3,858,806	3,688,999	3,287,812
Sales:					
Premium	$ 322,225	$ 533,091	$ 551,540	$ 517,510	$ 533,998
Unleaded	1,195,855	1,493,304	1,020,024	1,019,856	881,903
Regular	2,385,763	2,967,718	1,633,912	1,187,458	854,324
Lube	84,438	64,681	66,005	60,491	58,988
Heating oil	533,368	478,842	368,498	411,344	364,539
Diesel	397,663	410,090	332,637	345,317	310,858
Kerosene	92,252	119,845	117,952	162,359	147,066
Other products	53,960	10,757	48,261	140,259	177,768
Net sales	5,065,524	6,078,328	4,138,829	3,844,594	3,329,444
Cost of sales:					
Beginning inventory	77,420	84,927	84,804	136,862	131,592
Purchases net of discounts	4,725,693	5,691,682	3,885,577	3,528,264	2,942,582
	4,803,113	5,776,609	3,970,381	3,665,126	3,074,174
Ending inventory	84,927	84,804	136,862	131,592	149,007
Cost of sales	4,718,186	5,691,805	3,833,519	3,533,534	2,925,167
Gross profit	347,338	386,523	305,310	311,060	404,277
Selling, general and administrative expenses					
Licenses and nonincome taxes	22,447	22,462	18,472	22,604	8,917
Vehicle expense	23,362	41,510	36,837	43,950	32,583
Officers' salaries	68,248	63,370	53,970	52,952	50,780
Other salaries and wages	78,763	92,138	121,160	135,692	140,623
Other expenses	132,880	135,589	136,903	127,892	150,957
Depreciation	46,524	68,676	72,842	73,404	69,441
Interest on borrowing needs	6,457	7,410	11,232	11,999	9,299
Operating income (loss)	(31,343)	(44,632)	(146,106)	(157,433)	(58,323)
Earnings on marketable securities	4,456	2,853	3,009	2,943	3,739
Other income (for hauling)	83,587	112,425	103,109	144,878	85,038
Earnings before taxes	56,700	70,646	(39,988)	(9,612)	30,454
Provision for federal income taxes	6,590	11,870	(15,294)	(2,229)	2,485
Net income	$ 50,110	$ 58,776	$ (24,694)	$ (7,383)	$ 27,969

Note: Inventory is recorded on a LIFO basis.

depended more on financial considerations than marketing techniques because gasoline and oil products were generally considered commodities, and most distributors offered similar types of services. When a new gas station was about to be constructed (an event that had been occurring with decreasing frequency over the past 20 years), the operator would contact several distributors such as Walsh. The distributor would formulate a proposal based on expected sales gallonage. In return for an exclusive, long-term contract to supply the location with gasoline

Exhibit 2 WALSH PETROLEUM'S BALANCE SHEETS, 1981–85

	1981	1982	1983	1984	1985
Assets					
Current assets					
Cash	$ 36,305	$ 7,704	$ 38,510	$ 55,652	$ 14,003
Marketable securities	0	0	0	0	0
Accounts receivable	262,047	254,809	190,673	143,802	155,839
Inventories	84,927	84,804	136,862	131,592	149,007
Refundable taxes	3,964	0	27,194	2,665	200
Prepaid expenses	5,756	7,121	13,698	8,625	9,609
Notes receivable	0	0	0	0	9,368
Other current assets	0	0	0	0	116,607
Total current assets	392,999	354,438	406,937	342,336	454,633
Property plant and equipment					
Land	25,201	28,134	25,489	34,893	30,544
Equipment	154,029	140,493	163,011	130,797	144,965
Vehicles	51,930	60,678	42,367	37,032	24,604
Furniture and fixtures	5,544	3,730	3,449	4,102	3,425
Total	236,704	233,035	234,316	206,824	203,538
Long-term investments	677	1,202	1,202	1,202	1,202
Cash surrender value—officers life	30,970	35,117	690	3,116	0
Loan fees—net	370	277	195	0	0
Total other assets	32,017	36,596	2,087	4,318	1,202
Total assets	$661,720	$624,069	$643,340	$553,478	$659,373
Liabilities and Stockholders' Equity					
Current liabilities					
Accounts payable	$264,812	$155,012	$157,254	$ 80,624	$ 98,505
Notes payable	0	0	50,000	30,000	0
Current portion of long-term debt	18,163	18,315	18,204	17,900	50,675
Income taxes payable	334	4,506	0	235	2,485
Accrued expenses	42,834	45,944	55,125	44,424	40,724
Other current liabilities	0	0	522	846	0
Total current liabilities	326,143	223,777	281,105	174,029	192,389
Long-term debt	19,849	10,305	0	0	0
Other long-term	14,572	30,054	26,992	51,592	0
Total liabilities	360,564	264,136	308,097	225,621	192,389
Owners' equity	301,157	359,933	335,240	327,856	466,984
Total liabilities and owners' equity	$661,721	$624,069	$643,337	$553,477	$659,373

Note: Walsh has limited underground tank liability due to placing tanks in reseller's name and having installed double-walled tanks at the bulk plant over the past five years.

and oil products, the distributor provided the station with fuel storage tanks, pumps, remote consoles, and a canopy. Walsh's profit margin per gallon declined as the reseller's volume climbed based on a sliding scale. If up to 50,000 gallons a month were delivered, he received 4.5 cents over delivered cost (including freight). If 50,000 to 65,000 gallons a month were delivered he received 4.0 cents per gallon. For 65,000 to 75,000 gallons, he received 3.65 cents, and for over 75,000 gallons he received 3.5 cents per gallon. Over the course of the contract, the station operator could switch suppliers if he or she was willing to make a settlement on the equipment provided by the original distributor.

Exhibit 3 WALSH UNIT SALES TRENDS, 1984–87

Unit	Type	Average gallonage per month (000s)		
		1984	1985	1986 (est.)
1	4,000-square-foot rural grocery, owner change in 1984.	6.0	10.5	10.8
2	Village two-bay, financial problems, cash only, pool hall.	11.7	16.8	14.3
3	5,000-square-foot rural grocery in low-growth area.	—	—	8.2
4	C-store in growing rural area.	—	6.7	18.1
5	Two-bay station with marina service, new C-store competition.	20.3	17.9	20.7
6	Rehab two-bay on front of bulk plant property, owned by mother and leased to corporation, good location on four-lane with crossover access, growth area.	28.4	35.3	37.5
7	Three-bay station in low-growth rural area, father and son.	9.9	9.9	10.1
8	1,500-square-foot rural grocery with new owner, business recovery.	14.0	9.1	11.6
9	3,000-square-foot rural C-store with interceptor location, sell on consignment with Walsh controlling price, considering canopy to be leased by Walsh from owner.	17.6	18.8	20.0
10	3,000-square-foot rural C-store with interceptor location.	21.9	22.4	22.7

John had recently audited the profitability of his reseller accounts and found that many of the accounts yielded over a 20 percent after-tax internal rate of return. New reseller contracts also tended to be very lucrative, but there were relatively few high-gallonage locations left in Walsh's trading area, and only two or three new reseller accounts were out for bid each year. The capital requirements for such investments had grown over the years and ranged from $60,000 to $100,000. Exhibit 3 presents sales trends at the 10 contract locations.

In addition to the 10 contract locations, Walsh operated a reseller location on which it had constructed a convenience store (C-store). This diversification move was initiated by Mr. Walsh, Sr., in 1983. The C-store facility was located on 3 acres with 300 feet of road frontage on a four-lane U.S. highway. The property had been appraised at $356,000 and included not only the convenience store but also the bulk storage facilities (144,000 gallons). Mrs. Walsh owned the site and leased it to Walsh Petroleum at $4,000 per month ($2,500 for the bulk storage plant and $1,500 for the C-store). The property had a $100,000 note payable over five years at 9 percent.

Home Heating Oil.   Active accounts numbered 624, of which 325 were classified as automatic (with refills scheduled by the distributor). While the home heating oil business was relatively profitable, it was also highly seasonal, and, thus, efficient utilization of equipment and personnel was viewed as a problem. Some other distributors had taken on equipment sales and service, as well as related businesses such as air conditioning, in order to balance the seasonality of fuel oil sales. John had concluded that heating oil sales would have to double in order to justify the equipment investment and personnel training for an in-house sales/service department.

Commercial/Agricultural Accounts.   Approximately 120 businesses and/or farms maintained their own tanks and pumps for which Walsh supplied oil products. While these accounts had generally shown some loyalty to their petroleum supplier, there was no contractual relationship that would prevent them from changing suppliers.

Within Walsh Petroleum's trading area, there were three other gasoline and oil distributors. Competitive pressures were moderate for existing gasoline reseller and home heating oil accounts, but John had recently noticed an increased level of competition for the one or two new reseller locations constructed each year. None of the four distributors possessed a large competitive advantage over the others. Each competitor had about the same level of sales, and all possessed a similar amount of financial resources. Since gasoline and oil products have a significant freight-cost-to-value ratio, distributors of these products generally had a trading radius of approximately 75 miles around their terminal or distribution point. While the local competitors did not really worry John, some of the distributors that served the nearby metropolitan area were significantly larger than Walsh, and a move by one of these larger competitors into Walsh's trading area could well upset the competitive equilibrium that had evolved over the years.

FAMILY AND MANAGEMENT

Mrs. Walsh assumed the chairmanship of the company following the death of her husband, and she held 52 percent of the voting stock of the corporation (the remaining 48 percent being held equally by John and his two younger brothers). Having worked with her husband for several years, she was very knowledgeable about the firm's operations. While she held the title of chairman, Mrs. Walsh's duties consisted of supervising the convenience store adjacent to the distributorship and maintaining relationships with the fuel oil customers. A prominent citizen of the local community, Mrs. Walsh also served on the town council.

John Walsh had been employed as a geologist with an energy consulting firm in Denver before 1982. When he was visiting at home one weekend, he mentioned to his father that he was concerned his career would be hurt by the recent recession in the oil drilling business. Later that weekend, while having coffee together in the local doughnut shop, John, Sr., said, "John, our business here is changing rapidly, too. If you have any interest in joining the family business, you better make up your mind soon, because I may just sell the business rather than put up with all the changes that are occurring."

John returned to Denver, but after several months he decided the opportunity at Walsh Petroleum might offer a better future than his current job. John returned home in late 1982 and began to learn the business from his father. Not only did John assume many of the administrative duties, but he also managed the marketing relationships with the major accounts.

John's two younger brothers were not active in the management of the business at the time, although each held 16 percent of the corporate stock. Richard was 26 years old and was employed in another city. Daniel was a sophomore in college.

Aside from John and his mother, Walsh Petroleum employed three clerks and four driver/maintenance workers. The three clerks handled much of the administrative paperwork for both the oil distributorship and convenience store. Convenience stores have a multitude of vendors, all of which expect payment within 10 days. Managing the payables took a great deal of time, and Walsh's bookkeeping clerk had complained that she couldn't keep up with the work load. All the accounting was done manually, and John planned to install a computer system in the near future.

In addition, the convenience store employed two full-time and three part-time workers. Salaries and benefits for these workers corresponded to industry averages, and all employees were nonunionized. During the first quarter of 1986, John purchased a new tractor/trailer for $60,000 (9,000-gallon capacity). In addition, Walsh had three older "bobtail" trucks for short deliveries (2,000-gallon capacity) and two used service delivery vans.

THE OIL DISTRIBUTION INDUSTRY

Few industries have experienced the volatility and changes connected with the oil business in the past 15 years. In 1973 the Arab oil embargo resulted in a 119 percent increase in the price of crude oil during a 12-month period. While demand fell slightly from 1973 to 1981, prices were expected to continue climbing. Spurred by higher prices, oil exploration and refinery construction continued to increase. In 1981 President Reagan decontrolled gasoline and crude oil prices. The acquisition price of crude oil began to drop, and demand also fell as the world economy entered a recession.

The changes that occurred upstream in the oil production industry had a large impact on the independent petroleum market:

1. Between 1974 and 1985, American auto manufacturers doubled the miles per gallon of new cars, from 13.2 to 26.4.
2. During the same period, gasoline consumption of passenger cars declined from approximately 75 billion gallons to 65 billion.
3. The number of service stations (defined as outlets with 50 percent or more dollar volume from the sale of petroleum products) fell from 226,459 in 1972 to 121,000 in 1985.

In addition to these changes, oil distributors also faced declining margins, increased real estate costs, and a proliferation of environmental regulations.

News for distributors had not been all bad. The past two years had seen firmer gross profit margins and increased gallonage pumped. Although the market had not recovered to the volume levels of the late 1970s and early 1980s, gasoline gallonage used by motorists increased 1.5 percent in 1983, 1.5 percent in 1984, and 3.4 percent in 1985.[1] A significant portion of the increased demand had to be

---

[1] *1986 State of the Convenience Store Industry* (Alexandria, Va.: National Association of Convenience Stores, Inc.), p. 7.

attributed to the oversupply of world crude and, hence, to lower prices during each of the last three years (down 3.3 percent for 1983, 1.6 percent for 1984, and 1.6 percent for 1985).

Independent petroleum marketers are entrepreneurs involved in the sale and distribution of refined petroleum and ancillary products. While the exact number of the companies was unknown, one trade association report estimated their number between 11,000 and 12,000 in 1985.[2] The trade association membership is broken down in terms of size in Table 1.

Independent petroleum marketers have responded to the pressures in their industry in one of two ways: diversification or consolidation (mergers and acquisition). Table 2 shows how many oil distributors were engaged in various types of diversified activities.

Aside from diversifying into other areas, the number of acquisitions had increased in the past few years, spurred by industry decontrol. Independent marketers, particularly larger ones with the capital available to make acquisitions, had acquired other distributors to take advantage of economies of scale in storage, distribution, and other areas such as billing and general administrative services. A 1984 study found that 56 of 135 marketers had purchased one or more marketing companies within the last five years, and 24 of the 56 had purchased more than one.[3] Most of the acquisition activity occurred among marketers with assets greater than $1 million. Of the 90 firms in this category in the sample, 46 had acquired one or more businesses during the period.

Table 1 PERCENTAGE OF MARKETERS BY SIZE DISTRIBUTION

Millions of gallons sold	1984	1982
Less than 1.0	13.8%	18.0%
1.0–2.49	23.8	26.3
2.5–4.99	21.9	20.8
5.0–7.49	12.2	9.7
7.5–9.99	6.6	6.7
10.0–14.99	9.3	7.1
15.0–19.99	3.8	2.8
20.0–24.99	2.2	1.8
25.0–29.99	1.7	1.4
30.0–39.99	1.8	1.5
40.0–49.99	1.1	1.2
50.00 and above	1.8	2.7
Average volume	7.80	7.12
Median volume	3.91	3.18

Source: *1985 Petroleum Marketing Databook* (Alexandria, Va.: Petroleum Marketing Education Foundation, 1985), p. 12.

---

[2] *1985 Petroleum Marketing Databook* (Alexandria, Va.: Petroleum Marketing Education Foundation, 1985), p. 12.

[3] *1984 Petroleum Marketing Databook* (Alexandria, Va.: Petroleum Marketing Education Foundation, 1984), p. 19.

Table 2   TYPES OF DIVERSIFIED ACTIVITIES ENGAGED IN BY OIL DISTRIBUTORS

Types of diversified activities	Number of distributors
Auto repair/maintenance center	7,081
Auto/truck/trailer rentals	638
Beverage only stores	228
Car washes	2,961
Convenience stores	14,235
Fast-food operations	1,002
Heating/air-conditioning service	3,189
Kerosene heater sales	1,275
Lube centers	1,549
Plumbing service	501
Tires/tires, battery and accessory stores	3,507
Truck stops	1,734
Towing service	911
Coal sales	164
Other	1,000

Source: *1985 Petroleum Marketing Databook* (Alexandria, Va.: Petroleum Marketing Education Foundation, 1985), p. 15.

As a result of increasing profit pressure, a number of operating changes had occurred on the distribution level.[4] First, the total number of distributor-owned transportation vehicles had declined dramatically from 106,868 in 1982 to 96,972 in 1984. Second, distributors had decreased the amount of their storage facilities from a 2.3 billion-gallon capacity in 1982 to 1.7 billion in 1984. Finally, credit terms to distributors had tightened. In 1982, net 30-day payment terms were reported by 21 percent of trade association members, while in 1984 this percentage had dropped to 8.2 percent. These changes and others had led gasoline and oil distributors to redefine the term *good customer*. Whereas in the 1960s and 1970s, distributors were willing to inventory product and deliver relatively small amounts of gasoline on small bobtail trucks, the new market realities made these practices less attractive. Instead of inventorying product, successful distributors would now send a large transport truck (9,000-gallon capacity) to the terminal, or distribution point, and transport the gasoline directly to one service station. Since it was inefficient to have the large truck tied up making multiple deliveries, customer emphasis was on the volume gas station with tank capacity large enough to handle one large delivery. The "mom-and-pop" gasoline retailer was now considered undesirable. John Walsh stated, "In 1980 we considered a good account one that pumped 20,000 to 25,000 gallons per month, while in 1986 we consider a good account to be in the range of 40,000 to 50,000 gallons per month."

In addition to the deregulation of gasoline and crude oil prices in 1981, another regulatory development that affected oil distributors was the issuance of Environ-

---

[4] *1985 Petroleum Marketing Databook* (Alexandria, Va.: Petroleum Marketing Education Foundation, 1985), pp. 15–16.

mental Protection Agency (EPA) regulations regarding leakage of gasoline from underground steel storage tanks. According to one authority, as many as 30 percent of steel tanks currently in the ground might be leaking.[5] Since both past and present owners of property with underground tanks could be held legally liable for leakage pollution, many companies were completely removing older tanks (more than 10 to 15 years old) at a cost of approximately $1,000 for a 1,000- to -3,000-gallon tank. The cost of removing and then reinstalling a similar size tank cost approximately $6,000. If there was a minor leak, clean-up costs would be approximately $5,000 extra. Liability insurance for tank leakage had become exceedingly expensive and difficult to obtain, especially for older, single-wall steel tanks.

The Current Situation

From his study of trade journals and attendance at industry conferences, John Walsh concluded basic industry trends portended a bleak future for Walsh Petroleum unless the company's strategy was changed substantially. It seemed apparent to John that his company had to do something different or get out of the business. Being relatively young, John was confident he could start a career elsewhere, but he enjoyed living in his hometown of Lancaster and liked the idea of being his own boss. Furthermore, his mother was currently receiving an annual salary of $50,000 in addition to rent she received on the C-store. If they sold the company, would the proceeds generate sufficient income to replace his mother's current income?

If they decided not to sell the business, John wondered how the business could be changed? He had received an offer to purchase a competitor, Valley Oil, only weeks before.

THE VALLEY OIL ALTERNATIVE

In many respects, it seemed as though Valley Oil faced the same problems as Walsh. The two companies sold basically the same product lines, although Valley's percentage of heating fuel sales was higher than Walsh's. This aspect of Valley was attractive to John because heating fuel commanded higher margins than gasoline (25 cents per gallon versus 8 to 10 cents per gallon), and customers were a little less sensitive to price than gasoline resellers. Overall, though, Valley's unit sales were declining and unit profit margins were being squeezed. Many of Valley's contract resellers were low-volume accounts and had experienced declining sales volumes. Furthermore, their underground tanks were old.

The owner of Valley had died recently, and Valley's current 55-year-old CEO wanted to get out of the business. Valley's CEO had sent along a copy of the company's recent financial statements—see Exhibits 4 and 5. Valley's CEO said

---

[5] Plenn, Steffen W., *Underground Tankage: The Liability of Leaks* (Alexandria, Va.: Petroleum Marketing Education Foundation, 1986), pp. 9–12.

Exhibit 4 VALLEY OIL COMPANY'S INCOME STATEMENTS, 1981–85

	1981	1982	1983	1984	1985
Gallons:					
Premium	NA	NA	NA	NA	382,869
Unleaded	NA	NA	NA	NA	1,152,730
Regular	3,956,353	3,316,151	4,004,842	3,101,595	1,418,560
Lube	NA	NA	NA	NA	NA
Heating oil	978,113	1,004,000	1,057,131	1,137,072	1,267,011
Diesel	NA	NA	NA	NA	NA
Kerosene	286,870	286,430	262,802	310,066	315,739
Other products	NA	NA	NA	NA	NA
Total	5,221,336	4,606,581	5,324,775	4,548,733	4,536,909
Sales:					
Premium	NA	NA	NA	NA	$ 298,068
Unleaded	NA	NA	NA	NA	1,038,871
Regular	NA	NA	NA	$2,831,323	1,222,758
Lube	NA	NA	NA	95,781	100,922
Heating oil	NA	NA	NA	942,600	871,031
Diesel	NA	NA	NA	NA	295,955
Kerosene	NA	NA	NA	364,573	359,583
Other products	NA	NA	NA	NA	92,493
Net sales	$4,734,881	$4,332,049	$4,657,833	$4,234,277	$4,279,681
Cost of sales:					
Beginning inventory	211,832	210,000	192,449	153,639	160,344
Purchases net of discounts	4,292,934	3,873,798	4,138,784	3,752,969	3,714,003
	4,504,766	4,083,798	4,331,233	3,906,608	3,874,347
Ending inventory	210,000	192,449	153,639	160,344	153,135
Cost of sales	4,294,766	3,891,349	4,177,594	3,746,264	3,721,212
Gross profit	440,115	440,700	480,239	488,013	558,469
Selling, general and administrative expenses					
Licenses and nonincome taxes	23,584	24,450	25,943	25,810	22,252
Vehicle expense	100,471	61,397	85,365	74,066	81,748
Officers' salaries	45,500	49,414	48,700	51,000	53,100
Other salaries and wages	155,843	142,087	154,104	148,434	162,161
Other expenses	145,081	168,015	168,076	186,921	224,159
Depreciation	44,428	38,032	36,920	54,639	61,015
Interest on borrowing needs	10,025	3,496	5,272	7,144	11,203
Operating income (loss)	(84,817)	(46,191)	(44,141)	(60,001)	(57,169)
Earnings on marketable securities	8,746	14,493	5,134	6,426	8,103
Other income (for hauling)	72,552	74,672	90,703	96,501	95,066
Earnings before taxes	(3,519)	42,974	51,696	42,926	46,000
Provision for federal income taxes	(1,983)	4,942	10,776	707	9,049
Net income	$ (1,536)	$ 38,032	$ 40,920	$ 42,219	$ 36,951

Note: From 1981 to 1984, gallonage data are available only as aggregate gasoline sales—these are entered as regular. Likewise, during the entire five-year period, heating oil and diesel are combined under heating oil. During the same time period, dollar values are often unavailable.

that, while the company wasn't for sale on the open market yet, he believed an $800,000 offer would buy the company.

John thought that acquiring Valley Oil could offer some unique advantages—advantages that many other potential acquirers could not realize. First, many of the selling and administrative expenses that Valley incurred could be performed by Walsh's personnel. A potential buyer from outside the industry would probably have substantially higher operating costs than John would have.

Exhibit 5 VALLEY OIL COMPANY'S BALANCE SHEETS, 1981–85

	1981	1982	1983	1984	1985
Assets					
Current assets					
Cash	$ 64,468	$ 31,922	$ 24,076	$ 10,000	$ 26,558
Accounts receivable	656,187	579,313	471,803	470,120	421,308
Inventories	210,000	192,449	153,639	160,344	153,135
Refundable taxes	33,054	0	0	9,920	3,888
Prepaid expenses	2,636	1,535	1,526	1,766	25,883
Notes receivable	1,804	40,277	14,481	59,342	5,099
Total current assets	968,149	845,496	665,525	711,492	635,871
Property plant and equipment					
Land	79,942	79,942	79,942	79,942	79,942
Buildings	0	0	0	0	0
Equipment	207,463	216,139	208,116	207,873	227,444
Vehicles	247,339	274,634	253,153	279,634	255,355
Furniture and fixtures	5,032	21,588	22,393	24,388	30,464
Total	539,776	592,303	563,604	591,837	593,205
Less accumulated depreciation	392,800	430,332	427,310	392,465	422,781
Net property plant and equipment	146,976	161,971	136,294	199,372	170,424
Other assets					
Long-term investments	0	0	0	0	0
Deposits and licenses	0	0	0	0	0
Cash surrender value—officers life insurance	0	0	0	0	0
Loan fees—net	0	0	0	0	0
Advances to affiliated companies	0	0	0	0	0
Total other assets	0	0	0	0	0
Total assets	$1,115,125	$1,007,467	$801,819	$910,864	$806,295
Liabilities and Stockholders' Equity					
Current liabilities					
Accounts payable	$ 670,524	$ 474,892	$272,434	$295,092	$196,670
Notes payable	0	45,000	0	50,000	0
Income taxes payable	0	4,942	5,832	0	6,899
Total current liabilities	670,524	524,834	278,266	345,092	203,569
Long-term debt	0	0	0	0	0
Total liabilities	670,524	524,834	278,266	345,092	203,569
Owners' equity	444,601	482,633	523,553	565,772	602,726
Total liabilities and owners' equity	$1,115,125	$1,007,467	$801,819	$910,864	$806,295

Rather than beginning his analysis with what employees he would be able to eliminate from Valley's payroll, John decided to examine how many people he would have to add to Walsh Petroleum to serve Valley's customers. He figured that initially he would need at least two additional clerks to handle the scheduling and the billing for Valley accounts. Two additional full-time drivers would be needed for deliveries and two seasonal drivers for fuel oil. Salaries for clerks and drivers were estimated at $9,000 and $18,000 a year, respectively, and fringe benefits would probably add about 35 percent. John thought he could get someone to manage the new business at $30,000 (benefits included). John also felt that if he could get his computerized account system running within a year for approximately $40,000 he might be able to eventually eliminate one of the clerks. John was also pleased with the thought that the Valley acquisition would allow him to spread the significant upfront investment in hardware and software over a greater number of accounts, and by adding a delivery scheduling module to the computer system, he should be able to schedule his deliveries more efficiently. In addition, John's accountant recommended that he use a conservative tax rate of 30 percent in his analysis of Valley. Exhibit 6 shows the gallonages at Valley Oil's 18 locations. Exhibit 7 shows the age and capacity of the underground tanks at various Valley Oil locations.

Even with the operating savings John might be able to utilize, Valley would probably be an attractive acquisition to some of the large distributors in the nearby city. Compared to the fierce competition in that city, John's trading area would probably look very attractive to them. While John's knowledge of the local market gave him an advantage, the larger city-based distributors could achieve many of the operating cost savings John was contemplating. By purchasing Valley, John believed his gross profit margin would improve due to a reduced level of competition.

The more John thought about the possibility of combining Walsh and Valley, the more likely it seemed he wouldn't need most of Valley's physical assets to service the accounts he would be acquiring. John had scheduled a lunch with Valley's CEO to discuss the possible acquisition. John's hopes of acquiring Valley's customers only were quickly dashed. Valley's CEO stated that if he was getting out of the business, he was going to sell the whole business as a unit, not hold a "rummage sale." Moreover, he seemed firm about the price of $800,000. The rise in Valley's gross profit margin in 1985 had continued through the first half

Exhibit 6 GALLONS PUMPED AT VALLEY OIL'S 18 STATION LOCATIONS, 1985

Stations*	1985 Gallonages
1	346,279
2	160,316
3	128,620
4	111,702
5	105,036
6	116,286
7	37,894
8	19,746
9	121,440
10†	244,802
11	304,772
12	189,422
13	196,152
14	148,226
15	47,118
16	130,472
17	100,106
18	220,440
Total	2,728,829

* Reseller locations with contracts ranging from two to five years.
† Wholly owned by Valley Oil with appraised value of $100,000 (good potential, four-lane interceptor, C-store location).

Exhibit 7 CHARACTERISTICS OF UNDERGROUND TANKS AT VALLEY OIL SITES

Sites*	Capacity	Age	Type	Product
1	4,000 gallons	12 years	Steel	Gasoline
	4,000	12	Steel	Gasoline
	3,000	25	Steel	Gasoline
	4,000	25	Steel	Gasoline
	3,000	25	Steel	Gasoline
2	2,000	7	Steel	Gasoline
	2,000	7	Steel	Gasoline
	1,000	2	Steel	Gasoline
3	1,000	8	Steel	Gasoline
	1,000	8	Steel	Gasoline
4	1,000	10	Steel	Gasoline
	1,000	10	Steel	Gasoline
	1,000	10	Steel	Gasoline
5	2,000	20	Steel	Gasoline
	1,000	20	Steel	Gasoline
	1,000	20	Steel	Gasoline
6	1,000	12	Steel	Gasoline
	1,000	10	Steel	Diesel
	1,000	10	Steel	Diesel
7	1,000	15	Steel	Gasoline
	1,000	15	Steel	Gasoline
	2,000	10	Steel	Gasoline
	1,000	1	Steel	Gasoline
	1,000	1	Steel	Gasoline
8	1,000	25	Steel	Gasoline
	2,000	3	Steel	Gasoline
	2,000	3	Steel	Gasoline
	2,000	3	Steel	Gasoline
9	2,000	10	Steel	Gasoline
	4,000	11	Steel	Gasoline
	3,000	11	Steel	Gasoline
	3,000	11	Steel	Gasoline
	1,000	11	Steel	Gasoline
10	1,000	12	Steel	Gasoline
	1,000	5	Steel	Gasoline
11	1,000	15	Steel	Diesel
	1,000	15	Steel	Gasoline
12	10,000	15	Steel	Gasoline
	4,000	15	Steel	Gasoline
	4,000	15	Steel	Gasoline
	1,000	15	Steel	Kerosene
13	1,000	12	Steel	Gasoline
	1,000	12	Steel	Gasoline
	1,000	12	Steel	Gasoline

* Sites include reseller locations, large individual users, and bulk plant (number 21).

of 1986 because of the unprecedented drop in oil prices and "sticky" retail prices. However, John knew Valley's CEO would want to sell the business this year before long-term capital gains rates expired.

A big issue in John's mind was how to finance the acquisition. Neither he nor his mother had enough liquid funds outside the business to acquire Valley. Valley's owners indicated they might be willing to hold a note, but they would

Exhibit 7 *(concluded)*

Sites*	Capacity	Age	Type	Product
14	2,000	14	Steel	Gasoline
	1,000	14	Steel	Gasoline
15	1,000	12	Steel	Gasoline
	1,000	12	Steel	Diesel
	2,000	12	Steel	Fuel oil
16	10,000	10	Steel	Gasoline
	2,000	10	Steel	Gasoline
17	2,000	10	Steel	Gasoline
18	1,000	5	Steel	Gasoline
	1,000	5	Steel	Gasoline
19	1,000	9	Steel	Gasoline
	1,000	9	Steel	Gasoline
	1,000	9	Steel	Gasoline
20	10,000	35	Steel	Diesel
21	20,000	15	Steel	Fuel oil
	20,000	15	Steel	Fuel oil
	20,000	15	Steel	Fuel oil
	20,000	15	Steel	Fuel oil
	20,000	15	Steel	Gasoline
	20,000	15	Steel	Gasoline
	20,000	15	Steel	Gasoline
	20,000	15	Steel	Gasoline
	10,000	15	Steel	Gasoline
	6,266	35	Steel	Kerosene
	6,266	35	Steel	Kerosene
	5,631	35	Steel	Kerosene
	6,266	35	Steel	Kerosene
	6,266	35	Steel	Kerosene
	6,266	35	Steel	Kerosene
	6,769	35	Steel	Kerosene
22	4,000	10	Steel	Gasoline
	4,000	10	Steel	Gasoline
	3,000	10	Steel	Gasoline
	3,000	25	Steel	Gasoline
	3,000	25	Steel	Gasoline
23	1,000	20	Steel	Gasoline
	1,000	20	Steel	Gasoline
24	2,000	7	Steel	Gasoline
	1,000	7	Steel	Gasoline
	1,000	7	Steel	Gasoline
	1,000	7	Steel	Kerosene
25	2,000	11	Steel	Gasoline
	2,000	11	Steel	Gasoline

require certain covenants regarding Walsh Petroleum's financial condition in order to protect their position. Also, personal guarantees from John, his mother, and his brother would be required. John decided to try to get Valley's owners to finance 75 percent of the acquisition price over 10 years. While he would have to pay a premium over the prime rate, in his opinion it might still be a good investment.

To help him in his deliberations about the Valley Oil acquisition, John employed an independent consultant to Valley Oil. Excerpts from the consultant's report are shown in Exhibit 8. John was somewhat skeptical about the consul-

---

Exhibit 8   EXCERPTS FROM CONSULTANT'S REPORT ON THE VALUE OF VALLEY OIL COMPANY

Income-based value

In any discounted, income-based valuation, two factors must be determined: the discount rate and the earnings base. Theoretically, the discount rate can be assumed to be the rate of return an investor could earn on a portfolio of similar risk assets. As a starting point, one can consider that for the week of August 1, the Standard and Poor's 10-bond utility average yielded 9.03 percent. This range of 9 percent is consistent with performance over recent months and actually is low for the past decade. Working from this starting point, one can logically assume that there would have to be some risk premium; therefore, a minimum capitalization rate would be 10 percent. As an earnings base, one can use a weighted average of the last five years. This both eliminates any unusual blip in the last year and takes into account the overall trend.

Year	Weight factor	Income	W × I
1981	1	$ (1,536)	$ (1,536)
1982	2	38,032	76,064
1983	3	40,920	122,760
1984	4	42,219	168,876
1985	5	36,951	184,755
	15		$550,919

Weighted average earnings = $36,728

When this average earnings figure is capitalized at 10 percent, an income-based valuation of $367,280 emerges. Using a more reasonable discount rate of 12 percent yields a value of $306,067.

Adjusted asset value

Another step that must be taken in any valuation is an assessment of the asset value of the company. If the market-related asset value is higher than the income-based value, then the business has negative operating value and is worth more liquidated.

When this step is taken with Valley, the analysis is fairly simple. All of the current assets can be liquidated at their book value except for accounts receivables. These must be carried across to market less a 10% bad debt adjustment. This brings the value of total current assets to $620,557.

Adjustments for the fixed assets are a bit more complex. First, the land/buildings account must be adjusted to $100,000 market value. Equipment, with the exception of tanks, is valued at about $20,000 (79 pumps @ $250). The vehicles have an appraised market value of $156,500. The market value for furniture and fixtures is $7,050, giving a total market value to long-term assets of $283,550. The next step to be followed is to deduct any liabilities. These are deducted at book value of $203,569.

The final step in the adjusted asset valuation is to consider any hidden assets or liabilities. These can take several forms:

- Undervalued real estate which would actually bring much more than its book value.
- Exclusive distribution contracts or other market-related, hidden assets.
- Contingent liabilities such as pending lawsuits or potential lawsuits from sources such as leaking underground tanks.

The first of these is ruled out by the fact that Valley owns only one piece of real estate, which was recently appraised and is included in the valuation at its appraised value of $100,000. Neither does the second factor enter into the value—Valley has no unique market-related advantages.

The question of contingent liabilities is important; the possibility that one or more of the approximately 90 tanks could develop or already possess a leak is far from remote. According to Steffen Plenn, author of *Underground Tankage: The Liability of Leaks,* as many as 30 percent of the steel tanks currently in the ground may be leaking. What's worse, that number is expected to rise. The volatile nature of this problem is most clearly seen in its propensity to wind up in court. Plenn explains that these leaks, when discovered, are disasters of a magnitude that will not avoid court.* The most serious implication, however, is that the liability has historically extended to all owners of the tanks, both past and present, vis-a-vis the concept of joint and several liability. Thus,

---

* Plenn, Steffen W., *Underground Tankage: The Liability of Leaks* (Alexandria, Va.: Petroleum Marketing Education Foundation, 1986), pp. 9–12.

Exhibit 8 *(concluded)*

in the process of any rationally executed liquidation, the seller would have to remove each of the older tanks. In the case of Valley, this cost would amount to approximately $90,000. Deducting this contingent tank liability (cost of removal) from the previously computed values yields a liquidation value of $610,538.

Conclusion

This now presents us with two different values for consideration:

1. The income-based value of $367,280.
2. The adjusted asset liquidation basis of $610,538.

Realizing that

- The liquidation value exceeds the income-based value;
- There is a trend toward decreasing blue sky premiums;
- Good will is usually paid for growing or unusually profitable gallons, of which Valley has none;
- There is a significant contingent liability attached to the tanks, all of which cannot be eliminated by tank removal (due to potential for previous leaks); and
- Valley is a declining firm in a mature industry,

We recommend use of the adjusted asset liquidation value of $610,538 as our best estimate of market value.

---

tant's conclusions, however, because the consultant did not have experience in the petroleum business.

THE C-STORE ALTERNATIVE

One of the relative bright spots in Walsh Petroleum's operation had been the C-store. C-stores originated as a convenient alternative to the traditional grocery store, and the premise that consumers would pay higher than grocery store prices in exchange for convenience proved correct. Since customers typically bought only a few items, checkout lines were very short. C-stores carried a relatively limited product line of items generally regarded as necessities. Milk, bread, snack foods, cigarettes, beer, and soft drinks made up a substantial percentage of C-store sales. Although a majority of C-stores carried a very similar product mix, opportunities did exist for C-store operators to differentiate themselves. A number of operators offered video rentals, hot food service (hot dogs, pizza, and so on), and other amenities. Geographic location was also a critical success factor. Customers selected a C-store based on its proximity to their home or their daily route of travel.

Many motor fuel operators had taken the traditional gas station, closed the maintenance bays, and remodeled them into small convenience stores (800 to 1,200 square feet) with gasoline pumps out front. Likewise, convenience store operators, such as Southland (7-Eleven), added self-service gas pumps. According to the National Association of Convenience Stores, gasoline margins averaged 7.3 percent, while nongasoline margins averaged 32.2 percent.[6]

---

[6] "Why the C-store Image Race Could Lead to a Shakeout," *National Petroleum News,* September 1987, p. 40.

In early 1982 the Walshes had commissioned a marketing consulting group to conduct a feasibility study of a C-store location adjacent to the fuel oil distributorship. The location had approximately 300 feet of frontage on a major highway, and the traffic count looked as though it would make the operation feasible. Mr. Walsh, Sr., had remodeled an existing two-bay station, and within two years the unit was meeting and then exceeding the marketing consultants' projections.

Walsh Petroleum currently owned an unoccupied two-bay service station on a corner lot with good access from all directions and a stable traffic flow in a growing, nearby community. In the past the Walshes had leased the property to a number of service station operators. None of them had made a success of the operation, and it was John's opinion that the day of the traditional two-bay station was past its prime. Customers wanted either the pricing and convenience of a self-service station or a super-premium station that provided clearly superior maintenance and service. The turnover of operators was consuming much of Walsh's time, and the station would often sit empty.

John believed it might be possible to demolish the station and erect a C-store with self-serve gasoline pumps on the site. To investigate this possibility, John commissioned the same market research firm that had provided the feasibility study for the original C-store to analyze the new location. This firm had developed a forecasting model that would generate fairly accurate sales estimates for both gasoline and in-store sales for a C-store. Among the many variables included in the model were highway traffic flow, store size and layout, distance to the nearest existing C-store, as well as a variety of demographic data on the area. John's corner lot had a traffic count of 14,000 vehicles per day on the main road and 4,000 vehicles a day on the side street. The resulting sales forecast for gasoline was 915,000 gallons a year, reached by the end of year 2, and first year sales of 410,000 gallons. Kerosene sales were forecast at 7,500 gallons in year 1 and 10,000 gallons per annum thereafter. Inside sales items totaled $213,000 (year 1), $428,000 (year 2), maturing at $530,000 in year 3. Expected margins were 50 cents a gallon for kerosene, 8 cents a gallon for gasoline, and 32 percent for inside sales.

John also retained an architectural firm as a design consultant. Table 3 shows the costs that had been estimated under John's close supervision. Another option John had was to build a C-Store using his major oil supplier's generic C-store design plan. The generic design included a smaller C-store (40 by 50 feet) under a 90 by 40 feet canopy with pumps on either side of the store (35 feet from pump to entrance). The advantage to this design was that the major oil company would refund Walsh 2 cents per gallon on all gallons sold (up to 150,000 gallons per month) for 36 months and provide a detailed site plan without charge. John felt he would lose some inside sales with the oil supplier's fatter margins and he wouldn't get to build his own C-store identity and goodwill. The overall cost would be approximately the same for the two options, and John was uncertain which choice was best from a marketing point of view.

Based on those of his other store, John estimated the operating expenses per annum for the new store as follows: salaries and benefits for a 126-hour week at $80,000, utilities at $14,000, property taxes at $2,000, and other miscellaneous expenses at $20,000.

Table 3 C-STORE ESTIMATED COSTS	
Appraised value of lot	$100,000
Building (≈ $60 for 2,400 square feet of C-store)	144,400
Market research	1,000
Equipment costs	
Gas equipment	150,000
Food equipment	60,000
Canopy	17,500
Capitalized site plan (consultant)	20,000
Inventory	
Food	40,000
Fuel	14,500
Net operating capital	20,000
Total	$567,400
Salvage value	
Gas equipment	$13,500
Food equipment	6,000
Canopy	1,750
Capitalized site plan	0
Asset lives	
Gas equipment	5 years
Food equipment	7 years
Canopy	10 years
Site plan and building	31.5 years
Depreciation method	
Gas, food, and canopy equipment	Double declining balance
Site plan and building	Straight line

While the research pertaining to the original C-store had been highly accurate, John wondered how reliable the model could be in forecasting future sales for the proposed C-store. Because even the major highways were relatively undeveloped in his rural market, there were desirable road frontage locations near his site. A one-acre site directly across the street could be used for a C-store location. While he had considered buying the property as a defensive move, he felt he really couldn't afford to buy it at $150,000.

John felt that the threat of new C-store competitors was very real. Even though a half-million-dollar investment for a C-store was a substantial investment to John, this sum might look like a bargain to the major C-store chains that had been paying up to $1 million for prime suburban locations. Surely, John reasoned, a competing C-store within a mile or two of his location would hurt the validity of his financial projections. The design consultant had added a drive-in window at a cost of approximately $25,000 to differentiate the store and build customer loyalty. John felt a drive-in window would add 15 percent annually to projected inside sales.

At a recent petroleum distributors conference, John discussed his C-store plans with several fellow distributors. Most felt that the generic C-store designs offered by the major oil companies were too small to provide the maximum level of in-store sales, particularly in a rural market. They questioned the wisdom of the drive-in window, suggesting a car-wash operation instead.

While John believed the C-store alternative had potential, he also was aware that the move had its risks. Nationally, the number of C-stores had increased rapidly. At the end of 1981 there were 38,000 C-stores, and only 16,416 of these sold gasoline. Just four years later, the C-store population had reached 61,000, with 33,500 selling gasoline.[7]

There was general agreement in the industry that the danger of C-store saturation was greatest in suburban areas, but substantial opportunities remained in both urban and rural markets. One rural operator, who competed successfully in towns with as few as 1,000 residents, said, "For the rest of the industry, the mark-up on gas is 6 to 8 cents a gallon, while we get 8 to 10 cents. Often we are the only gas station in town."[8] While gas margins would be higher in rural areas, C-stores often increased margins on other products as well. Fast foods and video rentals were extremely profitable in the absence of strong competitors. Pizza, for example, carried a 70 percent profit margin. One C-store/pizza vendor said the pizza concept probably wouldn't work in cities where people could go to a Pizza Hut, "but out in the rural areas, there's no place else to get a good pizza."[9]

Until recently, most of the competitors in the C-store industry were convenience store chains, such as Southland, and locations operated by independent oil distributors. There were increasing indications that the big oil refiners were entering the industry in force. Eight refiner/supplier oil companies, such as Texaco, Mobil, and Exxon, were ranked in the top 50 C-store operators. Many industry observers expected that the entry of the big-oil-owned C-stores would touch off a price war in the industry, particularly in the in-store segment. The rationale behind this expectation was that oil companies would lower in-store merchandise mark-ups in order to increase pump gallonage. However, the major oil companies had tended to concentrate on the urban areas, leaving the rural markets to the distributors.

THE FUTURE OF WALSH OIL

During one of the recent executive education programs John had attended, a few sessions had been devoted to evaluating investment opportunities. He knew he should try to determine an appropriate hurdle rate to use. There were some discussions at these sessions about calculating a cost of capital, but that seemed too academic and complicated. Instead, he went to the library and looked up various interest rates and decided to add a couple of percentage points to them. He figured a small company like his would have to pay somewhere between 2 and 5 percent over the going rate. The interest rates as of August 1986 are listed in Table 4.

As he reviewed his notes from the training sessions, John found that real estate investments were evaluated differently from other types of investments.

---

[7] Ibid., p. 41.

[8] "Rural versus Urban: A Site Selection Dilemma," *Convenience Store News,* July 13–August 2, 1987, p. 54.

[9] Ibid.

Table 4 SELECTED INTEREST RATES, August 1986	
Prime rate charged by banks	7.75%
U.S. Treasury bonds—10 years	7.17%
Corporate bonds—Aaa seasoned	8.72%
Home mortgages—FHLBB	10.26%

Rather than using the total acquisition price as a measure of investment, real estate investments were analyzed on the basis of equity cash investment to determine the payback. One of John's friends in the real estate business told him that, rather than using the purchase price of the acquisition as a measure of its cost, he should use the down payment, or the immediate cash investment, as the cost measure and calculate a levered rate of return on investment.

John scheduled an initial meeting with his banker to see what type of financing he might be able to obtain. While the banker expressed interest in the C-store, he didn't believe the bank would be willing to lend funds for the acquisition of Valley Oil. "John, it's just too risky for us," he said. "Valley's assets just aren't liquid enough to qualify as high quality collateral. With those old tanks and trucks, we would never get our money out. Now the C-store is something I could sell to the loan committee. It's my guess that we could finance 80 percent of the land and building at 11.5 percent for 15 years.[10] In addition, we could finance 80 percent of the equipment including the site plan over 7 years at a 9.75 percent fixed rate."

The banker paused, as if unsure how to proceed. "You know, John, what I'm about to bring up is somewhat sensitive," he said, "so just tell me to stop if I'm out of line. I've watched you work like a dog over the past year to turn your business around, but at some point you have to start thinking about yourself. You can work like hell for 30 years and still only be a minority stockholder. If your mother and two brothers wanted to sell out at some point in the future, all your efforts, not to mention your career, are down the drain.

"Here's an alternative you might just think about," said the banker. "Walsh Petroleum owns the C-store site you are talking about developing. Why don't you buy the land personally and construct the C-store on it? We here at the bank would lend you the money, although we would probably have to have Walsh Petroleum guarantee the loan. You could then lease the C-store back to Walsh Petroleum and start building up some personal equity for yourself through the real estate investment."

As John Walsh pondered his alternatives, one thing seemed certain to him— he would have to act soon. Many of his friends he met at the trade association meetings seemed to be complacent about the pressure on their industry, but as John glanced at the financial statements again, he knew that a few more years like these past two would threaten not only his family's financial security, but his own as well. After all, he was really the only member of the family whose income was

---

[10] It should be noted that the bank is refinancing land that Walsh currently owns.

directly related to the future of Walsh Petroleum. He remembered the discussion of these issues at a recent dinner with his mother and brothers.

"John, I agree with the idea of expanding the business, and I think it would have pleased your dad," said Mrs. Walsh, "but you have to remember that Walsh Petroleum is really all I have. If we take on too much debt, and get into trouble, I don't know what I'll do in my old age."

"I see your point, Mom," said John, "but the fact is that I'm the only one in the family who is devoting the rest of my life to running the business. You already own C-store 1, and Richard and Daniel either don't want to be in the business or aren't sure yet. I don't want to sound selfish, but my interest in the business is only 16 percent. I don't want to wake up when I'm 50 and find that I've spent my whole life running this business for the rest of the family and have relatively little to show for it."

Richard puffed on his pipe and said, "John, I'm not sure the C-store alternative is a good idea for the family business. Sure, it's a good deal for you personally, but the rest of us have to guarantee your loan at the bank. I think Walsh Petroleum should give serious consideration to the Valley Oil deal."

"And why do you think that Valley is better than the C-store?" asked John.

"The main reason," Richard replied, "is that Walsh Petroleum is primarily a gasoline distributor. The original C-store was a great idea of Dad's, but the oil business is this family's cash cow. This is an opportunity to take out a competitor. We all agree there aren't a whole lot of new people going into this business, but if a big gasoline distributor in the region buys Valley, then Walsh Petroleum has got some major problems on its hands. The increased competition could certainly lower our gross margin 1-to-2 cents a gallon, and we all know that there are two large distributors that are interested in Valley."

"But, Richard, can't you see that we're in a declining industry?" said John. "If you looked at those financials I sent you, it should be obvious that our gallonage has been declining for several years."

"What do you think, Daniel?" asked Mrs. Walsh. "After all, it's as much your business as it is John's or Richard's."

"I think that John and Richard both have good points," said Daniel. "While John is the only one of us three in the business now, I may want to join the company when I finish school, and I really don't care to be a clerk in a convenience store. And while John certainly has a right to try to accumulate some wealth, I don't know that using the family business's credit rating to guarantee his personal investments is really fair to the rest of us. After all, John is at least getting a decent salary, and Richard and I don't even receive any dividends."

"Wait a second, Dan," said John, somewhat resentfully. "I'm not riding a gravy train here. My $30,000 salary at Walsh is no higher than what my market worth is, and especially the way things are going, my upside potential is much lower than I could get working for someone else. Even more importantly, the family couldn't find anyone else to do this job for any less than what I'm getting."

The family discussion had ended without resolving anything, but John was certain the business would be worth substantially less if he was unable to turn the operation around. Aside from the purely financial considerations, John knew that the major oil companies were now evaluating their distributors on sales levels and sales growth. A distributor in an attractive market who wasn't showing the appropriate level of sales or sales growth might soon find itself without a supply contract.

Further, while John was eager to stop the decline in the company's financial performance, he also felt strongly that the business plan he developed now should lay the foundation for the business growth for the next 5 to 10 years. The questions in his mind were, "How do we do it, and is it worth the trouble?"

ALLIED CORPORATION—SULFURIC ACID OPERATIONS*

In 1984 Allied Corporation had just come through five years of unprecedented change. The company's whole management approach had been overhauled from top to bottom and its business portfolio had been massively restructured by a series of acquisitions and divestitures. Within 10 days of being appointed Allied's chief executive officer in May 1979, Edward L. Hennessy, Jr., had formed an Acquisition Task Force. By the end of his second month, Hennessy had made a $598 million acquisition and had decided to divest several unprofitable businesses that he felt were in mature or unattractive industries. By the end of his fifth month, he had eliminated 700 corporate staff jobs, cut annual corporate overhead by $30 million, and decentralized authority for division operations, delegating far more autonomy to Allied's business-level managers than had his predecessors. After six months, Hennessy had negotiated settlements to three major lawsuits that had preoccupied Allied's top executives and was well into a program of corporate revitalization that included development of long-range strategies and comprehensive review of the company's internal policies and management practices. Two of Hennessy's long-run priorities were to build a strategically balanced business portfolio and to institute a new corporate culture at Allied. Exhibit 1 presents highlights of Allied's financial performance during the Hennessy years.

CORPORATE BACKGROUND

The company was first formed in 1920 as a merger of three complementary chemical and dye operations and a coal and coke producer; it operated under the name of Allied Chemical Corporation. By 1950, despite a long and tangled history of internal power struggles and management dissension, Allied had become an acknowledged leader in the U.S. chemical industry and was one of 30 "blue-chip" companies whose performance went into calculating the widely followed Dow Jones Industrial Average.

Between 1958 and 1968, Allied lost ground in the chemical industry principally because of (1) a weak research and development effort (Allied's conservative management never allocated more than a token percentage of revenues to research and development), (2) late entry into new specialty chemical markets (where profit margins were higher and proprietary technology and patents yielded a measure of protection from vigorous price competition), and (3) a top management leadership that spent more time on internal jockeying for power than on

---

* This case was prepared by Professor Arthur A. Thompson, with the assistance of graduate researchers Sharon Henson and Kem King, The University of Alabama. Copyright © 1985 by Allied Corporation and Arthur A. Thompson, Jr.

Years ended December 31	1979*	1980	1981*	1982*	1983*
For the year†					
Net sales	$ 4,160	$ 5,300	$ 6,142	$ 6,013	$ 10,022
Cost of goods sold	3,167	3,902	4,547	4,566	7,730
Income from operations	706	975	1,071	815	1,105
Nonrecurring items	(50)	(28)	84	(11)	—
Interest and other financial charges	(102)	(81)	(88)	(84)	(197)
Income from continuing operations before taxes on income	570	910	1,087	808	1,042
Taxes on income	391	630	711	524	592
Income from continuing operations	179	280	376	284	450
Discontinued operations:					
Operating income (losses), net of income taxes	(22)‡	9	(28)	(12)	(55)
Estimated loss on disposals, net of income taxes	(146)‡	—	—	—	(336)
Cumulative effect of change in accounting principle	—	—	—	—	39
Net income	11	289	348	272	98
Preferred stock dividend requirement	(5)	(23)	(38)	(68)	(91)
Earnings applicable to common stock	$ 6	$ 266	$ 310	$ 204	$ 7
Earnings per share of common stock:					
Income from continuing operations	$ 6.05	$ 7.85	$ 10.01	$ 6.59	$ 6.91
Income (losses) from discontinued operations	(5.85)‡	.30	(.84)	(.37)	(7.52)
Cumulative effect of change in accounting principle	—	—	—	—	.74
Net earnings	$ .20	$ 8.15	$ 9.17	$ 6.22	$ .13
Weighted average number of common shares outstanding (in millions)	28.7	32.6	33.8	32.8	52.0
Dividends per share of common stock	$ 2.00	$ 2.15	$ 2.35	$ 2.40	$ 2.40
Salaries and wages	660	804	992	1,121	2,400
Oil and gas exploration costs expensed	91	120	189	245	223
Property, plant, and equipment additions:					
Environmental improvement facilities	65	54	56	34	37
Capitalized oil and gas exploration and development	162	226	251	202	164
Plant improvements and additions	183	253	302	288	406
Total additions	409	533	609	524	607
At year-end					
Net working capital	$ 279	$ 467	$ 638	$ 416	$ 458
Property, plant, and equipment—net	$ 2,169	$ 2,384	$ 2,866	$ 2,858	$ 3,553
Total assets	$ 4,210	$ 4,538	$ 5,344	$ 6,272	$ 7,647
Long-term debt	$ 866	$ 814	$ 804	$ 669	$ 1,080
Limited recourse financing	$ 86	$ 71	$ 53	$ 31	$ 263
Preferred redeemable stock	$ 199	$ 260	$ 591	$ 586	$ 434
Capital stock and other shareholders' equity	$ 1,229	$ 1,664	$ 1,900	$ 2,013	$ 2,747
Book value per share of common stock	$ 42.65	$ 49.69	$ 56.30	$ 57.11	$ 45.92
Number of common shares outstanding (in millions)	28.8	33.5	33.7	35.2	53.5
Common shareholders	60,304	58,022	56,648	58,046	68,187
Employees	49,014	46,269	58,224	44,337	117,750
Financial statistics†					
Return on sales (pre-tax adjusted)	9.4%	11.2%	12.0%	8.9%	7.6%
Return on average assets:					
Pretax (adjusted)	12.4	15.5	16.9	11.1	11.1
After-tax	5.4	7.3	8.6	5.9	6.5
Return on shareholders' equity	14.2	15.4	17.8	10.7	14.0
Long-term debt as a percent of total capital	35.6	28.4	23.3	19.5	28.4
Interest coverage ratio	7.1×	9.9×	9.4×	7.3×	5.1×

* Includes the effect of acquisitions in the respective periods. The company acquired Eltra Corporation effective July 1, 1979, which was valued at approximately $598 million and was accounted for as a purchase.

† Restated to reflect discontinued operations. Sales applicable to discontinued operations before December 31, 1983, were as follows: 1983, $329 million; 1982, $154 million; 1981, $265 million; 1980, $219 million; and 1979, $172 million. Income taxes included in the caption "Discontinued operations: Operating income (losses), net of income taxes" for each period were: 1983, $(52) million; 1982, $(17) million; 1981, $(26) million; 1980, $7 million; and 1979, $(7) million.

‡ Substantially all of the amounts shown relate to businesses discontinued in 1979.

external jockeying for long-term position in the steadily changing markets for commodity and specialty chemicals. One business publication, commenting on this period, said:[1]

> Allied was a real blue chip. It was old . . . it was well established in chemicals that were basic to the entire economy. Spectacular, no. Solid, yes.
>
> Then it turned out that Allied wasn't solid at all. In fact, its basic structure was rotten. What looked to the outside like conservative management turned out, in fact, to be no management at all.

For a time, Allied's management was able to obscure the company's weakening market position from clear view by changing depreciation and tax accounting methods, capitalizing expenditures that had formerly been expensed currently, riding the crest of general chemical industry prosperity, and selling off unused land at a handsome profit. Between 1959 and 1965 Allied's revenues jumped almost 40 percent, yet its pretax operating income rose only 5 percent, a reflection of sharply lower margins on sales of basic commodity chemicals.

In January 1967 Allied's board of directors decided to act. John T. Connor, then secretary of commerce in Lyndon Johnson's administration, was hired as president and CEO. As Connor gradually saw through the mirage of his predecessors' creative accounting procedures and came to understand the deteriorating profit economics associated with Allied's chemical businesses, he realized the company was in deeper difficulty than had appeared when he took the job to see if he "could breathe some life into the wheezing corporate giant." Connor's probing ended with three important conclusions: (1) Allied's plants were in bad repair, were inefficient, and were scattered haphazardly across the United States and overseas; (2) the company's chemical products mix consisted mainly of standard low-margin products such as soda ash, sulfuric acid, dyestuffs, and biodegradable detergents—all subject to strong price competition, cyclical ups and downs, and slow rates of growth; and (3) Allied no longer enjoyed the market clout and respected status that came from being an acknowledged industry leader.

Connor tried to shore up Allied's position by selling several unprofitable businesses, diversifying into polyester, and investing heavily in oil and gas exploration and production. Connor's biggest strategic decision was to pump over $1 billion into Allied's Union Texas Petroleum subsidiary to prospect for and develop oil and gas reserves—a move that Connor helped finance by redeploying the $400 million Allied obtained from the sale of the marginal businesses Connor singled out for divestiture. Even so, Allied's performance under Connor was lackluster, partly because of only spotty profit improvements in Allied's chemical businesses and because large losses in the coal and coke division offset gains elsewhere. By 1979 oil and gas was Allied's top performing business, generating about 30 percent of sales and 76 percent of income.

Three major incidents during the 1970s compounded Connor's and Allied's problems. In 1975 Allied was sued for over $1 billion when employees of a subcontractor firm developed Kepone poisoning while producing the chemical

---

[1] "Allied Chemical: A Long Rough Road Back," *Forbes,* May 15, 1969, p. 205.

pesticide for Allied. It was discovered that the subcontractor firm was owned by former Allied employees and that Allied had discharged Kepone into the James River during the eight years it had produced the toxic chemical. The ordeal cost Allied $20 million in fines, settlements, and legal fees and also resulted in a qualified auditor's opinion for 1976 and 1977, diminished employee morale, and increased scrutiny of Allied's operations by government regulatory agencies such as the Environmental Protection Agency and the Occupational Safety and Health Administration.

The second incident took place in mid-1976 when Allied, responding to government pressure, closed a coke-producing facility in Kentucky to remedy environmental and safety problems. The plant's sole customer, Armco Steel, sued Allied for $217 million in damages for failure to meet its obligations to supply 95,000 tons of coke a month under a 10-year contract. Allied under Hennessy's guidance settled the suit out of court by giving Armco a coal mine with a $14 million book value and paying Armco $20 million in cash.

In 1979 Allied was indicted for allegedly conspiring to defraud the Internal Revenue Service. The company was charged with paying a General Tire and Rubber Company purchasing manager $220,000 for his assurance that General Tire would buy polyester cord yarn from Allied.

HENNESSY'S REVITALIZATION EFFORTS

Ed Hennessy began his business career as a junior accountant at Price Waterhouse—the worst job he ever had ("We had to wear straw hats and suits, and we spent days in warehouses" doing audits).[2] He held financial staff positions at Textron (five years), Lear Siegler (four years), ITT (four years under Harold Geneen, with exposure to Geneen's theories about making acquisitions and managing broad diversification), Colgate-Palmolive (one year), and Heublein (seven years, where he played a key role in Heublein's acquisition of Kentucky Fried Chicken). He then spent seven years at United Technologies, a large *Fortune 500* company noted for the aggressive way it pursued diversified growth via acquisition. At United Technologies, Hennessy rose through the ranks to occupy the number two post of executive vice president. At the time of his selection as Allied's CEO, he was perceived by some people as a strong-willed financial manager whose chief accomplishments had been engineering active acquisition campaigns on behalf of Heublein, Inc., and United Technologies. He was attracted to Allied by the opportunity to run his own show at a blue-chip company. Unlike Connor, when Hennessy came on board he was well aware that Allied was what one industry analyst described as "a doggy commodity chemical company . . . that was not growing or building stockholder value or even providing its employees with a very interesting place to work."[3]

---

[2] As quoted in Colin Leinster, "Allied-Signal's Tough Skipper," *Fortune*, June 24, 1985, p. 92.

[3] "Allied After Bendix: R&D is the Key," *Business Week*, December 12, 1983, p. 76.

Hennessy hit the ground running at Allied, not only because Allied's position was deteriorating, but also because there were signs that Allied might be the target of an acquisition takeover and because he learned that Standard & Poor's, a major bond rating agency, was considering lowering Allied's bond rating from A to BBB. Having just moved over to Allied, Hennessy had no interest in Allied's being acquired (having been on the other end many times during his days at United Technologies), and he feared a downgrading of Allied's bond rating would lessen the financial flexibility and maneuvering ability he would need to launch Allied on a new course. As it turned out, a takeover attempt never materialized and Hennessy convinced S&P to hold back on its bond downgrading until he had had a few months to turn Allied around.

In mid-June 1979, six weeks after taking command, Hennessy formed a policy and management committee consisting of Allied's 11 top managers. Over the next six months the committee discussed what changes to institute in Allied's operations. Through the committee Hennessy got widespread support for a revitalization plan consisting of four parts: (1) diversification by acquisition, (2) divestiture of businesses that were losing money or only marginally profitable, (3) decentralization of operating responsibilities to the business and division levels, and (4) upgrading internal administrative systems, incentive compensation, and the company's public image.

In early 1980 Hennessy started to concentrate on Allied's corporate strategy and strategic planning process. Quarterly strategic review sessions were initiated. While Allied's operating divisions had business strategies, some of which Hennessy felt were good, he still felt that the aggregate of the business strategies did not yield a coordinated or meaningful whole. Hennessy's probing into Allied's strategic management practices led him to several other conclusions:

- Allied's corporate management did not have a good overview of all the businesses the company was in and how attractive their future prospects were.
- Allied needed to have a strategic planning cycle whereby the managers of Allied's divisions and businesses would be motivated to make realistic assessments of the potential and attractiveness of the businesses they managed—a cycle and a discipline that would then lead to the development of sound business strategies and division-level (or business-level) accountability for successful strategy execution. Hennessy believed, based on his own personal experiences, that the managers of unattractive, poorly-performing business units could not be expected on their own initiative to document clearly the dim outlook for their divisions and to recommend it be divested; as Hennessy put it, "How many managers are going to say, 'This business will never get an 18 percent return so I think you better sell it and me.' It won't happen." Hence, Hennessy believed he had to push for the establishment of a strategic planning process that could be counted upon to expose the future prospects of each of Allied's businesses.
- The task of managing the formulation of a sound corporate strategy and the simultaneous formulation of sound business strategies in each business area was so big that consultants were needed to help.

Consultants were hired to come up with a new strategic planning process for Allied. The consultants trained Alied managers to "profile a business" and then spent three days with each of Allied's business areas helping them go through the profiling task. A standard profiling form was developed to facilitate comparing all of Allied's businesses. Using data from the business profiles, each Allied business was positioned on a corporatewide business portfolio matrix that used competitive standing and industry maturity as the variables on the two axes.

The profiling and business portfolio matrix analysis documented that 75 percent of Allied's businesses were in mature and aging industries. Hennessy and the rest of Allied's top management reached a consensus that Allied needed to be in more growth businesses. A financial objective of an 18 percent pretax return on assets was established for the corporation (at the time only Allied's fiber business and oil and gas business earned more than 18 percent target).

The corporate strategy that emerged centered around two themes. First, the company's business portfolio would consist of four or five groups of related core businesses. Hennessy often described the successful modern corporation as needing to be structured like a wheel with strong spokes. In his view, the three spokes that Allied had in 1980—chemicals, oil and gas, and polyester fibers—were not enough "to keep the wheel round and true and the company rolling along." Hence the need for Allied to diversify further, primarily through acquisition. The second strategic theme was that Allied's existing businesses in mature and aging industries were to be managed for long-term profit and cash flow. Resources were to be allocated to these units primarily for cost reductions, productivity improvements, and protection of assets. For any of these businesses to receive capital appropriations from corporate headquarters, Allied's senior management had to be convinced that the business had a good strategic plan with which they agreed, that the business plan was consistent with the corporate-level financial strategy, that the business had adequate long-run attractiveness, and that the business had realistic prospects for meeting the corporate objective of an 18 percent pretax return on assets. Insofar as Allied's chemical businesses were concerned, the strong preference of corporate management was to try over the long-run to diversify out of bulk chemicals into specialty chemicals and out of both into other faster-growing, more attractive industries. Hennessy stated:[4]

> Our goal is to become a leader—not necessarily number one but no worse than a close number two or three—in every business we're in. If we can't build a business to a leadership position—by becoming the low-cost producer or perhaps by extending our product line through acquisitions—then we should divest it.

By 1985 over 30 business units had been divested.

NEW ACQUISITIONS

Between 1979 and 1984, Hennessy spearheaded a series of important acquisitions that gave Allied's business portfolio a new look:

---

[4] As quoted in Allied Corporation (B), Harvard Case Services 0-383-078, p. 13.

Exhibit 2   ALLIED CORPORATION'S CORE BUSINESS GROUPS, 1983

Business groups	Principal products
Chemical sector Allied's chemical businesses produce a wide variety of commodity and specialty chemicals, synthetic fibers, and plastics for most of the key basic industries. The company is the largest producer of soda ash in North America and the world's largest producer of hydrofluoric acid, type 6 nylon, and fluorine-derived chemicals, one of which, fluorinated carbon, is packaged for use in lithium batteries.	Nylon filaments/staple fibers • nylon and polyester industrial fibers • nylon apparel fibers • fibers intermediates • ammonium sulfate • soda ash • fluorocarbons • fluorine, electronic, chrome, water treatment, and fine chemicals • tar products • hydrofluoric acid • sulfuric acid • uranium hexafluoride • engineered plastics • fluoropolymers • high-density polyethylene • low-molecular-weight polyethylene
Oil and gas sector Allied's oil and gas businesses are managed by its Union Texas Petroleum subsidiary, one of the largest independent oil and gas companies in the United States. UTP engages in worldwide oil and gas exploration and production such as in West Texas where this pipeline is part of a project to recover additional oil reserves at the Wellman Field. UTP also processes and distributes natural gas liquids, manufactures petrochemicals, and markets petroleum products.	Crude oil and condensate • natural gas • liquefied natural gas • liquefied petroleum gases • natural gasoline • residue gas • ethylene
Automotive sector Allied's automotive businesses, which include Bendix, Fram, Autolite, and Prestolite products, manufacture components and systems for passenger cars and trucks. Products are used in original equipment and as replacement parts. Bendix is the world's leading independent manufacturer of car and truck brake components and friction materials.	Disc/drum brakes • air/hydraulic disc and drum brakes • brake components • friction materials • air/oil/fuel filters • spark plugs • steering systems • engine controls • engine cooling fans • air cleaner assemblies • electric motors • wire products • ignition components • safety restraints • die castings and metal stampings
Aerospace sector Allied's aerospace businesses, primarily Bendix operations, manufacture products used in military and civil aircraft, spaceflight vehicles, missiles, and other national defense projects and space exploration, including the altitude pointing and control systems incorporated in the space telescope. Other aerospace units manage government-owned facilities and provide technical services for the Department of Energy and NASA.	Integrated avionic systems • weather radar systems • communications/navigation/identification systems • electronic cockpit displays • flight control systems • fuel control/ignition systems • electric generating systems • wheels/brakes • dynamic control systems • transmission shafts • test systems • gyroscopic guidance systems • tactical missile systems • antisubmarine systems • communications systems • technical services
Industrial and technology sector Allied's industrial and technology businesses were added to the corporation's portfolio largely through acquisitions since 1979. Among them are businesses in electronics and health care, whose markets have good growth potential.	Electrical/electronic connectors/components • flat ribbon cable/assemblies • seal lids/die attach preforms • analytical and measuring instruments/apparatus/appliances • biomedical instruments/supplies • reagent chemicals and diagnostics • glassware and plasticware • laboratory furniture • electronic information systems • phototypesetting equipment • batteries • refractory materials

Markets/industries	Year	Net sales	Percent of total sales	Income from operations	Percent of total profits
		1981–83 results of operations by sector (in millions of dollars)			
Carpet • automotive • cordage • lingerie, loungewear • fertilizer • glass • paper • nuclear • refrigeration • water treatment • semiconductor devices • electronics • plastics • packaging • metal finishing • aluminum and steel • wood treatment • additives • coatings	1983	$2,337	23%	$227	24%
	1982	2,143	36	136	22
	1981	2,387	39	199	24
Oil refining • gas pipelines • chemical feedstocks • home, farm, utility, and industrial fuels	1983	$1,989	20%	$413	43%
	1982	1,992	33	486	77
	1981	2,068	35	570	69
Passenger cars • light/medium/heavy trucks • industrial/off-road/recreational vehicles • aircraft • railway • powered equipment	1983	$2,370	24%	$203	21%
	1982	298	5	6	1
	1981	371	7	17	2
Military aircraft • civil aircraft • commercial aircraft • air traffic control • missiles and spacecraft • ships • oceanics • military land vehicles • refinery/industrial process control • industrial turbines	1983	$1,603	16%	$152	16%
	1982	48	2	—	0
	1981	42	2	(5)	(1)
Military/aerospace • telecommunications • computers • electronics • industrial/medical/government/educational institution laboratories • brokerage and banking • publishing • automotive • iron and steel	1983	$1,708	17%	$(43)	(4)%
	1982	1,392	24	1	0
	1981	963	17	49	6

1979   Acquired Eltra Corporation, a diversified manufacturer of consumer and industrial goods, including batteries, motors, cables, and athletic footwear. Eltra, with a net worth of almost $392 million, sales of $1 billion, and net income of $48 million, was acquired at a total cost to Allied of approximately $598 million. (Since the acquisition, some of Eltra's business divisions had been sold off and several others were up for sale in 1985.)

1981   Acquired Bunker Ramo Corporation, a producer of electrical and electronic connectors, information systems, and specialty textiles, with a net worth of $176.8 million, sales of $468 million, and net income of $27 million. Allied's total cost was approximately $347 million in cash, notes, and preferred stock.

Acquired Fisher Scientific Company, a manufacturer of scientific laboratory equipment and supplies, with a net worth of nearly $112 million, sales of $425 million, and net profit of $16 million. Allied's cost was approximately $311 million in preferred stock and cash.

1982   Acquired 50 percent of the Supron Energy Corporation, an oil and gas company with sales of $78 million and net profit of nearly $18 million. Allied's cost was $357 million.

1983   Acquired The Bendix Corporation, a diversified company whose operations consisted primarily of automotive components and aerospace-electronics and industrial tools, with a net worth of nearly $1.5 billion, sales over $4 billion, and net profit of $204.5 million. The merger (expected to reduce Allied's dependence upon oil and gas, diversify its operations into higher tech, higher value-added products, and make the company much less capital intensive) cost Allied approximately $1.8 billion.

Acquired Semi-Alloys, Inc., manufacturer of components for high-reliability semiconductor packages, to expand Allied's position as a leading supplier of chemicals and components to the semiconductor industry. Semi-Alloys' 1982 sales were $70 million. Allied paid approximately $97 million in cash and common stock.

Acquired Instrumentation Laboratory, Inc., producer of biomedical and analytical instruments, to add more high-technology products to the health and scientific products line acquired with Fisher Scientific. IL had 1982 revenues of $137.6 million and net income of $4.6 million. Allied paid approximately $115 million in cash and common stock.

These acquisitions led Allied in 1983 to organize into five core business groups (see Exhibit 2). To reflect the broader scope and corporate strategy that Hennessy was pursuing, the company's name was changed in 1981 from Allied Chemical Corporation to Allied Corporation.

ALLIED'S SULFURIC ACID BUSINESS

Spurred by Hennessy's drive to assess the long-term attractiveness of each of Allied's business units, in 1980 the managers in charge of Allied's sulfuric acid business area formed an internal task force, under the direction of the Chemical Company Planning Group, to reevaluate Allied's entire sulfuric acid operations and to make recommendations for improving the area's return on assets. The sulfuric acid area's pretax return on assets of 7.6 percent in 1980 was judged to be unacceptable. An in-depth study of the overall U.S. sulfuric acid industry was conducted as a basis for the evaluation; the rest of this section describes the findings and recommendations of the Sulfuric Task Force.

The U.S. Sulfuric Acid Industry in 1980

Sulfuric acid (H_2SO_4) was classified as a standard industrial commodity chemical and was commercially marketed in bulk railcar or tank truck lots. Three production methods existed; it could be (1) manufactured from Frasch mined sulfur (referred to as virgin or sulfur-burned sulfuric acid), (2) reconstituted from spent or waste acid, or (3) gathered as a by-product of metallic ore smelting (referred to as smelter or by-product acid). All three methods were in use in 1980. About 70 percent of total sulfuric acid production in the United States was consumed directly by the producer for intracompany use in making other products (referred to as the captive market). The remaining 30 percent was sold commercially to a wide variety of users (in what was known as the merchant market).

During the past two decades dramatic shifts in the end-use patterns for sulfuric acid had occurred. The use of sulfuric acid for manufacturing phosphoric acid (a basic fertilizer material) had mushroomed to over 60 percent of total demand. At the same time, demand for sulfuric acid had declined in many of the traditional end-use segments (such as steel pickling and manufacturing titanium dioxide—a paint pigment). The major end-use changes are shown in Exhibit 3.

A number of reasons accounted for the end-use declines in sulfuric acid demand:

Other fertilizers—The use of sulfuric acid in other fertilizers was on the decline due to their being replaced by newer, more concentrated fertilizers that used phosphoric acid as an ingredient.

Petroleum refining—The use of sulfuric acid was declining moderately because of refiners' preferences for using another chemical process to serve the same purpose.

Alcohols—Users were shifting to another process for making ethyl alcohol that did not use sulfuric acid.

Titanium dioxide—The sulfate process for making titanium dioxide (which required sulfuric acid) was being slowly replaced by the cloride process (which did not use sulfuric acid).

Hydrofluoric acid—The manufacturer of hydrofluoric acid was being shifted to new plants in Mexico and Canada, plus the use of hydrofluoric acid was waning because of sharp cutbacks in the use of fluorocarbons in aerosol packaging.

Rayon—Rayon demand had been declining because of competition from nylon and polyesters.

Exhibit 3 PERCENT OF TOTAL USE OF SULFURIC ACID

End uses	1960	1970	1978
Phosphoric acid	19.0%	41.0%	63.0%
Other fertilizers	14.0	3.8	2.5
Petroleum refining	9.0	7.0	6.5
Copper leaching	negl.	2.6	2.7
Ammonium sulfate	6.0	5.2	4.0
Alcohols	9.0	6.2	2.7
Titanium dioxide	9.0	5.5	2.2
Hydrofluoric acid	2.7	3.2	2.1
Uranium and vanadium	1.8	1.1	1.8
Aluminum	2.5	2.1	1.7
Rayon	3.6	2.2	1.3
Steel pickling	5.6	1.6	0.9
Surfectants	1.5	1.2	0.8
Batteries	0.5	0.4	0.5
Other	15.7	16.9	7.3
Total	100.0%	100.0%	100.0%

The only two industrial end-uses of sulfuric acid showing significant gains in demand from 1960–78 were for copper leaching and uranium ore processing.

From 1968 through 1978, overall use of sulfuric acid increased by about 30 percent—an average annual growth rate of 2.7 percent. The phosphoric acid end-use grew at an 8.1 percent annual rate; however, over 90 percent of the sulfuric acid used in making phosphoric acid was captively supplied. As a group, the other end-uses, mainly industrial, experienced a 23 percent decline over the 10-year period (see Exhibit 4).

Demand projections for the next five years indicated that phosphoric acid end-use would continue to expand and that industrial end-use demand for sulfuric acid would be essentially flat.

Although smelter acid was acceptable for some end-uses, it could not be used in many applications because of differences in quality, variations in concentration, and the presence of impurities. In 1979 smelter acid accounted for about 10 percent of the total end-use market; virgin and reconstituted acid producers

Exhibit 4 U.S. SULFURIC ACID DEMAND, 1968–78 (thousands of metric tons)

	Total	Phosphoric acid	All other uses
1968	27,514	10,358	17,156
1969	28,455	10,797	17,658
1970	28,462	11,581	16,881
1971	27,718	12,514	15,204
1972	29,708	14,410	15,298
1973	30,282	14,766	15,516
1974	32,375	15,433	16,942
1975	30,541	17,267	13,274
1976	31,733	18,028	13,705
1977	33,911	20,567	13,344
1978	35,766	22,540	13,226
10-year change	8,252	12,182	(3,930)

supplied the remaining 90 percent. Smelter acid producers netted about $5 to $15 per ton for their acid—a price that, after adding freight and handling charges, allowed smelter acid to compete favorably with the delivered prices of virgin acid at $50 to $75 per ton f.o.b. manufacturing plant, with the price being largely influenced by proximity to sulfur sourcing. Mining companies, the main source of smelter acid, were willing to unload their acid at very low prices because of the low-cost, by-product nature of smelter acid (any revenue they got for a largely unwanted by-product was considered as "gravy"); buyers of smelter acid bore the expensive freight charges (as much as $40 to $50 per ton depending on distance and freight rates) in transporting the substance.

Smelter acid had only recently become generally available in the merchant market, but low prices and growing availability had stimulated demand. Smelter acid production had grown from 1.6 million tons in 1955 to almost 4 million tons in 1979. A number of virgin acid producers bought smelter acid from mining companies for resale through their own marketing organization. Allied, in fact, was the dominant U.S. marketer of smelter acid with sales concentrated in the Northeast and the Midwest; this resale acid was marketed through Allied's distribution channels and was sold at a price just under the going market prices for virgin acid. Allied also purchased smelter acid for internal company use. The growing demand for smelter acid by price conscious end-users who were not concerned with its variable quality (because the nature of their use did not require pure acid) was having an adverse competitive effect on virgin sulfuric acid prices in 1980.

Industry Structure.   In 1980 the U.S. sulfuric acid industry consisted of about 5,000 customers served by over 50 producers. Domestic producers operated about 140 plants having a combined capacity of about 45 million tons. Industry revenues totaled about $2 billion. No producer supplied more than 8 percent of the total market and a number of producers had less than a 1 percent market share. Ten companies accounted for about 55 percent of the industry's production capacity, as shown in Exhibit 5.

Exhibit 5   MAJOR U.S. PRODUCERS OF SULFURIC ACID, 1979

Company	Annual capacity in tons (1979)	Percent of total U.S. capacity
Stauffer Chemical	3,800,000	8.4%
CF Industries*	3,430,000	7.6
Allied	2,532,000	5.6
Du Pont	2,445,000	5.4
Agrico Chemical*	2,400,000	5.3
Freeport Minerals*	2,296,000	5.1
Occidental Chemical*	2,184,000	4.9
Texasgulf*	2,072,000	4.6
IMC*	2,010,000	4.5
Beker Industries*	1,575,000	3.5

* Production capacity was almost exclusively dedicated to captive fertilizer requirements.

For the past 10 years the industry had suffered from substantial overcapacity. Excess supply conditions had resulted in industrywide capacity utilization rates in the 69 to 79 percent range—the 1968 through 1978 average was 73 percent.

In 1980, approximately 90 percent of all sulfuric acid shipments were made by truck; the remaining 10 percent of the shipments were carried by rail to final destinations. Truck shipments were favored over rail shipments because most acid was shipped only a short distance and because trucking could be arranged on shorter notice than could rail shipments.

Demand-Supply Conditions and Pricing. Because shipping costs were high relative to the actual production cost of acid, the output of most plants was marketed regionally. Historically, producers had located their plants close to end-use destinations. The supply network was more fully developed in the northeast, which for many years had had the strongest concentration of end-use demand. Plants had gradually been built in other regions as end-use demand sprung up in more and more geographic areas of the United States. By 1980, each major geographic region had developed its own unique characteristics of competition and pricing, largely based on supply-demand conditions in the region.

Regional demand patterns were in a state of flux. In recent years, some regions had experienced declines in demand (e.g., the northeast and midwest regions where much of Allied's capacity was located); two regions, the west and the southwest, had experienced growth in end-use demand. Meanwhile, continuing excess capacity conditions had caused shutdowns of older, higher cost plants and a number of producers had sold their sulfuric acid plants, either getting out of the business entirely or ridding themselves of unprofitable plants. Industrywide, however, companies had added nearly 5 million annual tons of new capacity since 1975—almost 2.5 million annual tons in the southwest region (1975–77), about 400,000 annual tons in the eastern region (1976–79), and about 2 million annual tons in eastern Canada (1977–79). Much of the new capacity, however, was being installed by end-users to put their own acid supply capability right next to their consuming operations; the rest of the expansion had been undertaken by smelters to collect sulfur dioxide gas that was causing an environmental problem.

Although reliable regional supply-demand figures were not available, regional production and merchant market sales figures were typically relied upon as reasonable proxies of regional market conditions. Examples of the regional production-merchant sales shifts during 1968–78 are shown in Exhibit 6.

The decline in production in the Northeast and North Central regions reflected declining end-use demand in these regions and growing availability of lower cost smelter acid entering the country from Canada. In 1955 Canadian imports of sulfuric acid were a fairly insignificant 28,000 tons, but, during the 1973–80 period, Canadian imports were in the 180,000 to 450,000 metric ton range. The major Canadian supplier to the U.S. market was CIL (Canadian Industries, Ltd.), an expansion-minded firm that manufactured and marketed Canadian smelter acid. Projections indicated Canadian production capacity would be more than ample to meet Canadian demand over the next five years and that the excess of about 325,000 net tons would likely be exported to the United States at least through 1984 and 1985.

Exhibit 6   SALES SHIFTS BETWEEN THE MERCHANT AND CAPTIVE SEGMENTS

Regional trends

Northeast:	Production—34 percent decline
	Merchant market shipments—35 percent decline
North central:	Production—25 percent decline
	Merchant market shipments—8 percent decline

Trends in selected states (where data were available)

States	Production	Approximate merchant market sales
Pennsylvania	37% decline	38% decline
Illinois	43% decline	11% decline
Virginia	10% increase	28% decline
Louisiana	203% increase	83% increase
California	27% decline	21% increase

In addition to the entry of Canadian imports, new sulfuric acid supplies were expected to come onto the market from electric utilities by 1985. Some coal-burning electric power plants, in response to new sulfur emission regulations, were projected to be equipped with sulfuric acid recovery systems. A minimum of 200,000 tons of acid was expected from these sources by 1985, and additional supplies were likely to be forthcoming after 1985. The collection of sulfuric acid by electric utilities was the result of desulfurizing flue gases, as opposed to turning the waste material into sludge to be disposed. Indications in 1980 were that the Environmental Protection Agency would institute regulations that would make sludge disposal so costly that the collection of sulfuric acid could become a more cost-efficient alternative for dealing with sulfur emissions. Even collection of a small fraction of the estimated potential of 49.4 million tons of sulfuric acid could have a dramatic effect on the competitive positions of traditional suppliers.

Sulfuric acid prices were historically determined largely by the cost of Frasch-mined sulfur, the major ingredient in producing virgin acid. As Frasch prices rose, sulfuric acid producers traditionally passed the higher costs through to end-users, explaining to customers that the price increases were a direct cause of the higher costs of Frasch-mined sulfur. 1980 projections showed a tightening of Frasch sulfur supply for several years and conditions were not expected to improve until 1983–85. The tight supply could be expected to push Frasch sulfur prices up again. According to the findings of Allied's Sulfuric Task Force:

> Sulfur is expected to remain in tight supply for the next few years with any substantial relief not expected to occur prior to the 1983–85 period. During this period, sulfur recovery projects from the Middle East, especially Saudi Arabia, could narrow the supply-demand gap sufficiently to begin some rebuilding of inventories. Recent curtailments in Iranian sulfur recovery illustrates, however, the vulnerability of supply from this area of the world. Tight supplies should continue to put upward pressure on price although some moderation is expected from recent sharp levels of escalation. Allied is continuing to try to minimize adverse cost effects by switching from costly Frasch sulfur to sulfur recovered from oil refineries or natural gas processing plants.

The regional nature of competition created variations in virgin sulfuric acid prices from region to region:

	Average annual price per ton of sulfuric acid	
Region	**1979**	**1980**
Northeast	$62.30	$81.92
Midwest	57.15	71.21
Gulf coast	55.75	74.81
Southwest	59.30	71.85

Because of the commodity nature of the product, if one major company changed its price to buyers in a region, other sellers in the region could be expected to follow the change.

Allied's Position in the U.S. Sulfuric Acid Industry

Over 75 percent of Allied's sulfuric acid capacity was located in the Northeast and Midwest, where the industrial market for sulfuric acid had steadily declined in the last 10 years. In 1980, Allied operated 10 sulfuric acid producing plants in the United States, as shown in Exhibit 7. Seven of the ten plants operated at a profit in 1979; their combined 1979 return on assets was 8 percent. In addition, between 1968 and 1978 Allied was the dominant domestic marketer of by-product acid, handling an average of 650,000 net tons annually; of this, 40 percent was consumed by other Allied businesses (captive use) and the balance was sold in the merchant market.

As of 1980, Allied had contracts with seven smelter acid producers to resell 772,000 tons per year:

Smelter acid producer	**Location**	**Tons per year**
Bunker Hill	Idaho	90,000
Phelps Dodge	New Mexico	157,000
Amax	Iowa	50,000
NJ Zinc	Pennsylvania	115,000
Getty Oil	Delaware	130,000
Amax	Pennsylvania	90,000
Noranda	Canada	140,000
Total		772,000

Allied estimated that in 1978–79 its pretax return on assets employed in resale operations was 29 percent.

The third segment of Allied's sulfuric operations involved spent acid conversion. Spent sulfuric acid was generated as a residual product when virgin acid was

		1979	1979
Plant location	**Capacity (tons/year)**	**Production volume (tons)**	**Sales (in 000s)**
Harrisburg, Pa.	145,000	122,550	$ 5,641
Philadelphia, Pa.	360,000	356,059	14,845
Pittsburgh, Pa.	160,000	112,166	5,319
Syracuse, N.Y.	114,000	93,823	4,443
Cumberland, Md.	130,000	85,654	3,057
Baltimore, Md.	153,000	133,404	4,953
Little Rock, Ark.	100,000	86,981	3,532
Toledo, Ohio	160,000	142,011	7,511
Sacramento, Caif.	150,000	92,728	3,749
Bakersfield, Calif.	90,000	80,677	2,788
Total	1,562,000	1,306,053	$55,838

Exhibit 7 ALLIED'S SULFURIC ACID PLANT OPERATIONS, 1979

not totally consumed during its use in a manufacturing process. The waste acid was typically contaminated with water, organics, or other impurities making it unsuitable for reuse directly in the same process. Spent acid regenerators, such as Allied, refortified, reprocessed, or resold these waste products for their customers. The charge for converting these spent acids coupled with the raw material and, in certain cases, fuel values contained in the waste acids made this business segment, in Allied's opinion, particularly attractive. Allied's Sulfuric Task Force concluded that recent sharp increases in the price of Frasch sulfur, together with tougher environmental and toxic regulations, would enhance future profitability of this segment. The Task Force reported:

> This is a service oriented, value added business. It is well protected from by-product incursions, has raw material supply protection, and is partially insulated from business cycles. Almost 90 percent of the business is done with oil companies which are strong financially and see sulfuric acid as a relatively small element of refinery costs. The seasonality of the business does require additional investment in storage in excess of that which normally supports the sulfuric businesses.

Allied operated seven plants to handle spent acid conversion; five were in the declining industrial areas of the northeast and north central regions.

A summary of the overall performance of Allied's sulfuric acid operations is contained in Exhibit 8.

Competition. In the virgin acid manufacturing and spent acid conversion segments, the number of Allied's competitors varied from plant to plant. At one plant Allied had to confront eight competitors; at another there were no nearby competitors. Most plants, however, had three to five competitors. Among Allied's biggest rivals were Du Pont, CIL, Essex, Stauffer, and American Cyanamid; lesser competitors included Coulton Chemical, National Distillers, Mobil, Esmark, Beker, and Monsanto. In the resale segment, Allied's primary competitor was Canadian Industries Limited (CIL). Allied considered it was the

Exhibit 8 PROFITABILITY OF ALLIED'S SULFURIC ACID OPERATIONS, 1970–78

	Volume (in thousands of tons)				Combined revenues ($ millions)	Pretax income ($ millions)	Pretax income as a percent of sales revenues
Year	Virgin acid production	Spent acid conversion	Resale of by-product acid	Total			
1970	1,590	498	568	2,656	$56.3	$ 8.1	14.4%
1971	1,542	486	563	2,591	51.7	5.6	10.8
1972	1,474	489	623	2,586	52.8	4.2	7.9
1973	1,359	429	707	2,495	54.9	5.4	9.9
1974	1,320	357	742	2,419	63.9	7.5	11.7
1975	1,025	284	510	1,819	68.8	12.3	17.9
1976	1,080	318	628	2,026	81.7	15.4	18.9
1977	1,123	328	714	2,165	86.3	8.9	10.3
1978	1,052	319	755	2,126	86.4	6.8	7.9

Source: Allied Corporation, Sulfuric Task Force Report.

leading U.S. marketer of by-product or smelter acid. CIL was the only other major acid producer with a significant by-product acid strategy; CIL handled about 1.6 million tons of by-product acid annually, about double Allied's 1980 volume, but much of CIL's volume was marketed to Canadian end-users. Allied expected CIL to challenge Allied's leadership in the resale segment in the United States. Other producers who competed with Allied in reselling by-product acid included Stauffer Chemical, Du Pont, Olin, and Esmark—all of which handled substantially smaller volumes than Allied.

The Sulfuric Task Force evaluated Allied's business characteristics and competitive strength in both virgin acid manufacture and the resale of by-product acid. The findings are summarized in Exhibits 9 and 10.

Allied's 1980 pretax return on assets for sulfuric acid operations was 7.6 percent. The Task Force came up with the capital requirements projections through 1984 as follows:

Allied's plants	Capital needs estimates (in thousands of dollars)				
	1980	1981	1982	1983	1984
Syracuse, New York	$ 440	$ 440	$ 440	$ 440	$ 440
Pittsburgh, Pennsylvania	765	825	795	1,545	1,320
Cumberland, Maryland	117	350	277	455	450
Toledo, Ohio	1,167	1,768	929	459	506
Philadelphia, Pennsylvania	1,800	2,695	1,450	1,795	4,755
Harrisburg, Pennsylvania	695	615	600	330	330
Little Rock, Arkansas	332	550	725	650	470
Bakersfield, California	570	489	335	457	300
Sacramento, California	950	1,000	700	200	375
Baltimore, Maryland	400	1,085	340	175	325
Total	$7,236	$9,817	$6,591	$6,506	$9,271

Exhibit 9 ALLIED'S BUSINESS CHARACTERISTICS AND COMPETITIVE STRENGTH, SULFURIC ACID MANUFACTURING OPERATIONS AND SPENT ACID CONVERSION OPERATIONS

Plant evaluations

Business characteristics	Philadelphia	Harris-burg	Syracuse	Pitts-burgh	Cumber-land	Toledo	Little Rock	Bakers-field	Sacra-mento	Balti-more
Number of competitors	5	4	3	3	2	8	5	0	3	2
Cyclicality	High	Moderate	High	High	High	High	High	Low	Low	High
Growth	Low	Low	Low	Low	Low	Low	Moderate	Low	Low	Low
Environmental problems	Moderate	High	High	Moderate	High	Moderate	High	Low	Moderate	High
Customer price concerns	Moderate	Moderate	Moderate	Moderate	Moderate	Moderate	Moderate	Low	Low	Moderate
Seasonality	Yes	Yes	Yes	No	No	Yes	No	Yes	Yes	No
Barriers to entry	High	High	High	High	High	High	High	High	High	High
Importance of capacity util.	High	High	High	High	High	High	High	High	High	High
Asset intensity	High	High	High	High	High	High	High	High	High	High
Raw material security	Concerns	No	Concerns	Concerns	Concerns	Concerns	Concerns	No	No	Concerns
Energy/labor intensity	Low	Low	Low	Low	Low	Low	Low	Low	Low	Low
Number—customer base	Moderate	Low	High	High	High	High	Moderate	Low	Moderate	Low
Product differentiation	Low	Low	Low	Low	Low	Low	Low	Low	Low	Low
Service content	High (spent acid)	High	High (spent acid)	High (spent acid)	Low	High (spent acid)	Low	High	High	Low
Marketing content	Low	Low	Low	Low	Low	Low (spent acid)	Low	Low	Low	Low
Competitive strengths										
Market share	Strong	Strong	Strong	Strong	Strong	Tenable	Weak	Strong	Equal	Strong
Cost	Equal	Weak	Tenable	Tenable	Tenable	Equal	Tenable	Strong	Strong	Equal
Raw material position	Strong (spent acid)	Strong	Strong (spent acid)	Equal	Weak	Strong (spent acid)	Equal	Strong	Strong	Equal
Base load	Strong	Strong	Equal	Strong	Strong	Strong	Strong	Strong	Strong	Strong
Facilities	Strong	Tenable	Tenable	Tenable	Equal	Equal	Tenable	Strong	Equal	Equal
Service	Equal	Equal	Equal	Equal	Equal	Equal	Equal	Strong	Strong	Strong
Environmental/ leg. impact	Strong	Weak	Weak	Strong	Tenable	Strong	Strong	Strong	Strong	Tenable
Labor	Equal	Tenable	Equal	Equal	Equal	Equal	Equal	Equal	Equal	Equal
Organization	Equal	Tenable	Equal	Equal	Equal	Equal	Equal	Equal	Equal	Equal
Financial	Tenable	Weak	Tenable	Weak	Equal	Equal	Tenable	Strong	Strong	Strong
Technology	Equal	Equal	Tenable	Tenable	Tenable	Equal	Tenable	Strong	Strong	Tenable

Source: Allied Corporation, Sulfuric Task Force Report.

Exhibit 10 ALLIED'S BUSINESS CHARACTERISTICS AND COMPETITIVE STRENGTH, RESALE OF BY-PRODUCT ACID SEGMENT

Business characteristics	Evaluation
Number of competitors	8
Cyclicality	High
Growth	Moderate
Environmental impact/concerns/problems	High
Application critical	Yes
Customer price concern	Moderate
Seasonality	No
Barriers to entry	Low
Capacity utilization importance	Low
Asset intensity	Moderate
Raw material security	Moderate concern
Energy/labor intensity	Low
Product differentiation	Low
Service content	Low
Material content	Low

Competitive strengths	Evaluation
Market share	Strong
Cost	Equal
Base load	Strong
Service	Strong
Environmental impact/concerns/problems	Equal
Labor	Equal
Organization	Equal
Financial	Strong
Market position/market niche	Strong
Product	Equal
Price	Equal
Selling	Equal
Distribution	Strong
Image	Strong
Product mix	Equal
Customer mix	Equal

Source: Allied Corporation, Sulfuric Task Force Report.

Sulfuric Task Force Recommendations

The Task Force concluded that the sulfuric acid industry, despite the problems of overcapacity and declining industrial end-use demand, was attractive—at least from Allied's standpoint. However, the Task Force recommended that Allied close several plants and consolidate operations to improve profitability in line with the corporate target of an 18 percent pretax return on assets. The specific plant-related recommendations were as follows:

1. *Harrisburg*—Shut the plant and serve customers on contract from Allied's Philadelphia plant. (The plant was incurring substantial financial losses.)

2. *Syracuse*—Continue to operate and maintain for the time being. (The economics for this location were integrated with Allied's production of nitric acid, ammonium thiosulfate, oxalic and metallic nitrates, all of which were attractively profitable. The Task Force noted that this plant's profitability could also be enhanced by shifting some production over from the Harrisburg and Pittsburgh plants.)

3. *Pittsburgh*—Shut the plant. (This plant had had an unacceptable ROA in the past and was projected to stay well below 18 percent in the future. The plant was at a competitive disadvantage and opportunities existed to shift a large part of the plant's output to other Allied plants where excess capacity existed.)

4. *Cumberland*—Continue to operate for the time being but find cheaper sulfur sources. To improve this plant's economics, the high-cost sulfur contract with Allied's Frasch sulfur supplier should be bought out at a $12 per ton penalty. Periodic make-buy analyses should be made to determine longer term viability.

5. *Little Rock*—Shut the plant and purchase Allied's captive acid requirements in the open market. (As an option, the Task Force indicated one of Allied's sister divisions, a major customer of this plant's output, could be approached to fund the operation at Little Rock at an adequate transfer price.)

6. *Toledo*—Operate for three years with restricted capital outlays (until mid-1983) while attempting to build a clientele and sales base for the plant with spent acid and other chemical products. If this is not successful, then take an orderly phase-out of operations.

7. *Philadelphia*—Attack the current low ROA by aggressively seeking more customers and by filling capacity through Harrisburg shutdown. Improved plant economics can be expected from absorbing activities formerly performed at Harrisburg and Pittsburgh plants.

8. *Other locations*—Continue to operate Baltimore, Bakersfield, and Sacramento plants, as all are operating at acceptable profit levels.

Because of weakening demand and forecasts of growing Canadian imports of by-product acid in the Northeast and North Central regions, the Task Force concluded that insofar as expansion of Allied's resale business was concerned, it would be best to pursue a Southwest strategy. The supporting reasons offered were:

1. Additional growth in the demand for smelter-produced by-product acid was anticipated in the Southwest and West regions.

2. Mining operations in the Southwest were expected to grow, thus offering good sources of smelter acid for resale.

3. Allied was recognized as a major marketer of sulfuric acid.

4. Allied's other divisions had a continuing need for sulfuric acid as a raw material.

5. A continuing position in the marketplace would insure Allied of a reliable and economic supply of acid.

The initial recommended action for the Southwest strategy was the negotiation of a contract with an Arizona mining operation to handle the resale of 500,000 tons of by-product acid. The Task Force developed a marketing plan and financial analysis for the proposed 500,000-ton arrangement, which projected a 24 percent pretax return on assets based on prevailing market conditions.

The Task Force identified three opportunity areas where Allied could expand profits in reprocessing spent acid, stating its findings as follows:

1. *Expansion into new spent acid opportunity areas*. Basically this area includes those waste acids previously disposed of by neutralizing disposal facilities or reused directly. Nitration spent acids containing nitrates and possibly halogen products, as well as those spents deemed unsuitable for the direct manufacture of fertilizers or other related products, will be forced into treatment and reprocessing over the next five years as tougher environmental standards are implemented. The company's technical and research efforts in this area will give us the expertise to initiate reprocessing of these acids in increasing quantities.

2. *The use of available excess capacity* at Allied's remaining plant (assuming the shutdown recommendation are followed) to achieve economies of scale and greater plant utilization economics. Opportunities exist to shift the spent acid operations at Harrisburg over to the Philadelphia plant, to de-bottleneck spent acid conversion at Pittsburgh once the Syracuse plant is closed, and to use the excess capacity at Toledo to handle spent acids currently serviced by Stauffer in Hammond, Indiana, and by U.S.I. in Kansas.

3. *The expansion of Allied into the Southwest market* by investing in spent acid facilities to serve an Arizona operation. This would enable Allied to share a portion of this growing market to counteract expected declines or lack of growth in Allied's existing Northern U.S. market areas.

The Task Force saw spent acid reprocessing as "an important area for future profit growth."

ALLIED'S RESPONSE TO THE TASK FORCE REPORT

Shortly after Allied's Sulfuric Task Force presented its recommendations, senior management took action. A $28 million pretax nonrecurring charge was made in the last quarter of 1980 to cover the write-off of sulfuric acid facilities that it was decided would be sold or shut down in 1981. In October 1981 the Toledo and Syracuse plants were sold and the Harrisburg plant was shut. In January 1982 the Pittsburgh plant was closed. In response to the Task Force's Southwest strategy recommendation, by mid-1982 Allied had implemented a major expansion of its West Coast sulfuric acid facility located at Bakersfield, California. Allied's strategy for the sulfuric acid area was revised and profiled in June 1982 (Exhibit 11). The Little Rock plant was shut down in December 1982.

Exhibit 11 ALLIED'S 1982 STRATEGIC PROFILE FOR ITS SULFURIC ACID UNIT

A. Situation analysis

1. *Statement of Scope:*

   - Sulfuric acid manufactured or purchased for resale is sold to domestic petroleum, fibers, steel, paint, paper, chemical, and agricultural industries.
   - Reprocessing sulfur-containing products for specialty markets.
   - Provide sulfur products for upgrading into other Allied products.

2. *Industry Description*

   1982: $2.3 billion: 34 metric tons (MM): 60 percent capacity.

   Approximately ⅔ of total industry volume is consumed captively for fertilizer manufacture.

   Major merchant market producers include:

	Capacity—MM Tons
Stauffer	3.7
Du Pont	2.5
Allied	1.9
Olin	1.1
American Cyanamid	1.1
Canadian Industries, Ltd.	0.6

   Sulfuric acid, the largest volume commodity chemical in the United States, is produced both by burning sulfur and as a recovered by-product. Historically, sulfuric acid has been manufactured from Frasch-mined sulfur, while selected locations have used spent acid regeneration and other sulfur bearing sources (e.g., H_2S: hydrogen sulfide) to augment raw material requirements. Frasch sulfur pricing has generally set acid pricing, but now environmentally dictated acid tends to sell at a lower price. The U.S. industry comprises 170 producing locations and about 5,000 customers. Markets are primarily regional in nature with minor exceptions involving movement of by-product acid.

   - Cyclicality: Linked to GNP
   - Timing: Coincident
   - Amplitude: Medium

3. *Industry Maturity*

   Current: *Aging*   Future: *Aging*

4. *Market Statistics (nonfertilizer segment)*

Nonfertilizer end-uses	U.S. MM	Allied MM	Allied growth rate	
			Past 5 years	Next 5 years
Chemicals	3.2	.5	−6.0	2.0
Petroleum	2.5	.2	−9.6	—
Other	7.6	.4	−4.4	2.0
Total	13.3	1.1	−5.8	1.7

5. *Market Description*

   Sulfuric acid is used to digest phosrock in the production of phosphate fertilizer. Most of the required sulfuric acid is produced captively. Chemical end uses are numerous; usually requiring high quality acid. Distribution systems and reliability of supply are important. In the petroleum industry it is used as a catalyst for alkylate and in other uses resulting in spent acids and sludges from which the acid must be recovered by decomposition techniques. Coke production by the steel industry requires large quantities of sulfuric acid for ammonium sulfate. Use for processing uranium ore in the West has grown; however, current demand for this use has slowed. Sulfuric acid supply has increased due to by-product acid recoveries in Canada and the Southwest. This by-product acid is sold throughout the United States.

Exhibit 11 *(continued)*

6. *Strategic Unit Description*

Allied's plants are managed to support captive requirements of about 316 million tons/year ($23 million) for upgraded Chemical group products, profitable service related reprocessing of sulfur containing materials, and stand-alone profitable locations which have defendable competitive positions.

Manufacturing plants include:

		Millions of net tons	
	Capacity	**1982 Volume estimate**	**Utilization**
Bakersfield	90	77	86%
Sacramento	150	100	67
Philadelphia	370	337	91
Baltimore	152	113	74
Total	762	627	82%

Additionally, approximately 450M tons/year of by-product acid is either resold or captively consumed.

  8 customers = 50% of Allied's total trade tons
24 customers = 80% of Allied's total trade tons

7. *Competitive Analysis*

	Du Pont	**Stauffer**	**CIL**	**AmCy**	**Essex**
Protected market position	+	=	+	+	+
Total cost	=	+	=	=	=
Profitability	=	=	+	=	−
Net cash throw-off	=	=	+	=	=
Location & size of facility	=	+	=	+	=

Summary: Equal/Favorable

8. *Past Strategies*

- Maintenance
- Market rationalization
- Product rationalization

B. Plan analysis

1. *Key Assumptions*

- Economic recovery in 1983.
- Decomposition volume remains stable.
- Contracts with big customers will continue.
- Increased competition—East Coast.
- No change in government regulations.
- By-product acid resale arrangements continue.

2. *Strategic Thrust and Positioning*

- Hold niche.
- Stand-alone manufacturing locations (product/market segments) will be managed to maximize return and cash flow. Resale arrangements will be continued wherever profitable.

Exhibit 11 *(concluded)*

3. *Acquisition Activities*
   None
4. *Current/Future Strategic Situation*

	Embryo	Growth	Mature	Aging
Leading				
Strong				
Favorable				X
Tenable				
Weak				

5. *Major Threats/Concerns*
   - East Coast competition will result in lower market share and margins.
   - Major customer plant closings could be announced.
   - By-product acid availability is growing.

Frank Biermann, marketing manager for Allied's sulfuric acid business, reflected on the changes that were implemented:

As a result of our actions in 1981, our sulfuric acid business is far healthier now and has the strong support of corporate management. Our current production locations, our captive demand, and our distribution systems have us well positioned to take advantage of further directional changes in both supply and demand for sulfuric acid in the years ahead.

I arrived on the scene in Spring 1981 to implement much of the plant rationalization strategy that had been formulated. Certainly the business is far healthier today because people made the tough decisions back in 1980 to shed assets that were marginal at best in markets that were to be increasingly dominated by smelter acid.

Our company's management has attained some notoriety in recent years for its aggressive acquisition program, but product or plant rationalization deserves even more credit because that is often a more difficult task. When Hennessy was brought aboard in 1979, he put renewed emphasis on ROA. The response by the Sulfuric Acid business group was right on target. Profit has been increased and assets have been reduced.

One of the ways that we have improved ROA is to put increased emphasis on individual asset bases. In the old days the Allied sulfuric business was viewed more as a nationwide "system" where profits were measured as a percentage of total business investment because of the number of plant locations and their intersecting shipping circles. This type of management approach can make a rationalization strategy difficult to conceive or implement because good locations can cover up poor ones when they are averaged. Nowadays, each location must stand on its own, either as a manufacturing plant or as a resale (smelter acid) location. Every location is expected to produce an acceptable ROA.

Exhibit 12 FINANCIAL PERFORMANCE OF ALLIED CORPORATION'S SULFUR PRODUCTS
OPERATIONS, 1981–83 (dollar figures in millions)

	Baltimore			Sacramento		
	1981	**1982**	**1983**	**1981**	**1982**	**1983**
Sales and operating revenue	$8.9	$7.7	$7.3	$7.8	$6.8	$8.9
Pretax income	$1.4	$0.7	$1.0	$2.9	$2.4	$2.4
Average assets	$4.6	$4.0	$4.1	$4.9	$5.3	$5.6
ROA	30.5%	17.5%	24.3%	59.2%	45.3%	42.8%
	Bakersfield			Philadelphia		
	1981	**1982**	**1983**	**1981**	**1982**	**1983**
Sales and operating revenue	$5.6	$5.5	$7.0	$33.1	$35.0	$33.6
Pretax income	$2.2	$2.4	$3.5	$ 3.5	$ 4.0	$ 3.7
Average assets	$6.1	$5.8	$5.7	$29.6	$26.4	$26.6
ROA	36.1%	41.4%	61.4%	11.8%	15.2%	13.9%
	Resale/Other			Discontinued		
	1981	**1982**	**1983**	**1981**	**1982**	**1983**
Sales and operating revenue	$24.8	$21.2	$19.8	$19.7		
Pretax income	$ 2.6	$ 0.9	$ 2.0	$ (4.4)		
Average assets	$ 2.7	$ 2.9	$ 2.0	$20.9		
ROA	96.3%	31.0%	100.0%	−21.1%		
	Total					
	1981	**1982**	**1983**			
Sales and operating revenue	$99.9	$76.2	$76.6			
Pretax income	$ 7.7	$10.3	$12.5			
Average assets	$68.8	$44.7	$44.0			
ROA	11.2%	23.1%	28.4%			

Source: Allied Corporation.

The real credit for Allied's strength today, from a marketing sense, probably belongs to my predecessors in the 1960s and early 1970s. They had the foresight to recognize that Allied should be in the business of marketing sulfuric acid, rather than merely manufacturing it. They recognized that copper smelters, electric utilities, and other environmentally related acid producers were going to need some help in marketing by-product acid. We now have in place the distribution systems (barges, rail fleet, tank trucks, order entry, sales force) to do the job . . . to provide a service where select opportunities allow us to earn an acceptable return on assets involved in selling by-product acid.

Exhibit 12 shows the 1981–83 operating results for Allied's sulfuric operations.

DEVELOPMENTS IN THE SULFURIC ACID INDUSTRY, 1982

In addition to the actions taken by Allied, several other sulfuric acid production facilities in the United States changed ownership during 1982 as shown in Exhibit 13.

Exhibit 13   SALES/PURCHASES OF U.S. SULFURIC ACID PLANTS, 1982

Buyer	Seller	Location	Annual capacity in tons
PVS Chemicals	Ozark-Mahoning	Tulsa, Okla.	90,000
PVS Chemicals	3M	Copley, Ohio	98,000
Koch Industries	N-Ren	Pine Bend, Minn.	98,000
Koch Industries	Northeast Chemical	Wilmington, N.C.	120,000
Smith-Douglas	Bordon, Inc.	Streator, Ill.	30,000
Amax Phosphate	Bordon, Inc.	Piney Point, Pa.	550,000
Mobil	Olin Corp.	Pasadena, Texas	500,000
J. R. Simplot Co.	Valley Nitrogen	Helm, Calif.	2,000,000
Tennessee Chemical	Cities Service Co.	Copperhill, Tenn.	1,260,000

Industry analysts attributed many of the plant sales to the growing strength of lower-priced smelter acid, as well as to the aggressive efforts of CIL to gain a bigger share of the U.S. market for both virgin and smelter acids. Also, virgin sulfuric acid profits were squeezed hard by depressed virgin acid prices, increased Frasch sulfur costs, and a significant economywide recession. Many companies began looking to dispose of unprofitable or out-of-date facilities.

There were a number of other developments in 1982:

July: Smelter acid producers began running low on inventories brought about by depressed copper, lead, and zinc markets. (Producers of these metals generated smelter acid as a by-product of their ore processing operations.) Many mining companies began to shut down for indefinite lengths of time in an effort to work off excess inventories and adjust production to reduced demand. However, the curtailment of smelter acid availability gave smelter acid producers an opening to boost prices, though not so much as to get above the posted prices on virgin sulfuric acid.

October: Frasch sulfur producers reduced prices by $12.50 per ton, which meant a cost savings for virgin sulfuric acid producers of around $3.80 per ton.

November: CIL Chemicals announced it would spend $1 million at its newly acquired Sayreville, New Jersey, operations to upgrade its acid storage capacity, sulfur delivery, and railway car loading facilities. This announcement was preceded by the U.S. Department of Transportation's decision to extend the amount of allowable loaded train movement between the United States and Canada.

November: Du Pont announced that it would drastically cut its sulfuric acid prices in an effort to reaffirm its market position, a move widely interpreted as signalling strong retaliation to CIL's aggressive attemps to grab market share. Du Pont's announced price cuts were as follows:

Market	Old price per ton	New price per ton
New Jersey	$95.90	$61.00
West Pennsylvania	80.25	55.80
Chicago	77.00	55.80
Gulf Coast	88.50	83.50
Virginia	95.90	90.90
Ohio Valley	80.25	75.25

November: CIL matched Du Pont's price cuts, despite having some operating problems in meeting its supply commitments from its Sayreville plant.

December: Other companies were slow to follow the deep price cuts announced by Du Pont and CIL. Industry observers speculated that this was because profit margins were already squeezed by a 10 to 20 percent falloff in demand in the Northeast.

SULFURIC ACID INDUSTRY DEVELOPMENTS, 1983

New competitive developments and capacity changes continued to keep the industry in a state of flux during 1983:

January: Sulfuric acid prices in the northeastern one-third of the United States began to stabilize around the Du Pont levels.

February: A slight increase in sulfuric acid demand occurred in the highly competitive Midwest and Northeast markets. The Southeast experienced some increase in demand, although not as much as was seen elsewhere; industry analysts suggested this might have been because the Southeast had not experienced the sharp price cuts that had hit the industrial Northeast and Midwest.

February: Chemical Marketing Services announced it would acquire two facilities that would have a combined production capacity of 75,000 tons of virgin sulfuric acid. (However, the acquisition never materialized.)

May: Frasch sulfur producers in Florida cut prices as much as $12.50 per long ton (2,240 pounds). Industry analysts familiar with the southeast region believed the price cuts were an effort to stave off the entry of Canadian-producer Frasch sulfur into the Gulf Coast mar-

ket. Canadian producers had begun shipping their sulfur to customers in the region just a few months earlier.

May: Japanese suppliers began exporting sulfuric acid to the Gulf Coast, adding to oversupply conditions in that area. The Japanese prices were said to be in the $35–39 per ton range; the posted prices of domestic producers selling in the Gulf Coast region were $48 to $52 per ton.

July: Phelps Dodge Corporation's copper mine workers went on strike and similar actions were being threatened at other major U.S. mines; the potential reduction in smelter acid supplies brought "a ray of hope" to producers plagued with general oversupply conditions. Without a steady stream of new smelter acid to handle, smelter acid suppliers were expected to be able to work off inventories to meet demand; inventories were said to be big enough to handle two months of sales.

August: Demand for sulfuric acid remained low, particularly in fertilizer end-uses where demand was not expected to recover until fall 1984. End-use demand in mining from 1981 to 1982 had fallen 800,000 tons.

August: Asarco, Incorporated, announced plans to increase daily capacity of smelter acid in the near future at its Hayden, Arizona, facility from its present 750 tons a day to 2,800 tons a day. Kennecott Corporation also announced plans to increase its daily smelter acid capacity approximately 65 percent to 600 tons a day.

September: Announcements indicated phosphate fertilizer exports were increasing and that by the spring of 1984 domestic sulfuric acid demand might in turn be boosted (sulfuric acid was needed to make phosphoric acid, which was a prime ingredient in producing phosphate fertilizers). The rise in phosphoric fertilizer production was also expected to assist in undergirding Frasch sulfur prices. Meanwhile, continued discounting of sulfuric acid on the Gulf Coast prompted Stauffer Chemical, the area's biggest producer, to drop its prices from $83.50 to $65 per ton. Prices in Houston remained between $95 and $100 per ton and Louisiana prices were about $5 higher. On the West Coast, increasing supply and limited demand prompted producers of sulfuric acid to turn to exporting their products. Exports had recently risen 65 percent and carried prices of $82 per ton.

October: Du Pont signed an agreement with Asarco, Inc., to purchase 300,000 tons of smelter acid per year from Asarco's Hayden, Arizona, plant. Speculations about the purchase were that Du Pont (1) might use the new supplies to cut back on its own sulfuric acid production, (2) might use the new supplies in place of other ways to meet its sulfuric requirements along the Gulf Coast, or (3) might have made the purchase to prevent another supplier from making that same purchase and using it to compete with Du Pont. Du Pont maintained the purchase was made in an effort to supply the midwest market that it presently could not serve.

October: Cutbacks in virgin sulfuric acid production, coupled with a growing optimism in the fertilizer industry, improved the outlook for bringing sulfuric acid demand and supply conditions into better balance in 1984. However, excess capacity and a dormant uranium end-use market continued to depress prices, particularly in the Gulf Coast area. Acid prices elsewhere were showing signs of firming up.

ALLIED'S STRATEGY IN SULFURIC ACID, 1984

Going into 1984 about 30 percent of Allied's sulfuric acid supplies were shipped to other Allied divisions and about 70 percent was sold in the merchant market. Allied had a base of approximately 600 customers for its various sulfur products. Overall U.S. consumption of sulfuric acid was projected to grow at an average annual rate of 2.5 percent from a 1984 base. Allied's strategy for the sulfuric acid business was reviewed and profiled in 1984 (Exhibit 14).

Frank Biermann, Allied's marketing manager for sulfuric acid products, indicated his thoughts about what future market conditions in the industry would be like:

The industry scene today is marked by the dominance of agricultural demand (largely captive supply) in certain geographical areas, continued retrenchment of producers who use Frasch to make virgin acid, and ambiguities in the supply of by-product acid.

Open market prices for sulfuric acid continue to be threatened by excess capacity among the fertilizer producers; the demand for agricultural fertilizers is down and some fertilizer producers are said to be considering selling sulfuric acid in the industrial market given that they temporarily do not need all of their acid-producing capacity in-house. However, their high concentration in Florida and the Gulf States, coupled with customer skepticism over just how long the fertilizer companies will be willing to commit their acid-making term commitment of capacity to outside merchant sales, has certainly minimized the impact of the current weak agricultural demand on industrial marketers such as Allied. Where it does hurt, though, is where large quantities of smelter acid are suddenly freed up because some of the fertilizer producers are no longer buying smelter acid on the open market to supplement their own in-house acid-producing capacity.

I expect to see some further shutdowns of sulfur based plants because of the impact of smelter acid. Generally, they are smaller plants that either have no specialty niche (upgrading to Oleum, regeneration of spent acids) or are facing large capital investments. Some of these plants are sold to smaller firms with presumably lower overhead who seem to hang in there longer than the larger companies. Sometimes they make very little sense from a marketing viewpoint. Large quantities of new sulfuric acid were predicted to arrive by the mid-80s as the acid rain issue received attention. This has just not happened anywhere near on-schedule. Electric utilities have just not moved to collect sulfur gases from their stacks via the sulfuric acid route to any degree at all. A number of copper smelters have improved their operations, resulting in more efficient collection of sulfur gases. While this has resulted in increased acid production at certain locations, in general the copper industry has been hurt badly by producers in South America and Africa who have higher grade ore deposits and often are accused of producing only to generate foreign exchange.

Exhibit 14 ALLIED'S 1984 STRATEGIC PLAN FOR ITS SULFURIC ACID BUSINESS

A. Situation analysis

1. *Statement of Scope*

   Sulfuric acid manufactured or purchased for resale is sold to domestic petroleum, fibers, steel, paint, paper, chemical, and agricultural industries. Related activities also include specialty reprocessing of sulfur-containing products.

   About 30 percent of Allied's sulfur products produced in this business unit are captively consumed in upgrade products (used by other Allied businesses), with the remaining 70 percent moving to the merchant market. Specifically excluded from the scope of this unit are sulfuric manufacturing facilities where product is totally consumed in captive on-site upgrading for fibers, agriculture, and Hydrofluoric Acid (HF) products.

2. *Industry Description*

   Sulfuric acid, the largest volume commodity chemical in the United States, is produced both by burning sulfur and as a recovered by-product. Total sulfuric acid production in the United States is valued at about $2.0 billion, typically representing 40 million net tons of product annually. Most sulfuric acid is consumed captively in production of other industrial chemicals, primarily fertilizers. Only about 30 percent of U.S. production moves to the merchant market. However, included in this percentage is acid use for alkylation and other sludge-producing operations that must be purchased from specific plants capable of recycling sludges. Historically, sulfuric acid has been manufactured from Frasch-mined sulfur, while selected locations have used spent acid regeneration and other sulfur bearing sources to augment raw material requirements. Frasch sulfur pricing has generally set acid pricing, but now environmentally-dictated acid tends to sell at a lower price. The U.S. industry comprises 140 producing locations with capacity of about 55 million net tons, and about 5,000 customers. Markets are primarily regional in nature with minor exceptions involving movement of by-product acid.

   Cyclicality: Linked to GNP; strong agricultural influences because of big fertilizer end-use.
   Timing: Coincident
   Amplitude: Medium

   There are 70 companies producing sulfuric acid in the United States at 140 producing locations.
   Major merchant market producers include:

	Capacity—MM tons
Stauffer	3.8
Du Pont	2.5
Allied	1.2
Tennessee Chemical	1.4
American Cyanamid	1.1
Canadian Industries, Ltd.	0.6
Essex Chemical	0.6

3. *Industry Maturity*

   Current: *Aging*   Future: *Aging*

Exhibit 14 *(continued)*

4. *Market Statistics*

Total consumption of sulfuric acid in the United States grew at an average annual rate of 3.0 percent from 1972 to 1981. Consumption declined significantly in 1982 and 1983 due to the general economic slowdown. This has been particularly true in the hard-hit fertilizer sector, which (excluding ammonium sulfate) accounts for some 60 percent of sulfuric acid consumption. Overall, U.S. consumption of sulfuric acid is projected to grow at an average annual rate of 2.5 percent from a 1984 base for the next several years, reflecting in part a recovery from the economic downturn. Growth in fertilizer use will exceed this rate, while other uses will be static or exhibit slower growth.

Nonfertilizer end uses	U.S. MM	Allied MM	Allied growth rate past 5 years
Chemicals	4.9	.6	−6.0
Petroleum	2.0	.2	−9.6
Other	7.5	.4	−4.4
Total	14.2	1.2	−5.8

5. *Market Description*

Sulfuric acid is used to digest phosrock in the production of phosphate fertilizer. Most of the required sulfuric acid is produced captively. Chemical end uses are numerous, usually requiring high quality acid. Distribution systems and reliability of supply are important. In the petroleum industry it is used as a catalyst for alkylate and in other uses resulting in spent acids and sludges from which the acid must be recovered by decomposition techniques. Coke production by the steel industry requires large quantities of sulfuric acid for ammonium sulfate. Use for processing uranium ore in the West has grown; however, current demand for this use has slowed. Sulfuric acid supply has increased due to by-product acid recoveries in Canada and the Southwest. This by-product acid is sold throughout the United States.

6. *Strategic Unit Description*

Regional business units, that is, producing location and/or resale arrangements, are managed to support captive requirements of about 300M tons/year for upgraded products, profitable service related reprocessing of sulfur containing materials, and stand-alone profitable locations which have defendable competitive positions.

Manufacturing plants include:

		Millions of net tons	
	Capacity	1984 estimate	Utili-zation
Bakersfield	100	89	89%
Sacramento	150	141	94
Philadelphia	370	275	74
Baltimore	152	126	83
Total	772	631	82%

Additionally, approximately 340M tons/year of by-product acid is either resold or captively consumed by Aliled.

  8 customers = 50% of Allied's total trade tons
  24 customers = 80% of Allied's total trade tons
Current Operating Rate: 82%

Exhibit 14 *(continued)*

7. *Competitive Analysis*

	Du Pont	Stauffer	CIL	AmCy	Essex
Protected market position	=	=	+	+	=
Total cost	=	=	+	=	=
Profitability	=	=	+	+	+
Net cash throw-off	=/+	=	+	+	=
Location and size of facility	=	+	+	+	=
Overall	=	=	+	+	=

Summary: Equal/Favorable

8. *Past Strategies*

- Maintenance
- Market rationalization
- Product rationalization

B. Plan analysis

1. *Key Assumptions*

- Economic recovery in 1984; fertilizer demand improves.
- Captive demand remains stable at 1984 levels.
- Decomposition volume remains constant on East Coast; customer mix changes.
- Avtex business continues viable.
- Continuation of long-term contractual arrangements.
- Continued supply/demand imbalance on East Coast limits margin improvement near term.
- Du Pont shutdown at Rapunto, New Jersey, facility 1984: Allied to supply.
- Additional production rationalization occurs within three to five years.
- By-product acid resale arrangements continue, but greater competitive pressure for participation.
- Acid rain issue resolution will not impact in plan period.

2. *Strategic Thrust and Positioning*

- Hold niche/defend position
- Stand-alone manufacturing locations (product/market segments) will be managed to maximize return and cash flow. Resale arrangements will be continued wherever profitable. Bakersfield and Sacramento will focus on maintaining existing niche, while Baltimore, Cumberland, and Philadelphia locations will orient to defending position based upon geographical advantage.

3. *Acquisition Activities*

None

4. *Current/Future Strategic Situation*

	Embryo	Growth	Mature	Aging
Leading				
Strong				
Favorable				X
Tenable				
Weak				

Exhibit 14 *(concluded)*

5. *Major Threats/Concerns*
- East Coast competition will result in lower market share and margins as new producers establish position and excess capacity continues.
- Major customer plant closings. Viability of Allied's chrome chemical business.
- Acceleration of resolution of acid rain issue could impact on sulfuric acid.
- Additional imported acid on East Coast (Canada, Europe).

6. *Major Action Programs*
- Maintenance of long-term contractual positions to defend positions.
- Continuation of cost reduction program at Philadelphia.
- Continue to explore potential change in Philadelphia customer/product mix to isolate from Northeast merchant market.
- Improve efficiencies on inventory and distribution management.

7. *Expected Competitive Response*

Expect continued price and margin pressures in East Coast market due to:
- CIL operation of Sayreville, New Jersey, plant (600 M tons) at one train rate to provide backup for smelter acid resale position.
- Essex operation of Baltimore, Maryland, plant (350 M tons) continues tenable near term.
- American Cyanamid will operate Warners, New Jersey, for energy value.
- Du Pont will consolidate capacity on East Coast.
- By-product acid (longer-term).
- Increased competition for Allied resale arrangements.

8. *Strategic Manufacturing Focus*

Objective is to be a dependable supplier with a competitive cost structure, including a secure sulfur raw material supply, while controlling investment in inventories and facilities.

9. *Strategic Technological Development Focus*

Research and development spending is focused on process improvement (spent decomposition efficiencies) and energy savings projects.

THE FUTURE OF THE SULFURIC ACID BUSINESS AT ALLIED

Although the profitability of Allied's sulfuric acid business had improved substantially since 1980, the review of the division's 1984 strategic plan (Exhibit 14) renewed debate over whether to keep or divest the company's sulfuric acid business. Hennessy listened intently as the arguments, pro and con, were presented.

D Strategy Implementation and Administration

INTERNATIONAL PHARMACEUTICALS INC. (A)*

By 1985 International Pharmaceuticals (IP) was emerging as one of the fastest growing, most diversified pharmaceutical companies in the United States. Its judicious avoidance of heavy external debt, made possible by its high relative profitability, had enabled IP to survive the high-interest, recession-prone early 1980s with a strong balance sheet and poised for further growth. Sales and profits of overseas affiliates exceeded domestic U.S. sales and profits for the first time in 1980, and the gap had widened since. However, all was not well on that international front. IP executives in New York were concerned that too much authority in the hands of country managers had made it difficult to penetrate international markets with some of the company's newer, more diversified product lines. The issue of international organization structure was brought to a head in the spring of 1985 by a specific proposal from the company's regional manager for Europe, Howard Anderson, to restructure European activities by product line rather than by country. It was a proposal that faced some significant opposition among IP's international executives.

PRODUCT MIX AND MARKETS

IP sales in 1984 exceeded $4 billion, of which over 55 percent were outside the United States. (See Exhibit 1 for abbreviated financial statements.) Sales of pharmaceutical products, the company's original area of emphasis, still accounted for 48 percent of sales. A further 13 percent took the form of agricultural and veterinary products, which shared similar R&D and production processes with

---

Exhibit 1 SUMMARY FINANCIAL DATA, 1980–84 (millions of dollars)

	1980	1982	1984
Consolidated net sales	$2,925	$3,150	$4,095
Percent from abroad*	49%	51%	56%
Consolidated net profit (after tax)	$ 275	$ 255	$ 410
Percent from abroad*	51%	54%	60%
Current assets	$ 750	$ 820	$1,100
Current liabilities	$ 350	$ 370	$ 500
Fixed assets	$1,075	$1,100	$1,450
Long-term debt	$ 200	$ 100	$ 300
Equity	$1,275	$1,450	$1,750

* Sales and profits from Canada were not included in percent from abroad.

---

* Prepared by Professor Harold Crookell of the University of Western Ontario. All names are disguised. Copyright © 1987, The University of Western Ontario.

Exhibit 2   PRODUCT MIX IN 1984

Product	% of IP Sales		R&D	Production	Marketing
	U.S.	Int'l.			
Pharmaceutical Products (proprietary medicines, antibiotics, stomach remedies, etc.)	49.9	46.5	Expensive centralized research. Some localized development work in packaging plants.	Fermentation-synthesis and other processes for active ingredient. Localized packaging plants.	Largely to doctor via detail men. No consumer advertising.
Agricultural and Veterinary Products (animal antibiotics, feed supplements, and pesticides)	11.0	14.5	Mostly derived from pharmaceutical R&D, but some overseas development work on local diseases.	Active ingredient same as for pharmaceuticals. Blending done largely by feed millers.	Largely to feed millers and veterinarians via direct sales force.
Chemical Products (fine chemicals, some plastics)	8.8	18.1	Emphasis on process technology and quality control. Modest expenditures.	Variety of processes. Some fermentation. Capital intensive, high-quality standards.	Largely to food processors. Little product differentiation among quality producers.
Cosmetics (men's and women's toiletries, perfumes, hand creams, etc.)	16.7	13.7	Minimal product-related R&D. Some market research.	Mixing and filling only. Raw materials and supplies purchased locally.	Mass marketing to multiple retail outlets. Heavy consumer advertising. Some door-to-door selling.
Medical Equipment (analytical equipment and prostheses)	13.6	7.2	Extensive research. Often cooperative effort with universities and medical professionals.	Exacting specifications in both equipment and prostheses.	Marketing to private and public hospitals. Advertising in professional magazines.

pharmaceuticals but sold to different markets. The other three divisions (fine chemicals, cosmetics, and medical equipment) came about through corporate acquisitions during the 1970s and, in the case of medical equipment, the early 1980s. Exhibit 2 summarizes pertinent information about each major product line's R&D, production, and marketing requirements. Sales of IP products by region were as follows in 1984:

IP SALES BY REGION IN 1984 (in millions of dollars)

	United States and Canada	Europe and Middle East	Latin America	Far East and Australia	Total
Pharmaceuticals	$ 897	$ 666	$175	$222	$1,960
Agricultural and veterinary products	198	190	68	75	531
Fine chemicals	158	285	61	68	572
Cosmetics	300	206	92	15	613
Medical equipment	244	83	12	70	409
Total	$1,797	$1,430	$408	$450	$4,085

Many factors explained the differences in sales penetration by region. Some attributed it to differences in product-market knowledge among country managers, others to differences in customer demand in different regions and cultures, and yet others to historical factors such as location of factories, evolution of world markets, and circumstances in place when acquisitions were made. It was nevertheless a source of concern to IP that its international operations could not achieve a more even distribution of sales between regions and countries.

EVOLUTION OF IP'S INTERNATIONAL OPERATIONS

IP had been involved in international business since 1952. Its first forays abroad were in Canada and England in pharmaceutical products. As sales developed in these countries, IP established R & D and production centers there, although its Canadian R & D center was folded back into the United States in 1970 when Canada introduced compulsory licensing for pharmaceuticals. The U.K. research center, however, continued over the years and generated a respectable share of new IP products. More importantly, as governments throughout the developed world established increasingly stringent testing requirements for new pharmaceutical products, the United Kingdom emerged as a preferred country for new-product introductions. U.K. regulations were thought to be less bureaucratic and less costly to comply with, while at the same time, test results in the United Kingdom were acceptable in other major markets. As a result, many new pharmaceutical products developed in IP's American laboratories were actually tested and introduced first in the United Kingdom, and for this purpose, the presence of the U.K. research center was very valuable.

As IP grew, both through acquisition and new-product development, the organization of the company in the United States evolved into five autonomous divisions along with a separate international division as follows:

IP CORPORATE STRUCTURE 1985

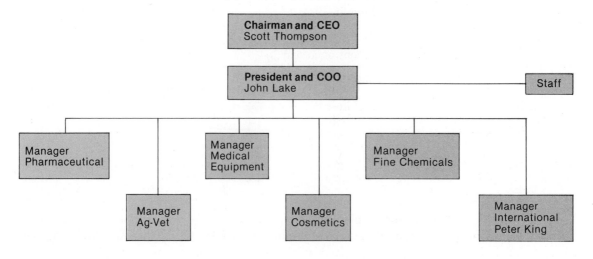

Each division was allowed broad operating freedom and was evaluated largely on sales growth and return on assets criteria. Peter King, manager of the international division and previously head of the European division, was expected to become president and chief operating officer in 1986 when Scott Thompson retired and John Lake moved up. King would be the first IP president with extensive international experience and his appointment, if it materialized, was expected to confirm an important message to the organization as a whole. Responding early to this message, Howard Anderson applied for and got the position of European region manager in 1982 when King moved up to head the international division. Anderson was previously head of the U.S. pharmaceuticals division, but lacked international experience.

The organization of international operations began with the establishment of country managers in Canada and the United Kingdom. As sales developed in other countries through the export marketing efforts of U.S. executives, additional country managers were appointed. Their initial task was to coordinate marketing activity, but success led quickly to the establishment of some manufacturing facilities in most major countries. Gradually, international business became less an exporting activity and more a foreign investment and technology transfer activity. As a consequence of these changes, IP decided in 1972 to form an international division from what previously was an export department serving the pharmaceutical and ag-vet divisions. At the same time, IP bought out an international fine chemicals manufacturer adding a third major division. The newly formed international division was given the responsibility of managing all non-U.S. business activity for all three divisions. With the passage of time, the cosmetics (1975) and medical equipment (late 1982) divisions were added, and international operations were broken into regions to facilitate control of growing worldwide activities. By 1985, the international division was organized as follows:

IP INTERNATIONAL DIVISION 1985

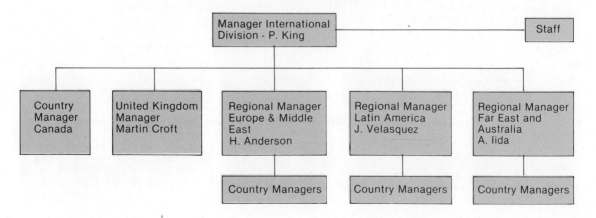

The Europe Reorganization Proposal

When Howard Anderson became regional manager for Europe in 1982, he was surprised at the relative untidiness of the organization he had inherited and at the relative sluggishness of the European economy. Sales for the European region in 1982 were below 1980 levels despite inflation averaging about 8 percent per year. Under Peter King's leadership, sales in the European region reached $1 billion in 1980, but two years later with Howard Anderson at the helm, they totaled $980 million. What upset Anderson more was that he had left behind a U.S. market on its way to major recovery and growth. Nevertheless, 1983 and 1984 proved very successful in Europe as sales climbed over 40 percent during the two years, due in part to the addition of the medical equipment division. Anderson's view was that sales could have climbed even faster if the expertise of the U.S. divisions could have been used more directly in Europe, and if the European region could have been reorganized to reflect the realities of the Common Market. Sales for 1984 by product and by country for Europe appear in Exhibit 3.

The structure of the European region Anderson inherited contained a number of historical anomalies. The U.K. area manager, Martin Croft, reported directly to New York rather than through Anderson. This was because of the presence of a major pharmaceutical research center in England that had to be coordinated with its U.S. counterpart and because the fine chemicals company acquired in 1972 had always run its European operations from the United Kingdom. As a result, the European region's structure in 1985 was roughly as follows:

IP EUROPEAN DIVISION 1985

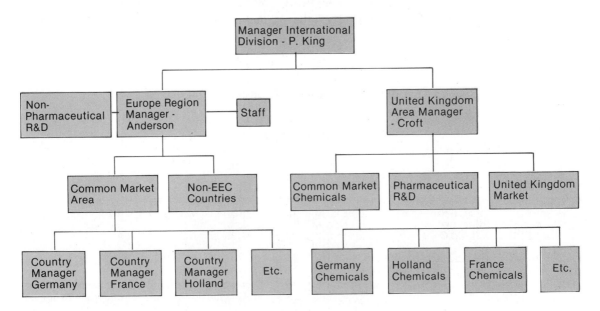

Exhibit 3 SALES BY PRODUCT AND BY COUNTRY, EUROPE REGION 1984
(millions of U.S. dollars)

	Pharma-ceuticals	Ag-Vet	Chemicals	Cosmetics	Medical equipment	Total
France	$ 65	$ 35	$ 40	$ 15	$25	$ 180
Germany	140	10	10	50	15	225
Holland	50	35	20	5	5	115
Italy	70	25	55	10	15	175
United Kingdom	170	30	105	35	5	345
Belgium	10	5	15	25	10	65
Norway	25	5	—	20	—	50
Spain	30	12	10	20	8	80
Portugal	25	7	—	10	—	42
Middle East	50	10	—	—	—	60
Other	31	16	30	16	—	93
Total	$666	$190	$285	$206	$83	$1430

As Anderson began to contemplate major changes to the structure of the European division, he decided it would be useful to explore his ideas with Croft and so invited him to a special meeting at European headquarters in Brussels.

Anderson: Fascinating city Brussels. It has more or less become the capital of the new Europe. You should visit us here more often.

Croft: The capital of the new bureaucracy perhaps, but not the heart of the commercial action. Still, I'm always happy to pay a visit. The restaurants are good.

Anderson: Hmm! Look Martin, I think we really need to think seriously about how we compete in Europe. Our organization structure is just a hodgepodge of historical precedents, and we really don't get a lot of help from the New York staff.

Croft: I agree. But then most staff people are not all that useful to line management. Never have been. I don't think New York has a monopoly on useless staff.

Anderson: But don't you think it's about time we considered reorganizing our division to reflect the Europe of the future rather than the Europe of the past. The Common Market really has created a sort of United States of Europe, and I think our organization structure should be tidied up to reflect this.

Croft: I see your point, but I'm more interested in whether our organization is effective than whether it is tidy. We have had two very good years, Howard. Why change a winning team?

Anderson: Because we could have done better, especially in chemicals.

Croft: Hey, now wait a minute! We got good growth in chemicals in a very competitive market. Surely you don't expect chemicals to match growth rates with pharmaceuticals. They're at different stages in their life cycles.

Exhibit 4 MEMORANDUM

to: Peter King, John Lake
from: Howard Anderson
copies: Martin Croft, Akio Iida, Jose Velasquez
subject: Corporate organization structure in Europe

The structure of our European organization is becoming an impediment to the future growth and profitability of our operations here. I have been concerned about it for a long time, but, although I can't claim unanimity of opinion among my colleagues, the time has come to act. Indeed, I have come to the view that a proposal as sweeping as the one I am about to make is never likely to obtain consensus. It is nevertheless vital and I am deeply committed to it.

What I propose is to restructure the company in Europe so that it resembles the U.S. structure—at least as far as the EEC is concerned. My main objective is to facilitate the flow of product-market know-how between the U.S. divisions and our divisions here in Europe. Furthermore, we need to encourage our own management throughout the EEC to think "Europe" rather than their own particular country or area. Detailed below is the organization structure I am proposing.

Proposed New Structure for Europe

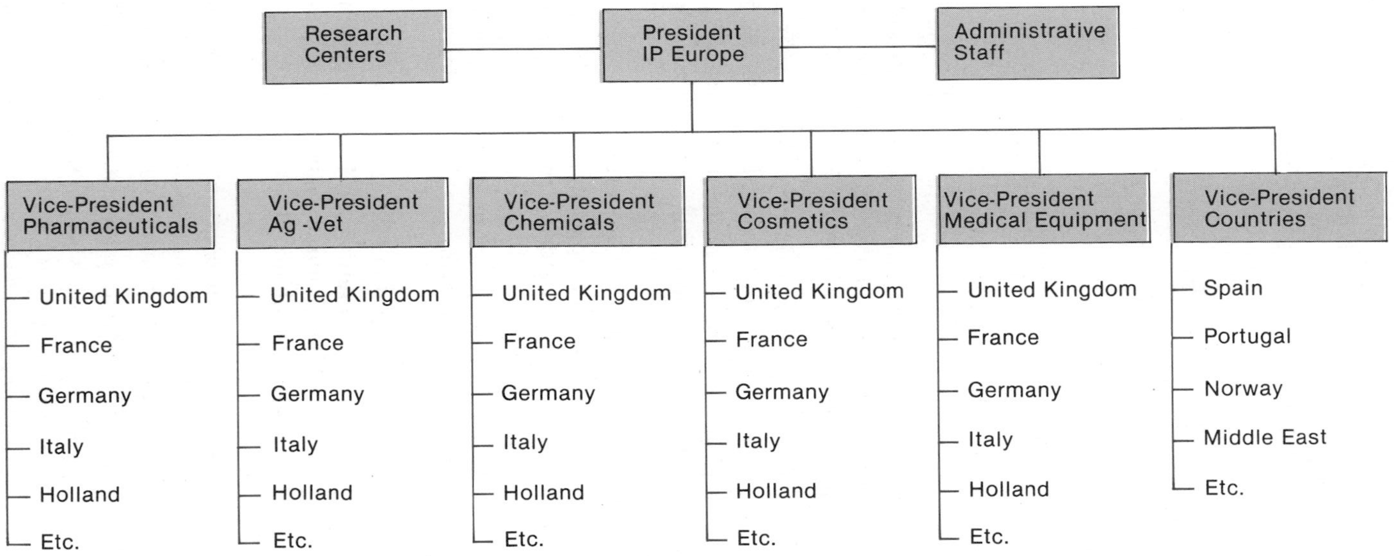

Our European sales level now is much higher than the U.S. sales level was when IP adopted the divisional structure for the U.S. market. The divisional structure has served the United States well, and its adoption in Europe is, in my view, long overdue. At this stage, I am proposing the divisional structure for the major EEC countries only. The smaller countries will remain under the existing area structure. However, as our sales in those markets expand they may be absorbed into the divisional system.

It is my hope that with this flexibility built in, the proposal might also be considered in our other regions. There are a number of other potential benefits to the proposal, but this memo is already long enough. Perhaps we could discuss it further on my next trip.

Anderson: OK! OK! Don't get so jumpy. I just think we could have done better in all products if we could have pulled more product-market ideas in from our divisional counterparts in the U.S. That's where we're missing the boat.

Croft: Maybe, you're just homesick, Howard. Ideas that work well in America don't always work here.

Anderson: Perhaps not, but some of them would. And we're just not well enough plugged in to find out which ones.

Croft: I suppose that's a two-way street. If the U.S. wanted to listen to some of our ideas in chemicals, they could be doing a lot better in the U.S. market. I mean, it's not as though they don't know where we are.

Some weeks later Croft was in a meeting in his London office with Akio Iida, the Japanese head of IP's Far East region. They were swapping ideas on how to increase sales of chemicals and medical equipment in their respective areas, and Iida wanted to visit specialists in the U.K. pharmaceutical lab. Their discussions were interrupted by Croft's second-in-command, John Allan, who had with him a copy of a just-received memorandum from Howard Anderson to Peter King and John Lake (see Exhibit 4).

Allan: I think you'd better look at this. It is copied to both of you.

Croft: (after digesting the memo) This is serious. He's out of his American mind.

Allan: I don't think so. He's addressed it to Lake as well. I think it's a direct challenge to the international division.

Croft: But the international division is doing so well. Why would anyone in his right mind want to do that? What do you think Aki?

Iida: You are in a difficult situation, Martin san. In my region, the countries differ from one another in important ways. The ASEAN bloc is not as close as the EEC. I think the proposal would not be good for my region. But for the EEC, who knows! You face a difficult choice, Martin san. Very difficult.

Croft: I have my regular quarterly review with Peter King in New York next week. I was really looking forward to it too. Our growth and profitability are way above budget. We look great on the numbers. But this memorandum of Anderson's is bound to be on the agenda. Any suggestions?

Allan: It looks like a typical power play to me. Anderson has gone too far this time. His motives are too transparent. You have to fight it, Martin. You have no choice.

Iida: The Anderson proposal will bring more U.S. involvement abroad. More management by numbers. More goals, and forecasts, and budgets, and reports. Very foolish! But also very clever. American leaders will be impressed. You fight and you might lose. My advice, Martin san, is do not fight this alone.

CASE 26	# INTERNATIONAL PHARMACEUTICALS INC. (B)*

Emil Gauthier was not easily annoyed, but when his wife told him that Tom Arthur of the New York office had called him at home three times that evening, sounding more irritable with each successive call, Gauthier's blood began to boil. "He wants you to call as soon as you can, regardless of the hour," his wife urged. He glanced at his watch. It was midnight in Paris, 6 P.M. in New York. He dialed but there was no reply either at Arthur's office or home.

At 9 A.M. the next morning, Gauthier asked his secretary to call Tom Arthur's home in New York. "But M. Gauthier, it is 3 A.M. in New York," she replied. "I'm aware of that," said Gauthier. "Let it ring till someone answers."

> **Arthur:** Hello.
>
> **Gauthier:** Tom. How are you this beautiful spring morning? Emil Gauthier, here.
>
> **Arthur:** Emil! What the hell time is it?
>
> **Gauthier:** It's 9 o'clock on a beautiful spring morning in Paris.
>
> **Arthur:** It's 3 in the morning, Emil! Do you hear me, it's three in the—morning!
>
> **Gauthier:** My wife told me you needed to talk to me urgently. This is the first chance I've had.
>
> **Arthur:** Just hang on a minute. I've got to find my glasses. (After a long pause.) Now look, Emil! All my files are in my office.
>
> **Gauthier:** *Moi aussi.*
>
> **Arthur:** What?
>
> **Gauthier:** I keep my files at the office too.
>
> **Arthur:** Is this some kind of a joke, Emil?
>
> **Gauthier:** *Mais non!* I too would rather not get business calls at home, but you said this was urgent.
>
> **Arthur:** Emil, I just got the first-quarter sales figures for 1987 and sales in France for Jasmine (a perfume in the IP cosmetics line) were only $1,250,000.
>
> **Gauthier:** *Mais oui!* Better than the first quarter of 1986 by 5 percent. Not spectacular, but OK.
>
> **Arthur:** Now come on, Emil. We just spent $70,000 in advertising and

---

* Prepared by Professor Harold Crookell of the University of Western Ontario. All names are disguised. Copyright © 1987, The University of Western Ontario.

there's practically nothing to show for it. How is the new distributor working out? Did we sell much outside the conventional shops?

Gauthier: No, not yet! We first need to invest in some new equipment to increase output before we actually take on a new distributor, and the investment has not been approved yet by M. deVille.

Arthur: What! You mean to tell me you guys haven't carried out your part of the strategy. As I recall it, the plan was to increase output, get a new distributor to move Jasmine into supermarkets and department stores, and spend $70,000 on advertising. The goal was sales of $8 to $10 million for 1987. Now you're telling me, we've spent the advertising money, *our* money, and that's it! We might just as well have poured it down the drain.

Gauthier: At least we know now that advertising alone does not increase sales much. I think that . . .

Arthur: Now, look Emil! We are just not reaching one another. I'm taking the Thursday morning flight to Paris. It should get to Orly airport at 8 P.M. Book us a table at the Grand Véfour, will you? I really like that place.

Gauthier: *Mais oui. Certainement!* But it is expensive.

Arthur: I know that. But you and I have to talk. If it takes the Grand Véfour for me to get through to you, then so be it.

THE ANDERSON PROPOSAL

International Pharmaceuticals underwent a major reorganization in 1986. It began with a controversial proposal by IP's European region manager, Howard Anderson, to change the way the company was organized in Europe. What he proposed (see Case 25, International Pharmaceuticals (A)) was to move away from the traditional region manager–country manager structure toward a structure based on product divisions. Furthermore, Anderson made his proposal not only to Peter King, head of the international division, but also to John Lake, the company president. When Anderson, King, and Lake met to discuss the idea, Anderson made the following major points in defense of his proposal.

1. The proposed change constituted a new way of linking the U.S. product divisions to IP's international operations and hence affected the company as a whole. (Anderson was manager of the pharmaceutical division in the United States before he became European region manager.)

2. The country managers in Europe were nowhere near as well informed about product technology or marketing techniques as the U.S. product divisions, and the organization structure impeded the transfer of this information.

3. The European Common Market had succeeded in bringing together a market of some 200 million people, but IP's European organization still thought and planned in terms of individual countries.

4. If U.S. division managers had worldwide responsibility for their products,

they would automatically pick up international experience along the way without having to be assigned abroad and would be better prepared for top management positions.

Lake found Anderson's arguments persuasive, but King prevailed on him to defer any decision until after he had heard from others who would be affected by the changes, particularly Martin Croft. "I know Martin won't like it," said Lake, "but progress has its costs and I think Anderson's proposal has merit. He's the first senior executive to get hands-on experience as both a division manager and a region manager. I'm impressed by him."

Within days, King had a formal meeting with Croft, at which Croft spelled out his concerns about Anderson's proposal. However, before the meeting, King received letters from both Jose Velasquez, region manager for Latin America, and Akio Iida, region manager for the Far East. Both of them expressed a specific and different concern about Anderson's proposal in the context of an otherwise balanced letter. Velasquez's concern was that Argentinians would not respond well to having a Brazilian or Mexican superior or vice versa, as the product line structure would require. Iida's concern was that the countries in his region had major cultural differences and needed strong country managers, whereas the product-line structure tended to weaken the role of the country manager. Croft was aware of these letters when he began his discussion with King.

> **King:** I was expecting your stubborn, grim-faced expression today, Martin. How come you're so cheerful?
>
> **Croft:** The results, Peter! We've had one of our best years ever in the U.K. area. Sales and profits were both up over 20 percent in 1984. Our targets have been exceeded easily for the second year in a row. Why shouldn't I be cheerful?
>
> **King:** I thought you might have the Anderson report on your mind.
>
> **Croft:** Oh, that! Well naturally I've read it. It's a very good document, actually. Not very practical, of course.
>
> **King:** What do you mean, not very practical?
>
> **Croft:** I should have thought the company would be more interested in results than organizational tidiness. The Anderson proposal has a lot of merit, but it would increase operating costs considerably, and the bottom line would suffer.
>
> **King:** Maybe! But if we got better sales performance by concentrating on each product division in each country, the higher costs could pay dividends.
>
> **Croft:** True! But who has had the best sales increases over the last two years—the European region or the U.S. divisions? What makes you think you'll get faster sales growth by giving the U.S. more control over Europe? They may know the products a little better than we do, but we know the market a lot better than they. What you may get is a nice combination of higher costs and slower sales growth.
>
> **King:** You make a strong point, but I . . .

Croft: It's much worse than you think, Peter. It's a direct threat to the international division itself. I mean, if we have divisions in Europe getting their marching orders from divisions in the United States, what happens to the role of the Europe region manager? And if we have divisions in the United Kingdom responsible to Italians, Germans, and French who get their marching orders from the United States, what happens to the country manager? And if the region and country managers lose power, what happens to the international division? Why it's a dog's breakfast! It's unthinkable! The U.S. divisions may be good, but they are very inexperienced abroad. No! Anderson's proposal sounds good in theory, but in practice it would be a disaster.

King: Actually, Iida and Velasquez have made some of these points, but not quite so strongly or persuasively.

Croft: Oh, really!

King: I think we need to talk to John Lake. He'll be interested in your views. Can you arrange to stay in New York an extra day or two?

THE 1986 REORGANIZATION

The result of Croft's prolonged stay was a stalemate on the Anderson proposal. Nothing was done until the spring of 1986, when Thompson retired, Lake became chairman of the board and chief executive officer, and King moved up to be president and chief operating officer. This left the international division open for new leadership or redefinition. As it happened, the U.S. divisions had a slightly better year in 1985 in terms of growth and profitability than did the international division. Lake and King decided to use Thompson's retirement to reorganize IP's approach to its international operations. They did so by preparing the following executive memorandum.

INTERNATIONAL PHARMACEUTICALS EXECUTIVE MEMORANDUM

To: All division managers, region and country managers.

From: John Lake and Peter King.

Subject: Reorganization of international activity.

   In recognition of the importance to IP of International markets now and in the future, we announce the formation of a new position—senior vice-president, international—and the appointment to this position of Mr. Martin Croft.
   We also announce the formation of a second new position—senior vice-president, divisions—and the appointment to this position of Mr. Howard Anderson. In future, product divisions will have world-wide responsibility for their product lines, specifically in the areas of technology transfer and international marketing. At the same time, country managers will have responsibility for all product lines within their markets, specifically in the areas of investment and adaptation to local market conditions.

Overlapping Responsibility

   We are aware that this reorganization creates a measure of overlapping responsibility. This is very deliberate. Both the product divisions and the country managers have important and different contributions to make in framing product strategy in any given country. It is hoped that through the dual accountability matrix structure we are now introducing, both sides will have equal input in a cooperative way into strategy formulation. Mr. Croft and Mr. Anderson have given their undertaking to do all they can to foster the necessary climate of understanding and cooperation.

Measures of Performance

Country managers will be evaluated primarily on the basis of return on assets employed (net profit after tax divided by working capital plus fixed assets). Division managers will be evaluated primarily on the basis of sales growth and return on sales (sales minus production marketing and distribution costs, divided by sales). The blending of product-line strategy and country strategy is to be accomplished by coordination meetings between product managers and country managers, with approval from appropriate area and division managers.

Movement of People

The movement of people between countries and divisions is encouraged. Division managers, however, have final authority for hiring decisions with the division, and region managers for hiring decisions within countries.

New Organization Structure

The decisions communicated in this memorandum constitute a major overhaul of our international thrust. The attached organization chart puts them in schematic form. Let's work together to make it work.

INTERNATIONAL PHARMACEUTICALS ORGANIZATION CHART, MAY 1986

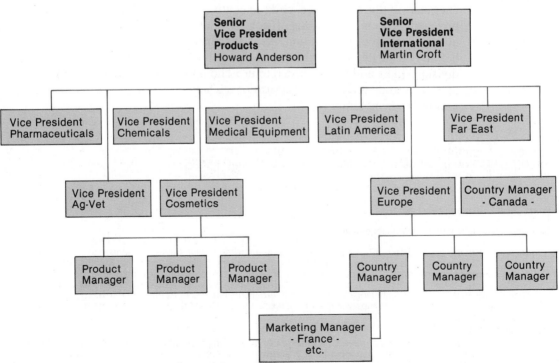

It was April 8, 1987, when Tom Arthur received his "wake-up" call from Emil Gauthier in Paris. He got into work late that morning and was 10 minutes late for a scheduled 9 A.M. meeting with his boss, Steve Hammond, VP cosmetics.

Hammond: Good morning, Tom. It is still morning, isn't it?

Arthur: Sorry I'm late, Steve. But you'll never guess what happened to me last night.

Hammond: What you do at night is your business, but whatever it was, it doesn't look like it did you much good. You look awful.

Arthur: That's pretty much the way I feel. I got a phone call this morning from Emil Gauthier at 3 A.M. "It's a beautiful spring morning in Paris," he says. I could have strangled him. Anyway when I got back to bed I couldn't sleep. It was about 5:30 when I finally dropped off, then I slept right through the alarm.

Hammond: What did he say about the Jasmine sales figures?

Arthur: You're not going to believe this, Steve, but they not only have no new distributor, they haven't even expanded production yet. The $70,000 advertising program was a complete waste. I'm flying out tomorrow to talk to Emil.

Hammond: I knew this new organization structure wasn't going to work. We got agreement on this strategy at the coordination meeting. They just haven't carried out their end. Look, Tom, if you can't persuade Emil to implement the strategy and put up the money for a second advertising campaign from his own budget, then I'm taking this up to the top.

Arthur: I'll do what I can. They'll certainly know I've made a visit. What I'm afraid of is that Emil is one of the problems. He looks after the medical equipment side too, and I think he puts more effort there because he just doesn't understand cosmetics. Maybe if I tell him about our success in Argentina with this strategy, it will help. We got sales up 80 percent in one year in Argentina.

Hammond: Let me know how you make out as soon as you get back. Oh, and be sure to check in with deVille.

Later the same day, Martin Croft received a phone call from John Allan, his new region manager for Europe.

Allan: I'm afraid we have a problem bubbling up that you're likely to hear about soon. Claude deVille is with me here in Brussels and he just got a call from Emil Gauthier in Paris. Apparently the cosmetics group is sending Tom Arthur over to lean on Emil about cosmetics strategy in France. He's coming tomorrow while Claude is here with me.

Croft: So why do I need to know?

Allan: Two reasons. First, we think he's going to recite their Argentine success story. Everyone's talking about it. Could you find out how the Argentine story sounds from our point of view? And second, we've had a bit of mix-up on timing, and the cosmetics group has spent advertising money in France before we lined up a new distributor and expanded output. It's not exactly a waste. We learned that advertising doesn't increase sales of Jasmine in France, but the cosmetics boys are likely to be upset.

Croft: Was the strategy for Jasmine approved at the coordination meeting?

Allan: It was discussed there. Tom Arthur and Steve Hammond pushed it very hard, so we agreed to look into it. What else could we do?

Croft: Did you sign off on a written strategy statement?

Allan: No! But a number of things have been done on the basis of a verbal understanding. This one just didn't sit well with Claude. The medical equipment side has a much better future and a much higher return than a ''me-too'' perfume in France.

Croft: Well at least we can claim a misunderstanding. Look, try to smooth things over with Tom. Get Emil to take him out for dinner. We really don't need a battle over this. Meanwhile, I'll have a word with Velasquez about Argentina.

Velasquez confirmed that the marketing strategy for Jasmine was a huge success in Argentina. Sales rose 80 percent in dollar terms, and the business was profitable. However, attractive credit terms were used as a selling device to retailers, which in high-inflation Argentina was a powerful weapon. As a result, working capital levels were high and the overall return on assets was not that attractive. As Croft pondered the implications of this new information, he received a phone call from his friend Aki Iida about some difficulties in the Far East. Once these had been resolved, Croft took the opportunity to sound out Iida about the new organization structure.

Iida: The structure is OK. It encourages people to share their skills and work together, and that is good. But it requires patience and careful listening. Sometimes the American divisions are too hurried. Their people need to slow down and stay longer. They need to put effort into learning about our markets as we have always done to learn about their products.

Croft: Do you have any specific suggestions for me Aki?

Iida: Perhaps, but you may not like to hear.

Croft: Try me! I've become an awesome listener.

Iida: I think the company's numerical performance measures are applied too often. We are too focused on the short term. We cannot develop patience and listening skills this way. People are always in a hurry, always trying to find a shortcut. Investment in technology always takes precedence over investment in people and relationships. Some things, I think, take longer to achieve the faster you go.

| CASE | 27 | # FOODSPLUS* |

Julius Mwanza, managing director of FoodsPlus, was considering a proposal to reorganize the company. FoodsPlus was an African holding company that managed investments in six operating companies. Three years ago, FoodsPlus had decentralized much of the management responsibility and control to the operating companies in order to reduce the influence of headquarters executives and to develop the local managers in the operating companies.

Decentralization had served its purpose, but Mwanza now was not certain it still was appropriate. He believed the operating companies were running away and that he no longer had sufficient control. Although his role now was more as a strategist, evaluator, and coordinator, he did not seem to be getting the information he needed to accomplish these tasks.

No standardized operating reports were coming to him, but that bothered him less than the intercompany coordination situation. No one seemed to have information on, or to be in control of, the numerous intercompany transfers of raw materials, by-products, or other transactions. All the operating companies wanted more capital, but he could not tell where it should be allocated. Mwanza now wondered whether these companies were being managed effectively. Maybe it was time to recentralize the whole corporation.

BACKGROUND

Before the creation of FoodsPlus, there had been one large company known as Premier Brands. Premier had been founded early in the colonial period by European and Indian businessmen to provide basic dietary foodstuffs: wheat and maize meal. Twenty years ago, Premier came to the financial aid of another company, Ace Bakeries Ltd., and shortly assumed control as majority owner. The acquisition was Premier's first major expansion. Several years later, because of the imminent retirement of some of the founders, controlling interest in Premier was sold to FoodsPlus, which had been incorporated by local African businessmen.

FoodsPlus and Ace Bakeries both traded on the national stock exchange. However, effective majority control of all operating companies was held by FoodsPlus (see Exhibit 1). Each company was a separate legal entity with separate management teams and separate (although with some overlap) boards of directors. The operating companies were all in the agri-processing and food industries.

* Prepared by Research Associate Steven Cox under the direction of Professors Harry Lane and Roderick White, all of The University of Western Ontario. Copyright © 1986, The University of Western Ontario.

Exhibit 1 THE FOODSPLUS HOLDING COMPANY STRUCTURE

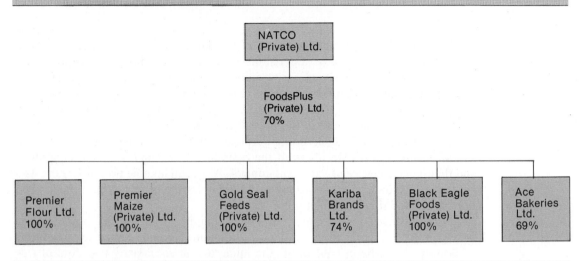

The FoodsPlus group of companies faced numerous challenges inherent in African good and agri-processing industries. Many of the company's products were staple food items and subject to rigorous government price control laws. Price controls were established on the raw materials, often its by-products, and the final product's selling price. These price control regulations affected the individual company's costs and revenues and were often cited by managers as the reasons for poor performance.

A continuing problem was shortages. Because of unpredictable weather, maize and wheat shortages occurred regularly. These commodities were controlled by the National Cereals Councils, which in turn sold them to processing companies. Many FoodsPlus products could become political in nature. When there were shortages, politics became severe. Accusations of windfall profits and black marketing often were levelled at the companies. The government would step in with its own teams and closely supervise the allocation and distribution of cereals. One recent example highlights this problem. The government had purchased spoiled yellow maize. The maize contained a toxic fungus that if consumed, could potentially harm humans. Very quickly, customers stopped buying maize as rumors circulated concerning its quality. One manager commented on the effect of shortages. "We lost good distributors. Some didn't come back to us." In times like these, Mwanza seemed to work continuously at managing relationships, between FoodsPlus and organizations in its external environment—government, suppliers, and customers.

The Former System

Until recently FoodsPlus had expatriates in the top management positions and had operated with a centralized management system. FoodsPlus also had large investments in companies in neighboring countries but had lost most of these as a result of nationalization or social turmoil. Supervision of these companies across national borders had required the skills of an experienced executive group; and a centralized management system was needed to coordinate communication, cooperation, and resource sharing among the widely dispersed companies. The former managing director staffed the group office with other expatriates to oversee the operating companies. Mwanza commented:

> After independence, most of the operating managers were new to their positions. Africans were finding their way into management jobs during the 1960s and 1970s, but because we lacked experience, we required specialized assistance to perform effectively. The experienced advisers provided guidance and advice.

The centralized structure is shown in Exhibit 2. It had been set up so the group managing director headed an office of 14 senior executives. These 14 executives had functional responsibility for the operating companies, but only in an advisory capacity. Direct line responsibility was between the group managing director and the various general managers of the operating companies. The centralized structure was designed to render assistance services, and FoodsPlus executive advisers had no power to implement policies, only to offer advice. FoodsPlus operated with its subsidiaries under revolving 10-year management agreements, whereby it earned a management fee of .5 percent of gross sales to cover its overhead.

This system began to fall apart. The nationalization of assets in neighboring countries took away much of the responsibility and work from the expatriate advisors. Although they supposedly had no implementation power, some tried to impose their authority. The group managing director attempted to police this behavior and to minimize its occurrence. However, some operating company general managers believed their authority was usurped by the advisory group. On occasion, an advisor would tell his counterpart in an operating company what to do without ever telling the general manager. Conflict was common. One of the original advisers still working with one of the operating companies recalled the old system:

> We supervised the assets in four countries from headquarters. At times, it was frustrating. The turnover rate amongst government personnel at some of those countries was high—a minister in the morning, a nobody after lunch. Also group advisers were expected to fill in for vacationing personnel at the subsidiary level in all the countries. There was frequent travel.
>
> In theory, we were supposed to communicate with our counterpart executives in the operating companies through the respective general manager. In practice, this was difficult. We had to talk directly since the talk was often too technically detailed for the general manager to understand. I suppose that is how a communications problem started.
>
> On routine technical and purchasing matters, our advice was usually taken. On controversial matters, that was another story. Controversy usually erupted over quality or pricing of by-products exchanged between the companies. In those days transfer prices were set at an agreed amount. Changes in these transfer prices were then related to the percentage change in the price of cereals. A 10

Exhibit 2   FOODSPLUS CENTRALIZED MANAGEMENT STRUCTURE (1963–1983)

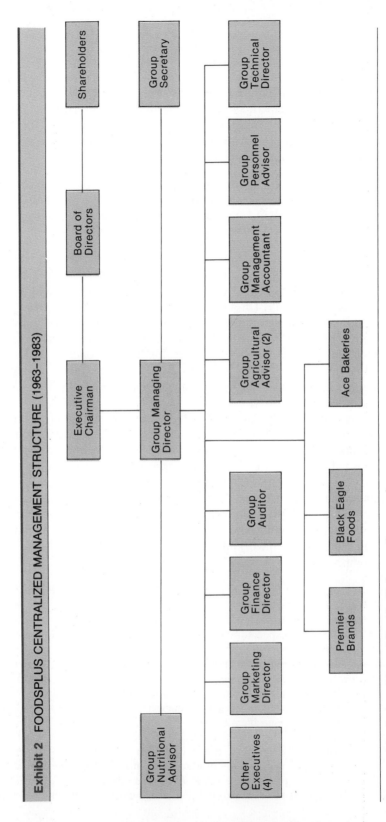

These executives had an advisory relationship with the operating companies.

percent price increase in maize translated to a 10 percent increase in the maize by-product.

Under the centralized system, there was no formal performance evaluation systems in place at either the holding company or operating company levels. Group advisers and general managers received their compensation increases from the group managing director, and general managers awarded increases to executives and staff at the operating company level.

Decentralization

Julius Mwanza began his career at Premier Brands and rose to the position of general manager. He was the first group managing director to be promoted to the holding company level from an operating company. Before his appointment, the group executives had been mostly expatriates. When Mwanza took over, he noticed there were roughly a dozen executives who did not have enough work and who occupied themselves criticizing the existing system, causing unnecessary conflict. Since he had been general manager of Premier Brands and had experienced the problem first hand, he felt strongly that the system had to be changed in order to improve organizational effectiveness.

The Structure

> Under the old system we were overcentralized: too many chiefs, and not enough tribesmen.
>
> *(Operating company executive)*

This feeling had been widely held at the operating company level. Julius Mwanza and the FoodsPlus board decided a change was necessary. They announced a policy of decentralization and disbanded the advisory group. All the advisory group executives were offered positions in the operating companies, and the practice of downward advice ended. They were promised that no one would lose their position or take a decrease in compensation as a result of the transition. Although some former group advisers earned more compensation than their respective general managers, this situation was gradually corrected. All of the secretarial staff members also were moved with their respective former group executive. The management agreements in place with the operating companies were nullified. All of the boards of the subsidiaries had outside directors removed, and the general manager and group managing director were installed together with an independent, outside chairman. The operating companies were to be given independence and autonomy.

Before the decentralization, Premier Brands had become very large and profitable. However, management did not know which of the four business areas profits were coming from (flour, maize, animal feeds, or food products) and whose performance was responsible for the profit. The company had grown too large and people did not have the time to pay attention to detailed operations. The solution was to split the company into four entities: Premier Flour, Premier Maize, Gold Seal Feeds (animal feeds), and Kariba Brands (consumer foodstuffs). Senior department managers at Premier were chosen to take charge of the new companies. The idea was to give these managers more responsibility and the time to manage smaller pieces of the company. The general managers would now have increased operating responsibility, and decision making would be located closer to the action in operations. One of these individuals spoke of the change:

> My mandate was to make my division a viable entity. If it made money, FoodsPlus would keep it. Otherwise, they might sell it off. I was told to go in there and if I made the company lose less money, I would be doing a good job. If I got it to break even, that would be really good. If it made money, that would be outstanding. I was given the privilege of picking the 10 best people from Premier to join my company with me.

For budgets and investment decisions, new executive committees (in operations, personnel, finance and marketing) were formed. They were comprised of the functional executives from each of the companies. These committees were chaired by the group managing director and took over the functions formerly held by the advisory officers. Approval for capital decisions rested at the board level of operating companies and then required ratification by the FoodsPlus board. FoodsPlus overhead was allocated approximately on the basis of company size and gross margins, not on the amount of FoodsPlus time or effort spent with the company.

Each company was responsible for preparing its own budgets for approval by FoodsPlus. General managers forecast revenue and expenses and set their profit budgets, which went to the company board for initial approval.

The new decentralized organization was monitored through the following reporting systems:

1. All general managers were required to submit a monthly written report to the group managing director. This report presented an overall assessment on profitability, budget variances, and other company issues such as security. During the times of shortages, the general managers reported once a week.

2. There was a monthly meeting of all general managers with the group managing director. The meeting discussed each of the subsidiaries and their current problems.

3. There was also a monthly meeting called the "finance and general purpose meeting." This was a meeting of the group managing director and group financial director with all of the senior executives of a subsidiary (general manager, production manager, finance manager, marketing manager). These meetings discussed management decisions specific to the subsidiary. Any capital asset that had to be bought, improved, or demolished was discussed and decided upon and then referred to the board of the subsidiary for approval.

Mwanza offered his views on the impact of change:

> The change was necessary and possible at that point because the subsidiary general managers were experienced enough to operate on their own and their management teams didn't need advisers.

However, 1983 was a very rough transitional year. The former group advisers still felt like group officers and tried to behave the same way. They continued to take the major decisions to the group managing director and go over the head of their respective general managers. Although there were no serious power struggles, I had to bridge a lot of meetings. Most of the 14 former group executives quit soon after the decentralization was announced. As of now, only four former group executives remain within the organization, and all are at the operating company level. None has yet been promoted to the general manager level.

On intracompany pricing, my role is to act as the arbitrator to make sure the boys are not killing each other. If there is a dispute over pricing, we will hold a special meeting.

One of the original group advisers, now an executive at one of the operating subsidiaries, talked about the new system:

When decentralization occurred, I was asked what position and title I wanted. My salary remained the same, and my salary and benefits were still paid by FoodsPlus, although this amount is crosscharged to the subsidiary company. I am classified as executive level. This distinction includes general managers, financial managers, and some marketing managers.

Now, in general terms, I report to the general manager, since part of my function is to help the general manager. I now have very limited contact with the group managing director.

Performance Evaluation

There were two levels of management employees: the executive level and the graded management staff. Appraisals were completed on a formal basis only for the graded management staff in grades 4 (middle grade) through 8 (top grade). The appraisals were done by the personnel manager.

On the other hand, executive level employees (production, finance, marketing, personnel managers) were responsible to the general manager. One general manager stated:

I cannot evaluate them. All I can do is "devaluate" them. I can only say that a certain executive in the company is not doing his job. If I don't say anything, then they are assumed to be doing their job by the FoodsPlus board.

Remuneration packages for executive-level employees included a base salary, house, car, servants, security service, and substantial educational allowances for children.

Mwanza shared his perspective on performance evaluation in the new system.

At present, there is no system for assessing the general managers at the subsidiary company level. Basically, to date, we have been surviving. It's very unfair to grade executives on corporate performance when most of the companies were just arbitrarily spun off from Premier Brands. They have no control over their raw material prices from the Cereal Councils.

A senior executive in one of the companies talked about his perception of performance evaluation.

I am paid by FoodsPlus. The FoodsPlus board determines my raises, but I have no idea how they are calculated. I don't even know that the increases have any relationship to performance. You just know if you are not performing—you'll be asked to leave.

The most rewarding thing I get is when the auditors have signed the accounts and I have shown a contribution to FoodsPlus and the board says thanks to us for getting their books done on time and operating within budget.

One former group advisor had not noticed a change in performance evaluation with the new system. "I have no idea how performance is assessed. My budgets are always approved without change. My annual salary review is signed by Julius Mwanza. I guess that means I am doing good work."

THE OPERATING COMPANIES

A brief description of each of the operating subsidiary companies' activities follows.

Premier Flour

Premier was the country's largest wheat milling company and had a 74 percent market share. Although market demand was relatively stable, wheat supply was unstable because of unpredictable drought and pestilence problems. Because bread was one of the country's major staple foods, it was strictly price controlled. Decisions on flour pricing, quality, and distribution were very sensitive. Premier had rebounded from recent losses in a year of drought and exhibited minor liquidity problems. Premier sold 54 percent of its annual flour production to a sister company, Ace Bakeries, at a small discount from *market price*[1] for bulk purchases. It also sold its entire by-product supply of wheat bran to another sister company, Gold Seal Feeds.

Premier Maize

Premier Maize was newly created from the breakup of Premier Brands. Its primary business was production of another staple food, maize meal. It held a 60 percent market share. The maize was milled to produce maize meal (83 percent), maize bran (7 percent), and maize germ (9 percent). Maize meal was price controlled. Its production and prices were scrutinized by politicians and the public, and this pressure had led to very small profit margins. Although profit margins were low, volumes were high. Premier Maize had just gone 10 months without operating because of a drought and the resulting maize shortage, but it still had earned a profit. At full capacity, this company was expected to be very profitable. It sold maize bran to a sister company, Gold Seal Feeds, at roughly 65

---

[1] *Market price* was defined as the price that a FoodsPlus subsidiary would receive from another nonrelated company, for both final products and by-products.

percent below its market price. Another by-product, maize germ, was sold to Black Eagle Foods for extraction of refined cooking oil.

Gold Seal Feeds

Gold Seal, founded two years ago, was the largest animal feeds company in the country. Its final products were not price controlled. In addition, Gold Seal produced animal veterinary products and mineral supplements. Most of its raw materials were by-products from sister companies' processes. These by-products were not price controlled. It purchased 100 percent of its wheat bran from Premier Flour at prices 16 to 18 percent below market price, 100 percent of its maize bran from Premier Maize at prices 65 percent below market price, and 100 percent of its maize cake from Black Eagle Foods. Gold Seal had the greatest return on capital largely because it benefited most from low intragroup prices. It also had a low equity base (mostly loans from other companies with low payback terms). In the view of FoodsPlus management, Gold Seal had outstanding long-term growth potential.

Kariba Brands

Kariba Brands started operations at the same time as Gold Seal and was the smallest company in the group. It produced breakfast cereals, pet foods, animal feeds, sausage filler, and other consumer food products. It also acted as distributor of Black Eagle oil, produced by its sister company. It purchased, at a discount, all of Ace Bakeries' stale bread for use in its animal feeds. It also was viewed as having very good potential for growth and increased profits.

Black Eagle Foods

Originally a joint venture with European businessman, Black Eagle was one of the older companies in the group. It produced spaghetti and other pastas and edible corn oil products. Corn oil products were especially sensitive to price control, and increases required approval. A recent price increase application had taken four years to get approved. Black Eagle purchased 100 percent of its maize germ needs from Premier Maize at prices 45 percent of market price, and sold all of its maize cake to Gold Seal Feeds at prices 52 percent less than market price.

Ace Bakeries

Ace was a long established company, acquired by Premier in 1960. It was the country's largest bakery. Although its market share hovered around 50 percent, there had been a steady decline over the decade. Ace produced only one product—a 500-gram loaf of bread. It had very small margins and was closely price controlled. Its performance was highly dependent on selling large volumes of bread and achieving operating economies of scale. Ace bought 100 percent of its wheat requirement from Premier Flour at bulk discount rates and sold all of its stale bread to Kariba at discounted rates. Ace's falling market share was a source of concern to the management of FoodsPlus.

Intercompany Transfers

FoodsPlus operating companies sold numerous final products and by-products between themselves. A flow chart indicating the flow of products and by-products between subsidiary companies can be found in Exhibit 3, and a chart indicating which products were price controlled can be found in Exhibit 4. Exhibit 5 lists a summary of each company's financial performance.

An important issue that FoodsPlus faced was intragroup pricing. The general managers were responsible for setting the price of their by-products. The operating companies sold significant products and by-products among each other at prices that ranged from market value (commercial prices) to as little as 35 percent of market value (preferential prices). Given that most sales were at preferential prices, it was difficult for FoodsPlus to accurately assess financial performance of the various group companies. Intragroup pricing methods were based on the two following methods:

1. *The negotiation method* normally produced a contract between two companies. Some of these contracts had been in place for long periods. Prices

---

Exhibit 3 FOODSPLUS (Pvt.) LTD. FLOW OF PRODUCTS AND BY-PRODUCTS

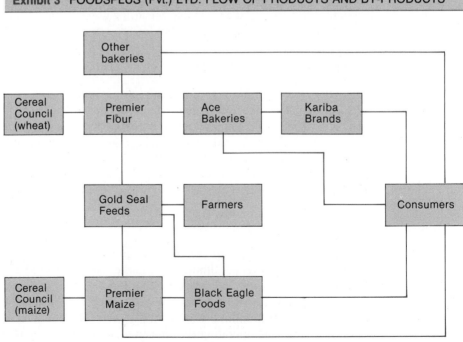

Exhibit 4 SCOPE OF PRICE CONTROLS IN FOODSPLUS COMPANIES

Company	Price controlled final products	Not subject to price controls		
		Final products	By-products sold	By-products purchased
Premier Flour (PF)	Flour		Wheat bran to GSF	
Premier Maize (PM)	Maize meal		Maize bran to GSF Maize germ to BE	
Gold Seal Feeds (GSF)		Animal feeds Animal veterinary products Mineral supplements		Wheat bran from PF Maize bran from PM Maize cake from BE
Kariba Brands (KB)	Black Eagle corn oil (distribution)	Breakfast cereals Pet foods Animal feeds Sausage filler Other consumer food products		Stale bread from Ace
Black Eagle (BE)	Black Eagle corn oil	Spaghetti, pastas	Maize cake to GSF	Maize germ from PM
Ace Bakeries	Bread		Stale bread to KB	

Exhibit 5 PERFORMANCE OF FOODSPLUS SUBSIDIARIES

	Return on capital		Profits after tax		Gross margin this year	Current ratio year ago
	This year	Year ago	This year	Year ago		
Premier Flour	11.53%	− 1.24%*	$25,372,440	$(2,731,420)*	13.6%	0.73
Premier Maize	25.50	N/A *	12,438,120	N/A *	8.9	1.45
Gold Seal Feeds†	71.28	17.86 *	3,777,860	946,320 *	13.1	1.00
Kariba Brands	1.85	− 12.30 *	46,760	(309,840)*	16.6	0.97
Black Eagle Foods	9.18	11.90	447,140	579,440	9.8	1.32
Ace Bakeries	11.17	45.30	3,825,860	15,519,180	7.2	1.00

* Figures are for seven-month period only from the date of the breakup of Premier into the four separate entities.
† The capital invested in Gold Seal was low, and a long-term loan, which was not being repaid, was regarded as quasi-equity. This inclusion would reduce the ROC figures.

were below market prices and were now in need of revision. These supply contracts set prices, quantities, mode of transportation, and costs of transportation. If agreement could not be achieved, then the directive method had to be used.

2. *The group directive method* was used in cases where an operating company requested raw material pricing assistance. For instance, in a case where Premier Flour applied for a price increase from FoodsPlus for by-products sold to Gold Seal Feeds, Gold Seal might be able to persuade FoodsPlus not to approve the increase.

A NEW ORGANIZATIONAL STRUCTURE?

In assessing the decentralized system, Mwanza worried that the change had led to too much general manager independence and that maybe FoodsPlus was too removed from its investments. He was aware of the serious implications another organizational change might have, but he wanted to come up with a structure that would operate smoothly and yet still allow him to monitor the overall corporate performance on behalf of the FoodsPlus Board of Directors. He was having difficulty keeping track of all the company data he was receiving and would probably need new staff to assist him. He wanted to improve communications and synergy across the various operating companies—in marketing, finance, production, and planning. Mwanza did not want to return to the bygone days of advisers; instead, coordinators or administrators might be a better head office group. But what would ensure that a repetition of the earlier dissatisfaction with a centralized system would not occur again?

Mwanza also wanted to formulate a policy on price control management, intragroup pricing, budgeting, capital investment, and long-term planning. FoodsPlus had long desired to diversify into new business ventures, but it lacked the organizational system to plan for them. A recent foray into real estate development had in Mwanza's words "taken a few years off my life." What industries should be investigated, and should the new business ventures be mergers, acquisitions, or new start-ups? Would it be better to shift emphasis out of price-controlled foods, or was FoodsPlus management too specialized in food-related industries?

TRW—OILWELL CABLE DIVISION*

It was July 5, 1983. Bill Russell had been expecting the phone call he had just received from the corporate office of TRW in Cleveland naming him general manager. Bill had been the acting general manager of the Oilwell Cable Division in Lawrence, Kansas, since January when Gino Strippoli left the division for another assignment. He had expected to be named general manager, but the second part of the call informing him that he must lay off 20 people or achieve an equivalent reduction in labor costs was greatly disturbing to him. It was now 8 A.M., and Bill had called an 8:15 A.M. meeting of all plant personnel to announce his appointment and, now, to also announce the mandate he had just gotten to reduce labor costs or else lay off 20 people. He was wondering how to handle the tough decisions that lay before him.

TRW

TRW is a diversified, multinational manufacturing firm that in 1983 had sales approaching $5.5 billion (see Table 1). Its roots can be found in the Cleveland Cap Screw Company, which was founded in 1901 with a total investment of $2,500 and employment of 29. Today, through a growth strategy of acquisition and diversification, the company employs 88,000 employees at over 300 locations in 17 countries. The original shareholders' investment of $2,500 in 1901 had grown to over $1.6 billion in 1983. As quoted from the company's 1983 Data Book, "This growth reflects the company's ability to anticipate promising new fields and to pioneer in their development—automotive, industrial, aircraft, aerospace, systems, electronics, and energy. We grew with these markets and helped create them."

The organization chart depicting TRW as it existed in 1983 is contained in Figure 1.

OILWELL CABLE DIVISION, LAWRENCE, KANSAS

The Oilwell Cable Division is part of the Industrial and Energy segment of TRW. In 1983, this segment of TRW's business represented 24 percent of its sales and 23 percent of its operating profits. The pumps, valves, and energy-services group, of which the Oilwell Cable Division is a part, accounted for 30 percent of the Industrial and Energy segment's net sales. The financial data for TRW by industry segment is contained in Table 2.

---

* Prepared by Michael G. Kolchin and Thomas J. Hyclak of Lehigh University and Sheree Demming of TRW. The authors gratefully acknowledge the financial support of the NET Ben Franklin Technology Center and the assistance of Mary Harhigh, our graduate research assistant.

Table 1   TRW FINANCIAL DATA FOR 1979–83

	Statement of consolidated earnings ($ millions except per share data)				
	1983	1982	1981	1980	1979
Net sales	$5,493.0	$5,131.9	$5,285.1	$4,983.9	$4,560.3
Other income	64.6	69.1	52.9	42.4	45.3
	5,557.6	5,201.0	5,338.0	5,026.3	4,605.6
Cost of sales	4,285.1	4,011.0	4,116.4	3,876.3	3,534.6
Administrative and selling expenses	840.6	791.0	734.9	693.1	61.6
Interest expense	29.7	51.2	65.9	66.5	52.3
Other expenses	37.3	7.8	34.8	27.0	32.2
	5,192.7	4,861.0	4,952.0	4,662.9	4,250.7
Earnings before income taxes	364.9	340.0	386.0	363.4	354.9
Income taxes	159.7	143.7	157.2	158.9	166.4
Net earnings	205.2	196.3	228.8	204.5	188.5
Preferred dividends	3.5	5.7	8.5	11.6	15.9
Earnings applicable to common stock	$ 201.7	$ 190.6	$ 220.3	$ 192.9	$ 172.6
Fully diluted earnings per share	$5.36	$5.20	$6.13	$5.49	$5.11
Primary earnings per share	5.53	5.49	6.60	6.15	5.86
Cash dividends paid per share	2.65	2.55	2.35	2.15	1.95
Fully diluted shares (millions)	38.3	37.8	37.3	37.3	36.9
Primary shares (millions)	36.5	34.7	33.4	31.4	29.5
Percent of sales					
Net sales	100.0%	100.0%	100.0%	100.0%	100.0%
Other income	1.2	1.3	1.0	0.8	1.0
	101.2	101.3	101.0	100.8	101.0
Cost of sales	78.0	78.2	77.9	77.8	77.5
Administrative and selling expenses	15.3	15.4	13.9	13.9	13.9
Interest expenses	0.6	1.0	1.2	1.3	1.1
Other expenses	0.7	0.1	0.7	0.5	0.7
	94.6	94.7	93.7	93.5	93.2
Earnings before income taxes	6.6	6.6	7.3	7.3	7.8
Income taxes	2.9	2.8	3.0	3.2	3.7
Net earnings	3.7	3.8	4.3	4.1	4.1
Preferred dividends	0.0	0.1	0.1	0.2	0.3
Earnings applicable to common stock	3.7%	3.7%	4.2%	3.9%	3.8%

Source: *TRW 1983 Data Book.*

The Oilwell Cable Division had its beginning as the Crescent Wire and Cable Company of Trenton, New Jersey. When TRW acquired Crescent, the company was losing money, occupied an outmoded plant, and had significant labor problems. In order to improve the profitability of the Crescent division, TRW decided to move its operations out of Trenton. The first decision was to move oilwell cable production to Lawrence, Kansas, in 1976. The line was moved into a new building

Figure 1 ORGANIZATIONAL STRUCTURE AT TRW.

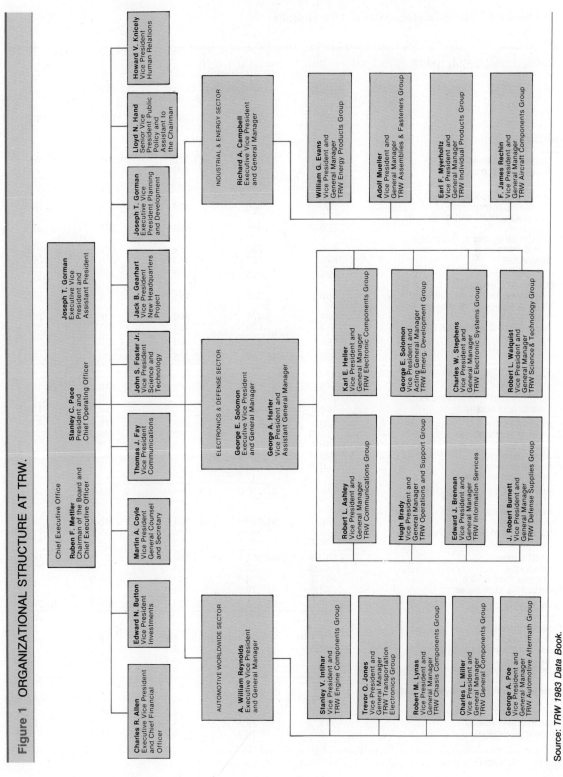

Source: *TRW 1983 Data Book.*

Table 2 FINANCIAL DATA FOR TRW

	Segments of business by industry ($ millions)				
	1983	**1982**	**1981**	**1980**	**1979**
Net Sales					
Car and truck					
Original equipment	$1,123	$1,052	$1,200	$1,291	$1,367
Replacement equipment	472	483	490	461	432
	1,595	1,535	1,690	1,752	1,799
Electronic and space systems					
Electronic components	396	406	437	419	363
Computer-based and analytical services	729	546	393	377	284
Electronic systems, equipment and services	851	787	772	648	552
Spacecraft	628	486	430	355	302
	2,604	2,205	2,032	1,799	1,501
Industrial and energy					
Fasteners, tools, and bearings	486	496	596	562	558
Pumps, valves, and energy services	394	471	506	436	380
Aircraft and components	414	425	461	435	322
	1,294	1,392	1,563	1,433	1,260
Net sales	$5,493	$5,132	$5,285	$4,984	$4,560
Operating profits					
Car and truck	$ 116.8	$ 129.2	$ 146.0	$ 149.4	$ 192.7
Electronics and space systems	212.2	170.0	123.3	133.3	88.9
Industrial and energy	98.2	126.9	219.9	193.9	156.8
Operating profit	429.2	426.1	489.2	476.6	438.4
Company staff expense	(56.0)	(53.9)	(48.5)	(49.4)	(43.3)
Interest income	15.1	15.4	12.6	1.4	3.1
Interest expense	(29.7)	(51.2)	(65.9)	(66.5)	(52.3)
Equity in affiliates	6.3	(14.0)	(1.4)	1.3	9.0
Gain on debt exchange	—	17.6	—	—	—
Earnings before income taxes	$ 346.9	$ 340.0	$ 386.0	$ 363.4	$ 354.9
Segment assets					
Car and truck	$ 968.6	$1,029.7	$1,101.3	$1,148.1	1,157.2
Electronics and space systems	1,113.7	1,000.6	888.3	865.1	779.9
Industrial and energy	886.2	921.6	915.0	808.2	752.4
Segment assets	2,968.5	2,951.9	2,904.6	2,821.4	2,689.5
Eliminations	(102.0)	(83.2)	(61.7)	(77.9)	(72.2)
Company staff assets	381.3	176.3	211.9	68.0	79.6
Investments in affiliates	73.6	79.8	71.8	74.3	52.2
Total assets	$3,321.4	$3,124.8	$3,126.6	$2,885.8	$2,749.1
Operating margin					
Car and truck	7.3%	8.4%	8.6%	8.5%	10.7%
Electronics and space systems	8.2	7.7	6.1	7.4	5.9
Industrial and energy	7.6	9.1	14.1	13.5	12.4
Company average	7.8	8.3	9.3	9.6	9.6
Operating return on segment assets					
Car and truck	12.1%	12.5%	13.3%	13.0%	16.7%
Electronics and space systems	19.2	17.0	13.9	15.4	11.4
Industrial and energy	11.1	13.8	24.0	24.0	20.8
Company average	14.5	14.4	16.8	16.9	16.3

Source: TRW 1983 Data Book.

and all new equipment was purchased. Only Gino Strippoli, the plant manager, and three other employees made the move from Trenton to Lawrence.

The reason for choosing Lawrence as the new site for Crescent division was fourfold. Most importantly, Lawrence was close to the customer base of the division in northeast Oklahoma. Second, Kansas was a right-to-work state and, given the labor problems of the Trenton plant, TRW was looking for a more supportive labor environment for its new operations. Third, the wage rates for the Lawrence area were very reasonable compared to Trenton. Finally, there was an already existing building that would allow for future expansion.

By just moving the oilwell cable line to Lawrence, TRW hoped to be able to focus on this product and make it more profitable before moving the other products from the Crescent plant in Trenton. By 1978, when the Oilwell Cable plant had reached division status, no further consideration was given to moving the rest of the Trenton plant. The remaining operations in Trenton were sold.

Team Management at Lawrence

When Gino Strippoli was given the task of starting up operations in Lawrence he saw a great opportunity to establish a new management system. With a new plant, new equipment and almost all new employees, the time seemed perfect to test the value of team management. Gino had long been a supporter of team management, and now a golden opportunity was being presented to him to set up an experiment to test his ideas.

Team management is a form of worker participation whereby team members are responsible for task-related decisions concerning their areas of responsibility. Teams are formed along functional lines. In the case of the TRW-Lawrence plant, 11 teams exist ranging in membership from 4 to 17. The title of the teams and brief descriptions of their makeup are shown in Table 3. Figure 2 depicts the current organization of the Oilwell Cable Division.

The five production teams listed in Table 3 are formed around the production process in use at TRW-Lawrence. Each of the teams meets on a weekly basis or as needed with exception of the resource team, which meets every two weeks.

Table 3 TEAM STRUCTURE

Team	Number of teams	Composition
Management	1	Members of management
Resource	1	Management information systems, design engineering, process engineering, employment, accounting, chemists, etc.
Technical	1	Nonexempt laboratory personnel
Administration	1	
Maintenance	1	Boiler, electrical, mechanical
Shipping and receiving	1	
Production	5	Extruding, armoring, braiding

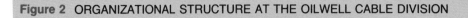

Figure 2 ORGANIZATIONAL STRUCTURE AT THE OILWELL CABLE DIVISION

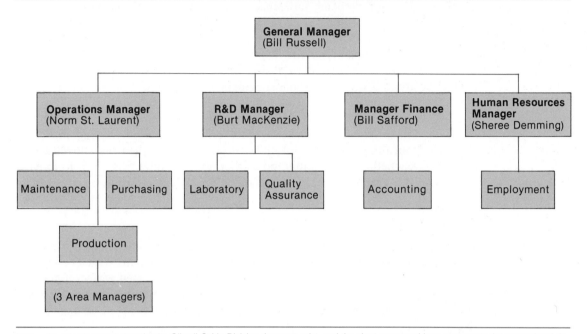

Note: An organizational chart for the Oilwell Cable Division does not exist, and the chart presented here represents the casewriters' depiction of the structure existing at TRW-Lawrence based on discussions with division personnel.

The typical meeting lasts an hour and a half to two hours. There is no formal structure for the team meeting, but most meetings would adhere to an agenda similar to the one described below:

1. Scheduling man hours and overtime.
2. Round-robin discussion/reporting from various plant committees (e.g., safety, gain-sharing, etc.).
3. Area manager's comments regarding scrap, labor efficiency, and any new information since the last meeting.

Other decisions made by the team are listed in Figure 3, which illustrates the roles of the various levels of management at the Oilwell Cable Division. Figure 3 also shows the relationships between levels. For instance, management has the responsibility for setting overall divisional goals and objectives and providing the resources necessary to the teams in order to attain these targets.

The role of the area manager is that of an intermediary. Area managers are present at most team meetings to act as facilitators and to provide the teams with information necessary to carry out their scheduling functions. In addition, the area managers fill a coordination function by meeting twice a week to discuss

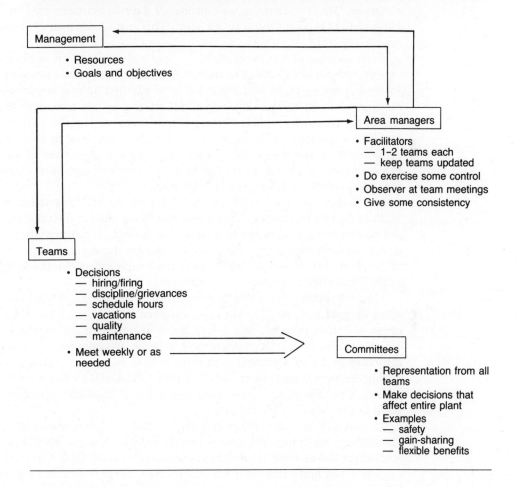

Figure 3 RELATIONSHIPS BETWEEN THE VARIOUS LEVELS IN THE TEAM MANAGEMENT CONCEPT

Management
- Resources
- Goals and objectives

Area managers
- Facilitators
  — 1–2 teams each
  — keep teams updated
- Do exercise some control
- Observer at team meetings
- Give some consistency

Teams
- Decisions
  — hiring/firing
  — discipline/grievances
  — schedule hours
  — vacations
  — quality
  — maintenance
- Meet weekly or as needed

Committees
- Representation from all teams
- Make decisions that affect entire plant
- Examples
  — safety
  — gain-sharing
  — flexible benefits

mutual problems and to discuss other items that should be presented at the weekly team meetings.

As can be seen in Figure 3, the teams are filling managerial roles, and the decisions they make are more typical of those made by supervisory levels in more traditional plants. In essence, the team members are given control over their work areas.

For decisions that affect the entire plant, a task force or a divisionwide committee is established that includes representatives from all of the teams. Examples of some of these divisionwide committees include safety, gain-sharing, and benefits.

Results from Team Management

After some initial start-up problems with the team management concept, the experiment started by Gino Strippoli in 1976 seemed to be a success. Gino observed, "In the beginning we considered it (team management) an experiment, but somewhere along the way we said, 'This is no longer an experiment; this is how we operate.'"[1]

The success of the experiment was not only written up in *Fortune* but also was the subject of several case studies.[2] But this success was not achieved easily. In the beginning, there was a good deal of mistrust among employees regarding management's motives. Also, when first starting up the Lawrence facility, there was only one union employee brought from Trenton. The rest of the people hired had little experience with the production process involved in making wire cable. As a result, there was a lot of frustration with a high level of turnover. The turnover rate of 12 percent in the first two years of operations compared to a national average of 3.8 percent at this time.[3]

But Gino was not to be deterred from seeing his experiment succeed. He realized that he was concentrating too heavily on team involvement concepts and not paying enough attention to technical concerns. A compensation scheme was developed that encouraged employees to master the various pieces of equipment in the plant. This action seemed to have the desired effect, for the division became profitable for the first time in January 1978.

In 1978, employment had dropped from a high of 132 to what seemed to be a more optimal level of 125. Turnover dropped from an excess of 12 percent to a range of 2 to 4 percent, which was more in line with the national average for manufacturing firms. More impressive was the absentee rate, which hovered in the range of 2.5 to 3 percent during the period 1978–1982. The national average during this period was closer to 6.5 percent.[4] Productivity was improving steadily as well. The Oilwell Cable Division now enjoyed the highest productivity of any plant in the oilwell cable industry.

It was not only the objective data that indicated that team management was succeeding, but comments from employees at the Oilwell Cable Division seemed to confirm this as well. By and large, employees rated TRW-Lawrence as a good company and preferred the team management concept to more traditional methods of management. Representative comments from the various levels of "management" indicated support for the system:

---

[1] Charles G. Burck, "What Happens when Workers Manage Themselves," *Fortune,* July 27, 1981, pp. 62–69.

[2] See Anil Verma, "Electrical Cable Plant," in *Human Resource Management and Industrial Relations,* Thomas A. Kochan and Thomas A. Barocci, ed. (Boston: Little, Brown and Company, 1985), pp. 425–35; and Cal W. Downs and Mary Lee Hummert, *Case History of TRW Oilwell Cable Division Team Management,* unpublished manuscript (Lawrence: University of Kansas, 1984).

[3] U.S. Department of Labor, *Handbook of Labor Statistics* (Washington, D.C.: Bureau of Labor Statistics, 1983), p. 180.

[4] Ibid., p. 136.

Team Members

". . . an excellent place to work."

"Team management gives employees a good deal of responsibility."

"Now at least we have some control over scheduling."

"The company gains as much as the employee because of the flexibility. Now there is little idle time."

"Team management gives the employee a feeling of equality."

"It allows for the maximum contribution of each member of the team."

Area Managers

"The plant is not a utopia, but I do feel better at the end of the day."

"Decision making is more difficult, but team management results in easier implementation and better understanding by team members."

Management

"It allows for crossing over lines of responsibility. There is not the turf issue that exists in traditionally structured plants."

"Team management concept has resulted in an excellent labor climate. TRW-Lawrence is a good place to work and the workers here are receptive to change."

"The major benefit of the team-management concept is flexibility while maintaining goal orientation."

Stripoli believed that the system had reduced the time he had to spend with day-to-day operating problems: "I really feel for the first time that I am managing rather than putting out fires. The teams are putting out the fires way down in the organization."[5]

From the worker's point of view, the major benefit of team management is their ability to control their job. This control has resulted in a high level of commitment by the employees, as evidenced by the numerous suggestions made by the teams that have resulted in significant improvement in quality and productivity.

It took two years for participants to become comfortable with the system and to accept the responsibility of managing themselves. However, after the settling-in period, productivity improved dramatically and has been maintained at that level through 1982—see Figure 4.

Although the current area managers still express some frustration at not being able to simply "tell" workers what to do, they do feel the team-management concept is a much more effective system than traditional supervisory systems and they would not want to go back to a traditional system. All in all, Gino was very

---

[5] "What Happens When Workers Manage Themselves," p. 69.

Figure 4 PRODUCTIVITY AT TRW-LAWRENCE, 1978–83

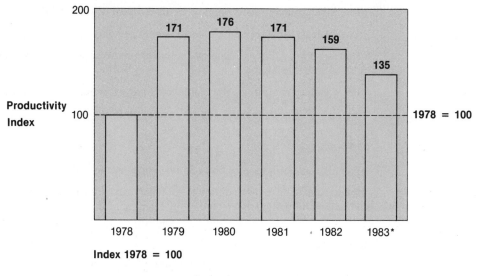

Index 1978 = 100

*Represents first six months only

pleased with the experiment. At the end of 1982, he left the Lawrence facility for another assignment and Bill Russell, who had been Gino's operations manager, replaced him as the acting general manager.

THE OILWELL CABLE DIVISION'S MARKET

The basic product produced by the Oilwell Cable Division is wire that provides power to submersible pumps used in oil drilling. As a result, demand is a function of the price of crude oil. As the price of oil increases, the demand for pumps increases as it became economically feasible to drill deeper wells.

Drilling deeper wells also produces a need for cables that are able to withstand the harsher environments found in such wells. For example, these wells often require the use of lead jackets to protect the cables from the corrosive effects of hydrogen sulfide.

With the Iranian oil crisis of 1979 and the resultant increase in oil prices, cable producers were able to sell pretty much all they were able to produce. Prices were determined on the basis of quality and delivery. Now, however, with the advent of an oil glut, demand for submersible pumps was dropping and the competitive factors in the market were determined more on the basis of price.

By the end of June 1983 the market for cable had fallen off dramatically. Bill Russell knew he had to do something soon if he were to maintain market share and profitability. Then came the phone call that forced his hand.

THE LAYOFF DECISION

As Bill Russell prepared to meet with all personnel at the Lawrence facility, he wondered how he would handle the process of laying off 16 percent of the current work force of 125. Two things particularly troubled him. First, his predecessor, Gino Strippoli, had implied that there would never be a layoff at the Oilwell Cable Division. Second, and perhaps more importantly, he had to decide whether the decision as to how to reduce labor costs was a decision he should make alone or one that the teams should undertake as their responsibility.

It was now 8:15 A.M. and Bill headed out to meet his employees.

PUBLIC SERVICE COMPANY OF NEW MEXICO (A)*

John Bundrant, president of Public Service Company of New Mexico's electric utility division, walked into his office shortly after 7 A.M. on a Friday in February 1986, sat down in his chair, and swung around to the computer terminal adjacent to his desk. He flipped on the switch, hit a few keys to "log on" to the system, hit another key to bring up the "PROFS" menu, and chose the "Open the Mail" option. Just over a year earlier, the company's ESBU (Electric Strategic Business Unit) had embarked on a program to install IBM's Professional Office System (PROFS) for 80 percent of its white-collar work force. The project had involved providing each of some 900 "knowledge workers" with a computer terminal connected to the company's mainframe computer. The PROFS software gave each user instant capability to (1) send notes and messages to other users (using the electronic mail option), (2) maintain daily calendars and schedule meetings (using the electronic calendaring and scheduling option), (3) create and process documents of all kinds (using the document and text processing features), (4) create and maintain files (via the electronic filing option), (5) arrange for automatic reminder messages, and (6) do a variety of other functions. Once the basic PROFS framework had been installed, the company had quickly followed up with an expanded menu, including spreadsheet analysis, graphing, daily operating reports, and access to other data bases on the mainframe.

Bundrant was pleased with ESBU's foray into office technology. Acceptance of the new office information system (OIS) had been enthusiastic. White-collar productivity had risen an estimated 11 percent, almost twice the original 6 percent projection. Virtually all of the OIS project's goals had been achieved. The previous week, Bundrant had gotten a status report on PROFS/OIS, outlining what had been done and achieved so far; a copy of the report is reproduced in Exhibit 1.

When Bundrant pressed the "Open the Mail" key, a short note from Jerry Geist, Public Service Company of New Mexico's chairman and chief executive officer, popped up on his screen. The message was terse: "John, if PNM is to make its corporate profit target for 1986, it looks like we are going to have to cut $27–$36 million out of the electric division's budgets for 1986 through 1988. Can you generate a proposed cutback plan for the corporate office to consider by the end of the month?" The note was not a big surprise; Bundrant and several other officers of the ESBU had concluded weeks ago that cutbacks were just a matter of time. The only question had been "how much." Now he knew. Bundrant hit a few

* Prepared by Professor Arthur A. Thompson, Jr., The University of Alabama. The author gratefully acknowledges the assistance, cooperation, and sponsorship of IBM Corporation and Public Service Company of New Mexico in preparing this material as a basis for analysis and discussion in an educational setting.

Exhibit 1 STATUS REPORT: OIS VALUE/BENEFIT/IMPACT IN PNM'S ESBU FEBRUARY 1986

1. *What is OIS?*
   - OIS is PNM's Office Information System. The backbone of OIS is IBM's Professional Office System (PROFS), which provides most of the functions of our system, plus a platform upon which our numerous enhancements and additions have been made.
   - Major non-PROFS OIS capabilities include Megacalc (a mainframe spreadsheet), Information Center/1, DisplayWrite/370.
   - OIS serves more than 900 internal users, a number which represents over 40% of the employees within ESBU and Corporate Office. OIS also serves a number of employees in Meadows, Sunbelt, and SDCW.

2. *Justification*
   - Original justification assumed 6% productivity gain; follow-up survey conducted at year-end 1985 showed 11% improvement.
   - Bulk of original justification based on productivity to be achieved from electronic mail, text processing, and calendar functions. Since that time many additional features have been added to OIS, without raising cost to the end-customer, Megacalc, InfoCenter/1, DisplayWrite/370, Easygraph, and many other customized features.
   - Also assumed 9% reduction in Word Processing Center traffic. Statistics show WPC production (number of lines) decreased by roughly 45% between 1983 and 1986. There have been several factors contributing to that decrease, and it is not possible to tell how much is directly attributable to OIS, but it is safe to assume that OIS has been a major factor.

3. *Cost—$140/month/user*
   - Flat fee has not increased since day 1, even though system is constantly being upgraded, enhanced, and includes extended features like Megacalc and IC/1 in addition to the original basic PROFS.
   - Operational cost of OIS is covered by monthly OIS charges; OIS is not being subsidized by other computer billings.

4. *Intangibles*
   - We are in the midst of the "information age," wherein information is an increasingly valuable corporate asset that only allows us to do our jobs properly, but may actually impact the financial bottom line. In many respects, accurate and timely information is a necessity in today's business world, not a luxury . . . OIS helps us collect, process, format, and disseminate that information.
   - Automation in general, and OIS specifically, helps us be more responsive to each other as employees, and by extension, to our customers.

   - OIS has put hundreds of computer terminals on admin/clerical/prof/exec desks . . . helped make hundreds of PNM employees more computer literate, aware of the power and productivity of automated systems . . . resulted in more use of the computer in general, not just OIS, for department/company productivity.
   - Value-added products on OIS (in addition to PROFS) such as Megacalc and IC/1 promote departmental computing and control over certain amount of information processing that would otherwise have to be analyzed, programmed, and maintained by our software group (or possibly not done at all). Existence of such tools may help reduce application backlog or provide information that otherwise would not exist.
   - Availability of text editor, spreadsheet, graphics, IC/1, etc., has reduced the number of personal computers required by individuals and/or departments.
   - Improved communication; impossible to put $ benefit on; can communicate with nearly half of the company within seconds, without paper expense of mailroom impact; greatly reduces "telephone tag"; has improved the timelines of communication since notes, documents, and messages can be sent, received, forwarded, replied to, all in a matter of minutes without waiting for copies, mail lag, etc.; great potential for making decisions more timely, based on the availability of timely info.

5. *Survey of other utilities with PROFS*
   - Per information supplied by IBM, approximately 50% of large utilities have office automation systems in place.

6. *Triggers for other automation*
   - Many OIS terminals are used for other applications as well.
   - Widespread availability of terminals as a result of OIS has made possible the development of certain applications dependent upon that availability, such as events reporting and online budget input. Such widespread availability of terminals also provides a foundation or basic level of equipment, already in place, that will benefit and support other online applications in the future.

7. *Reduced clerical support/word processing capacity*
   - Downsizing of word processing staff would have been very difficult without OIS in place. Example: clerical assistants were reduced from 5 to 2 in the Information Systems Department, an improbable accomplishment in the absence of OIS. Number of clericals now in place probably could not handle the work if OIS was to go away.

more keystrokes, automatically forwarding Geist's note to members of the electric division's top policy-making committee—a group known internally as USET (company shorthand for "Utility Sector Executive Team).

Bundrant quickly read through three other short messages on his mail list, then flipped through the calendar on his desk to see what next week's schedule looked like, pressed another key to reaccess the PROFS menu, and chose the "Schedule a Meeting" function from the options. He keyed in next Monday's date, then indicated he wanted a one-hour time slot. When the screen prompted him for names of the meeting participants, Bundrant typed in USET. A few seconds later the screen displayed two times when the other USET members could meet with Bundrant. He keyed in his preference for 10 A.M.; next the screen prompted him with the message "Send a notice of a meeting." He responded by typing in information on the location—eighth-floor conference room, along with the comment, "Let's bounce around our ideas on Jerry's note Monday at 10." Bundrant hit a key, automatically forwarding his message to all USET members.

Bundrant made a mental note of the fact that all this had been done in less than five minutes and that without OIS it probably would have taken his secretary 30 to 45 minutes to make copies of Jerry's note, distribute them to the others, and then go through the ritual of setting up a meeting—calling everybody on the telephone, catching the other people or their secretaries at their desks, communicating the purpose of the meeting, checking the calendars of everyone involved, calling back and forth to arrive at a mutually open time slot, typing a meeting notice, running off copies, and sending them out through the interoffice mail.

Had Bundrant's secretary been at her desk at the time, he would not have gone through the "Schedule a Meeting" routine himself. His usual practice was to let her handle such details; his personal use of the system was pretty much restricted to "Open the Mail," a feature he found convenient and efficient. Despite his engineering background, Bundrant did not use his computer terminal personally to the same degree that most other officers and managers did. While he suspected that some people thought this was because he was from "the old school" and wasn't comfortable with all the gadgetry of computers, the truth was that he thought the time-saving benefits accrued more to managers without a secretary and to clerical workers whose normal tasks could be done more quickly and easily using the capabilities built into PROFS. His secretary sometimes spent as much as four hours a day using various PROFS functions, and he had heard her praise the system. Bundrant saw the value of OIS to him personally as being faster, better communication between his office and the rest of the organization.

COMPANY BACKGROUND

With sales of $690 million and assets of $3 billion in 1985, Public Service Company of New Mexico (PNM) ranked among the 100 largest utility companies in the United States. Headquartered in Albuquerque, PNM's main business consisted of providing electric and gas service to about 65 percent of the state's population; the electric division served about 267,000 customers, and the gas division served over 322,000 customers. In addition to its electric and gas utility operations, PNM had several other business interests:

- Sangre de Cristo Water Co., which provided water utility services to the city of Sante Fe.
- Sunbelt Mining Co., which owned and operated coal and other mineral mining interests in New Mexico and Oklahoma and supplied coal to PNM's San Juan Generating Station and other electric utilities.
- Meadows Resources Inc., which had made a portfolio of financial investments in companies unrelated to utilities and had strategic goals of trying to attract new companies to locate in New Mexico, provide job opportunities to New Mexicans, enhance New Mexico's economic growth prospects, and broaden PNM's earnings base.
- Paragon Resources, which acquired water rights and property for future power plant projects and utility-related activities.

Exhibit 2 depicts PNM's corporate structure.

Electric and gas operations were PNM's principal revenue and profit producers. In 1985, 59 percent of PNM's revenues and 88 percent of its operating income came from electric operations. Gas operations accounted for 40 percent of operating revenues and 11 percent of operating earnings. About 1 percent of corporate revenues and operating income came from the other activities (however, Sunbelt Mining's sales of coal to the San Juan plant were included as a cost to the electric division and were recovered in the rates PNM charged its electric customers). Exhibit 3 shows a financial breakdown for 1985 by business segment.

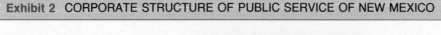

Exhibit 2 CORPORATE STRUCTURE OF PUBLIC SERVICE OF NEW MEXICO

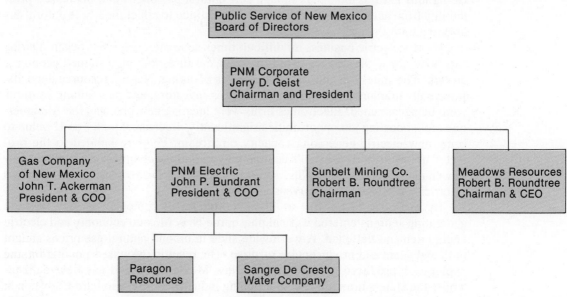

Exhibit 3 PUBLIC SERVICE COMPANY OF NEW MEXICO'S FINANCIAL SUMMARY, BY BUSINESS SEGMENT, 1985 (thousands of dollars)

	Electric	Gas	Other	Total
Operating revenues	$ 408,101	$273,737	$ 8,144	$ 689,982
Operating expenses excluding income taxes	227,228	250,899	4,891	483,018
Pretax operating income	180,873	22,838	3,253	206,964
Operating income tax	17,931	2,965	954	21,850
Operating income	$ 162,942	$ 19,873	$ 2,299	$ 185,114
Depreciation expense	$ 47,113	$ 7,515	$ 738	$ 55,366
Utility construction expenditure	$ 242,559	$ 17,675	$ 1,697	$ 261,931
Identifiable assets:				
Net utility plant	$1,923,939	$216,178	$ 31,340	$2,171,457
Other	460,514	92,352	285,915	838,781
Total assets	$2,384,453	$308,530	$317,255	$3,010,238

Source: *1985 Annual Report.*

The gas utility operations were a new business for PNM. The company had acquired the New Mexico natural gas utility assets of Southern Union Company in 1985 as part of a settlement of antitrust litigation brought against Southern Union by PNM and others. Falling natural gas prices, deregulation of the natural gas industry, and increased competition from the wellhead all the way to end-use customers were forcing PNM to find ways to protect the gas division's profitability and at the same time initiate the transition from being a traditional regulated gas utility to being a more price competitive, service-oriented operation. Going into 1986, it looked as though soft natural gas prices and depressed profitability from natural gas operations would continue to affect the whole natural gas industry until the early 1990s.

PNM's electric business hit difficult times soon after the 1980s began. During the 1970s, New Mexico appeared to be on the threshold of sustained economic growth. The state's oil and gas business was booming. Natural resource deposits, principally uranium and coal, were attracting investors, and new mining ventures were being launched. Electronics firms were locating new plants in the Albuquerque area, boosting job opportunities significantly. Because it took 8 to 12 years to bring new electric generating capacity on stream, PNM responded to the projected upturn in New Mexico's economy by initiating construction of several new power plants in the mid-1970s, so as to be in position to meet New Mexico's electricity needs in the mid-1980s and beyond.

By the early 1980s, just as PNM's program to complete the new electric generating stations entered its final phase, the New Mexico economy and electric energy demand flattened. A worldwide slide in oil and natural gas prices caught both end-users and producers by surprise. The resulting slowdown in drilling and exploration produced a depression in New Mexico's oil and gas fields. Meanwhile, the state's uranium and coal mining industries were also hard hit by slack demand and falling prices. Production cutbacks were so severe that, in early 1986,

PNM's uranium mining customers were using only 14 percent as much electricity as they used in 1979, and the peak load they placed on PNM's electric system was 97 percent below what had been projected; coal mining customers were using only 40 percent of the projected peak loads.

In Albuquerque, the electronics industry, hit hard by international competition, had not expanded to the expected degree. In fact, the largest electricity-using industrial facility to locate in PNM's service area during the 1980s was a small fiberboard plant that had been financed by PNM's Meadows Resources subsidiary.

As a consequence, PNM found itself with more electric generating capacity than its customers could use. In 1986 PNM had reserve generating capacity nearly 70 percent above that needed to meet its annual peak load requirement (the industry norm was a reserve margin about 20 percent above the annual peak). Completion of Unit 3 of the Palo Verde nuclear plant in 1987 would increase PNM's reserve margin by an additional 8 percent.

While PNM had been and still was trying to market its extra generating capacity to other electric utilities, the regional wholesale power market was temporarily glutted and buyers could bargain on price. Consequently, while 35 to 45 percent of PNM's total electric energy sales were coming from "off-system" sales to other electric utilities, the profit contributions on these sales were low. This threw the financial burden of PNM's construction program and the high fixed costs of underused plant capacity back on New Mexico ratepayers and the company's stockholders. The company's need to raise its retail electric rates to earn a decent return on its new construction investments had attracted much attention in the media and was emerging as an issue in New Mexico's gubernatorial campaign. With no turnaround in sight for the New Mexico economy, the company was projecting it would be deep into the 1990s before customers would need all the generating capacity available at the new Palo Verde and San Juan plants. All of this meant the electric division's sales were likely to be flat for the next five years and, in the absence of budget cuts and streamlining, the company's return on investment was in jeopardy.

In addition, adverse regulatory developments were brewing. PNM was using an innovative accounting treatment that kept the costs of PNM's Palo Verde nuclear generating plants out of the rate base, using an "Inventorying of Capacity" rate-making method, until the 1990s when higher rates would be phased in to cover the plant investment. However, proposed changes in national accounting standards would disallow the use of this rate-making methodology and require PNM to use accounting treatments that would severely dampen the company's reported earnings.

To make matters worse, the chances were good that the New Mexico Public Service Commission would soon decide to investigate the prudency of the costs incurred by PNM to construct the Palo Verde nuclear plant; hearings could be long. Any costs determined by the New Mexico PSC to be imprudent could end up being excluded from the rate base, effectively preventing PNM from recovering its investment through its electric rates and forcing the company to incur writeoffs against earnings. To ease the financial burden to its ownership interest in Palo Verde, PNM in 1985 initiated a sale and lease-back transaction for its part of

Exhibit 4 FACTS ABOUT PUBLIC SERVICE COMPANY OF NEW MEXICO

Average electric costs per residential kilowatt hour (dollars and cents)

Year	Costs	Change from previous year
1975	3.30¢	+38.1%
1976	3.54¢	+7.3%
1977	4.13¢	+16.7%
1978	5.14¢	+24.5%
1979	6.21¢	+20.8%
1980	6.66¢	+7.2%
1981	7.30¢	+9.6%
1982	8.02¢	+9.9%
1983	7.47¢	-6.9%
1984	8.39¢	+12.3%
1985	9.02¢	+7.5%

Distribution of the 1985 revenue dollar

Fuel and Purchased Power	9.02%
Dividends	20.81%
Taxes	14.16%
Payroll—Operations	11.47%
Other O&M	10.64%
Interest	21.84%
Depreciation & Amortization	8.75%
Reinvested Earnings	3.32%
	100.00%

1985 Revenues		% change from 1984
Electric	$408,100,965	-7%
Water	$8,143,722	28.2%
Total	$416,244,687	-6.5%

Electric plant investment

Year	Total (in millions)	Per customer
1970	$198	$1,300
1978	$829	$4,366
1979	$1,140	$5,352
1980	$1,412	$6,625
1981	$1,678	$7,781
1982	$1,966	$8,838
1983	$2,073	$9,108
1984	$2,333	$9,804
1985	$2,530	$10,079

Consumer demand

Year	Peak demand	Month/time/temp	% Change
1980	913 MW	June/3 pm/104°	
1981	992 MW	July/3 pm/100°	+8.65%
1982	957 MW	July/2 pm/98°	-3.53%
1983	998 MW	August/2 pm/94°	+4.28%
1984	976 MW	July/3 pm/96°	-2.2%
1985	861 MW	June/2 pm/95°	-11.8%

Miles of Transmission Lines — 2,739

Electric operations

Albuquerque Division
382 employees, 176,712 customers
Belen Division
44 employees, 15,652 customers
Bernalillo Division
42 employees, 15,442 customers
Clayton Division
9 employees, 1,662 customers
Deming Division
20 employees, 6,730 customers
Las Vegas Division
29 employees, 6,714 customers
Santa Fe Division (Includes Water)
186 employees, 50,451 customers
Power Supply
232 employees
San Juan
877 employees
System
818 employees
Total Company
2,639 employees full time, 273,363 customers

Electric usage (thousand kWhr)

Residential	1,319,529
Commercial	1,765,077
Industrial	788,880
Other Ultimate Customers	206,355
Sales for Resale	1,156,267
TOTAL	5,236,110
	(17% decrease from 1984)

Water plant investment

Year	Total	Per customers
1980	$38.6 million	$2,000
1981	$40.7 million	$2,065
1982	$34.4 million	$2,162
1983	$35.6 million	$2,176
1984	$36.6 million	$2,123
1985	$36.1 million	$1,978

PNM's role in New Mexico's 1985 economy (excluding subsidiaries)

—Payroll and other employee benefits: $86,918,172
—State, County and Local Taxes: $34,111,153
—City Franchise Fees: $8,313,533

Stockholders

Number of Common Shares Outstanding: 37,965,868
Number of Preferred Shares Outstanding: 3,220,800
Number of Common Shareholders: 67,524
Number of Preferred Shareholders: 2,526
Number of New Mexico Shareholders (Preferred and Common): 15,089

Electric generation on-line

Plant	Operating capacity	PNM's share	Fuel
Four Corners (Units 4 & 5)	1,478 MW	192 MW	Coal
San Juan (Units 1, 2, 3, & 4)	1,616 MW	834 MW	Coal
Palo Verde (Unit 1)	1,270 MW	130 MW	Nuclear
Person Station 4 Units	105 MW	105 MW	Gas/Oil
Reeves Station 3 Units	154 MW	154 MW	Gas/Oil
Las Vegas Comb. Turbine	20 MW	20 MW	Gas/Oil
TOTAL		1,435 MW	

Planned electric generating plants

Date	Plant	Est. capacity	PNM's share	Fuel
1986	Palo Verde #2	1,270 MW	130 MW	Nuclear
1987	Palo Verde #3	1,270 MW	130 MW	Nuclear

Units 1 and 2; this was the first such sale and lease-back transaction involving a nuclear plant.

Exhibit 4 is a "fact card" for PNM, summarizing a variety of company statistics.

THE OFFICE INFORMATION SYSTEMS PROJECT

Interest in considering office automation applications at PNM was sparked when an information systems manager saw PROFS demonstrated at a data processing conference in 1982. Soon after, David Bedford, then vice president for corporate services and considered something of a visionary by his peers, began to look into whether the company could benefit from "office of the future" technology. His first step was to call in a consultant to assess PNM's information systems needs; the consultant concluded the company needed to do something "regardless." Bedford recalled how the OIS project at PNM evolved in its formative stages:

> Our project really started as a way to reduce costs. I had heard pitches from IBM as to what their office systems would do. And because we had an IBM mainframe and a multitude of computer terminals already installed, I was interested in doing something that was compatible with the equipment investments we had already made.
>
> I asked our IBM representatives for information on PROFS and they got it for me. The more I learned, the more willing I became to try it. Of course, it wasn't a new product at that time, but it was new to us. We were among the first companies that IBM marketed PROFS to outside of their own organization.
>
> In 1983, we put together a joint company-IBM study team [known internally as the Application Transfer Team (ATT)] to evaluate the benefits and costs of going to office automation. My interest grew as the team dug out more facts about PROFS's capabilities and what the cost of installing it would be for different user levels. We looked very hard at the numbers and decided that the cost of office automation was in the range of something we could afford to experiment with. But it was the communications improvements, none of which were measureable directly, that convinced us to keep going ahead with our preliminary investigation. The communications features really turned me on.
>
> When the team made its report, they concluded we could realize a 6 percent gain in productivity. Not long thereafter, IBM came in and offered to bring in enough equipment for a 90-day pilot test for 32 users—it was all essentially free to the company except for the shipping cost. We decided that the pilot should be done in the offices of some of the executives and in the corporate services departments reporting to me. I got a terminal on my desk, my secretary got one, and all of the managers who reported directly to me got one. Then there were several managers one level down and some other staff members who participated. We created a pilot study team to evaluate the test and determine the technical feasibility and cost/benefit of implementing PROFS on a wider scale.

Exhibit 5 shows excerpts from the ATT study and pilot study reports. The supporting documentation for these two studies was over 3 inches thick. When questioned about why the benefit-cost studies and documentation were so extensive, Terry Othick, one of the key project managers, said:

Exhibit 5 EXCERPTS FROM THE REPORTS OF THE OFFICE AUTOMATION STUDY TEAMS

ATT STUDY—SUMMARY CONCLUSIONS

- Presently, the automated office functions which contribute most to potential dollar and time savings are text processing and electronic mail. Additional savings can be achieved through electronic calendaring.

- The estimated dollar value of time saved per year through installment of an office automation system ranges from $1.858 million (low estimate of time savings, 500 terminals) to $7.073 million (high estimate of time savings, 900 terminals).

- The dollar value of savings associated with reducing the work load of word processing, convenience copying, corporate manuals, internal mail, filing and micrographics is approximately $124,000 per year.

- There is a general willingness within PNM to accept office automation. This conclusion is based on the following factors:

  A generally high level of interest throughout the company in the topic of OA.

  The high response rate (approximately 55 percent) of people who responded to the invitation to participate in the questionnaire.

  The relatively high degree of familiarity with computer terminals and products of automated systems, which suggests an already existing degree of competence with and a willingness to use additional automated tools.

The main benefits projected are:

- A minimum weekly average reduction of 6.4% in administrative and management work hours. This represents a 3.1 hour per week reduction from 49.8 to 46.7 hours per person.

- A minimum weekly average reducton of 5.9% in administrative support work hours. This represents a 2.6 hour per week reduction from 45.5 to 42.9 hours per person.

- An approximate Word Processing Center volume reduction of 9%, or about 10,000 pages per month, which relates to a 15% labor reduction, or an annual savings of $79,000.

- An approximate monthly copying reduction of 149,000 pages from both the Reproduction Center and satellite copiers, representing an annual savings of $45,000.

OA PILOT STUDY—SUMMARY CONCLUSIONS

The on-site in-depth evaluation of the IBM/PROFS system as a solution to the office automation question produced the following conclusions:

- The PROFS system provides the basic as well as many advanced functions of an automated office and can technically support PNM's transition from a "manual" to an integrated office systems concept.

- IBM offers a complete solution to the OA question in terms of hardware, software, and necessary data communications technology.

- A full range of end user terminals is available to meet user requirements. These terminals range from relatively inexpensive "dumb" terminals to high resolution color graphics terminals and fully functional personal computers, all of which can access and use the Professional Office System (PROFS).

- A major commitment to the office automation concept has been made by IBM.

- Each user of PROFS needs his/her own terminal to maximize utilization and benefit.

- The IBM/PROFS system is not perfect. The basic functions of the system are easy to learn and use; however, the advanced functions are basically data processing oriented and require the user to understand some basic data processing concepts.

- Implementation of Office Automation implies that roughly one-third of all PNM's employees will adopt and use tools to accomplish their daily jobs. This will require a major shift in PNM's office work culture.

- A continuing user training and technical support program will be required to bring 900 non-data processing users up to a proficiency level adequate to achieve OA benefits. Computer operations, user training, and user support will require a permanent trained staff of 8 to 12 people (included in projected costs).

- The low benefit level cannot be achieved without an actual net reduction of ~ 55 jobs.

I think if it were redone today it wouldn't necessarily be as thick. The style of the senior vice president was very analytical, and people that went to him requesting to spend corporate funds expected to have to answer a lot of questions. Therefore, this document went into a significant amount of detail in anticipation of Mr. Bedford's probing questions.

In this particular instance, he really wanted to know what type of return the investment was going to get, what productivity gains from individuals we might expect, and what equipment costs and software costs would be incurred. He was also very concerned about what an OIS would do to the time and effort it took to process all the other computing jobs we had on the mainframe on a regular basis.

To get a handle on the productivity and other benefits, we did a survey of about 1000 employees who dealt with documents, spreadsheets, and the like. We asked them all kinds of questions about what they could do with an office automation system, how long they would use it daily, how much time they thought it might save—really, we asked just about everything we could think of. The survey was five pages long. Our estimates of potential productivity came pretty much directly out of the survey responses.

Othick saw Dave Bedford as the right person to champion OIS at the company:

He got turned on to this particular type of technology. He continued to push and prod and keep his hands more in this project than in many other projects. I think the reason was that he wanted very much to make it succeed. He kept asking questions dealing with security, training, use of the tools—everything he could think of. The questions were very hard and made us keep fine-tuning our approach.

Bill Wygant, who succeeded Dave Bedford as vice president for administrative services in early 1986 and who was heavily involved in the OIS project all along, echoed Othick's observation:

David was a young senior executive—single, very bright, technically competent. One of the things that he did was use systems. He discovered that most all systems except office systems were interconnected, and he felt that office systems would be more productive if connected through the mainframe. Our OIS proposal represented an opportunity to begin to do this. At the time, there were very few people who would approach office automation with a mainframe and dumb terminals. This was a very unusual route.

Dave normally built support for his decisions on very, very firm numbers. There were some soft spots in our benefit estimates, so Dave did the personal research necessary to convince himself that going to OIS was the proper thing to do. One of the major elements in that research was the ATT study, which he had me work through with IBM. That formed the basic justification for going ahead with the pilot. Then during the pilot, he was a very active user himself and he spent a lot of time listening to the reactions and opinions of the other trial users.

APPROVAL FOR THE OIS PROJECT

As the pilot project progressed, top management discussions about taking PROFS companywide began in earnest. Dave Bedford became convinced during the first 30 days of the pilot that PROFS delivered some very positive benefits and that the actual costs would be in line with the estimates. However, several senior executives were skeptical whether OIS was really cost justified. Bedford recalled the discussions:

> At the time, I was pushing all the other executives to hold the budgets in their areas down, yet here I was advocating that the company spend extra money installing PROFS. They argued that if an engineer or a surveyor became more productive using PROFS, the company would never see the cost-saving dollars because such people would just have more time to do their jobs thoroughly. They didn't deny that PROFS would be a plus. They just said they would never be able to capture the dollar savings in their budgets except in the case of clerical personnel—where it might be possible to get by with fewer people.
>
> To counter their arguments, I guaranteed enough actual dollar savings in the administrative services departments reporting to me to pay for installing the equipment companywide. In my service departments—about 700 people total—I could see that we could make enough reductions in bodies to recover the added costs of PROFS dollar for dollar from my own budget. Our forecasted benefits were two to three times the projected costs. My guarantee was what sold Jerry Geist, our CEO. There really wasn't any risk; it was all upside potential. I always had very good budget relations with Jerry. I never promised him something I couldn't deliver.
>
> But the hardest part of the process was getting my peers to install it in their own offices and getting agreement that we senior officers would pioneer the use of PROFS in our respective areas of responsibility. Some of them didn't want to be bothered because it was pretty much a break-even proposition in their departments. They didn't see where they could get the bucks back and they didn't want their budgets to go up. Jerry was the one who influenced the decision for all the senior executives and their direct reports to be the first ones to go on PROFS. He maintained that all the officers should give it a try since it wasn't going to be a drag on the bottom line and since no one's overall budget costs were at risk.

THE OIS IMPLEMENTATION PLAN

In February 1984 a top-level PNM policy group approved a full-scale OIS project to roll out PROFS companywide to 900 users by year-end 1985. The estimated payback period for the project was just under three years. The schedule called for new users to be brought onto the PROFS network at the rate of 40 per month. An IBM 4381 computer was installed to replace the company's 4341 model. A training program was put together to introduce new users to the functions available through PROFS; four training classes were offered—one that introduced the features of PROFS and how to use them and three advanced classes to enhance user proficiency in document creation, ad hoc tools, and expanded OIS applications.

When the capacity of the IBM 4381 model was fully taken up at the 500-user level, an IBM 3084 mainframe was installed, giving PNM not only enough computing power to handle all the foreseeable PROFS users but also enough to permit major enhancements to the basic PROFS functions and to handle most of PNM's other data processing needs as well.

Although the number of users brought onto the system ran slightly behind schedule for the first nine months, by fall 1984 users were being put on the system at rates above the scheduled 40 users per month. The OIS project reached its goal of 900 users in October 1985, approximately 10 weeks ahead of schedule and $350,000 under budget.

Almost immediately, efforts began to add enhancement functions and major non-PROFS OIS capabilities to the system, including Megacalc (a mainframe spreadsheet system with business graphics capability), Information Center/1 (for use in filing and reporting), Display Write/370 (a more sophisticated document composition software package), and Easygraph. An OIS user support program was established to provide several services on an ongoing basis:

- A telephone hot line available from 8 A.M. to 5 P.M. five days a week to give users quick problem resolution (the hot line was averaging 625 calls monthly).
- A consulting service that gave users one-on-one assistance to handle problems not able to be resolved over the phone.
- Training classes in using the new tools/functions.
- Periodic refresher courses in the use of PROFS and of the enhancements that had been added (for occasional users who might have forgotten or felt the need for more instructions and for users new to the system).
- A menu option on PROFS that provided "news bulletins" about upgrades to PROFS, dates for new classes, instructions for the newly introduced enhancements, and other information of value to users.

Terry Othick, one of the managers deeply involved in implementing the project companywide, commented on some of the factors that contributed to the OIS project being completed ahead of schedule and under budget:

> Doing the pilot was extremely important. It allowed us to gain knowledge and experience of how the operating system worked and get comfortable with running the system on a day-to-day basis. We were able to work out all of the bugs with a small, controlled, supportive audience.
>
> Another big thing was that the pilot project included the offices of the folks on USET. We saw them as a key group because they needed to see firsthand what PROFS could do and they, of course, in the end would either support the project or not. The pilot helped sell them. Then when USET approved full-scale implementation, the senior officers agreed among themselves that they would be the first group to adopt OIS, to go through training, and to begin to use the system. Their taking the lead on this sent a signal to all the managers below them that this was something they had better look at too.
>
> When we launched into marketing PROFS to the rest of the organization below USET, we did some things that surprised people. My I/S counterparts in other companies told me that their office automation implementation strategy was to offer OIS to managers and departments "free"—that is, the costs of OIS would either be added to their budgets automatically or else covered entirely in the I/S budget. What we did was go to each manager and ask if they wanted to try the system. If the answer was "yes," we would say "great, but, by the way, we're going to hit you with a $140 per month per user charge for it on your existing budget." That was the tough part of it. Many folks felt we shouldn't charge them for it. We explained that the way to absorb it was to do all those wonderful things

Exhibit 6   DISTRIBUTION OF USERS OF PNM'S OFFICE INFORMATION SYSTEM, DECEMBER 31, 1985

Area of company	Officials and managers	Professionals	Technicians	Office and clerical	Totals
Chairman and president (corporate office)	1	1	1		3
Meadows and Sunbelt	1			2	3
Corporate affairs	10	5		8	23
Corporate finance	27	16	1	13	57
Electric utility	297	360	55	112	824
Gas Company of New Mexico*	1			1	2
Totals	337	382	57	136	912†

* GCNM figures do *not* include approximately 75 PROFS IDs maintained on its own internal system.
† Total does *not* include 82 miscellaneous IDs (i.e., group-user IDs, lawyers, consultants, contractors, a doctor, etc.).

that they said they could do in the ATT survey when we asked them about all of the benefits and savings they could generate in their areas if they had OIS to work with. A number of managers said "OK, let's go ahead." This was surprising to some people, but we never pressured any manager to put in OIS and we never told them how many terminals they could have in their areas. We felt since they would be paying for it out of their budgets, they would not opt to put in any more terminals than they could really justify.

Our marketing plan worked. Almost from the start, we had a waiting list to go on the system and get employees into the next training class.

Exhibit 6 shows the distribution of PROFS/OIS users across the company.

INTERVIEWS WITH USERS

The reactions of users of the PROFS/OIS network at PNM were generally favorable. Below are excerpts of interviews conducted by the case researcher. The first interview was with Ernie C. de Baca, staff analyst.

Q: Could you tell us how enthusiastic a user of OIS you are?

A: I'm a real fan. In fact, one of the things that I would miss most if I left this company would be not having OIS. It is a very good communication tool. The best part of it is the way it holds notes for you until you can respond to them. It gives a good trail.

Q: How easy is the system to use?

A: OIS is scary at first to someone who has never seen it because it's so big, but it's really simple if you devote the time to it.

Q: How long did it take for you to become proficient with the system?

A: About a week of trying to make sure I really knew it.

Q: Tell us a little bit about how PROFS fits into your job?

A: I check every morning to see if there is any type of communication that I need to respond to. Our department needs to communicate with some of the higher management people who aren't readily available when you want them. Use of this tool provides access to them.

Q: What about the noncommunication aspects of PROFS and OIS?

A: I mostly use electronic mail, calendaring, document creation, and the spreadsheet functions. I have to look at a lot of data and work on many different reports. The OIS features help me gather data from other departments on a spreadsheet and not have to redo my spreadsheet every time I have a monthly report to turn out. It gives me quick access to that information without having to start over from scratch every time.

Q: How much time do you think that saves you?

A: It's just more efficient. It provides me a better way of doing my job.

Q: Do you think it allows you to get more done during the workday?

A: Yes. It provides a great amount of flexibility in my time.

Q: Does this system let you be your own secretary rather efficiently?

A: It can if you allow it to by doing all your own work. It also provides you with a way to let your secretary clean up things for you.

Q: Does your terminal stay on all day?

A: Yes.

Q: How long are you sitting at the terminal in a given day?

A: Three to four hours.

Q: Do you see your use going up, down, or staying about the same?

A: When you first become associated with OIS and its capabilities, usage goes up quite a bit. Then you plateau at a comfortable point for you.

The interview with Don Tidwell, design supervisor, generating engineering group follows:

Q: How enthusiastic a user of PROFS are you?

A: Probably more so than the average user.

Q: What are your favorite features?

A: Notes, messages, scheduling, and electronic mail. Our particular group is a matrix organization. We, in turn, support several different projects. Our people are assigned to four or five projects at a time. In trying to support all of these projects, there are many meetings that have to be attended and decisions made, and it turns into a lot of communicating. Many of the people we deal with work at our San Juan station 180 miles away. Prior to OIS, we mostly used the telephone. You'd have to call, leave a message, call back, and go through the telephone tag game. With OIS, I can send them a quick note that is concise, and they can easily respond. Scheduling is now a breeze. I used to have to go around and match up schedules, but now I can just send out a note and find out where everyone stands. I don't have a lot of secretarial support; one girl in my area covers 17 people, so I can't just turn over tasks like that to a secretary.

Q: Are there any other aspects of the PROFS system that you use frequently?

A: I take advantage of the fact that we do a lot of correspondence on PROFS. If I send out a particular question over the network to several people and I need their concurrence on some issue, when they respond, I stick it in Notes and file it for documentation. I would be doing it by hand otherwise. I do that 10 or 15 times a day.

Q: What about some of the add-on features like Megacalc?

A: We have used Megacalc. I used it for setting up a workload schedule for the people on my staff. One guy has five or six projects, and he has 20 or 30 hours a month committed to each, but they build up and taper off. I'd like to know three or four months ahead of time when he'll be free to take on another project. A spreadsheet does that and we used Megacalc for that purpose.

Q: What I've heard you saying is that OIS saves you a good bit of time, and it's low quality time that you've been saving. What have you done with the extra time now that you have PROFS?

A: It just means that I'm able to work on other things sooner. I can focus on the long-term needs of a project.

Q: So it allows you to spend more time managing instead of doing the administrative support things?

A: It does speed things up. That's just as big a benefit as the time saved. Things happen sooner because of the OIS user connections.

Q: Do you have any rough estimates of about how much time you spend on the system?

A: A couple of hours.

Q: What's the first thing you do when you come to work?

A: Log on.

Q: What's next?

A: I open the Mail.

Q: Then what?

A: I check the Schedule.

Q: Do you turn off the system or leave it on during the day when you're working?

A: I leave it on till I go to lunch, turn it off during lunch, then turn it back on for the afternoon.

Q: Do you use the Reminder feature?

A: Yes.

Q: If we were to go to the people that you supervise and ask them if you are a more impersonal manager than you used to be because you use this computer to talk to them, what do you think they would say?

A: That's tough. Probably they would say that there are times when they would rather talk to me face to face. On the other hand, they might say they'd rather get a note than have me barge in every 20 minutes interrupting them. I don't know, but that isn't a concern that I've heard expressed. A lot of my people prefer this to a personal confrontation. I try to utilize it when it's proper and speak in person when I should.

Q: Do you find it pretty easy to pick out the issues that need eyeball-to-eyeball communication as opposed to those that can be handled on this system?

A: Yes, because you know the people and how they communicate; you can read into their writing style and see what their concerns are.

The case writer's interview with Sherry Rice, clerical assistant follows:

Q: How enthusiastic are you about the PROFS/OIS system?

A: I use it about four hours a day. My favorite features are Mail, Document Creation, Notes, Calendar, Phone Directory, and Stock. I like this system of doing things; it saves a lot of time.

Q: Has PROFS changed the way you do your job?

A: Yes. I don't use the typewriter or shorthand like I used to.

Q: Has OIS changed the relationship you have with the person you're secretary to?

A: No, I don't think so. The thing that PROFS helps a lot is when they're out of the office you can still send them notes. That cuts down on phone calls.

Q: How has it changed filing?

A: There's a lot less physical filing because it's all right there in the PROFS system.

Q: Do you like using OIS for opening the Mail?

A: Yes, I think it's a lot quicker.

Q: Why do you use Stock?

A: I like to know what our stock price is doing. I have a few shares.

Q: What do you call your machine?

A: The tube or the terminal. Mostly the tube.

Q: Is that a complimentary term?

A: Just a term.

Q: What are your complaints about PROFS?

A: When the system goes down, we lose a lot of documents.

Q: Does that happen very often?

A: Not really, but it's very frustrating when it does.

Q: Do you think you've been given enough training in the use of OIS?

A: They've offered enough, but I don't think I've taken enough.

Q: Why?

A: I don't know; I schedule it and then just don't go. I think that's true of a lot of people.

The case writer found Ellen Wilson, manager of administrative services, San Juan plant, to be a real fan of the PROFS system:

Q: How enthusiastic a user of PROFS are you?

A: Quite enthusiastic. I couldn't get by without it.

Q: Can you tell us how you use it? What do you like?

A: I use Calendar. My secretary is quite comfortable and knowledgeable in the use of OIS because when I'm not there she checks all the Mail and the Calendar; we communicate that way rather than on the telephone. When I'm in Albuquerque, and I am quite a lot, we communicate via OIS. I use the basic memo and letter writing in Document Creation. I use the reminders on the calendar as well. I really believe that if my colleagues in Albuquerque and I didn't communicate a lot via this system, that we would find it very difficult to catch each other.

Q: Do you think this OIS communication saves you very much time?

A: Definitely. It's not more effective than the phone, but it is quicker and I utilize it to ask quick questions. It's not a substitute for the phone. I like face-to-face encounters, but it makes sure that when we talk, we're talking about something that we both need to have a discussion about.

Q: Does it change the way you communicate with your staff?

A: Yes. At my job in Albuquerque, I communicated with my staff on OIS a lot. We were all used to it and very comfortable with it. When I moved up to my present job at the San Juan plant, my staff was not used to it. I think it really changed the way they communicated with me. I use OIS for informal type things. Often I write a note to someone who has been on vacation saying I hope they've had a good time, and I usually use OIS to send holiday wishes to everyone. When I first came here I would send messages just to say hello and get marvelous messages back.

Q: When you went to San Juan and discovered that your staff members weren't using OIS, how did you handle introduction of it to them?

A: I started out incorrectly. I made the assumption that if I let them know that I was a strong OIS user that they would begin using it; that didn't work at all. After a short while I realized that they were not even opening the Mail and reading the messages I sent to them on OIS. I then explained why I liked OIS, why and how I used it, and how it could help them. I ended up asking them to check their mail twice a day and just try that much. There was quite a bit of resistance to that. It was a machine to them. So I went back and explained again how it helped me to save time. They pointed out that it was too impersonal, so I agreed not to use OIS in place of a real need to talk to them personally. After about six months, I began to get responses. We're now doing more of our business together on OIS, though not as much as I'd like.

Q: Have you noticed any impact of OIS on your personal productivity?

A: When I first got to the plant, I wasn't very certain of the scope of the job and I found myself not using OIS all that much. I was returning a lot of the phone calls instead of answering back on OIS. Slowly I realized that I couldn't possibly return all the calls and still do my job. Most of my time saving is in being able to communicate with a lot of people faster and quicker. I also can do the short drafts on memos and letters quicker than I could writing them out and going through my secretary.

Exhibit 7 USE STATISTICS FOR PNM's OIS/PROFS NETWORK FOR A TYPICAL MONTH (total number of users = 985)

OIS/PROFS functions	Times accessed this month	Total elapsed time (in seconds)	Average number of times accessed per (985) users	Average elasped time per use (in seconds)
Open the mail	87,080	36,578,531	88.4	420.06
Process notes and messages	33,247	10,369,303	32.7	311.89
Process schedules	14,900	3,927,451	15.3	263.59
Look at phone list	14,027	7,709,381	14.2	549.61
Prepare documents	7,784	9,497,960	7.9	1220.19
Look at current stock quote	7,430	1,183,067	7.5	159.23
Process postponed documents	6,294	7,776,956	6.4	1235.61
Facts	4,256	586,176	4.3	137.73
Megacalc	3,582	4,674,171	3.6	1304.91
Process the mail log	3,325	1,272,231	3.4	382.63
Add an automatic reminder	2,472	194	2.5	0.08
Job openings in PNM	2,019	323,710	2.0	160.33
Search for documents	945	133,040	1.0	140.78
IC/1 spreadsheet	730	941,251	.7	1289.38
List available commands	544	53,907	.6	99.09
Create author profile	530	65,907	.6	107.28
List note files	434	115,724	.4	266.65
Process distribution lists	420	98,666	.4	234.92
Process to do lists	346	125,518	.35	362.77
List all PROFS users	334	24,387	.34	73.01
Look at financial/operating statements	321	143,868	.33	448.19
Change nicknames	294	45,465	.30	154.64
Check status of outgoing mail	264	5,640	.27	21.36
Select individual printer list	215	14,487	.22	67.38
Change user password	205	6,272	.21	30.60
Listnews	90	3,162	.09	35.13
Easygraf	70	19,335	.07	276.21
Look at PNM OIS guidelines	51	7,827	.05	153.47
Process documents from other source	47	1	.05	0.02
Budget	21	552	.02	26.29
Forms	14	3,408	.01	243.43
Issues	11	2,873	.01	261.18
Invest	4	11	.004	2.75
Look at new PROFS functions	2	3	.002	1.50
All others combined	1,498	916,493	1.5	611.81

Source: Company records.

Ed Kist, manager of system planning, was more tempered in his enthusiasm for PROFS:

Q: How enthusiastic a user of OIS are you?

A: I'm enthusiastic about some uses of it. The parts that I like very much are Notes and the Calendar (which my secretary mostly uses for me). Things that I don't like about it are that it's frustratingly slow to me, the system seems to go down frequently, and there are functions that I don't feel are necessary to me as a manager that I'm probably paying for. It's expensive, too.

Q: How many people use this system in your group?

A: About 35.

Q: So that's a nice cut into your budget?

A: It makes a difference.

Q: About how much time is OIS saving you?

A: At least one half hour a day, I think. I used to run down the halls and try to leave messages. OIS stops that.

Q: Has OIS changed the way you communicate with your staff.

A: Not a lot. I believe in personal contact, but it leverages the current style that I have.

Q: Has OIS made your style better?

A: I think it has made it more efficient. Sometimes I'll get a message from someone that I want to pass along to my staff. It's very easy to do that.

Q: How many people report to you in your group?

A: About five.

Q: Do you think with your improved ability to communicate using OIS that you could handle seven direct reports rather than just five?

A: I don't think that the number of people who report to me would be a function of the machine. The choice of how I allocate my half-hour average of time savings a day isn't going to be affected in a major way by the number of people that I have reporting to me. If I could handle seven, then it would be because of what those seven were doing and what my capabilities are and not necessarily because I'm 5 percent more productive using OIS.

Exhibit 7 shows use statistics for PNM's office automation system for a typical month.

LINCOLN ELECTRIC COMPANY, 1989*

> People are our most valuable asset. They must feel secure, important, challenged, in control of their destiny, confident in their leadership, be responsive to common goals, believe they are being treated fairly, have easy access to authority and open lines of communication in all possible directions. Perhaps the most important task Lincoln employees face today is that of establishing an example for others in the Lincoln organization in other parts of the world. We need to maximize the benefits of cooperation and teamwork, fusing high technology with human talent, so that we here in the United States and all of our subsidiary and joint venture operations will be in a position to realize our full potential.
>
> *George Willis, CEO, the Lincoln Electric Company*

The Lincoln Electric Company is the world's largest manufacturer of welding products and a leading producer of industrial electric motors. The firm employs 2,400 workers in 2 U.S. factories near Cleveland and an equal number in 11 factories in other countries. This does not include the field sales force of more than 200. The company's U.S. market share (for arc-welding products) is estimated at more than 40 percent.

The Lincoln incentive management plan has been well known for many years. Many college management texts refer to the Lincoln plan as a model for achieving higher worker productivity. Certainly, the firm has been successful according to the usual measures.

James F. Lincoln died in 1965, and there was concern, even among employees, that the management system would fall into disarray, that profits would decline, and that year-end bonuses might be discontinued. Quite the contrary, 24 years after Lincoln's death, the company appears as strong as ever. Each year, except the recession years of 1982 and 1983, has seen higher profits and bonuses. Employee morale and productivity remain high. Employee turnover is almost nonexistent except for retirements. Lincoln's market share is stable. The historically high stock dividends continue.

HISTORICAL SKETCH

In 1895, after being frozen out of the depression-ravaged Elliott-Lincoln Company, a maker of Lincoln-designed electric motors, John C. Lincoln took out his second patent and began to manufacture his improved motor. He opened his new business, unincorporated, with $200 he had earned redesigning a motor for young Herbert Henry Dow, who later founded the Dow Chemical Company.

Started during an economic depression and cursed by a major fire afer only one year in business, the company grew, but hardly prospered, through its first

---

* Prepared by Professor Arthur D. Sharplin, McNeese State University.

quarter century. In 1906, John C. Lincoln incorporated the business and moved from his one-room, fourth-floor factory to a new three-story building he erected in east Cleveland. He expanded his work force to 30, and sales grew to over $50,000 a year. Lincoln preferred being an engineer and inventor rather than a manager, though, and it was another Lincoln who managed the company through its years of success.

In 1907, after a bout with typhoid fever forced him from Ohio State University in his senior year, James F. Lincoln, John's younger brother, joined the fledgling company. In 1914 he became active head of the firm, with the titles of general manager and vice president. John remained president of the company for some years but became more involved in other business ventures and in his work as an inventor.

One of James Lincoln's early actions was to ask the employees to elect representatives to a committee that would advise him on company operations. This advisory board has met with the chief executive officer every two weeks since then. This was only the first of a series of innovative personnel policies that have distinguished Lincoln Electric from its contemporaries.

The first year the advisory board was in existence, working hours were reduced from 55 per week, then standard, to 50. In 1915, the company gave each employee a paid-up life insurance policy. A welding school, which continues today, was begun in 1917. In 1918 an employee bonus plan was attempted. It was not continued, but the idea was to resurface.

The Lincoln Electric Employees' Association was formed in 1919 to provide health benefits and social activities. This organization continues today and has assumed several additional functions. In 1923 a piecework pay system was in effect, employees got two weeks' paid vacation each year, and wages were adjusted for changes in the consumer price index. Approximately 30 percent of the common stock was set aside for key employees in 1914. A stock purchase plan for all employees was begun in 1925.

The board of directors voted to start a suggestion system in 1929. The program is still in effect, but cash awards, a part of the early pogram, were discontinued several years ago. Now, suggestions are rewarded by additional "points," which affect year-end bonuses.

The legendary Lincoln bonus plan was proposed by the advisory board and accepted on a trial basis in 1934. The first annual bonus amounted to about 25 percent of wages. There has been a bonus every year since then. The bonus plan has been a cornerstone of the Lincoln management system, and recent bonuses have approximated annual wages.

By 1944 Lincoln employees enjoyed a pension plan, a policy of promotion from within, and continuous employment. Base pay rates were determined by formal job evaluation and a merit rating system was in effect. In the prologue of James F. Lincoln's last book, Charles G. Herbruck explains why these personnel practices were put in place:

> They were not to buy good behavior. They were not efforts to increase profits. They were not antidotes to labor difficulties. They did not constitute a "do-gooder" program. They were an expression of mutual respect for each person's

importance to the job to be done. All of them reflect the leadership of James Lincoln, under whom they were nurtured and propagated.

During World War II, Lincoln prospered as never before. By the start of the war, the company was the world's largest manufacturer of arc-welding products. Sales of about $4 million in 1934 grew to $24 million by 1941. Productivity per employee more than doubled during the same period. The Navy's Price Review Board challenged the high profits. And the Internal Revenue Service questioned the tax deductibility of employee bonuses, arguing they were not "ordinary and necessary" costs of doing business. But the forceful and articulate James Lincoln was able to overcome the objections.

Certainly since 1935 and probably for several years before that, Lincoln productivity has been well above the average for similar companies. The company claims levels of productivity more than twice those for other manufacturers from 1945 onward. Information available from outside sources tends to support these claims.

COMPANY PHILOSOPHY

James F. Lincoln was the son of a Congregational minister, and Christian principles were at the center of his business philosophy:

> The Christian ethic should control our acts. If it did control our acts, the savings in cost of distribution would be tremendous. Advertising would be a contact of the expert consultant with the customer, in order to give the customer the best product available when all of the customer's needs are considered. Competition then would be in improving the quality of products and increasing efficiency in producing and distributing them; not in deception, as is now too customary. Pricing would reflect efficiency of production; it would not be a selling dodge that the customer may well be sorry he accepted. It would be proper for all concerned and rewarding for the ability used in producing the product.

There is no indication that Lincoln attempted to evangelize his employees or customers—or the public for that matter. Neither the chairman of the board and chief executive, George Willis, nor the president, Donald F. Hastings, mention the Christian gospel in their recent speeches and interviews. The company motto, "The actual is limited, the possible is immense," is prominently displayed, but there is no display of religious slogans, and there is no company chapel.

Attitude toward the Customer

James Lincoln saw the customer's needs as the *raison d'etre* for every company. "When any company has achieved success so that it is attractive as an investment," he wrote, "all money usually needed for expansion is supplied by the customer in retained earnings. It is obvious that the customer's interests, not the stockholder's, should come first." In 1947 he said, "Care should be taken . . . not to rivet attention on profit. Between 'How much do I get?' and 'How do I make this better, cheaper, more useful?' the difference is fundamental and decisive."

Willis, too, ranks the customer as management's most important constituency. This is reflected in Lincoln's policy to "at all times price on the basis of cost and at all times keep pressure on our cost." Lincoln's goal is "to build a better and better product at a lower and lower price." "It is obvious," James Lincoln said, "that the customer's interests should be the first goal of industry."

Attitude toward Stockholders

Stockholders are given last priority at Lincoln. This is a continuation of James Lincoln's philosophy: "The last group to be considered is the stockholders who own stock because they think it will be more profitable than investing money in any other way." Concerning division of the largess produced by incentive management, he wrote, "The absentee stockholder also will get his share, even if undeserved, out of the greatly increased profit that the efficiency produces."

Attitude toward Unionism

There has never been a serious effort to organize Lincoln employees. While James Lincoln criticized the labor movement for "selfishly attempting to better its position at the expense of the people it must serve," he still had kind words for union members. He excused abuses of union power as "the natural reactions of human beings to the abuses to which management has subjected them." Lincoln's idea of the correct relationship between workers and managers is shown by this comment: "Labor and management are properly not warring camps; they are parts of one organization in which they must and should cooperate fully and happily."

Beliefs and Assumptions about Employees

If fulfilling customer needs is the desired goal of business, then employee performance and productivity are the means by which this goal can best be achieved. The Lincoln attitude toward employees, reflected in the following comments by James Lincoln, is credited by many with creating the company's success:

> The greatest fear of the worker, which is the same as the greatest fear of the industrialist in operating a company, is the lack of income. . . . The industrial manager is very conscious of his company's need of uninterrupted income. He is completely oblivious, evidently, of the fact that the worker has the same need.
>
> He is just as eager as any manager is to be part of a team that is properly organized and working for the advancement of our economy. . . . He has no desire to make profits for those who do not hold up their end in production, as is true of absentee stockholders and inactive people in the company.
>
> If money is to be used as an incentive, the program must provide that what is paid to the worker is what he has earned. The earnings of each must be in accordance with accomplishment.

Status is of great importance in all human relationships. The greatest incentive that money has, usually, is that it is a symbol of success. . . . The resulting status is the real incentive. . . . Money alone can be an incentive to the miser only.

There must be complete honesty and understanding between the hourly worker and management if high efficiency is to be obtained.

LINCOLN'S BUSINESS

Arc-welding has been the standard joining method in shipbuilding for decades. It is the predominant way of connecting steel in the construction industry. Most industrial plants have their own welding shops for maintenance and construction. Manufacturers of tractors and all kinds of heavy equipment use arc-welding extensively in the manufacturing process. Many hobbyists have their own welding machine and use them for making metal items such as patio furniture and barbecue pits. The popularity of welded sculpture as an art form is growing.

While advances in welding technology have been frequent, arc-welding products, in the main, have hardly changed. Lincoln's Innershield process is a notable exception. This process lowers welding cost and improves quality and speed in many applications. The most widely used Lincoln electrode, the Fleetweld 5P, has been virtually the same since the 1930s. The most popular engine-driven welder in the world, the Lincoln SA-200, has been a gray-colored assembly including a four-cylinder continental "Red Seal" engine and a 200-ampere direct-current generator with two current-control knobs for at least four decades. A 1989 model SA-200 even weighs almost the same as the 1950 model, and it certainly is little changed in appearance.

Lincoln's research and development expenditures have recently been less than 3 percent of sales. There is evidence that others spend several times as much as a percentage of sales.

The company's share of the U.S. arc-welding products market appears to have been about 40 percent for many years. The welding products market has grown somewhat faster than the level of industry in general. The market is highly price-competitive, with variations in prices of standard items normally amounting to only 1 percent or 2. Lincoln's products are sold directly by its engineering-oriented sales force and indirectly through its distribution organization. Advertising expenditures amount to less than three-fourths of one percent of sales.

The other major welding process, flame-welding, has not been competitive with arc-welding since the 1930s. However, plasma-arc-welding, a relatively new process that uses a conducting stream of super-heated gas (plasma) to confine the welding current to a small area, has recently made some inroads, especially in metal tubing manufacturing. Major advances in technology that will produce an alternative superior to arc-welding within the next decade or so appear unlikely. Also, it seems likely that changes in the machines and techniques used in arc-welding will be evolutionary rather than revolutionary.

Products

The company is primarily engaged in the manufacture and sale of arc-welding products—electric welding machines and metal electrodes. Lincoln also produces electric motors ranging from one half horsepower to 200 horsepower. Motors constitute about 8 to 10 percent of total sales.

The electric welding machines, some consisting of a transformer or motor and generator arrangement powered by commercial electricity and others consisting of an internal combustion engine and generator, are designed to produce 30 to 1,500 amperes of electrical power. This electrical current is used to melt a consumable metal electrode. The molten metal is transferred in super hot spray to the metal joint being welded. Very high temperatures and hot sparks are produced, and operators usually must wear special eye and face protection and leather gloves.

Lincoln and its competitors now market a wide range of general purpose and specialty electrodes for welding mild steel, aluminum, cast iron, and stainless and special steels. Most of these electrodes are designed to meet the standards of the American Welding Society, a trade association. The various electrodes on the market are essentially the same as to size and composition from one manufacturer to another. Every electrode manufacturer has a limited number of unique products, but these typically constitute only a small percentage of total sales.

Welding electrodes are of two basic types: (1) Coated "stick" electrodes, usually 14 inches long and smaller than a pencil in diameter, which are held in a special insulated holder by the operator, who must manipulate the electrode in order to maintain a proper arc-width and pattern of deposition of the metal being transferred. Stick electrodes are packaged in 6- to 50-pound boxes. (2) Coiled wire, ranging in diameter from .035 inches to 0.219 inches, which is designed to be fed continuously to the welding arc through a "gun" held by the operator or positioned by automatic positioning equipment. The wire is packaged in coils, reels, and drums weighing from 14 to 1,000 pounds.

Manufacturing Processes

The main plant is in Euclid, Ohio, an eastern Cleveland suburb. The layout of this plant is shown in Exhibit 1. There are no warehouses. Materials flow from the half-mile-long dock on the north side of the plant through the production lines to a very limited storage and loading area to the south side. Materials used on each workstation are stored as close as possible to the workstation. The administrative offices, near the center of the factory, are entirely functional. A corridor below the main level provides access to the factory floor from the main entrance near the center of the plan. *Fortune* magazine recently declared the Euclid facility one of America's 10 best-managed factories and compared it with a General Electric plant also on the list:

> Stepping into GE's spanking new dishwasher plant, an awed supplier said, is like stepping "into the Hyatt Regency." By comparison, stepping into Lincoln Electric's 33-year-old, cavernous, dimly lit factory is like stumbling into a dingy big-

Exhibit 1   MAIN FACTORY LAYOUT

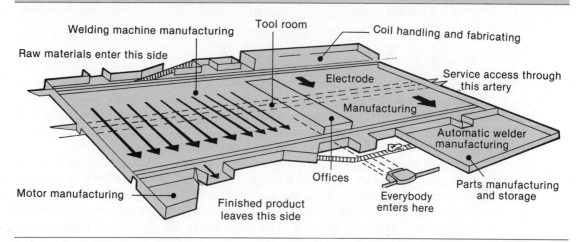

city YMCA. It's only when one starts looking at how these factories do things that similarities become apparent. They have found ways to merge design with manufacturing, build in quality, make wise choices about automation, get close to customers, and handle their work forces.

A new Lincoln plant in Mentor, Ohio, houses some of the electrode production operations, which were moved from the main plant.

Electrode manufacturing is highly capital intensive. Metal rods purchased from steel producers are drawn down to smaller diameters, cut to length, and coated with pressed-powder "flux" for stick electrodes or plated with copper (for conductivity) and put into coils or spools for wire. Lincoln's Innershield wire is hollow and filled with a material similar to that used to coat stick electrodes. This represented a major innovation in welding technology when it was introduced. The company is highly secretive about its electrode production processes, and outsiders are not given access to the details of those processes.

Lincoln welding machines and electric motors are made on a series of assembly lines. Gasoline and diesel engines are purchased partially assembled, but practically all other components are made from basic industrial products, for example, steel bars and sheets and bar copper conductor wire.

Individual components, such as gasoline tanks for engine-driven welders and steel shafts for motors and generators, are made by numerous small "factories within a factory." The shaft for a certain generator, for example, is made from raw steel bar by one operator who uses five large machines, all running continuously. A saw cuts the bar to length, a digital lathe machines different sections to varying diameters, a special milling machine cuts a slot for the keyway, and so forth, until a finished shaft is produced. The operator moves the shafts from machine to machine and makes necessary adjustments.

Another operator punches, shapes, and paints sheet-metal cowling parts. One assembles steel laminations onto a rotor shaft, then winds, insulates, and tests the rotors. Finished components are moved by crane operators to the nearby assembly lines.

Worker Performance and Attitudes

Exceptional worker performance at Lincoln is a matter of record. The typical Lincoln employee earns about twice as much as other factory workers in the Cleveland area. Yet the company's labor cost per sales dollar in 1989, 26 cents, is well below industry averages. Worker turnover is practically nonexistent except for retirements and departures by new employees.

Sales per Lincoln factory employee currently exceed $150,000. An observer at the factory quickly sees why this figure is so high. Each worker is proceeding busily and thoughtfully about the task at hand. There is no idle chatter. Most workers take no coffee breaks. Many operate several machines and make a substantial component unaided. The supervisors are busy with planning and record-keeping duties and hardly glance at the people they "supervise." The manufacturing procedures appear efficient—no unnecessary steps, no wasted motions, no wasted materials. Finished components move smoothly to subsequent workstations.

The appendix includes summaries of interviews with employees.

ORGANIZATION STRUCTURE

Lincoln has never allowed development of a formal organization chart. The objective of this policy is to insure maximum flexibility. An open-door policy is practiced throughout the company, and personnel are encouraged to take problems to the persons most capable of resolving them. Harvard Business School researchers once prepared an organization chart reflecting the implied relationships at Lincoln. The chart became available within the company, and present management believes that had a disruptive effect. Therefore, no organizational chart appears in this report.

Perhaps because of the quality and enthusiasm of the Lincoln work force, routine supervision is almost nonexistent. A typical production foreman, for example, supervises as many as 100 workers, a span of control that does not allow more than infrequent worker-supervisor interaction.

Position titles and traditional flows of authority do imply something of an organizational structure, however. For example, the vice president, sales, and the vice president, electrode division, report to the president, as do various staff assistants such as the personnel director and the director of purchasing. Using such implied relationships, it has been determined that production workers have two or, at most, three levels of supervision between themselves and the president.

PERSONNEL POLICIES

As mentioned earlier, Lincoln's remarkable personnel practices are credited by many with the company's success.

Recruitment and Selection

Every job opening is advertised internally on company bulletin boards, and any employee can apply for any job so advertised. External hiring is permitted only for entry-level positions. Selection for these jobs is done on the basis of personal interviews—there is no aptitude or psychological testing. Not even a high school diploma is required—except for engineering and sales positions, which are filled by graduate engineers. A committee consisting of vice presidents and supervisors interviews candidates initially cleared by the Personnel Department. Final selection is made by the supervisor who has a job opening. Out of more than 3,500 applicants interviewed by the Personnel Department during a recent period, fewer than 300 were hired.

Job Security

In 1958 Lincoln formalized its lifetime employment policy, which had been in effect for many years. There have been no layoffs since World War II. Since 1958, every worker with more than two years' longevity has been guaranteed at least 30 hours per week, 49 weeks per year.

The policy has never been so severely tested as during the 1981–83 recession. As a manufacturer of capital goods, Lincoln's business is highly cyclical. In previous recessions the company was able to avoid major sales declines. However, sales plummeted 32 percent in 1982 and another 16 percent the next year. Few companies would withstand such a revenue collapse and remain profitable. Yet, Lincoln not only earned profits, but also no employee was laid off and year-end incentive bonuses continued. To weather the storm, management cut most of the nonsalaried workers back to 30 hours a week for varying periods. Many employees were reassigned and the total work-force was slightly reduced through normal attrition and restricted hiring. Many employees grumbled at their unexpected misfortune, probably to the surprise and dismay of some Lincoln managers. However, sales and profits—and employee bonuses—soon rebounded and all was well again.

Performance Evaluations

Each supervisor formally evaluates subordinates twice a year using the cards shown in Exhibit 2. The employee performance criteria, "quality," "dependability," "ideas and cooperation," and "output," are considered to be independent of each other. Marks on the cards are converted to numerical scores that are forced to average 100 for each evaluating supervisor. Individual merit rating scores normally range from 80 to 110. Any score over 110 requires a special letter to top management. These scores (over 110) are not considered in computing the required 100-point average for each evaluating supervisor. Suggestions for improvements often result in recommendations for exceptionally high performance scores. Supervisors discuss individual performance marks with the employees concerned. Each warranty claim is traced to the individual employee whose work caused the defect. The employee's performance score may be reduced, or the

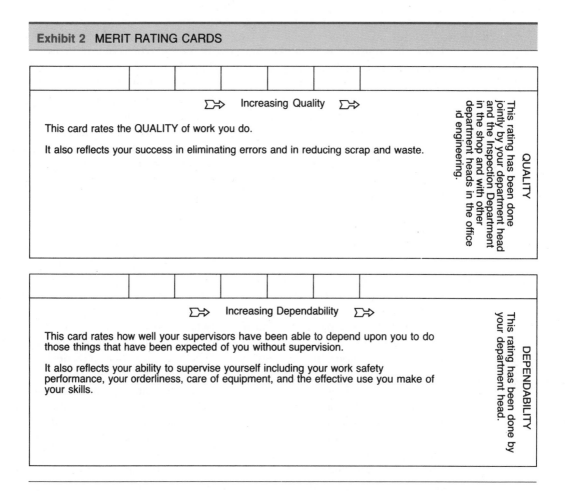

Exhibit 2 MERIT RATING CARDS

Increasing Quality

This card rates the QUALITY of work you do.

It also reflects your success in eliminating errors and in reducing scrap and waste.

QUALITY

This rating has been done jointly by your department head and the Inspection Department in the shop and with other department heads in the office id engineering.

Increasing Dependability

This card rates how well your supervisors have been able to depend upon you to do those things that have been expected of you without supervision.

It also reflects your ability to supervise yourself including your work safety performance, your orderliness, care of equipment, and the effective use you make of your skills.

DEPENDABILITY

This rating has been done by your department head.

worker may be required to repay the cost of servicing the warranty claim by working without pay.

Compensation

Basic wage levels for jobs at Lincoln are determined by a wage survey of similar jobs in the Cleveland area. These rates are adjusted quarterly in accordance with changes in the Cleveland area wage index. Insofar as possible, base wage rates are translated into piece rates. Practically all production workers and many others—for example, some forklift operators—are paid by piece rate. Once established, piece rates are never changed unless a substantive change in the way a job is done results from a source other than the worker doing the job.

In December of each year, a portion of annual profits is distributed to employees as bonuses. Incentive bonuses since 1934 have averaged about 90 percent of annual wages and somewhat more than aftertax profits. The average

Exhibit 2 *(concluded)*

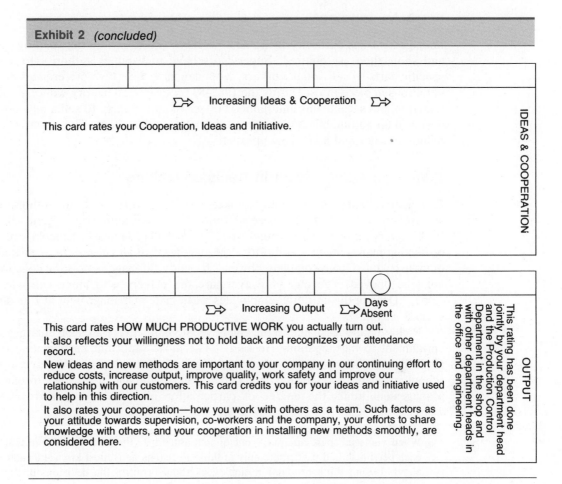

$\Longrightarrow$ Increasing Ideas & Cooperation $\Longrightarrow$

This card rates your Cooperation, Ideas and Initiative.

IDEAS & COOPERATION

$\Longrightarrow$ Increasing Output $\Longrightarrow$ Days Absent

This card rates HOW MUCH PRODUCTIVE WORK you actually turn out.

It also reflects your willingness not to hold back and recognizes your attendance record.

New ideas and new methods are important to your company in our continuing effort to reduce costs, increase output, improve quality, work safety and improve our relationship with our customers. This card credits you for your ideas and initiative used to help in this direction.

It also rates your cooperation—how you work with others as a team. Such factors as your attitude towards supervision, co-workers and the company, your efforts to share knowledge with others, and your cooperation in installing new methods smoothly, are considered here.

This rating has been done jointly by your department head and the Production Control Department in the shop and with other department heads in the office and engineering.

OUTPUT

bonus for 1988 was $21,258. Even for the recession years 1982 and 1983, bonuses had averaged $13,998 and $8,557, respectively. Individual bonuses are proportional to merit-rating scores. For example, assume the amount set aside for bonuses is 80 percent of total wages paid to eligible employees. A person whose performance score is 95 will receive a bonus of 76 percent (0.80 × 0.95) of annual wages.

Vacations

The company shuts down for two weeks in August and two weeks during the Christmas season. Vacations are taken during these periods. For employees with over 25 years of service, a fifth week of vacation may be taken at a time acceptable to superiors.

Work Assignment

Management has authority to transfer workers and to switch between overtime and short time as required. Supervisors have undisputed authority to assign specific parts to individual workers, who may have their own preferences due to variations in piece rates. During the 1982–83 recession, 50 factory workers volunteered to join sales teams and fanned out across the country to sell a new welder designed for automobile body shops and small machine shops. The result was $10 million in sales and a hot new product.

Employee Participation in Decision-Making

Participative mangement usually evokes a vision of a relaxed, nonauthoritarian atmosphere. This is not the case at Lincoln. Formal authority is quite strong. "We're very authoritarian around here," says Willis. James F. Lincoln stressed protecting management's authority. "Management in all successful departments of industry must have complete power," he said. "Management is the coach who must be obeyed. The men, however, are the players who alone can win the game." Despite this attitude, employees participate in management at Lincoln in several ways.

Richard Sabo, assistant to the chief executive officer, relates job enlargement/ enrichment to participation. He said, "The most important participative technique that we use is giving more responsibility to employees. We give a high school graduate more responsibility than other companies give their foremen." Management limits the degree of participation allowed, however. In Sabo's words:

> When you use "participation," put quotes around it. Because we believe that each person should participate only in those decisions he is most knowledgeable about. I don't think production employees should control the decisions of the chairman. They don't know as much as he does about the decisions he is involved in.

The advisory board, elected by the workers, meets with the chairman and the president every two weeks to discuss ways to improve operations. As noted earlier, this board has been in existence since 1914 and has contributed to many innovations. The incentive bonuses, for example, were first recommended by this committee. Every employee has access to advisory board members, and answers to all advisory board suggestions are promised by the following meeting. Both Willis and Hastings are quick to point out, though, that the advisory board only recommends actions. "They do not have direct authority," Willis says. "And when they bring up something that management thinks is not to the benefit of the company, it will be rejected."

Under the early suggestion program, employees were awarded one-half of the first year's savings attributable to their suggestions. Now, however, the value of suggestions is reflected in performance evaluation scores, which determine individual incentive bonus amounts.

Training and Education

Production workers are given a short period of on-the-job training and then placed on a piecework pay system. Lincoln does not pay for off-site education unless very specific company needs are identified. The idea behind this latter policy, according to Sabo, is that everyone cannot take advantage of such a program, and it is unfair to use company funds for an advantage to which there is unequal access. Recruits for sales jobs, already college graduates, are given on-the-job training in the plant followed by a period of work and training at one of the regional sales offices.

Fringe Benefits and Executive Perquisites

A medical plan and a company-paid retirement program have been in effect for many years. A plant cafeteria, operated on a break-even basis, serves meals at about 60 percent of usual costs. The Employee Association, to which the company does not contribute, provides disability insurance and social and athletic activities. The employee stock ownership program has resulted in employee ownership of about 50 percent of the common stock. Under this program, each employee with more than two years of service may purchase stock in the corporation. The price of these shares is established at book value. Stock purchased through this plan may be held by employees only. Dividends and voting rights are the same as for stock owned outside the plan. Approximately 75 percent of the employees own Lincoln stock.

As to executive perquisites, there are none—crowded, austere offices, no executive washrooms or lunchrooms, and no reserved parking spaces. Even the top executives pay for their own meals and eat in the employee cafeteria. On one recent day, Willis arrived at work late due to a breakfast speaking engagement and had to park far away from the factory entrance.

FINANCIAL POLICIES

James F. Lincoln strongly believed that financing for company growth should come from within the company—through initial cash investment by the founders, through retention of earnings, and through stock purchases by those who work in the business. He saw the following advantages of this approach:

1. Ownership of stock by employees strengthens team spirit. "If they are mutually anxious to make it succeed, the future of the company is bright."
2. Ownership of stock provides individual incentive because employees believe they will benefit from company profitability.
3. "Ownership is educational." Owners-employees "will know how profits are made and lost; how success is won and lost. . . . There are few socialists in the list of stockholders of the nation's industries."
4. "Capital available from within controls expansion." Unwarranted expansion would not occur, Lincoln believed, under his financing plan.

5. "The greatest advantage would be the development of the individual worker. Under the incentive of ownership, he would become a greater man."

6. "Stock ownership is one of the steps that can be taken that will make the worker feel that there is less of a gulf between him and the boss. . . . Stock ownership will help the worker to recognize his responsibility in the game and the importance of victory."

Exhibit 3 CONDENSED FINANCIAL STATEMENTS, LINCOLN ELECTRIC COMPANY, 1979–87 ($ in millions)*

	Balance sheets								
	1979	1980	1981	1982	1983	1984	1985	1986	1987
Assets									
Cash	$ 2	$ 1	$ 4	$ 1	$ 2	$ 4	$ 2	$ 1	$ 7
Bonds & CDs	38	47	63	72	78	57	55	45	41
Notes and accounts receivable	42	42	42	26	31	34	38	36	43
Inventories	38	36	46	38	31	37	34	26	40
Prepayments	1	3	4	5	5	5	7	8	7
Total current assets	121	129	157	143	146	138	135	116	137
Other assets†	24	24	26	30	30	29	29	33	40
Land	1	1	1	1	1	1	1	1	1
Net buildings	22	23	25	23	22	21	20	18	17
Net machinery and equipment	21	25	27	27	27	28	27	29	33
Total fixed assets	44	49	53	51	50	50	48	48	50
Total assets	$189	$202	$236	$224	$227	$217	$213	$197	$227
Liabilities and Stockholders' Equity									
Accounts payable	$ 17	$ 16	$ 15	$ 12	$ 16	$ 15	$ 13	$ 11	$ 20
Accrued wages	1	2	5	4	3	4	5	5	4
Accrued taxes	10	6	15	5	7	4	6	5	9
Accrued dividends	6	6	7	7	7	6	7	6	7
Total current liabilities	33	29	42	28	33	30	31	27	40
Long-term debt		4	5	6	8	10	11	8	8
Total debt	33	33	47	34	41	40	42	35	48
Common stock*	4	3	1	2	0	0	0	0	2
Retained earnings	152	167	189	188	186	176	171	161	177
Total stockholders' equity	156	170	190	190	186	176	171	161	179
Total liabilities and stockholders' equity	$189	$202	$236	$224	$227	$217	$213	$197	$227

	Income statements								
	1979	1980	1981	1982	1983	1984	1985	1986	1987
Revenues	$385	$401	$469	$329	$277	$334	$344	$326	$377
Cost of products sold	244	261	293	213	180	223	221	216	239
Selling, general, and administrative expenses‡	41	46	51	45	45	47	48	49	51
Incentive bonus	44	43	56	37	22	33	38	33	39
Pretax income	56	51	69	35	30	31	36	27	48
Income taxes	26	23	31	16	13	14	16	12	21
Net income	$ 30	$ 28	$ 37	$ 19	$ 17	$ 17	$ 20	$ 15	$ 27

* Columns totals may not check the amounts less than $500,000 (0.5) are shown as zero, due to rounding.
† Includes investment in foreign subsidiaries, $29 million in 1987.
‡ Includes pension expense and payroll taxes on incentive bonus.

Until 1980 Lincoln Electric borrowed no money. Even now, the company's liabilities consist mainly of accounts payable and short-term accruals.

The unusual pricing policy at Lincoln is succinctly stated by Willis: "At all times, price on the basis of cost, and at all times, keep pressure on our cost." This policy resulted in the price for the most popular welding electrode then in use going from 16 cents a pound in 1929 to 4.7 cents in 1938. More recently, the SA-200 Welder, Lincoln's largest-selling portable machine, decreased in price from 1958 through 1965. According to Dr. C. Jackson Grayson of the American Productivity Center in Houston, Texas, Lincoln's prices increased only one-fifth as fast as the consumer price index from 1934 to about 1970. This resulted in a welding products market in which Lincoln became the undisputed low-price seller of the products it manufactures. Not even the major Japanese manufacturers, such as Nippon Steel for welding electrodes and Osaka Transformer for welding machines, were able to penetrate the U.S. market in competition with Lincoln Electric.

Substantial cash balances are accumulated each year preparatory to paying the year-end bonuses. The bonuses totaled $54 million for 1988. The money is invested in short-term U.S. government securities and certificates of deposit until needed. Financial statements are shown in Exhibit 3. Exhibit 4 shows how company revenue was distributed in the late 1980s.

Exhibit 4   REVENUE DISTRIBUTION AT LINCOLN ELECTRIC, 1987

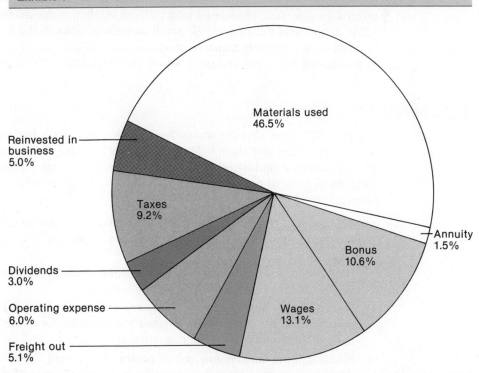

Materials used 46.5%
Reinvested in business 5.0%
Taxes 9.2%
Dividends 3.0%
Operating expense 6.0%
Freight out 5.1%
Wages 13.1%
Bonus 10.6%
Annuity 1.5%

HOW WELL DOES LINCOLN SERVE ITS STAKEHOLDERS?

Lincoln Electric differs from most other companies in the importance it assigns to each of the groups it serves. Willis identifies these groups, in the order of priority ascribed to them, as (1) customers, (2) employees, and (3) stockholders.

Certainly the firm's customers have fared well over the years. Lincoln prices for welding machines and welding electrodes are acknowledged to be the lowest in the marketplace. Quality has consistently been high. The cost of field failures for Lincoln products was recently determined to be a remarkable 0.04 percent of revenues. The "Fleetweld" electrodes and SA-200 welders have been the standard for decades in the pipeline and refinery construction industry, where price is hardly a criterion. A Lincoln distributor in Monroe, Louisiana, says he has sold several hundred of the popular AC-225 welders, which are warranted for one year, but has never handled a warranty claim.

Perhaps best-served of all management constituencies have been the employees. Not the least of their benefits are the year-end bonuses, which effectively double an already average compensation level.

While stockholders were relegated to an inferior status by James F. Lincoln, they have done very well. Recent dividends have exceeded $11 a share, and earnings per share have approached $30. In January 1980, the price of restricted stock, committed to employees, was $117 a share. In 1989, the stated value, at which the company will repurchase the stock if tendered, was $201. A check with the New York office of Merrill Lynch, Pierce, Fenner and Smith at that time revealed an estimated price on Lincoln stock of $270 a share, with none being offered for sale. Risk associated with Lincoln stock, a major determinant of stock value, is minimal because of the small amount of debt in the capital structure, because of an extremely stable earnings record, and because of Lincoln's practice of purchasing the restricted stock whenever employees offer it for sale.

A CONCLUDING COMMENT

It is easy to believe that the reason for Lincoln's success is the excellent attitude of the employees and their willingness to work harder, faster, and more intelligently than other industrial workers. However, Sabo suggests appropriate credit be given to Lincoln executives, whom he credits with carrying out the following policies:

1. Management has limited research, development, and manufacturing to a standard product line designed to meet the major needs of the welding industry.
2. New products must be reviewed by manufacturing and all producing costs verified before being approved by management.
3. Purchasing is challenged to not only procure materials at the lowest cost, but also to work closely with engineering and manufacturing to assure that the latest innovations are implemented.
4. Manufacturing supervision and all personnel are held accountable for reduction of scrap, energy conservation, and maintenance of product quality.

5. Production control, material handling, and methods engineering are closely supervised by top management.

6. Management has made cost reduction a way of life at Lincoln, and definite programs are established in many areas, including traffic and shipping, where tremendous savings can result.

7. Management has established a sales department that is technically trained to reduce customer welding costs. This sales approach and other real customer services have eliminated nonessential frills and resulted in long-term benefits to all concerned.

8. Management has encouraged education, technical publishing, and long-range programs that have resulted in industry growth, thereby assuring market potential for the Lincoln Electric Company.

Sabo writes:

> It is in a very real sense a personal and group experience in faith—a belief that together we can achieve results which alone would not be possible. It is not a perfect system and it is not easy. It requires tremendous dedication and hard work. However, it does work and the results are worth the effort.

....

APPENDIX A
Employee Interviews

Typical questions and answers from employee interviews are presented below. In order to maintain each employee's personal privacy, fictitious names are given to the interviewees.

Interview 1. Betty Stewart, a 52-year-old high school graduate who had been with Lincoln 13 years and who was working as a cost accounting clerk at the time of the interview.

Q: What jobs have you held here besides the one you have now?

A: I worked in payroll for a while, and then this job came open and I took it.

Q: How much money did you make last year, including your bonus?

A: I would say roughly around $25,000, but I was off for back surgery for a while.

Q: You weren't paid while you were off for back surgery?

A: No.

Q: Did the Employee Association help out?

A: Yes. The company doesn't furnish that, though. We pay $8 a month into the Employee Association. I think my check from them was $130.00 a week.

Q: How was your performance rating last year?

A: It was around 100 points, but I lost some points for attendance for my back problem.

Q: How did you get your job at Lincoln?

A: I was bored silly where I was working, and I had heard that Lincoln kept their people busy. So I applied and got the job the next day.

Q: Do you think you make more money than similar workers in Cleveland?

A: I know I do.

Q: What have you done with your money?

A: We have purchased a better home. Also, my son is going to the University of Chicago, which costs $13,000 a year. I buy the Lincoln stock which is offered each year, and I have a little bit of gold.

Q: Have you ever visited with any of the senior executives, like Mr. Willis or Mr. Hastings?

A: I have known Mr. Willis for a long time.

Q: Does he call you by name?

A: Yes. In fact he was very instrumental in my going to the doctor that I am going to with my back. He knows the director of the clinic.

Q: Do you know Mr. Hastings?

A: I know him to speak to him, and he always speaks, always. But I have known Mr. Willis for a good many years. When I did Plant Two accounting I did not understand how the plant operated. Of course you are not allowed in Plant Two, because that's the Electrode Division. I told my boss about the problem one day and the next thing I knew, Mr. Willis came by and said, "Come on, Betty, we're going to Plant Two." He spent an hour and a half showing me the plant.

Q: Do you think Lincoln employees produce more than those in other companies?

A: I think with the incentive program the way that it is, if you want to work and achieve, then you will do it. If you don't want to work and achieve, you will not do it no matter where you are. Just because you are merit rated and have a bonus, if you really don't want to work hard, then you're not going to. You will accept your 90 points or 92 or 85 because, even with that you make more money than people on the outside.

Q: Do you think Lincoln employees will ever join a union?

A: I don't know why they would.

Q: So you say that money is a very major advantage?

A: Money is a major advantage, but it's not just the money. It's the fact that having the incentive, you do wish to work a little harder. I'm sure that there are a lot of men here who, if they worked some other place, would not work as hard as they do here. Not that they are overworked—I don't mean that—but I'm sure they wouldn't push.

Q: Is there anything that you would like to add?

A: I do like working here. I am better off being pushed mentally. In another company, if you pushed too hard, you would feel a little bit of pressure, and someone might say, "Hey, slow down; don't try so hard." But here you are encouraged, not discouraged.

Interview 2. Ed Sanderson, a 23-year-old high school graduate who had been with Lincoln four years and who was a machine operator in the Electrode Division at the time of the interview.

Q: How did you happen to get this job?

A: My wife was pregnant, and I was making 3 bucks an hour and one day I came here and applied. That was it. I kept calling to let them know I was still interested.

Q: Roughly what were your earnings last year including your bonus?

A: $45,000.

Q: What have you done with your money since you have been here?

A: Well, we've lived pretty well and we bought a condominium.

Q: Have you paid for the condominium?

A: No, but I could.

Q: Have you bought your Lincoln stock this year?

A: No, I haven't bought any Lincoln stock yet.

Q: Do you get the feeling that the executives here are pretty well thought of?

A: I think they are. To get where they are today, they had to really work.

Q: Wouldn't that be true anywhere?

A: I think more so here because seniority really doesn't mean anything. If you work with a guy who has 20 years here, and you have two months and you're doing a better job, you will get advanced before he will.

Q: Are you paid on a piece-rate basis?

A: My gang does. There are nine of us who make the bare electrode, and the whole group gets paid based on how much electrode we make.

Q: Do you think you work harder than workers in other factories in the Cleveland area?

A: Yes, I would say I probably work harder.

Q: Do you think it hurts anybody?

A: No, a little hard work never hurts anybody.

Q: If you could choose, do you think you would be as happy earning a little less money and being able to slow down a little?

A: No, it doesn't bother me. If it bothered me, I wouldn't do it.

Q: Why do you think Lincoln employees produce more than workers in other plants?

A: That's the way the company is set up. The more you put out, the more you're going to make.

Q: Do you think it's the piece rate and bonus together?

A: I don't think people would work here if they didn't know that they would be rewarded at the end of the year.

Q: Do you think Lincoln employees will ever join a union?

A: No.

Q: What are the major advantages of working for Lincoln?

A: Money.

Q: Are there any other advantages?

A: Yes, we don't have a union shop. I don't think I could work in a union shop.

Q: Do you think you are a career man with Lincoln at this time?

A: Yes.

Interview 3.   Roger Lewis, a 23-year-old Purdue graduate in mechanical engineering who had been in the Lincoln sales program for 15 months and who was working in the Cleveland sales office at the time of the interview.

Q: How did you get your job at Lincoln?

A: I saw that Lincoln was interviewing on campus at Purdue, and I went by. I later came to Cleveland for a plant tour and was offered a job.

Q: Do you know any of the senior executives? Would they know you by name?

A: Yes, I know all of them—Mr. Hastings, Mr. Willis, Mr. Sabo.

Q: Do you think Lincoln salespeople work harder than those in other companies?

A: Yes. I don't think there are many salesmen for other companies who are putting in 50- to 60-hour weeks. Everybody here works harder. You can go out in the plant, or you can go upstairs, and there's nobody sitting around.

Q: Do you see any real disadvantage of working at Lincoln?

A: I don't know if it's a disadvantage, but Lincoln is a spartan company, a very thrifty company. I like that. The sales offices are functional, not fancy.

Q: Why do you think Lincoln employees have such high productivity?

A: Piecework has a lot to do with it. Lincoln is smaller than many plants, too; you can stand in one place and see the materials come in one side and the product go out the other. You feel a part of the company. The chance to get ahead is important, too. They have a strict policy of promoting from within, so you know you have a chance. I think in a lot of other places you may not get as fair a shake as you do here. The sales offices are on a smaller scale, too. I like that. I tell someone that we have two people in the Baltimore office, and they say, "You've got to be kidding." It's smaller and more personal. Pay is the most important thing. I have heard that this is the highest-paying factory in the world.

Interview 4.   Jimmy Roberts, a 47-year-old high school graduate who had been with Lincoln 17 years and who was working as a multiple-drill press operator at the time of the interview.

Q: What jobs have you had at Lincoln?

A: I started out cleaning the men's locker room in 1967. After about a year, I got a job in the flux department, where we make the coating for welding rods. I worked there for seven or eight years and then got my present job.

Q: Do you make one particular part?

A: No, there are a variety of parts I make—at least 25.

Q: Each one has a different piece rate attached to it?

A: Yes.

Q: Are some piece rates better than others?

A: Yes.

Q: How do you determine which ones you are going to do?

A: You don't. Your supervisor assigns them.

Q: How much money did you make last year?

A: $53,000.

Q: Have you ever received any kind of award or citation?

A: No.

Q: Was your rating ever over 110?

A: Yes. For the past five years, probably, I made over 110 points.

Q: Is there any attempt to let the others know?

A: The kind of points I get? No.

Q: Do you know what they are making?

A: No. There are some who might not be too happy with their points and they might make it known. The majority, though, do not make a point of telling other employees.

Q: Would you be just as happy earning a little less money and working a little slower?

A: I don't think I would—not at this point. I have done piecework all these years, and the fast pace doesn't really bother me.

Q: Why do you think Lincoln productivity is so high?

A: The incentive thing—the bonus distribution. I think that would be the main reason. The paycheck you get every two weeks is important too.

Q: Do you think Lincoln employees would ever join a union?

A: I don't think so. I have never heard anyone mention it.

Q: What is the most important advantage of working here?

A: Amount of money you make. I don't think I could make this type of money anywhere else, especially with only a high school education.

Q: As a black person, do you feel that Lincoln discriminates in any way against blacks?

A: No. I don't think any more so than any other job. Naturally, there is a certain amount of discrimination, regardless of where you are.

Interview 5.   Joe Trahan, 58-year-old high school graduate who had been with Lincoln 39 years and who was employed as a working supervisor in the tool room at the time of the interview.

Q: Roughly what was your pay last year?

A: Over $56,000; salary, bonus, stock dividends.

Q: How much was your bonus?

A: About $26,000.

Q: Have you ever gotten a special award of any kind?

A: Not really.

Q: What have you done with your money?

A: My house is paid for—and my two cars. I also have some bonds and the Lincoln stock.

Q: What do you think of the executives at Lincoln?

A: They're really top notch.

Q: What is the major disadvantage of working at Lincoln Electric?

A: I don't know of any disadvantage at all.

Q: Do you think you produce more than most people in similar jobs with other companies?

A: I do believe that.

Q: Why is that? Why do you believe that?

A: We are on the incentive system. Everything we do, we try to improve to make a better product with a minimum of outlay. We try to improve the bonus.

Q: Would you be just as happy making a little less money and not working quite so hard?

A: I don't think so.

Q: Do you think Lincoln employees would ever join a union?

A: I don't think they would ever consider it.

Q: What is the most important advantage of working at Lincoln?

A: Compensation.

Q: Tell me something about Mr. James Lincoln, who died in 1965.

A: You are talking about Jimmy Sr. He always strolled through the shop in his shirtsleeves. Big fellow. Always looked distinguished. Gray hair.

Friendly sort of guy. I was a member of the advisory board one year. He was there each time.

Q: Did he strike you as really caring?

A: I think he always cared for people.

Q: Did you get any sensation of a religious nature from him?

A: No, not really.

Q: And religion is not part of the program now?

A: No.

Q: Do you think Mr. Lincoln was a very intelligent man, or was he just a nice guy?

A: I would say he was pretty well educated. A great talker—always right off the top of his head. He knew what he was talking about all the time.

Q: When were bonuses for beneficial suggestions done away with?

A: About 18 years ago.

Q: Did that hurt very much.

A: I don't think so because suggestions are still rewarded through the merit rating system.

Q: Is there anything you would like to add?

A: It's a good place to work. The union kind of ties other places down. At other places, electricians only do electrical work, carpenters only do carpenter work. At Lincoln Electric, we all pitch in and do whatever needs to be done.

Q: So a major advantage is not having a union?

A: That's right.

MARY KAY COSMETICS, INC.*

In spring 1983 Mary Kay Cosmetics, Inc. (MKC), the second-largest direct-sales distributor of skin care products in the United States, encountered its first big slowdown in recruiting women to function as Mary Kay beauty consultants and market the Mary Kay cosmetic lines. As of April, MKC's sales force of about 195,000 beauty consultants was increasing at only a 13 percent annual rate, down from a 65 percent rate of increase in 1980. The dropoff in the percentage of new recruits jeopardized MKC's ability to sustain its reputation as a fast-growing company. MKC's strategy was predicated on getting even larger numbers of beauty consultants to arrange "skin care classes" at the home of a hostess and her three to five guests; at the classes consultants demonstrated the Mary Kay Cosmetics line, and usually sold anywhere from $50 to $200 worth of Mary Kay products. MKC's historically successful efforts to build up the size of its force of beauty consultants had given the company reliable access to a growing number of "showings" annually.

Even though MKC's annual turnover rate for salespeople was lower than that of several major competitors (including Avon Products), some 120,000 Mary Kay beauty consultants had quit or been terminated in 1982, making the task of recruiting a growing sales force of consultants a major, ongoing effort at MKC. Recruiting success was seen by management as strategically important. New recruits were encouraged to spend between $500 and $3,000 for sales kits and startup inventories; the initial orders of new recruits accounted for over one-third of MKC's annual sales. The newest recruits were also instrumental in helping identify and attract others to become Mary Kay beauty consultants.

Richard Rogers, MKC's cofounder and president, promptly reacted to the recruiting slowdown by announcing five changes in the company's sales force program:

- The financial incentives offered to active beauty consultants for bringing new recruits into the Mary Kay fold were increased by as much as 50 percent.
- A new program was instituted whereby beauty consultants who (1) placed $600 a month in wholesale order with the company for three consecutive months and (2) recruited five new consultants who together placed $3,000 in wholesale orders a month for three straight months would win the free use of a cream-colored Oldsmobile Firenza for a year (this program supplemented the existing programs whereby top-performing beauty consultants could win the use of a pink Cadillac or pink Buick Regal).

* Prepared by graduate researcher Robin Romblad and Professor Arthur A. Thompson, Jr., The University of Alabama. The assistance and cooperation provided by many people in the Mary Kay organization is gratefully acknowledged. Copyright © 1986 by Arthur A. Thompson, Jr.

- The minimum order size required of beauty consultants was increased from $400 to $600.
- The prices at which MKC wholesaled its products to consultants were raised by 4 percent.
- The requirements for attaining sales director status and heading up a sales unit were raised 25 percent; a sales director had to recruit 15 new consultants (instead of 12), and her sales unit was expected to maintain a monthly minimum of $4,000 in wholesale orders (up from $3,200).

In addition, MKC's 1984 corporate budget for recruiting was more than quadrupled and, as a special recruiting effort, the company staged a National Guest Night in September 1984 that consisted of a live closed-circuit telecast to 78 cities aired from Dallas, Texas, where MKC's corporate headquarters was located. Mary Kay salespeople all over the United States were urged to invite prospective recruits and go to one of the 78 simulcast sites.

NATIONAL GUEST NIGHT IN BIRMINGHAM

Jan Currier, senior sales director for MKC in the Tuscaloosa, Alabama, area, invited two other women and the casewriter to drive to Birmingham in her pink Buick Regal to attend what was billed as "The Salute to the Stars." On the way, Jan explained that as well as being entertaining, the evening's event would give everyone a chance to see firsthand just how exciting and rewarding the career opportunities were with MKC; she noted with pride that Mary Kay Cosmetics was one of the companies featured in the recent book *The 100 Best Companies to Work for in America.* As the Tuscaloosa entourage neared the auditorium in Birmingham, the casewriter observed numerous pink Cadillacs and pink Buick Regals in the flow of traffic and in the parking lot. Mary Kay sales directors were stationed at each door to the lobby enthusiastically greeting each person and presenting a gift of Mary Kay cosmetics. Guests were directed to a table to register for prizes to be awarded later in the evening.

Inside the auditorium over 1,500 people awaited the beginning of the evening's program. A large theater screen was located at center stage. The lights dimmed promptly at 7 P.M. and the show began. The casewriter used her tape recorder and took extensive notes to capture what went on:

Mark Dixon: [*national sales administrator for the south central division, appears on stage in Birmingham*]: Welcome, ladies and gentlemen, to National Guest Night, Mary Kay's Salute to the Stars. Tonight, you're going to be a part of the largest teleconference ever held by a U.S. corporation.

Now please help me welcome someone all of us at Mary Kay love very dearly, National Sales Director from Houston, Texas, Lovie Quinn. [*The crowd stands and greets Lovie with cheers and applause.*]

Lovie Quinn: [*comes out on stage in Birmingham to join Mark Dixon. Lovie is wearing this year's Mary Kay national sales director suit of red* *suede with black mink trim.*]: Good evening, ladies and gentlemen, and welcome to one of the most exciting events in the history of Mary Kay. An evening with Mary Kay as she Salutes the Stars. . . . During the evening you'll learn about career opportunities. There will be recognition of our stars. We'll see the salute to them with gifts and prizes you hear about at Mary Kay. You'll hear about . . . pink Cadillacs . . . pink Buick Regals, and Firenza Oldsmobiles.

You're going to hear about and see diamond rings and beautiful full-length mink coats. And of course we'll talk about MONEY.

If you've never attended a Mary Kay function you might very easily get the impression that we brag a lot. We like to think of it as recognition. . . . But we would not be able to give this recognition of success if you, the hostesses, our special guests, did not open up your homes so we may share with you and some of your selected friends the Mary Kay skin care program. For that reason we would like to show our appreciation at this time. Will all the special guests please stand up.

[*About 40 percent of the audience stands and the remainder applaud the guests.*]

Lovie Quinn: Now I need to have all our directors line up on stage. [*Each one is dressed in a navy blue suit with either a red, green, or white blouse—the color of the blouse signifies director, senior director, or future director status.*] Enthusiasm and excitement are at the root of the Mary Kay philosophy. This is why we always start a meeting like this with a song. We invite all of you to join with the directors and sing the theme song, "That Mary Kay Enthusiasm."

[*Lovie motions for the audience to stand; the choir of directors begins to clap and leads out in singing. The audience joins in quickly.*]

I've got that Mary Kay enthusiasm up in my
head, up in my head, up in my head.
I've got that Mary Kay enthusiasm up in my
head, up in my head to stay.
I've got that Mary Kay enthusiasm down in
my heart, down in my heart, down in my heart.
I've got that Mary Kay enthusiasm down in
my heart, down in my heart to stay.
I've got that Mary Kay enthusiasm down in
my feet, down in my feet, down in my feet.
I've got that Mary Kay enthusiasm down in
my feet, down in my feet to stay.
I've got that Mary Kay enthusiasm up in my
head, down in my heart, down in my feet.
I've got that Mary Kay enthusiasm all over
me, all over me to stay.

[*The song concludes to a round of applause. The crowd is spirited.*]

Lovie Quinn: Now we'd like to recognize a group of very special consultants. These ladies have accepted a challenge from Mary Kay and have held 10 beauty shows in one week. This is something really terrific. It demonstrates the successful achievement of a goal. We have found when you want to do something for our chairman of the board, Mary Kay Ash . . . you don't have to give furs. The most special gift you can give to Mary Kay is your own success. . . .

[*All of those recognized are seated in the first 10 rows with their guests; seating in the front rows is a special reward for meeting the challenge. The crowd applauds.*]

Lovie Quinn: It is almost time for the countdown to begin, but before it does one more special group must be recognized. These ladies are Mary Kay's Gold Medal winners. In one month they recruited *five* new consultants. [*A number of ladies stand; they beam with pride and each has been awarded a medal resembling an Olympic Gold. The audience gives them a nice round of applause.*]

Lovie Quinn [*Lovie continues to fill the crowd with excitement and anticipation.*]: The countdown is going to be in just a few moments. It will be a treat for those of you that have not met Mary Kay before. Please help me count down the final 10 seconds before the broadcast.

[*But the crowd is so excited it starts the countdown when one minute appears on the screen. As the seconds wind down, the crowd gets louder with anticipation and then gets in sync chanting: 10, 9, 8, 7, 6, 5, 4, 3, 2, 1. More screams and applause.*

On the screen a Gold Mary Kay medallion appears, then the production lines at the plant are shown, and then trucks shipping the products. The audience claps as they see these on the screen. Headquarters is shown. Now a number of the Mary Kay sales directors are shown framed in stars on the screen. People clap when they rcognize someone from their district. Loud applause fills the auditorium when Mary Kay Ash, MKC's chairman of the board and company cofounder, is shown in a star.

The Dallas-based part of the simulcast opens with female dancers dressed in pink and male dancers dressed in gray tuxedos. They perform the "Mary Kay Star Song," which includes a salute to various regions in the United States. The Birmingham crowd cheers when the South is highlighted.

A woman is chosen out of the audience in Dallas. Her name is Susan; the audience is told that at various intervals in the broadcast we will see her evolution into a successful Mary Kay Beauty consultant. Initially we see her get a feeling that maybe she can be a Mary Kay star. The message is that personal dreams of success can come true. Will she be successful? The answer comes back, "Yes, She Can Do It."

Mary Kay Ash is escorted on stage by her son Richard Rogers. She is elegantly dressed with accents of diamonds and feathers. The applause, the loudest so far, is genuinely enthusiastic and many in both the Dallas and Birmingham audiences are cheering loudly.]

Mary Kay Ash: Welcome everyone to our very first Salute to the Stars, National Guest Night. How exciting it is to think that right now over 100,000 people are watching this broadcast all over the United States. . . . Even though I can't see all of you, I can feel your warmth all the way to Dallas.

During the program this evening one expression you're going to hear over and over again is YOU CAN DO IT. . . . This is something we really believe in. What we have discovered is the seeds of greatness are planted in every human being. . . . Tonight we hope to inspire you, to get you to reach within yourself, to bring out some of those star qualities that I know you have. And no matter who you are and no matter where you live, I believe you can take those talents and go farther than you ever thought possible and we have a special place waiting just for you.

Now I would like to introduce someone who has a special place in my heart. Someone who has been beside me from the very beginning. Without him Mary Kay Cosmetics would not be what it is today. Please welcome your president and cofounder of our company, my son, Richard Rogers.

Richard Rogers [*steps to the microphone, accompanied by respectful applause*.]: When we started this company over 20 years ago my mother and I never dreamed we would be standing here talking live to over 100,000 of you all across the country. . . . Tonight we've planned a memorable evening just for you. A program that conveys the spirit of Mary Kay. Going back 21 years ago, Mary Kay saw a void in the cosmetics industry. The observation she made was that others were just selling products. No one was teaching women about their skin and how to care for it. . . . This is the concept on which she based her company. So on September 13, 1963, Mary Kay Cosmetics opened its doors in Dallas, Texas.

Throughout the decade Mary Kay's concepts continued to flourish. . . . By the end of the 60s, Mary Kay Cosmetics had become a fully integrated manufacturer and distributor of skin care products. In 1970 the sales force had grown to 7,000 consultants in Texas and four surrounding states.

California was the first state MKC designated for expansion. When we first went there, no one had ever heard of Mary Kay Cosmetics. Within three years California had more consultants selling Mary Kay Cosmetics than the state of Texas. . . . With this success, expansion continued throughout the United States. . . . By 1975 MKC had grown to 700 sales directors, 34,000 consultants, and $35 million in sales.

International expansion was initiated in 1978 by selling skin care products in Canada. In just 36 months MKC became the fourth-largest Canadian cosmetic company. . . . Since that time, Mary Kay has expanded to South America, Australia, and in September we opened for business in the United Kingdom.

At the end of 1983, MKC had over 195,000 consultants. Sales had reached over $600 million around the world. . . . With total commitment to excellence setting the pace, MKC is still working towards achieving the goal of being the finest teaching-oriented skin care organization in the world. . . . Mary Kay is proud to have the human resources necessary to meet this goal. At Mary Kay P&L means more than profit and loss. It also stands for People and Love. People have helped MKC reach where it is today, and they will play a big part in where it will be tomorrow.

Tonight we're proud to announce the arrival of a book that expresses the Mary Kay philosophy of Golden Rule management, a book that outlines the management style that has contributed to the success of Mary Kay Cosmetics. The new book is *Mary Kay on People Management*.

[*The crowd applauds at this announcement.*]

Mary Kay Ash [*reappears on stage.*]: We're so excited about the new book. I am pleased to have the opportunity to talk with you about it tonight. Actually, I started to write that book over 20 years ago. I had just retired from 25 years of direct sales. I wanted to share my experiences, so I wrote down my thoughts about the companies I had worked for. What had worked and what had not. . . . After expressing my ideas, I thought how wonderful it would be to put out these ideas of a company designed to meet women's needs into action. That is when Mary Kay Cosmetics was born. . . . The company helps women meet the goals they set for themselves. . . . I feel that is what has contributed to the success of the organization. Everyone at MKC starts at the same place, as a consultant, and everyone has the same opportunities for success.

[*The broadcast returns to the scenario of Susan as she becomes a new Mary Kay consultant. Susan sings about the doubts people have about her joining Mary Kay. She disregards this and decides to climb to success. At the end of the scene, she projects a positive, successful image that her friends and family recognize. The audience responds favorably.*]

Dale Alexander [*national sales administrator for Mary Kay Cosmetics appears on stage in Dallas.*]: It is a great honor to be with you tonight and I want to add my most sincere welcome. . . . Recognition is one of the original principles on which our company is based. It's an essential ingredient in the Mary Kay formula for success. . . . I want to start out by recognizing the largest group. The group of independent businesswomen who are out there every day holding beauty shows, teaching skin care, selling our products, and sharing the Mary Kay opportunity. At this time will all of the Mary Kay beauty consultants across the nation stand to be recognized? [*In Birmingham the lights go up and the crowd applauds the consultants in the audience.*] Next we want to recognize the Star Consultants. . . . Will these ladies stand?

Many of our people are wearing small golden ladders. This is our Ladder of Success. Each ladder has a number of different jewels awarded for specific accomplishments during a calendar quarter. Star consultants earn rubies, sapphires, and diamonds to go on their ladders. The higher they climb, the more dazzling their ladders become. A consultant with all diamonds is known at Mary Kay as a top Star Performer. It is like wearing a straight A report card on your lapel.

In addition to Ladders, consultants have an opportunity to earn great prizes each quarter. . . . This quarter's theme is Salute to the Stars . . . and these prizes are out of this world.

[The scene shifts to a description of the fall 1984 sales program; it utilizes a "Star Trek" theme, and across the screen is emblazoned "Starship Mary Kay in Search of the Prize Zone." Captain Kay appears with members of her crew on Starship Mary Kay. She remarks their mission is to seek out prizes to honor those that reach for the sky. They are approaching the prize zone. The awards and prizes are flashed onto the screen.

The Prize Zone
Bonus Prizes Available
Based on Fourth-Quarter Sales

$1,800 Wholesale sales	Cubic zirconia necklace and earnings or travel set with hair dryer
$2,400 Wholesale sales	Leather briefcase with matching umbrella
$3,000 Wholesale sales	Diamond earrings with 14K gold teardrops
$3,600 Wholesale sales	Telephone answering machine
$4,200 Wholesale sales	Sapphire ring
$4,800 Wholesale sales	Electronic printer by Brother—fits in a briefcase
$6,000 Wholesale sales	Diamond pendant—nine diamonds—.5 karat on a 18K gold chain

[Even though this "space" presentation of prizes is humorous, the ladies know that the rewards are real; they respond as the scene ends with a round of applause and a buzz of excitement. The scene concludes with the message, "When you reach for the sky you bring home a star."]

Mary Kay *[returns to the stage.]*: You can climb that ladder of success at Mary Kay. It is up to you to take that very first step. . . . There are so many rewards for being a Mary Kay consultant. There are top earnings, prizes, and lots of recognition. But there is even more to a Mary Kay career and that is the fulfillment of bringing beauty into the lives of others. . . .

When a woman joins our company she knows she can do it. But not alone. She'll receive support from many people. A big sister relationship will form between a new consultant and her recruiter. . . . Whoever invited you tonight thought you were a special person. She wanted to share this evening and introduce you to our company and let you see for yourself the excitement and enthusiasm Mary Kay people have when they are together. . . . The enthusiasm of our consultants and directors is responsible for our success.

[The vignette about Susan returns to the screen. This time she is thinking about concentrating her efforts on recruiting. After five recruits, she will become a team leader. A good goal to strive for, she thinks. A woman that had doubted Susan's career earlier is the first one recruited. Then four more ladies are recruited: a waitress, a teacher, a stewardess, and a

nurse. All kinds of people can be Mary Kay consultants. Susan has reached her goal—she is a team leader. The crowd applauds her success.]

Dale Alexander [*returns to the microphone in Dallas.*]: There is the perfect goal of a Mary Kay career. And now it is time to recognize a very special group of individuals who are proof of this point. Will all the team leaders please stand and remain standing for a few moments? [*The lights go up and team leaders stand. All are wearing red jackets.*]

To qualify for a team leader, each consultant must recruit five new consultants. . . . And now will you please recognize these ladies' achievements with a round of applause? [*The audience applauds.*] Now it is time to draw for the prizes. In each of the 75 locations, two names will be drawn. These lucky people will both win this exquisite 14K diamond earring and pendant set. [*The crowd oohs and aahs when the jewelry is shown on the screen.*] These two winners will also be eligible for the prize to be given by Mary Kay when the broadcast resumes.

[*The lights go up in the Birmingham auditorium. Lovie draws two tickets from a big box. When she calls out the names, the winners scream and run on stage to accept their gifts. The crowd applauds the winners.*]

Lovie Quinn [*on the stage in Birmingham*]: Please join me in counting down the final seconds left before we rejoin the broadcast.

[*Everyone stands and enthusiastically counts off "11, 10, 9, 8, 7, 6, 5, 4, 3, 2, 1." The crowd applauds and cheers.*]

Mary Kay [*appears on the screen as the broadcast from Dallas is rejoined.*]: I wish I could be there to congratulate each winner. . . . The two lucky winners in each of the 75 cities are eligible to win the grand prize. . . . It used to be you just drew a number out of a hat. Now that is considered old-fashioned. Tonight, we'll use a computer. All I have to do is push a button and a city will be randomly selected. The local winners in that city will also win this .75 carat diamond ring. [*The crowd buzzes as a close-up of the ring is shown on the giant screen.*] Are you ready? OK. Here goes. [*Mary Kay presses a button.*] The lucky city is Philadelphia. [*The crowd applauds.*] Congratulations, Philadelphia, and we will be sending each of you a ring real soon.

By the way, while we are talking about prizes, would you happen to have a spare finger for a diamond ring? [*The crowd cheers.*] Or could you squeeze into your closet room for a full-length mink coat? [*The crowd is really excited.*] Or is there by any chance a space in your driveway for a car? [*The crowd cheers and applauds. One member of the audience remarks how she would be glad to get rid of that old blue thing she is driving.*] Well, all you have to do is set your Mary Kay career goals high enough to achieve the recognition and rewards available just for you. . . .

I remember the first sales competition I set my goals to win. I worked so hard and all I won was a flounder light. [*The audience laughs.*] Does anyone know what you do with it? It is something you use when you put on waders and gig fish. [*The audience laughs again.*] I thought the prize was awful . . . but my manager was a fisherman and he thought it was great.

Winning that flounder light taught me a lesson. I decided if I was ever in a position to give awards, they would be things women appreciate, *not* flounder lights. . . . things women would love to have. Absolutely no washing machines and certainly no ironing boards. [*The audience shows their approval by cheers and applause.*] At MKC, you are rewarded for consistent sales and recruiting performance. . . . This past spring, a new program was added. . . . We call it our VIP program. It stands for Very Important Performer. . . . This program allows a person to win a cream-colored Oldsmobile Firenza with rich brown interior. . . . A consultant is eligible for this prize only three months after joining MKC. . . .

Mary Kay Cosmetics can offer several unique career opportunities:

- A 50 percent commission on everything you sell.
- Earnings of a 12 percent commission on your recruit's sales.
- You work your own hours.
- After three months, you can be eligible for a car. The car is free. MKC pays the insurance.
- When you do well, you get a lot of recognition. Not dumb old things like turkeys and hams. We're talking diamonds and furs.
- You work up to management because of your own efforts and merit.

Other companies would think these things are part of a dream world. At Mary Kay, we do live in a dream world and our dreams do come true.

[*The audience applauds loudly. The broadcast then returns to the scenario about Susan. She sets a goal to be a VIP. Through song and dance, her group illustrates setting goals and receiving recognition. Step by step they climb the ladder of recognition. The audience applauds this short scene on success.*]

Dale Alexander [*comes back to the Dallas stage.*]: We have some VIPs among us tonight. . . . Mary Kay's Very Import Performers. Will all the VIPs now stand? [*The lights go up in Birmingham; the VIPs stand and the audience applauds.*] Through her enthusiasm and hard work, each VIP has worked hard to achieve this status. And to recognize her accomplishments, she was awarded an Oldsmobile Firenza to show off her achievement of success. Now let's give all our VIPs a round of applause. [*The Birmingham and Dallas audiences respond with more applause.*]

Mary Kay Ash [*comes onto the stage in Dallas and the crowd in Birmingham turns its attention to the screen.*]: With Mary Kay you can achieve success. . . . All you have to do is break down your goals into small manageable steps. . . . You are able to move on to bigger accomplishments as you gain confidence in yourself.

Let's look at some of the provisions of the Mary Kay career plan and see how it works:

- Your products are purchased directly from the company.
- Generous discounts are offered on large orders.
- There are no territories. You can sell and recruit wherever you want.
- We provide our customers the best possible way to buy cosmetics. They can try the products in their own home before they buy.
- All Mary Kay products are backed by a full 100 percent money-back guarantee.

Mary Kay is a good opportunity to go into business for yourself. . . . There are many benefits of running your own business. . . . You meet new people and at the same time you enjoy the support of the Mary Kay sisterhood. . . . Plus you earn financial rewards as well as prizes. . . .

Now we need to talk about the position of Mary Kay sales director. Directors receive income not only from shows, facials, and reorders but also from recruit commissions. . . . In addition they earn unit and recruiting bonuses from Mary Kay. . . . Some earn the privilege to drive pink Regals and Cadillacs. . . . Each year, hundreds of sales directors earn over $30,000 a year. And today in our company we have more women earning over $50,000 a year than any other company in America. [*The audience applauds.*] At the very top are our national sales directors. . . . Their average is about $150,000 a year in commissions. How about that? [*The audience applauds.*] Everyone at Mary Kay starts at the same place with the same beauty showcase. I've always said you can have anything in this world if you want it badly enough and are willing to pay the price. With that kind of attitude anyone can succeed at Mary Kay.

[*The vignette about Susan comes back onto the screen. Susan sets a goal to achieve sales director. She sings about how invigorating her new career is and how she now wants to be a coach, a teacher, a counselor, and a friend to others. Everyone around her recognizes how her success has positively affected her whole life. The scene ends and the audience applauds.*]

Dale Alexander [*comes onto the screen from Dallas.*]: Those individuals that advance on to directorship lead our organizations. They set the pace for their units. Will all our sales directors please stand? [*The sales directors stand as the lights go up in Birmingham and the audience applauds.*] Among all our directors there are some that have reached a very special level. They have earned the privilege of driving one of Mary Kay's famous pink cars. . . . One thing is guaranteed. Whenever you see one of those pink cars on the road, you know there is a top achiever behind the wheel. At this time, we want to honor all these ladies. [*First the Regal drivers stand and then the Cadillac drivers. The audience recognizes each group* *with applause.*] Finally, there is one last group we want to recognize. A group whose members have already committed to a future with Mary Kay. . . . They are our DIQs or directors in qualification. They are working towards meeting the goals to qualify for directorship. . . . Will all the DIQs stand for a round of applause?

[*The lights go up and the DIQs stand. They are recognized with applause from the audience. The lights fade and the scene shifts back to Dallas.*]
Mary Kay: I want to congratulate these ladies. Next week I'll have the pleasure of hostessing our traditional tea for the DIQs at my home. [*The audience applauds.*] Our DIQs are a perfect example of one of the points we have tried to make this evening. . . . You can set your goals and achieve them if you want them badly enough.

I've always felt our most valuable asset is not our product but our people. . . . I wish I could tell you all the success stories of consultants at MKC. . . . We have chosen a few stories we think best represent Mary Kay consultants. The first person you'll meet is Rena.

[*The audience applauds; Rena is recognized by the Mary Kay people present. The narrator of the film clip tells us that Rena has been with MKC for 17 years. She has been Queen of Unit Sales four consecutive years, an honor that was earned when the sales unit she managed exceeded $1 million in sales in one year. Her reward was four $5,000 shopping sprees at Nieman-Marcus Co. in Dallas. When she started, she was living on $300 a month in government housing with her husband and three small children. One day a friend offered to buy her dinner and pay for a babysitter if she would attend a meeting. She couldn't pass up this offer so she went to the Mary Kay meeting. The meeting inspired her and she joined MKC. At the end, we learn that Rena has had cancer for the last eight years, a fact that is not well known; the point is made that it has never affected her ability to succeed with Mary Kay Cosmetics. The crowd applauds her success story.*

Next comes a film clip about Ruel; the audience is told that Ruel was raised in Arkansas, a daughter of a sharecropper. She joined Mary Kay in 1971. By 1976 she was a national sales director. A career with Mary Kay has given her confidence. She has two children in medical school and one of her sons just won a national honor, the Medal of Valor. All of this she attributes to Mary Kay. Her children saw her achieve and they knew they could too. Her career with Mary Kay has allowed her to climb up the scale from a poor sharecropper's daughter to become financially independent. Along the way, she has had the opportunity to meet many wonderful people. As her success story ends, the audience applauds.

The third story is about Arlene. Arlene has been a national sales director since 1976. She achieved this just five short years after joining MKC. She had been at home for 13 years and wanted to have her own business, set her own hours, and write her own checks. She found she could achieve these goals in a career with Mary Kay. Arlene, we are told, has been able to reach inside herself and achieve great success. Arlene testifies that one of her biggest rewards at Mary Kay has been helping other women achieve the goals they set. The audience loudly applauds the last of the success stories.]

Mary Kay: I am so proud of all these ladies. . . . It makes me feel good to be able to offer all these wonderful opportunities to so many women.

Every journey begins with a single step. All you have to do is make up your mind that YOU can do it! Isn't it exciting. You CAN do it.

All you need to start a Mary Kay career is a beauty case. It carries everything: vanity trays, mirrors, products, and product literature.

Tonight it becomes easier. . . . If you join us as a beauty consultant tonight, we will give you your beauty showcase. [*The audience interrupts with a round of applause.*] When you submit your Beauty Consultant agreement along with your first wholesale order, you will receive the beauty case free, an $85 value.

At Mary Kay you'll make lasting friends and you'll achieve a feeling of growth. . . . Tonight we wanted to give you a feel for Mary Kay Cosmetics. We have a place for you to shine. . . . Believe in yourself and you can do anything.

[*The broadcast from Dallas concludes; the audience stands and applauds the program.*]

Lovie Quinn [*comes on stage in Birmingham.*]: I started at Mary Kay just to earn money for Christmas. I told Mary Kay I could only work four hours a week. Believe it or not Mary Kay welcomed me into the organization.

Things were different then. There were no manuals or guides. I was given my first cosmetics in a shoe box. Mary Kay Cosmetics has come a long way. Each consultant has her own beauty case and is trained in skin care.

Last year I earned over $112,000. This does not include my personal sales. . . . I am now driving my 13th pink Cadillac. . . . For three years I have been in the half-million dollar club. The prizes for this honor include either a black mink, a white mink, or a diamond ring, all worth $10,000 each. I have all three.

Mary Kay Cosmetics offers many opportunities to women. . . . Tonight, if you join MKC, I would be honored to sign your agreement. This will let Mary Kay know you made your commitment tonight.

[*Lovie invites the new consultants to meet her up front. The audience applauds her. Many of the women eagerly go up to meet Lovie and have their agreements signed.*]

THE DIRECT SALES INDUSTRY

In 1984 Avon was the acknowledged leader among the handful of companies that chose to market cosmetics to U.S. consumers using direct sales techniques; Avon, with its door-to-door sales force of 400,000 representatives, had worldwide sales of about $2 billion. Mary Kay Cosmetics was the second-leading firm (see

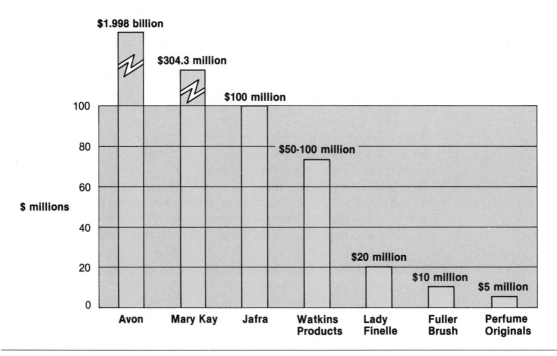

Exhibit 1   ESTIMATED SALES OF LEADING DIRECT SELLING COSMETIC COMPANIES, 1983

Source: "Reopening the Door to Door-to-Door Selling," *Chemical Business,* February 1984.

Exhibit 1). Other well-known companies whose salespeople went either door-to-door with their product or else held "parties" in the homes of prospective customers included Amway Corp. (home cleaning products), Shaklee Corp. (vitamins and health foods), Encyclopedia Britannica, Tupperware (plastic dishes and food containers), Consolidated Foods' Electrolux division (vacuum cleaners), and StanHome (parent of Fuller Brush). The direct sales industry also included scores of lesser known firms selling about every product imaginable—clothing, houseplants, toys, and financial services. Although Stanley Home Products invented the idea, Mary Kay and Tupperware were the best-known national companies using the "party plan" approach to direct selling.

The success enjoyed by Avon and Mary Kay was heavily dependent upon constantly replenishing and expanding their sales forces. New salespeople not only placed large initial orders for products but they also recruited new people into the organization. Revenues and revenue growth thus were a function of the number of representatives as well as the sales productivity of each salesperson. Market size was not seen as a limiting factor for growth because direct sales companies typically reached fewer than half the potential customer base.

Direct selling was grounded in capitalizing on networking relationships. Salespeople usually got their starts by selling first to relatives, friends, and neighbors, all the while looking for leads to new prospects. Direct sales specialists often believed that party plan selling was most successful among working class, ethnic, and small-town population groups where relationships were closer knit and where the social lives of women had a high carryover effect with work and high school. However, industry analysts saw several trends working against the networking approach and party plan type of direct-selling—rising divorce rates, the scattering of relatives and families across wider geographic areas, weakening ties to ethnic neighborhoods, declines in the number and strength of "the old girls" networks in many towns and neighborhoods, increased social mobility, the growing popularity of apartment and condominium living where acquaintances and relationships were more transient, and the springing up of bedroom communities and subdivisions populated by commuters and/or by families that stayed only a few years.

In the 1980s, direct selling companies began to have problems recruiting and retaining salespeople. During the two most recent recessionary periods in the United States, it was thought that the pool of potential saleswomen available for recruitment into direct sales careers would expand owing to above-normal unemployment rates. It didn't happen. As it turned out, many women became the sole family support and even greater numbers sought steady, better paying jobs in other fields. Part-time job opportunities mushroomed outside the direct-sales field as many service and retailing firms started hiring part-time permanent workers rather than full-time permanent staffs because part-time workers did not have to be paid the same extensive fringe benefits that full-time employees normally got. When the economy experienced upturns, the pool for direct-sales recruits shrank even more as people sought security in jobs offering regular hours and a salary; in 1983 all direct-sales companies reported increased difficulty in getting people to accept their part-time, sales-oriented, commission-only offers of employment.

Avon and Mary Kay were both caught offguard by these unpredicted events. Staffing plans at Avon had originally called for expansion in the number of sales force representatives from 400,000 in 1983 to 650,000 by 1987; in 1984 the company revised the 1987 goal down to 500,000 representatives. Four straight years of declining earnings convinced Avon that the traditional approach of depending on increasing the number of representatives for growth was not feasible any longer.

Sarah Coventry, a home party jewelry firm, decided in 1984 that relying solely upon direct selling approaches would not only be a continuing problem but also a growing problem. The company began to look for ways to supplement its direct-sales methods and shortly announced a plan to begin to sell Sarah Coventry products in retail stores. Fuller Brush, a long-standing door-to-door seller, began to distribute mail-order catalogs displaying a wider line of "househelper" products.

As of 1984, virtually every company in the direct-sales industry was critically evaluating the extent to which changes in the economy and in employment demographics would affect the success of direct selling. Many firms, including Avon and Mary Kay, were reviewing their incentive programs and sales organization methods. A number of industry observers as well as company officials believed some major changes would have to be made in the way the direct-sales industry did business.

MARY KAY ASH

Before she reached the age of 10, Mary Kay had the responsibility of cleaning, cooking, and caring for her invalid father, while her mother worked to support the family. During these years, Mary Kay's mother encouraged her daughter to excel. Whether at school or home, Mary Kay was urged to put forth her best efforts. By the time she was a teenager, Mary Kay had become a classic overachiever, intent on getting good grades and winning school contests. Over and over again, she heard her mother say "you can do it." Years later, Mary Kay noted on many occasions, "The confidence my mother instilled in me has been a tremendous help."[1]

Deserted by her husband of 11 years during the Great Depression, Mary Kay found herself with the responsibility of raising and supporting three children under the age of eight. Needing a job with flexible hours, she opted to try a career in direct sales with Stanley Home Products, a home party housewares firm. One of the first goals Mary Kay set at Stanley was to win Stanley's Miss Dallas Award, a ribbon honoring the employee who recruited the most new people in one week; she won the award during her first year with Stanley. After 13 years with Stanley, Mary Kay joined World Gift, a direct-sales company involved in decorative accessories; a few years later she was promoted to national training director. Her career and life were threatened in 1962 by a rare paralysis of one side of the face.

After recovery from surgery, she decided to retire from World Gift; by then she had remarried and lived in a comfortable Dallas neighborhood. She got so bored with retirement she decided to write a book on her direct-sales experiences. The more she wrote, the more she came to realize just how many problems women faced in the business world. Writing on a yellow legal pad at her kitchen table, Mary Kay listed everything she thought was wrong with male-run companies; on a second sheet she detailed how these wrongs could be righted, how a company could operate in ways that were responsive to the problems of working women and especially working mothers, and how women could reach their top potential in the business world. Being restless with retirement, she decided to do something about what she had written on the yellow pad and began immediately to plan how she might form a direct-sales company that had no sales quotas, few rules, flexible work hours, and plenty of autonomy for salespeople.

Finding a product to market was not a problem. In 1953, when she was conducting a Stanley home party at a house "on the wrong side of Dallas," she had noticed that all the ladies present had terrific-looking skin. It turned out that the hostess was a cosmetologist who was experimenting with a skin care product and all the guests were her guinea pigs. After the party, everyone gathered in the hostess's kitchen to get samples of her latest batch. The product was based on a formula that the woman's father, a hide tanner, developed when he accidentally discovered that some tanning lotions he made and used regularly had caused his hands to look much younger than his face. The tanner decided to apply these solutions to his face regularly, and after a short time his facial skin began looking more youthful too. The woman had since worked with her father's discovery for

---

[1] Mary Kay Ash, *Mary Kay* (New York: Harper & Row, 1981), p. 3.

17 years, making up batches that had the chemical smell of tanning solutions, putting portions in empty jars and bottles, and selling them as a sideline; she gave out instructions for use written in longhand on notebook paper. Mary Kay offered to try some of the hostess's latest batch and, despite the fact that it was smelly and messy, soon concluded that it was so good she wouldn't use anything else. Later, she became convinced that the only reason the woman hadn't made the product a commercial success was because she lacked marketing skills.

In 1963, using $5,000 in savings as working capital, she bought the formulas and proceeded to organize a beauty products company that integrated skin care instruction into its direct sales approach. The company was named Beauty by Mary Kay; the plan was for Mary Kay to take responsibility for the sales part of the company and for her second husband to serve as chief administrator. One month before operations were to start, he died from a heart attack. Her children persuaded her to go ahead with her plans, and Mary Kay's 20-year-old son, Richard Rogers, agreed to take on the job of administration of the new company. In September 1963, they opened a small store in Dallas with one shelf of inventory and nine of Mary Kay's friends as saleswomen. Mary Kay herself had limited expectations for the company and never dreamed that its sphere of operations would extend beyond Dallas.

All of Mary Kay's life-long philosophies and experiences were incorporated into how the company operated. The importance of encouragement became deeply ingrained in what was said and done. "You Can Do It" was expanded from a technique used by her mother to a daily theme at MKC. Mary Kay's style was to "praise people to success." She put into practice again the motivating role that positive encouragement had played in her own career; recognition and awards were made a highlight of the sales incentive programs that emerged. By 1984, recognition at MKC ranged from a single ribbon awarded for a consultant's first $100 show to a $5,000 shopping spree given to million-dollar producers.

The second important philosophy Mary Kay stressed concerned personal priorities: "Over the years, I have found that if you have your life in the proper perspective, with God first, your family second, and your career third, everything seems to work out."[2] She reiterated this belief again and again, regularly urging employees to take stock of their personal priorities and citing her own experience and belief as a positive example. She insisted on an all-out, firmwide effort to accommodate the plight of working mothers. Mary Kay particularly stressed giving beauty consultants enough control over how their selling efforts were scheduled so that problems with family matters and sick children were not incompatible with a Mary Kay career. A structure based on no sales quotas, few rules, and flexible hours was essential, Mary Kay believed, because working mothers from time to time needed the freedom to let work demands take a backseat to pressing problems at home.

Fairness and personal ethics were put in the forefront, too. The Golden Rule (treating others as you would have them treat you) was high on Mary Kay's list of management guidelines:

---

[2] Ibid., p. 56.

I believe in the Golden Rule and try to run the company on those principles. I believe that all you send into the lives of others will come back into your own. I like to see women reaching into themselves and coming out of their shells as the beautiful person that God intended them to be. In my company women do not have to claw their way to the top. The can get ahead based on the virtue of their own ethics because there's enough for everyone.[3]

To discourage interpersonal rivalry and jealousy, all rewards and incentives were pegged to reaching plateaus of achievements; everybody who reached the target level of performance became a winner. Sales contests based on declaring first place, second place, and third place winners were avoided.

MKC INC.

The company succeeded from the start. First-year wholesale sales were $198,000; in the second year, sales reached $800,000. At year-end 1983, wholesale revenues exceeded $320 million. Major geographical expansion was initiated during the 1970s. Distribution centers were opened in California, Georgia, New Jersey, and Illinois, and the company expanded its selling efforts internationally to Canada, Argentina, Australia, and the United Kingdom.

Early on, Mary Kay and Richard decided to consult a psychologist to learn more about their personalities. Testing revealed that Mary Kay was the type who, when encountering a person bleeding all over a fine carpet, would think of the person's plight first while Richard would think first of the carpet. This solidified their decision for Mary Kay to be the company's inspirational leader and for Richard to concentrate on overseeing all the business details.

In 1968 the company name was changed to Mary Kay Cosmetics, Inc. Also, during 1968, the company went public and its stock was traded in the over-the-counter market; in 1976 MKC's stock was listed on the New York Stock Exchange. Income per common share jumped from $0.16 in 1976 to $1.22 in 1983. A 10-year financial summary is presented in Exhibit 2; Exhibits 3 and 4 provide additional company data.

Richard Rogers, president, gave two basic reasons for the success of MKC:

We were filling a void in the industry when we began to teach skin care and makeup artistry and we're still doing that today. And second, our marketing system, through which proficient consultants achieve success by recruiting and building their own sales organization, was a stroke of genius because the by-product has been management. In other words, we didn't buy a full management team, they've been trained one by one.[4]

One of the biggest challenges MKC had to tackle during the 1970s was how to adapt its strategy and operating style in response to the influx of women into the labor force. Full- and part-time jobs interfered with attending beauty shows during normal working hours, and many working women with children at home had a

---

[3] As quoted in "The Beauty of Being Mary Kay," *Marketing and Media Decisions,* December 1982, pp. 150, 152.

[4] Mary Kay Cosmetics, Inc. "A Company and a Way of Life," company literature.

Exhibit 2 SELECTED FINANCIAL DATA, MARY KAY COSMETICS, INC., 1973–83 (in thousands except per share data)

	1973	1974	1975	1976	1977	1978	1979	1980	1981	1982	1983
Net sales	$22,199	$30,215	$34,947	$44,871	$47,856	$53,746	$91,400	$166,938	$235,296	$304,275	$323,758
Cost of sales	6,414	9,054	10,509	14,139	14,562	17,517	27,584	52,484	71,100	87,807	88,960
Selling, general, and administrative expenses	9,674	13,128	15,050	19,192	21,394	27,402	45,522	86,998	120,880	154,104	168,757
Operating income	6,111	8,033	9,388	11,540	11,900	8,827	18,304	27,456	43,316	62,364	66,041
Interest and other income, net	377	443	202	501	175	660	493	712	1,485	2,763	3,734
Interest expense	58	54	60	43	212	504	958	635	1,014	1,284	2,886
Income before income taxes	6,430	8,422	9,530	11,998	11,863	8,983	17,839	27,533	43,787	63,843	66,889
Provision for income taxes	3,035	3,973	4,480	5,854	5,711	4,110	8,207	12,398	19,632	28,471	30,235
Net income	$ 3,395	$ 4,449	$ 5,050	$ 6,144	$ 6,152	$ 4,873	$ 9,632	$ 15,135	$ 23,155	$ 35,372	$ 36,654
Net income per common share	$.09	$.11	$.13	$.16	$.17	$.15	$.33	$.52	$.82	$1.18	$1.22
Cash dividends per share	$.01	$.03	$.03	$.05	$.05	$.06	$.06	$.09	$.10	$.11	$.12
Average common shares	38,800	38,864	38,982	39,120	35,480	33,408	29,440	28,884	29,324	29,894	30,138
Total assets	$19,600	$24,743	$27,996	$34,331	$35,144	$36,305	$50,916	$ 74,431	$100,976	$152,457	$180,683
Long-term debt	$ 756	$ 87	$ 42	—	$ 5,592	$ 3,558	$ 4,000	$ 3,000	$ 2,366	$ 4,669	$ 3,915
Return on average stockholders' equity			21%	23%	24%	20%	38%	48%	48%	45%	32%
Stock prices											
Year high			2¾	2⅞	2⅝	1⅞	3⅞	8¾	18¾	28½	47⅞
Year low			1⅞	1¾	1½	1¼	1¼	3	6 1/18	8⅜	13⅛

Source: Mary Kay Cosmetics, Inc., *1983 Annual Report.*

Exhibit 3 GROWTH IN THE NUMBER OF MKC SALES DIRECTORS AND BEAUTY CONSULTANTS, 1973–83

Sales director growth

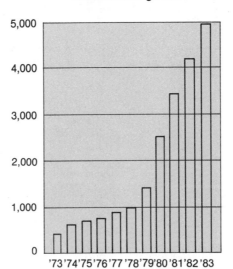

Beauty consultant growth

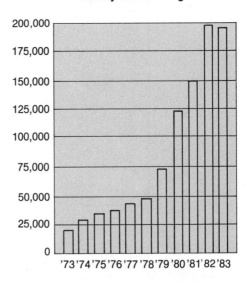

	Average number of consultants	Net sales ($000)	Average annual sales productivity per consultant
1983	195,671	$323,758	$1,655
1982	173,137	304,275	1,757
1981	134,831	235,296	1,745
1980	94,983	166,938	1,758
1979	57,989	91,400	1,576

Source: *1983 Annual Report.*

Exhibit 4 PERCENTAGE BREAKDOWN OF PRODUCT SALES AT MARY KAY COSMETICS, 1979–83

	1979	1980	1981	1982	1983
Skin care products for women	49%	52%	49%	46%	44%
Skin care products for men	1	2	1	1	1
Makeup items	26	22	26	26	30
Toiletry items for women	10	10	10	12	11
Toiletry items for men	2	2	2	2	2
Hair care	2	2	2	2	2
Accessories	10	10	10	11	10
Total	100%	100%	100%	100%	100%

Source: *1983 Annual Report.*

hard time fitting beauty shows on weeknights and weekends into their schedules. To make the beauty show sales approach more appealing to working women, the company began to supplement its standard "try before you buy" and "on-the-spot delivery" sales pitch themes. Consultants were trained to tout the ease with which MKC's scientifically formulated skin care system could be followed, the value of investing in good makeup and attractive appearance, the up-to-date glamor and wide selection associated with MKC's product line, the flexibility of deciding what and when to buy, and the time-saving convenience of having refills and "specials" delivered to their door instead of having to go out shopping. Mary Kay consultants quickly picked up on the growing popularity of having beauty shows on Tuesday, Wednesday, and Thursday nights; a lesser proportion of weekday hours were used for morning and afternoon showings, and a greater proportion came to be used for seeking and delivering reorders from ongoing users.

Exhibit 5 MARY KAY ASH IN 1983

Source: *1983 Annual Report* (picture on front cover).

MKC's corporate sales goal was to reach $500 million in revenues by 1990. As of 1984, about 65 percent of total sales were made to customers at beauty shows. However, it was expected that as the size of the company's customer base grew, the percentage of orders from repeat buyers would rise well above the present 35 percent level. MKC estimated that the average client spent over $200 a year on cosmetics. The company saw its target clientele as middle-class women in the 18–34 age group primarily and in the 35–44 age group secondarily and believed that a big percentage of its customers consisted of suburban housewives and white-collar clerical workers. The company's literature always pictured upscale women, dressed in a classy and elegant yet understated way, in either the role of a Mary Kay beauty consultant or the role of a user of Mary Kay cosmetics. As company figurehead, Mary Kay Ash personally made a point of being fashionably and expensively dressed, with perfect makeup and hairdo—a walking showcase for the company's products and a symbol of the professionally successful businesswoman (Exhibit 5).

MANUFACTURING

When Mary Kay Cosmetics commenced operations in 1963, the task of making the products was contracted out to a private Dallas-based manufacturing company. Mary Kay explained why:

> In 1963 I had no previous experience in the cosmetics industry; my forte was recruiting and training salespeople. After I acquired the formulas for the skin-care products, the first thing I did was seek out the most reputable cosmetics manufacturer I could find. Specifically I wanted a firm that not only made quality products, but observed the Food and Drug Administration's regulatory requirements to the letter. I knew it would be a fatal mistake to attempt to cut corners. With the right people in charge, we would never have to concern ourselves with that aspect of the business.[5]

In 1969, MKC built a 300,000-square-foot manufacturing and packaging facility adjacent to corporate headquarters. Packaging, warehousing, purchasing, and research labs were all housed in this location. Also included was a printing set-up that created Mary Kay labels in English, Spanish, and French. Many of the operations were automated.

The company's scientific approach to skin care was supported by a staff of laboratory technicians skilled in cosmetic chemistry, dermatology, physiology, microbiology, and package engineering. Ongoing tests were conducted to refine existing items and to develop new products. Laboratory staffs were provided with the comments and reactions about the products that came in from the beauty consultants and their customers. Consultants were strongly encouraged to report on their experiences with items and to relay any problems directly to the laboratory staff. About 80 percent of the R&D budget was earmarked for improving existing products.

---

[5] Mary Kay Ash, *Mary Kay on People Management* (New York: Warner Books, 1984), p. 13.

MKC believed that it was an industry leader in researching the properties of the skin (as concerned skin elasticity and moisture) and the anatomy of skin structure. Much of the research at MKC was performed in cooperation with academic institutions, particularly the University of Pennsylvania and the University of Texas Health Science Center.

PRODUCT LINE AND DISTRIBUTION POLICIES

As of 1984, the Mary Kay product line consisted of the Basic Skin Care Program for various skin types, the glamour collection, the body care products line, and a line of men's products called Mr. K. Most of the women's products were packaged in pink boxes and jars. When the company first began operations, Mary Kay personally put a lot of thought into packaging and appearance:

> Since people do leave their toiletries out, I wanted to package our cosmetics so beautifully that women would *want* to leave them out. So I was looking for a color that would make a beautiful display in all those white bathrooms. There were some shades of blue that were attractive, but the prettiest complementary color seemed to be a delicate pink. It also occurred to me that pink is considered a more feminine color. But my main reason for choosing it was that delicate pink seemed to look prettier than anything else in those white tile bathrooms. And from that I gained a *pink* reputation![6]

Mr. K, the men's line, was introduced in the 1960s in response to a number of confessions from men who used their wives' Mary Kay products. A rich chocolate brown package accented with silver was chosen for Mr. K. The men's line included a Basic Skin Care Program as well as lotions and colognes. The majority of Mr. K purchases were made by women for their husbands and boyfriends.

Consultants bought their supplies of products directly from MKC at wholesale prices and sold them at a 100 percent markup over wholesale. To make it more feasible for consultants to keep an adequate inventory on hand, the product line at MKC was kept streamlined, about 50 products. Mary Kay consultants were encouraged to carry enough products in their personal inventories that orders could be filled on the spot at the beauty shows. As an incentive to support this practice, MKC offered special awards and prizes when consultants placed orders of $1,500 or more.

A consultant could order as many or as few of the company's products as she chose to inventory. Most consultants stockpiled those items that sold especially well with their own individual clientele, and consultants also had the freedom to offer special promotions or discounts to customers. Nearly 50 percent of sales were for the skin care products that had evolved from the hide tanner's discovery. Consultants were required to pay for all orders with cashier's checks or money orders prior to delivery. MKC dealt only on a cash basis to minimize accounts receivables problems; according to Mary Kay, "Bad debts are a major reason for failure in other direct sales companies." In 1984, the average initial order of new

---

[6] Ash, *Mary Kay*, pp. 150–51.

consultants for inventory was about $1,000 ($2,000 in retail value). Consultants who decided to get out of the business could resell their inventories to MKC at 90 percent of cost.

During the company's early years, consultants were supplied only with an inventory of items to sell; shipments arrived in plain boxes. There were no sales kits and no instruction manuals to assist in sales presentations. However, by the 1970s, each new recruit received training in skin care techniques and was furnished with a number of sales aids. Later, new consultants were required to buy a beauty showcase containing everything needed to conduct a beauty show (samples, pink mirrors, pink trays used to distribute the samples, and a step-by-step sales manual that included suggested dialogue. In 1984 the showcase was sold to new consultants for $85. Along with the showcase came a supply of beauty profile forms to use at showings; guests filled out the form at the beginning of the show, and from the information supplied a consultant could readily prescribe which of the several product formulas was best suited for the individual's skin type.

In addition to the income earned from product sales, consultants earned bonuses or commissions on the sales made by all of the recruits they brought in. MKC paid consultants with one to four recruits a bonus commission equal to 4 percent in the wholesale orders of the recruits. A consultant with five or more recruits earned an 8 percent commission on the orders placed by recruits, or 12 percent if she also placed $600 a month in wholesale orders herself. MKC consultants who were entitled to a 12 percent commission and who had as many as 24 recruits were averaging about $950 monthly in bonuses and recruitment commissions as of 1984.

MKC'S SALES ORGANIZATION

The basic field organization unit for MKC's 195,000-person force of beauty consultants was the sales unit. Each sales unit was headed by a sales director who provided leadership and training for her group of beauty consultants. The top-performing sales directors were designated as national sales directors, a title that signified the ultimate achievement in the Mary Kay career sales ladder. A corporate staff of seven national sales administrators oversaw the activities of the sales directors in the field and their units of beauty consultants.

The sales units were not organized along strict geographical lines, and sales directors were free to recruit consultants anywhere; Mary Kay explained the logic for this approach:

> One of the first things I wanted my dream company to eliminate was assigned territories. I had worked for several direct-sales organizations in the past, and I knew how unfairly I had been treated when I had to move from Houston to St. Louis because of my husband's new job. I had been making $1,000 a month in commissions from the Houston sales unit that I had built over a period of eight years and I lost it all when I moved. I felt that it wasn't fair for someone else to inherit those Houston salespeople whom I had worked so hard to recruit and train.
>
>   Because we don't have territories at Mary Kay Cosmetics, a director who lives in Chicago can be vacationing in Florida or visiting a friend in Pittsburgh and recruit someone while there. It doesn't matter where she lives in the United

States; she will always draw a commission from the company on the wholesale purchases made by that recruit as long as they both remain with the company. The director in Pittsburgh will take the visiting director's new recruit under her wing and train her; the recruit will attend the Pittsburgh sales meetings and participate in the local sales contests. Although the Pittsburgh director will devote a lot of time and effort to the new recruit, the Chicago director will be paid the commissions. We call this our "adoptee" program.

The Pittsburgh recruit may go on to recruit new people on her own. No matter where she lives, she becomes the nucleus for bringing in additional people for the director who brought her into the business. As long as they're both active in the company, she will receive commissions from the company on her recruit's sales activity.

Today we have more than 5,000 sales directors, and most of them train and motivate people in their units who live outside their home states. Some have beauty consultants in a dozen or more states. Outsiders look at our company and say, "Your adoptee program can't possibly work!" But it does work. Each director reaps the benefits from her recruits in other cities and helps other recruits in return.[7]

THE BEAUTY CONSULTANT

Nearly all of MKC's beauty consultants had their first contact with the company as a guest at a beauty show. A discussion of career opportunities with Mary Kay was a standard part of the presentation at each beauty show. As many as 10 percent of the attendees at beauty shows were serious prospects as new recruits.

All beauty consultants were self-employed and worked on a commission basis. Everyone in the entire MKC sales organization started at the consultant level. The progression of each consultant up the "ladder of success" within the MKC sales organization was tightly linked to (1) the amount of wholesale orders the consultant placed with MKC, (2) her abilities to bring in new sales recruits, and (3) the size of the wholesale orders placed by these recruits. There were five rungs on the ladder of success for consultants, with qualifications and rewards as follows:

1. *New Beauty Consultant* (member of "Perfect Start Club").
   "Perfect Start Club" qualifications:

   Study and complete Perfect Start workbook.

   Observe three beauty shows.

   Book a minimum of eight shows within two weeks of receiving beauty showcase.

   Awards and recognition:

   Receives "Perfect Start" pin.

   Earns 50 percent commission on retail sales (less any discounts given to customers on "special promotions").

---

[7] Ash, *People Management*, pp. 2–3.

Becomes eligible for a 4 percent recruiting commission on wholesale orders placed by active personal recruits (to be considered active, a consultant had to place at least a $600 minimum wholesale order during the current quarter).

Is eligible for special prizes and bonuses given for current quarter's sales and recruiting contest.

2. *Star Consultant.*
    Qualifications:

    Must have three active recruits.

    Be an active beauty consultant (place a minimum wholesale order of $600 within the current calendar quarter).

Awards and recognition:

    Earns a red blazer.

    Earns a star pin.

    Earns "Ladder of Success" status by placing $1,800 in wholesale orders in a three-month period.

    Earns 50 percent commission on personal sales at beauty shows.

    Earns 4 percent personal recruiting commissions on wholesale orders placed by active personal recruits.

    Is eligible for special prizes and awards offered during quarterly contest.

    Receives a Star of Excellence ladder pin by qualifying as a star consultant for 8 quarters (or a Double Star of Excellence pin for 16 quarters).

3. *Team Leader.*
    Qualifications:

    Must have five or more active recruits.

    Be an active beauty consultant.

Awards and recognitions:

    Earns 50 percent commission on sales at own beauty shows.

    Earns a "Tender Loving Care" emblem for red blazer.

    Earns an 8 percent personal recruiting commission on wholesale orders of active personal recruits.

    Earns a 12 percent personal recruiting commission if (*a*) five or more active personal recruits place minimum $600 wholesale orders during the current month and (*b*) the team leader herself places a $600 wholesale order during the current month.

    Receives Team Leader pin in ladder of success program.

    Is eligible for quarterly contest prizes and bonuses.

4. *VIP (Very Important Performer).*
   Qualifications:

   Must have obtained Team Leader status.

   Must place wholesale orders of at least $600 for three consecutive months.

   Team must place wholesale orders of at least $3,000 each month for three consecutive months.

   Awards and recognition:

   Earns the use of an Oldsmobile Firenza.

   Earns 50 percent commission on sales at own beauty shows.

   Earns a 12 percent personal recruiting commission.

   Receives VIP pin in ladder of success program.

   Is eligible for quarterly contest prizes and bonuses.

5. *Future Director.*
   Qualifications:

   Must have qualified for Team Leader status.

   Must have 12 active recruits at time of application.

   Must make a commitment to Mary Kay to become a sales director by actually giving her letter of intent date.

   Awards and recognition:

   Earns a future director crest for red jacket.

   Plus all the benefits accorded team leaders and VIPs, as appropriate, for monthly and quarterly sales and recruiting performance.

New recruits were required to submit a signed Beauty Consultant Agreement, observe three beauty shows conducted by an experienced consultant, book a minimum of eight beauty shows, and hold at least five beauty shows within their first two weeks. Each consultant was asked to appear in attractive dress and makeup when in public and to project an image of knowledge and confidence about herself and the MKC product line. Mary Kay felt the stress on personal appearance was justified: "What we are selling is beauty. A woman is not going to buy from someone who is wearing jeans and has her hair up in curlers. We want our consultants to be the type of woman others will want to emulate."[8]

Consultants spent most of their work hours scheduling and giving beauty shows. A showing took about two hours (plus about an hour for travel time), and

---

[8] Rebecca Fannin, "The Beauty of Being Mary Kay," *Marketing & Media Decisions* 17 (December 1982), pp. 59–61.

many times the hostess and one or more of the guests turned out to be prospective recruits. New consultants were coached to start off by booking showings with friends, neighbors, and relatives and then network these into showings for friends of friends and relatives of relatives.

Consultants were instructed to follow up each beauty show by scheduling a second facial for each guest at the showing. Many times a customer would invite friends to her second facial and the result would be another beauty show. After the follow-up facial, consultants would call customers periodically to check on whether the customer was satisfied, to see if refills were needed, and to let the customer know about new products and special promotions. Under MKC's "dovetailing" plan, a consultant with an unexpected emergency at home could sell her prearranged beauty show to another consultant and the two would split the commissions generated by the show.

THE SALES DIRECTOR

Consultants who had climbed to the fifth rung of the consultants' ladder of success were eligible to become sales directors and head up a sales unit. In addition to conducting her own beauty shows, a sales director's responsibilities included training new recruits, leading weekly sales meetings, and providing assistance and advice to the members of her unit. Sales directors, besides receiving the commissions on sales made at their own showings, were paid a commission on the total sales of the unit they headed and a commission on the number of new sales recruits. In June 1984, the top 100 recruiting commissions paid to sales directors ranged from approximately $660 to $1,900. It was not uncommon for sales directors to have total annual earnings in the $50,000 to $100,000 range; in 1983, the average income of the 4,500 sales directors was between $25,000 and $30,000.

There were six achievement categories for sales directors, with qualifications and awards as shown below:

1. *Director in Qualification (DIQ).*
   Qualifications:

   Must have 15 active personal recruits.

   Submits a Letter of Intent to obtain Directorship.

   Gets the director of her sales unit to submit a letter of recommendation.

   Within three consecutive months:

   Must recruit an additional 15 consultants for a total of 30 personal active recruits.

   The unit of 30 personal active recruits must place combined wholesale orders of $4,000, $4,500, and $5,000 for months one, two, and three, respectively.

   Awards and recognition:

   Earns personal sales and personal recruiting commissions (as per schedules for at least team leader status).

   Eligible for prizes and bonuses in quarterly contests.

2. *Sales Director.*
   Qualifications:

   Sales unit must maintain a minimum of $4,000 in wholesale orders each month for the sales director to remain as head of her unit.

   Awards and recognition:

   Receives commissions of 9 percent to 13 percent on unit's wholesale orders.
   Receives monthly sales production bonuses:
   - A $300 monthly bonus if unit places monthly wholesale orders of $3,000–$4,999.
   - A $500 monthly bonus if unit places monthly wholesale orders of $5,000 and up.

   Receives a monthly recruiting bonus (for personal recruits or for recruits of other consultants in the sales unit):
   - $100 bonus if three to four new recruits come into unit.
   - $200 bonus if five to seven new recruits come into unit.
   - $300 bonus if 8 to 11 new recruits come into unit.
   - $400 bonus for 12 or more recruits.

   Is given a designer director suit.
   Is entitled to all commission schedules and incentives of future sales directors.

3. *Regal Director.*
   Qualifications:

   Members of sales unit must place wholesale orders of at least $24,000 for two consecutive quarters.
   Must qualify every two years.

   Awards and recognition:

   Earns the use of a pink Buick Regal.
   Is entitled to all the commission percentages, bonuses, and other incentives of a sales director.

4. *Cadillac Director.*
   Qualifications:

   Sales unit members must place at least $36,000 in wholesale orders for two consecutive quarters.
   Must qualify every two years.

   Awards and recognition:

   Earns the use of a pink Cadillac.
   Is entitled to all the commission percentages, bonuses, and other incentives of a sales director.

5. *Senior Sales Director.*
   Qualifications:

   > One to four sales directors emerge from her unit.

   Awards and recognition:

   > Earns a 4 percent commission on offspring director's consultants.
   > Is entitled to all the commission percentages, bonuses, and other incentives of at least a sales director.

6. *Future National Director.*
   Qualifications:

   > Five or more active directors emerge from her unit.

   Awards and recognition:

   > Is entitlted to all the commission percentages, bonuses, and other incentives of a senior sales director.

As of late 1983, the company had about 700 Regal directors and about 700 Cadillac directors; in one recent quarter, 81 sales directors had met the qualifications for driving a new pink Cadillac.

THE NATIONAL SALES DIRECTOR

Top-performing sales directors became eligible for designation as a national sales director, the highest recognition bestowed on field sales personnel. NSDs were inspirational leaders and managers of a group of sales directors and received commissions on the total dollar sales of the group of sales units they headed. In 1984, MKC's 50 national sales directors had total sales incomes averaging over $150,000 per year. A 1985 *Fortune* article featured Helen McVoy, a MKC national sales director since 1971, as one of the most successful salespeople in the United States; in 1984 she earned $375,000. McVoy began her career with Mary Kay in 1965 at the age of 45. Her family was on a tight budget, having lost all of their savings in a bad mining investment. To support her plant-collecting hobby, Helen started selling Mary Kay products on a part-time basis—two hours a week. Her original investment was for a beauty case; by the end of her first year she had made $17,000. From 1970 through 1984, she was the company's top volume producer.

TRAINING

Before holding a beauty show, a new consultant had to observe three beauty shows, attend orientation classes conducted by a sales director, and complete a self-study set of MKC training materials. This training covered the fundamentals of conducting skin care shows, booking future beauty shows, recruiting new Mary Kay consultants, personal appearance, and managing a small business. Active consultants were strongly encouraged to continue to improve their sales skills and product knowledge. In addition to weekly sales meetings and frequent one-on-one contact with other consultants and sales directors, each salesperson had access to a variety of company-prepared support materials—videotapes, films, slide shows, and brochures.

In 1983, a new educational curriculum was introduced to support each phase of a Mary Kay career. A back-to-basics orientation package provided a foundation for the first stage of career development. A recruitment notebook provided dialogue of mock recruiting conversations, and sales directors were provided with an organizational kit to help them make a smooth transition from being purely a consultant to being a sales manager as well as a consultant.

Additional learning opportunities were provided in the form of special product knowledge classes, regional workshops, and annual corporate-sponsored seminars.

MOTIVATION AND INCENTIVES

New sales contests were introduced every three months. Prizes and recognition awards were always tied to achievement plateaus rather than declaring first-, second-, and third-place winners. Top performers were spotlighted in the company's full-color monthly magazine, *Applause* (which had a circulation of several hundred thousand).

Mary Kay Ash described why MKC paid so much attention to recognition and praise:

> I believe praise is the best way for a manager to motivate people. At Mary Kay Cosmetics we think praise is so important that our entire marketing plan is based upon it.[9]

> Praise is an incredibly effective motivator; unfortunately, many managers are reluctant to employ it. Yet I can't help feeling that they know how much praise means, not only to others, but to themselves. . . . I believe that you should praise people whenever you can; it causes them to respond as a thirsty plant responds to water.[10]

> The power of positive motivation is a goal-oriented structure such as ours cannot be overstated. This is what inspires our consultants to maximize their true potentials.[11]

> As a manager you must recognize that everyone needs praise. But it must be given sincerely. You'll find numerous occasions for genuine praise if you'll only look for them.[12]

> Because we recognize the need for people to be praised, we make a concentrated effort to give as much recognition as possible. Of course with an organization as large as ours, not everyone can make a speech at our Seminars, but we do attempt to have many people appear on stage, if only for a few moments. During

---

[9] Ash, *People Management*, p. 21.

[10] Ibid., p. 23.

[11] Ibid., p. 26.

[12] Ibid., p. 27.

the Directors' March, for example, hundreds of directors parade on stage before thousands of their peers. In order to appear in the Director's March, a director must purchase a special designer suit. Likewise we have a Red Jacket March, in which only star recruiters, team leaders, and future directors participate. Again, a special uniform is required for participation.[13]

How important are these brief stage appearances? Frankly I think it means more for a woman to be recognized by her peers than to receive an expensive present in the mail that nobody knows about! And once she gets a taste of this recognition, she wants to come back next year for more![14]

SEMINAR

MKC staged an annual "Seminar" as a salute to the company and to the salespeople who contributed to its success. The first Seminar was held on September 13, 1964 (the company's first anniversary); the banquet menu consisted of chicken, jello salad, and an anniversary cake while a three-piece band provided entertainment. By 1984, Seminar had grown into a three-day spectacular repeated four consecutive times with a budget of $4 million and attended by 24,000 beauty consultants and sales directors who paid their own way to attend the event. The setting, the Convention Center in Dallas (see Exhibit 6), was decorated in red, white, and blue in order to emphasize the theme, "Share the Spirit." The climactic highlight of Seminar was Awards Night, when the biggest prizes were awarded to the people with the biggest sales. The company went to elaborate efforts to ensure the Awards Night was charged with excitement and emotion; as one observer of the 1984 Awards Night in Dallas described it, "The atmosphere there is electric, a cross between a Las Vegas revue and a revival meeting. Hands reach up to touch Mary Kay; a pink Cadillac revolves on a mist-shrouded pedestal; a 50-piece band plays; and women sob."

Mary Kay Ash customarily made personal appearances throughout the Seminar period. In addition to Awards Night, Seminar featured sessions consisting of informational and training workshops, motivational presentations by leading sales directors, and star entertainment (Paul Anka performed in 1984, and in previous years there had been performances by Tennesse Ernie Ford, John Davidson, and Johnny Mathis). Over the three days, Cadillacs, diamonds, mink coats, a $5,000 shopping spree at Nieman-Marcus for any director whose team sold $1 million worth of Mary Kay products, and lesser assorted prizes were awarded to the outstanding achievers of the past year. Gold-and-diamond bumblebee pins, each containing 21 diamonds and retailing for over $3,600, were presented to the Queen of Sales on Pageant Night; these pins were not only the company's ultimate badge of success, but Mary Kay felt they also had special symbolism:

It's a beautiful pin, but that isn't the whole story. We think the bumblebee is a marvelous symbol of woman. Because, as aerodynamic engineers found a long time ago, the bumblebee cannot fly! Its wings are too weak and its body is too

---

[13] Ibid., p. 25.

[14] Ibid., p. 26.

Exhibit 6 "SHARE THE SPIRIT," 1984 ANNUAL SEMINAR, MARY KAY COSMETICS

Source: Mary Kay Cosmetics, Inc., Interim Report, 1984.

heavy to fly, but fortunately, the bumblebee doesn't know that, and it goes right on flying. The bee has become a symbol of women who didn't know they could fly but they DID! I think the women who own these diamond bumblebees think of them in their own personal ways. For most of us, it's true that we refused to believe we couldn't do it. Maybe somebody said, "It's really impossible to get this thing off the ground." But somebody else told us, "You can do it!" So we did.[15]

On the final day of seminar, the Sue Z. Vickers Memorial Award—Miss Go Give—was presented. This honor was given to the individual who best demonstrated the Mary Kay spirit—a spirit described as loving, giving, and inspirational.

CORPORATE ENVIRONMENT

The company's eight-story, gold-glass corporate headquarters building in Dallas was occupied solely by Mary Kay executives. An open-door philosophy was

---

[15] Ash, *Mary Kay*, p. 9.

present at MKC. Everyone from the mailroom clerk to the chairman of the board was treated with respect. The door to Mary Kay Ash's office was rarely closed. Often people touring the building peeked in her office to get a glimpse of the pink and white decor. Mary Kay and all other corporate managers took the time to talk with any employee.

First names were always used at MKC. Mary Kay herself insisted on being addressed as Mary Kay; she felt people who called her Mrs. Ash were either angry at her or didn't know her. In keeping with this informal atmosphere, offices didn't have titles on the doors, executive restrooms didn't exist, and the company cafeteria was used by the executives (there was no executive dining room).

To further enhance the informal atmosphere and enthusiasm at MKC, all sales functions were stated with a group sing-along. Mary Kay offered several reasons for this policy:

> Nothing great is ever achieved with enthusiasm. . . . We have many of our own songs, and they're sung at all Mary Kay get-togethers, ranging from small weekly meetings to our annual Seminars. Our salespeople enjoy this activity, and I believe the singing creates a wonderful esprit de corps. Yet outsiders, especially men, often criticize our singing as being "strictly for women." I disagree. Singing unites people. It's like those "rah-rah-rah for our team" cheers. If someone is depressed, singing will often bring her out of it.[16]

The company sent Christmas cards, birthday cards, and anniversary cards to every single employee each year. Mary Kay personally designed the birthday cards for consultants. In addition, all the sales directors received Christmas and birthday presents from the company.

THE PEOPLE MANAGEMENT PHILOSOPHY AT MKC

Mary Kay Ash had some very definite ideas about how people ought to be managed, and she willingly shared them with employees and, through her books, with the public at large. Some excerpts from her book on *People Management* reveal the approach taken at Mary Kay Comsetics:

> People come first at Mary Kay Cosmetics—our beauty consultants, sales directors, and employees, our customers, and our suppliers. We pride ourselves as a "company known for the people it keeps." Our belief in caring for people, however, does not conflict with our need as a corporation to generate a profit. Yes, we keep our eye on the bottom line, but it's not an overriding obsession.[17]

> Ours is an organization with few middle management positions. In order to grow and progress, you don't move upward; you expand outward. This gives our independent sales organization a deep sense of personal worth. They know that they are not competing with one another for a spot in the company's managerial "pecking order." Therefore the contributions of each individual are of equal value. No one is fearful that his or her idea will be "stolen" by someone with

---

[16] Ash, *People Management*, p. 59.

[17] Ibid., p. xix.

more ability on the corporate ladder. And when someone—anyone—proposes a new thought, we all analyze it, improve upon it, and ultimately support it with the enthusiasm of a team.[18]

Every person is special! I sincerely believe this. Each of us wants to feel good about himself or herself, but to me it is just as important to make others feel the same way. Whenever I meet someone, I try to imagine him wearing an invisible sign that says: MAKE ME FEEL IMPORTANT! I respond to this sign immediately and it works wonders.[19]

At Mary Kay Cosmetics we believe in putting our beauty consultants and sales directors on a pedestal. Of all people, I most identify with them because I spent many years as a salesperson. My attitude of appreciation for them permeates the company. When our salespeople visit the home office, for example, we go out of our way to give them the red-carpet treatment. Every person in the company treats them royally.[20]

We go first class across the board, and although it's expensive, it's worth it because our people are made to feel important. For example, each year we take our top sales directors and their spouses on deluxe trips to Hong Kong, Bangkok, London, Paris, Geneva, and Athens to mention a few. We spare no expense, and although it costs a lot extra per person to fly the Concorde, cruise on the Love Boat, or book suites at the elegant Georges V in Paris, it is our way of telling them how important they are to our company.[21]

My experience with people is that they generally do what you expect them to do! If you expect them to perform well, they will; conversely, if you expect them to perform poorly, they'll probably oblige. I believe that average employees who try their hardest to live up to your high expectations of them will do better than above-average people with low self-esteem. Motivate your people to draw on that untapped 90 percent of their ability and their level of performance will soar![22]

A good people manager will never put someone down; not only is it nonproductive—it's counterproductive. You must remember that your job is to play the role of problem solver and that by taking this approach of criticizing people you'll accomplish considerably more.

While some managers try to forget problems they encounterd early in their careers, I make a conscious effort to remember the difficulties I've had along the way. I think it's vital for a manager to emphathize with the other people's problem, and the best way to have a clear understanding is to have been there yourself![23]

Interviews with Mary Kay consultants gave credibility to the company's approach and methods. One consultant described her experience thusly:

---

[18] Ibid., pp. 11–12.

[19] Ibid., p. 15.

[20] Ibid., p. 19.

[21] Ibid., p. 20.

[22] Ibid., p. 17.

[23] Ibid., p. 6.

I had a lot of ragged edges when I started. The first time I went to a Mary Kay seminar, I signed up for classes in diction and deportment; believe me, I needed them. I didn't even have the right clothes. You can only wear dresses and skirts to beauty shows, so I sank everything I had into one nice dress. I washed it out every night in Woolite and let it drip dry in the shower.

But I was determined to follow all the rules, even the ones I didn't understand—*especially* the ones I didn't understand. At times, it all seemed foolish, especially when you consider that all my clients were mill workers and didn't exactly appreciate my new grammar. But I kept telling myself to hang in there, that Mary Kay knew what was good for me.

When I first started, I won a pearl and ruby ring. A man or a man's company may say I'd have been better off with the cash, but I'm not so convinced. Mary Kay is on to something there. From the moment I won that ring, I began thinking of myself as a person who deserved a better standard of living. I built a new life to go with the ring.[24]

Another consultant observed:

The essential thing about Mary Kay is the quality of the company. When you go to Dallas, the food, the hotel, and the entertainment are all top notch. Nothing gaudy is allowed in Mary Kay.[25]

When asked if she didn't think pink Cadillacs were a tad gaudy, she responded in a low, level tone: "When people say that, I just ask them what color car their company gave them last year."

On the morning following Awards Night 1984, a group of Florida consultants was in the hotel lobby getting ready to go to the airport for the flight home.[26] One member had by chance met Mary Kay Ash in the ladies room a bit earlier and had managed to get a maid to snap a Polaroid photograph of them together. She proudly was showing her friends the snapshot and was the only one of the group who had actually met Mary Kay. The consultant said to her friends, "She told me she was sure I'd be up there on stage with her next year. She said she'd see me there." Her sales director, in noting the scene, observed, "She's got the vision now. She really did meet her. And you've got to understand that in Mary Kaydom that's a very big deal."

THE BEAUTY SHOW

It was a few minutes past 7 P.M. on a weeknight in Tuscaloosa, Alabama. Debbie Sessoms and three of her friends (including the casewriter) were seated around the dining room table in Debbie's house. In front of each woman was a pink tray, a mirror, a pencil, and a blank personal Beauty Profile form. Jan Currier stood at

---

[24] As quoted in Kim Wright Wiley, "Cold Cream and Hard Cash," *Savvy,* June 1985, p. 39.

[25] Ibid., p. 41.

[26] Ibid.

the head of the table. She welcomed each of the ladies and asked them to fill out the personal Beauty Profile form in front of them.

When they were finished, Jan started her formal presentation, leading off with how MKC's products were developed by a tanner. She used a large display board to illustrate the topics she discussed. Next Jan told the group about the company and the founder, Mary Kay Ash. She showed a picture of Mary Kay and explained she was believed to be in her 70s—though no one knew for sure because Mary Kay maintained that "A woman who will tell her age will tell anything." Jerri, one of the guests, remarked that she couldn't believe how good Mary Kay looked for her age. Jan told her that Mary Kay had been using her basic skin care formulas since the 1950s.

Jan went on to talk about the growth of the sales force from nine consultants to over 195,000 in 1984. She explained how the career opportunities at MKC could be adapted to each consultant's ambitions. A consultant, she said, determined her own work hours and could choose either a full-time or part-time career. Advancement was based on sales and recruiting abilities. The possible rewards included diamonds, minks, and pink Cadillacs.

Before explaining the basic skin care program, Jan told the women that with the Mary Kay money-back guarantee, products could be returned for any reason for a full refund. Jan distributed samples to each of the guests based on the information provided in the personal Beauty Profiles. Under Jan's guidance, the ladies proceeded through the complete facial process, learning each of the five basic skin care steps advocated by Mary Kay. There was a lot of discussion about the products and how they felt on everyone's skin.

When the presentation reached the glamour segment, each guest was asked her preference of makeup colors. Jan encouraged everyone to try as many of the products and colors as they wanted. Jan helped the guests experiment with different combinations and worked with each one personally, trying to make sure that everyone would end up satisfied with her own finished appearance.

After admiring each other's new looks, three of the women placed orders. Jan collected their payments and filled the orders on the spot. No one had to wait for delivery.

When she finished with the orders, Jan talked with Debbie's three guests about hostessing their own shows and receiving hostess gifts. Chris agreed to book a show the next week. Debbie was then given her choice of gifts based on the evening's sales and bookings. To close the show, Jan again highlighted the benefits of a Mary Kay career—being your own boss, setting your own hours—and invited anyone interested to talk with her about these opportunities. Debbie then served some refreshments. Shortly after 9 P.M., Jan and Debbie's three guests departed.

Walking to Jan's car, the casewriter asked Jan if the evening was a success. Jan replied that it had been "a pretty good night. Sales totaled $150, I got a booking for next Wednesday, I made $75 in commissions in a little over two hours, the guests learned about skin care and have some products they are going to like, and Debbie got a nice hostess gift."

THE WEEKLY SALES MEETING

Jan Currier, senior sales director, welcomed the consultants to the weekly Monday night meeting of the members of her sales unit.[27] After calling everyone's attention to a mimeographed handout on everybody's chair, she introduced the casewriter to the group and then invited everyone to stand and join in singing the Mary Kay enthusiasm song. As soon as the song was over, Jan started "the Crow Period" by asking Barbara, team leader, to stand and tell about her achievement of VIP (Very Important Performer) status. Barbara told of setting and achieving the goals necessary to win the use of an Oldsmobile Firenza. Her new goal was to assist and motivate everyone on her team to do the same. Jan recognized Barbara again for being both the Queen of Sales and the Queen of Recruiting for the previous month.

Jan began the educational segment by instructing the consultants on color analysis and how it related to glamour. She continued the instruction by explaining the proper techniques of a man's facial.

Next everyone who had at least a $100 week in sales was asked to stand. Jan began the countdown "110, 120, 130 . . . 190." Barbara sat down to a round of applause for her $190 week in sales. "200, 220 . . . 270." Melissa sat down. The ladies applauded her efforts. Mary was the only one left standing. There was anticipation of how high her sales reached as the countdown resumed. "280, 290, 300 . . . 335." Mary sat down. Everyone applauded this accomplishment of a consultant who had only been with MKC for four months and who held a 40-hour-week full-time job in addition to her Mary Kay sales efforts.

At this time Jan asked Linda and Susan to join her up front. She pinned each lady and congratulated them on joining her team. The Mary Kay pin was placed upside down on the new consultant's lapels. Jan explained this was so people would notice and ask about it. When they did, a consultant was to respond by saying; "My pin is upside down to remind me to ask you if you've had a Mary Kay facial." The pin would be turned right side up when the consultant got her first recruit. Each of the new consultants also received a pink ribbon. This marked their membership in the Jan's Beautiful People sales unit. Both Linda and Susan were given some material Jan had prepared (Exhibit 7); Jan said she would go over it with them after the meeting.

Next a new competition was announced. This contest focused on recruiting. For each new recruit, a consultant would receive one stem of Romanian crystal. So everyone could see how beautiful the rewards were, Jan showed a sample of the crystal.

A final reminder was made for attendance at the upcoming workshop on motivation. Jan sweetened the pot by providing a prize to the first one in her unit to register and pay for the seminar. Next week she would announce the winner.

The meeting was adjourned until next Monday evening.

---

[27] Most sales directors had their sales meeting on Monday night, a practice urged upon them by Mary Kay Ash. Mary Kay saw the Monday night meeting as a good way to start the week: "If you had a bad week—you need the sales meeting. If you had a good week, the sales meeting needs you! When a consultant leaves a Monday meeting excited, she has an entire week to let excitement work for her." Ash, *Mary Kay,* p. 40.

Exhibit 7 EXAMPLE OF MATERIAL PROVIDED TO NEW BEAUTY
CONSULTANTS AT WEEKLY SALES MEETING

The Mary Kay Opportunity

	Yearly Total
3 Shows per week with $150.00 sales per show Less 15 percent hostess credit = $191.25 profit (per week) Three persons buying per show, three shows per week	$ 9,945
468 prospective customers per year Average selling to 7 out of 10 327 new customers per year Call each customer at least six times per year Average $15.00 in sales per call Yearly reorder profits will be	14,715
1 Facial per week—52 prospective customers per year Average selling to 7 of 10, 36 new customers If each buys a basic, your facial profits will be	702
36 New customers from facials Call each customer six times per year Average $15.00 in sales per call Your yearly *reorder* profit will be	1,620
Recruit one person per month Each with at least a $1,500 initial order (wholesale) Ordering only $500.00 every month thereafter Your 4 percent—8 percent commission checks from these 12 recruits	3,490
Your yearly profits will be approximately	$30,472

This is a simple guidline designed to show you, in figures, approximately how much you can benefit from your Mary Kay career. These figures may vary a little, due to price changes. These totals are based on orders placed at our maximum discount level and do not include referrals, dovetail fees, and prizes.

Working hours per week for the above should not exceed 20 hours, if your work is well planned. Attitude and consistency are the keys to your success.

Jan Currier
Senior Sales Director

AN INTERVIEW WITH JAN CURRIER

One night shortly after attending the meeting of Jan's Beautiful People sales unit, the casewriter met with Jan to ask some questions.

Casewriter: How many are in your unit?

Jan: We're down right now. I had a small unit to start with. I only had 56. . . . A decent unit has got a hundred, 75 to 100 at least.

Casewriter: Is it the size of the town that hampers you?

Jan: No, no it's me who hampers me. The speed of the leader is the speed of the unit. If I'm not out there doing it, then they're not going to be doing it. If I'm recruiting, they're recruiting.

Casewriter: What about your leader, is your leader not fast?

Jan: No, it's me; see when you point a finger, three come back.

Casewriter: How do you handle a situation where a consultant would like to do well, but she doesn't put in the time necessary to do well?

Jan: You have to go back to that premise, that whole philosophy that you're in business for yourself but not by yourself. So if a girl comes in and says I want to make X number of dollars, then I will work with her and we will do it. I try to get them to set goals and really look at them every week and work for it. One gal comes in and wants to make $25 a week and another says, "I have to support my family." There's a big difference.

Casewriter: How do you handle those that only want to make $25 a week?

Jan: If you get rid of the piddlers, you wouldn't have a company. It's the piddlers that make up the company. There are only going to be one or two superstars.

Casewriter: How do you motivate the girls in your unit?

Jan: The only way you can really motivate is to call, encourage, write notes, and encourage recognition at the sales meetings and recognition in the newsletter. If they're not doing anything, they usually won't come to the sales meeting, but once in a while maybe, they'll find excuses.

Casewriter: What do you do when a girl hits that stage?

Jan: Everybody has to go through that phase. . . . If you're smart, you'll go to your director, read your book and go back to start where you were before—with what was working to begin with and you'll pull out of it. There are a lot of them who never pull out of it. They came in to have fun.

Casewriter: And the fun wears out.

Jan: Let's face it. This is a job. It's work, it's the best-paying hard work around, but it's work. I just finished with one gal last week who ended up saying, "Well, I just thought it would be fun. I thought it was just supposed to be fun." And I said, "Yes, but it's a job."

Casewriter: Can you tell before a girl starts if she'll be successful?

Jan: There's no way to predict who's going to make it; the one you think is going to be absolutely a superstar isn't. You give everybody a chance. I measure my time with their interest and I tell them that. I'll encourage them, but they are going to pretty much do what they want to do. I learned that the hard way. There is no point to laying guilt trips, no point pestering them to death, and pressure doesn't work.

Casewriter: Do you feel recognition is the best motivator?

Jan: Absolutely, recognition and appreciation. I think appreciation more than anything else. Little notes, I'm finally learning that too. Some of us are slow learners. . . . So I'll write little notes telling someone, I really appreciate your doing this, or I'm really proud of you for being a star consultant this quarter, or I'm so glad you went with us to Birmingham to the workshop.

Casewriter: Does it upset you when people don't come to the sales meetings?

Jan: I use to grieve when they wouldn't come to sales meetings. I'd ask what am I doing wrong. . . . Finally I realized that no matter how many people aren't there, the people who are there care and they are worth doing anything for. It's strange we seem to get a different batch every meeting.

Casewriter: I get the impression that you are always looking for new recruits.

Jan: Yes, I've gotten more picky. I'm looking more for directors. I'm looking for people who really want to work. I look for someone who is older, not just the 18-year-olds because they don't want to work. They want to make money, but they don't want to work. . . . I'd like to build more offspring directors.

Casewriter: What kind of people do you look for?

Jan: Not everybody's right for Mary Kay. It takes somebody who genuinely cares about other people.

Casewriter: Is there a common scenario that fits most new recruits?

Jan: Mary Kay attracts a lot of insecure women who are often married to insecure men. And that woman is told over and over by Mary Kay how wonderful she is and how terrific she is and how she can do anything with God's help. She can achieve anything. And like me she is dumb enough to believe it and go along with it.

Casewriter: What do you feel is the reason for the slowdown in recruiting at Mary Kay?

Jan: The key to this drop has been partly the economy, but partly a lot of people are weeding out. That's OK because the cream is going to rise to the top. I really believe that. We're going to have a stronger, much better company. I could see it at leadership (conference). The quality of people was much higher. It gets higher every year.

MKC'S FUTURE

MKC's sales in 1984 fell 14 percent to $278 million (down from $324 million in fiscal year 1983). The company's stock price, after a two for one split at about $44, tumbled from $22 in late 1983 to the $9–$12 range in 1984. Profits were down 8 percent to $33.8 million. The declines were blamed on a dropoff in recruiting and retention (owing to reduced attractiveness of part-time employment) and to the expense of starting up the European division. As of December 31, 1984, the company had about 152,000 beauty consultants and 4,500 sales directors as compared to 195,000 beauty consultants and 5,000 sales directors at year-end 1983. Average sales per consultant in 1984 was $1,603, versus $1,655 in 1983 and a 1980–82 average of $1,753; only 60,000 of the 152,000 consultants were thought to be significantly productive. A cosmetic analyst for one Wall Street securities firm, in talking about the company's prospects, said, "Brokers loved this stock because it had such a great story. But the glory days, for the time being, are certainly over."[28]

---

[28] As quoted in Wiley, "Cold Cream and Hard Cash," p. 40.

The company's mystique was upbeat, however. Mary Kay Ash was on the UPI list of the most interviewed women in America. And when the Republicans chose Dallas for its 1984 convention, the Chamber of Commerce had to persuade Mary Kay to change the date of the 1984 Seminar, which was slated for the same week in the same convention center. Positive anecdotes about Mary Kay Ash and how MKC was operated were cited in numerous books and articles.

Mary Kay Ash indicated that the company had no plans for changing the main thrust of company's sales and recruiting strategies:

> This is an excellent primary career for women, not just a way to get pin money. We see no need to alter our basic approach. It's taken us this far.[29]

> We have only 4 percent of the total retail cosmetics market. The way I see it 96 percent of the people in the United States are using the wrong product. There's no reason why we can't become the number one cosmetics company in the United States.[30]

---

[29] Ibid.

[30] As quoted in *Business Week,* March 28, 1983, p. 130.

WAL-MART STORES, INC.*

"Give me a W!" shouts Sam Walton, the founder and CEO of Wal-Mart Stores, Inc., to associates at the weekly Saturday morning headquarters meeting in Bentonville, Arkansas (population approximately 9,000). "W!" the crowd of some several hundred roars back. "Give me an A!" says Walton. And so it goes down to the last T. Then everyone joins in a final ringing chorus: "Wal-Mart, we're Number 1!" This rah-rah style keynoted the tone for each meeting, and the upbeat spirit carried over to the rest of the company's operations. Enthusiasm and dedication were factors in Wal-Mart's ranking as the second-largest national discount department store chain (Exhibit 1).

Sam Walton's goal for Wal-Mart was continued, controlled, profitable growth. During the 1976–85 period the company recorded average annual compound rates of growth of 38.5 percent in sales and 42.6 percent in profitability (see Exhibit 2 for a 10-year financial summary). This was good enough to firmly establish Wal-Mart as one of the fastest-developing major retailers in the nation and to cause its NYSE-listed common stock to command a price-earnings ratio that was far and away the highest among the leading discount chains. One Wall Street securities analyst noted, "Wal-Mart leads all other companies of its type in every quantitative measure I know."

The company opened 103 new discount stores, 8 Sam's Wholesale Clubs (a

Exhibit 1 DISCOUNT DEPARTMENT STORE RANKINGS, 1984

	General merchandise volume 1984*	Net earnings 1984*	Number of stores	Net selling space†
1. K mart Corp.	$21,040	$492.9	2,196	125,500
2. Wal-Mart Stores, Inc.	6,268	270.8	642	43,115
3. Target Stores	3,550	235.6	230	22,481
4. Best Products Co., Inc.	2,253	13.6	214	6,420
5. Zayre Corp.	2,195	122.2	325	17,907
6. T.G.&Y.	2,020	n/a	733	21,650
7. Toys "R" Us, Inc.	1,701	111.4	233	5,825
8. Service Merchandise	1,607	44.6	290	5,800
9. Bradlees	1,404	82.5	150	10,538
10. Gemco National, Inc.	1,247	12.7	80	6,400

* In millions of dollars.
† In thousands of square feet.

* Prepared by graduate researcher Kem A. King under the supervision of Professor Arthur A. Thompson, Jr., The University of Alabama.

Exhibit 2 TEN-YEAR FINANCIAL SUMMARY, WAL-MART STORES, INC. AND SUBSIDIARIES
(dollar amounts in thousands except per share data)

	1976	1977	1978	1979
Earnings				
Net sales	$340,331	$478,807	$678,456	$900,298
Licensed department rentals and other				
income—net	3,803	5,393	7,767	9,615
Cost of sales	251,473	352,669	503,825	661,062
Operating, selling, and general				
administrative expenses	66,427	95,488	134,718	182,365
Interest costs:				
Debt	1,758	1,680	2,068	3,119
Capital leases	2,419	3,506	4,765	6,595
Taxes on income	10,925	14,818	19,656	27,325
Net income	11,132	16,039	21,191	29,447
Per share of common stock:				
Net income				
Primary	.10	.15	.19	.24
Full diluted	.10	.14	.18	.24
Dividends	.008	.011	.02	.028
Stores in operation at the end of the period				
Wal-Mart Stores	125	153	195	229
Sam's Wholesale Clubs	—	—	—	—
Financial position				
Current assets	$ 76,070	$ 99,493	$150,986	$191,860
Net property, plant, equipment,				
and capital leases	48,744	68,134	100,550	131,403
Total assets	125,347	168,201	251,865	324,666
Current liabilities	33,953	43,289	74,891	98,868
Long-term debt	17,531	19,158	21,489	25,965
Long-term obligations under capital				
leases	26,534	41,190	59,003	72,357
Preferred stock with mandatory				
redemption provisions	—	—	—	—
Common stockholders' equity	47,195	4,417	96,482	127,476
Financial ratios				
Current ratio	2.2	2.3	2.0	1.9
Inventories/working capital	1.5	1.6	1.8	1.9
Return on assets*	11.2	12.8	12.6	11.7
Return on stockholders' equity*	30.9	34.0	32.9	30.6

* On beginning of year balances.
Source: *1985 Annual Report.*

wholesale outlet that sold in bulk on a membership-only basis), and 1 Helen's Arts & Crafts store during 1984. On January 31, 1985, Wal-Mart had 745 Discount Cities and 11 Sam's Wholesale Clubs in operation in 20 states in the Southeast and Midwest (see Exhibit 3); plans called for entering Colorado and Wisconsin next. The company's aggressive store opening program reflected a strategy of saturating target rural market areas first and then entering that area's major population center, a process Sam Walton dubbed "backwards expansion." About 80 percent of all Wal-Mart stores were located in towns with a resident population of 15,000 or less and a "shopping area" draw of about 25,000 people. Wal-Mart's small town focus was Sam Walton's brainchild; his idea was that if Wal-Mart offered prices as good or better than stores in cities that were several hours away by car, people would shop at home.

Exhibit 2 *(concluded)*

1980	1981	1982	1983	1984	1985
$1,248,176	$1,643,199	$2,444,997	$3,376,252	$4,666,909	$6,400,861
10,092	12,063	17,650	22,435	36,031	52,167
919,305	1,207,802	1,787,496	2,458,235	3,418,025	4,722,440
251,616	331,524	495,010	677,029	892,887	1,181,455
4,438	5,808	16,053	20,297	4,935	5,207
8,621	10,849	15,351	18,570	29,946	42,506
33,137	43,597	65,943	100,416	160,903	230,653
41,151	55,682	82,794	124,140	196,244	270,767
.33	.43	.63	.91	1.40	1.91
.33	.43	.63	.91	1.40	1.91
.038	.05	.065	.09	.14	.21
276	330	491	551	642	745
—	—	—	—	3	11
266,617	$ 345,204	$ 589,161	$ 720,537	$1,005,567	$1,303,254
190,562	245,942	333,026	457,509	628,151	870,309
457,879	592,345	937,513	1,187,448	1,652,254	2,205,229
170,221	177,601	339,961	347,318	502,763	688,968
24,862	30,184	104,581	106,465	40,866	41,237
97,212	134,896	154,196	222,610	339,930	449,886
—	—	7,438	6,861	6,411	5,874
164,844	248,309	323,942	488,109	737,503	984,672
1.6	1.9	1.7	2.1	2.0	1.9
2.4	1.7	2.0	1.5	1.5	1.8
12.7	12.2	14.0	13.2	16.5	16.4
32.3	33.8	33.3	38.3	40.2	36.7

Walton's backwards expansion strategy called first for building a cluster of 30 or 40 Discount City stores in a targeted rural area within a 600-mile radius of a distribution center. Once stores were opened in most of the selected towns around a more populous city, Wal-Mart would locate one or more stores in the metropolitan area and begin major market advertising. When a geographic area approached its store saturation target, the expansion effort shifted to penetrating adjoining market areas.

Complementing the store location strategy were a number of management practices concerning people, planning, discipline, and challenge. From its inception, Wal-Mart had followed participatory management practices, extending from decision-making to profit-sharing plans involving each of the 81,000 Wal-Mart employees (called "associates"). At the Saturday morning associates meetings in Bentonville, new action thrusts were regularly announced and mapped out for all

---

Exhibit 3   LOCATIONS OF WAL-MART FACILITIES

★ General office and three distribution centers in Bentonville, Arkansas.

♦ Distribution centers in Mt. Pleasant, Iowa; Searcy, Arkansas; Palestine, Texas; Cullman, Alabama; and Douglas, Georgia (under construction).

● Sam's Wholesale Clubs (11 units in eight cities)

▲ Dot Discount Drug store in Des Moines, Iowa.

■ Helen's Arts and Crafts store in Springfield, Missouri.

Figures indicate the number of Wal-Mart stores in each state.

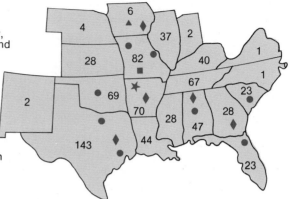

---

aspects of the business, ranging from what areas to expand in next, to what product lines to add, to how to better motivate associates. Wal-Mart believed it had to become a very cost-effective organization to reach its profit objectives via selling mostly name-brand merchandise at discount prices.

Driven by the need to be a low-cost operator, Wal-Mart modeled its warehouse-type, open-air store offices with two factors in mind: (1) to avoid the added cost of building and furnishing store offices and (2) to create a close feeling between store management and customers while promoting a better working bond between co-workers. Wal-Mart officers were so cost-control conscious that the company's total travel cost did not expand from 1983 to 1984 despite the opening of 95 new stores. Keeping costs low was also set up as a challenge for Wal-Mart associates to achieve, and Wal-Mart effectively used this challenge as a motivational technique. All stores were given the objective of achieving a 10 percent increase over the previous year's sales, and individual departments were pitted against one another to improve productivity in terms of sales per square foot. Sam Walton strongly advocated trying new ideas and suggestions, all the while recognizing that not all of what was tried would be successful.

SAM WALTON

> Sam Walton is the warmest, most genuine human being who's ever walked the face of the earth.
>
> *Bill Avery*
> *Wal-Mart management recruiter*

Walton graduated from the University of Missouri with a degree in business and began his retail career as a management trainee with the J.C. Penney Co., an experience that began to shape his thinking about department store retailing. His career with Penney's was interrupted by a stint in the military during World War II. When the war was over, Walton decided to open a Ben Franklin retail variety store in Newport, Arkansas, rather than return to Penney's. Five years later when the lease on the Newport building was lost, Walton relocated his Ben Franklin in Bentonville, Arkansas, where he bought a building and opened Walton's 5 & 10 as a Ben Franklin-affiliated store. During the next nine years, eight more Walton-owned Ben Franklin stores were opened in four states.

In 1961, Walton became very concerned about the long-term competitive threat to variety stores posed by the emerging popularity of giant supermarkets and discounters. Walton, an avid pilot, took off in his plane on a cross-country tour studying the changes in stores and retailing trends, then put together a plan for a discount store of his own. The first Wal-Mart Discount City was opened July 2, 1962, in Rogers, Arkansas. Twenty-three years later, Wal-Mart was a $6.4 billion company. In a 1985 *Forbes* magazine article, Sam Walton, at 67, was designated as the richest man in America based on his 39 percent ownership of Wal-Mart's common stock, worth about $2.8 billion at Wal-Mart's then current stock price of $51.

Despite his wealth and the demands placed upon his time as a result of the phenomenal growth of the Wal-Mart chain, Walton's outgoing personality and personal demeanor toward the Wal-Mart associates who worked for him were a source of admiration and inspiration. The comments of several associates indicated the regard and esteem he commanded:

> He's a beautiful man. I met him when this store opened. He came back two and one half years later and still remembered me. He walked over to this department and said, "Grace, you and I have been around a long time, I'm gonna hug your neck." That's just the type of guy he is. He's just a wonderful person.

> I was just . . . I was thrilled (to meet him). He's a very special person. He is a very outgoing person, and it kind of motivates you just to sit and listen to him talk. He listens—that's another thing.

> I think he's a fine person. He's just an everyday person like one of us. When you meet him he's just like one of us. You can talk to him. Anything you want to ask him—you can just go right up and ask.

> He's really down-to-earth. He'll put his arm around you, hug you, and tell you you're doing a good job.

> Mr. Walton cares about his employees. You get the feeling that you're working for him instead of Wal-Mart. And although he may not need the money, he's good to us and we try to be good to him.

WAL-MART'S NEAR-TERM GROWTH STRATEGY

Using Walton's backwards expansion strategy and aided by some acquisitions, Wal-Mart's 1-store operation in 1962 had become a 745-store operation in 1985, and the growth era seemed far from over. Wal-Mart's 1985 plans called for expanding in a number of directions simultaneously:

- Adding 20 percent more floor space in the form of 115 new store openings and the expansion of 60 existing stores (another 30 stores were scheduled for remodeling).
- Opening 10 to 12 new Sam's Wholesale Clubs and doubling the sales of this division.
- Adding several more units of Helen's Arts & Crafts.
- Opening one new DOT Discount Drug Store.
- Trying out 25,000- to 35,000-square-foot store prototypes in small communities (the regular Discount City store had 60,000 to 90,000 square feet of sales space).
- Installing electronic scanning devices at checkout counters in more than 200 stores so Universal Product Codes (UPC) could be used instead of price tags.
- Instituting a "Buy American" plan to give preference to stocking merchandise manufactured in the United States.

In mid-1985, Wal-Mart announced plans for capital expenditures of $250 million to construct 9 million square feet of additional retail space (a 22 percent increase over 1984). In terms of in-store sales growth, the company had a goal of $200 in sales per square foot (in 1985 Wal-Mart was realizing sales of $166 per square foot versus an industry average of around $100 per square foot). The company also began an "aggressive hospitality" program that featured a customer greeter at the front door of each store and enhanced efforts on the part of associates to "aggressively" make more contacts with shoppers, offering a cheerful word, a smile, help in finding items, and information about products.

NEW STORE INNOVATION

Wal-Mart's future was not dependent solely upon opening more Wal-Mart Discount Cities—Sam Walton was a strong advocate of continuously experimenting with new types of stores. Four new store prototypes were being explored. Wal-Mart intended to open several 25,000- to 30,000-square-foot Discount Cities in communities smaller than typical Wal-Mart towns. One Wal-Mart associate told the casewriter that since the smaller Discount City was only in the concept-testing phase, it was too early to know how it would mesh with other Wal-Mart growth options, but "it ought to be an interesting way to gain increased penetration of Wal-Mart's present geographic markets." The smaller stores were scheduled to carry a narrower selection of merchandise specially targeted to the tastes, incomes, and life-styles of rural area residents.

Another store prototype, Sam's Wholesale Club, a membership only, cash-and-carry warehouse, appeared in the Wal-Mart family in 1983. These stores were approximately 100,000 square feet in size and carried mostly best-selling brands of a particular item; a Sam's storefront is pictured in Exhibit 4. The concept of membership wholesale clubs represented a new retailing trend, and Wal-Mart was in the vanguard of companies trying to develop this segment (see Exhibit 5). Cash-and-carry warehouses were located in population centers and targeted the small-

Exhibit 4 SAMPLE LAYOUTS AND SCENES AT WAL-MART

Exhibit 5 MEMBERSHIP WAREHOUSE CLUBS				
	Volume in millions			
	Sales last fiscal year	**Sales previous fiscal year**	*Number of stores*	
Chain (headquarters)			**January 1985**	**January 1986**
Price Club (California)	$1,164	$643	19	25
Sam's Wholesale (Arkansas)	220	34	11	23
Makro (Ohio)	170	162	4	4
Warehouse Club (Illinois)	150	15	5	10
Value Club (Texas)	125	120	5	6
Costco (Washington)	102	0	12	21
Price Savers (Utah)	80	0	4	4
The Wholesale Club (Indiana)	46	11	3	5
BJ's Wholesale (Maryland)	40	0	3	6

business owner who was not able to buy directly from manufacturers or wholesalers in large enough quantities to receive bulk discounts. The merchandise mix stocked in Sam's was a variable because many products were bought whenever Wal-Mart ran across a special deal from suppliers. Expected operating margins were 8 to 9 percent of total sales. Three Sam's Wholesale Clubs were opened in 1983, and within two years 8 more were in operation, with plans to build another 10 to 12 by 1986. Small-business proprietors paid a $25 membership fee to join Sam's Wholesale Club; membership entitled them to buy materials at 10 percent above wholesale, prices that were cheaper than in the Wal-Mart Discount City stores. The idea of opening a Sam's Wholesale Club adjacent to a Wal-Mart Discount City was being considered as an experiment for 1986 or 1987.

In 1984 Wal-Mart opened its first Helen's Arts & Crafts store in Springfield, Missouri. The store carried a broader range of arts and crafts supplies than was generally found in a Wal-Mart store, plus assorted hobby equipment. Three more Helen's stores were opened in 1985, all with a full line of hobby equipment. The store sites selected were in free-standing or strip-store locations, not in connection with Wal-Mart Discount Cities, and were targeted to very selective markets. Although the markup in these stores was such that an excellent profit was made, plans for further expanding this prototype were not definite in 1986.

Wal-Mart also opened two DOT Discount Drug Stores in Des Moines and Kansas City. These were deep discount pharmacies that primarily carried a full line of drugs and personal care goods. As with the Helen's stores, the DOT stores were either free-standing or strip-stores and had no publicly visible Wal-Mart connection.

MARKETING POLICIES AND PROGRAMS

Leased Departments. Wal-Mart both owned and leased space for pharmacies and shoe departments in its Discount City stores. When Wal-Mart decided to add pharmacy departments to the Discount Cities, the strategy of leasing space to outside interests was a way of spreading the risk of adding previously untried lines of merchandise. But as one Wal-Marter put it, "We began leasing (pharmacies), and found we knew better than anyone else how to conduct our business—how to better enforce the Wal-Mart way, so we will continue to lease a few (pharmacies), but primarily will open our own." Plans called for deep discount pharmacies to be added to most existing stores. For similar reasons, all the leased shoe departments in the Discount Cities were scheduled to be acquired from Morse Shoe in three phases: 25 percent in February 1986; 25 percent in July 1986; and 50 percent in February 1987. Sales in leased-out departments totaled $117.2 million in 1985, $76.8 million in 1984, and $71.5 million in 1983; Wal-Mart's rental income from the leased space was $13.1 million in 1985, $10.2 million in 1984, and $7.3 million in 1983.

Products.   When customers walked into a Wal-Mart Discount City, it was very clear that Wal-Mart had a lot of merchandise to sell. Stock was stacked high along the walls and filled free-standing displays along narrow aisles. Wal-Mart tried to fully utilize the floor space in a Discount City without creating a cluttered look. In comparison to other well-known national chain stores, such as Sears and J.C. Penney, Wal-Mart was positioned as a deeper discounter and carried a narrower product line. In comparison to K mart, Wal-Mart stores had very much the same appearance, were somewhat smaller in square footage, packed more merchandise in a cleaner fashion into its sales spaces, and priced its merchandise at fractionally lower levels. The merchandise in Wal-Mart departments was a mixture of deeply discounted name brands and even lower priced off-brands. The front of every Wal-Mart store was emblazoned with the declaration "We Sell for Less" (see Exhibit 4).

In selecting which new items to carry and in experimenting with different merchandising techniques, Wal-Mart conducted tests in a selected market area to see if the new line or new merchandising technique was successful. If the item had successful sales figures in test stores, then it was "rolled out" or expanded to other stores.

Since the early 80s, Wal-Mart had increased the percentage of soft goods in its stores because of their higher gross margins. Wal-Mart also shifted toward more name brands. The women's clothing department began carrying more famous maker labels that appeared at lower-than-retail prices; plus-size and maternity-wear lines were also added.

A number of changes had recently been made to upgrade product offerings in the electronics department. The space given to LP records was cut back to make room for the addition of telephones. In larger stores, big-ticket items such as "boom-boxes" and home-and-go stereo units, with price tags ranging to $290 and $360, as well as videocassette recorders and cameras priced up to $1,000 were added. Some stores began to carry satellite dish TV receivers at prices exceeding $2,000. A film-processing plant was purchased in 1981 to support the camera department's activities and services. Name brand cameras, color video cameras, and videodisk players were added to lend credibility to the department and to help build customer traffic in the department.

These and other similar changes were all part of a "merchandise intensification" program that focused on adding more big-ticket items to the product mix. New lines added included paint, microwave ovens, jewelry, and an elementary education reading center. These complemented the merchandising of tried-and-true volume-producers such as housewares, garden supplies, auto supplies, health and beauty aids, and hardware. The newer "soft" items were added in expectation of producing both new store traffic and greater dollar sales per customer.

Customer Relations and Customer Service.   One store manager expressed to the casewriter that making the customer number one was what put Wal-Mart on top. He explained that Wal-Mart believed in standing behind the products it sold and said that it was much better for the company to replace a dissatisfied customer's merchandise and maintain a loyal patron than to chance incurring the wrath of the individual and the possibility of loss of future sales through negative publicity. Displayed above the door of every Wal-Mart store and even on the shopping bags was Wal-Mart's promise to its customers, "Satisfaction Guaranteed." Wal-Mart's newly instituted aggressive hospitality program represented an attempt by associates to provide "the warmest, most friendly, most helpful, and most appreciative environment in which to shop"—from the time the customers entered the store until they left.

When Wal-Mart associates were asked about their own customer relations activities, the following comments were made:

> The thing they teach us first is that the customer comes first and they pay our salaries, so always be nice to your customers, no matter what. That's the main thing, just always be nice to your customer. Always try to help your customer. Always go up to someone in your department and ask them if you can be of help— never be rude.

> That's one of our most important things—our customers. . . . We do our best to go out of our way for our customers.

> You're always supposed to drop what you're doing, the customer always comes first. Customer satisfaction—that's the Wal-Mart way. They start talking about that from day one.

> We're never supposed to point out where something is. We're supposed to take the customer to the item they're looking for.

> We try to please the customer. If they have any complaints we try to do something about it immediately. You know, the customers always come first at Wal-Mart.

PURCHASING AND WAREHOUSE DISTRIBUTION

Wal-Mart's buyers purchased merchandise in large quantities directly from the vendor and inventoried them in Wal-Mart distribution centers for shipment via Wal-Mart's own trucking fleet to Wal-Mart stores. Being able to receive bulk discount rates and to use its own distribution network gave Wal-Mart cost savings, which were in turn reflected in prices and profits. Approximately 70 to 80 percent of the merchandise was blanket ordered for all stores, although each store was allowed some latitude in stocking to meet differences in buying patterns. As one company official noted, "If you're in Cajun country in Louisiana and don't stock a crayfish pot, you're out of it."

Store managers telephoned their orders weekly into a central computer. Merchandise was then sorted by automated equipment onto the trucks and delivered to the stores, usually within a 24-to-48-hour period. Managers could swap stock between stores to assure that merchandise was sold and was in the best store location to meet customer demand.

The Buy American Plan.   One of Wal-Mart's newer purchasing programs was announced in 1985, the "Buy American" plan. In a letter sent to about 3,000 domestic vendors, dated March 14, 1985, Sam Walton discussed the "serious threat" of the nation's balance-of-trade deficit and conveyed his plans for carrying more U.S.-made goods in Wal-Mart's stores; yet, he assured the Buy American plan was not an anti-import effort:

> Our Wal-Mart company is firmly committed to the philosophy of buying everything possible from suppliers who manufacture their products in the United States. We are convinced that with proper planning and cooperation between retailers and manufacturers many products can be supplied to us that are comparable, or better, in value and quality to those we have been buying offshore.

In upholding his commitment to buying U.S.-manufactured goods, Walton offered longer lead times for placing orders and a willingness to take a lesser markup or to pay a slightly higher price for American-made goods. Walton added his own belief, "Wal-Mart believes our American workers can make the difference if management provides the leadership." Along with the Buy American program, Wal-Mart instituted a new promotional slogan: "Wal-Mart—Keeping America Working and Strong."

Projections by one store manager indicated that approximately 2,000 U.S. jobs had been saved as a result of the Buy American plan. In their search for American-made goods, Wal-Mart buyers located a flannel shirt maker in Arkansas who could supply shirts of an as good or better quality than those produced by the previous Hong Kong supplier; the Arkansas-made shirts were also obtained at a cost below what Wal-Mart was paying the Hong Kong supplier.

HUMAN RESOURCES

> The customer is Number 1; the sales associate is Number 2. You take care of those and the rest will just come along.
>
> *Bill Avery*
> *Wal-Mart management recruiter*

Wal-Mart's 81,000 employees were referred to as associates—a practice Walton insisted on from the outset. Walton preferred this term because it implied ownership, and Wal-Mart associates did have a stockholder interest through a profit-sharing plan that was transmitted to the associate through company stock. Walton believed when he first started Wal-Mart that if a partnership could be developed rather than an employer-employee relationship, the work would go a lot smoother. Associates were eligible to participate in the profit-sharing/stock ownership plan the month following one year of continuous full-time service in which the individual had worked 1,000 hours or more. At the end of an associate's second year of service, the company began contributing to the plan, in the associate's name, a certain percentage of its profits. The money, contributed solely by the company, became vested at the rate of 20 percent per year beginning the third year of participation in the plan. After seven years of continuous employment, the associate became fully vested; however, if the associate left the company prior to that time, the unvested portions were redirected into a company fund and redistributed to all remaining employees. As of January 1985, almost 2.2 million shares of stock had been issued under the profit-sharing/stock option plan.

Although only full-time associates were allowed to participate in Wal-Mart's benefits programs, one associate related that Wal-Mart did not try to hire a large ratio of part-time employees to avoid having to pay benefits. The associate indicated that in her store there was approximately a five-to-one full-time to part-time associate ratio.

Associates at Wal-Mart were hired at higher than minimum wage and could expect to receive a raise within the first year at one or both of two annual job evaluations. An associate told the casewriter that at least one raise was guaranteed in the first year if Wal-Mart planned to keep the individual on the staff. The other raise depended on how well the associate worked and improved during the year. At Wal-Mart, only the store managers were salaried. All other associates, including the department managers, were considered hourly employees.

Wal-Mart stressed participatory management from the top to the bottom, and listening was a very important part of each manager's job. It was not unusual to find Walton showing up on the loading docks at midnight with a bag of donuts to talk to the guys. One manager told the casewriter that up to 90 percent of his day was spent walking around the store communicating with the associates—praising them for a job well done, discussing how improvements could be made, listening to their comments, and soliciting suggestions. A steady stream of ideas from associates on how to improve performance was the rule rather than the exception. Moreover, Wal-Mart associates were encouraged to put their ideas into action, whether it was an associate contributing an idea for a sales contest or a corporate officer suggesting a new type of department or specialty store. According to Walton:

> Our philosophy is that management's role is simply to get the right people in the right places to do a job and then to encourage them to use their own inventiveness to accomplish the task at hand.

Task forces to evaluate ideas and to plan for future actions on those ideas were common; and it was not unusual for the person who developed the idea to be appointed the leader of the group. This encouraged a commitment to follow through on new ideas. Rewards for successful ideas took the form of companywide recognition such as mention in Saturday morning headquarters meetings and sometimes personal praise from Walton himself.

The planning process at Wal-Mart began with store management asking each associate what they could do individually or what could be changed to improve store operations. If anyone believed a policy or procedure detracted from operations, associates at all levels were encouraged to challenge and change it. "LTC" (low threshold for change) was a highly valued concept at Wal-Mart.

The Friday Morning Store Meetings.   On Friday morning, general store meetings were held in each Discount City store; associates at every level could ask questions and expect to get straightforward answers from management concerning departmental and store sales and cost figures, along with other pertinent store figures or information. The meeting might also include information on new company initiatives, policy change announcements, and perhaps video training films (the use of video films was a popular Wal-Mart training technique).

As David Glass, Wal-Mart's president and chief operating officer, said, "Most of us wear a button that says, 'Our People Make the Difference'—that is not a slogan at Wal-Mart, it is a way of life. Our people really do make a difference." Believing in this and encouraging superior performance was ingrained in all Wal-Mart staffers. Each week, department and store figures were posted on the back wall of the store. That way associates could see how their departments ranked against other departments and how the store was doing overall. If the figures were better than average, associates were praised verbally and given pats on the back; associates in departments that regularly outperformed the averages could expect annual bonuses and raises. When departmental per-

Exhibit 6   A SCENE FROM A WAL-MART SATURDAY MORNING MEETING AT HEADQUARTERS IN BENTONVILLE

formances came out lower than average, then the store manager would talk with department associates to see what was wrong and how it could be corrected.

The Saturday Morning Headquarters Meetings.   At 7:30 A.M. every Saturday morning since 1961, the top officers, the merchandising staff, the regional managers who oversaw the store districts, and the Bentonville headquarters' staff—over 100 people in all—gathered to discuss Wal-Mart issues (see Exhibit 6). Topics covered might include the week's sales, store payroll percentages, special promotion items, and any unusual problems. Reports on store construction, distribution centers, transportation, loss prevention, information systems, and so on were also given to keep everyone up-to-date.

The meetings were deliberately very informal and relaxed. Those attending might show up in tennis or hunting clothes so that when the meeting was over they could go on to their Saturday activities. The meetings, normally attended by Walton, were always up-beat and were sometimes begun by Walton "calling the hogs," a practice common in Arkansas razorback country. Walton used his cheerleading and hog-calling tactics to loosen everyone up, create some fun and excitement, and get things started on a stimulating note.

MANAGEMENT AND ASSOCIATE TRAINING

> At Wal-Mart we guarantee two things: Opportunity and hard work.
> *Bill Avery*
> *Wal-Mart management recruiter*

Management Training.   Wal-Mart managers were hired in one of three ways. Hourly associates could move up through the ranks from sales to department manager to manager of the check lanes into store management training. Second, people from other retail companies with outstanding merchandising skills were recruited to join the ranks of Wal-Mart managers. And third, Wal-Mart recruited college graduates to enter the company's management training program.

According to Wal-Mart's president:

> We create more opportunity for people in this company than most companies I know. If you want to advance, you can in Wal-Mart. If you want to do better, you can in Wal-Mart. If you don't like the area you are in and you want to try something else, the process we call crosspollinization, you can do that. If you have the desire and want to apply yourself, then we will work to help you do it. We involve our people in all of our areas.

Casewriter interviews with Wal-mart associates revealed a positive attitude concerning advancement opportunities and the company's work climate:

> You have the option to go as far as you want to go if you do a good job.

> It's up to you; if you do the work, you'll get the raises.

> I think it's a good place to work. There's a lot here (as far as advancement) if you want to work for it. It's a good open relationship with management. The benefits are good and the pay is above average for most discount stores.

The management training program involved two phases. In the first phase, the trainee completed a 16-week on-the-job training program:

Week 1	Checkouts/Service desk
Week 2	Cash office
Weeks 3 and 4	Receiving
Week 5	Invoicing
Weeks 6, 7, and 8	Hard-lines merchandising
Weeks 9 and 10	Merchandise office
Weeks 11, 12, and 13	Home and seasonal merchandising
Weeks 14, 15, and 16	Apparel merchandising

At designated times during Phase I, trainees were tested and evaluated by the store manager. During this time, the individual was encouraged to complete a "self-critique" of his or her own progress and the caliber of guidance being received from the training effort. At the end of Phase I, the trainee moved at once into Phase II.

The initial three weeks of Phase II were structured to cover such management topics as internal/external theft, scheduling, store staffing, retail math, merchandise replenishment, and the Wal-Mart "Keys to Supervision" series that dealt with interpersonal skills and personnel responsibilities. After completion of the first three weeks of Phase II, the trainee was given responsibility for an area of the store. The length of time during the remainder of Phase II varied according to the rate at which each trainee progressed. After showing good job performance, demonstrated leadership, and job knowledge, the trainee was promoted to an assistant manager. As an assistant manager, training continued with the Retail Management Training Seminar designed to complement the in-store training with other vital management fundamentals. With the quickly paced growth rate of Wal-Mart stores, the above-average trainee could progress to store manager within five years. Through bonuses for sales increases above projected amounts and company stock options, the highest-performing store managers earned salaries of around $70,000 to $80,000 annually.

To further promote management training, in November 1985 the Walton Institute of Retailing was opened in affiliation with the University of Arkansas. Within a year of its inception, every Wal-Mart manager from the stores, the distribution facilities, and the general office were expected to take part in special programs at the Walton Institute to strengthen and develop the company's mangerial capabilities.

Associate Training.   Wal-Mart did not provide a specialized training course for its hourly associates. Upon hiring, an associate was immediately placed in a position for on-the-job-training. From time to time, training films were shown in the Friday morning associates' meetings, but no other formalized training aids were provided by Wal-Mart headquarters. Store managers and department managers were expected to train and supervise the associates under them in whatever ways were needed.

A number of associates commented on the Wal-Mart training programs:

Mostly you learn by doing. They tell you a lot; but you learn your job every day.

They show you how to do your books. They show you how to order and help you get adjusted to your department.

We have tapes we watch that give us pointers on different things. They give you some training to start off—what you are and are not supposed to do.

The training program is not up to par. They bring new people in so fast. They try to show films, but it's just so hard in this kind of business. In my opinion you learn better just by experience. The training program itself is just not adequate. There's just not enough time.

We have all kinds of films and guidelines to go by, department managers' meetings every Monday, and sometimes we have quizzes to make sure we're learning what we need to know.

The most training you get is on the job—especially if you work with someone who has been around awhile.

MOTIVATION AND INCENTIVES

Developing new programs to encourage sales was one way Wal-Mart motivated its associates. One of Wal-Mart's most successful incentive programs was its VPI (Volume Producing Item) contests. In this contest, departments within the store were able to do special promotion and pricing on items they themselves wanted to feature. Management believed the VPI contests boosted sales, breathed new life into an otherwise slow-selling item, and helped keep associates thinking about how to help bolster sales; two sales associates commented on the VPI incentive scheme:

We have contests. You feature an item in your department and see how well it sells each week. If your feature wins, you get a half day off.

They have a lot of contests. If you're the top seller in the store you can win money. For four weeks in a row I've won money. That gives you a little incentive to do the very best you can. You kind of compete with other departments even though we're a big family in the long run. You like a little competition, but not too much.

Wal-Mart also had an incentive plan whereby associates received bonuses for "good ideas," such as how to reduce shoplifting or how to improve merchandising. As a result of the shoplifting reduction bonus plan, between 1977 and 1982 shrinkage dropped from 2.2 percent to 1.3 percent of total sales (as compared to an industrywide average of over 2 percent; in 1985 shrinkage dropped to a Wal-Mart record low of 1.06 percent). Fifty percent of the savings Wal-Mart realized from this shoplifting reduction plan was given to the associates as bonuses.

Another motivational tactic that Wal-Mart employed involved dress-up days in which associates dressed according to a theme (for instance, Western days or Halloween); these added fun and excitement for associates and the upbeat mood was transferred to the customer.

The Work Atmosphere at Wal-Mart.   Throughout company literature, comments could be found referring to Wal-Mart's "concern for the individual"; such slogans as "Our people make the difference," "We care about people," and "People helping People" were often repeated by Wal-Mart executives. "It's a lot of hard work, but it's so much fun," one Wal-Mart executive told this casewriter concerning his job with Wal-Mart. He indicated he enjoyed working for a company that promoted a concerned feeling toward its associates. He also stated that work at Wal-Mart was never dull. New challenges were always cropping up in the form of new products to be marketed or new merchandising techniques to be tested or implemented. In interviewing a number of Wal-Mart management associates, the casewriter was told several times that Wal-Mart was a wonderful place to work because of all the human resource practices carried out by the company.

> It's a special feeling you get when you walk in a Wal-Mart store. And when you're working there is when you really notice it because the people care about each other. It's like being with a successful football team, that feeling of togetherness, and everyone is willing to sacrifice in order to stay together.
>
> *Bill Avery*
> *Wal-Mart management recruiter*

In questioning Wal-Mart associates about how they liked working at Wal-Mart, a number of comments were made to the casewriter about the family-oriented atmosphere that was fostered at the store:

> There is no comparison between Wal-Mart and other places I've worked. Wal-Mart is far above. They just treat customers and associates really nice.

> It's more of a family-oriented place than anywhere I've ever worked. They seem to really care about their employees. It's not just the money they're making, but a true concern for the people working here.

> We're just like a family. Everybody cares for each other. The management is fantastic. You can go to them for anything and feel free to contradict them if you want to.

> They select such nice people to work with. We get along well.

> I care about my responsibilities. You're just more proud of it. You're more apt to care about it. You'll want people to come in and see what you've done. I guess the pats on the back let you know that what you've done is appreciated. And when they show their appreciation you're going to care more and do better.

> We're a united group. We may be from different walks of life, but once we get here we're a group. You may leave them at the door, but when you're in here you're part of a family. You help each other; you try to be everybody's friend. It's a united feeling.

To fire the managers up, Walton sent them and their spouses to a resort each year for strategy sessions and merchandising seminars. A highlight of the event was the spouses-only gripe-session. The program agenda was designed to reinforce Wal-Mart's down-home "concern for the individual" atmosphere.

Wal-Mart was founded and ingrained with old-fashioned beliefs that in 1985 still permeated the corporation. Restrictions on hiring persons over 65 were not formally lifted until Sam Walton himself approached the mandatory retirement age of 65. Other holdover practices that might seem out of step remained intact. For example, associates were not allowed to date one another without authorization from the executive committee. Women were rarely hired for executive positions. In 1985 only 12 (17 percent) of the merchandise buyers were women; and in 1984 Walton resisted naming a woman to the board of directors despite the urgings of Ferold G. Arend, a past president of Wal-Mart.

These old-line values did not seem to disturb any of the female associates at Wal-Mart. At the close of a number of interviews with the Wal-Mart associates, the casewriter asked the associate to relate what made Wal-Mart associates special and what made Wal-Mart so successful:

> They tell us that we are the best.

> I like working at Wal-Mart better than any other place. I'm freer to handle the work better. . . . I can go at my own speed and do the work the way I want to do it.

> I enjoy Wal-Mart; I've been here eight years. Of course, we work, but that's what we're here for. You've got potential with Wal-Mart.

> I think Wal-Mart is one of the best companies there is. I wouldn't want to work for anyone else.

> I think Wal-Mart is successful because it's geared to the needs of the average family from low-income families on up. And they have good merchandise. Since Wal-Mart has been here I've made very few trips to the city (30 miles away).

> Our low prices!!!

MANAGEMENT CHANGES AT WAL-MART HEADQUARTERS

Until 1984 Jack Shewmaker, 47, was president and chief operating officer. However, in late 1984 Shewmaker shifted to vice chairman and chief financial officer with responsibilities that included overseeing Sam's Wholesale Club, special divisions, data processing, real estate and construction, and finance and accounting. David Glass, 49, stepped in as president and chief operating officer at that time. The flip-flop in positions was explained as a means of giving both men an equal opportunity and the broad organizational experience for stepping into Walton's shoes when the time came. Robson Walton, 40, Sam Walton's eldest son, was also being prepared to assume the lead position.

FUTURE PROSPECTS AT WAL-MART

With a mind to the future, Wal-Mart planned to continue its established aggressive growth plans in terms of number of stores and sales increases. Two new southeastern distribution centers were to be completed in 1985, and a search was undertaken to locate a site for another distribution center in the western Wal-Mart territory. The western region distribution center would act as a springboard into greater western expansion. Top management indicated that people development would remain its number-one priority. Wal-Mart executives believed that in a growing company the decision-making process would have to be pushed to lower levels and that management at all levels would need to be broadened in preparation for that responsibility. Wal-Mart projected that sales would top $8 billion in fiscal 1986, up from $6.4 billion in 1985. During the bull market of early 1986, Wal-Mart's stock price set record highs and was selling at a price-earnings ratio of 34 to 1.

ELITE ELECTRIC COMPANY*

Elite Electric Company is a moderately small manufacturing subsidiary of a large European conglomerate. The company manufactures electric components supplied to its parent company for sale to consumer retail outlets as well as commercial distribution. Sales in 1978 were approximately $10 million and grew to $35 million in 1982. Elite Electric Company has two plants, one in Pennsylvania and the other in Massachusetts. The plant in Pennsylvania is relatively new and can manufacture three times the amount of units as the Massachusetts plant. The Massachusetts plant was established in the early 1920s and is on a large, beautifully manicured estate. The buildings are quite old, and the machinery is antiquated. However, the company headquarters is at the Massachusetts plant, and the company's president is insistent upon keeping both plants active. (See Exhibit 1 for the five-year production history of both plants.)

In order to cope with the growth of the company administratively, additional staff members were hired. However, there was no organized plan to establish systems and procedures for training, mechanization, etc., in anticipation of the increased work load and specialization of activities and functions that would eventually arise. People who had been with the company for a long time knew their assignments and, by and large, carried the company through its day-to-day activities. When many of these people left suddenly during a personnel reduction, an information void was created because there were few written procedures to guide those who remained and the replacement staff who were hired.

Another significant factor in the company's history was a very high level of employee turnover. Many of the losses in staff were in important positions, and all

---

Exhibit 1 FIVE-YEAR PRODUCTION HISTORY FOR ELITE ELECTRIC COMPANY (in units)

	1978	1979	1980 Mass.	1980 Penn.	1981 Mass.	1981 Penn.	1982 Mass.	1982 Penn.
Transistors (000s)	800	600	500	400	475	535	452	629
Large integrated circuit boards (000s)	475	479	325	201	300	227	248	325
Small integrated circuit boards (000s)	600	585	480	175	250	212	321	438
Large-capacity chips (millions)	1.2	1.1	700	506	600	700	571	927
Small-capacity chips (millions)	1.8	2.0	500	1.3	170	2.0	276	2.7
Cathode-ray tubes (000s)	325	250	210	22	126	46	147	63
Percent with defects	0.1	0.15	0.9	4.2	1.6	2.5	2.5	1.2

* New plant begins operations.

---

* Prepared by Barry R. Armandi, State University of New York, College at Old Westbury.

levels were affected. (Exhibits 2 and 3 show the organization charts for the company and the Massachusetts plant, respectively.)

THE MASSACHUSETTS PLANT

The president of the company, William White, originally came from LTV, which is located in Dallas, Texas. From there he was recruited to be plant operations manager in Massachusetts. When the original owners sold out to the European concern, White was made president. In early 1980, he opened the Pennsylvania plant.

As president, White developed a managerial philosophy based on six principles:

Make product quality and customer service a top priority.

Foster a human-oriented working atmosphere.

Maximize communication, interaction, and involvement.

Minimize the layers of organizational structure and control the growth of bureaucracy.

Value and respect our form of company organization.

Strive for excellence in our business performance.

Exhibit 2 ELITE ELECTRIC COMPANY ORGANIZATION CHART (1982)

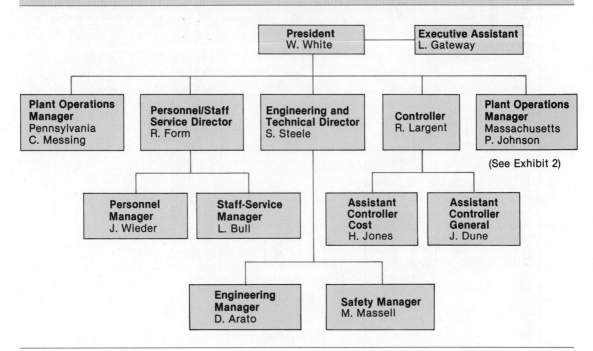

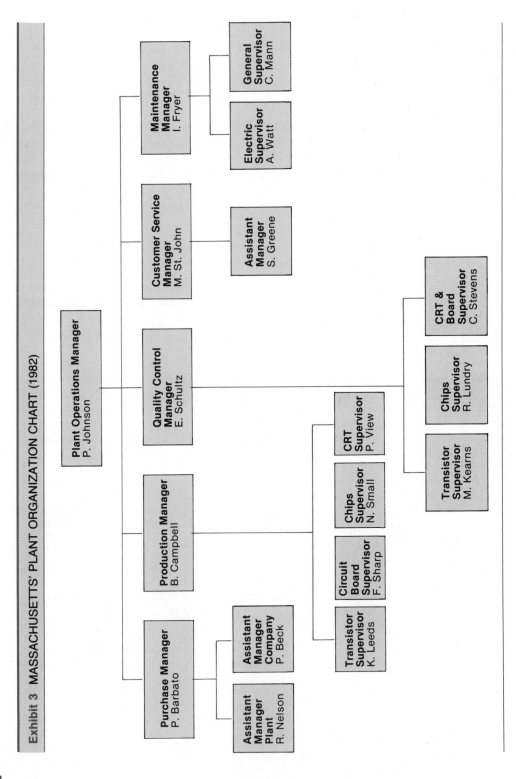

Exhibit 3 MASSACHUSETTS' PLANT ORGANIZATION CHART (1982)

Plant Operations Manager
P. Johnson

Purchase Manager
P. Barbato

Production Manager
B. Campbell

Quality Control Manager
E. Schultz

Customer Service Manager
M. St. John

Maintenance Manager
I. Fryer

Assistant Manager Plant
R. Nelson

Assistant Manager Company
P. Beck

Transistor Supervisor
K. Leeds

Circuit Board Supervisor
F. Sharp

Chips Supervisor
N. Small

CRT Supervisor
P. View

Transistor Supervisor
M. Kearns

Chips Supervisor
R. Lundry

CRT & Board Supervisor
C. Stevens

Assistant Manager
S. Greene

Electric Supervisor
A. Watt

General Supervisor
C. Mann

Upon being appointed president in 1979, White promoted Peter Johnson to the position of plant operations manager from his previous position of production manager. White told Johnson that he (Johnson) had a lot to learn about running a plant and to go easy with changes until he got "his feet wet." He also indicated that with the projected operation of the new plant the following year, Johnson should expect some reduction in production demand, but White felt this would be temporary. Further, White emphatically reminded Johnson of the company's philosophy and operating principles.

While White was plant operations manager, he initiated daily meetings with eight people: the purchasing manager (Paul Barbato); the production manager (Brian Campbell); the quality control manager (Elizabeth Schultz); the engineering manager (David Arato); the safety manager (Martin Massell); the personnel manager (Jane Wieder); a representative from customer service (Michael St. John); and an accounting representative (Harvey Jones).

When Johnson took over, he decide to continue the daily meetings. In 1979, after discussing problems of the company at an open meeting, it was decided that individuals from various other line and staff areas should attend the daily meetings. The transcript of a typical meeting is given below.

Peter Johnson: OK, everybody, it's 9 o'clock, let's get started. You all know what the agenda is, so let's start with safety first.

Martin Massell (safety manager): Well, Peter, I have a number of things to go over. First, we should look into feedback from maintenance. The other day we had an incident where the maintenance crew was washing down the walls and water leaked into the electrical wiring. Nobody was told about this, and subsequently seepage began Friday and smoke developed.

Peter Johnson: OK, we will have maintenance look into it and they will get back to you. What else, Marty?

Martin Massell: We found out that the operators of the fork lifts are operating them too fast in the plant. We are sending out a memo telling them to slow down.

David Arato (engineering manager): Why don't we just put some bumps in the floor so they can't speed over them.

Martin Massell: Well, we are looking at that. We may decide to do it, but we have to get some cost estimates and maintenance will have to fill us in.

Peter Johnson: By the way, where is the representative from maintenance . . . well, I will have to contact Irving (maintenance manager). Anything else, Marty?

Martin Massell: Oh yeah, I forgot to tell you yesterday the entire loading dock has been cleaned. We shouldn't be having any more problems. By the way, Brian, make sure you contact Irv about the spill in the area.

Brian Campbell: Oh, I forgot to tell you, Peter, but Irv said that we would have to close down machines 1 and 6 to get at the leak that is causing the oil spill. I have already gone ahead with that.

Peter Johnson: Gee, Brian, I wish you would clear these things with me first. How badly will this affect our production?

Brian Campbell: Not badly, we should be able to get away with a minimum of overtime this weekend.

Peter Johnson: Customer service is next. Mike, how are we doing with our parent company?

Michael St. John (customer service): Nothing much. We are starting to get flack for not taking that Japanese order, but the guys at the parent company understand. They may not like it, but they can deal with it. Oh, Paul, are you going to have enough transistors on hand to complete that order by next Tuesday?

Paul Barbato (purchasing manager): Sure, Mike, I sent you a memo on that yesterday.

Michael St. John: Sorry, but I haven't had a chance to get to my morning mail yet. I was too busy with some visitors from Europe.

Peter Johnson: Are these people being taken care of Mike? Is there anything we can do to make their stay here more comfortable?

Michael St. John: No, everything is fine.

Peter Johnson: OK, let's move on to employee relations, Jane.

Jane Wieder (personnel manager): I would like to introduce two guests from Training Programs, Inc. As you know, we will be embarking upon our final training program shortly. The grievance with Al Janow has been resolved. At the management/employee meeting last week, an agreement was reached that a representative from each department would attend. As you are aware, this meeting is once a month. It's funny, the biggest complaint at the meeting was an extra chair for the conference room (laughter). The interview workshop memo is done, Peter, and here it is. Also, Peter, we have to work on a posting of dates for the annual family get-together. I don't know if July will work out.

Michael St. John: July does not look that good. We have a great deal of overtime since that Australian order is due the beginning of August. Can we push it up to June?

Harvey Jones (accounting representative): Don't forget that in June, revised budgets are due. (The meeting continues to discuss the best date for the annual family get-together for another 15 minutes.)

Jane Wieder: One more thing, please notify us of any changes in marital status, address, etc. We have to keep our records up to date. Also, please be advised that the company cars can be purchased by employees. Sales will take place through a lottery system.

David Arato: Will we get a memo on this?

Jane Wieder: Yes, I will have one out by the end of the week.

Peter Johnson: Let's move on to quality control. Elizabeth?

Elizabeth Schultz (quality control manager): Our number 1 and 8 machines have been throwing out bent transistor leads. Over the weekend, these two machines will be down. Irv and Brian are aware of this. We have to straighten out this problem before we do the order from IBM. I have also noticed that the last gold shipment had some other metals in it. Paul, can you check this out to see what was the problem?

Paul Barbato: What amount of extraneous metals was present?

Elizabeth Schultz: We didn't do complete tests of the material, but it seems 5 ounces per 100 pounds.

Paul Barbato: That doesn't seem to be a significant amount.

Elizabeth Schultz: Well, it is according to our estimates, and I would like it to be checked out.

Peter Johnson: OK, Elizabeth, Paul will look into it. Now let's turn to production.

Brian Campbell: Last Monday we manufactured 3,000 transistors. Machines 1, 2, and 8 did 300, machines 2 and 4 were down, and the rest of the production was done by the remaining machines. On Tuesday we had to change to produce the larger integrated circuits that were needed by Control Data. We had two hours of down time to change the machines. Machines 6 and 7 did 20 percent out of the total production run of 5,000 boards. Machine 1 continued to manufacture the small transistorized chips, with machines 2 and 5 completing the rest of the integrated circuit board runs (at about this time, two people got up and walked out of the room as Brian was talking). Wednesday we switched back to the transistor runs on all machines. Unfortunately, machine 2 was down for the entire day, and machine 7 was up for preventive maintenance. We manufactured 2,700 transistors. Machines 4, 5, and 8 did approximately 60 percent of the work (a number of people started yawning). Thursday we produced only 1,000 transistors and had to ship part of our run to the cathode-ray tube production for Digital Equipment Corp. We produced 500 units for Digital. Machines 3, 4, and 5 were used for the DEC run, and machines 1, 2, and 8 were kept on the transistor production. Machine 7 was down. On Friday we had half a day and in the morning we had a blackout and were only able to get 100 transistors and 22 cathode-ray tubes done.

Peter Johnson: Brian, do you think you will be able to make up the rest of the order this week without much overtime?

Brian Campbell: I don't know. I think we should talk to Harry (Harry Brown was the union representative).

Peter Johnson: That may be difficult since Harry is on vacation, but I will try to get in touch with him. If I can't, let's go ahead with it anyway and we will take the consequences. All right, let's go around the room and see what anybody has to say.

Paul Barbato: Nothing.

Brian Campbell: Dave, I want to talk to you about the machine changeover and also if we can design a better ramp.

Elizabeth Schultz: Peter, can I see you after the meeting to discuss a personal matter?

David Arato: Nothing.

Martin Massell: I just wanted to let everyone know that we had a problem in one of the machine wells. It appears that while they were pouring some concrete around the well, some slipped in and it took us a couple of days to get it cleaned up.

Jane Wieder: Paul, see me on Mary Bernstein's problem.

Michael St. John: Just wanted to let you know we may be getting a very big order from Grumman.

Harvey Jones: The following people have not reported their exempt status to payroll (he lists about 12 individuals). Remember this was from Jane's memo about three weeks ago.

Peter Johnson: Brian, I want to take a tour with a couple of people from the university next week. I will call you and set something up. OK? Good meeting. See you tomorrow, same time, same place.

VILLAGE INN*

The Village Inn, located on Bermuda Boulevard in San Diego, was only a few blocks away from San Diego State University and was within several miles of some of California's largest tourist attractions. Visiting lecturers, speakers, professors interviewing for jobs, and people attending conferences at the university resulted in a considerable amount of business for Village Inn.

The inn was also near a concentrated area of light and heavy industry. The largest shopping mall in San Diego was under construction across the street from the inn. A relatively new Veterans Administration hospital and the University Community Hospital were both located within one mile. The inn's very favorable location, together with the fact that it was a franchise of a major national chain, had made it a profitable investment. During the past 12 months, the inn had an average occupancy rate of between 65 and 70 percent, some 15 or more percentage points above the break-even occupancy rate of 50 percent.

Although the Village Inn had only modest competition from other hotel or motel facilities in the immediate vicinity, a new Travelodge Inn was under construction next door. The other closest competitors were nearly three miles away at the intersection of Bermuda Boulevard and Interstate 8. Village Inn offered a full range of services to its guests, including a restaurant and bar. The new Travelodge next door was going to have just a coffee shop. Insofar as its restaurant/bar business was concerned, the Village Inn's strongest competitor was the popular priced University Restaurant, two blocks away. Village Inn did not consider its own food service operations to be in close competition with the area's fast-food franchises or with higher priced restaurants.

OWNERSHIP OF VILLAGE INN

Mr. Johnson, a native of Oregon, opened the first Village Inn in San Diego in 1958. Since that time he had shared ownership in 15 other Village Inns, several in the San Diego area. He opened the Bermuda Boulevard Inn in October 1966. Prior to his focusing on the motel and restaurant business, Johnson had owned and operated a furniture store and a casket manufacturing plant. A suggestion from a business associate in Oregon influenced his decision to seek Village Inn franchises and get into the motel business. In some of his Village Inn locations, Johnson leased the restaurant operations; however, the restaurant and bar at the Bermuda Boulevard Village Inn were not leased. Johnson felt that because the occupancy rate at his location was so favorable, it was more profitable to own and operate these facilities himself.

---

* Prepared by Diana Johnston, Russ King, and Professor Jay T. Knippen, the University of South Florida.

MANAGEMENT OF THE INN

Johnson had employed Mrs. Deeks as the innkeeper and manager of the entire operation. She had worked in Village Inns for the past seven and one-half years. Previously, Deeks had done administrative work for San Diego General Hospital and before that had been employed as a photo lab technician for two years. Her experience in the motel/restaurant business included working for several restaurants and lounges for five years as a cocktail waitress just before joining Village Inns.

Deeks stated that her main reason for going to work for Village Inns was because she felt there was more money to be made as a waitress than anything else she had tried. Her formal education for her present position of innkeeper consisted of a three-week training course at the Home Office Training Center in Louisville, Kentucky, and one-week refresher courses each year at the center.

Recently the assistant innkeeper had been promoted and transferred to another location. Both Johnson and Deeks agreed that there was a pressing need to fill the vacancy quickly. It was the assistant innkeeper's function to supervise the restaurant/bar area and this was the area that always presented the toughest problems to management. Unless the food was well prepared and the service was prompt, guests were quick to complain. Poor food service caused many of the frequent visitors to the area to prefer to stay at other motels. Moreover, it was hard to attract and maintain a sizable lunchtime clientele without having well-run restaurant facilities. With so many restaurant employees to supervise, menus to prepare, and food supplies to order, it was a constant day-to-day struggle to keep the restaurant operating smoothly and, equally important, to see that it made a profit. Deeks, with all of her other duties and responsibilities, simply did not have adequate time to give the restaurant/bar enough close supervision by herself.

While searching for a replacement, Johnson by chance happened to see a feature article in the *Village Inn Magazine,* a monthly publication of the Village Inns of America chain—copies of which were placed in all of the guest rooms of the inns. The article caught Johnson's attention because it described how a successful Village Inn in San Bernardino had gained popularity and acclaim from guests because of the good food and fast service provided by the head chef of the restaurant operations. After showing the article to Deeks, Johnson wasted no time in getting in touch with the head chef of that inn, Mr. Bernie, and persuading him to assume the new role of restaurant/bar manager for the Bermuda Boulevard Village Inn in San Diego.

FOOD SERVICE FACILITIES AND LAYOUT

Exhibit 1 depicts the arrangement of the lobby area and food service facilities at the inn. A brief description of the restaurant/bar area follows.

Restaurant. The restaurant itself consisted of a dining room that seated 74 people, a coffee shop that seated 62 persons, and a bar that seated 35 people. The inn's banquet facilities were just behind the main dining room and could seat 125 people.

MAIN BUILDING

The essential role of the restaurant and bar area was to provide pleasant and convenient facilities for the inn's guests. The contractual franchise agreements with the national chain required all owners to provide these services in conjunction with the overnight accommodations. There were periodic inspections of the facilities by a representative from Village Inn's corporate office. Village Inn required each franchisee to comply with minimum standards for its food service facilities in an effort to promote comparability and ensure attractiveness. Restaurant services were to be available to guests from 6:30 A.M. until 11 P.M.

Coffee Shop. The coffee shop was open from 6:30 A.M. to 11 A.M. to serve breakfast to motel guests. At 11 A.M., these facilities were closed and the main dining area was opened. The coffee shop was occasionally used beyond scheduled hours to serve customers for lunch and dinner when there was an overflow from the dinning area. Tables in both the coffee shop and the dining room were decorated and set uniformly.

Dining Room. The dining area was open from 11 A.M. until 11 P.M. It was located next to the lounge and was physically separated from the coffee shop by a wall. The lunch and dinner offerings featured a salad bar along with menu items that were somewhat uniform with other Village Inns and were prescribed by the franchise agreement. However, menu deviations were allowed if approved by corporate representatives from Village Inn's central office.

Bar. The bar, separated from the dining room by a partition, was open for business from 10 A.M. until 1 A.M. It had tables and booths, and customers who preferred to do so could have their food served to them in the bar area. A small dance floor was located in front of the entertainer stage near the front window; a juke box furnished music when there was no live entertainment. A small bar stockroom was located at one end of the bar counter. The cash register area was centrally located to receive payments from customers in all three areas—dining room, coffee shop, and bar.

Kitchen. The kitchen facilities, located beside the coffee shop and dining room, had a stainless steel counter at the entrance door from the restaurant area. It was here that waitresses turned orders in to the cooks and that the cooks served the orders up to the waitresses. The cooking area was located in the center of the room and sinks were located along the sides of the kitchen.

RESTAURANT OPERATIONS

As was to be expected, customer traffic in the restaurant fluctuated widely. Busy periods were generally at the traditional meal hours, but the peak load at any given mealtime period often varied by as much as an hour from one day to the next. At lunchtime, for example, customers sometimes seemed to come all at once, while on other days the arrival times were more evenly distributed throughout the 11:30 A.M. to 1:30 P.M. interval. Experience had shown that these peaks were hard to anticipate and that the staff had to be prepared for whatever occurred. Moreover, on Monday, Tuesday, Wednesday, and Thursday evenings, the customers were mostly businesspeople, sales representatives, and university visitors, whereas on weekends there were more family travelers. Because of the inn's location, its clientele consisted somewhat more of the former than the latter.

The inn's restaurant business was also subject to some seasonal fluctuations. There were always a certain number of people who spent the winter in Southern California to escape the harsh northern and Canadian winters; these included not only winter tourists but also the "Canadian Snow Birds" who came to Southern California to work in the late fall and returned to Canada in March or April. In addition, the inn's business picked up noticeably during the June graduation exercises at San Diego State University and during the week when the fall term opened. By and large, the daily fluctuations were harder to predict than the seasonal fluctuations.

RESTAURANT STAFFING

Because of the alternating between peak periods and slack periods, the employees in the food service area tended to work together, take breaks together, and eat their meals together. In commenting on the kind of people who tended to work in hotel-motel operations, Deeks indicated that employees were typically gregarious and were there because they wanted to be. They had to contend with an uneven work pace, a low-wage scale (often no more than the minimum wage), and irregular working hours. Since waitresses earned only a token wage and relied mainly on tips for their income, they could not afford many "slow days" or "bad days" at work. Their livelihood and degree of service was dependent upon how well they greeted customers, a friendly smile, prompt service, and, in general, an ability to make customers feel satisfied with the attention they received. When the food was cold or ill-prepared or the service less than expected, customers left smaller tips and the waitresses' disgruntlement carried over to the kitchen staff, the hostess, and the busboys. But even more disruptive than the loss of tips were the customers who complained directly to the inns' management; if this occurred frequently, then the pressure and anxiety felt by the restaurant staff increased noticeably. Deeks noted that people who could not adjust to the tempo and temperament of the restaurant business usually did not stay in it long. She noted further that it was extremely difficult to "standardize" the human service aspects of the restaurant business and that trying to attract and keep a good, experienced food service staff was a challenging task.

Deeks supplied the following job descriptions of the restaurant staff. These descriptions, however, came from her thoughts and perceptions and had never been formally set forth in writing to the inn's employees:

Bartender. Cut up fruit for drinks, wash glasses, serve counter drinks, clean behind bar, stock liquor and mixes, stock beer, fill room service orders, ring up checks, balance register, and help with inventory.

Hostess/Cashier. Take room service orders, seat guests, deliver menu, direct seating, supervise waitresses and busboys, perform any functions within their prescribed area that speeds service, check out customers from dining area, check out register, file cash register receipts, and assign stations.

Waitresses. Take food orders, deliver orders to kitchen, pick up and serve food orders, serve beverages, and perform any function that speeds service as directed by the hostess.

Busboys. Bus tables, put clean place settings on tables, clean dining rooms, stock supplies, take ice to all areas, get supplies for cooks, help set up banquets, deliver room service orders, help with maintenance, and perform any function that will speed service as directed by the hostess and manager.

Dishwasher. Wash dishes, pots, and pans, sweep and mop floors.

Cook. Prepare meals, schedule meals for prep cook, assist management in ordering supplies, receive food supplies, supervise and direct kitchen help, and assist management in menu changes. Report to management any changes or problems that occur.

Prep Cook.   Prepare all food that the cook needs for the dinner and evening meals. Assist cook in any meal preparation that is necessary to expedite service to guests. Inform cook of any problems that need attention and help cook see that facilities are clean at all times.

Breakfast Cook.   Open the kitchen in the morning. Prepare breakfast food for motel guests. Provide information necessary to maintain in-stock supplies.

MR. BERNIE

When Mr. Bernie arrived to assume his new duties as restaurant/bar manager, he wasted no time in demanding and receiving total obedience from the personnel under his direction. He made it clear that he would not tolerate insubordination and that the consequence would be immediate discharge. Although Bernie stayed in his new job less than three months (from January to March), he nonetheless created an almost instantaneous climate of ill will and hatred with his subordinates. The intense dislike for Bernie was voiced by nearly every employee. One example of this was a statement by Elaine, the day hostess/cashier who had been employed in this capacity for the past two and one-half years: "I enjoy my job because I like people. But Mr. Bernie was something else! I generally do not use this term in my vocabulary, but Mr. Bernie was a bastard from the day he arrived until the day he left."

Bernie's unpopularity was further brought out by a busboy's impromptu comment. Elaine was trying to possibly justify Bernie's temperament by pointing out that he was not of American nationality. Unable to recall his nationality she inquired of a nearby busboy if he could remember. The busboy immediately and sincerely replied, "He crawled out from under a rock."

Bernie spent considerable time trying to impress upon his staff the "right way" (his way) of accomplishing tasks (see Exhibits 2 and 3). Most of the employees resented Bernie's close supervision. Ann, a veteran employee and

---

Exhibit 2   MEMO NUMBER ONE FROM MR. BERNIE TO FOOD SERVICE STAFF

People,
> Please help keep the floor clean.
> If you drop something, pick it up.
> Wipe table off in a trash can.
> If you spill something the mops and brooms are outside.
> It's no fun scrubbing the floor Saturday, and if you don't believe it, be here Saturday night at 11:00 P.M.

Mr. "B"

Exhibit 3 MEMO NUMBER TWO FROM MR. BERNIE TO FOOD SERVICE STAFF

March 11

TO ALL FOOD AND BEVERAGE EMPLOYEES:

I wish to thank each and every one of you for the very good job you have done in the past two weeks. The service has greatly improved on both shifts. There has been a better customer/employee relationship, but there is a long way to go yet. We are nearing the end of our winter season so it is most important to all of us that we concentrate on more service in order to obtain a local year-round business. Appearance, neatness, and good conduct on the floor will obtain this, along with good food.

A waitress and busboy are like salesmen. The hostess/cashier can determine the quality of service in this organization.

I expect my waitresses while on duty to be on the dining room cafe floor at all times. I should find waitresses and busboys at the cashier stand only when getting a ticket or paying a check.

I smoke myself—probably more than the rest of you put together. Your service area is beginning to look like a cigarette factory. I do not expect people to give up their smoking habits, but I do expect them to conform to the rules and regulations of Village Inn, Inc., and those of the health department, "No Smoking on Premises." I would not like to enforce the law.

In the last two weeks I have walked into the operation after a busy breakfast or dinner and found everyone sitting around the first three booths of the cafe. I do not say it cannot be used, but when I find no waitresses on either floor day or night and customers have to call for service because waitresses are off the floor, I believe each waitress and busboy on all shifts should ask themselves one thing; what kind of service would I like if I were a guest? There is only one thing I know, in this part of California when the tourist is gone, half of the employees work on a part-time basis, which is not good on anyone's pocketbook. Therefore, I say let's not be second best but let's be first.

With regard to employees taking their meal breaks, I do not wish to schedule them but I cannot have everyone eating at once. Busboys will eat one at a time.

Thank you once again for your good performance.

Mr. "B"

---

waitress, describing her resentment, said, "No one really needs to supervise us, especially the way Mr. Bernie stood over us. Usually the hostess is the supervisor, but all the old girls know what they are doing and everyone does their job."

Although an intense dislike for Bernie was foremost in the minds of the employees, he did make a number of improvements and innovations. Physical changes became obvious within all departments under his authority. In the kitchen, a general cleanup campaign was instituted, an order spindle was added, and new oven equipment installed. In the coffee shop and restaurant, new silverware, china, and glasses were purchased, and the menu was improved and complemented by the use of a salad bar. Explicit work duties were written and verbally defined to all employees under Bernie.

Bernie separated the cashier/hostess function into two distinct jobs. The cashier was confined to the cash register station and given instructions as to the duties she was to perform in that area. The hostess was given instructions to greet people, seat them, and supply menus. When Bernie was absent, he instructed the hostess to see that the waitresses and busboys carried out their jobs efficiently and effectively. According to Gay, one of the two day hostesses:

When Mr. Bernie was here I never had any employee problems. Waitresses and busboys did what I asked. But now if we have a busboy absent or we are crowded, some of the waitresses inform me they will not bus tables. Today there's no one in charge of anything. We need more employees here. It is always better to have more help than not enough. That's one thing Mr. Bernie did, he doubled the help the day he came.

The changes that Bernie instituted regarding the waitresses were significant in several aspects. All waitresses were required to wear fitted uniforms. This necessitated them driving across town for a uniform fitting. Bernie's detailed scrutinizing consisted of specific instructions on how to serve customers and which station locations each waitress would serve. He even went as far as to show them how to wrap the silverware and the napkins and gave explicit instructions to veteran waitresses on how to fill out the order tickets.

Bernie had the wall between the dining room and bar taken down. He then brought in an entertainer who supplied dinner music for both the restaurant and bar guests. Today the waitresses are getting some dysfunctional effects from this innovation; according to one:

Mr. Bernie brought in an organ player. While this was conducive to a more pleasant dining atmosphere, the organist was not good enough to keep the people beyond their meal. But now that Mr. Bernie is gone our new entertainer is causing some serious problems. For example, last night I had a family of five sit at a table in my station for two and a half hours after their dinner. If people won't leave and they won't buy drinks, I can't make tips.

Bernie instilled an atmosphere of insecurity and day-to-day doubt in the minds of the employees as to how long they could weather the barrage of innovation and directives. To some, just remaining on the job became a challenge in itself. Elaine (the day hostess) phrased it in this manner:

I have been employed with the Villiage Inn for almost two and one half years. I have worked most of my life and have never felt insecure in any of my jobs. The last job I held was a swimming instructor for 10 years with the Academy of Holy Names in San Diego. The reason I had to leave there was because of the change in the educational background requirement, which called for a college degree.

My children are all college graduates with highly responsible positions. They achieved this by hard work. I instilled this in their minds because I am a hard worker. But when Mr. Bernie was here, I experienced for the first time in my life the feeling of not knowing from one day to the next if my job would be there when I came to work. What few personnel he failed to drive away, he fired.

Linda, who was a bartender in the lounge area, commented further on Bernie's supervisory tactics:

Bernie was a rover. When he walked into an area, including my area, the bar, he could not stand to see someone not involved with busy work. He even made me clean under the bar on the customer's side. I'm not a maid and I often wanted to tell him so. But the way he was hiring and firing employees, I just kept my mouth closed and did as he told me. My experiences with Mr. Bernie were nothing compared to the relationship he had with the busboys. From the bar he would sneak around and watch them in the dining area. If they did anything the least bit out of line, he would call them aside and give them lectures that could last for half an hour. He really treated the busboys like the scum of the earth. When the boys did get a break, they would come over to the bar and get a coke and ice. You know, he even started charging them 25 cents for that!

Sam, a cook hired by Bernie, offered a slightly different perspective view of Bernie:

My wife was working here as a hostess and I used to bring her to work everyday. One day I came in with her and for some reason they were short of help in the kitchen. They needed a dishwasher. I was sitting in the coffee shop and Mr. Bernie walked over and asked me if I could use a job. I had been interested in cooking ever since I was in the Navy. There are two things you can do in your spare time in the Navy . . . drink and chase women or find a hobby. I found a hobby, which was cooking. On my two days off, I used to go down to the galley and help the cooks. There I learned everything I know today. When I got out of the service I worked as a prep cook in a restaurant in Pennsylvania for a year or so. My real specialty is soups, though. Anyway, I had been a dishwasher here for about two days when the cook walked off the job after three years of service here. Mr. Bernie came in and asked how I'd like to be the new cook and here I am today. Mr. Bernie really taught me a lot. He taught me that a restaurant has three things it must give a customer: service, good food, and a pleasing environment to dine. If you have these three, customers will return.

I've spent most of my working career in the automotive business doing such things as driving trucks. But I'm really into this cooking thing. Mr. Bernie taught me that about 50 percent of the customers who come in and order from the menu have no idea what they are ordering. The menu is too complicated. The customer doesn't know what he thinks he ordered and what you think he ordered. Another thing that fascinates me is trying to think like the customer. His definition of rare, medium, and well done is altogether different from my idea of how it should be. One addition by Mr. Bernie was the salad bar. This is a tremendous help to my job. If the waitress can get to the customer before they go to the salad bar and take their order, this gives me plenty of lead time to be sure the meal will be cooked right and served in the attractive manner that Mr. Bernie was so particular about. This lead time is especially important on those days that we are unusually busy. For example, I have prepared as many as 250 meals on some days and as few as 40 on others.

The employees who left or were dismissed by Bernie included two hostesses, two waitresses (one had an employment record at the inn that dated back five years), and two busboys. Two of the personnel that Bernie fired have since returned to their old jobs. One of the waitresses that subsequently was rehired described her reason for leaving as follows:

I really enjoy being a waitress and have been here for about five years. The work isn't really too hard and the pay is good. I took all the "directives" I could take from Mr. Bernie! A week before he left, I gave my resignation and took a vacation. When I returned, I learned of his departure and here I am again. I'm really glad things have worked out as they did.

Deeks' opinion of Bernie's performance was one of general dissatisfaction with the way he handled his dealings with employees:

> Mr. Bernie was highly trained, but he was an introvert who stood over his subordinates and supervised everything they did. Cooks are a rare breed of people all to themselves. The help situation has changed greatly in the past few years. It used to be that you could give orders and tell people what they were supposed to do. Now, you have to treat them with "kid gloves" or they'll just quit and get a job down the street. This problem is particularly true with cooks. They are very tempermental and introverted and they expect to be treated like "prima donnas."
>
> Mr. Johnson and I really tried to work with Mr. Bernie during his 90-day trial period. We knew that terminating him without a replacement would be hard on us, but we had no choice. We are now without a restaurant/bar manager or assistant inn-keeper. We have been looking for a replacement, but finding a person that is knowledgeable in both the hotel and restaurant management is something of a chore.

CONDITIONS AFTER MR. BERNIE'S DEPARTURE

Since Bernie had departed, the restaurant personnel were in general agreement that their operation was understaffed. Often guests were seated in both the dining area and coffee shop waiting to be served; even though the waitresses were apparently busy, many customers experienced waits of 20 to 30 minutes. Elaine, one of the two hostesses, explained the lack of prompt service as follows:

> The coffee shop is supposed to take care of the guests until 11 A.M. and then the restaurant part is to be opened. Mr. Bernie handled the situation differently than we do now. When he was here, he would not open the dining hall in the morning no matter how crowded the coffee shop was. I can remember mornings when people were lined into the hallway and all the way outside the front door. I guess he knew two girls and two busboys could not handle two rooms.
>
> But today we handle the situations differently. If the coffee shop gets crowded or we have many dirty tables, we open up both rooms. This really makes it hard on the girls trying to serve both rooms. What we generally have when this happens is poor service to all concerned and consequently some guests leave unhappy and without tipping the waitresses.

Ralph, a busboy, indicated the problem was not exclusively felt in the restaurant only. He seemed to feel the lack or absence of a manager was the primary problem:

> Mrs. Deeks just can't run this operation by herself. It is physically impossible for her to be here seven days a week from 6:30 A.M. until 11 P.M. and manage the kitchen, restaurant, bar, coffee shop, front desk, maid service, and maintenance crew all at the same time.

Some of the employees perceived their duties and functions differently. For instance, the restaurant's two day hostesses alternated work shifts. Elaine would seat customers, give them their menu, take beverages to customers to help out the waitresses, help out busing tables when it was very busy, and had very little to say in supervising the waitresses and busboys. On the other hand, the other day hostess, Gay, would seat customers and give them menus but would not do what she perceived to be the duties of waitresses and busboys. Instead, she exercised supervisory authority over these personnel and when they were not able to get everything done, she would try to find out why not, rather than doing them herself.

There were similar discrepancies in the ways the waitresses and busboys performed their duties. In some cases, waitresses would help busboys clear tables during over-crowded periods and busboys would also help out the waitresses by bringing water and coffee to the people who were waiting to be served. The other side of the coin occurred also. Some of the waitresses, particularly those who had been employed for some time, felt that it was the busboys' responsibility to clear tables and would not lift a finger to help them. In these instances, the busboys did not go out of their way to help the waitresses.

Gene, the other bartender, offered yet another view of the inn's problems:

> You know, I could tell management a few things about the restaurant business if they asked me. I knew from the first day Mr. Bernie arrived that he wouldn't work out. But Mr. Bernie is not the only problem they had. One of the biggest problems they have with this restaurant is in the banquets they have. We have a luncheon here every week with such clubs as the Sertoma, Kiwanis, and the like. Their luncheons start at noon and last until 1:30 or so. Have you ever noticed how they park outside? Well, I'll tell you they park all over the front parking lot and when local people drive by they assume our restaurant is full and go on down the street. These businessmen tie up most of our help and yet the dining room may be empty. These banquet people don't buy drinks with lunch like the local businessmen do who take clients out to lunch and often have a bigger bar bill than their restaurant checks. There's only one successful way to have a banquet business and that's not next to your dining room. If the banquet room was on the opposite side of the restaurant, then it would be OK.

EMPLOYEE TRAINING

The Village Inn provided a minimal amount of job training for employees with the exception of the management staff. The contractual agreement between franchise owners and Village Inns of America required all innkeepers, assistant innkeepers, and restaurant managers to attend the Home Office Training Center within a year of being hired. They also had to attend refresher courses on a yearly basis.

The restaurant personnel, in contrast, were given little job training. Instead, efforts were made to hire cooks, waitresses, and bartenders who had previous experience in the field. But in practice, this policy was not always adhered to—as was exemplified by the way Linda became a bartender:

> My training on the job was really short and sweet. Mr. Bernie came in one day and inquired, "How would you like to be a bartender?" At the same time he handed me a book on mixing drinks. I went home and studied it and "poof" I was a bartender.

Within a short time on the job, I began getting a lot of help and advice from the waitresses who came over to the bar for drink orders. Sometimes when we do get a drink mixup they are very nice about it. I've even had people from other departments in the inn to help me when the situation called for it. One night I had two ladies in here, one from the "crazy house" and the other her bodyguard. After a few "shooters" as they referred to the drinks, they asked for their check. They wanted to use a credit card instead of paying cash. This was not a problem, but so I would get my tip I offered to carry the check and credit card to the front desk. Then they said I would cheat them on their bill once I was out of their sight. The front desk man heard the hassle and came in and escorted the ladies to the desk. This type of working together happens here all the time. Mrs. Deeks, my boss, is really a nice person to work for. She doesn't come around very much, except if she needs information or to advise me about something.

PAY SCALES

Management indicated that there was a shortage of good employees and that a low pay scale was characteristic of the restaurant business. Some of the employees expressed their awareness of this also.

(Bartender) Linda: The pay scale is really low compared to other areas. My first job as a cocktail waitress in San Diego was in a dive downtown. They paid us $2 an hour plus tips, but the tips were lousy. Here they're paying $3 an hour plus tips, which is somewhat better, but it's still way below the wages elsewhere. I really don't feel like I'm suited for this work, but I make more money at the bar than I did as a cocktail waitress.

(Hostess) Gay: I make $4 an hour here. With all the responsibility and experience I've had, the pay scale here compared to other parts of the country is deplorable. The busboys make almost as much as I do. They make $3.50 an hour plus 15 percent of the waitress's tips. Even though the pay scale is low, there is always overtime available to most of all of the employees who want it. My husband who is a cook here has worked 145 hours so far in this two-week pay period and he still has five more days to go.

Barb, one of the waitresses, further substantiated the availability of overtime by saying she got at least one hour overtime each day. She attributed the extra hours of overtime to the fact that the inn's restaurant staff always seemed to have at least one person unexpectedly absent each day.

The problem in the restaurant was apparently compounded by the fact that it was operating with a minimum number of employees. Timmy, a busboy, indicated the wide range of activities that were expected of him and the other busboys:

We do everything; I clean and bus tables, sweep floors, and do janitorial work. I don't mean in just my area either. If the front desk needs a porter or runner or if some type of room service is needed, I do that too. Mr. Bernie was really hard to work under, but he always confined us to restaurant duties. When he was here, we didn't do all those jobs outside our area. Those duties were handled by a front-desk porter. But, I'd still rather have to do things all over the place than have to put up with Mr. Bernie.

SEARCHING FOR MR. BERNIE'S REPLACEMENT

In outlining her thoughts on trying to replace Bernie, Deeks stated:

I really had a good track record with personnel before Mr. Bernie came along. I strongly objected to his dictatorial supervision. In my experience I have learned employees perform their jobs better when left alone most of the time. I once tried to set up off-job activities for my employees. I reserved a room at the hotel for employees to meet together after working hours to play cards and drink coffee. Unfortunately, the room was not used enough to merit keeping it on reserve. However, I still support functions that the employees suggest. We are presently sponsoring a bowling team that two of my waitresses belong to.

Most of the waitresses would rather work night shifts if they have their choice. Some of the girls have children and husbands that require them to be home at night. This balances the shifts real well. One reason I prefer to schedule the waitresses is because of peculiar problems which occur. For example, I have two extremely good waitresses that will not work on Saturdays and Sundays. The other waitresses do not know this, and I feel if I were to allow the hostess to do the scheduling I would have some immediate personnel problems. To further complicate any benefits that might be derived by allowing the hostesses to make out schedules, it would be necessary to reveal my awareness of the slower waitresses we have which I schedule on Saturday and Sunday—our slower business days.

I am really more active in managment and day-to-day problems that most of the employees realize. Any significant changes in rules or policies are usually passed in the form of a written memo. I prefer to handle communication in this way for two reasons: first, there is no room for distortion, and second, it does not give the employees a feeling that they are being closely supervised. However, I do need an assistant to help me manage this place. I have verbally put the word out to other inns and motels. I'm really not concerned whether I get a restaurant manager or an assistant innkeeper so long as he has a knowledge of the food and beverage service. I'm really going to be cautious in the selection of this person as I don't want to jump out of the frying pan into the fire.

E Strategy and Ethics Management

TDK DE MEXICO*

"I want to be the main supplier base of magnets for South and North America," proclaimed Fumio Inouye, general manager of TDK de Mexico, located in Cd. Juarez, a border city of millions close to El Paso, Texas. "To help gain this status, our operating targets need to be met, and that might include expansion of present plant facilities and more automation. Increasingly I feel, though, that people here don't want to see expansion. . . . They seem to enjoy excuses! Whether you call it Japanese or American management, I cannot accept delays, wastes, and excuses! Culture to me is important only when the process of production and the importance of work are clearly understood. Make no mistake, my parent company (TDK of Japan) wouldn't stand for anything other than making acceptable margins. I am having difficulty in putting the reasons for all the problems on culture. . . . I refuse to take it as a dumping ground."

PRODUCTION METHODS AND TECHNOLOGY

TDK de Mexico produced ceramic ferrite magnets of various shapes and sizes that were used for speakers, generators, and motors. It was one of the few plants in its area that produced a final product from the raw material. Production was based on job orders—in other words, production was scheduled as TDK de Mexico received orders for X number of Y type of magnet. Exhibit 1 shows TDK's plant layout and production process. The raw material used to make the final product was black powder called ferrite powder. The ferrite powder, a critical raw material, was imported although it was available in the Mexican market. But to ensure quality, TDK of Japan insisted on using ferrite powder from Japan. The manufacturing process started by wetting and mixing the powder in large containers. The mixture was dried and then was fed into the press machines that gave the shape to the magnets. The shape was determined by the mold inserted into the press machine (Exhibit 2). All of the molds used also came from Japan. The various molds for the different shapes and sizes were stored at the plant and used as needed.

Two distinct methods were used during the press stage of the production process, the dry method and the wet method. The basic difference between the two was that the wet method, installed at TDK de Mexico in 1983 after Inouye took charge, utilized water during the pressing of the raw material. It made stronger magnets, but it took more time. With the wet method, the worker collected the magnets just pressed and placed them in a temporary drying area before they were baked in the ovens. With the dry method, the worker collected the magnets just pressed, and they were sent straight to the ovens for baking.

---

* Prepared by Professor Manab Thakur, California State University, Fresno.

Exhibit 1 PLANT LAYOUT AND PRODUCTION PROCESS

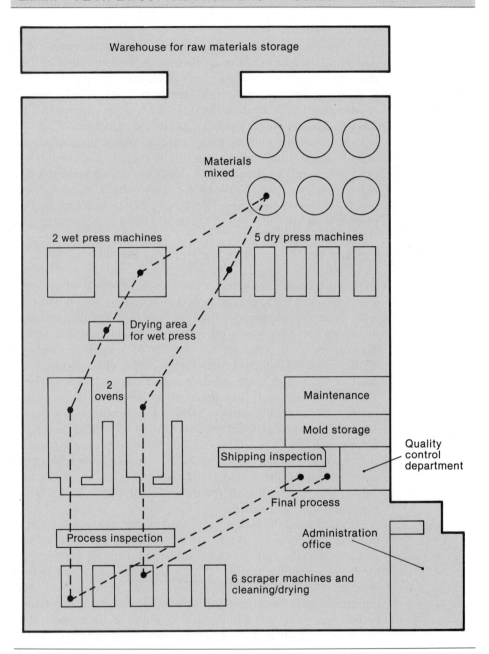

Exhibit 2 PRODUCTION TECHNOLOGY

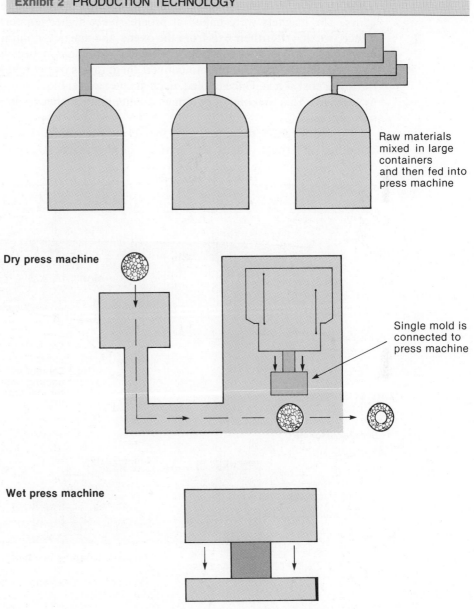

Raw materials mixed in large containers and then fed into press machine

Dry press machine

Single mold is connected to press machine

Wet press machine

While collecting the magnets, the worker visually checked each magnet for cracks or other defects. Defective ones were thrown out for scrap. It was important to spot defective magnets at this stage because it was much harder to convert them into scrap after they were baked. All scrap materials were broken down and used again in the raw material mixture.

After pressing, the magnets were mechanically moved through a series of ovens (Exhibit 3). One set of pressed magnets was placed in the oven every 12 hours. The magnets were baked at progressively higher temperatures from entrance to exit. After their exit from the ovens, the magnets continued moving to a temporary storage area to cool. The ovens presently in use were electrically powered, but there was a plan to convert them to gas ovens to take advantage of the lower cost of gas. Once cooled, each magnet was subject to process inspection by workers. This was one of two main quality control checkpoints in the production process.

Cooled magnets were taken to the scraper machine. The scraper machine smoothed the rough edges and surface of the magnets. The scrapings were

Exhibit 3 PRODUCTION TECHNOLOGY AND MAGNETS MADE

Oven

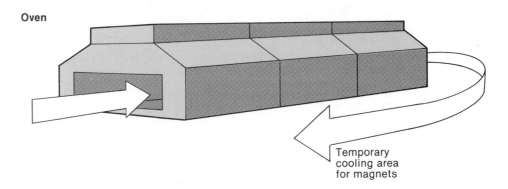

Temporary
cooling area
for magnets

Scraper machine

Encased scraping machine

Magnets made

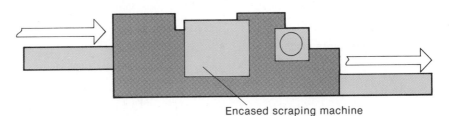

For speakers   For generators   For motors

collected and used again in the raw material mixture. From the scraper machine, the workers placed the magnets in water to be cleaned. After cleaning, the magnets were sent through the drying machine. At the exit point of the drying machine, the magnets were collected by workers and placed in boxes. The boxes of magnets were taken to the final process department where each magnet was given a final check. This stage was called the shipping inspection, and it represented the second main quality control checkpoint. Quality control and specification requirements adhered to at this stage included measurement of weight, length, and appearance of magnets.

About 85 percent of production was exported to the United States—to TDK of America facilities in Chicago, Los Angeles, New York, and Indiana. The remaining 15 percent was exported to Hong Kong. The sales offices and warehouse facilities in these cities were in charge of all selling, shipping, and billing functions. TDK of America sold most of its products to Briggs and Stratton of Milwaukee, Wisconsin, and to Buehler Products of Kingston, North Carolina.

TDK de Mexico had encountered no bureaucratic delays or customs problems in shipping out final products, even though other companies in the area were having difficulties arranging for timely shipment of their merchandise out of Mexico. Inouye was proud that he had been able to secure the necessary clearances and paperwork for getting the product out of the country without much hassle. His explanation was, "You don't create systems when you simply need some people who can do things for you.' You need to get out and find them. You create systems where systems are accepted. . . . It is not here!"

Hiratzuka, TDK's production manager, commented, "We hear that the Mexican government may change the rules of the game. There are rumors that we may have to buy 20 to 25 percent of our raw materials from Mexican suppliers." He went on, "Other than what the government will and will not do, I think you also need to understand that our primary concern is to attract quality labor, since our production process demands it. . . . We can't just hire anyone who walks in."

TDK de Mexico had not looked into possible changes in the Mexican government's local procurement rules to any extent, but had expressed its apprehension to Mexican officials if the firm was forced to buy ferrite powder locally. On another issue, Hiratzuka stated, "As you know, border plants in Mexico like ours have a 'no sale' rule where all goods produced must be exported. But the government is considering a compulsory selling rule whereby 20 percent of a border plant's goods must be sold locally." Such a rule was potentially more troublesome to TDK de Mexico because it was not clear that there was much of a market in Mexico for TDK's products.

THE MEXICAN MAQUILADORAS

In 1965 the United States, working in conjunction with the Mexican government, set up the *maquiladora* program to create jobs for unemployed and underemployed Mexican workers. The idea was to get U.S. companies to open light assembly plants just across the Mexican border and to use cheap Mexican labor to assemble American-made parts into finished goods. In many cases, the components were manufactured in plants located on the U.S. side of the border; this allowed the components to be easily and quickly transported to the Mexican side for final assembly. The effect was to create twin plants a few miles apart—the U.S. plant being used for capital-intensive/skilled-labor operations and the Mexican plant being used for labor-intensive, assembly operations.

When the finished products were shipped back into the United States, U.S. companies were taxed only on the value added in Mexico (mostly labor costs) rather than on the total value of the goods being imported. When the Mexican government experienced a debt crisis in 1982 and the value of the Mexican peso collapsed against the dollar, cheap Mexican wages triggered a *maquiladora* explosion. By early 1987, there were over 630 plants employing over 178,000 people along the Mexican side of the U.S. border. These plants, known as *maquiladoras* (or "in-bond" or twin plants), were all engaged in assembling components in Mexico for re-export in the United States and elsewhere and had become an important economic force along the U.S.-Mexican border. Juarez, where TDK de Mexico's plant was located, had a big concentration of *maquilas*. Exhibit 4 presents some of the features of the *maquiladoras* program.

Maquiladoras operated within a highly volatile political environment, one that affected every aspect of their existence. They were dependent upon the Mexican government continuing to permit raw materials and components to enter duty free and the U.S. government simultaneously permitting finished products to return with duty paid only on the value added in Mexico. Any major change in these policies by either country could shut down most *maquiladoras* overnight by making assembly operations on the Mexican side of the border uneconomical. Both countries had strong political groups opposed to the *maquiladora* concept. Opponents labeled such operations as *sweatshops* and claimed that workers were being exploited by capitalistic interests.

The average age of the *maquiladora* workers was 24, with a relative dearth of workers over 30. Seventy percent were young women and teenage girls. Workers lived under crowded conditions—the mean household size of *maquiladora* workers was 7.8 persons. Their wages averaged about $0.80 per hour, barely more than half the 1987 average Mexican manufacturing wage of $1.57 an hour (including benefits). The low wages made it very attractive for mass assembly operations requiring low-skill labor to be located on the Mexican side of the U.S. border. Managers of the *maquiladoras* expressed a preference for hiring "fresh or unspoiled" workers that had not acquired "bad habits" in other organizations. The work was so low-skilled that workers received very little training. The turnover rate ran 59 percent to 100 percent a year in many plants.

However, many of the large multinational companies with *maquiladoras* paid more than the wage minimums, and their overall compensation package was more attractive than the lowest-paying operations. Some of the multinationals also spent substantial amounts in training and employee development.

The location of twin (or *maquiladora*) plants along the northern border of Mexico was increasing at a phenomenal speed, and unemployed Mexicans were flocking to northern border towns to fill the rapidly expanding number of job openings. By the end of 1988, it was predicted that *maquiladoras* would employ 350,000 workers, one-tenth of Mexico's industrial work force, and that the plants

Exhibit 4 THE MAQUILADORA PROGRAM: LEGAL AND REGULATORY REQUIREMENTS IMPOSED BY THE MEXICAN GOVERNMENT

A. Foreign investment

As a rule, a foreign company may subscribe and own only up to 49 percent of the stock in Mexican corporations with the exception of maquilas, which may be totally owned by foreigners. Except wearing apparel, all items may be produced by in-bond assembly enterprises. Wearing apparel, due to the restriction of textile imports into the United States, is subject to a quota.

B. Import duties

In-bond plants are not required to pay import duties, but the product assembled or manufactured may not be sold in Mexico. Bonds are generally posted by bonding companies and are renewed yearly.

C. Taxes

The maximum income tax on corporate profits is 42 percent on taxable income of P$$500,000 or more in a fiscal year, and employees' share in profits before taxes is at the rate of 8 percent. There are other taxes such as the Social Security Tax based on salaries earned and state taxes.

D. Maquiladora versus Joint Venture

A comparison of the different rules and practices for joint ventures between Mexican and foreign companies is summarized below:

Concept	Maquiladora	Joint venture
1. Doing business in Mexico	To operate in Mexico under a maquila program, a company must be incorporated under Mexican laws (i.e., Sociedad Anonima).	To carry out industrial or commercial activities for the Mexican market, a corporation or other recognized corporate entity must be organized.
2. Equity ownership	100% foreign ownership is allowed.	The general rule is that foreigners may not hold more than 49% of the stock of a corporation doing business in the Mexican market. Exceptions to allow higher percentages of foreign ownership, up to 100%, may be authorized by the Mexican government under special circumstances.
3. Special operating authorizations	To operate under maquila (in-bond) status, the Ministry of Commerce (SOCOFIN) must authorize a maquila program, setting forth the products or activities the company may manufacture/assemble or carry out. Certain committments must be made, the compliance with which shall be reviewed periodically.	Unless the company intends to work within a branch of regulated industry, a joint venture company may freely operate without the need to obtain any special operating permits.
4. Importation of equipment	All production equipment may be imported free of all duties, under bond, subject to it being exported once the company ceases to operate under its maquila program.	The importation of equipment for the production of items that are to be sold in the Mexican market requires an import permit to be obtained and normal duties to be paid thereon.
5. Importation of raw materials	All raw materials and supplies may be imported free of all duties under bond, subject to it being exported within an extendable six-month period, shrinkage and wastage excepted. Under special circumstances, maquiladoras may be authorized to sell up to 20% of a specific product within the Mexican market.	The importation of raw materials and supplies for the production of items that are to be sold in the Mexican market requires an import permit to be obtained and normal duties to be paid thereon. In all cases, import permits are granted on an absolutely discretionary basis. Currently such permits are quite restricted. Under certain conditions, the negotiation of a manufacturing or integration program with the government may be required.

Exhibit 4 *(concluded)*	

Concept	Maquiladora	Joint venture
6. Currency exchange controls	Any operating expense, including rent, payroll, taxes, etc., must be paid in Mexican pesos that must be obtained from a Mexican bank by selling dollars thereto at the controlled rate of exchange. Fixed assets may be paid for in dollars at the free rate of exchange.	There are no specific exchange controls on domestic transactions. If the company exports, it will, in general, be required to sell foreign currencies received to a Mexican bank at the controlled rate of exchange.
7. Labor law requirements	Subject to the Federal Labor Law.	Equally subject to the Federal Labor Law.
8. Acquisition of real estate	Real estate to establish a production facility may be freely bought in the interior of the country. In the border areas or coasts, it may be acquired through a trust.	Same as a maquiladora.
9. Leasing of real estate	Real estate may be leased under freely negotiated items, up to a maximum of 10 years.	Same as a maquiladora, although the term may be longer.
10. Immigration requirements	Foreign technical or management personnel are readily granted work visas, subject to very lenient requirements.	Work visas for foreign technical or management personnel are granted on a very limited basis. Requirements for the obtainment thereof are significantly more stringent.
11. Transfer of technology	For tax purposes it is advisable that a Technical and/or Management Assistance Agreement be executed between the maquiladora and its parent. Such agreement would need to be registered with the National Transfer of Technology Registry (NTTR), which registration would be readily obtained.	If technical or management assistance is granted to a domestic company from a foreign source and royalties or fees are to be paid therefor, an agreement must be registered with the NTTR. To obtain such registration the agreement must meet certain criteria and the amounts which may be charged are limited.
12. Taxes	A maquiladora is in principle subject to the payment of all Mexican taxes. However, since such operations are intended to be cost centers rather than profit centers, the income taxes to be paid are limited. Also, any value added tax paid by the maquiladora shall be refunded to it upon its request.	A domestic company is subject to all normal taxes such as income tax and value added tax (maximum corporate income tax rate = 42%).

would import $8 billion in U.S. components, add $2 billion in value (mostly labor), and ship $10 billion in finished goods back to the United States for sale in the United States and other world markets. A number of Japanese-based companies had begun to set up *maquila* operations to handle the production and sale of their products in U.S. markets—TDK de Mexico was one of these companies.

Despite concerns over the *maquiladoras,* the program was central to the Mexican government's economic revival plans. Mexican leaders were most enthusiastic about a new kind of *maquiladora.* These were plants built in the interior of Mexico that were geared to exports, like the border plants, but unlike the border operations, they undertook in-house manufacture of many of the components used in the final assembly process. These plants used higher-skilled employees and paid wages much closer to the average manufacturing wage in Mexico, and they did not rely so heavily on the use of female labor. They also relied more heavily on Mexican companies for raw material supplies and services.

TDK'S INTERNAL MANAGEMENT

TDK de Mexico had 183 employees (158 women and 25 men). Inouye, before he came to TDK de Mexico, operated machines in a Taiwan plant to help gain a better understanding of workers at that level. After his move to Mexico in 1983, Inouye organized the work force into teams consisting of workers, subleaders, and leaders. Leaders were not entrusted with the job of supervision; all supervisory responsibilities remained with individuals having a title of supervisor. It took an average of two years for a worker to become a subleader. All subleaders at TDK de Mexico were Mexican; they had a median age of 28.2 years. Only three were women.

There were 11 leaders. The specifics of their job were dependent upon their department. Generally, they oversaw workers and machines in their respective departments but were given little authority and were not accountable for achieving set objectives. They were also in charge of training new workers. The leaders at TDK de Mexico had been at the company for an average of 6.4 years. The average time it took to become a leader was about three years. All of the leaders at TDK de Mexico were Mexican. Very few had ever been promoted to the supervisory level.

Five Japanese filled the 12 positions of supervisors and assistant supervisors (Exhibit 5). Like the leaders, their jobs varied based on the department they supervised. Primarily their duties included supervision of the leaders as well as the teams under the leaders. They determined production plans for their respective departments. Although there were Mexican nationals in higher positions, all Japanese employees, irrespective of their job titles, reported directly to Inouye. Because most of the Japanese could not speak Spanish, Inouye thought it was wise to have this direct reporting relationship. However, some of the managers of Mexican origin did not accept this line of reasoning (one manager called it "clannish behavior"); their protests to Inouye had not met with much success.

WAGE POLICIES

TDK de Mexico paid higher wages than most other companies located in the Juarez industrial park plants. TDK de Mexico had several pay incentives available to the workers. They received a bonus after 30 days on the job. There was extra pay for overtime, night shifts, weekend work, and also generous incentives for attendance. Yet, Alfred Gomez, personnel manager for TDK de Mexico, stated, "Absenteeism and lateness are becoming problems. In some cases, when a worker decides to leave her job, she just stops coming to work without any notice. One reason for this problem is that the Juarez public health hospital gives out medical excuses to workers to miss work for the slightest illness. . . . There is very little we can do about it."

Exhibit 5 TDK DE MEXICO ORGANIZATION CHART

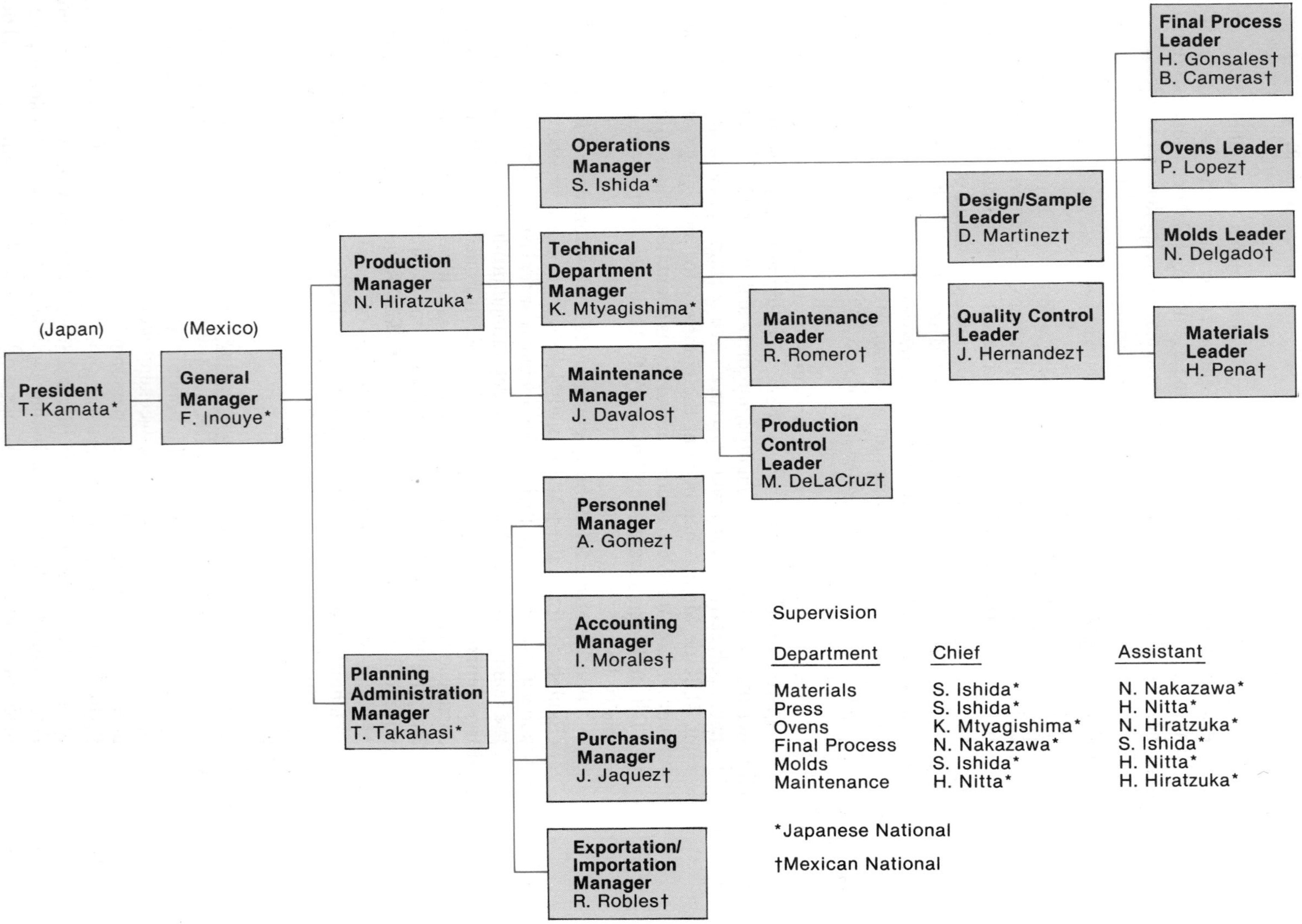

(Japan)

President
T. Kamata*

(Mexico)

General Manager
F. Inouye*

Production Manager
N. Hiratzuka*

Planning Administration Manager
T. Takahasi*

Operations Manager
S. Ishida*

Technical Department Manager
K. Mtyagishima*

Maintenance Manager
J. Davalos†

Personnel Manager
A. Gomez†

Accounting Manager
I. Morales†

Purchasing Manager
J. Jaquez†

Exportation/ Importation Manager
R. Robles†

Design/Sample Leader
D. Martinez†

Quality Control Leader
J. Hernandez†

Maintenance Leader
R. Romero†

Production Control Leader
M. DeLaCruz†

Final Process Leader
H. Gonsales†
B. Cameras†

Ovens Leader
P. Lopez†

Molds Leader
N. Delgado†

Materials Leader
H. Pena†

Supervision

Department	Chief	Assistant
Materials	S. Ishida*	N. Nakazawa*
Press	S. Ishida*	H. Nitta*
Ovens	K. Mtyagishima*	N. Hiratzuka*
Final Process	N. Nakazawa*	S. Ishida*
Molds	S. Ishida*	H. Nitta*
Maintenance	H. Nitta*	H. Hiratzuka*

*Japanese National

†Mexican National

TRAINING

TDK had invested a lot of resources in training its employees; most of its training, however, had been confined to leaders and subleaders. Gomez, the head of personnel, did not go through any systematic training need analysis but professed to know "who needed training and who did not by sight." Inouye's position was, "We will spend money on training, of course, but only with those who show promise." Asked how did he see promise, he replied, "I have been working for 25 years. . . . I know!" A leader who had just finished an in-house training program on motivation commented, "Whenever we face a major crisis, the six Japanese managers get together with Mr. Inouye and decide what course of action to take. It seems like the only decisions I am allowed to participate in are of routine nature that are easily solved. What do I do with what I learned from the training sessions?"

FUMIO INOUYE'S CONCERNS

In March 1988, Inouye met with all the managers (Mexican and Japanese) and presented the plant's most recent operating statistics (Exhibit 6). He was clearly unhappy with the data. A senior manager from Japanese headquarters also attended the meeting along with two other managers from TDK of America. Inouye laid out several options that could be pursued:

1. Downsize the labor force, to correct for the decline in sales and the increase in expenses.
2. Try to avoid downsizing and try to reduce operating costs by buying ferrite powder locally. Since it was not known where and how ferrite powder could be obtained from Mexican sources, Inouye suggested that immediate consideration be given to making the material locally or acquiring a native company.

Exhibit 6 OPERATING STATISTICS OF TDK DE MEXICO, 1984–87

	1984	1985	1986	1987
Total sales (U.S. dollars)	$4,168,000	$3,774,000	$3,837,000	$3,168,000*
Employees	112	128	140	183
Sales per person	$ 29,000	$ 22,000	$ 20,000	$ 23,000
Efficiency rate	82%	81%	80%	80%
Labor turnover rate	16%	47%	46%	39%†
Selling/adm. expenses	$1,623,000	$1,529,000	$1,698,000	$1,878,000
Cost of raw materials	$1,052,000	$1,071,000	$1,099,000	$1,181,000

Shipping cost = .01¢ per gram or 2–10% of total costs.
Price of magnets = .05¢ per gram.
Average production for a year = 5,100,000 grams.
Production figure for 1987 = 6,900,000 grams.
Plant is presently at full capacity.

* Based on the then exchange rate.
† Other maquilas in the park ranged from 25 to 170 percent per year.

3. Send some senior managers (Inouye emphasized Mexican nationals) to Japan for further training.

The Mexican managers thought the concerns expressed in the meeting were addressed specifically to them. One Mexican manager said after the meeting, "If these people would live in Mexico and not run to their comfortable homes on the other side of the border after 5 o'clock, maybe they would understand us a little better!"

Several Mexican managers again suggested to Inouye that the Japanese managers learn the language and work closely with the workers. Inouye was sympathetic to the suggestion but questioned whether learning the language was essential. He advised them to examine "the pockets of inefficiency" and lectured them about the value of hard work.

The manager from TDK Japan left with a stern warning for imminent improvement or else. He explained to the casewriter:

> You see, I came over here in late 1983, after spending years in Singapore, Taiwan, and Hong Kong. I don't know how useful it is to have a grand strategy or any plan per se for an operation like this. . . . What is boils down to is SHOOTEN (focus), SHITSU (quality), and BUNAI (distribution). . . . I'm not about to give up because of cultural differences or any such nonsense. Maybe, and just maybe, I will ask these people here: what do you have to do to earn more money! And if the answer is anything but work harder, I have problem!

Inouye began to contemplate what actions he should take.

JOHNSON & BURGESS LIMITED*

On November 4, 1985, Peter Johnson, president of Johnson & Burgess Limited (J & B), one of Canada's fastest-growing advertising agencies, faced a complex and potentially explosive situation. Jack Kelly, CEO of the Regal Tobacco Company, a large Canadian cigarette manufacturer, had personally contacted Johnson to request that J & B make a speculative bid for a $5 million piece of Regal's $12 million account.

Since Kelly was a longtime friend, Johnson had been able to probe the reasons for moving the account from the incumbent agency. He concluded it had gone stale creatively and was experiencing internal problems arising from weak leadership and excessive turnover of account executives.

Over lunch and in a confirming letter, Kelly had stated that his top marketing people were very much sold on J & B because they were aware of the agency's outstanding work and reputation. He had strongly implied that the switch to J & B would be simply a formality if they really wanted the business and if the presentation for the Regal marketing management group went as expected. Kelly asked for an answer in three days.

Johnson was conscious of the irony of his situation. Two weeks previously, he had received an application for employment from a recently graduated MBA, who had asked in her covering letter if J & B handled a cigarette account. He remembered dictating in his reply that J & B did not. Now he was coming to grips with a decision that might change that.

His decision was not as straightforward as it once might have been but was complicated by other recent experiences. In September, while undergoing a routine medical checkup, he and his doctor happened to discuss smoking. In the conversation, his doctor had pointedly mentioned cigarette advertising: "The sooner the government stops these companies from advertising, the better off we'll all be." Johnson would normally have countered with a defensive retort and put the matter out of his mind, but because the doctor was a personal friend and a smoker as well, the statement stuck with him for several days.

Another circumstance disturbed Johnson even more. In mid-October he learned that a close friend, who had been a heavy smoker, was dying of lung cancer. In many ways he was surprising himself with his quandary. "Last year," he thought, "I would have jumped at the chance to take this business. I better put these second thoughts out of my mind and get with it. I'm running an ad agency, not a charitable society." Moreover, he could easily predict what his older partner, Tony Burgess, would say: "Cigarette smoking is legal. It brings people

---

* Prepared by Professor Donald H. Thain with the assistance of Joseph C. Shlesinger, both of The University of Western Ontario. Copyright © 1985. The University of Western Ontario. Revised 1986.

pleasure. Nobody's forcing them to smoke. Therefore, I don't give a damn what effect smoking has on health. If we can make a buck advertising cigarettes, let's go for it!''

He knew that there were mixed feelings about smoking within the agency. It was made a nonsmoking office[1] just six months after a sometimes bitter struggle during which two key creative people threatened to quit. He knew some of his staff would not really care about the issue, but many, if not most, would. And he also knew it was his job to think of the agency's future and balance the rights of all his employees to have their personal values respected in such an important decision.

THE ADVERTISING AGENCY BUSINESS IN CANADA

The Canadian advertising scene was characterized by corporate, customer, and geographic concentration. There were about 400 agencies in Canada in 1985. The vast majority were located in Toronto, although Montreal and, more recently, Vancouver were also major centers. Of those 400 agencies, 20 accounted for 48 percent of total industry billings of $2 billion. Moreover, the top 10 advertisers (see Exhibit 1) accounted for nearly one-fifth of industry revenues.

The business was changing. There was a growing tendency for multinational companies to advertise with multinational agencies based in the United States. This was distressing for independent Canadian agencies that were in jeopardy of losing U.S. subsidiary accounts as a result of head office decisions beyond their control. At the same time, their opportunity to land such accounts was diminishing. For example, Colgate-Palmolive had just decided to advertise Colgate toothpaste in 45 countries with Young and Rubicam of New York, one of the largest

---

Exhibit 1 TOP 10 NATIONAL ADVERTISERS, 1984

Rank	Company (head office)	Advertising spending ($ millions)
1	Government of Canada (Ottawa)	$ 95.8
2	Procter & Gamble (Toronto)	46.3
3	John Labatt Ltd. (London)	37.6
4	The Molson Companies (Montreal)	35.3
5	Kraft Ltd. (Montreal)	32.5
6	Government of Ontario (Toronto)	32.1
7	Rothmans of Pall Mall Canada (Toronto)	31.0
8	General Motors of Canada (Oshawa)	30.0
9	Nabisco Brands Ltd. (Toronto)	24.5
10	General Foods Inc. (Toronto)	22.9
Total		$388.0

Source: *Marketing,* May 13, 1985, Page 1.

---

[1] Smoking was prohibited in public areas as a result of a decision voted by employees encouraged by a Canadian government Department of Health and Welfare-sponsored antismoking program.

worldwide agencies. There was no way an independent Canadian agency could get that type of account.

Competition was stiff in the advertising agency business. As account turnover was a never-ending concern of management, aggressive new-business solicitation was a basic activity in all well-run agencies. New account selling began with finding potential prospects that could be encouraged to switch agencies. The process developed through building relationships, communicating the competence and value added by the agency, and convincing the marketing people of the potential new client that they should replace the incumbent agency. When this process reached the point of a formal review and appraisal by the client, efforts often reached a fever pitch, culminating in a formal presentation selling the agency, its client service team, marketing expertise, advertising ideas and creativity. While elaborate and costly speculative presentations were frowned upon by the advertising agency association, the final pitch for a major account was usually an elaborate, all-out affair with suggested marketing plans, sample advertisements, and whatever else was thought to be necessary to convince the potential client.

Eroding margins presented another problem. As competition increased, pressures mounted to provide more comprehensive services at lower costs, including marketing planning, marketing and advertising research, sales promotion, and public relations. Although most agencies made a conscious effort to keep salaries below 56 percent of total revenue (see Exhibit 2), agency cost structures generally showed wages at 59 percent of revenue.

Although agencies aimed for a 20 percent pretax profit, most were closer to 15 percent. Those that got close to 20 percent were generally the smaller agencies. Larger agencies typically had larger clients that were more sophisticated, more bureaucratic, and more demanding. With smaller accounts, it was usually easier and less expensive for the agency to service client needs and get approval of a given ad campaign.

Exhibit 2 AGENCY COST STRUCTURE TARGET

Revenue (15% commission and fees)		100%
Expenses		
Payroll		
Management	9	
Client contact	16	
Creative	10	
Other services	20	
Total	55	
Travel and entertainment	5	
Office facilities	10	
General office expenses	10	
Total expenses		80
Net profit before tax		20
		100%

Source: Casewriter's estimate.

SMOKING IN CANADA

In 1985, 33 percent of Canadians regularly smoked cigarettes, down from 50 percent in 1965. The smoking rate was highest among teenage girls. Industry research indicated cigarette smoking rates were relatively higher among the following market segments: marital status—separated or divorced; income—low; occupation—blue collar; sex—female; and age—younger and older. One result of the declining market was that manufacturers were, for the first time, initiating and pursuing aggressive price competition. The 8 percent sales decline in 1985 led to major promotional campaigns with producers sometimes selling products at or below cost. Another outcome was that tobacco growers were being hit hard by falling sales and prices. In 1985, the Canadian federal government allocated $90 million for financial help for tobacco growers to inventory their crop until prices rebounded.

Tobacco industry sales were about $3 billion in 1984, and it was estimated that nearly $6 billion was spent on smoking-related health care. Cigarettes were blamed for 30,000 deaths a year in Canada. In fact, more Canadians died from smoking every 18 months than died in World War II.[2]

Criticism of smoking by the medical profession began in earnest with the 1964 report of the U.S. Surgeon General's Advisory Committee on smoking and health, which argued that smoking was a major cause of lung cancer and several other diseases. In July 1985, *The New York Journal of Medicine* published a 200-page report stating that the tremendous marketing efforts by cigarette manufacturers to create a strong, favorable image (by sponsoring sporting events and art shows) dwarfed attempts made to combat smoking. It included a report showing that the industry was attracting females by advertising in women's magazines and sponsoring women's tennis tournaments at which samples were often distributed.

The Canadian Council on Smoking and Health and the Non-Smokers Rights Association had lobbied against tobacco for several years. However, the closest the federal government had come to regulating tobacco was in 1969 when a parliamentary committee recommended elimination of all cigarette advertising. In response to this threat, tobacco manufacturers voluntarily withdrew all television and radio ads.

The only restriction on tobacco marketing was a voluntary code (see Exhibit 3) administered by the Canadian Tobacco Manufacturers' Council. Except for political pressure through the Minister of Health and Welfare, the public had no say in the development, enforcement, or interpretation of the code.

Only two Canadian newspapers—*The Kingston Whig-Standard* and *The Brockville Intelligencer*—had banned cigarette advertising. In May 1985, *The London Free Press* had been pressured by the Non-Smokers Rights Association to drop it but refused to do so. Addressing the issues, Bob Turnbull, the paper's president and associate publisher, wrote:

> The problem here is a medical problem. It has nothing to do with our integrity or anything else. . . . All of these (pressure) tactics are directed, I think, the wrong way. They should be directed at the smoking problem.

---

[2] *The London Free Press, Encounter,* May 6, 1985, p. 6.

Exhibit 3 CIGARETTE AND CIGARETTE TOBACCO ADVERTISING AND PROMOTION CODE (of the Canadian Tobacco Manufacturers' Council)

Rule 1
There will be no cigarette or cigarette tobacco advertising on radio or television, nor will such media be used for the promotion of sponsorships of sports or other popular events whether through the use of brand or corporate name or logo.

Rule 2
The industry will limit total cigarette and cigarette tobacco advertising, promotion and sponsorship expenditures for any year to 1971 levels. The limits will be revised annually to compensate for cost increases or declines.

Rule 3
Advertising of sponsored events associated with a brand or corporate name or logo will be limited to non-broadcast media and such advertising together with promotional material will not include package identification, product selling line or slogan, or the words "cigarette" or "tobacco."

Rule 4
No cigarette or cigarette tobacco brand shall be promoted by incentive programs offering to the consumer cash or other prizes. Coupons redeemable for gifts and related gift catalogues will not be advertised.

Rule 5
Direct mail advertising will not be used as a medium to promote the sale of cigarettes or cigarette tobacco.

Rule 6
All advertising will be in conformity with the Canadian Code of Advertising standards as issued in 1967 by the Canadian Advertising Advisory Board.

Rule 7
Cigarette or cigarette tobacco advertising will be addressed to adults 18 years of age or over and will be directed solely to the increase of cigarette brand shares.

Rule 8
No advertising will state or imply that smoking the brand advertised promotes physical health or that smoking a particular brand is better for health than smoking any other brand of cigarettes, or is essential to romance, prominence, success or personal advancement.

Rule 9
No advertising will use, as endorsers, athletes or celebrities in the entertainment world.

Rule 10
All models used in cigarette and cigarette tobacco advertising will be at least 25 years of age.

Rule 11
No cigarette or cigarette tobacco product will be advertised on posters or bulletin boards located in the immediate vicinity of primary or secondary schools.

Rule 12
All cigarette packages, cigarette tobacco packages and containers will bear, clearly and prominently displayed on one side thereof, the following words:

"WARNING: Health and Welfare Canada advises that danger to health increases with amount smoked—avoid inhaling.

AVIS: Santé et Bien-être social Canada considère que le danger pour la santé croît avec l'usage—èviter d'inhaler."

Rule 13
The foregoing words will also be used in cigarette and cigarette tobacco print advertising (see Appendix 1 for size and location). Furthermore, it will be prominently displayed on all transit advertising (interior and exterior), airport signs, subway advertising and market place advertising (interior and exterior) and point-of-sale material over 144 square inches in size but only in the language of the advertising message.

Rule 14
Average tar and nicotine content of cigarette smoke from any brand of cigarettes will not exceed, within normal tolerances, 22 milligrams of tar, moisture free weight, and 1.6 milligrams of nicotine per cigarette.

Rule 15
The average tar and nicotine content of smoke per cigarette will be shown on all cigarette packages and in print media advertising.

Rule 16
Labels carrying the warning noted in Rule 12 are available through the Council to operators of cigarette vending machines. No cigarette brand advertising or Corporate symbol except for package facsimiles will appear on cigarette vending machines.

Rule 17
Consumer sampling of cigarettes or cigarette tobacco free of charge will be limited to new products or existing products in which significant technological changes have been made. Such free sampling will be limited to a period not exceeding twelve months from the date of introduction of the said product in any given area, and the function of sampling limited to those areas in which cigarettes are normally purchased and only to persons who may legally purchase the product and are perceived as in the act of making a purchase. Furthermore, the sampling function will be carried out only by regular employees of the Manufacturer. These restrictions will not preclude free distribution of cigarettes by manufacturers to their employees for their personal use, or to consumers in answer to complaints.

Rule 18
No cigarette or cigarette tobacco brand names will be used on future cigar or pipe tobacco products nor will cigar or pipe tobacco brand names be used on future cigarette or cigarette tobacco products.

Rule 19
The parties to this Code agree that adherence to the Code's provision will be subject to review by a Board of Arbitration and that the Board will have power to impose sanctions on an offending party or parties.

I just can't be convinced that tobacco advertising in daily newspapers would have a significant impact on the medical problem. It is not our role to make these rules.[3]

To the best of Johnson's knowledge, there were only two Canadian advertising agencies that had an explicit policy of no tobacco advertising. In the case of one, he suspected it was a matter of "sour grapes" because it had lost a major cigarette account.

A group called Physicians for a Smoke Free Canada, was demanding a ban on all tobacco advertising within two years. Some experts predicted all forms of cigarette advertising would be banned by the year 2000.

The most threatening trend in the industry, many experts said, was the increasing frequency of cigarette advertising aimed at the youth market. RJR MacDonald Inc., a large Canadian cigarette producer, brought this issue to the forefront with its "Tempo" campaign (see Exhibit 4). Its apparent focus on the young was accused of being purposely controversial. In response, the Federal Ministry of Health and Welfare, a nonsmoking office, began a $1.5 million campaign aimed at the young to counter such advertising.

JOHNSON & BURGESS LTD.

J & B was one of the largest Canadian-owned agencies, with commissionable billings of $60 million in 1984. The agency was known for its talented people and had recently won several creative awards. It was considered by many creative people in the industry to be a rising star. J & B had 160 employees, of whom 145 worked in the firm's offices in Toronto and Montreal, both of which were designated nonsmoking.

Over the past 10 years, J & B had grown rapidly. According to Peter Johnson, the strategy had been to "overspend on people so that our creative product and client service are second to none." With strong political connections, a first-class marketing research group, and some widely publicized work in public opinion polling, the agency had also attracted significant public relations business from three large companies with extensive public affairs activities. Several staff members had worked hard for the PC party in the last federal election. Consequently, the agency had picked up over $3 million in federal government advertising.

The agency was earning a profit and in good shape financially (see Exhibit 5). However, there was significant slack in the organization as a result of learning curve improvements, particularly on two large accounts the agency had taken over two years previously after fierce competition with several other agencies. Management was concerned about the need to either add more business or reduce salaries and wages.

Management also intended at some point to make a public offering of equity shares in order to build a financial base for diversification into communication ventures. Management shareholdings are outlined in Exhibit 6.

---

[3] *The London Free Press*, May 29, 1985, p. A3.

Exhibit 4 NEWSPAPER ARTICLE: "Cigaret Firms Try New Marketing"

In what may be the beginning of a cigaret packaging revolution similar in scope to changes that have affected the brewing industry, two leading cigaret manufacturers have adopted more aggressive marketing techniques.

RJR-Macdonald Inc. has introduced Tempo brand, a mid-strength cigaret in a trendy package, and Rothmans Inc. has begun selling its Number 7 brand in packages containing 30 cigarets for the price of a 25-pack.

Spokesmen for both Toronto-based companies said the changes are designed to capture market share from the competition and not to increase the over-all size of the smoking market.

Jeffrey Goodman, vice-president of corporate affairs at RJR-Macdonald, said Tempo "breaks the mold" for cigaret packaging because of its "very contemporary nature."

"We are going after smokers of competitive brands, but we're not reacting to declining markets," he said.

He said Tempo's marketing strategy, developed by J. Walter Thompson Co. Ltd. of Toronto, is not aimed at young people, as anti-smoking lobbyists have charged, but at mid-strength cigaret smokers, who make up about half the market.

The Tempo advertisements, currently in Toronto only but planned for all of Canada eventually, use bright colors in the background and young-looking people in the foreground who are perhaps best described as appearing to be "hip."

Mr. Goodman said his company has no plans as yet to follow Rothmans' lead in offering different package sizes. He said his company suspected some time ago that Rothmans was going to introduce Number 7s in the 30-pack.

RJR-Macdonald has been expanding its current lines and will probably digest such changes before introducing more changes, he said.

The company currently holds about 18 percent of the Canadian market, Mr. Goodman said, with annual sales of about $400 million. RJR-Macdonald produces more than a dozen different cigaret brands as well as cigars and cigaret sundries.

The 30-pack introduced by Rothmans is likely to have even more impact than changes at RJR-Macdonald if smokers jump at what amounts to a price cut. "Obviously the competition won't stand by and watch us make a success of it," Peter Bone, a spokesman at Rothmans, said.

Mr. Bone said there are so many different varieties of cigaret packages on the market already he is not entirely sure what will happen next. He said an Ontario provincial "stick tax" limits what manufacturers can do economically.

He pointed out that Rothmans once sold cigarets in a variety of package sizes and even gave away packages of five cigarets for promotional purposes. He said no plans exist for repeating such schemes beyond the 30-pack. "But someone may do something."

Rothmans sold more than $550 million worth of to-bacco products last year, but profit was just over $17.4 million, down about $2 million from the previous year. The company paid almost $300 million in sales and excise taxes.

Mr. Bone said that many years ago, the Canadian cigaret industry agreed to adopt its fairly staid packaging format because such items as five-packs were un-economical. The changes made by RJR-Macdonald and Rothmans effectively end that agreement.

The same kind of agreement existed in the beer industry until a couple of years ago, when the traditional stubby bottle gave way to a torrent of different shapes and sizes, all designed to increase lagging sales.

Mr. Bone said it "is awfully hard to tell" at this stage whether cigaret marketing will undergo a similar revolu-tion, but Rothmans said recently, after major manage-ment changes, that it planned a major market offensive to increase market share.

Source: Adam Corelli, "Cigaret Firms Try New Marketing," *The Globe and Mail,* October 2, 1985.

The Key Players

A chart of the J & B organization indicating the main areas of the business and the top managers responsible is presented in Exhibit 7. The six key managers in the agency were described as follows:

Tony Burgess, Chairman. Tony was a good advertising agency man, but his greatest asset had always been his friendly, outgoing personality. He had many friends and an amazing network of contacts. For retirement income he was counting heavily on cashing in his J & B stock, which was currently worth about $2.25 million. He was very much aware that the agency's average five-year earnings per share figure could improve rapidly because earnings had been low in 1980 and 1981. Johnson knew that Burgess very much wanted to buy an attractive home in a prime Florida real estate development and that he would not be able to

Exhibit 5   PROFIT AND LOSS STATEMENT, JOHNSON & BURGESS, 1984

	($000's)	Percent
Revenues		
Gross commissionable billings	$60,000	
Commission	9,000	
Service and other fees	8,000	
Gross revenue	$17,000	100.0
Expenses		
Client contact	$ 3,400	20.0
Management	1,700	10.0
Creative	1,700	10.0
TV and radio	1,020	6.0
Public relations	680	4.0
Marketing	510	3.0
Research	340	2.0
Other	1,530	9.0
Total	$10,800	64.0
Office facilities		
Rent	$ 969	5.7
Amortization/leasehold facilities	51	.3
Depreciation/furniture, fixtures and equipment	136	.8
Heat, light, water	34	.2
Maintenance and repairs	102	.6
Municipal taxes	68	.4
Other	170	1.0
Total	$ 1,530	9.0
General office expenses		
Postage and courier	$ 68	.4
Supplies and stationery	255	1.5
Telephone and telegraph	289	1.7
Donations	136	.8
Doubtful accounts	34	.2
Company contribution to pension plan	153	.9
Group insurance	102	.6
Unemployment insurance and other benefits	34	.2
Miscellaneous	289	1.7
Total	$ 1,360	8.0
Travel and entertainment	$ 850	5.0
Total expenses	$14,620	86.0
Net profit before tax	2,380	14.0
Income tax	1,190	7.0
Net profit	1,190	7.0
EPS (100,000 shares)	11.90	

Johnson & Burgess' profit-sharing plan called for 40% of earnings to be distributed to 52 plan participants on a basis proportional to salaries.
Another 40% of earnings was customarily paid out in dividends.

finance it unless the agency did very well in Burgess's remaining two years. A former college rugger player, Burgess had a strong constitution and had smoked since he was a teenager.

Peter Johnson, President.   Several industry observers attributed the success of J & B primarily to Johnson's unfailingly pragmatic, open, and positive leadership; his education, training, and experience; his ability to attract and hold good people; and his sincerity and honesty in dealing with clients and staff alike.

A reformed smoker, he stayed in good shape by jogging all year and playing in an old-timers hockey league from September to April. While he was idealistic and

Exhibit 6 SHAREHOLDERS, JOHNSON & BURGESS, LTD.

	Number of shares	Percent
Tony Burgess	25,000	25
Peter Johnson	20,000	20
Bill Nugent	12,000	12
Jack Spitzer	10,000	10
Wally Bick	5,000	5
Lou Destino	5,000	5
21 others	23,000	28
Total	100,000	100

Shares were valued at 6 times average earnings per share for last 5 years plus $33 per share to cover per share portion of earned surplus and deemed good will.

Earnings per share for the past 5 years had been as follows:

1980	$ 6.80
1981	7.10
1982	10.25
1983	11.20
1984	11.90

Past 5-year average = $9.45.
1985 EPS forecast = $15.25.

Exhibit 7 J & B's ORGANIZATION CHART (age)

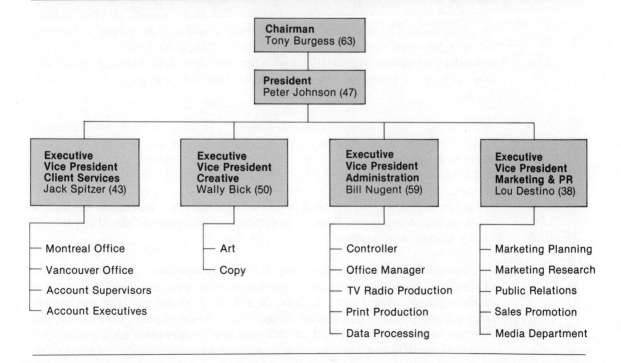

socially responsible, he seemed to rationalize easily a wide variety of questionable behaviors as being necessary because advertising agencies were in a competitive, personal service business.

Bill Nugent, Vice President, Administration.   Bill was an unflappable but disorganized workaholic. Of medium height and noticeably overweight, he was a heavy smoker who drank more than his share. Bill was everyone's friend and the confidant of many. His grown children were all married, and his wife, the daughter of a once-prominent politician, was involved in many charitable and social activities. Bill worked many evenings, and after working hours his door was always open. Anyone from Tony Burgess to a junior copywriter might be found in his office chatting about personal or business affairs.

Wally Bick, Vice President, Creative.   With an excess of brilliant creative talent, Wally was the key idea man and a driving force of the agency. He was well known as an active member of a large downtown church. A health food devotee, he neither smoked nor drank. On the request of a bishop of his church, he had given many hours of professional help to a group of parents organizing a political action group to fight drunken driving. The creative work for beer and liquor accounts was his general responsibility, but he showed little interest in them beyond seeing that they were handled by top-rated people. Client services personnel, particularly on the beer account, occasionally complained privately to Jack Spitzer that they did not have Bick's full commitment. Johnson hoped that despite Bick's condemnation of smoking, he would still see that the creative work on a cigarette account was handled professionally. Johnson worried, however, about what he would tell Kelly if he specifically asked for Bick to be heavily involved on the Regal account. He expected that while Bick would oppose taking a cigarette account, he would stop short of outright action to block the freedom of colleagues to work on what they wished. Bick had in the past mentioned informally that there was no way he would accept any direct or indirect benefits from a cigarette account.

Jack Spitzer, Vice President, Client Services.   Pleasant, capable, and efficient, Jack knew and stayed in close touch with client top-management personnel and made sure they got what they wanted. Sometimes accused of being too political and pragmatic in giving in to client pressures, he nevertheless was widely respected. Jack had been the hard-driving leader of the agency's new-business campaign and took great personal pride in its growth record. Johnson knew Jack would be a vociferous and devastating opponent of anyone who raised any barrier to any kind of new business.

Lou Destino, Vice President, Marketing and Public Relations.   A business school graduate with good training and experience, Lou was the able leader of the marketing and public relations thrust in J & B. Lou did much of the market targeting and planning that guided Spitzer's new-business push. Foresighted and strategic in his thinking, he doubted that cigarette business was good for the long term because of falling sales, growing government reaction against tobacco products, medical opposition, and mounting product liability legal claims (none successful), which he was afraid might eventually involve the ad agencies that did cigarette advertising.

However, he had no real personal hangups about working on a cigarette account. While he occasionally smoked cigars and a pipe, he was opposed to cigarette smoking and had told several friends about how happy he had been when his wife, who was a heavy smoker, quit smoking because of the pressure their young children had focused on her. As he recounted the story, the children had appealed to his wife by saying: "Mom, our teacher at school told us that you might die if you keep on smoking."

The Meeting

Since Johnson had to make up his mind immediately regarding his reply to Kelly, he called a special meeting of the Management Committee for the next Saturday morning. Casually dressed, they assembled around the boardroom table. The meeting had been called for 10 A.M., and Johnson thought it might take an hour and a half at most. As usual, Nugent and Spitzer smoked throughout. Johnson started off by describing Kelly's request and his subsequent meeting, telephone discussions, and letter; then he asked for their input to his decision. Excerpts representing the various points of view expressed in what became a no-holds-barred exchange are as follows:

Bick: There is no way we can get around the fact that smoking is just plain bad for everybody and lethal for many. We all know the terrible numbers—10,000 die from lung cancer alone and that's only one of the many possible side effects. And we all know that's just the beginning—bronchitis, emphysema, cancer of the larynx, bladder, esophagus, mouth, lip, and reproductive systems—you name them, they're all attributable to smoking. There's no way we should take this account. We should all be worried about ourselves for even giving it serious consideration.

Spitzer: Come on, Wally, that's a lot of antismoking medical propaganda. The scientists working for the tobacco industry deny those things have ever been proved. For the big majority—must be way over 90 percent—of smokers there's no problem at all. If all that medical crap is really true, how come so many doctors smoke?

Burgess: Regardless of the medical arguments, it's legal and fits in with today's life-style. Advertising simply informs people about what they obviously want. We can't make anyone smoke who doesn't want to! And we have no right or responsibility to set ourselves up as judges of what's good for society. That's the job of government. As long as the government raises taxes from cigarettes and openly supports tobacco farmers, how can we be so self-righteous as to make moral judgments against the business?

Spitzer: If we're going to get on a soap box and make public moral "statements," what about some of our other businesses. . . . Our beer and liquor business is almost $6 million this year. Our automotive business includes a sports car with such incredible performance that four out of five buyers—especially teenagers—are a danger everytime they get behind the wheel. Incidentally, yesterday, when I was out at . . . , they told me they've got over $200 million worth of consumer liability legal actions going in North America. We all know that you just can't waste time thinking about this kind of stuff. And why should we? There's no business in the world that's perfect. . . .

Nugent: I don't see what harm cigarette advertising does anyway. The tobacco industry says that it's all brand advertising to defend share of market and not to promote primary demand. We all know that cigarette sales are falling in spite of all the advertising that's being done.

Burgess: I think we've got to look at the positive side of this opportunity. It would be the biggest piece of new business we've ever picked up. We'll get some great publication and trade exposure because it will be the biggest account to move this year. That means momentum, reputation, and success. And there's a good chance for a lot more of Kelly's business if we do an excellent job. I'd be less than frank if I didn't admit that it would be a tremendous benefit to me and my wife. I've given my total commitment for 27 years to this team and to making our operation the best. The boost this would give to the price of my stock in a couple of years when I cash out would have to be one of the bigger breaks in my career. Not to speak of what it means in profit sharing for all of us!

Destino: I'm not sure this would be good for us in the longer-term future. Sure, it's morally objectionable and it's going to cause internal conflict. But the real problem is the opportunity cost. There is lots of better business out there. If we take this account, we'll have no capacity for another big account for quite a while. I wouldn't want to take this at the cost of having to pass on some better business a month or two from now.

Spitzer: Do you have anything specific in mind?

Destino: Not right now.

Spitzer: Well then, let's take what we can get right now and worry about our next new account when the time comes.

Destino: Yeah, but if we land this account, we might lose some government advertising because of it.

Spitzer: So what if we do? Government can deal with some other agency. They've got too big a bureaucracy anyway—you need client approval at five levels, and it's taking a lot more time than we planned for in our budgets.

Johnson: OK, but what about the internal consequences? What team will we put on the account.

Spitzer: For an account this size, we'll need eight people: an account supervisor, an account executive, two assistant account executives, two artists, and two copywriters. They would all work for Regal pretty well full time. I'd like to make sure we'd put our best people on this account, since it's so important.

Bick: But some of our best people, like Jim, Marie, and Jan (three of J & B's best copywriters and artists) say they'd have nothing to do with cigarette advertising. In fact, I wouldn't be surprised to find that Jim would quit before we took this account.

Burgess: Look, I can't tell you what to do, but if we don't take this account, someone else will. Then what has our "statement" meant? Only a big loss for us in terms of dollars and exposure. Think about it. Look at what it would mean to our profit-sharing plan. We owe it to all our staff, now and in the future, to go after this account as hard as we can.

Johnson: Maybe we do. But you're making our short-term advances more important than long-term stability. What if we do lose some of our best talent, and don't actually get the account? What effect will that have on our future? Some of these idealistic young people will think we're prostituting the whole agency for a few more bucks. Who'd want to come work for us thinking we cared only about the bottom line? If Kelly's people weren't known to be such a professional and classy organization, it'd be easier to make this decision.

Nugent: Let's put the staff problem in a little perspective. Out of our total of 160 people, I'd say only 4 or 5 at the very most would ever quit over this. Another 15 or 20 would be strongly against it and drag their feet or not give their top effort. Another 25 or 30 would be against it but forget about the problem in a week or so. At the other end of the spectrum, we would have our 35 to 40 smokers and quite a few nonsmokers who would think we are crazy for even thinking about passing up such a great piece of business. Many of them would think they are being shafted by a bunch of do-gooders.

After lasting for over three hours, the meeting broke up when Lou Destino and Bill Nugent had to leave. Destino's parting comment to Peter Johnson: "You and Tony better take the rest of the afternoon and decide what we should do. I gotta leave. See you tommorrow.

Johnson knew he had to make up his mind quickly. However, after a long talk with Tony Burgess, he was even more confused about what he should do. As he reviewed the file of notes he had accumulated on the problem, he assessed the pros and cons of his options. The organization was strong and cohesive, but he worried that the agency job market was good for experienced, high performers. The tangible costs and benefits were fairly clear, but the intangibles were difficult to assess. The longer he pondered his dilemma the more he realized there were going to be serious consequences no matter what he decided.

DUN & BRADSTREET CORPORATION*

Dun & Bradstreet (D & B) possessed one of the best-known names in American business. The company owed much of its reputation to its flagship division, Dun & Bradstreet Credit Services, whose legendary credit reports were a relied upon source of information about how quickly a company paid its bills and about its creditworthiness.

Founded in 1841, Dun & Bradstreet had developed a very extensive data base of financial, credit, and marketing-related information on more than 13 million businesses worldwide. D & B processed more than 90,000 inquiries a day from some 80,000 clients who subscribed to its credit services and needed information about companies they were doing or considering doing business with. Clients used D & B credit reports in making loans or extending credit to customers, in evaluating suppliers they were considering buying from, in developing lists of potential new customers, and in an assortment of other financial assessment decisions. D & B was the world's largest provider of services to support commercial credit risk assessment.

DUN & BRADSTREET'S BUSINESSES

Dun & Bradstreet ranked 14th on *Fortune's* 1988 list of the 50 largest diversified service companies; the company had 1988 sales of $4.3 billion and employed 69,500 persons. A 10-year financial summary is presented in Exhibit 1. D & B had three main business groups: business information services, publishing, and marketing services.

Business Information Services. This group contributed 35 percent of 1988 revenues and had grown 13 percent annually for the past three years. The key division in this group was D & B Credit Services, which provided customers with credit risk assessment information on 9 million U.S. businesses and 1 million international firms through its credit ratings and its business information reports.

The credit reports provided balance sheet and income data, payment analyses, and profiles of top managers, officers, and directors. The business information reports contained commercial credit information on a specific company—a brief history, operating statistics, financial statement information, payment data, and banking relationships. The *Dun & Bradstreet Reference Book,* published six times a year, contained listings on over 3.5 million businesses in the United States and Puerto Rico, arranged alphabetically by city or town within each state. D & B Credit Services faced competition from in-house operations of businesses, as well

---

* Prepared by Professor A. J. Strickland III, The University of Alabama.

Exhibit 1   SELECTED FINANCIAL DATA FOR THE DUN & BRADSTREET CORP., 1979–88 (all amounts except per share data, average number of shares outstanding, and percentages are in millions)

	1988	1987	1986	1985	1984	1983	1982	1981	1980	1979
Continuing operations:										
Operating revenue	$4,267.4	$3,788.5	$3,463.2	$3,022.0	$2,624.6	$2,267.0	$2,040.1	$1,818.1	$1,566.0	$1,274.3
Costs and expenses	3,463.9	3,075.1	2,840.6	2,467.2	2,173.1	1,881.3	1,703.6	1,515.9	1,315.2	1,079.0
Operating income	803.5	713.4	622.6	554.8	451.5	385.7	336.5	302.2	250.8	195.3
Nonoperating (expense) income—net	(12.8)	20.4	24.3	25.8	35.5	9.7	1.5	(0.6)	3.4	10.3
Income from continuing operations before provision for income taxes	790.7	733.8	646.9	580.6	487.0	395.4	338.0	301.6	254.2	205.6
Provision for income taxes	291.7	295.4	270.0	257.3	210.5	188.2	161.5	148.2	123.6	101.5
Income from continuing operations	499.0	438.4	376.9	323.3	276.5	207.2	176.5	153.4	130.6	104.1
Income from discontinued operations, net of income taxes	.0	.6	2.3	1.5	4.1	27.7	22.8	17.3	13.6	20.6
Income from operations, net of income taxes	499.0	439.0	379.2	324.8	280.6	234.9	199.3	170.7	144.2	124.7
Dividends	288.1	226.8	193.2	164.5	126.1	104.1	88.9	76.9	65.6	55.9
Earnings per share of common stock:										
Continuing operations	$ 2.67	$ 2.36	$ 2.03	$ 1.74	$ 1.49	$ 1.12	$ .96	$ .84	$ .72	$ .58
Discontinued operations	.00	.00	.01	.01	.02	.15	.12	.09	.07	.11
Income from operations	2.67	2.36	2.04	1.75	1.51	1.27	1.08	.93	.79	.69
Dividends per share	$ 1.68	$ 1.445	$ 1.235	$ 1.06	$ .905	$ .773	$ .665	$ .57	$ .493	$ .418
Average number of shares outstanding (in millions)	187.1	186.1	185.9	185.7	185.5	185.0	183.6	183.1	182.0	180.1
As a % of operating revenue:										
Operating income	18.8	18.8	18.0	18.4	17.2	17.0	16.5	16.6	16.0	15.3
Income from operations, net of income taxes	11.7	11.6	10.9	10.7	10.7	10.4	9.8	9.4	9.2	9.8
Return on average shareowners' equity %	25.2	25.0	24.4	23.6	23.0	27.5	26.5	25.7	24.6	24.3
Shareowners' equity	$2,093.2	$1,899.3	$1,650.9	$1,474.0	$1,311.8	$ 910.5	$ 807.6	$ 703.0	$ 632.7	$ 546.8
Total assets	$5,023.8	$3,753.7	$3,484.0	$2,949.5	$2,486.8	$1,843.3	$1,583.4	$1,443.9	$1,241.7	$1,038.2

Source: 1988 Annual Report.

as numerous other general and specialized reporting services and the credit departments of banks.

Customers could receive their information from D & B in printed formats, via a toll-free telephone call, via on-line computer terminals, or via push-button telephone access to a computer-generated voice system. More than 80 percent of the inquiries were being handled electronically. The credit services division sponsored customer workshops and seminars to explain its array of services and to obtain customer suggestions on new information and services they would like to see provided. The division had appointed a customer advisory group and solicited members' advice and suggestions at regularly scheduled meetings. A bankers advisory council had been formed to provide an opportunity for senior officers of major U.S. banks to suggest product modifications, to discuss specific industry data requirements, and to provide input to new product development initiatives. The division was continually assessing customers' needs for new and enhanced products and services that would help D & B users reduce their credit risks and better manage their businesses.

Division sales representatives called on existing and potential customers regularly to apprise them of new products and services and to promote greater use of D & B's widening range of business information services. In the United States, five new products/services were introduced in 1987, and internationally, 35 new products and services were introduced in 11 countries (France, Great Britain, West Germany, the Netherlands, Italy, Israel, Australia, Hong Kong, Canada, Argentina, and Brazil). D & B International provided credit services and financial information to customers in 25 countries.

Also included in the business information services group were units that provided on-line investment information on the international securities industry, econometric and portfolio accounting services, claims payment services for underwriters of group insurance programs for small and medium-sized companies, and accounts receivable services (to assist in the collection of past due accounts). The McCormack and Dodge division supplied financial and human resource applications software systems, tools, and services. Represented in 40 countries, McCormack and Dodge had more than 10,000 systems installed throughout the world for customers, including more than one-half of the Fortune 500 companies.

Publishing. Dun & Bradstreet's two big divisions in the publishing group were Donnelley Directory and Moody's Investors Service. Donnelley Directory compiled, published, and served as sales representative for the Yellow Pages and telephone directories of two of the regional Bell operating companies, Ameritech and NYNEX, plus 28 other small telephone company clients throughout the United States. These directories represented about 18 percent of the total U.S. Yellow Pages market.

Moody's Investors Service was one of the nation's major financial publishers, providing a variety of corporate and financial data on over 22,000 major U.S. and foreign corporations plus 28,000 municipalities and government agencies. It issued ratings on corporate and municipal bonds, Eurobonds, and commercial paper and was striving to become the major bond ratings provider in the global financial marketplace. Moody's biggest competitor was Standard & Poor's. A third major subsidiary, the Official Airline Guides division, was sold in 1988 at a pretax gain of $752 million. Another business in this group was Thomas Cook Travel U.S.A., acquired in 1985. D & B's publishing businesses accounted for 19 percent of 1988 revenues; it was the slowest growing of the three groups.

Market Services. The best-known division in the market services group was Nielsen Media Research, the provider of television-rating information for the major networks, independent TV stations, and television advertisers. Nielsen Marketing Research measured consumer response to sales promotion campaigns in retail stores and provided market share data to suppliers of grocery items,

Exhibit 2 D & B's FINANCIAL PERFORMANCE BY BUSINESS SEGMENT, 1986–88

Year ended December 31, 1988	Business information services	Publishing	Market services	Total
Operating revenue	$1,504,946,000	$ 800,397,000	$1,962,034,000	$4,267,377,000
Restructuring (expense) income— net	$ (248,400,000)	$ 705,348,000	$ (447,100,000)	$ 9,848,000
Segment operating income (loss)	$ 76,077,000	$1,016,750,000	$ (123,272,000)	$ 969,555,000
General corporate expenses				(166,041,000)
Nonoperating (expense)—net				(12,846,000)
Income before provision for income taxes				$ 790,668,000
Segment depreciation and amortization	$ 97,216,000	$ 20,899,000	$ 94,003,000	$ 212,118,000
Segment capital expenditures	$ 101,182,000	$ 26,786,000	$ 188,816,000	$ 316,784,000
Identifiable assets at December 31, 1988	$1,377,226,000	$ 526,291,000	$1,740,295,000	$3,643,812,000
Year ended December 31, 1987				
Operating revenue	$1,302,847,000	$ 765,334,000	$1,720,321,000	$3,788,502,000
Restructuring expense—net	$ 0	$ (35,300,000)	$ 0	$ (35,300,000)
Segment operating income	$ 297,007,000	$ 220,392,000	$ 308,847,000	$ 826,246,000
General corporate expenses				(112,853,000)
Nonoperating income—net				20,444,000
Income before provision for income taxes				$ 733,837,000
Segment depreciation and amortization	$ 76,962,000	$ 16,467,000	$ 79,951,000	$ 173,380,000
Segment capital expenditures	$ 109,004,000	$ 17,552,000	$ 130,764,000	$ 257,320,000
Identifiable assets at December 31, 1987	$1,050,656,000	$ 522,610,000	$1,561,021,000	$3,134,287,000
Year ended December 31, 1986				
Operating revenue	$1,181,209,000	$ 837,984,000	$1,443,958,000	$3,463,151,000
Restructuring (expense) income— net	$ (98,010,000)	$ 162,047,000	$ (113,674,000)	$ (49,637,000)
Segment operating income	$ 135,965,000	$ 458,727,000	$ 132,058,000	$ 726,750,000
General corporate expenses				(104,165,000)
Nonoperating income—net				24,341,000
Income before provision for income taxes				$ 646,926,000
Segment depreciation and amortization	$ 74,446,000	$ 12,450,000	$ 70,494,000	$ 157,390,000
Segment capital expenditures	$ 68,995,000	$ 26,131,000	$ 95,049,000	$ 190,175,000
Identifiable assets at December 31, 1986	$ 895,543,000	$ 509,569,000	$1,360,983,000	$2,766,095,000

Source: *1988 Annual Report.*

health and beauty aids, and other packaged goods in retail markets in 27 countries. Nielsen Clearing House provided cents-off coupon administration and management services to retailers and provided research services to manufacturers. Four other business units provided a variety of other marketing and information services to business-to-business marketers, consumer goods marketers, and magazine publishers. The market services group accounted for 46 percent of 1988 corporatewide revenues and had grown 26 percent annually since 1985.

Exhibit 2 provides a financial breakdown on the operations of Dun & Bradstreet's three business groups.

GUIDING PRINCIPLES, MISSION, AND BELIEFS

Dun & Bradstreet's senior management proclaimed that the company's performance was driven by five fundamental principles:

1. Concentrating on providing products and services that meet the information needs of customers and prospects worldwide.
2. Sustaining Dun & Bradstreet's position as the world leader among information services companies.
3. Maintaining a record of profitability and growth.
4. Organizing to keep Dun & Bradstreet's rapid growth manageable, both strategically and operationally.
5. Creating and maintaining an environment that maximized the contributions of all its employees.

The company's publicly stated mission was "creating value for customers." The following statement, which appeared in D & B's *1987 Annual Report,* explained how D & B endeavored to create value for its customers:

> The Dun & Bradstreet Corporation produces and markets information products and services designed to help customers achieve fundamental goals: to reduce their risks of doing business; to market their products more effectively; and to lower their costs, enhance their productivity and improve their profits.
>
> Dun & Bradstreet's broad array of information products and services is designed to represent value—the ratio of benefits to price—as defined by the customer.

Some of the specific values to customers that D & B's divisions tried to provide are shown in Exhibit 3.

Management stated that customers were central to the company's strategy. References were often made to D & B's customer focus principle: "listening to, hearing, and heeding our customers." Internally, top management stressed that strict adherence to the customer focus principle was "the only way of doing business." In the company's *1986 Annual Report,* the two highest-ranking officers of the company asserted that from initial product development to customer billing, each D & B employee was committed to providing value to customers.

Exhibit 3 EXAMPLES OF THE VALUES TO CUSTOMERS WHICH D & B's DIVISIONS WERE TRYING TO PROVIDE	
D & B division	**Intended customer value**
D & B Credit Services	Accurate, quick decision-making that minimizes risk
D & B International	Business information on-line for measuring creditworthiness
D & B Plan Services	Affordable employee benefits for small businesses
D & B Receivable Management Services	Improved management of accounts receivable
McCormack and Dodge	Faster, simpler data processing and lower computing costs
Donnelley Directory	Enhanced Yellow Pages that link buyers and sellers effectively
Moody's Investors Service	Making wise investments and borrowing money at minimum cost
Nielsen Marketing Research	Better marketing and merchandising of packaged goods
Nielsen Media Research	Targeted placement of television advertisements

Source: *1987 Annual Report.*

QUESTIONABLE COMPANY PRACTICES

On March 19, 1989, the following article appeared on the front page of *The Wall Street Journal:*

Dun & Bradstreet Faces Flap over How It Sells Reports on Businesses

It Is Accused of Misleading Customers So They Buy More Than They Need—Rising Demands for Refunds

In early 1987, several Pittsburgh-area customers of Dun & Bradstreet Corp. received a mysterious call from a man who would identify himself only as an employee of the company.

The caller made a disturbing claim. Dun & Bradstreet, he said, was using deceptive methods in selling its credit reports—records of companies' creditworthiness that are a vital business tool for tens of thousands of American businesses.

Prompted by the call, several Dun & Bradstreet customers began looking into their purchases of credit reports. One customer, Black Box Corp., was buying a package of services costing $60,000 to $70,000 a year, on the advice of a D & B salesman. It discovered it was actually using service worth less than half

that. Dun & Bradstreet eventually made refunds to three customers, including $23,000 to Black Box. The whistle blower, identified by an internal investigation, still works at the company, but a salesman was fired for misleading customers.

Several Settlements

Several months later, dozens of Dun & Bradstreet's Philadelphia customers received an unsigned letter that began, "Webster's Dictionary defines embezzlement as . . . " Noting the Pittsburgh settlements, the writer told customers they, too, were being misled into paying for far more credit data than they were using. Dun & Bradstreet ultimately settled with 11 customers who received the letter.

After consulting a handwriting expert, the company accused a veteran Philadelphia salesman of writing the letter. He later took early retirement and, according to a former colleague, has agreed not to discuss the case publicly. No one was fired after the refunds, Dun & Bradstreet says.

But its problems didn't end in Philadelphia, either. The company, which has close to a monopoly on the sale of corporate credit information, now is being questioned by customers around the country, large and small, about their purchases of credit reports. Though there are other allegations, the main one is that Dun & Bradstreet salesmen have managed to sell customers larger credit-data packages than they needed by keeping them in the dark about their actual usage and misleading them about that usage when asked.

Denial from Company

Dun & Bradstreet vigorously denies any wrongdoing, except in rare cases that it has addressed. But a four-month investigation by this newspaper, involving court testimony, company records and interviews with numerous customers and current and former employees, suggests a broader problem. These documents and interviews indicate that the total amount of disputed and potentially disputed charges could be millions of dollars.

In New York, Manufacturers Hanover Trust Co. is among customers reviewing their accounts. Interbank Leasing Co. of North Hollywood, Calif., is suing Dun & Bradstreet after failing to reach a settlement. In New Jersey, Hertz Corp.'s former leasing unit did reach a settlement, giving it over $200,000 in free service. In Greensboro, N.C., a concern called Disston Co. is seeking a $200,000 refund.

In Cincinnati, the U.S. Postal Inspection Service, with the cooperation of the U.S. Attorney, is investigating whether Dun & Bradstreet's operations in Ohio violated federal mail-fraud law. They have subpoenaed 200,000 pages of company records. The inquiry grew out of a federal suit in Cincinnati filed by a salesman, since fired, who alleges that D & B deceived clients.

Sterling Reputation

The growing controversy threatens to tarnish the reputation of Dun & Bradstreet, one of the oldest (it was founded in 1841) and most respected of U.S. corporations. It could also rattle the finances of the information giant. Analysts estimate that Dun & Bradstreet Credit Services, after rapid growth over the past 15

years, contributes roughly a quarter of the company's nearly $500 million in annual profits. D & B also owns the Moody's debt-rating business, the audience-measuring firm of A. C. Nielsen and Yellow-pages publisher Donnelley.

Dun & Bradstreet's credit reports play a central role in American commerce. Each outlines a company's credit history, giving a running account of how quickly it pays its bills. It lists any court judgments or bankruptcy filings and provides brief biograhies of owners and officers. Clients use the data and related services in making a wide variety of business decisions, such as making loans, selling insurance, evaluating vendors and developing marketing plans.

With credit information on more than 9 million U.S. companies, Dun & Bradstreet's data base is the largest of its kind. The company delivers services to 62,000 customers, who contact it 90,000 times a day. While Dun & Bradstreet has some competition from regional concerns and from TRW Inc., it has almost "a lock on this business," says Jed Laird, a senior investment analyst at Hambrecht & Quist. D & B puts its market share at about 90 percent.

The company has long prided itself on its emphasis on ethics and integrity. "Truth is the best defense against slander," John P. Kunz, president of the credit-services division, recently said in a memo to employees about the controversy. He was quoting Abraham Lincoln, who once worked for D & B as a correspondent-reporter. And certainly many customers feel the trust is earned. "I'm very happy with what they do," said Terry Strohl, credit manager for Robert Bruce Industries Inc. in Philadelphia.

Dun & Bradstreet says it will provide "satisfactory solutions" to any customers who may have "overpurchased" services because they were misled. Customers have begun receiving usage statements without demanding them, and the pricing system is being altered somewhat. If there is a problem, says Mr. Kunz, the credit-services president, during a two-hour-plus interview, it is due to the isolated and uncondoned activities of a few renegade salesmen. Seven or eight out salesmen—of a total of over 600—have been fired in recent years, Mr. Kunz says.

Yet Dun & Bradstreet managers also knew when customers were consistently paying more than necessary for credit information. Managers have to approve contracts submitted by the sales force. Salesman Gary Mertz says he gave up a management position partly because he was expected to pressure salesmen to mislead customers. "I couldn't condone it, and I couldn't tell my people to do it," says Mr. Mertz who works in Columbus, Ohio. Dun & Bradstreet denies that managers had to do any such thing.

Management was certainly aware of some problems, though. In 1984, D & B gave Tennessee Valley Authority a refund of $97,000 for services, on three separate contracts, that TVA says it hadn't ordered or received. D & B won't comment on the case. Also in 1984, Mr. Kunz, who had just become president of the credit-services operation, wrote employees that several customers had complained of being misled.

He conceded in the memo that two customers had in fact been misled and sternly warned salesmen to avoid doing so. Nevertheless, misleading of customers about their usage continued, and it wasn't until last spring that the company began routinely giving customers statements that could help them see where they stood.

The Unit System

The roots of the problem go back to 1976, when Dun & Bradstreet changed its system for selling credit reports. Instead of simply ordering reports as they needed them, customers would buy an annual subscription of "units," which they then traded for credit reports or other services.

Unused units generally weren't refunded, and only a small number could be carried over to the next year. Even so, the system encouraged customers to load up when ordering units. That's because they had to pay a substantial premium for additional units if they ran out before the end of the year.

The system is still much the same. The advance-purchase price this year is $15.65 per unit, and the price for supplemental units is $19.75. One change, starting this year, permits customers in certain cases to carry over more units, but then they wind up paying a steep $27 a unit for what they actually use.

The package-of-units system, combined with a growing array of new products (each with its own pricing structure), made it very difficult for credit managers to keep track of what they were using. Usage statements could

be obtained on request, but Dun & Bradstreet did little to make customers aware of that and, by some accounts, its employees discouraged them from getting such statements.

"If a customer called into the office and wanted to know their usage, we weren't allowed to give it to him," says a former secretary in the Greensboro office, Kay Hiatt. "You could look at the usage reports and see customers were buying outrageous amounts," she adds. "You would think they would cut, but instead they would renew for the same, increase or in some cases supplement during the year when they had plenty of units left." Ms. Hiatt says customers wanting usage figures were referred to salesmen.

Just Say No

But often that didn't help. "We were instructed by our superiors to never, never divulge the actual number of reports a customer uses," says John R. Glazier, a former sales manager in the East. "The only way a customer ever received the actual figures [was] by threatening to drop the service," Mr. Glazier says in a letter to a plaintiff's lawyer, adding that when asked about usage, "salesmen were instructed to use such phrases as 'about the same as last year' or 'ahead of last year's pace' etc. They made a joke out of it."

As a result, Mr. Glazier charges, "customers of Dun & Bradstreet have been sending in millions of dollars for years, for service they have never even begun to utilize." Dun & Bradstreet calls Mr. Glazier's allegations "defamatory" and says it fired him for cause in 1977.

The company contends that "it was common knowledge" among customers that if they wanted to know their usage, they could request a report of it. Nevertheless, at least two-thirds of customers weren't getting such information. Many simply relied on the D & B salesmen to tell them how many units they needed, based on prior experience, when reordering.

"I trusted them to do what they were supposed to do," says Janis Stephenson, controller for Glass Unlimited Inc. in High Point, N.C.

Commission Structure

But the D & B compensation setup gives salesmen an incentive to mislead customers about their needs. A salesman gets no commission for an account's annual renewal unless the customer is spending more money than the year before. So even if a renewing corporation has used only a fraction of the service paid for in the old contract, the salesman still has to try to sell it expanded service. If a customer cuts its level of service, the salesman has to repay commissions previously earned.

"You basically had to lie to your customers," says Michael Parrs, a former D & B salesman in Harrisburg, Pa. "Either you lie or you're gone."

Jim Rawls, credit manager at Carolina Enterprises Inc. in Tarboro, N.C., says his D & B salesman regularly urged him to increase his order. "The rep would always come in and normally say, 'It's time to renew,' and [that] the reports were used up," Mr. Rawls recalls. "He implied that they were all used up, and one time he said, 'You are all used up.'"

Mr. Rawls didn't increase his order. Last year, he says, he did his own study of his company's credit-report usage and found that Carolina had been using less than half of the 900 units it had been ordering and paying for every year.

Suits Are Filed

Black Box, the Pittsburgh company that received a $23,000 settlement from Dun & Bradstreet, tells a similar story. "They were selling us a yacht when they knew we needed a rowboat," says David Hughes, general counsel.

In January, Interbank of North Hollywood, Calif., sued in federal court in Cincinnati after failing to reach a settlement with Dun & Bradstreet. Two weeks later, W. M. Hershman Inc. of Cincinnati filed a similar suit in the same court. The suits, both designed as class actions, are pending.

Dun & Bradstreet was asked to comment on these cases and on other companies mentioned in this article. On Interbank, D & B provided a copy of a memo Mr. Kunz wrote to employees, showing that that firm used between 60 percent and 106 percent of its units in recent years. "I want to demonstrate my point that allegations . . . are not facts," he wrote.

For the other cases, Dun & Bradstreet would only provide summaries of its conversations with the companies, not identifying them. Some of the companies told this newspaper they were happy with Dun & Bradstreet. But many customers, particularly small ones, ap-

pear afraid of offending the information giant that is virtually the only source for the credit reports they need. According to Dun & Bradstreet's summaries, one customer apologized to it for granting a reporter an interview and pledged never to do so again. The customer added: "We need you guys and I'm satisfied you're the only game in town."

One customer told Dun & Bradstreet that she had asked this reporter, "How did you ever get all that information about my usage? I always wanted that information from D & B and could not get it. Now a reporter gives me the information! If I knew I was so underused, I would have never renewed for that amount."

Other companies also say they had trouble getting usage reports. "Many times I asked the salesman to get me an accounting. He would say, 'They are still trying to calculate it.' It was pointless," says Paul Sechrist, credit manager for Henley Paper Co. in Greensboro, N.C.

Extent of Overbuying

Documents from the Greensboro Dun & Bradstreet office—one of its 55 district and divisional offices—suggest the extent of the overbuying by customers. During the 1980s, Greensboro's 500 to 600 customers purchased as much as $700,000 of credit services a year that they didn't use, the documents indicate.

Some overordering is unavoidable. The company generally requires customers to buy at least 100 units a year, which is more than some small ones need. Also, a customer might order more in anticipation of adding new accounts that ultimately don't materialize, or might end up needing fewer reports than ordered because it decides to ease credit policies. Salesmen were supposed to monitor accounts for usage and, if they noticed customers weren't using their units, try to suggest other ways to use up units.

But like Carolina Enterprises, many Greensboro customers were consistently buying 50 percent to 300 percent more than the level of services they used. For example, according to the documents, Tie Right Neckwear of Asheboro, N.C., has bought 700 to 800 units annually since 1981, even though it never used more than 300 units a year. Asked about the figures, a stunned official of Carolina Enterprises says, "This is the first I'm aware of this. We didn't get enough feedback."

The records show that from 1982 to at least 1987, Henley Paper was sold 2,100 to

2,800 units annually—but used as few as 690 and never more than 1,160. Henley also was sold 800 to 2,000 "Dunsdial" units, for retrieving credit reports by phone, of which it never used more than 532 a year. Says Mr. Sechrist, the credit manager, "With what they would read out to me, it did sound like we needed more."

Appeal to Salesmen's Spouses

Salesmen and managers in the Greensboro office were under severe pressure to increase revenues. An internal memo from 1986 notes that Dun & Bradstreet even sent letters to the spouses of sales representatives "to get them involved with increasing the Reps. performance." The memo says contracts being renewed without an increase "must be looked at as cuts."

In a June 1986 memo to sales reps, John G. Parrish, then Greensboro district manager, complained that "subscribers are 'making money' from our reference books. . . . We need to get some of that money they are saving." The frequently updated books are directories of firms on which D & B maintains credit reports.

Mr. Parrish commanded his sales team to "start quoting a 3 book minimum new contract" even though Dun & Bradstreet's policy was and is that customers need order only two. Two days later, an assistant vice president for the Southeast region sent a memo to district managers lauding Mr. Parrish's tactic: "This looks like an excellent campaign which some of you might want to copy."

When contacted, Mr. Parrish said, "I really don't have anything to say."

Last year, a saleswoman in the Greensboro office quit after complaining to management that customers were routinely being misled. According to her and other employees, the company sent a top auditor to Greensboro to check. The investigation hasn't resulted in any changes at the regional office, employees say. The auditor and Dun & Bradstreet decline to comment.

Further evidence that overbuying was widespread comes from a case in federal court in Cincinnati. Joseph Davidoski, a former D & B salesman who is accusing the company of harassment, testified that some $750,000 of service sold annually by the Cincinnati office wasn't used. Four of his colleagues also testi-

fied, at a hearing for a preliminary injunction, that many of their customers had been misled.

Mr. Davidoski testified that at a sales meeting a senior executive put the number of unused units companywide at 4 million in 1986. At today's discounted price of $15.65, their value would be $62.6 million. The senior executive, Pamela V. Alden, didn't respond to a telephone message.

Saleswoman Linda Teeter testified at the hearing that managers coached her on how to evade customers on the usage issue. She was congratulated, she said, if she could renew a much-underused account without its being cut. If the customer "had 500 [units] last year and used 100 and took 500 again this year, you have done an excellent job," she testified.

Late in January, Dun & Bradstreet fired Ms. Teeter, along with another salesman who testified, William Lewis Jr. It says it dismissed Ms. Teeter for lying to a customer about usage and Mr. Lewis for insubordination. Ms. Teeter couldn't be reached. Mr. Lewis says he was fired because he was telling customers how they had been misled by salesmen.

A Dun & Bradstreet manager in the Columbus office, Aloysius J. Carl, when asked if he had ever been instructed to mislead customers about how much service they were using, invoked the Fifth Amendment and declined to answer. He won't talk to a reporter.

Dun & Bradstreet dismisses Mr. Davidoski's suit as the act of a disgruntled employee who wasn't performing and was trying to save his job. Yet until recently, he was one of the company's top salesmen. In 1987, he was made a national account manager, one of a dozen or so salesmen who call on the biggest accounts.

Letter to Superior

But Mr. Davidoski was unhappy with the sales system and began to complain internally. According to his testimony, he raised the subject repeatedly with his managers, at national sales meetings and with Bain & Co., a management consultant retained by D & B (Bain won't comment).

On June 30, 1988, shortly after a law to protect "whistle blowers" went into effect in Ohio, Mr. Davidoski and another salesman wrote a letter to their supervisor accusing management of encouraging salesmen to deceive customers into buying more units than needed.

The letter also alleged that some employees were using customers' account numbers to order reports without their permission and thus inflate their apparent usage.

Within hours, superiors had the locks to Mr. Davidoski's office changed. The salesman, who despite his strong past record had recently been warned about his performance, was put on probation for being well under his sales quota. His biggest accounts were reassigned to the coauthor of the letter, Gary Mertz (the man who says he gave up a management job partly because he didn't want to pressure salesmen to mislead employees).

In September Mr. Davidoski sued, initially asking the court to order the company to stop harassing him. The court rejected the injunction, and Dun & Bradstreet dismissed Mr. Davidoski in late December. The rest of his case is pending.

Mr. Mertz, still at Dun & Bradstreet, says he raised the issue of deception with his superior when he was a manager. His conversation with this reporter came before Dun & Bradstreet sent a memo warning employees not to discuss the company with the news media.

Pressing the Claims

Dun & Bradstreet has another problem in a small New Jersey company formed last spring by two former salesmen. Credit Adivsors Inc., based in New Brunswick, alerts customers who may have bought unnecessary credit services and helps them seek refunds. Its founders, Frederick Paley and his son Thomas, were both fired from the Dun & Bradstreet sales force last year. The senior Mr. Paley was dismissed for "wrongfully manipulating the usage records of a customer," their ex-employer says, and his son for giving "false usage information to a customer."

Source: Johnnie L. Roberts, "Credit Squeeze," *The Wall Street Journal*, March 19, 1989.

E. & J. GALLO WINERY*

In the mid-1980s, alcohol consumption in the United States had been declining in virtually every category except low-priced wines. A number of producers in the wine industry did not believe they should be producing what they called skid-row wines (wines fortified with additional alcohol and sweetener and sold in screw-top, half-pint bottles). Richard Maher, president of Christian Brothers Winery in St. Helena, California, who once was with E. & J. Gallo Winery, said he didn't think Christian Brothers should market a product to people, including many alcoholics, who were down on their luck. "Fortified wines lack any socially redeeming values," he said.

Major producers of the low-end category of wines, called "dessert" or "fortified" (sweet wines with at least 14 percent alcohol), saw their customers otherwise. Robert Hunington, vice president of strategic planning at Canandaigue (a national wine producer whose product, Wild Irish Rose, was the number one low-end wine), said 60 percent to 75 percent of its "pure grape" Wild Irish Rose was sold in primarily black, inner-city markets. Hunington described Wild Irish Rose's customer in this $500 million market as "not super-sophisticated", lower middle-class, and low-income blue-collar workers and mostly men. However, Canandaigua also estimated the annual national market for dessert category wine to be 55 million gallons; low-end brands accounted for 43 million gallons, with as much as 50 percent sold in pints (typically the purchase choice of winos—alcoholics with a dependency on wine). Daniel Solomon, a Gallo spokesman, said Gallo's Thunderbird had lost its former popularity in the black and skid-row areas and was consumed mainly by retired and older people who didn't like the taste of hard distilled products or beer.[1]

Tony Mayes, area sales representative for Montgomery Beverage Company, Montgomery, Alabama, said one-third of the total revenue from wine sales in the state of Alabama was from the sale of one wine product—Gallo's Thunderbird. Sales crossed all demographic lines. According to Mayes, a consumer developed a taste for wine through an education process that usually began with the purchase of sweet wines from the dessert category. He attributed the high sales of Thunderbird to the fact that the typical wine drinker in Alabama was generally not the sophisticated wine drinker found in California or New York.

---

* Prepared by Daniel C. Thurman, doctoral student, under the supervision of A. J. Strickland III, both of The University of Alabama.

[1] Alix M. Freedman, "Misery Market—Winos & Thunderbird Are a Subject Gallo Doesn't Like to Discuss," The Wall Street Journal, February 25, 1988, pp. 1, 18.

COMPANY HISTORY AND BACKGROUND

The E. & J. Gallo Winery, America's biggest winery, was founded by Ernest and Julio Gallo in 1933. More than 55 years later, the Gallo Winery was still a privately owned and family-operated corporation actively managed by the two brothers. The Gallo family had been dedicated to both building their brands and the California wine industry.

The Gallos started in the wine business working during their spare time in the vineyard for their father, Joseph Gallo. Joseph Gallo, an immigrant from the Piedmont region in northwest Italy, was a small-time grape grower and shipper. He survived Prohibition because the government permitted wine for medicinal and religious purposes, but his company almost went under during the Depression. During the spring of 1933, Joseph Gallo killed his wife and chased Ernest and Julio with a shotgun. He killed himself following their escape. Prohibition ended that same year, and the Gallos, both in their early 20s and neither knowing how to make wine, decided to switch from growing grapes to making wine. With $5,900 to their names, Ernest and Julio found two thin pamphlets on wine-making in the Modesto Public Library and began making wine.[2]

The Gallos had always been interested in quality and began researching varietal grapes in 1946. They planted more than 400 varieties in experimental vineyards during the 1950s and 1960s, testing each variety in the different growing regions of California for its ability to produce fine table wines. Their greatest difficulty was to persuade growers to convert from common grape varieties to the delicate, thin-skinned varietals because it took at least four years for a vine to begin bearing and perhaps two more years to develop typical, varietal characteristics. As an incentive, in 1967, Gallo offered long-term contracts to growers, guaranteeing the prices for their grapes every year, provided they met Gallo quality standards. With a guaranteed long-term "home" for their crops, growers could borrow the needed capital to finance the costly replanting, and the winery was assured a long-term supply of fine wine grapes. In 1965, Julio established a grower relations staff of skilled viticulturists to aid contract growers. This staff still counsels growers on the latest viticultural techniques.[3]

Private ownership and mass production were the major competitive advantages contributing to Gallo's success. Gallo could get market share from paper-thin margins and absorb occasional losses that stockholders of publicly held companies would not tolerate. Gallo was vertically integrated, and wine was its only business. While Gallo bought about 95 percent of its grapes, it virtually controlled its 1,500 growers through long-term contracts. Gallo's 200 trucks and 500 trailers constantly hauled wine out of Modesto and raw materials in. Gallo was the only winery to make its own bottles (2 million a day) and screw-top caps. Also, while most of the competition concentrated on production, Gallo participated in

---

[2] Jaclyn Fierman, "How Gallo Crushes the Competition," *Fortune,* September 1, 1986, pp. 24–31.

[3] "The Wine Cellars of Ernest & Julio Gallo, a Brief History," a pamphlet produced by Ernest & Julio Gallo, Modesto, Calif.

every aspect of selling its product. Julio was president and oversaw production, while Ernest was chairman and ruled over marketing, sales, and distribution. Gallo owned its distributors in about a dozen markets and probably would have bought many of the more than 300 independents handling its wines if laws in most states had not prohibited it.

Gallo's major competitive weakness over the years had been an image associated with screw tops and bottles in paper bags that developed because of its low-end dessert wine, Thunderbird.[4] There were stories, which Gallo denied, that Gallo got the idea for citrus-flavored Thunderbird from reports that liquor stores in Oakland, California, were catering to the tastes of certain customers by attaching packages of lemon Kool-Aid to bottles of white wine to be mixed at home.[5]

Thunderbird became Gallo's first phenomenal success. It was a high-alcohol, lemon-flavored beverage introduced in the late 1950s. A radio jingle sent Thunderbird sales to the top of the charts on skid rows across the country: "What's the word? Thunderbird. How's it sold? Good and cold. What's the jive? Bird's alive. What's the price? Thirty twice." Thunderbird has remained a brand leader in its category ever since. In 1986, Ernest Gallo poured $40 million into advertising aimed at changing Gallo's image to one associated with quality wines.

Information on Gallo's finances were not publicly available, and the brothers maintained a tight lid on financial details. In a 1986 article, *Fortune* estimated that Gallo earned at least $50 million a year on sales of $1 billion. By comparison, the second leading winery, Seagram's (also the nation's largest distillery), had approximately $350 million in 1985 wine revenues and lost money on its best-selling table wines. *Fortune* stated that several of the other major Gallo competitors made money, but not much.[6]

Gallo produced the top-selling red and white table wines in the country. Its Blush Chablis became the best-selling blush-style wine within the first year of its national introduction. Gallo's award-winning varietal wines were among the top sellers in their classification. The company's Carlo Rossi brand outsold all other popular-priced wines. Gallo's André Champagne was by far the country's best-selling champagne, and E & J Brandy has outsold the number two and three brands combined. Gallo's Bartles & Jaymes brand was one of the leaders in the new wine cooler market.[7]

THE U.S. WINE INDUSTRY

Wine sales in the United States grew from about 72 million gallons in 1940 to over 600 million gallons, accounting for retail sales in excess of $9 billion (see Exhibit 1). This retail sales volume had exceeded such major established grocery catego-

---

[4] Jaclyn Fierman, "How Gallo Crushes the Competition."

[5] Alix M. Freedman, "Misery Market."

[6] Jaclyn Fierman, "How Gallo Crushes the Competition."

[7] "Gallo Sales Development Program," a pamphlet produced by Ernest & Julio Gallo, Modesto, Calif.

Exhibit 1 THE NATIONAL WINE MARKET (1977–86)

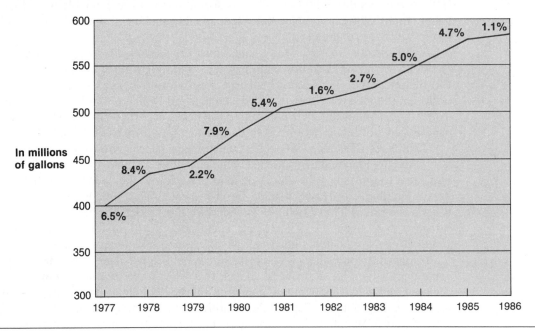

Source: *National Beverage Marketing Directory,* 10th ed., 1988.

ries as detergents, pet foods, paper products, and canned vegetables. While wine consumption had grown at an astonishing rate, trends toward moderation and alcohol-free life-styles made this growth rate impossible to maintain. Nevertheless, annual growth was projected to be 3.2 percent through 1995.

Per capita consumption of wine was low in the late 1950s and early 1960s because wine drinking was perceived as either the domain of the very wealthy or the extreme opposite. "Fortified" dessert wines were the top-selling wines of the period. The first surge in consumption in the late 1960s was the result of the introduction of "pop" wines, such as Boones Farm, Cold Duck, and Sangrias. These wines were bought by baby boomers, who were now young adults. Their palates were unaccustomed to wine drinking and these wines were suited to them. By the mid-1970s, the pop wine drinkers were ready to move up to Lambruscos and white wine "cocktails," and per capita consumption increased (see Exhibit 2). The wine spritzer became the trend, still the alternative to more serious wines for immature palates. Just as this surge began to wane, wine coolers were introduced in 1982 and exploded on the market in 1983. Wine coolers were responsible for a 5 percent market surge in 1984 and experienced four consecutive years of very high growth rates, rising 6 percent in 1987 to 72.6 million nine-liter cases.

Exhibit 2 PER CAPITA CONSUMPTION OF WINE IN THE U.S.

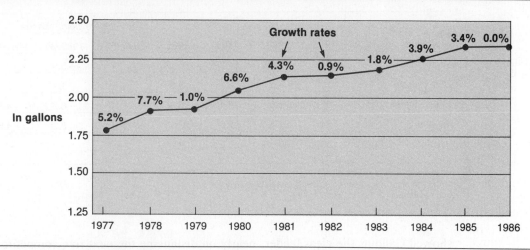

Source: *National Beverage Marketing Directory*, 10th ed., 1988.

The imported wines category enjoyed an upward growth rate from 6.6 percent of the market in 1960 to a high of 27.6 percent in 1985 (see Exhibits 3 and 4). The category lost market share to 23.1 percent in 1986 primarily because of the shift from Lambruscos to wine coolers. Additional factors were the weakening dollar and an overall improved reputation for domestic wines.

There were about 1,300 wineries in the United States. *Fortune* identified the major market-share holders in the U.S. market in a September 1986 article. It

Exhibit 3 WINE PRODUCTION BY PLACE OF ORIGIN (millions of nine-liter cases)

Origin	1970	1975	1980	1985	1986	Average annual compound growth rate			Percent change 1985–86
						1970–75	1975–80	1980–85	
California	82	115	139.5	133.2	133.3	7.0%	3.9%	−0.9%	0.1%
Other states*	18	19	18.7	16.9	17.3	1.4	−0.3	−2.0	2.4
United States	100	134	158.2	150.1	150.6	6.1	3.3	−1.0	0.3
Imports	13	21	43.1	57.2	45.3	10.5	15.8	5.8	−20.8
Total†	113	115	201.3	207.3	195.9	6.6%	5.4%	0.6%	−5.5%

* Includes bulk table wine shipped from California and blended with other state wines.
† Addition of columns may not agree because of rounding.
Source: *Impact* 17, no. 11 (June 1, 1987), p. 4.

Exhibit 4 MARKET SHARE TRENDS IN WINE PRODUCTION

Place produced	1970	1975	1980	1985	1986	Share point change		
						1970–80*	1980–85	1985–86
California	73%	74%	69.3%	64.3%	68.0%	4	−5.0	3.8
Other states	16	12	9.3	8.2	8.8	−7	1.1	0.7
United States	88	86	78.6	72.4	76.9	−10	−6.2	4.5
Imports	12	14	21.4	27.6	23.1	9	6.2	−4.5
Total†	100%	100%	100.0%	100.0%	100.0%	—	—	—

* 1980 based on unrounded data.
† Addition of columns may not agree because of rounding.
Source: *Impact* 17, no. 11 (June 1, 1987), p. 4.

showed Gallo as the clear leader, nearly outdistancing the next five competitors combined (see Exhibit 5).

A number of threats had faced the wine industry, not the least of which had been the national obsession with fitness and the crackdown on drunken driving. Americans drank 6.5 percent less table wine in 1985 than in 1984 (see Exhibits 6 and 7), and consumption was projected to be down another 5 percent in 1986. The industry answer to this problem had been introduction of wine coolers. Gallo's Bartles and Jaymes Coolers were number one until they lost the lead by only a slight margin to a Seagram's brand in 1987.

Another trend had been a shift toward a demand for quality premium wines made from the finest grapes. Premium wines increased market share from 8 percent in 1980 to 20 percent in 1986. Again, Gallo had sold more premium wine

Exhibit 5 1985 SHARE OF U.S. WINE MARKET

Company	Percent
E. & J. Gallo Winery	26.1%
Seagram & Sons	8.3
Canandiagua Wine	5.4
Brown-Forman	5.1
National Distillers	4.0
Heublein	3.7
Imports	23.4
All Others	24.0
Total	100.0%

Source: Jaclyn Fierman, "How Gallo Crushes the Competition," *Fortune*, September 1, 1986, p. 27.

Exhibit 6 SHIPMENTS OF WINE ENTERING U.S. TRADE CHANNELS BY TYPE (millions of nine-liter cases)

| Type | 1970 | 1975 | 1980 | 1984 | 1985 | 1986 | Average annual compound growth rate | | | Percent change* 1985–86 |
							1970–75	1975–80	1980–85	
Table	55.9	88.9	150.8	170.9	159.2	147.1	9.9%	11.2%	1.1%	−7.4%
Dessert	31.1	28.2	19.1	15.5	14.3	14.7	−2.0	−7.5	−5.7	3.2
Vermouth	4.2	4.2	3.7	3.0	2.9	2.7	—	−2.5	−4.8	−6.9
Sparkling	9.3	8.4	12.7	19.7	19.4	18.7	−1.9	8.6	8.6	−4.5
Special natural	11.8	24.0	13.6	10.9	10.7	10.9	15.3	−10.7	−4.7	1.9
Imported specialty†	0.3	1.0	1.5	1.0	0.9	1.8	25.4	8.1	−9.7	104.7
Total‡	112.6	154.7	201.3	220.1	207.3	195.9	6.6%	5.4%	0.6%	−5.5%

* Based on unrounded data.
† Imported fruit wines and wine specialties (includes sangria and fruit-flavored wines).
‡ Addition of columns may not agree because of rounding.
Source: *Impact* 17, no. 11 (June 1, 1987), p. 3.

Exhibit 7 SHARE OF MARKET TRENDS IN SHIPMENTS OF WINE ENTERING U.S. TRADE CHANNELS BY TYPE

| Type | 1970 | 1975 | 1980 | 1984 | 1985 | 1986 | Share point change | | |
							1970–80*	1980–85	1985–86
Table	50%	57%	74.9%	77.2%	76.8%	75.1%	25	1.9	−1.7
Dessert	28	18	9.5	7.0	6.9	7.5	−18	−2.6	0.6
Vermouth	4	3	1.8	1.4	1.4	1.4	−2	−0.4	†
Sparkling	8	5	6.3	9.0	9.4	9.5	−2	3.0	0.2
Special natural	10	16	6.8	5.0	5.2	5.6	−3	−1.6	0.4
Imported specialty	‡	1	0.7	0.5	0.4	0.9	+	−0.3	0.5
Total	100%	100%	100.0%	100.0%	100.0%	100.0%	—	—	—

* 1980 based on unrounded data.
† Addition of columns may not agree because of rounding.
‡ Less than 0.05%.
Source: *Impact* 17, no. 11 (June 1, 1987), p. 3.

than any other producer, but Gallo's growth had been limited by its lack of snob appeal.[8]

Although more than 80 percent of the U.S. adult population enjoyed wine occasionally, Gallo's research indicated most Americans were still infrequent wine drinkers by global standards. Only about one in four Americans drank wine as often as once a week. Per capita consumption in the United States was less than 2.5 gallons per year, compared to about 20 gallons in some Western European countries.[9]

Though the health-consciousness and alcohol-awareness of the 1980s had a moderating influence on wine growth patterns as consumers traded up in quality and drank less, long-term growth was expected to be steady but slower than that of the 1970s and early 1980s. Exhibit 8 provides drinking patterns for 1986. Personal disposable income was expected to grow in the United States through 1995; busy life-styles contributed to more dining out; and sale of wine in restaurants was expected to increase. As the aging baby boomers grew in number and importance, their wine purchases were expected to increase. All these factors contributed to the projected average yearly increase in growth rate of 3.2 percent through 1995.[10]

THE DESSERT WINE INDUSTRY

Dessert wine represented a 55 million-gallon, $500 million industry. The dessert wine category, also called fortified wines, included wines that contained more than 14 percent alcohol, usually 18 percent to 21 percent. They were called fortified because they usually contained added alcohol and additional sugar or sweetener. This category included a group of low-end priced brands that had been the brunt of significant controversy. Canandaigua's Wild Irish Rose had been the leading seller in this category, with Gallo's Thunderbird claiming second place, followed by Mogen David Wine's MD 20/20.[11]

Dessert wines had shown a decreasing trend both in amount of wine consumed and in market share from 1970 through 1985. However, the trend changed in 1986 when dessert wine's market share rose six-tenths of a share point to 7.5 percent of the total wine market (see Exhibit 7). The rise was attributed in large measure to the 19 percent federal excise tax increase on distilled spirits. An additional factor in the increase in the dessert wine category was the shift to fruit-flavored drinks, which also affected the soft drink industry and wine coolers.[12]

---

[8] Jaclyn Fierman, "How Gallo Crushes the Competition."

[9] "Gallo Sales Development Program."

[10] "Coolers Providing Stable Growth," *Beverage Industry Annual Manual,* 1987.

[11] Alix M. Freedman, "Misery Market."

[12] "U.S. News and Research for the Wine, Spirits and Beer, Executive," *IMPACT,* 17, no. 11 (June 1, 1987); and *IMPACT* 17, no. 18 (September 15, 1987).

Exhibit 8 BEVERAGE CONSUMPTION PATTERNS

1986 National beverage consumption by gender (% of volume)

Gender	Malt beverages	Wine	Distilled spirits	Coolers	Total nonalcoholic beverages	Total beverages
Male	80.8%	51.6%	62.6%	44.9%	51.1%	52.7%
Female	19.2	48.4	37.4	55.1	48.9	47.3
Total	100.0%	100.0%	100.0%	100.0%	100.0%	100.0%

1986 National alcoholic beverage consumption by household income (% of volume)

Household income	Malt beverages	Wine	Distilled spirits	Coolers	Total alcoholic beverages
Under $15,000	26.1%	11.7%	19.7%	22.3%	26.5%
$15,000–$24,999	19.1	13.9	18.1	19.5	21.3
$25,000–$29,999	10.8	14.2	6.6	10.9	12.1
$30,000–$34,999	11.7	9.9	14.7	7.9	10.3
$35,000 & over	32.3	50.3	40.9	39.4	29.8
Total	100.0%	100.0%	100.0%	100.0%	100.0%

1986 National beverage consumption by time of day (% of volume)

Time of day	Malt beverages	Wine	Distilled spirits	Coolers	Total nonalcoholic beverages	Total beverages
Breakfast/morning	2.7%	2.1%	4.6%	1.5%	32.7%	30.6%
Lunch	6.8	5.8	4.2	4.4	20.8	19.8
Snack	27.5	19.0	31.9	27.0	10.9	12.0
Dinner	14.2	45.8	15.5	13.7	22.9	22.6
Evening	48.8	27.3	43.8	53.4	12.7	15.0
Total	100.0%	100.0%	100.0%	100.0%	100.0%	100.0%

1986 National beverage consumption by location of consumption (% of volume)

Location	Malt beverages	Wine	Distilled spirits	Coolers	Total nonalcoholic beverages	Total beverages
Total home	64.6%	75.8%	61.4%	76.9%	76.1%	75.5%
Total away from home	35.4%	24.2%	38.6%	23.1%	23.9%	24.5%

Source: *Impact* 17, no. 18 (September 15, 1987), pp. 3–4.

A number of factors indicated that the growth trend would continue for the $500 million dessert wine category. The desire to consume beverages that contained less alcohol than distilled spirits and were less expensive than distilled spirits, the desire for fruit flavor, and the American trend toward eating out at restaurants more often contributed to the trend toward increased consumption of dessert wines. Additionally, the dessert wine category had survived relatively well with virtually no promotion or advertising. This had been possible because, of the category's 55 million gallons, low-end brands accounted for 43 million gallons, approximately 50 percent of which was sold in half pints; and this market had not been accessible by traditional advertising or promotion.

The dessert wine category had been a profitable venture because many of the wines in this category were made with less expensive ingredients, packaged in less expensive containers, and had usually been sold without promotion. Canandaigua estimated that profit margins in this category were as much as 10 percent higher than those of ordinary table wines. Gallo said this was not true for its products, but it would not reveal the figures.

The low-end dessert wines were a solid business. *The Wall Street Journal* reported that, of all the wine brands sold in America, Wild Irish Rose was the number 6 best seller, Thunderbird was 10th, and MD 20/20 was 16th. In contrast to the growth expectations of other brands and categories, sales of these low-end brands were expected to be up almost 10 percent. Yet the producers of these top-selling wines distanced themselves from their products by leaving their corporate names off the labels, obscuring any link to their products. Paul Gillette, publisher of the *Wine Investor,* was quoted in a discussion of this unsavory market as saying: "Makers of skid-row wines are the dope pushers of the wine industry."[13]

---

[13] Alix Freedman, "Misery Market."

III

Instructions for Using the STRAT-ANALYST™ Software Package

STRAT-ANALYST™ software is designed to accompany the fifth edition of STRATEGIC MANAGEMENT: CONCEPTS AND CASES by Arthur A. Thompson, Jr. and A. J. Strickland III. The STRAT-ANALYST™ computer program (disks) may be included with this text or the disks may be purchased separately. If you wish to purchase the software, contact your instructor or your college/university bookstore.

INSTRUCTIONS FOR USING STRAT-ANALYST™

STRAT-ANALYST™ is user-friendly. Even if you are a novice on the personal computer, you can learn to use STRAT-ANALYST successfully in less than an hour. STRAT-ANALYST gives you the capability to *quickly* and *easily*:

1. Obtain calculations showing financial ratios, profit margins and rates of return, the percentage composition of income statements and balance sheets, annual compound growth rates, and Altman's bankruptcy index (a predictor of impending financial crisis).
2. Construct line graphs, bar graphs, pie charts, and scatter diagrams using any of the case data or calculations on file.
3. Do "what-if" scenarios and compare the projected outcomes for one strategic option versus another.
4. Make five-year best-case, expected-case, and worst-case projections of a company's performance.
5. Get report-ready printouts of all these calculations and graphs.
6. Go through an easy-to-use procedure for doing:

    • Industry and competitive situation analysis.
    • Company situation analysis.

    Then get report-ready printouts of all your work.
7. Develop a set of action recommendations for:

    • Revising/improving a company's strategy and competitive position (a particularly useful option for Cases 6–19).
    • Improving strategy implementation and addressing internal problems/issues (a particularly useful option for Cases 1–5 and 25–34).

    You again will be able to get report-ready printouts of your recommended action plan.

Complete step-by-step instructions for using all of these capabilities are provided on the two STRAT-ANALYST disks. You will find that the STRAT-ANALYST software package will give you a major assist in doing higher-caliber strategic analysis, and it will significantly cut the time it takes to do the number-crunching needed for first-rate preparation of a case assignment.

PART I: STRAT-ANALYST START-UP PROCEDURES

STRAT-ANALYST can be used on any personal computer with at least one floppy disk drive, 512K (or greater) memory, and the capability to run Release

2.01 or higher of Lotus 1-2-3® or the Student Edition of Lotus 1-2-3. Due to the variety of personal computer setups you may be working with, we have provided separate start-up instructions for each of the three basic types of personal computer configurations: (1) systems with two removable (floppy) disk drives, (2) fixed disk systems with one removable (floppy) disk drive, and (3) fixed disk systems with STRAT-ANALYST installed on the fixed disk. Consult the set of step-by-step instructions appropriate for the system you are using.

A. Step-by-step instructions for systems with two removable (floppy) disk drives

1. To begin, you will need a DOS disk of version 2.1 or later (DOS stands for Disk Operating System), a Lotus 1-2-3 System Disk (Release 2.01 or higher) and the two STRAT-ANALYST disks.

2. Insert the DOS disk (label side up) into Drive A of the personal computer and close the drive door. Turn the computer on and wait for it to start. The red drive light is the signal that the disk drive is running. DO NOT OPEN THE DRIVE DOOR, INSERT OR REMOVE A DISK, OR STRIKE ANY KEY ON THE KEYBOARD WHEN THE RED DRIVE LIGHT IS ON.

3. You will be prompted to enter the date and the time. Type the date and the time if necessary—you may be able to get around this by simply pressing [Return] when prompted to enter the date and time.

4. At this point the A prompt (A>) will appear somewhere on the left side of the screen. A> is your signal that the computer is ready for a command.

5. Remove the DOS from Drive A, insert in its place a Lotus 1-2-3 System Disk (label side up), and close the door to Drive A.

6. Insert Disk 1 of STRAT-ANALYST (label side up) into the B drive and close the drive door.

7. At the A prompt (A>), type in 123 and press [Return]. The red drive light will come on again, signaling that Disk 1 of the STRAT-ANALYST and Lotus 1-2-3 are being loaded into the computer.

8. After a few seconds, the Lotus 1-2-3 introductory screen will appear, and then the STRAT-ANALYST title screen will appear soon after.

   Note: If the STRAT-ANALYST title screen does NOT appear within a few seconds, follow this procedure:

   a. Make sure Disk 1 of the STRAT-ANALYST is in the B disk drive and that the drive door is closed.

   b. Type the following Lotus command sequence:

   /FD B: [Return]

   Then type:

   /FRAUTO123 [Return]

   The red light of drive B will come on indicating that STRAT-ANALYST is being loaded into the computer, and the opening STRAT-ANALYST screen will appear soon after.

9. You are now "in," STRAT-ANALYST is "booted up," and you are ready to begin your session on STRAT-ANALYST. Proceed to Part II below.

B. Step-by-step instructions for fixed disk systems with one removable (floppy) disk drive

If you are using a fixed disk system in a PC lab with Lotus 1-2-3 (Release 2.01 or higher) installed on the fixed disk, follow this procedure to start up STRAT-ANALYST.

1. Turn on the computer and wait a few seconds for it to come on.
2. Enter the time and date if required. The C prompt (C>) character will appear on the screen. C> is your signal that the computer is ready for a command.
3. Insert Disk 1 of STRAT-ANALYST into the removable (floppy) disk drive and close the drive door.
4. Load Lotus 1-2-3 from the fixed disk using the procedures appropriate for the setup you have.
5. If the STRAT-ANALYST title screen does NOT appear within a few seconds of the time that you load Lotus 1-2-3, you will need to make sure that Disk 1 of STRAT-ANALYST is in the floppy disk drive and then type the following Lotus command sequence:

/FD A: [Return]

Then type:

/FRAUTO123 [Return]

The red drive light will come on indicating that STRAT-ANALYST is being loaded in to the computer, and the opening STRAT-ANALYST screen will appear soon thereafter. DO NOT OPEN THE DRIVE DOOR, INSERT OR REMOVE A DISK, OR PRESS ANY KEY ON THE KEYBOARD WHEN THE RED DRIVE LIGHT IS ON.

6. You are now "in," STRAT-ANALYST is "booted up," and you are ready to begin your session on STRAT-ANALYST. Proceed to Part II below.

C. Instructions for installing and running STRAT-ANALYST on a fixed disk

If you have your own fixed-disk PC, you can either use the removable (floppy) disks provided (following the procedures in section B above) or copy the removable (floppy) disk files directly onto your own fixed disk. You may find it a bit quicker and more convenient to run STRAT-ANALYST entirely from your fixed disk. The following is a set of step-by-step instructions for installing and running STRAT-ANALYST on your fixed disk:

1. Begin by checking the STRAT-ANALYST file directory against your fixed-disk directory to see if you have any other files on your fixed disk that

have the same name as any of the following 22 file names we used to create STRAT-ANALYST:

AUTO123.WK1	MARYKAY.WK1
TURNER.WK1	CAMPBELL.WK1
CARMIKE.WK1	NUCOR.WK1
WESTMIN.WK1	EXXON.WK1
COPE.WK1	LINCOLN.WK1
WTD.WK1	WALSH.WK1
TIRE.WK1	WAL-MART.WK1
UNIROYAL.WK1	SITUATAN.WK1
ICECREAM.WK1	RECS.WK1
MENU_1.WK1	GRAPHS.WK1
FOODLION.WK1	MENU_2.WK1

The STRAT-ANALYST file name that is most likely to be a duplicate of a file name on your fixed disk directory is AUTO123.WK1. If you do have a file of the same name as a STRAT-ANALYST file and it is in the same directory as that to which you are copying STRAT-ANALYST, your file will be overwritten (lost) when you copy STRAT-ANALYST onto the fixed disk. To prevent your file from being overwritten, you will need to create a subdirectory on your fixed disk in which to copy the STRAT-ANALYST files. To create a subdirectory and to install STRAT-ANALYST on your fixed disk, follow this one-time procedure:

a. With the C> on the screen type:

MD\STRATA

and press [Return]. This creates a subdirectory called STRATA.

b. Then type

A:

and press [Return] to get the A on the screen.

c. At the A>, insert STRAT-ANALYST Disk 1 into the A drive and type:

COPY*.* C:\STRATA

and press [Return].

d. Repeat step (c) above using Disk 2 of STRAT-ANALYST to complete the installation of STRAT-ANALYST on your fixed disk.

e. Check to see that all of the STRAT-ANALYST files from both disks were copied onto your fixed disk by calling up a file listing of the STRATA directory.

f. Now that STRAT-ANALYST is installed on your fixed disk, you will not need to use this procedure again unless you want to install STRAT-ANALYST on another fixed disk computer.

2. Once STRAT-ANALYST is installed on your fixed disk, you should use the following procedures each time you want to load and run STRAT-ANALYST:

a. The current C drive directory must contain your Lotus 1-2-3 system files, so type CD \ and the name of the directory containing your Lotus 1-2-3 system files, and press [Return].

b. When the C> appears, type in 123 and press [Return].

c. A blank Lotus 1-2-3 spreadsheet will appear shortly after. At this point, type the following Lotus command sequence:

/FD C:\STRATA [Return]

Then type:

/FRAUTO123 [Return]

This loads STRAT-ANALYST and the first STRAT-ANALYST screen will then appear.

d. You are now "in," STRAT-ANALYST is "booted up," and you are ready to begin your session on STRAT-ANALYST. Proceed to Part II below.

PART II: PERSONALIZING AND PROTECTING YOUR STRAT-ANALYST DISKS

The first time you boot up STRAT-ANALYST and go past the first two introductory screens, you will come to a series of screens involving how to personalize and protect your disks. Please read the screens that appear in this phase carefully.

1. Begin your first use of STRAT-ANALYST by reading the two opening screens, pressing [Return] after each one. (Every time you use STRAT-ANALYST, you will enter through these screens.)

2. On the third screen, STRAT-ANALYST asks you for your first name. We recommend that you press the [CAPS LOCK] key at this point (the reason will become apparent shortly). When the "CAPS" indicator appears at the bottom of the screen, you are ready to proceed as follows: Type your first name and press [Return].

3. Your name will appear in bold letters in the middle of the screen. If you made a typing error or otherwise do not like the way your name appears on the screen, press [Esc], retype your name, and press [Return].

4. When your name is typed in the way you want it, press [Return] again and it will become a permanent part of your STRAT-ANALYST program.

5. Next, STRAT-ANALYST will ask you to create our own password. Decide on a password that is easy for you to type and easy to remember. WRITE YOUR PASSWORD DOWN SOMEWHERE.

   NOTE ON PASSWORDS: Every time you re-enter STRAT-ANALYST, it will ask you for your password. The password you enter must match EXACTLY the password you are about to create; this includes the use of capital and lower-case characters. If you always type with the [CAPS LOCK] on, it will be a bit easier to match the password each time you re-enter STRAT-ANALYST. STRAT-ANALYST gives you three tries to match the password. If on the third try you fail to enter the correct password, you will be "kicked out" of STRAT-ANALYST. You will then have to restart STRAT-ANALYST and try again.

6. Type in the password you have decided to use and press [Return].

7. Your password will appear in bold letters in the middle of the screen. If you have made a mistake or otherwise do not like the way your password appears on the screen, press [Esc], retype your password, and press [Return].

8. When your password appears the way you want it, press [Return] again. The red drive light will come on, indicating that your password is becoming a permanent part of your STRAT-ANALYST program.

9. Read the screen that comes up, then press [Return] and the STRAT-ANALYST Main Menu will appear.

Notice to removable floppy disk users on protecting your disks against erasure. After you have (1) personalized your STRAT-ANALYST disks with your name and password and (2) completed your first session on STRAT-ANALYST, we recommend you make a duplicate copy of STRAT-ANALYST (see the instructions in Part IV below) and that you put write-protect tabs on both of the STRAT-ANALYST disks (see item 6 of the instructions for Part V). The write-protect tabs will prevent you from inadvertently copying over or erasing the material on the STRAT-ANALYST disks.

PART III: STRAT-ANALYST MENUS

Moving from file to file from screen to screen is easy with STRAT-ANALYST menus. STRAT-ANALYST menus appear in two forms: (1) in a column on the screen or (2) in a line at the top of the screen. To make a menu selection from either of these types of menus, simply press the letter corresponding to your menu selection.

Some STRAT-ANALYST screens will have no menu. These screens will always present instructions as to how to proceed (the usual procedure is to press [Return]).

Unless otherwise indicated, the [Esc] key will send you to the first screen (usually the main menu) for the particular file you are in. Use the [Esc] key to "escape" from any screen you have accessed; it will return you to the Main Menu of the current file. [Esc] will NOT cause you to leave the STRAT-ANALYST file you are currently using.

When accessing files with the STRAT-ANALYST Main Menu, you will occasionally be prompted by STRAT-ANALYST to replace Disk 1 with Disk 2 or vice versa. This occurs when the computer needs to access a file stored on the other STRAT-ANALYST disk—i.e., the one NOT currently in the machine. When you encounter this screen, instructions for proceeding will appear.

FIXED DISK USERS: If you have loaded all of the STRAT-ANALYST disks onto your hard disk and the program prompts you to exchange disks, simply press [Return] to continue the execution of your menu selection.

Important Notice. All other instructions you will need to use STRAT-ANA-LYST's capabilities successfully are self-contained on STRAT-ANALYST Disks 1 and 2.

PART IV: MAKING A BACKUP COPY OF STRAT-ANALYST

It is always good practice to make backup copies of your working disks. In the event that your original STRAT-ANALYST disks are lost or damaged, your backup copies will serve as replacements. Get two blank disks and proceed to make a backup copy of each STRAT-ANALYST disk as follows:

1. Insert a DOS disk into Drive A and turn the computer on.
2. Enter the date and time if necessary.
3. The A> will appear on the left side of the screen.
4. At the A> type:

   Diskcopy A: B:

   and press [Return].
5. The computer will load the Diskcopy program from DOS and prompt you as follows:

   Insert SOURCE Diskette in Drive A:

   Insert TARGET Diskette in Drive B:

   Press any key when ready. . . .
6. Remove the DOS disk from Drive A, insert a STRAT-ANALYST disk into Drive A and your own double-sided, double-density blank disk into Drive B and press any key to start the copy procedure.
7. After about one minute, the computer will complete the copy procedure. Now label the backup disk with the number of the STRAT-ANALYST disk you just copied from.
8. Repeat steps 1 through 7 with the remaining STRAT-ANALYST disk and you will have a backup copy of your STRAT-ANALYST disks. Be sure to label your disks, so you will know which is which.
9. Store your labeled backup disks in a safe place, observing the disk-handling procedures in Part V below.

PART V: DISK HANDLING PROCEDURE AND USE OF WRITE-PROTECT TABS

Special care should always be taken when handling the STRAT-ANALYST disks.

1. Do not touch or otherwise contaminate the exposed magnetic surfaces of the disks.
2. Do not expose the disks to magnetized objects such as televisions, radios, metal detectors, or library theft control systems.

3. Keep the disks in their paper sleeves when not in use and store them in a protective plastic case.

4. Do not bend or fold the disks.

5. Do not expose the disks to excessive heat or sunlight (the safe operating and storage temperature ranges from 50 degrees F to 120 degrees F).

6. SPECIAL NOTE: After you have gone through the procedure of entering your name and password on your STRAT-ANALYST disk, we recommend that you put a write-protect tab on each of the two STRAT-ANALYST disks. The advantage of write-protect tabs is that they prevent you from inadvertently copying over or erasing any of the material on the STRAT-ANALYST disks. Write-protect tabs come with boxes of disks; if you don't have any tabs, see if you can borrow two and/or consult the personnel in the PC lab for advice.

If you will always observe these six basic disk-handling rules, then the integrity of your disks and their programming will be ensured.

Name Index

Subject Index